P9-CQZ-251

# Psychology

Fourth Edition

# Psychology

*David G. Myers*

Hope College
Holland, Michigan

WORTH PUBLISHERS

**To Laura**

**Psychology**, Fourth Edition

Copyright © 1995, 1992, 1989, 1986 by Worth Publishers, Inc.
All rights reserved

Manufactured in the United States of America
Library of Congress Catalog Card Number: 94-60649
ISBN: 0-87901-644-2
Printing: 5 4
Year: 99 98 97 96 95

Development editor: Christine Brune
Design: Malcolm Grear Designers
Art director: George Touloumes
Production editor: Barbara B. Toniolo
Production supervisor: Sarah Segal
Layout: Matthew Dvorozniak
Picture editor: June Lundborg Whitworth
Line art: Bruce P. Maddocks, Warren Budd, and Demetrios Zangos

Composition and separations: TSI Graphics, Inc.
Printing and binding: Von Hoffmann Press, Inc.

Illustration credits begin on page IC-1, and constitute an extension of the copyright page.

All royalties from the sale of this book are assigned to the David and Carol Myers Foundation, which exists to receive and distribute funds to other charitable organizations.

**Worth Publishers**
33 Irving Place
New York, NY 10003

*Also Available for Students*

Richard O. Straub, **Study Guide** (0-87901-645-0)

Richard O. Straub, **Study Guide for Discovering Psychology Telecourse** (0-87901-777-5)

Jane S. Halonen, **Critical Thinking Companion for Introductory Psychology** (1-57259-018-1)

**Psychology 4E** plus **Study Guide** (shrink-wrapped) (1-57259-029-7)

**Psychology 4E** plus **Critical Thinking Companion for Introductory Psychology** (shrink-wrapped) (1-57259-028-9)

**Psychology 4E** plus **Study Guide** plus **Critical Thinking Companion for Introductory Psychology** (shrink-wrapped) (1-57259-036-x)

**CD-ROM** (0-87901-764-3)

Richard O. Straub and Thomas Ludwig, **Computerized Study Guide**
(DOS 3.5) (0-87901-779-1)
(DOS 5.25) (0-87901-790-2)
(Macintosh) (0-87901-791-0)

**Psychology 4E** plus **Computerized Study Guide**
(DOS 3.5) (shrink-wrapped) (1-57259-021-1)
(DOS 5.25) (shrink-wrapped) (1-57259-022-x)
(Macintosh) (shrink-wrapped) (1-57259-025-4)

# Contents in Brief

# Contents

# Preface

Throughout its four editions, my vision for *Psychology* has remained the same: *to merge rigorous science with a broad human perspective in a book that engages both mind and heart.* Across the dozen years spent shaping this book, my aim has been to create a state of the art introduction to psychology's methods and findings, written with sensitivity to students' needs and interests. I aspire to help students gain insight into, and appreciate the wonder of, important phenomena of their everyday lives. I also want to convey the inquisitive, critical, and compassionate spirit in which psychologists *do* psychology. Believing with Thoreau that "Anything living is easily and naturally expressed in popular language," I seek to communicate today's scholarship with crisp narrative and vivid storytelling.

## New to the Fourth Edition

This new edition retains the voice, and much of the organization and content of its predecessors. It is, however, the most effortful and significant revision to date.

### Enhanced "Thinking Critically" Theme

New Chapter 1, Thinking Critically With Psychological Science, takes an innovative critical thinking approach to teaching methods (see table of contents at right). The chapter shows how psychology's methods address everyday questions of behavior with a set of formal procedures for gathering and evaluating evidence that diminish the errors of everyday intuition. It looks at how psychology's methods can help us answer many significant questions and think more intelligently. Later chapters reinforce the "thinking critically" theme, often with boxes that model critical analysis. A Critical Thinking Exercise at the end of each chapter tests student understanding of the principles, with sample answers in an end-of-book appendix. These creative exercises use the model established by well-known critical thinking researcher Jane Halonen, whose new *Critical Thinking Companion for Introductory Psychology* is available from Worth Publishers for use with this text. By the book's end, students should not only have learned psychology's most important concepts and findings, but also how and why we play the science game.

## Strengthened Neuroscience Perspective

Chapter 2, now titled Neuroscience and Behavior, offers increased and updated coverage of psychology's neuroscience foundations. The art program has been enhanced and expanded so that it more effectively helps students visualize what is presented in the text (for example, see Figure 2–2 below). On the stated assumption that "everything psychological is simultaneously biological," information on the neurobiology and genetics of behavior, cognition, and emotion is also integrated throughout the text at more than three dozen locations (see cross-reference guide, page 74).

**Figure 2–2**

**Axonal Transmission** *A neuron fires an impulse when stimulated by pressure, heat, light, or chemical messages from adjacent neurons. This brief electrical charge, called an action potential, travels down the axon, beginning (a) at the juncture of the cell body and the axon. A thousandth of a second later (b), the electrical change produces another action potential a little farther along the axon, and the first section begins to recharge. After another thousandth of a second (c), the action potential appears to have moved farther along the axon, and the first section has completely recharged.*

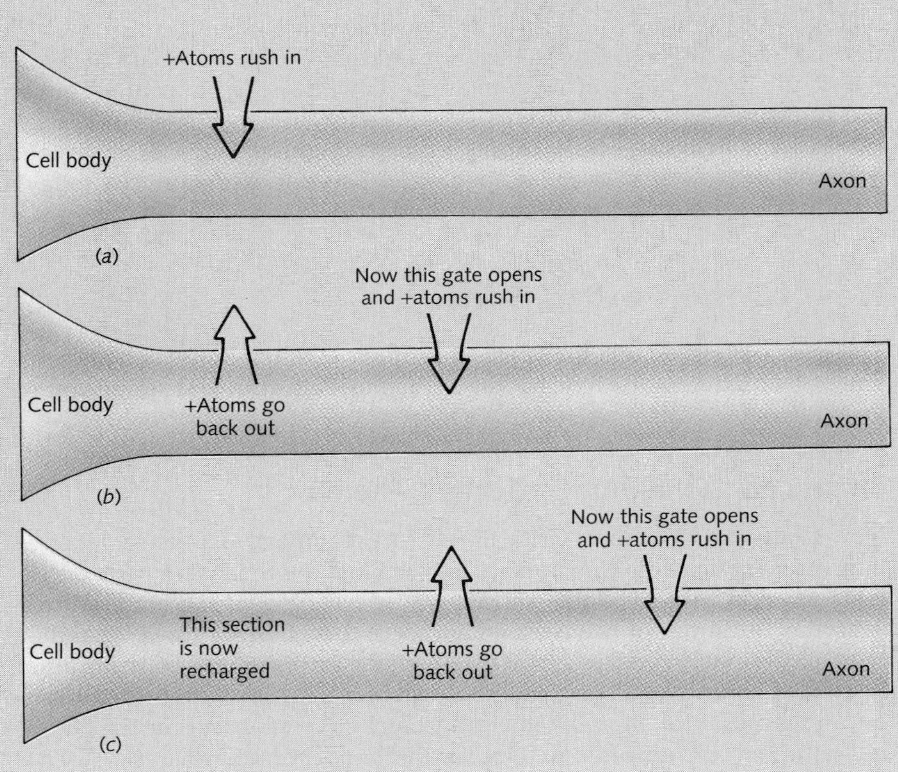

## New Pedagogical Aids

A new system of study aids has been introduced—**PRTR.** Major chapter sections now begin with a "**P**review" that helps focus student reading on each section's overarching concepts (see sample below from Chapter 5 section on Hearing). Chapters have been broken down into more digestible sections to help students chart their **R**eading. Critical **T**hinking is incorporated as a theme throughout the book—within the narrative, in "Thinking Critically About . . ." boxes, and in end-of-chapter exercises. Each major section ends with a "**S**umming Up" that **R**eviews the most important concepts (see sample below). To enhance student review, the key terms are now defined and organized by major chapter section at the end of each chapter.

*Samples of "Preview" and "Summing Up"*

## Hearing

*Somewhat less mysterious than sight, but still pretty amazing, is another aspect of our ordinary experience: the process by which we convert air pressure waves into neural messages that the brain interprets as a meaningful symphony of sound. How do we do it? What breaks in the system typically cause hearing loss? What is it like to live without hearing?*

### Summing Up

**The Stimulus Input: Sound Waves** The pressure waves we experience as sound vary in frequency and amplitude, and correspondingly in perceived pitch and loudness.

**The Ear** Through a mechanical chain of events, sound waves traveling through the auditory canal cause minuscule vibrations in the eardrum. Transmitted via the bones of the middle ear to the fluid-filled cochlea, these vibrations create movement in tiny hair cells, triggering neural messages to the brain.

Research on how we hear pitch supports both the place theory, which best explains the sensation of high-pitched sounds, and frequency theory, which best explains the sensation of low-pitched sounds. We localize sound by detecting minute differences in the loudness and timing of the sounds received by each ear.

**Hearing Loss and Deaf Culture** Hearing losses linked to conduction and nerve disorders can be caused by prolonged exposure to loud noise and by diseases and age-related disorders. Those who live with hearing loss face social challenges.

## Thorough Updating

A 3-year search of tens of thousands of article titles led to nearly 3000 filed items, which were winnowed to 829 new citations (32 percent of the book's references). I aim not to drown the reader with bibliography, but to credit and make available both classic and current information.

## Integrated and Focused Coverage of Culture and Gender

Introductory text authors wrestle with whether to cover topics such as culture, ethnicity, and gender as an in-depth focus or whether to distribute such coverage in smaller bites throughout the text. This book pursues both strategies.

- *Focused coverage* of diversity in the book's capstone chapter addresses one of the great issues of our time: As people of differing cultures, ethnicities, and genders, how are we different and how we are alike? How can we understand and accept our diversity while affirming our human kinship? And how in a world torn asunder by differences can we define shared values? How can we realize the ideal of *community incorporating diversity?*
- *Integrated coverage* of diversity permeates the other chapters (see cross-references, below). For example, 60 percent of the book's 391 references to "culture" and "cultural" appear *before* Chapter 19. Countless additional mentions are made of specific ethnic and cultural groups. An inclusive illustration program makes human diversity visible. For this and succeeding editions my aim is more and more to offer a world-based psychology for a worldwide student body. Rather than covering multicultural and gender issues exclusively in boxes or special sections, all this is naturally embedded in the ongoing flow.

### Integrated Cultural Diversity

**From the Introduction to Chapter 18 the integrated coverage of cultural diversity permeates the book in discussions of culture and:**

**Integrated Gender Diversity**

**The psychology of women and men is similarly integrated into the book's ongoing narrative at dozens of points <u>before</u> Chapter 19:**



## Goals for the Fourth Edition

Throughout this revision, I have steadfastly followed eight principles:

1. ***To exemplify the process of inquiry*** I strive to show students not just the outcome of research, but how the research process works. Throughout, the book tries to excite the reader's curiosity. It invites readers to imagine themselves as participants in classic experiments. Several chapters introduce research stories as mysteries that progressively unravel as one clue after another falls into place.
2. ***To teach critical thinking*** By presenting research as intellectual detective work, I exemplify an inquiring, analytical mind-set. Whether students are studying development, cognition, or statistics, they will become involved in, and see the rewards of, critical reasoning. Moreover, they will discover how an empirical approach can help them evaluate competing ideas and claims for highly publicized phenomena—ranging from subliminal persuasion, ESP, and facilitated communication to astrology, basketball streak-shooting, and repressed and recovered memories.
3. ***To put facts in the service of concepts*** My intention is not to fill students' intellectual file drawers with facts, but to reveal psychology's major concepts—to teach students how to think, and to offer psychological ideas worth thinking about. In each chapter I place emphasis on those concepts I hope students will carry with them long after they complete the course. Always, I try to follow Albert Einstein's dictum that "Everything should be made as simple as possible, but not simpler."
4. ***To be as up-to-date as possible*** Few things dampen students' interests as quickly as the sense that they are reading stale news. While re-

taining psychology's classic studies and concepts, I also present the discipline's most important recent developments. Twenty-three percent of the references in this edition are dated 1992 to 1995.

5. ***To integrate principles and applications*** Throughout—by means of anecdotes, case histories, and the posing of hypothetical situations—I relate the findings of basic research to their applications and implications. Where psychology can illuminate pressing human issues—be they racism and sexism, health and happiness, or violence and war—I have not hesitated to shine its light.
6. ***To enhance comprehension by providing continuity*** Many chapters have a significant issue or theme that links subtopics, forming a thread that ties the chapter together. The Learning chapter conveys the idea that bold thinkers can serve as intellectual pioneers. The Thinking and Language chapter raises the issue of human rationality and irrationality. The Psychological Disorders chapter conveys empathy for, and understanding of, troubled lives. "The uniformity of a work," observed Edward Gibbon, "denotes the hand of a single artist." Because the book has a single author, other threads, such as nature-nurture interaction and cultural diversity, weave throughout the *whole* book, and students hear a consistent voice.
7. ***To reinforce learning at every step*** Everyday examples and rhetorical questions encourage students to process the material actively. Concepts presented earlier are frequently applied, and thereby reinforced, in later chapters. Marginal pedagogical aids augment learning without interrupting the text narrative. Major sections begin with previews and end with summaries that highlight the organization and key concepts. Chapters conclude with defined key terms (grouped by major chapter section), and suggested readings attuned to students' interests and abilities.
8. ***To convey respect for human unity and diversity*** Time and again, readers will see evidence of our human kinship—our shared biological heritage, our common mechanisms of seeing and learning, hungering and feeling, loving and hating. They will also better understand the dimensions of our diversity—our *individual* diversity in development and aptitudes, temperament and personality, and disorder and health; and our *cultural* diversity in attitudes and expressive styles, childrearing and care for the elderly, and life priorities.

## The Supplements Package

*Psychology* is accompanied by widely acclaimed materials to enhance teaching and learning. For students who desire additional help mastering the text, there is Richard O. Straub's (University of Michigan, Dearborn) *Study Guide.* Each chapter uses the *PRTR: Preview/Read/Think Critically/Review* format to guide students at each step of their study. For each section of the text chapter, a list is provided of the idioms and other phrases potentially unfamiliar to students for whom English is a second language. Each word or phrase is carefully explained and related to the text material. The list of words and phrases appears in the Guided Study section, and the definitions are provided at the back of the chapter in a clearly defined box. Progress tests help students check their mastery of the material. The study guide is also computerized in a highly interactive program for use on IBM PC or Macintosh computers.

The *Instructor's Resources*, created by Martin Bolt (Calvin College) for *Psychology*, has been hailed as the finest set of psychology teaching resources ever assembled. With 25 percent new items in this edition, it features dozens of ready-to-use demonstration handouts, along with learning objectives, lecture/discussion ideas, student projects, classroom exercises, and video and film suggestions. Martin Bolt's *Lecture Guides*, which come in both printed and easily modifiable IBM PC and Macintosh formats, offer instructors an additional resource for lecture preparation.

The award-winning computer software developed by Thomas Ludwig (Hope College) brings some of psychology's most important concepts and methods to life. *PsychSim: Interactive Graphic Simulations for Psychology* contains 20 programs, including four new to this edition, for use in the Macintosh or IBM Windows formats. Some simulations engage the student as experimenter—conditioning a rat, electrically probing the hypothalamus, or working in a sleep lab. Others engage the student as subject—responding to tests of memory or visual illusions, or interpreting facial expressions. Still others provide a dynamic tutorial/demonstration of, say, hemispheric processing or cognitive development principles. Student worksheets are provided. The *PsychSim* programs for this edition are significantly enhanced over an earlier version that received the 1990 Educom/NCRIPTAL Higher Education Software Award for "Best Psychology Software"—marking the first time that software specifically designed for introductory psychology has been so honored.

The *Test Bank*, by John Brink (Calvin College), provides a minimum of 150 questions per chapter for a total of 3150 multiple-choice questions, plus essay questions. Each question is keyed to a learning objective, page-referenced to the textbook, and rated in level of difficulty. (Optional questions are also included for the *PsychSim* programs and *The Brain* and *The Mind* modules, see below.) The *Test Bank* is available in test-generation systems for IBM PC, Macintosh, and the Apple II family of microcomputers.

Our *Psychology Videodisc* will help you bring to life for your students all of the major topics in *Psychology*, combining brief, exciting video clips and animated segments with a library of stills. This two-sided CAV videodisc is accompanied by an extensive *Instructor's Guide*, by Martin Bolt and Richard O. Straub, complete with bar codes, descriptions of each item and suggestions for how to incorporate the material into your lecture, and a subject index that references and cross-references all items by topic across chapters. A software package by Thomas Ludwig, for use on IBM-PC or Macintosh computers, includes an indexing program as well as slide show and lecture template programs. The indexing program makes it easy to assemble a list of relevant videodisc clips and stills for any lecture topic. Instructors may print this list for use with a remote control keypad or barcode reader, or may control the videodisc player directly from the computer to display the clips and stills in "slide show" fashion or as part of a complete computerized lecture.

For users of the *Discovering Psychology* telecourse, we now have a *Discovering Psychology* Study Guide. This Study Guide is designed for use with the text and with the *Discovering Psychology* telecourse, narrated by Philip Zimbardo and produced by the Annenberg/CPB Project. Based on the idea that learning is most effective when it is active, this Study Guide contains objectives to be answered as the student reads the text and views the video. Progress tests, including a minimum of 50 multiple-choice questions, help students to check their mastery of the material. The questions for the two media are carefully integrated to make the text and program work together.

In addition, Worth Publishers has produced 38 video modules from *The Mind* series, in association with WNET. These modules were edited by

Frank Vattano (Colorado State University) with the consultation of Charles Brewer (Furman University) and myself. Rather than displace the instructor, as do longer films, these brief clips (which can be dubbed onto individual cassettes) dramatically enhance and illustrate lectures. They do so in ways that written and spoken words cannot—by introducing students to a split-brain patient being tested, a sleeping subject being monitored in a lab, a patient suffering the ravages of schizophrenia, and so forth. In addition to the 38 modules on videocassettes available from Worth Publishers, there is now a two-sided CAV videodisc that includes 14 highlights from *The Mind* modules. These are also available from Worth Publishers, accompanied by a bar-coded Faculty Guide.

Finally, an exciting new CD-ROM version of *Psychology* will be available for students in the fall of 1995. This interactive product will include the text of the book as well as its illustrations, the *PsychSim* modules, the Study Guide, and a set of video and audio clips.

## In Appreciation

If it is true that "whoever walks with the wise becomes wise" then I am wiser for all the wisdom and advice received from expert colleagues. Aided by some 300 consultants and reviewers over the last decade, this has become a better, more accurate book than one author alone (this author, at least) could write. My indebtedness continues to each of the teacher-scholars whose influence I acknowledged in the three previous editions.

My gratitude now extends to the colleagues who contributed criticism, corrections, and creative ideas to this new edition. For this expertise and encouragement, I thank the following reviewers:

**Emir Andrews,** *Memorial University*

**Michael L. Atkinson,** *University of Western Ontario*

**Marvin Brown,** *University of Saskatchewan*

**Kaye K. Diefenderfer,** *Seminole Community College*

**Bruce Earhard,** *Dalhousie University*

**Gail A. Eskes,** *Victoria General Hospital*

**Julie Felender,** *Fullerton College*

**Geoffrey T. Fong,** *University of Waterloo*

**Bennett G. Galef, Jr.,** *McMaster University*

**Meg Gerrard,** *Iowa State University*

**Phillip Goernert,** *Mankato State University*

**John P. Governale,** *Clark College*

**Richard A. Griggs,** *University of Florida*

**Elaine Hauff,** *Minneapolis Community College*

**Bryan Hendricks,** *University of Wisconsin*

**John Hinchy**, *Deakin University*

**Patricia Keith-Spiegel,** *Ball State University*

**Lynn Kiorpes,** *New York University*

**Peter K. Leppmann,** *University of Guelph*

**Thomas W. Lombardo,** *University of Mississippi*

**Thomas Ludwig,** *Hope College*

**William Moorcroft,** *Luther College*

**Joel Morgovsky**, *Brookdale Community College*

**Darwin Muir,** *Queen's University*

**Linden L. Nelson,** *California Polytechnic State University*

**Elizabeth Weiss Ozorak,** *Allegheny College*

**Les Parrott,** *Seattle Pacific University*

**Robert Patterson,** *Washington State University*

**Sergio M. Pellis,** *University of Lethbridge*

**Jeffrey E. Pfeifer,** *University of Regina*

**Peter Platenius,** *Queen's University*

**Leon Rappoport,** *Kansas State University*

**Robert D. Ridge,** *Brigham Young University*

**Greg Robinson-Riegler,** *University of St. Thomas*

**Patricia Roehling,** *Hope College*

**John Shaughnessy,** *Hope College*

**Charles M. Slem,** *California Polytechnic State University*

**James R. Stellar,** *Northeastern University*

**Jonathan Tudge,** *University of North Carolina-Greensboro*

**Scott Vrana,** *Purdue University*

**William P. Wallace,** *University of Nevada-Reno*

**Dennis Wanamaker,** *Bellevue Community College*

**Joyann Ward,** *Spokane Community College*

**John E. Williams,** *Wake Forest University*

**Gordon Wood,** *Michigan State University*

**Mary Lou Zanich,** *Indiana University of Pennsylvania*

**Otto Zinser,** *East Tennessee State University*

Charles Brewer (Furman University) enhanced this book with meticulous critiques, probing questions, and spirit-sustaining encouragement through its first three editions, and helped define priorities as a special consultant at the planning stage of this new edition.

At Worth Publishers—a company with a passion for excellence—a host of people played key roles. Alison Meersschaert commissioned the book and helped me envision its goals. Managing editor Anne Vinnicombe brought the first two editions to fulfillment while painstakingly scrutinizing the accuracy, logic, and clarity of every page.

Christine Brune, chief editor for the last two editions, is a wonder worker. She offers just the right mix of encouragement, gentle admonition, and attention to detail, while coordinating the whole team of reviewers, editors, and supplements authors. An author could not ask for more.

Other Worth staff also played essential roles. Freelance copyeditor Nancy Fleming sensitively fine-tuned the final manuscript. Production editor Barbara B. Toniolo effectively guided the transformation of manuscript into book. And Worth's gifted artistic and production team, including George Touloumes, Sarah Segal, Demetrios Zangos, and Matthew Dvorozniak again crafted the elegant product before you.

At Hope College, the supporting team members for this edition included Kim Ebright and Mary Lee Pikey, who researched countless bits of information and proofed hundreds of pages. In this effort, they were supported by my endlessly supportive librarian colleagues. Mary Lee Pikey also prepared the name index. With infectious good cheer, Kathy Adamski composed my awkward dictation into hundreds of letters to researchers. Typesetters Phyllis and Richard Vandervelde met or exceeded all deadlines, often by working into the wee hours to enter or revise every one of the more than 400,000 words, and finally to code them for electronic delivery.

Again, I gratefully acknowledge the influence of my writing coach, poet Jack Ridl, whose influence lingers in the voice you will be hearing in the pages that follow. He more than anyone cultivated my delight in dancing with the language, and taught me to approach writing as a craft that shades into art.

After hearing countless dozens of people say that this book's supplements have taken their teaching to a new level, I reflect on how fortunate I am to be a part of a team on which everyone has produced on-time work marked by the highest professional standards. For their remarkable talents, their dedication, and their friendship, I thank Martin Bolt, John Brink, Thomas Ludwig, and Richard Straub. Martin also played a key role in inspiring and guiding the formation of the new Introduction and Chapter 1. And Rick Straub authored the critical thinking exercises that appear at the end of each chapter.

Finally, my gratitude extends to the students and instructors who have written to offer suggestions, or just an encouraging word. It is for them, and those about to begin their study of psychology, that I have done my best to introduce the field I love.

When those who paint the Golden Gate Bridge finish, it is time to start over again. So with this book. The ink is barely dry before one begins envisioning the next edition. By the time you read this, I will be gathering information for the fifth edition. Letters and now electronic mail will again influence how this book continues to evolve. So, please, do share your thoughts.

David G. Myers

Hope College
Holland, Michigan 49422-9000
USA
E-mail: myers@hope.edu

# Psychology

Psychology's Roots

Psychology's Big Issues

Psychology's Subfields

Studying Psychology

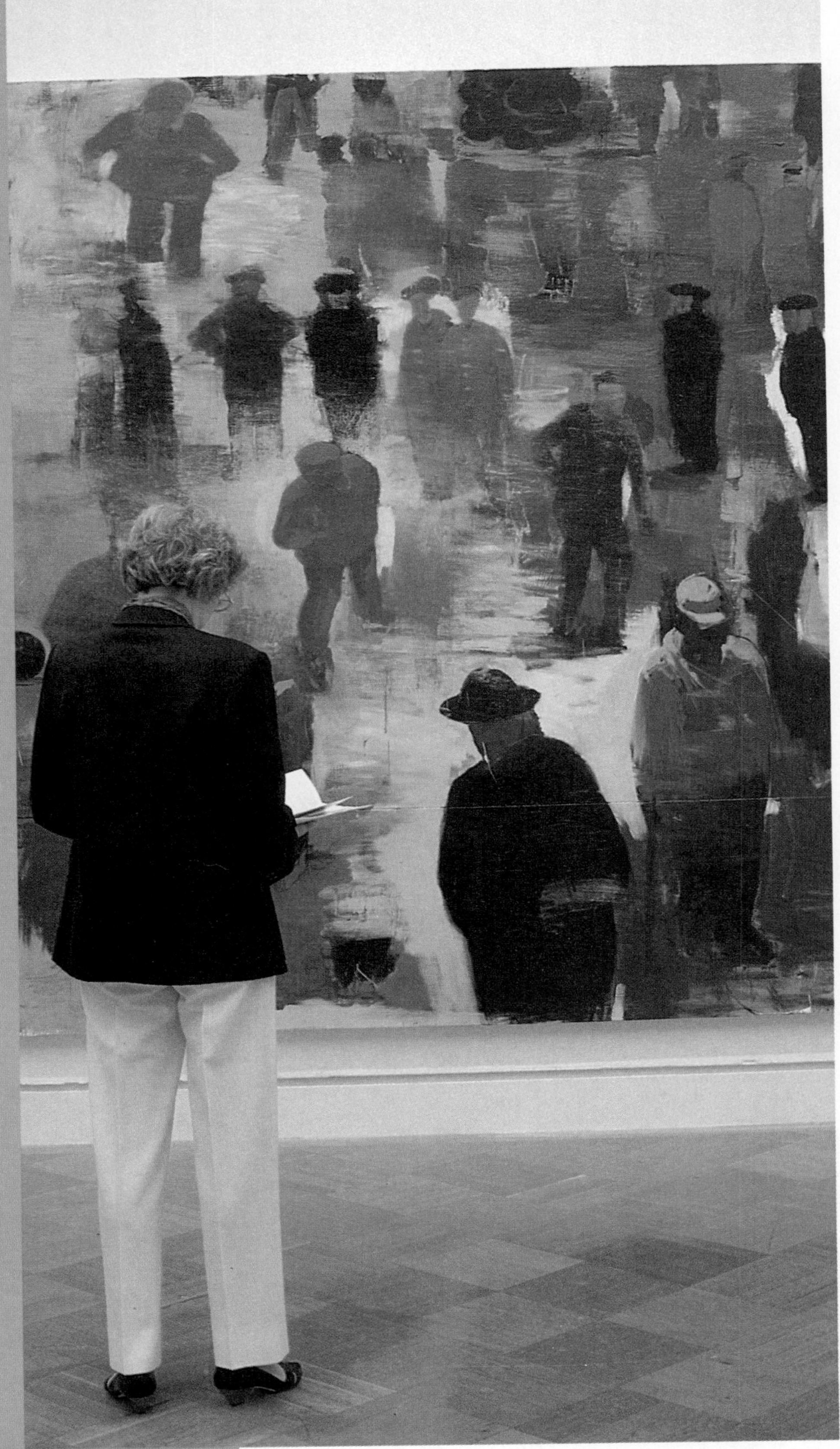

# Introduction

I was relaxing in the barber's black leather chair, enjoying my last haircut before leaving Seattle, when the barber struck up a conversation:

*"What do you do?"*

*"Next week I'll be moving to Iowa to begin graduate school," I replied.*

*"What are you studying?"*

*"Psychology."*

The haircutting ceased as the friendly barber took a step back and timidly wondered aloud:

*"So what do you think of me?"*

For my barber, as for many people whose exposure to psychology comes mostly from popular books, magazines, and TV, psychologists analyze personality, practice psychotherapy, and dispense child-rearing advice.

Do they? Yes, and much more. Consider some of psychology's questions, questions that from time to time you may wonder about:

Have you ever found yourself reacting to something just as one of your parents would—perhaps in a way you vowed you never would—and then wondered how much of your personality you inherited? To what degree are you really like your mother or your father? *To what extent is your parents' influence transmitted through their genes? To what extent through the environment they gave you?*

Have you ever played peekaboo with a 6-month-old infant and wondered why the baby finds the game so delightful? The baby reacts as though, when you momentarily move behind a door, you actually disappear—only to reappear later out of thin air. *What do babies actually perceive and think?*

Have you ever awakened from a nightmare and, with a wave of relief, wondered why we have such crazy dreams? *How often, and why, do we dream?*

Have you ever been to a circus and wondered how they trained the poodles to dance, the lions to jump through hoops, the chimps to ride bikes? *What are the limits on what we can train animals to do?*

Do you ever get depressed or anxious and wonder whether you'll ever feel "normal"? *What triggers our bad moods—and our good ones?*

Have you ever worried about how to act among people of a different culture, race, or sex? In what ways are we alike as members of the human family? How do we differ? As citizens of multicultural countries and a shrinking global village, *how can we build community while accepting our diversity?*

Such questions provide grist for psychology's mill, for psychology is a science that seeks to answer all sorts of questions about us all: how we think, feel, and act.

## Psychology's Roots

*Psychology has developed from international and multidisciplinary roots to become a science that aims to describe and explain how we think, feel, and act. This book shows how smart thinking people can apply psychology's strategies, and it highlights psychology's most humanly significant findings.*

Psychology is a young science with roots in many disciplines, from physiology to philosophy. Wilhelm Wundt, who founded the first psychology laboratory in 1879 at Germany's University of Leipzig, was both a physiologist and a philosopher. Ivan Pavlov, who pioneered the study of learning, was a Russian physiologist. Sigmund Freud, renowned personality theorist, was an Austrian physician. Jean Piaget, this century's most influential observer of children, was a Swiss biologist. William James, author of an important 1890 psychology textbook, was an American philosopher.

"I'm a social scientist, Michael. That means I can't explain electricity or anything like that, but if you ever want to know about people I'm your man."

Drawing by Handelsman; ©1986 The New Yorker Magazine, Inc.

This list of pioneering psychologists—"Magellans of the mind," as Morton Hunt (1993) calls them—illustrates that psychology has its origins not only in many disciplines but also in many countries. Today, psychology's researchers and students, like its historic pioneers, are citizens of many lands. In the last few decades, psychology has flourished more in North America, where there are now about 200,000 psychologists, than in Third World countries such as China (2000 psychologists), Nicaragua (500 psychologists), or Nigeria (fewer than 100 psychologists) (Akin-Ogundeji, 1991; Antaki, 1989; DeAngelis, 1988; Vetter, 1989). Nevertheless, the field is thriving, from Australia to Western Europe to the developing nations. Worldwide, the number of psychologists—now well over 500,000 men and women—has doubled since 1980 (Rosenzweig, 1992).

So what is psychology? With research ranging from recording nerve cell activity to studying psychotherapy's effectiveness, psychology is not easily defined. Psychology began as the science of mental life. Just over a century ago, Wilhelm Wundt's basic research tool was introspection—self-examination of one's own emotional states and mental processes. Wundt focused on *inner* sensations, feelings, and thoughts. Thus, until the 1920s, psychology was defined as "the science of mental life."

From the 1920s into the 1960s, American psychologists redefined psychology as "the science of observable behavior." After all, they said, science is rooted in observation. You cannot observe a sensation, a feeling, or a thought, but you *can* observe people's *behavior* as they respond to different situations.

In the 1960s, psychology began to recapture its initial interest in mental processes through studies of how our minds process and retain information. To encompass psychology's concern both with overt behavior and with covert thoughts and feelings, **psychology** has become *the science of behavior and mental processes.*

*Throughout this book, important concepts are set in boldface type. As you study, you can find these terms with their definitions both at the end of each chapter and at the end of the book. Information sources are cited in parentheses, with name and date, then provided fully in the References section at the book's end.*

Let's unpack this definition. *Behavior* is anything an organism *does*—any action we can observe and record. Yelling, smiling, blinking, sweating, talking, and questionnaire-marking are all observable behaviors. *Mental processes* are the internal subjective experiences we infer from behavior—the sensations, perceptions, dreams, thoughts, beliefs, and feelings.

For many psychologists, the key word in psychology's definition is *science.* Psychology, as I will emphasize in Chapter 1 and throughout this book, is less a set of findings than a way of asking and answering questions. As a *science*, psychology aims to sift opinions and evaluate ideas with careful observation and rigorous analysis. In its quest to describe and explain nature (human nature included), psychological science welcomes hunches and plausible-sounding theories. And it puts them to the test. If a theory works—if the data support its predictions—so much the better for it. If the predictions fail, the theory gets rejected or revised.

My aim in this text, then, is not merely to report results but to show you how we play the game. How do research psychologists sift contesting opinions and ideas? And how might all of us, whether scientists or simply curious people, think smarter when describing and explaining the events of our lives?

Of course, psychology also has content: Its scientific sifting of ideas has produced a smorgasbord of concepts and findings, from which we can only sample the fare. Once aware of psychology's well-researched ideas—about how body and mind connect, how a child's mind grows, how we construct our perceptions, how we remember (and misremember) our experiences, how people across the world differ (and are alike)—your mind may never again be quite the same.

*"Once expanded to the dimensions of a larger idea, [the mind] never returns to its original size."*

Jurist Oliver Wendell Holmes, 1841–1935

## Psychology's Big Issues

*Several issues cut across psychology, the most persistent of which concerns the impact of biological nature and experienced nurture. Differing perspectives on such issues often prove complementary.*

During its short history, psychology has wrestled with some issues that will reappear throughout this book. One such issue concerns *stability versus change.* Do our individual traits persist as we age? Do we become older versions of our same old selves? Does a reactive infant become a volatile adult? Or do people change? Can shy preschoolers become senior class clowns? Can troubled teens become mature executives? Do people exhibit apparently differing personalities in different situations?

Another issue concerns human *rationality versus irrationality.* How deserving are we of our name *homo sapiens*—wise humans? We will see that in some ways— recognizing patterns, handling language, processing abstract ideas—we outstrip the smartest computers. The simple act of perceiving this book involves disassembling visual stimuli into millions of nerve impulses, distributing them for processing in different brain regions, and then, in an imperceptible instant, reassembling the information into a colorful image. As human observers we all have an urge to explain behavior, to attribute it to some cause. Indeed, using certain rules of thumb, we make snap judgments with amazing efficiency and sufficient rationality. "How noble in reason!" declared Shakespeare's Hamlet.

But we are prone to err. We sometimes shoehorn reality into our preconceptions. We deceive ourselves about the accuracy of our memories. We overestimate our judgments. We often are swayed more by compelling anecdotes than by statistical reality. We "see" causes and associations that don't exist. We treat others in ways that lead them to confirm our mistaken ideas about them. These limits to human rationality—also spelled out in the pages to come—caused philosopher Bertrand Russell to lament that "most people would sooner die than think; in fact, they do so."

**Like Peas in a Pod** *Because identical twins have the same genes, they are ideal subjects for studies designed to shed light on hereditary and environmental influences on temperament, intelligence, and other traits. Studies of identical and fraternal twins have provided a rich array of findings—described in later chapters—that underscore the importance of both* nature *and* nurture.

The biggest and most persistent issue, however, concerns the relative contributions of biology and experience. This **nature-nurture** debate is long-standing. The ancient Greek philosopher Plato assumed that character and intelligence are largely inherited and that certain ideas are inborn. Aristotle replied that there is nothing in the mind that does not first come in from the external world through the senses. In the 1600s, philosophers rekindled the debate. John Locke believed that the mind is a blank slate at birth and that most knowledge comes in through the senses. René Descartes believed that some ideas are innate.

The nature-nurture debate weaves a thread from the distant past to our time. Today's psychologists have continued the debate by asking these and other questions:

- Are intelligence, personality, obesity, and psychological disorders more influenced by heredity or by environment?
- Is children's grammar innate or shaped by experience?
- Are eating and sexual behavior more "pushed" by inner biology or "pulled" by external incentives?
- Is depression a brain disorder or a thought disorder?
- How are humans alike (thanks to their common biology) and different (thanks to their differing cultures)?
- Are gender differences biologically predisposed or socially constructed?

Over and over again we will see the nature-nurture tension dissolve: Nurture works on what nature endows. Unlike reptiles, our species is biologically endowed with an enormous capacity to learn and adapt. Moreover, every psychological event (every thought, every emotion) is simultaneously a biological event. Thus depression can be *both* a brain disorder and a thought disorder.

Take an emotion such as anger. Someone working from a *biological perspective* might study the brain circuits that trigger the physical state of being "red in the face" and "hot under the collar." But as Table 1 shows, there are other perspectives as well. Someone working from a *behavioral perspective* might study the facial expressions and body gestures that accompany anger, or might attempt to determine which external stimuli result in angry responses or aggressive acts. Someone working from a *cognitive perspective* might study how our interpretation of a situation affects our anger and how our anger affects our thinking. Someone working from a *social-cultural perspective* might explore which situations produce the most anger, and how expressions of anger vary across cultural contexts.

Such perspectives needn't contradict one another. Rather, they are complementary outlooks on the same biological state. It's like explaining why grizzly bears hibernate. Is it because their inner physiology drives them to do so? Because cold environments hinder food gathering during winter? Both perspectives are useful, and they complement each other.

This important point—that different perspectives on the big issues can complement one another—is also true of the different academic disciplines. Each provides a particular perspective on nature and our place in it. The basic sciences investigate nature's building blocks, seeking principles based on objective observation. The humanities (literature, philosophy, and the like) address questions of life's meaning and value, using more subjective methods. Psychology lies near the middle of this continuum; it uses scientific methods to explore our thoughts and actions.

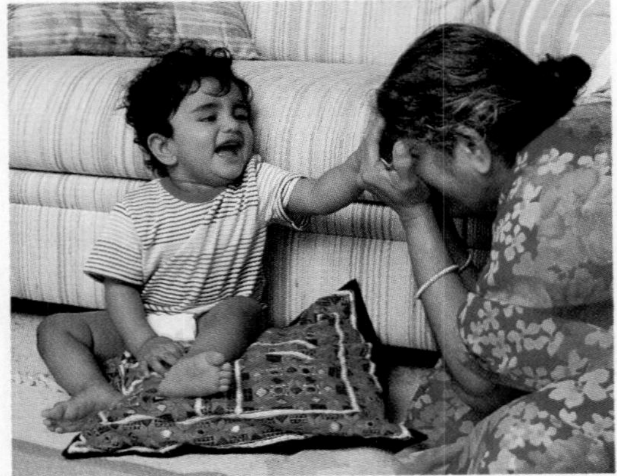

**I See You!** *A biological psychologist might view this child's delighted response as evidence for brain maturation. A cognitive psychologist might see it as a demonstration of the baby's growing knowledge of his surroundings. For a cross-cultural psychologist the role of grandparents in different societies might be the issue of interest. As you will see throughout this book, different perspectives offer complementary views of behavior.*

**Table 1 Psychology's Current Perspectives**

| Perspective | Focus | Sample Issues |
|---|---|---|
| *Biological* | How the body and brain create emotions, memories, and sensory experiences | How do evolution and heredity influence behavior? How are messages transmitted within the body? How is blood chemistry linked with moods and motives? |
| *Behavioral* | How we learn observable responses | How do we learn to fear particular objects or situations? What is the most effective way to alter our behavior, say, to lose weight or stop smoking? |
| *Cognitive* | How we process, store, and retrieve information | How do we use information in remembering? Reasoning? Solving problems? |
| *Social-cultural* | How behavior and thinking vary across situations and cultures | How are we—as Africans, Asians, Australians, or North Americans—alike as members of one human family? As products of different environmental contexts, how do we differ? |

Each perspective has its questions and its limits. Differing perspectives are like different two-dimensional views of a three-dimensional object (Figure 1). Each two-dimensional perspective is helpful, but none by itself reveals the whole picture.

So bear in mind psychology's limits. Don't expect psychology to answer the ultimate questions posed by Russian novelist Leo Tolstoy (1904): "Why should I live? Why should I do anything? Is there in life any purpose which the inevitable death that awaits me does not undo and destroy?" Instead, expect that psychology will help you understand why people think, feel, and act as they do. Then you should find the study of psychology both fascinating and useful.

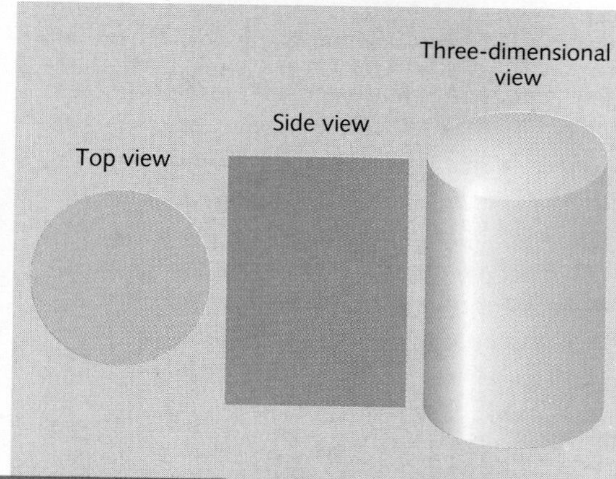


**Figure 1**

**Complementary Perspectives** *What is this object? One person, looking down from the top, sees a disk. Another, looking at it from the side, sees a rectangle. Their differing perspectives seem contradictory. In fact, they are complementary, for we can assemble these images into a three-dimensional view of the object, a cylinder. The views offered by psychology's different perspectives are often like this: A lot depends on your point of view.*

## Psychology's Subfields

*Psychology is a collection of diverse subfields. Some psychologists do basic research, some do applied research, and some provide professional services.*

Picturing a chemist at work, you probably envision a white-coated scientist surrounded by glassware and high-tech equipment. Picture a psychologist at work and you would be right to envision

- a white-coated scientist probing a rat's brain.
- an intelligence researcher measuring how quickly an infant becomes bored with (looks away from) a familiar picture.
- an executive proposing a new "healthy lifestyles" employee-training program.

- someone at a computer keyboard, analyzing data on whether adopted teens have temperaments more like their adoptive parents or like their biological parents.
- a traveler en route to collecting data on human values and behaviors in different cultures.
- a therapist, listening carefully to a client's depressed thoughts.

The conglomeration of subfields that we call psychology has less unity than most other sciences. But there is a payoff: Psychology is a meeting ground for different disciplines, and thus a perfect home for those with wide-ranging interests. In their diverse activities, from biological experimentation to cultural comparisons, psychologists share a common quest: describing and explaining behavior and the mental processes that underlie it.

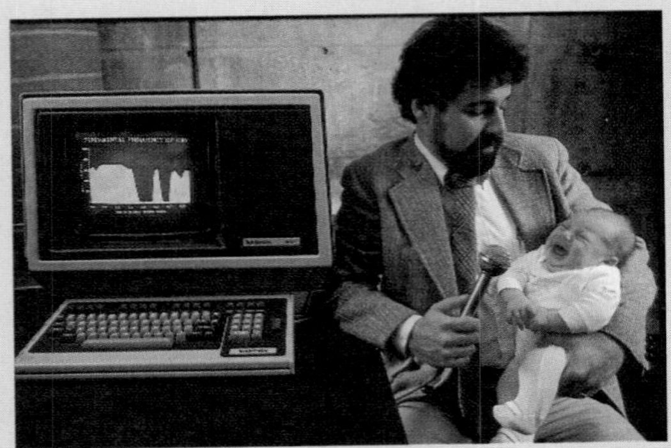

**Psychology: A Science and a Profession** *In their laboratories and consulting rooms, psychologists study and treat a wide range of human conditions. Here you can see sound-analyzing technology being used to monitor infant brain development, a graduate student running a laboratory experiment on social judgment, and a face-to-face encounter typical of psychotherapy.*

Some psychologists conduct **basic research** that builds psychology's knowledge base. In the pages to follow we will meet a wide variety of such researchers: *biological psychologists* exploring the links between brain and mind; *developmental psychologists* studying our changing abilities from womb to tomb; *personality psychologists* investigating our inner traits.

Other psychologists conduct **applied research** that tackles practical problems. For example, *industrial/organizational psychologists* study and advise on behavior in the workplace. They use psychology's concepts and methods to help organizations select and train employees, boost morale and productivity, and design products and assess people's responses to them.

Although all introductory psychology texts focus on the methods and results of psychological science, psychology is also a helping profession devoted to such practical issues as how to have a happy marriage, how to overcome anxiety or depression, and how to raise children. **Clinical psychologists** study, assess, and treat troubled people. After graduate school training, they administer and interpret tests, provide psychotherapy, manage mental health programs, and conduct research. By contrast, **psychiatrists**, who also often provide psychotherapy, are medical doctors licensed to prescribe drugs and otherwise treat physical causes of psychological disorders. In both of these mental health professions, some practitioners are influenced by Sigmund Freud's *psychoanalytic perspective*, which saw problems arising from unconscious desires and unresolved childhood conflicts.

With perspectives ranging from the biological to the social, and with settings from the clinic to the laboratory, psychology has become a meeting place for many disciplines. More and more, psychology connects with fields ranging from mathematics and biology to sociology and philosophy. And more and more, psychology's methods and findings aid other disciplines. Psychologists teach in medical schools, law schools, and theological seminaries, and they work in hospitals, factories, and corporate offices. They engage in interdisciplinary studies, such as psychohistory—the psychological analysis of historical characters—and psycholinguistics—the study of the relationship between language and its users' thinking and behavior.

*Not yet an interdisciplinary field: psychoceramics, the study of crackpots.*

Psychology's influence also penetrates into modern culture. Knowledge transforms. Learning to read, to understand the solar system, and to comprehend the germ theory of disease alters the way people think and act. Learning psychology's findings also changes people: They no longer judge psychological disorders as a moral failing, treatable by punishment and ostracism. They less often regard and treat women as men's mental inferiors. They no longer view and rear children as ignorant, willful beasts in need of taming. "In each case," notes Morton Hunt (1990, p. 206), "knowledge has modified attitudes, and, through them, behavior."

## Studying Psychology

*Although psychology has much to offer, mastering it requires active study. A preview-read-think-review study method, supplemented by other effective study principles, should boost your learning and performance.*

The investment you are making in studying psychology has the potential to enrich your life and enlarge your vision. Although many of life's significant questions are beyond psychology, some very important ones are illuminated by even a first psychology course. Through painstaking research, psychologists have gained insights into brain and mind, depression and joy, dreams and memories. Even the unanswered questions can enrich us, by renewing our sense of mystery about "things too wonderful" for us yet to understand. What is more, your study of psychology can help teach you *how to ask and answer important questions*—how to think critically as you evaluate competing ideas and claims.

Having your life enriched and your vision enlarged (and getting a decent grade, too) requires effective study. As you will see in Chapter 9, to master any subject you must *actively process* it. Your mind is not like your stomach, something to be filled passively; it is more like a muscle, which grows stronger with exercise. Countless experiments reveal that people learn and remember material best when they put it in their own words, rehearse it, and then review and rehearse it again.

A simple study method incorporates these principles. You can remember it as PRTR: *P*review, *R*ead, *T*hink critically, and *R*eview.

First, *preview* what you're about to read. Note its organization (as hinted in the italicized preview sentences that begin most main sections). This provides a framework on which you can hang the information to come. We remember organized information more easily than we remember disorganized facts.

Second, *read* the section you have previewed. Usually a single main chapter section will be as much as you can absorb without tiring. Treat each main chapter section as if it were a whole chapter.

Third, *think actively and critically.* Ask questions. Make notes. Reflect on implications: How does what you've read support or challenge your assumptions? How does it relate to your own life?

Fourth, *review.* To drive a section's organization more deeply into your memory, rescan the section or read its Summing Up paragraphs. Glance over your notes or highlighting. Then stop and let it all sink in.

Preview, read, think, review. I have organized the chapters to facilitate your using the PRTR study method. Each chapter begins with an outline that helps you to preview upcoming material, and each main section begins with an italicized two- or three-sentence preview. I have divided chapters into three to five main sections of readable length. To assist your reviewing of what you've read, each main section ends with a summary (as if it were a little chapter). Then the whole chapter ends with an organized reminder of key terms and their definitions. Preview, read, think, review.

Four additional study hints may further boost your learning:

1. ***Distribute your study time.*** One of psychology's oldest findings is that "spaced practice" promotes better retention than "massed practice." You'll remember material better if you space your time over several study periods—perhaps 1 hour a day, 6 days a week—rather than cram it into one long study blitz. Spacing your study sessions requires a disciplined approach to managing your time. (Richard O. Straub explains time management in the *Study Guide* that accompanies this text.) For example, rather than trying to read a whole chapter in a single sitting, read just one of the chapter's main sections and then turn to something else.
2. ***In class, listen actively.*** As psychologist William James urged nearly 100 years ago, *"No reception without reaction, no impression without . . . expression."* Listen for the main idea and sub-ideas in lectures. *Write them down.* Ask questions during and after class. In class, as in your private study, process the information actively and you will understand and retain it better.
3. ***Overlearn.*** Psychology tells us that "overlearning improves retention." The more often students read a chapter and the fewer classes they miss, the better their exam scores are (Woehr & Cavell, 1993). Students frequently stop short of overlearning and overestimate how much they know. You may understand a chapter as you read it, but if you devote extra study time to rereading, to testing yourself, and to reviewing what you think you know, you will retain your new knowledge farther into the future.
4. ***Be a smart test-taker.*** If a test contains both multiple-choice questions and an essay question, turn first to the essay. Read the question carefully, noting exactly what the instructor is asking. On the back of a page, pencil in a list of points you'd like to make, and then organize them. Before writing, put the essay aside and work through the multiple-choice questions. (As you do so, you may continue to mull over the essay question. Sometimes the objective questions will bring per-

tinent thoughts to mind.) Then reread the essay question, rethink your answer, and start writing. When you finish, proofread your work to eliminate spelling and grammatical errors that make you look less competent than you are.

When reading multiple-choice questions, don't confuse yourself by trying to imagine how each choice might be the right one. Try instead to answer the question as if it were a fill-in-the-blank. First, cover the answers, recall what you know, and complete the sentence in your mind. Then read the answers on the test and find the alternative that best matches your own answer.

As you read psychology, you will learn much more than effective study techniques. Psychology teaches us how to ask important questions—how to think critically as we evaluate competing ideas and popular claims. It deepens our appreciation for how we humans perceive, think, feel, and act. By so doing it can enrich our lives and enlarge our vision. Through this book I hope to help guide you toward that end. As educator Charles Eliot said a century ago, "Books are the quietest and most constant of friends, and the most patient of teachers."

## Terms and Concepts to Remember

**psychology** The science of behavior and mental processes.

**nature-nurture issue** The long-standing controversy over the relative contributions that genes and experience make to the development of psychological traits and behaviors.

**basic research** Pure science that aims to increase the scientific knowledge base.

**applied research** Scientific study that aims to solve practical problems.

**clinical psychology** A branch of psychology involving the assessment and treatment of those who suffer psychological disorders.

**psychiatry** A branch of medicine dealing with psychological disorders; practiced by physicians and sometimes involving medical (for example, drug) treatments as well as psychological therapy.

# CHAPTER 1



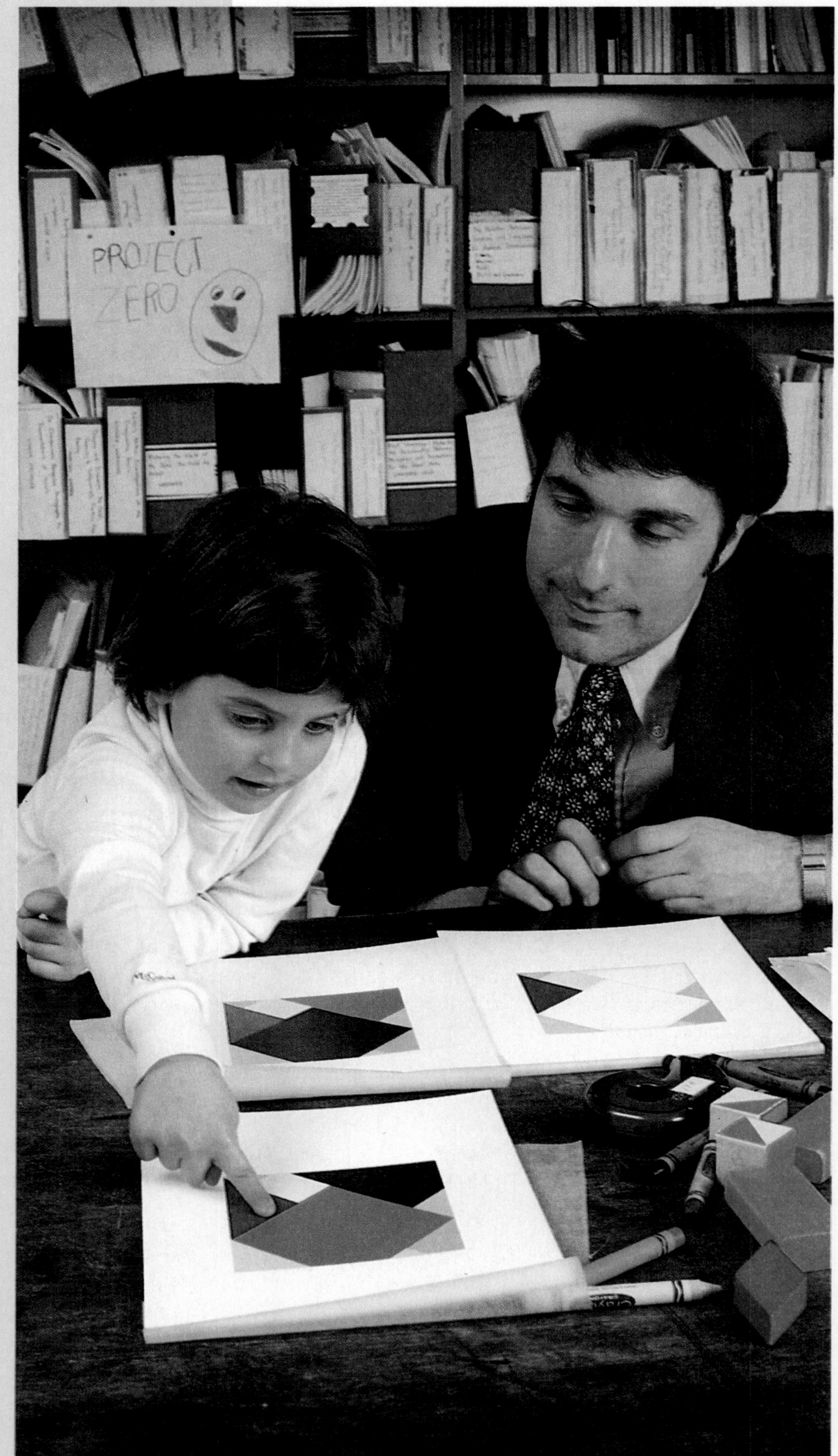

# Thinking Critically With Psychological Science

*What good fortune for those in power that people do not think.*

Adolph Hitler, 1889–1945

*Although in some ways we outsmart the smartest computers, our intuition often goes awry. To err is human. Enter psychological science. With its procedures for gathering and sifting evidence, science restrains error. As we familiarize ourselves with its strategies and incorporate its underlying principles into our daily thinking, we can think smarter.*

Hoping to satisfy their curiosity about people and to remedy their woes, millions of people turn to "psychology." They listen to talk shows featuring over-the-air counseling, read magazine columns on harnessing psychic powers, attend seminars on how to stop smoking through hypnosis, and browse self-help books on the meaning of dreams, the secrets of ecstatic love, the roots of personal happiness.

Others, intrigued by claims of psychological truth, wonder: Do mothers and infants bond in the first hours after birth? Should we trust memories, "recovered" in adulthood, of child sexual abuse—and prosecute the alleged predators? Are first-born children more driven to achieve? Does handwriting give clues to personality? Does psychotherapy help?

In answering such questions, how can we separate pseudopsychology from the science of behavior and mental processes? Mere opinions from examined conclusions? *How can we use psychology to understand why people think, feel, and act as they do?*

## The Scientific Attitude

*A scientific approach to nature and to life is undergirded by curious* skepticism *and open-minded* humility. *The critical inquiry that flows from such attitudes helps winnow sense from nonsense.*

Underlying all science is a hard-headed curiosity, a passion to explore and understand without fooling or being fooled. Some questions (Is there life after death?) are beyond science. To answer them either way requires a leap of faith. With many other ideas, the proof is in the pudding. No matter how sensible or crazy-sounding an idea, the hard-headed question is, Does it work? When put to the test, can we confirm its predictions?

This scientific approach has a long history. How to evaluate a self-proclaimed prophet? Moses' answer: Put the prophet to the test. If the predicted event "does not take place or prove true," then so much the worse

**The Amazing Randi** *The magician James Randi, shown here with the "Alexander the Man Who Knows" machine, is an exemplar of skepticism. He has tested and effectively debunked a variety of psychic phenomena.*

for the prophet (Deuteronomy 18:22). Magician James Randi uses Moses' approach when testing those claiming to see auras around people's bodies:

**Randi:** *Do you see an aura around my head?*

**Aura-seer:** *Yes, indeed.*

**Randi:** *Can you still see the aura if I put this magazine in front of my face?*

**Aura-seer:** *Of course.*

**Randi:** *Then if I were to step behind a wall barely taller than I am, you could determine my location from the aura visible above my head, right?*

Randi tells me that no aura-seer has yet agreed to take this simple test.

When subjected to such scrutiny, crazy-sounding ideas sometimes find support. During the 1700s, scientists scoffed at the notion that meteorites had extraterrestrial origins. When two Yale scientists dared to deviate from the conventional opinion, Thomas Jefferson jeered, "Gentlemen, I would rather believe that those two Yankee Professors would lie than to believe that stones fell from heaven." Sometimes scientific inquiry refutes skeptics.

More often, it relegates crazy-sounding ideas to the mountain of forgotten claims of perpetual motion machines, cancer cures, and out-of-body travels into centuries past. To sift reality from fantasy, sense from nonsense, therefore requires a scientific attitude: being skeptical but not cynical, humbly open but not gullible.

*"A skeptic is one who is willing to question any truth claim, asking for clarity in definition, consistency in logic, and adequacy of evidence."*

Philosopher Paul Kurtz
*The Skeptical Inquirer*, 1994

As scientists, psychologists aim to approach the world of behavior with a curious *skepticism.* They persistently ask two questions: What do you mean? and How do you know? Consider some familiar claims. Can a theater owner make you hungry by flashing an imperceptibly brief message—EAT POPCORN? Do lie detectors tell the truth? Can astrologers analyze your character and predict your future based on the position of the planets at the moment of your birth? As you will see in the chapters to follow, we can test all such claims. In the arena of competing ideas, skeptical testing can reveal which ones best match the facts.

Putting a scientific attitude into practice requires *humility,* because it means that we may have to reject our own ideas. In the last analysis, what matters is not my opinion or yours, but whatever truths nature reveals in response to our questioning. If animals or people don't behave as our ideas predict, then so much the worse for our ideas. As Agatha Christie's Miss Marple explained, "It wasn't what I expected. But facts are facts, and if one is proved to be wrong, one must just be humble about it and start again." This is the humble attitude expressed in one of psychology's early mottos: "The rat is always right."

*"My deeply held belief is that if a god anything like the traditional sort exists, our curiosity and intelligence are provided by such a god. We would be unappreciative of those gifts . . . if we suppressed our passion to explore the universe and ourselves."*

Carl Sagan (1979a)

Historians of science tell us that these attitudes of curious skepticism and open-minded humility helped make modern science possible. Many of its founders were people whose religious convictions made them humble before nature and skeptical of any human authority (Hooykaas, 1972; Merton, 1938). Of course, scientists, like anyone else, can have big egos and may cling stubbornly to their preconceptions. We all view nature through the spectacles of our preconceived ideas. Still, the ideal that unifies psychologists with all scientists is the skeptical yet humble scrutiny of competing ideas.

This attitude, armed with scientific principles for sifting reality from illusion, prepares us to think smarter. Smart thinking, called **critical thinking**, examines assumptions, discerns hidden values, evaluates evidence, and assesses conclusions. Whether reading news reports or listening to conversation, critical thinkers ask questions. They wonder, How do they know that? and What axe is this person grinding? Is the conclusion based on mere anecdote and gut feelings? Or on trustworthy evidence? Does the evidence justify a cause-effect conclusion? What alternative explanations are possible? Carried to an extreme, healthy skepticism can degenerate into a negative cynicism that scorns any unproven idea. But when also applied to our own thinking, a critical attitude instead produces humility—an awareness of our own vulnerability to error and an openness to surprises and new perspectives.

Has psychology's own critical inquiry indeed been open to surprising findings? The answer, as ensuing chapters illustrate, is plainly yes. Believe it or not . . .

- Massive losses of brain tissue early in life may have minimal long-term effects (see page 87).
- Newborn infants come equipped with remarkable perceptual abilities (see page 83).
- On average, any two children from the same family (children reared under the same parental philosophy and in the same schools, neighborhood, and social class) have personalities nearly as different as any two children picked at random (see page 113).
- Prolonged stress hinders the body's disease-fighting immune system, making people more vulnerable to physical illness (see pages 583–584).
- Men and women, old and young, rich and working class, blacks and whites, with disabilities and without—all report roughly comparable levels of personal happiness (see page 451).
- Electroconvulsive ("shock") therapy is often an effective treatment for severe depression (see page 567).

And has critical inquiry convincingly debunked popular presumptions? The answer, as ensuing chapters also illustrate, is again yes. The available evidence contradicts beliefs that . . .

- As part of their passage to middle adulthood, men in their early forties undergo a traumatic midlife crisis (see page 139).
- Most mothers are depressed for a time after their children grow up, leave home, and marry (see page 141).
- Some people seldom dream; sleepwalkers are acting out their dreams; sleeptalkers are verbalizing their dreams (see Chapter 7).
- Our past experiences are all recorded in our brains; with brain stimulation or hypnosis, one can "play the tape" and relive long-buried or repressed memories (see Chapter 9).
- Most people suffer from unrealistically low self-esteem (see pages 483–484).
- Opposites attract (see page 647).

## The Limits of Intuition and Common Sense

*Two reliable phenomena—hindsight bias and judgmental overconfidence—illustrate why Madeline L'Engle was right: "The naked intellect is an extraordinarily inaccurate instrument."*

Skeptical inquiry and humility before nature are well and good for science. But don't intuition and plain common sense suffice for everyday life? In sifting reality from illusion, do we need the scientific attitude that drives critical thinking?

Some doubt it. They say psychology merely documents what people already know and dresses it in jargon: "So what else is new—you get paid for using fancy methods to prove what my grandmother knew?"

Others scorn a scientific approach because of their faith in human intuition. Advocates of "intuitive management" urge us to tune into our hunches. When hiring, firing, and investing, we should distrust statistical predictors and listen to our premonitions. We should follow *Star Wars'* Luke Skywalker by trusting the force within.

Actually, intuition sometimes blunders. Consider, for example, two situations in which our statistical intuition might lead us astray. (See page 15 for the answers.)

- Imagine (or ask someone to imagine) folding a sheet of paper on itself 100 times. Roughly how thick would it then be?
- Given our year with 365 days, a group needs 366 people to ensure that at least two people share the same birthday; how big should the class be to have a 50 percent chance of finding a birthday match?

Our notions of common sense similarly err. We're all Monday morning quarterbacks, presuming we could have foreseen what we know happened.

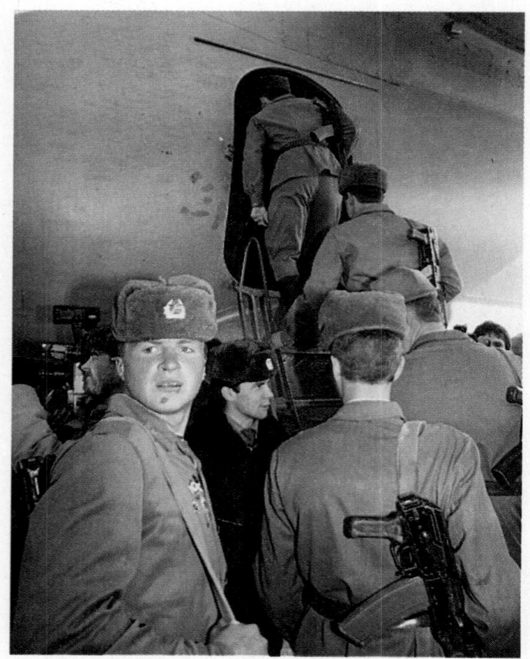

**Looking Backward** *These Soviet troops were among the last to leave Afghanistan in 1989, after a decade-long, inconclusive military intervention. With the "wisdom" of hindsight, it is hard to see how the Soviets could have made such an "obvious" policy blunder. But then, after Pearl Harbor and the Vietnam War, people asked similar questions about U.S. foreign policy.*

## Did We Know It All Along? The Hindsight Bias

Psychologist Baruch Fischhoff and others (Slovic & Fischhoff, 1977; Wood, 1979) have shown how scientific results and historical happenings can indeed seem like obvious common sense. They discovered that events that don't seem obvious beforehand seem quite predictable in hindsight. Once people learn the outcome of an experiment or an historical episode, it suddenly seems less surprising to them than to people asked to guess the outcome. Finding out that something has happened makes it seem inevitable. Psychologists call this 20/20 hindsight vision the **hindsight bias**, also known as the *I-knew-it-all-along phenomenon.*

The phenomenon is easy to demonstrate. Give half the members of a group some purported psychological finding and the other half an opposite result. For example, imagine reading, "Psychologists have found that separation weakens romantic attraction. As the saying goes, 'Out of sight, out of mind.'" Could you imagine why this might be? Most people can, and nearly all will then regard the finding as unsurprising.

But what if you had read the opposite: "Psychologists have found that separation strengthens romantic attraction. As the saying goes, 'Absence makes the heart grow fonder.'" People given this result can also easily explain it, and they overwhelmingly see it as unsurprising common sense. Obviously, when both a supposed finding and its opposite seem like common sense, there is a problem.

*"Life is lived forwards, but understood backwards."*
Søren Kierkegaard, 1813–1855

We also experience hindsight bias while looking back on history. In contrast to other people's preelection uncertainty, people *after* a presidential election exude confidence that they could have told you how it would turn out (Powell, 1988). To doctors given case information plus an autopsy report, a cause of death may seem obvious—something they easily could have foreseen, knowing the symptoms. But it is not so obvious to doctors told the same symptoms without the autopsy report (Dawson & others, 1988). From our 1990s vantage point, it may in hindsight seem obvious that Eastern European countries would exchange communism for democracy. But it wasn't obvious to United Nations ambassador Jeanne Kirkpatrick in 1980 when she warned, "The history of this century provides no grounds for expecting that radical totalitarian regimes will transform themselves." So, the point is *not* that common sense is usually wrong, but that it is after the fact. Common sense describes what's happened more easily than it predicts what will happen. As Dr. Watson said to Sherlock Holmes, "Anything seems commonplace, once explained."

Nevertheless, Grandmother is often right. As baseball great Yogi Berra once said, "You can observe a lot by watching." (We have Berra to thank for other gems, such as "Nobody ever comes here—it's too crowded," and "If the people don't want to come out to the park, nobody's gonna stop 'em.") Because we're all behavior-watchers, it would be surprising if many of psychology's findings had *not* been foreseen.

But some research findings *do* jolt our common sense. Sometimes Grandmother's intuition has it wrong. Informed by countless casual observations, our intuition may tell us that familiarity breeds contempt, that dreams predict the future, and that emotions coincide with menstrual phase. As we will see in later chapters, the available evidence suggests that these common sense ideas are wrong, wrong, and wrong. Throughout this book we will see how research has both inspired and overturned popular ideas—about aging, about sleep and dreams, about personality—and how it has surprised us with discoveries about how the brain's chemical messengers control our moods and memories, about animal abilities, about the effects of stress on our capacity to fight disease.

© 1988 by Sidney Harris/*American Scientist Magazine.*

*Answers to page 14: Given a 0.1-millimeter-thick sheet, the thickness after 100 folds would be 800 trillion times the distance between the earth and the sun (Gilovich, 1991). Only 23 people are needed to give better than even odds of any two people having the same birthday.*

## Overconfidence

Our everyday thinking is limited not only by our after-the-fact common sense but also by our human tendency toward overconfidence. As Chapter 10 explains, we tend to think we know more than we do. Asked how sure we are of our answers to factual questions (is Boston north or south of Paris?), we tend to be more confident than correct.[1] Or consider these three anagrams, which Richard Goranson (1978) asked people to unscramble.

*"It ain't so much the things we don't know that get us into trouble. It's the things we know that just ain't so."*

Artemus Ward, 1834–1867

WREAT → WATER
ETRYN → ENTRY
GRABE → BARGE

Reflect for a moment: About how many seconds do you think it would have taken you to unscramble each of these?

Once people know the target word, hindsight makes it seem obvious—so much so that they become overconfident. They think they would have seen the solution in only 10 seconds or so, when in reality the average subject spent 3 minutes, as you also might, given an anagram without the solution: OCHSA (see page 16).

Are we any better at predicting our social behavior? To find out, Robert Vallone and his associates (1990) had students predict at the beginning of the school year whether they would drop a course, vote in the November election, call their parents more than twice a month, and so forth. On average, the students felt 84 percent confident in making these self-predictions. Later quizzes about their actual behavior showed their predictions were correct only 71 percent of the time. Even when they were 100 percent sure of themselves, their self-predictions erred 15 percent of the time.

*"We don't like their sound. Groups of guitars are on their way out."*

Decca Records, in turning down a recording contract with the Beatles

Or consider the confidence of new collegians about their college future: As they begin college, only 2 percent of American students say there is a very good chance they will drop out permanently or temporarily (Astin &

[1] Boston is south of Paris.

others, 1993). But the optimism of the other 98 percent is unrealistic. Nearly half of the students entering a 4-year college or university do not earn a degree within 5 years.

Overconfidence stems partly from our human tendency to seek information that *confirms* our ideas (a phenomenon that Chapter 10 will label "confirmation bias"). When assessing our ideas, we prefer to look at evidence that might confirm rather than disconfirm them. Reflecting on many experiments, P. C. Wason (1981) reports that once people have a wrong idea they often will not budge from their illogic: "Ordinary people evade facts, become inconsistent, or systematically defend themselves against the threat of new information relevant to the issue."

*"They couldn't hit an elephant at this dist—."*

General John Sedgwick's last words, uttered during a Civil War battle, 1864

Our quest for positive instances of an idea biases our thinking even when we're neutral on an issue. In one study, people reflected on which pair of countries was most similar: East and West Germany, or Sri Lanka and Nepal. Scanning their memories for examples that would confirm similarity, most people answered East and West Germany. Others considered which of these same pairs of countries was most dissimilar. Again, after scanning their memories most people answered East and West Germany (Tversky & Gati, 1978). Obviously, something was awry here: The same pair of countries couldn't be both more similar and more dissimilar. People in both groups had looked for—and found—more German examples that confirmed whatever idea they were assessing.

*Solution to anagram on page 15: CHAOS.*

## Summing Up

Scientific inquiry begins with an attitude—an eagerness to skeptically scrutinize competing ideas and an open-minded humility before nature. Putting ideas, even crazy-sounding ideas, to the test helps us winnow sense from nonsense. The curiosity that drives us to test ideas and to expose their underlying assumptions carries into everyday life as *critical thinking*.

If intuition and common sense were trustworthy, we would have less need for scientific inquiry and critical thinking. But without such thinking we readily succumb to *hindsight bias*, also called the I-knew-it-all-along phenomenon. Learning the outcome of a study (or of an everyday happening) can make it seem like obvious common sense. But things seldom seem so obvious before the fact. We also are routinely *overconfident* of our judgments, thanks partly to our bias to seek information that confirms them. Such biases lead us to overestimate our unaided intuition. Although limited by the testable questions it can address, a scientific approach can help us sift reality from illusion, taking us beyond the horizons of our intuition and common sense.

## Research Strategies: How Psychologists Ask and Answer Questions

*Like all scientists, psychologists construct theories that organize observations and imply testable hypotheses. To describe, predict, and explain behavior and mental processes, psychologists use three methods: They describe behavior using case studies, surveys, and naturalistic observations. They predict behavior from correlational studies. And they seek cause-effect explanations through experiments that manipulate one or more factors under controlled conditions.*

Psychologists arm their scientific attitude with the scientific method: They make observations, form theories, and then refine their theories in the light of new observations.

## The Scientific Method

In everyday conversation, we sometimes use "theory" to mean "mere hunch." In science, "theory" is linked with observation. A creative **theory** *explains* through an integrated set of principles that *organize* and *predict* observable behaviors or events. By organizing isolated facts, a theory simplifies things. There are now so many known facts about behavior—Nobel-laureate psychologist Allen Newell (1988) estimated 3000, including 29 that govern behavior while typing at a keyboard—that we could never hope to remember them all. By linking observations and bridging them to deeper principles, a theory offers a useful summary. G. E. Morton (1994) likens theory construction to solving a connect-the-dots puzzle; as lines are drawn linking the isolated dots, a coherent picture emerges.

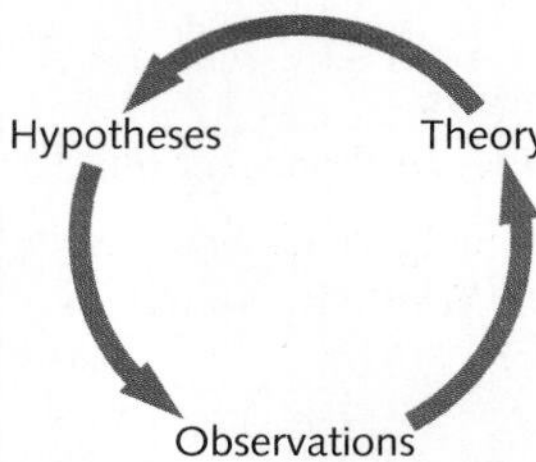


**The Ongoing Process of Science** *A theory implies hypotheses, which predict observations, which in turn we use to refine the theory.*

A good theory of depression, for example, will first help us organize countless observations concerning depression into a much shorter list of principles. Say we observe over and over that depressed people recall their past, describe their present, and predict their future in gloomy terms. We might therefore theorize that low self-esteem contributes to depression. So far so good: Our self-esteem principle neatly summarizes a long list of facts about depressed people.

Yet no matter how reasonable a theory may sound—and low self-esteem certainly seems a reasonable explanation of depression—we must put it to the test. A good theory implies testable predictions, called **hypotheses**. By enabling us to test and reject or revise the theory, such predictions give direction to research. They specify in advance what results would support the theory and what results would disconfirm it. To test our self-esteem theory of depression we might give people a test of self-esteem and see whether, as we hypothesized, people who report poorer self-images are indeed more depressed (Figure 1–1).

In doing so, we should be aware that our theory can bias our observations. Having theorized that depression springs from low self-esteem, we may see what we expect to see. We may be tempted to perceive depressed people's comments as self-disparaging.

As one check on their biases, psychologists report their research precisely enough to allow others to **replicate** (repeat) our observations. If other researchers recreate the essence of a study with different subjects and materials and get similar results, then our confidence in the reliability of our finding grows. The first study of hindsight bias aroused psychologists' curiosity. Now, after many successful replications with differing people and questions, we feel quite sure of the phenomenon's power.

In the end, our theory will be useful if it powerfully organizes and predicts—if it (1) effectively organizes a range of observations and (2) implies clear predictions that anyone can use to check the theory or to derive practical applications. (If we boost people's self-esteem, will their depression lift?) Eventually, our research will probably lead to a revised theory (such as the one on page 522) that better organizes and predicts what we know about depression.

The alternative research strategies include descriptive, correlational, and experimental methods. We test hypotheses and refine our theories by making *observations* that *describe* behavior, detecting correlations that predict behavior, and doing experiments that help explain behavior. To think criti-

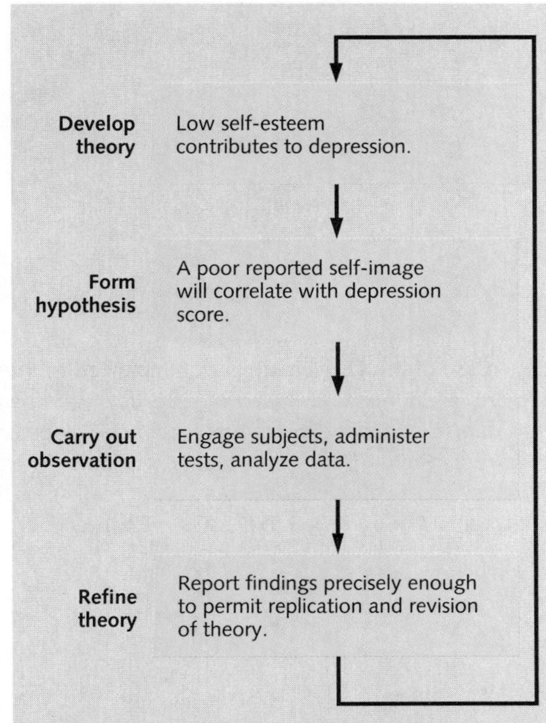


**Figure 1–1**

**Steps in the Scientific Method** *Researchers systematically follow a self-correcting process of creating, testing, and refining a theory.*

*Good theories explain by*
*1. organizing and linking observed facts.*
*2. implying hypotheses which offer testable predictions and sometimes practical applications.*

cally about popularized psychology claims, we need to recognize these designs and to know how we can use them to sharpen our everyday thinking.

## Description

*Research strategies:*
***1. Description***
*2. Correlation*
*3. Experimentation*

The starting point of any science is description. In everyday life, all of us observe and describe people, often forming hunches about why they behave as they do. Professional psychologists are doing much the same, only more objectively and systematically.

### The Case Study

Among the oldest research methods is the **case study**, in which psychologists study one or more individuals in great depth in the hope of revealing things true of us all. Much of our early knowledge about the brain came from case studies of individuals who suffered a particular impairment after damage to a particular brain region. Sigmund Freud constructed his theory of personality from a handful of case studies. Developmental psychologist Jean Piaget taught us about children's thinking after carefully observing and questioning his own three children. Studies of but a handful of chimpanzees have revealed their capacity for understanding and using language. Intensive case studies are sometimes very revealing.

*"'Well my dear,' said Miss Marple, 'human nature is very much the same everywhere, and of course, one has opportunities of observing it at closer quarters in a village.'"*

Agatha Christie
*The Tuesday Club Murders,* 1933

Although case studies can also suggest hypotheses for further study, they sometimes have a problem: Any given individual may be atypical, making the case misleading. Our tendency to leap from unrepresentative information is a common source of mistaken judgment. Indeed, anytime a researcher mentions a finding (smokers die younger: 95 percent of men over 85 are nonsmokers) someone is sure to offer a contradictory case ("Well, I have an uncle who smoked two packs a day and lived to be 89"). As every psychology instructor knows, anecdotal cases—dramatic stories, personal experiences, even psychological case examples—have a way of overwhelming general truths. Numbers are numbing (in one study of 1300 dream reports concerning a kidnapped child, only 5 percent correctly envisioned the child as dead—see page 213). Anecdotes are alarming ("but I know a person who dreamed her sister was in a car accident and 2 days later she was badly injured").

**The Case of the Conversational Chimpanzee** *In intensive case studies of chimpanzees, psychologists have explored the intriguing question of whether language is uniquely human. Here Nim Chimpsky signs "hug" as his trainer, psychologist Herbert Terrace, shows him the puppet Ernie. But is Nim really capable of using language? We'll explore that issue in Chapter 10.*

After 12-year-old Polly Klaas was kidnapped from her California bedroom and murdered, and after 2-year-old James Bulger was abducted from a Liverpool shopping mall and bludgeoned to death, children and parents in both countries became noticeably "scared" (as a 1994 *Newsweek* cover story put it)—much more scared than they were of car accidents or cancer, which cause hundreds of times more child deaths than kidnapping. The brutal kidnappings were impressed on people's memories, and people intuitively judge various risks based on how easily they remember examples of them. As psychologist Gordon Allport said, "Given a thimbleful of [dramatic] facts we rush to make generalizations as large as a tub."

So, individual cases can suggest fruitful ideas. But to discern the general truths that cover individual cases requires other methods of answering questions.

### The Survey

The **survey** method, which is commonly used in both descriptive and correlational studies, looks at many cases in less depth. A survey asks people to report their behavior or opinions. Questions about everything from sexual practices to political opinions get put to the public. It's hard to think of a significant question that survey researchers have not asked. In the United States, for example, recent Harris and Gallup polls reveal that 72 percent of people think there is too much TV violence, 80 percent favor equal job opportunities for homosexuals, 89 percent say they face high stress, 95 percent believe in God, and 96 percent would like to change something about their appearance.

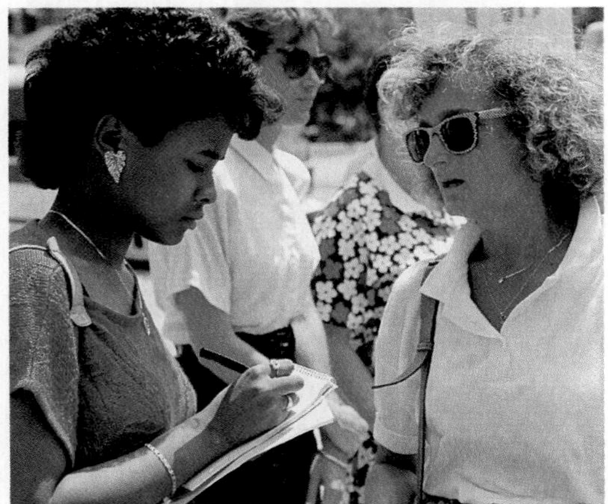

**What Do You Know?** *Like this interviewer, psychologists using the survey method ask people to describe their behavior or opinions. The way the researcher frames the questions can bias answers, but accuracy also depends on respondents' memory and honesty.*

**Wording Effects** Asking questions is tricky, because even subtle changes in the order or wording of questions can have big effects. For example, 8 in 10 Americans agree that "women with young children should be able to work outside the home." But 7 in 10 also agree that "women should stay home if they have young preschool children" (*Public Opinion*, 1984, 1985). Should cigarette ads or pornography be allowed on television? People are much more likely to approve "not allowing" such things than "forbidding" or "censoring" them. They are similarly much more approving of "aid to the needy" than of "welfare." Because wording questions is such a delicate matter, critical thinkers will reflect on how the phrasing of a question might have affected the opinions respondents expressed.

**Sampling** In everyday experience we are exposed to a biased sample of people. We associate mostly with those who share our attitudes and habits. Thus, when we are guessing how many people hold a particular belief, those who think as we do come to mind most readily. This tendency to overestimate others' agreement with us is the **false consensus effect** (Ross & others, 1977). Vegetarians will think more people are vegetarians than will meat-eaters, and conservatives will perceive more support for conservative views than will liberals. To restrain this bias, we can gather a more representative sample of people.

Most surveys sample a target group. If you wished to survey the students at your college you could question them all, but probably there are too many to do so. Instead, you could survey a representative sample of the total student **population**—the whole group you wanted to study and describe. How could you make your sample representative of this population? By making it a **random sample**, one in which every person in the entire group has an equal chance of participating.

To sample the students at your institution randomly, you would *not* send them all a questionnaire. (The conscientious people who return it would not represent a random sample.) Rather, you would aim for a representative sample by, say, using a table of random numbers to pick participants from a student listing and then making sure you get responses from as many as possible. Large, representative samples are better than small

"How would you like me to answer that question? As a member of my ethnic group, educational class, income group, or religious category?"

Drawing by D. Fradon; © 1969 The New Yorker Magazine, Inc.

ones; but it is better to have a small, representative sample of 100 than a haphazard, unrepresentative sample of 500.

The random-sampling principle also works in national surveys. Imagine that you had a giant barrel containing 60 million white beans thoroughly mixed with 40 million green beans. A scoop that randomly sampled 1500 of them would contain about 60 percent white and 40 percent green beans, give or take 2 or 3 percent. Sampling voters in a national election survey is like sampling the beans; 1500 randomly sampled people provide a remarkably accurate snapshot of the opinions of a nation.

Because gathering a random sample can be a huge task, some survey takers don't make the effort. Shere Hite's book *Women and Love* reported survey findings based on only a 4.5 percent response rate from mailings to an unrepresentative sample of 100,000 women. The response was doubly unrepresentative, because not only did she have a modest, self-selected return, but the women initially contacted were members of women's organizations. Nonetheless, "It's 4500 people. That's enough for me," reported Hite. And it was apparently enough for *Time* magazine, which made a cover story of her findings—that 70 percent of women married 5 years or more were having affairs, and that 95 percent of women feel emotionally harassed by the men they love (Wallis, 1987). Evidently it didn't matter that on less publicized surveys, *randomly* sampled women express much higher levels of satisfaction: Half or more report feeling "very happy" or "completely satisfied" with their marriage; only 3 percent say they are "not at all happy" (Peplau & Gordon, 1985). And only 1 in 10 reports having had an affair during their current marriage (Greeley, 1991). (Other unrepresentative surveys give differing, but still high, numbers of married people having affairs—54 percent of 106,000 married women readers of *Cosmopolitan*, 35 percent of married men and 25 percent of married women in the 1993 *Janus Report on Sexual Behavior*, again featured by *Time*.) Without random sampling, larger samples merely give better estimates of a misleading number (a number that does not represent the population of interest—in this case, all married women).

You can forecast the weather by taking a haphazard sample—by looking at the clouds and holding your finger in the wind—or you can look at weather maps based on comprehensive reporting. You can describe human experience using common sense, dramatic anecdotes, personal experience, and haphazard samples. But for an accurate picture of the experiences and attitudes of a whole population there's only one game in town—the representative survey.

*The moral:* Before believing survey findings, think critically: Consider the sample. You cannot compensate for an unrepresentative sample by adding more people.

We can extend the moral to everyday thinking, as we generalize from samples we observe. We meet a few students and attend a few classes during a visit to a college and infer from those instances how friendly the campus is and how good the teaching is. We observe the weather during a week-long visit to Seattle and then tell our friends about the climate there.

It is often tempting to overgeneralize from such select samples, especially so when the extremes are vivid cases. Given (a) a statistical summary of a professor's student evaluations and (b) the vivid comments of two irate students, an administrator's impression of the professor may be influenced as much by the two unhappy students as by the many favorable evaluations in the statistical summary. Driving into Chicago from the south, many people see the miles of tenement houses near the highway and think, "What an ugly city this is." Standing in the checkout line at the su-

THIS MODERN WORLD by Tom Tomorrow © 1991.

permarket, George sees the woman in front of him pay with food stamps, and then watches with dismay as she drives away in a Cadillac. In each of these situations, the temptation to generalize from a few vivid but unrepresentative cases is nearly irresistible.

*The moral:* The best basis for generalizing is not from the exceptional cases one finds at the extremes, but from a representative sample of cases.

### Naturalistic Observation

Watching and recording the behavior of organisms in their natural environment is known as **naturalistic observation**. Naturalistic observations range from watching chimpanzee societies in the jungle, to "unobtrusive measures" of parent-child interactions in different cultures, to recording students' self-seating patterns in the lunchrooms of desegregated schools.

Like the case study and survey methods, naturalistic observation does not *explain* behavior. It *describes* it. Nevertheless, description can be revealing. We once thought, for example, that only humans use tools. Then naturalistic observation revealed that chimpanzees sometimes insert a stick in a termite mound and withdraw it, eating the stick's load of termites. Chimps and baboons also use deception to achieve their aims. Psychologists Andrew Whiten and Richard Byrne (1988) repeatedly saw one young baboon pretending to have been attacked by another as a tactic to get its mother to drive the other baboon away from its food.

**Naturalistic Observation** *By unobtrusively watching and recording behavior in natural environments, cross-cultural psychologists have discovered significant variations in human child-rearing patterns. Here in Zaire's rain forest, psychologist Gilda Morelli and her research assistant gather data on Efe children's involvement in community routines.*

Through naturalistic observations we have also learned that culture shapes child-rearing. In Japan, children learn to "get along" and "go along" with their group. Western child-rearing more often emphasizes individual achievement and rewards assertiveness. Naturalistic observation also reveals that at school, students of different races often shun each other outside the classroom (page 688). This suggests that special efforts to engage students in cooperative play and work may be needed to foster social integration.

## Correlation

*Research strategies:*
*1. Description*
***2. Correlation***
*3. Experimentation*

Describing behavior is a first step toward predicting it. When surveys and naturalistic observation reveal that one trait or behavior accompanies another, we say the two correlate. A **correlation** is a statistical measure of relationship: It reveals how closely two things vary together and thus how well one *predicts,* the other. Knowing how much high school grades *correlate* with college grades tells us how well high school grades *predict* college grades.

A *positive* correlation (between 0 and +1.00) indicates a *direct* relationship, meaning that two things increase together or decrease together. If amount of violence viewed on television correlates positively with aggressive social behavior (which it does), then people's TV-viewing habits will predict their aggressiveness. Likewise, high school grade averages correlate about +.6 with college grade averages, meaning that high school performance is a rough predictor of college performance. A *negative* correlation—equally predictive—indicates an *inverse* relationship: As one thing increases, the other decreases. Our findings on self-esteem and depression illustrate a negative correlation: People who score *low* on self-esteem tend to score *high* on depression. Negative correlations could go as low as –1.00, which means that one set of scores goes down precisely as the other goes up.

| | Cloud-seeding | No cloud-seeding |
|---|---|---|
| Rainfall | a | b |
| No rainfall | c | d |

**Figure 1–2**

**Confirmation Bias Produces Illusory Correlation** *Evaluating the correlation between cloud-seeding and rainfall requires data from all four cells in the figure. People tend to focus on instances (from cells a and d) that confirm their expectation of a correlation.*

### Illusory Correlations

Correlations make visible relationships that the naked eye would miss. They also help us stop "seeing" relationships that actually don't exist. A perceived correlation that does not really exist is an **illusory correlation**. When we *believe* there is a relationship between two things, we are likely to *notice* and *recall* instances that confirm our belief (Troilier & Hamilton, 1986). In one experiment, people saw the results of a hypothetical, 50-day experiment (Ward & Jenkins, 1965). For each of the 50 days, the subjects learned whether the clouds had been "seeded" to produce rain and whether it had rained. The "results" given were actually random; they showed no relationship between cloud-seeding and rainfall. Nevertheless, the subjects typically perceived—in keeping with what they expected—a positive relationship between cloud-seeding and rainfall (see Figure 1–2).

Such illusory correlations help explain many a superstitious belief, such as the presumption that more babies are born when the moon is full or that infertile couples who adopt become more likely to conceive (Gilovich, 1991). Those who conceive after adopting capture our attention. Those who adopt and never conceive, or who conceive without adopting, we're less likely to notice. In other words, illusory correlations occur when we overrely on cell a of Figure 1–3, ignoring equally essential information in cells b, c, and d.

Because we are sensitive to dramatic or unusual events, we are especially likely to notice and remember the occurrence of two such events in sequence—say, a premonition of an unlikely phone call followed by the call. When the call does not follow the premonition, we are less likely to note and remember the nonevent.

Likewise, instances of positive-thinking people being cured of cancer impress those who believe positive attitudes counter disease. But to assess whether positive thinking actually affects cancer, we need three more types of information. First, we need an estimate of how many positive thinkers *weren't* cured. And among those *not* trying to heal themselves through positive thinking, we need to know how many were and were not cured. Without these comparison figures, positive examples of a few hope-filled people tell us nothing about the actual correlation between attitudes and disease.

*The moral:* When we notice random coincidences, we may forget that they are random and see them as correlated. Thus, we can easily deceive ourselves by seeing what is not there.

| | Conceive | Do not conceive |
|---|---|---|
| Adopt | a | b |
| Do not adopt | c | d |

**Figure 1–3**

**Illusory Correlation in Everyday Life** *Many people notice infertile couples who conceive after adopting. They are vulnerable to an illusory correlation if they ignore other pertinent information, especially from cells b and c. This information is needed to compute the likelihood of conceiving after adopting versus after not adopting. (From Gilovich, 1991.)*

### Perceiving Order in Random Events

Illusory correlations arise from our natural eagerness to make sense of our world. Given even random data, we look for order, for meaningful patterns. And we usually find it, because *random sequences often don't look random.* If someone flipped a coin six times, would one of the following sequences of heads (H) and tails (T) be more likely than the other two: HHHTTT or HTTHTH or HHHHHH?

Daniel Kahneman and Amos Tversky (1972) found that most people believe HTTHTH would be the most likely random sequence. Actually, all possible sequences are equally likely (or, you might say, equally unlikely) to occur. A bridge or poker hand of 10 through Ace, all of hearts, would seem extraordinary; actually, it would be no more or less likely than any other specific hand of cards.

Psychologists Thomas Holtgraves and James Skeel (1992) exposed people's perceptions of randomness in their bets placed in Indiana's Pick-3 Lottery. You can play, too: Pick any three-digit number from 0 to 999.

Did your number have a repeated digit (as in 525)? Probably not. Only

14 percent of 2.24 million number strings chosen in July 1991 had a repeated digit. Although repeated digits occur in 28 percent of the available numbers, such numbers *look* less random (and people prefer to bet random-looking series). In actual random sequences, seeming patterns and streaks (such as repeating digits) occur more often than people expect. Thus, shown random data, scientists and psychics alike can often "see" an interesting pattern (Guion, 1992). Seek and you shall find.

The failure to recognize random occurrences for what they are can predispose people to seek extraordinary explanations for ordinary events. Imagine that on one warm spring day 4000 college students gather for a coin-tossing contest. Their task is to flip heads. On the first toss, 2000 students do so and remain standing for a second round. As you might expect, about 1000 of these progress to a third round, 500 to a fourth, 250 to a fifth, 125 to a sixth, 62 to a seventh, 31 to an eighth, 15 to a ninth, and 8 amazing individuals, having flipped heads nine times in a row with ever-increasing displays of concentration and effort, remain standing for the tenth round.

**Two Random Sequences** *Your chances of being dealt either of these hands is precisely the same: 1 in 2,598,960.*

By now, the crowd of losers is in awestruck silence as these expert coin tossers prepare to display their amazing ability yet again. The proceedings are temporarily halted so that a panel of impartial scientists can observe and document the incredible achievement of these gifted individuals. Alas, on succeeding tosses half of those remaining flip a tail, until all have sat down. "But, of course," their admirers say, "coin tossing is a highly sensitive skill. The tense, pressured atmosphere created by the scientific scrutiny has disturbed their fragile gift."

Some happenings, though, seem so extraordinary that we struggle to conceive an ordinary, chance-related explanation (as applies to our coin-tosses). In such cases, statisticians often are less mystified. When Evelyn Marie Adams won the New Jersey lottery *twice*, newspapers reported the odds of her feat as 1 in 17 trillion. Bizarre? Actually, 1 in 17 trillion are the odds that a given person who buys a single ticket for two New Jersey lotteries will win both times. But statisticians Stephen Samuels and George McCabe (1989) report that, given the millions of people who buy U.S. state lottery tickets, it was "practically a sure thing" that someday, somewhere, someone would hit a state jackpot twice. Indeed, say fellow statisticians Persi Diaconis and Frederick Mosteller (1989), "With a large enough sample, any outrageous thing is likely to happen."

We all experience enough events that we're sure to feel astonished now and then. One day when my daughter bought two pairs of shoes, we later were astounded to discover that the two brand names were her first and last names. Checking out a Xerox copy counter from our library, I confused the clerk when giving him my six-digit department charge number—which just happened at that moment to be identical to the counter's one-in-a-million number on which the last user finished. Watching the end of two Chicago Cubs baseball games at Pittsburgh in the same weekend, I was astonished as slugger Andre Dawson hit, for only the fifth and sixth time in his long career, bases-loaded home runs. Weirder yet, both came in the last inning, both with two outs, both gave his team a lead and likely victory—and both were overcome by Pittsburgh in the last half of the same final inning. (You gotta love those Cubs.)

© 1990 by Sidney Harris/*American Scientist Magazine.*

*Bizarre-looking, perhaps. But actually no more unlikely than any other number sequence.*

Baseball fan Ron Vachon was even more astounded during a September 1990 game in Boston. Oakland A's outfielder Rickey Henderson hit two foul balls right to him, on successive pitches. That something like that should have happened to Vachon (who dropped them both) was incredibly unlikely. That it sometime would happen to someone was not. An event that happens to but 1 in 1 billion people every day occurs about six times a day, 2000 times a year.

## *Thinking Critically About* Hot and Cold Streaks—Random Sequences That Don't Look Random

Every basketball player and every fan intuitively "knows" that players have hot and cold streaks. Players who have "hot hands" can't seem to miss, while those who have "cold" ones can't find the center of the hoop. When Thomas Gilovich, Robert Vallone, and Amos Tversky (1985) interviewed team members of the Philadelphia 76ers, the players estimated they were about 25 percent more likely to make a shot after they had just made one than after a miss. In one survey, 9 in 10 basketball fans agreed that a player "has a better chance of making a shot after having just *made* his last two or three shots than he does after having just *missed* his last two or three shots." Believing in shooting streaks, players will feed the ball to a teammate who has just made two or three shots in a row, and many coaches will bench the player who has just missed three in a row.

The only trouble is (believe it or not), it isn't true. When Gilovich and his collaborators studied detailed individual shooting records, they found that the 76ers—and the Boston Celtics, the New Jersey Nets, the New York Knicks, and Cornell University's men's and women's basketball players—were equally likely to score after a miss and after a basket. A typical 50 percent shooter averages 50 percent after just missing three shots, and 50 percent after just making three shots. It works with free throws, too. Celtic star Larry Bird made 88 percent of his free throws after making a free throw and 91 percent after missing.

Why, then, do players and fans alike believe that players are more likely to score after scoring and miss after missing? It's because streaks do occur, more than people expect in random sequences. In any series of 20 shots by a 50 percent shooter (or 20 flips of a coin), there is a 50-50 chance of four baskets (or heads) in a row, and it is quite possible that 1 person out of 5 will have a streak of five or six. Players and fans notice these random streaks and so form the myth that "when you're hot you're hot" (Figure 1–4).

The same misinterpretation of random sequences is common in other settings. Hospital workers sometimes notice streaks of male births or female births. On August 11, 1993, the infant-intensive-care staff at the Grand Rapids, Michigan, Blodgett Hospital was astounded to find its unit filled with 17 baby boys—and no girls. Not realizing that random sequences can contain such streaks, people may attribute them to mysterious forces, such as phases of the moon.

Likewise, many investors believe that a mutual fund that has had a string of good years will likely outperform one that has had a string of bad years. Based on that assumption, investment magazines report mutual funds' performance. But, as economist Burton Malkiel (1989 ) documents, past performances of mutual funds do not predict their future performance. When funds have streaks of several good or bad years, we may nevertheless be fooled into thinking that past success predicts future success. "Randomness is a difficult notion for people to accept," notes Malkiel. "When events come in clusters and streaks, people look for explanations and patterns. They refuse to believe that such patterns—which frequently occur in random data—could equally well be derived from tossing a coin. So it is in the stock market as well."

*The moral:* Whether watching basketball, choosing stocks, or flipping coins, remember: Our intuition often deceives us. Random sequences frequently don't look random. Expect streaks.

**Figure 1–4**

**Who Is the Chance Shooter?** *Here are 21 consecutive shots, each scoring either a basket or a miss, by two players who each make 50 percent. Within this sample of shots, which player's sequence looks more like what we would expect in a random sequence? (See page 25.) (Adapted from Barry Ross,* Discover, *1987.)*

## Correlation and Causation

So far we've seen that correlation enables prediction and restrains the illusions of our flawed intuition. Violence-viewing correlates with (and therefore predicts) aggression. But does it *cause* aggression? Does low self-esteem *cause* depression? If, based on the correlational evidence, you assume that they do, you have much company. Perhaps the most irresistible thinking error made both by lay people and by professional psychologists is assuming that correlation proves causation. No matter how strong the relationship, it does not! If watching TV violence correlates positively with aggressiveness, does this mean that watching TV violence influences aggressive behavior? It may. Or does it mean that aggressive people prefer violent programs?

And what about the negative correlation between self-esteem and depression? Perhaps low self-esteem does cause depression. But as Figure 1–5 suggests, we'd get the same coincidence of low self-esteem and depression if depression caused people to be down on themselves or if something else—a third factor such as heredity or brain chemistry—caused both low self-esteem and depression. Among men, length of marriage correlates positively with hair loss—because both are associated with a third factor, age.

*The moral:* Correlation enables prediction and may hint at possible cause-effect relationships. But it does not provide a causal explanation. Knowing that two events are correlated need not tell us anything about causation. *Correlation does not prove causation.* Remember this principle and you will be wiser as you see reports of scientific studies in the news and in this book.

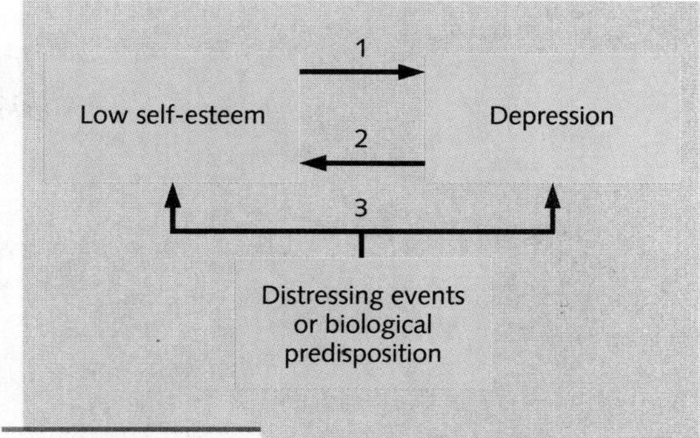


**Figure 1–5**

**Three Possible Cause-Effect Relationships**
*People low in self-esteem tend to be more depressed than those high in self-esteem. One possible explanation of this correlation is that a bad self-image causes depressed feelings. But as the diagram indicates, other cause-effect relationships are possible.*

## Experimentation

*Research strategies:*
*1. Description*
*2. Correlation*
***3. Experimentation***

Happy are they "who have been able to perceive the causes of things," remarked the Roman poet Virgil. We endlessly wonder and debate *why* people act as they do. As I write, the day's newspapers are filled with such wonderings: What caused two English schoolboys to bludgeon a 2-year-old to death? Why do people smoke? Have babies as unmarried teens? Do stupid things when drunk? Psychology can't answer these questions directly, but it has helped us to understand what influences aggression, drug use, sexual attitudes, and thinking when drinking.

In everyday life, many factors influence behavior. To isolate cause and effect—to explain what helps cause, say, depression—psychologists conduct **experiments**. Experiments enable a researcher to focus on the possible effects of one or more factors by (a) *manipulating the factors of interest* and (b) *holding constant ("controlling") other factors*. Imagine that some researchers wanted to study the effect of alcohol consumption on thinking ability. Before giving a thinking test, they would *manipulate* alcohol consumption (by giving some people a strong-tasting drink laced with alcohol, others the same drink without alcohol). By randomly assigning people to the two conditions, which otherwise are similar, they would hold all other factors constant. This would eliminate alternative explanations for why thinking might vary with drinking.

If behavior changes when we vary an experimental factor, such as alcohol, then the factor is having an effect. To repeat, unlike correlational studies, which uncover naturally occurring relationships, an experiment manipulates a factor to see its effect. To illustrate, let's consider two actual experiments.

*Answer to Figure 1–4 (page 24): Player B, whose outcomes may look more random, actually has fewer streaks than would be expected by chance. For these players, chance shooting, like chance coin tossing, should produce a change in outcome about 50 percent of the time. But 70 percent of the time (14 times out of 20) Player B's outcome changes on successive shots. Player A, on the other hand, is scoring more as we would expect from a 50 percent shooter; 10 times out of 20, Player A's next outcome is different.*

## Do Black Sports Uniforms Affect Perceptions?

Cornell University psychologists Mark Frank and Thomas Gilovich (1988) noticed that in virtually all cultures from central Africa to the Orient to Western Europe, the color black connotes evil. In movies, the bad guys wear black. It's a "black day" when we get "blackballed" or "blackmailed." Iran's Ayatollah Khomeini reportedly referred to the residence of the U.S. president as the "Black House."

*The color effect is not race-related. Instead, believes cross-cultural researcher John Williams (1992), it stems from our ancestors' associations with the black of night and light of day. Thus, in many African societies, "black" magic is bad magic.*

Summarizing these varied observations, Frank and Gilovich proposed a simple, small-scale theory: Black garb suggests evil, cuing us to *perceive* people dressed in black as evil and cuing those who wear black to *act out* their evil image. Frank and Gilovich knew that a useful theory must offer testable predictions. So they derived several hypotheses. First, they predicted that people unfamiliar with football and hockey would rate the black uniforms of National Football League and National Hockey League teams as seeming more evil than nonblack uniforms. Indeed, for both sports, people rated black uniforms as bad, mean, and aggressive.

Second, Frank and Gilovich hypothesized, and found, a positive correlation between black team uniforms and total penalties for aggressive play. In all but 1 of the 17 seasons between 1970 and 1986, the football teams with black uniforms were penalized a disproportionate number of yards. Likewise, in all 16 hockey seasons between 1970–1971 and 1985–1986, the teams wearing black uniforms spent more time in the penalty box. Moreover, when the Pittsburgh Penguins switched to black uniforms during the middle of the 1979–1980 season, their penalties increased from an average of 8 minutes per game to 12 minutes. So, in these two sports at least, there definitely has been a correlation between black uniforms and penalized play.

**Bad Guys Wear Black Hats** *Since the early days of motion pictures, directors have dressed their villains in black so that viewers can easily tell the good guys from the bad. This tactic capitalizes on a common human bias that experimenters have recently documented: We see what we expect to see. When we see black, we expect aggression.*

Remember, a correlation is simply a relationship between two factors—in this case, uniform color and penalties. Correlation cannot prove a cause-effect relationship. Maybe there is no cause-effect connection; maybe organizations wanting an aggressive image simply choose black outfits and hire aggressive players. (For the Hell's Angels, white outfits just won't do.) But can you imagine *possible* causes of this correlation? Frank and Gilovich suggested two: The correlation occurs because referees *perceive* acts by players in black as more violent than similar acts by players not wearing black. Or, players who wear black uniforms *enact* the expected tough image.

In experimenting to evaluate these two possibilities, Frank and Gilovich found, first, that uniform color did indeed affect perceptions. They videotaped two staged football plays in which black- or white-clad defenders either drove the ball carrier back several yards and then threw him to the ground or hit the ball carrier violently in midair. The experimenters then manipulated the jersey-color factor. People were randomly assigned to either an experimental condition or a control condition. In the **experimental condition**, raters saw the same videotape in full color. With the color on, the raters (fans and professional referees) were more likely to judge the tackles as aggressive and illegal when committed by players wearing black (Figure 1–6). For comparison, the experimenters took the color out of the picture to create a **control condition**—a condition that contrasts with the experimental treatment. When all the players' jerseys appeared dull gray, raters judged the tackles of the white- and black-clad defenders as equally illegal. Thus, the control condition of an experiment provides a baseline against which we can compare the effect of the treatment found in the experimental condition.

*Note the distinction between random sampling in surveys and random* assignment *in experiments. Random sampling helps us generalize to a larger population. Random assignment controls extraneous influences, which helps us infer cause and effect.*

Note that a key feature of experiments is **random assignment**. If enough individuals of different ages and opinions are randomly assigned to two groups, the random assignment will roughly equalize the two groups in age, opinion, and every other characteristic that could possibly affect the results. With random assignment, we can therefore say that if the two groups behave or feel differently at the end of the experiment, it very probably is due to the experiment's independent variable. Without random assignment, the groups might differ in ways that could affect the results. If the researchers asked people from one dorm to view the color video and people from another dorm to view the no-color video, they wouldn't know for sure whether the color or the dorm population made the difference.

In a second experiment, Cornell students came to a study of "the psychology of competition." Frank and Gilovich randomly assigned them to wear either black or white jerseys and then invited them to choose some games. When the students donned black rather than white jerseys, they preferred more aggressive games. On average (such findings tell us only about group trends), wearing black affected not only perceptions but behavior as well.

The Frank and Gilovich experiments were fairly simple. They manipulated just one factor, jersey color. We call this experimental factor the **independent variable** because we can vary it independently of the other factors, such as the age or size of the players. Experimenters examine the effect of one or more independent variables on some measurable behavior, called the **dependent variable** because it can vary depending on what takes place during the experiment. Both variables are given precise **operational definitions**. Operational definitions specify the procedures that create the independent variable or measure the dependent variable. Thus they answer the "what do you mean?" question with an exactness that allows others to repeat the study. In Frank and Gilovich's first experiment, the dependent variable was the subjects' ratings of illegal aggression in response to (a) the control condition (videotape with dull gray jerseys) and (b) the experimental condition (videotape showing the black versus white jerseys). Table 1–1 shows the independent and dependent variables in their second experiment.

Let's recap: An experiment has at least two different conditions, a comparison or control condition and an experimental condition. Random assignment equates the conditions before any treatment effects. In this way, the experiment tests the effect of at least one independent variable (the experimental factor) on at least one dependent variable (the response that is measured).

Note, too, that in this series of studies a very simple theory, inspired by everyday observations, generated hypotheses. These predictions were con-

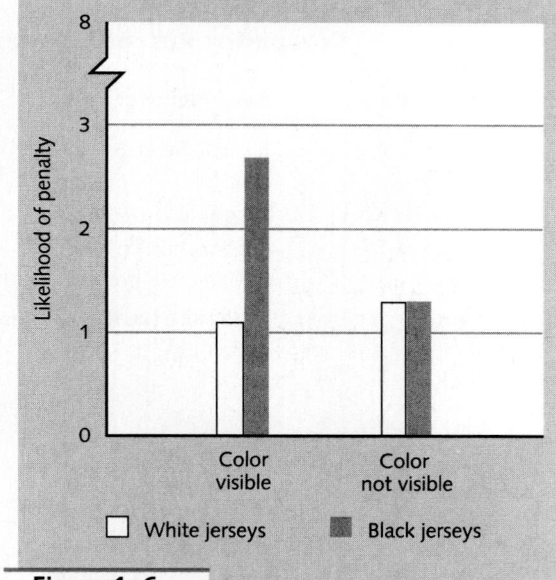


**Figure 1–6**

**Perceptions of Violence** *People judged videotaped midair tackles as more likely illegal when enacted by a player wearing black—but only when the color of the jersey was visible. (From Frank & Gilovich, 1988.)*

*Note again the importance of random assignment. If people had chosen their jersey color, the results might merely reflect a greater natural aggressiveness among those who prefer black.*

***Summary of Experimental Design***

***Independent variable*** *The experimental factor you manipulate; the treatment itself.*

***Dependent variable*** *The behavior measured; the factor that might be affected by changes in the independent variable.*

***Experimental condition*** *The condition that exposes subjects to one version of the independent variable.*

***Control condition*** *A condition identical to the experimental one, except the independent variable has a different value, such as zero.*

***Random assignment*** *Assigning subjects to conditions by chance, thus minimizing preexisting differences between those in the different conditions.*

**Table 1–1** **The Design of the Second Frank and Gilovich Experiment**

| | Condition | Manipulation of Independent Variable | Measurement of Dependent Variable |
|---|---|---|---|
| Random assignment of subjects | Experimental | Wear black jerseys | Aggressiveness (game choice) |
| | Control | Not wear black jerseys (wear white) | Aggressiveness (game choice) |

**Table 1–2 Comparing Research Methods**

| Research Method | Basic Purpose | How Conducted | What Is Manipulated |
|---|---|---|---|
| *Descriptive* | To observe and record behavior | Case studies, surveys, and naturalistic observations | Nothing |
| *Correlational* | To detect naturally occurring relationshps; to assess how well one variable predicts another | Computing statistical association, sometimes among survey responses | Nothing |
| *Experimental* | To explore cause and effect | Manipulating one or more factors and using random assignment to eliminate preexisting differences among subjects | The independent variable |

firmed by the correlation between uniforms and penalties, which in turn stimulated experiments that examined causation. Table 1–2 compares the features of psychology's research methods.

How freely can we generalize Frank and Gilovich's findings? Surely we don't perceive Catholic priests and nuns as aggressive, nor does it seem that wearing black causes them to act aggressively. Frank and Gilovich suspect, and wonder: Do the effects occur only in situations involving competition and aggressive confrontation? As so often happens, answering one question has led to asking another. Scientific inquiry is a voyage of discovery toward a horizon, beyond which yet another horizon beckons.

*"In solving one discovery we never fail to get an imperfect knowledge of others of which we had no idea before, so that we cannot solve one doubt without creating several new ones."*

Joseph Priestly
*Experiments and Observations on Different Kinds of Air,* 1775–1786

These concepts—experimental and control conditions, independent and dependent variables, random assignment—are important, yet easily confused. So let's put them to work with another intriguing set of experiments.

### Can Subliminal Tapes Improve Your Life?

A new generation of entrepreneurs would have you believe so. Mail order catalogs, cable television ads, and bookstores offer tapes with imperceptibly faint messages that will "reprogram your unconscious mind for success and happiness." While underachieving students listen to soothing music, subliminal messages (below one's threshold for hearing) persuade the unconscious that "I am a good student. I love learning." Procrastinators can be similarly reprogrammed to think "I set my priorities. I get things done ahead of time!"

Is there *anything* to these wild and sometimes wacky claims? Might positive subliminal messages help us, even a little? In Chapter 5, we will see that subliminal sensation is for real. We do process much information without conscious awareness. And under certain conditions, a stimulus too weak to recognize can subtly affect us.

But does this subtle, fleeting effect extend to the powerful, enduring effects claimed by the subliminal tape merchants? Anthony Greenwald, Eric Spangenberg, Anthony Pratkanis, and Jay Eskenazi (1991) decided to find out. They randomly assigned eager university students to listen daily for 5 weeks to commercial subliminal tapes designed to improve either self-esteem or memory. Then the researchers manipulated an experimental factor. On half the tapes the researchers switched the labels. People given

*In this experiment, what was the independent variable? The dependent variable? (See page 30.)*

these tapes *thought* they were receiving affirmations of self-esteem, when, actually, they heard the memory enhancement tape. Or they got the memory tape but *thought* their self-esteem was being recharged (Figure 1–7).

Were the tapes effective? Scores on both self-esteem and memory tests, taken before and after the 5 weeks, revealed no effects. Zilch. Nevertheless, those who *thought* they had heard a memory tape *believed* their memories had improved. Same for those who thought they had heard a self-esteem tape. Although the tapes had no effects, people *perceived* themselves receiving the benefits they expected. Reading this research, we can hear echoes of the testimonies that adorn the mail order tape catalogs. Having bought something that is not supposed to be heard, and having indeed not heard it, many customers are impressed. "I really know that your tapes were invaluable in reprogramming my mind," wrote one thankful customer.

*"There is no evidence that commercially available subliminary auditory tapes have any genuine utility. . . . We do not recommend purchasing them."*

British Psychological Society
*Subliminal Messages*, 1992

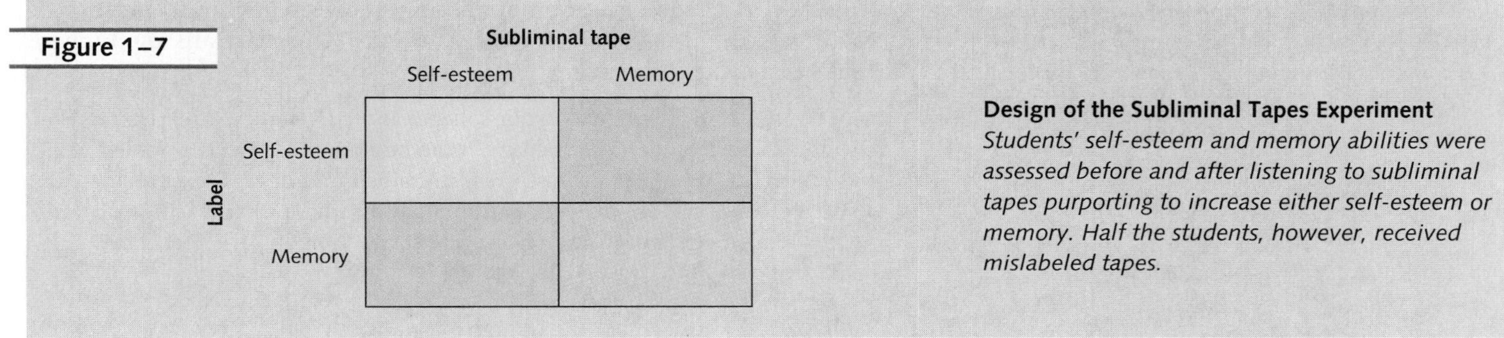


**Design of the Subliminal Tapes Experiment** *Students' self-esteem and memory abilities were assessed before and after listening to subliminal tapes purporting to increase either self-esteem or memory. Half the students, however, received mislabeled tapes.*

Our natural tendencies to try new remedies when we are in an emotional down can further distort a testimony. When our emotions rebound to normal, we attribute the rebound to something we have done. If 3 days into a cold we start taking vitamin C tablets and find our cold symptoms lessening, the pills may seem more potent than they are (an illusion of control). If, after doing exceptionally poorly on the first exam, we listen to a "peak learning" subliminal tape and find our next exam score rebounds ("regresses") toward our average, we may be deceived into crediting the tape. In the 1700s, even blood-letting *seemed* effective. Sometimes people improved after the treatment; when they didn't, the practitioner inferred the disease was too far advanced to be reversed. So, whether or not a remedy is effective, enthusiastic users will probably endorse it. To find out whether it actually is effective we must experiment.

And that is precisely how we evaluate new drug treatments and new methods of psychological therapy (see Chapter 16). In many of these studies, the subjects are "blind" (uninformed) about what treatment, if any, they are receiving. One group might receive the treatment (say, a particular subliminal message or a new drug). Others receive a pseudotreatment—an inert **placebo** (a tape without the expected message, a pill with no drug in it). Often both the subject and the research assistant who collects the data will not know which condition the subject is in. This **double-blind procedure** allows researchers to check the actual effects of a treatment apart from their subjects' and their own enthusiasm for it. In the last 10 years, 16 double-blind experiments have evaluated subliminal self-help tapes. Their results are uniform: Not one has found any therapeutic effect (Greenwald, 1992).

Experiments can also help us evaluate social programs. Do early childhood education programs boost impoverished children's chances for success? What are the effects of different anti-smoking appeals? Do school sex education programs reduce teen pregnancies? To answer such questions, we can experiment: If a treatment is welcomed but resources are scarce, we could use a lottery to randomly assign some people (or regions) to experience the new program and others to a control condition. If later the two groups differ, there will be much less to argue about (Passell, 1993).

Using the principles discussed in this chapter can also help us think critically—to see more clearly what we might otherwise miss or misinterpret and to generalize more accurately from our observations. People do think smarter when they understand and use the principles of research methods and statistics (Fong & others, 1986; Lehman & others, 1988; Vander Stoep & Shaughnessy, 1991). It requires training and practice, but developing the ability to think clearly and critically is part of becoming an educated person. The report of the Project on Redefining the Meaning and Purpose of Baccalaureate Degrees (1985) eloquently asserts why there are few higher priorities in a college education:

*Answer to question on page 28: In the subliminal tapes experiment, the primary independent variable was the type of subliminal message, self-esteem versus memory. (This experiment actually had a second independent variable as well: people's beliefs about which tape they received.) The primary dependent variable was improvement on the self-esteem and memory measures.*

> If anything is paid attention to in our colleges and universities, thinking must be it. Unfortunately, thinking can be lazy. It can be sloppy. . . . It can be fooled, misled, bullied. . . . Students possess great untrained and untapped capacities for logical thinking, critical analysis, and inquiry, but these are capacities that are not spontaneous: They grow out of wide instruction, experience, encouragement, correction, and constant use.

## Summing Up

**The Scientific Method** Research stimulates the construction of *theories*, which organize the *observations* and imply predictive *hypotheses*. These hypotheses (predictions) are then tested to validate and refine the theory and to suggest practical applications.

**Description** Through individual case studies, surveys among random samples of a population, and naturalistic observations, psychologists observe and describe behavior and mental processes. In generalizing from observations, remember: Representative samples are a better guide than vivid examples.

**Correlation** The strength of relationship between one factor and another is expressed in their *correlation.* Correlations help us to see relationships that the naked eye might miss and to discount illusory correlations and random events that might otherwise look significant. Knowing how closely two things are positively or negatively correlated tells us how much one predicts the other. But correlation is only a measure of relationship; it does not reveal cause and effect.

**Experimentation** To discover cause-and-effect relationships, psychologists conduct *experiments.* By constructing a controlled reality, experimenters can manipulate one or more factors and discover how these independent variables affect a particular behavior, the dependent variable. In many experiments, control is achieved by randomly assigning people either to be experimental subjects, who are exposed to the treatment, or control subjects, who experience no treatment or a different version of the treatment.

## Commonly Asked Questions About Psychology

*A scientific approach can restrain our flawed intuition while satisfying our curiosity about what predicts or causes behavior. But for many thoughtful students the idea of applying science to human affairs raises concerns about how well experiments relate to life, how experimenters treat human and animal subjects, and how psychologists' values influence their work and its applications.*

We have seen how case studies, surveys, and naturalistic observations allow us to describe behavior. We have noted that correlational studies assess the relationship between two factors, indicating how well we can predict one thing, knowing another. We have examined the logic that underlies experiments, which use control conditions and random assignment of subjects to isolate the effects of an independent variable on a dependent variable. And we have reflected on how a scientific approach can restrain the biases of our unaided intuition.

This is reasonable preparation for understanding what lies ahead and for thinking critically about psychological matters. Yet, knowing this much, students often approach psychology with a mixture of curiosity and apprehension. So before we plunge in, let's confront some typical questions and concerns.

### Can Laboratory Experiments Illuminate Everyday Life?

When you see or hear a report of psychological research, do you ever wonder whether people's behavior in the laboratory has "external validity"—whether it predicts their behavior in real life? Does detecting the blink of a faint red light in a dark room have anything useful to say about flying a plane at night? Does our tendency to remember best the first and last items in a list of unrelated words tell us anything about how we remember the names of people we meet at a party? After viewing a violent, sexually explicit film, does an angered man's increased willingness to push buttons he thinks electrically shock a woman really say anything about whether violent pornography makes men more likely to abuse women? Where on earth but a psychological laboratory does someone squint at red lights in a dark room, watch unrelated words flash on a video screen, or push buttons that supposedly deliver electric shocks?

Before you answer, consider the intent of laboratory experiments. Far from considering artificiality a problem, the experimenter *intends* the laboratory environment to be a simplified reality—one in which important features of everyday life can be simulated and controlled. Like an aeronautical wind tunnel that recreates atmospheric forces under controlled conditions, an experiment enables a psychologist to recreate psychological forces under controlled conditions.

Obviously, deciding whether to push a button that delivers shock is not literally the same as slapping someone in the face. But the principle is the same. The experiment's purpose is not to recreate the exact behaviors of everyday life but to test theoretical principles, notes Douglas Mook (1983). *It is the resulting principles—not the specific findings—that help explain everyday behaviors.* When psychologists apply laboratory research on aggression to actual violence, they are applying theoretical *principles* of aggressive behavior, principles refined through many experiments. Similarly, it is the principles of the visual system, developed from experiments in artificial settings (such as looking at red lights in the dark), that we apply to more complex behaviors such as night flying.

**A Cultured Greeting** *Because culture shapes people's understanding of social behavior, actions that seem ordinary to us may seem quite odd to visitors from far away. Yet, underlying these differences are powerful similarities. School children everywhere greet their teachers with respect, although not necessarily with the formality of this young Japanese schoolgirl.*

*"All people are the same; only their habits differ."*
Confucius, 551–479 B.C.

The point to remember: As psychologists, our concerns lie less with particular behaviors than with general principles that help explain many behaviors.

## Doesn't Behavior Depend on One's Culture?

If culture shapes behavior, what can psychological studies done with North Americans—often with white North Americans—really tell us about people in general? As we will see time and again, culture matters. Our culture influences our standards of promptness and frankness, our attitudes toward premarital sex and differing body shapes, our tendencies to be casual or formal, and much more. Being aware of such differences can restrain our assuming that others will, or should, think and act as we do. Given the growing mixing and clashing of cultures, the need for such awareness becomes urgent.

Yet our shared biological heritage unites us as members of a universal human family. The same underlying processes guide people everywhere. Varying languages—spoken and gestured—may impede communication across cultures. Yet all languages share deep principles of grammar, and people from opposite sides of the globe can communicate with a smile or a frown. People in different cultures vary in feelings of loneliness, yet across cultures shyness and low self-esteem magnify loneliness (Jones & others, 1985). Japanese prefer their fish raw while North Americans prefer theirs cooked, but the same principles of hunger and taste influence both. It is truly said that we are each in certain respects like all others, like some others, and like no other. Studying people of all races, sexes, and cultures helps us discern our similarities and differences.

The point to remember: Even when specific attitudes and behaviors vary across cultures, as they often do, the underlying processes are much the same.

## Doesn't Behavior Vary With Gender?

At your birth, people immediately wondered which of the two human types you were: male or female. Given how basic our sex is to our identity and to others' perceptions of us, do we need a different psychology for women and for men?

As you will see throughout this book, gender issues penetrate psychology. For instance, researchers report gender differences in what we dream, how we express and detect emotions, and in our risk of alcoholism, depression, and eating disorders. Studying such differences is not only interesting, but potentially beneficial. Many researchers believe, for example, that women converse more readily to build relationships, and that men talk more to give information and advice (Tannen, 1990). Knowing this difference can help prevent conflicts and misunderstandings on the job and in everyday relationships.

Nevertheless, it's important to remember that psychologically as well as biologically, women and men are overwhelmingly similar. Whether female or male, we learn to walk about the same age; experience the same sensations of light and sound; feel the same pangs of hunger, desire, and fear; and exhibit similar overall intelligence and happiness. Moreover, we tend to exhibit and perceive the very behaviors our culture *expects* of males and females.

So, gender matters. Biology determines our sex, and then culture further bends the genders. But viewing life through the lens of gender can exaggerate the differences. The lesson of research embedded throughout this book is expressed by a children's song: "We're all the same and different."

### What Do Animal Experiments Tell Us About People?

Many psychologists study animals because they find them fascinating. Psychologists also study animals to learn about people, by doing experiments that are permissible only with animals. Human physiology resembles that of many other animals. That is why animal experiments have led to treatments for human diseases—insulin for diabetes, vaccines to prevent polio and rabies, transplants to replace defective organs.

Likewise, the processes by which humans see, exhibit emotion, and become obese operate in rats and monkeys. To discover more about the basics of human learning, researchers are even studying sea slugs. To understand how a combustion engine works, you would do better to study a lawn mower's engine than a Mercedes'. Humans, like Mercedes, are more complex. But it is precisely the simplicity of the sea slug's nervous system that makes it so revealing of the neural mechanisms of learning.

### Is It Ethical to Experiment on Animals?

If we share important similarities with other animals, then should we not respect them? "We cannot defend our scientific work with animals on the basis of the similarities between them and ourselves and then defend it morally on the basis of differences," notes Roger Ulrich (1991). The animal protection movement protests the use of animals in psychological, biological, and medical research—some 20 million animals annually, according to the National Academy of Sciences (1991). Researchers remind us that these 20 million animals are less than 1 percent of the 5 billion animals killed annually in the United States as a source of food (which means the average American eats 20 animals a year without allowing for imported meat). While researchers each year conduct experiments on some 200,000 dogs and cats cared for under humane regulations, animal shelters kill 50 times that many.

**A Question of Ethics** *Is it right to use animals to advance our understanding of humans? For animal rights activists, no purpose justifies hurting, frightening, or (as shown here) manipulating an animal. For most psychologists and medical researchers, animal research is ethically justified so long as researchers observe strict standards and inflict no unnecessary pain.*

Mobilization for Animals, a network of some 400 animal protection organizations, is nevertheless concerned. It has declared that in psychological experiments animals are shocked "until they lose the ability to even scream in pain, . . . deprived of food and water to suffer and die slowly from hunger and thirst, . . . put in total isolation chambers until they are driven insane or even die from despair and terror," and made "the victims of extreme pain and stress, inflicted upon them out of idle curiosity." Psychologists Caroline Coile and Neal Miller (1984) analyzed every animal research article published in the American Psychological Association's journals during the preceding 5 years. They found not one study in which any of these allegations was true. Even when researchers used shock, it usually was of a mild intensity that humans can easily endure on their fingers. Only 7 percent of psychology's studies have involved animals, 95 percent of which are rats, mice, rabbits, or birds. About 10 percent of these animal studies involved electric shock (Coile & Miller, 1984; Gallup & Suarez, 1985). In British psychology departments, where animal use has dropped by two-thirds since 1977, electric shock is used in but 4 percent of animal studies—all involving rats (Thomas & Blackman, 1991).

*"I believe that to prevent, cripple, or needlessly complicate the research that can relieve animal and human suffering is profoundly inhuman, cruel, and immoral."*

Psychologist Neal Miller (1983)

Moreover, say researchers, this is not the morality of good versus evil but of compassion (for animals) versus compassion (for people). How many of us would have attacked Pasteur's experiments with rabies, which in causing some dogs to suffer led to a vaccine that spared millions of people, and dogs, from agonizing death? And would we really wish to have deprived ourselves of the animal research that led to effective methods of training retarded children; of relieving fears and depression; and of controlling obesity, alcoholism, and stress-related pain and disease?

Out of the heated debate on this subject, two issues emerge. The basic one is whether it is right to place the well-being of humans above that of animals. In experiments on stress and cancer, is it right that mice get tumors so that people might not? Should some monkeys be exposed to an HIV-like virus in the search for developing an AIDS vaccine? Is the human use of other animals as natural and moral as the behavior of carnivorous hawks, cats, and whales? (Animals themselves do not assign rights to other animals lower on the food chain.) Defenders of research on animals argue that anyone who has eaten a hamburger, worn leather shoes, tolerated hunting and fishing, or supported the extermination of crop-destroying or plague-carrying pests has already agreed that, yes, it is sometimes permissible to sacrifice animals for the sake of human well-being. After all, the most fundamental right is the right not to be eaten.

*"Please do not forget those of us who suffer from incurable diseases or disabilities who hope for a cure through research that requires the use of animals."*

Paraplegic psychologist Dennis Feeney (1987)

Scott Plous (1993) notes that our compassion for animals varies, as does our compassion for people, based on their perceived similarity to us. As Chapter 18 explains, we feel more attraction, give more help, and act less aggressively toward similar others. Likewise, we value animals according to their perceived kinship with us. Few people equate all animals as does Ingrid Newkirk, the director of People for the Ethical Treatment of Animals: "A rat is a pig is a dog is a boy" (quoted by Baldwin, 1993). Primates and companion pets get top priority. (Western people raise or trap mink and foxes for their fur, but not dogs or cats.) Other mammals occupy the second rung on the privilege ladder, followed by birds, fish, and reptiles on the third rung, with insects at the bottom. In human-animal relations, a cockroach is not a crow is not a cow is not a collie or chimpanzee. In deciding which animals have rights we must draw a cut-off line somewhere across the animal kingdom.

*"The righteous know the needs of their animals."*

Proverbs 12:10

If we give human life first priority, the second issue is the priority given the well-being of animals. What safeguards should protect animals? Most researchers today feel ethically obligated to enhance the well-being of captive animals and protect them from needless suffering. They also believe that humane care is good science, because pain and stress would distort animals' behavior during experiments. Thus, they welcomed national animal protection legislation updated by the United States in 1985 and Britain in 1986 and the accompanying regulations and laboratory inspections (Cherfas, 1990; Johnson, 1990). The American Psychological Association, for example, has developed extensive guidelines for the care and justified use of animals.

Ironically, animals have themselves benefitted from animal research. Studies have helped improve their care in laboratories and zoos. By revealing our behavioral kinship with animals and the remarkable intelligence of some animals, experiments have also increased our empathy with them. At its best, a psychology that is concerned for humans and sensitive to animals can serve the welfare of both.

*"The greatness of a nation can be judged by the way its animals are treated."*

Mahatma Gandhi, 1869–1948

### Is It Ethical to Experiment on People?

If the image of animals or people receiving supposed electric shocks troubles you, you may find it reassuring that most psychological research involves no such stress. Blinking lights, flashing words, and pleasant social interactions are the rule.

Occasionally, though, researchers temporarily stress or deceive people. This is done only when judged essential to a justifiable end, such as understanding and controlling violent behavior or studying mood swings. Such experiments wouldn't work if the participants knew all there was to know about the experiment beforehand. Either the procedures would be ineffective or the participants, wanting to be helpful, might try to confirm the researchers' predictions.

Ethical principles developed by the American Psychological Association (1992) and the British Psychological Society (1993) urge investigators to (1) obtain the informed consent of potential participants, (2) protect them from harm and discomfort, (3) treat information about individual participants confidentially, and (4) fully explain the research afterward. Moreover, most universities today screen research proposals through an ethics committee that safeguards participants' well-being.

### Is Psychology Free of Value Judgments?

Psychology is definitely not value-free. Values affect what we study, how we study it, and how we interpret results. Consider: Researchers' values influence their choice of research topics—whether to study worker productivity or worker morale, sex discrimination or sex differences, conformity or independence. Values can also color "the facts." Our preconceptions can bias our observations and interpretations; sometimes we see what we want or expect to see. Even the words we use to describe a phenomenon can reflect our values. Whether we label sex acts we do not practice as "perversions" or as "sexual variations" conveys a value judgment. The same holds true in everyday speech, as when one person's "terrorists" are another's "freedom fighters," or one person's "faith" is another's "fanaticism." Our labeling someone as "firm" or "stubborn," "careful" or "picky," "discreet" or "secretive" reveals our feelings. Both in and out of psychology, labels describe and labels evaluate.

*"It is doubtless impossible to approach any human problem with a mind free from bias."*

Simone de Beauvoir
*The Second Sex,* 1953

Popular applications of psychology also contain hidden values. When people defer to "professional" guidance about how to live—how to raise children, how to achieve self-fulfillment, what to do with sexual feelings,

**What Do You See?** *People interpret ambiguous information to fit their preconceptions. Did you see a duck or a rabbit? What influenced your first impression? (From Shepard, 1990.)*

how to get ahead at work—they are accepting value-laden advice. A science of behavior and mental processes can help us reach our goals, but it cannot decide them.

### Is Psychology Potentially Dangerous?

If some people see psychology as mere common sense, others have an opposite concern—that it is becoming dangerously powerful. Is it an accident, someone once wondered, that astronomy is the oldest science and psychology the youngest? Exploring the external universe is one thing, but exploring our own inner universe is even more dangerous and threatening. Might psychology be used to manipulate people? Might it become the tool of someone seeking to create a totalitarian *Brave New World* or *Nineteen Eighty-Four?*

Knowledge is a power that, like all powers, we can use for good or evil. Nuclear power has been used to light up cities—and to demolish them. Persuasive power has been used to educate people—and to deceive them. The power of mind-altering drugs has been used to restore sanity—and to destroy it.

Although it has the power to deceive, psychology strives to enlighten. Psychologists are exploring ways to enhance moral development, perceptual accuracy, learning, creativity, and compassion. And psychology speaks to many of the world's great problems—war, overpopulation, prejudice, family dysfunction, crime—all of which involve attitudes and behaviors. Psychology also speaks to humanity's deepest longings—for love, for happiness, even for food and water. Psychology cannot address all the great questions of life, but it speaks to some mighty important ones.

## Summing Up

**Can Laboratory Experiments Illuminate Everyday Life?** By intentionally creating a controlled, artificial environment in the lab, researchers aim to test theoretical principles. These principles help us to understand, describe, explain, and predict everyday behaviors.

**Doesn't Behavior Depend on One's Culture?** Although attitudes and behaviors vary across cultures, the principles that underlie them vary much less. Cross-cultural psychology explores both our cultural differences and the universal similarities that define our human kinship.

**Doesn't Behavior Vary With Gender?** Gender is a basic fact of life. Although gender differences tend to capture attention, it is important to remember our greater gender similarities.

**What Do Animal Experiments Tell Us About People?** Some psychologists study animals out of an interest in animal behavior. Others do so because knowledge of the physiological and psychological processes of animals gives them a better understanding of the similar processes operating in humans.

**Is It Ethical to Experiment on Animals?** Only about 7 percent of all psychological experiments involve animals, and under ethical and legal guidelines these animals rarely experience pain. Nevertheless, animal rights groups raise an important issue: Is an animal's temporary suffering justified if it leads to the relief of human suffering?

**Is It Ethical to Experiment on People?** Occasionally researchers temporarily stress or deceive people in order to learn something important. Professional ethical standards provide guidelines concerning the treatment of human as well as animal participants.

**Is Psychology Free of Value Judgments?** Psychology is not value-free. Psychologists' own values influence their choice of research topics, their theories and observations, their labels for behavior, and their professional advice.

**Is Psychology Potentially Dangerous?** Knowledge is power that can be used for good or evil. Applications of psychology's principles have so far been mostly for the good, and psychology addresses some of humanity's greatest problems and deepest longings.

## Terms and Concepts to Remember

### The Scientific Attitude

**critical thinking** Thinking that does not blindly accept arguments and conclusions. Rather, it examines assumptions, discerns hidden values, evaluates evidence, and assesses conclusions.

### The Limits of Intuition and Common Sense

**hindsight bias** The tendency to believe, after learning an outcome, that one would have foreseen it. (Also known as the I-knew-it-all-along phenomenon.)

### Research Strategies: How Psychologists Ask and Answer Questions

**theory** An explanation via an integrated set of principles that organizes and predicts observations.

**hypothesis** A testable prediction, often implied by a theory.

**replication** Repeating the essence of a research study, usually with different subjects in different situations, to see whether the basic finding generalizes to other subjects and circumstances.

**survey** A technique for ascertaining the self-reported attitudes or behaviors of people, usually by questioning a representative, random sample of them.

**case study** An observation technique in which one person is studied in depth in the hopes of revealing universal principles.

**false consensus effect** The tendency to overestimate the extent to which others share our beliefs and behaviors.

**population** All the cases in a group, from which samples may be drawn for a study.

**random sample** A sample that fairly represents a population because each member has an equal chance of inclusion.

**naturalistic observation** Observing and recording behavior in naturally occurring situations without trying to manipulate and control the situation.

**correlation** A statistical measure that indicates the extent to which two factors vary together and thus how well either factor predicts the other.

**illusory correlation** The perception of a relationship where none exists.

**experiment** A research method in which the investigator manipulates one or more factors (independent variables) to observe their effect on some behavior or mental process (the dependent variable) while controlling other relevant factors by random assignment of subjects.

**experimental condition** The condition of an experiment that exposes subjects to the treatment, that is, to one version of the independent variable.

**control condition** The condition of an experiment that contrasts with the experimental treatment and serves as a comparison for evaluating the effect of the treatment.

**random assignment** Assigning subjects to experimental and control conditions by chance, thus minimizing preexisting differences between those assigned to the different groups.

**independent variable** The experimental factor that is manipulated; the variable whose effect is being studied.

**dependent variable** The experimental factor—in psychology, the behavior or mental process—that is being measured; the variable that may change in response to manipulations of the independent variable.

**operational definition** A statement of the procedures (operations) used to define research variables.

**placebo** [pluh-SEE-bo] An inert substance or condition that may be administered instead of a presumed active agent, such as a drug, to see if it triggers the effects believed to characterize the active agent.

**double-blind procedure** An experimental procedure in which both the subject and the research staff are ignorant (blind) about whether the subject has received the treatment or a placebo. Commonly used in drug evaluation studies.

## Critical Thinking Exercise*

Now that you have read and reviewed Chapter 1, take your learning a step further by testing your critical thinking skills on this scientific problem solving exercise. For an introduction to these exercises, turn to Appendix B before working this exercise.

> Philip, who teaches first grade, believes that educational television programs such as *Sesame Street* promote reading ability in young children. He announces his hunch to his students and tells their parents about his idea during a P.T.A. meeting. Some parents respond enthusiastically when he asks for volunteers to participate in a 3-month experiment to test his hypothesis. Ten volunteers are assigned to the experimental group and instructed to have their children watch the 1-hour *Sesame Street* program each day after school. The parents of 10 other students, who are picked at random from the remaining members of the class, receive the same instructions except that the target program is a 1-hour, noneducational cartoon. After the 3-month period, Philip administers a standardized reading test to both groups. He is delighted to find that students in the experimental group have a substantially higher average test score than students in the comparison group.

1. What is the *focal behavior* of the study?
2. What is Philip's *hypothesis*?
3. What is the *independent variable*?
4. What is the *dependent variable*?
5. List three variables that are controlled in the experiment.
6. List three variables that aren't controlled and explain how they might have affected Philip's findings.
7. Was the research a valid test of the hypothesis? Explain your reasoning.

Check your progress on becoming a critical thinker by comparing your answers to the sample answers found in Appendix B.

*The Critical Thinking Exercise at the end of each chapter was prepared by Richard O. Straub, University of Michigan, Dearborn.

## For Further Reading

*The best effect of any book is that it excites the reader to self-activity.*

Thomas Carlyle, 1795–1881

At the conclusion of each chapter I suggest several books or articles you could explore for further information.

For many students, the most helpful supplementary source will be the innovative *Study Guide* by Richard O. Straub that accompanies this text. It begins with a guide to managing your time and improving the productivity of your study. For each text chapter, the *Study Guide* provides learning objectives; a programmed review of the chapter; multiple-choice practice quizzes (with answers—including explanations of what is wrong with the incorrect choices); a discussion of key terms; and an explanation of difficult words and phrases for those whose first language is not English. My students who have trouble with exams find it a valuable study aid—almost like a tutor.

For an informative free booklet that describes psychology's fields and careers, you can write the American Psychological Association, 750 First Street, N.E., Washington, D.C. 20002-4242, and request "Careers in Psychology."

Here are some other items of possible interest:

**American Psychological Association** (1993). *Guidelines for ethical conduct in the care and use of animals.* Washington, D.C.

*An 11-page pamphlet from the American Psychological Association's Committee on Animal Research and Ethics (CARE) offers standards for the acquisition, care, and use of animals. For a free copy, write Science Directorate, American Psychological Association, 750 First Street, N.E., Washington, D.C. 20002-4242.*

**Paulos, J. A.** (1988). *Innumeracy: Mathematical illiteracy and its consequences.* New York: Hill and Wang.

*A delightful book filled with humorous examples of how our mathematical intuition fails us and why we need to become more mathematically and statistically literate.*

**Shaughnessy, J. J., & Zechmeister, E. B.** (1994). *Research methods in psychology* (3rd ed.). New York: McGraw-Hill.

*An excellent, gentle introduction to basic statistical methods and procedures used by psychologists; shows how our everyday use of them can sharpen our reasoning.*

**Stanovich, K. E.** (1992). *How to think straight about psychology* (3rd ed.). Glenview, IL: Scott Foresman.

*A delightful read for those who want to think straight about many things; alerts us to how popular media mislead and how we deceive ourselves.*

# CHAPTER 2



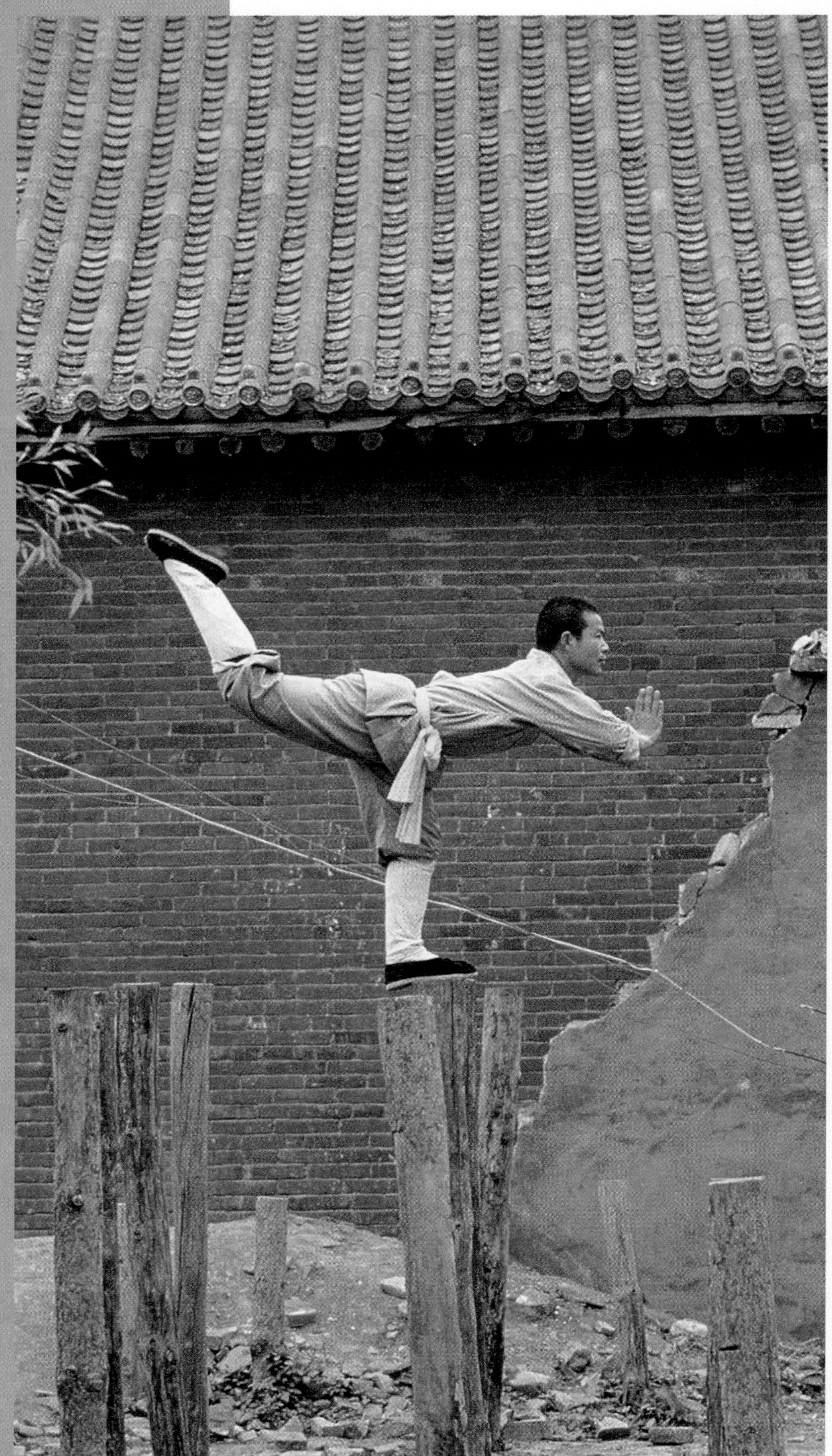

# Neuroscience and Behavior

No principle is more central to today's psychology, or to this book, than this: *Everything psychological is simultaneously biological.* Your every idea, every mood, every urge is a biological happening. You are a body. You think, feel, and act with your body. You relate to the world through your body. (Try laughing, crying, or loving without it.) Your body—your genes, your brain, your body chemistry, your inner organs, your appearance—is you. Without your body, you are, indeed, nobody. Although we find it convenient to talk separately of biological and psychological influences on behavior, let us not forget: To think, feel, or act without a body is as plausible as running without legs.

As we finish this century, scientific attention is riveted on this chapter's focus—the most amazing part of our body: our brain and its component neural systems. The brain's ultimate challenge is to understand itself. How does the brain communicate with itself? How does experience modify it? How do its various parts process the information needed for a basketball player's jump shot? A poet's rhythm of words? A lover's memory of the first kiss?

To appreciate the excitement that pervades this "decade of the brain" (as declared by the U.S. Congress), consider the explosion in our understanding of how the brain enables the mind. On the time scale of human existence, the last 150 years are only a few ticks of the clock. But that's how recently a scientific understanding of the brain-mind connection began to emerge. We have come far since the early 1800s, when a German physician named Franz Gall invented *phrenology*, an ill-fated theory that bumps on the skull could reveal our mental abilities and character traits. At one point, Great Britain had 29 phrenological societies, and phrenologists traveled North America giving skull readings (Hunt, 1993).

**A Wrongheaded Theory** *Despite initial acceptance of Gall's speculations, bumps on the skull tell us nothing about how the brain works. Nevertheless, some of his assumptions have been found to hold true: Different parts of the brain do control different aspects of behavior.*

Despite its wrong-headedness, phrenology focused attention on the idea that various brain regions have particular functions. In little more than a century, we have also realized that the body is composed of cells; that among these are nerve cells that conduct electricity and "talk" to one another by sending chemical messages across a tiny gap that separates them; that specific brain systems serve specific functions (though not the functions that Gall supposed); and that from the information processed in these different brain systems we construct our experience of sights and sounds, meanings and memories, pain and passion. You and I are privileged to live in a time when discoveries about the interplay of our biology and behavior are occurring at an exhilarating pace.

Throughout this book you will find examples of how our biology underlies our behavior and mental processes. By studying the links between biological activity and psychological events, **biological psychologists** are gaining a better understanding of sleep and dreams, depression and schizophrenia, hunger and sex, stress and disease. We therefore begin our study of psychology with a look at its biological roots. Chapter 2 explores the neuroscience revolution, and Chapter 3 examines genetic influences on behavior.

## Neural Communication

*The body's information system is built from billions of interconnected cells called neurons. To fathom our thoughts and actions, memories and moods, we must first understand how neurons work and communicate.*

We are each a system, composed of subsystems that are parts of larger systems. Body organs such as the stomach, heart, and brain form larger systems for digestion, circulation, and information processing, which are part of an even larger system—you, which in turn forms a part of your family, community, and culture. Your organs, in turn, are composed of subsystems—cells—that operate biochemically. At every level, then, our existence is both part of a larger system and a combination of smaller systems. For a deep understanding of behavior, we must study how biological, psychological, and social systems work and interact.

In this chapter, we start small and begin building—up to the brain (and, by Chapters 18 and 19, to the social and cultural influences that interact with our biology). At all levels, psychologists examine how we process information—how we get information in; how we organize, interpret, and store it; and how we use it. For scientists, it is a happy fact of nature that the information systems of humans and other animals operate similarly. So similarly, in fact, that you could not distinguish between small samples of brain tissue from a person and a monkey. This similarity allows researchers to study simple animals, such as squids and sea slugs, to discover how their neural systems operate and to study mammals' brains to understand the organization of our own. Human brains are more complex, but they follow principles that govern the rest of the animal world.

### Neurons

Our body's neural information system is complexity built from simplicity. Its building blocks are **neurons**, or nerve cells. Each neuron consists of a cell body and its branching fibers (Figure 2–1). The fibers are of two types:

The bushy **dendrites** receive information. The **axon** passes it along to other neurons or to muscles or glands. Unlike the short dendrites, axons may be short or may project through the body up to several feet. The cell body and axon of a motor neuron are roughly on the scale of a basketball attached to a rope 4 miles long. A layer of fatty cells, called the **myelin sheath**, insulates the axons of some neurons and helps speed their impulses. The importance of the myelin sheath can be seen in the disease multiple sclerosis, in which the myelin sheath degenerates, with resulting slowdown of communication to muscles and loss of muscle control.

*"Dendrite" is derived from the Greek word* dendron, *meaning tree.*

Figure 2–1

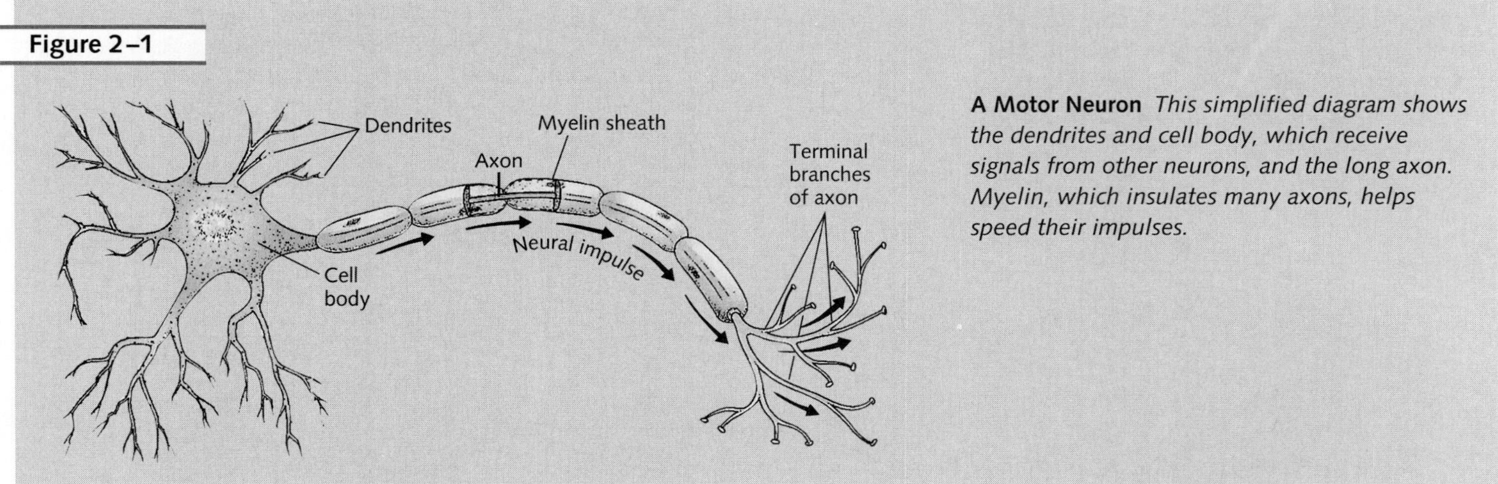


**A Motor Neuron** *This simplified diagram shows the dendrites and cell body, which receive signals from other neurons, and the long axon. Myelin, which insulates many axons, helps speed their impulses.*

Depending on the type of fiber, the neural impulse travels at speeds ranging from a sluggish 2 miles per hour to, in some myelinated fibers, a breakneck 200 or more miles per hour. But even this top speed is 3 million times slower than the speed of electricity through a wire. That helps to explain why, unlike the nearly instantaneous reactions of a high-speed computer, it may take a quarter-second or more for you to react to a sudden event, such as a child darting in front of your car.

A neuron fires an impulse when stimulated by pressure, heat, light, or chemical messages from adjacent neurons. The impulse, called the **action potential**, is a brief electrical charge that travels down the axon, rather like a line of dominoes falling. As batteries generate electricity from chemical events, so the neuron's electrical impulse arises from chemical events.

*"I sing the body electric."*
Walt Whitman
"Children of Adam," 1855

The chemistry-to-electricity process works roughly like this: The fluid interior of a resting axon carries mostly negatively charged atoms, while the fluid outside the axon membrane has mostly positively charged atoms (Figure 2–2, page 44). This positive-outside/negative-inside polarization occurs because the cell's membrane is selectively permeable—it has gates that the positive atoms cannot pass through. When a neuron fires, the first bit of the axon opens its gates, allowing the positively charged atoms to rush in through a channel. This *depolarizes* that part of the axon, which causes the axon's next channel to open, and then the next, like dominoes falling. During a resting pause (the *refractory period*), the neuron pumps positively charged atoms back outside. Then it can fire again. Although the mind boggles when imagining this electrochemical process repeating 100 times a second, this is but the first of many astonishments.

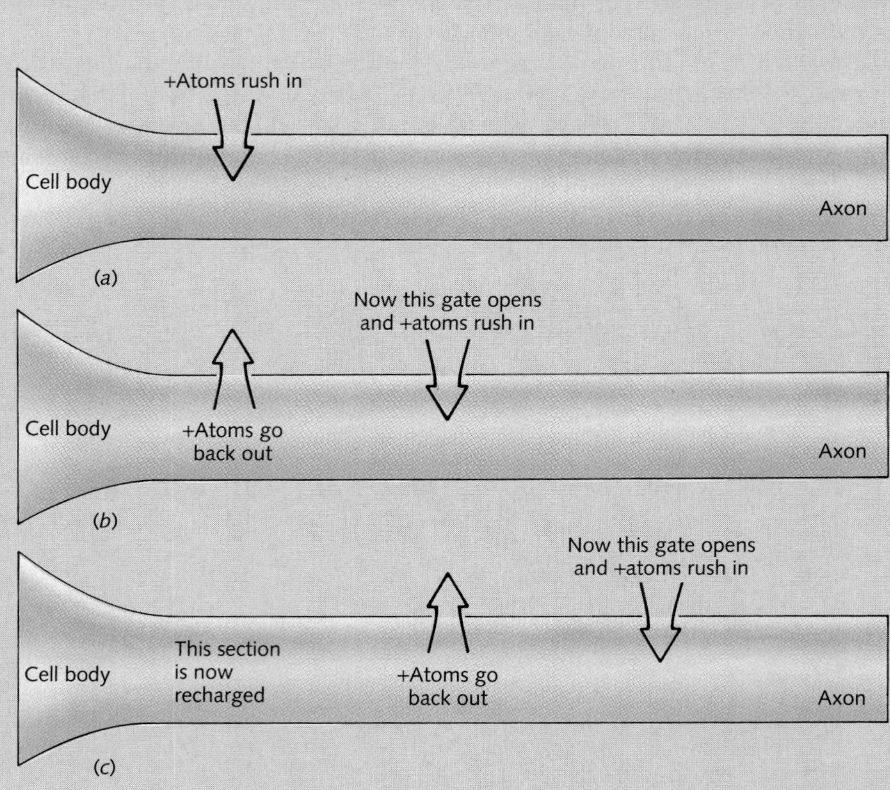


**Figure 2–2**

**Axonal Transmission** *A neuron fires an impulse when stimulated by pressure, heat, light, or chemical messages from adjacent neurons. This brief electrical charge, called an action potential, travels down the axon, beginning (a) at the juncture of the cell body and the axon. A thousandth of a second later (b), the electrical change produces another action potential a little farther along the axon, and the first section begins to recharge. After another thousandth of a second (c), the action potential appears to have moved farther along the axon, and the first section has completely recharged.*

*You can remember the dendrite-axon sequence as DA—District Attorney.*

The neuron, a miniature decision-making device, receives signals on its dendrites and cell body from hundreds or even thousands of other neurons. Some of these signals are excitatory, rather like pushing a neuron's accelerator. Other signals are inhibitory, rather like pushing its brake. The combined signals trigger an impulse if excitatory signals minus inhibitory signals exceed a minimum intensity, called the **threshold**. If excitatory inputs exceed the threshold, the neuron transmits an electrical impulse down its axon, which branches into junctions with hundreds or thousands of other neurons and with the body's muscles and glands.

Increasing the stimulus above the threshold, however, will not increase the impulse's intensity. (The neuron's reaction is an *all-or-none response*; like guns, neurons either fire or they don't.) Nor does the strength of the stimulus affect the impulse's speed.

How then do we detect the intensity of a stimulus? How do we distinguish a gentle touch from a firm hug? Although a strong stimulus cannot trigger a stronger or faster impulse in a neuron, it can trigger more neurons to fire, and to fire more often.

## How Neurons Communicate

Neurons interweave so intricately that even with a microscope it is hard to see where one neuron ends and another begins. A hundred years ago many scientists believed that the branching axon of one cell fused with the dendrites of another in an uninterrupted fabric. But then British physiologist

Sir Charles Sherrington (1857–1952) noticed that neural impulses were taking more time to travel a neural pathway than they should. Sherrington inferred there must be a brief interruption in the transmission.

We now know that the axon terminal of one neuron is indeed separated from the receiving neuron by a tiny gap less than a millionth of an inch wide. This junction Sherrington called the **synapse**, and the gap is called the *synaptic gap* or cleft. To the Nobel laureate, Spanish neuroanatomist Santiago Ramón y Cajal (1832–1934), these near-unions of neurons—"protoplasmic kisses," he called them—were another of nature's marvels. How does the nerve impulse execute the protoplasmic kiss? How does it cross the tiny synaptic gap? The answer is one of the important scientific discoveries of our age.

*"All information processing in the brain involves neurons 'talking to' each other at synapses."*

Neuroscientist Solomon H. Snyder (1984)

When the action potential reaches the knoblike terminals at an axon's end, it triggers the release of chemical messengers, called **neurotransmitters** (Figure 2–3). Within 1/10,000th of a second, the neurotransmitter molecules cross the synaptic gap and bind to receptor sites on the receiving neuron—as precisely as a key fits a lock. For an instant, the neurotransmitter unlocks tiny channels at the receiving site. This allows ions (electrically charged atoms) to enter the receiving neuron, thereby either exciting or inhibiting its readiness to fire.

**Figure 2–3**

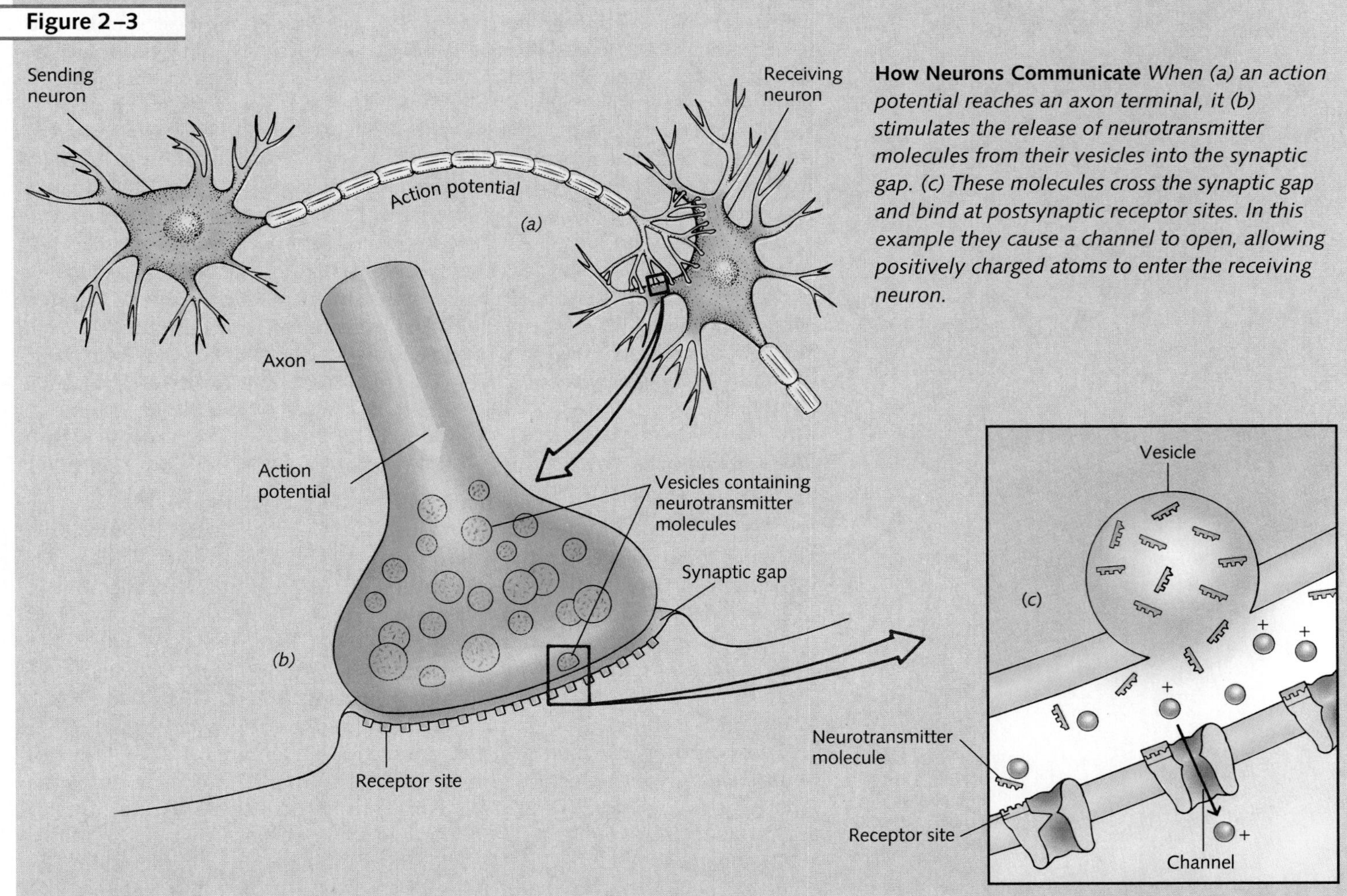


**How Neurons Communicate** *When (a) an action potential reaches an axon terminal, it (b) stimulates the release of neurotransmitter molecules from their vesicles into the synaptic gap. (c) These molecules cross the synaptic gap and bind at postsynaptic receptor sites. In this example they cause a channel to open, allowing positively charged atoms to enter the receiving neuron.*

Most neurons have a resting rate of random firing that increases or decreases with input from other neurons and from chemicals that affect their sensitivity. Roughly speaking, the neuron is democratic: If it receives many more excitatory than inhibitory messages, the cell fires often. More electrical impulses flash down its axon, releasing more packets of neurotransmitters, which diffuse across their synaptic gaps to other neurons.

## How Neurotransmitters Influence Us

The discovery of some 75 different neurotransmitters raises a host of questions: Are certain neurotransmitters found only in specific places? What are their effects? Can we boost or diminish these effects through drugs or diet? Could such changes affect our moods, memories, or mental abilities? Such questions intrigue neuroscience researchers—stimulating reports on 3000 new neurotransmitter studies at the 1992 Society for Neuroscience meeting—and fascinate those of us who are their spectators.

*"When it comes to the brain, if you want to see the action, follow the neurotransmitters."*
Neuroscientist Floyd Bloom (1993)

Later chapters explain the role of neurotransmitters in depression and euphoria, hunger and thinking, addictions and therapy. For now, let's glimpse how neurotransmitters influence our motions and emotions. We now know that a particular neural pathway in the brain may use only one or two neurotransmitters, and that particular neurotransmitters may have particular effects on behavior and emotions. One of the best understood neurotransmitters, **acetylcholine (ACh)**, is the messenger at every junction between a motor neuron and muscle. With powerful electron microscopes, neurobiologists can magnify thinly sliced specimens of tissue enough to see the sacs that store and release ACh molecules. When ACh is released to the muscle cells, the muscle contracts.

If the transmission of ACh is blocked, muscles cannot contract. Curare, a poison that certain South American Indians put on the tips of their hunting darts, occupies and blocks ACh receptor sites, leaving the neurotransmitter unable to affect the muscles. Struck by one of these darts, an animal becomes paralyzed. Botulin, a poison that can form in improperly canned food, causes paralysis by blocking ACh release from the sending neuron. By contrast, the venom of the black widow spider causes a synaptic flood of ACh. The result? Violent muscle contractions, convulsions, and possible death.

### The Endorphins

An exciting discovery about neurotransmitters occurred when Candace Pert and Solomon Snyder (1973) attached a radioactive tracer to morphine, allowing them to see exactly where in an animal's brain it was taken up. (Morphine, an opiate drug, elevates mood and eases pain.) Pert and Snyder discovered that the morphine was taken up by receptors in areas linked with mood and pain sensations.

It was hard to imagine why the brain would contain these "opiate receptors" unless it had its own naturally occurring opiates. Why would the brain have a chemical lock, unless it also had a corresponding key? Researchers soon confirmed that the brain indeed contains several types of neurotransmitter molecules similar to morphine. Named **endorphins** (short for *endo*genous [produced within] m*orphine*), these natural opiates are released in response to pain and vigorous exercise (Farrell & others, 1982; Lagerweij & others, 1984). They may therefore help explain all sorts of good feelings, such as the "runner's high," the pain-killing effects of acupuncture, and the indifference to pain in some injured people, such as David Livingstone reported in his 1857 *Missionary Travels*:

> I heard a shout. Starting, and looking half round, I saw the lion just in the act of springing upon me. I was upon a little height, he caught my shoulder as he sprang, and we both came to the ground below together. Growling horribly close to my ear, he shook me as a terrier does a rat. The shock produced a stupor similar to that which seems to be felt by a mouse after the first shake of the cat. It caused a sort of dreaminess in which there was no sense of pain nor feeling of terror, though [I was] quite conscious of all that was happening. . . . This peculiar state is probably produced in all animals killed by the carnivora; and if so, is a merciful provision by our benevolent creator for lessening the pain of death.

*Physician Lewis Thomas on the endorphins: "There it is, a biologically universal act of mercy. I cannot explain it, except to say that I would have put it in had I been around at the very beginning, sitting as a member of a planning committee."*

*The Youngest Science*, 1983

### How Drugs Alter Neurotransmission

If indeed the endorphins lessen pain and boost mood, why not flood the brain with artificial opiates, thereby intensifying the brain's own "feel good" chemistry? One problem is that when flooded with opiate drugs such as heroin and morphine, the brain may stop producing its own natural opiates. When the drug is withdrawn, the brain may therefore be deprived of any form of opiate. For a drug addict, the result is agony that persists until the brain resumes production of its natural opiates or receives more of the drug. As we will see in later chapters, mood-altering drugs, from alcohol to nicotine to heroin, share a common effect: They trigger unpleasant, lingering aftereffects. For suppressing the body's own neurotransmitter production, nature charges a price.

The good news is that neurotransmitter research is enabling the creation of new therapeutic drugs, such as those used to alleviate depression and schizophrenia. Some work by mimicking or blocking a particular neurotransmitter (Figure 2–4). Others work by hampering the neurotransmitter's natural breakdown or its reabsorption. But designing a drug can be harder than it sounds, because some chemicals don't have the right shape to slither through the *blood-brain barrier* by which the brain fences out unwanted chemicals circulating in the blood. For example, scientists know that the tremors of Parkinson's disease result from the death of nerve cells that produce a neurotransmitter called *dopamine*. Giving the patient dopamine as a drug doesn't help, though, because dopamine cannot cross the blood-brain barrier. But L-dopa, a raw material the brain can convert to dopamine, can sneak through. Given L-dopa, the patients' healthy, dopamine-making neurons produce extra dopamine, helping them regain control over their muscles.

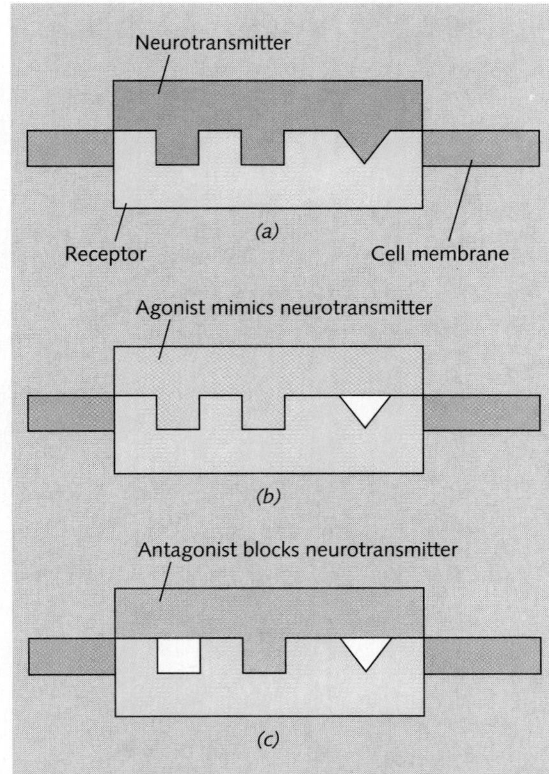


**Figure 2–4**

**Drugs That Mimic or Block Natural Neurotransmitters** *Part (a) shows a neurotransmitter molecule stimulating a receptor. Part (b) shows a drug molecule (an "agonist") similar enough to the neurotransmitter to mimic its effects. This may, for example, produce a temporary "high" by amplifying normal sensations of arousal or pleasure (as with opiate drugs). Part (c) shows a drug molecule (an "antagonist") enough like the natural neurotransmitter to occupy its receptor site and block its effect but not similar enough to stimulate the receptor. Some poison and snake venoms paralyze by blocking acetylcholine receptors that produce muscle movement.*

## Summing Up

The body's circuitry, the nervous system, consists of billions of individual cells called *neurons*. A neuron receives signals from other neurons through its branching dendrites and cell body, combines these signals in the cell body, and transmits an electrical impulse (the action potential) down its axon. When these signals reach the end of the axon, they stimulate the release of chemical messengers called *neurotransmitters*. These molecules pass on their excitatory or inhibitory messages as they traverse the tiny synaptic gap between neurons and combine with receptor sites on neighboring neurons. Researchers are studying neurotransmitters to discern their role in behavior and emotion.

# Neural and Hormonal Systems

*To live is to take information in from the world and the body's tissues, to make decisions, and to send information and orders back to the body's tissues. Neurons are the elementary components of our nervous system, our body's speedy electrochemical information system. Hormones released by the endocrine glands form the body's slower information system.*

Neurons communicating with other neurons form our body's primary information system, the **nervous system** (Figure 2–5). The brain and spinal cord form the **central nervous system**. The **peripheral nervous system** links the central nervous system with the body's sense receptors, muscles, and glands. The sensory and motor axons carrying this information are bundled into the electrical cables that we know as **nerves**. The optic nerve, for example, bundles nearly a million axon fibers into a single cable carrying the information that each eye sends to the brain.

Figure 2–5

The Functional Divisions of the Human Nervous System

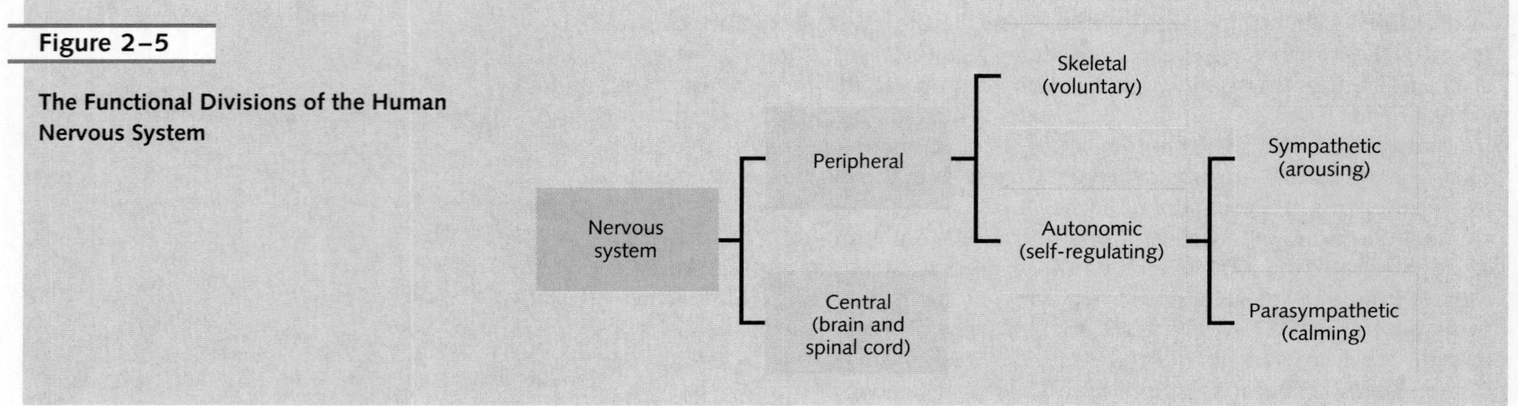


Information travels in the nervous system through three types of neurons. The **sensory neurons** send information from the body's tissues and sensory organs inward to the brain and spinal cord, which process the information. This processing involves a second class of neurons, the central nervous system's own **interneurons**, which enable its internal communication. The central nervous system then sends instructions out to the body's tissues via the **motor neurons**. Our complexity, though, resides mostly in our interneuron systems. Our nervous system has a few million sensory neurons, a few million motor neurons, and billions and billions of interneurons.

## The Peripheral Nervous System

Our peripheral nervous system has two components—skeletal and autonomic. The **skeletal nervous system** controls the voluntary movements of our skeletal muscles. As you reach the bottom of the next page, the skeletal nervous system will report to your brain the current state of your skeletal muscles and carry instructions back, triggering your hand to turn the page.

Our **autonomic nervous system** controls the glands and the muscles of our internal organs. Like an automatic pilot, it can be consciously overridden. But usually it operates on its own (autonomously) to influence our internal functioning, including our heartbeat, digestion, and glandular activity.

Figure 2–6

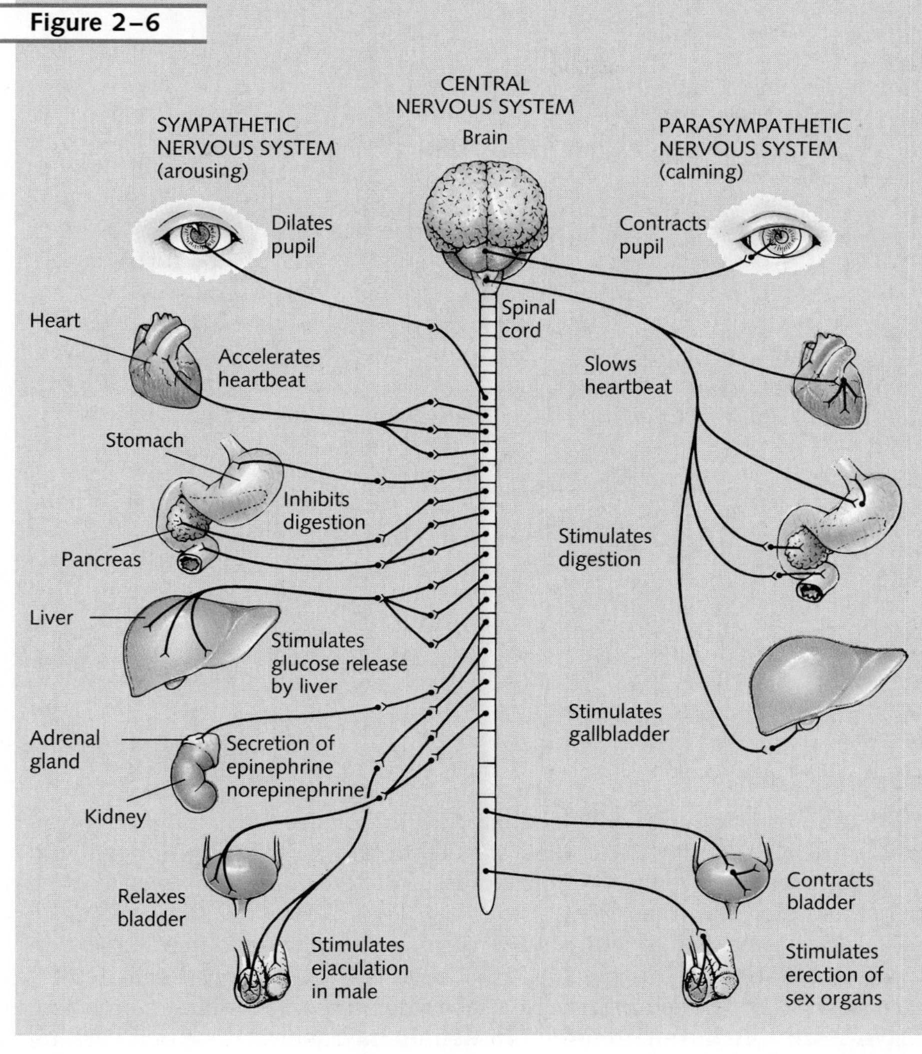


**The Dual Functions of the Autonomic Nervous System** *The autonomic nervous system controls the more autonomous (or self-regulating) internal functions, including those shown here. Its sympathetic division arouses and expends energy. Its parasympathetic division calms and conserves energy, allowing routine maintenance activity. Most organs are affected by both divisions. For example, sympathetic stimulation accelerates heartbeat, while parasympathetic stimulation slows it.*

The autonomic nervous system is a dual system (Figure 2–6). The **sympathetic nervous system** arouses us for defensive action. If something alarms or enrages you, the sympathetic system will accelerate your heartbeat, slow your digestion, raise your blood sugar, dilate your arteries, and cool you with perspiration, making you alert and ready for action. When the stress subsides, the **parasympathetic nervous system** produces opposite effects. It conserves energy as it calms you by decreasing your heartbeat, lowering your blood sugar, and so forth. In everyday situations, the sympathetic and parasympathetic nervous systems work together to keep us in a steady internal state.

## The Central Nervous System

From the simplicity of neurons "talking" to other neurons arises the complexity of the central nervous system, which enables our humanity—our thinking, feeling, and acting. Tens of billions of neurons, each in communication with thousands of other neurons, would yield an ever-changing wiring diagram that dwarfs the biggest computer.

Figure 2–7

**A Simple Reflex** *Information from the skin receptors travels inward via a sensory neuron to a spinal cord interneuron, which sends a signal outward to the arm muscles via a motor neuron. Because this reflex involves only the spinal cord, the hand jerks away from the candle flame before the brain creates an experience of pain.*

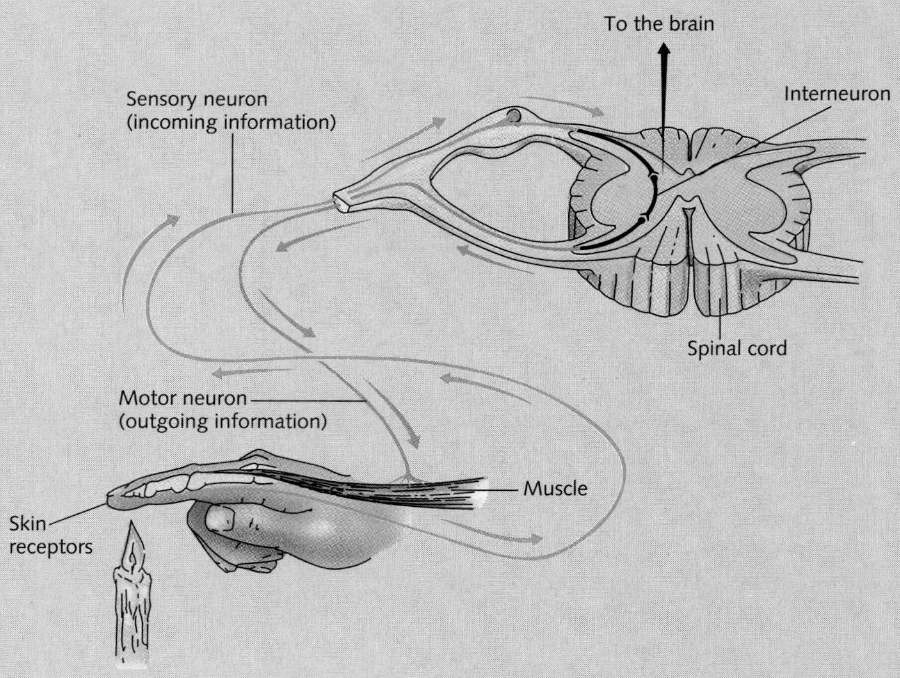

## Spinal Cord

The central nervous system's spinal cord is an information highway connecting the peripheral nervous system to the brain. Ascending neural "tracts" send up sensory information, and descending tracts send back motor-control information.

A look at the neural pathways governing our **reflexes**, our automatic responses to stimuli, illustrates the spinal cord's work. A simple spinal reflex pathway is composed of a single sensory neuron and a single motor neuron, which often communicate through an interneuron. The knee-jerk response is one example; a headless warm body could do it.

Another such pathway enables the pain reflex (Figure 2–7). When your fingers touch a hot stove, neural activity excited by the heat travels via sensory neurons to interneurons in your spinal cord. These interneurons respond by activating motor neurons to the muscles in your arm, causing you to jerk your hand away.

Because the simple pain reflex pathway runs through the spinal cord and out, you jerk your hand from the hot stove *before* your brain receives and responds to the information that causes you to feel pain. Information travels to and from the brain by way of the spinal cord. Were the top of your spinal cord severed, you would not feel such pain. Or pleasure. Your brain would literally be out of touch with your body. Thus, you would lose all sensation and voluntary movement in body regions whose sensory and motor neurons connect with the spinal cord below its point of injury. Male paraplegics (whose legs are paralyzed) are usually capable of an erection (a simple reflex) if their genitals are stimulated. But, depending on where and how completely the spinal cord is severed, they may have no genital feeling and be genitally unresponsive to erotic images (Kennedy & Over, 1990). To produce bodily pain or pleasure, the sensory information must reach the brain.

*"If the nervous system be cut off between the brain and other parts, the experiences of those other parts are nonexistent for the mind. The eye is blind, the ear deaf, the hand insensible and motionless."*

William James
*Principles of Psychology*, 1890

Figure 2–8

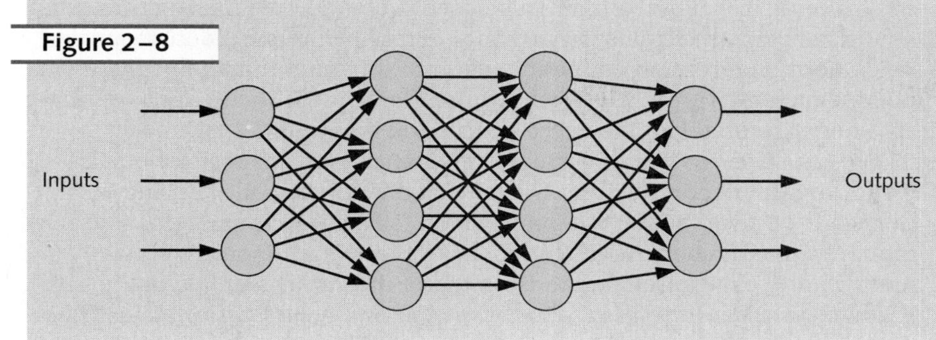


**A Simulated Neural Network** *Each unit, or cell, connects with each unit of the next layer. Given feedback, the network can strengthen connections that produce a given output in response to a given pattern of inputs.*

### Neural Networks

The other part of your central nervous system, your brain, receives information, interprets it, and decides responses. In doing so, the brain functions rather like a computing machine. It receives images of an object from the two eyes, computes their difference, and instantly infers how far the object must be to project such a difference. As basketball star Michael Jordan would shoot a falling-away jump shot, his agile brain was performing an incredible number of instant computations, adjusting for body position and movement, distance, and angle.

How do our brains perform such computations? First, our neurons cluster into work groups or **neural networks**. To understand why neurons tend to connect with nearby neurons, Stephen Kosslyn and Olivier Koenig (1992, p. 12) invite us to "think about why cities exist; why don't people distribute themselves more evenly across the countryside?" Like people networking with people, neurons network with nearby neurons with which they can have short, fast connections. As in Figure 2–8, the cells in each layer of a neural network connect with various cells in the next layer. Learning occurs as feedback strengthens connections that produce certain results. New computer models simulate neural networks, complete with excitatory and inhibitory connections that gain strength with experience—and mimic the brain's capacity for learning.

Of course, the system inside each of us is more complicated than depicted in Figure 2–8, because one neural network is interconnected with other networks that do different things. There are no arrows to tell us where one network ends and the next begins; what distinguishes them is their specific functions. Each is a subnetwork, contributing its little bit of information to the whole information-processing system we call the brain.

## The Endocrine System

Interconnected with the nervous system is the second of the body's communication systems, the **endocrine system** (Figure 2–9). The endocrine system's glands secrete **hormones**, chemical messengers that are produced in one tissue and travel through the bloodstream and affect other tissues, including the brain. Hormones acting on the brain influence our interest in sex, food, and aggression.

Some hormones are chemically identical to neurotransmitters (those chemical messengers that diffuse across a synapse and excite or inhibit an adjacent neuron). The endocrine system and nervous system are therefore kindred systems: They both secrete molecules that activate receptors elsewhere. But unlike the speedy nervous system, which zips messages from

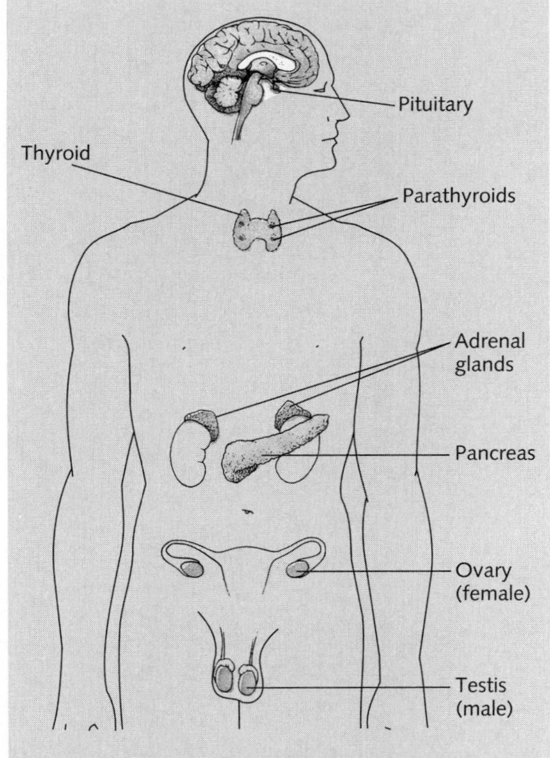


Figure 2–9

**The Body's Major Endocrine Glands** *The pituitary releases hormones that, in turn, regulate the hormone secretions of other glands.*

eyes to brain to hand in a fraction of a second, endocrine messages use the slow lane. Several seconds or more may elapse before the bloodstream carries a hormone from an endocrine gland to its target tissue. But these endocrine messages are often worth waiting for, because their effects are usually longer-lasting than the effects of a neural message.

The endocrine system's hormones influence many aspects of our lives, from growth to reproduction, from metabolism to mood, keeping everything in balance while we respond to stress, exertion, and internal thoughts. In a moment of danger, for example, the autonomic nervous system will order the **adrenal glands** on top of the kidneys to release *epinephrine* and *norepinephrine* (also called *adrenaline* and *noradrenaline*). These hormones increase heart rate, blood pressure, and blood sugar, providing us with a surge of energy. When the emergency passes, the hormones—and the feelings of excitement—linger a while.

The most influential endocrine gland is the **pituitary gland**, a pea-sized structure located in the base of the brain, where it can be controlled by an adjacent brain area. The pituitary releases hormones that influence growth. Its secretions also influence the release of hormones by other endocrine glands. This makes the pituitary a sort of master gland. For example, under the brain's influence the pituitary triggers your sex glands to release sex hormones, which may in turn influence your brain and behavior.

This feedback system (brain → pituitary → other glands → hormones → brain) illustrates the intimate connection of the nervous and endocrine systems. The nervous system directs endocrine secretions, which affect the nervous system. Moreover, the discovery that neurotransmitters can drift in the brain's fluid to nerve receptors at distant sites, affecting overall alertness or mood, blurs the distinction between certain neurotransmitters and their chemical twins, called hormones when released by glands (Agnati & others, 1992; Pert, 1986). Conducting and coordinating this whole electrochemical orchestra is that maestro we call the brain.

### Summing Up

The central nervous system's neurons in the brain and spinal cord communicate with the peripheral nervous system's sensory and motor neurons. The peripheral nervous system has two main divisions. The skeletal nervous system directs voluntary movements and reflexes. The autonomic nervous system, through its sympathetic and parasympathetic divisions, controls our involuntary muscles and the glands of our endocrine system. Hormones released by endocrine glands travel through the bloodstream and affect other tissues, including the brain.

## The Brain

*In this "decade of the brain," the known universe's most amazing organ is being probed and mapped by a new generation of neural cartographers. Lower level brain networks sustain basic life functions and enable memory, emotions, and basic drives. Atop the brain, neural networks within the cerebral hemispheres form specialized work teams that enable our perceiving, thinking, and speaking.*

In a jar on a display shelf in Cornell University's psychology department resides the well-preserved brain of Edward Bradford Titchener, a great turn-of-the-century experimental psychologist and proponent of the study of consciousness. Imagine yourself gazing at that wrinkled mass of grayish tissue. Is there any sense in which Titchener is still in there?[1]

You might answer that without the living whir of electrochemical activity there could be nothing of Titchener in his preserved brain. Consider then an experiment about which the inquisitive Titchener himself might have daydreamed. Imagine that just moments before his death, someone removed Titchener's brain from his body and kept it alive by pumping enriched blood through it as it floated in a tank of cerebral fluid. Would Titchener now still be in there? Further imagine, to carry our fantasy to its limit, that someone transplanted the still-living brain into the body of a badly brain-damaged person. To whose home should the recovered patient return?

That we can imagine such questions illustrates how convinced we are that we live in our heads. And for good reason: As Woody Allen has said, the brain is a very important organ. The brain enables the mind: seeing, hearing, remembering, thinking, feeling, speaking, dreaming. Indeed, say neuroscientists, *the mind is what the brain does*. But precisely where and how are mind functions tied to the brain? Let's first see how scientists explore such questions.

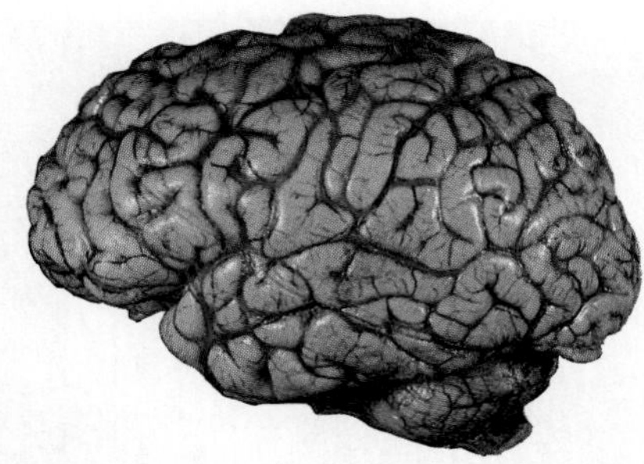

**The Human Brain** *This small, wrinkled organ is far more complex than the most sophisticated computer. What you see here is only a portion of the brain's outer layer. Most of its surface lies hidden within its convoluted folds.*

*"I am a brain, Watson. The rest of me is a mere appendix."*

Sherlock Holmes, in Arthur Conan Doyle's *The Adventure of the Mazarin Stone*

## The Tools of Discovery

It is exciting to consider how fast and how far the neurosciences have progressed within a lifetime. For centuries, the human brain lay largely beyond the reach of science. The neuron was too small to study with the naked eye, its impulses too faint to record with ordinary electrodes. We were able to feel bumps on the skull, dissect and analyze lifeless brains, and observe the effects of specific brain diseases and injuries. But there were no tools high-powered yet gentle enough to explore the living brain. Now, that has changed. Whether in the interests of science or medicine, we can selectively destroy tiny clusters of normal or defective brain cells, leaving their surroundings unharmed. We can probe the brain with tiny electrical pulses. We can snoop on the messages of individual neurons and on the mass action of billions. We can see color representations of the brain's energy-consuming activity. These new tools and techniques have made possible a neuroscientific revolution.

### Clinical Observations

The oldest method of studying brain-mind connections is to observe the effects of brain diseases and injuries. Such observations were first recorded some 5000 years ago. But it was not until the last two centuries that physicians began systematically to record the results of damage to specific brain areas. Some noted that damage to one side of the brain often caused numbness or paralysis on the body's opposite side, suggesting that the right side of the body is wired to the brain's left side, and vice versa. Others noticed that damage to the back of the brain disrupted vision, and that damage to the left front part of the brain produced speech difficulties. Gradually, the brain was being mapped. Today, records of some 1500 brain-injured patients have been assembled by University of Iowa researchers into the largest-ever brain-damage registry.

**THE FAR SIDE**

*"That's a lie, Morty! . . . Mom says you might have got the brains in the family, but I got the looks!"*

THE FAR SIDE © 1987 FARWORKS, INC./Dist. by UNIVERSAL PRESS SYNDICATE. Reprinted with permission. All rights reserved.

### Manipulating the Brain

Scientists need not wait for brain injuries. They can also electrically, chemically, or magnetically stimulate various parts of the brain, noting the ef-

[1] Carl Sagan's *Broca's Brain* (1979a) inspired this question.

**Figure 2–10**

**An Electroencephalograph Providing Amplified Tracings of Waves of Electrical Activity in the Brain** *Here it is detecting brain response to sound, making possible an early evaluation of what may be a hearing impairment.*

fects. Or they can surgically **lesion** (destroy) tissue in specific brain areas in animals. For example, a lesion destroying the region of a rat's brain called the hypothalamus reduces eating, causing the rat to starve unless force-fed. Conversely, a lesion in a nearby area produces overeating.

### Recording the Brain's Electrical Activity

Modern researchers have also learned to eavesdrop on the brain. Electrical activity in the brain's billions of neurons sweeps in regular waves across its surface. The **electroencephalogram (EEG)** is an amplified tracing of such waves by an instrument called an electroencephalograph. Studying an EEG of the gross activity of the whole brain is like studying the activity of a car engine by listening to the hum of its motor. However, by presenting a stimulus repeatedly and having a computer filter out electrical activity unrelated to the stimulus, one can identify the electrical wave evoked by the stimulus (Figure 2–10).

In addition, modern microelectrodes have tips so small they can detect the electrical pulse in a single neuron, making possible some astonishingly precise findings. For example, we can now detect exactly where the information goes after someone strokes a cat's whisker.

### Brain-Imaging Techniques

Other new windows into the brain give us a Supermanlike ability to see inside the brain without lesioning it. For example, the **CAT (computerized axial tomograph) scan** examines the brain by taking x-ray photographs that can reveal brain damage. Even more dramatic is the **PET (positron emission tomograph) scan** (Figure 2–11). A PET scan depicts the activity of different brain areas by showing each area's consumption of its chemical fuel, the sugar glucose (see illustration, page 63). Active neurons burn more glucose. When a person is given a temporarily radioactive form of glucose, the PET scan measures and locates the radioactivity, thereby detecting where this "food for thought" goes. In this way, researchers can see which brain areas are most active as the person performs mathematical calculations, listens to music, or daydreams.

Another new way of looking into the living brain exploits the fact that the centers of atoms, including those in our brains, spin like tops. In **MRI (magnetic resonance imaging)** the head is put in a strong magnetic field, which aligns the spinning atoms. Then a brief pulse of radio waves disorients the atoms momentarily. When the atoms return to their normal spin they release detectable signals, which become computer-generated images

**Figure 2–11**

**The PET Scan** *To obtain a PET scan, researchers inject volunteers with a low and harmless dose of a short-lived radioactive sugar. Detectors around the subject's head pick up the release of gamma rays from the sugar, which has concentrated in active brain areas. A computer then processes and translates these signals into a map of the brain at work.*

of their concentrations. The result is a detailed picture of the brain's soft tissues. For example, MRI scans reveal enlarged fluid-filled brain areas in some patients suffering from schizophrenia, a disabling psychological disorder (Figure 2–12).

By taking pictures less than a second apart, MRI scans can now show the brain lighting up (with increased oxygen-laden blood flow) as a person performs different mental functions (Kwong & others, 1992). As a person sees a light turn on, a "fast MRI" machine (also called "functional" or "dynamic" MRI) detects blood rushing to the back of the brain, which processes visual information (Figure 2–20, page 62). Ask the person to solve a verbal analogy problem, and the part of the brain's left side near the front will light up. Such snapshots of the brain's mind-making activity may enable new insights into how and where the brain divides its labor.

What the microscope did for biology and the telescope for astronomy, these new brain-imaging instruments may do for psychological science. The tools are triggering a scientific revolution. To be learning about the neurosciences now is like studying world geography while Magellan was exploring the seas. Every year the explorers announce new discoveries, which also generate new interpretations of old discoveries. With data from different brain-imaging techniques appearing faster than anyone can read and remember them, researchers are now assembling the information in computer databases (Gibbons, 1992). This brain cartography will give all researchers instant access through electronic networks to PET or MRI studies that reveal activity in a particular brain area while a person, for example, solves math problems. Clearly, this *is* the decade of the brain, the golden age of brain science.

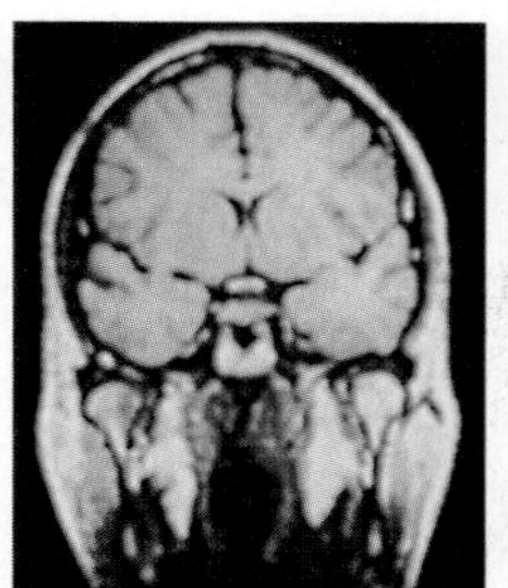
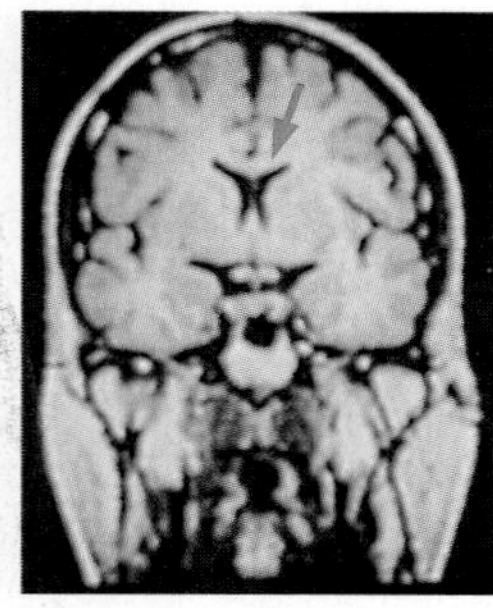

**Figure 2–12**

**MRI Scan of a Normal Person (Left) and a Schizophrenia Patient (Right)** *Note the enlarged fluid-filled brain region in the brain on the right.*

**THE FAR SIDE**

*"The picture's pretty bleak, gentlemen. . . . The world's climates are changing, the mammals are taking over, and we all have a brain about the size of a walnut."*

THE FAR SIDE © 1985 FARWORKS, INC./ Dist. by UNIVERSAL PRESS SYNDICATE. Reprinted with permission. All rights reserved.

## Lower Level Brain Structures

If you could open the skull and look inside, the first thing you might notice is the brain's size. In dinosaurs the brain represents 1/100,000th of the body's weight, in whales 1/10,000th, in elephants 1/600th, in humans 1/45th. It looks as though a principle is emerging. But keep on. In mice the brain is 1/40th the body's weight, and in marmosets 1/25th. So there are exceptions to the rule of thumb that the ratio of brain to body weight provides a clue to a species' intelligence.

More useful clues to an animal's capacities come from the brain's structures. In primitive vertebrate (backboned) animals, such as sharks, the brain primarily regulates basic survival functions: breathing, resting, and feeding. In lower mammals, such as rodents, a more complex brain enables emotion and greater memory. In advanced mammals, such as humans, the brain processes more information, enabling us to act with foresight.

Brain evolution has not greatly altered the basic mechanisms for survival. Rather, as the English neurologist John Hughlings Jackson recognized a century ago, evolution has elaborated new brain systems on top of the old, much as the earth's landscape covers the old with the new. Digging down, one discovers the fossil remnants of the past—brainstem components still performing much as they did for our distant ancestors. Let's now explore the brain, starting here and working up.

### The Brainstem

The **brainstem** is the brain's oldest and innermost region. It begins where the spinal cord enters the skull and swells slightly, forming the **medulla**. Here lie the controls for your heartbeat and breathing. If the top of a cat's brainstem is severed from the rest of the brain above it, the animal will still

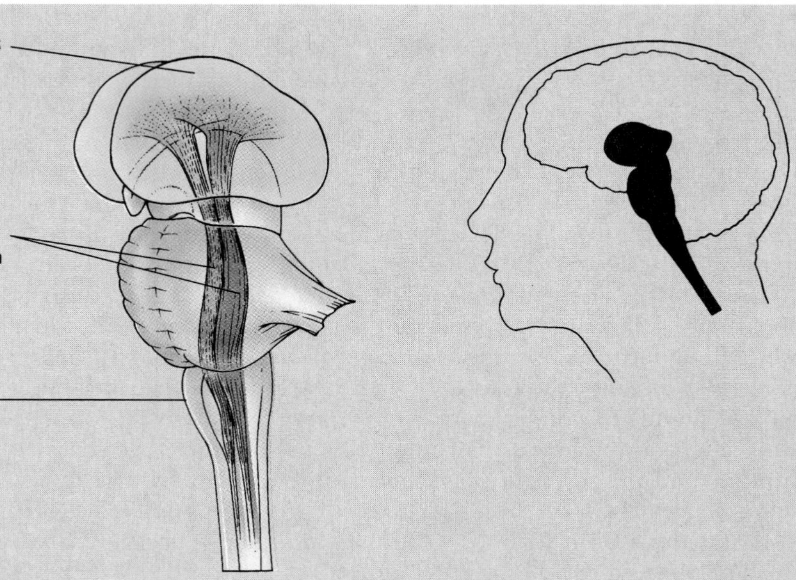

Figure 2–13

**The Brainstem and Thalamus** *In this figure you can see the parts of the brainstem, the thalamus attached to its top, and the reticular formation, which passes through both structures.*

breathe and live—and even run, climb, and groom (Klemm, 1990). But cut off from the brain's higher region it won't purposefully run or climb to get food.

Here in the brainstem is also the crossover point, where most nerves to and from each side of the brain connect with the body's opposite side. This peculiar cross-wiring is but one of many surprises the brain has to offer.

*"No one has the remotest idea why there should be this amazing tendency for nervous system pathways to cross."*

David H. Hubel and Torsten N. Wiesel (1979)

Inside the brainstem, the **reticular** ("netlike") **formation**, a finger-shaped network of neurons, extends from the spinal cord right up to the thalamus (Figure 2–13). As the spinal cord's sensory input travels up to the thalamus, some of it branches off to the reticular formation, which filters incoming stimuli and relays important information to other areas of the brain. Among its other functions, the reticular formation helps control arousal.

In 1949, Giuseppe Moruzzi and Horace Magoun discovered that electrically stimulating the reticular formation of a sleeping cat almost instantly produced an awake, alert animal. Magoun also severed a cat's reticular formation from higher brain regions without damaging the nearby sensory pathways. The effect? The cat lapsed into a coma from which it never awakened. Magoun could clap his hands in the cat's ear, even pinch it; still, no response. This established the reticular formation's involvement in arousal. Later, though, it was discovered that elsewhere in the brainstem are neurons whose *activity* is needed for sleep. (As we will see, the brain is not idle during sleep.)

### The Thalamus

Atop the brainstem sits a joined pair of egg-shaped structures called the **thalamus** (Figure 2–13). This is the brain's sensory switchboard: It receives information from the sensory neurons and routes it to the higher brain regions that deal with seeing, hearing, tasting, and touching. We can think of the thalamus as being to neural traffic what London is to England's train traffic: Sensory input passes through it en route to various destinations. The thalamus also receives some of the higher brain's replies, which it directs to the cerebellum and medulla.

*You can challenge your understanding of the essential functions of lower level brain areas by considering these questions: Within what brain region would damage be most likely to disrupt your ability to skip rope? Your ability to sense tastes or sounds? In what brain region would damage perhaps leave you in a coma? Without the very breath and heartbeat of life?* *(See page 59.)*

## The Cerebellum

Extending from the rear of the brainstem is the **cerebellum**, meaning little brain, which is rather what its two wrinkled hemispheres look like (Figure 2–14). The cerebellum influences learning and memory, but its most obvious function is coordinating voluntary movement. If you injured your cerebellum, you would probably have difficulty walking, keeping your balance, or shaking hands. Your movements would be jerky and exaggerated.

Note that these lower brain functions all occur without any conscious effort. This illustrates another of this book's recurring themes: *Our brain processes much information outside of our awareness*. We are aware of the *results* of our brain's labor (say, our current visual experience) but not of *how* we construct the visual image. Likewise, whether we are asleep or awake, our brainstem manages its life-sustaining functions, freeing our higher brain regions to dream, to think, to talk, to savor a memory.

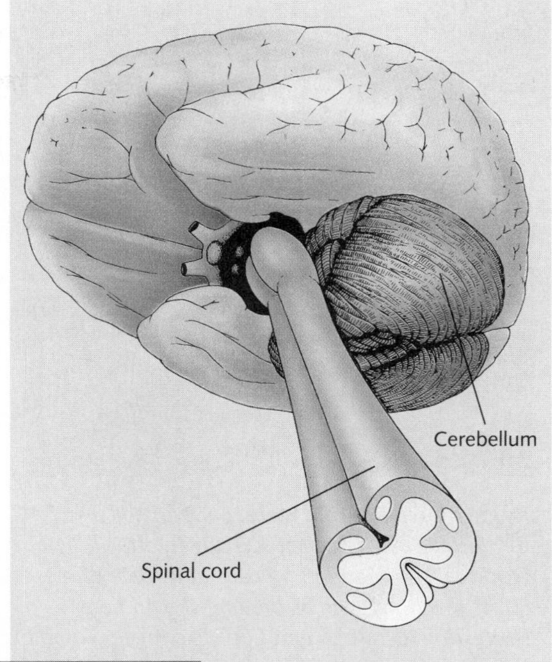


**Figure 2–14**

**The Cerebellum** *Hanging at the back of the brain, this "little brain" coordinates our movements.*

## The Limbic System

At the border ("limbus") of the brain's older parts and the cerebral hemispheres is a doughnut-shaped neural system called the **limbic system** (Figure 2–15). We will see in Chapter 9 how one limbic system component, the *hippocampus*, processes memory. (When animals or humans lose their hippocampus to surgery or injury, they become unable to lay down new memories of facts and experiences.) For now, let's look at the limbic system's links to emotions, such as fear and anger, and to basic motives, such as those for food and sex. As we will see, the limbic system's influence on emotions and motives occurs partly through its control of the body's hormones.

**The Amygdala** Two almond-shaped neural clusters in the limbic system, called the **amygdala**, influence aggression and fear. In 1939, psychologist Heinrich Klüver and neurosurgeon Paul Bucy surgically lesioned part of a rhesus monkey's brain that included the amygdala. The operation transformed the normally ill-tempered monkey into the most mellow of creatures. Poke it, pinch it, do virtually anything that normally would trigger a

**Figure 2–15**

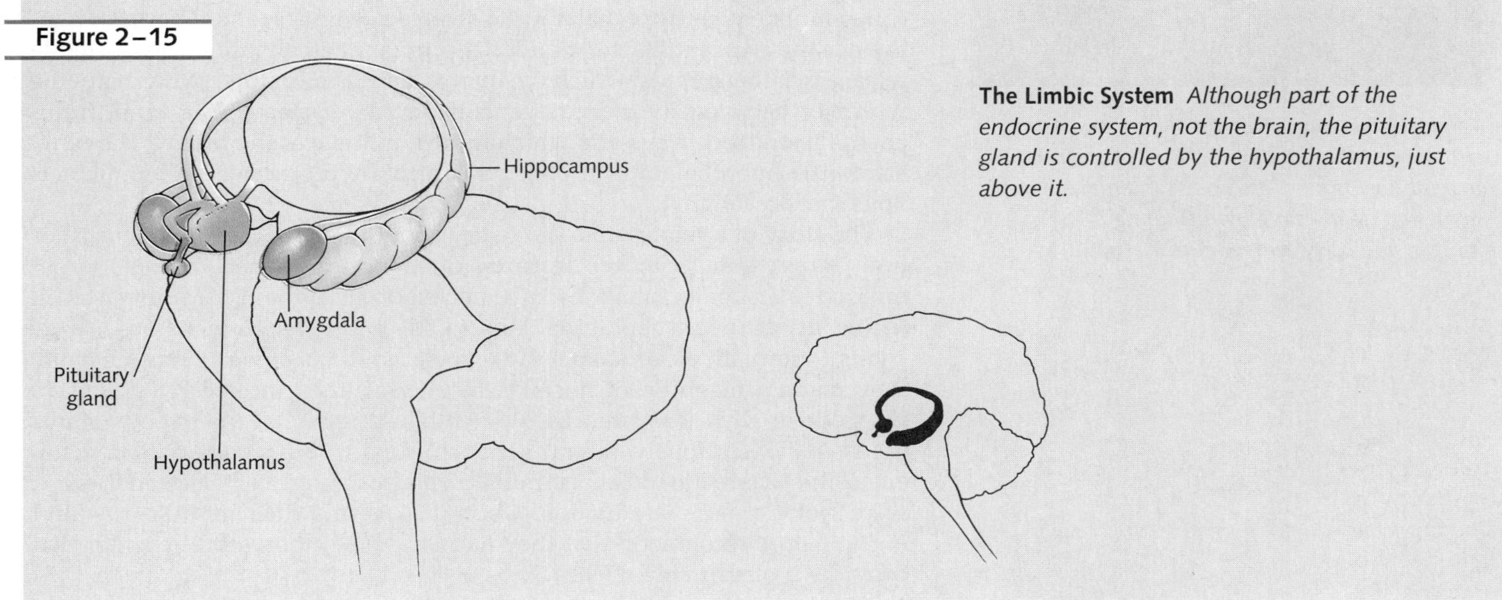


**The Limbic System** *Although part of the endocrine system, not the brain, the pituitary gland is controlled by the hypothalamus, just above it.*

**Aggression as a Brain State** *Back arched and fur fluffed, this fierce cat is ready to attack. Electrical stimulation of a cat's amygdala provokes reactions such as the one shown here, suggesting its role in emotions like rage. Which division of the autonomic nervous system is activated by such stimulation? (See page 61.)*

ferocious response, and still the animal remained placid. In later studies with other wild animals, including the lynx, wolverine, and wild rat, researchers noted the same effect. What then might happen if we electrically stimulated the amygdala in a normally placid domestic animal, such as a cat? Do so in one spot and the cat prepares to attack, hissing with its back arched, its pupils dilated, its hair on end. Move the electrode only slightly within the amygdala and the cat cowers in terror when caged with a small mouse.

These experiments testify to the amygdala's role in such emotions as rage and fear. Still, we must be careful not to think of the amygdala as *the* control center for aggression and fear. The brain is *not* neatly organized into structures that correspond to our categories of behavior. Aggressive and fearful behavior involve neural activity in all levels of the brain. Even within the limbic system, stimulating neural structures other than the amygdala can evoke such behavior. Similarly, if you manipulate your car's carburetor, you can affect how the car runs, but that doesn't mean that the carburetor by itself runs the car. It is merely one link in an integrated system.

Given that amygdala lesions can change violent monkeys into mellow ones, might such lesions do the same in violent humans? Such "psychosurgery" has produced varied results (Mark & Ervin, 1970; Valenstein, 1986). In a few cases involving patients who suffered brain abnormalities, it reduced fits of rage, though sometimes with devastating side effects on the patient's everyday functioning. For ethical reasons, and because of the uncertainties involved, drastic psychosurgery is highly controversial and seldom used. Perhaps, though, as we learn more about how the brain controls behavior, we will learn to alleviate brain disorders without creating new ones.

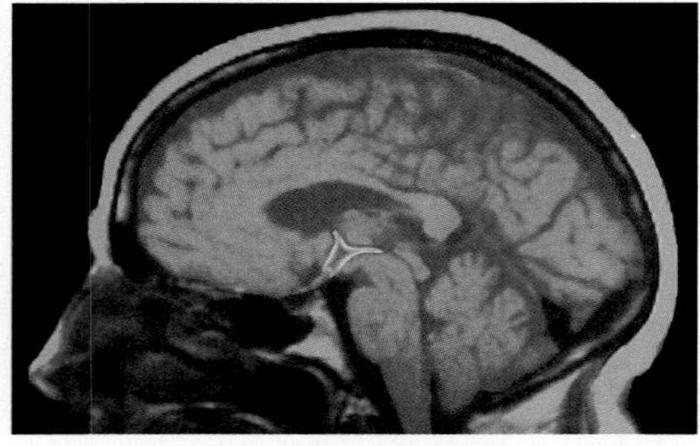

**The Hypothalamus** *This small but important structure, colored red in this MRI brain scan photograph, helps keep the body's internal environment in a steady state by regulating thirst, hunger, and body temperature.*

**The Hypothalamus** Another of the limbic system's fascinating structures lies just below (*hypo*) the thalamus, and so is called the **hypothalamus**. By lesioning or stimulating different areas in the hypothalamus, neuroscientists have isolated within it neuron networks that perform specific bodily maintenance duties. Some of these neural clusters influence hunger; still others regulate thirst, body temperature, and sexual behavior.

The hypothalamus monitors blood chemistry and takes orders from other parts of the brain. Thinking about sex (in your brain's cerebral cortex) can stimulate your hypothalamus to secrete hormones. These hormones influence the adjacent master gland, the pituitary, which influences hormone release by other glands, which the hypothalamus monitors. (Note again the interplay between the nervous and endocrine systems: The brain influences the endocrine system, which in turn influences the brain.) The powerful little hypothalamus also exerts control by triggering autonomic nervous system activity.

The story of a remarkable discovery about the hypothalamus illustrates how progress in scientific research often occurs—when curious, open-minded investigators make an unexpected observation. Two young McGill University neuropsychologists, James Olds and Peter Milner (1954), were trying to implant electrodes in the reticular systems of white rats. One day they made a magnificent mistake. In one rat, they incorrectly placed an electrode in what was later discovered to be a region of the hypothalamus (Olds, 1975). Curiously, the rat kept returning to the place on its tabletop enclosure where it had been stimulated by this misplaced electrode, as if it were seeking more stimulation. Upon discovering their mistake, the alert investigators recognized that they had stumbled upon a brain center that provides a pleasurable reward.

Figure 2–16

**Rat With an Implanted Electrode** *With an electrode implanted in a reward center of its hypothalamus, the rat readily crosses an electrified grid, accepting the painful shocks, to press a lever that sends electrical impulses to its "pleasure centers."*

In a meticulous series of experiments, Olds (1958) then went on to locate other "pleasure centers," as he called them. (What the rats actually experience only they know, and they aren't telling. Not wanting to attribute human feelings to the rat, today's scientists seldom refer to "pleasure centers.") When Olds allowed rats to trigger their own stimulation in these areas by pressing a pedal, they would sometimes do so at a feverish pace—up to 7000 times per hour—until they dropped from exhaustion. Moreover, they would do anything to get this stimulation, even cross an electrified floor that a starving rat would not cross to reach food (Figure 2–16).

Similar reward centers in or near the hypothalamus were later discovered in many other species, including goldfish, dolphins, and monkeys. In fact, animal research reveals both a general reward system that triggers the release of the neurotransmitter dopamine, and specific centers associated with the pleasures of eating, drinking, sex, and addictive drugs. Animals, it seems, come equipped with built-in reward systems for activities essential to survival.

*"If you were designing a robot vehicle to walk into the future and survive, . . . you'd wire it up so that behavior that ensured the survival of the self or the species—like sex and eating—would be naturally reinforcing."*

Candace Pert (1986)

These dramatic findings made people wonder whether humans, too, might have limbic centers for pleasure. Indeed they do. One neurosurgeon has used electrodes to calm violent patients. Stimulated patients report mild pleasure; unlike rats, they are not driven to a frenzy by it (Deutsch, 1972; Hooper & Teresi, 1986).

## The Cerebral Cortex

With the elaboration of the cerebral cortex, tight genetic controls relax and the organism's adaptability increases. Thus, amphibians, such as frogs, have a small cortex and operate extensively on preprogrammed genetic instructions; the larger cortex of mammals offers increased capacities for learning and thinking, enabling them to be more adaptable. Most of what makes us distinctively human arises from the complex functions of our highly developed cerebral cortex.

### Structure of the Cortex

Opening a human skull and exposing the brain, we would see a wrinkled organ, shaped rather like the meat of an oversized walnut. Eighty percent of the brain's weight lies in the ballooning left and right cerebral hemispheres, which are mostly filled with axon connections between the brain's surface and its other regions. The thin surface layer of the cerebral hemispheres is the **cerebral cortex**, a ⅛-inch sheet of cells composed of some 30

*Answers to questions at bottom of page 56: the cerebellum, the thalamus, the reticular formation, and the medulla.*

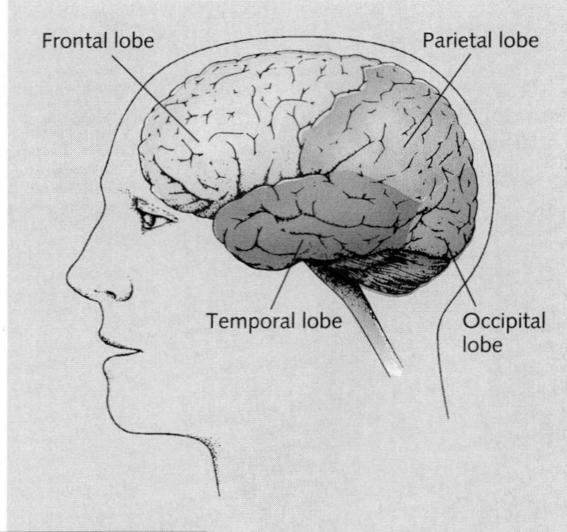


**Figure 2–17**

**The Basic Subdivisions of the Cortex** *We can view the cortex as divided into four lobes in each hemisphere, separated by fissures, or grooves.*

billion nerve cells. (A square millimeter speck of cortical tissue is packed with nearly 150,000 neurons—Ornstein, 1991.) Each neuron connects with thousands of others. To get a feel for the complexity of these interconnections, consider that you could join two 8-studded Lego bricks 24 ways and six bricks nearly 103 million ways. With some 30 billion neurons, each having roughly 10,000 contacts with other neurons, we end up with something like 300 trillion cortical synaptic connections. Being human takes a lot of nerve.

The first thing you would notice about the cerebral cortex is its wrinkled appearance, which leaves only about one-third of it visible on the surface. These folds greatly increase the brain's surface area, which would be roughly the size of a newspaper page if flattened out. In rats and other lower mammals, the surface of the cortex is much smoother, which means there is less of this neural fabric.

We can view each brain hemisphere as divided into four regions, or *lobes*. Starting at the front of your brain and going around over the top, there are the **frontal lobes** (behind your forehead), the **parietal lobes** (at the top and to the rear), the **occipital lobes** (at the back of your head), and the **temporal lobes** (just above your ears). These lobes are convenient geographic subdivisions separated by prominent folds (Figure 2–17). As we will see, the lobes are not distinct operating units. Each lobe carries out many functions, and some functions require the interplay of several lobes.

### Functions of the Cortex

More than a century ago, autopsies of partially paralyzed or speechless people revealed damage to specific areas of the cortex. But this rather crude evidence did not prove that specific parts of the cortex perform specific functions. After all, if control of speech and movement were diffused across the entire cortex, damage to almost any area might produce the same effect. Likewise, a television would go dead with its power cord cut, but we would be deluding ourselves if we were to think we had "localized" the source of the picture in the cord. This analogy suggests how easy it is to err when trying to localize brain functions.

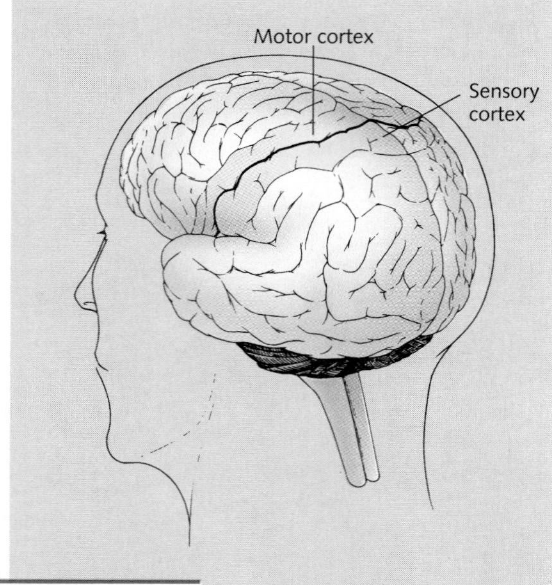


**Figure 2–18**

**The Motor and Sensory Cortex** *The motor cortex controls voluntary muscle movements. The sensory cortex, to the rear of the central fissure, receives input from the skin and muscles.*

**Motor Functions** In 1870, German physicians Gustav Fritsch and Eduard Hitzig applied mild electrical stimulation to the cortexes of dogs and made an important discovery: They could make different body parts move. The effects were selective: Stimulation caused movement only when applied to an arch-shaped region at the back of the frontal lobe, running roughly from ear to ear across the top of the brain. This arch we now call the **motor cortex** (Figure 2–18). Moreover, when the researchers stimulated specific parts of this region in the left or right hemisphere, specific body parts moved on the *opposite* side of the body.

A half century ago, neurosurgeons Otfrid Foerster in Germany and Wilder Penfield in Montreal mapped the motor cortex in hundreds of wide-awake patients. The surgeons needed to know the possible side effects of removing different parts of the cortex. So, before putting the knife to the brain, they would painlessly (the brain has no sensory receptors) stimulate different cortical areas and note body responses. Like Fritsch and Hitzig, they found that when they stimulated different areas of the motor cortex at the back of the frontal lobe, different body parts moved. They were therefore able to map the motor cortex according to the body parts it controlled (Figure 2–19). Interestingly, those areas of the body requiring precise control, such as the fingers and mouth, occupied the greatest amount of cortical space.

Figure 2–19

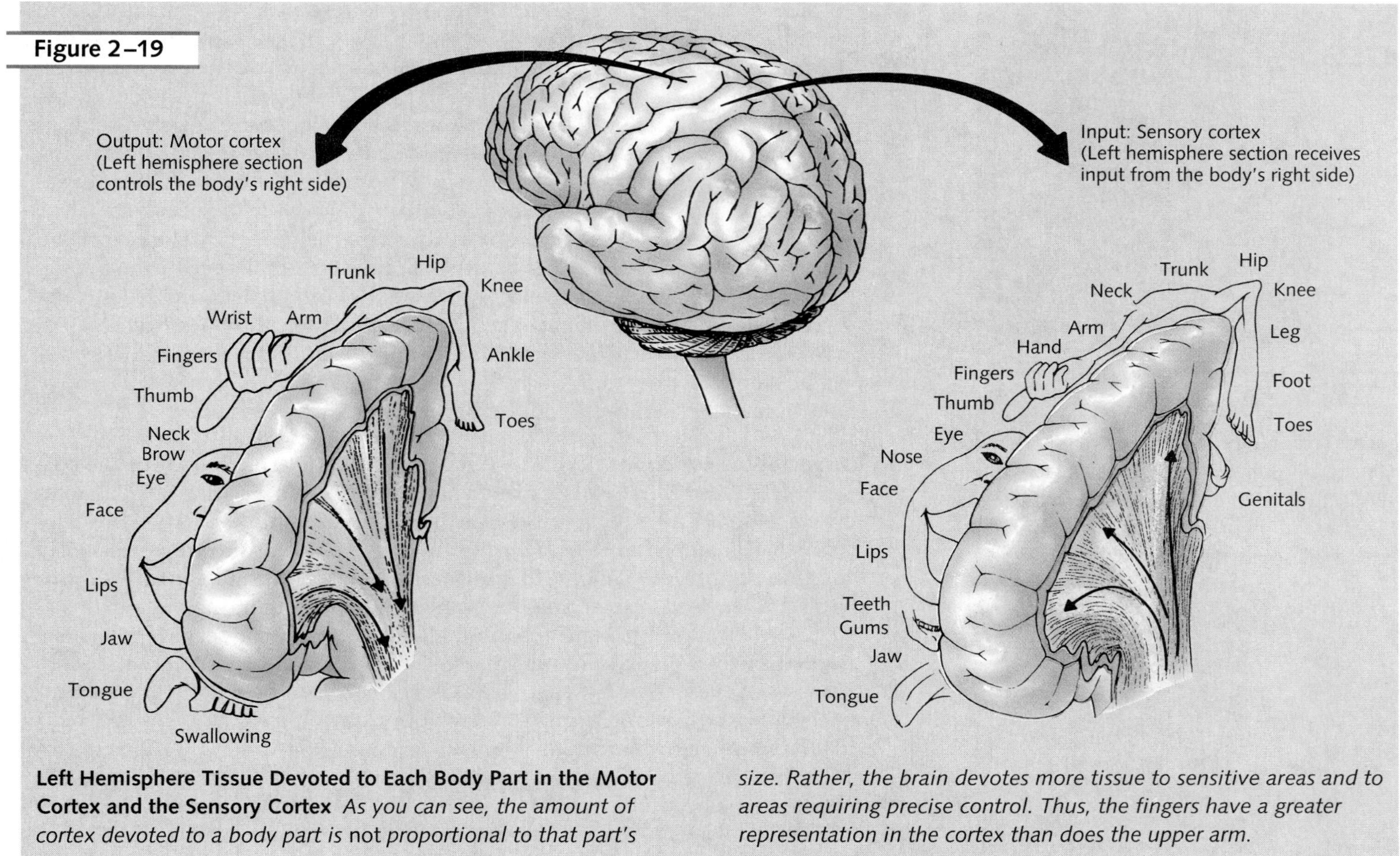


**Left Hemisphere Tissue Devoted to Each Body Part in the Motor Cortex and the Sensory Cortex** *As you can see, the amount of cortex devoted to a body part is* not *proportional to that part's size. Rather, the brain devotes more tissue to sensitive areas and to areas requiring precise control. Thus, the fingers have a greater representation in the cortex than does the upper arm.*

Neuroscientist José Delgado demonstrated the mechanics of motor behavior. In one monkey, he evoked a smiling response over 400,000 times. In a human patient, stimulation of a certain spot on the left motor cortex triggered the right hand to make a fist. Asked to keep the fingers open during the next stimulation, the patient, whose fingers closed despite his best efforts, remarked, "I guess, Doctor, that your electricity is stronger than my will" (Delgado, 1969, p. 114).

*The cat on page 58 is aroused via its sympathetic nervous system.*

**Sensory Functions** If the motor cortex sends messages out to the body, where do *incoming* messages reach the cortex? Penfield identified a cortical area that specializes in receiving information from the skin senses and from the movement of body parts. This area, parallel to the motor cortex and just behind it at the front of the parietal lobes, we now call the **sensory cortex** (Figure 2–18). Stimulate a point on the top of this band of tissue, and the person may report being touched on the shoulder; stimulate some point on the side, and the person may feel something on the face.

The more sensitive a body region, the greater the area of the sensory cortex devoted to it; your supersensitive lips project to a larger brain area than do your toes (Figure 2–19). Similarly, rats have a large area of the brain devoted to whisker sensations, owls to hearing sensations, and so forth. If a monkey or a human loses a finger, the region of the sensory cortex devoted

*The people who first dissected and labeled the brain used the language of scholars, Latin and Greek. Their words are actually attempts at graphic description: For example, "cortex" means bark, "cerebellum" is little brain, and "thalamus" is inner chamber.*

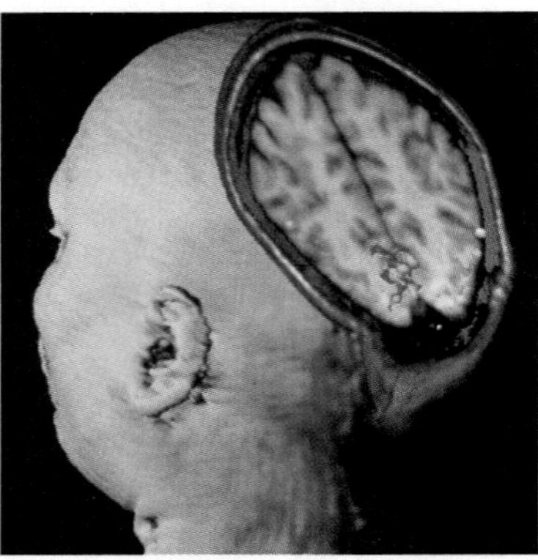

**Figure 2–20**

**New Technology Shows the Brain in Action** *In this composite sketch and photograph, a fast MRI scan shows the visual cortex activated (color representation of increased blood flow), as researchers shine a light into a subject's eyes. If the light is switched off, the region instantly calms down.*

to receiving input from that finger branches to receive sensory input from the adjacent fingers, which now become more sensitive (Fox, 1984). As this illustrates, the brain is sculpted not only by our genes but also by our experience.

Further exploration identified areas where the cortex receives input from the other senses. At this moment you are receiving visual information in the occipital lobes at the very back of your brain (Figure 2–20). Stimulated there, you might see flashes of light or dashes of color. So, in a sense, we *do* have eyes in the back of our head. From there the visual information you are now processing goes to other brain areas that specialize in tasks such as identifying words, detecting emotions, and recognizing faces.

Any sound you are hearing you processed with the auditory areas in your temporal lobes (Figure 2–21). Most of this auditory information travels a circuitous route from one ear to the auditory receiving area above your opposite ear. Stimulated there, you might hear a sound.

*"Scientists and psychologists tell us we use only about 10 percent of our brain power."*
*World Almanac*, 1929

**Association Functions** So far we have pointed out small areas of the cortex that either receive sensory information or direct muscular responses. In humans, that leaves some three-fourths of the thin wrinkled layer, the cerebral cortex, uncommitted. Neurons in these **association areas** (the gray areas in Figure 2–22) integrate information. They associate various sensory inputs with stored memories—an important part of thinking.

Electrically probing the association areas doesn't trigger any response. So, unlike the sensory and motor areas, we can't so neatly specify the functions of the association areas. Their silence seems to be what someone had in mind when formulating one of pop psychology's most widespread myths: that we ordinarily use only 10 percent of our brains. The myth implies that if we could activate our whole brain, we would be far smarter than those who drudge along on 10 percent brain power. But from observing surgically lesioned animals and brain-damaged humans, we know that the association areas are not dormant. Rather, they interpret, integrate, and act on information processed by the sensory areas.

Association areas in the frontal lobe enable judging and planning. People with damaged frontal lobes may have intact memories, score high on intelligence tests, and be well able to bake a cake—yet they may be unable to plan ahead to *begin* baking the cake for a birthday party.

Frontal lobe damage can also alter personality, removing a person's inhibitions. Consider the classic case of railroad worker Phineas Gage. One afternoon in 1848, 25-year-old Gage was packing gunpowder into a rock with a tamping iron. A spark ignited the gunpowder, shooting the rod up through his left cheek and out the top of his skull, leaving his left frontal lobe massively damaged. To everyone's amazement, Gage was still able to sit up and speak, and after the wound healed he returned to work. Although his mental abilities and memories were intact, his personality was not. The affable, soft-spoken Phineas Gage was now an irritable, profane, capricious person who eventually lost his job and ended up earning his living as a fairground exhibit. This person, said his friends, was "no longer Gage."

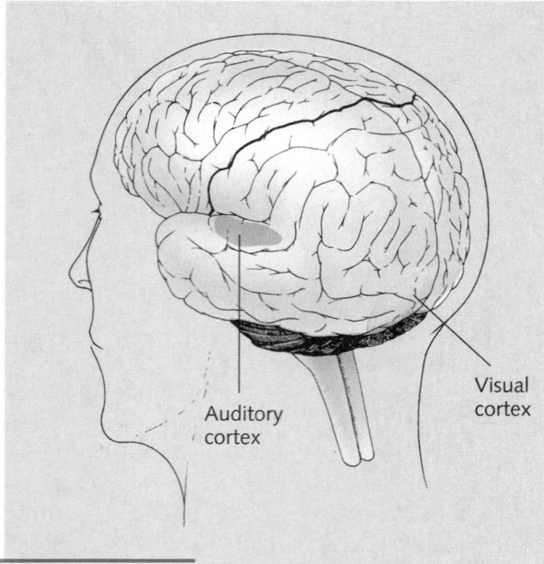


**Figure 2–21**

**The Visual and Auditory Cortex** *The occipital lobes at the rear receive input from the eyes. An auditory area of the temporal lobes receives information from the ears.*

The association areas of the other lobes also perform mental functions. For example, an area on the underside of the right temporal lobe enables us to recognize faces. If a stroke or head injury destroyed this area of your brain, you would still be able to describe facial features and to recognize someone's sex and approximate age, yet be strangely unable to identify the person as, say, Boris Yeltsin, your next-door neighbor, or even your spouse. But by and large, complex mental functions such as learning and memory

Figure 2–22

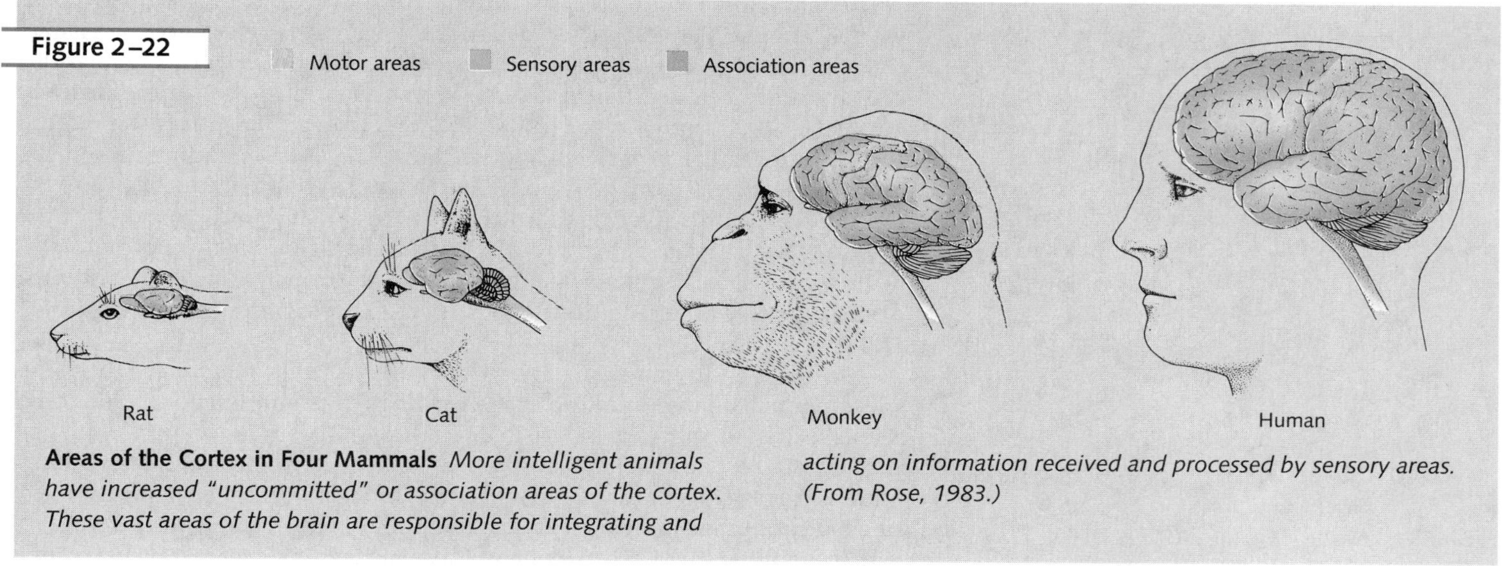


**Areas of the Cortex in Four Mammals** *More intelligent animals have increased "uncommitted" or association areas of the cortex. These vast areas of the brain are responsible for integrating and acting on information received and processed by sensory areas. (From Rose, 1983.)*

don't reside in any one place. There is no one spot in a rat's small association cortex that, when damaged, will obliterate its ability to learn or remember a maze. Such functions seem spread throughout much of the cortex.

**Language** Complex human abilities, such as language, result from the intricate coordination of many brain areas. For example, consider the curious finding that damage to any one of several cortical areas can cause **aphasia**, an impaired use of language. It is even more curious that some aphasic people can speak fluently but are unable to read (despite good vision), while others can comprehend what they read but are unable to speak. Still others can write but not read, read but not write, read numbers but not letters, or sing but not speak. These observations are puzzling because we think of speaking and reading, or writing and reading, or singing and speaking as merely different examples of the same general ability. Consider the clues that helped lead to the solving of this mystery of language:

*Clue 1* In 1865, French physician Paul Broca reported that damage to a specific area of the left frontal lobe, later called **Broca's area**, left a person struggling to form words yet able to sing familiar songs and comprehend speech.

*Clue 2* In 1874, German investigator Carl Wernicke discovered that damage to a specific area of the left temporal lobe (**Wernicke's area**) left people able to speak words but in a meaningless way. Asked to describe a picture that showed two boys stealing cookies behind a woman's back, one patient responded: "Mother is away her working her work to get her better, but when she's looking the two boys looking the other part. She's working another time" (Geschwind, 1979).

*Clue 3* It was later discovered that reading aloud involves a third brain area. The *angular gyrus* receives the visual information from the visual area and recodes it into the auditory form from which Wernicke's area derives its meaning.

*Clue 4* Nerve fibers interconnect these brain areas.

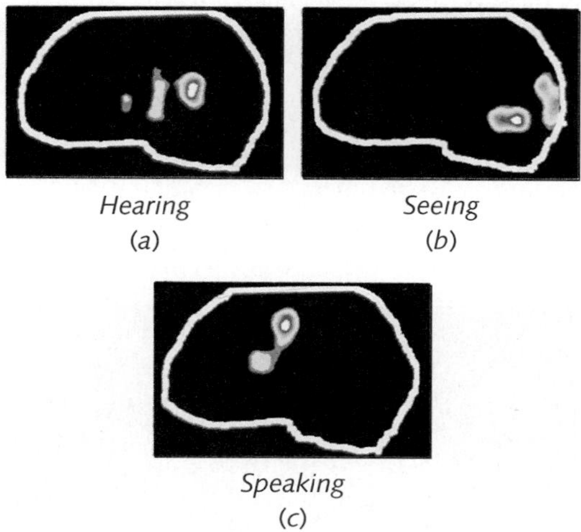


**PET Scan Images of Language Processing** *PET scans such as these detect the activity of different areas of the brain by measuring their relative consumption of a temporarily radioactive form of the brain's normal fuel, glucose. This series of side-view PET scans of left-facing patients shows levels of increased brain activity in specific areas: (a) when hearing a word—auditory cortex and Wernicke's area; (b) when seeing a word—visual cortex and angular gyrus; and (c) when repeating a word—Broca's area and the motor cortex. The red blotches show where the brain is rapidly consuming glucose.*

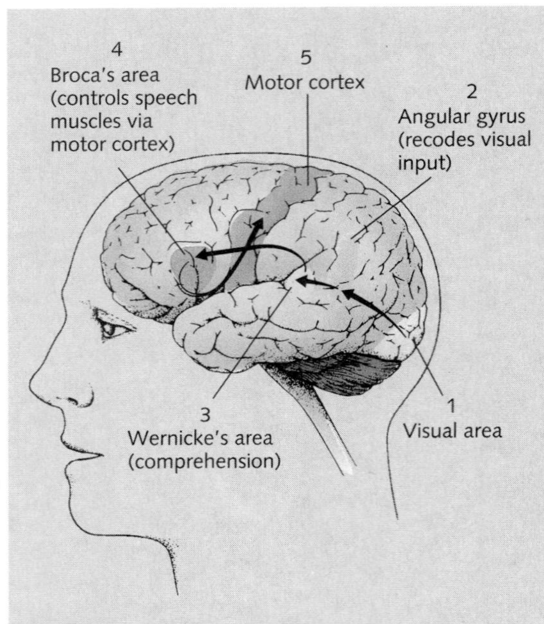


**Figure 2–23**

**Specialization and Integration** *Reading aloud requires the coordination of several brain areas. The arrows show the movement of information in the brain from the time a word is read until it is spoken. (Adapted from "Specialization of the human brain" by N. Geschwind. Copyright © 1979 Scientific American, Inc. All rights reserved.)*

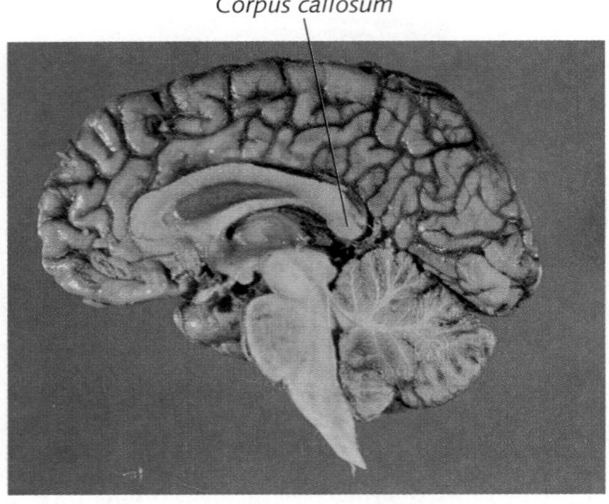


**Figure 2–24**

**The Corpus Callosum** *This large band of neural fibers connects the two brain hemispheres. To photograph the half brain shown here, the hemispheres were separated by cutting through the corpus callosum and lower brain regions.*

Norman Geschwind assembled these clues into an explanation of how we use language. When you read aloud, the words (1) register in the visual area, (2) are relayed to the angular gyrus, which then transforms the words into an auditory code that is (3) received and understood in the nearby Wernicke's area, and (4) sent to Broca's area, which (5) controls the motor cortex, creating the pronounced word (Figure 2–23). Depending on which link in this chain is damaged, a different form of aphasia occurs. Damage to the angular gyrus leaves the person able to speak and understand but unable to read. Damage to Wernicke's area disrupts understanding. Damage to Broca's area disrupts speaking. The general principle bears repeating: Complex abilities result from the intricate coordination of many brain areas.

Said differently, the brain operates by dividing its mental functions—speaking, perceiving, thinking, remembering—into subfunctions. Our conscious experience *seems* indivisible. Right now you are experiencing a whole visual scene as if your eyes were video cameras projecting the scene into your brain. Actually, as we will see, your brain breaks vision into specialized subdimensions, such as color, depth, movement, and form. (After a localized stroke that destroys one of these neural work teams, people may lose just one aspect of vision, such as the ability to perceive movement.) These specialized neural networks, each having done its own thing, then feed their information to "higher level" networks that combine the atoms of experience and relay them to progressively higher level association areas, enabling us to recognize a face as "Grandmother." The same is true of reading a word: The brain computes the word's form, sound, and meaning using different neural networks (Posner & Carr, 1992). Think about it: What you experience as a continuous, indivisible stream of perception is actually but the visible tip of the information-processing iceberg, most of which lies beneath the surface of your conscious awareness.

To sum up, the mind's subsystems are localized in particular brain regions, yet the brain acts as a unified whole. Moving your hand; recognizing faces; even perceiving color, motion, and depth all depend on specific neural networks. Yet complex functions such as language, learning, and loving involve the coordination of many brain areas. Both principles—specialization and integration—appear in research on the two brain hemispheres.

## Our Divided Brains

For more than a century, clinical evidence has shown that the brain's two sides serve differing functions. Accidents, strokes, and tumors in the left hemisphere generally impair reading, writing, speaking, arithmetic reasoning, and understanding. Similar lesions in the right hemisphere do not have such dramatic effects. Small wonder, then, that the left hemisphere became known as the "dominant" or "major" hemisphere, and its silent companion to the right as the "subordinate" or "minor" hemisphere. The left, verbal hemisphere is rather like the moon's facing side—the one easiest to observe and study. The other side is there, of course, but less visibly noticeable. (With some left-handers, speech is processed in the right hemisphere—see page 68.)

By 1960, the assumption of left hemisphere superiority was well accepted. But then the "minor" right hemisphere was found to be not so limited after all. As with the moon in recent years, we have reached and come to appreciate the other side. The story of this discovery is a fascinating chapter in psychology's history.

## Splitting the Brain

In 1961, two Los Angeles neurosurgeons, Philip Vogel and Joseph Bogen, were considering surgery for several patients who suffered from epilepsy. The surgeons speculated that major epileptic seizures were caused by an amplification of abnormal brain activity that reverberated between the two hemispheres. They therefore wondered whether they might control severe epilepsy by cutting communication between the hemispheres. To do so, the surgeons would have to sever the **corpus callosum**, the wide band of axon fibers connecting the two hemispheres (Figure 2–24).

*Question: If your Broca's area were damaged, could you write a letter?* *(See page 66.)*

They had reason to believe such an operation would not be incapacitating. Psychologists Roger Sperry, Ronald Myers, and Michael Gazzaniga had divided the brains of cats and monkeys in this manner, without serious ill effects. So Vogel and Bogen operated. The result? The seizures were nearly eliminated and the patients were surprisingly normal, their personalities and intellect hardly affected. Waking from the surgery, one patient even managed to quip that he had a "splitting headache" (Gazzaniga, 1967).

If you chatted with one of these **split-brain** patients you probably would not notice anything unusual. You could understand why only a decade earlier neuropsychologist Karl Lashley jested that maybe the corpus callosum served only "to keep the hemispheres from sagging." But surely a broad band of 200 million nerve fibers capable of transferring more than a billion bits of information per second between the hemispheres must have a more significant purpose. It does, and the ingenious experiments of Sperry and Gazzaniga revealed its purpose and provided a key to understanding the two hemispheres' special functions.

After one of the split-brain operations, the researchers placed an unseen object in a patient's left hand. He denied it was there. This came as no surprise to Sperry or Gazzaniga. They knew that information from the left hand went to the right hemisphere, and their animal experiments suggested that the right hemisphere would be unable to send this information to the left hemisphere (which in most humans controls speech). More extraordinary results came when Sperry and Gazzaniga conducted some perceptual tests.

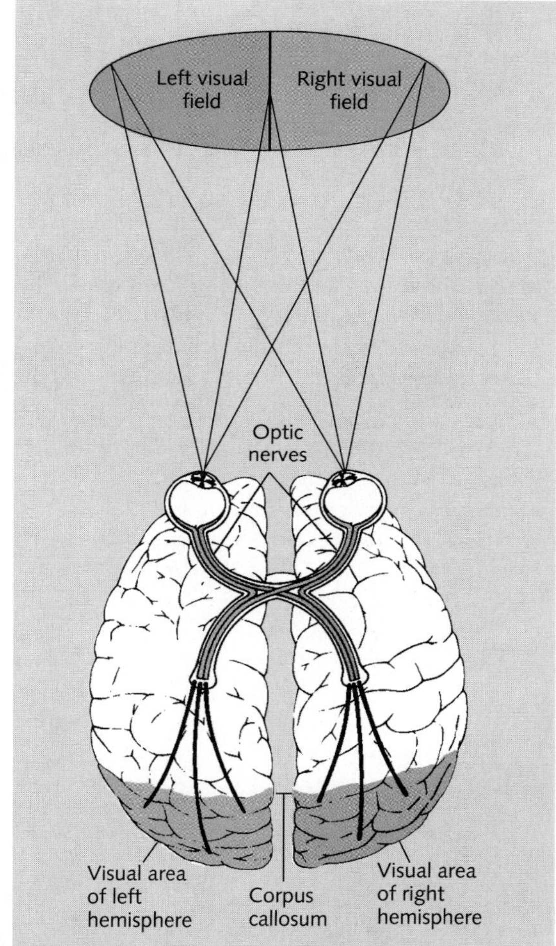


**Figure 2–25**

**The Information Highway From Eye to Brain** *Information from the left half of your field of vision is received only by your right hemisphere, and information from the right half of your visual field is received only by your left hemisphere. (Note, however, that each eye receives sensory information from* both *the right and left visual fields.) The data received by either hemisphere are quickly transmitted to the other across the corpus callosum. In a split-brain patient with a severed corpus callosum, this information sharing does not take place.*

Our eyes connect to our brains in such a way that, when we look straight ahead, the left half of our field of vision transmits through both eyes to our right hemisphere (Figure 2–25). Likewise, the right side of our field of vision transmits only to our left hemisphere. One woman, who had lost a vision-related part of her *right* hemisphere to a massive stroke but was otherwise normal, sometimes complained that nurses had not put dessert or coffee on her tray. A nurse would then turn the woman's head so that the tray came into view in the right half of her field of vision (where her *left* visual cortex could detect it). She then would say, "Oh, there it is—it wasn't there before" (Sacks, 1985, p. 73).

In those of us with healthy, intact brains, information presented only to our right hemisphere is quickly sent to our left hemisphere, which names it. But what happens in a person whose corpus callosum has been severed? To find out, experimenters ask a split-brain patient to look at a designated spot. Then they send information to either the left or right hemisphere (by flashing it to the spot's right or left). Finally, they quiz each hemisphere separately.

See if you can guess the results of an experiment using this procedure (Gazzaniga, 1967). While the patients stared at a dot, the word HEART was flashed across the visual field with HE in the left visual field and ART in the right. First, what did the patients *say* they saw? Second, asked to iden-

*Answer to question on page 65: Yes. Broca's area produces a program for controlling the muscles of speech. If the area is damaged, a victim can still understand speech and communicate through gestures or writing.*

tify with their *left* hands what they had seen, HE or ART, what did they *point* to?

As Figure 2–26 shows, the patients *said* they saw ART and so were startled when their left hands *pointed* to HE. When given an opportunity to express itself, each hemisphere reported only what *it* had seen.

Similarly, when a picture of a spoon was flashed to the right hemisphere, the patients could not say what they saw; but when asked to identify what they had seen by feeling with their left hands an assortment of objects hidden behind a screen, they readily selected the spoon (Figure 2–27). If the experimenter said, "Right!" the patient might reply, "What? Right? How could I possibly pick out the right object when I don't know what I saw?" It is, of course, the left hemisphere doing the talking here, bewildered by what its other half knows. It was as if the patients had "two separate inner visual worlds," noted Sperry (1968).

The left hemisphere, which acts as the brain's press agent, does mental gymnastics to rationalize reactions it does not understand. If the patient followed an order sent to the right hemisphere ("Walk"), the interpretive left hemisphere would offer a ready explanation ("I'm going into the house to get a Coke"). Thus, Michael Gazzaniga (1988) concludes that the left hemisphere is an "interpreter" that instantly constructs theories to explain our behavior.

*Question: If we flashed a red light to the right hemisphere of a split-brain patient and a green light to the left hemisphere, would each observe its own color? Would the person be aware that the colors differ? What would the person verbally report seeing? (Answers on page 68.)*

These experiments demonstrate that the right hemisphere understands simple requests and easily perceives objects. In fact, the right hemisphere is superior to the left at copying drawings, recognizing faces, reading emotions, and expressing emotion (through the more expressive left side of the face—Hauser, 1993; Skinner & Mullen, 1991). Most of the body's paired organs—kidneys, lungs, breasts—perform identical functions, providing a backup system should one side fail. Not so the brain's two halves, which serve differing functions.

**Figure 2–26**

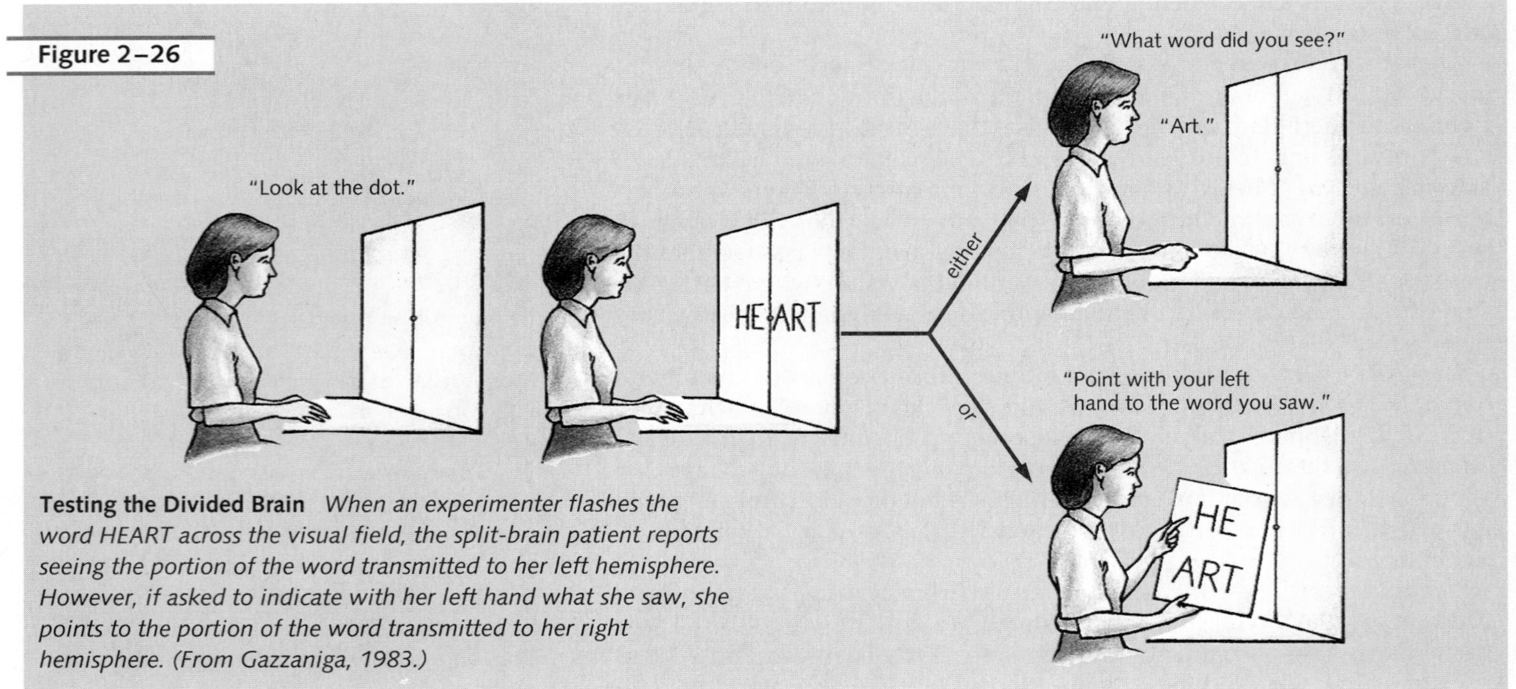
"Look at the dot."
HE•ART
either
or
"What word did you see?"
"Art."
"Point with your left hand to the word you saw."
HE
ART

**Testing the Divided Brain** *When an experimenter flashes the word HEART across the visual field, the split-brain patient reports seeing the portion of the word transmitted to her left hemisphere. However, if asked to indicate with her left hand what she saw, she points to the portion of the word transmitted to her right hemisphere. (From Gazzaniga, 1983.)*

**Figure 2–27**

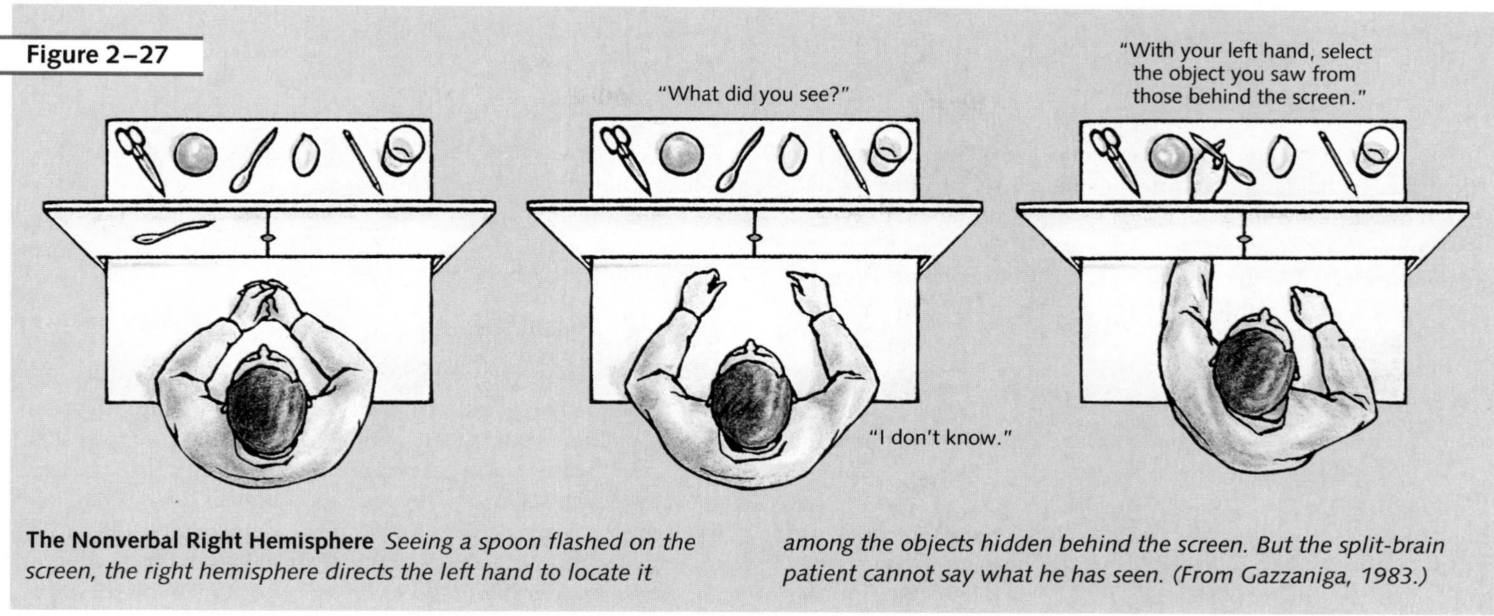
"What did you see?"
"With your left hand, select the object you saw from those behind the screen."
"I don't know."

**The Nonverbal Right Hemisphere** *Seeing a spoon flashed on the screen, the right hemisphere directs the left hand to locate it among the objects hidden behind the screen. But the split-brain patient cannot say what he has seen. (From Gazzaniga, 1983.)*

The right hemisphere's perceptual superiority is apparent in one of Sperry's films. A split-brain patient's left hand (directed by the right hemisphere) easily rearranges some blocks to match a drawing. When the right hand (directed by the left hemisphere) tries to perform the same perceptual task, it makes many errors. The bumbling performance frustrates the right hemisphere, which is observing all this. So it triggers the left hand to interrupt the bumbling right hand, but the persistent right hand pushes the left hand away. Outside the laboratory, a few split-brain patients have been for a time bothered by the unruly independence of their left hand, which would unbutton a shirt while the right hand buttoned it. It was as if each hemisphere had a mind of its own, perhaps thinking "I've half a mind to wear my green (blue) shirt today," said Sperry (1964). Indeed, split-brain surgery leaves people "with two separate minds."

*"Do not let your left hand know what your right hand is doing."*

Matthew 6:3

## Studying Hemispheric Differences in the Intact Brain

What about the 99.99+ percent of us with undivided brains? Have scientists found our hemispheres similarly specialized? They have indeed, in several different types of studies. For example, when a person performs a *perceptual* task, brain waves, blood flow, and glucose consumption reveal increased activity in the *right* hemisphere; when a person speaks or calculates, activity increases in the left hemisphere.

On occasion, hemispheric specialization has been even more dramatically shown by briefly sedating an entire hemisphere. To check for the locus of language before surgery, a physician may inject a sedative into the neck artery that feeds blood to the hemisphere on its side of the body. Before the drug is injected, the patient is lying down, arms in the air, conversing easily. Can you predict what happens when the drug flows into the artery going to the left hemisphere? Within seconds, the right arm falls limp and, assuming the person's left hemisphere controls language, the subject becomes speechless until the drug wears off. When the drug goes into the artery to the right hemisphere, the *left* arm falls limp, but speech is still possible.

**THE FAR SIDE**

8-27
© 1990 Universal Press Syndicate
Memo: Tonight I strike! Death to the left hand! Death! Death!

*Innocent and carefree, Stuart's left hand didn't know what the right was doing.*

THE FAR SIDE © 1990 FARWORKS, INC./Dist. by UNIVERSAL PRESS SYNDICATE. Reprinted with permission. All rights reserved.

## Close-Up: Left-Handedness—Is Being a Lefty All Right?

Judging by our everyday conversation, left-handedness is not all right. To be "coming from left field," or to offer a "left-handed compliment" is hardly more complimentary than to be "sinister" or "gauche" (words derived from the Latin and French for left). On the other hand, right-handedness is "right on," which any "righteous" "right-hand man" "in his right mind" usually is.

### How Many People Are Left-handed?

About 10 percent (somewhat more among males, somewhat less among females) of the human population is left-handed. Judging from cave drawings and the tools of prehistoric humans, this veer to the right occurred long ago in the development of our species. Thus, right-handedness prevails today in all human cultures (Corballis, 1989). Moreover, it appears prior to culture's impact: Ultrasound observations of fetal thumb-sucking reveal that more than 9 in 10 fetuses suck the right hand's thumb (Hepper & others, 1990). This right-hand bias is uniquely human; other primates are more ambidextrous.

### Is Handedness Inherited?

There is no simple genetic code for handedness, which is one of but a few traits that genetically identical twins aren't especially likely to share (Halpern & Coren, 1990). Nevertheless, observing 150 babies during the first 2 days after birth, George Michel (1981) found that two-thirds consistently preferred to lie with their heads turned to the right. When he restudied a sample of these babies at age 5 months, almost all of the "head right" babies reached for things with their right hands, and almost all of the "head left" babies reached with their left hands. Such findings, along with the universal prevalence of right-handers, indicate that either genes or some prenatal factor have an influence on handedness.

### Is the Brain Organization of Left-Handers Opposite That of Right-Handers?

Tests reveal that about 95 percent of right-handers process speech primarily in the left hemisphere (Springer & Deutsch, 1985). Left-handers are more diverse. More than half process speech in the left hemisphere, as right-handers do. About one-quarter process language in the right hemisphere; the other quarter use both hemispheres more or less equally. Such left-handers may therefore require better communication between the hemispheres. This might explain the discovery that the corpus callosum averages 11 percent larger in left-handers (Witelson, 1985).

### So, Is It All Right to Be Left-Handed?

Left-handers are more numerous among people with reading disabilities, allergies, and migraine headaches (Geschwind & Behan, 1984). But left-handedness is also more common among musicians, mathematicians, professional baseball and cricket players, architects, and artists, including such luminaries as Michelangelo, Leonardo da Vinci, and Picasso. Although left-handers must tolerate elbow-jostling at dinner parties, right-handed desks, and awkward scissors, it seems the pros and cons of being a lefty are roughly equal.

*In sports, strategic factors explain the higher-than-normal percentage of lefties. For example, it helps a soccer team to have left-footed players play the left side of the field (Wood & Aggleton, 1989).*

Other tests confirm hemispheric specialization. Most people recognize pictures faster and more accurately when flashed to the right hemisphere, but recognize words faster and more accurately when flashed to the left hemisphere. If a word is flashed to your right hemisphere, perception takes a fraction of a second longer—the length of time it takes to send the information through the corpus callosum to the more verbal left hemisphere.

Finally, which hemisphere would you suppose enables sign language among the deaf? Is it the right hemisphere, because of its visual-spatial superiority? Or the left, because of its preparedness to process language? Studies reveal that just as hearing people use the left hemisphere to process speech, deaf people use the left hemisphere to read signs (Corina & others, 1992). A stroke in the left hemisphere therefore disrupts a deaf person's ability to sign much as it would disrupt a hearing person's use of spoken language. To the brain, language is language, whether spoken or signed.

*Answers to questions on page 66: Yes. No. Green.*

So, a variety of observations—of people with "split" brains and people with "normal" brains—converge beautifully. There is now little doubt that we have unified brains with specialized parts. Although language requires the left hemisphere, the right hemisphere helps us modulate our speech to make meaning clear—asking "What's that in the road ahead?" instead of "What's that in the road, a head?" (Heller, 1990). From looking at the two hemispheres, which look alike to the naked eye, who would suppose that they contribute so uniquely to the harmony of the whole?

We have glimpsed the truth of our overriding principle: Everything psychological is simultaneously biological. This chapter has focused on some ways in which our thoughts, feelings, and actions arise from our specialized yet integrated brain. Chapters to come will further explore the significance of the biological revolution in psychology. We will see, for example, how

- brain development underlies a child's mental development.
- the brain compensates for brain damage that occurs early in life.
- genes and experience jointly influence our personality, emotions, gender, and intelligence.
- our sense organs and brains enable us to see and hear.
- the brain records memories.
- aberrant brain anatomy and chemistry influence depression and schizophrenia, and how biological treatments can alleviate these conditions.
- our brains and bodies work to create our experiences of hunger and sexuality, anger and fear, sleep and dreams.
- mind and body together influence our vulnerability to disease and our capacity for healing.
- our species' evolutionary history may predispose us to hurt, help, or sexually love certain others.

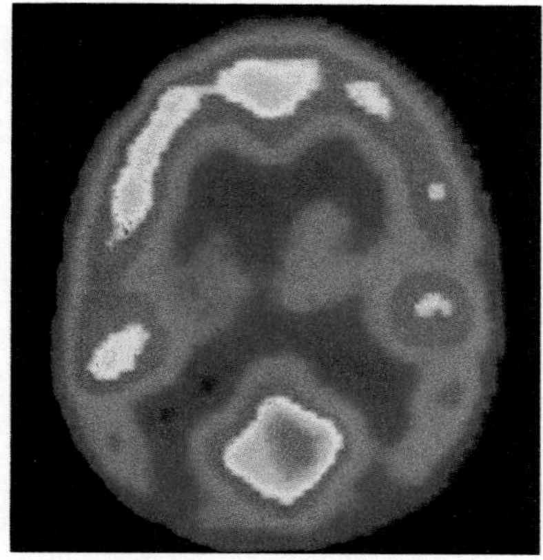

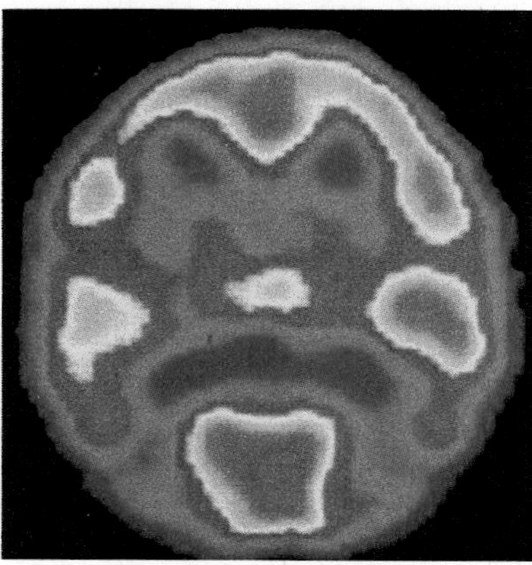

**PET Scan Images of Hemispheric Differences** *These PET scans show how active the right hemisphere becomes when the subject is listening to music (bottom) compared to resting (top). Red signifies the most activity, blue the least.*

From nineteenth-century phrenology to today's neuroscience we have come a long way. Yet what is unknown still dwarfs what is known. We can describe the brain. We can learn the functions of its parts. We can study how the parts communicate. But how does this electrochemical whir give rise to a feeling of elation, a creative idea, or a memory of Grandmother's freshly baked cookies?

The mind boggles both at what is known and what is not comprehended. To judge from interviews with leading brain scientists, feelings of wonder are commonplace and sometimes lead to mystical and spiritual inspirations. In the words of Candace Pert (1986, p. 390), "I see in the brain all the beauty of the universe and its order—constant signs of God's presence." Others ponder philosophical mysteries: How does the material brain give rise to consciousness? And to what extent can a thing understand itself? The mind seeking to understand the brain—that is indeed the ultimate scientific challenge.

*"If the human brain were so simple that we could understand it, we would be so simple that we couldn't."*

Emerson M. Pugh, quoted by George E. Pugh
*The Biological Origin of Human Values*, 1977

## Summing Up

**The Tools of Discovery** Clinical observations have long revealed the general effects of damage to various brain areas. But powerful new technologies now reveal brain structures and activities in the living brain. By surgically lesioning or electrically stimulating specific brain areas, by recording the brain's surface electrical activity, and by displaying neural activity with computer-aided brain scans, neuroscientists explore the connections among brain, mind, and behavior.

## *Thinking Critically About* **Left Brain/Right Brain**

*"Error flies from mouth to mouth, from pen to pen, and to destroy it takes ages."*
Voltaire, 1694–1778

You've heard or read it many times: Some people are "left-brained," others "right-brained." Leaping from the new research on split and intact brains, educators, management advisers, and self-help writers urge us to harness our undeveloped half brain. Are you lacking in creativity, music appreciation, or emotional empathy? Well, get your brain in balance. Awaken your dormant right hemisphere. Advocate "whole brain" education in your schools. Unleash intuitive, right-brained management from the chains of cold logic and statistics. Try *Drawing on the Right Side of the Brain* (the title of a million-copy best-seller translated into 10 languages).

What should we make of all this? By calling my friend Elsie "right-brained" have I explained why she's such a zany free spirit? And why her "left-brained" husband Bill is so coolly analytical? We've seen that research does show that each hemisphere serves special functions. The left is more logical, verbal, and able to deal with things in sequence. The right is more emotionally intuitive and expressive, skilled at spatial relations, and able to deal with things all at once. But neuroscientists offer a caution flag: Beware the fad of locating complex human abilities such as science or art in either hemisphere. "The left-right dichotomy in cognitive mode is an idea with which it is very easy to run wild," warned Sperry (1982). Complex activities such as doing science or creating art require the *integrated* activity of both hemispheres. Even when we just read a story, both hemispheres are active—the left processing the words and finding meaning, the right appreciating humor, imagery, and emotional content (Hellige, 1993; Levy, 1985).

Why, then, do the popularizations of brain research so greatly exaggerate the findings? In *The Left-Hander Syndrome*, University of British Columbia psychologist Stanley Coren (1993) illustrates how journalism often oversimplifies and embellishes science. He recalls hearing a convention talk by Doreen Kimura, a psychologist at the University of Western Ontario in London, Ontario. Kimura reported that melodies fed to the left ear were more easily recognized than melodies fed to the right ear. Knowing that the left ear sends most of its information to the right hemisphere, she concluded that, among her right-handed student volunteers, the right brain was better at recognizing melodies.

A few days later, the *New York Times* reported that "Doreen Kimura, a psychologist from London, Ontario, has found that musical *ability* is controlled by the right side of the brain" (italics highlight the embellishment). Apparently drawing from the *Times* story, a syndicated newspaper story then reported that "London psychologist, Dr. Doreen Kimura, claims that musicians are right-brained!" (But Kimura studied university students, not musicians.) Later, a follow-up newspaper article further distorted the study: "An English psychologist has finally explained why there are so many great left-handed musicians. Dr. Doreen Kimura has found. . . ."

Knowing that Kimura is not English, did not study musicians, and did not study left-handers, Coren recalled the words of an American editor: "Everything you read in the newspaper is absolutely true, except for the rare story of which you happen to have first-hand knowledge."

What can happen is this: As information flows from scientist to reader, it gets simplified and embellished, much as gossip does in passing from one person to the next. A TV network picks up an interesting finding, reduces it to a 30-second report with an 11-second sound bite from the researcher. This alerts a major newspaper to a story angle, which in turn gets picked up by popular science magazines and, eventually, by supermarket magazines and tabloids.

At each step, notes Coren, "Ideas become more speculative and more distant from the actual research. . . . After a while, the neuropsychologist is no longer even visible in the communication chain." Eventually, the rumors grow, accumulate, and evolve into scientific myths that become "'accepted truths,' which show up in conversation and writing in sentences that begin with, 'As everybody knows . . . ,' or 'Scientists have shown that. . . .'" In the end, sighs Coren, the public myth drowns the weak voices of dissenting scientists.

The moral is not to disbelieve everything you read. Surely Oscar Wilde was too cynical when expressing gratitude "for modern journalism. By giving us the opinions of the uneducated, it keeps us in touch with the ignorance of the community." (Although few journalists check the accuracy of their draft articles with those they've interviewed, some do.) Rather, beware that reporters want their stories to be newsworthy. At their best, their ideal (and mine, in writing this book) is to extract the essence—to simplify without oversimplifying. At their worst, they distort pretzel-shaped findings into a breadstick-shaped story: Some people are left-brained, others right-brained. . . .

**How the Brain Governs Behavior** The brainstem begins where the spinal cord swells to form the medulla, which controls heartbeat and breathing. Within the brainstem, the reticular formation has control over arousal. Atop the brainstem is the thalamus, the brain's sensory switchboard. The cerebellum, attached to the rear of the brainstem, coordinates muscle movement.

Between the brainstem and cerebral cortex is the limbic system, which is linked to memory, emotions, and drives. One of its neural centers, the amygdala, is involved in aggressive and fearful responses. Another, the hypothalamus, is involved in various bodily maintenance functions, pleasurable rewards, and the control of the endocrine system.

Each hemisphere of the cerebral cortex—the neural fabric that covers the hemispheres—has four geographical areas: the frontal, parietal, occipital, and temporal lobes. Small, well-defined regions within these lobes control muscle movement and receive information from the body senses. However, most of the cortex—its association areas—is uncommitted to such functions and is therefore free to process other information.

Some brain regions serve specific functions (Figure 2–28). The brain divides its labor into specialized subtasks and then integrates the outputs from its neural networks. Thus human emotions, thoughts, and behaviors result from the intricate coordination of many brain areas. Language, for example, depends on a chain of events in several brain regions.

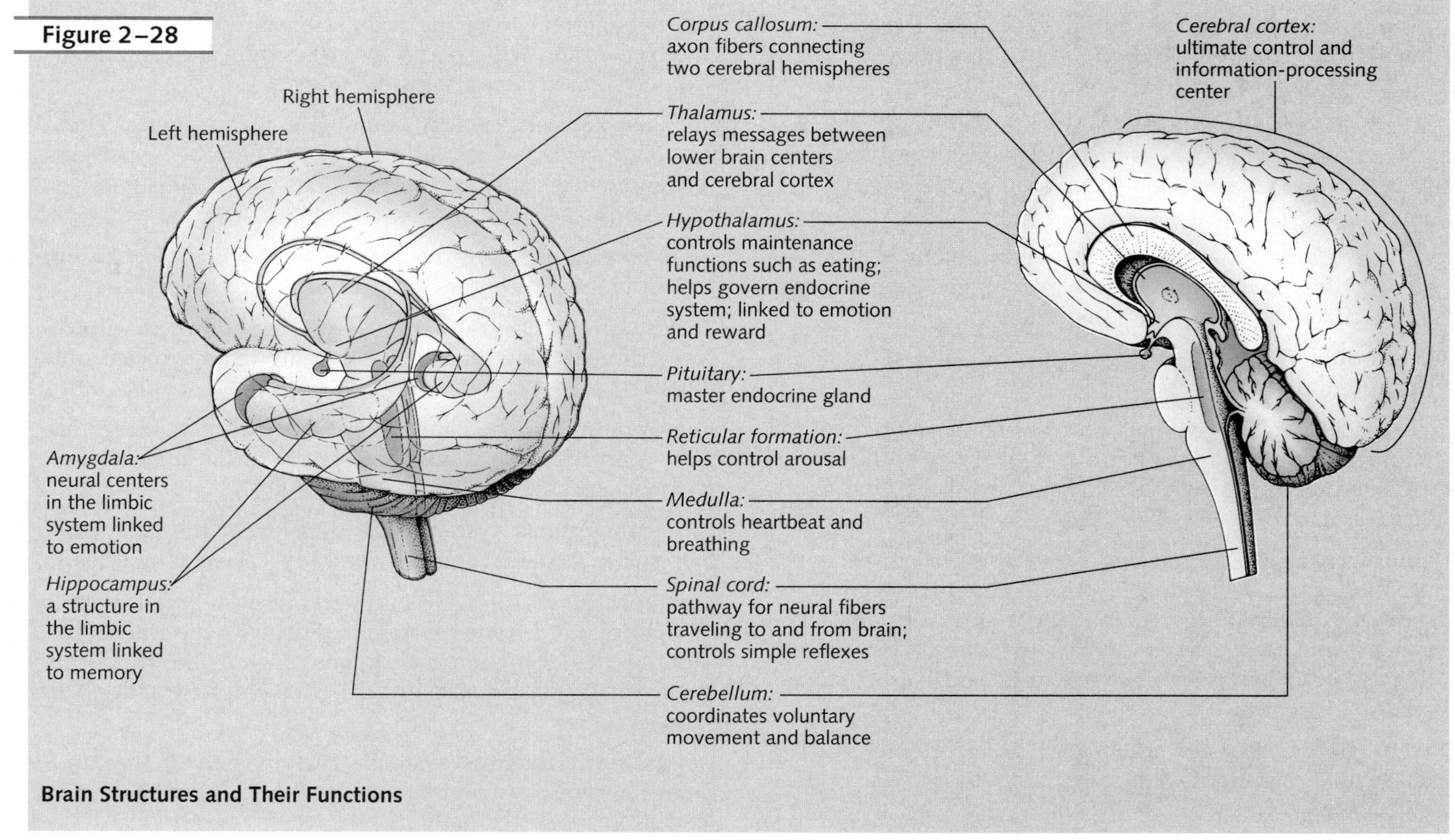


**Figure 2–28**

**Brain Structures and Their Functions**

**Our Divided Brains** Clinical observations long ago revealed that the left cerebral hemisphere is crucial for language. Experiments on split-brain patients have refined our knowledge of each hemisphere's special functions. By testing the two hemispheres separately, researchers have confirmed that in most people the left hemisphere is the more verbal, and that the right hemisphere excels in visual perception and the recognition of emotion. Studies of normal people with intact brains confirm that each hemisphere makes unique contributions to the integrated functioning of the brain.

## Terms and Concepts to Remember

**biological psychology** A branch of psychology concerned with the links between biology and behavior. (Some biological psychologists call themselves *behavioral neuroscientists, neuropsychologists, physiological psychologists,* or *biopsychologists.*)

### Neural Communication

**neuron** A nerve cell; the basic building block of the nervous system.

**dendrite** The bushy, branching extensions of a neuron that receive messages and conduct impulses toward the cell body.

**axon** The extension of a neuron, ending in branching terminal fibers, through which messages are sent to other neurons or to muscles or glands.

**myelin** [MY-uh-lin] **sheath** A layer of fatty cells segmentally encasing the fibers of many neurons; makes possible vastly greater transmission speed of neural impulses.

**action potential** A neural impulse; a brief electrical charge that travels down an axon. The action potential is generated by the movement of positively charged atoms in and out of channels in the axon's membrane.

**threshold** The level of stimulation required to trigger a neural impulse.

**synapse** [SIN-aps] The junction between the axon tip of the sending neuron and the dendrite or cell body of the receiving neuron. The tiny gap at this junction is called the *synaptic gap* or cleft.

**neurotransmitters** Chemical messengers that traverse the synaptic gaps between neurons. When released by the sending neuron, neurotransmitters travel across the synapse and bind to receptor sites on the receiving neuron, thereby influencing whether it will generate a neural impulse.

**acetylcholine** [ah-seat-el-KO-leen] **(ACh)** A neurotransmitter that, among its functions, triggers muscle contraction.

**endorphins** [en-DOR-fins] "Morphine within"—natural, opiatelike neurotransmitters linked to pain control and to pleasure.

### Neural and Hormonal Systems

**nervous system** The body's speedy, electrochemical communication system, consisting of all the nerve cells of the peripheral and central nervous systems.

**central nervous system** The brain and spinal cord.

**peripheral nervous system** The neurons that connect the central nervous system to the rest of the body. It consists of the sensory neurons, which carry messages to the central nervous system from the body's sense receptors, and the motor neurons, which carry messages from the central nervous system to the muscles and glands.

**nerves** Neural "cables" containing many axons. These bundled axons, which are part of the peripheral nervous system, connect the central nervous system with muscles, glands, and sense organs.

**sensory neurons** Neurons that carry incoming information from the sense receptors to the central nervous system.

**interneurons** Central nervous system neurons that intervene directly between the sensory inputs and motor outputs.

**motor neurons** The neurons that carry outgoing information from the central nervous system to the muscles and glands.

**skeletal nervous system** The division of the peripheral nervous system that controls the body's skeletal muscles.

**autonomic** [aw-tuh-NAHM-ik] **nervous system** The part of the peripheral nervous system that controls the glands and the muscles of the internal organs (such as the heart). Its sympathetic division arouses; its parasympathetic division calms.

**sympathetic nervous system** The division of the autonomic nervous system that arouses the body, mobilizing its energy in stressful situations.

**parasympathetic nervous system** The division of the autonomic nervous system that calms the body, conserving its energy.

**reflex** A simple, automatic, inborn response to a sensory stimulus, such as the knee-jerk response.

**neural networks** Interconnected neural cells. With experience, networks can learn, as feedback strengthens or inhibits connections that produce certain results. Computer simulations of neural networks show analagous learning.

**endocrine** [EN-duh-krin] **system** The body's "slow" chemical communication system; a set of glands that secrete hormones into the bloodstream.

**hormones** Chemical messengers, mostly those manufactured by the endocrine glands, that are produced in one tissue and affect another.

**adrenal** [ah-DREEN-el] **glands** A pair of endocrine glands just above the kidneys. The adrenals secrete the hormones epinephrine (adrenaline) and norepinephrine (noradrenaline), which help to arouse the body in times of stress.

**pituitary gland** The endocrine system's most influential gland. Under the influence of the hypothalamus, the pituitary regulates growth and controls other endocrine glands.

## The Brain

**lesion** [LEE-zhuhn] Tissue destruction. A brain lesion is a naturally or experimentally caused destruction of brain tissue.

**electroencephalogram (EEG)** An amplified recording of the waves of electrical activity that sweep across the brain's surface. These waves are measured by placing electrodes on the scalp.

**CAT (computerized axial tomograph) scan** A series of x-ray photographs taken from different angles and combined by computer into a composite three-dimensional representation of a slice through the body.

**PET (positron emission tomograph) scan** A visual display of brain activity that detects where a radioactive form of glucose goes while the brain performs a given task.

**MRI (magnetic resonance imaging)** A technique that uses magnetic fields and radio waves to produce computer-generated images that distinguish among different types of soft tissue; allows us to see structures within the brain.

**brainstem** The oldest part and central core of the brain, beginning where the spinal cord swells as it enters the skull; it is responsible for automatic survival functions.

**medulla** [muh-DUL-uh] The base of the brainstem; controls heartbeat and breathing.

**reticular formation** A nerve network in the brainstem that plays an important role in controlling arousal.

**thalamus** [THAL-uh-muss] The brain's sensory switchboard, located on top of the brainstem; it directs messages to the sensory receiving areas in the cortex and transmits replies to the cerebellum and medulla.

**cerebellum** [sehr-uh-BELL-um] The "little brain" attached to the rear of the brainstem; it helps coordinate voluntary movement and balance.

**limbic system** A doughnut-shaped system of neural structures at the border of the brainstem and cerebral hemispheres; associated with emotions such as fear and aggression and drives such as those for food and sex.

**amygdala** [ah-MIG-dah-la] Two almond-shaped neural centers in the limbic system that are linked to emotion.

**hypothalamus** [hi-po-THAL-uh-muss] A neural structure lying below (*hypo*) the thalamus; it directs several maintenance activities (eating, drinking, body temperature), helps govern the endocrine system via the pituitary gland, and is linked to emotion.

**cerebral** [seh-REE-bruhl] **cortex** The intricate fabric of interconnected neural cells that covers the cerebral hemispheres; the body's ultimate control and information-processing center.

**frontal lobes** The portion of the cerebral cortex lying just behind the forehead; involved in speaking and muscle movements and in making plans and judgments.

**parietal** [puh-RYE-uh-tuhl] **lobes** The portion of the cerebral cortex lying at the top of the head and toward the rear; includes the sensory cortex.

**occipital** [ahk-SIP-uh-tuhl] **lobes** The portion of the cerebral cortex lying at the back of the head; includes the visual areas, each of which receives visual information from the opposite visual field.

**temporal lobes** The portion of the cerebral cortex lying roughly above the ears; includes the auditory areas, each of which receives auditory information primarily from the opposite ear.

**motor cortex** An area at the rear of the frontal lobes that controls voluntary movements.

**sensory cortex** The area at the front of the parietal lobes that registers and processes body sensations.

**association areas** Areas of the cerebral cortex that are not involved in primary motor or sensory functions; rather, they are involved in higher mental functions such as learning, remembering, thinking, and speaking.

**aphasia** Impairment of language, usually caused by left hemisphere damage either to Broca's area (impairing speaking) or to Wernicke's area (impairing understanding).

**Broca's area** An area of the left frontal lobe that directs the muscle movements involved in speech.

**Wernicke's area** An area of the left temporal lobe involved in language comprehension.

**corpus callosum** [KOR-pus kah-LOW-sum] The largest bundle of neural fibers connecting and carrying messages between the two brain hemispheres.

**split brain** A condition in which the two hemispheres of the brain are isolated by cutting the connecting fibers (mainly those of the corpus callosum) between them.

## Critical Thinking Exercise

Now that you have read and reviewed Chapter 2, take your learning a step further by testing your critical thinking skills on this pattern recognition exercise.

Playing a musical instrument is a complicated skill that involves every major aspect of behavior and cognition. To be proficient, musicians must have honed their fine motor skills. In addition, many aspects of thinking come into play, including *memory* of how to play the instrument and of musical scales and time signatures, and the planning and *decision making* inherent in translating a piece of sheet music into sound. Equally important are the musician's *motivation* and *emotion,* which influence many aspects of a musical performance.

In this exercise you will develop a map describing how various parts of the brain enable a musician to perform a piece of music. Using the following grid, identify three lower level brain structures and three upper level structures and then describe how each structure is involved in musical performance.

| Lower Level Brain Structures | How the Structures Are Involved in Musical Performance |
|---|---|
| ______________ | ______________ |
| ______________ | ______________ |
| ______________ | ______________ |
| ______________ | ______________ |

| Upper Level Brain Structures | How the Structures Are Involved in Musical Performance |
|---|---|
| ______________ | ______________ |
| ______________ | ______________ |
| ______________ | ______________ |
| ______________ | ______________ |

Check your progress on becoming a critical thinker by comparing your answers to the sample answers found in Appendix B.

## For Further Information

*You can find more information regarding neuroscience on the following text pages:*

Genes and
- aggression, p. 632
- altruism, p. 643
- depression, pp. 518–519
- development, pp. 78, 80, 107–111
- fearfulness, p. 445
- gender, pp. 673–675
- intelligence, pp. 383–386
- learning, pp. 264–265
- obesity, p. 606
- schizophrenia, pp. 527–528
- sociobiology, p. 643

Neurology and
- intelligence, pp. 375–377

Neurotransmitters and
- depression, p. 519
- drugs, pp. 243–245
- exercise, pp. 593–594
- hunger, p. 403
- memory, pp. 303–304
- smoking, p. 601
- therapy, pp. 565–567

Hormones and
- aggression, p. 633
- development, pp. 80, 118–119
- emotion, p. 434
- gender, pp. 673–674
- hunger, p. 402
- memory, p. 304
- sex, pp. 410–411
- stress, pp. 575–576, 582

Brain activity and
- aggression, pp. 632–633
- development, pp. 84–87
- dreams, pp. 228–230
- emotion, p. 435
- hunger, p. 403
- intelligence, p. 375
- memory, pp. 302–307
- sensation, Chapter 5
- psychosurgery, p. 568
- sex, p. 411
- sleep, pp. 221–224
- stress and health, Chapter 17

## For Further Reading

**Bloom, F. E., Lazerson, A., & Hofstadter, L.** (1988). *Brain, mind, and behavior* (2nd ed.). New York: Freeman.

*A lavishly illustrated summary of brain research written to accompany the PBS television series "The Brain."*

**Coren, S.** (1993). *The left-hander syndrome: The causes and consequences of left-handedness*. New York: Free Press.

*How, and why, do left- and right-handers differ in intelligence, personality, creativity, and longevity? This captivating book offers well-researched answers.*

**Kosslyn, S. M., & Koenig, O.** (1992). *Wet mind: The new cognitive neuroscience*. New York: Free Press.

*"The mind is what the brain does," say Kosslyn and Koenig. But how does the brain do it? A challenging but state-of-the-art introduction to how the brain processes the information needed to see, read, speak, move, and remember.*

**Sacks, O.** (1985). *The man who mistook his wife for a hat*. New York: Summit Books.

*Fascinating case studies of people whose disorders reveal the brain's workings.*

**Springer, S. P., & Deutsch, G.** (1994). *Left brain, right brain* (4th ed.). New York: Freeman.

*An award-winning description of research on the two hemispheres of brain-damaged, split-brain, and normal subjects. Discusses handedness, gender differences, learning disabilities, and theories of consciousness.*

# CHAPTER 3



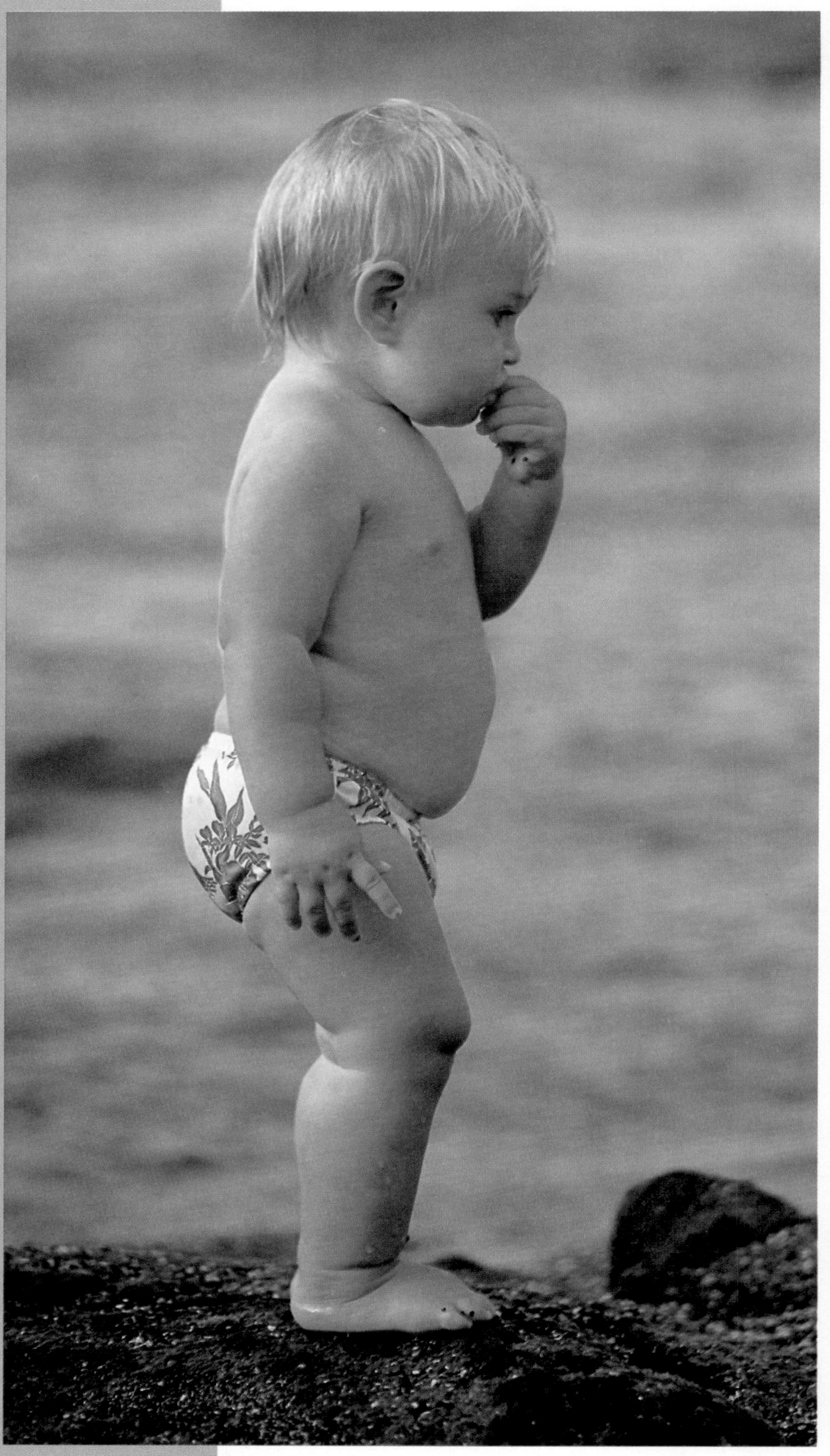

# The Developing Child

*In mid-1978, the newest astonishment in medicine, covering all the front pages, was the birth of an English baby nine months after conception in a dish. The older surprise, which should still be fazing us all, is that a solitary sperm and a single egg can fuse and become a human being under any circumstance, and that, however implanted, [this multiplied] cell affixed to the uterine wall will grow and differentiate into eight pounds of baby; this has been going on under our eyes for so long a time that we've gotten used to it; hence the outcries of amazement at this really minor technical modification of the general procedure—nothing much, really, beyond relocating the beginning of the process from the fallopian tube to a plastic container.*

Lewis Thomas
*The Medusa and Snail*, 1979

The developing person is no less a wonder after birth than in the womb. Physically, mentally, socially, we are always in the process of becoming. As we journey through life from womb to tomb, when and how do we change?

Usually we notice how we differ. To developmental psychologists our commonalities are just as important. Virtually all of us began walking around age 1 and talking by age 2. As children we all engaged in social play in preparation for life's serious work. We all smile and cry, love and hate, and occasionally ponder the fact that someday we will die.

## Developmental Issues

Unlike most other chapters in this book, this one and the next focus not so much on a topic—the brain, memory, thinking, personality, social behavior—as on a *perspective*. The developmental perspective examines how all such things *change* over the life span. **Developmental psychologists** study physical, mental, and social changes occurring throughout the life cycle. Much of their work centers on three major issues:

1. ***Nature/nurture*** How is our development influenced by our genetic inheritance and by our experience? Do children in different cultures travel down the same developmental highway (thanks to their shared human nature)? Or does their physical, mental, and social growth unfold differently, depending on their cultural nurture?
2. ***Continuity/stages*** Is developmental change gradual and continuous? Or does it proceed in spurts, through a sequence of separate stages?

3. ***Stability/change*** How much do we change? Do our individual traits persist? Or do we become different persons as we age?

## Nature/Nurture

*More than 98 percent of our genes are identical to those of chimpanzees. But what a difference that 2 percent makes—enabling not only our art and science but also our power to destroy all our achievements.*

Our **genes** are the biochemical units of heredity that make each of us a distinctive human being. The genes we share are what make us people rather than dogs or tulips. Do our individual genetic makeups also explain why one person is outgoing, another shy? Why one person is slow-witted and another smart? Are human traits, like eye color, pretty much fixed? Or are they changeable?

Our answers affect how we view certain social policies. Those who presume that people are the way they are "by nature" typically place little faith in programs that try to compensate for educational disadvantage or to rehabilitate prisoners. They tend to agree with the developmental psychologists who emphasize the influence of our genes. As a flower unfolds in accord with its genetic blueprint, so our genes design an orderly sequence of biological growth processes called **maturation**. Maturation decrees many of our commonalities: standing before walking, using nouns before adjectives. Although extreme deprivation or abuse will retard development, the genetic growth tendencies are inborn. Maturation sets the basic course of development and experience adjusts it.

*"Nature is all that a man brings with him into the world; nurture is every influence that affects him after his birth."*

Francis Galton
*English Men of Science*, 1874

Those who favor the nurture side of the debate agree with the developmentalists who emphasize learning and external influences. As a potter shapes a lump of clay, our experiences shape us. Families matter. Culture matters. Children do not develop in isolation from their surroundings.

These surroundings shape us in many ways, as emphasized by Lev Vygotsky (1896–1934), a Russian psychologist whose sociocultural theories have recently inspired many Western developmentalists. According to Vygotsky, parents and other teachers transmit to every child whatever skills, values, and perspectives are needed in that society. The skill might be knowing how to catch and store salmon in a Native Alaskan coastal village or how to transmit electronic mail in a modern metropolis. The value might be modest self-effacement or brash self-assurance. The perspective might be that women are inferior, superior, or equal to men. The social context that surrounds each of us from earliest infancy is the source for many of our thoughts, beliefs, and behaviors.

In reality, almost everyone agrees that our behaviors are a product of the *interaction* of our genes and our experiences. If an attractive, athletic teenage boy is treated as a leader and sought out by girls, shall we say his positive self-image is due to his genes or to his environment? It's both, because his environment is reacting to his genetic endowment. Asking which factor is more important is like asking whether the area of a soccer field is due more to its length or to its width. Genes predispose behaviors that surface in a particular social context.

## Continuity/Stages

Change happens: Adults are vastly different from infants. But do they differ as a giant redwood differs from its seedling—a difference created by gradual, cumulative growth? Or do they differ as a butterfly differs from a caterpillar—a difference of distinct stages? In short, is development a slow, continuous process, or does it occur in spurts that define distinct stages?

Generally speaking, researchers who emphasize experience and learning see development as a slow, *continuous* shaping process. Those who emphasize biological maturation tend to see development as a sequence of genetically predetermined *stages* or steps; although progress through the various stages may be quick or slow, everyone passes through the stages in the same order.

## Stability/Change

Change happens, but how changeable are we? And at what ages? For much of this century, psychologists took the position that once a person's personality forms, it hardens like clay and remains set for life. Researchers who have followed lives through time are now debating the extent to which our past reaches into our future. Is development characterized more by *stability* over time or by *change*? Are the effects of early experience enduring or temporary? Will the cranky infant grow up to be an irritable adult? Or is such a child as likely to become a placid, patient person? Do differences among classmates in, say, aggressiveness, aptitude, or strivings for achievement persist throughout the life span? In short, to what degree do we grow to be merely older versions of our early selves, and to what degree do we become new persons?

**It Runs in the Family** *Whitney Houston (left), her aunt Dionne Warwick (right), and her mother Cissy Houston, a gospel singer (center), have all made their mark in the world of music. The existence of such exceptional talent across generations raises intriguing questions about the relative impact of our genes, our experience, and how they interact.*

Most developmentalists now believe that for certain traits, such as emotional intensity, there is an underlying continuity, especially in the years following early childhood. Yet as we age we also change—physically, mentally, socially. Thus, we have today's life-span view: Human development is a lifelong process.

At the end of this chapter and the next we will reflect on these three developmental issues. But first, our main agenda: to examine human development across the life span, beginning where life begins and ending where life ends.

## Prenatal Development and the Newborn

*How, over time, did we come to be who we are? From the union of sperm and egg to birth of the newborn, development progresses in an orderly, though fragile, sequence. By birth, infants are equipped with perceptual and behavioral abilities that facilitate their survival.*

### From Life Comes Life

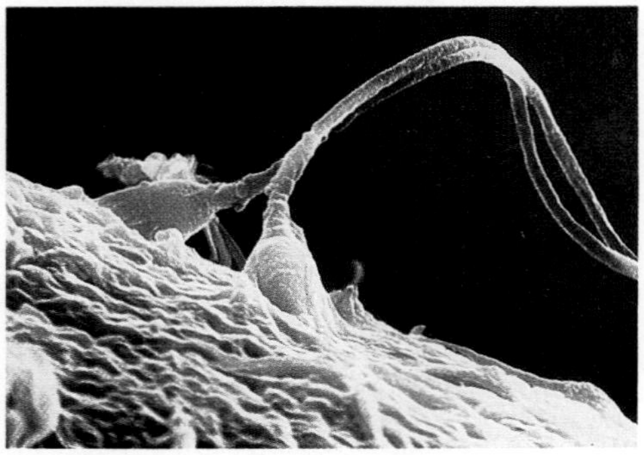

Nothing is more natural than a species reproducing itself. Yet nothing is more wondrous. Consider human reproduction. The process starts when a woman's ovary releases a mature egg, a cell roughly the size of the period at the end of this sentence, and the 200 million or more sperm deposited during intercourse begin their race upstream toward it. A girl is born with all the immature ova she will ever have, although only 1 in 5000 will ever mature and be released. A boy, in contrast, begins producing sperm cells at puberty. The manufacturing process continues 24 hours a day for the rest of his life, although the rate of production—more than 1000 sperm during the second it takes to read this phrase—does slow down with age.

Like space voyagers approaching a huge planet, the sperm approach a cell 85,000 times their own size. The relatively few sperm that make it to the egg release digestive enzymes that eat away the egg's protective coating, allowing a sperm to penetrate (Figure 3–1). But the egg is hardly passive. Rather, as a sperm begins to penetrate, an electric charge shoots across the egg's surface, blocking out all other sperm during the minute or so that it takes the egg to form a protective barrier. Meanwhile, fingerlike projections sprout around the successful sperm and pull it inward. The egg nucleus and the sperm move toward each other and, before half a day elapses, fuse. The two have become one.

**Figure 3–1**

**Sperm and Egg Unite** *With this union, development begins. If all goes well, the resulting single cell will emerge 9 months later as a 100-trillion-cell human being.*

Consider it your luckiest of moments. Among 200 million sperm, the one needed to make you, in combination with that one particular egg, won the race. A 7-year-old boy was overheard explaining the idea to a friend: "Robbie, do you know how many sperm were trying to be you? (Robbie shook his head.) Well, there were millions. I saw it on *Nova*. They were all racing against you, but *you* won. Anybody who is alive won. So you're a winner and I'm a winner; everybody's a winner" (Mahoney, 1989).

When egg and sperm unite, the 23 **chromosomes** carried in the egg pair up with the 23 chromosomes brought to it by the sperm. These 46 chromosomes contain the master plan for your body. Each chromosome is composed of long threads of a molecule called **DNA (deoxyribonucleic acid)**. DNA in turn is made of thousands of genes, functional segments capable of synthesizing specific proteins (the biochemical building blocks of life, including our neural information system) (Figure 3–2).

Your sex is determined by your twenty-third pair of chromosomes, the sex chromosomes. The member of the pair that came from your mother was an ***X* chromosome**. From your father, you received either an *X* chromosome, making you a girl, or a ***Y* chromosome**, making you a boy. The *Y* chromosome contains a single gene that throws a master switch triggering the testes to develop and produce the principal male hormone, **testosterone**, which in turn triggers the development of external male sex organs. Inject this gene fragment of the *Y* chromosome into female mouse embryos carrying a normal pair of *X* chromosomes and they may grow up as males (Koopman & others, 1991).

Figure 3–2

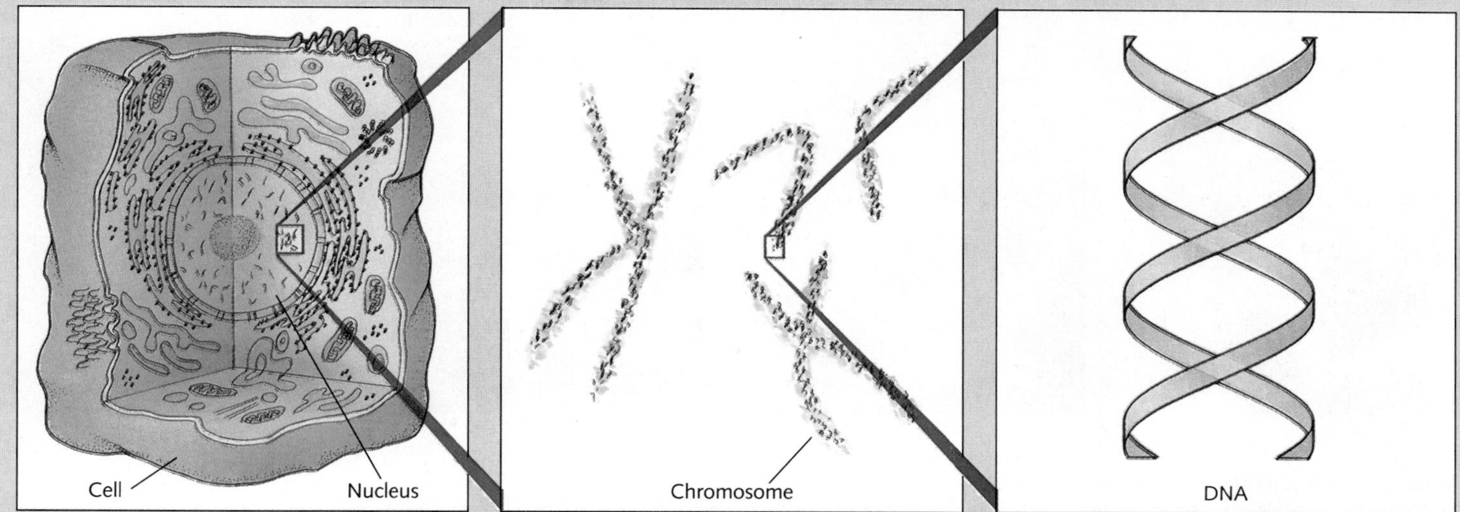


**The Genes: Their Location and Composition** *Contained in the nucleus of each of the trillions of cells in your body are chromosomes. Each chromosome is composed in part of the molecule DNA. Genes are segments of DNA that form templates for the production of proteins. By directing the manufacture of proteins, the genes determine our individual biological development.*

## Prenatal Development

Even at your fortunate moment when one lucky sperm won the race, your destiny was not assured. Fewer than half of fertilized eggs, called **zygotes**, survive beyond the first 2 weeks (Grobstein, 1979). If human life begins at conception, then most people die without being born.

*"From the very moment that the sperm hits the egg, a precarious trip on the thin edge of biological extinction has begun."*

Ralph Blair
*Nevertheless Joy!*, 1989

But for you and me good fortune prevailed. Beginning as one cell, each of us became two cells, then four—each cell just like the first. Then, within the first week, when this cell division had produced a zygote of some 100 cells, the cells began to *differentiate*—to specialize in structure and function. About 10 days after conception, the increasingly diverse cells became attached to the mother's uterine wall, beginning approximately 37 weeks of the closest human relationship (Figure 3–3, page 82).

The zygote's outer part attaches to the uterine wall and becomes the placenta, through which nourishment passes. In this second prenatal stage, the inner cells become the **embryo**. During the next 6 weeks, the embryo's body organs begin to form and function. The heart begins to beat and the liver begins to make red blood cells. Embryos carrying a *Y* chromosome begin to secrete testosterone, diverting them down the road to maleness.

By 9 weeks after conception, the embryo looks unmistakably human and is now a **fetus**. By the end of the sixth month, internal organs such as the stomach have become sufficiently formed and functional to allow a prematurely born fetus a chance of survival. By that time, the developing fetus also becomes responsive to sound. Microphone readings taken inside the uterus reveal that the fetus is, for example, exposed to its mother's voice via bone conduction, diaphragm movements, and air conduction (Ecklund-Flores, 1992). Immediately after birth, infants prefer this familiar

***Prenatal development***
***zygote:*** *conception to 2 weeks*
***embryo:*** *2 weeks through 8 weeks*
***fetus:*** *9 weeks to birth*

Figure 3–3

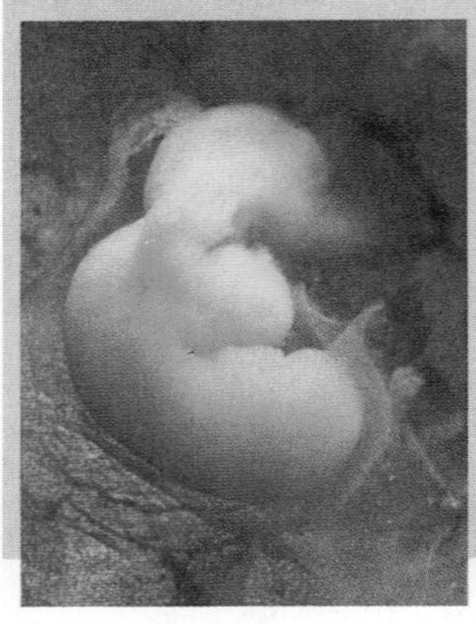
(a)

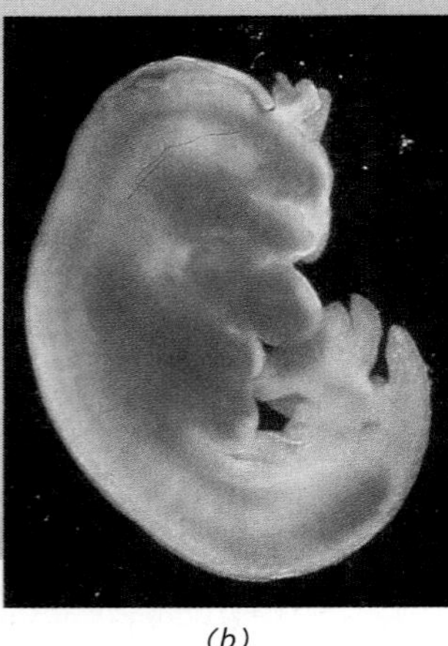
(b)

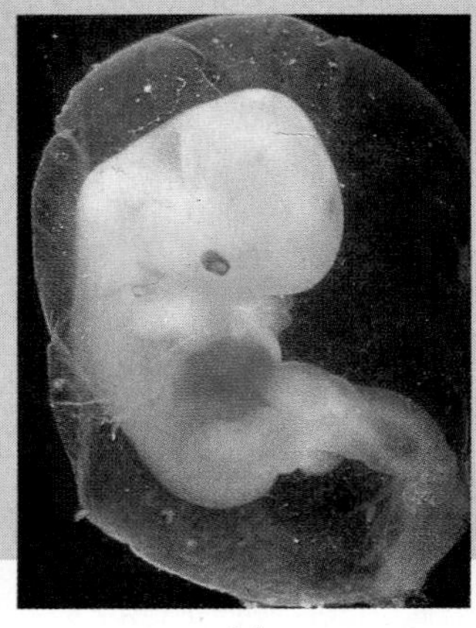
(c)

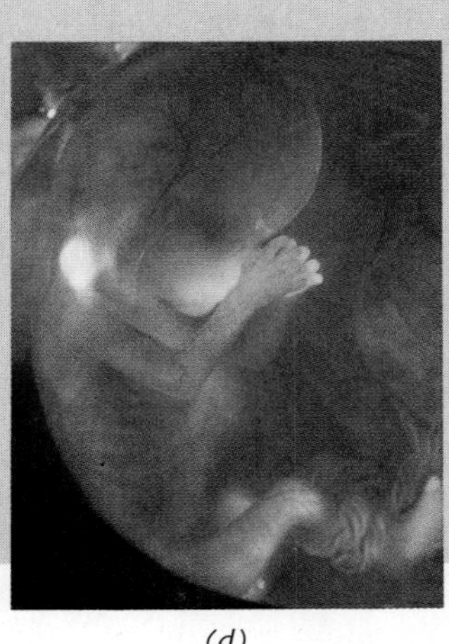
(d)

**Prenatal Development** *(a) The embryo grows and develops rapidly. At 40 days, the spine is visible and the arms and legs are beginning to grow. (b) Five days later the inch-long embryo's proportions have begun to change. The rest of the body is now bigger than the head, and the arms and legs have grown noticeably. (c) By the end of the second month, when the fetal period begins, facial features, hands, and feet have formed. (d) As the fetus enters the fourth month, it weighs about 3 ounces.*

voice to another woman's voice or their father's voice (Busnel & others, 1992; DeCasper & others, 1980, 1984, 1986).

At each prenatal stage, genetic *and* environmental factors affect development. The placenta screens out many potentially harmful substances, while allowing nutrients and oxygen to pass through. But nourishment isn't all that passes the placental screen. Devastating effects may follow when the placenta admits **teratogens**—harmful agents, such as certain viruses and drugs. A pregnant woman never smokes alone. When she puffs on a cigarette, she and her fetus both experience reduced blood oxygen and a shot of nicotine. If she is a heavy smoker, her newborn probably will be underweight, sometimes dangerously so. If she is a heroin addict, her baby will be born a heroin addict. If she carries the AIDS virus, her baby often does too. And if the mother uses crack, her baby, having been deprived of nutrients and oxygen while in the womb, may suffer deformities and growth impairment. In the early 1990s, as the first wave of a new "crack baby" generation began school, urban special education programs braced for a surge in the numbers of withdrawn, impulsive, hyperactive children.

Tera *means "monster"; teratogens are "monstrous" agents, such as chemicals and viruses, that may harm the fetus.*

When a pregnant woman takes a drink, alcohol enters her bloodstream—and her fetus's—and depresses activity in both their central nervous systems. If she drinks heavily, her baby will be at risk for birth defects and mental retardation. For 1 in 750 infants, the effects are visible as **fetal alcohol syndrome (FAS)**, which involves small, misproportioned heads and lifelong brain abnormalities, making it now the leading cause of mental retardation (Streissguth & others, 1988). Although there is no known safe amount of alcohol for a pregnant woman, children of alcoholic mothers are especially at risk. About 4 in 10 alcoholic mothers who drink during pregnancy have babies who suffer the enduring damage of fetal alcohol syndrome. Where maternal drinking is common—as in France and among Native Americans—more children suffer from FAS (Dorozyaski, 1993; Dorris, 1989). "If women didn't drink anymore during pregnancy," notes researcher Ann Streissguth (1993), "there would *never* be another baby born with fetal alcohol syndrome."

*"You shall conceive and bear a son. So then drink no wine or strong drink."*

Judges 13:7

## The Competent Newborn

Having survived prenatal hazards, newborns come equipped with reflexes ideally suited for survival. Infants will withdraw a limb to escape pain. Put a cloth over their faces, interfering with their breathing, and they will turn their heads from side to side and swipe at it. New parents are often awed by the coordinated sequence of reflexes by which babies get food. The **rooting reflex** illustrates this: When something touches their cheeks, babies will open their mouths and vigorously "root" for a nipple. Finding one, they will automatically close on it and begin sucking—which itself requires a coordinated sequence of tonguing, swallowing, and breathing. Failing to find satisfaction, the hungry baby may cry—a behavior parents are predisposed to find highly unpleasant to hear and very rewarding to relieve.

The pioneering American psychologist William James (who once said, "The first lecture on psychology I ever heard was the first I ever gave") presumed that the newborn experiences a "blooming, buzzing confusion." Until the 1960s, few people disagreed. It was said that, apart from a blur of meaningless light and dark shades, newborns could not see. Then, just as the development of new technology led to progress in the neurosciences, so too did new investigative techniques enhance the study of infants. Scientists discovered that babies can tell you a lot—if you know how to ask. To ask, you must capitalize on what the baby can do—gaze, suck, turn the head. So, equipped with eye-tracking machines, pacifiers wired to electronic gear, and other such devices, researchers set out to answer parents' age-old questions: What can my baby see, hear, smell, and think?

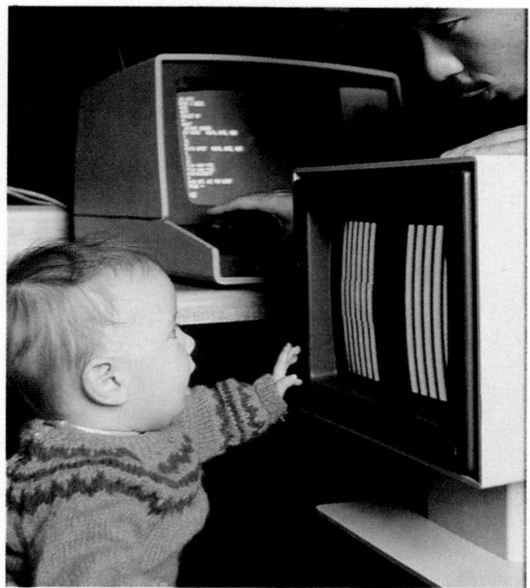

**You've Come a Long Way, Baby** *Studies like the one underway in this M.I.T. laboratory are exploring infants' abilities to perceive and remember. Experiments show that young infants are capable of sophisticated visual discrimination and will look much longer at an unfamiliar than a familiar pattern. Such tests have changed psychologists' ideas of what the world looks like to a baby.*

They discovered that infants are born preferring sights and sounds that facilitate social responsiveness. Newborns turn their heads in the direction of human voices. They gaze longer at a drawing of a human face than at a bull's-eye pattern; yet they gaze more at a bull's-eye pattern—which has contrasts much like that of the human eye—than at a solid disk (Fantz, 1961). They prefer to look at objects 8 to 12 inches away, which, wonder of wonders, just happens to be the approximate distance between a nursing infant's eyes and the mother's (Maurer & Maurer, 1988). Newborns, it seems, arrive perfectly designed to see their mothers' eyes.

Babies' perceptual abilities are continuously developing during the first months of life. Within days of birth, babies can distinguish their mothers' odor and voice. The infant's brain is an absorbent sponge, its neural networks stamped immediately with the smell of its mother's body. Thus, a week-old nursing baby, placed between a gauze pad from its mother's bra and one from another nursing mother, will usually turn toward the smell of its own mother's pad (MacFarlane, 1978). At 3 weeks of age, an infant who sucks on a pacifier that sometimes turns on recordings of its mother's voice and sometimes that of a female stranger will suck more vigorously when it hears its now-familiar mother's voice (Mills & Melhuish, 1974). Newborns can also learn to turn their heads to the left or right to receive a sugar solution when their forehead is stroked (Lancioni, 1980). So not only can young infants see what they need to see, and smell and hear well, but they are already using their sensory equipment to learn.

Researcher Tiffany Field (1987) notes, "Our knowledge of infancy was in its infancy 20 years ago, but what we have learned since then has dramatically changed the way we perceive and treat infants." More and more, she goes on to say, psychologists see the baby as "a very sophisticated perceiver of the world." The "helpless infant" of a generation ago has become today's "amazing newborn."

## Summing Up

By studying the human life span from conception to death, developmental psychologists examine how we develop physically, cognitively, and socially. The life cycle begins when one sperm cell, out of the some 200 million ejaculated, unites with an egg to form a zygote. Attached to the uterine wall, the developing embryo begins to form body organs. By 9 weeks, the fetus becomes recognizably human. Along with nutrients, teratogens ingested by the mother can reach the developing child and place it at risk.

With the aid of new methods for studying babies, researchers have discovered that newborns are surprisingly competent. They are born with sensory equipment and reflexes that facilitate their interacting with adults and securing nourishment. For example, they quickly learn to discriminate the smell and sound of their mothers.

# Infancy and Childhood

*"It is a rare privilege to watch the birth, growth, and first feeble struggles of a living human mind."*
Annie Sullivan, in Helen Keller's *The Story of My Life*, 1903

During infancy, a baby grows from newborn to toddler, and during childhood from toddler to teenager. Beginning in this chapter with infancy and childhood and continuing in the next chapter with adolescence through old age, we will see how people of all ages develop—physically, cognitively, and socially.

## Physical Development

*Infants' biological development enables their psychological development. The brain's maturing neural networks are sculpted by experience. The developing brain fosters developing motor skills.*

### Brain Development

While you resided in your mother's womb, your body was forming nerve cells at the rate of about one-quarter million per *minute*. On the day you were born you had essentially all the brain cells you will ever have. However, at birth the human nervous system is immature: After birth, the neural *networks* that enable us to walk, talk, and remember have a wild growth spurt (Figure 3–4).

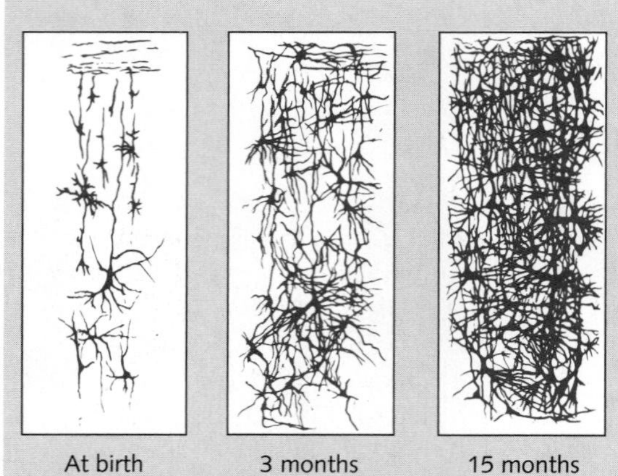


**Figure 3–4**

**Drawings of Human Brain Cerebral Cortex Sections** *In humans, the brain is immature at birth. As the child matures, the neural networks grow increasingly more complex.*

**Maturation and Infant Memory** The lack of neural connections (and of language and a sense of self) helps explain why our earliest memories seldom predate our third birthdays (Howe & Courage, 1993; Nelson, 1993). For parents, this "infantile amnesia," as Freud called it, can be disconcerting. After all the hours we spend with our babies—after all the frolicking on the rug, all the diapering, feeding, and rocking to sleep—what would they consciously remember of us if we died before they reached age 3? Virtually nothing!

But if little is consciously recalled, something has still been gained. Given occasional reminders, 3-month-old infants who learn that moving their leg propels a mobile will remember the association for at least a month (Figure 3–5). Two-and-a-half-year-olds in a pitch-dark room are more likely to reach for and grasp a squeaking Big Bird toy if they experienced the same situation 2 years earlier (Perris & others, 1990). Such memories are not of words but of images, sounds, and emotions.

Animals such as guinea pigs, whose brains are mature at birth, more readily form permanent memories in infancy than do animals with immature brains, such as rats (Campbell & Coulter, 1976). These findings cast doubt on the idea that humans, whose brains are also immature at birth, subconsciously remember their prenatal life or the trauma of their birth.

Because of changes after age 5 in how memories are organized, most people also have few memories of their preschool years. Elizabeth Loftus and Leah Kaufman (1992) note that trying to access our preschool memories is like trying to read a diskette that was formatted by an earlier version of a computer operating system.

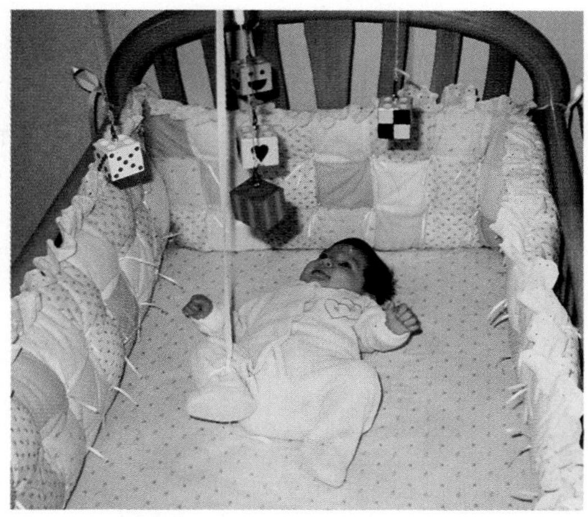

**Figure 3–5**

**Infant at Work** *Babies only 3 months old can learn that kicking moves a mobile—and can retain that learning for a month.*

**Experience and Brain Development** Experience, as well as biological maturation, helps develop the brain's neural connections. Although "forgotten," early learning is not all erased. Rather, it helps prepare our brains for thought and language, and also for later experiences.

How do early experiences leave their "marks" in the brain? Mark Rosenzweig and David Krech reared some young rats in solitary confinement and others in a communal playground (Figure 3–6). Rats living in the deprived environment usually developed a lighter and thinner brain cortex. Rosenzweig (1984; Renner & Rosenzweig, 1987) reported being so surprised by these effects of experience on brain tissue that he repeated the experiment several times before publishing his findings. Rats are not people, but these findings are consistent with what we know about the importance of active involvement for human development. These and other results have helped encourage improvement in the environments provided for laboratory, farm, and zoo animals—and for children in institutions.

Several research teams have found that infant rats and premature babies benefit from the stimulation of being touched or massaged (Field & others, 1986; Meaney & others, 1988). "Handled" infants of both species gain weight more rapidly and develop faster neurologically. William Greenough and his University of Illinois colleagues (1987) further discovered that repeated experiences sculpt a rat's neural tissue—at the very spot in the brain that processes the experience. After brain maturation provides an abundance of neural connections, sculpting preserves activated connections while allowing unused connections to degenerate, resulting in a massive loss of unemployed connections by puberty.

Here, then, at the juncture of nurture and nature, is where a child's enriched environment activates and preserves connections that, given impov-

**Figure 3–6**

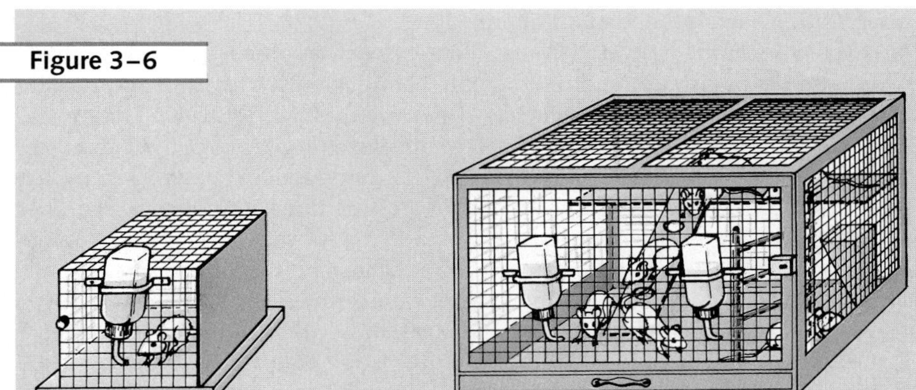


**Experience Affects Brain Development** *Mark Rosenzweig and David Krech reared rats either alone in an environment without playthings or with others in an environment enriched with playthings that were changed daily. In 14 of 16 repetitions of this basic experiment, the rats placed in the enriched environment developed significantly more cerebral cortex (relative to the rest of the brain's tissue) than did those in the impoverished environment. (From "Brain changes in response to experience" by M. R. Rosenzweig, E. L. Bennett, and M. C. Diamond. Copyright © 1972 Scientific American, Inc. All rights reserved.)*

erished experiences, may die off from disuse. There is a biological reality to early childhood education. Given stimulating infant care, children from impoverished environments have higher intelligence scores at age 12 than those of similar children in a control group (Ramey & Ramey, 1992). It is during these early childhood years—while the excess connections still are on call—that youngsters can most easily master the grammar and accent of another language. Lacking any exposure to language (written or signed) before adolescence, the person will never master any language (see page 346). Lacking visual experience during the early years, people whose vision is restored by cataract removal never achieve normal perceptions (see page 203). The brain cells normally assigned to vision have died or been diverted to other uses. For optimum brain development, the early years are critical. With the maturing brain, the rule seems to be use it or lose it.

The brain's development does not, however, end with childhood. Throughout life our neural tissue is changing. Sights and smells, touches and tugs activate and strengthen some neural pathways, while others weaken from disuse. Like pathways through a forest, less traveled paths are abandoned, popular paths are broadened. Our genes dictate our overall brain architecture, but experience directs the details. If a monkey is trained to push a lever with a finger several thousand times a day, the brain tissue that controls the finger changes to reflect the experience. Human brains work similarly. The wiring of Michael Jordan's brain reflects the thousands of hours he spent shooting baskets. Experience nurtures nature.

**Brain Reorganization** Nurture's sculpting of the ever-changing brain is evident in studies of the brain's **plasticity**. Although severed neurons will not regenerate (if your spinal cord is severed you are permanently paralyzed), neural tissue can reorganize in response to damage.

In one experiment, neuroscientists surgically cut the neural pathways for incoming information from a monkey's arm. The area of the sensory cortex that formerly received this input gradually shifted its function and began to respond when researchers touched the animal's face (Pons & others, 1991). Similarly, if a laser beam damages a spot in a cat's eye, the brain area that received input from that spot will soon begin responding to stimulation from nearby areas in the cat's eye. If blind people use one finger to read Braille, the brain area dedicated to that finger expands (Barinaga, 1992a). And among deaf people who communicate visually, with sign language, the temporal lobe area normally dedicated to auditory information waits in vain for stimulation. Finally, it looks for other signals to process, such as those from the visual system.

Thus, the brain may not be as "hard-wired" as once thought. Unlike fixed computer circuits, brain hardware changes with time. In response to changing stimulation, the brain can either rewire itself with new synapses or (according to another theory) select new uses for its prewired circuits (Gazzaniga, 1992). When one brain area is damaged, other areas may in time reorganize and take over some of its functions. If neurons are destroyed, nearby neurons may partly compensate for the damage by making new connections that replace the lost ones. These new connections are one way the brain struggles to recover from, say, a minor stroke. They are also the brain's way of compensating for the gradual loss of neurons with age.

Our brains are most plastic when we are young children—before cortical regions' functions become fixed (Kolb, 1989). Children are born with a surplus of neurons. If an injury destroys one part of a child's brain, the brain will compensate by putting other surplus areas to work. Thus, if the speech areas of an infant's left hemisphere are damaged, the right hemisphere will take over much of its language function. After age 5, left hemisphere damage permanently and severely disrupts language.

As an extreme example of plasticity, consider a 5-year-old boy whose severe seizures, caused by a deteriorating left hemisphere, require removing the *entire* hemisphere. What hope for the future would such a child have? Is there any chance he might attend school and lead a normal life, or would he suffer permanent retardation?

Astonishingly, one such individual was at last report an executive. Half his skull is filled with nothing but cerebrospinal fluid—functionally it might as well be sawdust—yet he has scored well above average on intelligence tests, has completed college, and at last report was attending graduate school part-time (Smith & Sugar, 1975; A. Smith, 1987). Although paralyzed on the right side, this man (along with other such cases of "hemispherectomy") testifies to the brain's extraordinary powers of reorganization when damaged before it is fully developed.

### Motor Development

As the infant's muscles and nervous system mature, more complicated skills emerge. With minor exceptions, the sequence of these skills is universal. Babies roll over before they sit unsupported, and creep on all fours before walking.

**A Triumphant Toddler** *Before 12-month-old Christopher achieved this major milestone, his motor development proceeded in the orderly sequence typical of infant locomotion. At about 6 to 7 months, most babies sit without support. At about 9 months, they stand and walk holding on. At about 1 year, they begin to walk unaided.*

But there are individual differences in timing of this sequence. In America, one in four babies walks by age 11 months, half within a week after their first birthday, and 90 percent by age 15 months (Frankenburg & others, 1992). And there are cultural differences. In Uganda, a healthy baby usually walks before age 10 months. In France, walking usually begins after age 1. African-American infants, too, tend to walk earlier than European-American infants (Rosser & Randolph, 1989).

Nurture may influence motor development. Compared with babies who spend much of the day lying in a crib, Ugandan babies experience more intimate physical contact, along with the parent's rhythmic gait, while being carried upright on the back (Bril, 1986). But nature (genes) plays a major role. Identical twins typically begin sitting up and walking on nearly the same day (Wilson, 1979). Biological maturation—including the rapid development of the cerebellum at the brain's rear—creates a readiness to learn walking at about 1 year of age. Experience before that time has a limited effect. This is true for other physical skills, including bowel and bladder control. Until the necessary muscular and neural maturation occurs, no amount of pleading, harassment, or punishment will produce successful toilet training.

After a spurt during the first 2 years, growth slows to a steady 2 to 3 inches per year through childhood. With all of the neurons and most of their interconnections in place, brain development after age 2 similarly proceeds at a slower pace. The sensory and motor cortex areas continue to mature, enabling fine motor skills to develop further (Wilson, 1978).

## Summing Up

Within the brain, nerve cells form before birth. Sculpted by experience, their interconnections continue to multiply after birth. If one hemisphere is damaged early in life, the other will pick up many of its functions, thus demonstrating the brain's plasticity. The brain becomes less plastic later in life. Frequently, however, nearby neurons can partially compensate for damaged ones, as when a person recovers from a stroke or brain injury.

*To predict a girl's adult height, double her height at 18 months. To predict a boy's adult height, double his height at 2 years.*

Infants' more complex physical skills—sitting, standing, walking—develop in a predictable sequence whose actual timing is a function of individual maturation rate and culture. Childhood—from toddlerhood to the teen years—is a period of slow, steady physical development.

**Jean Piaget** *"If we examine the intellectual development of the individual or of the whole of humanity, we shall find that the human spirit goes through a certain number of stages, each different from the other" (1930).*

## Cognitive Development

*As a newborn, you confronted a sea of sensations and began making sense of them with greater speed and ease than psychologists once believed possible. By 6 months you comprehended permanence, number, and simple physical laws. From these beginnings blossomed your capacity for taking another's perspective, for logic, and for all that defines the mature mind.*

The association areas of the cortex—those linked with thinking, memory, and language—are the last brain areas to develop. As they do, the child's mental abilities surge ahead (Chugani & Phelps, 1986; Thatcher & others, 1987). Brain and mind, neural hardware and cognitive software, develop together. **Cognition** refers to all the mental activities associated with thinking, knowing, and remembering. Few questions intrigue developmental psychologists more than these concerning cognitive development: When and how do children begin to see things from another's point of view? Reason logically? Think symbolically? Simply put, how does a child's mind grow? Such were the questions posed by developmental psychologist Jean Piaget (pronounced Pee-ah-ZHAY).

"Who knows the thoughts of a child?" wondered poet Nora Perry. As much as anyone of his generation, Piaget knew. His interest began in 1920, when he was working in Paris to develop questions for children's intelligence tests. While administering tests to find out at what age children could answer certain questions correctly, Piaget became intrigued by children's *wrong* answers. Where others saw childish mistakes, Piaget saw intelligence at work. The errors made by children of a given age, he noted, were often strikingly similar.

The half century Piaget spent with children convinced him that the child's mind is not a miniature model of the adult's. Young children understand the world in radically different ways than adults do, a fact that we sometimes overlook when teaching children. Piaget further believed that the child's mind develops through a series of stages, in an upward march from the newborn's simple reflexes to the adult's abstract reasoning power. An 8-year-old child therefore comprehends things that a 3-year-old cannot. An 8-year-old might grasp the analogy "getting an idea is like having a light turn on in your head," but trying to teach the same analogy to a 3-year-old would be fruitless.

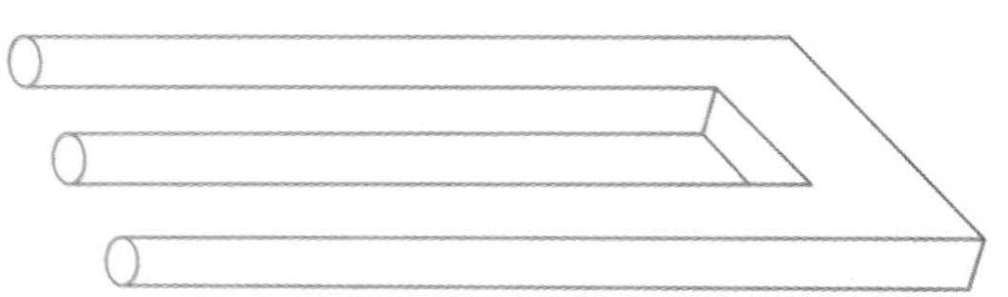

**An Impossible Object** *Look carefully at the "devil's tuning fork" above. Now look away—no, better first study it some more—and then look away and draw it. Not so easy, is it? Because this tuning fork is an impossible object, you have no schema into which you can assimilate what you see.*

### How the Mind of a Child Grows

The driving force behind this intellectual progression is our unceasing struggle to make sense of our experience. To this end, the maturing brain builds concepts, which Piaget called **schemas**. Schemas (or schemes) are mental molds into which we pour our experience. By adulthood we have built countless schemas that range from knowing how to tie a knot to our concept of love.

Piaget proposed two concepts to explain how we use and adjust our schemas. First, we interpret our experience in terms of our current understandings. In Piaget's terms, we use our schemas to incorporate, or **assimilate**, new experiences. Given a simple schema for *dog*, a toddler may call all four-legged animals *doggies*. But we also adjust, or **accommodate**, our schemas to fit the particulars of new experiences. The child soon learns that the original *doggie* schema is too broad and accommodates by refining the category. As children interact with the world, they construct and modify their understanding of it.

### Piaget's Theory and Current Thinking on Cognitive Stages

Science itself is a process of assimilation and accommodation. Scientists use their preconceived theories (for example, that newborns are passive, incompetent creatures) to assimilate (incorporate) their observations. Then, as new observations collide with these theories, the theories change to accommodate (adjust to) the findings. Thus, the new concept of the newborn as competent replaces the old schema. That, Piaget believed, is how children (and adults) construct reality. And that is how Piaget's own concepts have functioned—first by helping us understand children's behavior and then by changing to accommodate new findings.

Piaget described cognitive development as occurring in four stages (Table 3–1). Developing children, he believed, experience spurts of change followed by greater stability as they move from one developmental plateau to the next. Each plateau has distinctive characteristics that permit specific kinds of thinking. To appreciate how the mind of a child grows, let's look at each of Piaget's stages in light of current thinking about cognitive development.

**Table 3–1 Piaget's Stages of Cognitive Development**

| Typical Age Range | Description of Stage | Developmental Milestones |
|---|---|---|
| Birth to nearly 2 years | *Sensorimotor*<br>Experiencing the world through senses and actions (looking, touching, mouthing) | • Object permanence<br>• Stranger anxiety |
| About 2 to 6 years | *Preoperational*<br>Representing things with words and images but lacking logical reasoning | • Ability to pretend<br>• Egocentrism |
| About 7 to 11 years | *Concrete operational*<br>Thinking logically about concrete events; grasping concrete analogies and performing arithmetical operations | • Conservation<br>• Mathematical transformations |
| About 12 through adulthood | *Formal operational*<br>Abstract reasoning | • Abstract logic<br>• Potential for mature moral reasoning |

**Sensorimotor Stage** During the **sensorimotor stage**, from birth to nearly age 2, babies understand the world through their sensory and motor interactions with objects—through looking, touching, mouthing, and grasping. At first they seem unaware that things continue to exist apart from their perceptions.

In one of his tests, Piaget would show an infant an appealing toy and

**The Process of Assimilation** *When we experience something new and it fits roughly with our existing understandings, we assimilate that experience (to use Piaget's term). What is your reaction to these two pictures of Pablo Picasso's wife Françoise Gilot? If you are a lover of modern art, you may easily assimilate his abstract painting as a glorious representation of a beautiful woman. For most of us, however, the realistic photograph is more readily assimilated because it better fits our available schemas of beauty.*

**The Beginnings of Logical Thought** *During the sensorimotor stage, from birth until about 2 years of age, children understand the world mainly through their actions and sensations. They enjoy smelling, feeling, and tasting almost anything they can get their hands on. As children reach the preoperational stage, which lasts from about 2 to 6 years of age, pretending becomes possible.*

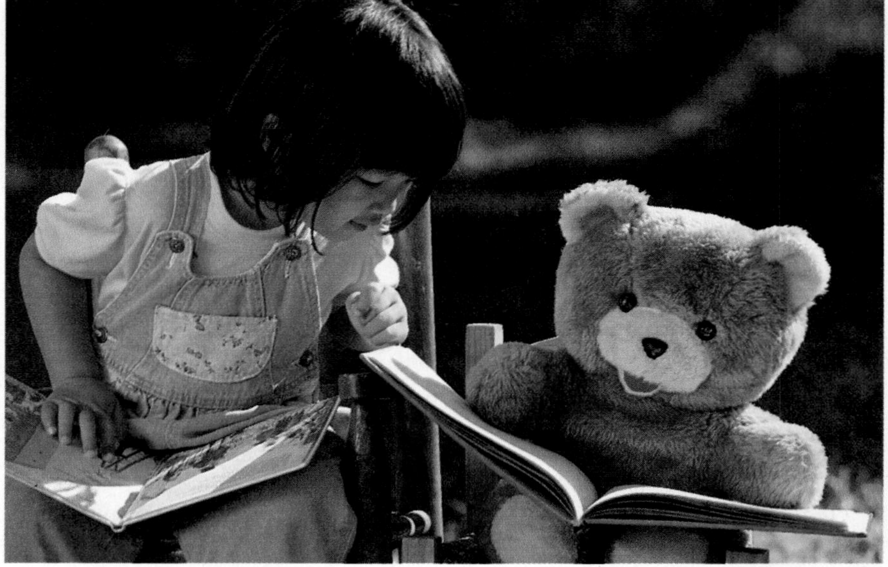

then flop his beret over it to see whether the infant searched for the toy. Much before the age of 8 months, they did not. They lacked **object permanence**—the awareness that objects continue to exist when not perceived. The infant lives in the present. What is out of sight is out of mind. By 8 months, infants begin to exhibit memory for things no longer seen. Hide the toy and the infant will momentarily look for it. Within another month or two, the infant will look for it even after being restrained for several seconds.

But today's researchers wonder: Do children's cognitive abilities really grow through distinct *stages*? Does object permanence in fact blossom by 8 months, much as a tulip blossoms in spring? Today's researchers see development as more continuous than did Piaget. For example, they now view object permanence as unfolding gradually, beginning with young infants' looking for a toy where they saw it hidden a second before.

Researchers believe that Piaget and his followers underestimated young children's competence. Before age 2, Piaget assumed, infants cannot think. They can recognize things, smile at them, crawl to them, manipulate them. But they have no abstract concepts or ideas. Theirs is a life not thought about, only lived.

**Object Permanence** *Infants younger than 6 months do not understand that things continue to exist when they are out of sight. But for this infant, out of sight is definitely not out of mind.*

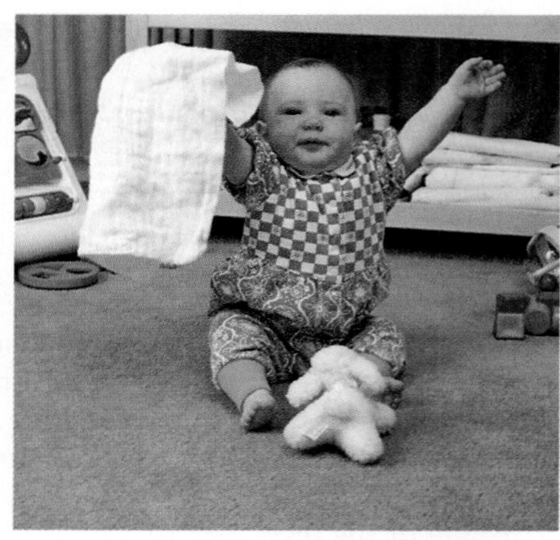

## Thinking Critically About **Infants' Thinking**

Can a newborn see well enough to distinguish shapes? Can a 3-month-old recognize faces? Does a 5-month-old have a concept of number? If only babies could talk, we would ask them.

Might there nevertheless be ways to ask such questions without words? Psychology, the science of behavior and mental processes, often lets behavior do the talking. Developmental researchers, for example, exploit a simple form of learning called **habituation**—decreasing responsiveness with repeated stimulation. A novel stimulus gets attention when first presented. But the more it is presented, the weaker the response becomes. This seeming boredom with familiar stimuli provides a way to assess what infants see and remember.

Alan Slater and his University of Exeter colleagues (1988) illustrated the strategy when they asked newborns as young as 7 hours old what they could see. When first shown a stimulus like the one in Figure 3–7, the newborns gazed intently for an average 41 seconds. With repeated presentations, their interest soon waned.

What if the figure were rotated 90° to a new position? Could the infants *remember* the initial stimulus and perceive it as different from the new one? As Figure 3–8 indicates, they could indeed. Shown a stimulus with lines oriented as already seen, plus another stimulus with the novel, rotated orientation, the infants looked three times as long at the new one. Their behavior indicated they *could* remember and discriminate between differing visual stimuli. Using the habituation phenomenon, other researchers report that infants can also discriminate colors, shapes, and sounds and can understand some basic concepts of numbers and physics. In all these studies, researchers assume that infants' greater attention to some stimuli reveals their ability to distinguish different stimuli.

Given the elegant simplicity of such studies, why have they been done only recently? Researcher Slater (1994) explains: To recognize a new stimulus as different an infant must remember the initial stimulus. Until the early 1980s, researchers assumed a newborn's brain was too immature to enable such memory. Thus, they never tested for habituation. Then, as appreciation for the newborn's abilities began to grow, investigators created new ways to test the scope of their cognition.

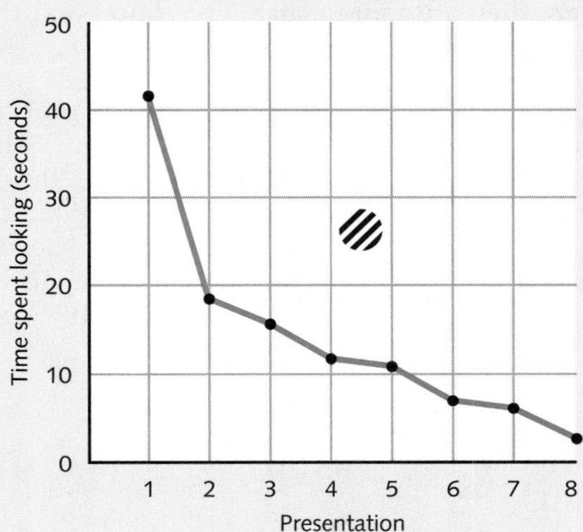


**Figure 3–7**

**Habituation** *Newborns' looking times with repeated presentation of a visual stimulus. (Data from Slater & others, 1988.)*

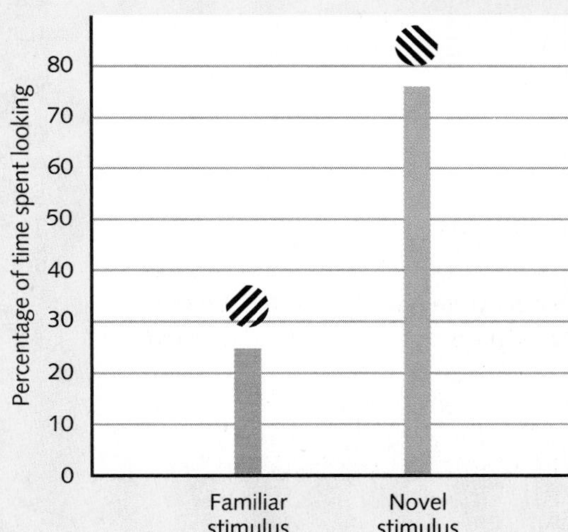


**Figure 3–8**

**Novelty Preference** *Having habituated to the old stimulus, newborns preferred gazing at a new one—thus revealing their visual ability. (Data from Slater & others, 1988.)*

Consider, however, a simple experiment. Karen Wynn (1992) showed 5-month-old infants one or two objects (Figure 3–9). Then she hid the objects behind a screen, sometimes removing or adding one through a trap door. When she lifted the screen, the infants sometimes did a double take, staring longer when shown a wrong number of objects.

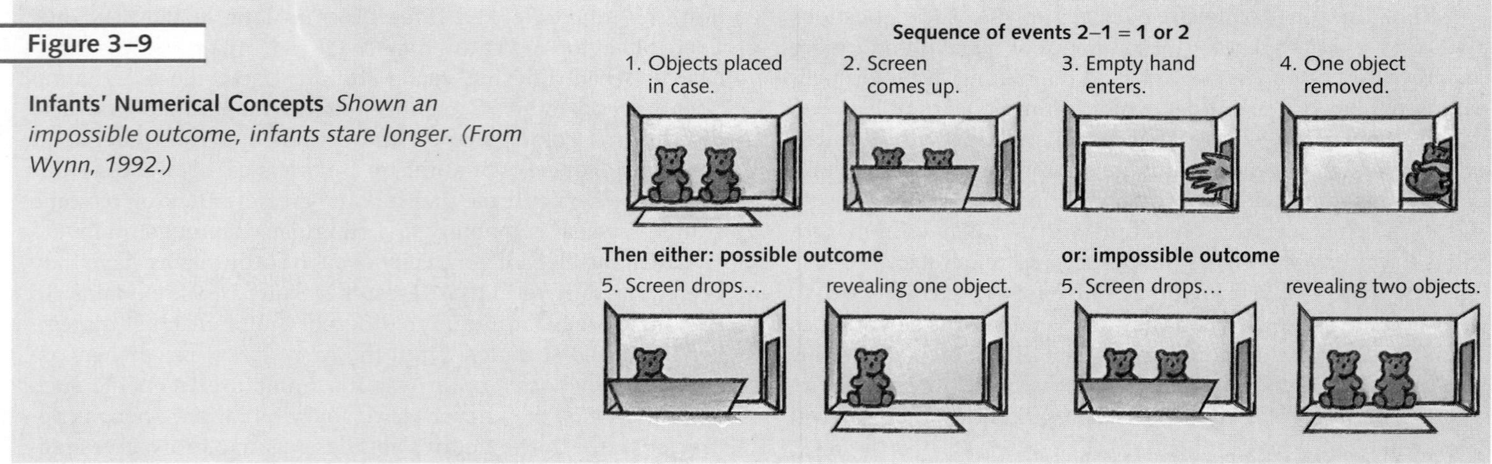
Sequence of events 2–1 = 1 or 2
1. Objects placed in case.
2. Screen comes up.
3. Empty hand enters.
4. One object removed.
Then either: possible outcome
5. Screen drops...
revealing one object.
or: impossible outcome
5. Screen drops...
revealing two objects.

Figure 3–9

**Infants' Numerical Concepts** *Shown an impossible outcome, infants stare longer. (From Wynn, 1992.)*

Babies show not only an intuitive grasp of number but also of simple laws of physics. For example, they look longer when viewing an unexpected scene of a car seeming to pass through a solid object or a ball stopping in midair (Baillargeon, 1992; Spelke & others, 1992; Wellman & Gelman, 1992). Clearly, then, they are more capable of conceptual thinking than Piaget realized.

**Preoperational Stage** Seen through the eyes of Piaget, preschool children are still unable to reason and to take another's point of view. Although aware of themselves, of time, and of the permanence of objects, they are, he said, **egocentric**: They cannot perceive things from another's point of view. Three-year-old Rebecca hides under a table, assuming that if she can't see someone's eyes they can't see her. Children's conversations also reveal their egocentrism, as one young boy demonstrated (Phillips, 1969, p. 61):

*"Do you have a brother?"*

*"Yes."*

*"What's his name?"*

*"Jim."*

*"Does Jim have a brother?"*

*"No."*

Preschool TV-watchers who block your view of the television assume that you see what they see. Preschoolers who ask a question while you are on the phone assume that you hear what they hear. When relating to a young child, you may find it helpful to remember that such behaviors reflect a cognitive limitation: The egocentric preschooler is not intentionally "selfish" or "inconsiderate" but rather has difficulty taking another's viewpoint.

Preschoolers also find it easier to follow positive instructions ("Hold the puppy gently") than negative ones ("Don't squeeze the puppy"). Parents who abuse their children generally have no understanding of these limits. They see their children as junior adults who are in control of their behavior (Larrance & Twentyman, 1983). Thus, they perceive children who stand in the way, spill food, disobey negative instructions, or cry as willfully malicious.

Although Piaget's concept of egocentrism is important, preschoolers are *not* purely egocentric. Given very simple tasks, 4-year-olds will adjust their explanations to make them clearer to a blindfolded listener and will show a toy or picture with the front side facing the viewer (Gelman, 1979; Siegel & Hodkin, 1982).

Piaget believed that during this preschool period and up to about age 7, children are in what he called the **preoperational stage** to perform mental operations. For a 5-year-old, the quantity of milk that is "too much" in a tall, narrow glass may become an acceptable amount if poured into a short, wide glass. This is because the child focuses only on the height dimension and is incapable of performing the *operation* of mentally pouring it back. The child lacks the concept of **conservation**—the principle that quantity remains the same despite changes in shape.

**Piaget's Test of Conservation** *This preoperational child does not yet understand the principle of conservation of substance. Closed beakers with identical volumes seem suddenly to hold different amounts after one is merely inverted.*

Although Piaget did not view the stage transitions as abrupt, the rudiments of conservation can be found at an earlier age than he supposed. If questioned in a way that makes sense to them, 5- and 6-year-olds will exhibit some understanding of conservation (Donaldson, 1979). Likewise, more than Piaget realized, preoperational children are capable of thinking symbolically. Judy DeLoache (1987) discovered this when she showed a group of 2-year-olds a model of a room and hid a model toy in it (say, a miniature stuffed dog behind a miniature couch). The children could easily remember where to find the miniature toy. But they could not readily use that model to locate an actual stuffed dog behind a couch in a real room. Only 6 months older, 3-year-olds usually went right to the actual stuffed animal in the real room, showing that they could think of the model as a symbol for the room. Thus, the abilities to take another's perspective, to perform mental operations, and to think symbolically are not absent in the preoperational stage—and then present at some later time. Rather, these abilities begin early and develop gradually.

Preoperational children are also developing other important mental abilities. The Soviet psychologist Lev Vygotsky (1932) noted that by age 7 children stop thinking aloud and instead rely on inner speech. By internalizing their culture's language, children become more capable of verbal thinking and of using it to work out solutions to problems.

**DENNIS THE MENACE**

*"Cut it up into a LOT of slices, Mom. I'm really hungry!"*

DENNIS THE MENACE ® used by permission of Hank Ketcham and ©1992 by North America Syndicate.

**Concrete Operational Stage** By about 7 years of age, children enter the **concrete operational stage**. Given concrete materials, they begin to grasp that a given quantity remains the same no matter how its shape changes. By age 11, children can mentally pour the milk back and forth between different-shaped glasses. They realize that change in shape does not mean change in quantity. They also enjoy jokes that allow them to use their new concepts, such as conservation:

> Mr. Jones went into a restaurant and ordered a whole pizza for his dinner. When the waiter asked if he wanted it cut into 6 or 8 pieces, Mr. Jones said, "Oh, you'd better make it 6, I could never eat 8 pieces!" (McGhee, 1976).

During the concrete operational stage, said Piaget, children fully gain the mental ability to comprehend mathematical transformations and conservation. When my daughter Laura was 6, I was astonished at her inability to reverse arithmetic operations—until considering Piaget. Asked, "What is eight plus four?" she required 5 seconds to compute "twelve," and another 5 seconds to then compute twelve minus four. By age 8, she could reverse the process and answer the second question instantly.

If Piaget was correct—if children construct their understandings and think differently than adults—what are the implications for preschool and elementary school teachers? Piaget contended that teachers should build on what children already know, give them concrete demonstrations, and stimulate them to think for themselves. Future teachers, remember: Young children are incapable of adult logic. Understand how children think. Realize that what is simple and obvious to you—that, say, subtraction is the reverse of addition—may be incomprehensible to a 6-year-old. Accept children's cognitive immaturity as adaptive—as nature's strategy for keeping children close to protective adults and providing time for learning and socialization (Bjorklund & Green, 1992).

**Formal Operational Stage** By age 12, reasoning expands from the purely concrete (involving actual experience) to encompass abstract thinking (involving imagined realities and symbols). As they approach adolescence, said Piaget, many children become capable of solving hypothetical propositions and deducing consequences: *If* this, *then* that. Systematic reasoning, which Piaget called **formal operational** thinking, is now within their grasp.

But are younger children incapable of abstract logic? Consider this simple problem:

> If John is in school, then Mary is in school. John is in school. What can you say about Mary?

Many 7-year-olds have no trouble answering correctly (Suppes, 1982). This illustrates why, once again, critics say the rudiments of Piaget's cognitive stages begin earlier than he realized.

*For more information on formal operational reasoning, see Chapter 4, Adolescence and Adulthood.*

**Reflections on Piaget's Theory** Piaget's stage theory is controversial. In some ways it gets high marks. Studies around the globe, from aboriginal Australia to Algeria to North America, reveal that human cognition everywhere unfolds basically in the sequence he proposed (Segall & others, 1990). Today's researchers do, however, see development as more continuous than did Piaget. By detecting the beginnings of each type of thinking at earlier ages, they have revealed conceptual abilities that Piaget missed.

What remains of Piaget's ideas about the child's mind? Plenty. Piaget identified important cognitive milestones and stimulated interest in how the mind develops. That we today are adapting his ideas to accommodate new findings surely would not surprise him.

## Summing Up

Jean Piaget's observations of children convinced him—and almost everyone else—that the mind of the child is not that of a miniature adult. Piaget theorized that the mind develops by forming schemas that help us assimilate our experiences and that must occasionally be altered to accommodate new information. In this way, children progress from the sensorimotor simplicity of the infant to more complex stages of thinking. For example, by about 8 months, an infant becomes aware that things still exist even when out of sight.

Piaget believed that preschool children are egocentric and unable to perform simple logical operations. However, he thought that at about age 7 children become capable of performing concrete operations, such as those required to comprehend the principle of conservation. Recent research shows that young children are more capable, and development more continuous, than Piaget believed. The cognitive abilities that emerge at each stage have begun developing in a rudimentary form in the previous stage.

## Social Development

*A human is, as Aristotle said, "a social animal," destined to live in close relationship with important others. How, then, do the bonds of attachment form? What happens when they form securely or when they are missing or broken? And how do parents and culture influence a child's self-concept?*

Babies are social creatures from birth. Almost from the start, parent and baby communicate through eye contact, touch, smiles, and voice. Even when interacting over life-size, closed-circuit TV, 9-week-old babies and their mothers have a comfortable synchrony—until a tape of the mother is rewound and replayed. Now, with the same mother no longer responsive to them, the babies turn away and fidget. When real-time interaction resumes, they cheer up again (Murray & Trevarthen, 1986). Such interactions promote infants' survival and their emerging sense of self, so that they, too, eventually may bear and nurture a new generation.

In all cultures, infants develop an intense bond with those who care for them. Beginning with newborns' attraction to humans in general, infants soon come to prefer familiar faces and voices and then to coo and gurgle when given their mothers' or fathers' attention. By 8 months, object permanence emerges simultaneously with a fear of strangers, called **stranger anxiety**. Watch how infants of different ages react when handed over to a stranger and you will notice that, beginning at 8 or 9 months, they often will cry and reach for their familiar caregivers. Is it a mere coincidence that object permanence and stranger anxiety develop together? Probably not. After about 8 months of age, children have schemas for familiar faces; when they can't assimilate a new face into these remembered schemas, they become distressed (Kagan, 1984). This illustrates an important principle: The brain, the mind, and social-emotional behavior develop together.

At 12 months many infants cling tightly to a parent when frightened or expecting separation. Reunited, they shower the parent with smiles and hugs. No social behavior is more striking than this intense and mutual infant-parent love, called **attachment**—a powerful survival impulse that keeps infants close to their caregivers. Among the early social responses—love, fear, aggression—the first and greatest is this bond of love.

### Origins of Attachment

A number of elements work to create the parent-infant bond.

**Figure 3–10**

**Harlow's Mothers** *Harry Harlow reared monkeys with two artificial mothers—one a bare wire cylinder with a wooden head and an attached feeding bottle, the other a cylinder covered with foam rubber and wrapped with terry cloth but without a feeding bottle. Harlow surprised many psychologists when he reported that the monkeys much preferred contact with the comfortable cloth mother even while feeding from the nourishing mother.*

**Body Contact** For many years, developmental psychologists reasoned that infants became attached to those who satisfied their need for nourishment. It made perfect sense. But an accidental finding revealed that this explanation of attachment is incomplete. During the 1950s, University of Wisconsin psychologist Harry Harlow bred monkeys for his learning studies. To equalize the infant monkeys' experiences and to prevent the spread of disease, he separated the monkeys from their mothers shortly after birth and raised them in sanitary, individual cages, which included a cheesecloth baby blanket (Harlow & others, 1971). Surprisingly, the infants became intensely attached to their blankets: When the blankets were taken to be laundered, the monkeys became distressed.

Harlow soon recognized that this attachment to the blanket contradicted the idea that attachment derives from the association with nourishment. But could he show this more convincingly? To pit the drawing power of a food source against the contact comfort of the blanket, Harlow created two artificial mothers. One was a bare wire cylinder with a wooden head, the other a cylinder wrapped with foam rubber and terry cloth. He could associate either with nourishment by attaching a bottle.

When reared with both a nourishing wire mother and a non-nourishing cloth mother, the monkeys overwhelmingly preferred the cloth mother (Figure 3–10). Like human infants clinging to their mothers, the monkeys would cling to their cloth mothers when anxious. They also used her as a secure base from which to venture into the environment, as if attached to the mother by an invisible elastic band that stretches so far and then pulls the infant back. Further studies with Margaret Harlow and others revealed that other qualities—rocking, warmth, and feeding—could make the cloth mother even more appealing.

In human infants, too, attachment usually grows from body contact with parents who are soft and warm and who rock, feed, and pat. All this should reassure the fathers of breast-fed infants: Attachment does not depend on feeding alone.

Moreover, for humans, too, attachment consists of one person providing another with a *secure base* from which to explore the world and a *safe haven* in times of stress. As we mature, our attachments change. Our secure base and safe haven shift from parents to peers and partners. But at all ages we are social creatures. We gain strength when someone says to us, by words and actions, "I am here. I will be here. I am interested in what you do and what you think and feel. I will actively support you" (Crowell & Waters, 1994). We are "happiest and able to deploy [our] talents to best advantage," said attachment researcher John Bowlby (1979), when we know that one or more trusted friends are standing behind us, come what may.

*Lee Kirkpatrick (1994) reports that for some people a perceived relationship with God functions as do other attachments—by providing a secure base for exploration and a safe haven when threatened.*

**Familiarity** Another key to attachment is familiarity (Rheingold, 1985). In many animals, attachments based on familiarity form during a sensitive, **critical period**—an optimal period shortly after birth when certain events must take place if proper development is to occur (Bornstein, 1989). The first moving object a gosling, duckling, or chick sees during the hours shortly after hatching is normally its mother. Thereafter the young fowl trails after her, and her alone.

Konrad Lorenz (1937) explored this rigid attachment process, called **imprinting**. He wondered what ducklings would do if *he* was the first moving creature they observed. What they did was follow him around: Everywhere that Konrad went, the ducks were sure to go. Further tests revealed that although baby birds imprint best to their own species, they also will imprint to a variety of moving objects—an animal of another species, a box on wheels, a bouncing ball (Colombo, 1982; Johnson, 1992). Once formed, this attachment is difficult to reverse.

Proponents of a critical "bonding" period argue that for humans, too, contact during the first hours after birth boosts parent-infant attachment (Kennell & Klaus, 1982). Believing this, many hospitals now have "bonding rooms" where staff members seek to ensure that bonding occurs before mother and infant leave. Is this very early contact essential? If so, are adoptive parents, and mothers who have had cesarean deliveries, poorly bonded with their children?

Developmental psychologists are unconvinced (Eyer, 1992). Human infants do prefer familiar faces and objects, but they *don't* have a precise critical period for becoming attached. Although psychologists welcome the trend toward humanizing childbirth, parents who miss their child's birth needn't feel deficient. Attachment in humans develops more gradually, allowing plenty of time for parents and their infants to come to know and love each other.

Although children—unlike ducklings—do not imprint, they do become attached to what they've known. "Mere exposure" to people and things fosters fondness (see page 644). Thus, children like to reread the same books, rewatch the same movies, reenact the same family traditions. They prefer to eat familiar foods, live in the same familiar neighborhood, attend school with the same old friends. Familiarity breeds content.

**THE FAR SIDE**

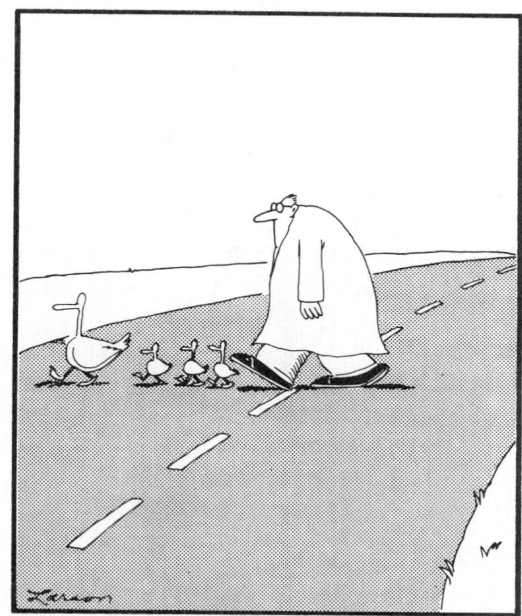

*When imprinting studies go awry . . .*

"The Far Side" cartoon is reprinted by permission of Chronicle Features, San Francisco.

**Temperament** In studies the world over, some babies seem more disposed to forming a secure attachment. Placed in a strange situation (usually a laboratory playroom), some infants show *secure attachment*. In their mother's presence they play comfortably, happily exploring their new environment. When she leaves, they are distressed; when she returns, they seek contact with her. Other infants show *insecure attachment*. They are less likely to explore their surroundings and may even cling to their mother. When she leaves, they cry loudly; when she returns, they may be indifferent or even hostile toward her (Ainsworth, 1973, 1989; van IJzendoorn & Kroonenberg, 1988). What accounts for these differences?

Might the infants' differences be inborn? An infant's **temperament** includes the inborn rudiments of personality, especially the child's emotional excitability—whether reactive, intense, and fidgety or easygoing, quiet, and placid. From the first weeks of life, "easy" babies are cheerful, relaxed, and predictable in feeding and sleeping. "Difficult" babies are more irritable, intense, and unpredictable (Chess & Thomas, 1987).

Temperament endures. The most emotionally reactive newborns tend also to be the most reactive 9-month-olds (Wilson & Matheny, 1986; Worobey & Blajda, 1989). And 4-month-olds who react to changing scenes with arched back, pumping legs, and crying are usually fearful and inhibited in their second year. Those who react with relaxed smiles are usually fearless and sociable in their second year (Kagan, 1990). Exceptionally inhibited and fearful 2-year-olds often are still relatively shy as 8-year-olds

(Kagan & others, 1992). And the most emotionally intense preschoolers tend to be relatively intense as young adults (Larsen & Diener, 1987). With age, many shy, inhibited infants relax, but few fearless, spontaneous infants become shy.

Infant monkeys also vary in temperament. Some are timid and fearful, others more relaxed. When researcher Stephen Suomi (1987) placed genetically predisposed "uptight" or "easygoing" infant monkeys with foster mothers who were themselves uptight or easygoing, heredity overrode rearing. Compared with the naturally easygoing monkeys, the uptight monkeys reacted more anxiously to the stress of separation from the mother, even when they were being raised by easygoing, nurturant foster mothers.

Physiological tests reveal that anxious, high-strung human infants have high and variable heart rates and a reactive nervous system (Kagan & others, 1992). They become more physiologically aroused when facing new or strange situations. Heredity seems to predispose the human differences, too. Twins who share identical genes are more likely to have similar temperaments than are nonidentical twins (Emde & others, 1992; Gabbay, 1992; Robinson & others, 1992).

**Figure 3–11**

**Social Deprivation and Fear** *Monkeys raised by artificial mothers were terror stricken when placed in strange situations without their surrogate mothers.*

**Responsive Parenting** But there is more to infant attachment differences than inherited temperament. Another possible influence on attachment is the mother's behavior. Mary Ainsworth (1979) observed mother-infant pairs at home during their first 6 months and then later observed the 1-year-old infants in a strange situation without their mothers. Sensitive, responsive mothers—mothers who continually noticed what their babies were doing and who responded appropriately—had infants who usually became securely attached. Insensitive, unresponsive mothers—mothers who attended to their babies when they felt like doing so but ignored them at other times—had infants who often became insecurely attached. The Harlows' monkey studies, in which the artificial mothers were the ultimate in unresponsiveness, produced even more striking effects. When put in strange situations without their artificial mothers, the deprived infants were more than distressed—they were terrified (Figure 3–11).

To see whether infants' attachments are a product of parenting and not just of biologically disposed temperaments, Dutch researcher Dymphna van den Boom (1990) varied parenting while controlling temperament. (Pause and think: If you were the researcher, how might you have done this?) Van den Boom's solution was to randomly assign one hundred 6- to 9-month-old temperamentally difficult infants to either an experimental condition, in which mothers received personal training in sensitive responding, or to an untreated control condition. At age one, 68 percent of the experimental condition infants were rated securely attached, as were only 28 percent of the control condition infants.

The attachments of early childhood eventually relax. Whether children are raised entirely at home or also in a day care center, whether they live in North America, Guatemala, or the Kalahari Desert, anxiety over separation from parents peaks at around 13 months and then gradually declines (Kagan, 1976) (Figure 3–12). With time, children become familiar with a wider range of situations and communicate with strangers more freely.

Does this mean that, as we develop, our need for and love of others fades away? Hardly. In other ways our capacity for love grows, and our pleasure in touching and holding those we love never ceases. The power of early attachment nonetheless gradually relaxes, allowing children to move out into the world. One might even say that much of the life cycle story boils down to a poignant rhythm of attachment and separation—from the attachment of fetal life to the separation of birth, from infant attachment to adolescent separation, from the attachment of marriage and parenthood to the separation of death.

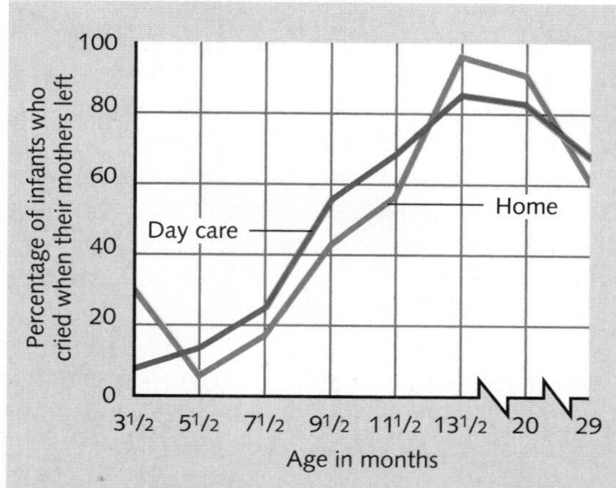


**Figure 3–12**

**Infants' Anxiety Over Separation From Parents** *In an experiment, groups of infants who had and had not experienced day care were left alone by their mothers in an unfamiliar room. In both groups, the percentage who cried when the mother left peaked at about 13 months. (From Kagan, 1976.)*

### Effects of Attachment

Does a trusting, secure attachment have lasting benefits? And does the quality of an infant's attachment predict the child's social competence in the years that follow?

**Secure Attachment Predicts Social Competence** At the University of Minnesota, Alan Sroufe and his colleagues (1983) identified infants who were securely attached at 12 to 18 months of age—those who used their mother as a base for comfortably exploring the world and as a haven when distressed. When Sroufe restudied these infants as 2- to 3-year-olds, he saw them functioning more confidently than other toddlers. Given challenging tasks, they were more enthusiastic and persistent. With other children they were more outgoing and responsive.

Developmental theorist Erik Erikson (1902–1994) said that securely attached children approach life with a sense of **basic trust**—a sense that the world is predictable and reliable. A child who will let parents leave is a child who trusts they will return. Erikson attributed basic trust not to one's continuing positive environment or inborn temperament, but to early parenting. He theorized that infants blessed with sensitive, loving caregivers form a lifelong attitude of trust rather than fear. Erikson would not have been surprised that as adults, our romantic love styles exhibit either secure, trusting attachment; insecure, anxious attachment; or the avoidance of attachment (Feeney & Noller, 1990; Shaver & Hazan, 1993; Simpson & others, 1992). Our early attachment styles, it seems, form a foundation for our future relationships.

*"Out of the conflict between trust and mistrust, the infant develops hope, which is the earliest form of what gradually becomes faith in adults."*
Erik Erikson (1983)

**Deprivation of Attachment** If secure attachment nurtures social competence, what happens when circumstances prevent children from forming attachments? In all of psychology, no research literature is more saddening. Children reared in institutions without the stimulation and attention of a regular caregiver, or locked away at home under conditions of abuse or extreme neglect, are often withdrawn, frightened, even speechless. Adopted during infancy or childhood into a loving home, they usually progress rapidly, especially in their cognitive development. Nevertheless, they frequently bear scars from their early mistreatment (Malinosky-Rummell & Hansen, 1993; Rutter, 1979).

So, too, did the Harlows' monkeys if reared in total isolation, without even an artificial mother. As adults they either cowered in fright or lashed out in aggression when placed with other monkeys their age. Upon reaching sexual maturity, most were incapable of mating. Artificially impregnated females often were neglectful, abusive, or even murderous toward their firstborn offspring. The unloved had become the unloving.

Most abusive human parents, too, report being neglected or battered as children (Kempe & Kempe, 1978). Many condemned murderers report the same. One study of 14 young men awaiting execution for juvenile crimes found that all but two had histories of brutal physical abuse (Lewis & others, 1988).

So, do most victims of child abuse become abusive? Is today's victim predictably tomorrow's predator? No. Most abused children do *not* later become violent criminals or abusive parents. But 30 percent of those

## Close-Up

## Father Care

Perhaps you are wondering why mothers are the focus of so much developmental research. Why not fathers, too? The common assumption, long seen in child-custody decisions, has been that fathers are less interested and less competent in child care than mothers. Due to increased divorce and nonmarital births, half of today's American children and increasing numbers in other countries will spend time in a single-parent family. In seven out of eight cases, such children do not live with their father and usually see him only rarely (Bureau of the Census, 1993; Whitehead, 1993). In subtle ways, psychologists, too, have sometimes assumed that fathers matter little. Infants who lack mother care are said to suffer "maternal deprivation"; those lacking father care are said merely to experience "father absence."

Across the world mothers do assume more responsibility for infant care, and young children more quickly turn to their mothers for comfort and support (Hartup, 1989). Moreover, a breast-feeding mother and nursing infant have wonderfully coordinated biological systems that predispose their responsiveness to one another.

Thus, in 37 percent of 186 cultures studied, fathers are in close proximity to their infants only occasionally; in 20 percent, fathers are rarely or never with them (Hewlett, 1991). Nevertheless, in 43 percent of cultures, fathers are frequently with their infants. As many modern fathers have become more involved in infant care, researchers have become more interested in fathers.

One of the leading father-watchers, Ross Parke (1981), reports that fathers can be as interested in, sensitive to, and affectionate toward their infants as mothers typically are. Although most infants prefer their mothers when anxious, when left alone they are as distressed by their father's departure as by their mother's. Moreover, infants whose fathers have shared in their diapering, bathing, and feeding are more secure when left with a stranger. Preschoolers with involved fathers tend to become adults who are especially concerned with being kind, sensitive, and warmhearted (Koestner & others, 1990). On the down side, just as mothers' psychological problems correlate with problems among their children, so do fathers' problems (Phares & Compas, 1992).

Looking for differences, research psychologists have also uncovered several distinctive ways in which fathers and mothers interact with their infants. Fathers smile less at their babies. (Males smile less at everyone.) They spend more of their interaction in play rather than in caregiving (especially with sons). And they play with more physical excitement (Parke, 1981).

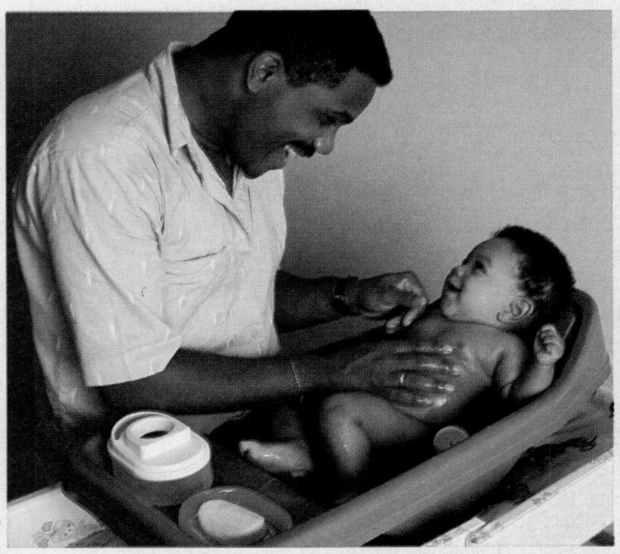

**Fathering a Child** *Although fathers and mothers interact with their infants in distinctive ways, they are more similar than different when it comes to nurturing. As this man demonstrates, men, too, can provide sensitive infant care.*

However, fathers who are the primary caregivers interact with their babies as mothers typically do. This suggests that father-mother differences are not biologically fixed, but have social roots as well. Animal research confirms this. When the Harlows caged monkey mothers and fathers with their infants, the fathers, too, were protective and affectionate toward their infants.

Within two-parent families, both parents have yet another gift to offer: their support of one another. Mothers and fathers who support one another and who sense this mutual support and agreement in child-rearing are more responsive to their infants and feel more competent as parents (Dickie, 1987).

Thanks partly to such research, "fathering" is shifting meaning. "Fathering a child" once meant impregnating, "mothering" meant nurturing. More and more these days, people appreciate that fathers are not just mobile sperm banks. Thus, fathering and mothering both mean parenting.

abused do abuse their children—a rate four times higher than the national rate of child abuse (Kaufman & Zigler, 1987; Widom, 1989a,b). Moreover, young children terrorized through sexual abuse or wartime atrocities (being beaten, witnessing torture, and living in constant fear) may suffer other scars—often nightmares, depression, and a troubled adolescence (Kendall-Tackett & others, 1993).

**Disruption of Attachment** What happens to an infant when attachment is disrupted? Separated from their families, both monkey and human infants become upset and, before long, withdrawn and even despairing (Bowlby, 1973; Mineka & Suomi, 1978). Fearing that such extreme stress might cause lasting damage (and when in doubt, acting to protect parents' rights), courts are usually reluctant to remove children from their homes.

However, if placed in a more positive and stable environment, most infants recover from the distress of separation. In studies of adopted children, Leon Yarrow and his co-workers (1973) found that when children between 6 and 16 months of age were removed from their foster mothers, they initially had difficulties eating, sleeping, and relating to their new mothers. But when these children were studied at age 10, little visible effect remained. Thus, they fared no worse than children placed before the age of 6 months (with little accompanying distress). Most year-old infants form new attachments without permanent emotional scars. Foster care that moves a child through a series of foster families and thereby prevents attachment can be very disruptive, however, as can repeated removals from a mother and reunions with her.

For adults, too, severed attachment bonds, whether through death or separation, produce a predictable sequence of agitated preoccupation with the lost partner, followed by deep sadness and, eventually, the beginnings of emotional detachment and a return to normal living (Hazan & Shaver, 1994). Even newly separated couples who have long ago ceased feeling affection are often surprised at their desire to be near the former partner. Deep and longstanding attachments seldom break quickly; detaching is a process, not an event.

**Does Day Care Affect Attachment?** During the fifties and sixties, when Mom-at-home was the social norm, researchers asked, "Is day care bad for children? Does it disrupt children's attachments to their parents?" For the high-quality day care programs usually studied, the answers were no (Belsky, 1990). In *Mother Care/Other Care*, developmental psychologist Sandra Scarr (1986) explained that children are "biologically sturdy individuals . . . who can thrive in a wide variety of life situations." Scarr speaks for many developmental psychologists, whose research has uncovered no major impact of maternal employment on children's development (Hoffman, 1989; Mott, 1991).

That issue settled, and with slightly over half of mothers of preschoolers now employed, the research questions have shifted to the effects of different forms of day care on different types and ages of children. We now know enough to distinguish good day care from poor. Scarr and Richard Weinberg (1986) explain: "Good care means three or four infants and toddlers per caregiver and six to eight preschoolers. . . . Good care also means a cheerful, stimulating, and safe physical environment." The ideal, then, is a verbally stimulating environment in which any child frequently talks with an adult caregiver. In this regard, quality day care offers a child more intellectual boost and opportunity for social development than does, say, home care with a sitter (Clarke-Stewart, 1991; Zaslow, 1991).

*One-third of preschoolers with working parents are cared for in someone else's home, one-third are in nursery schools and day care centers, and one-third are cared for by someone in their own homes. In compiling these data, the National Center for Health Statistics (1990) lumps in-home father care with other forms of nonmaternal child care. Perhaps some day such care will instead be called parenting.*

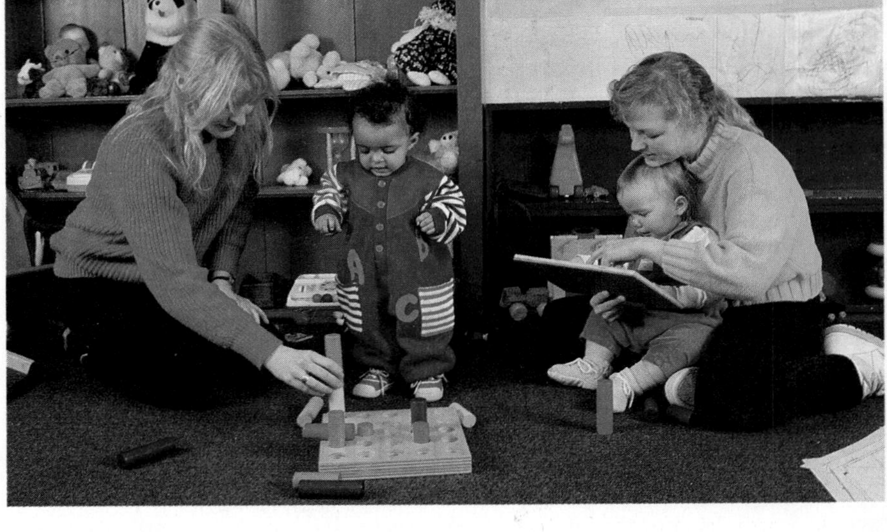

**An Example of High-Quality Day Care** *Forms of day care differ widely in philosophy and quality. Research has shown that in safe, stimulating environments like this day care center, toddlers thrive both socially and intellectually. A ratio of about one caregiver for every three or four children is especially important in producing this outcome.*

Parents of children 2 years and older may gain some relief from knowing that day care *can* mean high-quality child care. But the scientific jury is still debating infant day care. Developmental psychologists Jay Belsky (1988) and Edward Zigler (1986) express concern. In Belsky's words, "Children growing up in families using more than 20 hours per week of nonparental care in their first year of life are at heightened risk of seeming insecure as 1-year-olds and of being disobedient and aggressive at older ages."

Many developmentalists believe, however, that *quality* infant day care does not hinder secure attachment. They find support in two recent studies of enriched infant day care in the United States and Sweden (Andersson, 1989; Field, 1991). In both, schoolchildren who had experienced quality day care during their first 6 months were more outgoing, popular, and academically successful than those who hadn't.

A striking outcome of research on parent care and day care is how *little* quality time children receive from parents, employed or not. One national survey revealed that employed mothers average only 11 minutes and fathers only 8 minutes per weekday in child-centered activities such as reading, conversing, and playing with their children. Homemaker mothers devote not much more to such activities—only about 30 minutes per day (Timmer & others, 1985-1986).

*"There is near consensus among developmental psychologists and early childhood experts that child care per se does not constitute a risk factor in children's lives; rather, poor quality care and poor family environments can conspire to produce poor developmental outcomes."*

Sandra Scarr, Deborah Phillips, and Kathleen McCartney (1990)

There is little disagreement that the half million preschool children actually left *alone* for part of the time their parents are at work deserve better. So do those children who merely exist for 9 hours a day in minimally equipped, understaffed centers with untrained and poorly paid caregivers. What all children need is a consistent, warm relationship with people whom they can learn to trust. What they often get in a society that places a much lower value on workers who care for its future citizens than for its leaky pipes is an annual staff turnover rate approaching 50 percent (Wingert & Kantrowitz, 1990).

**Children and Divorce** Nearly half of marriages in Western countries (slightly more than half in the United States) end in divorce. That's double the proportion of 30 years ago. This fact makes people wonder and worry: Are children casualties of divorce? Does the stress of divorce and its aftermath erode children's well-being?

To answer these questions, researchers have not only compared children from divided and intact families but also followed children from before divorce to after it. Mavis Hetherington and her colleagues (1989, 1992) summarize the results: Divorce places "children at increased risk for developing social, psychological, behavioral and academic problems." Yet, they report, children's responses are diverse. Whether children cope well after divorce or develop behavior problems depends on such factors as the child's temperament, the intensity of parental conflict, and the continuity of other relationships, such as those with familiar friends and classmates. If the child is easygoing, if divorce enables the custodial parent to escape a traumatic or abusive situation, and if other relationships are preserved, the adjustment is most likely to go well.

One recent study had British parents and teachers rate the behavior of 12,000 children as 7-year-olds and again 4 years later (Cherlin & others, 1991). At the second rating, boys whose parents had divorced during the 4 years had about one-fourth more behavior problems (tantrums, fights, sleep problems, and so forth) than those whose families remained intact. But the apparent effect of divorce on boys was nearly halved when allowance was made for predivorce behavior differences between the two groups. (For girls, adjusting for preexisting behavior problems did not reduce the apparent divorce effect.) For boys, it seems, family troubles begin taking a toll in advance of divorce.

Typically, divorce provides children with a double dose of stress. The first occurs immediately following the parents' divorce, when many children feel angry, resentful, and depressed. Young children may blame themselves. Older children may exhibit heightened aggression and noncompliance. Within 2 or 3 years, life typically settles back to a more comfortable equilibrium. Then, often 3 to 5 years after the divorce, a second dose of stress may follow: the custodial parent's remarriage. Because 75 percent of divorced mothers and 80 percent of divorced fathers remarry, most children of divorce will gain a stepparent. Especially for girls, the new stepfather's entering the home may at first be an unwelcome event, disrupting the single mother-daughter relationship and necessitating another period of readjustment.

Data amassed from 92 studies suggest that this double stress does leave its mark on some children (Amato & Keith, 1991; Wallerstein, 1991). Compared with those who grew up in intact families, children of divorce grow up with a diminished feeling of well-being. As adults they are more likely to divorce and less likely to say they are "very happy."

But are their problems caused by divorce per se? Consider the results of one study of more than 17,000 children by the U.S. Census Bureau for the National Center for Health Statistics (1991). The researchers knew that intact and divided families can differ in many ways (parental education, race, income, and so forth), so they statistically adjusted their results to remove such influences. Still, children of divided parents were about twice as likely to experience a variety of social, psychological, or academic problems (Figure 3–13). Although they are more at risk for difficulty, most such children, however, do fine—especially if endowed with an easygoing temperament and the love and support of relatives and friends.

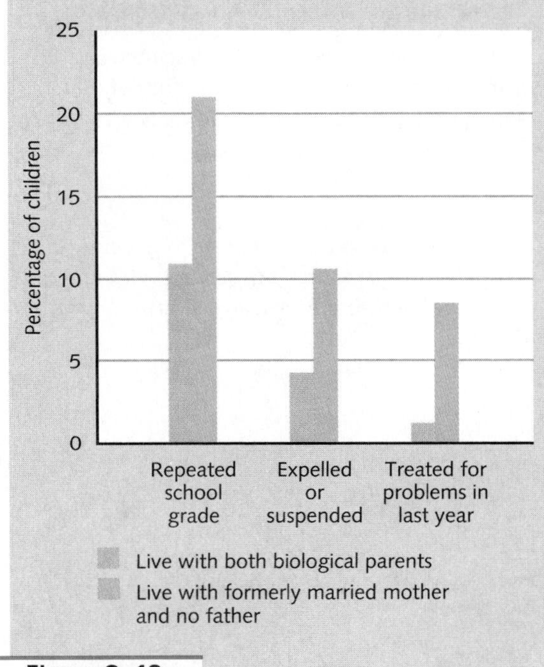


**Figure 3–13**

**Percentage of Children Experiencing School Problems in the Previous Year** *In the 1988 National Health Survey, conducted by the U.S. Census Bureau for the National Center for Health Statistics (1991), children living with both their biological parents had fewer problems. Note, however, that these problems affected a minority of children.*

## Self-Concept

Infancy's number one social achievement is attachment. Childhood's major social achievement is a positive sense of self. By the end of childhood, at about age 12, most children have developed a self-concept—a sense of their own identity and personal worth. Parents wonder when and how this sense of self develops. "Is my baby aware of herself—does she know she is a person distinct from others?"

Although we cannot ask the baby directly, we can again capitalize on

**Self-Awareness** *Mirror images fascinate infants from the age of about 6 months, but not until about 18 months does this child recognize that the image in the mirror is "me."*

*Only three other species—chimpanzees, orangutans, and dolphins—have similarly demonstrated self-recognition of their mirror-image (Marino & others, in press).*

what she can do—letting her *behavior* provide clues to the beginnings of her self-awareness. In 1877, biologist Charles Darwin offered one idea: Self-awareness begins when a child recognizes herself in a mirror. By this indicator, self-recognition emerges gradually over about a year, starting in roughly the sixth month, when the child reaches toward the mirror to touch her image as if it were another child (Damon & Hart, 1982, 1988).

How can we know when the child recognizes that the girl in the mirror is indeed herself and not just an agreeable playmate? In a simple variation of the mirror procedure, researchers sneakily dabbed rouge on children's noses before placing them in front of the mirror. Beginning by 15 to 18 months, children will touch their own noses when they see the red spot in the mirror (Butterworth, 1992; Gallup & Suarez, 1986). Apparently, 18-month-olds have a schema of how their faces should look. It's as if they wonder, "What is that spot doing on *my* face?"

Beginning with this simple self-recognition, the child's self-concept gradually becomes stronger. By school age, children begin to describe themselves in terms of their gender, their group memberships, and their psychological traits. They come to see themselves as good and skillful in some ways but not others. They form a concept of which traits, ideally, they would like to have. By age 8 or 10, their self-images have become quite stable.

Children's views of themselves affect their actions. Children who form a positive self-concept are more confident, independent, optimistic, assertive, and sociable (Maccoby, 1980). This raises an important question: How can parents encourage a positive self-concept? How does parenting style affect children?

## Child-Rearing Practices

Parenting styles vary. Some parents spank, some reason. Some parents are strict, some are lax. Some parents seem indifferent to their children, some liberally hug and kiss them. Do such differences affect children?

The most heavily researched aspect of parenting has been how, and to what extent, parents seek to control their children. Several investigators have identified four parenting styles:

1. *Authoritarian* parents impose rules and expect obedience: "Don't interrupt." "Don't leave your room a mess." "Don't stay out late or you'll be grounded." "Why? Because I said so."
2. *Authoritative* parents are both demanding and responsive. They exert control not only by setting rules and consistently enforcing them but also by explaining the reasons and, especially with older children, encouraging open discussion when making the rules.
3. *Permissive* parents submit to their children's desires, make few demands, and use little punishment.
4. *Rejecting-neglecting* parents are disengaged. They expect little and invest little.

Studies by Stanley Coopersmith (1967), Diana Baumrind (1983, 1991), and John Buri and others (1988) reveal that children with the highest self-esteem, self-reliance, and social competence usually have warm, concerned, *authoritative* parents. Although in most studies the subjects have been middle-class white families, studies with families of other races and in more than 200 cultures worldwide confirm the social and academic benefits of loving and authoritative parenting (Baumrind, 1991; Rohner, 1994).

What accounts for this finding? As later chapters will explain, people given *control* over their lives become motivated and self-confident. Those who experience little control more often see themselves as helpless and incompetent. Likewise, children who sense enough control to attribute their behaviors to their choices ("I obey because I am good") internalize their behaviors. Coerced children ("I obey or I get in bad trouble") tend not to internalize their actions.

Of the four parenting styles, authoritative parenting provides children with the greatest sense of control, and it does so for two reasons. First, authoritative parents openly discuss family rules, by explaining them to younger children and reasoning about them with older children. When rules seem more negotiated than imposed, older children feel more self-control (Baumrind, 1983; Lewis, 1981). Second, when parents enforce rules with consistent, predictable consequences, the child controls the outcome.

**Authoritative Parenting** *Studies suggest that consistency in enforcing rules, combined with calm discussion and explanation, helps children achieve self-control.*

Before jumping to conclusions about the results of different parenting styles, we must heed a caution. The evidence is correlational. It tells us that certain parenting styles (say, being firm but open) are associated with certain childhood outcomes (say, social competence). But remember: Correlation need not reveal cause and effect. There may be other possible explanations (Figure 3–14). Perhaps socially mature, agreeable children *elicit* greater trust and more reasonable treatment from their parents than do less competent and less cooperative children.

Or consider this: Authoritative parents are more often well educated and less often stressed by poverty or recent divorce—factors that can affect children's competence (Hetherington, 1979). Or maybe competent parents and their competent children share genes that predispose social competence. Knowing that parents' behavior relates to their children's behavior does not prove cause and effect.

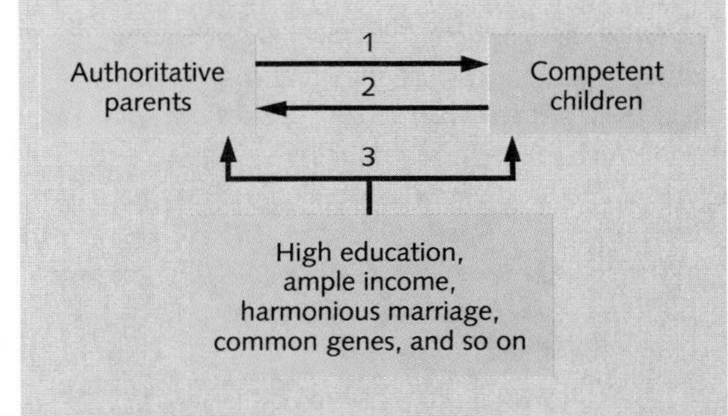


**Figure 3–14**

**The Correlation Between Authoritative Parenting and Social Competence in Children** *Three possible explanations are: (1) parenting may influence children's competence; (2) children's social competence may influence parenting; or (3) both may be influenced by an underlying third factor.*

When considering "expert" child-rearing advice we should also remember that all advice reflects the advice-giver's values. For those who prize unquestioning obedience from a child, an authoritarian style may have the desired effect. For those who value children's sociability and self-reliance, authoritative firm-but-open parenting is advisable. Different experts have different values, which helps explain their disagreements.

Parents struggle with conflicting advice and with the stresses of child-rearing. Indeed, the tens of thousands of dollars it costs to raise a child buy many years not only of joy and love but of worry and irritation. Yet for most parents, a child is one's biological and social legacy—one's personal investment in the human future. To paraphrase psychiatrist Carl Jung, we reach backward into our parents and forward into our children, and through their children into a future we will never see, but about which we must therefore care.

## Culture and Child-Rearing

Social values differ not only from expert to expert but also from one time and place to another. Do you prefer children who are independent or who respect authority?

If you live in Western Europe or North America, the odds are you prefer the former. Most parents in Western societies want their children to think for themselves. "You are responsible for yourself," our families and schools tell us. "Follow your conscience. Be true to yourself. Define your gifts. Satisfy your personal needs." But cultural values change over time. A half century ago, Western parents placed greater priority on obedience, respect, and sensitivity to others (Alwin, 1990; Remley, 1988). "Be true to your traditions," they taught their children. "Be loyal to your heritage and country. Show respect toward your parents and superiors."

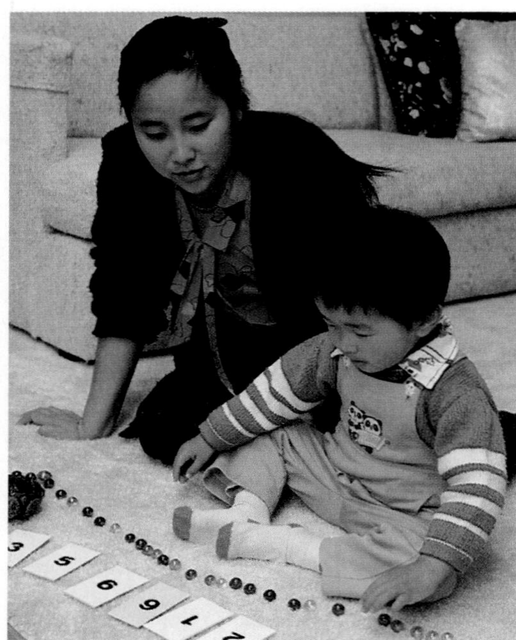

**Parental Involvement Promotes Development** *Parents in every culture facilitate their children's discovery of their world, but cultures differ in what they deem to be important. Asian cultures place more emphasis on school and hard work than does North American culture. This may help explain why Japanese and Taiwanese children get higher scores on mathematics achievement tests.*

Unlike most Westerners, who now raise their children to be independent, many Asians and Africans live in communal cultures, which focus on cultivating emotional closeness. Rather than being given their own bedrooms and sent off to day care or nursery school, infants typically sleep with their mothers and spend their days close to a family member (Morelli & others, 1992; Whiting & Edwards, 1988). Children of communal cultures grow up with a stronger sense of "family self"—a feeling that what shames the child shames the family. Compared with Westerners, people in Japanese and Chinese cultures, for example, exhibit greater shyness toward strangers and greater concern for social harmony and loyalty (Bond, 1988; Cheek & Melchior, 1990; Triandis, 1994). "My parents will be disappointed in me" is a concern of 7 percent of American and Italian teenagers, 14 percent of Australian teens, but nearly 25 percent of teens in Taiwan and Japan (Atkinson, 1988).

After people immigrate to a contrasting culture, such differences often diminish, but they seldom disappear. For example, Mary Stopes-Roe and Raymond Cochrane (1990) invited British parents to rate the importance of 13 character traits in children. Two-thirds of West Asian immigrant parents, but only one-fifth of native white parents, rated "obedience" among the three most important qualities. Among younger people, the cultural difference was somewhat less but still substantial. Such social diversity can challenge us—whatever our culture—to rethink the benefits and costs of our own assumed values.

### Developmental Similarities Across Groups

Mindful of how others differ from us, we often fail to notice the similarities predisposed by our shared biology. As Chapter 19 explains, cross-cultural research helps us appreciate both our cultural diversity *and* our human kinship. Compared to person-to-person differences within groups, differences between groups are small. Thus, regardless of our culture, we humans share the same life cycle. We all speak to our infants in similar ways and respond similarly to their coos and cries (Bornstein & others, 1992a,b). Across the world, parents who are warm and supportive have children who feel better about themselves and are less hostile toward others than do punitive and rejecting parents (Rohner, 1986; Scott & others, 1991).

Within a culture, ethnic groups may differ in their behavior, yet be influenced by the same underlying processes. Differences sometimes attributed to race may therefore actually result from other factors. David Rowe, Alexander Vazsonyi, and Daniel Flannery (1994) illustrate with an analogy: Black men tend to have higher blood pressure than white men. Suppose that (1) in both groups salt consumption correlates with blood pressure, and (2) blacks consume more salt than whites. What then might we expect? A blood pressure "race difference" that may actually be a *diet* difference. (Even if the relation of dietary salt to blood pressure is identical in blacks and whites, differing dietary inputs could produce differing results.)

And that, say Rowe and his colleagues, parallels psychological findings: Behavior differences, like blood pressure differences, can result from differing inputs to the same process. Or so they conclude after distilling data from six major investigations of ethnic differences in behavior. Although American Hispanic, Asian, black, and white ethnic groups differed in levels of school achievement and delinquency, the differences were "no more than skin deep." The factors that influenced adolescent behavior in different ethnic groups were "statistically indistinguishable." To the extent that variables such as family structure, peer influences, and parental education predicted behavior in one ethnic group, they did so for other groups as well.

The available data so far come from the United States. But "it bodes well," say the researchers, "that developmental processes are alike in many subgroups of *Homo sapiens*." In surface ways we may differ, but as members together of one species we seem subject to the same psychological forces. As members of different ethnic and cultural groups, our languages vary, yet reflect universal principles of grammar (Chapter 10). Our tastes vary, yet reflect common principles of hunger (Chapter 12). Our social behaviors vary, yet reflect pervasive principles of human influence (Chapters 18 and 19).

*When someone "has discovered why men on Bond Street wear black hats he will at the same moment have discovered why men in Timbuctoo wear red feathers."*

G. K. Chesterton, 1874–1936

## Summing Up

Although the experiences of infancy are not consciously remembered for long and their effects may be reversed by later experiences, they can nevertheless have a lasting influence on social development.

Attachment style in infancy predicts later social development. Infants become attached to their mothers and fathers not simply because mothers and fathers gratify biological needs but, more important, because they are comfortable, familiar, and responsive. If denied such care, both monkey and human infants may become pathetically withdrawn, anxious, and eventually abusive. Once an attachment forms, infants who are separated from their caregivers will, for a time, be distressed. Human infants who display secure attachment to their mothers generally become socially competent preschoolers. Infants' differing attachment styles reflect both their individual temperaments and the responsiveness of their parents and child care providers.

As with cognitive abilities, a self-concept develops gradually. By 18 months, infants will recognize themselves in a mirror. By age 8 or 10, children's self-images are quite stable and are linked with their independence, optimism, and sociability. Children who develop a positive self-image and a happy, self-reliant manner tend to have been reared by parents who are neither permissive nor authoritarian, but authoritative without depriving their children of a sense of control over their own lives. Decisions about child-rearing involve value judgments about what traits to encourage in children. Cultural differences, such as between the communalism of Asian families and the individualism of Euro-American families, illustrate the impact of parental values. Cultural and ethnic differences in behavior may, however, arise from the same underlying forces.

## Reflections on the Nature-Nurture Issue

*To what extent is our development influenced by our genetically disposed nature? By our experienced nurture? And what does it mean to say that nature and nurture interact? Studies of twins and adoptees provide some answers.*

Everyone agrees: We are all influenced by genes *and* experience. The question is, how important is each and how do their influences interact? For physical attributes such as hair color, the genetic factor predominates. For psychological attributes, the answer is less obvious. In Chapter 11, we will examine the thorny debate over genetic and environmental determinants of intelligence. Here we will consider some provocative findings on how nature and nurture influence the developing personality.

## Twin Studies

To discern the effect of environment, apart from hereditary differences between children, it would be nice if we could hold heredity constant while varying the environment. Happily for our purposes, nature has given us ready-made subjects for this experiment: twins. **Identical twins**, who develop from a single fertilized egg that splits in two, are genetically identical (Figure 3–15). **Fraternal twins**, who develop from separate eggs, are genetically no more similar than ordinary brothers and sisters.

*Curiously, twinning rates vary by race. The rate among Caucasians is roughly twice that of Asians and half that of Africans (Diamond, 1986).*

**Figure 3–15**

**Same Egg, Same Genes; Different Eggs, Different Genes** *Identical twins develop from a single fertilized egg, fraternal twins from two.*

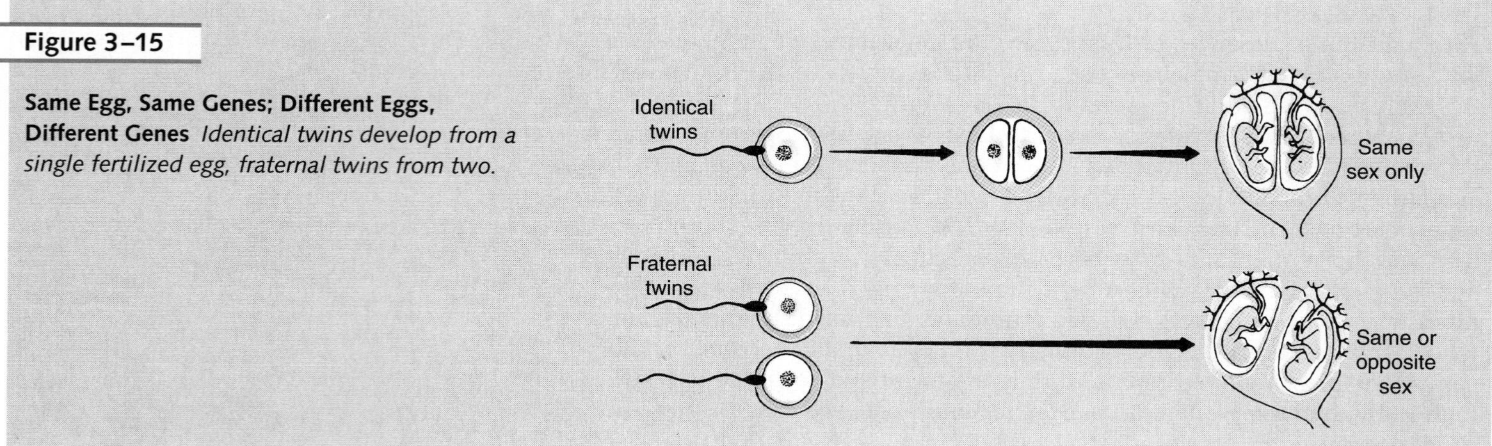


Do identical twins, being genetic replicas of one another, develop more personality similarities than fraternal twins? To find out, Birgitta Floderus-Myrhed and her colleagues (1980) gave tests of extraversion (outgoingness) and neuroticism (emotional instability) to nearly 13,000 pairs of Swedish identical and fraternal twins, as did Richard Rose and his colleagues (1988) to 7000 Finnish twin pairs, and A. C. Heath and colleagues (1989) to 3810 Australian twin pairs. Their consistent findings: On both extraversion and neuroticism, identical twins were much more similar than fraternal twins, suggesting a substantial genetic influence on both traits.

If genes influence traits such as emotional instability, might they also influence the social effects of such traits? To find out, Matt McGue and David Lykken (1992) studied divorce rates among 1500 same-sex, middle-aged twin pairs. Their result: If you have a fraternal twin who has divorced, the odds of your divorcing go up 1.6 times (the same rate as for those whose parents have divorced). If you have an identical twin who has divorced, the odds of your divorcing go up 5.5 times. From such data McGue and Lykken estimated that divorce risk is about 50 percent attributable to genetic factors. Another study of 2315 twin pairs confirms that identical twins' recent troubles at home, work, and elsewhere are more alike than fraternal twins' troubles (Kendler & others, 1993). Although identical twins also experience greater similarity in their childhood environments, the effect seems mostly genetic; twins who report more similar childhood environments are not more likely to have experienced similar upsets.

Other dimensions of personality also reflect genetic influences. John Loehlin and Robert Nichols (1976) gave a battery of questionnaires to 850 U.S. twin pairs. Once again, identical twins were much more similar, and in a variety of ways—in abilities, personality, even interests. However, the identical twins, more than fraternal twins, also reported being treated alike.

So, did their experience rather than their genes account for their similarity? No, said Loehlin and Nichols. Identical twins whose parents treated them alike were *not* psychologically more alike than identical twins who were treated less similarly.

## Separated Twins

Imagine a science fiction experiment in which someone, driven by curiosity, decides to separate identical twins at birth and rear them in differing environments. Would such twins differ from each other more than twins reared together? If so, our mad scientist reasons, one could only credit their differing environments. In reality, circumstances occasionally set up just these conditions.

Thus, in 1979 when University of Minnesota psychologist Thomas Bouchard read a newspaper account of the reuniting of 39-year-old twins who had been separated from infancy, he seized the opportunity and flew them to Minneapolis for extensive tests. Bouchard was looking for differences. What "the Jim twins," Jim Lewis and Jim Springer, presented were amazing similarities (Holden, 1980a,b). Both had married and divorced women named Linda and had later married women named Betty. One had a son James Alan, the other a son James Allan. Both had dogs named Toy, chain-smoked Salems, served as sheriff's deputies, drove Chevrolets, chewed their fingernails to the nub, enjoyed stock car racing, had basement workshops, and had built circular white benches around trees in their yards. They also had similar medical histories: Both gained 10 pounds at about the same time and then lost it. Both suffered what they mistakenly believed were heart attacks, and both began having late-afternoon headaches at age 18.

**How Heritable Are Personality Traits?** *Identical twins Gerald Levey and Mark Newman were separated at birth and raised in different homes. When reunited at age 31, they discovered they had chosen the same vocation. Research has shown remarkable similarities in the life choices of separated twins, lending support to the idea that at least some aspects of personality are genetically influenced.*

Identical twins Oskar Stohr and Jack Yufe presented equally striking similarities. One was raised by his grandmother in Germany as a Catholic and a Nazi, while the other was raised by his father in the Caribbean as a Jew. Nevertheless, they share traits and habits galore. They like spicy foods and sweet liqueurs, have a habit of falling asleep in front of the television, flush the toilet before using it, store rubber bands on their wrists, and dip buttered toast in their coffee. Stohr is domineering toward women and yells at his wife, as did Yufe before he and his wife separated.

Aided by publicity in magazine and newspaper stories, Bouchard and his colleagues (1990; Lykken & others, 1993) have now located and studied 71 pairs of identical twins reared apart. They continue to be impressed by the similarities not only of tastes and physical attributes but also of personality, abilities, attitudes, interests, and even fears. In Sweden, which has a national registry of 25,000 pairs of adult twins, Nancy Pedersen and her coworkers (1988) identified 99 separated identical twin pairs and more than 200 separated fraternal twin pairs. Compared with equivalent samples of identical twins reared together, the separated identical twins had more dissimilar personalities. Still, separated twins were more alike when genetically identical rather than fraternal. And separation shortly after birth (rather than, say, at age 8) didn't amplify their personality differences.

The more bizarre similarities—such as flushing the toilet before using it—exist not because we have genes for specific behaviors, cautions Bouchard. Rather, presented with a similar range of options, similarly disposed people often make similar choices. Even on traits for which heredity strongly influences personality (such as "social potency"—having an assertive, take-charge nature), it does so not through a single gene but through a complex combination of genes. Influencing a complex trait requires a very large number of genes, each having very small effects (Plomin, 1990a).

*"In some domains it looks as though our identical twins reared apart are . . . just as similar as identical twins reared together. Now that's an amazing finding and I can assure you none of us would have expected that degree of similarity."*

Thomas Bouchard (1981)

*Coincidences are not unique to twins. Patricia Kern of Colorado was born March 13, 1941, and named Patricia Ann Campbell. Patricia DiBiasi of Oregon also was born March 13, 1941, and named Patricia Ann Campbell. Both had fathers named Robert, worked as bookkeepers, and have children ages 21 and 19. Both studied cosmetology, enjoy oil painting as a hobby, and married military men, within 11 days of each other. They are not genetically related. (From an AP report, May 2, 1983.)*

The cute stories do not impress Bouchard's critics. They contend that if any two strangers of the same sex and age were to spend hours comparing their behaviors and life histories, they would probably discover many coincidental similarities. Even the more impressive data from the personality assessments are clouded by the reunion of many of the separated twins for some years before being tested. Moreover, adoption agencies tend to place separated twins in similar homes. When environments are similar, the impact of environment looks smaller relative to heredity. As twins age, differing experiences often make their personality differences more noticeable (McCartney & others, 1990). Nevertheless, the twin studies illustrate why scientific opinion has shifted toward a greater appreciation of genetic influences.

## Adoption Studies

Adoption studies offer additional clues. For any given trait we can ask whether adopted children are more like their adoptive parents, who contribute a home environment, or their biological parents, who contributed their genes. While sharing the same home environment, do adopted siblings come to share traits? The stunning finding from studies of hundreds of adoptive families in Minnesota, Texas, and Colorado is that people who grow up together do not much resemble one another in personality, whether biologically related or not (Rowe, 1990). Moreover, the personalities of parents have been astonishingly unrelated to the personalities of their children. Sandra Scarr and her colleagues (1981) summarized the findings vividly:

> It would have to be concluded that upper-middle-class brothers who attended the same school and whose parents took them to the same plays, sporting events, music lessons, and therapists and used similar child-rearing practices on them would be found to be only slightly more similar to each other in personality measures than to working-class or farm boys, whose lives would be totally different.

*"All parents are environmentalists—until the birth of their second child."*

Anonymous

What we have here is developmental psychology's biggest puzzle: Why are children in the same family so different? Why do the shared genes and the shared family environment (the family's social class, the parents' personalities and marital status, day care versus home care, the neighborhood) have so little discernible effect on children's personalities? Is it because siblings—despite sharing half their genes—have very different combinations of genes (Lykken & others, 1992)? Is it because each sibling experiences a different environment—differing peer influences, birth orders, life events (Dunn & Plomin, 1990; Hetherington & others, 1993)?

Twin and adoption studies reveal that genetic influences account for nearly 50 percent of person-to-person differences in traits such as outgoingness and emotional instability. What accounts for the other 50 percent? Because siblings are *not* appreciably influenced by their shared home environment (shocking as that may sound), researchers assume they *are* influenced by their *non*shared experiences—their own unique experiences. Apparently what affects each child is not so much the parents per se as how the child interacts with and experiences them, plus other peer and cultural influences. The same parental influence may affect an easygoing child one way, a reactive child another. Family environment can matter, even if siblings differ, notes Lois Hoffman (1991). The same fire that tempers steel melts butter.

Adoption studies also show that, although the personalities of adopted children do not much resemble those of their adoptive parents, adoption has many effects (Brodzinsky & Schechter, 1990). First, the home environment influences adopted children's values, beliefs, and social attitudes. Second, in adoptive homes, child neglect and abuse are rare. (Adoptive parents are carefully screened; natural parents are not.) So it is not surprising that, despite somewhat greater risk of psychological disorder (Wierzbicki, 1993) most adopted children thrive. They score higher than their biological parents on intelligence tests, and they generally become happier and more stable people than they would have in a stressed or neglectful environment. Children need not resemble their adoptive parents to have benefitted from adoption.

**A Family by Choice** *Studies of adoptive families have provided new clues to hereditary and environmental influences on development. How similar would you expect adopted children to be to their adoptive parents? To their biological parents?*

## How Much Credit (or Blame) Do Parents Deserve?

Parents typically feel enormous pride in their children's successes, and guilt or shame over their failures. They beam when folks offer congratulations for the child who wins an award. They wonder where they went wrong with the child who repeatedly is called into the principal's office. Psychiatry and Freudian psychology have at times been the source of such ideas, by blaming problems from asthma to schizophrenia on "bad mothering." Society reinforces such parent-blaming: Believing that parents shape their children as a potter molds clay, people readily praise parents for their children's virtues and blame them for their children's vices. Even among chimpanzees, when one infant is hurt by another, the victim's mother will often attack the offender's mother (Goodall, 1968).

**CALVIN AND HOBBES**

WHAT ASSURANCE DO I HAVE THAT YOUR PARENTING ISN'T SCREWING ME UP?


CALVIN AND HOBBES ©1993 Watterson. Dist. by UNIVERSAL PRESS SYNDICATE. Reprinted with permission. All rights reserved.

This chapter provides confirmation of the power of parenting. The extremes provide the sharpest examples—the abused who become abusive, the neglected who become neglectful, the loved but firmly handled children who become self-confident and socially competent. Recall, too, the effects of environmental deprivation versus enrichment on the developing neural network, and the effects of parental conflict and divorce on children's social and academic outcomes. Consider the remarkable academic and vocational successes of children of the refugee Asian boat people—successes attributed to close-knit, supportive, even demanding families (Caplan & others, 1992). Parents also noticeably influence their children's attitudes, values, faith, and politics. Parenting matters.

## *Thinking Critically About* "Dysfunctional Families"

Popular culture of the 1990s endlessly tells us of the psychological harm that parents inflict on their fragile children. "The major source of human misery" is the "neglected, wounded child" within each of us, claims author-lecturer John Bradshaw (1990, p. 7). Having survived our "toxic" parents, today's "adult children" have swarmed to "recovery groups." It's about time, contend some leaders of today's recovery movement, given that most of us come from "dysfunctional families." (If you think your family isn't or wasn't dysfunctional, they might add, that probably indicates you're "in denial.")

What should we make of all this? If parental slips—being occasionally shouted at or ignored—constitute "abuse," then, yes, we can hold our parents to blame for our resulting vices ("addictions"). And if we occasionally feel anxious, inadequate, or alienated, that might indicate we experienced emotional abuse or neglect. Given today's problem, we could infer a childhood cause.

But do parents produce future adults having a wounded child within by being (take your pick from the toxic lists): overbearing—or uninvolved? Pushy—or ineffectual? Overprotective—or distant? Are children indeed easily wounded by well-meaning but occasionally exhausted parents who don't successfully navigate the psychological tightrope? If so, should we blame our parents for our failings, and ourselves for our children's failings? Or does talk of wounding fragile children (through variations within the normal range of parenting) trivialize the brutality of real abuse and the force of real addictions?

Consider: How might research shed light on these questions? To make the issue testable, we might ask whether parents' behaviors correlate with their children's traits. As we have seen, loving homes do produce outcomes noticeably different from those generated by abusive or neglectful homes. Likewise, differences are sometimes observed in the children of authoritarian and authoritative parents, and in the children of two-parent and father-absent homes. The social context matters.

But we must remember that correlations between parental behavior and child personality mirror not only parents' influence on children but children's influence on their parents (Bell, 1977). Children's easygoing or reactive dispositions influence their parents' childrearing tactics.

The extreme environmentalism of 1990s pop psychology, say its critics, is also built on ignorance of a shocking but consistent finding. If millions of toxic, dysfunctional parents have predictably damaged their children, shouldn't children who grow up in the same home be noticeably alike? Shouldn't the children of "toxic" parents be wounded and the children of healthy parents be healthy?

That presumption is refuted by the most astonishing recent finding of developmental psychology. In the words of behavior geneticists Robert Plomin and Denise Daniels (1987), "Two children in the same family [are on average] as different from one another as are pairs of children selected randomly from the population." To developmental psychologist Sandra Scarr (1993), this implies that "parents should be given less credit for kids who turn out great and blamed less for kids who don't." Although environments matter, "Extreme environmentalism is cruel," contends Michael Gazzaniga (1992, p. 202), "because it suggests to the parents that their child has been warped by something they did."

*"It's a mistake to look at a child and say, 'I'm going to make this child X or Y.' I say . . . let's see what that child does well at and enjoys. Then let's reinforce those kinds of things . . . what people in the past have called gifts."*

Thomas Bouchard (1990)

Nevertheless, given our readiness to praise or blame and to feel pride or shame, we would do well to remember a simple principle: Within the normal range of environments, children's genetically predisposed tendencies will assert themselves. Children are not so easily molded as clay. Moreover, as the next chapter illustrates, lives also are formed by environmental influences beyond parents' control—by peer influences, chance events, and all sorts of life experiences.

It may be scary to realize how risky is the business of having and raising children. In procreation a woman and a man shuffle their gene decks and deal a life-forming hand to their child-to-be, who is then subject to countless influences beyond their control. Keeping in mind that lives are formed by influences both under and beyond parents' control, we should, perhaps, be slower to credit parents for their children's achievements and slower still to blame them for their children's traits.

To say that genes and experience are *both* important is true but oversimplified. More precisely, their effects intertwine. Imagine two babies, one genetically predisposed to be attractive, sociable, and easygoing, the other less so. Assume further that the first baby attracts more affectionate and stimulating care than the second and so develops into a warmer and more outgoing person. As the two children grow older, the more naturally outgoing one seeks activities and friends that encourage further social confidence.

*"Heredity deals the cards; environment plays the hand."*

Charles L. Brewer (1990)

What has caused their resulting personality difference? We cannot say that their personalities are *x* percent due to genes and *y* percent to experience, for the gene-experience effect is combined. In fact, genes influence experience. As we grow older we *select* environments well suited to our natures. Moreover, as in our imaginary example, our genetically influenced traits *evoke* significant responses in others. This helps explain why identical twins reared in *different* families recall their parents' warmth as remarkably similar—almost as similar as if they had the same parents (Plomin & others, 1988, 1991, 1994). Fraternal twins recall their early family life more differently—even if reared in the same family! "Children experience us as different parents, depending on their own qualities," notes Scarr (1990). Our genes affect not only us but how our environment reacts to and influences us.

*The moral*: Our genes influence the experiences that shape us. The correct view, say behavior genetics researchers, is not nature *versus* nurture, but nature *via* nurture.

## Summing Up

Studies of the inheritance of temperament, and of twins and adopted children, provide scientific support for the idea that nature *and* nurture influence one's developing personality. Developmentalists generally agree that genes and environment, biological and social factors, direct our life courses and that their effects intertwine.

## Terms and Concepts to Remember

### Developmental Issues

**developmental psychology** A branch of psychology that studies physical, cognitive, and social change throughout the life span.

**genes** The biochemical units of heredity that make up the chromosomes; a segment of DNA capable of synthesizing a protein.

**maturation** Biological growth processes that enable orderly changes in behavior, relatively uninfluenced by experience.

### Prenatal Development and the Newborn

**chromosomes** Threadlike structures made of DNA molecules that contain the genes.

**DNA (deoxyribonucleic acid)** A complex molecule containing the genetic information that makes up the chromosomes.

***X* chromosome** The sex chromosome found in both men and women. Females have two *X* chromosomes; males have one. An *X* chromosome from each parent produces a female.

***Y* chromosome** The sex chromosome found only in males. When paired with an *X* sex chromosome from the mother, it produces a male child.

**testosterone** The most important of the male sex hormones. Both males and females have it, but the additional testosterone in males stimulates the growth of the male sex organs in the fetus and the development of the male sex characteristics during puberty.

**zygote** The fertilized egg; it enters a 2-week period of rapid cell division and develops into an embryo.

**embryo** The developing human organism from about 2 weeks after fertilization through the second month.

**fetus** The developing human organism from 9 weeks after conception to birth.

**teratogens** Agents, such as chemicals and viruses, that can reach the embryo or fetus during prenatal development and cause harm.

**fetal alcohol syndrome (FAS)** Physical and cognitive abnormalities in children caused by a pregnant woman's heavy drinking. In severe cases, symptoms include noticeable facial misproportions.

**rooting reflex** A baby's tendency, when touched on the cheek, to open the mouth and search for the nipple.

## Infancy and Childhood

**plasticity** The brain's capacity for modification, as evident in brain reorganization following damage (especially in children) and in experiments on the effects of experience on brain development.

**cognition** All the mental activities associated with thinking, knowing, and remembering.

**schema** A concept or framework that organizes and interprets information.

**assimilation** Interpreting one's new experience in terms of one's existing schemas.

**accommodation** Adapting one's current understandings (schemas) to incorporate new information.

**sensorimotor stage** In Piaget's theory, the stage (from birth to about 2 years of age) during which infants know the world mostly in terms of their sensory impressions and motor activities.

**object permanence** The awareness that things continue to exist even when not perceived.

**habituation** Decreasing responsiveness with repeated stimulation. For example, as infants gain familiarity with repeated exposure to a visual stimulus, their interest wanes and they look away sooner.

**egocentrism** In Piaget's theory, the inability of the preoperational child to take another's point of view.

**preoperational stage** In Piaget's theory, the stage (from about 2 to 6 or 7 years of age) during which a child learns to use language but does not yet comprehend the mental operations of concrete logic.

**conservation** The principle (which Piaget believed to be a part of concrete operational reasoning) that properties such as mass, volume, and number remain the same despite changes in the forms of objects.

**concrete operational stage** In Piaget's theory, the stage of cognitive development (from about 6 or 7 to 11 years of age) during which children gain the mental operations that enable them to think logically about concrete events.

**formal operational stage** In Piaget's theory, the stage of cognitive development (normally beginning about age 12) during which people begin to think logically about abstract concepts.

**stranger anxiety** The fear of strangers that infants commonly display, beginning by about 8 months of age.

**attachment** An emotional tie with another person; shown in young children by their seeking closeness to the caregiver and showing distress on separation.

**critical period** An optimal period shortly after birth when an organism's exposure to certain influences produces proper development.

**imprinting** The process by which certain animals form attachments during a critical period very early in life.

**temperament** A person's characteristic emotional reactivity and intensity.

**basic trust** According to Erik Erikson, a sense that the world is predictable and trustworthy; said to be formed during infancy by appropriate experiences with responsive caregivers.

## Reflections on the Nature-Nurture Issue

**identical twins** Twins who develop from a single zygote (fertilized egg) that splits in two, creating two genetic replicas.

**fraternal twins** Twins who develop from separate zygotes. They are genetically no closer than brothers and sisters, but they share the fetal environment.

## Critical Thinking Exercise

Now that you have read and reviewed Chapter 3, take your learning a step further by testing your critical thinking skills on this perspective taking exercise.

You have decided to open a baby-sitting service for children from 18 months to 12 years of age. Your advertising campaign is based on your intention to provide children with intellectually stimulating activities. To design activities that will be appropriate for children of different ages, you decide to follow Piaget's stage theory of cognitive development.

Your task in this exercise is to imagine the viewpoint of children at various stages of cognitive development. For the moment, set aside what you *think* about the intellectual abilities of children of various ages and try to *identify* with the unique ways in which they experience the world. Then describe two or three intellectually stimulating activities that would be appropriate for each group.

1. How does an 18-month-old child experience the world?
2. What activities would you plan for an 18-month-old child?
3. How does a 5-year-old child experience the world?
4. What activities would you plan for a 5-year-old child?
5. How does an 8-year-old child experience the world?
6. What activities would you plan for an 8-year-old child?
7. How does a 12-year-old child view the world?
8. What activities would you plan for a 12-year-old child?

Check your progress on becoming a critical thinker by comparing your answers to the sample answers found in Appendix B.

## For Further Reading

**Berger, K. (with the assistance of Ross A. Thompson)** (1991). *The developing person through childhood and adolescence* (3rd ed.). New York: Worth.

*A comprehensive and readable textbook summarizing what we know about infancy, childhood, and adolescence.*

**Dunn, J., & Plomin, R.** (1990). *Separate lives: Why siblings are so different*. New York: Basic Books.

*Examines sibling differences by interweaving research with the life stories of famous authors and their siblings.*

**Field, T.** (1990). *Infancy*. Cambridge, MA: Harvard University Press.

*An expert's introduction to how babies develop physically, cognitively, and socially—with special attention to infants at risk.*

**Maurer, D., & Maurer, C.** (1988). *The world of the newborn*. New York: Basic Books.

*An award-winning look at how the world looks, sounds, smells, and feels to a newborn.*

**Plomin, R., & McClearn, G. E.** (1993). *Nature, nurture, and psychology*. Washington, DC: American Psychological Association.

*Top investigators summarize the contributions of nature and nurture to intelligence, personality and temperament, and disorder.*

**Scarr, S.** (1986). *Mother care/Other care*. New York: Basic Books.

*An award-winning guide to child care by a leading developmental researcher.*

# CHAPTER 4



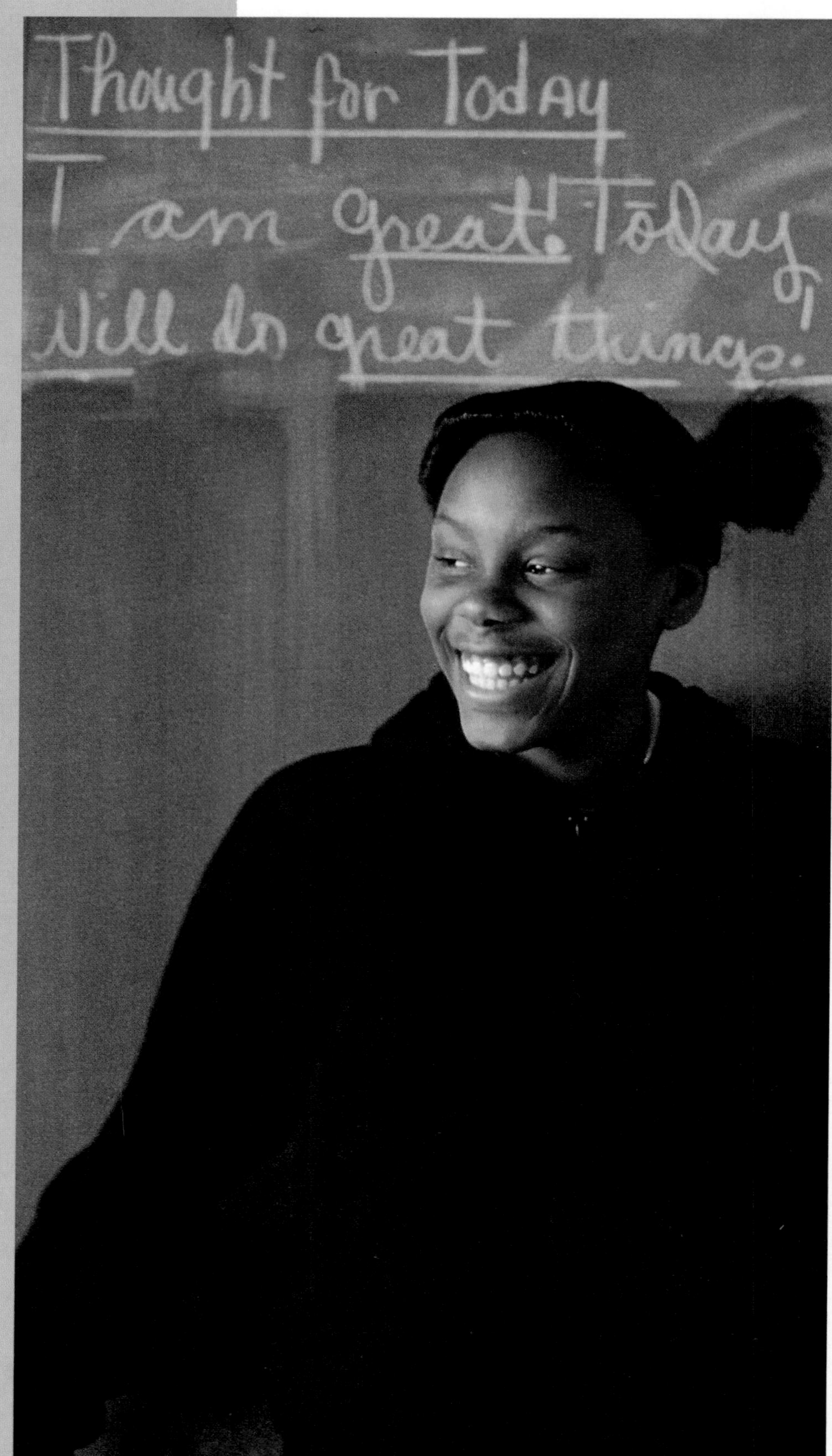

# Adolescence and Adulthood

For much of this century, psychologists echoed poet Alexander Pope's sentiment that "as the twig is bent the tree's inclined." Developmental experts focused on the "critical" early years, reasoning that by the end of childhood our traits have nearly set, like clay. Life experiences will smooth the rough edges, but the pliable period is over. With our traits formed, the legacy of infancy and childhood will reach decades into the future.

Now, among a new generation of developmental psychologists, the belief that no important changes in personality occur after childhood has given way to an awareness that development is *lifelong*. As today's life-span perspective emerged, psychologists began to look at how maturation and experience shape us in infancy and childhood—*and* in adolescence and beyond. At a 5-year high school reunion, friends may be surprised at the divergence of their paths. A decade after college, two former soul mates may have trouble keeping a conversation going. As long as we live, we develop.

## Adolescence

*What defines adolescence? How are adolescents influenced by their physical maturation and their cognitive development? What tasks and challenges do they face en route to mature adulthood?*

**Adolescence** is life between childhood and adulthood. It starts with the physical beginnings of sexual maturity and ends with the social achievement of independent adult status, a time period that in the Western world roughly corresponds to the teen years.

Adolescence is a time of transition. At earlier times in Western societies (and in some developing countries today), adolescence was but a brief interlude between the dependence of childhood and the responsibilities of adulthood (Baumeister & Tice, 1986). Adult status and responsibilities were bestowed shortly after sexual maturity, often marked by an elaborate initiation. The new adult worked, married, and had children.

Then, thanks to improved nutrition, sexual maturity began occurring earlier. And thanks to compulsory schooling, adult independence began occurring later. The resulting gap between biological maturity and social independence is adolescence.

What are the teen years like? To St. Augustine, these years were a time of fiery passions involving "the hot imagination of puberty. . . . Both love and lust boiled within me and swept my youthful immaturity over the precipice." In Leo Tolstoy's *Anna Karenina*, the teen years were, rather, "that blissful time when childhood is just coming to an end, and out of that vast circle, happy and gay, a path takes shape." In her diary, written as she and her family hid from the Nazis, teenager Anne Frank observed,

> My treatment varies so much. One day Anne is so sensible and is allowed to know everything; and the next day I hear that Anne is just a silly little goat who doesn't know anything at all and imagines that she's learned a wonderful lot from books. . . . Oh, so many things bubble up inside me as I lie in bed, having to put up with people I'm fed up with, who always misinterpret my intentions.

*How will you look back on your life 10 years from now? Are you doing the things and making the choices that someday you will recollect with satisfaction?*

To G. Stanley Hall (1904), one of the first psychologists to describe adolescence, the tension between biological maturity and social dependence created—no surprise to Augustine—a period of "storm and stress." Indeed, after age 30, many people look back on their teenage years as a time they would not like to relive, a time when the social approval of peers was imperative, one's sense of direction in life was in flux, and alienation from parents was deepest (Macfarlane, 1964).

Today's psychologists note that adolescence is, indeed, often marked by mood swings. Yet for many it is also as Tolstoy described it—a time of vitality without the cares of adulthood, a time of rewarding friendships, a time of heightened idealism and a growing sense of life's exciting possibilities (Coleman, 1980). These psychologists would not be surprised that 9 of 10 high school seniors agree with the statement, "On the whole, I'm satisfied with myself" (*Public Opinion*, 1987).

## Physical Development

Adolescence begins at **puberty**, when one first becomes capable of reproducing. Puberty follows a surge of hormones, which may intensify moods and which trigger a 2-year period of rapid physical development that usually begins in girls at about age 11 and in boys at about age 13. About the time of puberty, boys grow as much as 5 inches a year, compared with about 3 inches for girls—propelling the average male, for the first time, to greater height than the average female (Figure 4–1). During this growth spurt, the reproductive organs, or **primary sex characteristics**, develop dramatically. So do the **secondary sex characteristics**, the nonreproductive traits of females and males, such as enlarged breasts and hips in girls, facial hair and a deepened voice in boys, pubic and underarm hair in both sexes (Figure 4–2).

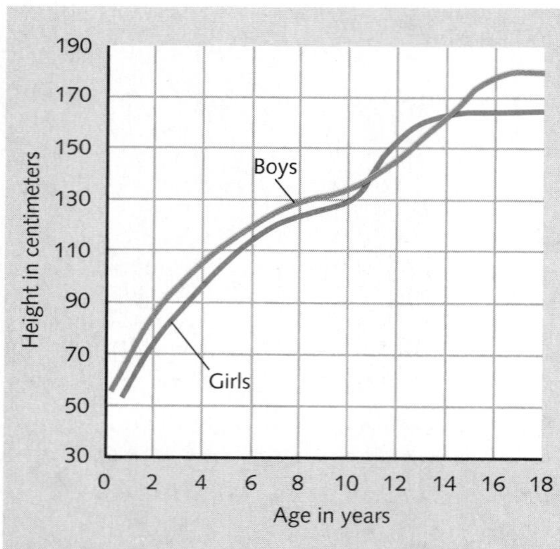


**Figure 4–1**

**Height Differences** *Throughout childhood, boys and girls are similar in height. At puberty, girls surge ahead briefly, but then boys overtake them at about age 14. (Data from Tanner, 1978.)*

The landmarks of puberty are the first ejaculation in boys, which usually occurs by about age 14, and the first menstrual period in girls, by about age 13. (These events need not signify fertility; it may be another year or more before ejaculations contain sufficient live sperm and the menstrual cycle includes ovulation [Tanner, 1978].)

The first menstrual period, called **menarche** (meh-NAR-key), is a memorable event, one that is recalled by nearly all adult women. Most experience and later recall a mixture of feelings—pride, excitement, embarrassment, and apprehension (Greif & Ulman, 1982; Woods & others, 1983). For the first few months many keep it a secret from friends, and very few discuss it with their fathers (Brooks-Gunn, 1989). Girls well prepared for menarche usually experience it as a positive life transition. And a transition it is. Regardless of their age, girls afterward increasingly see and present themselves as different from boys and function more independently of their parents (Golub, 1983). Most men similarly recall their first ejaculation, which usually occurs as a nocturnal emission (Fuller & Downs, 1990).

Figure 4–2

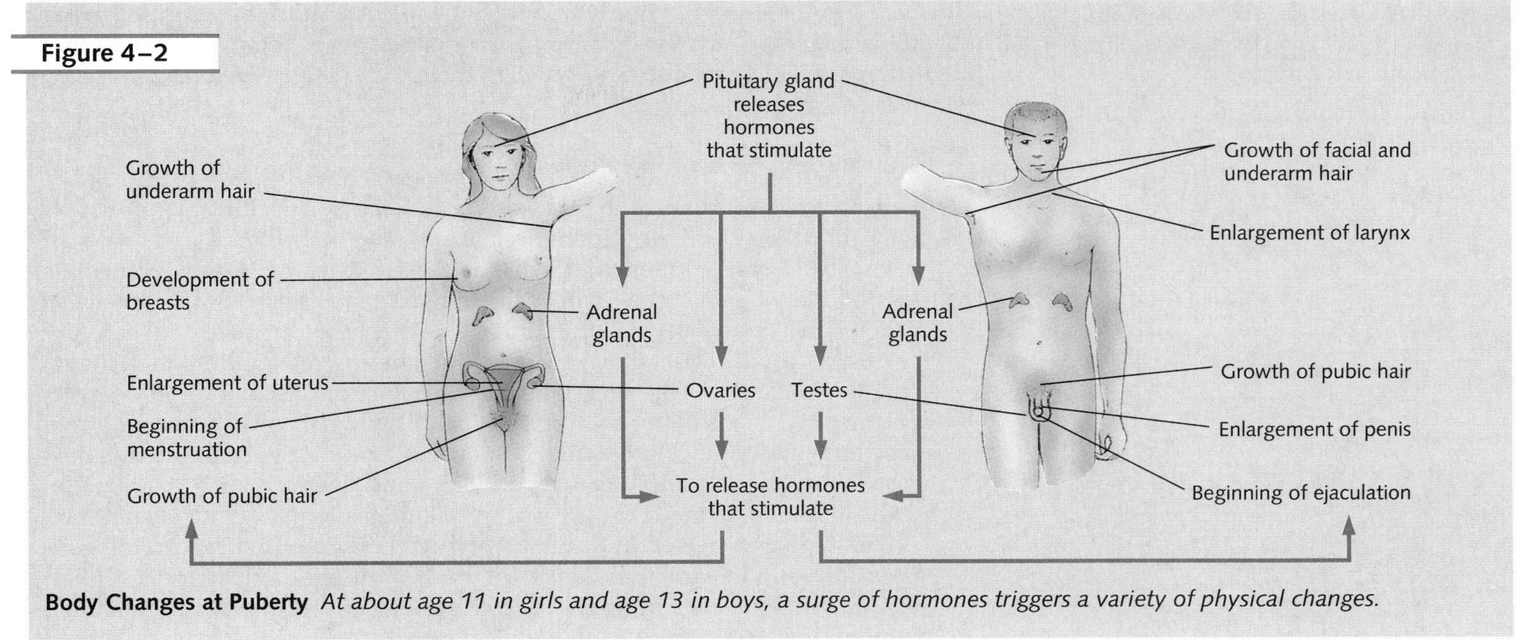


**Body Changes at Puberty** *At about age 11 in girls and age 13 in boys, a surge of hormones triggers a variety of physical changes.*

As in the earlier life stages, the *sequence* of physical changes (for example, breast buds before visible pubic hair before menarche) is far more predictable than their *timing*. Some girls start their growth spurt at 9, some boys as late as age 16. Such variations have little effect on height at maturity, but they may have psychological consequences. Studies performed in the 1950s by Mary Cover Jones and her colleagues revealed that early maturation pays dividends for boys. Early-maturing boys, being stronger and more athletic during their early teen years and seemingly less childlike, tend to be more popular, self-assured, and independent.

For girls, early maturation can be stressful. In Sweden, North America, and New Zealand, studies of girls whose menarche comes either early (before age 12) or late (at age 14 or after) reveal that early maturation can amplify preexisting problems (Caspi & Moffitt, 1991; Simmons & Blyth, 1987; Stattin & Magnusson, 1990). If a young girl's body is out of sync with her emotional maturity and with what her friends are experiencing, she may begin associating with older friends and doing things considered out of bounds for girls her age. Moreover, the 11-year-old who towers over her classmates and becomes the object of sexual attention may temporarily suffer embarrassment and be the object of teasing (Petersen, 1987). But as her peers catch up, in junior and senior high school, her postpubertal experience may help her to enjoy greater prestige and self-confidence.

For smooth adjustment it's not only when we mature that counts, but also how people around us react to our physical development. Remember: *Heredity and environment interact*. In this case, how the environment responds to the youngster depends on the timing of maturation, as influenced by heredity.

**Timing Is Everything** *Some girls and boys mature relatively early or late. This variation from the norm can produce feelings of social awkwardness, especially for early-maturing girls and for late-maturing boys. As this friendly pair makes clear, however, not all early and late bloomers suffer social embarrassment.*

## Cognitive Development

Adolescents' developing ability to reason gives them a new level of social awareness and moral judgment. As young teenagers become capable of thinking about their thinking, and of thinking about other people's think-

*"When the pilot told us to brace and grab our ankles, the first thing that went through my mind was that we must all look pretty stupid."*

Jeremiah Rawlings, 12, after a 1989 DC-10 crash in Sioux City, Iowa

ing, they begin imagining what other people are thinking about *them*. As their cognitive abilities mature, many adolescents begin to think about what is ideally possible and criticize their society, their parents, and even their own shortcomings.

## Developing Reasoning Power

During the early teen years, reasoning is often self-focused. Adolescents may think their private experiences are unique, and that their parents or friends just can't understand what it feels like to be dating or to hate school. The adolescent in love for the first time may sigh, "But, Mother, *you* don't really know how it feels to be in love" (Elkind, 1978).

*"Ben is in his first year of high school, and he's questioning all the right things."*

Drawing by Koren; ©1992 The New Yorker Magazine, Inc.

Gradually, though, most achieve the intellectual summit that Piaget called *formal operations*. Preadolescents reason concretely, but adolescents become more capable of abstract, logical thinking. They can reason hypothetically and deduce consequences: *If* this, *then* that. We can see this new reasoning power in adolescents' pondering and debating such abstract topics as human nature, good and evil, truth and justice. Having perhaps envisioned God as a person in the clouds when they were first capable of symbolic thinking in early childhood, they may now seek a deeper conception of God and existence (Elkind, 1970; Worthington, 1989). Adolescents' logical thinking also enables them to detect inconsistencies in others' reasoning and between their ideals and their actions. Indeed, their newfound ability to spot hypocrisy can lead to heated debates with parents and silent vows never to lose sight of their own ideals (Peterson & others, 1986). The new understanding of hypocrisy and possible solutions (or lack of them) to personal problems helps explain why suicide rates rise to adult levels during the teen years.

*"When I was a boy of 14 my father was so ignorant I could hardly stand to have the old man around. But when I got to be 21, I was astonished at how much he had learnt in 7 years."*

Mark Twain, 1835–1910

Piaget (1972) may have underestimated the role of culture and schooling and therefore overestimated the number of people who attain formal logic. If uneducated in the logic of science and mathematics, some adolescents and adults don't achieve formal operational reasoning. Consider this conversation between researcher Sylvia Scribner (1977) and an illiterate Kpelle farmer in a Liberian village:

**Sylvia Scribner:** *All Kpelle men are rice farmers. Mr. Smith is not a rice farmer. Is he a Kpelle man?*

**Kpelle farmer:** *I don't know the man. I have not laid eyes on the man myself.*

Kpelle villagers who did have formal schooling could respond in kind to Scribner's formal logic.

**Demonstrating Their Reasoning Ability** *These adolescents are on opposite sides of the abortion debate. The idealism that brings them to the picket lines is part of their newfound ability to think logically about abstract topics. According to Piaget, they are in the final cognitive stage, formal operations.*

### Developing Morality

A crucial task of childhood and adolescence is learning right from wrong and developing character—the psychological muscles for controlling impulses. To be a moral person is to *think* morally and *act* accordingly. Although as the French essayist Montaigne said, "It is a delightful harmony when doing and saying go together," such harmony often eludes us. "To put one's thoughts into action," noted the German poet Goethe, is "the most difficult thing in the world."

**Moral Thinking** Piaget (1932) believed that children's moral judgments build on their cognitive development. Accordingly, Lawrence Kohlberg (1981, 1984) sought to describe the development stages of *moral reasoning*, the thinking processes that occur when we consider right and wrong. In his research Kohlberg posed stories to children, adolescents, and adults in which the characters face a moral dilemma. He then analyzed their answers for evidence of different stages of moral thinking. Ponder for a moment his best-known dilemma:

> In Europe, a woman was near death from a very bad disease, a special kind of cancer. There was one drug that the doctors thought might save her. It was a form of radium that a druggist in the same town had recently discovered. The drug was expensive to make, but the druggist was charging ten times what the drug cost him to make. He paid $200 for the radium and charged $2,000 for a small dose of the drug. The sick woman's husband, Heinz, went to everyone he knew to borrow the money, but he could get together only about $1,000, which was half of what it cost. He told the druggist that his wife was dying and asked him to sell it cheaper or let him pay later. But the druggist said, "No, I discovered the drug and I'm going to make money from it." Heinz got desperate and broke into the man's store to steal the drug for his wife.

What do you think: Should Heinz have stolen the drug? Why was what he did right or wrong? Kohlberg would not have been interested in whether you judged Heinz's behavior as right or wrong—either answer could be justified—but rather in the *reasoning process* by which you arrived at your judgment. We all are moral philosophers, Kohlberg proposed, and our moral reasoning helps guide our judgments and behavior. Kohlberg himself discussed with a friend the moral dilemma of suicide before, nearing 60 and racked by pain, he committed suicide (Hunt, 1993).

Kohlberg argued that as we develop intellectually we pass through as many as six stages of moral thinking, moving from the simplistic and concrete toward more abstract and principled reasoning. He clustered these six stages into three basic levels: preconventional, conventional, and postconventional.

Before age 9, most children have a *preconventional* morality of self-interest: They obey either to avoid punishment ("If you let your wife die, you will get in trouble") or to gain concrete rewards.

By early adolescence, morality usually evolves to a more *conventional* level that upholds laws and social rules simply because they are the laws and rules. Being able to take others' perspectives, adolescents may approve actions that will gain social approval or that will help maintain the social order ("If you steal the drug, everyone will think you are a criminal").

Those who develop the abstract reasoning of formal operational thought may come to a third level. *Postconventional* morality affirms people's agreed-upon rights ("People have a right to live") or follows what one personally perceives as basic ethical principles ("If you steal the drug, you won't have lived up to your own ideals").

**Martin Luther King, Jr.** *Those who conform to society's rules often do not take kindly to those who seek to change those rules. Kohlberg contended that postconventional moral thinking, embodied here by Martin Luther King, Jr., may be rejected by those who do not comprehend it.*

*Should we agree that Kohlberg's postconventional, Western morality is indeed the "highest" and most "mature" level? Would society benefit if we all disregarded conventions and followed our own perceptions of universal ethical principles?*

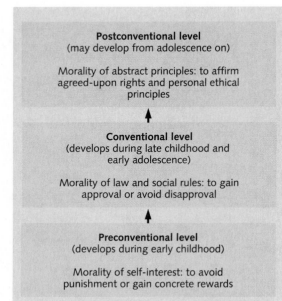

**Postconventional level**
(may develop from adolescence on)

Morality of abstract principles: to affirm agreed-upon rights and personal ethical principles

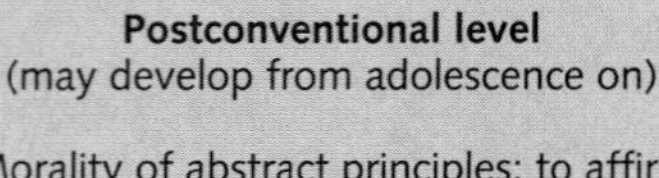

**Conventional level**
(develops during late childhood and early adolescence)

Morality of law and social rules: to gain approval or avoid disapproval

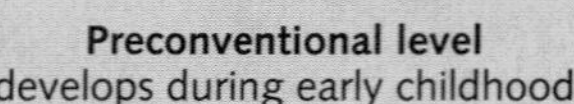

**Preconventional level**
(develops during early childhood)

Morality of self-interest: to avoid punishment or gain concrete rewards

**Figure 4–3**

**Kohlberg's Moral Ladder** *As moral development progresses, the focus of concern moves from the self to the wider social world.*

Kohlberg's controversial claim was that these levels form a moral ladder (Figure 4–3). The rungs extend from a young child's immature, preconventional morality at the bottom to, at the top, an adult's self-defined ethical principles. As with all stage theories, the sequence does not vary. We begin on the bottom rung and ascend to varying heights.

Research confirms that children in various cultures do progress sequentially from the level Kohlberg called preconventional into the stages of his conventional level (Edwards, 1981, 1982; Snarey, 1985, 1987). However, the postconventional level appears mostly in the European and North American educated middle class, which prizes individualism—giving priority to one's own goals rather than group goals (Eckensberger, 1994). Critics therefore contend the theory is biased against the moral reasoning of those in communal societies such as China and Papua, New Guinea—and also against women, whose morality may be less a matter of abstract, impersonal principles and more a matter of caring relationships (see Chapter 19).

**Moral Action** Our moral reasoning surely influences our moral talk, but sometimes talk is cheap. Morality is also *doing* the right thing, and what we do depends not only on our thinking but on social influences.

During World War II, many Nazi concentration camp guards were ordinary "moral" people who were corrupted by a powerfully evil situation (Arendt, 1963). Because of social influences, people's willingness to cheat, to discriminate racially, and to smoke marijuana are not neatly determined by their attitudes toward cheating, race, and drugs. The best predictor of whether a high school student smokes marijuana, for instance, is simply how many of the student's friends smoke it (Oetting & Beauvais, 1987).

Given the slack between thinking and acting, effective moral education must focus on both. We can stimulate children's moral development through discussions of moral issues and their implications. We can also teach children to restrain their impulses, to delay small gratifications now for the sake of bigger gratifications later. Those who learn to do so become more socially responsible, academically successful, and productive (Funder & Block, 1989; Mischel & others, 1988, 1989).

And we can focus directly on just and caring moral commitments by teaching and modeling such behaviors. When parents set high moral standards and practice what they preach, their moral principles become forceful. Such was true of the caring parents of those morally courageous people who protected Jews in Nazi Europe (Oliner & Oliner, 1988).

Moral ideas grow stronger when acted on. As we will see in Chapter 18, our actions feed our attitudes. We are as likely to act ourselves into a way of thinking as to think ourselves into action. To develop deeper moral principles, people can act on the ones they have. To stand up and be counted, to explain and defend our convictions, to commit money and energy, is then to believe our convictions more strongly.

*"This might not be ethical. Is that a problem for anybody?"*

Drawing by Vietor; ©1987 The New Yorker Magazine, Inc.

## Social Development

Theorist Erik Erikson (1963) contended that each stage of life has its own "psychosocial" task, a crisis that needs resolution. Young children wrestle with issues of *trust* (page 99), then *autonomy* (independence), then *initiative* (Table 4–1). School-age children develop *competence*, the sense that they are able and productive human beings. In adolescence, the task is to synthesize past, present, and future possibilities into a clearer sense of self. Adolescents wonder: "Who am I as an individual? What do I want to do with my life? What values should I live by? What do I believe in?" Erikson called

**Table 4–1 Erikson's Stages of Psychosocial Development**

| Approximate Age | Description of Task |
|---|---|
| *Infancy* (1st year) | *Trust vs. mistrust* If needs are dependably met, infants develop a sense of basic trust. |
| *Toddler* (2nd year) | *Autonomy vs. shame and doubt* Toddlers learn to exercise will and do things for themselves, or they will doubt their abilities. |
| *Preschooler* (3–5 years) | *Initiative vs. guilt* Preschoolers learn to initiate tasks and carry out plans, or they will feel guilty about efforts to be independent. |
| *Elementary school* (6 years to puberty) | *Competence vs. inferiority* Children learn the pleasure of applying themselves to tasks, or they will feel inferior. |
| *Adolescence* (teen years into 20s) | *Identity vs. role confusion* Teenagers work at refining a sense of self by testing roles and then integrating them to form a single identity, or they become confused about who they are. |
| *Young adulthood* (20s to early 40s) | *Intimacy vs. isolation* Young adults struggle to form close relationships and to gain the capacity for intimate love, or they will feel socially isolated. |
| *Middle adulthood* (40s to 60s) | *Generativity vs. stagnation* The middle-aged discover a sense of contributing to the world, such as through family and work, or they may feel a lack of purpose. |
| *Late adulthood* (late 60s and up) | *Integrity vs. despair* When reflecting on his or her life, the older adult may feel a sense of satisfaction or failure. |

this quest to more deeply define one's sense of self the adolescent's "search for identity."

As sometimes happens in psychology, Erikson's interests were bred by his life experience. As the son of a Jewish mother and stepfather, Erikson was "doubly an outsider," reports Morton Hunt (1993, p. 391). He was "scorned as a Jew in school but mocked as a Gentile in the synagogue because of his blond hair and blue eyes" (from his Danish biological father). Such episodes fueled his interest in the adolescent struggle for identity.

### Forming an Identity

To refine their sense of identity, adolescents in Western cultures usually try out different "selves" in different situations—perhaps acting out one self at home, another with friends, and still another at school and work. If two of these situations overlap—as when a teenager brings home friends with whom he is Joe Cool—the discomfort can be considerable. The teen asks, "Which self should I be? Which is the real me?" Often, this role confusion is resolved by the gradual reshaping of a self-definition that unifies the various selves into a consistent and comfortable sense of who one is—an **identity**.

But not always. Erikson noticed that some adolescents forge their identity early, simply by taking on their parents' values and expectations. (Traditional, less individualistic cultures tell adolescents who they are rather than letting them decide on their own.) Other adolescents may adopt a negative identity that defines itself in opposition to parents and society but in conformity with a particular peer group—complete, perhaps, with shaved head or multicolored, spiked hair. Still others never quite seem to find themselves or to develop strong commitments. For most, the identity question—Who am I?—continues past the teen years and reappears at turning points during adult life.

**Who Shall I Be Today?** *By varying the way they look, adolescents try out different "selves." Although we eventually form a consistent and stable sense of identity, the "self" we present may change with the situation.*

The late teen years, when many people begin attending college or working full time, provide new opportunities for trying out possible roles. As college seniors, many students have achieved a clearer identity than they had as first-year students (Waterman, 1988). Their identity typically incorporates an increasingly positive self-concept. In several nationwide studies, researchers have given young Americans tests of self-esteem. (Sample item: "I am able to do things as well as most other people.") Between ages 13 and 23, the self-concept usually becomes more positive, especially among boys and among those who belong to a satisfying peer group. A clearer, more self-affirming identity is forming, and with it comes a greater sense of control over one's future (Baumgardner, 1990; O'Malley & Bachman, 1983; Strange & Forsyth, 1993).

*"I am becoming still more independent of my parents; young as I am, I face life with more courage than Mummy; my feeling for justice is immovable, and truer than hers. I know what I want, I have a goal, an opinion, I have a religion, and love. Let me be myself and then I am satisfied. I know that I'm a woman, a woman with inward strength and plenty of courage."*

Anne Frank
*Diary of a Young Girl*, 1947

During the teen years, identity also becomes more personalized. Daniel Hart (1988) asked youths of various ages to imagine a machine that would clone (a) what you think and feel, (b) your exact appearance, or (c) your relationships with friends and family. He then asked them (and you might pause to ask yourself) which of these clones "is closest to being you?" Among seventh-graders, three-fourths chose (c), the one with the same social network. Among ninth-graders, three-fourths chose (a), the clone with their individual thoughts and feelings.

## Developing Intimacy

Erikson contended that the adolescent identity stage is followed in young adulthood by a developing capacity for **intimacy**, the ability to form emotionally close relationships. Once you have a clear and comfortable sense of who you are, said Erikson, you are ready for close relationships. But to Carol Gilligan and her colleagues (1982, 1990), the "normal" struggle to create one's separate identity describes individualist males more than relationship-oriented females. Gilligan believes females are less concerned than males are with viewing themselves as separate individuals, and are more concerned with "making connections."

As adolescents seek to form their own identities, they begin to separate themselves from their parents (Paikoff & Brooks-Gunn, 1991). What their friends are—what "everybody's doing"—they often become. In Western cultures, adolescence is typically a time of growing peer influence and diminishing parental influence, especially on matters of personal taste and life-style. One study asked teens to report their emotions when beeped by electronic pagers at random times. Most reported feeling more free and open with friends than with family (Larson & Bradney, 1988).

For a small minority of parents and their adolescents, differences mean estrangement. But for most, disagreement at the level of bickering is not destructive. A study of 6000 adolescents in 10 countries, from Australia to Bangladesh to Turkey, found that most liked their parents (Offer & others, 1988). "We usually get along but . . . ," adolescents often report (Galambos, 1992; Steinberg, 1987). In a recent Gallup Poll (1993) of American teens, 95 percent said they were more "happy" than "not that happy" with how things were going in their home. Positive relations with parents support positive peer relations. High school girls who have the most affectionate relationships with their mothers tend also to enjoy the most intimate friendships with girlfriends (Gold & Yanof, 1985).

Moreover, most families easily bridge the generation gap, because it is rather narrow. Only 5 percent of U.S. teens report not getting on with their parents at all (Gallup Organization, 1988). Indeed, most adolescents closely reflect the social, political, and religious views of their parents (Gallatin, 1980). As often as not, "generation gaps" on such issues merely involve differences in the degree to which adolescents and their parents hold their shared views (Figure 4–4).

As identity and intimacy mature during the twenties, emotional ties between parents and children continue to loosen. During their early twenties, many still lean heavily on their parents. By their late twenties, most feel more comfortably independent of their parents and better able to empathize with them as fellow adults (Frank, 1988; White, 1983). As the twentieth century winds down, this graduation from adolescence to adulthood is taking longer. Adolescents in Europe and North America are taking longer to finish college, to leave the nest, to establish their careers. From 1960 to 1990, Americans' average age at first marriage increased nearly 4 years (to 26 for men, 24 for women).

**Family Intimacy** *Relationships with parents are a vital part of adolescence. Although there may be differences over values, relationships, and responsibilities, most teenagers, like the young woman shown here, are on good terms with their parents.*

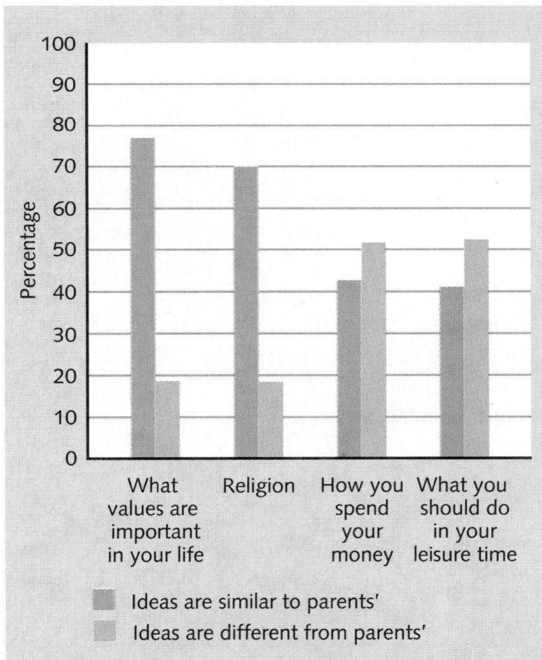


**Figure 4–4**

**High School Seniors' Attitudes Versus Their Parents'** *As this study found, high school seniors' attitudes appear to be in much closer agreement with their parents' than many suppose. Agreement is greater, however, on basic values than on life-style choices. (From Bachman & others, 1987.)*

## Adolescent Sexuality and Pregnancy

Adolescents' physical maturation fosters a sexual dimension to their emerging identity. How and when that gets expressed differs with time and culture. In the United States, the percentage of ninth- to twelfth-graders reporting having sexual intercourse rose during the 1970s and 1980s to a peak of 59 percent in 1989. Then, with greater awareness of sexually transmitted diseases such as AIDS, it declined to 54 percent in 1991

*"Will your child learn to multiply before she learns to subtract?"*

Anti–teen-pregnancy poster for the Children's Defense Fund

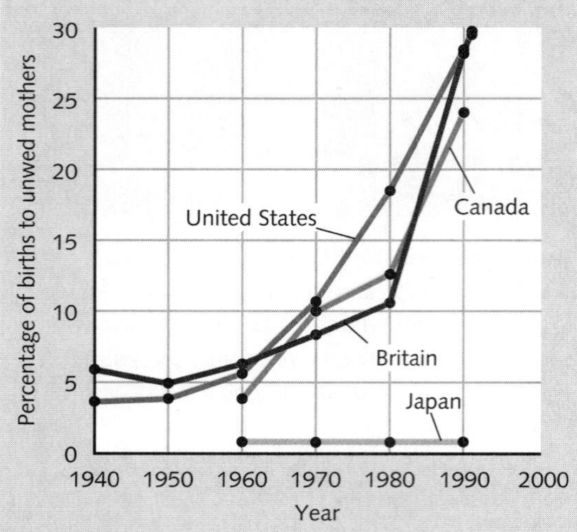


**Figure 4–5**

**Births to Unwed Parents** *Since 1960, the percentage of babies born to unmarried Canadian, British, and American women—one-third of whom were teens—has more than quintupled. This increase stems from two trends: a decreasing birth rate among married women and a doubling of the birth rate among unmarried women. (Data from National Center for Health Statistics; Bureau of the Census [1993], Table 1380; and British Central Statistical Office, 1993.)*

*"All of us who make motion pictures are teachers, teachers with very loud voices."*

Film producer George Lucas
Academy Award ceremonies, 1992

(Kann & others, 1993). Teen intercourse rates are higher in western Europe but much lower in Arab and Asian countries (Buss, 1989; Toufexis, 1993). These varying sexual standards help explain the changes and culture differences in rates of nonmarital childbearing (Figure 4–5).

The increased adolescent pregnancy rate and the often impoverished futures of teenage mothers and of children abandoned by their biological fathers have prompted new research on teen sexuality and adolescents' use of contraceptives. Short of "just saying no," contraceptives are the surest strategy of preventing pregnancy. Although the number of American teenagers using condoms doubled during the 1980s, half of teen sexual acts were unprotected. Only one-third of sexually active male teens used condoms consistently (Sonenstein, 1992). Why? Among the contributing factors are these:

1. ***Ignorance*** In eight surveys, fewer than half the adolescents could correctly identify the safe and risky times of the menstrual cycle (Morrison, 1985). Thus, most unwed teen mothers report surprise at finding themselves pregnant (Brooks-Gunn & Furstenberg, 1989). They didn't choose to become pregnant; rather, they and their partners failed to prevent pregnancy. In the 1990s, ignorance may also involve a failure to realize one's risk of contracting a sexually transmitted disease.
2. ***High sex guilt*** Although sexual inhibitions reduce sexual activity, they also result in lack of planned birth control for those who do engage in sex (Byrne & others, 1993). Not wanting to appear deliberately sexual or promiscuous, teens may hesitate to carry and produce a condom. When, as sometimes happens, passion overwhelms intentions, the result may be conception.
3. ***Minimal communication about birth control*** Many teenagers are uncomfortable discussing contraception with parents, partners, and peers (Kotva & Schneider, 1990; Milan & Kilmann, 1987). Teens are more likely to use contraceptives if they talk freely with friends or parents and are in an exclusive relationship with a partner with whom they communicate openly.
4. ***Alcohol use*** Sexually active teens are typically alcohol-using teens (National Research Council, 1987). By depressing brain centers that control judgment, inhibition, and self-awareness, alcohol tends to break down normal restraints, a phenomenon well known to sexually coercive males (page 241).
5. ***Mass media norms of unprotected promiscuity*** The Planned Parenthood Federation (1986) has complained that television and movies help define sexual norms, which today are "Go for it *now*. . . . Don't worry about anything." An average hour of prime-time television on the three major American networks contains approximately 15 sexual acts, words, and innuendos—one every 4 minutes—nearly all involving unmarried persons and rarely communicating any concern for birth control or sexually transmitted disease (Sapolsky & Tabarlet, 1991). Planned Parenthood contends that repeated portrayals of unsafe sex, without consequence, amounts to a campaign of sex *dis*information.

With teen pregnancy rising despite increased sex education, the United States national health objectives for the year 2000 now include a dual aim: increasing condom use to 90 percent among those sexually active, and re-

**FEIFFER**

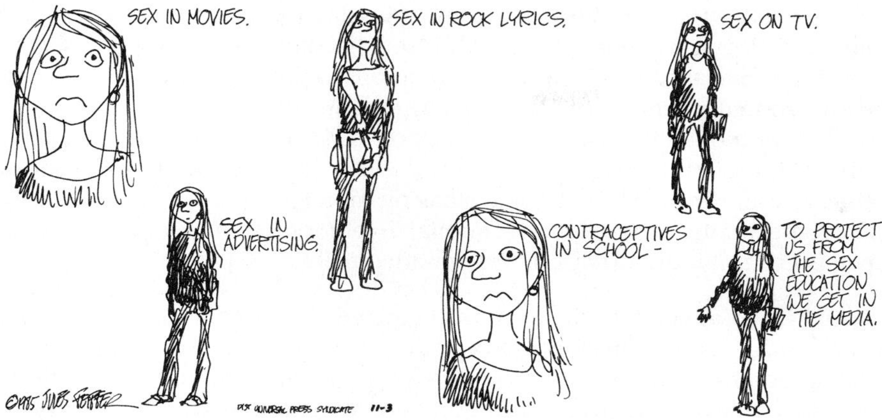

SEX IN MOVIES.
SEX IN ROCK LYRICS.
SEX ON TV.
SEX IN ADVERTISING.
CONTRACEPTIVES IN SCHOOL -
TO PROTECT US FROM THE SEX EDUCATION WE GET IN THE MEDIA.


FEIFFER copyright 1985 Jules Feiffer. Reprinted with permission of UNIVERSAL PRESS SYNDICATE. All rights reserved.

ducing the proportion of 17-year-olds who have had intercourse from approximately 70 percent to under 40 percent (Centers for Disease Control, 1992). This two-pronged emphasis on contraception ("safe sex") and abstinence ("saved sex") is reflected in changing sex education, which is shifting toward the linking of sex with commitment, or at least with self-protection.

The shift responds to declining adolescent well-being (Myers, 1994). In the United States, the number of children not living with two parents has more than doubled since 1960. As elsewhere in the industrialized world, teen and young adult depression rates have soared. Teen suicide has tripled. Teen arrests for violent crime have increased sixfold. "Never before," declared a 1990 National Association of State Boards of Education report, "has one generation of American teenagers been less healthy, less cared for, or less prepared for life than their parents were at the same age."

Throughout history, the pendulum of sexual values has swung—from the European eroticism of the early 1800s to the conservative Victorian era of the late 1800s, from the libertine flapper era of the 1920s to the family values of the 1950s. With new 1990s voices decrying family disintegration and calling for a balance between sexual expression and restraint, and with teen intercourse rates beginning to decline, the pendulum may have begun a new swing toward commitment.

*"We cannot renew our country when within a decade more than half of our children will be born into families where there is no marriage."*

Bill Clinton
State of the Union Address, 1994

## Summing Up

Due to earlier maturation and prolonged education, adolescence—the transition years between biological maturity and social independence—has lengthened in many countries.

**Physical Development** Adolescence extends from the sexual maturity of puberty and the growth spurt to the achievement of adult independence. Depending on how other people react, early or late maturation can influence adjustment which again illustrates how genes and environment interact in shaping us.

**Cognitive Development** Piaget theorized that adolescents develop the capacity for formal operations, which enables them to reason abstractly. However, some developmentalists believe that the development of formal logic depends on schooling as well, and that the rudiments of logic appear earlier than Piaget believed.

Following Piaget's lead, Lawrence Kohlberg contended that moral thinking likewise proceeds through a sequence of stages, from a preconventional morality of self-interest, to a conventional morality concerned with gaining others' approval or doing one's duty, to (in some people) a postconventional morality of agreed-upon rights or universal ethical principles. But morality also lies in actions, which are influenced by the social situation and inner attitudes as well as by moral reasoning. Moreover, say Kohlberg's critics, the postconventional level represents morality from the perspective of individualist, liberal-minded males.

**Social Development** Erik Erikson theorized that a chief task of adolescence is solidifying one's sense of self—one's identity. For many people, this struggle continues into the adult years as new relationships emerge and new roles are assumed. Although adolescence has traditionally been viewed as a time of storm and stress, researchers have found that most teenagers relate to their parents reasonably well and generally affirm their parents' beliefs and attitudes. In the Western world, the last 30 years have been a time of changing sexual standards and increasing risk of teen pregnancy.

## Adulthood

*As we age, our paths diverge. Yet we all continue to develop physically, cognitively, and socially. What sensory and neural changes mark the aging process? In what ways do memory and intelligence change? Is the journey from adolescence to death marked by stages that serve as developmental milestones?*

At one time, psychologists viewed adulthood, especially the center-of-life years between adolescence and old age, as one long plateau. No longer. Those who follow the unfolding of people's adult lives now believe development continues. Physically, cognitively, and especially socially, people at age 50 are different from their 25-year-old selves.

Recognizing that adults do change, developmental theorists have proposed various stages of adult development, complete with transition periods. When people become independent of their parents and assume work roles, a transition from adolescence to *early adulthood* occurs. This extends from the twenties (or earlier, depending on the culture and the individual) into the forties, when *middle adulthood* begins. Some developmentalists now distinguish the "young-old" years (age 65 to 75) of *later adulthood* from the "old-old" years (after age 75) of more rapid physical decline.

Labeling life's phases is a convenient way to organize the adult years. But the labels are arbitrary, and the transition points are fuzzy. Moreover, by itself age causes nothing. People do not get wiser with age, they get wiser with experience. People do not die of old age, they die of the physical deterioration that accompanies aging. And during adulthood, age predicts people's traits only modestly. If you know only that Maria is a 1-year-old and Meredith is a 10-year-old, you could say a great deal about each. Not so with adults who differ by 10 years. The boss may be 30 or 60; the marathon runner may be 20 or 50; your classmates may be teenagers or grandparents. Likewise, a 19-year-old can be a parent who supports a child or a student who still gets an allowance.

*"I am still learning."*

Michelangelo's motto, 1560, at age 85

It's also harder to generalize about adulthood stages than about life's early years. During the first months of life, biological maturation narrowly restricts our life course. The infant who is strapped on a cradleboard and the one who moves freely will both walk and talk within a few weeks of each other. As the years pass, we sail a widening channel in which the winds of individual experience cause our courses to diverge more and more. Yet our life courses are in some ways similar. Our bodies, our minds, and our relationships undergo some changes in common with those of childhood friends, who in other ways now seem so very different.

## Physical Changes

Although few of us are aware of it at the time, our physical abilities peak in early adulthood. Muscular strength, reaction time, sensory keenness, and cardiac output all crest by the mid-twenties. Like the declining daylight after the summer solstice, declining physical prowess begins imperceptibly. Athletes are often the first to notice. World-class sprinters and swimmers peak in their teens or early twenties. Women, because they mature earlier than men, also peak earlier. But most people—especially those whose daily lives do not require peak physical performance—hardly perceive the early signs of decline.

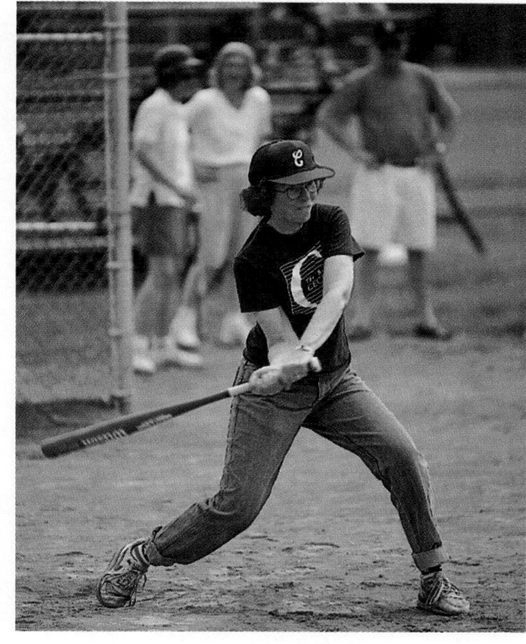

**A Good Sport** *Whether they choose baseball or tennis, jogging or walking, middle-aged adults who exercise maintain their physical vigor. In fact, exercise is one of the best ways to stay healthy in later life.*

### Physical Changes in Middle Adulthood

As middle-aged athletes know well, physical decline gradually accelerates (Figure 4–6). "I feel like a 15-year-old trapped in an aging 47-year-old body," said one middle-aged basketball player. But even diminished vigor is sufficient for normal activities. Moreover, during early and middle adulthood physical vigor has less to do with age than with a person's health and exercise habits. Many of today's physically fit 50-year-olds can run 4 miles with ease, while sedentary 25-year-olds find themselves huffing and puffing on a jog around the block.

As in adolescence, the physical changes of adult life may trigger psychological responses, which vary depending on how one views growing older. In some Eastern cultures, where respect and power come with age, outward signs of advancing years are accepted and even welcomed. In Western cultures, where the perceived ideal is smooth skin and a slim torso, the wrinkles and bulges that frequently accompany middle age can threaten self-esteem. But nature will not be denied; despite efforts to preserve youthful appearance, the lines appear and the youthful form begins to change its shape.

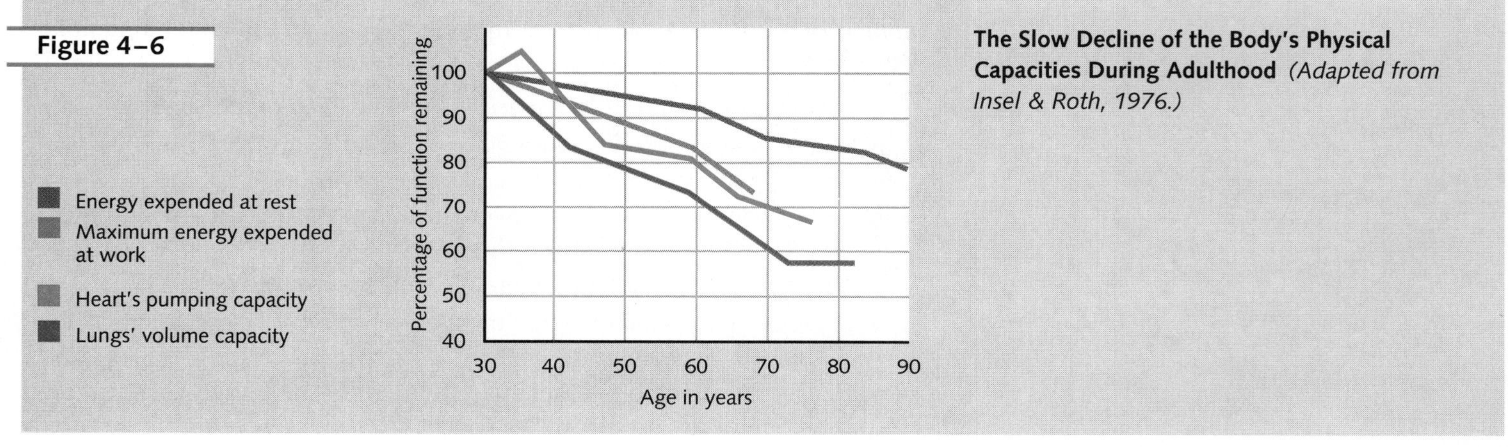


**The Slow Decline of the Body's Physical Capacities During Adulthood** *(Adapted from Insel & Roth, 1976.)*

*Although menstruation begins earlier today than in centuries past, menopause has been occurring around age 50 for at least 1500 years (Matthews, 1992).*

For women, the foremost biological change related to aging is **menopause**, the ending of the menstrual cycle, usually beginning within a few years of age 50. Menopause and its occasional physical symptoms, such as hot flashes in some women, accompany a reduction in the hormone estrogen. Like the stereotype of adolescent storm and stress, the image of menopausal emotionality and depression clashes with reality: Menopause usually does *not* create psychological problems for women. One survey of 2500 middle-aged Massachusetts women, and another that followed 541 middle-aged Pennsylvania women for 3 years, found them no more or less depressed if experiencing menopause (McKinlay & others, 1987a,b; Matthews, 1992). Apart from occasional stiff shoulders and headaches, Japanese women, too, report few symptoms of menopause (Lock & others, 1988).

A woman's expectations and attitudes regarding menopause influence its emotional impact. Does she see menopause as a sign that she is losing her femininity and sexual attractiveness and beginning to grow old? Or does she look on it as liberation from contraceptives, menstrual periods, fears of pregnancy, and the demands of children?

To learn women's attitudes toward menopause, Bernice Neugarten and her colleagues (1963) did what, amazingly, no one had bothered to do: They questioned women whose experience of menopause had not led them to seek treatment. When asked whether it is true that after menopause "women generally feel better than they have for years," only one-fourth of the premenopausal women under age 45 guessed yes. Of the older women who had experienced menopause, two-thirds said yes. As one woman said, "I can remember my mother saying that after her menopause she really got her vigor, and I can say the same thing myself." Social psychologist Jacqueline Goodchilds (1987) quips: "If the truth were known, we'd have to diagnose [older women] as having P.M.F.—Post-Menstrual Freedom."

Men experience no equivalent to the menopause—no cessation of fertility, no sharp drop in sex hormones. But they do experience a more gradual decline in sperm count, testosterone level, and speed of erection and ejaculation. Some may also experience psychological distress related to their perception of decreased virility and declining physical capacities. Nevertheless, after middle age most men and women remain capable of satisfying sexual activity.

### Physical Changes in Later Life

Is old age "more to be feared than death" (Juvenal, *Satires*)? Or is life "most delightful when it is on the downward slope" (Seneca, *Epistulae ad Lucilium*)? What is it like to grow old? To gauge your own understanding, take the following true/false quiz:

1. By the year 2050, 1 in 10 Americans will be 65 or older (see page 131).
2. Older people become more susceptible to short-term illnesses (see page 133).
3. About one-fourth of people over age 65 live in nursing homes, hospitals, homes for the aged, or other institutions (see page 133).
4. During old age many of the brain's neurons die (see page 133).
5. If they live to be 90 or older, most elderly people eventually become senile (see page 133).
6. Recognition memory—the ability to identify things previously experienced—declines with age (see page 135).

7. Life satisfaction peaks in the fifties and then gradually declines after age 65 (see page 142).
8. Among the elderly, there are twice as many widows as widowers (see page 143).
9. A fear of death preoccupies many older people (see page 144).

**Life Expectancy** The above statements—all false—are among the myths about aging exploded by recent research on the world's most rapidly growing population group. The post-65-year-old population rose from fewer than 1 in 100 in 1900 to 1 in 16 in 1992, en route to 1 in 5 by 2050 (Figure 4–7). In developing countries, the proportionately small elderly population will double between 1980 and 2000. In China, where there were five children per elderly person in 1955, there will be but two children per elderly person in 2040 (Hugo, 1987). Clearly, countries that depend on children to care for the aged are destined for major social changes.

Although 126 male embryos begin life for every 100 females, males are more death-prone ever after (Strickland, 1992). By birth the sex ratio is down to 105 males for every 100 females. During the first year, male infants' death rates exceed females' by one-fourth. Worldwide, women outlive men—by nearly 7 years in Canada, the United States, and Australia. (Rather than marrying a man older than themselves, 20-year-old women who want a husband who shares their life expectancy should wait for the 14-year-old boys to mature.) By age 100, females outnumber males 5 to 1.

*The risk of death doubles every 8 years after age 30. Despite greater life expectancy today than a century ago, a 48-year-old still is twice as likely to die as a 40-year-old (National Center for Health Statistics, 1992; Olshansky & others, 1993).*

But few of us live to 100, because even in the absence of a fatal disease or accident, the body senesces: it ages. Its cells stop reproducing. It becomes frail. It becomes vulnerable to tiny insults—hot weather, a fall, a mild flu bug—that would have been trivial at age 20. Even if no one died before age 50, and cancer, heart disease, and infectious illness were eliminated, life ex-

*The oldest known person ever to have lived was Shirechiyo Izumi of Japan, who died in 1986 at age 120 years, 237 days (National Institute on Aging, 1993).*

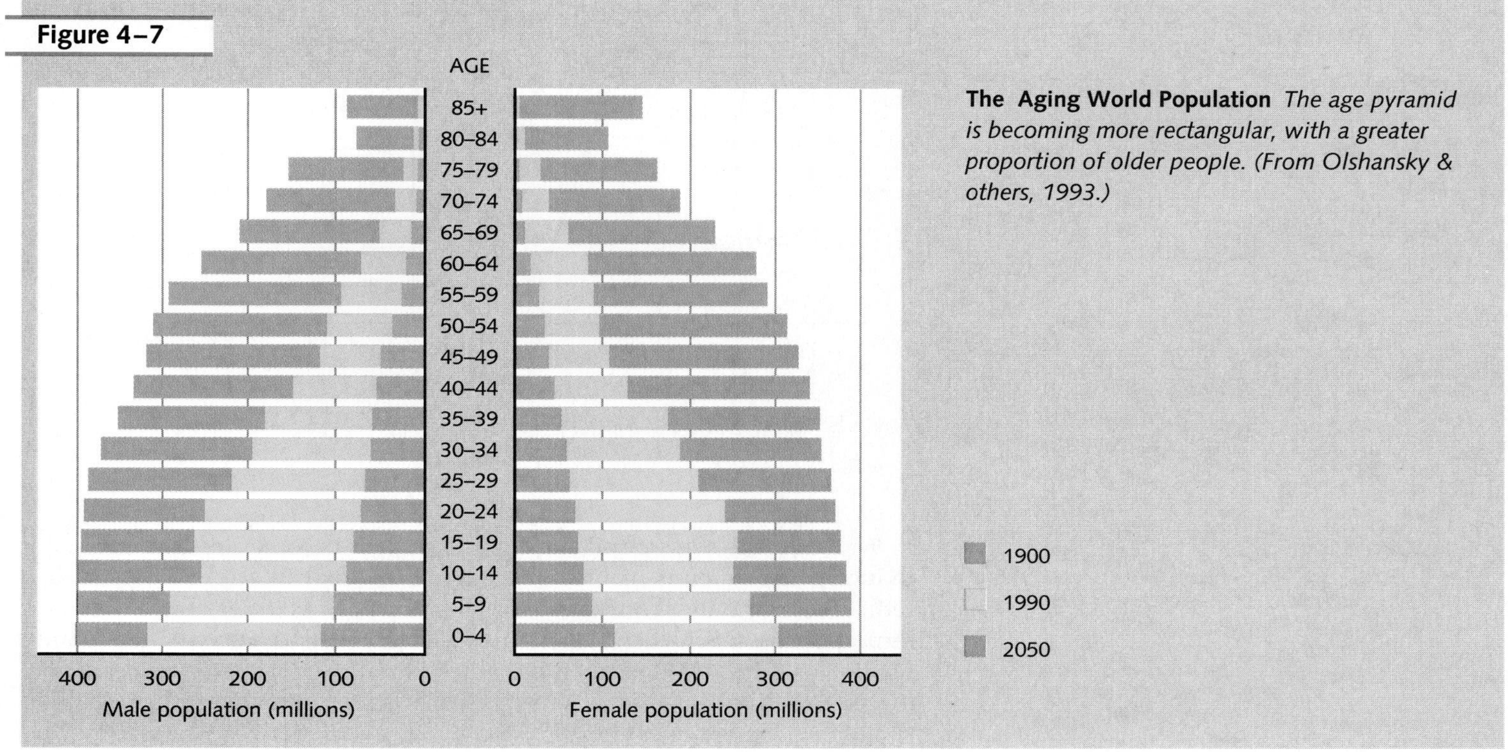


**Figure 4–7**

**The Aging World Population** *The age pyramid is becoming more rectangular, with a greater proportion of older people. (From Olshansky & others, 1993.)*

pectancy would still increase only to 85, by some estimates, or a few years beyond that, by other estimates (Barinaga, 1991).

But why do we age, eventually wearing out? Why don't we, like the bristlecone pine trees, rockfish, and some social insect queens, grow older without withering? One theory, proposed by evolutionary biologists, speculates that the answer relates to our survival as a species: We pass on our genes most successfully when we raise our young and then stop consuming resources. Moreover, once we've fulfilled our reproductive potential, there are no natural selection pressures against genes that cause degeneration in later life (Sapolsky & Finch, 1991; Olshansky & others, 1993).

*Question: How much priority should medicine and your nation's health policy devote to extending the life span (for example, with heart surgeries for 80-year-olds) even if this increases the years of frailty and disability?*

**Sensory Abilities** As we have seen, physical decline begins in early adulthood, but not until later life do people become acutely aware of it. As visual sharpness diminishes and adaptation to changes in light level slows, older people have more accidents. Most stairway falls taken by older persons occur on the top step, precisely where the person typically descends from a window-lit hallway into the darker stairwell (Fozard & Popkin, 1978). By using what we know about aging when designing environments, we could reduce such accidents (National Research Council, 1990). Muscle strength, hearing, distance perception, reaction time, and stamina also diminish noticeably (Figure 4–8). In later life, the stairs get steeper, the newsprint smaller, and people seem to mumble more. After age 70, car accident rates per mile increase, reaching the relatively high teenage level by age 75 (National Research Council, 1990).

**Figure 4–8**

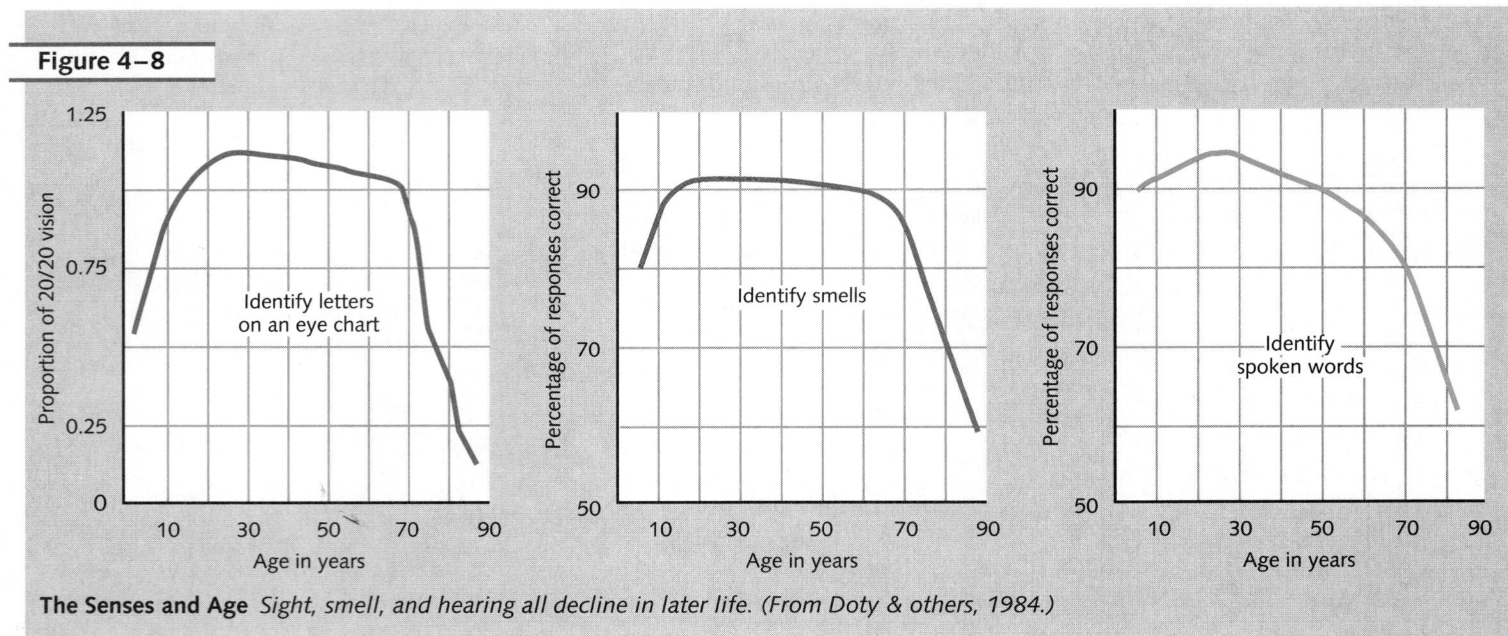


**The Senses and Age** *Sight, smell, and hearing all decline in later life. (From Doty & others, 1984.)*

With age, the eye's pupil shrinks and its lens becomes less transparent, reducing the amount of light reaching the retina. In fact, a 65-year-old retina receives only about one-third as much light as its 20-year-old counterpart (Kline & Schieber, 1985). Thus, to see as well as a 20-year-old when reading, a 65-year-old needs three times as much light—a reason for buying cars with untinted windshields. That also explains why older people sometimes ask younger people, "Don't you need better light for reading?"

**Health** For those growing older, there is both bad and good news about health. The bad news: The body's disease-fighting immune system weakens, making the elderly more susceptible to life-threatening ailments such as cancer and pneumonia. It's as if the very old have a very mild case of AIDS—the immune deficiency that hampers the body's ability to fight infections.

The good news: Thanks to a lifetime's accumulation of antibodies, older people *less* often suffer short-term ailments, such as common flu and cold viruses. For example, those over 65 are half as likely as 20-year-olds and one-fifth as likely as preschoolers to suffer upper respiratory flu each year (U.S. National Center for Health Statistics, 1990). This is one reason why older workers have lower absenteeism rates (Rhodes, 1983). Also, 96 studies of 40,000 workers indicate that older workers are not, as a general rule, less productive (McEvoy & Cascio, 1989).

One survey revealed that most elderly people believe the majority of their peers suffer serious health problems. But when asked about their own health, fewer than one in four reported that *they* have such a problem (National Council on the Aging, 1976). So it shouldn't surprise us that only 5 percent of all those over 65 live in hospitals, nursing homes, and other such institutions.

Aging does, however, slow neural processes. During the early years of life, up to the teen years, we process information more and more speedily (Kail, 1991). But compared with teens and young adults, older people take a bit more time to react, to solve perceptual puzzles, even to remember names (Salthouse, 1992; Schaie, 1989). Speed slows especially when the task becomes complex (Cerella, 1985; Poon, 1987). At video games, most 70-year-olds are no match for a 20-year-old. (Nor, as I discovered in play with my daughter, is a 48-year-old a match for a 14-year-old at Nintendo's perceptual speed game, Tetris.) As we age, we become aware of a growing gap between what we were and what we are becoming.

Beginning in young adulthood, there is also a small, gradual loss of brain cells, contributing to a 5 percent or so reduction of brain weight by age 80. But the proliferation of neural connections, especially in people who remain active, helps compensate for the cell loss (Coleman & Flood, 1986). This helps explain the common finding that adults who remain active—physically, sexually, and mentally—retain more of their capacity for such activities in later years (Jarvik, 1975; Pfeiffer, 1977). "Use it or lose it" is sound advice. We are more likely to rust from disuse than to wear out from overuse.

*"Everything I've got is 93. You don't see as well. You can't kick the back of your head. Your mind doesn't get old—your body does."*

George Burns, 1990

**Keeping the Biological Clock Running Smoothly** *How quickly people age depends in part on their health habits. As this cheerful group makes clear, the more active people remain, the more vigor they retain.*

**Senility and Alzheimer's Disease** Some adults do, unfortunately, suffer a substantial loss of brain cells. A series of small strokes, a brain tumor, or alcoholism can progressively damage the brain, causing that mental erosion we call senility (Figure 4–9). So, too, can the most feared of all brain ailments, **Alzheimer's disease**, which strikes 3 percent of the world's population by age 75. Up to age 95, the incidence doubles roughly every 5 years. Alzheimer's symptoms are *not* the same as normal aging. (Occasionally forgetting where you laid the car keys or losing someone's name is no cause for alarm.)

Alzheimer's destroys even the brightest of minds. First memory, then reasoning and language deteriorate. Robert Sayre (1979) recalls his father shouting at his afflicted mother to "think harder" when she could not remember where she had put something, while his mother, confused, embarrassed, on the verge of tears, randomly searched the house. As the disease runs its course, after 5 to 20 years, the patient becomes disoriented, then in-

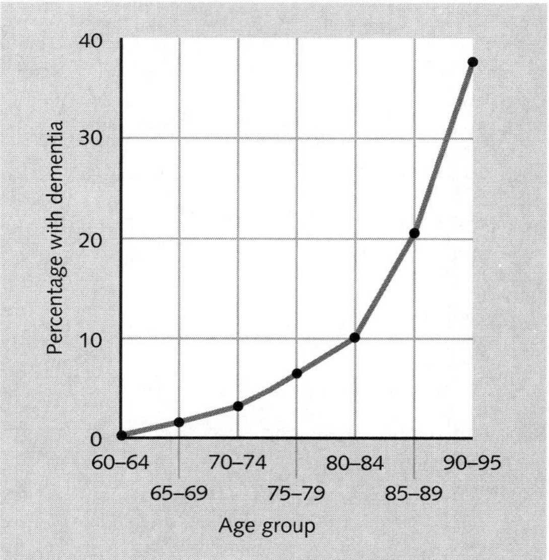


**Figure 4–9**

**Incidence of Dementia (Mental Disintegration) by Age** *Risk of mental loss due to Alzheimer's disease or a series of strokes doubles about every 5 years in later life. (From Jorm & others, 1987, based on 22 studies in industrialized nations.)*

continent, finally mentally vacant—a sort of living death, a mere body stripped of its humanity. Caregiving family members of increasingly confused and helpless sufferers themselves often become the disease's exasperated and exhausted victims.

Underlying the symptoms is a deterioration of neurons that produce the neurotransmitter acetylcholine. Deprived of this vital chemical messenger, memory and thinking suffer. An autopsy reveals two telltale abnormalities in these acetylcholine-producing neurons: shriveled protein filaments in the cell body and placques (globs of degenerating tissue) at the tips of neuron branches. At least three forms of Alzheimer's disease are hereditary, linked to three different chromosomes (Marx, 1992). With continuing advances in our understanding of the chemical, neural, and genetic roots of Alzheimer's, hopes grow for eventual control of this dread disease.

Some hopes reside in work on transplanting brain tissue. Recall that, especially in the early years, the brain is to some extent plastic—it can reorganize its functions after damage. In the later years, could we enhance the brain's self-repair by transplanting brain tissue? Even in this era of heart transplants and skin grafts, transplanting neural tissue still sounds like science fiction. But in experiments with animals, neuroscientists are now trying, with some success, to mend the brain by replacing destroyed nerve cells with healthy ones (Dunnett, 1989; Gash & others, 1986).

*If transplanted brain tissue indeed alleviates Parkinson's disease, would you favor or oppose the use of brain tissue from aborted fetuses?*

Might such transplants someday enable neurosurgeons to repair the human brain? The tremors of Parkinson's disease, like the progressive deterioration of Alzheimer's disease, involve a degeneration of brain tissue that normally produces vital neurotransmitters—dopamine, in Parkinson's disease. If we transplant dopamine-producing tissue into the brain of a Parkinson's patient, would the tissue survive and release the needed neurotransmitters? Using such tissue from patients' own adrenal glands or, more effectively, from 6- to 8-week-old fetuses, experimental surgery on dozens of patients in Sweden, Mexico, the United States, and elsewhere has raised hopes that it might (Thompson, 1992). Some patients have been able to reduce their medication and even to regain the ability to drive, cook, and talk on the phone.

## Cognitive Changes

One of the most controversial questions in the study of the human life span is whether adult cognitive abilities, such as memory, creativity, and intelligence, parallel the gradually accelerating decline of physical abilities. Employers, for example, may wonder whether to encourage their senior workers to retire—or to capitalize on their experience. In general, people perceive the elderly as mentally less sharp (Kite & Johnson, 1988). Is this stereotype accurate? Is there truth in the old proverb, "You can't teach an old dog new tricks"? Or does truth lie with another old proverb: "You're never too old to learn"?

### Aging and Memory

Early adulthood is the peak time for some types of learning and remembering. In one experiment, Thomas Crook and Robin West (1990) invited 1205 people to learn some names. Fourteen videotaped people said his or her name using a common format: "Hi, I'm Larry." Then the 14 individuals reappeared saying, for example, "I'm from Philadelphia"—providing a visual and voice cue to remember the person's name. As Figure 4–10 shows, everyone remembered more names after a second and third replay of the introductions, but younger adults' recall for the names consistently sur-

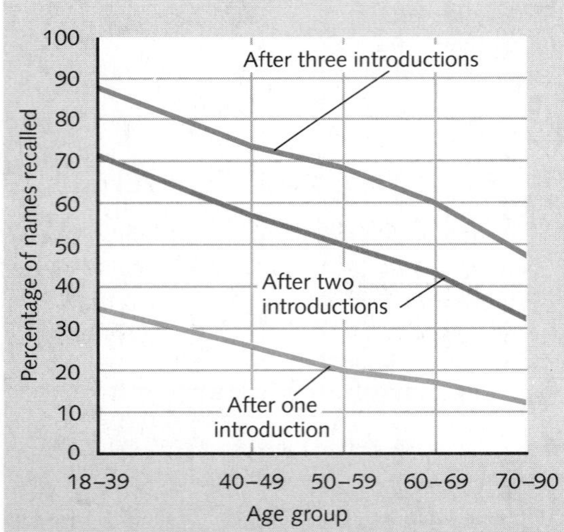


**Figure 4–10**

**Tests of Recall** *Recalling new names introduced once, twice, or three times is easier for younger adults than for older ones. (Data from Crook & West, 1990.)*

passed that of older adults. Quicker learning by younger adults is not restricted to human beings. Aging monkeys, too, take progressively more time to master new tasks (Bachevalier & others, 1991, 1992).

But consider another experiment. David Schonfield and Betty-Anne Robertson (1966) asked adults of various ages to learn a list of 24 words. Without giving any clues, the researchers asked some to recall as many words as they could from the list. As Figure 4–11 shows, younger adults had better recall. Others, given multiple-choice questions that asked them simply to *recognize* the words they had seen, exhibited no memory decline with age. This type of memory is especially good when older adults are tested early rather than late in the day (May & others, 1993). So, how well older people remember depends: Are they being asked simply to *recognize* what they have tried to memorize (minimal decline) or to *recall* it without clues (greater decline).

Part of the memory difficulty older adults complain of may be normal forgetfulness. When a 20-year-old mislays her car keys, she gets frustrated; when her grandfather mislays his, he gets frustrated and blames his age. But forgetting—or remembering—seems also to depend on the type of information. If you are asked to recall meaningless information—remembering nonsense syllables or unimportant events—then the older you are, the more errors you are likely to make. However, if the information is meaningful, older people's rich web of existing knowledge helps them catch it. Thus, their capacity to learn and remember skills and *meaningful* material shows less decline (Graf, 1990; Labouvie-Vief & Schell, 1982; Perlmutter, 1983). There also seems to be little decline with age in people's "prospective" memory—a type of memory involved in remembering *to do* something, such as taking a pill with meals or picking up bread on the way home (Einstein & McDaniel, 1990).

One other important complication: Right through their later years, people continue to diverge. If you think 20-year-olds differ widely in their abilities to learn and remember, consider this: 70-year-olds differ much more. Some 70-year-olds perform below nearly all 20-year-olds; other 70-year-olds match or outdo the average 20-year-old. Neuropsychologist Michela Gallagher (1990) has found that aging rats, too, vary much more than do young rats. Some old rats are as quick-witted as the smartest of young rats; others, for reasons related to brain deterioration, show their age.

*"I don't recall."*

Seventy-nine-year-old Ronald Reagan's repeated answer when testifying at the trial of his adviser John Poindexter

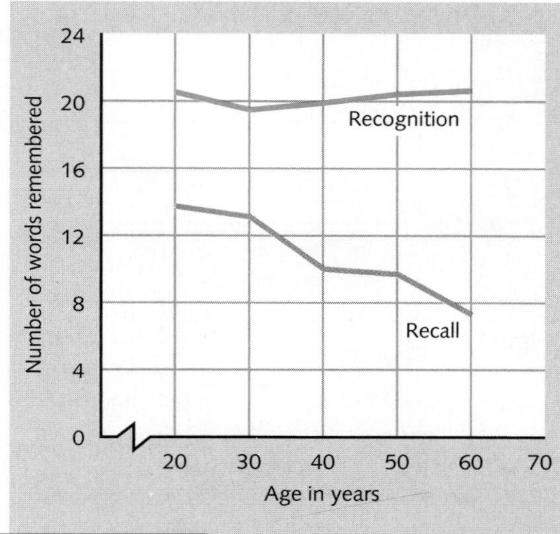


**Figure 4–11**

**Recall and Recognition in Adulthood** *In this experiment, the ability to* recall *new information declined during early and middle adulthood but the ability to* recognize *new information did not. (From Schonfield & Robertson, 1966.)*

**Still Answering the Call to Serve** *At the age of 100, Jim Grote, shown here with his collection of firefighting mementos, was still actively employed as a fire marshal, inspecting buildings and investigating fires for the town of Chester, Connecticut. As Grote demonstrates, activities and interests contribute to intellectual stability in the later years.*

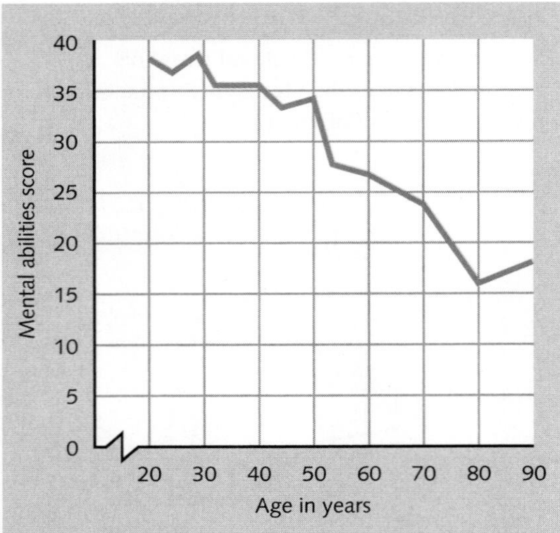


**Figure 4–12**

**Cross-Sectional Comparison of Intelligence**
*On intelligence tests older adults get fewer questions correct than younger adults. But see Figure 4–13. (From Geiwitz, 1980.)*

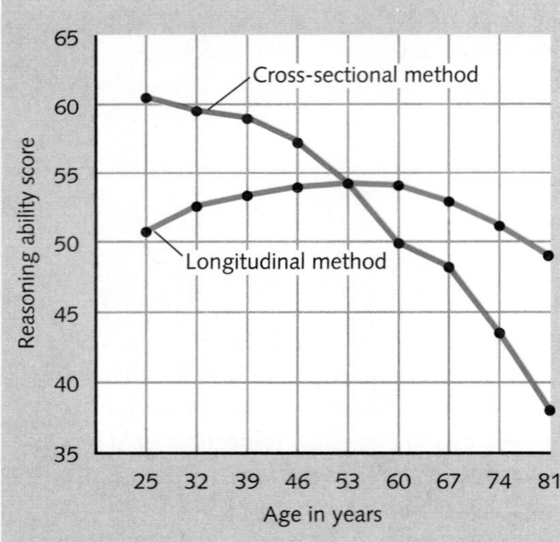


**Figure 4–13**

**Cross-Sectional Versus Longitudinal Methods**
*In this test of one type of verbal intelligence (inductive reasoning), the cross-sectional method produced declining scores with age. The longitudinal method (in which the same people were retested over a period of years) produced a slight rise in scores well into adulthood. (Adapted from Schaie, 1994.)*

Adults' learning skills can be seen in classrooms. In recent years, more and more adults have returned to school and turned to leisure education programs. By 1990, 41 percent of American college students were age 25 and older (Bureau of the Census, 1993). Despite occasional difficulties in adjusting to the demands of course work and testing, most older students do better than the typical 18-year-old, perhaps because they have clearer goals (Badenhoop & Johansen, 1980).

## Aging and Intelligence

What happens to our broader intellectual powers as we age? Do they gradually decline, as does our ability to recall new material? Or do they remain constant, as does our ability to recognize meaningful material? The evolving answer to this question makes an interesting research story that illustrates psychology's self-correcting process (Woodruff-Pak, 1989).

**Phase I: Cross-Sectional Evidence for Intellectual Decline** In **cross-sectional studies**, researchers test people of various ages at the same time. When giving intelligence tests to representative samples of people, researchers consistently find that older adults give fewer correct answers than do younger adults (Figure 4–12). David Wechsler (1972), creator of the most widely used adult intelligence test, therefore concluded that "the decline of mental ability with age is part of the general [aging] process of the organism as a whole."

Until the 1950s, this rather dismal view of mental decline was unchallenged. Many executives established mandatory retirement policies, assuming their companies would benefit by replacing aging workers with younger, presumably more capable, employees. As everyone "knew," you couldn't teach an old dog new tricks.

**Phase II: Longitudinal Evidence for Intellectual Stability** Colleges began giving intelligence tests to entering students about 1920, making it possible to retest older people who had taken an intelligence test years earlier. Several psychologists saw their chance to study intelligence **longitudinally**, by retesting the same people over a period of years. What they expected to find was the usual decrease in intelligence after about age 30 (Schaie & Geiwitz, 1982). What they actually found was a surprise: Until late in life, intelligence remained stable (Figure 4–13). On some tests, it even increased.

How then are we to account for the findings from the cross-sectional studies? In retrospect, researchers saw the problem. When a cross-sectional study compares 70- and 30-year-olds, it compares people not only of two different ages but of two different eras. It compares generally less educated people (born, say, in the early 1900s) with more educated people (born after 1950), people raised in large families with people raised in smaller families, people growing up in less affluent families with people raised in more affluent families.

According to this more optimistic view, the myth that intelligence sharply declines with age is laid to rest. As everyone "knows," given good health you're never too old to learn. At age 70, John Rock developed the birth control pill. At age 78, Grandma Moses took up painting and was still painting after age 100. At age 81—and 17 years from the end of his college football coaching career—Amos Alozo Stagg was named coach of the year. At age 89, architect Frank Lloyd Wright designed New York City's Guggenheim Museum. Moreover, when people have kept alive their expertise—typing, playing chess, playing the piano—their abilities often remain intact well into their eighties (Schaie, 1987). As psychologist David Krech (1978) said, "He who lives by his wits, dies with his wits."

**Phase III: It All Depends** But the controversy continues. For one thing, longitudinal studies have their own pitfalls. Those who survive to the end of longitudinal studies may be bright, healthy people whose intelligence is least likely to decline. If so, such studies underestimate the average decline in intelligence.

Research is further complicated by the finding that intelligence is not a single trait (see Chapter 11). Intelligence tests that assess speed of thinking may place older adults at a disadvantage because of their slower neural mechanisms for processing information. But slower need not mean less intelligent. Given other tests that assess general vocabulary, knowledge, and ability to integrate information, older adults generally hold their own. Older Canadians surpass younger Canadians at answering questions such as, "Which province was once called New Caledonia?" (Told the right answer on missed questions, younger Canadians, though, have the edge a week later at recalling these answers [Craik, 1986].)

German researcher Paul Baltes (1993) has developed "wisdom" tests that assess traits such as expertise and sound judgment on important matters of life. Their results suggest that older adults more than hold their own on such tests. As we age, our neural networks store more and more of the decisions we've made, and their associated results. This accumulation of experience enables us to generalize when making future decisions (Kosslyn & Koenig, 1992). Thus, despite 30-year-olds' quick-thinking smarts, we usually select older people to be president of the company, the college, or the country. Age is sage. Other researchers note that with age there also comes the wisdom to reflect with greater detachment about the limits of one's knowing and the unpredictability of life (Birren & Fisher, 1990). This helps account for the consistent finding that religious commitment tends to increase with age (Benson, 1992).

*"In youth we learn, in age we understand."*
Marie von Ebner-Eschenbach
*Aphorisms*, 1883

So, whether intelligence increases or decreases with age depends on what type of intellectual performance we measure. **Crystallized intelligence**—one's accumulated knowledge as reflected in vocabulary and analogies tests—*increases* up to old age. **Fluid intelligence**—one's ability to reason speedily and abstractly, as when solving novel logic problems—*decreases* with age (Cattell, 1963; Horn, 1982). We can see this pattern in the intelligence scores of a national sample of adults. After adjusting for education, verbal scores (reflecting crystallized intelligence) held relatively steady from ages 20 to 74, while nonverbal, puzzle-solving intelligence declined (Figure 4–14).

**Figure 4–14**

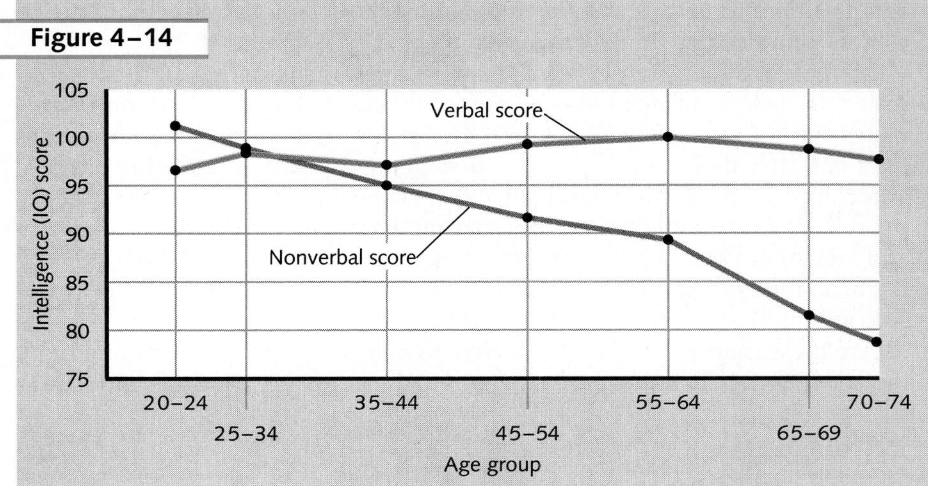


**IQ Scores and Age** *After adjustments for education, verbal intelligence scores hold steady with age, while nonverbal intelligence scores decline. (IQ scores from standardization sample of the Wechsler Adult Intelligence Scale, based on norms for 25- to 34-year-olds.) (Adapted from Kaufman & others, 1989.)*

This helps explain why mathematicians and scientists produce much of their most creative work during their late twenties or early thirties, while those in literature, history, and philosophy tend to produce their best work later—in their forties, fifties, and beyond, after accumulating more knowledge (Simonton, 1988, 1990). History bears out this finding. For example, poets reach their peak output earlier than prose authors (who need a deeper knowledge reservoir)—a finding observed in every major literary tradition, for both living and dead languages. So, whether intellectual performance increases or decreases with age depends on how we assess it. And whether a worker's performance improves, declines, or is steady with age may depend on the extent to which the job requires continued learning of new technology and procedures (Park, 1992).

## Social Changes

**Resetting the Social Clock** *To meet the demands of a changing economy, many adults have returned to school to acquire new skills. The social clock once "dictated" that college graduation should occur between ages 21 and 23. For this proud graduate, standard time is no longer the only setting.*

Many differences between younger and older adults are created not by the physical and cognitive changes that accompany aging but by life events associated with family relationships and work. A new job means new relationships, new expectations, and new demands. Marriage brings the joy of intimacy and the stress of merging your life with another's. The birth of a child introduces responsibilities and significantly alters your life focus. The death of a loved one creates a sense of irreplaceable loss and a need to reaffirm your own life. Do these normal events of adult life shape a predictable sequence of life changes?

### Adulthood's Ages and Stages

Some psychologists describe the human journey through adulthood by intensively studying small samples of people. Daniel Levinson and others (1978, 1986) conducted lengthy interviews with 85 successful, middle-aged men and women. Based partly on their recollections, Levinson concluded that adults progress through periods of stability punctuated by times of upheaval and change. For example, he believes that as people enter their forties, they undergo a "midlife transition" to middle adulthood, which for many is a crisis, a time of great struggle or even of feeling struck down by life. They give up their dreams of fame and fortune (or the illusion that such bring happiness) and question their work and family commitments. The result, says Levinson, is often turmoil and despair. Fortyish people realize they no longer are starting out but rather are drawing closer to the end. When this painful growth period concludes at about age 45, they again settle into new or deepened attachments, set about completing their careers, and become more compassionate and reflective.

Many researchers are skeptical about such efforts to define adult life as a series of neatly packaged stages, especially stages based merely on interviews with a select few people. To generalize from their career-oriented lives or to use their "midlife crises" to explain or justify renouncing old relationships is misleading (Gilligan, 1982). The fact—from large samples of people—is that job dissatisfaction, marital dissatisfaction, divorce, anxiety, and suicide do *not* surge during the early forties (Hunter & Sundel, 1989). Divorce, for example, is most common among those in their twenties, suicide among those in their seventies and eighties.

*"Midway in the journey of our life I found myself in a dark wood, for the straight way was lost."*

Dante
*The Divine Comedy*, 1300–1321

Are these markers of crisis too crude to detect a more subtle midlife turmoil? National Institute of Aging researchers Robert McCrae and Paul

Costa (1990) gave 350 men between the ages of 30 and 60 a "Midlife Crisis Scale," assessing sense of meaninglessness and mortality, job and family dissatisfaction, and inner turmoil and confusion. They could find "no evidence at all" that such concerns peak at midlife. Surprised, they gave their scale to a new group of 300 men and supplemented it with a measure of emotional instability, which they gave to nearly 10,000 men and women. "The results were an exact reconfirmation: There was not the slightest evidence" that distress peaks anywhere in the midlife age range (Figure 4–15).

There is another reason skeptics question age-linked stage theories. The **social clock**—the cultural prescription of "the right time" to leave home, get a job, marry, have children, and retire—varies from culture to culture and era to era. In Jordan, 40 percent of brides are in their teens; in Hong Kong, only 3 percent are (United Nations, 1992). In Western Europe, fewer than 10 percent of men over 65 remain in the work force as do 16 percent in the United States; but 36 percent remain in the work force in Japan, and 69 percent in Mexico (Davies & others, 1991). In contemporary Western nations, the 1950s sequence from student to worker to wife to at-home mom to older worker has loosened. Modern women occupy these roles in any order or all at once. Given variations in the social clock and individual experience, the stage theory critics suspect any proposed timetable of adult ages and stages.

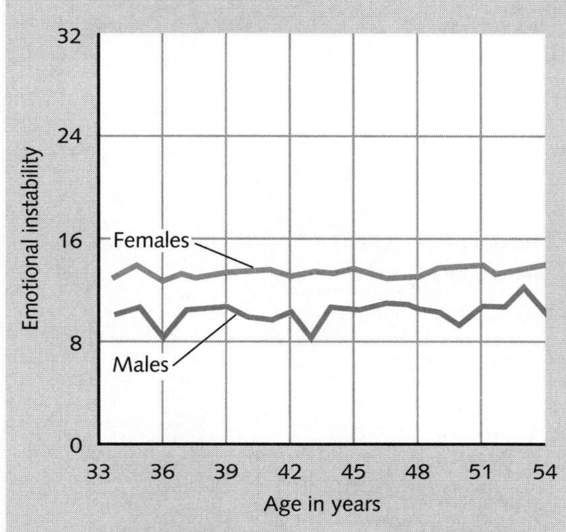


**Figure 4–15**

**Early Forties Midlife Crises?** *Among 10,000 people responding to a national health survey, there was no early forties increase in emotional instability ("neuroticism") scores. (From McCrae & Costa, 1990.)*

### Life Events and Chance Encounters

More important than one's chronological age are life events. Marriage, parenthood, vocational changes, divorce, nest-emptying, relocation, and retirement mark transitions to new life stages whenever they occur—and increasingly they are occurring at unpredictable ages. The social clock is still ticking, but people feel freer to be out of sync with it.

Even chance encounters and events can have lasting significance, deflecting us down one road rather than another (Bandura, 1982). In the 1950s, actress Nancy Davis might never have met her future husband had she not, through a mix-up, begun to receive Communist party mailings intended for another woman of the same name. During those early Cold War days of Hollywood blacklisting, Davis feared her career might be jeopardized by this mistaken identity. She went to see the president of the Screen Actors Guild, Ronald Reagan, and the rest is history (Reagan & Libby, 1980). Given the impact of chance encounters, it is small wonder that researcher Bernice Neugarten (1979, 1980) concludes that "adults change far more, and far less predictably, than the oversimplified stage theories suggest."

The influence of chance encounters on romantic attraction is implied by a recent study of identical twins and their spouses. Twins, especially identical twins, make similar choices of friends, clothes, vacations, jobs, and so on. So, if your identical twin became engaged to someone, wouldn't you (being in so many ways the same as your twin) expect to feel attracted to this person? Surprisingly, only half the identical twins recalled really liking their co-twin's selection, and only 5 percent said "I could have fallen for my twin's fiancée." Researchers David Lykken and Auke Tellegen (1993) surmise that romantic love is rather like ducklings' imprinting: Given repeated exposure to someone after childhood, one may form a bond (infatuation) with almost any available person who has a roughly similar background and level of attractiveness and who reciprocates one's affections.

## Adulthood's Commitments

Two basic aspects of our lives do, however, dominate adulthood. Erik Erikson called them *intimacy* (forming close relationships) and *generativity* (being productive and supporting future generations). Researchers have chosen various terms—*affiliation* and *achievement*, *attachment* and *productivity*, *commitment* and *competence*. But Sigmund Freud (1935) put it most simply: The healthy adult, he said, is one who can *love* and *work*. For most adults, love centers on family commitments toward partner, parents, and children. Work encompasses our productive activities, whether for pay or not.

*"One can live magnificently in this world if one knows how to work and how to love."*

Leo Tolstoy, 1856

**Love** Across time and place, human societies have nearly always included a relatively monogamous bond between men and women and a bond between parents and their children. We flirt, fall in love, and marry—one person at a time. "Pair-bonding is a trademark of the human animal," notes anthropologist Helen Fisher (1993). The arrangement makes biological sense. Parents who cooperated to nurture their children to maturity were more likely to pass their genes along to posterity than parents who didn't.

The bond of love is most satisfying and enduring when marked by a similarity of interests and values, a sharing of emotional and material support, and intimate self-disclosure (see Chapter 18). Marriage bonds are usually lasting when couples also marry after age 20 and are well-educated. Compared with their counterparts of 30 years ago, people in Western countries *are* better educated and marrying later. In the United States, for example, the average man isn't marrying until age 26 (up from 23 in 1960) and the average woman until age 24 (up from 20 in 1960).

Ironically, people are nevertheless divorcing more. When marrying, whether for the first time or the second, nearly everyone hopes for a satisfying, enduring bond. Yet marriages today are twice as likely to end in divorce as they were in 1960. To judge from the divorce rate—roughly 40 percent of Canadian marriages and half of U.S. marriages end in divorce—marriage has become a union that often defies management. In Europe, divorce is nearly as common, after increasing 400 percent since 1960 (Inglehart, 1990).

Although rocked by increased divorce and cohabitation (page 417), the institution of marriage endures. More than 9 in 10 adults marry. Of those who divorce, 75 percent remarry—and their second marriages are virtually as happy as the average first marriage (Vemer & others, 1989). Although the relatively few people who feel trapped in an unhappy marriage typically feel miserable, most married Europeans and North Americans generally feel happier than those unmarried, especially when compared with others who are separated and divorced (Inglehart, 1990). In the United States, for example, fewer than 25 percent of unmarried adults, but nearly 40 percent of married adults, have reported being "very happy" (Lee & others, 1991).

Marriages that last are not always devoid of conflict. Some couples fight but also shower one another with affection afterwards. Other couples never raise their voices yet also seldom praise or nuzzle. Both styles can last. After observing the interactions of 2000 couples, John Gottman (1994) reports a better indicator of likely marital success: at least a 5 to 1 ratio of positive to negative interactions. Stable marriages provide five times more smiling, touching, complimenting, and laughing than sarcasm, criticism, and insults. And if you want to predict which newlyweds will stay together, don't pay attention to how passionately they are in love. The couples who make it are more often those who restrain the number of putdowns that, unchecked, can take over a relationship (Notarius & Markman, 1993). To prevent a cancerous negativity, successful couples learn to fight fair (to state feelings without insulting) and to steer conflict away from chaos with comments like "I know it's not your fault" or "Be quiet for a moment and listen."

Often, love bears children. The most enduring of life changes, having a child, is for most people a happy event. As children begin to absorb time, money, and emotional energy, however, satisfaction with the marriage itself often declines. This is especially so among those employed women who, more than they expected, bear the traditional burden of increased chores at home (Belsky & others, 1986; Hackel & Ruble, 1992).

Another significant event in family life happens when children leave home. If you have left home, consider your parents' experience: Did they suffer an "empty nest syndrome"—a feeling of distress focusing on a loss of purpose and relationship? Or did your parents discover renewed freedom, relaxation, and satisfaction with their own relationship?

Seven national surveys reveal that the empty nest is for most people a happy place (Adelmann & others, 1989; Glenn, 1975). Compared with middle-aged women who still have children at home, those whose nest has emptied report greater happiness and greater enjoyment of their marriage. Many parents therefore experience what sociologists Lynn White and John Edwards (1990) call a "post-launch honeymoon," especially if they maintain close relationships with their children. One such mother, 50-year-old Phoebe, explains: "Our family is very close. When my two sons come home I can't wait till they get here, I stay excited throughout their stay, and I'm in tears after they leave. Yet within a day or two we're back to enjoying our freedom—none of the aggravations of kids in the house, and our time is ours!" Bernice Neugarten (1974) would say that Phoebe speaks for many:

> Just as the major problem of middle-aged women is not the menopause, it is also not the empty nest. Most women are glad to see their children grow up, leave home, marry, and have their careers. The notion that they mourn the loss of their reproductive ability and their mother role does not seem to fit modern reality. No matter what the stereotypes tell us, it is not the way women talk when you listen.

**Work** For adults, a large part of the answer to "Who are you?" is the answer to "What do you do?" For most, to feel productive and competent is to raise children and to undertake a career.

Because it often takes time for people to settle on an occupation and because the impact of chance encounters can be very great, career choices are hard to predict. During the first 2 years of college, most students cannot predict their later career path. Most shift from their initially intended majors while in college, many find their postcollege employment in fields not directly related to their majors, and most will change careers (Rothstein, 1980). To many career counselors, this unpredictability means that the best education is not a narrow vocational training, but rather a broad liberal education, an education that fosters "the critical qualities of mind and the durable qualities of character that will serve [people] in circumstances we cannot now even predict" (Gardner, 1984).

Does work, including a career, indeed contribute to fulfillment, as Freud supposed? One approach to answering this question has been to compare the roughly equal numbers of North American women who are or are not

**Job Satisfaction and Life Satisfaction** *Work provides people with a sense of identity and competence and opportunities for accomplishment. Perhaps this is why a challenging and interesting occupation enhances people's happiness.*

Drawing by M. Stevens; ©1989 The New Yorker Magazine, Inc.

employed. From their studies at the Wellesley College Center for Research on Women, Grace Baruch and Rosaline Barnett (1986) conclude that what matters is not which roles a woman occupies—as paid worker, wife, and/or mother—but the quality of her experience in those roles. Happiness is having work that fits your interests and provides a sense of competence and accomplishment; having a partner who is a close, supportive companion and who sees you as special; and/or having loving children whom you like and feel proud of.

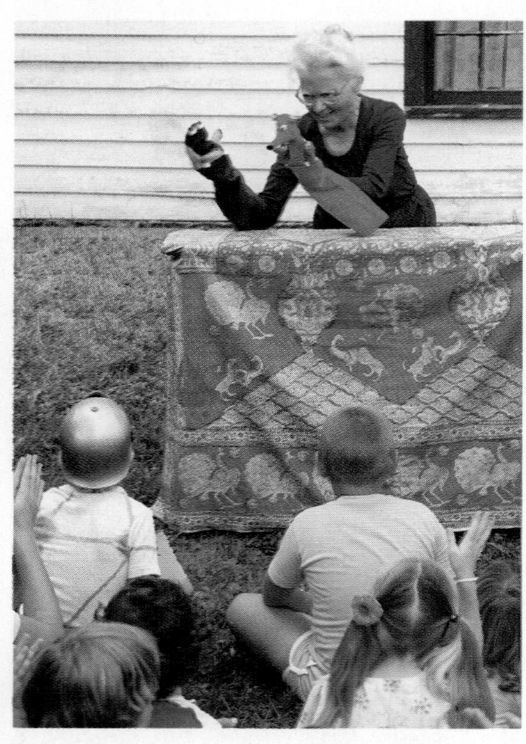

**Time for Fun** *With the tasks of the earlier adult years behind them, many older adults have more time to enjoy pursuing their personal interests. No wonder their satisfaction with life usually remains high, especially if they are healthy and active.*

### Well-Being Across the Life Span

Researchers have compared the sense of well-being among young and old. Who do you suppose are the happiest? The carefree youth? The up-and-coming young adults? The successful and secure middle-aged? Or those enjoying the leisure of retired life? The answer may surprise you.

To live is to grow older, which means that we all can look backward with satisfaction or sorrow, and forward with hope or dread. People see adolescents as buffeted by mood swings and insecurity, parental power and peer pressures, identity confusion and career worries. In later life, income shrinks, work is taken away, the body deteriorates, recall fades, energy wanes, family members and friends die or move away, and the great enemy, death, looms ever closer. Small wonder that many presume the teen and over-65 years to be the worst of times (Freedman, 1978).

But they are not. People of all ages report similar feelings of happiness and satisfaction with life. Individuals vary, but more than 100 studies reveal that less than 1 percent of their variation in well-being relates to age (Stock & others, 1983). Ronald Inglehart (1990) confirmed this when he amassed interviews conducted during the 1980s with representative samples of nearly 170,000 people in 16 nations. As Figure 4–16 illustrates, age differences in life satisfaction are trivial.

Whatever the explanation—reduced stress, lowered aspirations, satisfaction over accomplishments, newfound sources of pleasure—the bottom line is this: Older people report as much happiness and satisfaction with life as younger people do. Given that growing older is one sure consequence of living, an outcome most of us prefer to its alternative, we can all take comfort in this finding.

The astonishing stability of well-being across the life span obscures some interesting age-related emotional differences. As the years go by, feelings mellow (Costa & others, 1987; Diener & others, 1986). Highs become less high, lows less low. Thus, although the *average* feeling level may remain stable, with age we find ourselves less often feeling excited, intensely proud, and on top of the world, but also less often depressed. Compliments provoke less elation and criticisms less despair as both become merely additional feedback atop a mountain of accumulated praise and blame. Psychologists Mihaly Csikszentmihalyi and Reed Larson (1984) mapped people's emotional terrain by periodically signaling them with electronic beepers to report their current activities and feelings. They found that teenagers typically come down from elation or up from gloom in less than an hour. Adult moods are less extreme but more enduring. For most people, old age offers less intense joy but greater contentment. As we age, life's emotional roller coaster provides a smoother ride.

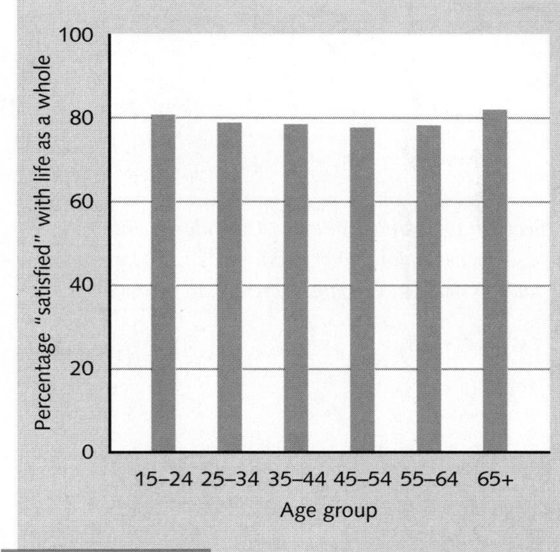


**Figure 4–16**

**Age and Life Satisfaction** *Does well-being align itself with any particular age group? Multinational surveys reveal that age differences in life satisfaction (and happiness) are trivial. (Data from Inglehart, 1990.)*

## Death and Dying

Most of us will suffer and cope with the deaths of relatives and friends. Usually, the most difficult separation is from one's spouse—a loss suffered by five times more women than men. Grief is especially severe when the death of a loved one comes suddenly and before its expected time on the social clock. The accidental death of a child or the sudden illness that claims a 45-year-old spouse may trigger a year or more of mourning flooded with memories, eventually subsiding to a mild depression that sometimes continues for several years (Lehman & others, 1987). Because AIDS so often strikes down people in midlife and younger, it has left countless family members and friends in a state of intense grief.

The normal range of reactions to a loved one's death is wider than most people suppose. Some cultures encourage public weeping and wailing, others hide grief. Within any culture some individuals grieve more intensely and openly. Contrary to a popular myth, those who express the strongest grief immediately do not resolve their grief more quickly (Wortman & Silver, 1989).

Those who suffer a terminal illness live with the awareness of their impending death. In analyzing how people cope with the prospect of death, the stage theorists have once again arrived ahead of us. From her interviews with dying patients, Elisabeth Kübler-Ross (1969) proposed that the terminally ill pass through a sequence of five stages: *denial* of the terminal condition; *anger* and resentment ("Why me?"); *bargaining* with God (or physicians) for more time; *depression* stemming from the impending loss of everything and everyone; and, finally, peaceful *acceptance* of one's fate. Others propose similar stages for coping with a sudden physical impairment—disbelief, protest, depression, recovery (Fitzgerald, 1970).

*"Do not go gentle into that good night,*
*Old age should burn and rave at close of day;*
*Rage, rage against the dying of the light."*

Dylan Thomas
"Do Not Go Gentle into That Good Night," 1952, a poem written to his father as he lay dying peacefully

Critics question the generality of all such stages, stressing that each person's experience is unique. Real people, they say, don't fit into these neat boxes. Moreover, they argue, the simplified stages ignore many important factors—for example, that people who are old usually view death with minimal fear and resentment (Wass & others, 1978–1979). Critics also voice concern about the eagerness with which courses and books have popularized the death-and-dying formula. The danger, they fear, is that rather than having their feelings respected, dying people may be analyzed or manipulated in terms of the stereotyped stages: "She's just going through the anger stage."

*"How many of us older persons have really been . . . prepared for the second half of life, for old age, death and eternity?"*

Carl Jung
*Modern Man in Search of a Soul*, 1933

Nevertheless, the death-education movement has enabled us to deal more openly and humanely with death and grief. A growing number of individuals are aided by **hospice** organizations, whose staff and volunteers work in special facilities and in people's homes to support and comfort the terminally ill and their families. Hospice aims to help make dying a meaningful time "when good-byes can be said, when broken relationships can be healed, when forgiveness can be given or received" (Magno, 1989).

*Scottish tombstone epitaph: "Consider, friend, as you pass by, as you are now, so once was I. As I am now, you too shall be. Prepare, therefore, to follow me."*

We can be grateful for the waning of death-denying attitudes. Facing death with dignity and openness helps people complete the life cycle with a sense of life's meaningfulness and unity—the sense that their existence has been good and that life and death are parts of an ongoing cycle. Although death may be unwelcome, life itself can be affirmed even at death. This is especially so for people who review their lives not with despair but with what Erik Erikson called a sense of *integrity*—a feeling that one's life has been meaningful and worthwhile.

## Summing Up

During early life, we sail a narrow channel, constrained by biological maturation. As the years pass, the channel widens, allowing us to diverge more and more. By adulthood, age no longer neatly predicts a person's life experience and traits. Yet in some ways our bodies, minds, and relationships still undergo predictable changes. As long as we live, we adapt.

**Physical Changes** The barely perceptible physical declines of early adulthood begin to accelerate during middle adulthood. For women, a significant physical change of adult life is menopause, which generally seems to be a smooth rather than rough transition. After 65, perceptual acuity, strength, and stamina decline, but short-term ailments are fewer. Neural processes slow, but the brain remains healthy, except for those who suffer brain disease, such as the progressive deterioration of Alzheimer's disease.

**Cognitive Changes** As the years pass, recognition memory remains strong, although recall begins to decline, especially for meaningless information. Research on how intelligence changes with age has progressed through several phases: cross-sectional studies suggesting a steady intellectual decline after early adulthood; longitudinal studies suggesting intellectual stability until very late in life; and today's view that fluid intelligence declines in later life, but crystallized intelligence does not.

**Social Changes** From close study of small samples of individuals, some theorists maintain that adults pass through an orderly sequence of life stages. Daniel Levinson contends that moving from one stage to the next entails recurring times of crisis, such as the early-forties time of transition to midlife. But people are not so predictable. Not only life events involving love and work but also even chance occurrences influence adult life in unanticipated ways. Since 1960, marriage has been in decline, as reflected in later marriages, increased cohabitation, and doubled divorce rates.

Although few people grow old gratefully, most age gracefully, retaining a sense of well-being throughout life. Those who live to old age must, however, cope with the deaths of friends and family members and with the prospect of their own deaths.

## Reflections on Life-Span Development

*We conclude our womb-to-tomb journey where we began in Chapter 3, with two of developmental psychology's big questions: Does life unfold through predictable stages? And as we develop do our traits typically change or remain consistent?*

Our survey of developmental psychology began in Chapter 3 by identifying three pervasive issues: (1) whether development is steered more by genes or experience; (2) whether development is a gradual, continuous process or a discrete series of stages; and (3) whether the life span is characterized more by stability over time or by change. We noted there how heredity and environment jointly affect human development. Let's now take stock of current thinking on the latter two issues.

### Continuity and Stages

We have considered several stage theorists: Jean Piaget on cognitive development, Lawrence Kohlberg on moral development, and Erik Erikson and Daniel Levinson on psychosocial development. And we have seen their stage theories criticized: Young children have some abilities that Piaget attributed to later stages. Kohlberg assumed a worldview characteristic of educated males in individualistic cultures. The ideas of Erikson and Levinson are contradicted by research showing that adult life does not progress through a fixed, predictable series of steps.

Although research casts doubt on the idea that life proceeds through neatly defined, age-linked stages, the concept of stage remains useful. There are spurts of brain growth during childhood and puberty that correspond roughly to Piaget's stages (Thatcher & others, 1987). And stage theories contribute a developmental perspective on the whole life span. They show the order in which abilities develop and suggest how people of one age think and act differently when they arrive at a later age.

### Stability and Change

This leads us to the final question: Over time, are people's personalities and social skills consistent, or do they change? If reunited with a long-lost grade-school friend, would you instantly recognize that "it's the same old Andy"? Or is a person during one period of life likely to seem like a different person at a later period?

Obviously, either extreme is false: If there were no stability, we could not hope that the person we marry today would be the same person a decade later, or that the promising management trainee would remain suited for management. If there were no change, all juvenile delinquents would become career criminals; all alcoholics would drink themselves into the grave; life would be one long rut.

Still, the issue is real: Do infants' traits predict their childhood characteristics? Is the troubled adolescent likely to have a rocky adulthood? Will the assertive young woman still be noticeably assertive at age 60? Researchers who follow lives through time are debating the extent to which our past reaches into our future.

A generation ago, most psychologists and lay people assumed that once genes and early experience form our personalities, they remain set for life.

*"In most of us, by the age of thirty, the character has set like plaster, and will never soften again."*

William James
*Principles of Psychology*, 1890

Then, during the 1960s and 1970s, new findings suggested that throughout much of life personality evolves. For example, Jean Macfarlane (1964) followed 166 people from babyhood to age 30 and discovered that "many of our most mature and competent adults had severely troubled and confusing childhoods and adolescences." Often, the unhappy, rebellious adolescent became a stable, successful, happy adult. Alexander Thomas and Stella Chess (1986) similarly followed 133 people from infancy to early adulthood and found that the troubled children among them usually became stable adults.

Some researchers have found that even adults frequently undergo surprising and unpredictable changes. Reflecting on her studies of such changes during the life cycle, Bernice Neugarten (1980) reported that "the primary consistency we have found is a lack of consistency." After following college students from age 20 to 42, Susan Krauss Whitbourne and her colleagues (1992) were similarly impressed by how much more self-confident they had become. Many a professor, too, has been amazed at the 20-year-old goof-offs who mature into 40-year-old business and cultural leaders.

So, shall we conclude that later experience copies over early experience, erasing the voices of the past? If so, we can counsel parents of difficult babies and teenagers to be patient and hopeful. We can reassure the depressed, lonely young adult that development never ends: The struggles of the present may lay the base for a happier future.

On the other hand, much recent research reveals a consistency to personality. After painstakingly comparing people in their forties with ratings of the same people as junior high students, Jack Block (1981) concluded that there is an underlying stability to our basic social and emotional style. The troubled adolescent often turned out better than we would have guessed, but it was usually a cheerful teenager who became the very cheerful 40-year-old.

Similarly, Avshalom Caspi and his colleagues (1987) found that, compared with milder-mannered boys, 9-year-old boys with explosive temper tantrums are more likely as adults to have trouble keeping good jobs and are twice as likely to have divorced by age 40. Leonard Eron (1987) and others found that the most physically aggressive 8-year-olds tended to become the most aggressive (and potentially violent) 30-year-olds (Figure 4–17). And David Magnusson and L. R. Bergman (1990) found that hyperaggressive Swedish 13-year-olds often developed adult records of crime and alcohol abuse.

Once people reach adulthood, their dispositions become even more stable. From their periodic retesting of Boston and Baltimore area adults, Robert McCrae and Paul Costa (1982) concluded, "For the great majority of people, the self-concept at age 30 is a good guide to personality at age 80." During the adult years, people's outgoingness, emotional stability, openness, agreeableness, and conscientiousness are persistent (Conley, 1985; Costa & McCrae, 1993; Finn, 1986). Part of our consistency comes from our selecting environments and marrying people who help sustain our traits (Caspi & Herbener, 1990). Outgoing people, for instance, are more likely to seek social encounters that nourish their outgoingness and to marry sociable people.

So, should we conclude that throughout life we change, but our basic social and emotional styles become more stable as we grow older? Whatever their apparent disagreements, researchers do agree that:

Figure 4–17

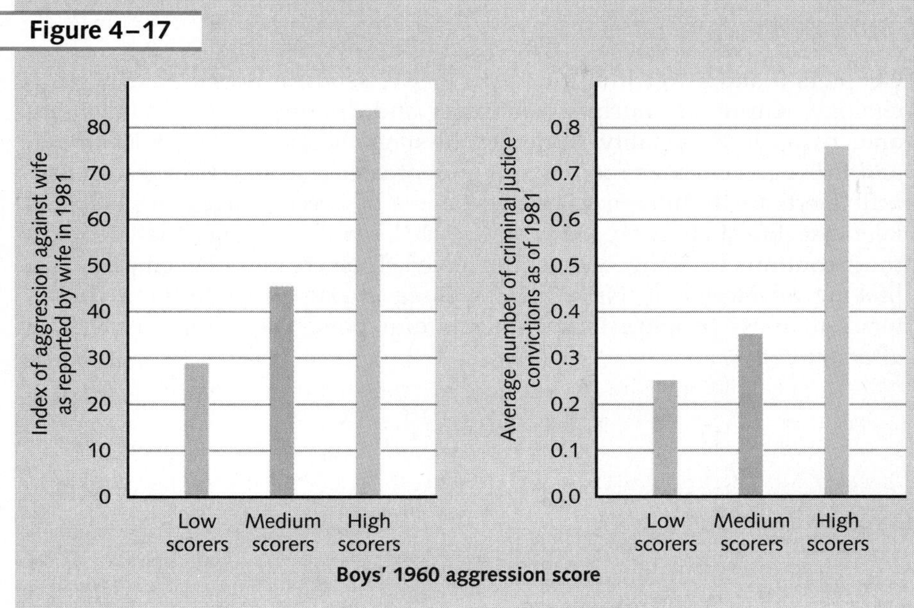


**The Stability of Aggressiveness** *Leonard Eron and Rowell Huesmann (1984) found that the aggressiveness displayed by 8-year-old boys (low, medium, or high) helped predict their aggressiveness 2 decades later, as revealed by their wives' reports and by their criminal convictions.*

1. The first 2 years of life provide a poor basis for predicting a person's eventual traits. As people grow older, predictability increases. There is less stability from age 14 to 18 than from 18 to 22 (Stein & others, 1986) and less stability from 20 to 30 than from 30 to 40 (Costa & McCrae, 1989).
2. The greater the span of years between assessments, the greater the likelihood that personality will have changed. From assessing the traits of 25-year-olds, psychologists can better predict their personalities as 26-year-olds than as 40-year-olds (Schuerger & others, 1989).
3. Some characteristics, such as temperament, are more stable than others, such as social attitudes (Moss & Susman, 1980). But attitudes, too, become more stable with age (Krosnick & Alwin, 1989).
4. In some ways, we all change with age. Most shy, fearful toddlers begin opening up by age 4, and during adulthood most of us mellow. In the years after college, most people become calmer and quieter (Costa & McCrae, 1989). Such changes can occur without changing a person's position *relative* to others of the same age. The hard-driving young adult may mellow by later life yet still be a relatively hard-driving senior citizen.

*"At 70, I would say the advantage is that you take life more calmly. You know that 'this, too, shall pass!'"*
Eleanor Roosevelt, 1954

Finally, we should remember that life contains *both* stability and change. Stability enables us to depend on others. It motivates our concern for children's healthy formation. And it provides our identity. Change motivates our concerns about present influences. It sustains our hope for a brighter future when we are depressed. And it enables us to adapt and grow with experience.

## Summing Up

Chapters 3 and 4 touch on three pervasive issues in developmental psychology: nature and nurture, continuity and discrete stages, and stability and change in personality. Although the stage theories of Piaget, Kohlberg, and Erikson have been modified in light of later research, each theory usefully alerts us to differences among people of different ages and helps us keep the life-span perspective in view. Research findings that people's traits continue to change in later life have helped create a new emphasis on lifelong development. Nevertheless, there is also an underlying consistency to most people's temperaments and personality traits, especially after age 30.

## Terms and Concepts to Remember

### Adolescence

**adolescence** The transition period from childhood to adulthood, extending from puberty to independence.

**puberty** The time of sexual maturation, when one first becomes capable of reproducing.

**primary sex characteristics** The body structures (ovaries and testes) that make sexual reproduction possible.

**secondary sex characteristics** Nonreproductive sexual characteristics, such as female breasts and hips, male voice quality, and body hair.

**menarche** [meh-NAR-key] The first menstrual period.

**identity** One's sense of self; according to Erikson, the adolescent's task is to solidify a sense of self by testing and integrating various roles.

**intimacy** In Erikson's theory, the ability to form close, loving relationships; a primary developmental task in late adolescence and early adulthood.

### Adulthood

**menopause** The time of natural cessation of menstruation; also refers to the biological changes experienced during a woman's years of declining ability to reproduce.

**Alzheimer's disease** A progressive and irreversible brain disorder characterized by gradual deterioration of memory, reasoning, language, and, finally, physical functioning.

**cross-sectional study** A study in which people of different ages are tested or observed at the same point in time.

**longitudinal study** Research in which the same people are restudied and retested over a long time period.

**crystallized intelligence** One's accumulated knowledge and verbal skills; tends to increase with age.

**fluid intelligence** One's ability to reason speedily and abstractly; tends to decrease during late adulthood.

**social clock** The culturally preferred timing of social events such as marriage, parenthood, and retirement.

**hospice** An organization whose largely volunteer staff provides support for dying people and their families either in special facilities or in people's own homes.

## Critical Thinking Exercise

Now that you have read and reviewed Chapter 4, take your learning a step further by testing your critical thinking skills on the following psychological reasoning exercise.

Since he retired as a college professor 5 years ago, 65-year-old Bentley has suffered numerous health problems, including high blood pressure, chest pains, and muscle tremors. Once very active physically, Bentley has not been able to take his daily 30-minute jog for the past 3 years. For the first time in his life Bentley takes several prescription drugs daily, including one that controls his muscle tremors by blocking the neurotransmitter acetylcholine. Bentley's biggest complaint, however, is that he is bored and misses the intellectual stimulation of his former students and colleagues.

Bentley's daughter Mary recently read a magazine article on Alzheimer's disease and is worried that something may be seriously wrong with her father's mind. For a man who once prided himself on his infallible memory and the quickness of his thinking, Bentley's memory now occasionally falters, and his reactions are slower. Fearing that her father may be suffering from Alzheimer's disease, Mary decides to conduct an experiment. Pretending that she is stumped while working on a "brain teaser," she asks her father to help her identify the next letter in the series *d f i m r x e*. When Bentley becomes flustered and cannot quickly come up with the answer, Mary is crestfallen, certain that her father is in the early stages of a devastating disease.

1. State Mary's argument in your own words.
2. Describe the evidence on which Mary has based her argument.
3. State three reasons why Mary's evidence is not strong enough to support her argument.

Check your progress on becoming a critical thinker by comparing your answers to the sample answers found in Appendix B.

## For Further Reading

**Berger, K., with the assistance of Thompson, R.** (1994). *The developing person through the life span* (3rd ed.). New York: Worth.

*A comprehensive, current, and readable textbook summary of what we know about infancy, childhood, adolescence, and adulthood.*

**Coles, R.** (1990). *The spiritual life of children*. Boston: Houghton Mifflin.

*The eighth and final volume in psychiatrist Coles's exploration of children's lives. Using a case study approach, Coles's books record and reflect upon his extended conversations with children and their families.*

**Damon, W.** (1988). *The moral child: Nurturing children's natural moral growth*. New York: Free Press.

*Drawing on recent research, a developmental psychologist charts the course of moral development, stressing the value of authoritative rather than authoritarian parenting.*

**Silverstone, B., & Hyman, H. K.** (1981). *You and your aging parent: The modern family's guide to emotional, physical, and financial problems* (2nd ed.). New York: Pantheon.

*A useful book that provides information and practical advice on how to care responsibly for one's aging parents without feeling trapped.*

# CHAPTER 5

# Sensation

In the outer world, innumerable stimuli bombard your body. In a silent, cushioned, inner world of utter darkness floats your brain. These facts raise a question that predates psychology by thousands of years and helped inspire its beginnings a century ago: *How does the world out there get in?*

To modernize the question: How do we construct our representations of the external world? How do we represent a campfire's flicker, crackle, and odor as patterns of active neural connections? And how from this living neurochemistry do we create our conscious experience of its motion and temperature, its aroma and beauty?

To represent the world in our head, we must detect physical energy from the environment and encode it as neural signals, a process traditionally called **sensation**. And we must select, organize, and interpret our sensations, a process traditionally called **perception**. In our everyday experiences, sensation and perception blend indetectably into one continuous process. In Chapters 5 and 6, we slow down that process to study its parts.

In this chapter we start with the sensory receptors and work up to higher levels of processing. Psychologists refer to sensory analysis that starts at the entry level and works up as *bottom-up* processing. The next chapter focuses on how our minds interpret what our senses detect. We construct perceptions drawing not only on sensations coming "up" to the brain but also on our experience and expectations, which psychologists call *top-down* processing.

Failures of perception may occur anywhere between sensory detection and perceptual interpretation. For example, the eyes of a person born with cataracts may be unable to detect light. Without the light stimulus, the brain's higher-level visual processing equipment is useless. Studying brain-damaged patients reveals the importance of other links in the sensation-perception process. After losing a temporal lobe area essential to recognizing faces, patient "E. H." suffers from a condition called *prosopagnosia*. She has complete sensation but incomplete perception. She can sense visual information—indeed may accurately report the features of a face—yet be unable to recognize it. Shown an unfamiliar face, she is unreactive. Shown a familiar face, her autonomic nervous system responds with measurable perspiration. Still, she hasn't a clue to who the person is. Shown her own face in a mirror she is again stumped. Because of her brain damage, she is unable to process from the top down; she cannot relate her stored knowledge to the sensory input.

**What's Going on Here?** *Our sensory and perceptual processes work together to help us sort out the complex images in this Bev Doolittle painting, "The Forest Has Eyes." Processing from the bottom up, our sensory systems detect the lines, angles, and colors that form the horses, rider, and surroundings. From the top down, we consider the painting's title, notice the apprehensive expressions, and then direct our attention to aspects of the painting that will give those observations meaning. (Detail, "The Forest Has Eyes" by Bev Doolittle © The Greenwich Workshop, Inc., Trumball, CT.)*

## Sensing the World: Some Basic Principles

*We begin with questions that cut across all our sensory systems: What stimuli cross our threshold for conscious awareness? Could we unknowingly be influenced by "subliminal" stimuli that are too weak to be perceived? Why are we unaware of unchanging stimuli, such as the watch pressing against our wrist?*

Sensory systems enable organisms to obtain the information they need to function and survive. A frog, which feeds on flying insects, has eyes with receptor cells that fire only in response to small, dark, moving objects. A frog could starve to death knee-deep in motionless flies. But let one zoom by and the frog's "bug detector" cells snap awake. A male silkworm moth has receptors so sensitive to the odor of the female sex-attractant that a single female silkworm moth need release only a billionth of an ounce per second to attract every male silkworm moth within a mile. Which is why there continue to be silkworms. We humans are similarly designed to detect what are, for us, the important features of our environments. Our ears are most sensitive to the sound frequencies of the human voice. Nature's sensory gifts suit the needs of each particular recipient.

### Thresholds

We exist in a sea of energy. At this moment, you and I are being struck by x-rays and radio waves, ultraviolet and infrared light, and sound waves of very high and very low frequencies. But to all of them we are blind and deaf. The shades on our senses are open just a crack, allowing us only a restricted awareness of this vast sea. **Psychophysics** is the study of the relationship between this physical energy and our psychological experience. What stimuli can we detect? At what levels of intensity? How sensitive are we to changing stimulation?

#### Absolute Thresholds

To some kinds of stimuli we are exquisitely sensitive. Standing at the top of a mountain on an utterly dark, clear night, we can, given normal senses, see a candle flame atop another mountain 30 miles away. In a silent room, we can hear a watch ticking 20 feet away. We can feel the wing of a bee falling on our cheek. We can smell a single drop of perfume in a three-room apartment (Galanter, 1962).

Our awareness of these faint stimuli illustrates our **absolute thresholds**—the minimum stimulation necessary to detect a particular stimulus (light, sound, pressure, taste, odor). Psychologists usually measure absolute threshold by recording the stimulation needed for detection 50 percent of the time. To test your absolute threshold for sounds, a hearing specialist exposes each ear to varying sound levels. For each pitch, the hearing test defines where half the time you correctly detect the sound and half the time you do not. For each of the senses, that 50–50 point defines your absolute threshold.

(*a*)

(*b*)

**On a Different Wavelength** *Sensory capacities are not the same across species, perhaps because different ecological niches demand sensitivity to different kinds of energy. Compare, for example, the way a flower is registered by (a) a human eye and (b) a bee's eye. The bee can detect differences in ultraviolet wavelengths reflected by the flower, enabling it to see the "landing field" that makes possible more efficient food-gathering.*

### Signal Detection

Detecting a weak stimulus, or signal, depends not only on the signal's strength (such as the tone on a hearing test), but also on our psychological state—our experience, expectations, motivation, and fatigue. Thus, those who study **signal detection** contend that there is no single absolute threshold. Exhausted parents of a newborn will notice the faintest whimper from the cradle, while louder, unimportant sounds go unnoticed. In a horror-filled wartime situation, failure to detect an intruder may mean death. A sentry standing guard alone at night may therefore notice—and fire at—an almost imperceptible noise. With heightened responsiveness come more false alarms. In peacetime, when survival is not threatened, the same sentry requires a stronger signal before sensing danger.

Signal detection theorists seek to understand why people respond differently to the same stimuli, and why the same person's reactions vary as circumstances change. Signal detection can have life-or-death consequences when people are responsible for detecting blips on a radar screen, weapons at an airport security checkpoint, or the monitoring equipment at an intensive care nursing station. Studies of signal detection, in which people must judge whether a faint stimulus is present, have shown, for example, that after about 30 minutes of performing such tasks, people's vigilance diminishes. But this depends on the task, on the time of day, and even on whether the subjects are given a chance to exercise (Warm & Dember, 1986).

### Subliminal Stimulation

In 1956, controversy erupted over a (false) report that New Jersey movie audiences were unwittingly being influenced by imperceptible flashed messages to DRINK COCA-COLA and EAT POPCORN (Pratkanis, 1992).

## Thinking Critically About Unconscious Influence: Backward Messages in Rock Albums

The influences on how we think and act are often subtle, even unrecognized. Might it therefore be possible for unperceived backward messages, implanted on rock albums, to corrupt unwitting listeners? In the 1980s, concerns about such messages led to political efforts in the Canadian parliament and several American states to contain the supposed powers of "backmasking."

Are these concerns warranted? Assuming that such backward messages exist, could they have any influence? If indeed people are unconsciously influenced by a message they can't perceive, how might psychologists detect such influence?

Confronted with such questions and armed with the methods of psychological science, University of Alberta psychologists John Vokey and Don Read (1985) decided to investigate. They began by recording some simple sentences from Lewis Carroll's "Jabberwocky" and from the Twenty-third Psalm and then rerecorded them backward. This retained the pauses and pitches, producing a recording that sounded rather like a foreign language.

But it was meaningless gibberish. Listeners could not detect whether a given word was or wasn't present, whether they had heard a declarative sentence or a question, or whether the sentence was meaningful or nonsensical. When simple messages such as "Jesus loves me, this I know" were played backward, people couldn't surpass chance when guessing whether the words were Satanic, Christian, pornographic, advertising, or from a nursery rhyme.

Might meaningless backward information nevertheless have a subtle influence? Research psychologists have invented clever methods for uncovering such influences, including one that uses homophones—words that sound alike but differ in spelling and meaning. Imagine, for example, hearing the sentence, "Climbing a mountain is a remarkable *feat*." Later, even after you had forgotten the sentence, you would probably be more likely to spell the italicized word as f-e-a-t rather than f-e-e-t. This effect occurs without people realizing why they have chosen a particular spelling. But you must hear the homophone normally, not backward. When Vokey and Read buried the homophone in a backward message the unconscious influence disappeared.

In continued quest of unconscious influence, Ian Begg and his McMaster University colleagues (1993) adapted "the illusory truth effect"—the tendency for repeated statements, such as "The most prevalent infection in the world today is cholera" to seem true. As usual, people became more accepting of such statements when played forward. But the phenomenon disappeared when they played the statements backward.

Once again, a popular idea collapsed when tested experimentally. Those concerned about backward messages in rock music can relax. Rock music's influence just doesn't leak through in backward messages.

*How to think uncritically without psychology: James Vicary, an unemployed marketing researcher, masterminded the EAT POPCORN subliminal advertising hoax with the help of uncritical reporters and broadcasters. Vicary reportedly collected big fees from advertising firms for his promised services—and then disappeared (Rogers, 1993, 1994).*

More than 35 years later, the controversy has erupted anew. Advertisers are said to manipulate consumers by imperceptibly printing the word *sex* on crackers and by embedding erotic images in liquor ads. Rock recordings are said to contain "satanic messages" that can be heard if the recordings are played backward and that can unconsciously persuade the unwitting listener, even when played normally. Entrepreneurs offer to help us lose weight, stop smoking, or improve our memories with audiotapes of soothing ocean sounds that contain unheard messages such as, "I am thin," "Smoke tastes bad," and "I do well on tests. I have total recall of information." These claims make two assumptions: that unconsciously we can sense **subliminal** (literally, "below threshold") stimuli, and that, without our awareness, these stimuli have extraordinary suggestive powers. Can we? Do they?

Can we sense stimuli that are below our absolute thresholds? In one sense, the answer is clearly yes. Remember that the "absolute" threshold is merely the point at which we detect a stimulus half the time (Figure 5–1). At or slightly below this threshold we will still detect the stimulus some of the time. The answer is yes in another sense, too. People who plead total ignorance when asked to make some perceptual judgment—for example, when deciding which of two very similar weights is heavier—usually beat chance. Sometimes we know more than we think.

Can we be affected by stimuli too weak for us *ever* to notice? Recent experiments hint that, under certain conditions, the answer may again be yes. One experiment subliminally flashed either emotionally positive scenes (such as kittens or a romantic couple) or negative scenes (such as a werewolf or a dead body) an instant before subjects viewed slides of nine people (Krosnick & others, 1992). Although the subjects consciously perceived only a flash of light, they gave more positive ratings to people whose photos had been associated with positive scenes. People somehow looked nicer if their photo immediately followed unperceived kittens rather than unperceived werewolves. Chinese characters, too, seem nicer if preceded by a flashed but unperceived smiling face rather than a scowling face (Murphy & Zajonc, 1993). And consider how invisible words can "prime" your response to a later question. If the word *bread* were flashed so quickly that you could detect only the flash, you might then detect a related word such as *butter* faster than unrelated words such as *bottle* or *bubble* (Bornstein & Pittman, 1992; Carr & others, 1987; Marcel, 1983). Sometimes we feel what we do not know and cannot describe.

So, we *can* process information without being aware of it. A weak stimulus evidently triggers a weak response that evokes a feeling, though not a conscious awareness of the stimulus. What the conscious mind can't recognize, the heart may know.

But does the fact of subliminal *sensation* verify entrepreneurial claims of subliminal *persuasion*? Can advertisers or diabolical rock groups really manipulate us with "hidden persuasion"? The near-consensus among research psychologists is no. Their verdict is like that of astronomers who say that, yes, astrologers are right that stars and planets are out there, but no, they don't directly affect us.

Consider: The laboratory research reveals a *subtle, fleeting* effect on *thinking*. Subliminal tape hucksters claim something different: a *powerful, enduring* effect on *behavior*. Moreover, experiments, such as one described in Chapter 1, show that commercial subliminal tapes have no effect beyond one's belief in them (the placebo effect).

Earlier studies produced similar results, discounting the threat of "hidden persuasion" through subliminal ads (Moore, 1988). Shortly after news of the supposed EAT POPCORN effect swept North America, the Canadian Broadcasting Corporation used a popular Sunday night TV show to flash a subliminal message 352 times (*Advertising Age*, 1958). Asked to guess the message, none of the almost 500 letter-writers did so. Nearly half, however, did report feeling strangely hungry or thirsty during the show. But this was merely an effect of expectations. The actual message was TELEPHONE NOW. The effect of these 352 subliminal messages on Canadian telephone usage? Zilch. All the evidence considered, say researchers Anthony Pratkanis and Anthony Greenwald (1988), "Subliminal procedures offer little or nothing of value to the marketing practitioner."

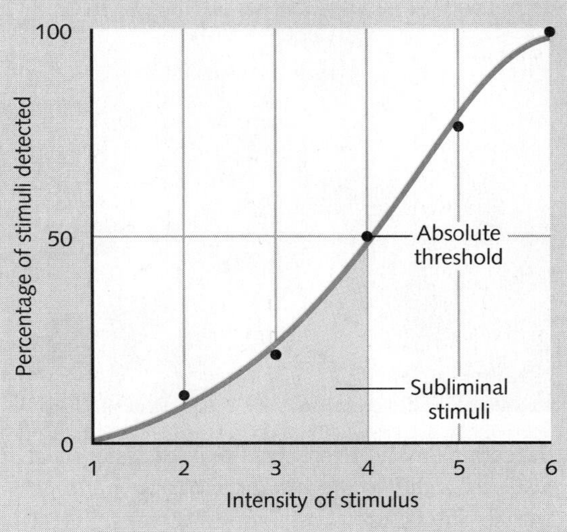


**Figure 5–1**

**The Absolute Threshold** *Absolute threshold is arbitrarily measured as the intensity at which we perceive a stimulus 50 percent of the time. By this definition, stimuli that are perceived less than 50 percent of the time are subliminal.*

The LORD is my shepherd;
I shall not want.
He maketh me to lie down
in green pastures:
he leadeth me
beside the still waters.
He restoreth my soul:
he leadeth me
in the paths of righteousness
for his name's sake.
Yea, though I walk through the valley
of the shadow of death,
I will fear no evil:
for thou art with me;
thy rod and thy staff
they comfort me.
Thou preparest a table before me
in the presence of mine enemies:
thou anointest my head with oil,
my cup runneth over.
Surely goodness and mercy
shall follow me
all the days of my life:
and I will dwell
in the house of the LORD
for ever.

**The Difference Threshold** *In this computer-generated copy of the Twenty-third Psalm, each line of the typeface changes imperceptibly. How many lines are required for you to experience a just noticeable difference?*

## Difference Thresholds

To function effectively, we need absolute thresholds low enough to allow us to detect important sights, sounds, textures, tastes, and smells. We also need to detect small differences among stimuli. A musician must detect minute discrepancies in an instrument's tuning. A wine taster must detect the slight flavor difference between two vintage wines.

**Detecting Small Differences** *This tea taster must distinguish minuscule variations in flavor and aroma. The task requires exquisitely sensitive senses of taste and smell and considerable learning, too.*

The **difference threshold** (also called the **just noticeable difference**, or **jnd)** is the minimum difference a person can detect between any two stimuli 50 percent of the time. The difference threshold increases with the magnitude of the stimulus. Add 1 ounce to a 10-ounce weight and you will detect the difference; add 1 ounce to a 10-*pound* weight and you will not, because the difference threshold has increased. More than a century ago, Ernst Weber noted that regardless of their magnitude, two stimuli must differ by a constant proportion for their difference to be perceptible. This principle—that the difference threshold is not a constant amount but some constant *proportion* of the stimulus—is so simple and so widely applicable that we still refer to it as **Weber's law**. The exact proportion varies, depending on the stimulus. For the average person to perceive their differences, two lights must differ in intensity by 8 percent, two objects must differ in weight by 2 percent, and two tones must differ in frequency by only 0.3 percent (Teghtsoonian, 1971).

Weber's law is a rough approximation that works well for nonextreme sensory stimuli. It also parallels some of our life experiences. If the price of a 50-cent candy bar goes up by a nickel, shoppers might notice the change; similarly, it might take a $5000 price hike in a $50,000 Mercedes-Benz to raise the eyebrows of its potential buyers. In both cases, the price went up by 10 percent. Weber's principle: Our thresholds for detecting differences are a roughly constant proportion of the size of the original stimulus.

## Sensory Adaptation

Entering your neighbor's living room, you smell an unpleasant odor. You wonder how she tolerates the stench, but within minutes you no longer notice it. Jumping into a swimming pool, you shiver and complain how cold it is. A short while later a friend arrives and you exclaim, "C'mon in. Water's lovely!" These examples illustrate **sensory adaptation**—our diminishing sensitivity to an unchanging stimulus. (To experience this phenomenon, move your watch up your wrist an inch: You will feel it—but only for a few moments.) After constant exposure to a stimulus, our nerve cells fire less frequently.

*"We need above all to know about changes; no one wants or needs to be reminded 16 hours a day that his shoes are on."*

Neuroscientist David Hubel (1979)

Why, then, if we stare at an object without flinching, does it not vanish from sight? Because, unnoticed by us, our eyes are always moving, quivering just enough to guarantee that the retinal image continually changes.

*For 9 in 10 people—but, curiously, for only 1 in 3 schizophrenia patients—this eye flutter turns off when the eye is following a moving target (Holzman & Matthysse, 1990).*

What if we could stop our eyes from moving? Would sights seem to vanish, as odors do? To find out, psychologists have devised ingenious instruments for maintaining a constant image on the retina. Imagine that we fitted a subject, Mary, with one of these instruments—a miniature projector mounted on a contact lens (Figure 5–2[*a*]). When Mary's eye moves, the image from the projector moves as well. Thus, everywhere that Mary looks the scene is sure to go.

If we project the profile of a face through such an instrument, what will Mary see? At first she will see the complete profile. But within a few seconds, as her sense receptors begin to fatigue, things get weird. Bit by bit, the image vanishes, only later to reappear and then disappear—in recognizable fragments or as a whole (Figure 5–2[*b*]). Interestingly, the disappearance and reappearance of an image occurs in meaningful units. If a person is shown a word, it will disappear, and new words made up of parts of that word will appear and then vanish. This phenomenon anticipates the next chapter's major conclusion: Our perceptions are organized by the meanings that our minds impose.

*"My suspicion is that the universe is not only queerer than we suppose, but queerer than we can suppose."*

J. B. S. Haldane
*Possible Worlds*, 1927

Although sensory adaptation reduces our sensitivity, it offers an important benefit: It enables us to focus our attention on *informative* changes in our environment without being distracted by the uninformative, constant stimulation of garments, odors, and street noise. Our sense receptors are alert to novelty; bore them with repetition and they free our attention for things more interesting. This reinforces a fundamental lesson: We perceive the world not exactly as it is, but as it is useful for us to perceive it.

Sensory thresholds and adaptation are not the only commonalities among the senses. All the senses receive sensory stimulation, transform it into neural information, and deliver that information to the brain. How do the senses work? How do we see? Hear? Smell? Taste? Feel pain? Let's start with vision, the sense most people prize the most.

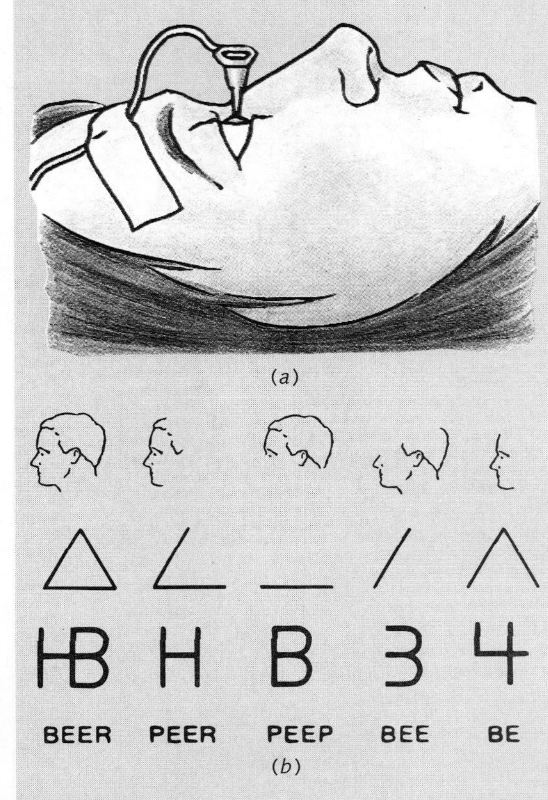


**Figure 5–2**

**A Stabilized Image** *(a) A projector mounted on a contact lens makes the projected image move with the eye. (b) Initially the subject sees the stabilized image, but soon she sees fragments fading and reappearing. (From "Stabilized images on the retina" by R. M. Pritchard. Copyright © 1961 Scientific American, Inc. All rights reserved.)*

## Summing Up

To study sensation is to study an ageless question: How does the world out there get represented inside our heads? Put another way, how are the external stimuli that strike our bodies transformed into messages that our brains comprehend?

**Thresholds** Each species comes equipped with sensitivities that enable it to survive and thrive. We sense only a portion of the sea of energy that surrounds us, but to this portion we are exquisitely sensitive. Our absolute threshold for any stimulus is the minimum stimulation necessary for us to detect it. Signal detection researchers report that our individual absolute thresholds vary with our psychological state.

Can we react to stimuli that are not only subthreshold (subliminal) but so weak that we could never consciously perceive them? Recent experiments reveal that we *can* process some information from stimuli too weak to recognize. But the restricted conditions under which this occurs would not enable unscrupulous opportunists to exploit us with subliminal messages. Nor is there any evidence or plausible theory that we can effortlessly "reprogram" our minds with subliminal tapes.

To survive and thrive, an organism must also have difference thresholds low enough to detect minute changes in important stimuli. In humans, difference thresholds (also called *just noticeable differences*, or *jnd's*) increase in proportion to the size of the stimulus—a principle known as Weber's Law.

**Sensory Adaptation** The phenomenon of sensory adaptation focuses our attention on changing stimulation by diminishing our sensitivity to constant or routine odors, sounds, and touches.

# Vision

*One of nature's greatest wonders is neither bizarre nor remote, but commonplace: How does our material body construct our conscious visual experience? How do we transform particles of light energy into colorful sights?*

*"The most commonplace crime is often the most mysterious. . . . Life is infinitely stranger than anything which the mind of man could invent."*

Sherlock Holmes, in Arthur Conan Doyle's *A Study in Scarlet*, 1888

Part of your taken-for-granted genius is your body's ability to convert one sort of energy to another. Sensory **transduction** is the process by which our sensory systems convert stimulus energy into neural messages. Your eyes, for example, receive light energy and transduce (transform) the energy into neural messages, which ultimately we process into what we consciously see. Let's consider how.

## The Stimulus Input: Light Energy

Scientifically speaking, what strikes our eyes is not color but pulses of electromagnetic energy that our visual system experiences as color. What we see as visible light is but a thin slice of the whole spectrum of electromagnetic radiation. As Figure 5–3 illustrates, this *electromagnetic spectrum* ranges from the imperceptibly short pulses or waves of gamma rays to the narrow band that we see as visible light to the long waves of radio transmission. Other organisms are sensitive to differing portions of the spectrum. As we noted earlier, bees cannot see red but can see ultraviolet light, the part of the spectrum that causes sunburn in humans.

Two physical characteristics of light help determine our sensory experience of it. Its **wavelength**—the distance from one wave peak to the next (Figure 5–4[*a*]—determines its **hue** (the color we experience, such as blue or green). **Intensity**, the amount of energy in light waves (determined by a wave's *amplitude*, or height), influences brightness (Figure 5–4[*b*]). To understand *how* we transform physical energy into a sensation of color, we first need to understand our mind's window, the eye.

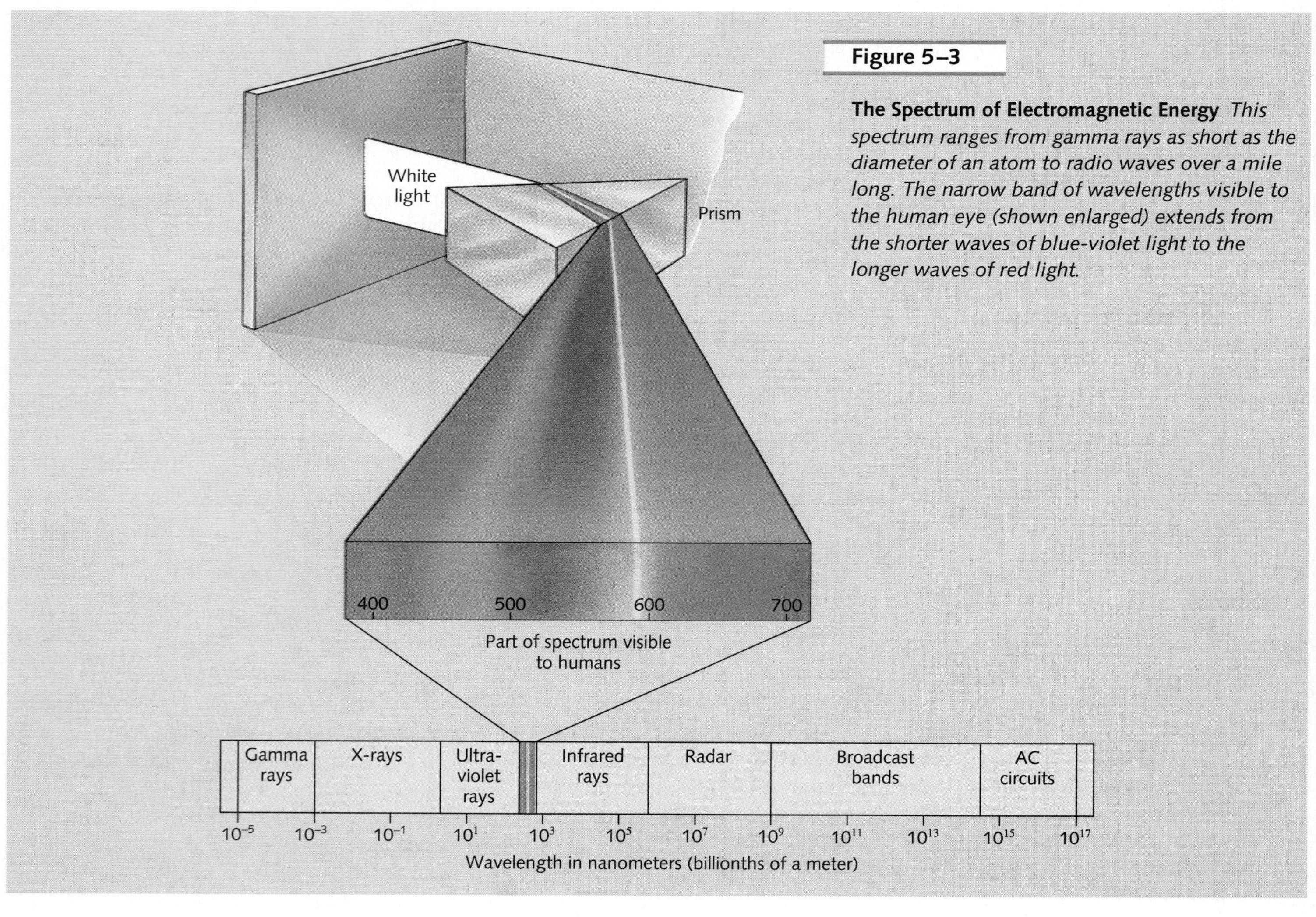


**Figure 5–3**

**The Spectrum of Electromagnetic Energy** *This spectrum ranges from gamma rays as short as the diameter of an atom to radio waves over a mile long. The narrow band of wavelengths visible to the human eye (shown enlarged) extends from the shorter waves of blue-violet light to the longer waves of red light.*

Figure 5–4

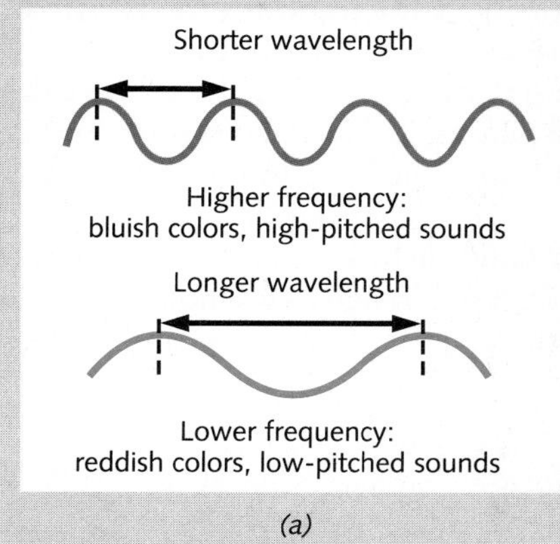


(a)

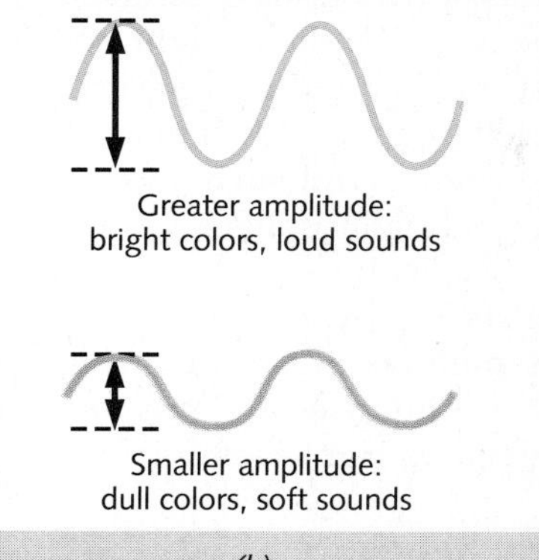


(b)

**The Physical Properties of Waves** *(a) Waves vary in wavelength, the distance between successive peaks. Frequency, the number of complete wavelengths that can pass a point in a given time, depends on the wavelength. The shorter the wavelength, the higher the frequency.* *(b) Waves also vary in amplitude, the height from peak to trough. Wave amplitude determines the intensity of colors and sounds.*

## The Eye

Light enters the eye through the **pupil**, a small adjustable opening (Figure 5–5). The pupil's size, and therefore the amount of light entering the eye, is regulated by the **iris**, a colored muscle surrounding the pupil. Behind the pupil is a **lens** which focuses the incoming rays into an image on a light-sensitive surface. It does so by changing its curvature in a process called **accommodation**. The light-sensitive surface on which the rays focus is the **retina**, the multilayered tissue that lines the inside of the back of the eyeball.

For centuries, scientists have known that when the image of a candle passed through a small opening, its mirror image appeared inverted on a dark wall behind (like the inverted rose in Figure 5–5). This fact had schol-

Figure 5–5

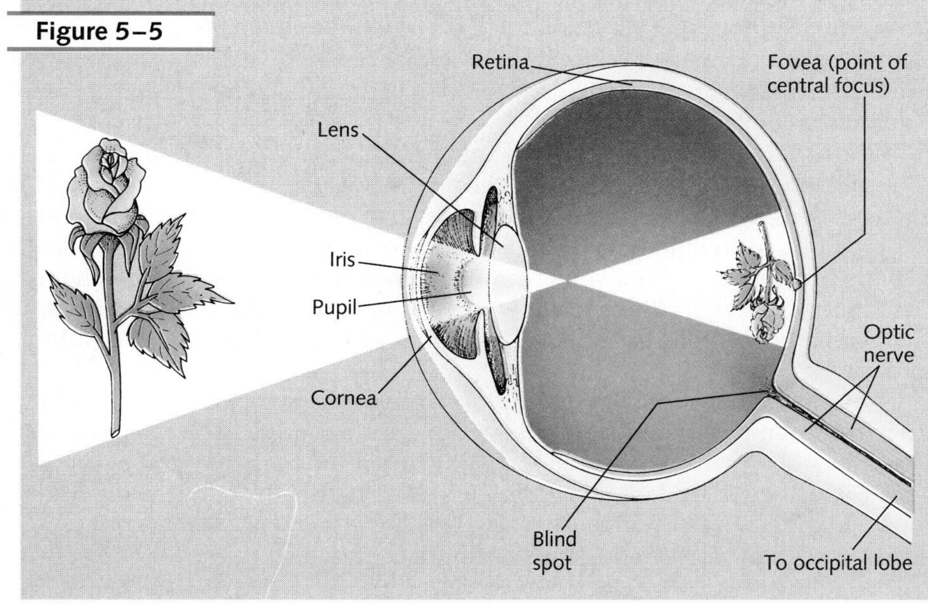


**The Eye** *Light rays reflected from the rose pass through the cornea, pupil, and lens. The curvature and thickness of the lens change to bring either nearby or distant objects into focus on the retina. Light rays travel in straight lines. So rays from the top of the rose strike the bottom of the retina and those from the left side of the rose strike the right side of the retina. The rose's retinal image is thus upside-down and reversed.*

ars baffled. If the retina receives an upside-down image, how can we see the world right side up? One idea was that the eye's sensing device is the lens. Realizing this wasn't so, the ever-curious Leonardo da Vinci had another idea: Perhaps the eye's watery fluids bent the lightrays, reinverting the image to the upright position as it reached the retina. But in 1604, the astronomer and optics expert Johannes Kepler showed that the retina did receive upside-down images of the world (Crombie, 1964). And how could we understand such a world? "I leave it," said the befuddled Kepler, "to natural philosophers."

The "natural philosophers," who eventually included research psychologists, discovered that the retina doesn't read the image as a whole. Rather, its millions of receptor cells convert light energy into neural impulses. These impulses are sent to the brain and assembled *there* to create a perceived, upright-seeming image.

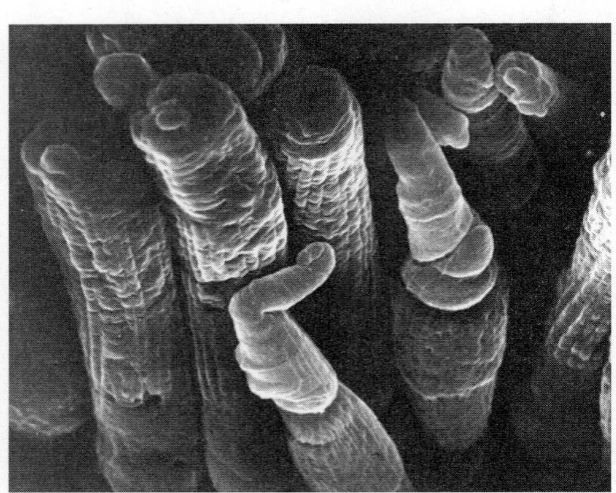

**Rod-Shaped Rods and Cone-Shaped Cones** *As the scanning electron microscope shows, rods and cones are well named. Rods are more light-sensitive than the color-sensitive cones, which is why the world looks colorless at night. Some nocturnal animals, such as toads, mice, rats, and bats, have retinas made up almost entirely of rods, allowing them to function well in dim light. These creatures probably have very poor color vision.*

### The Retina

If we were to follow a single particle of light energy into the eye, we would see that it first makes its way through the retina's outer layer of cells to its buried receptor cells, the **rods** and **cones** (Figure 5–6). When struck by light energy, chemical changes in the rods and cones generate neural signals that activate the neighboring *bipolar cells*, which in turn activate the neighboring *ganglion cells*. The axons from the network of ganglion cells converge like the strands of a rope to form an **optic nerve** that carries information to the brain. Nearly a million messages can be sent by the optic nerve at once, through nearly 1 million ganglion fibers. (The auditory nerve, which enables hearing, carries much less information through its mere 30,000 fibers.) Where the optic nerve leaves the eye there are no receptor cells—creating a **blind spot** (Figure 5–7).

Most cones are clustered around the **fovea**, the retina's area of central focus (Figure 5–6). In fact, the fovea contains only cones, no rods. Unlike rods, many cones have their own bipolar cells to help relay their individual messages to the cortex, which devotes a large amount of its area to impulses from the fovea. This preserves the cones' precise information, making them better able to detect fine detail. (Rods have no such hotline to the brain; they share bipolar cells with other rods, so their individual messages get combined.) To illustrate, if you pick a word in this sentence and stare directly at it, focusing its image on the cones in your fovea, you will see that words a few inches off to the side appear blurred. This is because their image strikes the more peripheral region of your retina, where the rods predominate (Table 5–1).

**Table 5–1 The Human Eye**

| | Cones | Rods |
|---|---|---|
| *Number* | 6 million | 120 million |
| *Location in retina* | Center | Periphery |
| *Sensitivity in dim light* | Low | High |
| *Color sensitive?* | Yes | No |

Rods enable black-and-white vision; cones enable you to see color. As illumination diminishes, the cones become ineffectual. The rods, however, remain sensitive in dim light, because several rods will funnel their faint energy from dim light onto a single bipolar cell. That is why you don't see colors in dim light. When you enter a darkened theater or turn off the light at night, your pupils dilate to allow more light to reach the rods in the retina's periphery. Typically it takes 20 minutes or more before our eyes fully adapt.

You can demonstrate dark adaptation by closing or covering one eye for up to 20 minutes, then making the room light not quite bright enough to read this book with your open eye. Now open the dark-adapted eye and read. This period of dark adaptation is yet another instance of the remarkable adaptiveness of our sensory systems, for it parallels the natural twilight transition between the sun's setting and darkness.

Figure 5–6

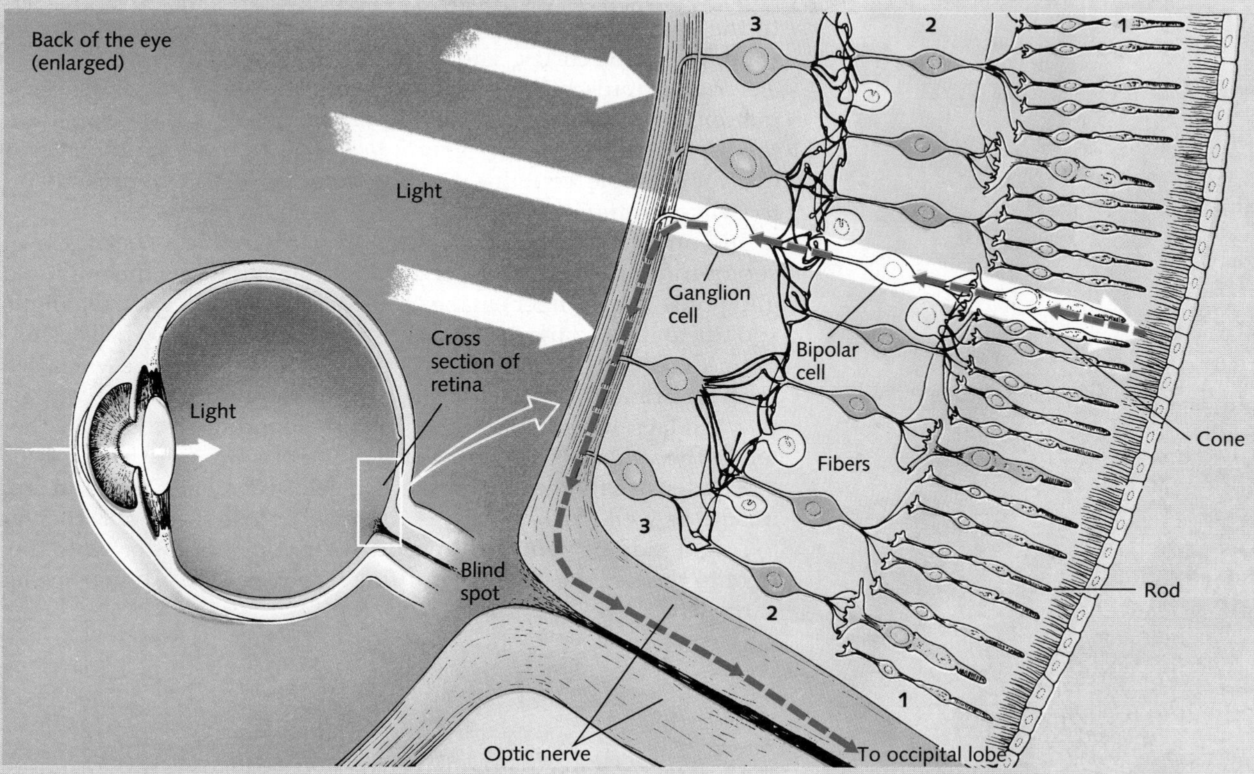


**The Path of Light Through the Eye** *Before signals from the retina reach the brain, they pass through a switchboard of neural cells. A ray of light entering the eye triggers a photochemical reaction in the rods and cones (1) at the back of the retina behind the other neural layers. This chemical reaction in turn triggers the bipolar cells (2). The bipolar cells then activate the ganglion cells (3), which converge to form the optic nerve. The optic nerve transmits information to the brain's occipital lobe.*

Knowing just this much about the eye, can you imagine why a cat sees so much better at night than you do? There are at least two reasons: A cat's pupils can open much wider than yours, letting in more light; and a cat has a higher proportion of light-sensitive rods (Moser, 1987). But there is a trade-off: With fewer cones, a cat can't see details or color as well as you do.

Figure 5–7

●

**The Blind Spot** *Where the optic nerve leaves the eye (Figure 5–6), there are no receptor cells. This creates a blind spot in our vision. To demonstrate, close your left eye, look at the spot, and move the page to a distance from your face (about a foot) at which the car disappears. In everyday vision the blind spot doesn't impair your vision because your eyes are moving and because one eye covers what the other misses.*

## Visual Information Processing

We process visual information at progressively more abstract levels. At the entry level, the retina—which is actually a piece of the brain that migrates to the eye during early fetal development—processes information before routing it to the cortex. The retina's neural layers are not just passing along electrical impulses; they also help to encode and analyze the sensory information. Indeed, much of the important processing of visual information takes place in the retina's neural tissues. The third neural layer in a frog's eye, for example, contains the "bug detector" cells that fire only in response to flylike stimuli.

In human eyes, the information from the retina's nearly 130 million receptor rods and cones is received and transmitted by the million or so ganglion cells, whose fibers make up the optic nerve. A typical ganglion cell responds to light/dark contrasts revealed by its receptor cells. This helps the brain detect edges and other important features of the visual world. But most information processing occurs in the brain. Any given area of the retina relays its information to a corresponding location in the occipital lobe—the visual cortex at the back of the brain (Figure 5–8).

The sensitivity that enables retinal cells to fire messages can lead them to misfire as well. Turn your eyes to the left, close them, and then gently rub the right side of your right eyelid with your fingertip. Note the patch of light to the left, moving as your finger moves. Why do you see light? Why at the left?

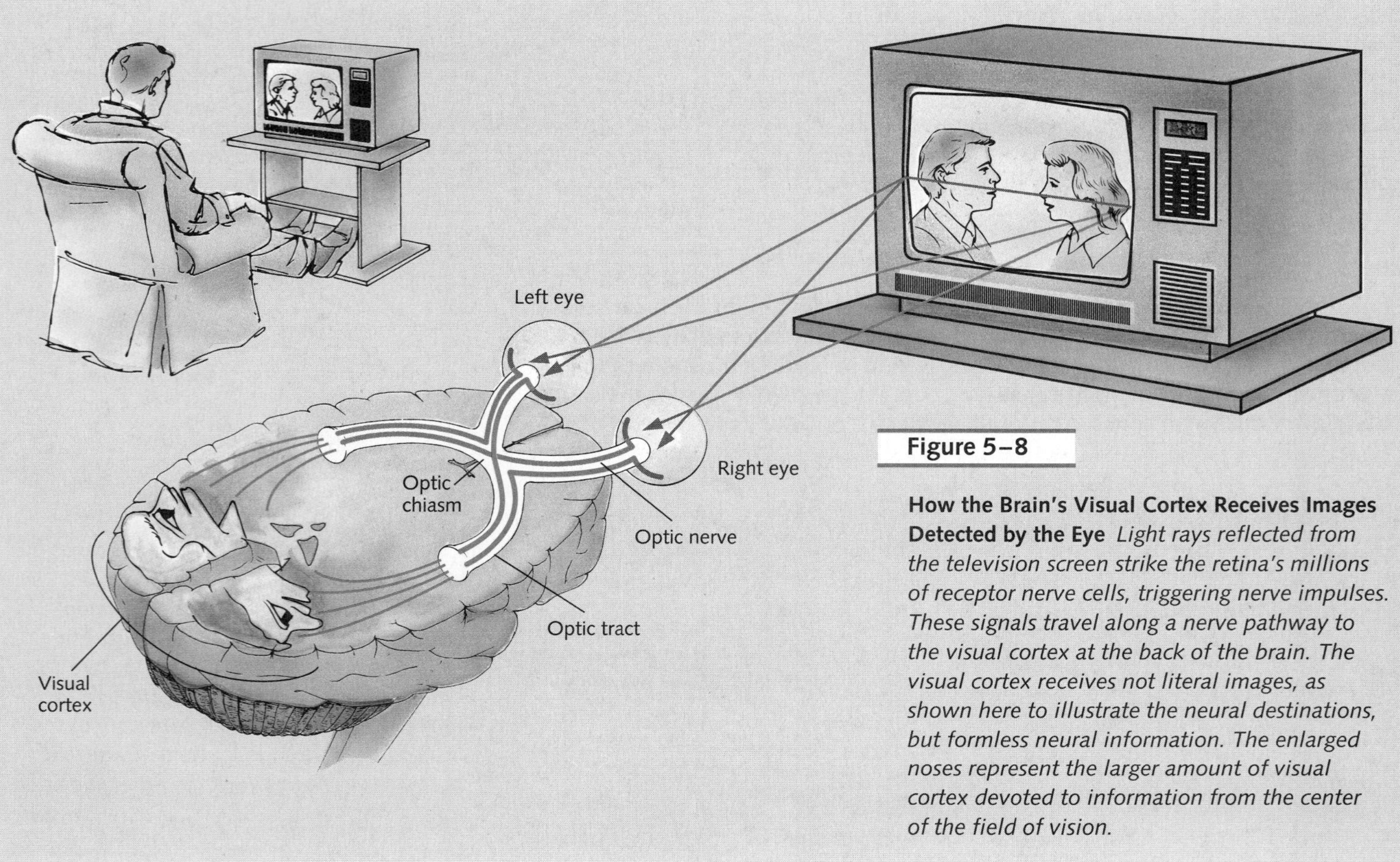


**Figure 5–8**

**How the Brain's Visual Cortex Receives Images Detected by the Eye** *Light rays reflected from the television screen strike the retina's millions of receptor nerve cells, triggering nerve impulses. These signals travel along a nerve pathway to the visual cortex at the back of the brain. The visual cortex receives not literal images, as shown here to illustrate the neural destinations, but formless neural information. The enlarged noses represent the larger amount of visual cortex devoted to information from the center of the field of vision.*

Your retinal cells are so responsive that even pressure triggers them. But your brain interprets their firing as light. Moreover, it interprets the light as coming from the left—which is where light normally comes from when it activates the right side of the retina.

## Feature Detection

When individual ganglion cells register information in their region of the visual field, they send signals to the visual cortex. Nobelists David Hubel and Torsten Wiesel (1979) demonstrated that when certain cortical neurons, called **feature detectors**, receive this information, they respond to specific features of a scene—to particular edges, lines, and angles. From these elements the brain assembles the perceived image.

For example, Hubel and Wiesel report that a given brain cell might respond maximally to a line flashed at a particular tilt (Figure 5–9). If the line is tilted further—say, from a 2 o'clock to a 3 o'clock or 1 o'clock position—the cell quiets down. Thus, the feature detector cells record amazingly specific features taken in by the eye. Feature detector cells pass this information to other cells that respond only to more complex patterns. The basic idea is that perceptions arise from the interaction of many neurons, each performing a simple task.

Figure 5–9

**Electrodes Record How Individual Cells in This Monkey's Visual Cortex Respond to Different Visual Stimuli** *Hubel and Wiesel won the Nobel prize for their discovery that most cells in the visual cortex respond only to particular features—for example, to the edge of a surface, or to a line at a 30-degree angle in the upper right part of the field of vision. More complex features trigger higher-level detector cells, which integrate information from these simpler ones.*

Some higher-level brain cells respond only to specific visual stimuli, such as a face or an arm movement in a particular direction. Psychologist David Perrett and his colleagues (1988) report that for biologically important objects and events, monkey brains (and surely ours as well) have a "vast visual encyclopedia" distributed as cells that respond to one stimulus but not others. Researchers also have identified nerve cells that may fire or not, depending on how a monkey *perceives* an image, even when physical input is constant. Special goggles give the monkey's two eyes contradictory information about an object that can be perceived as moving either up or down. If the image appears to be moving up (as "reported" by the monkey's eye movements), certain cells become active; if, a moment later, it seems to be moving down, other cells become active (Logothetis & Schall, 1989).

Researchers debate the precise nature of the features and patterns that brain cells detect. New research suggests that any image, such as a face, can be broken down into patterns of changing light intensity that can be described mathematically. Thus, in seeing, the brain may actually be processing mathematical-like codes that represent a perceived image (Kosslyn & Koenig, 1992; Marr, 1982).

## Parallel Processing

Neural impulses travel a million times slower than a computer's internal messages, yet the brain humbles any computer by recognizing a familiar face instantly. Unlike most computers, which do step-by-step serial processing, we do **parallel processing**, which means we can do several things at once. Our brain divides a visual scene into subdimensions such as color, depth, movement, and form and works on each aspect simultaneously (Livingstone & Hubel, 1988). As David Rumelhart (1989) explains, this division of labor to specialized neural networks more than makes up for the brain's slowness:

> Although the brain has *slow* components, it has *very many* of them. The human brain contains billions of such processing elements. Rather than organize computation with many, many serial steps, as we do with [computer] systems whose steps are very fast, the brain must deploy many, many processing elements cooperatively and in parallel to carry out its activities.

**Parallel Processing** *Studies of brain-damaged patients suggest that the brain delegates the work of processing color, motion, form, and depth to different areas. After taking a scene apart, how does the brain integrate these subdimensions into the perceived image? The answer to this question is the Holy Grail of vision research.*

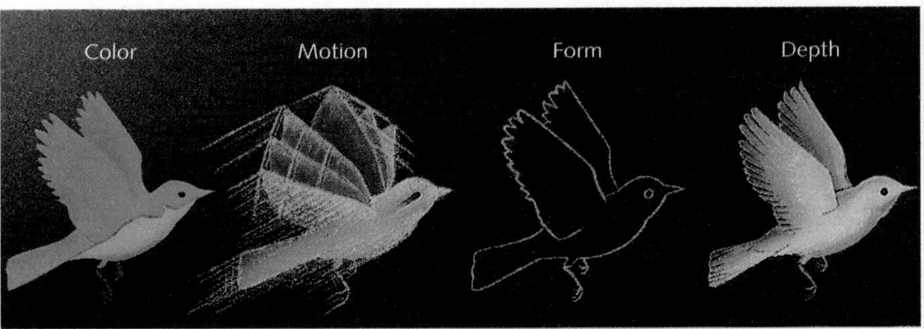
Color
Motion
Form
Depth

Thus the retina projects not just to one visual cortex area but to several areas, each of which becomes active in response to retinal stimulation. When this visual information is integrated, further processing in another cortex area, the temporal lobe, enables us to recognize an image as, say, Mother. The whole process of facial recognition requires tremendous brain power—30 percent of the cortex, 10 times what the brain devotes to hearing. The computations required for sensory-motor coordination dwarf even those involved in reasoning. We now have computers that can play chess with champion Garry Kasparov, but we're a long way from computer-driven robots that can play tennis with Monica Seles.

The distribution of visual tasks to different neural work teams explains a strange phenomenon. After a stroke, people may lose just one aspect of vision. A person may perceive color but not movement. If something moves, it disappears until it stops. Other brain-damaged victims can tell you all about the subdimensions of an object—the size and color of a rose, for instance—without recognizing the object or the person.

Still others have lost a neural area involved in consciously perceiving some aspect of their field of vision. One such woman was shown two drawings of a house—identical except that the house's left side was on fire in one drawing. Asked to select which house she would prefer to live in, she thought the question silly, "because they're the same." Yet she consistently chose the house that was not burning (Marshall & Halligan, 1988). This uncanny ability to respond to something not consciously perceived, called *blindsight*, reminds us once again of the startling truth: Our brains are doing many things at once, automatically and without our awareness.

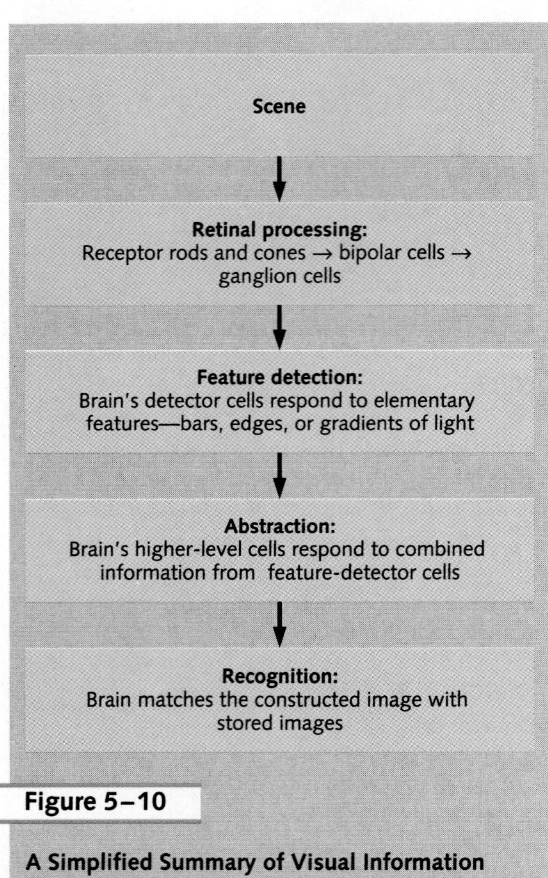
Scene
Retinal processing:
Receptor rods and cones → bipolar cells → ganglion cells
Feature detection:
Brain's detector cells respond to elementary features—bars, edges, or gradients of light
Abstraction:
Brain's higher-level cells respond to combined information from feature-detector cells
Recognition:
Brain matches the constructed image with stored images

**Figure 5–10**

**A Simplified Summary of Visual Information Processing**

The other senses process information with similar speed and intricacy. Opening the back door, you recognize the aroma wafting from the kitchen even before you step inside. Answering the phone, you recognize the friend calling from the moment she says "Hi." Within a fraction of a second after such events stimulate the senses, millions of neurons have simultaneously coordinated in extracting the essential features, comparing them with past experience, and identifying the stimulus (Freeman, 1991).

This emerging scientific understanding of sensation illustrates neuropsychologist Roger Sperry's (1985) reflection: The "insights of science give added, not lessened, reasons for awe, respect, and reverence." Think about it: As you look at someone, the visual information is sent to your brain as millions of neural impulses, then reassembled into its component features, and finally, in some as yet mysterious way, composed into a consciously perceived image, which is then compared with previously stored images and recognized as, for example, your grandmother. The whole process (Figure 5–10) is as complex as taking a car apart, piece by piece, transporting it to a different location, then having specialized workers reconstruct it. That all of this happens instantly, effortlessly, and continuously is indeed awesome.

*"I am fearfully and wonderfully made."*

King David
Psalms 139:14

## Color Vision

People talk as if objects *possess* color. We say, "The tomato is red." Perhaps you have pondered the old question, "If a tree falls in the forest and no one hears it, does it make a sound?" We can ask the same of color: If no one sees the tomato, is it red?

The answer is no. First, the tomato is everything *but* red, because it *rejects* (reflects) the long wavelengths of red. Second, the tomato's color is our mental construction. As Isaac Newton (1704) noted, "The [light] rays are not coloured." Color, like all aspects of vision, resides not in the object but in the theater of our brains. Even while dreaming, we may perceive things in color.

*"Only mind has sight and hearing; all things else are deaf and blind."*

Epicharmus
*Fragments*, 550 B.C.

In the study of vision, one of the most basic and intriguing mysteries is how we see the world in color. How, from the light energy striking the retina, does the brain manufacture our experience of color—and of such a multitude of colors? Our difference threshold for colors is so low that we can discriminate some 7 million different color variations (Geldard, 1972).

At least most of us can. For about 1 in 50 people, vision is color-deficient—and that person is probably male, because the defect is genetically sex-linked. To understand why some people have color-deficient vision we must first understand how normal color vision works.

Modern detective work on the mystery of color vision began in the nineteenth century when Hermann von Helmholtz built on the insights of an English physicist, Thomas Young. They recognized a clue in the fact that any color can be created by combining the light waves of three primary colors—red, green, and blue (Figure 5–11). Young and Helmholtz inferred that the eye must have three types of receptors, one for each primary color.

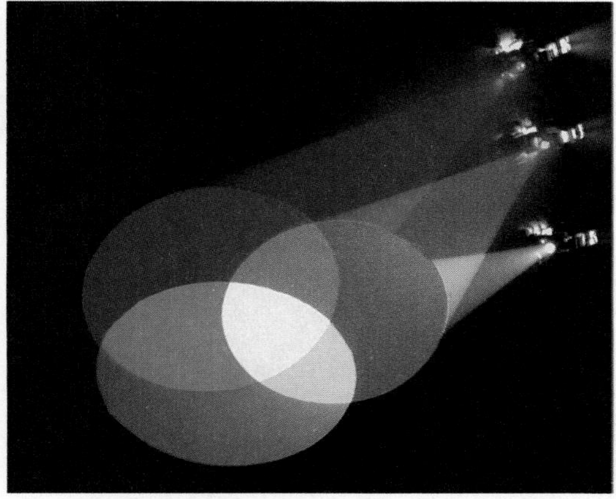

**Figure 5–11**

**The Three Primary Colors of Light** *The primary colors mix to create other colors. For example, red and green combine to create yellow. All three—red, green, and blue—combine to create white.*

Many years later, researchers measured the response of various cones to different color stimuli and confirmed the **Young-Helmholtz trichromatic (three-color) theory**, which simply states that the retina has three types of color receptors, each especially sensitive to one of three colors. And surprise! Those colors are, indeed, red, green, or blue. When we stimulate combinations of these cones, we see other colors. For example, there are no receptors especially sensitive to yellow. Yet when both red- and green-sensitive cones are stimulated, we see yellow.

Most color-deficient people are not actually "color blind." Rather, they simply lack functioning red- or green-sensitive cones. Their vision is dichromatic instead of trichromatic, making it difficult to distinguish red and green, as in Figure 5–12 (Boynton, 1979). Dogs, too, lack receptors for the wavelengths of red, giving them only limited, dichromatic color vision (Neitz & others, 1989).

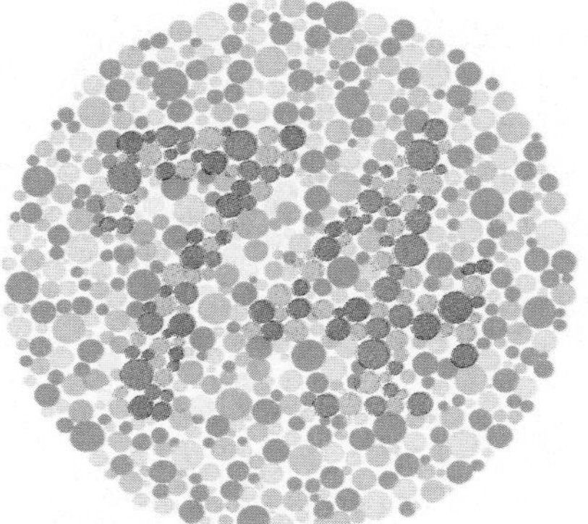

**Figure 5–12**

**Color-Deficient Vision** *People who suffer red-green blindness have trouble perceiving the number within the design.*

**Figure 5–13**

**Afterimage Effect** *Stare at the center of the flag for a minute and then shift your eyes to the dot in the white space beside it. What do you see? (After tiring your neural response to black, green, and yellow, you should see their opponent colors.)*

Soon after Young and Helmholtz proposed the trichromatic theory, physiologist Ewald Hering pointed out that other parts of the color vision mystery remained unsolved. For example, we see yellow when mixing red and green light. But how is it that people blind to red and green can often still see yellow? And why does yellow appear to be a pure color and not a mixture of red and green, as purple does of red and blue?

Hering found a clue in the well-known occurrence of *afterimages*. When you stare at a green square for a while and then look at a white sheet of paper, you see red, green's "opponent color." Stare at a yellow square and you will later see its opponent color, blue, on the white paper (as in the flag demonstration in Figure 5–13). Hering surmised that there were two additional color processes, one responsible for red versus green perception, and one for blue versus yellow.

A century later, researchers confirmed Hering's **opponent-process theory**. *After* leaving the receptor cells, visual information is analyzed in terms of the opponent colors red and green, blue and yellow, and also black and white. In the thalamus (where impulses from the retina are relayed en route to the visual cortex) some neurons are turned "on" by red but turned "off" by green. Others are turned on by green but off by red (DeValois & DeValois, 1975). So if you detect one of these colors at a particular point on the retina, you cannot simultaneously detect the opposing color at the same point; you therefore cannot see a greenish red.

Opponent processes explain afterimages, such as in the flag demonstration, in which we tire our green response by staring at green. When we then stare at white (which contains all colors, including red), only the red part of the green/red pairing will fire normally.

The present solution to the mystery of color vision is therefore roughly this: Color processing occurs in two stages. The retina's red, green, and blue cones respond in varying degrees to different color stimuli, as the Young-Helmholtz trichromatic theory suggested. Their signals are then processed by the nervous system's opponent-process cells, en route to the visual cortex.

*"Is it not stirring to understand how the world actually works—that white light is made of colors, that color measures light waves, that transparent air reflects light. . . ? It does no harm to the romance of the sunset to know a little about it."*

Carl Sagan
*Skies of Other Worlds*, 1988

## Color Constancy

Our experience of color depends on something more than the wavelength information received by our trichromatic cones and transmitted through the opponent-process cells of our thalamus.

That something more is the surrounding *context*. If you view only part of a tomato, without knowing what it is, its color will seem to change as the light changes. But if you see the whole tomato as one item in a bowl of fresh vegetables, its color will remain roughly constant as the lighting shifts—a phenomenon known as **color constancy**. Dorothea Jameson (1985) notes that a chip colored blue under indoor lighting matches the wavelengths reflected by a gold chip in the sunlight. Yet bring a bluebird indoors and it won't look like a goldfinch. Likewise, a green leaf hanging from a brown branch may, when the illumination changes, now reflect the same light energy that formerly came from the brown branch. Yet to us the leaf stays greenish and the branch stays brownish.

We take this color constancy for granted, but the phenomenon is remarkable. It demonstrates that our experience of color comes not just from the object—the color is not in the isolated leaf—but from everything around it as well. You and I see color thanks to our brains' computations of the light reflected by any object *relative to its surrounding objects*.

In an unvarying context, we maintain color constancy. But what if we change the context? Because the brain computes the color of an object relative to its context, the perceived color changes (as is dramatically apparent in Figure 5–14). This principle—that we perceive objects not in isolation but in their environmental context—is especially significant for artists, interior decorators, and clothing designers. The color of a wall or of a swatch of paint on a canvas is determined not just by the paint in the can but by the surrounding colors.

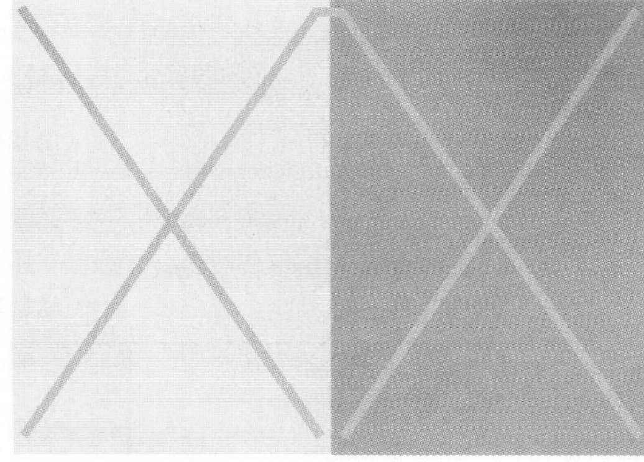

**Figure 5–14**

**Color Depends on Context** *In this painting by Joseph Albers (1975), the unchanging line* seems *to vary from gray to yellow as its surrounding context changes.*

## Summing Up

The task of our visual sense, as of each of our senses, is to receive stimulation, transduce it into neural signals, and send these neural messages to the brain.

**The Stimulus Input: Light Energy** The energies we experience as visible light are a thin slice from the broad spectrum of electromagnetic radiation. Their perceived hue and brightness of light depends on the wavelength and intensity.

**The Eye** After entering the eye through a cameralike lens, light waves strike the retina. The retina's light-sensitive rods and color-sensitive cones convert the light energy into neural impulses, which are coded by the retina before traveling up the optic nerve to the brain.

**Visual Information Processing** In the cortex, individual neurons respond to specific features of a visual stimulus, and their information is pooled by higher-level brain cells for interpretation. Subdimensions of vision (color, movement, depth, and form) are processed separately and simultaneously, illustrating our brain's capacity for parallel processing.

**Color Vision** Research on how we see color supports two nineteenth-century theories. First, as the Young-Helmholtz three-color theory suggests, the retina contains three types of cones. Each is most sensitive to the wavelengths of one of the three primary colors (red, green, or blue). Second, as opponent-process theory maintains, the nervous system codes the color-related information from the cones into pairs of opponent colors, as demonstrated by the phenomenon of afterimages and as confirmed by measuring opponent processes within visual neurons of the thalamus. As illustrated by the phenomenon of color constancy under varying illumination, our brains construct our experience of color.

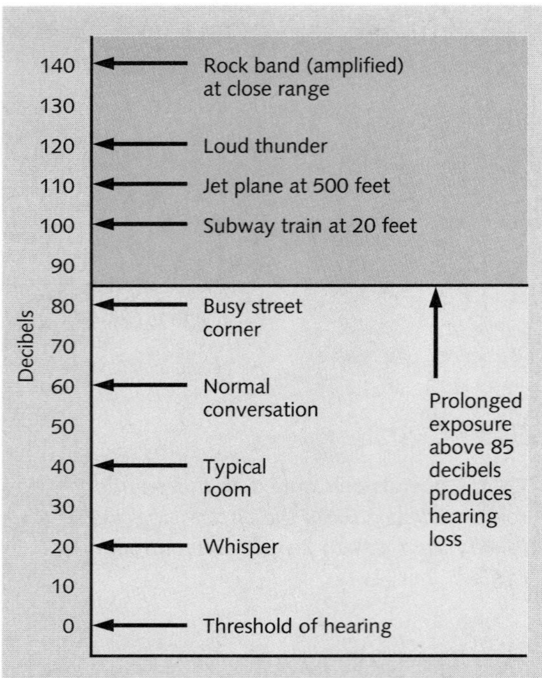


**Figure 5–15**

**The Intensity of Some Common Sounds, Measured in Decibels**

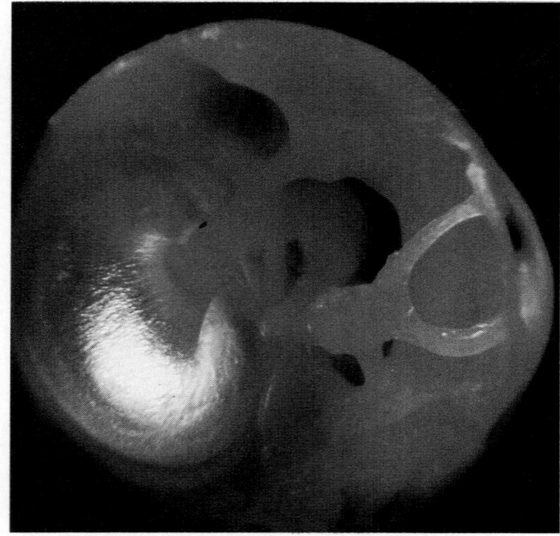

**The Middle Ear** *This remarkable photo of the middle ear (see Figure 5–16) shows the eardrum (at left, curving in a bit), the round window (black spot at far right), the stirrup (just left of the round window), and the oval window (covered by the stirrup). The actual distance from eardrum to oval window is less than 1 centimeter.*

# Hearing

*Somewhat less mysterious, but still pretty amazing, is another aspect of our ordinary experience: the process by which we convert air pressure waves into neural messages that the brain interprets as a meaningful symphony of sound. How do we do it? What breaks in the system typically cause hearing loss? What is it like to live without hearing?*

Like our other senses, our hearing, or **audition**, is highly adaptive. We hear a wide range of sounds, but we are best able to hear sounds having frequencies within a range that corresponds to the range of the human voice. We also are remarkably sensitive to faint sounds, an obvious boon to our ancestors' survival when hunting or being hunted. (If our ears were much more sensitive, we would hear a constant hiss from the movement of air molecules.) Moreover, we are acutely sensitive to differences in sounds. We can easily detect differences among thousands of human voices, which helps us instantly recognize the voice of almost anyone we know.

For hearing as for seeing, the fundamental question is: How do we do it? How do we transduce sound energy into neural messages that the brain interprets as a particular sound coming from a particular place?

## The Stimulus Input: Sound Waves

Hit a piano key and the resulting stimulus energy is sound waves—jostling molecules of air, each bumping into the next, like a shove being transmitted through the crowded exit tunnel of a football stadium. The resulting waves of compressed and expanded air are like the ripples on a pond circling out from where a tossed stone has broken the surface of the water. The strength, or amplitude, of sound waves determines their *loudness*. Waves also vary in length, and therefore in **frequency** (recall Figure 5–4, page 159). Their frequency determines their **pitch**: The longer the waves (thus, the lower their frequency), the lower the pitch; the shorter the waves (thus, the higher their frequency), the higher the pitch. A piccolo produces much shorter sound waves than does a kettledrum.

*Decibels* are the measuring unit for sound energy. The absolute threshold for hearing is arbitrarily defined as 0 decibels. Every 10 decibels correspond to a tenfold increase in sound. Thus, normal conversation (60 decibels) is about 100 times louder than a whisper (40 decibels). And a tolerable 90 decibel sound is a trillion times louder than the faintest detectable sound. (For light, too, we can tolerate a stimulus a trillion times more intense than a barely noticeable glimmer.) When prolonged, however, exposure to sounds above 85 decibels can produce hearing loss (Figure 5–15).

## The Ear

To hear, we must somehow convert sound waves into neural activity. The human ear accomplishes this feat through an intricate mechanical chain reaction (Figure 5–16). First, the visible outer ear channels sound waves through the auditory canal to the *eardrum*, a tight membrane that vibrates with the waves. The **middle ear** transmits the eardrum's vibrations through a piston made of three tiny bones (the *hammer*, *anvil*, and *stirrup*) to a snail-shaped tube in the **inner ear** called the **cochlea** (KOHK-lee-uh). The incoming vibrations cause the cochlea's membrane (the *oval window*) to vibrate the fluid that fills this tube. This motion causes ripples in the *basilar membrane*, which is lined with *hair cells*, so named because of their tiny hairlike projections. At the end of this sequence, the rippling of the basilar

Figure 5–16

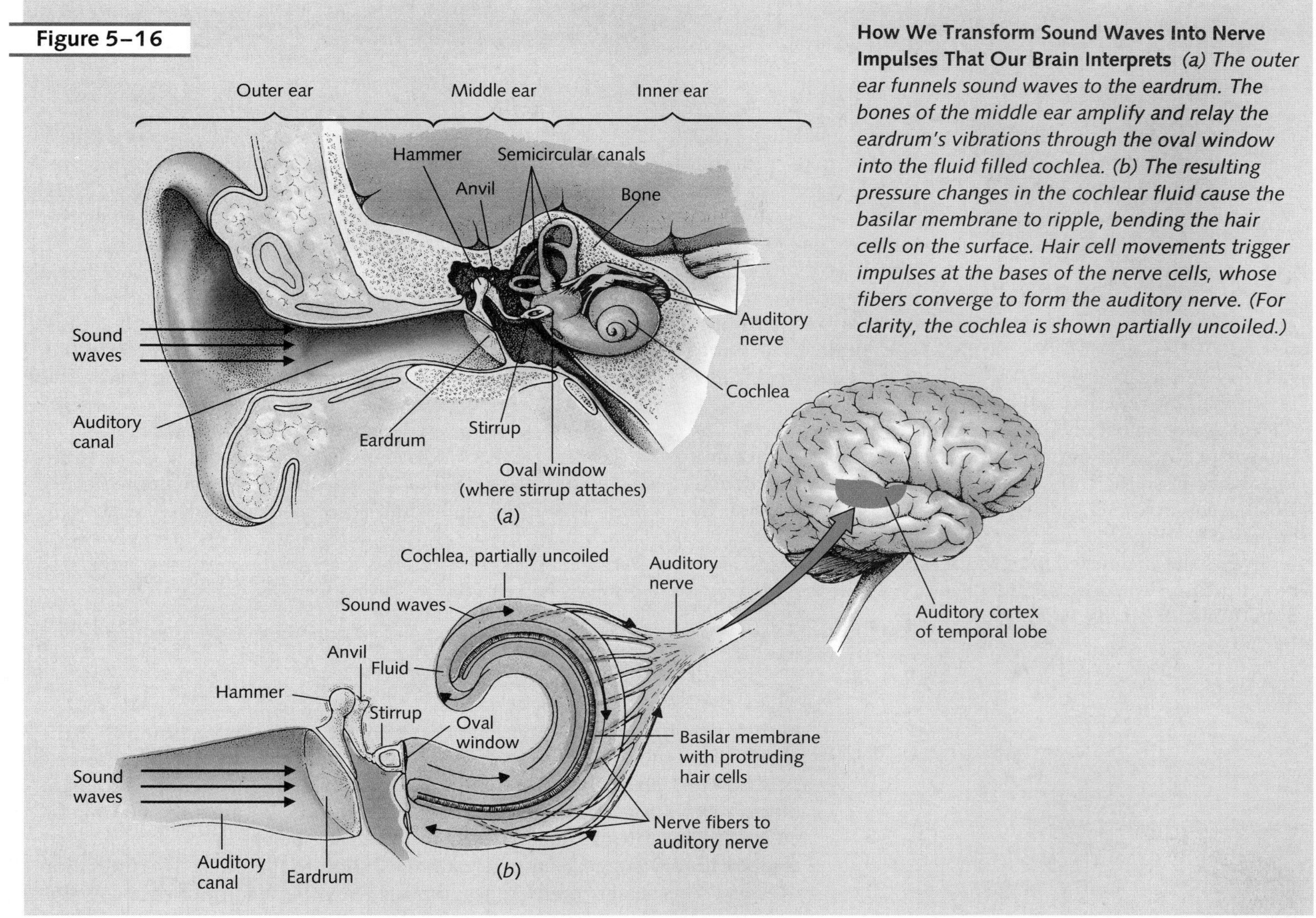


**How We Transform Sound Waves Into Nerve Impulses That Our Brain Interprets** *(a) The outer ear funnels sound waves to the eardrum. The bones of the middle ear amplify and relay the eardrum's vibrations through the oval window into the fluid filled cochlea. (b) The resulting pressure changes in the cochlear fluid cause the basilar membrane to ripple, bending the hair cells on the surface. Hair cell movements trigger impulses at the bases of the nerve cells, whose fibers converge to form the auditory nerve. (For clarity, the cochlea is shown partially uncoiled.)*

membrane bends these hair cells, rather like the wind bending a wheat field. This hair cell movement triggers impulses in the adjacent nerve fibers, which converge to form the auditory nerve. Through this mechanical chain of events, sound waves cause the hair cells of the inner ear to send neural messages up to the temporal lobe's auditory cortex. From vibrating air to moving piston to fluid waves to electrical impulses to the brain: We hear.

### How Do We Perceive Pitch?

How do we know whether a sound is the high-frequency, high-pitched chirp of a bird or the low-frequency, low-pitched roar of a truck? Current thinking on how we discriminate pitch, like current thinking on how we discriminate color, combines two theories.

**Place theory** presumes that we hear different pitches because different sound waves trigger activity at different places along the cochlea's basilar membrane. Thus, the brain can determine a sound's pitch by recognizing the place on the membrane from which it receives neural signals. When Georg von Békésy (1957) cut holes in the cochleas of guinea pigs and human cadavers and looked inside with a microscope, he discovered that

## Close-Up Noise

Urban life is noisy. Traffic roars. Factory machines clatter. Jackhammers tear up pavement. Escaping to more pleasant sounds, runners stride to the beat of intense music on their headsets.

But the intensity of that sound may cause a problem. Brief exposure to extremely intense sounds, such as gunfire near one's ear, and prolonged exposure to intense sounds, such as amplified music, can damage receptor cells and auditory nerves (Backus, 1977; West & Evans, 1990). Although rock and roll may be here to stay, the sad truth for some rock musicians is that their hearing may not be.

Noise affects not only our hearing but also our behavior. On tasks requiring alert performance, people in noisy surroundings work less efficiently and make more errors (Broadbent, 1978). People who live with continual noise in factories, in homes near airports, and in apartments next to trains and highways suffer elevated rates of stress-related disorders; high blood pressure, anxiety, and feelings of helplessness are common (Cohen & others, 1986).

But is it the noise that causes the stress? Laboratory experiments on the psychological effects of noise suggest an answer. In one such experiment, David Glass and Jerome Singer (1972) recreated the noise of city life by taperecording the chattering of office machines and of people speaking various languages. While working at various tasks, people heard this noise, played either loudly or softly, either at predictable or unpredictable intervals. Regardless of the conditions, the people soon adapted to the noise and performed well on most tasks. However, having coped with the noise, those exposed to the *unpredictable* loud noise later made more errors on a proofreading task and reacted more quickly to frustration.

The conclusion: Noise is especially stressful when unanticipated or uncontrollable. That explains why the unpredictable and uncontrollable blaring of someone else's stereo can be so much more upsetting than the same decibels from your own. At such times we may wish that, as our eyes have eyelids, so our ears had earlids.

high-frequency waves triggered activity mostly near the beginning of the cochlea's membrane, a discovery that contributed to his 1961 Nobel prize.

Although place theory explains how we hear high-pitched sounds, it doesn't explain how we hear low-pitched sounds, because the neural signals they generate are not so neatly localized on the basilar membrane. **Frequency theory** suggests an alternative solution to the pitch-discrimination mystery. The basilar membrane vibrates with the incoming sound wave. This triggers neural impulses to the brain at the same rate as the sound wave. If the sound wave has a frequency of 100 waves per second, then 100 pulses per second travel up the auditory nerve. Thus, the brain can read pitch from the frequency of neural impulses.

Frequency theory can explain how we perceive low-pitched sounds. But individual neurons cannot fire faster than 1000 times per second, so how can it explain our sensing sounds with frequencies above 1000 waves per second (roughly the upper third of a piano keyboard and above)? Enter the *volley principle*: Like soldiers who alternate firing so that some can shoot while others reload, neural cells can alternate firing and thereby achieve a combined frequency well above 1000 times per second.

Place theory best explains how we sense the high pitches and frequency theory the lower pitches. Some combination of the two processes seems to handle the intermediate-range pitches.

### How Do We Locate Sounds?

The slightly different messages sensed by the two microphones used in creating a stereophonic recording mimic the slightly different sound messages received by our two ears. As the placement of our eyes allows us to sense depth visually (page 194), the placement of our two ears allows us to enjoy stereophonic ("three-dimensional") hearing.

For at least two reasons, two ears are better than one. If a car to the right honks, your right ear receives a more *intense* sound slightly *sooner* than your left ear. Because sound travels 750 miles per hour and our ears are but 6 inches apart, the loudness difference and time lag are extremely small. But our auditory system is so sensitive that our two ears can detect such minute differences (Brown & Deffenbacher, 1979; Middlebrooks & Green, 1991). A just noticeable difference in the direction from which two sounds come corresponds to a time difference of just 0.000027 second! With auditory as with visual information, the brain uses parallel processing—by putting specialized neural teams to work simultaneously on different subtasks. Owls (and probably humans, too) process timing differences in one neural pathway and intensity differences in another before converging their information to pinpoint a sound's location (Konishi, 1993).

So how well do you suppose we do at locating a sound that is equidistant from our two ears, such as those that come from directly ahead, behind, overhead, or beneath us? Not very well, because such sounds strike the two ears simultaneously. You can experience this by sitting with closed eyes while a friend snaps fingers at various locations around your head. You will easily point to the sound when it comes from either side, but you will probably make mistakes when it comes from directly ahead, behind, above, or below. That is why, when trying to pinpoint a sound, you cock your head, so that your two ears receive slightly different messages.

**How Owls Localize Sounds** *The barn owl hardly has to cock its head to ensure that each ear receives a different message. The right ear and its opening are directed slightly upward; the left ear and its opening, slightly downward. The built-in asymmetry enables it to pinpoint the location of a sound both horizontally and vertically, making this species the successful nighttime hunter that it is. Even the faint sound of a field mouse scurrying through grass allows the owl to locate its prey with deadly accuracy.*

## Hearing Loss and Deaf Culture

The ear's intricate and delicate structure makes it vulnerable to damage. Problems with the mechanical system that conducts sound waves to the cochlea cause **conduction deafness**. If the eardrum is punctured or if the tiny bones of the middle ear lose their ability to vibrate, the ear's ability to conduct vibrations diminishes. A hearing aid may restore hearing by amplifying the vibrations.

Damage to the cochlea's hair cell receptors or their associated nerves can cause **nerve deafness**. Occasionally, disease causes nerve deafness, but more often biological changes linked with aging (Figure 5–17) and prolonged exposure to ear-splitting noise or music are the culprits. Once de-

**Figure 5–17**

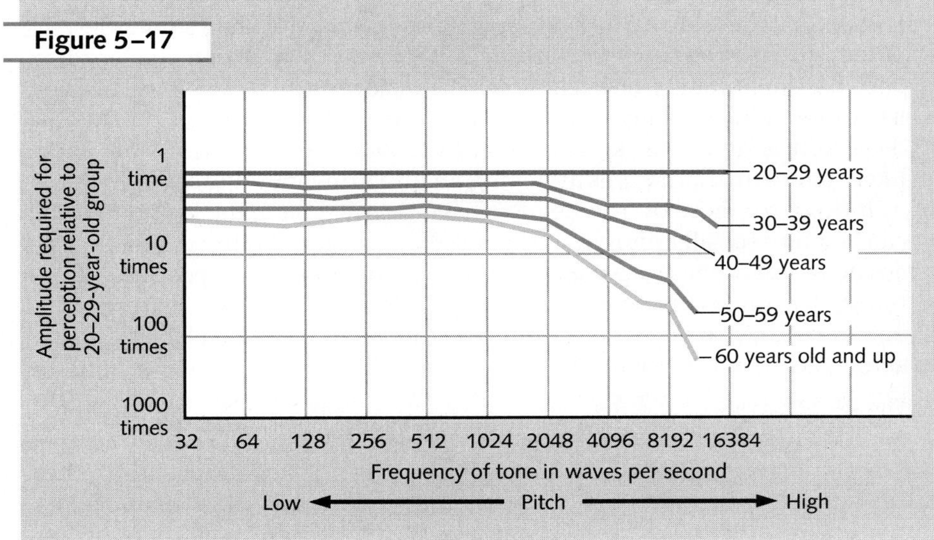


**Older People Tend to Hear Low Frequencies Well But Suffer Hearing Loss for High Frequencies** *This high-frequency loss results from nerve degeneration near the beginning of the basilar membrane. Which explanation of hearing does this confirm, place or frequency theory? (From Wever, 1949.)*

**Good Vibrations** *Scotland's Evelyn Glennie, who has been profoundly deaf since she was 12 years old, is a full-time percussion soloist. In performance she relates to her instruments through her sense of touch and to the conductor through her keen visual sense.*

stroyed in the human ear, these tissues remain dead, though a hearing aid may amplify sound to stimulate other hair cells. In other animals, such as sharks and birds, hair cells can regenerate. And recently, scientists have discovered ways to chemically stimulate hair cell regeneration in guinea pigs and rat pups (Forge & others, 1993; Warchol & others, 1993). This finding raises hopes that a way might someday be found to trick the human cochlea into regenerating hair cells—and thereby to restore hearing among those with nerve deafness.

Until then, the only game in town for restoring hearing among nerve-deafened people is a sort of bionic ear—a *cochlear implant*. This electronic device translates sounds into electrical signals, which are wired into the cochlea's nerves, conveying some information about sound to the brain. The typical result is a rough approximation of hearing—usually not enough to understand sentences with eyes closed but sufficient to assist lipreading and to hear a dog's bark or a horn's honk. More than 90 percent of deaf children have hearing parents, most of whom want to give their children this window on the world of sound and talk.

However, the National Association of the Deaf, which takes pride in deaf language and culture, objects to using the implants on children deafened before learning to speak. Deafness, the Association argues, is *not* a disability. Native signers, for example, are not linguistically disabled. Gallaudet University linguist William Stokoe confirmed this in his 1960 book, *Sign Language Structure*. He showed what native signers, like the proverbial fish who are the last to recognize water, had until then not fully understood: Sign is a complete language with its own grammar, syntax, and semantics.

Some deaf-culture advocates further contend that deafness could as well be considered "vision enhancement" as "hearing impairment." People who lose one channel of sensation seem to compensate with a slight enhancement of their other sensory abilities (Backman & Dixon, 1992; Levy & Langer, 1992). As a result of her blindness and deafness, Helen Keller's brain had regions normally dedicated to visual and auditory inputs available for other uses, such as discriminating touch sensations. Although deaf people don't generally have superior reading ability, visual compensation may help explain why so many of them are visually skilled engineers, architects, and mathematicians.

*"By placing my hand on a person's lips and throat, I gain an idea of many specific vibrations, and interpret them: a boy's chuckle, a man's 'Whew!' of surprise, the 'Hem!' of annoyance or perplexity, the moan of pain, a scream, a whisper, a rasp, a sob, a choke, and a gasp."*

Helen Keller (1908)

Of the 21 million Americans who experience hearing loss, the National Center for Health Statistics estimates that only 250,000 were born deaf. Losses that develop with age are greatest in the higher frequencies. To older adults, birds seem to chirp more softly and whispered conversation becomes frustratingly unintelligible. The majority of people whose hearing has diminished with age or after illness—those of us who live outside the deaf culture and have known, then lost, some or all hearing—are more likely to describe ourselves as having an impairment or disability.

Indeed, for those of us who have never learned Sign, the loss of hearing can be more socially disabling. Helen Keller said she "found deafness to be a much greater handicap than blindness. . . . Blindness cuts people off from things. Deafness cuts people off from people." Those whose hearing is impaired needn't think of themselves as disabled *people* (which labels the person) to acknowledge that they are persons with a disability (describing the impairment). Thus, the celebrated 1992 civil rights act was called not the Disabled Americans Act but the Americans with Disabilities Act.

## *Close-Up* Living in a Silent World

Those who live with hearing loss are a diverse group. Some are profoundly deaf; others have limited hearing. Some were deaf "prelingually" (before developing language); others have known the hearing world. Some communicate with sign language and identify with the language-based culture of deafness; others, especially those postlingually deaf, are "oral" and converse with the hearing world by reading lips. Still others move between the deaf and hearing cultures. If raised in a signing household, whether by deaf or hearing parents, deaf children often feel more accepted and express higher self-esteem (Bat-Chava, 1993).

Among deaf children, about one-fourth attend residential schools, half attend special education programs in public schools, and the remaining fourth are partially or wholly mainstreamed into regular classrooms, sometimes aided by sign language interpreters (Kirk & Gallagher, 1989). Among the deaf as among the hearing, some of these students are slow learners, others are brilliant. Essentially all children, whether deaf or hearing, whether signers or speakers, display a remarkable ability to learn language (Meier, 1991).

Still, all deaf people face challenges. Because academic subjects are rooted in spoken languages, academic achievement may suffer. The social challenges are even greater. Unable to communicate in customary ways, deaf children and their playmates struggle to coordinate their play. Adolescents may suffer social exclusion and resulting low self-confidence. Even adults whose hearing becomes impaired later in life may find the difficulties of social interaction producing a sort of shyness. "It's almost universal among the deaf to want to cause hearing people as little fuss as possible," reports Henry Kisor (1990, p. 244), a Chicago newspaper editor and columnist who lost his hearing at age 3. "We can be self-effacing and diffident to the point of invisibility. Sometimes this tendency can be crippling. I must fight it all the time."

I know. My 85-year-old mother, with whom we communicate by writing notes on an erasable "magic pad," lives in a silent world, long ago having withdrawn from the stress and strain of trying to interact with people outside a small circle of family and old friends. With my own hearing now declining on a trajectory toward hers, I find myself sitting front and center at plays and meetings, seeking quiet corners in restaurants, asking my wife to make necessary calls to friends whose accents differ from ours, using a special volume-controllable telephone. But the greatest frustration comes when, with or without a hearing aid, I can't hear the joke that everyone else is guffawing over; when, after repeated tries, I just can't catch that exasperated person's question and can't fake my way around it; when I can't hear the low frequencies of the bass that my son is playing in the school orchestra; when family members give up and say, "Oh, never mind" after trying three times to tell me something unimportant.

**Cracking the Code** *With the help of a computer at the Lexington Center in New York, this profoundly deaf young man is learning to speak. The computer screen displays for him the position of his teacher's tongue, the vibration of her nose, and the intensity of her voice. By matching her speech patterns, this boy will learn to speak more clearly.*

As my mother aged, she came to feel that seeking social interaction was just not worth the effort. But for newspaper columnist Kisor, communication *is* worth the effort. "So, for the most part, I will grit my teeth and plunge ahead" (p. 246). To reach out, to connect, to communicate with others, even across a chasm of silence, is to affirm our humanity as social creatures.

## Summing Up

**The Stimulus Input: Sound Waves** The pressure waves we experience as sound vary in frequency and amplitude, and correspondingly in perceived pitch and loudness.

**The Ear** Through a mechanical chain of events, sound waves traveling through the auditory canal cause minuscule vibrations in the eardrum. Transmitted via the bones of the middle ear to the fluid-filled cochlea, these vibrations create movement in tiny hair cells, triggering neural messages to the brain.

Research on how we hear pitch supports both the place theory, which best explains the sensation of high-pitched sounds, and frequency theory, which best explains the sensation of low-pitched sounds. We localize sound by detecting minute differences in the loudness and timing of the sounds received by each ear.

**Hearing Loss and Deaf Culture** Hearing losses linked to conduction and nerve disorders can be caused by prolonged exposure to loud noise and by diseases and age-related disorders. Those who live with hearing loss face social challenges.

# The Other Senses

*Extraordinary happenings are hidden within four other ordinary senses: touch, taste, smell, and our sense of body position and movement. What are these happenings? And what happens if we restrict input from any or all the senses?*

For humans, seeing and hearing are the major senses. We depend on them, particularly for communication. Our brains give these two senses priority in the allocation of cortical tissue. For other animals, the priorities differ. Sharks and dogs rely on their extraordinary senses of smell, aided by the large segment of their cortexes devoted to it. Nevertheless, without our sense of touch, our senses of taste and smell, and our senses of body motion and position, we humans would be seriously handicapped, and our capacities for enjoying the world would be devastatingly diminished.

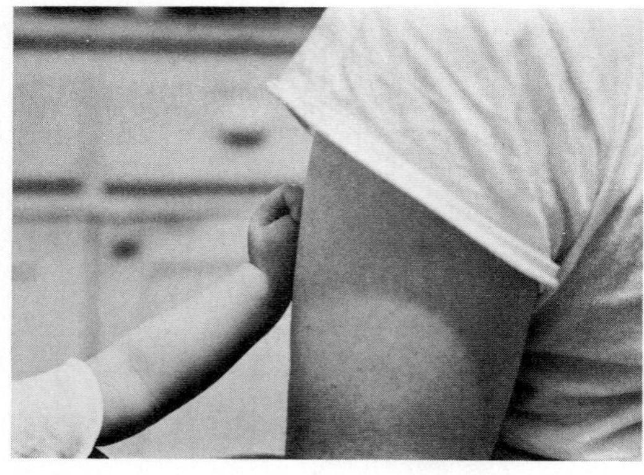

**The Precious Sense of Touch** *As William James wrote in his* Principles of Psychology *(1890), "Touch is both the alpha and omega of affection."*

## Touch

If you had to give up one sense, which would it be? If you could retain only one sense, which would it be?

Touch would be a good candidate for retention. Right from the start, touch is strangely essential to our development. As we noted in Chapter 3, premature babies gain weight faster and go home sooner if stimulated by hand massage. Infant rats deprived of their mothers' grooming touch produce less growth hormone and have a lower metabolic rate—a good way to keep alive until the mother returns, but one that will result in stunted growth if she's delayed. Infant monkeys allowed to see, hear, and smell—but not touch—their mothers are desperately unhappy; much less so are those separated by a screen with holes that allow touching. As lovers, we yearn to touch—to kiss, to stroke, to snuggle like spoons.

Dave Barry is perhaps right to say of the skin that it "keeps people from seeing the inside of your body, which is repulsive, and it prevents your organs from falling onto the ground." But skin does more. Our "sense of touch" is actually a mix of at least four distinct skin senses—pressure, warmth, cold, and pain. Touching various spots on the skin with a soft hair, a warm or cool wire, and the point of a pin reveals that some spots are especially sensitive to pressure, others to warmth, others to cold, still others to pain. Within the skin are different types of specialized nerve endings. Does that mean that each type is a receptor for one of the basic skin senses, much as the eye's cone receptors correspond to light's basic colors?

Surprisingly, there is no simple relationship between what we feel at a given spot and the type of specialized nerve ending found there. Except for pressure, which does have identifiable receptors, the relationship between warmth, cold, and pain and the receptors that respond to them remains a mystery. Other skin sensations are variations of the basic four (pressure, warmth, cold, and pain):

Stroking adjacent pressure spots creates a tickle.

Repeated gentle stroking of a pain spot will create an itching sensation.

Touching adjacent cold and pressure spots triggers a sense of wetness, which you can experience by touching dry, cold metal.

Stimulating nearby cold and warmth spots produces a feeling of "hot." Cold spots respond either to very low or very high temperatures. We sense hot when a high temperature activates both warm and cold spots (Figure 5–18).

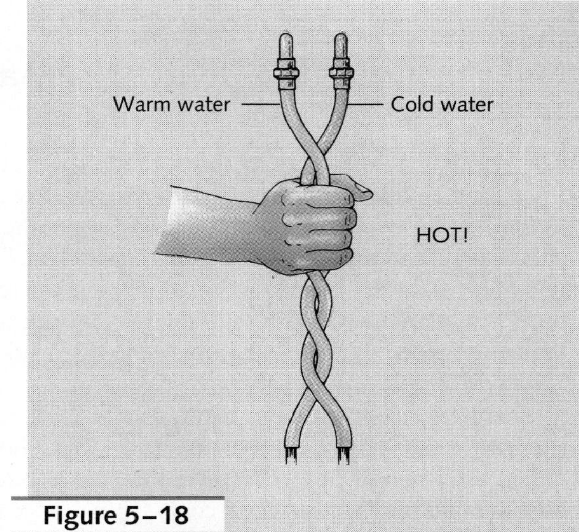


**Figure 5–18**

**Warm + Cold = Hot** *When ice-cold water passes through one coil and comfortably warm water through another, we perceive the combined sensation as burning hot.*

## Pain

Be thankful for occasional pain. Pain is your body's way of telling you that something has gone wrong. It draws your attention to a burn, a break, or a rupture and tells you to change your behavior immediately. The rare people who are born without the ability to feel pain may experience severe injury without ever being alerted by pain's danger signals. Usually, they die by early adulthood. Without the discomfort that makes us occasionally shift position, their joints fail from excess strain. Without pain, the effects of unchecked infections and injuries accumulate (Neese, 1991). More numerous are those who endure chronic pain. The suffering of people with persistent or recurring backaches, arthritis, headaches, and cancer-related pain prompts two questions: What is pain? How might it be controlled?

*"When belly with bad pains doth swell,*
*It matters naught what else goes well."*

Sadi
*The Gulistan*, 1258

**What Is Pain?** Pain is not only a property of the senses—of the region where we feel it—but of the brain as well. As the dreamer sees with eyes closed and the listener hears a ringing during utter silence, so some 7 in 10 amputees may feel pain in their nonexistent limbs (Melzack, 1992). These "phantom limb sensations" indicate that with pain, as with sights and sounds, the brain can misinterpret the spontaneous central nervous system activity that occurs in the absence of normal sensory input. To see, hear, and feel, we require not a body but a brain.

Unlike vision, however, the pain system is not located in a simple neural cord running from a sensing device to a definable area in the brain. Moreover, there is no one type of stimulus that triggers pains (as light triggers vision), and there are no special receptors (like the retina's rods and cones) for pain. At low intensities, the stimuli that produce pain cause other sensations, including warmth or coolness, smoothness or roughness.

Although no theory of pain explains all the available findings, psychologist Ronald Melzack and biologist Patrick Wall's (1965, 1983) **gate-control theory** provides a useful model. Melzack and Wall believe that the spinal cord contains a sort of neurological "gate" that either blocks or allows pain

## *Thinking Critically About* Matter Over Mind: Firewalking

The popular media have at times made the phenomenon of firewalking a hot topic. For $60 or so we can take a "mind over matter" class that supposedly enables us to alter our body's chemistry. The "proof": walking on red-hot coals without feeling pain or being burned. The psychological result: a newfound capacity to conquer one's fears. "If I can do something that's supposed to be impossible," says the elated firewalker, "I can do almost anything."

Skeptical scientists have taken a cool look at firewalking (Leikind & McCarthy, 1985, 1988). The secret, they report, lies not in any mental power to alter the senses but in the poor heat conductivity of the wood coals. Think of a cake baking in a 350° oven. Touch the aluminum cake tin and you'll get burned; touch the cake—like wood, a poor heat conductor—and you'll be okay. Cakes and coals do conduct some heat, so you'd better not stay in touch with them too long or you will get burned. Some have learned the hard way that he (or she) who hesitates is lost. But the 2 seconds or less that it takes to quick-step across hot embers puts each foot in contact with the coals for only a fraction of a second and for less than a second in total time per foot. Wetting the feet on damp grass or in water before the firewalk provides further insulation (a phenomenon familiar to anyone who has used wet fingers to snuff a candle or test a hot iron). Confident of these facts, skeptical scientists have themselves performed the feat without the "mind over matter" training.

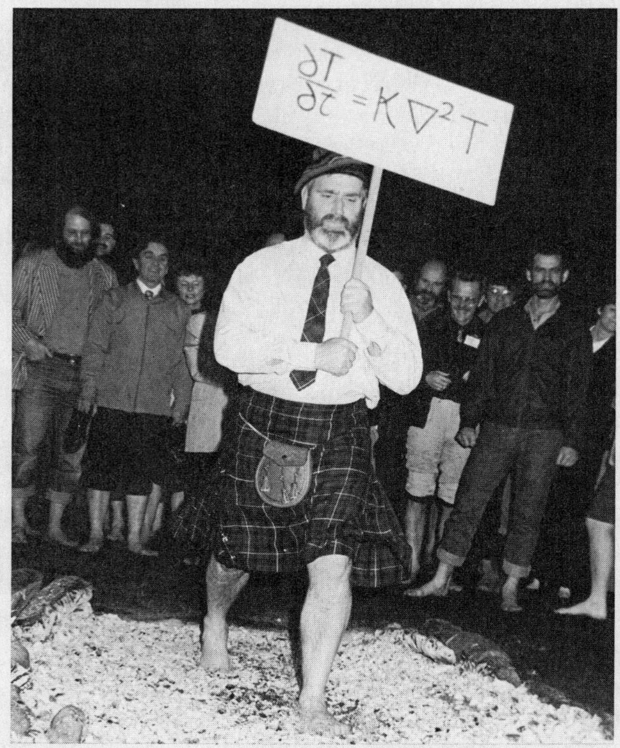


**Some Like It Hot** *At a New Zealand skeptics' meeting, University of Canterbury physicist John Campbell explained heat diffusion principles that permit firewalking, then put his feet where his mouth was by leading 80 people across 12 feet of hot coals.*

signals to pass on to the brain. The spinal cord contains small nerve fibers that conduct most pain signals, and larger fibers that conduct most other sensory signals. When tissue is injured, the small fibers activate and open the neural gate, and you feel pain. Large-fiber activity closes the pain gate, turning pain off.

Thus, one way to treat chronic pain is to stimulate (electrically, by massage, or even by acupuncture) "gate-closing" activity in the large neural fibers. Rubbing the area around your stubbed toe creates competing stimulation that will block some of the pain messages. Placing ice on a bruise serves not only to control swelling but also to trigger cold messages that close the gate on the pain signals. Some arthritic patients wear a small portable electrical stimulation unit next to a painful area. When the unit stimulates nerves in the area, the patient feels a vibrating sensation rather than pain (T. Murphy, 1982).

Melzack and Wall believe the pain gate can also be closed by information from the brain. These brain-to-spinal cord messages help explain some striking psychological influences on pain. When distracted from pain signals and soothed by the release of endorphins, our experience of pain may be greatly diminished. Sports injuries may be unnoticed, until taking the after-game shower. During a 1989 basketball game, Ohio State University guard Jay Burson broke his neck—and kept playing. Clearly, there is more to pain than what stimulates the sense receptors.

*"Pain is increased by attending to it."*
Charles Darwin
*Expression of Emotions in Man and Animals*, 1872

There is also more to our memories of pain than the pain we experience. In experiments, and after medical procedures, people overlook a pain's duration. Their memory snapshots instead record its peak moment and how much pain they felt at the end. Daniel Kahneman and his co-researchers (1993) discovered this when they asked people to immerse one hand in painfully cold water for 60 seconds, and then the other hand in the same painfully cold water for 60 seconds followed by a slightly less painful 30 seconds more. Curiously, when asked which trial they would prefer to repeat, most preferred the longer trial, with more net pain—but less pain at the end. When patients recalled the pain of a colon examination a month later, their memories were similarly dominated by the final (and the worst) moments, not by how long the pain lasted. It's better, it seems, for medical personnel to taper down a painful procedure than to switch it off abruptly.

*"From there to here, from here to there, funny things are everywhere."*
Dr. Seuss
*One Fish, Two Fish, Red Fish, Blue Fish*

**Pain Control** If pain is indeed a physical and a psychological phenomenon, then it should be treatable both physically and psychologically. Depending on the type of symptoms, pain control clinics select one or more therapies from a list that includes drugs, surgery, acupuncture, electrical stimulation, massage, exercise, hypnosis, relaxation training, and thought distraction.

The widely practiced Lamaze method of childbirth combines several of these pain control techniques. Among them are relaxation (through deep breathing and muscle relaxation), counterstimulation (through gentle massage), and distraction (through focusing attention on, say, a pleasant photograph). After Everett Worthington and his colleagues (1983) trained women in the use of such techniques, the women could more easily tolerate the pain of having their hand in ice water. The women's pain tolerance was even greater when a trusted "coach" encouraged them, as husbands or an intimate friend encourage Lamaze-trained women during childbirth.

*Although Lamaze training reduces labor pain, most Lamaze patients request a local anesthetic during labor. Some—having expected a "natural, painless birth"—feel needless guilt and failure (Melzack, 1984). Melzack therefore advocates—as does the Lamaze program itself—childbirth training that prepares a woman "to cope with an event which is often extremely painful and, at the same time, one of the most fulfilling peak experiences in her life."*

Distracting people with pleasant images ("Think of a warm, comfortable environment") or drawing their attention away from the painful stimulation ("Count backward by 3's") is an especially effective way to increase pain tolerance (Fernandez & Turk, 1989; McCaul & Malott, 1984). The principle works in health care situations. A nurse will distract needle-shy patients with chatter and may ask them to look away when inserting the needle. For hospitalized patients, a pleasing window view of natural vegetation may have a similarly relaxing and distracting effect. In examining the records of one Pennsylvania hospital, Roger Ulrich (1984) discovered that surgery patients assigned to rooms looking out on trees required less pain medication and had shorter stays than did those assigned to identical rooms overlooking a brick wall.

## Taste

Like touch, our sense of taste involves four basic sensations—sweet, sour, salty, and bitter (McBurney & Gent, 1979). All other tastes are mixtures of these. Investigators have, however, been frustrated in their search for specialized nerve fibers for each of the four basic taste sensations.

Taste is a chemical sense. Inside the little bumps on the top and sides of your tongue are 200 or more taste buds. Each contains a pore that catches food chemicals. These molecules are sensed by 50 taste receptor cells that project antennalike hairs into the pore. Some of these receptors respond mostly to sweet-tasting molecules, others to salty- , sour- , or bitter-tasting ones. It doesn't take much to trigger a response. When a stream of water is pumped across the tongue, the addition of a concentrated salty or sweet taste for but one-tenth of a second gets noticed (Kelling & Halpern, 1983). When a friend asks for "just a taste" of your soft drink, you can squeeze off the straw after a mere fraction of a second.

Taste receptors reproduce themselves every week, so if you burn your tongue with hot food it matters little. However, as you grow older, the number of taste buds decreases, as does taste sensitivity (Cowart, 1981). (No wonder adults enjoy strong-tasting foods that children resist.) Heavy smoking and alcohol use accelerate the decline in taste buds and sensitivities.

Although taste buds are essential for taste, there is more to taste than meets the tongue. Hold your nose, close your eyes, and have someone feed you various foods. A piece of apple may then be indistinguishable from a piece of raw potato; a piece of steak may taste like cardboard. To savor a taste, we normally breathe the aroma through our nose—which is why eating is not much fun when you have a bad cold, and why people who lose their sense of smell may think they have also lost their sense of taste. Smell not only adds to our perception of taste, it also changes it. A drink's strawberry odor enhances our perception of its sweetness. This is **sensory interaction** at work—the principle that one sense may influence another. Smell plus taste equals flavor. Similarly, we correctly perceive the location of the voice directly in front of us partly because we also see that the person is in front of us, not behind, above, or beneath us.

Taste researcher Linda Bartoshuk (1993) offers other fascinating facts about taste:

- Our emotional responses to taste are hard-wired. Put a sweet or bitter substance on newborns' tongues and their tongues and faces react like adults'.
- People without tongues can still taste—through receptors in the back and roof of the mouth.
- If you lose taste sensation from one side of your tongue you probably won't notice. That's because the other side will become correspondingly supersensitive. Also, the brain doesn't localize taste well: Although the middle of our tongue has few taste receptors, we perceive taste as coming from the whole tongue.
- We can neither taste nor smell most nutrients—fat, protein, starch, and food vitamins. (Sugar is an exception.) But we do quickly associate the taste and smell of other food components with a food's nutritional or poisonous significance (see pages 264–265).

## Smell

Breaths come in pairs—inhale, exhale—except at two moments: birth and death. Each day, as you inhale and exhale nearly 20,000 breaths of life-sustaining air, you bathe your nostrils in a stream of scent-laden molecules. More than you may realize, your resulting experiences of smell (*olfaction*) are intimate ones. To smell someone you inhale something of the person.

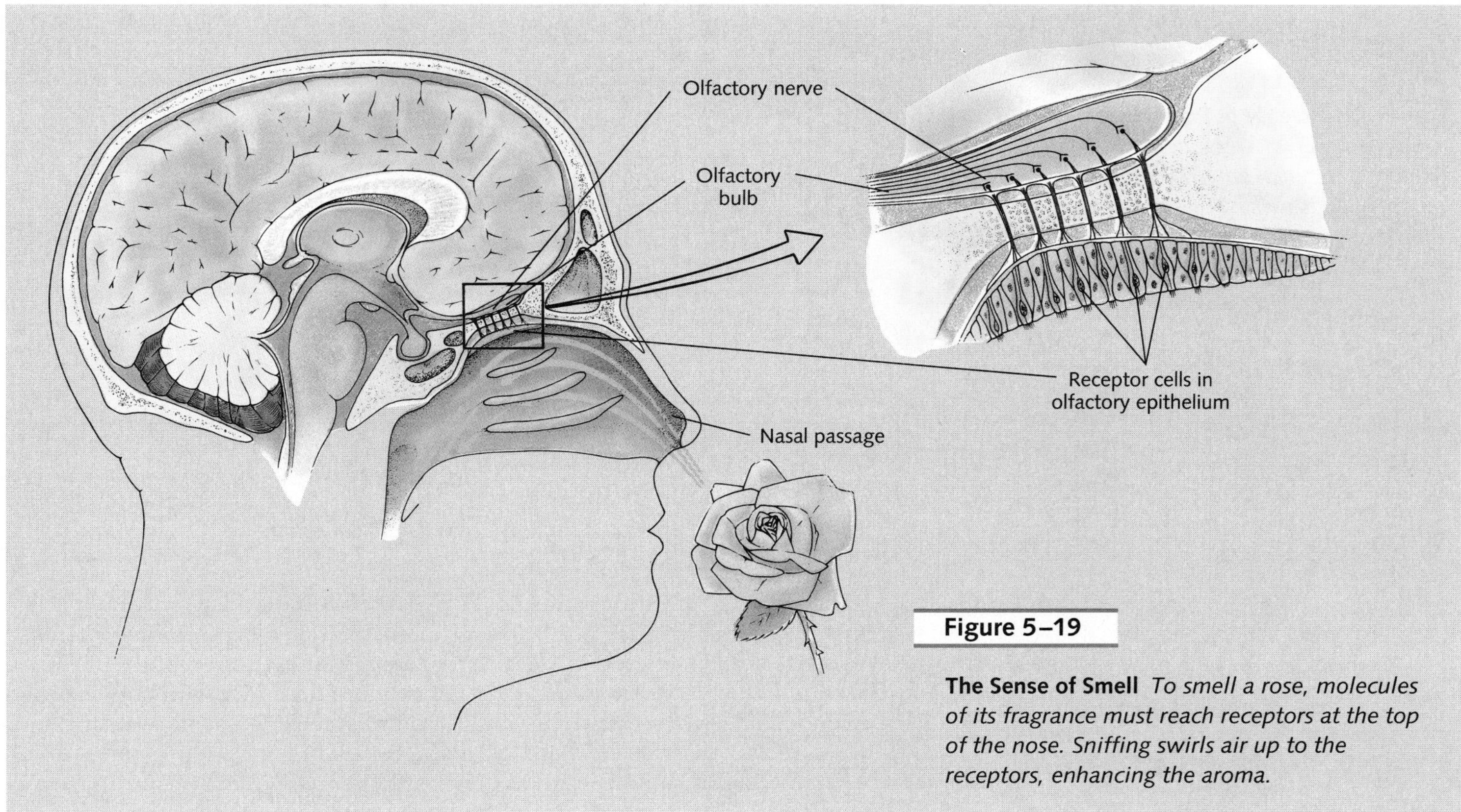


**Figure 5–19**

**The Sense of Smell** *To smell a rose, molecules of its fragrance must reach receptors at the top of the nose. Sniffing swirls air up to the receptors, enhancing the aroma.*

Like taste, smell is a chemical sense. We smell something when air-carried molecules of a substance reach a tiny cluster of 5 million receptor cells at the top of each nasal cavity (Figure 5–19). These olfactory receptor cells, waving like sea anemones on a reef, respond selectively to the aroma of brownies baking, to a wisp of smoke, to a friend's fragrance, and instantly alert the brain. Even nursing infants and mothers have a literal chemistry to their relationship, as they quickly learn to recognize each others' scents (McCarthy, 1986). Aided by smell, a mother fur seal returning to a beach crowded with pups will find her own. Yet, unlike that of the mother fur seal, our sense of smell is less impressive than the acuteness of our seeing and hearing (within the stimulus ranges we detect). Looking out across a garden we see its forms and colors in exquisite detail and hear its singing birds, yet smell little of it without jamming our nose into the flowers.

Precisely how olfactory receptors work is a mystery. Unlike light, which can be separated into its spectral colors, an odor cannot be separated into more elemental odors. Thus, the olfaction system has no parallel to the retina, which detects myriad colors with sensory cells dedicated to red, green, or blue. Olfactory receptors recognize odors individually.

Odor molecules come in so many shapes and sizes that it takes lots of different receptors to detect them. A large family of genes design receptor proteins that recognize particular molecules (Buck & Axel, 1991). As a key slips into a lock, so odor molecules slip into these receptors. Yet we seem not to have a distinct receptor for each of the some 10,000 odors we can detect. This hints that some odors trigger a combination of receptors.

**Figure 5–20**

**Age, Sex, and Sense of Smell** *Among the 1.2 million people who responded to a* National Geographic *scratch and sniff survey, women and younger adults most successfully identified six sample odors. (From Wysocki & Gilbert, 1989.)*

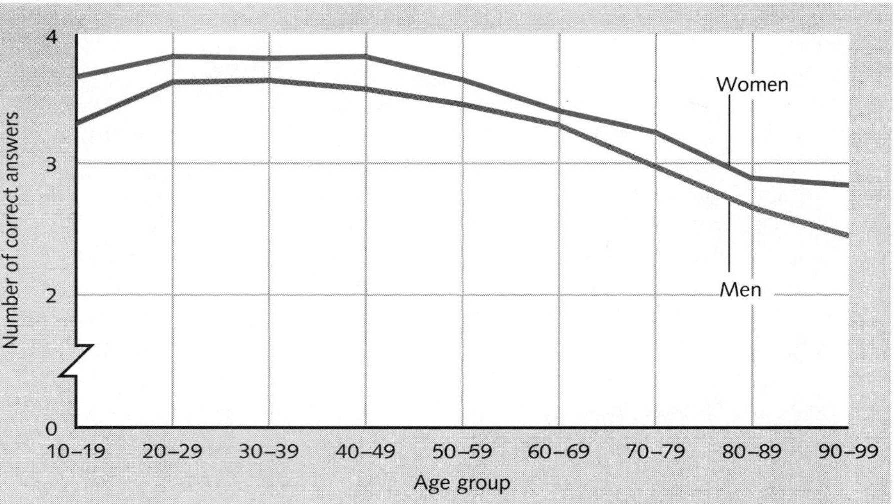

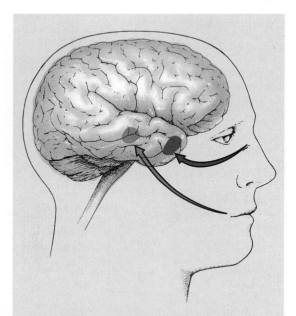

**The Olfactory Brain** *Information from the taste buds (orange arrow) travels to an area of the temporal lobe not far from that where olfactory information is received. The brain's circuitry for smell (magenta arrow) also connects with areas involved in memory storage, which helps explain why a smell can trigger a memory explosion.*

The ability to identify scents peaks in early adulthood and gradually declines thereafter (Figure 5–20). Despite our skill at discriminating scents, we aren't nearly so good at describing them. Words more readily portray the sound of a piccolo than the aroma of coffee. Compared with how we experience and remember sights and sounds, smells seem more primitive and harder to describe (Richardson & Zucco, 1989).

As any dog or cat with a good nose could tell us, we each have our own identifiable chemical signature. (One noteworthy exception: A dog will follow the tracks of one identical twin as though they had been made by the other [Thomas, 1974].) Animals that have many times more olfactory receptors than we do also use their sense of smell to communicate and navigate. Long before the shark can see its prey, or the moth its mate, odors direct the way.

Odors also have the power to evoke memories and feelings. In *Remembrance of Things Past*, the French novelist Marcel Proust described how the aroma and flavor of a bit of cake soaked in tea resurrected long-forgotten memories of his aunt's bedroom in the old family house. "The smell and taste of things," he noted, "bears unfaltering, in the tiny and almost impalpable drop of their essence, the vast structure of recollection."

Laboratory studies confirm that, though it's difficult to recall odors by name, we do indeed have a remarkable capacity to recognize long-forgotten odors and their associated personal episodes (Engen, 1987; Schab, 1991). Students who do a word exercise while smelling the aroma of chocolate remember the words better the next day if the chocolate aroma is again present (Schab, 1990). And pleasant odors evoke pleasant memories (Ehrlichman & Halpern, 1988). The smell of the sea, the scent of a perfume, or an aroma like the floorwax smell in Grandma's kitchen bring to mind happy memories.

Pleasant moods produced by pleasant scents may also give a boost to workers' performance. That's what Robert Baron (1990) surmised after having students work in rooms with or without pleasant air scents. Pleasant scents boosted the subjects' moods and self-confidence, leading them to set slightly higher work goals on a clerical task and to negotiate more aggressively on a bargaining task. Such is the power of odors to switch on memories and to retrieve associated emotions.

## Body Position and Movement

With only the five familiar senses we have so far considered, we would be helpless. We could not put food in our mouths, stand up, or reach out and touch someone. To know just how to move your arms to grasp someone's hand, you first need to know the current position of your arms and hands and then be aware of their changing positions as you move them. To take just one step requires feedback from and instructions to some 200 muscles.

Humans come equipped with millions of such position and motion sensors. They are all over our bodies—in the muscles, tendons, and joints—and they are continually providing our brains with information. If we twist our wrists 1 degree, the sensors immediately report it. This sense of our body parts' position and movement is **kinesthesis** (kin-ehs-THEE-sehs).

Have you ever considered life without kinesthesis, without, say, being able to sense the positions of your limbs when awakening during the night? Such is the experience of Christina, whose nerve fibers carrying information from muscles, tendons, and joints were destroyed by disease, leaving her floppy as a rag doll (Sacks, 1985). What does it feel like? Like she is disembodied, her body dead, not real, not hers. Against all odds, Christina has, however, learned to walk and eat—by visually attending to her limbs and directing them accordingly.

A companion sense called **equilibrium** monitors the position and movement of the whole body. The biological gyroscopes for our sense of equilibrium are in the inner ear. In the *semicircular canals,* which look like a three-dimensional pretzel (Figure 5–16[*a*], page 169), and the *vestibular sacs,* which connect the canals with the cochlea, are substances that move when the head rotates or tilts. This movement stimulates hairlike receptors in these organs of the inner ear. The receptors then send to the brain messages that enable us continually to sense our body position and maintain our balance.

If you've been twirling around and come to an abrupt halt, the fluid in your semicircular canals and your kinesthetic receptors does not immediately return to its neutral state. The aftereffect fools your dizzy brain with the sensation that you're still spinning. This illustrates a principle that underlies the next chapter's discussion of perceptual illusions. Mechanisms that normally give us an accurate experience of the world can, under special conditions, fool us. Understanding how we get fooled provides clues to how our perceptual system works.

# Sensory Restriction

Imagine that one of your sensory windows on the world snapped shut. Could your other senses partially make up for the loss? People with sensory deficits show us the rich potential of each sense. Blind people cope by making greater use of their hearing—for example, by locating obstacles while attending to echoes bouncing off them. Helen Keller, blind *and* deaf, vividly experienced life's aromas, tastes, and touches.

Close your eyes and immediately you, too, will notice your attention being drawn to your other senses. When kissing, lovers minimize distraction and increase their touch sensitivity by closing their eyes. People with aphasia—having lost the ability to comprehend language—typically become acutely sensitive to nonlanguage cues. You and I might miss the meaning conveyed by someone's intonation and gestures, but the aphasic reads these messages readily.

**Sensory Compensation** *"Ears are eyes to the blind," wrote Sophocles. Cortney Glonk, blind since birth, uses her clicker's echoes to navigate the hallways at her Detroit school.*

The loss of a sense is but one type of sensory restriction. Another is sensory monotony—the relatively unchanging sensory input experienced by prisoners in solitary confinement, nighttime truck drivers and airline pilots, and animals in barren zoos.

To investigate how sensory restriction affects us, experimenters have put thousands of people through controlled, temporary simulations of such conditions. Some have spent several days in monotonous environments—small rooms in which light and sound are unchanging. Others have passed time in dark, silent rooms, deprived of normal sensory input. Initial "sensory deprivation" experiments produced bizarre and widely publicized findings (Heron, 1957). The subjects, lying on beds and wearing translucent goggles to diffuse the light, typically began the experiment in good spirits. Here was a chance to make some easy money while enjoying a time for relaxation and creative thinking. Before long, however, they became disoriented. Many experienced hallucinations, and some became susceptible to piped-in messages arguing for the reality of ghosts.

As often happens in science, manipulating one factor simultaneously changes other factors. Are the effects of a monotonous environment caused by the sensory restriction or by the social isolation or stress of confinement? The dramatic reports from early experiments prompted many more investigations, most of which produced less newsworthy results (Suedfeld & Kristeller, 1982).

In fact, researchers have found sensory restriction does not disturb most people. More often, the experience reduces stress and helps people become more open to positive influence. In experiments with smokers and overweight people at the University of British Columbia, Peter Suedfeld (1980) found that restricted sensory input helps people modify their behavior. People wanting to alter their behavior were often able to increase their self-control after 24 hours of what he aptly calls REST—Restricted Environmental Stimulation Therapy.

In one such experiment conducted by Allan Best and Suedfeld (1982), smokers listened to antismoking messages while spending 24 hours lying on beds in quiet, dark rooms (rising only to drink a liquid diet available through tubes or to use toilets next to the beds). In the week that followed, none relapsed to smoking. A year later, two-thirds were still abstaining—double the number of abstainers who had received the instruction without the day of REST.

Shorter REST periods can also pay dividends. In one experiment, heavy-drinking college students spent 2½ hours in REST. After 1½ hours, a 5-minute message gave factual information about alcohol's negative effects. Unlike those in control conditions, the REST-plus-message group decreased their alcohol consumption by 55 percent during the ensuing 6 months (Cooper & others, 1988).

In other times and places, periods of solitude and sensory restriction have fostered human fulfillment. Sensory restriction is a traditional component of the "quiet therapies" of Japan (Reynolds, 1982, 1986). For example, Morita therapy for depressed or anxious people sometimes begins with a week of bed rest and meditation and then progresses to assigned light tasks. The religious visions of Moses, Mohammed, and Buddha reportedly occurred during times of solitude and contemplation. As living creatures we require sensory stimulation, but there are also times when we benefit from the peace and relaxation of restricted stimulation.

*"It is in silence and not in commotion, in solitude and not in crowds that God best likes to reveal Himself."*

Thomas Merton
*The Silent Life*, 1957

In this chapter we have taken a "bottom-up" look at how we experience the world, starting with how our ingenious sense receptors transduce physical energy into neural messages sent to our brain. We've also taken a "top-down" look at how our mind, too, shapes our experiences. Pain, for example, is a response to information coming both up the spinal cord's small nerves and down from what our mind is paying attention to. Our experiences are in the brain—so much so that the brain can choose how to interpret neural activity or may even conjure up perceived sights, sounds, and pains without external stimulation. Sensation and perception are different aspects of one whole fabric—how we experience the world around us.

## Summing Up

**Touch** Our sense of touch is actually four senses—pressure, warmth, cold, and pain—that combine to produce other sensations, such as "hot." One theory of pain is that a "gate" in the spinal cord either opens to permit pain signals traveling up small nerve fibers to reach the brain or closes to prevent their passage. Because pain is both a physiological and psychological phenomenon, it often can be controlled through a combination of medical and psychological treatments.

**Taste** Taste, a chemical sense, is likewise a composite of four basic sensations—sweet, sour, salty, and bitter—and of the aromas that interact with information from the taste buds.

**Smell** Like taste, smell is a chemical sense, but there are no basic sensations for smell, as there are for touch and taste. Like other stimuli, odors can spontaneously evoke memories and feelings.

**Body Position and Movement** Finally, our effective functioning requires a kinesthetic sense, which notifies the brain of the position and movement of body parts, and a sense of equilibrium, which monitors the position and movement of the whole body.

**Sensory Restriction** People temporarily or permanently deprived of one of their senses typically compensate by becoming more acutely aware of information from the other senses. Temporary experiences of sensory restriction often evoke a heightened awareness of all forms of sensation. Under supervision, sensory restriction may provide a therapeutic boost for those seeking control over problems such as smoking.

## Terms and Concepts to Remember

**sensation** The process by which our sense receptors and nervous system receive and represent stimulus energies from our environment.

**perception** The process of organizing and interpreting sensory information, enabling us to recognize meaningful objects and events.

### Sensing the World: Some Basic Principles

**psychophysics** The study of relationships between the physical characteristics of stimuli and our psychological experience of them.

**absolute threshold** The minimum stimulation needed to detect a particular stimulus.

**signal detection** The task of judging the presence of a faint stimulus ("signal"). Signal detection researchers assume there is no single absolute threshold, because the detection of a weak signal depends partly on a person's experience, expectation, motivation, and level of fatigue.

**subliminal** Below one's absolute threshold for conscious awareness.

**difference threshold** The minimum difference that a subject can detect between two stimuli 50 percent of the time. We experience the difference threshold as a just noticeable difference (jnd).

**just noticeable difference (jnd)** See *difference threshold*.

**Weber's law** The principle that, to perceive their difference, two stimuli must differ by a constant minimum percentage (rather than a constant amount).

**sensory adaptation** Diminished sensitivity that is a consequence of constant stimulation.

## Vision

**transduction** Conversion of one form of energy into another. In sensation, the transforming of stimulus energies into neural impulses.

**wavelength** The distance from the peak of one light or sound wave to the peak of the next. Electromagnetic wavelengths vary from the long pulses of radio transmission to the short blips of cosmic rays.

**hue** The dimension of color that is determined by the wavelength of light; what we know as the color names "blue," "green," and so forth.

**intensity** The amount of energy in a light or sound wave, which we perceive as brightness or loudness, as determined by the wave's amplitude.

**pupil** The adjustable opening in the center of the eye through which light enters.

**iris** A ring of muscle tissue that forms the colored portion of the eye around the pupil and controls the size of the pupil opening.

**lens** The transparent structure behind the pupil that changes shape to focus images on the retina.

**accommodation** The process by which the eye's lens changes shape to focus the image of near objects on the retina.

**retina** The light-sensitive inner surface of the eye, containing the receptor rods and cones plus layers of neurons that begin the processing of visual information.

**rods** Retinal receptors that detect black, white, and gray; necessary for peripheral and twilight vision, when cones don't respond.

**cones** Receptor cells that are concentrated near the center of the retina and that function in daylight or in well-lit conditions. The cones detect fine detail and give rise to color sensations.

**optic nerve** The nerve that carries neural impulses from the eye to the brain.

**blind spot** The point at which the optic nerve leaves the eye, creating a "blind" spot because no receptor cells are located there.

**fovea** The central focal point in the retina, around which the eye's cones cluster.

**feature detectors** Nerve cells in the brain that respond to specific features of the stimulus, such as movement, angle, or shape.

**parallel processing** Information processing in which several aspects of a problem are processed simultaneously. The brain's natural mode of information processing for many functions, including vision; contrasts with the step-by-step (serial) processing of most computers and of conscious problem-solving.

**Young-Helmholtz trichromatic (three-color) theory** The theory that the retina contains three different color receptors—one most sensitive to red, one to green, one to blue—which combined can produce the perception of any color.

**opponent-process theory** The theory that opposing retinal processes (red-green, yellow-blue, white-black) enable color vision. For example, some cells are stimulated by green and inhibited by red; others are stimulated by red and inhibited by green.

**color constancy** Perceiving familiar objects as having consistent color, even if changing illumination alters the wavelengths reflected by the object.

## Hearing

**audition** The sense of hearing.

**frequency** The number of complete wavelengths that pass a point in a given time (for example, per second).

**pitch** A tone's highness or lowness; depends on frequency.

**middle ear** The chamber between the eardrum and cochlea containing three tiny bones (hammer, anvil, and stirrup) that concentrate the vibrations of the eardrum on the cochlea's oval window.

**inner ear** The innermost part of the ear, containing the cochlea, semicircular canals, and vestibular sacs.

**cochlea** [KOHK-lee-uh] A coiled, bony, fluid-filled tube in the inner ear through which sound waves trigger nerve impulses.

**place theory** In hearing, the theory that links the pitch we hear with the place where the cochlea's membrane is stimulated.

**frequency theory** In hearing, the theory that the rate of nerve impulses traveling up the auditory nerve matches the frequency of a tone, thus enabling us to sense its pitch.

**conduction deafness** Hearing loss caused by damage to the mechanical system that conducts sound waves to the cochlea.

**nerve deafness** Hearing loss caused by damage to the cochlea's receptor cells or to the auditory nerves.

### The Other Senses

**gate-control theory** Melzack and Wall's theory that the spinal cord contains a neurological "gate" that blocks or allows pain signals to pass on to the brain. The "gate" is opened by the activity of pain signals traveling up small nerve fibers and closed by activity in larger fibers or by information coming from the brain.

**sensory interaction** The principle that one sense may influence another, as when the smell of food influences its taste.

**kinesthesis** [kin-ehs-THEE-sehs] The system for sensing the position and movement of individual body parts.

**equilibrium** The sense of body movement and position, including the sense of balance.

## Critical Thinking Exercise

Now that you have read and reviewed Chapter 5, take your learning a step further by testing your critical thinking skills on the following psychological reasoning exercise.

> Carlos, who is determined to quit smoking, today purchased a subliminal persuasion audio/videotape package. The booklet accompanying the tapes claims that subliminal suggestions "harness the power of the unconscious mind to [help you increase motivation to] quit smoking." Carlos is skeptical, but he decides to try the demonstration included on the videotape. The instructions are to turn off room lights, start the videotape, and stare at a fixation point (a plus sign that appears in the center of the television screen) until the screen goes blank. During the demonstration, which lasts about 5 minutes, Carlos occasionally perceives a flash of light on the screen just above the fixation point. Shortly after the screen goes blank, several geometric figures, including a square, a circle, a triangle, and a rectangle, appear above the question, "Which of these figures is most pleasing to you?" Although he is not sure why, Carlos picks the triangle. The tape ends with the following message: "If you picked the triangle, subliminal persuasion will work for you! During the demonstration, what appeared to be flashes of light were actually subliminal presentations of triangles. The triangles, which appeared too briefly to be perceived by your conscious mind, *were* perceived by your unconscious mind. Since familiarity breeds fondness, your unconsciousness persuaded you that smoking is unhealthy, unflattering, and something you definitely do not want to continue doing."

1. What assertions about subliminal persuasion are made in the booklet and videotape? Be sure to define all important concepts and terms as they are used in this example.
2. What evidence is presented that the subliminal suggestions will help Carlos quit smoking? Is this evidence trustworthy?
3. How else could you explain Carlos's preference for the triangle?

Check your progress on becoming a critical thinker by comparing your answers to the sample answers found in Appendix B.

## For Further Reading

**Ackerman, D.** (1990). *A natural history of the senses.* New York: Random House.

*A sensuous book about how, and especially what, we can sense.*

**Frisby, J. P.** (1980). *Seeing: Illusion, brain and mind.* Oxford: Oxford University Press.

*A wonderfully illustrated introduction to the visual system.*

**Hubel, D. H.** (1988). *Eye, brain and vision.* New York: Scientific American Library.

*A careful look at how we see the world.*

**Kisor, H.** (1990). *What's that pig outdoors: A memoir of deafness.* New York: Hill and Wang.

*A Chicago newspaper columnist provides a fascinating perspective on the worlds of the deaf and the hearing as he recalls the ups and downs of growing up deaf in a hearing culture.*

CHAPTER

# 6

# Perception

Some 2400 years ago, the philosopher Plato rightly discerned that we perceive objects through the senses, with the mind. As we saw in Chapter 5, to construct the world in our heads we must detect physical energy from the environment and encode it as neural signals (a process traditionally called *sensation*). And we must select, organize, and interpret our sensations (a process traditionally called *perception*). We not only sense raw sights and sounds, tastes and smells, we *perceive*. We hear not just a mix of pitches and rhythms but a child's cry of pain, the hum of distant traffic, a symphony. In short, we transform meaningless sensations into meaningful perceptions.

## Selective Attention

Perceptions come to us moment by moment, one perception vanishing as the next appears. Note how Figure 6–1 evokes more than one perception. The circles can be organized into several coherent images, each equally plausible, and the mind switches back and forth from one to the next. Although you *know* that two interpretations of this figure, known as a

**Figure 6–1**

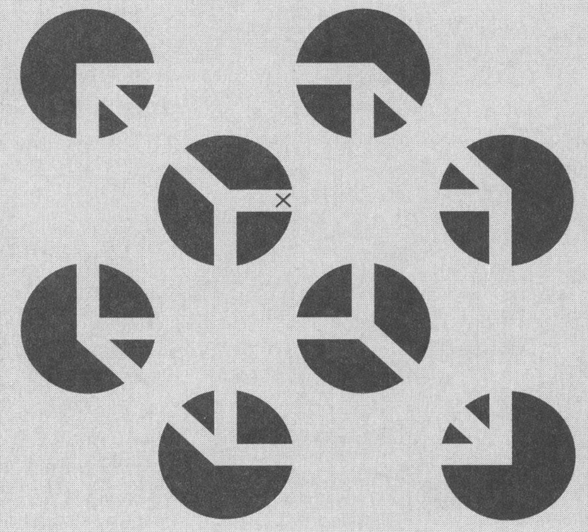

**Selective Attention** *What do you see: circles with gray lines, or a cube? If you stare at the cube, you may notice that it reverses location, moving the tiny X in the center from the front edge to the back. At times the cube may seem to float in front of the page, with circles behind it; at other times the circles may become holes in the page through which the cube appears, as though it were floating behind the page. You can't see both interpretations at once, because attention is selective. (From Bradley & others, 1976.)*

**Attention** *With experience, tasks such as driving become mostly automatic, freeing our conscious attention for other matters. However, in an emergency, a driver immersed in a phone conversation may run into trouble.*

"Necker Cube," are possible, you can consciously experience only one of them at any moment. This illustrates an important principle: Our conscious attention is *selective*.

**Selective attention** means that at any moment we focus our awareness on only a limited aspect of all that we are capable of experiencing. Until reading this sentence, you have been unaware that your shoes are pressing against your feet or that your nose is in your line of vision. Now, suddenly, your attentional spotlight shifts and your feet feel encased, your nose stubbornly intrudes on the page before you. While attending to these words, you've also been blocking from awareness information coming from your peripheral vision. But you can change that. While staring at the X below, notice what surrounds the book (the edges of the page, your desk top, and so forth).

X

Another example of selective attention is the *cocktail party effect*—the ability to attend selectively to only one voice among many. Imagine hearing two conversations over a headset, one in each ear, and being asked to repeat the left-ear message as it is spoken. When you pay attention to what's being said in your left ear, you won't perceive what is said in your right ear. If later you are asked what language your right ear heard, you may draw a blank (though you could report the speaker's sex and loudness). At the level of conscious awareness, whatever has your attention has your undivided attention.

It's true of other senses, too. From the immense array of visual stimuli that are constantly before us, we can select only a few for processing. Ulric Neisser (1979) and Robert Becklen and Daniel Cervone (1983) demonstrated this dramatically. They showed people a 1-minute videotape in which the images of three men in black shirts passing a basketball were superimposed over the images of three men in white shirts doing the same thing. They asked the viewers to press a key every time the black-shirted players passed the ball. Midway through the tape, a young woman carrying an umbrella sauntered across the screen (Figure 6–2). Most of the viewers focused their attention so completely on the black-shirted players that they failed to notice the woman. When the researcher replayed the tape for them, they were astonished to see her.

**Figure 6–2**

**Testing Selective Attention** *In this experiment on selective attention, viewers who were attending to basketball tosses among the black-shirted players usually failed to notice the woman with an umbrella sauntering through. (From Neisser, 1979.)*

Can unnoticed stimuli affect us? Indeed yes. In one experiment, women students listened through headphones as a prose passage played in one ear. Their task was to repeat its words out loud and to check them against a written transcript (Wilson, 1979). Meanwhile, some simple, novel tunes played in the other ear. The tunes were not subliminal—the women could hear them easily. But with their attention selectively focused on the passage, the women were no more aware of the tunes than you normally are of your shoes. Thus, when they later heard these tunes interspersed among new ones, they could not recognize them (just as people cannot recall a conversation to which they paid no attention). Nevertheless, when asked to rate their fondness for each tune, they *preferred* the ones previously played. Their preferences revealed what their conscious memories could not.

In other experiments, listeners attended to a message piped into one ear (such as, "We stood by the bank"). When a pertinent word ("river" or "money") is simultaneously sent to the unattended ear the listeners do not consciously perceive it, yet the word influences their interpretation of the ambiguous sentence (Baars & McGovern, 1994). So perception requires attention, but even unattended stimuli sometimes have subtle effects.

## Perceptual Illusions

Once we have attended to certain stimuli, how do we organize them into meaningful perceptions? During the late 1800s, when psychology was emerging as a distinct discipline, perceptual illusions fascinated scientists. And they still do, because illusions reveal the ways we normally organize and interpret our sensations. Consider five such perceptual puzzles:

***Puzzle 1*** To the right is an adaptation of a classic illusion created in 1889 by Franz Müller-Lyer. Does either line segment, *AB* or *BC*, appear longer? To most people the two segments appear the same length. Surprise! They are not. As your ruler can verify, line *AB* is a full one-third longer than line *BC*. Why do our eyes deceive us? (On page 199 we will discover one explanation.)

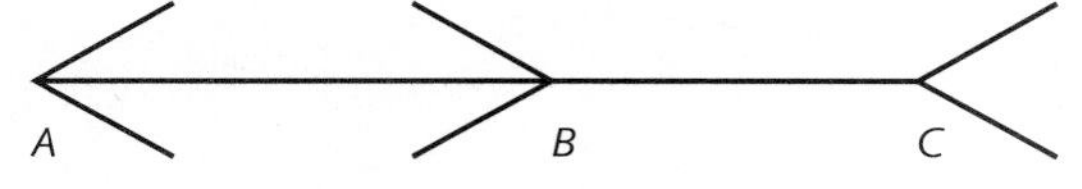


***Puzzle 2*** Below we have two unretouched photos of the same two girls, in the same room. The camera shows you these scenes much as you would see them if you were looking into the room through a single peephole. Why do the girls seem to change size when they switch places? (Pages 200–201 will reveal why.)

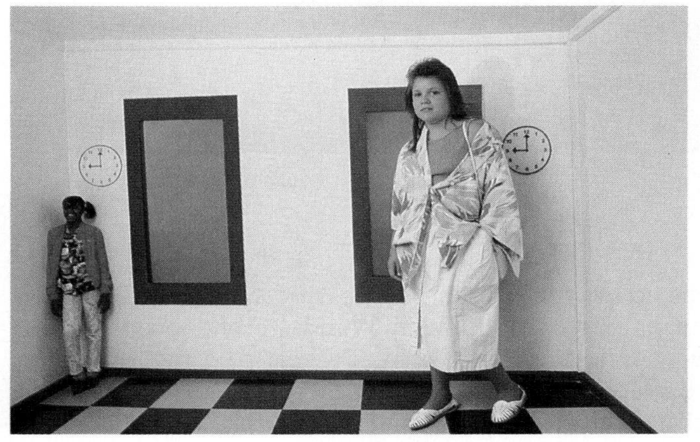

*Puzzle 3* Is Gateway Arch in St. Louis taller than it is wide? Or vice versa? To most it appears taller. In truth, its height and width are equal. Once again, seeing is deceiving. Why? (On page 195 we will meet this phenomenon again.)

*Puzzle 4* Aircraft pilots, ship captains, and car drivers perceive their surroundings under varying visibility. When their perceptions or reactions err—as happens in most commercial airplane accidents (Adler, 1989)—the results can be devastating. To simulate distance judgments, psychologist Helen Ross (1975) asked passersby to estimate the distances of white disks she had placed on the lawn at Britain's Hull University. Those who judged the distance in the thick morning fog perceived the disks to be farther away than did those who made their estimates in the midday sunshine. What does this suggest about how we normally judge distances? (Pages 193–197 explain distance perception.)

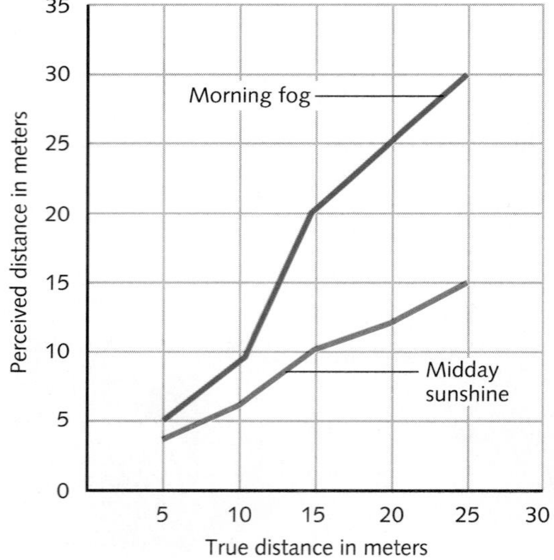

Morning fog

Midday sunshine

*Puzzle 5* Illusions occur with the other senses, too. More than a century ago, the German psychologist Wilhelm Wundt (pronounced Vooont) was puzzled by people's hearing the steady beat of a metronome or clock as if it were a repeating rhythm of two, three, or four beats—not as an unaccented click-click-click-click, which it is, but as, say, CLICK-click

CLICK-click CLICK-click. From the steady beat that strikes the ear, each listener unconsciously shapes an auditory pattern. What perceptual principle is at work here? (See page 202 to find out.)

The emphasis on *visual* illusions reflects vision's preeminence among our senses. When there is conflict between vision and other sensations, vision usually dominates—a phenomenon called **visual capture**. When the sound of a movie comes from a projector behind us, we nevertheless perceive it as coming from the screen, where we *see* the actors talking (much as we perceive a voice from the ventriloquist's dummy). While viewing a roller coaster ride on a wraparound movie screen, we may brace ourselves, though our other senses tell us we're not moving. In both cases, vision *captures* the other senses.

## Perceptual Organization

*To transform sensory information into meaningful perceptions we must organize it: We must perceive objects as distinct from their surroundings, see them as having a meaningful and constant form, and discern their distance and motion. The brain's rules for constructing perceptions explain some puzzling illusions.*

Early in this century, a group of German psychologists became intrigued with how the mind organizes sensations into perceptions. Given a cluster of sensations, the human perceiver organizes them into a **gestalt**, a German word meaning a "form" or a "whole." The Gestalt psychologists provided compelling demonstrations of gestalt perception. Look again at Figure 6–1 on page 187. Note that the individual elements of the figure are really nothing but eight blue circles, each containing three converging gray lines. But when we view them all together, we see a *whole* form, a "Necker cube."

As the Gestalt psychologists were fond of saying, in perception the whole may exceed the sum of its parts. Combine sodium, a corrosive metal, with chlorine, a poison gas, and something very different emerges—table salt. Likewise, a unique perceived form emerges from an object's components (Rock & Palmer, 1990). There is far more to perception than meets the senses.

Such demonstrations led the Gestalt psychologists to describe principles by which we organize our sensations into perceptions. As you read about these organizational principles, keep in mind the fundamental truth they illustrate: Our brains do more than merely register information about the world. Perception is not just opening a shutter and letting a picture print itself on the brain. Always, we are filtering sensory information and inferring perceptions in ways that make sense to us. Mind matters.

Our human yen for assembling visual features into complete forms involves the *bottom-up* processing starting with entry level sensory analysis as well as the *top-down* processing that uses our experiences and expectations to interpret those sensations. Monkey brains have cells that respond to "illusory contours" as in Figure 6–3 (Winckelgren, 1992; Wenderoth, 1992). Surprisingly, these cells have now been found in a visual cortex area that receives signals from the eyes, before much cognitive processing could have occurred (Grosof & others, 1993). The Gestalt principles are a clear example of the interpretive powers of the mind. Sensation and perception blend into one continuous process, progressing upward from specialized detector cells and downward from our assumptions.

**Figure 6–3**

**Illusory Contours** *The primary visual cortex of monkey brains contains cells which respond to subjective contours such as those perceived at the border between two sets of lines.*

Figure 6–4

**Reversible Figure and Ground** *Vase or two faces?*

## Form Perception

Imagine that you wanted to design a video/computer system that, like your eye/brain system, could read handwritten addresses or recognize faces at a glance. (The U.S. Postal Service is, in fact, investing millions of dollars hoping to develop such a scanner.) What abilities would it need?

### Figure and Ground

To start with, the system would need to recognize the addresses and faces as distinct from their backgrounds. Likewise, our first task in perception is to perceive any object, called the *figure,* as distinct from its surroundings, called the *ground.* Among the voices you hear at a party, the one you attend to becomes the figure, all others part of the ground. As you read, the words are the figure; the white paper, the ground. In Figure 6–4, the **figure-ground** relationship continually reverses—but always we organize the stimulus into a figure seen against a ground. (Is it a vase, or the profiles of two faces?) Such reversible figure and ground illustrations demonstrate again that the same stimulus can trigger more than one perception.

### Grouping

Having discriminated figure from ground, we (and our video/computer system) must then organize the figure into a meaningful form. Some basic features of a scene—such as color, movement, and light-dark contrast—we process instantly and automatically (Treisman, 1987). To bring order and form to these basic sensations, our minds follow certain rules for **grouping** stimuli together. These rules, identified by the Gestalt psychologists, illustrate their idea that the perceived whole differs from the mere sum of its parts (Rock & Palmer, 1990):

**Proximity** We group nearby figures together. We see not six separate lines, but three sets of two lines.

**Similarity** If figures are similar to each other, we group them together. We see the triangles and circles as vertical columns of similar shapes, not as horizontal rows of dissimilar shapes.

**Continuity** We perceive smooth, continuous patterns rather than discontinuous ones. This pattern could be a series of alternating semicircles, but we perceive it as a wavy line and a straight line.

**Closure** If a figure has gaps, we complete it, filling in the gaps to create a complete, whole object. We easily fill the gaps in this figure's outline and see a complete triangle.

**Connectedness** We perceive spots, lines, or areas as a single unit when uniform and linked.

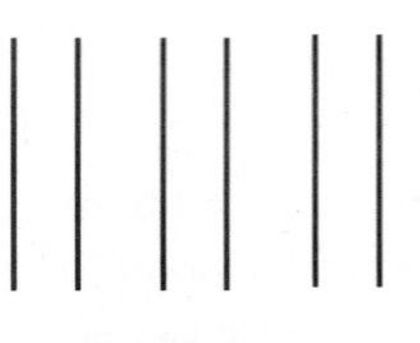

Proximity

Similarity

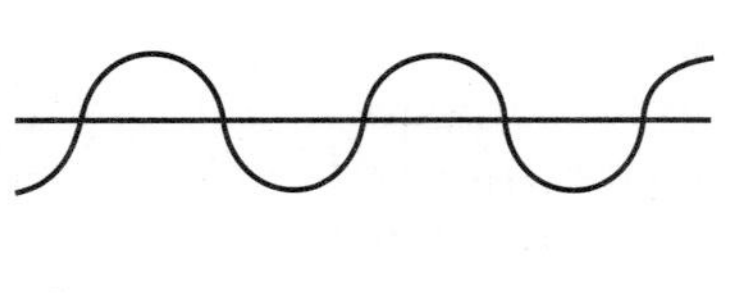

Continuity

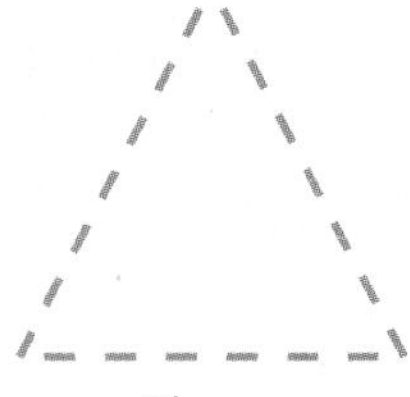

Closure

Connectedness

The grouping principles usually help us perceive reality, but sometimes they lead us astray, as when viewing the doghouse in Figure 6–5.

## Depth Perception

From the two-dimensional images that fall on our retinas we somehow organize three-dimensional perceptions. Seeing objects in three dimensions, called **depth perception**, allows us to estimate their distance from us. At a glance, we estimate the distance of an oncoming car or the height of a cliff. This ability is partly innate. Eleanor Gibson and Richard Walk (1960) discovered this using a miniature cliff with a drop-off covered by sturdy glass. The inspiration for these experiments occurred to Gibson as she was eating a picnic lunch on the rim of the Grand Canyon. She wondered: Would a toddler peering over the rim perceive the dangerous drop-off and draw back?

Back in their Cornell University laboratory, Gibson and Walk placed 6- to 14-month-old infants on the edge of a **visual cliff** (Figure 6–6). Their mothers then coaxed them to crawl out on the glass. Most refused to do so, indicating that they could perceive depth. Perhaps by crawling age they had *learned* to perceive depth. Yet newborn animals with virtually no visual experience—including young kittens, a day-old goat, and newly hatched chicks—respond similarly. What is more, during the first month of life, human infants turn to avoid objects coming directly at them but are unbothered by objects approaching at an angle that would not hit them (Ball & Tronick, 1971).

Although biological maturation predisposes our wariness of heights, experience amplifies it. Infants' wariness increases with crawling experience, at whatever age crawling begins. Given the enhanced locomotion made possible by a walker, infants become even more wary of heights (Campos & others, 1992).

How do we do it? How do we transform two-dimensional retinal images into three-dimensional perceptions? Some depth cues require both eyes—**binocular cues**. Others are available to each eye separately—**monocular cues**.

**Figure 6–5**

**Grouping Principles** *You probably perceive this doghouse as a gestalt—a whole (though impossible) structure. As the photo on page 210 shows, Gestalt grouping principles are at work here. (Reprinted from GAMES Magazine [810 Seventh Avenue, New York, NY 10019]. Copyright © 1983 PSC Games Limited Partnership.)*

**Figure 6–6**

**Visual Cliff** *Eleanor Gibson and Richard Walk devised this miniature cliff with a glass-covered drop-off to determine whether crawling infants and newborn animals can perceive depth. Even when coaxed, infants are reluctant to venture onto the glass over the cliff.*

### Binocular Cues

Because our eyes are about 2½ inches apart, our retinas receive slightly different images of the world. When the brain compares these two images, their **retinal disparity** (the difference in the two images) provides an important cue to the relative distance of different objects. When you hold your finger directly in front of your nose, your retinas receive quite different views. (You can see this if you close one eye and then the other, or create a finger sausage as in Figure 6–7.) At greater distance—say, when you hold your finger at arm's length—the disparity is smaller.

Figure 6–7

**The Floating Finger Sausage** *Hold your two index fingers about 5 inches in front of your eyes, with their tips half an inch apart. Now look at the other side of the room, beyond them, and note the weird result. Move your fingers out further and the retinal disparity—and the finger sausage—will shrink.*

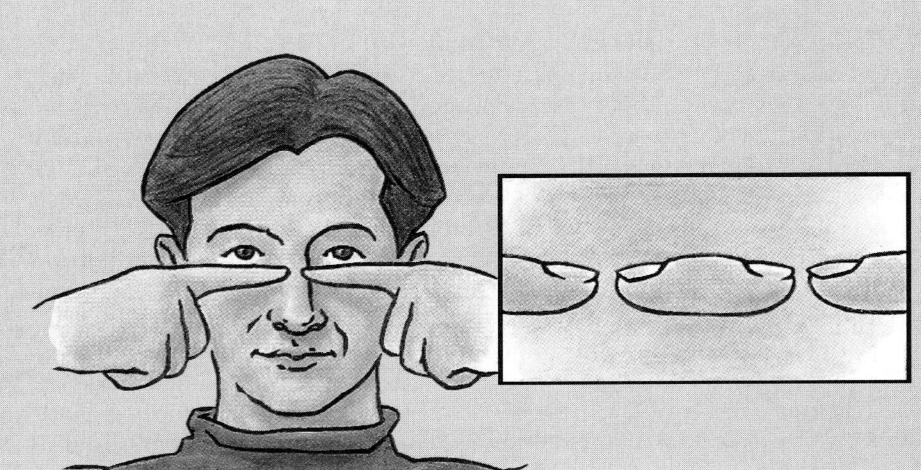

The creators of 3-D movies and "Viewmaster" 3-D scenes simulate retinal disparity by photographing a scene with two cameras placed a few inches apart (a feature we might want to build into our seeing computer). When viewed through spectacles or a device that allows the left eye to see only the image from the left camera and the right eye the image from the right camera, the 3-D effect mimics normal retinal disparity.

Another binocular cue to distance is **convergence**, a neuromuscular cue from the greater inward turn when the eyes view a near object. By noting the angle of convergence, the brain can compute whether you are focusing on this printed page or on the person across the room.

Relative size

### Monocular Cues

With both eyes open, we can readily and precisely touch the tip of a pen held in front of us; with one eye closed, the task becomes noticeably more difficult. This demonstrates the importance of binocular cues in judging the distance of nearby objects. Two eyes are better than one. How then do we judge whether a person is 100 feet or 100 yards away? In both cases, the retinal disparity while looking straight ahead is slight. At such distances we depend on monocular cues such as the following:

**Relative size** If we assume that two objects are similar in size, we perceive the one that casts the smaller image on the retina as farther away.

**Interposition** If one object partially blocks our view of another, we perceive it as closer. We perceive the interposed young deer as closer than its partially obscured mother.

Interposition

**Relative clarity** We perceive hazy objects as farther away than sharp, clear objects. (Recall from Puzzle 4, page 190, the effects of fog on judging distance.)

**Texture gradient** A gradual change from a coarse, distinct texture to a fine, indistinct texture signals increasing distance.

Texture gradient

**Relative height** We perceive objects higher in our field of vision as farther away. This may contribute to the illusion that vertical dimensions are longer than identical horizontal dimensions (as we saw in Puzzle 3, page 190, the St. Louis Arch). Is the vertical line here longer, shorter, or equal in length to the horizontal line? Measure and see.

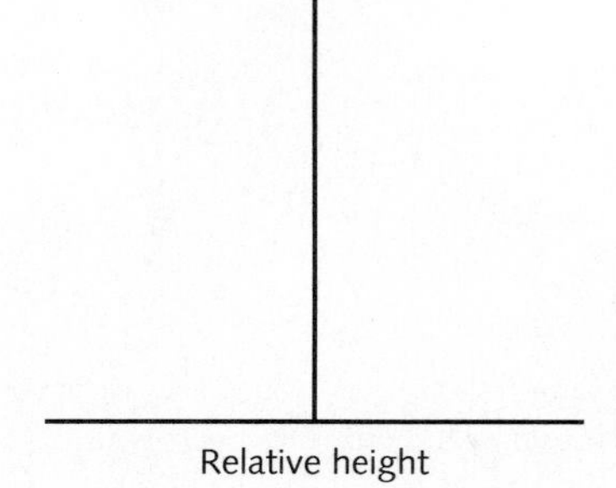

Relative height

**Relative motion** As we move, stable objects appear to move relative to us. If while riding in a train you fix your gaze on some object—say, a tree—you see the objects closer than the tree (the fixation point) appear to move backward. The nearer an object is, the faster it seems to move.

Relative motion

Objects beyond the fixation point appear to move with you at a decreasing speed as the object gets farther away. Your brain uses these speed and direction clues to compute the objects' relative distances.

**Linear perspective** Parallel lines, such as railroad tracks, appear to converge with distance. The more the lines converge, the greater their perceived distance. Linear perspective can contribute to rail-crossing accidents, by leading people to overestimate a train's distance (Leibowitz, 1985). (A train's massive size also makes it appear to be moving more slowly than it is.)

Linear perspective

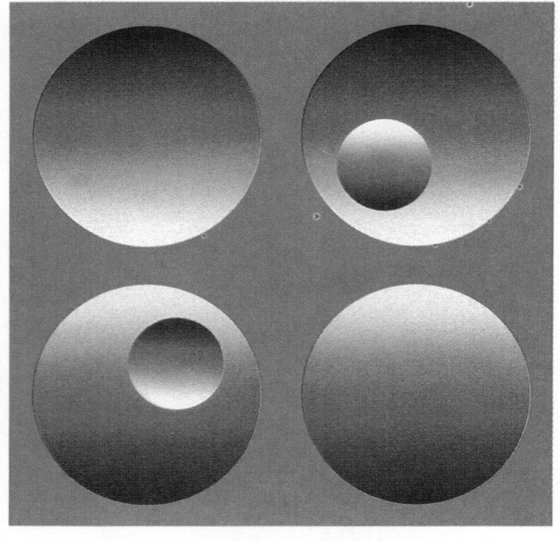
Relative brightness

From "Perceiving Shape from Shading" by Vilayanur S. Ramachandran. Copyright © 1988 by Scientific American, Inc. All rights reserved.

**Relative brightness** Nearby objects reflect more light to our eyes. Thus, given two identical objects, the dimmer one seems farther away. This illusion also contributes to accidents, as when a fog-shrouded vehicle, or one with only its parking lights on, seems farther away than it is. Shading, too, produces a sense of depth consistent with the assumed light source. Invert the illustration at the left and the hollow becomes a hill, because we assume that light comes from above.

To convey depth on a flat canvas (Figure 6–8), artists use these monocular cues, as do people who must gauge depth with but one eye. In 1960, the

Figure 6–8

**Perspective Techniques** *By the time that "Bristol, Broad Quay" was painted (c. 1730, Anonymous), the techniques for showing perspective were well established. Note the effective use of distance cues such as texture gradient, interposition, linear perspective, and relative size and height.*

University of Washington football team won the Rose Bowl, thanks partly to the superb passing of quarterback Bob Schloredt. Schloredt, who was obviously skilled at judging his receiver's distance, must be supersensitive to monocular cues for distance, because he is blind in his left eye.

## Motion Perception

Imagine that you could perceive the world as having color, form, and depth but could not see motion. Not only could you not play tennis or drive a car, you might have trouble writing, eating, and walking.

Our brain computes motion based partly on its assumption that shrinking objects are retreating (not getting smaller) and enlarging objects are approaching. But the changing size and position of a retinal image isn't our only clue to motion. Nod your head and the visual field's retinal position changes, but nothing appears to move—unless body movement can't account for the changing image. (Close your right eye and gently move your left eyeball by pushing on the upper eyelid. Now the brain reads the changing retinal image as a moving world.)

As film animation artists know well, the brain will also interpret a rapid series of slightly varying images as movement (a phenomenon called *stroboscopic movement*). By flashing 24 still pictures a second, a motion picture creates perceived movement. The motion we see is not in the film, which is just a superfast slide show, but constructed in our heads. (Recall the famous EAT POPCORN/DRINK COCA-COLA subliminal persuasion hoax described on page 153. We know such an experiment never occurred not only because the reported site—the Fort Lee, New Jersey, theater—could not have held the number of people supposedly tested, and not only because the theater manager at the time denied such an experiment was ever conducted, but also because the briefest possible movie image, a 1/24th second frame, would *not* have been subliminal [Rogers, 1994].)

Theater and restaurant marquees sometimes create another illusion of movement, using the **phi phenomenon**. When two adjacent stationary lights blink on and off in quick succession we perceive a single light moving back and forth between them. Lighted signs exploit the phi phenomenon with a succession of lights that create the impression of, say, a moving arrow.

## Perceptual Constancy

So far we have noted that our video/computer system must first perceive objects as we do—as having a distinct form, location, and perhaps motion. Its next task is even more challenging: to recognize the object without being deceived by changes in its size, shape, brightness, or color. **Perceptual constancy** allows us to perceive an object as unchanging while the stimuli we receive from it change. Thus, we can identify things regardless of viewing angle, distance, and illumination. You glance at someone ahead of you on the sidewalk and instantly recognize a classmate. In less time than it takes to draw a breath, information reaching your eyes has been sent to your brain, where work teams comprising millions of neurons have extracted the essential features, compared them with stored images, and identified the person. Replicating this human perceptual feat, which has intrigued perception researchers for decades, provides a monumental challenge for our seeing computer.

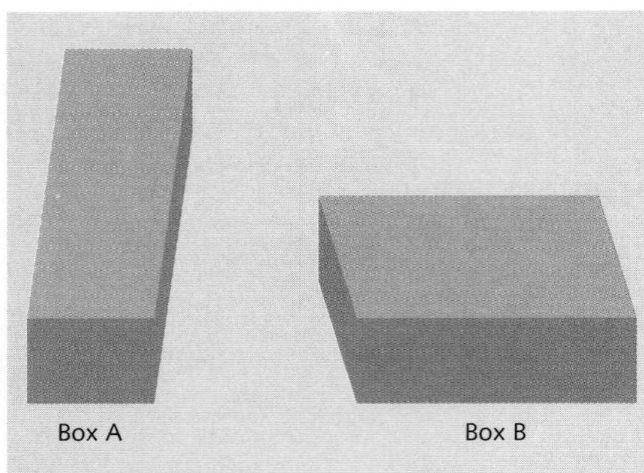


**Figure 6–9**

**Perceiving Shape** *Do the tops of boxes A and B have different dimensions? They appear to. But—believe it or not—they are identical. (Measure and see.) With both boxes we adjust our perceptions relative to our viewing angle. (From Shepard, 1981.)*

### Shape and Size Constancies

Sometimes an object's actual shape is unchanging, but the object *seems* to change shape with our viewing angle (Figure 6–9). More often, thanks to *shape constancy*, we perceive familiar objects as having a constant form even while our retinal images of them change. When a door opens, it casts a changing shape on our retinas, yet we manage to perceive the door as having a constant doorlike shape (Figure 6–10).

Thanks to *size constancy* we perceive objects as having a constant size, even while our distance from them varies. Size constancy allows us to perceive a car as big enough to carry people, even when we see its tiny image from two blocks away. This illustrates the close connection between an object's perceived *distance* and perceived *size*. Perceiving an object's distance gives us cues to its size. Likewise, knowing its general size—that the object is, say, a car—provides us with cues to its distance.

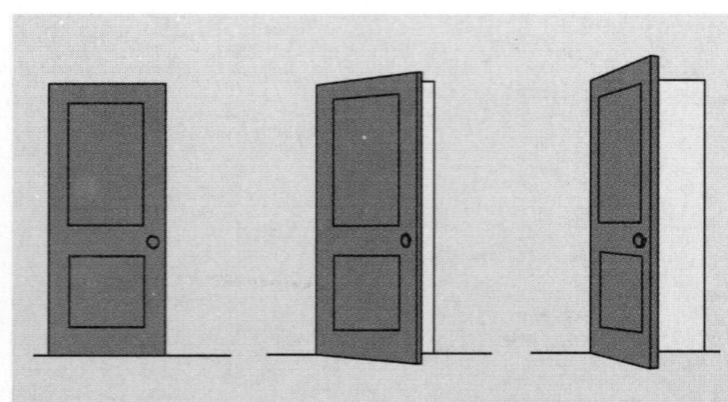

**Figure 6–10**

**Shape Constancy** *A door casts an increasingly trapezoidal image on our retinas as it opens, yet we still perceive it as rectangular.*

**Size-Distance Relationship** The marvel of size perception is how effortlessly it occurs. Given the perceived distance of an object and the size of its image on our retinas, we instantly and unconsciously infer the object's size. Although the monsters in Figure 6–11(*a*) cast the same retinal images, the linear perspective tells our brain that the monster in pursuit is farther away. We therefore perceive it as larger.

This interplay between perceived size and perceived distance helps explain several well-known illusions. For example, can you imagine why the moon looks up to 50 percent larger near the horizon than when high in the sky? For at least 22 centuries, scholars have wondered and argued about the causes of the *moon illusion* (Hershenson, 1989). Researchers have not yet found a fully satisfactory explanation. A suggested partial reason is that cues to objects' distances at the horizon make the moon behind them seem farther away (Kaufman & Rock, 1962). Thus, the moon on the horizon seems larger (like the distant monster in Figure 6–11[*a*] and the distant bar in Figure 6–11[*b*]). Take away these distance cues—by looking at the horizon moon (or the monsters) through a paper tube—and it immediately shrinks.

Figure 6–11

(a)

(b)

**The Interplay Between Perceived Size and Distance** *(a) The monocular cues for distance make the pursuing monster look larger than the pursued. It isn't. (From Shepard, 1990.) (b) The Ponzo illusion. The two identical orange bars cast identical images on our retinas. But our experience tells us that a more distant object can create the same-sized image only if it is larger. Thus, we perceive the bar that seems more distant as larger.*

The size-distance relationship helps us understand two illusions demonstrated earlier. Puzzle 1, the Müller-Lyer illusion concerning the lengths of straight lines between arrow tips, has been the subject of more than 1250 scientific publications, yet psychologists still debate its explanation. One is that our experience with the corners of rooms or buildings prompts us to interpret the vertical line on the ticket booth in Figure 6–12(*a*) as closer to us and therefore shorter, and the vertical line by the door as farther away and therefore longer.

Figure 6–12

(a)

(b)

**The Müller-Lyer Illusion** *(a) Richard L. Gregory (1968) suggested that the corners in our rectangularly carpentered world teach us to interpret "outward" or "inward" pointing arrowheads at the ends of a line as a cue to the line's distance from us and so to its length. The red line defined by the corner at the ticket windows looks shorter than the red line defined by the corner to the right. But if you measure them, you will see that both are the same length. (b) There is more to the Müller-Lyer illusion than size constancy, however, for if we replace the arrowheads with circles and judge whether the black or blue line segment seems longer, we still get much the same effect. Here the two line segments are equal. Most people judge the black line as longer, apparently because they perceptually adjust the lengths of the lines toward the distance separating the figures. (From Day, 1984.)*

Supporting this theory, people are more susceptible to the Müller-Lyer illusion if, unlike many rural Africans, they have lived in a carpentered world of rectangular shapes (Segall & others, 1990). The phenomenon reflects cultural experience, not race, for the same study showed that Africans who live in carpentered cities are more vulnerable to the illusion than Africans in uncarpentered environments. Our experience in carpentered contexts provides a perspective that helps us construct our perceptions, top-down.

Anthropologist Colin Turnbull (1961, p. 252) noted another effect of experience on perception when he took an African Pygmy guide, Kenge, on his first trip out of the dense forest. As they were crossing a wide plain, buffalo loomed several miles away. Kenge, unaccustomed to judging size over unbroken distances, wondered, "What insects are those?" "When I told Kenge that the insects were buffalo, he roared with laughter and told me not to tell such stupid lies," Turnbull reported. As they drove on, the mystified Kenge became frightened as the buffalo grew bigger and bigger.

Anthropologists, missionaries, and cross-cultural psychologists also report that people who have never before seen photos or drawings may initially find them confusing (Deregowski, 1989). Shown a painting or a black-and-white picture of a familiar animal such as a tortoise, the inexperienced person may at first just not get it. This, too, reminds us that, more than we realize, our taken-for-granted perceptions of the world depend on our experience. We perceive the world not just as it is, but as we are.

**Culture and Depth Perception** *The spear points at which animal? People who have never seen two-dimensional drawings or photos of three-dimensional scenes often have difficulty seeing depth in a figure such as this. (Adapted from Jean B. Deregowski, "Pictorial Perception and Culture," November 1972, p. 83. Copyright 1972 by Scientic American, Inc. All rights reserved.)*

Size-distance relationships also explain Puzzle 2, the shrinking and growing girls. As Figure 6–13 reveals, the room is distorted. But viewed with one eye through a peephole, its trapezoidal walls produce the same images as those of a normal rectangular room viewed with both eyes. Presented with the camera's one-eyed view, the brain makes the reasonable assumption that the room *is* normal and perceives the girls as changing in size.

Our occasional misperceptions demonstrate the workings of our normally effective perceptual processes. The perceived relationship between distance and size is generally valid, but under special circumstances it can lead us astray—as when helping to create the moon illusion, the Müller-

Figure 6–13

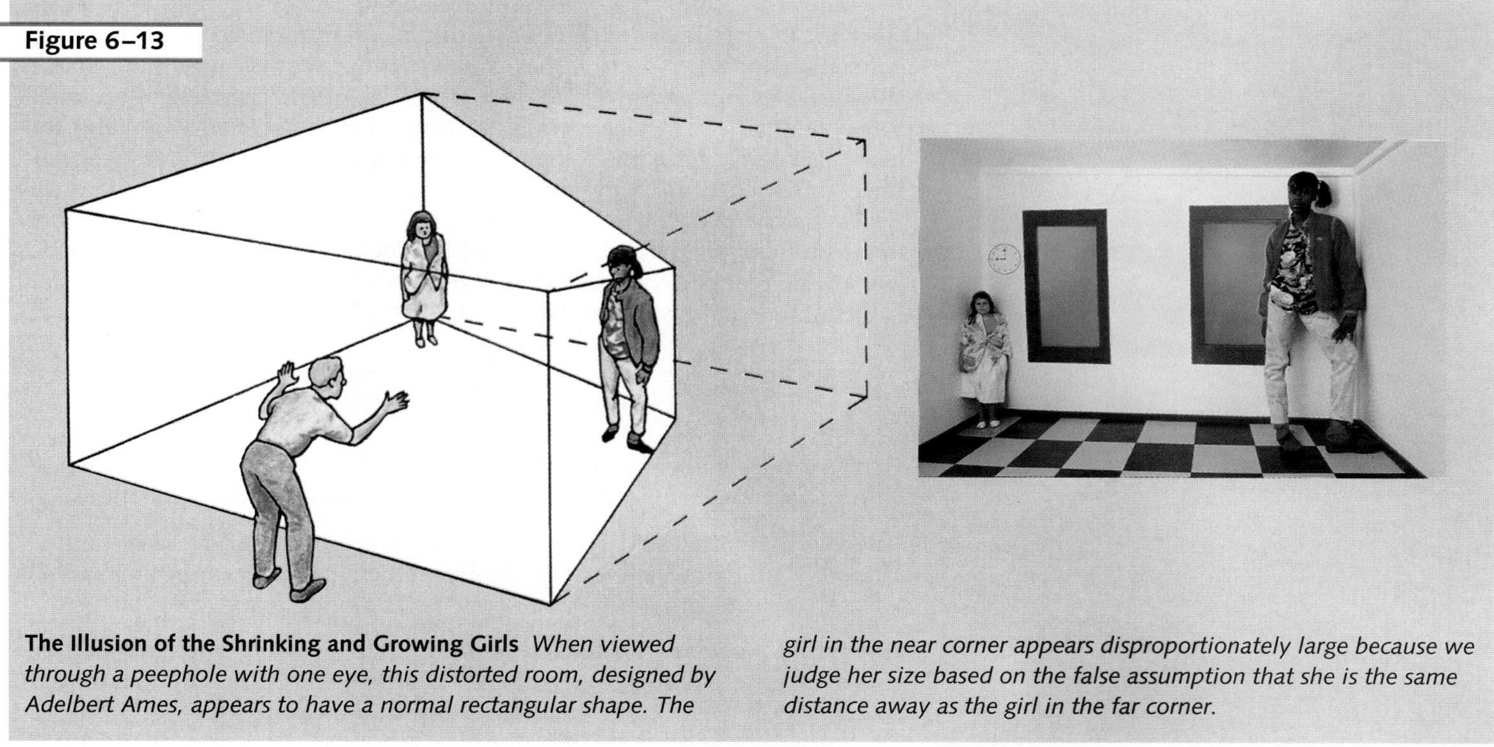

**The Illusion of the Shrinking and Growing Girls** *When viewed through a peephole with one eye, this distorted room, designed by Adelbert Ames, appears to have a normal rectangular shape. The girl in the near corner appears disproportionately large because we judge her size based on the false assumption that she is the same distance away as the girl in the far corner.*

Lyer illusion, and the distorted room illusion. Using distance cues to assess perceived size triggers illusions only if we aren't familiar with the object or if the distance cues are misleading. When we correctly interpret the distance cues—which we normally do—we perceive the size of objects correctly.

## Lightness Constancy

White paper reflects 90 percent of the light falling on it; black paper, only 10 percent. In sunlight the black paper may reflect 100 times more light than does the white paper indoors, but it still looks black (McBurney & Collings, 1984). This illustrates *lightness constancy* (also called *brightness constancy*), our perceiving an object as having a constant lightness even while its illumination varies. Perceived lightness depends on *relative luminance*—the amount of light an object reflects relative to its surroundings. If you view sunlit black paper through a narrow tube so nothing else is visible, it may look gray, because in bright sunshine it reflects a fair amount of light. View it without the tube and it is again black, because it reflects much less light than the objects around it. The phenomenon is similar to that of color constancy (pages 166–167). A red apple in a fruit bowl retains its redness as the light changes, because our brain computes the light reflected by any object relative to its surrounding objects.

If perceived lightness stays roughly constant, given an unchanging context, what happens when the surrounding context changes? As Figure 6–14 shows, the brain computes brightness and color relative to surrounding objects. Thus perceived lightness changes with context.

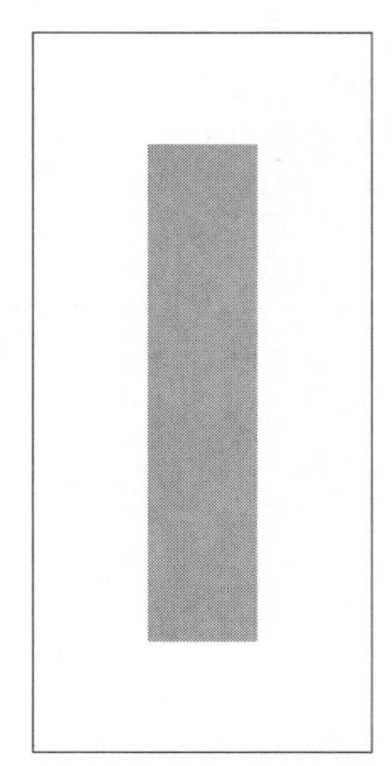

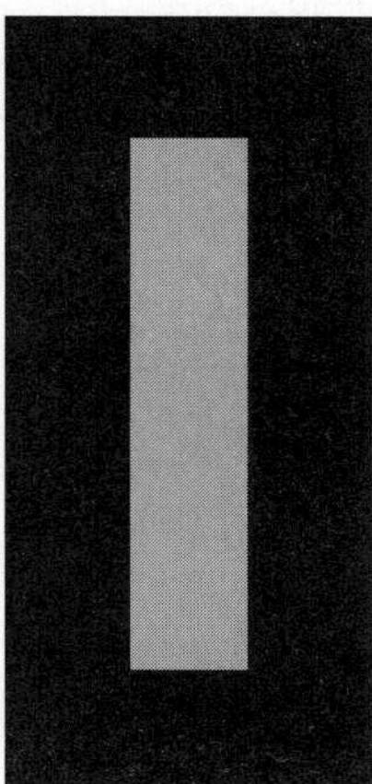

Figure 6–14

**Brightness Contrast** *Although they are in fact identical, the perceived lightness of the interior rectangles differs depending on their surroundings. Like color constancy (pages 166–167), this phenomenon has great significance for artists and interior designers.*

Form perception, depth perception, motion perception, and perceptual constancy illustrate how we organize our visual experiences. Perceptual organization applies to other senses, too. It explains why we group the clock's steady clicks into patterns (Puzzle 5, pages 190–191). Listening to an unfamiliar language, we have trouble hearing where one word stops and the next one begins. Listening to our own language, we automatically hear distinct words. This, too, is a form of perceptual organization. But it is more, for we even organize a string of letters—THEDOGATEMEAT—into words that make an intelligible phrase, more likely "The dog ate meat" than "The do gate me at" (McBurney & Collings, 1984). This process involves not only organization but *interpretation*—finding meaning in what we perceive.

## Summing Up

From a top-down perspective, we see how, aided by knowledge and expectations, we transform sensory information into meaningful perceptions.

**Selective Attention** At any moment we are conscious of a very limited amount of all that we are capable of experiencing. One example is the cocktail party effect—attending to only one voice among many.

**Perceptual Illusions** Visual and auditory illusions were fascinating scientists even as psychology emerged. Explaining illusions required an understanding of how we transform sensations into meaningful perceptions, so the study of perception became one of psychology's first concerns. Conflict between visual and other sensory information is usually resolved with the mind accepting the visual data, a tendency known as *visual capture*.

**Perceptual Organization** The early Gestalt psychologists were impressed with the seemingly innate way in which we organize fragmentary sensory data into whole perceptions. Our minds structure the information that comes to us in several demonstrable ways:

*Form Perception* To recognize an object, we must first perceive it (see it as a figure) as distinct from surrounding stimuli (the ground). We must also organize the figure into a meaningful form. Several Gestalt principles—proximity, similarity, continuity, closure, and connectedness—describe this process.

*Depth Perception* Research on the visual cliff reveals that many species perceive the world in three dimensions at, or very soon after, birth. We transform two-dimensional retinal images into three-dimensional perceptions by using binocular cues, such as retinal disparity, and monocular cues, such as the relative sizes of objects.

*Motion Perception* Our brain computes motion as objects move across or toward the retina. A quick succession of images, as in a motion picture or on a lighted sign, can also create an illusion of movement.

*Perceptual Constancy* Having perceived an object as a coherent figure and located it in space, how do we recognize it—despite the varying images that it may cast on our retinas? Size, shape, and lightness constancies describe how objects appear to have unchanging characteristics regardless of their distance, shape, or motion. These constancies explain several of the well-known visual illusions. For example, familiarity with the size-distance relationships in a carpentered world of rectangular shapes makes people more susceptible to the Müller-Lyer illusion.

## Interpretation

*To what extent do we learn to perceive? If our eyes were covered with blinders or cataracts during our early years, would we enjoy normal perceptions when such were removed? If given glasses that displaced or inverted the world, could we adapt? To what extent do our assumptions and beliefs shape our interpretations, and thus our perceptions?*

Philosophers have debated the origins of our perceptual abilities: Is it nature or nurture? German philosopher Immanuel Kant (1724–1804) maintained that knowledge comes from our *inborn* ways of organizing sensory experiences. Indeed, we come equipped to process sensory information. But British philosopher John Locke (1632–1704) argued that through our experiences we also *learn* to perceive the world. Indeed, we learn to link an object's distance with its size. But just how important is experience? How radically does it shape our perceptual interpretations?

### Sensory Restriction and Restored Vision

Writing to John Locke (1690), William Molyneux wondered whether "a man *born* blind, and now adult, taught by his *touch* to distinguish between a cube and a sphere" could, if made to see, visually distinguish the two. Locke's answer was no, because the man would never have *learned* to see.

Molyneux's hypothetical case has since been put to the test with dozens of adults who, though blind from birth, have gained sight (Gregory, 1978; Senden, 1932). Most were patients born with cataracts—clouded lenses that enabled them to see only diffused light, rather as you or I might see a diffuse fog through a Ping-Pong ball sliced in half. When their cataracts were surgically removed, the patients could distinguish figure from ground and could sense colors—suggesting that these aspects of perception are innate. But much as Locke supposed, the formerly blind patients often could not visually recognize objects that were familiar by touch.

*"Let us then suppose the mind to be, as we say, white paper void of all characters, without any ideas: How comes it to be furnished? . . . To this I answer, in one word, from EXPERIENCE."*

John Locke
*An Essay Concerning Human Understanding*, 1690

Perhaps in these cases the surgery didn't completely restore the patients' visual equipment. Seeking to gain more control than is provided by clinical cases, researchers have conducted Molyneux's imaginary experiment with animals. To discover whether altering a young animal's normal visual experience would permanently alter its perceptual abilities, they stitched closed the eyelids of infant kittens and monkeys or outfitted them with goggles through which the animals could see only diffuse, unpatterned light (Wiesel, 1982). After infancy, when their visual impairments were removed, these animals exhibited perceptual limitations much like those of human patients born with cataracts. They could distinguish color and brightness, but not the form of a circle from that of a square. Their eyes had not degenerated; their retinas still relayed signals to their visual cortex. But lacking stimulation, the cortical cells had not developed normal connections. Thus, the animals remained functionally blind to shape.

In both humans and animals, a similar period of sensory restriction does no permanent harm if it occurs later in life. Cover the eye of an animal for several months during adulthood, and vision will be unaffected after removing the eye patch. Remove cataracts that develop after early childhood, and a human, too, will enjoy normal vision. The effects of visual experiences during infancy in cats, monkeys, and humans suggest there is a *critical period* (pages 96–97) for normal sensory and perceptual development. Experience guides the organization of the brain's neural connections.

**Figure 6–15**

**The Experimental Apparatus for the Blakemore and Cooper Studies** *From the time their eyes first opened up to age 5 months, these kittens were removed from darkness each day to spend 5 hours alone in a black-and-white striped cylinder with a clear glass floor. A stiff collar prevented the kittens from seeing anything else, even their own bodies. Afterward, these kittens were less sensitive to horizontal forms. (From Blakemore & Cooper, 1970.)*

We can also see the profound effects of early visual experience in experiments with young animals who were reared with severely restricted visual input. Cambridge University researchers Colin Blakemore and Grahame Cooper (1970) reared kittens in darkness, except for 5 hours each day during which they were placed in a horizontally or vertically striped environment (as in Figure 6–15). Remarkably, kittens raised without exposure to horizontal lines later had difficulty perceiving horizontal bars, and those raised without vertical lines had difficulty seeing vertical bars. While two of these kittens played, a researcher playfully shook a long black rod. The kitten reared in a world of vertical lines would play with the rod only when it was held upright. When the rod was held flat, that kitten ignored it while its companion—reared in a world of horizontal lines—ran to play with it. Eventually, their selective blindness diminished, but the kittens never regained normal sensitivity. By sampling the activity of the kittens' feature-detecting brain cells, Blakemore and Cooper found that whether such cells responded mostly to horizontal or vertical lines depended on the kittens' early visual experience.

Experiments on perceptual limitations produced by early sensory deprivation provide a partial answer to a question debated in Chapter 4: Does the effect of early experience last a lifetime? For some aspects of visual perception, the answer is clearly yes: We retain the imprint of early visual experiences far into the future.

## Perceptual Adaptation

Given a new pair of glasses, we may feel slightly disoriented and dizzy. Within a day or two, we adjust. Our **perceptual adaptation** to changed visual input makes the world seem normal again. Now imagine a far more dramatic new pair of glasses—one that shifts the apparent location of objects 40 degrees to the left. When you first put them on and toss a ball to a friend, it sails off to the left. Walking forward to shake hands with the person, you veer to the left.

Could you adapt to this distorted world? Chicks cannot. When fitted with such lenses, they continue to peck where food grains *seem* to be (Hess, 1956; Rossi, 1968). But humans adapt to distorting lenses quickly. Within a few minutes your throws would again be accurate, your stride on target. Remove the lenses and you would experience an aftereffect: At first your throws would err in the *opposite* direction, sailing off to the right; but again, within minutes you would readapt.

Now imagine an even more radical pair of glasses—one that literally turns the world upside down. The ground is up, the sky is down. Could you adapt? Fish, frogs, and salamanders cannot. When Roger Sperry (1956) surgically turned their eyes upside down, they thereafter reacted to objects by moving in the wrong direction. But, believe it or not, kittens, monkeys, and humans can adapt to an inverted world. Turn-of-the-century psychologist George Stratton (1896) experienced this when he invented and wore for 8 days optical headgear that flipped left to right *and* up to down, making him the first person to experience a right-side-up retinal image while standing upright.

**Perceptual Adaptation** *Dr. Hubert Dolezal views the world through inverting goggles. Remarkably, people can learn to adapt to an upside-down visual world.*

At first, Stratton was disoriented. When he wanted to walk, he had to search for his feet, which were now "up." Eating was nearly impossible. He became nauseated and depressed. But Stratton persisted, and by the eighth day he could comfortably reach for something in the right direction and walk without bumping into things. When Stratton finally removed the headgear, he readapted quickly.

Later experiments replicated Stratton's experience (Dolezal, 1982; Kohler, 1962). After a period of adjustment, people wearing the optical gear have even been able to ride a motorcycle, ski the Alps, and fly an airplane. Is this because through experience they perceptually reinvert their upside-down world to an upright position? No, the street, ski slopes, and runway still seem above their heads. But by actively moving about in this topsy-turvy world, they adapt to the context and learn to coordinate their movements.

## Perceptual Set

As everyone knows, to see is to believe. As many people also know, but do not fully appreciate, to believe is to see. Our experiences, assumptions, and expectations may give us a **perceptual set**, or mental predisposition, that greatly influences what we perceive. Is the person in the center picture of Figure 6–16 a man playing the saxophone or a woman's face? What we see in such a drawing can be influenced by first viewing either of two unambiguous versions (Boring, 1930).

Knowing this much, see if you can explain the results of another experiment. A slightly blurred picture was identified correctly by 73 percent of first-time viewers, but by only 25 percent of those who had previously been shown a *badly* blurred version of the same picture (Bruner & Potter, 1964). Why do you suppose the second group had such trouble perceiving the image?

**Figure 6–16**

**Perceptual Set** *Which do you see in the center picture: the male saxophonist or the woman's face? Glancing first at one of the two unambiguous versions of the picture is likely to influence your interpretation. (From Shepard, 1990.)*

It's because people cannot resist imposing a pattern on unpatterned stimuli. Shown a hopelessly blurred picture, people automatically form a preliminary hunch (perceptual set), which then interferes with their later perceptions. Thus, it is much harder to recognize a photo coming into focus than to "hang on" to the same photo going out of focus. Once we have formed a wrong idea about reality, we have more difficulty seeing the truth. Even scientists, striving for objectivity, perceive reality through the lenses of their theories. When first viewing the "canals" on Mars through telescopes, some astronomers and writers perceived them as the product of intelligent life. They were—but the intelligence was on the viewing end of the telescope.

*"The temptation to form premature theories upon insufficient data is the bane of our profession."*

Sherlock Holmes in Arthur Conan Doyle's *The Valley of Fear*, 1914

Everyday examples of perceptual set abound. In 1972, a British newspaper published genuine, unretouched photographs of a "monster" in Scotland's Loch Ness—"the most amazing pictures ever taken," stated the paper. If this information creates in you the same perceptual set it did in most of the paper's readers, you, too, will see the monster in the photo reproduced in Figure 6–17(*a*). But when Steuart Campbell (1986) approached the photos with a different perceptual set, he saw a curved tree trunk—very likely the same tree trunk others had seen in the lake the day the photo was shot. Moreover, with this different perceptual set, you may now notice that the object is floating motionless, without any water disturbance or wake around it—hardly what we would expect of a lively monster.

**Figure 6–17**

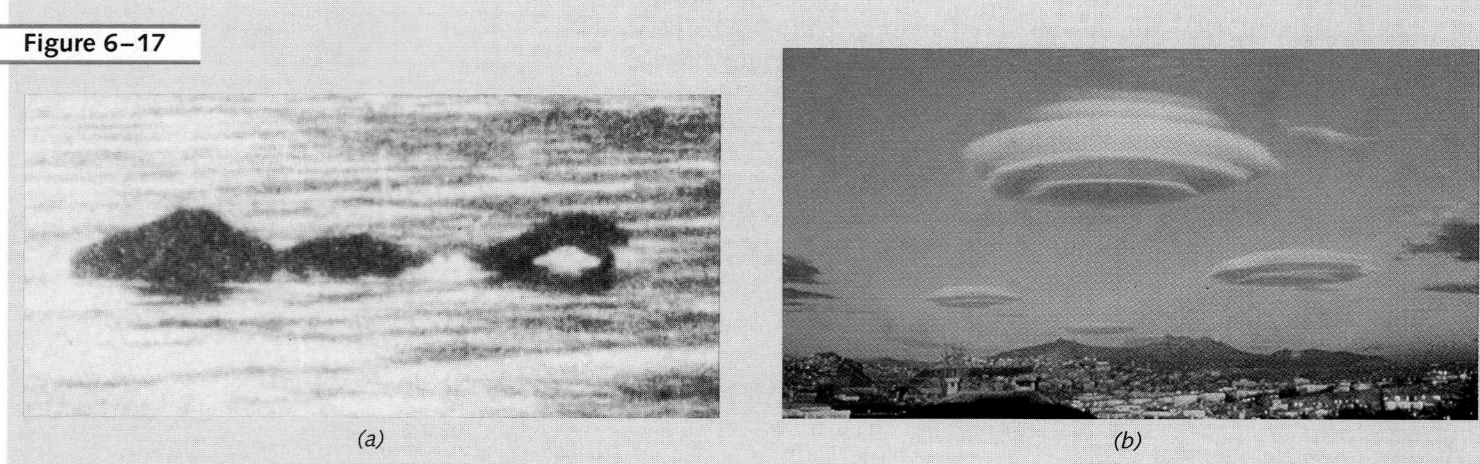

*(a)* *(b)*

**Believing Is Seeing** *(a) Is this the Loch Ness monster or a log? (b) Are these flying saucers or clouds? We often see what we expect to see.*

Our perceptual set can influence what we hear as well as what we see. Witness the kindly airline pilot who, on a takeoff run, looked over at his depressed co-pilot and said, "Cheer up." The co-pilot heard the usual "Gear up" and promptly raised the wheels—before they had left the ground (Reason & Mycielska, 1982). When listening to rock music played backward, people often perceive an evil message *if* specifically told what to listen to (Vokey & Read, 1985). When observing presidential campaign debates, most Americans perceive their favorite candidate as being the better debator (Gallup, 1992). Clearly, much of what we perceive comes not just from the world "out there" but also from what's behind our eyes and between our ears.

What determines our perceptual set? Through experience we form concepts, or *schemas*, which organize and interpret unfamiliar information. Our preexisting schemas for male saxophonists and women's faces, for monsters and tree trunks, for airplane lights and UFOs, all help us interpret ambiguous sensations with top-down processing. Confronted with an ambiguous moving object in the sky, different people may therefore apply different schemas: "It's a bird." "It's a plane." "It's Superman!"

Children's drawings allow us to glimpse their developing perceptual schemas. A preschooler can draw circles and angled lines but cannot combine them to create an elaborate human figure. The child's problem is not clumsiness. A right-handed adult asked to draw with the left hand will create an awkward drawing, but it will be unlike the child's drawing in Figure 6–18. Part of the difference lies in children's difficulty representing visually what they see. The main difference, however, lies in the child's simplified schema for essential human characteristics. To a 3-year-old, a face is a more essential human feature than a body. From ages 3 to 8, children's schemas for bodies become more elaborate, and so do their drawings.

Our schemas for faces prime us to see facial patterns in cartoonists' caricatures and even in random configurations, such as the lunar landscape. Peter Thompson (1980) at the University of York discovered that our face recognition is especially attuned to the expressive eyes and mouth. Thus, we have trouble imagining what U.S. President Bill Clinton's inverted eyes and mouth will look like when we turn his face upright (Figure 6–19).

**Figure 6–18**

**Schemas** *Children's drawings reflect their schemas of reality, as well as their abilities to represent what they see. This drawing by a 3-year-old illustrates that the face has far greater importance than the body in young children's schemas of essential human characteristics.*

**Figure 6–19**

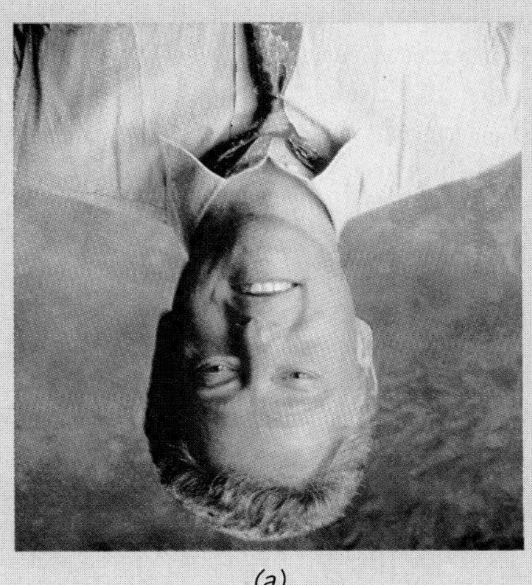

*(a)*

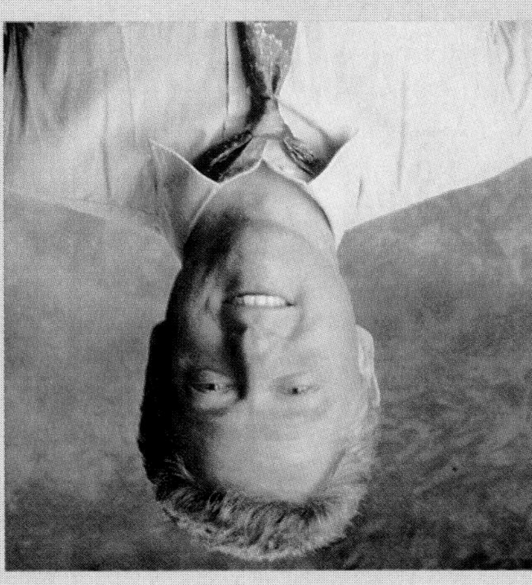

*(b)*

**Face Schemas** *Look at President Clinton's reconstructed face (a) and try to imagine what his face will look like when you turn it upright.*

### Context Effects

A given stimulus may trigger radically different perceptions, partly because of our differing schemas, but also because of the immediate context. Some quick examples:

Did the speaker say "cults and sects" or "cults and sex"? Did the critic advocate "attacks" or "a tax" on our politicians? We must discern from the surrounding words.

Did the pursuing monster in Figure 6–11 on page 199 look aggressive? Did the pursued one seem frightened? If so, you are experiencing a context effect. The two monsters are the same.

Figure 6–20

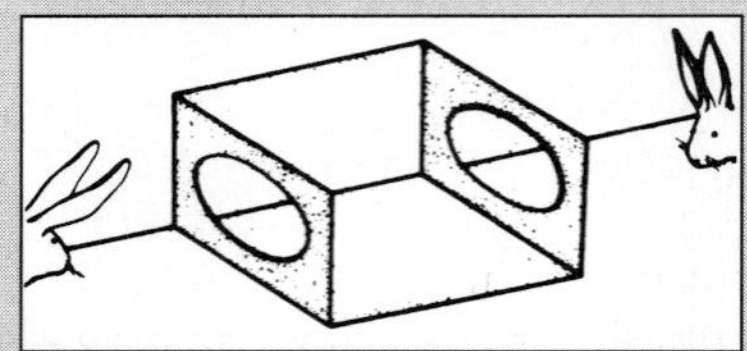

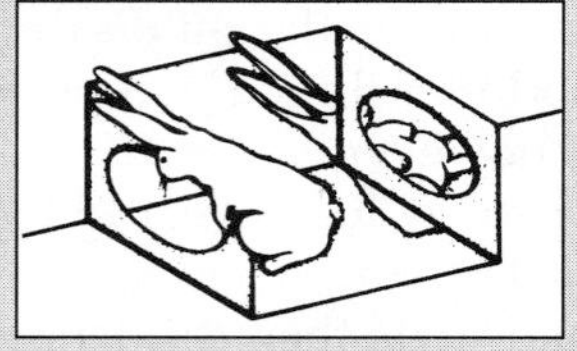

**Context Effects** *Is the box in the far left frame lying on the floor or hanging from the ceiling? The context defined by the inquisitive bunnies guides our perceptions. (From Shepard, 1990.)*

Is the "Magician's Cabinet" in Figure 6–20 sitting on the floor or hanging from the ceiling? How we perceive it depends on the context defined by the bunnies.

Soviet film director Lew Kulechov believed that skilled directors create audience emotion by defining a context in which viewers interpret an actor's expressions. He once produced three short films, each depicting one of three contexts, followed by identical clips of an actor with a neutral expression (Wallbott, 1988). Shown a dead woman, viewers were struck by the actor's sadness. Shown a dish of soup, viewers judged the actor thoughtful. Shown a playing child, viewers said the actor appeared happy.

In Seattle's county hospital where I was once an orderly, we occasionally faced the task of transporting a dead body through crowded hallways without alarming the patients or their visitors. Our solution was to exploit the "Kulechov effect" by creating a context that matched people's schemas for sleeping and sedated patients: With the body's face uncovered and the sheet turned down in normal fashion, we could wheel an apparently "sleeping" body past the unsuspecting.

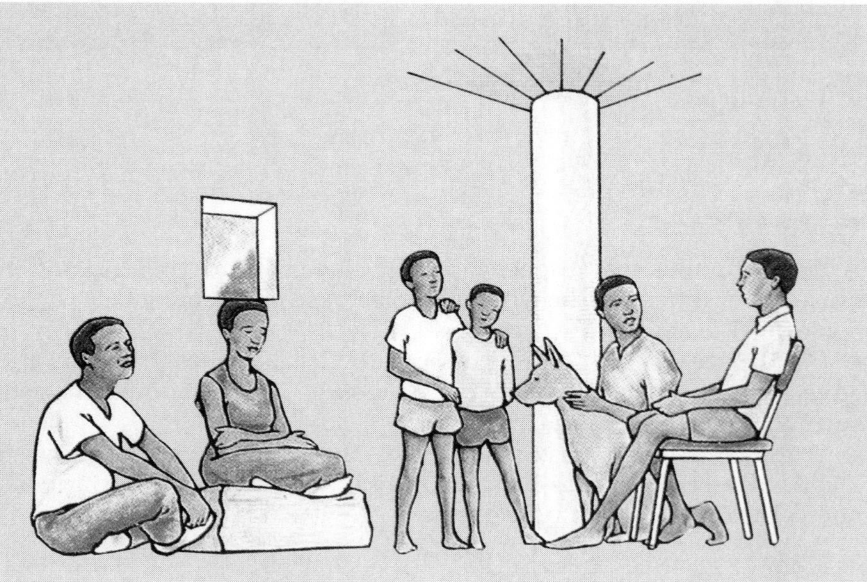

**Culture and Context Effects** *What is above the woman's head? In this experiment, nearly all the participants from East Africa thought she was balancing a metal box or can on her head and that the family was sitting under a tree. Westerners, to whom corners and boxlike architecture are more common, were more likely to perceive the family as being indoors, with the woman sitting under a window. (Adapted from Gregory & Gombrich, 1973.)*

## *Close-Up* The Human Factor in Operating Machines

At the 1991 Cal Tech commencement, then-President George Bush proposed a national goal: "By the turn of the century, Americans must be able to get their VCRs to stop flashing 12:00." Democrat Tipper Gore could agree with Republican Bush on that much: She finally covered her VCR clock with black masking tape to hide the relentless blinking. Like her ABC-News colleague Peter Jennings, Barbara Walters also can't program any of her three VCRs. "I'm reduced to asking friends to tape for me," she has said. "I am deeply ashamed" (Zoglin, 1992).

I love our VCR, though I still haven't figured out how to make it "express record." Our stove is wonderful, except for the moments I spend puzzling over which control works which burner. The push-bar doors on our campus buildings are safe and easy, though occasionally frustrating when I push the wrong end. The extra buttons on my computer-linked phone are handy, though when transferring a call I still must look up which button to press.

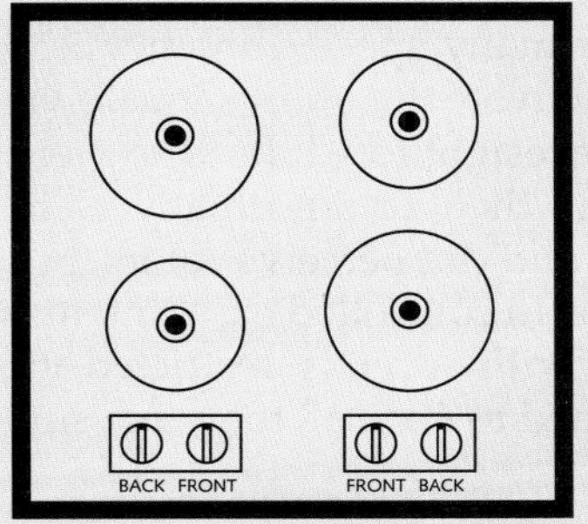


(*a*) Traditional labeling

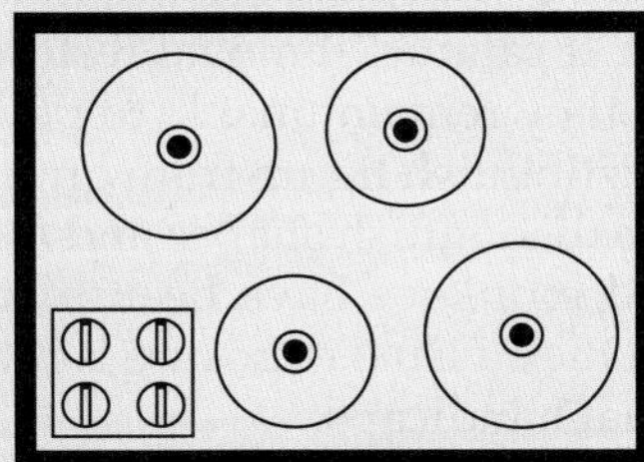

(*b*) Natural map

**Good Design** *Common stove controls require labeling, as in (a). By using a natural map (b), we needn't read labels. (From Norman, 1988.)*

*Human factors psychologists* help to design appliances, machines, and work settings that harness rather than confound our natural perceptions. Psychologist Donald Norman (1988) suggests how simple design changes could reduce some of our frustrations. For example, by exploiting "natural mapping," we could design stove controls that require no labels.

Understanding human factors can do more than design for reduced frustration; it can help avoid disaster. After beginning commercial flights in the late 1960s, the Boeing 727 was involved in several landing accidents caused by pilot error. Psychologist Conrad Kraft (1978) noted a common setting for these accidents: All took place at night and involved landing short of the runway after crossing a dark stretch of water or unilluminated ground. Beyond the runway, city lights would project a larger retinal image if on a rising terrain. This would make the ground seem closer than it was. By recreating these conditions in flight simulations, Kraft discovered that pilots were deceived into thinking they were flying safely higher than they were (Figure 6–21). Aided by Kraft's finding, the airlines began corrective measures (such as requiring the co-pilot to monitor the altimeter and call out altitudes) and the accidents diminished.

**Figure 6–21**

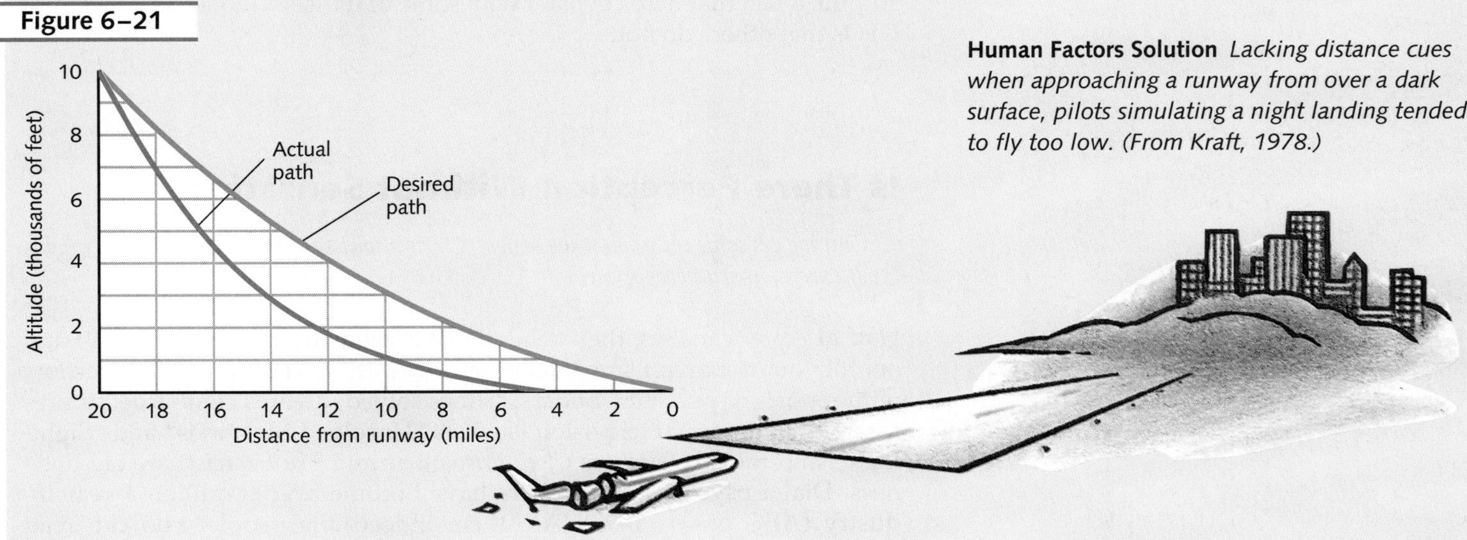


**Human Factors Solution** *Lacking distance cues when approaching a runway from over a dark surface, pilots simulating a night landing tended to fly too low. (From Kraft, 1978.)*

**The Solution** *Another view of the impossible doghouse in Figure 6–5 (page 193) reveals the secrets of this illusion. From the photo angle in Figure 6–5, the grouping principle of closure leads us to perceive the boards as continuous.*

*Reprinted from GAMES Magazine (810 Seventh Avenue, New York, NY 10019). Copyright © 1983 PSC Games Limited Partnership.*

In everyday life, perceptual sets—for example, stereotypes about gender or culture—can color the context. Without the obvious clues of pink or blue, people will struggle over whether to call the new baby a "he" or a "she." But told an infant is "David," people (especially children) may perceive "him" as bigger and stronger than if the same infant is called "Diana" (Stern & Karraker, 1989). Some gender differences, it seems, exist merely in the eyes of their beholders.

The effects of perceptual sets and context show how experience helps us construct perception. "We hear and apprehend only what we already half know," said Thoreau. The river of perception is fed by two streams, sensation and cognition. To return to the question—is perception innate or learned?—we can answer simply: It's both.

## Summing Up

The most direct tests of the nature-nurture issue come from experiments that modify human perceptions.

**Sensory Restriction and Restored Vision** For many species, infancy is a critical period during which experience must activate the brain's innate visual mechanisms. If cataract removal restores eyesight to adults who were blind from birth, they remain unable to perceive the world normally. Generally, they can distinguish figure from ground and can perceive colors, but they are unable to distinguish shapes and forms. In controlled experiments, infant kittens and monkeys have been reared with severely restricted visual input. When their visual exposure is returned to normal, they, too, suffer enduring visual handicaps.

**Perceptual Adaptation** Human vision is remarkably adaptable. Given glasses that shift the world slightly to the left or right, or even turn it upside down, people manage to adapt their movements and, with practice, to move about with ease.

**Perceptual Set** Clear evidence that perception is influenced by our experience—our learned assumptions and beliefs—as well as by sensory input comes from the many demonstrations of perceptual set and context effects. The schemas we have learned help us to interpret otherwise ambiguous stimuli, a fact that helps explain why some of us "see" monsters, faces, and UFOs that others do not.

# Is There Perception Without Sensation?

*Can we perceive only what we sense? Or, without sensory input, are we capable of extrasensory perception?*

Half of Americans say they believe in **extrasensory perception (ESP)** and another quarter aren't sure (Gallup & Newport, 1991). The media overflow with reports of psychic wonders: crimes solved, dreams come true, futures foretold. Paranormal television (such as "Unsolved Mysteries" and "Sightings") and movies (such as *Close Encounters* and *The Exorcist*) are big business. Dial-a-psychic 900 numbers have become a $100 million-a-year industry (ABC News, 1993). Are there indeed *any* people who can read minds, see through walls, or foretell the future?

In laboratory experiments, **parapsychologists**—those who study paranormal (literally, beyond the normal) happenings—have sometimes been astonished at psychics who seem capable of discerning the contents of sealed envelopes, influencing the roll of a die, or drawing a picture of what someone else is viewing at an unknown remote location. But other research psychologists and scientists—including 96 percent of scientists in the National Academy of Sciences—are skeptical (McConnell, 1991). If ESP is real, we would need to overturn the scientific understanding that we are creatures whose minds are tied to our physical brains and whose perceptual experiences of the world are built of sensations. Sometimes new evidence does overturn our scientific preconceptions. So let's look at some claims for ESP, and then see why scientists remain dubious.

## Claims of ESP

Claims of paranormal phenomena include astrological predictions, psychic healing, reincarnation, communication with the dead, and out-of-body frequent flyer programs. Of these, the most respectable, testable, and—for a chapter on perception—relevant claims are for three varieties of ESP:

*Telepathy*, or mind-to-mind communication—one person sending thoughts to another or perceiving another's thoughts.

*Clairvoyance*, or perceiving remote events, such as sensing that a friend's house is on fire.

*Precognition*, or perceiving future events, such as a political leader's death or a sporting event's outcome.

Closely linked with these are claims of *psychokinesis*, or "mind over matter," such as levitating a table or influencing the roll of a die.

On stage, the "psychic," like a magician, controls what the audience sees and hears. In the laboratory, the experimenter controls what the psychic sees and hears. Consider one careful experiment conducted by Bruce Layton and Bill Turnbull (1975) at the University of North Carolina. Layton and Turnbull had a computer generate a randomized 100-item list of the digits 1, 2, 3, 4, and 5 for each of their 179 student participants. They gave each student such a list in a sealed envelope and asked the student to guess which number was in each of the 100 positions.

By chance, 1 guess in 5, or 20 guesses out of the 100, should be correct. When told beforehand that ESP was beneficial, subjects averaged 20.66 correct out of 100. When told that ESP was harmful, they averaged only 19.49 correct. The difference might seem insignificant—indeed, you would never notice so small an effect while observing an experiment. But a statistical analysis revealed that a difference that large among so many participants would seldom occur by chance. So Layton and Turnbull concluded that an ESP effect had occurred.

Bolstered by such experiments, believers in ESP accuse research psychologists of the same sort of skepticism that led eighteenth-century scientists to scoff at the idea that meteorites come from outer space. Novelist Arthur Koestler, who in 1983 left more than $700,000 to fund a British professorship in parapsychology, once complained that today's skeptical scientists resemble the Italian philosophers who refused to look at Jupiter's moons through Galileo's telescope—because they "knew" that such moons did not exist. Stubborn skepticism sometimes blinds people to surprising truth.

The Quigmans by Buddy Hickerson; © 1990, Los Angeles Times Syndicate. Reprinted with permission.

*Which supposed psychic ability does the sportscaster claim?*

*"A man does not attain the status of Galileo merely because he is persecuted; he must also be right."*

Stephen Jay Gould
*Ever Since Darwin*, 1973

## Skepticism About ESP

The skeptics reply that an uncritical mind is a gullible mind. Time and again, they point out, so-called psychics have exploited unquestioning audiences with amazing performances in which they *appeared* to communicate with the spirits of the dead, read minds, or levitate objects—only to have it revealed that their acts were a hoax, nothing more than the illusions of stage magicians. Indeed, many psychic deceptions have been exposed by magicians, who resent the exploitation of their arts in the name of psychic powers.

*"A psychic is an actor playing the role of a psychic."*
Psychologist-magician Daryl Bem (1984)

Even scientists get hoodwinked. A notable case involved two teenage magicians, Steve Shaw and Michael Edwards (Randi, 1983a,b). In 1979, this young pair approached Washington University's new parapsychology laboratory, offering to demonstrate their "psychic powers." Over the next 3 years, the two pretended to defy the laws of nature. They appeared to project mental images onto film, cause clocks to slide across a table, effortlessly bend metal objects, and move objects in sealed jars. Forewarned against trickery by James Randi, the youngsters' magician-adviser, the laboratory director nevertheless ignored the warnings and for a time proclaimed that "these two kids are the most reliable of the people that we've studied" ("Psychic Abscam," 1983).

*"The most eminent scientist, untrained in magic, is putty in the hands of a clever charlatan."*
Martin Gardner (1983)

This parapsychologist's gullibility illustrates how tempting it is to label phenomena *we* don't understand as beyond explanation: "What other explanation could there possibly be but ESP?" the awestruck observer asks. Thus, before bats' echolocation ability was discovered, many people attributed bats' ability to avoid wires in complete darkness to clairvoyance (Gibson, 1979). When the bats were blinded, when their noses were sealed, when their wings were coated with varnish, they still could navigate, so what other explanation could there be but ESP?

### Premonitions or Pretensions?

Can psychics see into the future? Although one might wish for a psychic stock forecaster, the tallied forecasts of "leading psychics" reveal meager accuracy. Between 1978 and 1985, the New Year's predictions of the *National Enquirer's* favorite psychics yielded 2 accurate predictions out of 486 (Strentz, 1986). During the early 1990s, tabloid psychics were all wrong in predicting surprising events (Madonna did not become a gospel singer, a UFO base was not found in the Mexican desert, Queen Elizabeth did not abdicate her throne to enter a convent). And they again missed all the significant unexpected events, such as the dissolution of the Soviet Union, Saddam Hussein's assault on Kuwait, and the World Trade Center bombing.

**OUT THERE by Rob Pudim**

*The National Star has a winner at last.*
Reprinted with permission of the Skeptical Inquirer.

Analyses of psychic visions offered to police departments reveal that these, too, are no more accurate than guesses made by others (Reiser, 1982). Psychics working with the police do, however, generate dozens or even hundreds of predictions; this increases the odds of an occasional correct guess, which psychics can then report to the media. Moreover, vague predictions can later be interpreted to match events, which provide a perceptual set for interpreting them. Nostradamus, a sixteenth-century French psychic, explained in an unguarded moment that his ambiguous prophecies "could not possibly be understood till they were interpreted after the event and by it." Police departments are wise to all this. When Jane Ayers Sweat and Mark Durm (1993) asked the police departments of America's 50 largest cities whether they ever used psychics, 65 percent said they never had. Of those that had, not one had found it helpful.

Are the spontaneous "visions" of ordinary people any more accurate? Consider our dreams. Do they foretell the future, as about half of university students believe (Messer & Griggs, 1989)? Or do they only seem to because we are more likely to recall or reconstruct dreams that seem to have come true? Sixty years ago, two Harvard psychologists (Murray & Wheeler, 1937) tested the prophetic power of dreams. After aviator Charles Lindbergh's baby son was kidnapped and murdered but before the body was discovered, the researchers invited the public to report their dreams about the child. Of the 1300 dream reports submitted, how many accurately envisioned the child dead? A mere 5 percent. And how many also correctly anticipated the body's location—buried among trees? Only 4 of the 1300. Although this number was surely no better than chance, to those 4 dreamers the accuracy of their *apparent* precognitions must have seemed uncanny.

*More recent experiments in which people attempted to send mental images to dreamers produced some intriguing initial results, but these could not be replicated even with the same subjects. Dream telepathy experiments therefore were discontinued (Hyman, 1986).*

Every day each of us imagines many events. Occasionally an unlikely imagined event is bound to occur and to astonish us when it does. If you tell everyone in a group of 100 people to think "heads" before each tosses six coins, someone is likely to get all heads (whether thinking heads or not) and to feel eerie afterwards. As Chapter 1 explained, random sequences will sometimes contain weird conjunctions or streaks. Given the billions of events that occur in the world each day, and given enough days, some stunning coincidences are sure to occur. "Time converts the improbable to the inevitable," notes Stephen Jay Gould.

Finally, consider this, say the skeptics: After tens of thousands of experiments, *there has never been discovered a reproducible ESP phenomenon, nor any individual who can convincingly demonstrate psychic ability* (Marks, 1986). A National Research Council investigation of ESP similarly concludes that "the best available evidence does not support the contention that these phenomena exist" (Druckman & Swets, 1988).

*"There comes a point where one has to accept the message of the data, that absence of evidence is evidence of absence."*

Frank Close
*Too Hot to Handle: The Race for Cold Fusion*, 1991

One skeptic, magician James Randi, has offered $10,000 to anyone who can demonstrate "*any* paranormal ability" before a group of competent experts. Other similar offers total more than a third of a million dollars (Jones, 1985–1986; Karr, 1993). To anyone whose claims could be authenticated, the scientific seal of approval would be worth far more. Randi's offer has been publicized for well over two decades, and dozens of people have been tested, sometimes under the scrutiny of an independent panel of judges. To refute those who say there is no ESP, one need only produce a single person who can demonstrate a single reproducible ESP phenomenon. As yet, no one has exhibited any such power.

Lacking such, and faced with increasing skepticism, the Parapsychological Association has recently been losing membership, and several major parapsychological laboratories lost their funding and closed during the 1980s (Hess, 1993). Even while fascination with ESP grows in some parts of the world, doubts about ESP are increasing among American teens. The 67 percent who told the 1978 Gallup Youth Survey they believed in ESP declined to 43 percent in 1992.

### Thinking Critically About ESP

In times past, there have been all kinds of crazy ideas—that bumps on the head reveal character traits, that bloodletting is a cure-all, that each sperm cell contains a miniature person inside. When faced with such claims—or with claims of mind-reading or out-of-body travel or mind-over-matter—how can we separate crazy ideas from those that sound crazy but are true? At the heart of science we find a simple answer: Test them to see if they work. If they do, so much the worse for our skepticism. If they don't, so much the worse for the ideas.

*"At the heart of science is an essential tension between two seemingly contradictory attitudes—an openness to new ideas, no matter how bizarre or counterintuitive they may be, and the most ruthless skeptical scrutiny of all ideas, old and new."*

Carl Sagan (1987)

This scientific attitude appears in the agreement of believers and skeptics that what parapsychology needs to give it credibility is a reproducible phenomenon and a theory to explain it. Could the Layton and Turnbull clairvoyance experiment (in which students beat chance in guessing numbers in sealed envelopes) provide such a reproducible phenomenon? The skeptical editor of the *Journal of Experimental Social Psychology*, to which Layton and Turnbull submitted their results for publication, wondered. So he and the authors reached an unusual agreement: The researchers would repeat their experiment, and the journal would then publish the results of both, regardless of the new outcome. (As this illustrates, both ESP researchers and skeptics genuinely seek truth.) The result of the second experiment? Layton and Turnbull summarized honestly and succinctly: "No [statistically] significant effects were present."

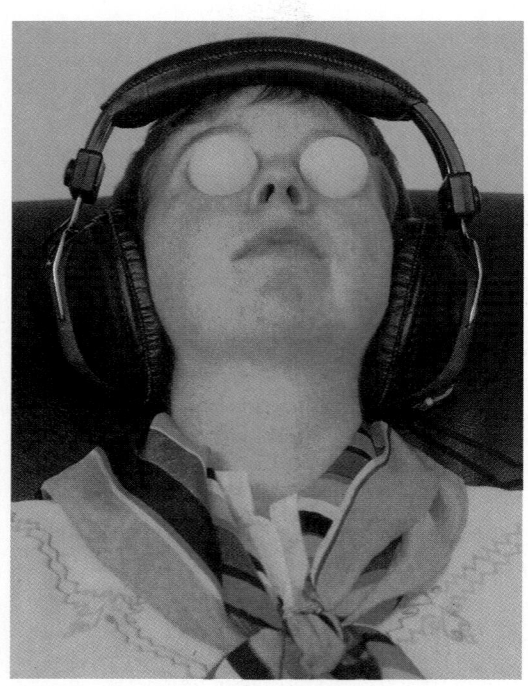

**The Ganzfeld Procedure** *Hoping to detect faint telepathy signals, parapsychologists are using sensory deprivation to minimize distractions.*

Knowing how easily people are deceived, and lacking reproducible results, most research psychologists remain skeptical. Indeed, they are dismayed by all the shows, books, and magazines on paranormal topics. But some are newly intrigued by findings recently published by social psychologist Daryl Bem and parapsychologist Charles Honorton (1994) using the "ganzfeld procedure." The procedure places the subject in a reclining chair, plays hissing white noise through headphones, and shines diffuse red light through translucent ping-pong ball halves taped over the eyes. Ostensibly, this reduction of external distractions enables subjects better to hear still small voices within. Building on earlier studies using this procedure, Bem and Honorton isolated a "sender" and "receiver" in separate, shielded chambers and had the sender concentrate on a randomly selected visual image. Over 11 studies, the receivers beat chance by a small but reliable margin (32 percent versus 25 percent chance) when rating which of four images best matched the images they experienced during the session.

Recall that psychology-based critical inquiry asks two questions: What do you mean? And how do you know (what's your evidence)? Parapsychologists say these ganzfeld tests of ESP offer clear answers to both questions. Skeptic Ray Hyman (1994) grants that their methodology surpasses that of previous ESP experiments, but he questions certain procedural details that may have introduced bias. Intrigued, other researchers are now at work replicating these experiments. Will this be the first reliable ESP phenomenon? Or one more dashed hope, one more "phenomenon" that later will be refuted and abandoned? Stay tuned, and remember: The scientific attitude blends curious skepticism with open-minded humility. It demands that extraordinary claims be supported by clear and reliable evidence; given such evidence, it is open to nature's occasional surprises.

As critical thinkers, this can be our attitude, too. We, too, can be skeptical, but without closing ourselves to all startling claims. We can be open to new ideas without being gullible, discerning without being cynical. We can be critical thinkers; yet, knowing that our understanding of nature is incomplete, we can agree with Shakespeare's Hamlet that "there are more things in heaven and earth, Horatio, than are dreamt of in your philosophy."

Some things that we assume to be true—the reality of another's love, the existence or nonexistence of God, the finality of death or the reality of life after death—are beyond science. That is one reason why, after clearing the decks of tested and rejected pseudomysteries, we can retain a humble sense of wonder regarding life's untestable mysteries.

Why are so many people predisposed to believe that ESP exists? Why do sensational claims so often race ahead of simple facts? In part, such beliefs may stem from understandable misperceptions, misinterpretations, and selective recall. But for some people there also exists an unsatisfied hunger for wonderment, an itch to experience the magical. In Britain and the United States, the founders of parapsychology were mostly people who, having lost their religious faith, were searching for a scientific basis for believing in the meaningfulness of life and the possibility of life after death (Alcock, 1985; Beloff, 1985). In the upheaval since the collapse of autocratic rule in Russia, there has come an "avalanche of the mystical, occult and pseudoscientific" (Kapitza, 1991). "Extrasensorial" healers, astrologers, and seers fascinate the awestruck public.

To feel awe and to gain a deep reverence for life, we need look no further than our own perceptual system and its capacity for organizing formless nerve impulses into colorful sights, vivid sounds, and evocative smells. Within our ordinary perceptual experiences lies much that is truly extraordinary—surely much more than has so far been dreamt of in our psychology. A century of research has revealed many of the secrets of sensation and perception, but for future generations of researchers there remain profound and genuine mysteries to explore.

*"I have uttered what I did not understand, things too wonderful for me."*

Job 42:3

We have now examined the first steps in our processing of information, from receiving sensory input to constructing meaningful perceptions. But our skull's three-pound information processing system does much more: Under the influence of sleep, hypnosis, or drugs, it will construct unreal images (Chapter 7). It learns from our experiences, recalling them long afterward (Chapters 8 and 9). It thinks and makes intelligent plans (Chapters 10 and 11). Between our sensing and acting lies an unimaginably complex information system that, more than ever, beckons explorers of our mind's inner space.

## Summing Up

Many people believe in or claim to experience extrasensory perception. Parapsychologists have tried to document several forms of ESP—telepathy, clairvoyance, and precognition. But for several reasons, especially the lack of a reproducible ESP effect, most research psychologists remain skeptical. New studies using the ganzfeld procedure have recently raised hopes of a possible telepathy phenomenon. Follow-up studies should soon indicate the phenomenon's reliability.

## Terms and Concepts to Remember

### Selective Attention

**selective attention** The focusing of conscious awareness on a particular stimulus, as in the cocktail party effect.

### Perceptual Illusions

**visual capture** The tendency for vision to dominate the other senses; we perceive filmed voices as coming from the screen we see rather than from the projector behind us.

### Perceptual Organization

**gestalt** An organized whole. Gestalt psychologists emphasize our tendency to integrate pieces of information into meaningful wholes.

**figure-ground** The organization of the visual field into objects (the *figures*) that stand out from their surroundings (the *ground*).

**grouping** The perceptual tendency to organize stimuli into coherent groups.

**proximity** The perceptual tendency to group together visual and auditory events that are near each other.

**similarity** The perceptual tendency to group together similar elements.

**continuity** The perceptual tendency to group stimuli into smooth, continuous patterns.

**closure** The perceptual tendency to fill in gaps, thus enabling one to perceive disconnected parts as a whole object.

**connectedness** The perceptual tendency to perceive features, such as dots, as a single unit when uniform and linked.

**depth perception** The ability to see objects in three dimensions although the images that strike the retina are two-dimensional; allows us to judge distance.

**visual cliff** A laboratory device for testing depth perception in infants and young animals.

**binocular cues** Depth cues, such as retinal disparity and convergence, that depend on the use of two eyes.

**monocular cues** Distance cues, such as aerial and linear perspective and overlap, available to either eye alone.

**retinal disparity** A binocular cue for perceiving depth; the greater the disparity (difference) between the two images the retina receives of an object, the closer the object is to us.

**convergence** A binocular cue for perceiving depth; the extent to which the eyes converge inward when looking at an object.

**relative size** A monocular cue for perceiving distance; when we assume two objects are the same size, the one that produces the smaller image appears more distant.

**interposition** A monocular cue for perceiving distance; nearby objects partially block our view of more distant objects.

**relative clarity** A monocular cue for perceiving distance; hazier objects appear more distant.

**texture gradient** A monocular cue for perceiving distance; a gradual change to a less distinct texture suggests increasing distance.

**relative height** A monocular cue for perceiving distance; higher objects appear more distant.

**relative motion** A monocular cue for perceiving distance; when we move, objects at different distances change their relative positions in our visual image, with those closest moving most.

**linear perspective** A monocular cue for perceiving distance; we perceive the converging of what we know to be parallel lines as indicating increasing distance.

**relative brightness** A monocular cue for perceiving distance; dimmer objects appear more distant.

**phi phenomenon** An illusion of movement created when two or more adjacent lights blink on and off in succession.

**perceptual constancy** Perceiving objects as unchanging (having consistent lightness, color, shape, and size) even as illumination and retinal images change.

### Interpretation

**perceptual adaptation** In vision, the ability to adjust to an artificially displaced or even inverted visual field.

**perceptual set** A mental predisposition to perceive one thing and not another.

### Is There Perception Without Sensation?

**extrasensory perception (ESP)** The controversial claim that perception can occur apart from sensory input. Said to include *telepathy*, *clairvoyance*, and *precognition*.

**parapsychology** The study of paranormal phenomena including ESP and psychokinesis.

## Critical Thinking Exercise

Now that you have read and reviewed Chapter 6, take your learning a step further by testing your critical thinking skills on the following practical problem solving exercise.

> Air traffic controllers face the difficult task of guiding pilots in making safe departures and landings. To complicate matters, at any moment several airplanes may be simultaneously approaching different runways at similar angles and altitudes while other airplanes are in various stages of taking off from nearby runways. To assist them in their task, the controllers monitor air traffic in two ways: (1) by visually observing from a high tower, and (2) by monitoring airplanes as they appear as "blips" on a radar screen.
>
> The air traffic controller's task can be construed as a practical problem involving perceptual organization. For example, when the image of an airplane first appears in the sky or on the radar screen, it must be differentiated from other objects. Once it is recognized as an airplane, its distance, altitude, and angle of approach must be discerned.
>
> Psychology offers principles of perceptual organization for grouping stimuli together into recognizable forms and for determining their distance. The principle of relative clarity, for example, states that hazy objects are perceived as farther away than sharp, clear objects. Can you envision how air traffic controllers use each of the following principles of perceptual organization? In framing your answers, first indicate *what* the principle enables air controllers to do and then say *how* this ability helps them.

*Figure-ground:*

*Relative size:*

*Continuity:*

*Relative height:*

Check your progress on becoming a critical thinker by comparing your answers to the sample answers found in Appendix B.

## For Further Reading

**Alcock, J. E.** (1990). *Science and supernature: A critical appraisal of parapsychology*. Buffalo, NY: Prometheus Books.

*A research psychologist's critique of parapsychology.*

**Fineman, M.** (1981). *The inquisitive eye*. New York: Oxford University Press.

*Written for students in psychology, art, design, and photography, this entertaining book discusses and demonstrates many perceptual phenomena.*

**Rock, I.** (1984). *Perception*. New York: Scientific American Books.

*A beautifully illustrated treatment of many of the classic concerns of perception.*

**Shepard, R. N.** (1990). *Mind sights*. New York: Freeman.

*A delightful collection of original visual illusions and ambiguities, with commentary on how the mind perceives.*

***The Skeptical Inquirer***

*An entertaining quarterly periodical that analyzes ongoing paranormal claims, from astrology and ESP to UFOs and psychic healers.*

**Wolman, B. B., Dale, L. A., Schmeidler, G. R., & Ullman, M.** (Eds.). (1985). *Handbook of parapsychology*. New York: Van Nostrand Reinhold.

*Parapsychologists summarize their field's research.*

# CHAPTER 7

# States of Consciousness

Now playing at an inner theater near you: the premiere showing of some sleeping person's vivid dream. This never-before-seen mental movie features captivating characters wrapped in a plot so original and unlikely, yet so intricate and real-seeming, that the viewer later marvels at its creation. Awakening from a troubling dream, wrenched by its emotions, who among us has not wondered about this weird state of consciousness? How does our brain so creatively, colorfully, and completely construct this alternative conscious world? In the shadowland between our dreaming and waking consciousness, we may even wonder for a moment which realm represents reality. And what shall we make of other altered states of consciousness—of daydreaming, hypnosis, and drug-altered hallucinations?

But first questions first: What is consciousness? In every science there are concepts so fundamental they are nearly impossible to define. Biologists agree on what is alive but not on precisely what life is. In physics, matter and energy elude simple definition. To psychologists, consciousness is similarly a fundamental yet slippery concept.

## Studying Consciousness

*Psychologists have long explored consciousness, at first eagerly, then warily, and now with renewed vigor. What explains these swings of interest? And what are the levels and functions of consciousness?*

At its beginning, psychology was sometimes defined as "the description and explanation of states of consciousness" (Ladd, 1887). But the difficulty of scientifically studying consciousness led many psychologists during the first half of this century to turn to direct observations of behavior—an approach favored by an emerging school of psychology called *behaviorism* (page 259). At midcentury, psychology was no longer defined as the study of consciousness or "mental life" but rather as the science of behavior. Psychology had nearly lost consciousness. Consciousness was viewed like a car's speedometer: "It doesn't make the car go, it just reflects what's happening" (Seligman, 1991, p. 24).

By 1960, mental concepts began to reenter psychology. Advances in neuroscience made it possible to relate brain activity to various mental states—waking, sleeping, dreaming. Researchers were beginning to study altered states of consciousness induced by hypnosis and drugs. Psychologists of all persuasions were affirming the importance of mental processes (cognition). Psychology was regaining consciousness.

*"Psychology must discard all reference to consciousness."*

Behaviorist John B. Watson (1913)

For most psychologists today, **consciousness** is our awareness of ourselves and our environment. When we learn a complex concept or behavior—say, driving a car—consciousness focuses our concentration on the car and the traffic. This awareness varies with our attentional spotlight though. With practice, driving becomes automatic and does not require our undivided attention—freeing our consciousness to focus on other tasks.

## Levels of Information Processing

Many of this book's other chapters (Perception, Learning, Memory, Thinking and Language, Emotion) involve the study of normal waking consciousness. Research in each of these areas reveals that we process much information outside of awareness. We register and react to stimuli we do not consciously perceive. We type without paying attention to where the letters are on the keyboard. We change our attitudes and reconstruct our memories with no awareness of doing so. We are influenced by our past in ways we don't know (Greenwald & Banaji, 1995).

So, as far as our information processing is concerned, *conscious* awareness is but the tip of the iceberg. It is the part that enables us to exert voluntary control and to communicate our mental states to others (Kihlstrom, 1987). Beneath the surface, subconscious information processing occurs simultaneously on many parallel tracks. When we look at a flying bird, we are consciously aware of the result of our cognitive processing but not of our subprocessing of the bird's color, form, movement, distance, and identity. Yet consciousness arises from these brain events that immediately precede it. Stephen Kosslyn and Olivier Koenig (1992) suggest that brain events are to consciousness as a guitar's individual notes are to a chord. As a chord emerges from the interaction of different notes, so consciousness emerges from the interaction of individual brain events. As we experience the chord an instant *after* all the notes are present, so consciousness is known to lag the brain events that evoke it (Libet, 1985). And just as a consonant or dissonant chord tells us whether the instrument is in tune, so consciousness serves as a check that different brain subsystems are meshing properly.

*For a recap of serial and parallel processing, see pages 163–164.*

Unlike the parallel processing of subconscious information, conscious processing takes place in sequence (serially), is relatively slow, and has limited capacity. Consciousness is like a chief executive officer. Its many assistants automatically take care of routine business without bothering the CEO. This allows the CEO to monitor the whole system and deal with new challenges. Thus, in a familiar place we can talk politics while driving "on automatic."

Less habitual tasks require our conscious attention. When first arriving in a country where cars go on the other side of the road, driving commands one's full attention. Or try this: You can move your right foot in a smooth counterclockwise circle, and you can write the number 3 repeatedly with your right hand—but not at the same time. (If you are musically inclined, try something equally impossible: Tap a steady three times with your left hand while tapping four times with your right hand.) Both tasks require conscious attention, which can only be in one place at a time. If time is nature's way of keeping everything from happening at once, then consciousness is nature's way of keeping us from thinking and doing everything at once.

Consciousness occurs in varied states. We have not only normal seeing and hearing, reasoning and remembering, but also the altered consciousness of sleep dreams and daydreams, hypnotic states, chemically-induced hallucinations, and near-death visions.

## Summing Up

Psychology began as the study of consciousness, then turned to the study of observable behavior. Today, scientific investigation of states of mind is again one of psychology's pursuits. Speedy, parallel processing handles subconscious information; conscious processing is serial and much slower.

# Sleep and Dreams

*Sleep—sweet, renewing, mysterious sleep. Sleep—the irresistible tempter to whom we must all succumb. Sleep—the mantle that covers human thought. What is it? Why must we have it? Why do we spend a third of our lives—some 25 years, on average—sleeping? What and why do we dream?*

Sleep's age-old mysteries have intrigued humans for centuries. Now, some of these mysteries are being solved. In laboratories throughout the world, thousands have slept attached to recording devices while others observe. By recording sleepers' brain waves and muscle movements, by observing and awakening them from time to time, the sleep-watchers glimpse things that a thousand years of common sense never told us. Perhaps you can anticipate some of their discoveries. Are the following statements true or false?

*"I love to sleep. Do you? Isn't it great? It really is the best of both worlds. You get to be alive and unconscious."*

Comedian Rita Rudner, 1993

1. When people dream of performing some activity, their limbs often move in concert with the dream (pages 223–224).
2. Older adults sleep more than young adults (page 225 and Figure 7–6).
3. After 2 or 3 sleepless days, a person's performance on a brief but demanding intellectual task suffers (page 225).
4. Sleepwalkers are acting out their dreams (pages 223–224).
5. Sleep experts recommend treating insomnia with an occasional sleeping pill (page 226).
6. The dreams we have before awakening in the morning are similar to those we have soon after falling asleep (page 228).
7. Some people dream every night; others seldom dream at all (page 224).

All these statements (adapted from Palladino & Carducci, 1983) are false. Let's see why.

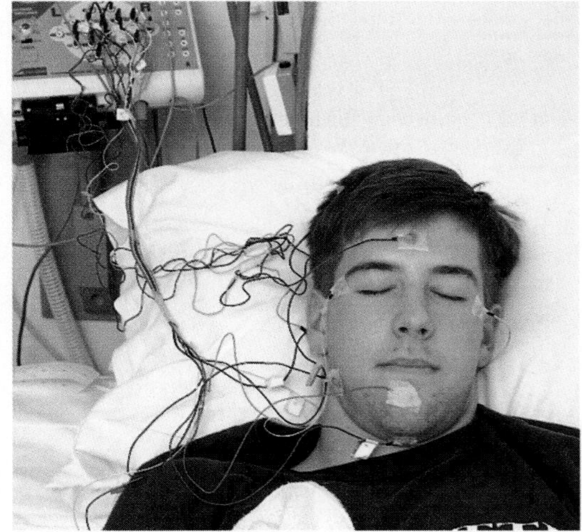

**A Study in Sleep** *In a sleep laboratory at Brigham and Woman's Hospital in Boston, recording equipment monitors a man's physiological state. The electrodes pasted to his face and scalp pick up weak electrical signals from his brain, as well as his eye movements and muscle tension. These patterns will vary with his sleep rhythm.*

## The Rhythm of Sleep

The rhythm of the day parallels the rhythm of life—from our waking to a new day's birth to our nightly return to what Shakespeare called "death's counterfeit." Our bodies synchronize with the 24-hour cycle of day and night through a biological clock called the **circadian rhythm** (from the Latin *circa*, "about," and *dies*, "day"). Our body temperature, for example, rises as morning approaches, peaks during the day, and then begins to drop before we go to sleep. Awake at 4:00 A.M. with a depressed body, we may fret over concerns: Does a lover's spat signal a split? Does a child's moodiness mean more trouble ahead? By midday, our body energized, we fret less. Pulling an all-nighter, we feel groggiest about 4:00 A.M. but we feel a second wind as our normal wake-up time arrives.

A transcontinental flight disrupts our circadian rhythm and we experience jet lag, mainly because we are awake when our circadian rhythm cries, "Sleep!" If we stay up late and sleep in on weekends, our biological clock begins to reset itself. When the weekend ends, the result may be "Sunday night insomnia" and "Monday morning blues." (Those who sleep till noon on Sunday and then go to bed just 11 hours later in preparation for the new workweek often find sleep elusive.)

Mysteriously, young adults isolated without clocks or daylight typically adopt a 25-hour day. This helps explain why many people find it easier to jet west, with an extended day, than east; why rotating shift workers adapt better to progressively later shifts than to earlier shifts; why until our later years we must discipline ourselves to get to bed on time and force ourselves to get up. When placed in a time-free environment under constant illumination, most animals, too, exceed a 24-hour day.

*If our natural circadian rhythm was attuned to a 23-hour cycle, would we instead need to discipline ourselves to stay up later at night and sleep in longer in the morning?*

There is also a biological rhythm during our sleep. About every 90 or 100 minutes we pass through a cycle of five distinct sleep stages. This elementary fact was unknown until 8-year-old Armond Aserinsky went to bed one night in 1952. His father, Eugene, a University of Chicago graduate student, needed to test an electroencephalograph he had been repairing during the day (Aserinsky, 1988; Seligman & Yellen, 1987). He placed electrodes near Armond's eyes to record the rolling eye movements believed to occur during sleep. Before long, the machine went wild, tracing deep zigzags on the graph paper. Aserinsky thought the machine was still broken. But as the night proceeded, the activity periodically recurred, indicating, Aserinsky finally realized, fast, jerky eye movements accompanied by energetic brain activity. When he awakened Armond during one such episode of *r*apid *e*ye *m*ovement sleep (**REM sleep**), the boy reported he was having a dream.

To find out if similar cycles occur during adult sleep, Nathaniel Kleitman (1960) and Aserinsky pioneered procedures that have now been used with thousands of volunteers. To appreciate both their methods and findings, imagine yourself as a subject. As the hour grows late you yawn in response to reduced brain metabolism. Yawning stretches your neck muscles and increases your heart rate, thus increasing the blood flow to your brain, and your alertness (Moorcroft, 1993). When you are ready for bed, the researcher glues electrodes to your scalp (to detect your brain waves), just outside the corners of your eyes (to detect eye movements), and on your chin (to detect muscle tension) (Figure 7–1). Other devices allow the researcher to record your heart rate, your respiration rate, and even the degree of your genital arousal.

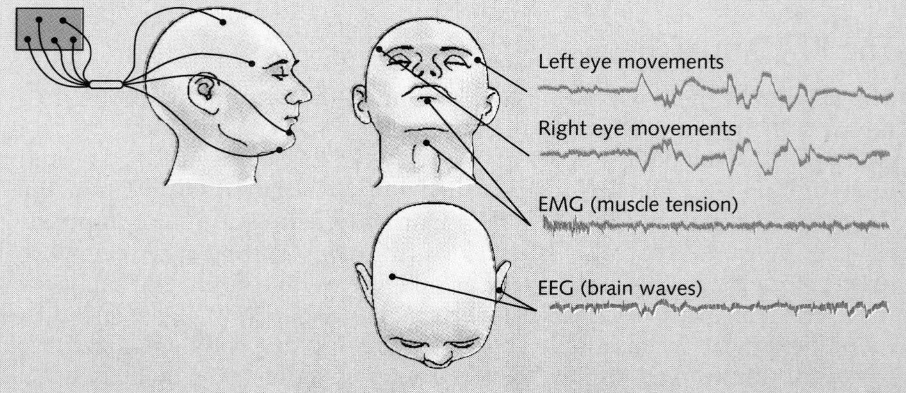


**Figure 7–1**

**Measuring Sleep Activity** *Sleep researchers measure brain-wave activity, eye movements, and muscle tension by electrodes that pick up weak electrical signals from the brain, eye, and facial muscles. (From Dement, 1978.)*

When you are in bed with your eyes closed, the researcher in the next room sees on the EEG the relatively slow **alpha waves** of your awake but relaxed state (Figure 7–2). As you adapt to all this equipment and grow tired, you slip into sleep and begin your deep-sea dive toward deeper and deeper levels. Your breathing rate slows and your brain waves slow further and show the irregular waves of Stage 1 sleep. During this light sleep, which lasts about 2 minutes, you may experience fantastic images, which are like **hallucinations**—sensory experiences that occur without a sensory stimulus. You may have a sensation of falling (at which moment your body may suddenly jerk) or of floating weightlessly.

Soon, you relax more deeply and begin about 20 minutes of Stage 2 sleep, characterized by the periodic appearance of *sleep spindles*—bursts of rapid, rhythmic brain-wave activity. Although you can still be awakened without too much difficulty during this phase, you are now clearly asleep. Sleeptalking—usually garbled or nonsensical—can occur during any sleep stage but seldom appears during deep sleep. More often it occurs during Stage 2 sleep or in the Stage 1 borderline between sleeping and waking.

Then for the next few minutes you go through the transitional Stage 3 to the deep sleep of Stage 4. Starting in Stage 3 and increasingly in Stage 4, your brain emits large, slow **delta waves**. These stages together are therefore called *slow-wave sleep*. They last for about 30 minutes, during which you are hard to awaken. Curiously, it is during the deep sleep of Stage 4 that we may begin walking in our sleep, or (as children) wet the bed. Moreover, even when we are deeply asleep, our brains somehow process the meaning of certain stimuli. We move around on our beds, but we manage not to fall out of them. The occasional roar of passing vehicles may leave deep sleep undisturbed, but the cry from a baby's nursery quickly interrupts it. EEG recordings confirm that our brain's auditory cortex responds to sound stimuli even while we sleep (Kutas, 1990).

About an hour after you first fall asleep, a strange thing happens. Rather than continuing in deep slumber, you ascend from your initial sleep dive. Returning through Stage 3 and Stage 2 (where you spend about half your night), you enter the most intriguing sleep phase of all—REM sleep (Figure 7–3). For about 10 minutes, your brain waves become rapid and saw-

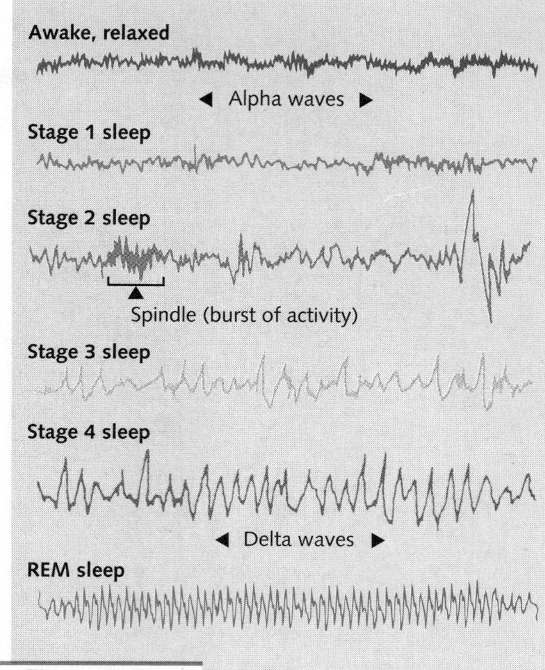


**Figure 7–2**

**Brain Waves and Sleep Stages** *The regular alpha waves of an awake, relaxed stage are quite different from the slower, larger delta waves of deep Stage 4 sleep. Although the rapid REM sleep waves resemble the near-waking Stage 1 sleep, the body is more aroused during REM sleep than during Stage 1 sleep. (From Dement, 1978.)*

**Figure 7–3**

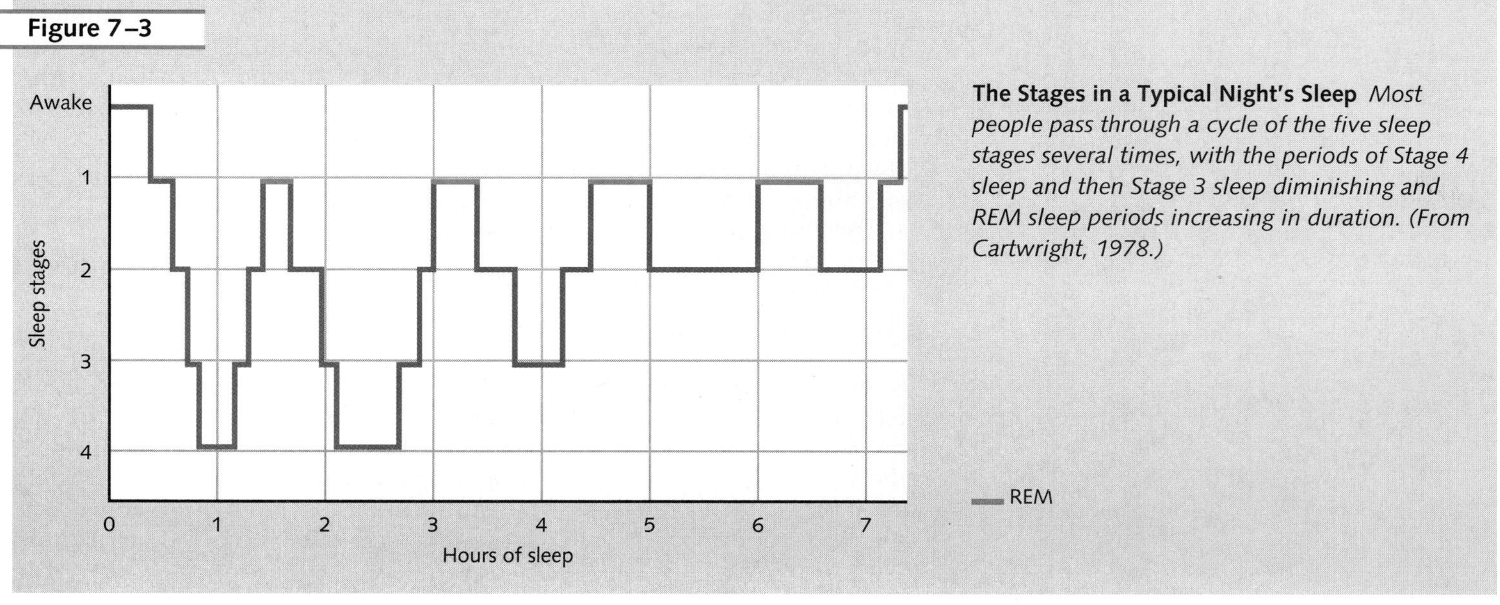


**The Stages in a Typical Night's Sleep** *Most people pass through a cycle of the five sleep stages several times, with the periods of Stage 4 sleep and then Stage 3 sleep diminishing and REM sleep periods increasing in duration. (From Cartwright, 1978.)*

*"Boy are my eyes tired! I had REM sleep all night long."*

© 1994 by Sidney Harris.

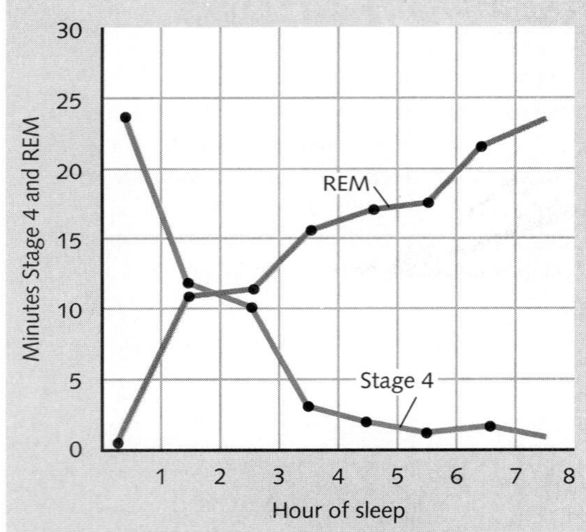


**Figure 7–4**

**The Progression of Stage 4 and REM Sleep Across a Night's Sleep** *(Data averaged from 30 young adults by Webb, 1992.)*

*People rarely snore during dreams. When REM starts, snoring stops.*

toothed, more like those of the nearly awake Stage 1 sleep. But unlike Stage 1 sleep, REM sleep is a time when your heart rate rises, your breathing becomes more rapid and irregular, and every half minute or so your eyes dart around in a momentary burst of activity behind closed lids. Because anyone watching a sleeper's eyes can notice these REM bursts, it is amazing that science was ignorant of REM sleep until 1952.

During REM sleep, your genitals become aroused (an erection or increased vaginal lubrication). The common "morning erection" stems from the night's last REM period, often just before waking. Except during very scary dreams, genital arousal always occurs, regardless of whether the dream's content is sexual (Karacan & others, 1966). In young men, sleep-related erections outlast REM periods, lasting 30 to 45 minutes on average (Karacan & others, 1983; Schiavi & Schreiner-Engel, 1988). A typical 25-year-old man therefore has an erection during nearly half his night's sleep, a 65-year-old man for one-quarter. Many men troubled by "erectile disorder" (impotence) have morning erections, which suggests that their problem is not with their genitals.

Although your brain's motor cortex is active during REM sleep, your brain stem blocks its messages, leaving your muscles relaxed—so relaxed that, except for an occasional finger, toe, or facial twitch, you are essentially paralyzed. Moreover, you cannot easily be awakened. Thus, REM sleep is sometimes called *paradoxical sleep* because internally the body is aroused but externally it appears calm.

Even more intriguing than the paradoxical nature of REM sleep is what the rapid eye movements announce: the beginning of a dream. Even those who claim they never dream will, more than 80 percent of the time, recall a dream after being awakened during REM sleep. Unlike the fleeting images of Stage 1 sleep, REM sleep dreams are often emotional and usually storylike. (People occasionally recall dreams when awakened from stages other than REM sleep, but these dreams usually contain a single vague image, such as, "I was trying to borrow something from someone.")

Are the eye movements linked to a dream's visual aspects? Is the dreamer "watching" the dream as if it were a private movie projected in the mind's inner theater? Most researchers believe not: The darting eyes, like the occasional twitching of muscles, may merely reflect the overflow of the dreamer's active nervous system (Chase & Morales, 1983).

As the night wears on, this sleep cycle repeats itself about every 90 minutes. Curiously, small animals have shorter sleep cycles (rats, 10 minutes) than big animals (elephants, 100+ minutes) (Hobson, 1989). During the night, deep Stage 4 sleep gets progressively briefer and then disappears, and the REM sleep period gets longer (Figure 7–4). By morning, 20 to 25 percent of our average night's sleep—some 100 minutes—has been REM sleep. This means that those who say, "I never dream" actually spend about 600 hours a year experiencing some 1500 dreams, which totals more than 100,000 dreams over a typical lifetime.

## Why Do We Sleep?

Sleep commands roughly one-third of our lives. Deprived of it, we begin to feel terrible; our bodies yearn for it. You can know you are sleep-deprived—as many college students are (Levine & others, 1988)—if most of the following are true: You need an alarm clock to shorten your natural sleep pattern; you feel sleepy while sitting in class or you lack vigor needed for peak performance; you collapse into sleep almost immediately after your head hits the pillow. How much sleep do you need? The answer is simple, says sleep researcher William Moorcroft (1993): enough so you will not feel tired the next day.

Obviously, we need sleep. But why? It seems an easy question to answer: Just keep people awake for several days and note how they deteriorate. If you were a subject in such an experiment, how do you think it would affect your body and mind?

Of course, you would become terribly drowsy at times—especially during the hours when your biological clock programs you to sleep. But could lack of sleep physically damage you? Would it noticeably alter your biochemistry or body organs? Would you become emotionally disturbed? Intellectually disoriented?

*A few of the unanswered questions about sleep: Why do we sleep more when we are young? Why do some animals sleep most of the day, others not at all? Why, when REM sleep paralyzes our muscles, do we twitch and jerk? Most important, what is sleep's function?*

Adapted from UCLA Brain Research Institute, 1989

The major effect, as fatigued college students know, is sleepiness, and sometimes a general malaise (Mikulincer & others, 1989). Owing to modern light bulbs, TV, shift work, and social diversions, people today more than ever suffer from sleep patterns that thwart their having an energized feeling of well-being. Teenagers typically need 8 or 9 hours sleep but now average nearly 2 hours less sleep a night than their counterparts of 80 years ago (Holden, 1993). Many fill this need by using home room for their first siesta and after-lunch study hall for a slumber party. As sleep researcher William Dement (1990) laments, "The national sleep debt is larger and more important than the national debt."

Other effects are more subtle: impaired creativity and concentration, diminished immunity to disease, slight hand tremors, irritability, slowed performance, occasional misperceptions on monotonous tasks (Horne, 1989; Koslowsky & Babkoff, 1992). With some tasks, such as truck driving and controlling air traffic, these effects can be devastating. "Rest. That's what I need is rest," said Eastern Airlines Captain James Reeves to the control tower on a September, 1974, morning—30 minutes before crashing his airliner at low altitude, killing the crew and all 68 passengers (Moorcroft, 1993). The *Exxon Valdez* oil spill, Union Carbide's Bhopal, India, disaster; and the Three Mile Island and Chernobyl nuclear accidents all occurred after midnight, when operators were likely to be drowsiest.

On short, highly motivating tasks, however, sleep deprivation has little effect. When 17-year-old Randy Gardner made his way into the *Guinness Book of World Records* by staying awake for 11 days, he at times had to keep moving to stay awake. Nevertheless, during his final night of sleeplessness, Gardner managed to beat researcher Dement 100 straight times in a pinball game. He then slept 15 hours and awoke feeling fine (Gulevich & others, 1966).

*The current record holder, Robert ("Ramblin Rob") McDonald, reportedly stayed awake for 18 days, 22 hours in a 1986 rocking chair marathon.*

Why, then, must we sleep? We have few answers, but sleep may have evolved for at least two reasons: First, it hides us out of harm's way. Our ancestors were safer if asleep at night. Animals with the least reason to fear predation or the most need to graze tend to sleep less. Elephants and horses sleep 3 to 4 hours a day. Second, sleep helps us recuperate. It helps restore body tissues, especially those of the brain. As we sleep, our brain is actively repairing and reorganizing itself and consolidating memories. Our lowered body temperature during sleep also conserves energy for the daytime hours.

*"Sleep faster, we need the pillows."*

Yiddish proverb

Sleep may additionally play a role in the growth process. During deep sleep, the pituitary gland releases a growth hormone. As adults grow older, they release less of this hormone, and they spend less time in deep sleep (Pekkanen, 1982). These physiological discoveries are only beginning to solve the ongoing riddle of sleep. As researcher Dement (1978, p. 83) deadpanned, "We have miles to go before we sleep."

*1993 Time/CNN poll:*
*"How many hours do you sleep each night?"*

| | |
|---|---|
| *Under six* | *12%* |
| *Six* | *26* |
| *Seven* | *30* |
| *Eight* | *28* |
| *Over eight* | *3* |

*"The lion and the lamb shall lie down together, but the lamb will not be very sleepy."*

Woody Allen in the movie *Love and Death*, 1975

## Sleep Disorders

The idea that "everyone needs 8 hours of sleep" is untrue. Newborns spend nearly two-thirds of their day asleep, adults barely more than one-fourth. Age-related differences in average time spent sleeping are rivaled by differences in the normal amount of sleep among individuals at any age. Some people thrive with fewer than 6 hours of sleep per night; others regularly sleep 9 hours or more. Sleep patterns may be genetically influenced. When Wilse Webb and Scott Campbell (1983) checked the pattern and duration of sleep among fraternal and identical twins, only the identical twins were strikingly similar.

Whatever their normal need for sleep, some 10 to 15 percent of adults complain of **insomnia**—persistent problems in falling or staying asleep. True insomnia is not the occasional inability to sleep that we experience when anxious or excited. When stressed, alertness is a natural and adaptive response. We commonly underestimate the amount of sleep we get on restless nights. Even if we've been awake only an hour, we may *think* we've had insomnia much of the night, because that's the part we remember. From middle age on, sleep is seldom uninterrupted. Occasional awakenings become the norm, not something to fret over or treat with medication.

The most common quick fixes for true insomnia, sleeping pills and alcohol, can aggravate the problem. Both reduce REM sleep and can leave a person with next-day blahs. With continued use it takes bigger doses to get an effect, and when the drug is discontinued the insomnia may worsen. Sleep experts offer other alternatives:

1. Relax before bedtime.
2. Avoid caffeine (this includes chocolate) after late afternoon and avoid rich foods before bedtime. A glass of milk may help. (Milk provides raw materials for the manufacture of serotonin, a neurotransmitter that facilitates sleep.)
3. Sleep on a regular schedule (rise at the same time even after a restless night) and avoid naps.
4. Exercise regularly but not in the late evening (best in the late afternoon).
5. Reassure yourself that the temporary loss of sleep causes no great harm, certainly nothing worth losing sleep over. "Sleep is like love or happiness," notes Wilse Webb (1992, p. 170). "If you pursue it too ardently it will elude you." One experimenter offered subjects $10 for every minute they fell asleep faster than the night before. Not a single person made money.
6. If nothing else works, aim for less sleep; go to bed later or get up earlier.

Rarer but more severe than insomnia are the sleep disorders narcolepsy and sleep apnea. People with **narcolepsy** (*narco* = numbness, *lepsy* = seizure) suffer periodic, overwhelming sleepiness, sometimes at the most inopportune times, perhaps just after taking a terrific swing at a softball or when laughing loudly or shouting angrily (Dement, 1978). The person collapses directly into a brief period of REM sleep, with its accompanying loss of muscular tension. Those who suffer from narcolepsy—1 in 1000 people, estimates the National Commission on Sleep Disorders Research—must live with extra caution. As a traffic menace, "snoozing is second only to boozing," says the American Sleep Disorders Association, and those with narcolepsy are especially at risk (Aldrich, 1989).

The National Heart, Lung, and Blood Institute reports that 1 in 25 people (mostly overweight men) suffer from **sleep apnea**—a disorder that was unknown before modern sleep research. They intermittently stop breathing during sleep. (*Apnea* means "stopping respiration.") After an airless minute or so, decreased blood oxygen arouses the sleeper to awaken and snort in air for a few seconds. The process can repeat more than 400 times a night, depriving the person of slow-wave sleep. Apart from complaints of sleepiness and irritability during the day—and their mates' complaints about their loud "snoring"—apnea sufferers are often unaware of their disorder.

Still other sleepers, mostly children, experience **night terrors**. The person might sit up or walk around, talk incoherently, experience a doubling of heart and breathing rates, and appear terrified (Hartmann, 1981). The night-terror sufferer very seldom awakens fully and recalls little or nothing the next morning—at most, a fleeting, frightening image. Night terrors are not nightmares, which typically occur during early morning REM sleep. Like sleepwalking, night terrors usually occur during the first few hours of sleep and begin during Stage 4 sleep (Figure 7–5). Family members will usually guide a sleepwalker back to bed or try to awaken and reassure the person. As we grow older we have less of the deep Stage 4 sleep, but for some this also means an end to sleepwalking and night terrors.

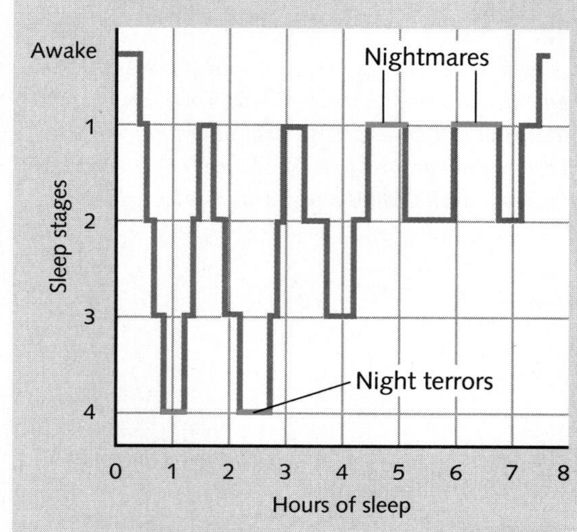


**Figure 7–5**

**Night Terrors and Nightmares** *Night terrors occur within 2 or 3 hours of falling asleep, during Stage 4 sleep. Nightmares occur toward morning, during REM sleep. (From Hartmann, 1984.)*

## Dreams

Discovering the link between REM sleep and dreaming opened a new era in dream research. Instead of relying on someone's hazy recall hours or days after having a dream, researchers could catch dreams as they happen. They could awaken their subjects during a REM sleep period, or within 3 minutes afterward, and hear a vivid account of the dream.

### What Do We Dream?

Compared with daydreams, REM dreams are more vivid, more emotional, more bizarre. Several times a night, you are the creator and producer of a surrealistic mental movie, in which events frequently occur in a jumbled sequence, scenes change suddenly, people appear and disappear, and physical laws, such as gravity, may be violated. Yet dreams are so vivid we may confuse them with reality. Occasionally, we may be sufficiently aware during a dream to wonder whether we are, in fact, dreaming. When experiencing such *lucid dreams*, some people are able to test their state of consciousness. If they can perform some absurd act, such as floating in the air, then they know they are dreaming.

*"I do not believe that I am now dreaming, but I cannot prove that I am not."*

Philosopher Bertrand Russell, 1872–1970

Although we are more likely to be awakened by and to remember our most emotional dreams, many dreams are rather ordinary. When awakened during REM sleep, people report dreams with sexual imagery less often than you might think. In one study, only 1 in 10 dreams among young men and 1 in 30 among young women had sexual overtones (Hall & Van de Castle, 1966). (Recall that genital arousal typically accompanies REM sleep, so it is usually *not* caused by sexual dreams.)

*Would you suppose that people dream if blind from birth? Studies of blind people in France, Hungary, and Egypt all found them dreaming of using their nonvisual senses—hearing, touching, smelling, tasting* (Buquet, 1988; Taha, 1972; Vekassy, 1977).

More commonly, we dream of daily life events, such as a meeting at work or taking an exam. In the month after the San Francisco earthquake, 4

*A popular sleep myth: If you dream you are falling and hit the ground (or if you dream of dying), you die. (Unfortunately, those who could confirm these ideas are not around to do so. Some people, however, have had such dreams and are alive to report them.)*

*"For what one has dwelt on by day, these things are seen in visions of the night."*

Menander of Athens, 342–292 B.C.
*Fragments*

in 10 college students in the area (but only 1 in 20 students elsewhere) had one or more nightmares about an earthquake (Wood & others, 1992). Six years of our life we spend dreaming, most of which is anything but sweet: People commonly dream of repeatedly failing in an attempt to do something; of being attacked, pursued, or rejected; or of experiencing misfortune (Hall & others, 1982).

Across the world, people of all ages show a curious gender difference in dream content. Women dream of males and females equally often, whereas 65 percent of the characters in men's dreams are males. No one is sure why. Whatever its significance, dream researcher Calvin Hall (1984) believed we can add this fact to the short list of psychological gender differences (see Chapter 19).

The story line of our dreams—what Sigmund Freud called their **manifest content**—often incorporates experiences and preoccupations from the day's events, especially in our first dreams of the night. The sensory stimuli of our sleeping environment may also intrude. A particular odor or the telephone's ringing may be instantly and ingeniously woven into the dream story. In one experiment, William Dement and Edward Wolpert (1958) lightly sprayed cold water on dreamers' faces. Compared with sleepers who did not get the cold water treatment, these subjects were more likely to dream about water—about waterfalls, leaky roofs, or even about being sprayed by someone. Even while in REM sleep, focused on internal stimuli, we maintain some awareness of changes in our external environment.

So, could we learn a foreign language by listening to tapes during sleep? If only it were so easy. While sleeping we can learn to associate a sound with a mild electric shock (and to react to the sound accordingly). But we do not remember taped information played while we are soundly asleep (Eich, 1990; Wyatt & Bootzin, 1994). In fact, experiences that occur during the 5 minutes just before falling asleep are typically lost from memory (Roth & others, 1988). This helps explain why dreams that momentarily awaken us are mostly forgotten by morning. To remember a dream, get up and stay awake for a while.

**Nocturnal Mysteries** *Everyone dreams, and the content is sometimes as bizarre as these images from Francisco de Goya's "The Dream of Reason Produces Monsters." Our fascination with dreams has led to some interesting theories about their function.*

### Why Do We Dream?

In his landmark book *The Interpretation of Dreams*, published in 1900, Freud argued that by fulfilling wishes a dream is a psychic safety valve that harmlessly discharges otherwise unacceptable feelings. According to Freud, a dream's manifest content is but a censored, symbolic version of its **latent content**, which consists of unconscious drives and wishes that would be threatening if expressed directly. Although most dreams have no overt sexual imagery, Freud nevertheless believed that most adult dreams can be "traced back by analysis to *erotic wishes*." In Freud's view, a gun, for example, might be a disguised representation of a penis.

Although Freud considered dreams the key to understanding our inner conflicts, his critics say that dream interpretation leads down a blind alley. Some contend that even if dreams are symbolic, they can be interpreted almost any way one wishes. Others maintain there is nothing hidden in dreams. A dream about a gun, they say, is a dream about a gun. Even Freud, who loved to smoke cigars, acknowledged that "sometimes, a cigar is just a cigar."

Freud's theory of dreams is giving way to newer theories. One of these sees dreams as *information processing*: Dreams may help sift, sort, and fix in memory our day's experiences. Following stressful experiences or intense learning periods, REM sleep increases (Palumbo, 1978). What is more, there is "consistent and compelling evidence" that REM sleep facilitates memory for unusual or anxiety-arousing material (McGrath & Cohen, 1978). In one experiment, people heard unusual phrases before bedtime and then were given a memory test the next morning. If awakened every time they began REM sleep, they remembered less than if awakened during other sleep stages (Empson & Clarke, 1970). A night of solid sleep (and dreaming) does, it seems, have an important place in a student's life.

Another explanation of dreams proposes that they may also serve a physiological function. Perhaps dreams—or the associated brain activity of REM sleep—provide the sleeping brain with periodic stimulation. As you may recall from Chapter 3, stimulating experiences develop and preserve the brain's neural pathways. This theory makes sense from a developmental point of view. Infants, whose neural networks are just developing, spend a great deal of time in REM sleep (Figure 7–6).

**Figure 7–6**

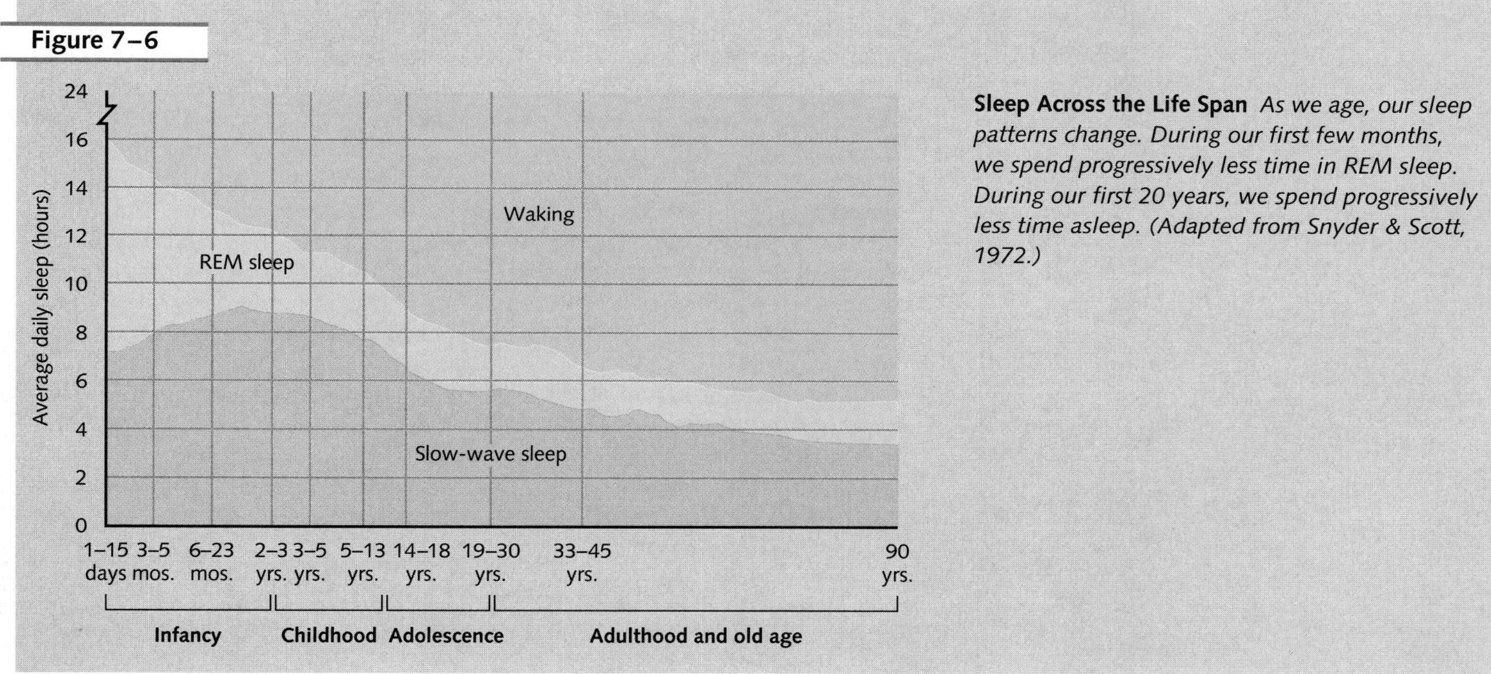


**Sleep Across the Life Span** *As we age, our sleep patterns change. During our first few months, we spend progressively less time in REM sleep. During our first 20 years, we spend progressively less time asleep. (Adapted from Snyder & Scott, 1972.)*

Still other physiological theories propose that dreams erupt from neural activity that spreads upward from the brainstem (Antrobus, 1991; Hobson, 1988). According to one version, this neural activity is random, and dreams are the brain's attempt to make sense of it. Much as a neurosurgeon can produce hallucinations by stimulating different parts of the cortex, so can stimulation originating within the brain. Psychologists Martin Seligman and Amy Yellen (1987) note that the seconds-long bursts of rapid eye movements during REM sleep coincide with bursts of activity in the visual cortex. If awakened during one of these bursts of brain activity, people report vivid experiences, usually dramatic hallucinations.

Given these visual scenes, how does our cognitive machinery react? It does what it usually does with meaningless stimuli—it imposes meaning. (Recall from Chapter 2 how split-brain patients instantly "explain" puzzling actions commanded by their right hemisphere. And recall from

Chapter 6 how readily we can "see" flying saucers in clouds and monsters in dead, floating trees.) Thus, say Seligman and Yellen, our ever-active brain weaves a story line from whatever is available—residues from the day's experiences, the alarm clock's ringing, or the brief visual hallucinations triggered by the brainstem. The emotion-related limbic system also becomes active during REM sleep. Add its activity to the brain's commotion and—voila!—we dream.

The theory, then, is that dreams spring from the mind's relentless effort to make sense of unrelated visual bursts, which are given their emotional tone by the limbic system. This helps explain many of our dream experiences, such as the sudden and bizarre changes in scene (triggered by a new visual burst). Dream reports by Seligman's University of Pennsylvania students confirm that the most vivid dream images are the surprising, discontinuous aspects of the dream; other, less vivid images we presumably conjure up to string the visual bursts together.

The function of dreams provokes vigorous debate, but the disputants all agree that we *need* REM sleep. Deprived of it by repeated awakenings, people return more and more quickly to the REM stage after falling back to sleep. When finally allowed to sleep undisturbed, they literally sleep like babies, with increased REM sleep—a phenomenon called **REM rebound**. The withdrawal of REM-suppressing sleeping medications also increases REM sleep, but with accompanying nightmares. Most other mammals also experience REM sleep and REM rebound. Animals' need for REM sleep suggests that its causes and functions are deeply biological. That REM sleep occurs in mammals (and not in animals such as fish, whose behavior is less influenced by learning) also fits the information-processing theory of dreams. All of which serves to remind us once again of a basic lesson: Biological and psychological explanations of behavior are partners, not competitors.

But if dreams serve physiological functions and lack the disguised meanings that Freud supposed, are they psychologically meaningless? Not necessarily. Every psychologically meaningful experience involves an active brain. Moreover, say advocates of dream reflection, dreams may be akin to abstract art—amenable to more than one meaningful interpretation, and illuminating to ponder.

## Summing Up

**The Rhythm of Sleep** Our daily schedule of waking and sleeping is timed by a body clock known as circadian rhythm. Each night's sleep also has a rhythm of its own, running from transitional Stage 1 sleep to deep Stage 4 sleep and back up to the more internally active REM sleep stage. This cycle repeats several times during a normal night's sleep, with periods of Stage 4 sleep progressively shortening and of REM sleep lengthening.

**Why Do We Sleep?** Depriving people of sleep has failed to reveal why, physiologically, we need sleep. Recent research reveals that sleep is linked with the release of pituitary growth hormone and that it may help to restore brain tissues and consolidate memories.

**Sleep Disorders** The disorders of sleep include insomnia (recurring wakefulness), narcolepsy (uncontrollable lapsing into REM sleep), and sleep apnea (the stopping of breathing while sleeping).

**Dreams** Although conscious thoughts can occur during any sleep stage, awakening people during REM sleep yields predictable "dreamlike" reports; awakening during other sleep stages yields a fleeting image only occasionally. Our dreams are mostly of ordinary events; they often relate to everyday experiences and involve anxiety or misfortune more frequently than triumphant achievements.

Freud believed that a dream's manifest content is a censored version of its latent content, which gratifies our unconscious wishes. Newer explanations of why we dream suggest that dreams (*a*) help process information from the day and fix it in memory, (*b*) serve a physiological function, and/or (*c*) are the brain's efforts to string periodic hallucinations (from activity bursts in the visual cortex) into a story line. Despite their differences, most theorists agree that REM sleep and its associated dreams serve an important function, as shown by the REM rebound that occurs following REM deprivation.

## Daydreams and Fantasies

*The dazed consciousness of daydreams and fantasies can absorb us for stretches of time. Does such reverie serve a purpose?*

In James Thurber's classic story "The Secret Life of Walter Mitty," the bland existence of mild-mannered Walter Mitty is spiced with gratifying fantasies. As he drives past a hospital, Mitty imagines himself as Dr. Mitty, rushing to an operating room where two renowned specialists plead for his help. Again and again, the bumbling Walter Mitty relieves the tedium of his life by imagining himself as the triumphant Walter Mitty—now the world's greatest target shooter, now a heroic pilot.

Thurber's story became a classic because most of us can identify with Walter Mitty. From interview and questionnaire studies with hundreds of adults, clinical psychologist Jerome L. Singer (1975) reported that nearly everyone has daydreams or waking fantasies every day—on the job, in the classroom, walking down the street—in fact, almost anywhere at any time. Compared with older adults, young adults spend more time daydreaming and admit to more sexual fantasies (Cameron & Biber, 1973; Giambra, 1974).

Not all daydreaming is as overtly escapist or dramatic as Walter Mitty's. Mostly it involves the familiar details of our lives—perhaps imagining an alternative approach to a task we are performing, or picturing ourselves explaining to an instructor why a paper will be late, or replaying in our minds personal encounters that we relish or wish had gone differently.

**Looking Into the Inner World** *Daydreams and fantasies are a constructive part of everyone's repertory of behavior. For these Dutch commuters, daydreams may release tension, increase creativity, illuminate solutions to problems—and even lessen boredom.*

Some individuals—perhaps 4 percent of the population—fantasize so vividly they are called **fantasy-prone personalities**. One study of 26 such women found that as children they had enjoyed unusually intense make-believe play with their dolls, stuffed animals, or imaginary companions (Wilson & Barber, 1983). As adults, they reported spending more than half their time fantasizing. They would relive experiences or imagine scenes so vividly that occasionally they later had trouble sorting out their remembered fantasies from their memories of actual events. When watching or imagining violent or scary scenes, they sometimes felt ill. Many reported profound mystical or religious experiences. Three-fourths had experienced orgasms solely by sexual fantasy.

*"When I examined myself, and my methods of thought, I came to the conclusion that the gift of fantasy has meant more to me than my talent for absorbing positive knowledge."*

Albert Einstein, 1879–1955

Are the hours we spend in fantasy merely a way of escaping rather than facing reality? Sometimes. But daydreaming can also be adaptive. Some daydreams help us prepare for future events by keeping us aware of unfinished business and serving as mental rehearsals. Playful fantasies enhance the creativity of scientists, artists, and writers. For children, daydreaming in the form of imaginative play is believed important to social and cognitive development—a fact that makes the diversion of television watching a matter of concern to some child psychologists (Singer, 1986).

*"The art of living requires us to steer a course between the two extremes of external and internal stimulation."*

Psychologist Jerome L. Singer (1976)

Daydreams may also substitute for impulsive behavior. People who are prone to delinquency and violence or who seek the artificial highs of dangerous drugs have fewer vivid fantasies (Singer, 1976). Perhaps Walter Mitty's imaginative reveries not only rescued him from boredom but also allowed him to indulge his impulses within the safety of his inner world.

## Summing Up

Virtually everyone daydreams, especially fantasy-prone people and especially in times when attention can be freed from the tasks at hand. Daydreaming can be adaptive; it can help us prepare for future events and may substitute for impulsive behavior.

## Hypnosis

*What is it like to be hypnotized? What powers does hypnosis have? And what really is hypnosis—a special state of consciousness? Or an extension of normal consciousness?*

Imagine you are about to be hypnotized. The hypnotist invites you to sit back, fix your gaze on a spot high on the wall, and relax. In a quiet, low voice the hypnotist suggests, "Your eyes are growing tired. . . . Your eyelids are becoming heavy . . . now heavier and heavier. . . . They are beginning to close. . . . You are becoming more deeply relaxed. . . . Your breathing is now deep and regular. . . . Your muscles are becoming more and more relaxed. Your whole body is beginning to feel like lead."

After a few minutes of this hypnotic induction, your eyes are probably closed and you may undergo **hypnosis**—an apparently heightened suggestibility that enables a hypnotist's coaxings and directions to trigger specific behaviors, perceptions, and perhaps even memories. When the hypnotist suggests, "Your eyelids are shutting so tight that you cannot open them even if you try," your eyelids may seem beyond your control and may remain closed. Told to forget the number 6, you may be puzzled when you count 11 fingers on your hands. Invited to smell a sensuous perfume that is actually ammonia, you may linger delightedly over its pungent odor. Asked to describe a nonexistent picture the hypnotist claims to be holding, you may talk about it in detail. Told that you cannot see a certain object, such as a chair, you may indeed report that it is not there, although, curiously, you may manage to avoid the chair when walking around.

And if instructed to forget all these happenings once you are out of the hypnotic state, you may later report **posthypnotic amnesia**, a temporary

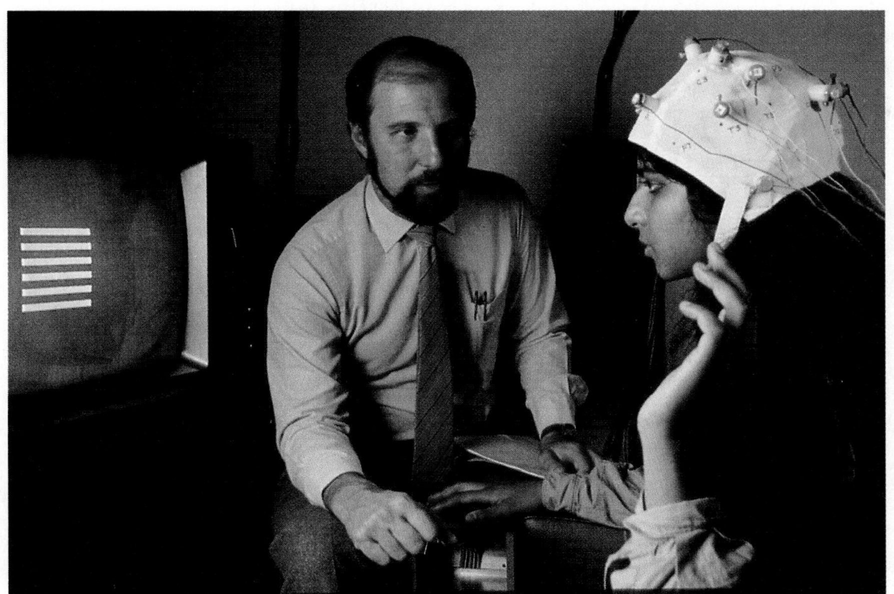

**Subject to Influence** *As a deeply hypnotized subject sits before a TV screen, researcher David Spiegel asks her to imagine that a cardboard box is blocking the screen. When a stimulus appears on the screen, her brain waves do not display the normal response to the stimulus. Findings like this, Spiegel argues, suggest that hypnosis can alter brain functioning.*

memory loss rather like being unable to recall a familiar name. Although people *say* they don't remember "forgotten" material, subtle tests lead skeptics to doubt their reported amnesia (Coe, 1989a). The material must be "in there," for it can affect later behavior and be recalled at a prearranged signal (Kihlstrom, 1985; Spanos & others, 1985). A critical issue, then, is whether people are genuinely *unable* to recall the "forgotten" material, or whether people distract themselves or withhold information to meet the hypnotist's expectations.

Hypnotic techniques have been used since antiquity, but credit for their modern popularity goes to an Austrian physician, Anton Mesmer, 1734–1815, who mistakenly thought he had discovered an "animal magnetism." With great flourish, Mesmer passed magnets over the bodies of ailing people, some of whom would lapse into a trancelike ("mesmerized") state and awaken much improved. A French commission chaired by Benjamin Franklin found no evidence of animal magnetism and attributed Mesmer's "cures" to "mere imagination." Thus, hypnosis—or mesmerism, as it was then called—became linked with quackery.

Also working against the respectability of hypnosis were the grand claims made by its practitioners. Supposedly, mesmerized people could see with the backs of their heads, perceive others' internal organs, and communicate with the dead. Researchers now agree that hypnotized persons can perform no such feats (Figure 7–7). Like unhypnotized people, those under hypnosis cannot leap tall buildings, run faster than a speeding bullet, or display superhuman strength. Hypnotized subjects may surprise you by, say, extending their arms for 6 minutes straight—but so can unhypnotized subjects.

Before considering whether the hypnotic state is actually an altered state of consciousness, let's first consider some areas of general agreement. Then, with the facts of hypnosis in mind, we can ponder two perplexing questions: What is hypnosis? What does hypnosis tell us about human consciousness?

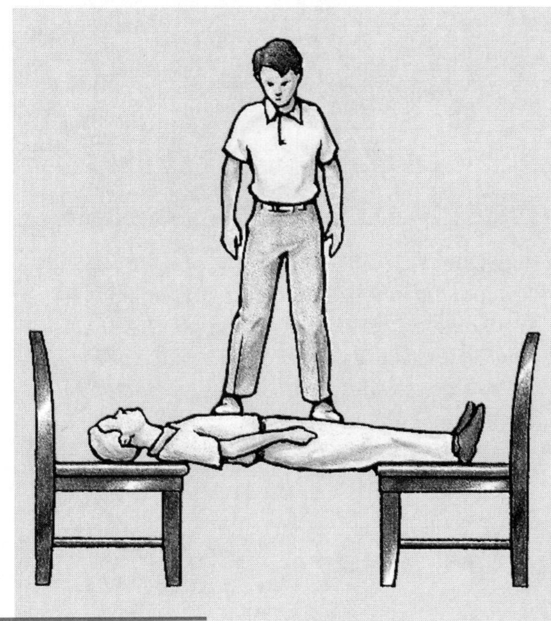

**Figure 7–7**

**The "Amazing" Hypnotized "Human Plank"** *Actually, unhypnotized people can also perform this feat.*

## Facts and Falsehoods

### Can Hypnosis Work for Anyone?

Those who study hypnosis agree that its power resides not in the hypnotist but in the subject's openness to suggestion (Bowers, 1984). To some extent, nearly everyone is suggestible. When people standing upright with their eyes closed are told repeatedly that they are swaying back and forth, most will indeed sway a little. In fact, postural sway is one of the items on the Stanford Hypnotic Susceptibility Scale that assesses a person's hypnotizability. During the assessment, a hypnotist gives a brief hypnotic induction and then presents a series of suggested experiences that range from easy (one's outstretched arms will move together) to difficult (with eyes open one will see a nonexistent person).

Those who are highly hypnotizable—say, the 20 percent who can carry out a suggestion not to smell or react to a bottle of ammonia held under the nose—are still likely to be the most hypnotizable 25 years later (Piccione & others, 1989). These hypnotically susceptible people, like the fantasy-prone people described earlier, frequently become deeply absorbed in imaginative activities (Lynn & Rhue, 1986; Silva & Kirsch, 1992). Typically, they have rich fantasy lives and easily become absorbed in the imaginary events of a novel or movie. Many researchers therefore refer to hypnotic "susceptibility" as hypnotic *ability*, giving it a label with more positive connotations. Few of us would care to be "susceptible" to hypnosis, but most of us would be glad to have the "ability" to focus our attention totally on a task, to become imaginatively absorbed in it, to entertain fanciful possibilities. And that is what fantasy-prone people with hypnotic ability can do.

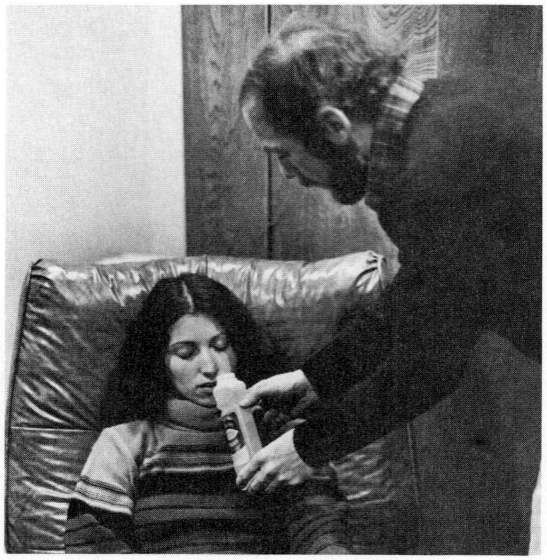

**How Does It Smell?** *Only a person with highly developed hypnotic abilities could remain outwardly unperturbed over an open bottle of ammonia. Researchers have found a range of hypnotic responsiveness, with fantasy-prone people being among the best subjects.*

Actually, anyone who can turn attention inward, relax, and imagine can experience some degree of hypnosis—because that's what hypnosis is. And virtually anyone will experience hypnotic responsiveness, if led to *expect* it. To convince even skeptical University of Connecticut students that they were hypnotizable, Cynthia Wickless and Irving Kirsch (1989) played a clever stunt on them. After a standard hypnotic induction, they suggested to the students that they would see red, then see green, hear music, and so forth. After each suggestion, the merry prankster experimenters subtly projected appropriate stimuli—a very faint red or green light, or faint eerie music. Fooled by this weird experience of seeing and hearing what the hypnotist suggested, there were no doubters left. Thus, unlike those in control conditions not similarly persuaded, most scored as *highly* hypnotizable when later given the suggestions of the Stanford Hypnotic Susceptibility Scale; virtually none scored low.

Any real-life hypnotist does much the same in suggesting that "your eyes are growing tired . . . your eyelids are becoming heavy" after having people strain their eyes by staring at a high spot. Anyone's eyes would get tired. But if the hypnotist is successful, the subject will attribute the heavy eyelids to the hypnotist's powers.

### Can Hypnosis Enhance Recall of Forgotten Events?

Can hypnotic procedures enable people to relive earlier experiences? To recall kindergarten classmates? To retrieve forgotten or suppressed details of a crime? Should testimony obtained under hypnosis be admissible in court?

Most people believe—wrongly, as Chapter 9 will explain—that our experiences are all "in there," that everything that happens to us gets recorded in our brains and can be recalled if only we can break through our own defenses (Loftus, 1980). Most university students, for example, agree that "under hypnosis a person [can] recall childhood events with very high accuracy" (Furnham, 1993). Testimonies to this come from **age regression** demonstrations, in which subjects supposedly relive experiences from their childhood. But 60 years of research dispute claims of age regression: Hypnotized people are *not* more genuinely childlike than unhypnotized people who are asked to feign childlike behavior (Nash, 1987). Age-regressed people act as they *believe* children would, but they typically miss the mark by outperforming real children of the specified age (Silverman & Retzlaff, 1986). Age-regressed people may, for example, *feel* childlike and may print much as they know a 6-year-old would, but they sometimes do so with perfect spelling and typically without any change in their adult brain waves, reflexes, and perceptions.

On rare occasions, the relaxed, focused state of hypnosis has enabled witnesses to produce leads in criminal investigations. One instance occurred in 1977, when 26 children and their bus driver, Ed Ray, were kidnapped and forced into an abandoned trailer truck buried 6 feet underground. After their rescue, Ray, under hypnosis, recalled all but one digit of the kidnapper's license plate. With this crucial information, police tracked down the abductors. This anecdote is atypical, and it is unclear whether hypnosis enabled the memory retrieval. Nevertheless, many researchers believe that hypnotic procedures may have value—or at least do little harm—when used as an investigative tool.

The problem comes in putting on the witness stand someone whose memories are "hypnotically refreshed." Because researchers have found that hypnotically refreshed memories combine fact with fiction, a growing list of state courts ban testimony from witnesses who have been hypnotized. Hypnosis has unpredictable effects, sometimes boosting recall, but sometimes contaminating memory with false recollections or increasing confidence in false memories (McConkey, 1992). When pressed under hypnosis to recall details, perhaps to "zoom in on your visual memory screen," people use their imaginations to construct their memories. Without either person being aware of what is going on, the hypnotist's hints—"Did you hear loud noises?"—can become the subject's memory. Thus, previously hypnotized witnesses may end up testifying confidently to events they never experienced (Laurence & Perry, 1988). And whether hypnotized or not, highly hypnotizable (fantasy-prone) people are especially vulnerable to false memory suggestions (Barnier & McConkey, 1992). "Hypnosis is not a psychological truth serum," concludes researcher Kenneth Bowers (1987), "and to regard it as such has been a source of considerable mischief."

### Can Hypnosis Force People to Act Against Their Will?

Researchers Martin Orne and Frederick Evans (1965) demonstrated that hypnotized subjects *could* be induced to perform an apparently dangerous act. For example, they followed a request to dip a hand briefly in fuming acid and then throw the "acid" in a research assistant's face. When interviewed a day later, they exhibited no memory of their acts and emphatically denied they would follow orders to commit such actions.

Had hypnosis given the hypnotist a special power to control these people against their will? To find out, Orne and Evans unleashed that enemy of so many illusory beliefs—the control group: Orne asked some additional subjects to *pretend* they had been hypnotized. The laboratory experimenter, unaware that these control subjects had not been hypnotized, treated all subjects in the same manner. The result? All the *un*hypnotized subjects performed the same acts as the hypnotized ones. Similarly, most hypnotized subjects can be induced to cut up their country's flag or deface a Bible, and a few will even cooperate in stealing an exam or selling illegal drugs. But people asked to simulate hypnosis are no less likely to perform the same acts (Levitt, 1986).

This illustrates a principle that Chapter 18, Social Psychology, emphasizes: An authoritative person in a legitimate context can induce people—hypnotized or not—to perform some unlikely acts. Hypnosis researcher Spanos (1982) puts it simply: "The overt behaviors of hypnotic subjects are well within normal limits."

### Can Hypnosis Be Therapeutic?

The clinical use of hypnosis is mushrooming. Hypnotherapists do nothing magical. Rather, they try to help patients harness their own healing powers (Baker, 1987). **Posthypnotic suggestions** (suggestions to be carried out after the hypnosis session has ended) have helped alleviate headaches, asthma, warts, and stress-related skin disorders. One woman, who suffered open sores all over her body for more than 20 years, was asked to imagine herself swimming in shimmering, sunlit liquids that would cleanse her skin and to experience her skin as smooth and unblemished. Within 3 months her sores had disappeared (Bowers, 1984).

When applied to bad habits such as nail biting and smoking, hypnosis is not more helpful to those most hypnotizable than to those least so. This suggests that any benefits are not due to the hypnosis per se (Bowers & LeBaron, 1986). With problems unrelated to willpower, such as skin disorders, is hypnosis the therapeutic agent? Do its benefits surpass those of merely encouraging people to relax and form positive images? The answer remains in doubt. For example, hypnosis speeds the disappearance of warts. But in controlled studies, so do the same positive suggestions given without hypnosis (Spanos, 1991).

### Can Hypnosis Alleviate Pain?

Yes, hypnosis can relieve pain (Kihlstrom, 1985). When unhypnotized subjects put their arms in an ice bath, they feel intense pain within 25 seconds. When hypnotizable subjects do the same after being given suggestions to feel no pain, they indeed report feeling little pain. As some dentists know, even light hypnosis can reduce fear, and thus hypersensitivity to pain. And some 10 percent of us can become so deeply hypnotized that even surgery can be performed without anesthesia.

How can this be? One theory of hypnotic pain relief involves **dissociation**, a split between different levels of consciousness. Hypnosis, it suggests, dissociates the sensation of the pain stimulus (of which the subject is still aware) from the emotional suffering that defines our pain experience. The ice water therefore feels very cold but not painful.

Another theory proposes that hypnotic pain relief is due to selective attention, as when an injured athlete, caught up in the competition, feels little or no pain until the game ends. Support for this view comes from several studies showing that hypnosis relieves pain no better than does merely relaxing and distracting people (Chaves, 1989). With their attention distracted during hypnosis, some women can experience childbirth with minimal pain; but so can some women without hypnosis, especially if given childbirth training (D'Eon, 1989).

## Thinking Critically About Hypnotic Age-Regression: A True Story

### Remembrances of Christmases Past?

What shall we make of a clever study by Robert True (1949)? He regressed hypnotized volunteers back to their Christmases and birthday parties at ages 10, 7, and 4. In each case, he asked them what day of the week it was. Without hypnosis, the odds that a person could name offhand the day of a long-ago date are but 1 in 7. Remarkably, the hypnotized subjects' answers were 82 percent correct.

Other investigators were unable to replicate True's results. When Martin Orne (1982) asked True why, he replied that *Science*, the journal that published his article, had shortened his key question to "What day is this?" Actually, he had asked his age-regressed subjects, "Is it Monday? Is it Tuesday?" and so forth until the subject stopped him with a yes. When Orne asked True if he knew the actual day of the week while posing the questions, True granted that he did but was puzzled why Orne would ask.

Can you see why? True's experiment appears to be a beautiful example of how hypnotists can subtly influence their subjects' memories (and, more generally, of how experimenters can subtly communicate their expectations). "Given the eagerness of the hypnotized subject to fulfill the demands placed upon him," surmised Orne, it takes only the slightest change of inflection (in asking "Is it Wednesday?") for the subject to respond, "Yes."

The final blow to True's experiment came when Orne simply asked ten 4-year-olds what day of the week it was. To his surprise, none knew. If 4-year-olds typically do not know the day of the week, then True's adults were reporting information they probably didn't know when they were 4.

Drawing by M. Stevens; © 1987 The New Yorker Magazine, Inc.

### Remembrances of Lives Past?

If people's hypnotic regressions to childhood are partly imagined, then how believable are claims of hypnotic "regression to past lives"? Can the 1 in 4 Americans who believe in reincarnation (*Gallup Poll Monthly*, 1991) find support in such reports? Nicholas Spanos (1987–1988; Spanos & others, 1991) reports that when hypnotized, fantasy-prone people who believe in reincarnation will offer vivid details of "past lives." But they nearly always report being their same race—unless the researcher has informed them that different races are common. They often report being someone famous rather than one of the countless "nobodies." Some contradict one another by claiming to have been the same person, such as King Henry VIII (Reveen, 1987–1988). Moreover, they typically do not know things that any person of that historical time would have known. One subject who "regressed" to a "previous life" as a Japanese fighter pilot in 1940 could not name the emperor of Japan and did not know that Japan was already at war. Hypnotic regressions to past lives thus offer no credible evidence of reincarnation.

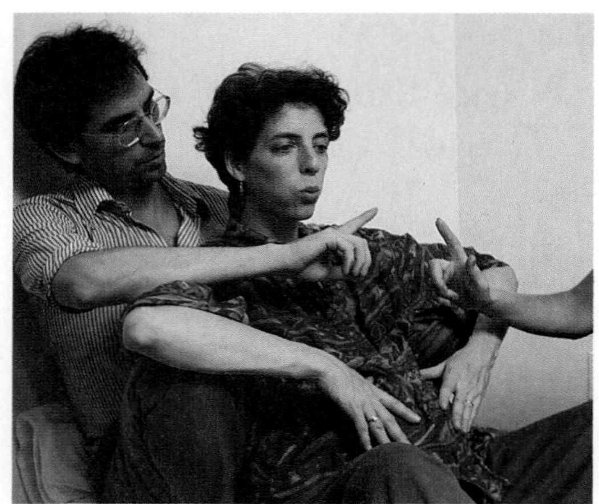

**The Lamaze Method of Childbirth** *Like hypnosis, the Lamaze method involves breathing and concentration techniques that draw attention away from pain. Women for whom the method works tend to have high hypnotic ability (Venn, 1986).*

Both views of pain assume that at some level a hypnotized person does experience the pain stimulus. Indeed, people who report feeling no pain will nevertheless perspire with pounding heart in response to electric shock or a surgeon's knife. Likewise, following a suggestion of deafness, hypnotized people will deny being able to hear their own voices. But when they hear their voice over a headset with a half-second delay, they respond as unhypnotized people do: The delayed feedback disrupts their ability to speak fluently. If told they are color blind, hypnotized people do not respond to color blindness tests as do people with actual color-deficient vision. In each of these cases, the hypnotized subjects *report* perceiving no pain, sound, or color. Yet the stimuli have quite obviously registered within their sensory systems. Thus, hypnosis does *not* block sensory input. What people *say* they experience just doesn't fit with their behavior.

The unanswered question of how hypnosis relieves pain—by *dissociating* the pain sensation from conscious awareness, or merely by focusing *attention* on other things—brings us to the basic issue: Is hypnosis a unique psychological state?

## Is Hypnosis an Altered State of Consciousness?

We have seen that hypnosis involves heightened suggestibility. We have also seen that hypnotic procedures do not endow a person with special powers. But they can sometimes enhance recall of real (and unreal) past events, aid in overcoming psychologically influenced ailments, and help alleviate pain. So, just what is hypnosis? Does it qualify as an altered—out-of-the-ordinary—state of consciousness?

### Hypnosis as a Social Phenomenon

Skeptics note that hypnosis is not a unique physiological state. Moreover, behaviors produced through hypnotic procedures can also be produced without them. This suggests that hypnotic phenomena may be nothing more than the workings of normal consciousness (Lynn & others, 1990; Spanos & Coe, 1992).

In Chapter 6 we saw how powerfully our interpretations influence ordinary perceptions. Especially in the case of pain, for which the effects of hypnosis seem most dramatic, our perceptions follow our attention. Moreover, imaginative people can manufacture vivid perceptions without hypnosis. Perhaps, then, "hypnotized" people are just acting the role of "good hypnotic subjects" and allowing the hypnotist to direct their fantasies.

It's not that people are consciously faking hypnosis. Rather, they're doing and reporting what's expected of them. Like actors who get caught up in their roles, they begin to feel and behave in ways appropriate to the hypnotic role. The more they like and trust the hypnotist and feel motivated to demonstrate hypnotic behavior, the more they do so (Gfeller & others, 1987). If an experimenter eliminates the motivation for acting hypnotized—by telling subjects that hypnosis reveals "gullibility"—they become unresponsive. If told later to scratch their ear when they hear the word *psychology*, subjects will likely do so only if they think the experiment is still under way (and scratching is therefore expected). Based on such findings, advocates of the social influence theory contend that hypnotic phenomena are *not* unique to hypnosis. Like other supposed altered states, such as multiple personality (page 512) and spirit or demon possession (Spanos, 1994), hypnotic phenomena are instead an extension of everyday social behavior. Hypnotic subjects, say skeptics, are imaginative actors caught up in playing the role of hypnotic subject.

### Hypnosis as Divided Consciousness

Most hypnosis researchers grant that normal social and cognitive processes play a part in hypnosis, but they believe hypnosis is more than imaginative acting. For one thing, hypnotized subjects will *sometimes* carry out suggested behaviors on cue, even when they believe no one is watching. Their doing so shows that more may be at work than merely trying to be a "good subject." Moreover, many practitioners remain convinced that certain phenomena *are* unique to hypnosis. What else explains hypnotic experiences such as the reduction of pain and the compelling hallucinations (Bowers, 1990)? Skeptics reply that hypnotists' livelihoods depend on maintaining an aura of mysterious power (Coe, 1989b).

To veteran researcher Ernest Hilgard (1986, 1992), hypnosis is a special state of dissociated consciousness. Hilgard views hypnotic dissociation as a more extreme form of everyday mind splits. Putting a child to bed, we might read *Goodnight Moon* for the fourteenth time while mentally organizing a busy schedule for the next day. Under the influence of my dentist's nitrous oxide—a real gas—I hear her ask me to "open wide." As my conscious self contemplates her request, my mouth, much to my surprise, immediately obeys. "Turn toward me," she says. Again, as if controlled by some strange force, my head instantly complies. With practice, it is even possible to read and comprehend a short story while copying dictated words, much as you can doodle while listening to a lecture, or much as a skilled pianist can converse while playing a familiar piece (Hirst & others, 1978). Thus, when hypnotized subjects write answers to questions about one topic while talking or reading about a different topic, they display an accentuated form of normal cognitive dissociation.

*"The total possible consciousness may be split into parts which co-exist but mutually ignore each other."*
William James
*Principles of Psychology*, 1890

Hilgard's discovery of hypnotic dissociation occurred dramatically. During a class demonstration of hypnosis, he induced deafness in a subject and then set about showing the class that the person was now utterly unresponsive to questions, taunts, and even sudden loud sounds. When a student asked whether some part of the subject might still be able to hear, Hilgard decided to show that the answer was no. He quietly asked the subject to raise his right index finger if some part of him could still hear. To everyone's surprise—including Hilgard's and the subject's—the finger rose. When the subject's hearing was restored, he explained that "it was a little boring just sitting here . . . when I suddenly felt my finger lift; that is what I want you to explain to me."

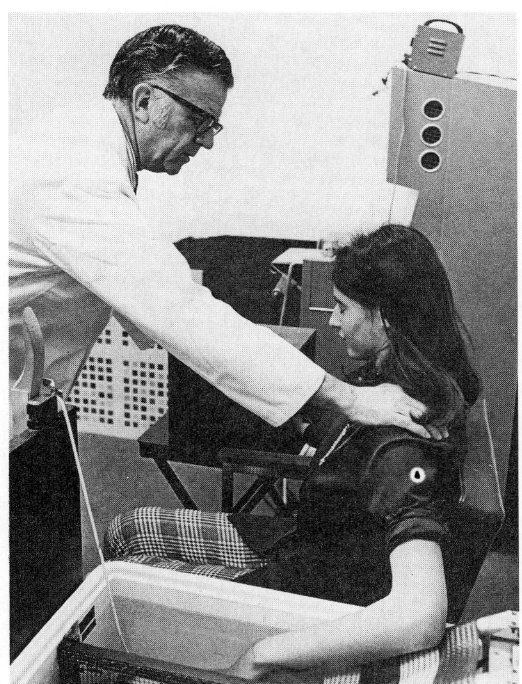

**Demonstrating the "Hidden Observer"** *A hypnotized subject being tested by Ernest Hilgard exhibits no pain when her arm is placed in an ice bath. But asked to press a key if some part of her feels the pain, she does so. To Hilgard, this suggests that hypnosis divides consciousness into one part that is unaware of pain and another part—a "hidden observer"—that is aware of it.*

This phenomenon spurred further inquiry. Hypnotized subjects, as we noted earlier, report far less pain than others when they place their arms in ice water. But when asked to press a key if "some part" of them does feel the pain, they invariably press the key. To Hilgard, this suggests that a dissociated consciousness, a **hidden observer**, is passively aware of what is happening.

The divided-consciousness theory of hypnosis is controversial, because what the "hidden observer" reports varies with what the experimenter seems to want. But this much seems clear: You and I process much information without conscious awareness. We have seen examples of unconscious information processing in the chapters on sensation and perception, and we will see more in later chapters on learning, memory, and thinking. Without doubt, there is more to thinking than we are conscious of.

Then again, there is little doubt that social influences do play an important role in hypnosis. So, might the two views—social influence and divided consciousness—be bridged? Researchers John Kihlstrom and Kevin McConkey (1990) believe there is no contradiction between the two approaches, which may eventually converge into a "unified account of hypnosis." Until then, they suggest, we can understand hypnosis as an extension *both* of normal principles of social influence *and* of everyday splits in consciousness.

## Summing Up

**Facts and Falsehoods** Although hypnosis was historically linked with quackery, it has more recently become the subject of serious research. Psychologists now agree that hypnosis is a state of heightened suggestibility to which people are subject in varying degrees, and that, although hypnotic procedures may help someone to recall something, the hypnotist's beliefs frequently work their way into the subject's recollections. They also agree that hypnotized people cannot be made to act against their will any more than nonhypnotized people can. Hypnosis can be at least temporarily therapeutic, and hypnotizable people can enjoy significant pain relief.

**Is Hypnosis an Altered State of Consciousness?** There is debate, however, on whether hypnosis is a by-product of normal social and cognitive processes or whether it is an altered state of consciousness, perhaps involving a dissociation between levels of consciousness.

## Drugs and Consciousness

*What types of drugs influence consciousness? Do they work by changing the user's brain chemistry? The user's expectations? Both? Why do some people become regular users of consciousness-altering drugs?*

If there is controversy about whether hypnosis alters consciousness, there is little dispute that drugs do. **Psychoactive drugs** are chemicals that change perceptions and moods. An imaginary drug user's day dramatizes the widespread use of legal psychoactive drugs: It begins with a wake-up cup of strong coffee. By midday, several cigarettes and a prescription tranquilizer have calmed the nerves. An early exit from work makes time for a happy-hour cocktail, providing a relaxing and sociable prelude to a dental appointment, where nitrous oxide makes an otherwise painful experience mildly pleasurable. A diet pill before dinner helps stem the appetite, and its stimulating effects can later be partially offset with a sleeping pill. Before drifting off into REM-depressed sleep, our hypothetical drug user is dismayed by a news report of "rising drug abuse."

*"Just tell me where you kids got the idea to take so many drugs."*
© 1992 by Sidney Harris.

Continued use of a psychoactive drug produces **tolerance**: The user requires larger and larger doses to experience the drug's effect. A person who rarely drinks alcohol might get tipsy on one can of beer, but an experienced drinker may not get tipsy until the second six-pack. Despite the connotations of "tolerance," alcoholics' brains, hearts, and livers suffer damage from the excessive alcohol they are "tolerating."

Users who stop taking psychoactive drugs may experience the undesirable side effects of **withdrawal**. As the body responds to the drug's absence, the user may feel physical pain and intense cravings for a dose. This indicates a **physical dependence** on the drug. People can also develop **psychological dependence**, particularly for drugs used to relieve stress. Although the drug may not be physically addictive, it nevertheless becomes an important part of the user's life, often as a way of relieving negative emotions. With either physical addiction or psychological dependence, the user's primary focus becomes obtaining and using the drug.

There are three types of psychoactive drugs: **depressants**, or "downers," which calm neural activity and slow down body functions; **stimulants**, or "uppers," which temporarily excite neural activity and arouse body functions; and **hallucinogens**, which distort perception and evoke sensory images without sensory input. Drugs in all three categories do their work at the brain's synapses, by stimulating, inhibiting, or mimicking the activity of neurotransmitters, the brain's chemical messengers.

## Depressants

Let's look first at drugs such as alcohol, tranquilizers, and opiates, which slow down body functions.

### Alcohol

True or false? In large amounts, alcohol is a depressant; in small amounts, it is a stimulant.

False. Small doses of "spirits" may, indeed, enliven a drinker, but they do so by slowing brain activity that controls judgment and inhibitions. If provoked, people under alcohol's influence respond more aggressively than usual. If asked to help, people under alcohol's influence respond more helpfully than usual. In everyday life, alcohol *increases* both harmful tendencies—as when sexually coercive college men try to disinhibit their dates by getting them to drink (Abbey, 1991; Mosher & Anderson, 1986)—and helpful tendencies—as when restaurant patrons tip more when tipsy (M. Lynn, 1988). Thus, alcohol makes us more aggressive or helpful, or self-disclosing or sexually daring, when such tendencies are present. Whatever urges you feel when sober, you are more likely to act upon if intoxicated.

*A University of Illinois campus survey showed that before sexual assaults, 80 percent of the male assailants and 70 percent of the female victims had been drinking (Camper, 1990).*

Low doses of alcohol relax the drinker by slowing sympathetic nervous system activity. With larger doses, alcohol can become a staggering problem: Reactions slow, speech slurs, and skilled performance deteriorates. These physical effects, combined with the lowering of inhibitions, contribute to alcohol's worst consequences—to several hundred thousand lives claimed annually worldwide in alcohol-related accidents and violent crime. Accidents occur despite drinkers' belief (when sober) that it is wrong to drive impaired and despite their insisting they wouldn't do so. Yet under alcohol's influence, people's moral judgments become more immature, their qualms about drinking and driving lessen—and virtually all will drive home from a bar, even if given a breathalyzer test and told they are intoxicated (Denton & Krebs, 1990).

Alcohol has an intriguing effect on memory. It impairs neither short-term recall for what just happened nor existing long-term memories. Rather, it disrupts the *processing* of recent experiences into long-term memories. Thus, the day after being intoxicated, heavy drinkers may not recall whom they met or what they said or did the night before. This memory blackout stems partly from an inability to transfer memories from the intoxicated to the sober state (Eich, 1980). Blackouts after drinking may also result from alcohol's suppression of REM sleep. (Recall that people deprived of REM sleep have difficulty fixing their day's experiences into permanent memories.)

***Fact:*** *College students drink more alcohol than their noncollege peers, and fraternity and sorority members drink three times as much as other students (Atwell, 1986; Malloy & others, 1994). Although few university students believe they have an alcohol problem, many meet the criteria for alcohol abuse (Marlatt, 1991).*

Alcohol has another intriguing effect on consciousness: It reduces self-awareness (Hull & others, 1986). Compared with people who feel good about themselves, those who want to suppress their awareness of failures or shortcomings are more likely to drink. The Nazi doctors who selected "unfit" inmates for the gas chambers often did so while drunk, or got drunk afterwards (Lifton, 1986). By focusing attention on the immediate situation and away from future consequences, alcohol also facilitates urges that the individual might otherwise resist (Steele & Josephs, 1990).

**Don't Drink and Drive** *With billboards like this one that shows the appalling consequences of driving under the influence of alcohol, Mothers Against Drunk Driving (MADD) has vigorously promoted awareness of the dangers of alcohol abuse. They have also lobbied for stiffer penalties for drunk drivers.*

***Fact:*** *Binge drinking—the consumption of five or more drinks on some occasion during the last month—is reported by 22 percent of American adults. The highest rate of binge drinking—52 percent—is among 18- to 24-year-old males (Centers for Disease Control, 1983).*

As with other psychoactive drugs, alcohol's behavioral effects stem not only from its alteration of brain chemistry but also from the user's expectations. Many studies have found that when people *believe* that alcohol affects social behavior in certain ways, and *believe*, rightly or wrongly, that they have been drinking alcohol, they will behave accordingly (Leigh, 1989). In a driving simulator, sensation-seeking people drive more recklessly when they *believe* they have consumed alcohol (McMillen & others, 1989).

***Fact:*** *A survey of 56,000 college students found that* D *and* F *students imbibe three times as much as* A *students (Presley & Meilman, 1992).*

Another example: Alcohol per se has some effect on sexual arousal, by decreasing cognitive inhibitions (Crowe & George, 1989). But people become even more responsive to sexual stimuli if they believe alcohol promotes arousal and believe they have been drinking. From their review of research, Jay Hull and Charles Bond (1986) concluded that for some people alcohol serves "as an excuse to become sexually aroused."

***Fact:*** *Ten percent of drinkers account for half of the alcohol consumed (Centers for Disease Control, 1989).*

Consider one such experiment by David Abrams and Terence Wilson (1983). They gave Rutgers University men who volunteered for a study on "alcohol and sexual stimulation" either an alcoholic or a nonalcoholic drink. (Both drinks had a strong taste that masked any alcohol.) In each group, half the subjects thought they were drinking alcohol and half thought they were not. Regardless of what they drank, after being shown an erotic movie clip, the men who *thought* they had consumed alcohol were more likely to report having strong sexual fantasies and feeling guilt-free. Being able to *attribute* their sexual responses to alcohol released their inhibitions—whether they actually had drunk alcohol or not.

***Fact:*** *Anheuser-Busch Brewery's annual advertising budget has been seven times the budget of the National Institute on Alcohol Abuse and Alcoholism (McCarthy, 1988).*

***Fact:*** *Alcohol kills more people than all illegal drugs combined. So does tobacco (Siegel, 1990).*

This research illustrates an important principle: A drug's psychological effects are powerfully influenced by the user's expectations. And that explains why drug experiences vary with cultures (Ward, 1994). If one culture assumes that a particular drug produces euphoria (or aggression or sexual arousal) and another does not, each culture may find its expectations fulfilled.

### Barbiturates

The **barbiturate** drugs, or *tranquilizers*, mimic the effects of alcohol. Because they depress sympathetic nervous system activity, barbiturates such as Nembutal and Seconal are sometimes prescribed to induce sleep or reduce anxiety. In larger doses, they can lead to impaired memory and judgment. In combination with alcohol—as when people take a sleeping pill after an evening of drinking—the total depressive effect on body functions can be lethal. With sufficient doses, barbiturates by themselves can also cause death, which makes them the drugs often chosen by those attempting suicide.

### Opiates

The **opiates**—opium and its derivatives, morphine and heroin—also depress neural functioning. The pupils constrict, the breathing slows, and the user becomes lethargic. For a few hours, blissful pleasure replaces pain and anxiety. But for pleasure one pays a price, which for the heroin user is the gnawing craving for another fix, the need for progressively larger doses, the week-long physical anguish of withdrawal—and for some the ultimate price, death by overdose.

The pathway to addiction is treacherous. When repeatedly flooded with artificial opiates, the brain eventually stops producing its own opiates, the endorphins. Then, when the drug is withdrawn, the brain lacks the normal level of these painkilling neurotransmitters. The result is the agony of withdrawal.

## Stimulants

The most widely used stimulants are caffeine, nicotine, the powerful **amphetamines**, and the even more powerful cocaine. Stimulants speed up body functions, hence the nickname "speed" for amphetamines. Strong stimulants increase heart and breathing rates. The pupils dilate, appetite diminishes (because blood sugar rises), and energy and self-confidence rise. For these reasons, people use stimulants to stay awake, lose weight, or boost mood or athletic performance. As with other drugs, the benefits come with a price. When drug stimulation ends, the user experiences a compensating slowdown and may "crash" into tiredness, headaches, irritability, and depression. Like the depressants, stimulants, including coffee, can be addictive (Silverman & others, 1992). (For information on nicotine addiction, see pages 600–601.)

*The recipe for Coca-Cola originally included an extract of the coca plant, creating a cocaine tonic for tired elderly people. Between 1896 and 1905, Coke was indeed "the real thing."*

In national surveys, 3 percent of adults and 3 percent of high school seniors reported having tried cocaine during the past year (National Institute on Drug Abuse, 1992; Johnston & others, 1994). Of the seniors, 1.5 percent said they had smoked *crack*, a potent form of cocaine. By the early 1990s the decade-long cocaine epidemic began subsiding. Credit goes partly to increased treatment and awareness but also to the impoverishment, imprisonment, and deaths of so many cocaine victims (Hamid, 1992).

When animals and people chew coca leaves, small amounts of cocaine enter the bloodstream gradually, without seeming ill effects (Siegel, 1990). But when extracted cocaine is sniffed ("snorted"), and especially when smoked ("free-based") or injected, it enters the bloodstream quickly. The result: a "rush" of euphoria that lasts 15 to 30 minutes. Because the rush depletes the brain's supply of the neurotransmitters dopamine and norepinephrine, a crash of agitated depression occurs as the drug's effect wears off (Figure 7–8). Crack works even faster and produces a briefer but more intense high, a more intense crash, and a craving for more crack, which wanes after several hours and then returns several days later (Gawin, 1991).

**Figure 7–8**

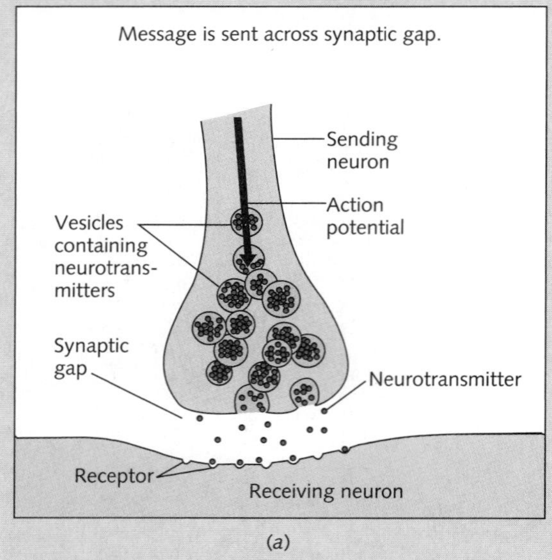
Message is sent across synaptic gap.
Sending neuron
Action potential
Vesicles containing neurotrans-mitters
Synaptic gap
Neurotransmitter
Receptor
Receiving neuron

(a)

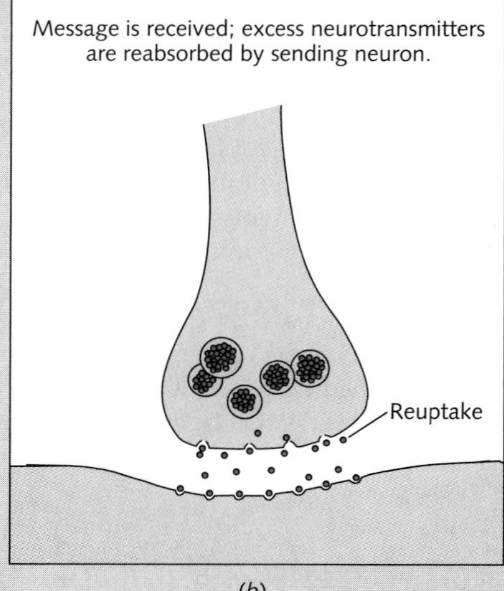
Message is received; excess neurotransmitters are reabsorbed by sending neuron.
Reuptake

(b)

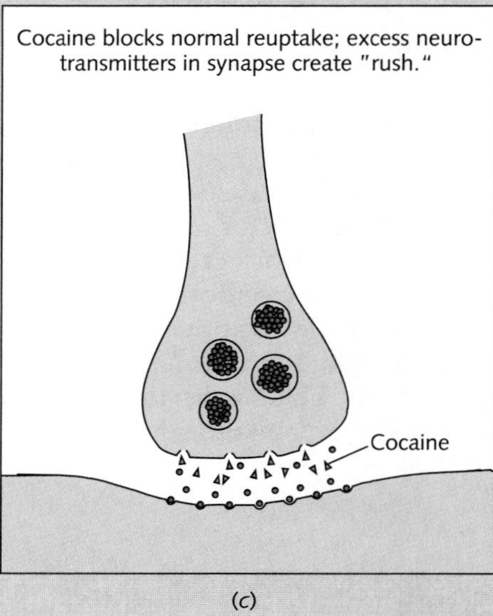
Cocaine blocks normal reuptake; excess neuro-transmitters in synapse create "rush."
Cocaine

(c)

**Cocaine Euphoria and Crash** *After neurotransmitters carry a message across a synapse (a), the sending nerve cell normally reabsorbs excess neurotransmitters (a process called reuptake) (b). Cocaine blocks reuptake of three neurotransmitters: dopamine, norepinephrine, and serotonin (Ray & Ksir, 1990). The extra neurotransmitter molecules therefore remain in the synapse, intensifying their normal mood-altering effects and producing a euphoric rush (c). When the cocaine is metabolized out of the body, the absence of these neurotransmitters produces a crash. Amphetamines act differently—by stimulating the release of excess norepinephrine.*

Regular cocaine users become addicted—monkeys so strongly addicted that they have pressed a lever more than 12,000 times to gain each cocaine injection (Siegel, 1990). Human and animal cocaine users may experience emotional disturbance, suspiciousness, convulsions, cardiac arrest, or respiratory failure. In situations that often trigger aggression, ingesting cocaine may increase aggressive reactions. Caged rats fight when given foot shocks, and they fight even more when given foot shocks and cocaine. Asked to determine how much electric shock one's opponent will receive in a laboratory competition, those who have ingested high-dose cocaine rather than a placebo set higher levels (Licata & others, 1993). As with all psychoactive drugs, cocaine's psychological effects depend not only on the dosage and form in which one takes the drug but also on one's expectations, one's personality, and the situation—a mix of factors. Given a placebo, cocaine users who *think* they are taking cocaine often have a cocaine-like experience (Van Dyke & Byck, 1982).

## Hallucinogens

Hallucinogens are psychoactive drugs that distort perceptions and evoke vivid images without sensory input (which is why they are also called *psychedelics*, meaning "mind-manifesting"). Some hallucinogens are natural substances, such as marijuana, which is sometimes classified as a mild hallucinogen. Others are synthetic. Of the synthetics, the two best known are PCP ("angel dust"), a potent and illegal pain killer that has highly unpredictable and sometimes devastating psychological effects, and LSD.

### LSD

The first "acid trip" was taken in 1943 by chemist Albert Hofmann, the creator of **LSD** (*lysergic acid diethylamide*). After accidentally ingesting some of the chemical, Hofmann reported that he "perceived an uninterrupted stream of fantastic pictures, extraordinary shapes with intense, kaleidoscopic play of colors" (Siegel, 1984). LSD and other powerful hallucinogens are chemically similar to (and therefore block the actions of) a subtype of the neurotransmitter serotonin (Jacobs, 1987). The emotions of an LSD trip vary from euphoria to detachment to panic.

As with all drug use, a person's current mood and expectations color the LSD experience. Despite emotional variations, the resulting perceptual distortions and hallucinations have commonalities. Psychologist Ronald Siegel (1982) reports that whether you provoke your brain to hallucinate by loss of oxygen, extreme sensory deprivation, or drugs, "it will hallucinate in basically the same way." The experience typically begins with simple geometric forms, such as a lattice, a cobweb, or a spiral (Figure 7–9). The next phase consists of more meaningful images; some may be superimposed on a tunnel or funnel, others may involve the replay of past emotional experiences. When the hallucinogenic experience peaks, people frequently feel separated from their bodies and experience dreamlike scenes as if they were real—so real that users may become panic-stricken or may harm themselves.

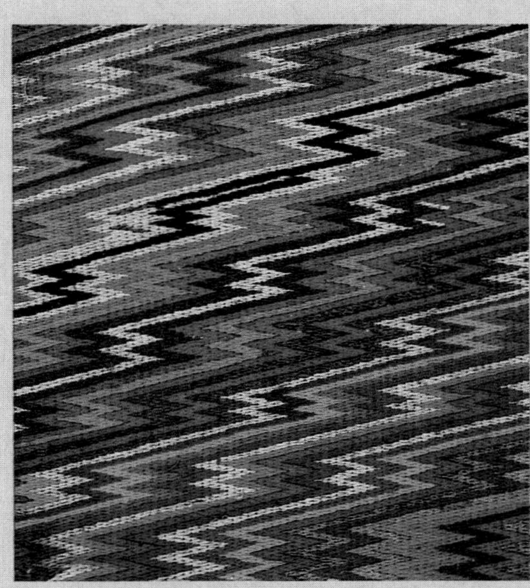

**Figure 7–9**

**Hallucination-like Patterns** *Geometric forms, such as those experienced by drug users during drug-induced hallucinations, can be seen in the embroidery of the Huichol, Mexican Indians who used peyote, from which the hallucinogen mescaline derives.*

### Marijuana

Marijuana consists of the leaves and flowers of the hemp plant, which for 5000 years has been cultivated for its fiber. Marijuana's major active ingredient is **THC**, the everyday name of the complex organic molecule delta-9-tetrahydrocannabinol. Whether smoked or eaten in such foods as brownies, THC produces a mix of effects that makes the drug difficult to classify. (Smoking gets the drug into the brain in about 7 seconds; this produces a greater effect than does eating the drug, which causes its peak concentration to be reached at a slower, unpredictable rate.) Like alcohol, marijuana relaxes, disinhibits, and may produce a euphoric high. But marijuana also acts as a mild hallucinogen by amplifying sensitivity to colors, sounds, tastes, and smells.

As with other drugs, the marijuana user's experience varies, depending on the situation. If the person feels anxious or depressed, taking the drug may intensify these feelings. In other situations, using marijuana can be not only pleasurable but therapeutic. For those who suffer the pain of glaucoma (caused by pressure within the eyeball) or the nausea that sometimes accompanies cancer chemotherapy, marijuana may spell relief. In acknowledging such benefits, a review of marijuana research published by the National Academy of Sciences (1982) also identified some not-so-pleasant consequences. Like alcohol, marijuana impairs the motor coordination,

## Close-Up

## Misconceptions About Addiction

An *addiction* has traditionally meant a craving for a substance, with physical symptoms such as aches, nausea, and distress following sudden withdrawal. In recent pop psychology, the supposedly irresistible seduction of addiction has been extended to cover many behaviors formerly considered bad habits or even sins. Has the concept been stretched too far? Are addictions as irresistible as commonly believed? Many drug researchers believe the following three myths about addiction are false:

1. *Addictive drugs quickly corrupt; for example, morphine taken to control pain is powerfully addictive and often leads to heroin abuse.* After taking a psychoactive drug, some people—perhaps 10 percent—do indeed have a hard time using it in moderation or stopping altogether. However, there are many more controlled, occasional users than addicts of drugs such as alcohol, marijuana, and cocaine (Gazzaniga, 1988; Siegel, 1990). The crazed user who will do anything to get more of the drug is more the exception than the rule. Moreover, people typically don't become addicted when using drugs medically. Those given morphine to control pain rarely develop the cravings of the addict who uses morphine as a mood-altering drug (Melzack, 1990). Thus, taking a psychoactive drug is necessary, but usually not sufficient, to cause addiction.

2. *Addictions can't be overcome voluntarily; therapy is a must.* The thriving addiction-treatment business promotes the notion that we're helpless without them. True, some addicts do benefit from treatment programs. Alcoholics Anonymous, for example, has supported many people in overcoming their alcohol dependence. But, say critics, the recovery rates of treated and untreated groups differ less than one might suppose.

Moreover, viewing addiction as a disease, as diabetes is a disease, can undermine self-confidence and the will to change cravings that, without treatment, "one can't fight." And that, critics say, would be unfortunate, for many people do voluntarily stop using addictive drugs, without treatment. Some 70 percent of smokers who seek treatment for their addiction later return to smoking, whereas most of America's 41 million ex-smokers kicked the habit on their own (page 601). Half of the American soldiers in Vietnam tried heroin or opium, and 20 percent became regular users. Worried about an influx of returning addicts, the U. S. Department of Defense commissioned a research team led by Lee Robins (1974) to follow nearly 500 men whose urine revealed narcotic use upon their departure from Vietnam. Back home, one-third of this group did try narcotics again. Yet, removed from the war's stressful setting and all the stimulus cues associated with their drug use (the place, the friends, the circumstances), only 7 percent of the 500 became readdicted. The rest—all but the relatively few hard-core addicts—left their dependence behind.

3. *We can extend the concept of addiction to cover not just drug dependencies, but a whole spectrum of repetitive, pleasure-seeking behaviors.* We can, and we have, but should we? How far should we stretch the concept of addiction?

The addiction-as-disease-needing-treatment idea has been extended to cover a host of driven behaviors, including overeating, shopping, exercise, gambling, work, and sex. Initially, we may use the term metaphorically. "I'm a ski addict" is just a way of saying, "I love skiing." But when people begin taking the metaphor as reality, addiction becomes an all-purpose excuse. Those who embezzle to feed their "gambling addiction," or who abuse or betray to indulge their "sex addiction" can protest that "I can't help it" and seek sympathy and treatment rather than judgment and jail. They follow the example of Marion Barry, former mayor of Washington, D.C.

perceptual skills, and reaction time necessary for safe driving and machine operation. "THC causes animals to misjudge events," reports Ronald Siegel (1990, p. 163). "Pigeons wait too long to respond to buzzers or lights that tell them food is available for brief periods; and rats turn the wrong way in mazes." Marijuana also disrupts memory formation and interferes with immediate recall of information learned only a few minutes before. Clearly, being stoned is not conducive to learning.

Unlike alcohol, which the body eliminates within hours, THC and its byproducts linger in the body for a month or more. Thus, contrary to the usual tolerance phenomenon, regular users may achieve a high with smaller amounts of the drug than occasional users would take to get the same effect.

Asked why he lied about being "chemically dependent," Barry replied, "That was the disease talking. I did not purposely do that to you. I was a victim" (Leo, 1991).

Sometimes, though, behaviors such as gambling do become compulsive and dysfunctional, much like abusive drug-taking. So is there justification for stretching the addiction concept to cover social behaviors? (What do you think?)

Some critics also chide bookstores that now carry whole sections of books on addictive relationships, also known as "co-dependence." A supposedly co-dependent person—usually a woman—is said to be addicted to, or dependent on, a dysfunctional partner. For this dependency she pays a price: the loss of her own identity and self-fulfillment. Indeed, daughters of alcoholic parents may learn to meet exploitive people's expectations (Lyon & Greenberg, 1991). And women who live with a substance abuser do experience great stress and sometimes help hide the abuser's addiction from public view. But, say critics, our individualistic culture often stretches "co-dependence" to include the lost freedoms of normal, mutually dependent wife-husband or parent-child relationships (Kaminer, 1992). Moreover, the co-dependent person often is *blamed* for sharing and supporting the partner's dysfunctional behavior. His shame becomes hers as well. If people derive meaning from supporting and loving a troubled family member, are they really blameworthy or socially ill?

If the addiction-as-disease-needing-treatment model is controversial even with drug dependencies, it is doubly controversial when extended to other excessive behaviors.

**CALVIN AND HOBBES**

CALVIN AND HOBBES copyright 1993 Watterson. Dist. by UNIVERSAL PRESS SYNDICATE. Reprinted with permission. All rights reserved.

Uncertainty persists about marijuana's physical effects, but medical research suggests that long-term marijuana use may depress male sex hormone and sperm levels and damage the lungs more than cigarette smoking (Wu & others, 1988). Large doses hasten the loss of brain cells (Landfield & others, 1988). Although marijuana is not as addictive as cocaine or nicotine, one study that followed 654 junior high students into their early twenties found that adolescents who heavily used marijuana developed more health and family problems than did nonusers (Newcomb & Bentler, 1988).

Despite their differences, the psychoactive drugs summarized in Table 7–1 (page 248) share a common feature: They trigger negative aftereffects that offset their immediate positive effects. The aftereffects illustrate the more general principle that emotions tend to produce opposing emotions,

**Table 7–1 A Guide to Selected Psychoactive Drugs**

| Drug | Type | Pleasurable Effects | Adverse Effects |
|---|---|---|---|
| *Alcohol* | Depressant | Initial high followed by relaxation and disinhibition | Depression, memory loss, organic damage, impaired reactions |
| *Heroin* | Depressant | Rush of euphoria, relief from pain | Depressed physiology, agonizing withdrawal |
| *Cocaine* | Stimulant | Rush of euphoria, confidence, energy | Cardiovascular stress, suspiciousness, depressive crash |
| *Marijuana* | Mild hallucinogen | Enhances sensation, relieves pain, distorts time, relaxed high | Lowered sex hormones, disrupted memory, lung damage |
| *Nicotine* | Stimulant | Arouses and relaxes, sense of well-being | Heart disease, cancer (from tars) |

*"How strange would appear to be this thing that men call pleasure! And how curiously it is related to what is thought to be its opposite, pain! . . . Wherever the one is found, the other follows up behind."*

Plato
*Phaedo,* Fourth century B.C.

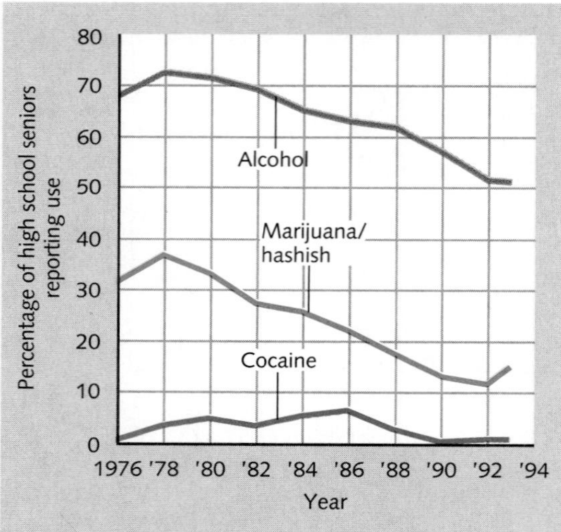


**Figure 7–10**

**Trends in Drug Use** *The percentage of high school seniors who report having used alcohol, marijuana, or cocaine during the past 30 days has declined since the late 1970s. (From Johnston & others, 1994.)*

*"Outlawing drugs in order to solve drug problems is much like outlawing sex in order to win the war against AIDS."*

Ronald Siegel
*Intoxication,* 1990

which linger after the original emotions disappear. With repetition, the opposing emotions grow stronger (page 450). This emotions-trigger-opposing-emotions principle parallels that of drug-induced pleasures; the pleasures wane as the drug exacts its compensatory price. That helps explain both tolerance and withdrawal. Because the opposing, negative aftereffects are getting stronger, it takes larger and larger doses to produce the desired high (tolerance), causing the aftereffects to worsen in the drug's absence (withdrawal). This in turn creates a need to switch off the withdrawal symptoms by taking yet more of the drug.

## Influences on Drug Use

Drug use by North American youth increased during the 1970s and declined during the 1980s. In the University of Michigan's annual survey of 16,000 high school seniors, the proportion who believed there is "great risk" in regular marijuana use rose from 35 percent in 1978 to 73 percent in 1993 (Johnston & others, 1994). After peaking in 1978, marijuana use by this age group declined until 1992 (Figure 7–10). In the UCLA/American Council on Education annual survey of new college students, support for the legalization of marijuana dropped from 53 percent in 1977 to 28 percent in 1993 (Astin & others, 1987, 1993). Similar attitude and usage changes appear in surveys of Canadian teens. Between the late 1970s and early 1990s, Ontario teens, for example, became less and less likely to report using marijuana, tobacco, and alcohol (Smart & others, 1991).

Other studies reveal a changing national attitude toward alcohol. More than at any time since prohibition, health- and safety-conscious people see alcohol less as a cheerful beverage than as a drug to be shunned. The number of new American collegians who reported abstinence from beer during the past year increased from 25 percent in 1981 to 46 percent in 1993. For any given month, 49 percent of Americans report having abstained from all alcohol use (National Institute on Drug Abuse, 1991). Hard liquor sales from 1980 to 1991 dropped 33 percent (Bureau of the Census, 1993). When the alcohol industry started substituting wine coolers for wine, and nonalcoholic beer for alcoholic, you knew attitudes were changing.

Cigarette smoking, though addictive, has similarly plummeted (see page 601). This is especially so among highly educated people, the vast majority of whom have never started or have stopped. Effectively inform people about the health hazards of using cocaine, marijuana, alcohol, or tobacco and—without therapy, support groups, or medicines—many will simply stop.

Why, then, do some people continue to use psychoactive drugs? Why, for example, do nearly one-third of American high school seniors report having tried an illegal drug during the past year (Johnston & others, 1994)? For some adolescents, occasional drug use represents thrill-seeking. Such experimentation is uncorrelated with maladjustment (Shedler & Block, 1990). Other adolescents become regular drug users. Why?

In the case of alcohol, some people may be biologically vulnerable. For example, evidence accumulates that heredity influences alcoholic tendencies. Consider:

- Adopted individuals are more susceptible to alcoholism if one or both of their biological parents is alcoholic (Mirin & Weiss, 1989).
- Having an alcoholic identical twin puts a male at increased risk for alcohol problems by age 20 (Heath & others, 1989; McGue & others, 1992).
- Compared with children of nonalcoholics, children of alcoholics have a higher tolerance for multiple alcoholic drinks over an hour or two (Schuckit, 1994). They also show a smaller evoked brain response to certain types of sensory stimulation (Polich & others, 1994).
- Researchers have bred rats that prefer alcoholic drinks to water (Holden, 1991).
- Molecular geneticists have recently identified a gene on chromosome 11 that is more common among alcoholics, especially severe alcoholics (Noble, 1993).

Such findings have fueled the search for a better understanding of genetic and biochemical influences on addiction. The biggest study yet—a $25 million, 5-year analysis of 600 alcoholics and their relatives—is under way. If biological markers of addiction-proneness can be found, then perhaps young people at risk for specific addictions can be identified and counseled.

But psychological and social factors may also have an influence. In their studies of New Jersey and California youth and young adults, Michael Newcomb and L. L. Harlow (1986) found that one psychological factor is the feeling that one's life is meaningless and directionless, a common feeling among school dropouts who subsist without job skills, without privilege, with little hope.

Other studies reveal that heavy users of alcohol, marijuana, and cocaine often have experienced significant stress or failure and are depressed. As we noted earlier, alcohol temporarily dulls the pain of self-awareness; by so doing, it may offer a way to avoid having to cope with depression, anger, anxiety, or insomnia. The relief may be temporary, but as Chapter 8 explains, behavior is often controlled more by its immediate than by its later consequences.

*Some warning signs of alcoholism:*

- *Drinking binges*
- *Regretting things done or said when drunk*
- *Feeling low or guilty after drinking*
- *Failing to honor a resolve to drink less*
- *Drinking to alleviate depression or anxiety*
- *Avoiding family or friends when drinking*

Especially for teenagers, drug use also has social roots, evident in differing rates of drug use across cultural groups. Alcohol and other drug addiction rates are extremely low among the Amish, Mennonites, Mormons, and orthodox Jews (Trimble, 1994). And what do you suppose is the rate of drug usage among African-American students—low or high? One of psy-

*In the real world, alcohol accounts for one-sixth or less of beverage use. In television's world, alcohol drinking occurs more often than the combined drinking of coffee, tea, soft drinks, and water (Gerbner, 1990).*

chology's best-kept secrets is that, contrary to popular stereotypes, African-American high school seniors "report the lowest rates of use for virtually all drugs" (Johnston & others, 1994). For example, nearly a third of white seniors, but only 13 percent of black seniors, report recent heavy drinking. Monthly smoking rates are 33 percent among white seniors but only 10 percent among black seniors. Although these data exclude high school dropouts, independent government studies of drug use in households nationwide and among 12,272 high schoolers in all 50 states confirms the finding: African-American teens have sharply lower rates of drinking, smoking, and cocaine use (Bass & Kane-Williams, 1993; Kann & others, 1993).

Social influences are transmitted largely through the peer culture. By their words and examples, peers influence attitudes about drugs. They also provide the drugs and the parties for their use. If an adolescent's friends use drugs, the odds are that he or she will, too. If the friends don't, the temptation may not even arise. Indeed, the peer factor is so powerful that other predictors of adolescent drug use, such as family strength, religiousness, and school adjustment, seem to operate through their effects on peer associations.

Peer influence is a matter not just of what friends do and say but also of what adolescents *believe* their friends are doing and favoring. Young adolescents consume more alcohol when, as often happens, they overestimate their friends' use (Aas & Klepp, 1992; Graham & others, 1991). At the university level, drinking dominates social occasions partly because students overestimate their fellow students' enthusiasm for alcohol use (Prentice & Miller, 1993). Thinking that few students share their concerns about the risks associated with alcohol, most students surrender to the perceived norm.

Those who use drugs are more likely to stop if indeed their drug use was peer influenced (Kandel & Raveis, 1989). When the friends stop or the social network changes, usage typically ceases. Teenagers who come from happy families and do well in school seldom use drugs, largely because they rarely associate with those who do (Oetting & Beauvais, 1987, 1990).

Correlations between drug use and these other factors—dropping out, hopelessness, and drug-using peers—don't prove cause and effect. (Does failure lead to drug use, or drug use lead to failure?) But the findings do suggest three possible channels of influence for drug prevention and treatment programs: (1) education about the long-term costs of a drug's temporary pleasures, (2) efforts to boost people's self-esteem and purpose in life, and (3) attempts to modify peer associations or to "inoculate" youth against peer pressures, by training "refusal skills." Said differently, people are *very* unlikely to abuse drugs if they understand the physical and psychological costs, feel good about themselves and the direction their lives are taking, and are in a peer group that disapproves of drug use.

## Summing Up

Psychoactive drugs, including depressants, stimulants, and hallucinogens, also alter consciousness. Drugs often trigger negative aftereffects that oppose and offset their temporary pleasure.

**Depressants** Alcohol, barbiturates, and the opiates act by depressing neural functioning. Each offers its pleasures, but at the cost of impaired memory and self-awareness or other physical consequences.

**Stimulants** Caffeine, nicotine, the amphetamines, and cocaine act by stimulating neural functioning. As with nearly all psychoactive drugs, they act at the synapses by influencing the brain's neurotransmitters, and their effects depend on dosage and the user's personality and expectations.

**Hallucinogens** LSD and marijuana can distort the user's judgments of time and, depending on the setting, can alter sensations and perceptions.

**Influences on Drug Use** Drug use among teenagers and young adults declined during the 1980s, as attitudes changed. Nevertheless, psychological factors (such as stress, depression, and hopelessness) and social factors (such as peer pressure) combine to lead many people to experiment with—and become dependent on—drugs. Some people also appear to have a greater biological susceptibility to dependence on drugs such as alcohol.

## Near-Death Experiences

*What should we make of the reports of people who describe mystical experiences after close brushes with death? Do they prove that we can look forward to bliss on the other side of death? Do they confirm Plato's doctrine that mind—or soul—is separable from body? Do those facing death reliably experience such flights of mind?*

> A man . . . hears himself pronounced dead by his doctor. He begins to hear an uncomfortable noise, a loud ringing or buzzing, and at the same time feels himself moving very rapidly through a long dark tunnel. After this, he suddenly finds himself outside of his own physical body . . . and sees his own body from a distance, as though he is a spectator. . . . Soon other things begin to happen. Others come to meet and to help him. He glimpses the spirits of relatives and friends who have already died, and a loving, warm spirit of a kind he has never encountered before—a being of light—appears before him. . . . He is overwhelmed by intense feelings of joy, love, and peace. Despite his attitude, though, he somehow reunites with his physical body and lives. (Moody, 1976, pp. 23, 24)

This passage from Raymond Moody's best-selling book, *Life After Life*, is a composite description of a **near-death experience**. Near-death experiences are more common than you might suspect. Several investigators each interviewed a hundred or more people who had come close to death through such physical traumas as cardiac arrest. In each study, 30 to 40 percent of such patients recalled a near-death experience (Ring, 1980; Schnaper, 1980). When George Gallup, Jr. (1982; Gallup & O'Connell, 1986) interviewed a national sample of Americans, 15 percent reported having experienced a close brush with death. One-third of these people—representing some 8 million people by Gallup's estimate—reported an accompanying mystical experience. Some claimed to recall things said while they lay unconscious and near death. (But then, some anesthetized patients undergoing major surgery later display similar recall of operating room conversation or of obscure facts presented over headphones [Hilgard, 1986; Jelicic & others, 1992].)

Did Moody's description of the "complete" near-death experience sound familiar? The parallels with Ronald Siegel's (1977) descriptions of the typical hallucinogenic experience are striking: replay of old memories, out-of-body sensations, and visions of tunnels or funnels and bright lights or beings of light (Figure 7–11). In short, the content of the near-death experience is just what one would expect from a knowledge of hallucinations. More-

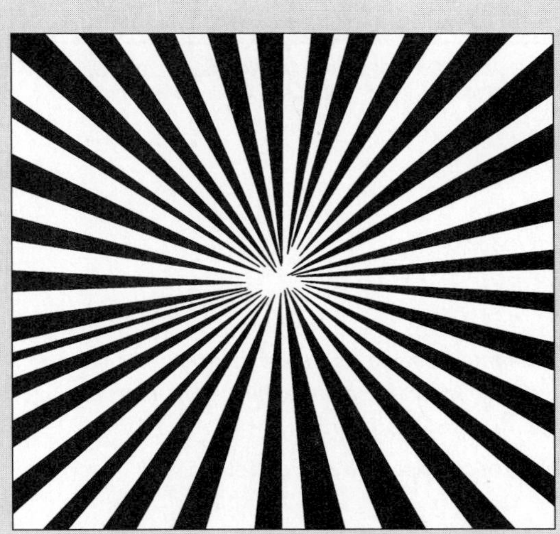

**Figure 7–11**

**Near-Death Vision or Hallucination?** *Psychologist Ronald Siegel (1977) reports that people under the influence of hallucinogenic drugs often see "a bright light in the center of the field of vision. . . . The location of this point of light create[s] a tunnel-like perspective." Susan Blackmore (1991, 1993) offers an explanation of similar light during a near-death experience: As oxygen deprivation turns off the brain's inhibitory cells, neural activity increases in the visual cortex. The result is a growing patch of light, which looks much like what you would see moving through a tunnel. (From "Hallucinations" by R. K. Siegel. Copyright © 1977 Scientific American, Inc. All rights reserved.)*

**THE FAR SIDE**

THE FAR SIDE © 1992 FARWORKS, INC./Dist. by UNIVERSAL PRESS SYNDICATE. Reprinted by permission. All rights reserved.

over, oxygen deprivation and other insults to the brain are known to produce hallucinations.

Perhaps, then, the brain under stress manufactures the near-death experience. Patients who experience temporal lobe seizures often report similarly profound mystical experiences, as have solitary sailors and polar explorers while enduring monotony, isolation, and cold (Suedfeld & Mocellin, 1987). Even the twilight state between waking and sleeping may produce sensations of floating up off the bed. Fantasy-prone persons are especially susceptible to near-death and other out-of-body experiences, such as believing one has encountered or been abducted by aliens (Ring, 1992; Wilson & Barber, 1983).

Siegel (1980) concluded that the near-death experience is best understood "as a dissociative hallucinatory activity of the brain": When external input dims, the brain's own interior activity becomes perceptible. He illustrates with an analogy: When gazing out a window at dusk, we begin to see the reflected interior of the room as if it were outside, either because the light from outside is dimming (as in the near-death experience) or because the inside light is being amplified (as with LSD). When projected on our perceptual window, says Siegel, our mind's internal images appear real. Those having a near-death experience, like those on an LSD trip, explore "the beyond within."

Some investigators of near-death experiences object. People who have experienced both hallucinations and the near-death phenomenon typically deny their similarity. Moreover, a near-death experience may change people in ways that a drug trip doesn't. They become kinder, more spiritual, more believing in life after death. Skeptics reply that these effects stem from the death-related context of the experience.

The controversy over interpreting near-death experiences raises a basic mind-body issue: Is the mind immaterial? Can it exist separate from the body? **Dualists** answer yes. They believe that the mind and body are two distinct entities—the mind nonphysical, the body physical—that somehow interact with each other. As Socrates says in Plato's *Phaedo*, "Does not death mean that the body comes to exist by itself, separated from the soul, and that the soul exists by herself, separated from the body? What is death but that?" For Socrates, as for those today who believe that near-death experiences are proof of immortality, death is not really the death of the person. Death is merely a person's liberation from the bodily prison, an occasion for rejoicing. (Carried to its extreme, this dualist view has given rise to glorifications of the afterlife trip under such titles as "The Thrill of Dying" and "The Wonderful World of Death.")

*"The mind seems to act independently of the brain in the same sense that a programmer acts independently of his computer."*

Neuroscientist Wilder Penfield (1975)

**Monists** answer no to the separation of mind and body. They contend that mind and body are different aspects of the same thing. In the Western world, monists include scientists who assume the inseparability of mind and brain and theologians who hold to an afterlife that involves some form of bodily resurrection. Such monists generally believe that death is real and that without bodies we truly are nobodies.

*"Everything in science to date seems to indicate that conscious awareness is a property of the living functioning brain and inseparable from it."*

Neuroscientist Roger W. Sperry (1985)

As debates over the significance of dreams, fantasy, hypnotic states, drug-induced hallucinations, and near-death experiences illustrate, science informs our wondering about human consciousness and human nature. Although there remain questions that it cannot answer, science nevertheless helps fashion our image of who we are—of our human potentials and our human limits.

## Summing Up

About one-third of those who have survived a brush with death, such as through cardiac arrest, later recall visionary near-death experiences. Dualists interpret these experiences as evidence of human immortality. Monists point out that reports of such experiences closely parallel reports of hallucinations.

## Terms and Concepts to Remember

### Studying Consciousness

**consciousness** Our awareness of ourselves and our environments.

### Sleep and Dreams

**circadian rhythm** [ser-KAY-dee-an] The biological clock; regular bodily rhythms (for example, of temperature and wakefulness) that occur on a 24-hour cycle.

**REM sleep** Rapid eye movement sleep, a recurring sleep stage during which vivid dreams commonly occur. Also known as *paradoxical sleep* because the muscles are relaxed (except for minor twitches) but other body systems are active.

**alpha waves** The relatively slow brain waves of a relaxed, awake state.

**hallucinations** False sensory experiences, such as seeing something without any external visual stimulus.

**delta waves** The large, slow brain waves associated with deep sleep.

**insomnia** A sleep disorder involving recurring problems in falling or staying asleep.

**narcolepsy** A sleep disorder characterized by uncontrollable sleep attacks in which the sufferer lapses directly into REM sleep, often at inopportune times.

**sleep apnea** A sleep disorder characterized by temporary cessations of breathing during sleep and consequent momentary reawakenings.

**night terrors** A sleep disorder characterized by high arousal and an appearance of being terrified; unlike nightmares, night terrors occur during Stage 4 sleep, within 2 or 3 hours of falling asleep, and are seldom remembered.

**manifest content** According to Freud, the remembered story line of a dream (as distinct from its latent content).

**latent content** According to Freud, the underlying but censored meaning of a dream (as distinct from its manifest content). Freud believed that a dream's latent content functions as a safety valve.

**REM rebound** The tendency for REM sleep to increase following REM sleep deprivation (created by repeated awakenings during REM sleep).

### Daydreams and Fantasies

**fantasy-prone personality** Someone who imagines and recalls experiences with lifelike vividness and who spends considerable time fantasizing.

### Hypnosis

**hypnosis** An apparently heightened suggestibility in which some people narrow their focus of attention and claim to experience imaginary happenings as if they were real.

**posthypnotic amnesia** Supposed inability to recall what one experienced during hypnosis; induced by the hypnotist's suggestion.

**age regression** In hypnosis, the supposed reliving of earlier experiences, such as in early childhood; greatly susceptible to false recollections.

**posthypnotic suggestion** A suggestion, made during a hypnosis session, to be carried out after the subject is no longer hypnotized; used by some clinicians to help control undesired symptoms and behaviors.

**dissociation** A split in consciousness, which allows some thoughts and behaviors to occur simultaneously with others.

**hidden observer** Hilgard's term describing a hypnotized subject's awareness of experiences, such as pain, that go unreported during hypnosis.

### Drugs and Consciousness

**psychoactive drug** A chemical substance that alters mood and perceptions.

**tolerance** The diminishing of a drug's effect with regular use of the same dose, requiring the user to take larger and larger doses before experiencing the drug's effect.

**withdrawal** The discomfort and distress that follow the discontinued use of addictive drugs.

**physical dependence** A physiological need for a drug, with unpleasant withdrawal symptoms when discontinued.

**psychological dependence** A psychological need to use a drug, such as to relieve negative emotions.

**depressants** Drugs (such as alcohol, barbiturates, and opiates) that reduce neural activity and slow body functions.

**stimulants** Drugs (such as caffeine, nicotine, and the more powerful amphetamines and cocaine) that excite neural activity and speed up body functions.

**hallucinogens** Psychedelic ("mind-manifesting") drugs, such as LSD, that distort perceptions and evoke sensory images in the absence of sensory input.

**barbiturates** Drugs that depress the activity of the central nervous system, reducing anxiety but impairing memory and judgment.

**opiates** Opium and its derivatives, such as morphine and heroin; they depress neural activity, temporarily lessening pain and anxiety.

**amphetamines** Drugs that stimulate neural activity, causing speeded-up body functions and associated energy and mood changes.

**LSD** (*lysergic acid diethylamide*) A powerful hallucinogenic drug; also known as *acid*.

**THC** The major active ingredient in marijuana; triggers a variety of effects, including mild hallucinations.

### Near-Death Experiences

**near-death experience** An altered state of consciousness reported after a close brush with death (such as through cardiac arrest); often similar to drug-induced hallucinations.

**dualism** The presumption that mind and body are two distinct entities that interact.

**monism** The presumption that mind and body are different aspects of the same thing.

## Critical Thinking Exercise

Now that you have read and reviewed Chapter 7, take your learning a step further by testing your critical thinking skills on the following scientific problem solving exercise.

> Consider the following hypnosis experiment. "Geraldo the hypnotist" is invited to demonstrate hypnosis to your psychology class. He brings along three volunteers currently enrolled in his hypnosis certification course and claims that hypnosis can trigger specific behaviors, perceptions, and memories. He then hypnotizes the volunteers and begins a demonstration of age regression. The volunteers are brought back to their first day of kindergarten. Remarkably, their behavior and speech seem childlike. After instructing them to forget everything that happened, Geraldo brings the subjects out of the hypnotic state and invites you and your classmates to question them. To your amazement, the subjects report no memory of the incident. Geraldo argues that his experiment demonstrates that hypnotic age regression actually causes subjects to relive earlier experiences, while the suggestion of posthypnotic amnesia erases memory of the hypnosis from the brain.

1. Geraldo's "experiment" has at least three major flaws. Can you identify them?
2. What explanation does Geraldo offer for the behavior of the subjects in the hypnosis demonstration?
3. Does this explanation make sense based on the evidence?
4. How else might the behavior of the hypnotized subjects be explained?
5. Suggest a more valid test of hypnosis.

Check your progress on becoming a critical thinker by comparing your answers to the sample answers found in Appendix B.

## For Further Information

*You can find further information in this text regarding drugs on the following pages:*



## For Further Reading

### Consciousness

**Ornstein, R.** (1991). *The evolution of consciousness: The origins of the way we think*. Boston: Houghton Mifflin.

*Argues that our brain-mind systems evolved not to reason but to help us survive—to avoid danger, obtain food, perpetuate our genes.*

**Wallace, B., & Fisher, L. E.** (1991). *Consciousness and behavior* (3rd ed.). Boston: Allyn & Bacon.

*A useful, in-depth overview of the psychology of consciousness and its altered states.*

### Sleep and Dreams

**Moorcroft, W.** (1993). *Sleep, dreaming, and sleep disorders: An introduction* (2nd ed.). Landam, MD: University Press of America.

*A comprehensive and lucid overview of all that's known about sleep and dreams.*

**Webb, W. B.** (1992). *Sleep: The gentle tyrant*. (2nd ed.). Bolton, MA: Anker Publishing.

*Wilse Webb, a gentle giant among sleep researchers, offers a first-hand look at the new sleep research.*

### Hypnosis

**Spanos, N. P., & Chaves, J. F.** (1989). *Hypnosis: The cognitive-behavioral perspective*. Buffalo: Prometheus Books.

*A survey of ingenious testing procedures for getting at the truth about what hypnosis is and how it affects people.*

**Zilbergeld, B., Edelstien, M. G., & Araoz, D. L.** (1986). *Hypnosis: Questions and answers*. New York: Norton.

*Here 85 experts answer 78 questions, from "Are stage hypnotists really doing hypnosis?" to "Can hypnosis enhance athletic performance?"*

### Drugs

**Siegel, R. K.** (1990). *Intoxication*. New York: Pocket Books.

*A guide to intoxicants, how animals and people use them, and with what effects.*

**Snyder, S. H.** (1986). *Drugs and the brain*. New York: Scientific American Library.

*An authoritative and beautifully illustrated summary of how psychoactive drugs, both therapeutic and illicit, affect the brain.*

# CHAPTER 8

## Classical Conditioning

**Pavlov's Experiments**
- Acquisition
- Extinction and Spontaneous Recovery
- Generalization
- Discrimination

**Updating Pavlov's Understanding**
- Cognitive Processes
- Biological Predispositions

**Pavlov's Legacy**
- Applications of Classical Conditioning

## Operant Conditioning

**Skinner's Experiments**
- Shaping
- Principles of Reinforcement
- Punishment

**Updating Skinner's Understanding**
- Cognition and Operant Conditioning
- Biological Predispositions

**Skinner's Legacy**
- Applications of Operant Conditioning

**Contrasting Conditioning Techniques**

## Learning by Observation

**Bandura's Experiments**

**Applications of Observational Learning**

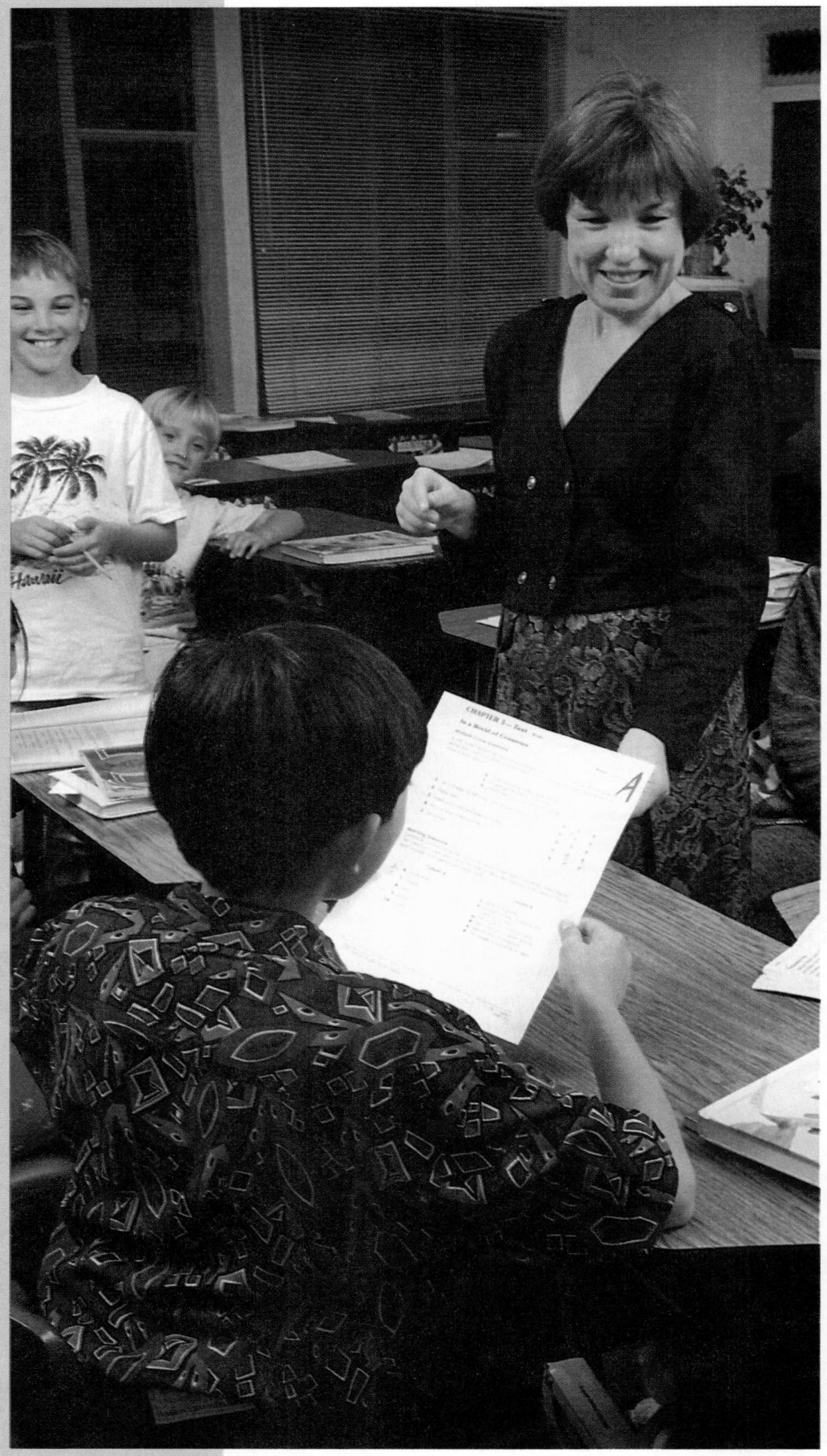

# Learning

*All animals, especially humans, adapt to their environments aided by learning. The process of learning associations between events is called conditioning. Through classical conditioning, we learn to anticipate important events, such as impending food or pain. Through operant conditioning, we learn to repeat acts that bring desired results and to avoid acts that bring punishment. Through observational learning, we learn from the experience and example of others.*

When a chinook salmon first emerges from its egg in the gravel bed of a stream, its genes provide many of the behavioral instructions it needs for life. It instinctively knows how and where to swim, what to eat, and how to protect itself from predators. Following this built-in plan, the young salmon soon begins a trek to the sea. After some 4 years in the ocean, instinct drives the mature salmon back to its birthplace. It navigates hundreds of miles to the mouth of its home river and then, guided by the scent of its home stream, begins an upstream odyssey to its ancestral spawning ground. Once there, the salmon seeks out the exact conditions of temperature, gravel, and water flow that will facilitate its breeding, and then mates.

"Actually, sex just isn't that important to me."

©1984 by Sidney Harris; *American Scientist Magazine.*

Unlike the salmon, we are not born with a genetic blueprint for life. Much of what we do we must learn from experience. Although we must struggle to find the life direction a salmon is born with, our learning gives us vastly more flexibility. We can learn how to build igloos or grass huts or submarines and thereby adapt to almost any environment. Indeed, nature's most important gift to us may be our *adaptability*—our capacity to learn new behaviors that enable us to cope with ever-changing circumstances.

No topic is closer to the heart of psychology than **learning**, *a relatively permanent change in an organism's behavior due to experience.* In earlier chapters we considered the learning of moral ideas, of self-concept, of visual perceptions. In later chapters we will consider how learning shapes our thought and language, our motivations and emotions, our personalities and attitudes.

Learning in all such realms breeds hope. What is learnable we can potentially teach—a fact that encourages parents, educators, athletic coaches, and animal trainers. What has been learned we can potentially change by new learning—an assumption that underlies counseling, psychotherapy, and rehabilitation. No matter how unhappy, unsuccessful, or unloving we are, that need not be the end of our story. Of all the world's creatures, we humans are the most capable of changing our behavior through learning.

*"Learning is the eye of the mind."*

Thomas Drake
*Bibliotheca Scholastica Instructissima*, 1633

By definition, experience is key to learning. More than 200 years ago, philosophers such as John Locke and David Hume echoed Aristotle's conclusion from 2000 years earlier: We learn by association. Our minds naturally connect events that occur in sequence: We *associate* them. If, after seeing and smelling freshly baked bread, you eat some and find it satisfying, then the next time you see and smell fresh bread, your experience will lead you to expect that eating some will be satisfying again. And if you associate a sound with a frightening consequence, then your fear may be aroused by the sound itself. As one 4-year-old exclaimed after watching a TV character get mugged, "If I had heard that music, I wouldn't have gone around the corner!" (Wells, 1981).

Simple animals can learn simple associations. When disturbed by a squirt of water, the sea snail *Aplysia* will protectively withdraw its gill. If the squirts continue, as happens naturally in choppy water, the withdrawal response diminishes. (The snail "habituates.") But if the sea snail repeatedly receives a shock just after being squirted, its withdrawal response to the squirt alone becomes stronger. Somehow the animal learns to associate the squirt with the impending shock. More complex animals can learn more complex associations, especially those that bring favorable consequences. Sea lions in an aquarium will repeat behaviors, such as slapping and barking, that prompt people to toss them a herring.

By linking two events that occur close together, both the sea snail and the sea lion exhibit **associative learning**. The sea snail associates the squirt with impending shock; the sea lion associates slapping and barking with receiving a herring. In both cases, the animals learned something important to their survival: to associate the past with the immediate future.

Event 1 ⟶ Event 2
Squirt ⟶ Tail shock
Bark ⟶ Herring

Learned associations influence people, too, sometimes in weird ways. In one experiment, people rated neutral stimuli (Chinese characters) more positively when pressing their arms upward (as when lifting food) rather than when pressing them downward (as when pushing something or someone away). The positive associations of upward flexion imbued the stimuli with more positive overtones (Cacioppo & others, 1993). (Can you feel a subtle emotional difference while lifting a table edge with upturned hands rather than pressing it down?)

*Conditioning* is the process of learning associations. In *classical conditioning*, we learn to associate two stimuli (as when we learn that a nearby flash of lightning signals an impending crack of thunder):

Event 1 ⟶ Event 2
Stimulus (lightning) ⟶ Stimulus (thunder)

In *operant conditioning*, we learn to associate a response and its consequence (as when we learn that the pull on a vending machine lever relates to the delivery of a candy bar).

Event 1 ⟶ Event 2
Response (pull) ⟶ Stimulus—rewarding or punishing (candy)

To simplify things, we will consider these two types of associative learning separately. Often, though, they occur together in the same situation. A clever Japanese rancher reportedly herds cattle by outfitting them with electronic pagers, which he calls from his portable phone. After a week of training, the cows learned to associate two stimuli—the beep on their pager and the arrival of food (classical conditioning). But they also learn to associate their hustling to the food trough with the pleasure of eating (operant conditioning).

This, however, leaves many questions: What principles influence the learning and the loss of associations? How can we apply these principles? And what really are the associations: Do neural networks develop as different brain neurons are activated together? Do associations form between neurons that are simultaneously active, such that firing one neuron cluster activates another? If so, does the first event also trigger a mental representation of the second? Does the beep on the cow's pager evoke a cognitive representation of food, to which the cow responds by coming to the trough? Or does it make little sense to explain conditioned associations in terms of cognitive processes?

Conditioning is not the only form of learning. Complex animals, such as chimpanzees, sometimes learn behaviors merely by observing others perform them. If one animal learns to solve a puzzle that gains a food reward while another watches, the second animal may perform the trick more quickly. We humans learn in all these ways—by learning to associate events (as in classical and operant conditioning) and by observation. Through language, we also learn things we have neither experienced nor observed.

All these ways of learning enable us to adapt to our environments. As this chapter will explain, we learn to expect and prepare for significant events such as food or pain (classical conditioning). We also learn to repeat acts that bring good results and to avoid acts that bring bad results (operant conditioning). And by watching others, we gain new behaviors indirectly (observational learning).

In searching for laws underlying such learning, psychologist John B. Watson (1913) urged his colleagues to discard reference to inner thoughts, feelings, and motives. Forget the mind, said Watson. Psychology should instead study how organisms respond to stimuli in their environments. "Its theoretical goal is the prediction and control of behavior. Introspection forms no essential part of its methods." Simply said, psychology should be an objective science based on *observable behavior*. This view, which influenced American psychology during the first half of this century, Watson called **behaviorism**. American academic culture, with its concerns for scientific objectivity and for the created equality of all, proved fertile soil for the new behaviorism.

*Most of us would be unable to name the order of the songs on our favorite CD. Yet hearing the end of one piece cues (by association) an anticipatory mental representation of the next. Likewise, when singing your national anthem, you associate the end of each line with the beginning of the next. (Pick a line out of the middle and notice how much harder it is to recall the* previous *line.)*

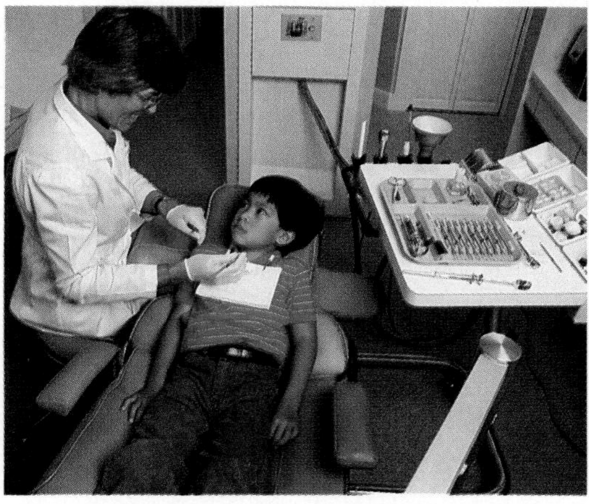

**Conditioned Fear** *The dentist's smile does nothing to allay the apprehension of this young patient. Because of pain experienced during previous experiences in the dentist chair, he has learned to expect discomfort.*

*Psychology's "factual and theoretical developments in this century—which have changed the study of mind and behavior as radically as genetics changed the study of heredity—have all been the product of objective analysis—that is to say, behavioristic analysis."*

Psychologist D. O. Hebb (1980)

## Classical Conditioning

*Russian physiologist Ivan Pavlov explored one important form of learning in his classic experiments on conditioning dogs. Pavlov showed how scientific research can reveal learning principles that apply across species. Others have modified Pavlov's understandings by demonstrating the importance of cognition and of biological predispositions to learn certain associations.*

Although the idea of learning associations had long generated philosophical discussion, it was not until this century that psychology's most famous research verified it. For many people, the name Ivan Pavlov rings a bell. His experiments are classics, and the phenomenon he explored we justly call **classical conditioning** (or *Pavlovian conditioning*).

**Ivan Pavlov** *"Experimental investigation . . . should lay a solid foundation for a future true science of psychology" (1927).*

## Pavlov's Experiments

Pavlov was driven by a lifelong passion for research. After receiving a medical degree at age 33, he spent the next 2 decades studying the digestive system, work that earned him Russia's first Nobel prize in 1904. But it was his novel experiments on learning, to which he devoted the last 3 decades of his life, that earned this feisty scientist his place in history.

Pavlov's new direction came when his creative mind seized on an incidental finding. After studying salivary secretion in dogs, he knew that when he put food in a dog's mouth the animal would invariably salivate. He also noticed that when he worked with the same dog repeatedly, the dog began salivating to stimuli associated with food—to the mere sight of the food, to the food dish, to the presence of the person who regularly brought the food, or even to the sound of that person's approaching footsteps. Because these "psychic secretions" interfered with his experiments on digestion, Pavlov considered them an annoyance—until he realized they pointed to a simple but important form of learning. From that time on, Pavlov studied learning, which he hoped might enable him to understand better the workings of the brain.

At first, Pavlov and his assistants tried to imagine what the dog was thinking and feeling as it drooled in anticipation of the food. This only led them into fruitless debates. So to attack the phenomenon more objectively, they experimented. They paired various neutral stimuli with food in the mouth to see if the dog would begin salivating to the neutral stimuli alone. To eliminate the possible influence of extraneous stimuli, they isolated the dog in a small room, secured it in a harness, and attached a device that diverted its saliva to a measuring instrument (Figure 8–1). From an adjacent room they could present food—at first by sliding in a food bowl, later by blowing meat powder into the dog's mouth at a precise moment. If a neutral stimulus—something the dog could see or hear—now regularly signaled the arrival of food, would the dog associate the two stimuli? If so, would it begin salivating to the neutral stimulus in anticipation of the food?

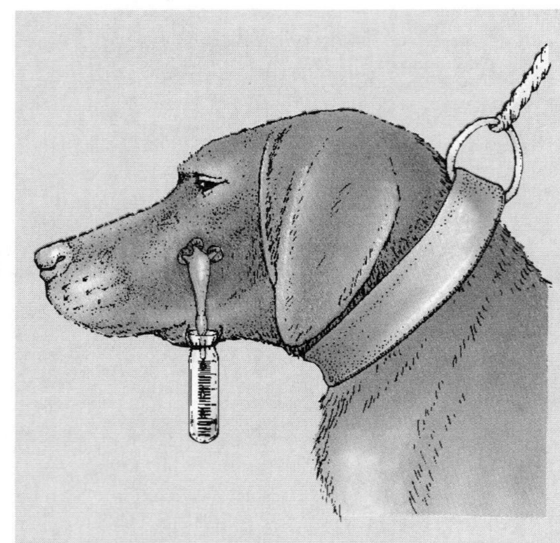

**Figure 8–1**

**Pavlov's Device for Recording Salivation** *The isolated dog's saliva was collected drop by drop in a tube. (Adapted from Goodwin, 1991.)*

The answers proved to be yes. Just before placing food in the dog's mouth to produce salivation, Pavlov would sound a tone. After several pairings of tone and food, the dog began salivating to the tone alone in anticipation of the meat powder. Using this procedure, Pavlov conditioned dogs to salivate to other stimuli—a buzzer, a light, a touch on the leg, even the sight of a circle.

Now for some necessary terminology: Because salivation in response to food in the mouth was unlearned, Pavlov called it an **unconditioned response (UCR)**. Food in the mouth automatically, *unconditionally*, triggers a dog's salivary reflex (Figure 8–2). Thus, Pavlov called the food stimulus an **unconditioned stimulus (UCS)**.

Salivation in response to the tone was conditional upon the dog's learning the association between the tone and the food. This learned response we therefore call the **conditioned response (CR)**. The previously neutral tone stimulus that now triggered the conditional salivation we call the **conditioned stimulus (CS)**. It's easy to distinguish these two kinds of stimuli and responses. Just remember: conditioned = learned; *un*conditioned = *un*learned.

If this demonstration of associative learning was so simple, what did Pavlov do for the next 3 decades? He and his associates explored the causes and effects of classical conditioning. Their experiments identified five major conditioning processes: acquisition, extinction, spontaneous recovery, generalization, and discrimination.

**Figure 8–2**

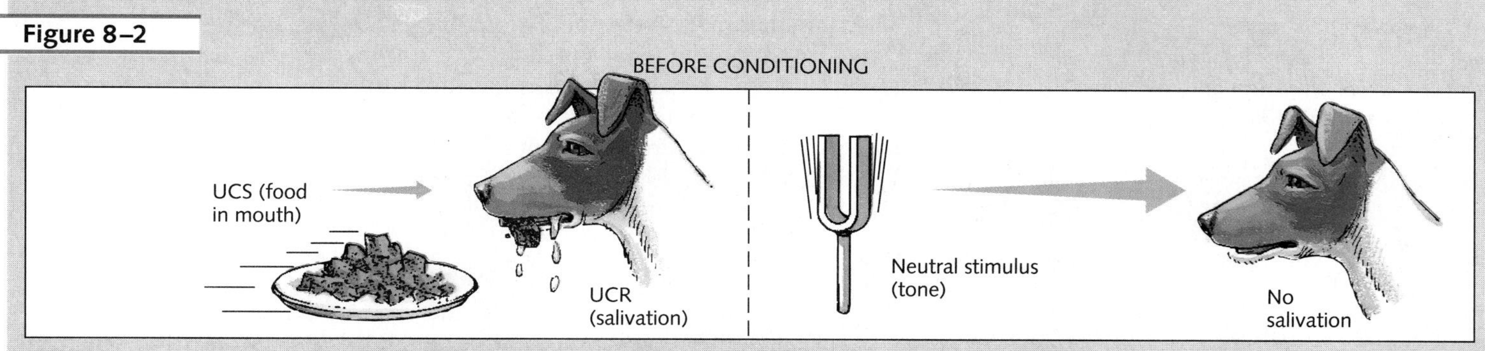


An unconditioned stimulus (UCS) produces an unconditioned response (UCR). A neutral stimulus produces no response.

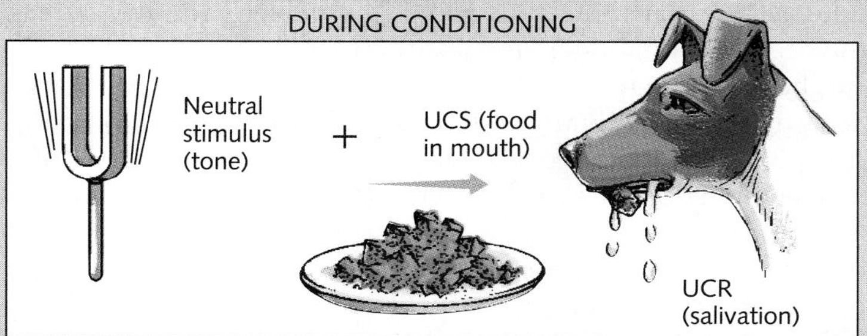


The unconditioned stimulus is presented just after a neutral stimulus. The unconditioned stimulus continues to produce an unconditioned response.

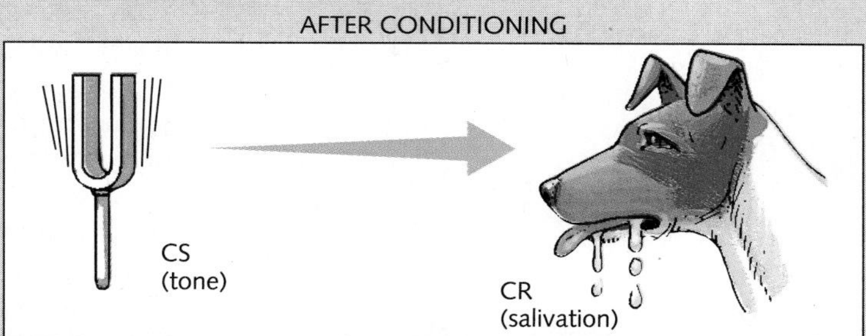


The neutral stimulus now produces a conditioned response (CR), thereby becoming a conditioned stimulus (CS).

**Pavlov's Classic Experiment** *By presenting a neutral stimulus (a tone) just before an unconditioned stimulus (food in mouth), the neutral stimulus becomes a conditioned stimulus. The previously neutral stimulus, now a conditioned stimulus, produces a conditioned response.*

## Acquisition

Regarding the **acquisition**, or initial learning, of the response, there was first a question of timing: How much time should elapse between presenting the neutral stimulus (the tone, the light, the touch, or whatever) and the unconditioned stimulus? In most cases, not much. With many species and procedures, half a second works well. What do you suppose would happen if the food (UCS) appeared *before* the tone (CS) rather than after? Do you think conditioning would occur?

*Check yourself: If the aroma of brownies baking sets your mouth to watering, what is the UCS? The CS? The CR? (See page 263.)*

Not likely. Although there are exceptions, conditioning seldom occurs when the CS comes after the UCS. This finding fits the presumption that classical conditioning is biologically adaptive. It helps organisms *prepare* for good or bad events. Pavlov's tone (CS) signals an important biological event—the arrival of food (UCS). To a deer in the forest, the sound of a snapping twig (CS) may come to signal danger (UCS). If the good or bad event had already occurred, the CS would not likely signal anything significant.

Michael Domjan (1992) showed how this works by conditioning the sexual arousal of male Japanese quail. The researchers turned on a red light before presenting an approachable female. Over time, the quail developed a liking for their cage's red-light district. Moreover, when the red light heralded a female's impending arrival, the male quail became excited (began copulating with her more quickly).

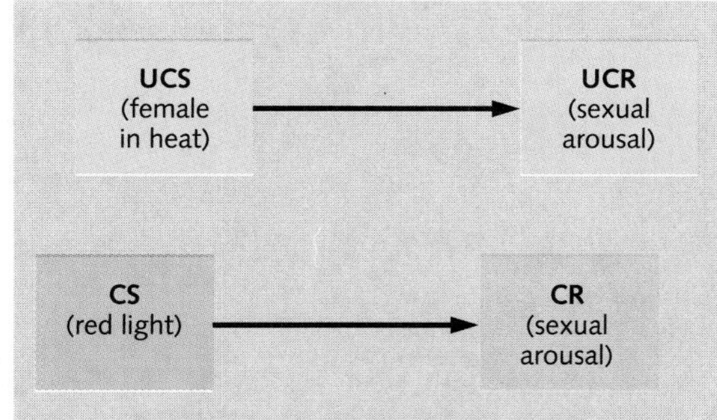


**The Quail's Sexual Conditioning** *As in Figure 8–2, the top row indicates events* before *conditioning, and the bottom row* after *conditioning.*

In humans, too, objects, smells, and sights associated with sexual pleasure become conditioned stimuli for sexual arousal. Psychologist Michael

*Remember:*
***UCS** = **U**n**C**onditioned **S**timulus*
***UCR** = **U**n**C**onditioned **R**esponse*
***CS** = **C**onditioned **S**timulus*
***CR** = **C**onditioned **R**esponse*

Tirrell (1990) recalls: "My first girlfriend loved onions, so I came to associate onion breath with kissing. Before long, onion breath sent tingles up and down my spine. Oh what a feeling!" (Questions: What is the unconditioned stimulus here? What is the conditioned response?) In laboratory experiments, even a geometric figure can become sexually arousing if repeatedly associated with an erotic stimulus (Byrne, 1982). (Note that in this case the figure is a CS, which gains its power to arouse by repeated pairing with a naturally erotic stimulus.)

### Extinction and Spontaneous Recovery

After conditioning, what happens if the CS occurs repeatedly without the UCS? Will the CS continue to elicit the CR? Pavlov found that when he sounded the tone again and again without presenting food, the dogs salivated less and less. Their declining salivation illustrates **extinction**, which occurs when the CS (tone) no longer signals an impending UCS (food).

Pavlov found, however, that if he allowed several hours to elapse before sounding the tone again, the salivation to the tone would reappear spontaneously (Figure 8–3). This **spontaneous recovery**—the reappearance of a (weakened) CR after a rest pause—suggested to Pavlov that extinction was suppressing the CR rather than eliminating it.

After breaking up with his fire-breathing heartthrob, Tirrell also experienced extinction and spontaneous recovery. He recalls that "the smell of onion breath (CS), no longer paired with the kissing (UCS), lost its ability to shiver my timbers. Occasionally, though, after not sensing the aroma for a long while, smelling onion breath awakens a small version of the emotional response I once felt."

**Figure 8–3**

**Idealized Curve of Acquisition, Extinction, and Spontaneous Recovery** *The rising curve shows that the CR rapidly grows stronger as the CS and UCS are repeatedly paired (acquisition), then wanes as the CS is presented alone (extinction). After a rest pause the CR reappears (spontaneous recovery).*

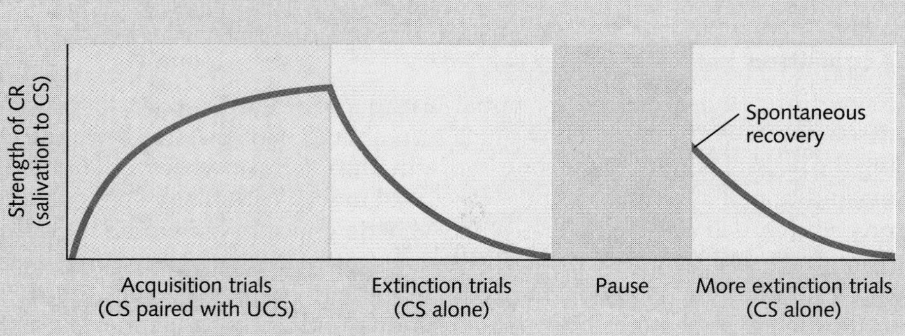


### Generalization

Pavlov and his students noticed that a dog conditioned to the sound of one tone also responded somewhat to the sound of a different tone or even to a buzzer never paired with food. Likewise, a dog conditioned to salivate when rubbed would also salivate some when scratched (Windholz, 1989) or when stimulated on a different body part (Figure 8–4). This tendency to respond to stimuli similar to the CS is called **generalization**. Generalization can be adaptive, as when toddlers taught to fear moving cars in the street respond similarly to trucks and motorcycles.

Because of generalization, stimuli that are similar to naturally disgusting or appealing objects will, by association, evoke some disgust or liking. Normally desirable foods, such as fudge, are unappealing when presented in a disgusting form, as when shaped to resemble dog feces (Rozin & others, 1986). We perceive adults with childlike facial features (round face, large forehead, small chin, large eyes) as having childlike warmth, submissiveness, and naiveté (Berry & McArthur, 1986). In both cases, people's emotional reactions to one stimulus generalize to similar stimuli.

### Discrimination

Pavlov's dogs also learned to respond to the sound of a particular tone and *not* to other tones. This learned ability to *distinguish* between a conditioned stimulus and similar but irrelevant stimuli is **discrimination**. Like generalization, discrimination has survival value. Slightly different stimuli are at times followed by vastly different consequences. Being able to recognize these differences is adaptive. Confronted by a pit bull, your heart may race; confronted by a cocker spaniel, it does not. Facing an approaching group of skinheads, you may cross the street; approaching some bald gentlemen, you don't.

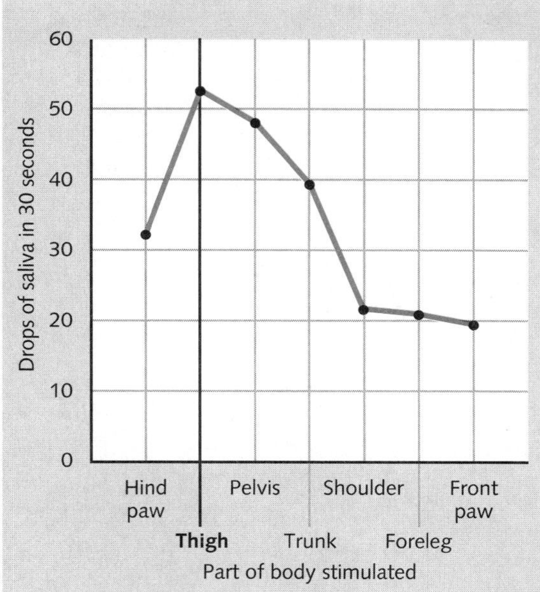


**Figure 8–4**

**Generalization** *Pavlov demonstrated generalization after attaching miniature vibrators to various parts of a dog's body. After conditioning salivation to stimulation of the thigh, he stimulated other areas. The closer they were to the original site of stimulation, the stronger the conditioned response. (From Pavlov, 1927.)*

*Answer to questions on page 261: Brownies (and their taste) are the UCS. The associated aroma is the CS. Salivation to the aroma is the CR.*

## Updating Pavlov's Understanding

Pavlov and Watson's disdain for "mentalistic" concepts such as consciousness has given way to a growing realization that they underestimated the importance of cognitive processes (thoughts, perceptions, expectations) and of biological constraints on an organism's capacity for learning.

### Cognitive Processes

The early behaviorists believed that the learned behaviors of various organisms could be reduced to mindless stimulus-response mechanisms. The idea that rats and dogs exhibit cognition therefore struck many psychologists as silly. No longer. Classical conditioning experiments by Robert Rescorla and Allan Wagner (1972) revealed that when two significant events occur close together in time, an animal learns the *predictability* of the second event, given the first. What matters is not how *often* an electric shock, say, follows a tone, but how predictably. The more predictable the association, the stronger the conditioned response.

It's as if the animal learns an *expectancy*, an awareness of how likely it is that the UCS will follow the CS. Rescorla (1988) surmises that classical conditioning "is not a stupid process by which the organism willy-nilly forms associations between any two stimuli that happen to occur." Rather, the organism is an information seeker, using relations among events to form its own adaptive representation of the world. Indeed, says Rescorla, a simple rule of thumb summarizes a host of facts about classical conditioning: Conditioning occurs best when the CS and UCS have just the sort of relationship that would lead a scientist to conclude that the CS *causes* the UCS.

This analysis helps to explain why classical conditioning treatments that ignore cognitive appraisals often have limited success. For example, therapy for alcoholics sometimes includes giving them alcohol spiked with a nauseating drug. Will they then associate alcohol with sickness? If classical conditioning were merely a matter of "stamping in" stimulus-response associations, we might hope so, and—to some extent—this does occur (as we will see on page 549). However, alcoholics are aware that they can blame their nausea on the drug, not on the alcohol. This cognition often weakens the association between alcohol and sickness. So, even in classical conditioning, it is not only the simple stimulus-response association but also the thought that counts.

### Biological Predispositions

Ever since Darwin, scientists have assumed that animals share both a common evolutionary history and resulting commonalities in their make-up and functioning. Pavlov and Watson, for example, believed the basic laws of learning were essentially similar in all animals. So it should make little difference whether one studied pigeons or people. Moreover, it seemed that any natural response could be conditioned to any neutral stimulus. As learning researcher Gregory Kimble proclaimed in 1956, "Just about any activity of which the organism is capable can be conditioned and . . . these responses can be conditioned to any stimulus that the organism can perceive" (p. 195).

Twenty-five years later, Kimble (1981) humbly acknowledged that "half a thousand" scientific reports had proven him wrong. More than the early behaviorists realized, an animal's capacity for conditioning is constrained by its biology. The biological predispositions of each species dispose it to learn the particular associations that enhance its survival.

The person most responsible for challenging the prevailing behaviorist view was John Garcia. While researching the effects of radiation on laboratory animals, Garcia and Robert Koelling (1966) noticed that rats began to avoid drinking water from the plastic bottles in the radiation chambers. They wondered whether classical conditioning might be the culprit. Might the rats have linked the plastic-tasting water (a CS) to the sickness (UCR) induced by the radiation (UCS)?

To test their hunch, Garcia and Koelling gave the rats a particular taste, sight, or sound (CS) and later also gave them radiation or drugs (UCS) causing nausea (UCR). Two startling findings emerged: First, even if sickened as late as several hours after tasting a particular flavor, the rats thereafter avoided that flavor. This appeared to violate the notion that for conditioning to occur, the UCS must follow the CS immediately.

**John Garcia (1917– )** *As the laboring child of California farmworkers, Garcia's early schooling occurred in the off-season. After entering junior college in his late twenties, and earning his Ph.D. in his late forties, he received the American Psychological Association's Distinguished Scientific Contribution Award "for his highly original, pioneering research in conditioning and learning."*

Second, the sickened rats developed aversions to the tastes but not to the sights or sounds. This contradicted the behaviorists' idea that any perceivable stimulus could serve as a CS. But it made adaptive sense, because for rats the easiest way to identify tainted food is to taste it. Birds, which hunt by sight, appear biologically primed to develop aversions to the *sight* of tainted food (Nicolaus & others, 1983). Humans, too, seem biologically prepared to learn some things rather than others. We more readily learn to fear snakes and spiders than to fear flowers (Cook & others, 1986). It makes sense: Such animals harm us more frequently than do flowers. We learn an aversion to alcohol better by associating its taste with nausea than with something unrelated to consumption, such as electric shock.

All these cases support Darwin's principle that natural selection favors traits that aid survival. Nature prepares the members of each species to learn those things crucial to its survival. Someone who readily learns a taste aversion is unlikely to eat the same toxic food again and is more likely to survive and leave descendants. Indeed, all sorts of bad feelings, from nausea to anxiety to pain, serve good purposes. Like the low-oil light on a car dashboard, each alerts the body to a threat (Neese, 1991).

The philosopher Schopenhauer once said that important ideas are first ridiculed, then attacked, and finally taken for granted. So it was with Garcia's findings on taste aversion. At first, the leading journals refused to publish his work. The findings were impossible, said some critics. But as often happens in science, Garcia's provocative findings stimulated new research, which confirmed his surprising findings and extended them to other species. For example, when coyotes and wolves are tempted into eating sheep carcasses laced with a sickening poison, they develop an aversion to sheep meat (Gustavson & others, 1974, 1976). Two wolves later penned with a live sheep seemed actually to fear it. Such research suggests possible humane ways for controlling predators and agricultural pests. This is but one instance in which psychological research that began with the discomfort of some laboratory animals enhanced the welfare of many more animals. In this case it saved the sheep from the coyotes. The coyotes in turn were saved from angry ranchers and farmers who, with their livestock no longer endangered, were less adamant about destroying the coyotes.

*"Once bitten, twice shy."*
G. F. Northall
*Folk-Phrases*, 1894

Has research on biological constraints compelled researchers to abandon the search for universal principles of learning that generalize across species? No, biological predispositions affirm a deeper principle: *Learning enables animals to adapt to their environments.* Adaptation shows us why animals would be responsive to stimuli that announce significant events, such as food or pain. Animals are predisposed to associate a CS with a UCS that follows predictably and immediately—for causes often immediately precede effects.

Adaptation also helps explain exceptions, such as the taste-aversion finding. In this case, cause need not precede effect immediately—bad food usually causes sickness quite a while after it has been consumed. Similarly, cancer patients who suffer nausea and vomiting beginning more than an hour following chemotherapy often develop classically conditioned nausea to stimuli associated with taking the drug. The conditioned stimuli evoke a cognitive representation of the unconditioned stimulus and the associated nausea. Thus, merely returning to the clinic or seeing the nurses can provoke sick feelings (Burish & Carey, 1986; Davey, 1992).

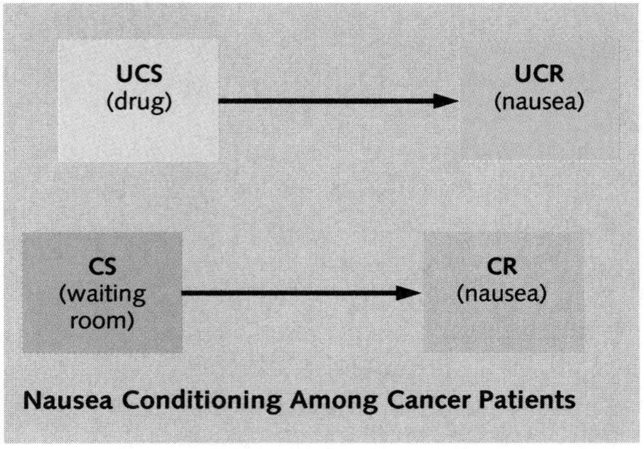

**Nausea Conditioning Among Cancer Patients**

## Pavlov's Legacy

What, then, remains of Pavlov's ideas about conditioning? A great deal. All the researchers we have met so far in this chapter agree that classical conditioning is a basic form of learning. Judged by today's knowledge of cognitive processes and biological predispositions, Pavlov's ideas were incomplete. But if we see further than Pavlov did, it is because we stand on his shoulders.

Why is Pavlov's work so important? If he had taught us only that old dogs can learn new tricks, his experiments would have long ago been forgotten. Why should anyone care that a dog can be conditioned to drool at the sound of a tone? The importance lies first in this fact: Many other responses to many other stimuli can be classically conditioned in many other organisms—in fact, in every species tested, from earthworms to fish to dogs to monkeys to people (Schwartz, 1984). Thus, classical conditioning is one way that virtually all organisms learn to adapt to their environment.

Second, Pavlov showed us how an internal process such as learning can be studied objectively. Pavlov was proud that his methods involved virtually no subjective judgments or guesses about what went on in the dogs' minds. The salivary response is an overt behavior measurable as so many drops or cubic centimeters of saliva. Pavlov's success therefore suggested a scientific model for how the young discipline of psychology might proceed—by isolating the elementary building blocks of complex behaviors and studying them with objective laboratory procedures.

**John B. Watson** *In 1924, Watson admitted to "going beyond my facts" when offering his famous boast: "Give me a dozen healthy infants, well-formed, and my own specified world to bring them up in and I'll guarantee to take any one at random and train him to become any type of specialist I might select—doctor, lawyer, artist, merchant-chief, and, yes, even beggar-man and thief, regardless of his talents, penchants, tendencies, abilities, vocations, and race of his ancestors."*

### Applications of Classical Conditioning

In later chapters on motivation, emotion, psychological disorders, therapy, and health, we will see how Pavlov's principles of classical conditioning apply to human health and well-being. For example, former crack cocaine users often feel a craving when they again encounter cues (people, places) associated with previous highs. Thus, drug counselors advise addicts to steer clear of settings associated with the euphoria of previous drug use. And alcoholics are given experiences that reverse their associations with alcohol (page 549). Classical conditioning even works on the body's disease-fighting immune system. When, say, a particular taste accompanies a drug that influences immune responses, the taste by itself may come to produce an immune response (page 588).

Pavlov's work provided a basis for John Watson's idea that human behavior, though biologically influenced, is also a bundle of conditioned responses. In one famous though ethically troublesome study, Watson and Rosalie Rayner (1920; Harris, 1979) showed how specific fears might be conditioned. Their subject was an 11-month-old infant named Albert. Like most infants, "Little Albert" feared loud noises but not white rats. Watson and Rayner presented him with a white rat and, as he reached to touch it, struck a hammer against a steel bar just behind his head. After seven repetitions of seeing the rat and then hearing the frightening noise, Albert burst into tears at the mere sight of the rat. What is more, 5 days later Albert showed generalization of his conditioned response by reacting with fear when presented with a rabbit, a dog, and a sealskin coat, but not to dissimilar objects such as toys.

Although Little Albert's fate is unknown, Watson's is not. After losing his professorship at Johns Hopkins University over an affair with Rayner (whom he later married), he became the J. Walter Thompson advertising agency's resident psychologist. There he used his knowledge of associative learning to conceive many successful campaigns, including one for Maxwell House that helped make the "coffee break" an American custom (Hunt, 1993).

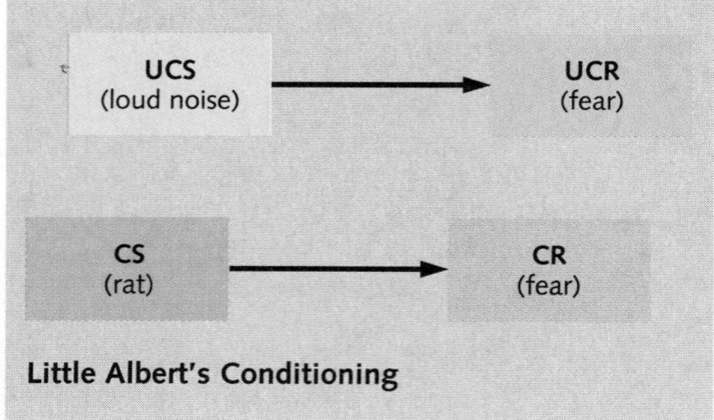


**Little Albert's Conditioning**

Although some psychologists had difficulty repeating Watson and Rayner's findings with other children, the work with Little Albert has had legendary significance for many psychologists. Some have wondered if each of us might not be a walking repository of conditioned emotions. Might our less adaptive emotions be controlled by the application of extinction procedures or by conditioning new responses to emotion-arousing stimuli? One therapist told a patient, who for 30 years had feared going into an elevator alone, to force himself to enter 20 elevators a day. Within 10 days, his fear nearly vanished (Ellis & Becker, 1982). In Chapter 16, Therapy, we will see more examples of how psychologists use behavioral techniques to treat emotional disorders.

## Summing Up

Although learning by association had been discussed for centuries, it remained for Ivan Pavlov to capture the phenomenon in his classic experiments on conditioning.

**Pavlov's Experiments** Pavlov repeatedly presented a neutral stimulus (such as a tone) just before an unconditioned stimulus (UCS, food) triggered an unconditioned response (UCS, salivation). After several repetitions, the tone alone (now the conditioned stimulus, CS) began triggering a

## Close-Up Rape as Classical Conditioning

"A burnt child dreads the fire," says a medieval proverb. Experiments with dogs reveal that, indeed, if a painful stimulus is sufficiently powerful, a single event is sometimes enough to traumatize the animal when it again faces the situation. The human counterparts to these experiments can be tragic, as illustrated by one woman's experience of being attacked and raped, and thereby conditioned to a life of fear. Her fear (CR) is most powerfully associated with particular locations and people (CS), but it generalizes to other places and people. Note, too, how her traumatic experience has robbed her of the normally relaxing associations with such stimuli as home and bed.

> Four months ago I was raped. In the middle of the night I awoke to the sound of someone outside my bedroom. Thinking my housemate was coming home, I called out her name. Someone began walking slowly toward me, and then I realized. I screamed and fought, but there were two of them. One held my legs, while the other put a hand over my mouth and a knife to my throat and said, "Shut up, bitch, or we'll kill you." Never have I been so terrified and helpless. They both raped me, one brutally. As they then searched my room for money and valuables, my housemate came home. They brought her into my room, raped her, and left us both tied up on my bed.
>
> We never slept another night in that apartment. We were too terrified. Still, when I go to bed at night—always with the bedroom light left on—the memory of them entering my room repeats itself endlessly. I was an independent person who had lived alone or with other women for 4 years; now I can't even think about spending a night alone. When I drive by our old apartment, or when I have to go into an empty house, my heart pounds and I sweat. I am afraid of strangers, especially men, and the more they resemble my attackers the more I fear them. My housemate shares many of my fears, and is frightened when entering our new apartment. I'm afraid to stay in the same town, I'm afraid it will happen again, I'm afraid to go to bed. I dread falling asleep.

Eleven years later this woman could report that her conditioned fears are gradually extinguishing:

> The frequency and intensity of my fears have subsided. Still, I remain cautious about personal safety and occasionally have nightmares about my experience. But more important is my renewed ability to laugh, love, and trust—both old friends and new. Life is once again joyful. I have survived. (From personal correspondence, with permission.)

conditioned response (CR, salivation). Further experiments on acquisition revealed that classical conditioning was usually greatest when the CS was presented just before the UCS, thus preparing the organism for what was coming. Other experiments explored the phenomena of extinction, spontaneous recovery, generalization, and discrimination.

Pavlov's work laid a foundation for John B. Watson's emerging belief that, to be an objective science, psychology should study only overt behavior, without considering unobservable mental activity. Watson called this position *behaviorism.*

*In Watson and Rayner's experiment, what was the UCS? The UCR? The CS? The CR? (See page 268.)*

**Updating Pavlov's Understanding** The behaviorists' optimism that learning principles would generalize from one response to another and from one species to another has been tempered. Conditioning principles, we now know, are cognitively and biologically constrained. In classical conditioning, animals learn when to "expect" an unconditioned stimulus. Moreover, rats are biologically prepared to learn associations between a peculiar taste and a sickness-producing drink, which they will then avoid. But they don't learn to avoid a sickening drink announced by a noise.

*Psychologist Gregory Razran (1940) found that associating political slogans (a CS) with the eating of food (a UCS) made people more approving of them. Similarly, advertisers like to associate their products with naturally pleasing images, such as a sexually appealing model.*

**Pavlov's Legacy** Pavlov taught us that principles of learning apply across species, that significant psychological phenomena can be studied objectively, and that conditioning principles have important practical applications.

## Operant Conditioning

*Through classical (Pavlovian) conditioning, an organism associates different stimuli that it does not control. Through operant conditioning, the organism associates its behaviors with consequences. Behaviors followed by reinforcers increase; those followed by punishment decrease. This simple but powerful principle has many applications, but also several important qualifications.*

*Answer to question on page 267: The UCS was the loud noise; the UCR was the startled fear response; the CS was the rat; the CR was fear.*

Classical conditioning associates neutral stimuli with important stimuli that produce responses which often are automatic, involving the autonomic nervous system. It's one thing to teach an animal to salivate at the sound of a tone or a child to fear cars in the street. It's quite another to teach an elephant to walk on its hind legs or a child to say please. Another type of associative learning explains—and trains—such behaviors. Through **operant conditioning** subjects associate behaviors with their consequences. Thus, they become more likely to repeat rewarded (reinforced) behaviors and less likely to repeat punished behaviors.

**DENNIS THE MENACE**

*"I think Mom's using the can opener."*

DENNIS THE MENACE ® used by permission of Hank Ketcham and © by North America Syndicate.

**The Law of Effect** *Having previously been rewarded when running to the food dish at the sound of the can opener, the dog's behavior recurs.*

***Respondent behavior*** *responds to stimuli.*

***Operant behavior*** *operates to produce stimuli.*

Classical and operant conditioning both involve acquisition, extinction, spontaneous recovery, generalization, and discrimination. Yet their difference is straightforward: Classical conditioning cognitively associates stimuli (a CS and the UCS it signals). It also involves **respondent behavior**—behavior that occurs as an automatic *response* to some stimulus (such as salivating in response to meat powder and later in response to tone). Operant conditioning involves **operant behavior**, so-called because the act *operates* on the environment to produce rewarding or punishing stimuli. It therefore associates an action with a resulting stimulus. We can therefore distinguish classical from operant conditioning by asking: *Is the organism learning associations between events that it doesn't control (classical conditioning)? Or is it learning associations between its behavior and resulting events (operant conditioning)?*

## Skinner's Experiments

B. F. Skinner (1904–1990) was a college English major and aspiring writer who, seeking a new direction, entered graduate school in psychology and went on to become modern behaviorism's most influential and controversial figure. Skinner's work elaborated a simple fact of life that turn-of-the-century psychologist Edward L. Thorndike called the *law of effect*: Rewarded behavior is likely to recur. Using Thorndike's law of effect as a starting point, Skinner developed a "behavioral technology" that enabled him to teach pigeons such unpigeonlike behaviors as walking in a figure 8, playing Ping-Pong, and keeping a guided missile on course by pecking at a moving target displayed on a screen.

For his pioneering studies with rats and later with pigeons, Skinner designed the now famous **Skinner box** (Figure 8–5). The box is typically a soundproof chamber with a bar or key that an animal presses or pecks to release a food or water reward, and with a device that records these responses. Experiments by Skinner and other operant researchers did far more than teach us how to pull habits out of a rat. They explored the precise conditions that foster efficient and enduring learning.

**Figure 8–5**

**A Skinner Box** *Inside the box, the rat presses a bar for a food reward. Outside, a measuring device records the animal's accumulated responses.*

### Shaping

In his experiments, Skinner used **shaping**, a procedure in which rewards, such as food, gradually guide an animal's behavior toward a desired behavior. Imagine that you wanted to condition a rat to press a bar. After observing how the animal naturally behaves before training, you would build on its existing behaviors. You might give the rat a food reward each time it approaches the bar. Once the rat is approaching regularly, you would require it to move closer before rewarding it; then closer still, and finally to touch the bar before giving it the food. With this method of *successive approximations*, you reward responses that are ever-closer to the final desired behavior and ignore all other responses. In this way, researchers and animal trainers gradually shape complex behaviors.

By shaping nonverbal organisms to discriminate between stimuli, a psychologist can also determine what they perceive. Can a dog distinguish colors? Can a baby discriminate sounds? If we can shape them to respond to one stimulus and not to another, then obviously they can perceive the difference. Experiments show that some animals are remarkably capable of forming concepts; they demonstrate this by discriminating between classes of events or objects (Hackenberg & Hineline, 1990). If an experimenter reinforces a pigeon for pecking after seeing a human face, but not after seeing other images, the pigeon will learn to recognize faces (Herrnstein & Loveland, 1964). After being trained to discriminate among flowers, people, cars, and chairs, pigeons can usually identify in which of these categories a new pictured object belongs (Bhatt & others, 1988; Wasserman, 1993). With training, pigeons have even been taught to discriminate between Bach's music and Stravinsky's (Porter & Neuringer, 1984).

**A Discriminating Creature** *University of Windsor psychologist Dale Woodyard uses a food reward to train this manatee to discriminate between objects of different shapes, colors, and sizes. A manatee can remember such responses for as long as a year.*

Parents may use rewards to shape good table manners by praising eating behavior that is more and more adultlike. This sounds simple, but let's compare the essential features of shaping to what often happens at home and at school. In the shaping procedure, the trainer builds on the individual's existing behaviors by expecting and immediately rewarding successively closer approximations of a desired behavior. In everyday life, too, we continually reward and shape the behavior of others, said Skinner, but we often do so unintentionally. Sometimes we even reward offensive behavior.

Billy's whining annoys his mystified parents. But look how they typically deal with Billy—by rewarding the very behavior they find so annoying:

**Billy:** *Could you tie my shoes?*

**Father:** *(Continues reading paper.)*

**Billy:** *Dad, I need my shoes tied.*

**Father:** *Uh, yeah, just a minute.*

**Billy:** *DAAAAD! TIE MY SHOES!*

**Father:** *How many times have I told you not to whine? Now, which shoe do we do first?*

**HI AND LOIS**

Reprinted with special permission of King Features Syndicate.

Or compare the way psychologists shape behavior—by rewarding small improvements—to the way some teachers use rewards. On a wall chart, the teacher pastes gold stars after the names of children scoring 100 percent on spelling tests. All children take the same tests. As everyone can then see, some children, the academic all-stars, easily get 100 percent. The others, no matter how hard they try or how much they improve, get no reward. The teacher would be better advised to reward poor spellers for gradual improvement (successive approximations toward their potential) or for doing their best.

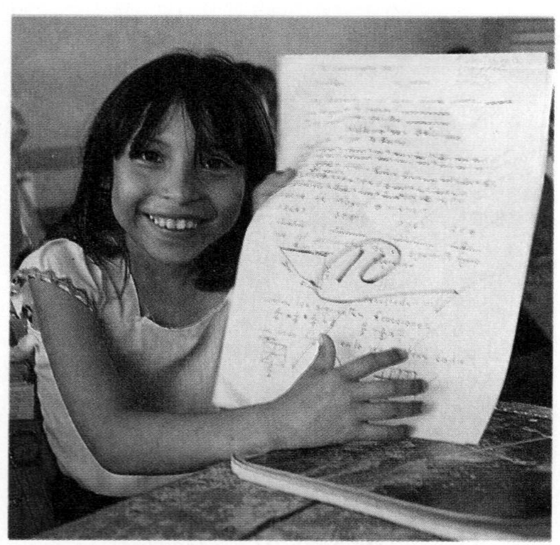

**Positive Reinforcement** *The good score has positively reinforced this young girl for her hard work in school. Its "arrival" increases the likelihood that she will continue to study hard. Praise from her parents may further reinforce her good study habits.*

## Principles of Reinforcement

So far, we have referred rather loosely to the power of "rewards." This idea gains a more precise meaning in Skinner's concept of the **reinforcer**, any event that increases the frequency of a preceding response. A reinforcer may be a tangible reward. It may be praise or attention. Or it may be an activity—being able to use the car when the dishes are done or to have recess after an hour of study (Timberlake & Farmer-Dougan, 1991).

Although most people think of reinforcers as rewards, there actually are two kinds of reinforcers. One type (positive reinforcer) strengthens a response by presenting a positive stimulus after a response. Food is a positive reinforcer for animals; attention, approval, and money are positive reinforcers for most people. The other type (negative reinforcer) strengthens a response by reducing or removing an aversive (unpleasant) stimulus. Imagine that alien invaders put you in an electrified cage, but that you could reduce or remove the electric shock by pressing a bar. You would surely press the bar, and feel (negatively) reinforced for doing so. When a barely awake person pushes the snooze button, the silencing of the annoying alarm is similarly a reinforcer. When someone stops nagging or whining, that, too, is a reinforcer. (Note that contrary to popular usage, a negative reinforcer is not a punishing event; it is the *removal* of a punishing event.)

So imagine that whenever a child throws a tantrum, the parent gives in for the sake of peace and quiet. The child's tantrums will be reinforced when the parent gives in. And the parent's behavior will be reinforced when the child stops screaming. Or imagine a worried student who, after goofing off and getting a bad exam grade, studies harder for the next exam. The student may be reinforced by reduced anxiety and by a better grade. Whether it works by giving something positive or by reducing something negative, *a reinforcer always strengthens behavior*.

**Primary and Secondary Reinforcers** **Primary reinforcers**—getting food or being relieved of shock—are innately satisfying. We need not learn to like them. **Secondary reinforcers** are learned. They get their power through association with primary reinforcers. If a rat in a Skinner box learns that a light reliably signals that food is coming, the rat will work to turn on the light. The light has become a secondary reinforcer associated with food. Our lives are filled with secondary reinforcers—money, good grades, a pleasant tone of voice, a word of praise—each of which has been linked with more basic rewards. Secondary reinforcers greatly enhance our ability to influence one another.

**Immediate and Delayed Reinforcers** Consider a typical shaping experiment. Before performing a "wanted" behavior such as pressing the bar, an animal will engage in a sequence of "unwanted" behaviors—scratching, sniffing, and moving around. Whichever of these behaviors immediately precedes the reinforcer becomes more likely to recur. If we delay the reinforcer for bar pressing for as long as 30 seconds, allowing other behaviors to intervene and be reinforced, virtually no learning of the bar pressing occurs.

Humans, though, do respond to reinforcers that are greatly delayed: the paycheck at the end of the week, the grade at the end of the semester, the trophy at the end of the season. Indeed, to function effectively we must learn to postpone immediate rewards for greater long-term rewards. Four-year-old children who in laboratory testing show an ability to delay gratification—who'd sooner have a big reward tomorrow than a small one right now—become more socially competent and more likely to be high achievers as adolescents (Mischel & others, 1989).

The immediacy of reinforcement does influence our behavior, however. Smokers, alcoholics, and other drug users may know that their immediate pleasure—the kick that often comes within seconds—is more than offset by future ill effects. Still, immediate reinforcement prevails. Indeed, drugs such as nicotine and cocaine that provide the most immediate reinforcement are the most strongly addictive (Marlatt, 1991). Likewise, for many teens the immediate gratification of risky, unprotected sex in passionate moments prevails over the delayed gratifications of safe sex or saved sex (Loewenstein & Furstenberg, 1991). And the hour-long enjoyment of staying up to watch another TV show may seem to outweigh the prospect of tomorrow's day-long sluggishness. To our detriment, small but immediate reinforcements are sometimes more alluring than big but delayed reinforcements.

*"Oh, not bad. The light comes on, I press the bar, they write me a check. How about you?"*

Drawing by Cheney; © 1993 The New Yorker Magazine, Inc.

**Reinforcement Schedules** So far, most of our examples assume **continuous reinforcement**: The desired response is reinforced every time it occurs. Under such conditions, learning occurs rapidly. But when the reinforcement stops—when we disconnect the food delivery chute—extinction also occurs rapidly. The rat soon stops pressing the bar. If a normally dependable candy machine fails to deliver a candy bar twice in a row, we stop putting money into it (although a week later we may exhibit spontaneous recovery by trying again).

In real life, continuous reinforcement is rare. A salesperson does not make a sale with every pitch, nor does an angler get a bite with every cast. But they persist because their efforts have occasionally been rewarded. Researchers have explored several **partial reinforcement** schedules in which responses are sometimes reinforced, sometimes not (Nevin, 1988). Initial learning is typically slower with partial reinforcement, which makes continuous reinforcement preferable until a behavior is mastered. But partial reinforcement produces greater persistence—greater *resistance to extinction*—than is found with continuous reinforcement. Imagine a pigeon that has learned to peck a key to obtain food. When the experimenter gradually fades out the delivery of food until it occurs only rarely and unpredictably, pigeons may peck 150,000 times without a reward (Skinner, 1953). With partial reinforcement, hope springs eternal.

*"The charm of fishing is that it is the pursuit of what is elusive but attainable, a perpetual series of occasions for hope."*

Scottish author John Buchan, 1875–1940

Corresponding human examples come readily to mind. Slot machines reward gamblers occasionally and unpredictably. This partial reinforcement affects them much as it affects pigeons: They keep trying, sometimes interminably. There is also a valuable lesson here for parents. *Occasionally* giving in to children's tantrums for the sake of peace and quiet puts the child on a partial reinforcement schedule. That's the very best procedure for making a behavior persist.

Skinner (1961) and his collaborators compared four schedules of partial reinforcement. Some are rigidly fixed, some unpredictably variable.

**Fixed-ratio schedules** reinforce behavior after a set number of responses. Like people paid on a piecework basis—say, for every 30 pieces—laboratory animals may be reinforced on a fixed ratio of, say, one reinforcer for every 30 responses. Once conditioned, the animal will pause only briefly after a reinforcer and will then return to a high rate of responding (Figure 8–6). Because resting while on a fixed-ratio schedule reduces re-

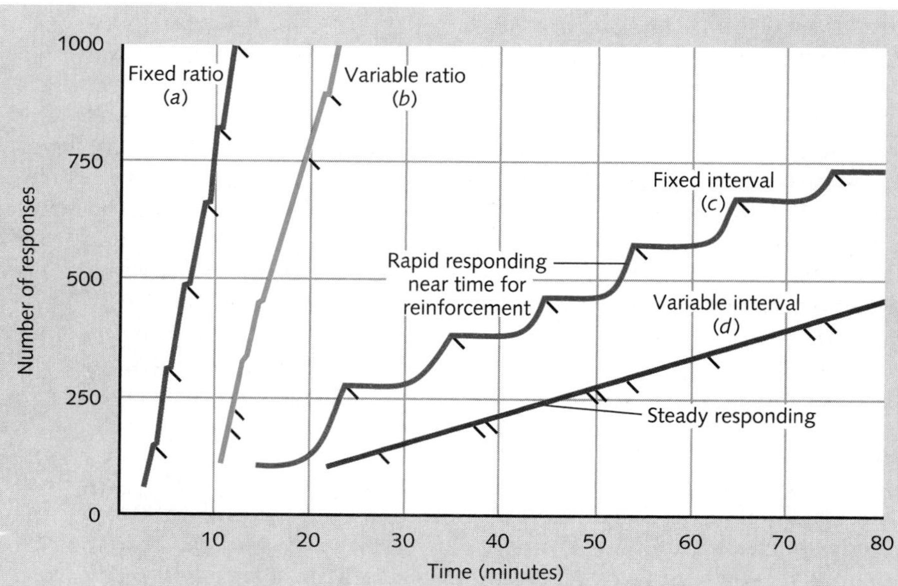


**Figure 8–6**

**Partial Reinforcement Schedules** *Skinner's laboratory pigeons produced these response patterns to each of four reinforcement schedules. For people as for pigeons, reinforcers (diagonal marks on the graph) linked to responses—whether to a fixed number (a) or a variable number (b)—produce higher response rates. Reinforcers linked to time intervals—either fixed (c) or variable (d)—produce lower response rates than reinforcers linked to either (a) or (b). Fixed schedules produce higher response rates than the related variable schedules. (Adapted from "Teaching Machines" by B.F. Skinner. Copyright © 1961 Scientific American, Inc. All rights reserved.)*

wards, employees often find such arrangements tiring. Unions have therefore pressured employers to replace piecework pay with hourly wage schedules.

**Variable-ratio schedules** provide reinforcers after an unpredictable number of responses. This is what gamblers and fly casters experience—unpredictable reinforcement—and what makes gambling and fishing behavior so hard to extinguish. Like the fixed-ratio schedule, it produces high rates of responding, because reinforcers increase as the responding increases.

**Fixed-interval schedules** provide an equal pause after each reinforcer. During this time no reinforcers are available. When the fixed interval ends, the next response is reinforced. Like people checking more frequently for the mail as the delivery time approaches, pigeons on a fixed-interval schedule peck a key more frequently as the anticipated time for reward draws near, producing a choppy stop-start pattern.

**Variable-interval schedules** reinforce the first response after *varying* time intervals. Like the unpredictable pop quiz that reinforces studying or the "hello" that finally rewards persistence in redialing a busy phone number, variable-interval schedules tend to produce slow, steady responding. This makes sense, because there is no knowing when the waiting will be over. Should the pop quiz become predictable, students will begin the stop-start work pattern that characterizes fixed-interval schedules.

*Question: Airline frequent-flyer programs that offer a free flight after every 20,000 miles of travel use which reinforcement schedule? Door-to-door sales people are reinforced by which schedule? (See page 274.)*

Animal behaviors differ, yet Skinner (1956) contended that these reinforcement principles of operant conditioning are universal. It matters little, he said, what response, what reinforcer, or what species you use. The effect of a given reinforcement schedule is pretty much the same: "Pigeon, rat, monkey, which is which? It doesn't matter. . . . Behavior shows astonishingly similar properties."

### Punishment

The effect of **punishment** is opposite that of reinforcement. Reinforcement increases a behavior; punishment decreases it. Thus, a punisher is an aversive consequence that *decreases* the frequency of a preceding behavior. Swift and sure punishers can powerfully restrain unwanted behavior. The dog that learns to come running at the sound of the electric can opener will learn to hide if its master starts using the can opener to catch it and banish it to the basement. The rat that is shocked after touching the forbidden object and the child who loses a treat after running into the street will learn not to repeat the behavior.

Nevertheless, punishment has drawbacks. As powerful as punishment can be, punished behavior is not forgotten; it is suppressed. This temporary suppression may reinforce the people who do the punishing. But if the punishment is avoidable, the punished behavior may reappear in safe settings. The child who learns through spankings not to swear around the house may swear elsewhere. The driver who is hit with a couple of speeding tickets may buy a radar detector and speed freely when no radar patrol is around.

Opponents of punishment also say that it increases aggressiveness by demonstrating that aggression is a way to cope with problems. This helps explain why so many aggressive delinquents and abusive parents come from abusive families (Straus & Gelles, 1980). Moreover, punishment can create fear; the person receiving the punishment may associate the fear not only with the undesirable behavior but also with the person who administers it or with the situation in which it occurs. Thus, a child may come to fear the punitive teacher and want to avoid school. Worse, when punishments are unpredictable and inescapable, both animals and people may de-

**The Problem With Punishment** *Swift and sure punishment can decrease unwanted behavior, but it can also evoke undesired responses, such as anger, fear, or resistance.*

velop the sense that events are beyond their control. As a result, they may come to feel helpless and depressed. For these reasons, most European countries have banned hitting children in schools and child care institutions (Leach, 1993, 1994). The Scandinavian countries and Austria have further outlawed physical punishment by parents (thus extending to children the same legal protection given to spouses).

Even when punishment suppresses unwanted behavior, it often does not guide one toward more desirable behavior. Punishment tells you what *not* to do; reinforcement tells you what *to* do. (Children more easily understand positive instructions than negative ones—see page 93.) Thus, punishment combined with reinforcement is usually more effective than punishment alone. This approach has been used with children who bite themselves or bang their heads. They may be mildly punished (say, with a squirt of water in the face) whenever they bite themselves, while also rewarded with positive attention and food when behaving well. The approach also works in the classroom. The teacher whose feedback on a paper says, "No, but try this . . . " and "Yes, that's it!" reduces unwanted behavior by reinforcing alternative behaviors.

To sum up, swift and sure punishment can be effective, and it may on occasion cause less pain than does the self-destructive behavior it suppresses. However, punished behavior may reappear if the threatened punishment can be avoided. (What punishment often teaches, said Skinner, is how to avoid it.) Punishment can also have undesirable side effects, such as creating fear and teaching aggression, and it often fails to teach how to act positively. Thus, like Skinner, most psychologists favor an emphasis on reinforcement rather than punishment. Catch people doing something right and affirm them for it.

*Answer to question on page 273: Frequent-flyer programs use a fixed-ratio schedule. Door-to-door sales people are reinforced on a variable ratio schedule (after varying numbers of rings).*

Parents of delinquent youth often lack this awareness of how to reinforce desirable behavior without screaming or hitting (Patterson & others, 1982). Training programs for such parents help them reframe contingencies from dire threats to positive incentives—from "You clean up your room this minute or no dinner!" to "You're welcome at the dinner table after you get the room cleaned up." When you stop to think about it, many threats of punishment are just as forceful, and perhaps more effective, if rephrased positively. Thus, "If you don't get your homework done, there'll be no TV" would better be phrased as. . .

## Updating Skinner's Understanding

Although Skinner granted both the existence of mental processes and the biological underpinnings of behavior, many psychologists criticized him for discounting the importance of these factors.

## Thinking Critically About Applying Research—Does Arrest Deter Repeated Domestic Violence?

If swift and sure punishment can inhibit unwanted behavior, would swift arrest of abusive husbands and boyfriends deter repeated abuse? To find out, Lawrence Sherman and Richard Berk (1984) enlisted the cooperation of the Minneapolis Police Department. In response to complaints of abuse, they randomly assigned officers either to arrest or not to arrest the offender. (Those not arrested were either offered advice or told to leave the premises for 8 hours.) Police records revealed that in the next 6 months about 20 percent of those not arrested were repeat offenders, compared with only 10 percent of those arrested.

Reflecting on their soon-to-be-publicized results, Sherman and Berk questioned the laws of 22 states that prohibited warrantless arrest in misdemeanor domestic violence cases. But they also cautioned that it would be "premature" for legislatures, based on their single experiment, to pass new laws that *required* arrest. Rather, they advised *replicating* the study with larger samples in other cities.

Ignoring this caution, big-city police departments, impressed by their finding, reversed their arrest policies. In the ensuing 5 years the percentage of departments encouraging or requiring their officers to make immediate arrests in domestic violence cases mushroomed—from 10 percent to 84 percent (Sherman, 1992).

Meanwhile, researchers, including Sherman and Berk, were doing the painstaking work of repeating the experiment in five cities. The results were a wash. In Miami and Colorado Springs, as in Minneapolis, repeated violence was less likely among those arrested. But in Milwaukee, Omaha, and Charlotte, repeated violence was less likely among those *not* arrested. The only consistent finding, reports Sherman (1992), was an interaction between arrest and employment: Employed offenders less often repeated their violence if arrested, while unemployed offenders less often repeated their violence if not arrested.

From this unfinished story, we can draw several lessons:

***Much as we might wish for simple results, the social world is complex.*** Often, the effect of one variable (arrest) depends on ("interacts with") another (employment status).

***The world is not dispassionately neutral.*** Sherman reports that the initial Minneapolis results supported the emerging get-tough-on-abusive-spouses view. Thus, these results were uncritically publicized as a "breakthrough" and were quickly applied, whereas the failures to replicate were grudgingly accepted, ignored, or attacked. *The moral:* A study's impact may depend on whether its results support current opinion.

***Conflicting results motivate further research.*** Would the arrest effect be greater if custody lasted longer than the mere 2 to 24 hours, as in these studies? Could guidelines be developed as to what sorts of communities, and what sorts of offenders and victims, benefit most from get-tough arrest policies? Do police policies affect the rate of first offenses, too?

***To evaluate the reliability of a phenomenon in different contexts, replication is essential.*** Critical thinkers know that an experiment is a better basis for deciding what works than are mere anecdote and opinion. But they also know that repeating a provocative experiment under differing circumstances enables us to assess its applicability in a particular situation.

### Cognition and Operant Conditioning

A mere 8 days before dying of leukemia, Skinner (1990) stood before the American Psychological Association convention for one final blast at "cognitive science," which he viewed as a throwback to turn-of-the-century introspectionism. Skinner died resisting the growing belief that cognitive processes—thoughts, perceptions, expectations—have a necessary place in the science of psychology and even in our understanding of conditioning. Yet we have seen several hints that cognitive processes are at work in operant learning. For example, animals on a fixed-interval reinforcement schedule respond more and more frequently as the time approaches when a response will produce a reinforcer. The animals behave as if they expect that repeating the response will soon produce the reward.

*For more information on animal behavior, see books by (I'm not making this up) Robin Fox and Lionel Tiger.*

Drawing by Nurit; © 1985 The New Yorker Magazine, Inc.

**Latent Learning** Other evidence of cognitive processes comes from studies of rats in mazes. Rats exploring a maze, with no obvious reward, are like people driving around a new town. The rats develop a **cognitive map**, a mental representation of the maze. This occurs even if the rats are carried passively through the maze in a wire basket. When an experimenter then places a reward in the maze's goal box, the rats immediately perform as well as rats that have been reinforced with food for running the maze (Figure 8–7). During their explorations, the rats seemingly experience **latent learning**—learning that becomes apparent only when there is some incentive to demonstrate it. The unavoidable conclusion: Learning can occur without reinforcement. As the cognitive mapping experiments suggest, there is more to learning than associating a response with receiving a tangible consequence. There is also cognition. In Chapter 10, Thinking and Language, we will encounter striking evidence of animals' cognitive abilities in solving problems and using aspects of language.

**Figure 8–7**

**Latent Learning** *Animals, like people, can learn from experience, with or without reinforcement. After exploring a maze for 10 days, rats received a food reward at the end of the maze. They quickly demonstrated their prior learning of the maze—by immediately doing as well as (and even better than) rats that had been reinforced for running the maze. (From Tolman & Honzik, 1930.)*

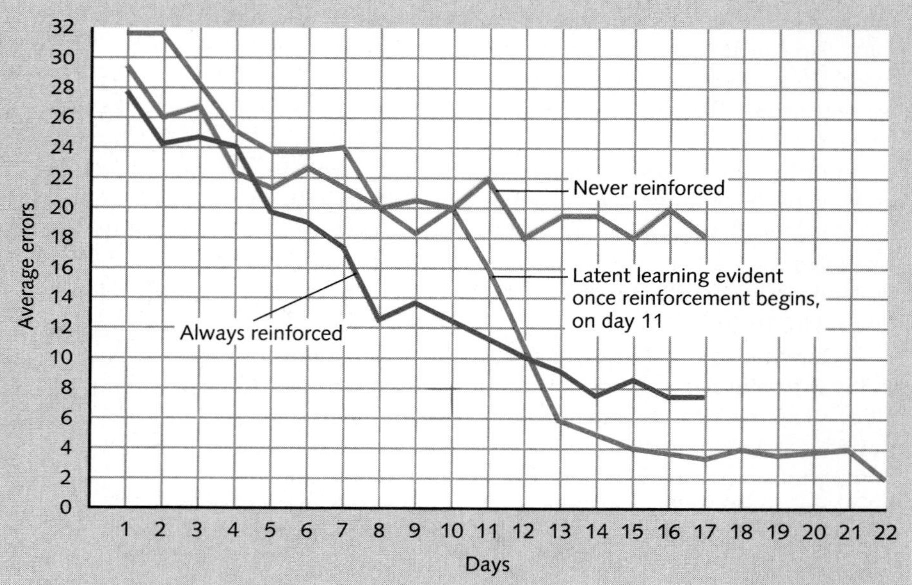


**Overjustification** The cognitive perspective has also led to an important qualification concerning the power of rewards: Unnecessary rewards carry hidden costs. Most people think that offering tangible rewards will boost anyone's interest in a task (Boggiano & others, 1987). Actually, promising children a reward for a task they already enjoy can backfire. People who begin to see the reward as their motive for performing the task may lose their intrinsic interest in it. This phenomenon is called the **overjustification effect**, because an already justifiable activity becomes *over*justified by the promise of added reward.

In experiments, children promised a payoff for playing with an interesting puzzle or toy later play with the toy less than do children who are not paid to play (Tang & Hall, 1994). It is as if the children think, "If I have to be bribed into doing this, then it must not be worth doing for its own sake."

*If a teacher offered candy each day to children who did their homework, how might this affect their natural eagerness to do schoolwork?*

Wendy Grolnick and Richard Ryan (1987) showed how overjustification can affect teaching and learning. They invited fifth graders to read a passage from a social studies book. Some they instructed in a controlling way: "I'll be grading you on the test to see if you're learning enough." Others, treated in a less controlling manner ("You won't be graded on [the questions]—I'm just interested in what children can remember"), learned as much *and found the passage more interesting*. Interest also survives when rewards are used not to bribe or control but to signal a job well done (Boggiano & others, 1985). If a reward boosts your feeling of competence after doing good work, your liking of the task may increase.

*Have you ever thought you'd enjoy learning more if you didn't have to do it for a grade?*

### Biological Predispositions

As with classical conditioning, an animal's natural predispositions constrain its capacity for operant conditioning. When you reinforce its behavior with food, you can easily condition a golden hamster to dig or to rear up, because these actions are among the animal's natural behaviors when searching for food. But it's much harder to use food reinforcers to shape hamster behaviors, such as face washing, that aren't normally associated with food or hunger (Shettleworth, 1973). Pigeons easily learn to flap their wings to avoid shock and to peck to obtain food, because they naturally flee with their wings and eat with their beaks. But they have a hard time learning to peck to avoid shock or to flap to obtain food. Biological constraints predispose organisms to learn associations that are naturally adaptive.

**A Natural Athlete** *Animals can most easily learn and retain behaviors that draw on their biological predispositions, such as a raccoon's inborn tendency to manipulate objects with its paws.*

Skinner's former associates, Keller Breland and Marian Breland (1961), came to appreciate biological predispositions while using operant procedures to train animals for circuses, TV shows, and movies. The Brelands had originally assumed that operant principles would work on almost any response that any animal could make. But after training 6000 animals of 38 different species, from chickens to whales, they concluded that biological predispositions were more important than they had supposed. In one act, they trained pigs to pick up large wooden "dollars" and deposit them in a piggy bank. After learning this behavior, however, the animals began to drift back to their natural ways. They would drop the coin, push it with their snouts as pigs are prone to do, pick it up again, and then repeat the sequence—delaying their food reinforcer. As this "instinctive drift" illustrates, "misbehaviors" occurred when the animals reverted to their biologically predisposed patterns.

*"Never try to teach a pig to sing. It wastes your time and annoys the pig."*

Mark Twain

## Skinner's Legacy

B. F. Skinner was one of the most controversial intellectual figures of our time. He stirred a hornet's nest by repeatedly insisting that external influences, not internal thoughts and feelings, shape behavior and by urging the use of operant principles to influence people's behavior at school, work, and home. To help or manage people effectively, Skinner said, we should worry less about their illusions of freedom and dignity. Recognizing that behavior is shaped by its consequences, we should administer rewards in ways that promote more desirable behavior.

Skinner's critics objected: They said he dehumanized people by neglecting their personal freedom and by seeking to control their actions. Skinner's reply: People's behavior is already haphazardly controlled by external consequences, so why not administer those consequences for human betterment? In place of the punishments used in homes, schools, and prisons, would not reinforcers be more humanitarian? And if it is humbling to think that we are shaped by our histories, this very idea also enables hope that we can shape our future.

**B. F. Skinner** *"I am sometimes asked, 'Do you think of yourself as you think of the organisms you study?' The answer is yes. So far as I know, my behavior at any given moment has been nothing more than the product of my genetic endowment, my personal history, and the current setting" (1983).*

## Applications of Operant Conditioning

We have seen applications of operant conditioning principles, and in later chapters we will see how psychologists apply these principles to problems ranging from high blood pressure to social withdrawal. Reinforcement technologies are also at work in schools, businesses, and homes.

**At School** A generation ago, Skinner and others advocated teaching machines and textbooks that would shape learning in small steps and provide immediate reinforcement for correct responses. These machines and texts, they said, would revolutionize education and free teachers to concentrate on their students' special needs.

To envision Skinner's dream, imagine two math teachers. Faced with a class of academically diverse students, Teacher *A* gives the whole class the same math lesson. The teacher knows that some students already understand the concepts and that others will be frustrated by their inability to comprehend. But with so many different children, how can one teacher guide them individually? When test time comes, the whiz kids breeze through unchallenged, and the slower learners again experience failure. Faced with a similar class, Teacher *B* paces the material according to each student's rate of learning and provides prompt feedback with positive reinforcement to slow and fast learners. Does the individualized instruction of Teacher *B* sound like an impossible ideal?

Although the predicted revolution has not occurred, to the end of his life Skinner (1986, 1988, 1989) believed the ideal was achievable. "Good instruction demands two things," he said. "Students must be told immediately whether what they do is right or wrong and, when right, they must be directed to the step to be taken next." To do this, and to free teachers for uniquely human tasks, computers were his final hope. For reading and math drills, the computer could be Teacher *B*—engaging the student actively, pacing material according to the student's rate of learning, quizzing the student to find gaps in understanding, providing immediate feedback, and keeping flawless records for the supervising teacher.

Experiments comparing computer-assisted instruction (CAI) to traditional classroom instruction suggest that, for some drill and practice tasks, the computer can indeed be more effective (Kulik & others, 1980, 1985). As microcomputers have become more widely available, so too have new techniques of CAI. A computer can effectively train students to type or play the piano, while tracking progress and providing positive reinforcements. Educational games and simulations can entice students to explore and discover principles on their own. Computer-driven laser disks can retrieve video segments that teach to a student's need.

Reinforcement principles can also enhance sports abilities. Again, the secret is to shape behavior. Start by reinforcing small successes, then gradually up the challenge. Thomas Simek and Richard O'Brien (1981, 1988) apply this to teaching golf and baseball by starting with responses that are easily reinforced. Golf students begin with very short putts. As they build mastery, they eventually step back farther and farther until taking full swings off the tee. Likewise, novice baseball players begin with half swings at an oversized ball pitched from 10 feet away, which immediately gives them the pleasure of smacking the ball. As their confidence builds with success and they achieve mastery at each level, the pitcher gradually moves back to 15 feet, then 22 feet, 30 feet, and 40.5 feet, and eventually introduces a regular ball. Compared to children taught by conventional methods, those trained by this behavioral method show faster skill improvement in both testing and game situations.

*"You mene I've bin spending this whol term with a defektiv reeding machin?"*

© 1992 by Sidney Harris.

**At Work** Believing that reinforcers influence productivity, business managers have capitalized on psychological research. Many companies now enable their employees to share profits, or even to participate in company ownership. When workers' productivity boosts rewards for all, their motivation, morale, and cooperative spirit often increase (Deutsch, 1991). Reinforcement for jobs well done is especially effective in boosting productivity when the desired performance is *well-defined and achievable*. Reward specific behaviors, not vaguely defined merit. Criticism, too, triggers the least resentment and the greatest performance boost when it is considerate and specific (Baron, 1988).

It's also a good idea to make the reinforcement *immediate*. Thomas Watson, who led IBM during its tremendous growth, would write out a check on the spot for achievements he observed (Peters & Waterman, 1982). But rewards need not be material, nor should they be so big that they become political and a source of discouragement to those who don't receive them. An effective manager may simply walk the floor and praise people for good work, or write unexpected notes of appreciation for a completed project. As Skinner said, "How much richer would the whole world be if the reinforcers in daily life were more effectively contingent on productive work?"

Drawing by Ziegler; © 1989 The New Yorker Magazine, Inc.

Animals, too, can be trained to perform useful work. Imagine a self-propelled marine vehicle with a sonar system and on-board computer suitable for detecting, classifying, and manipulating targets. That pretty well describes how the U.S. Navy once viewed its dolphins and sea lions, which at various times have been trained to perform salvage duties, serve as watch dogs around a submarine base, or seek out explosive mines in the Persian Gulf. The animals' training used food reinforcements to shape them toward ever-closer approximations of the desired behavior (Holing, 1988; Morrison, 1988).

**At Home** Many economists and psychologists view people's spending behavior as controlled by its consequences (its costs and benefits). Compared with people who rent apartments in buildings where energy costs are paid by the landlord, those who live in comparable buildings but pay their own energy costs (therefore reaping the rewards of their own energy savings) use about 20 percent less energy. Similarly, home electricity users on an "energy diet" are helped by frequent feedback that shows their current usage compared with their past consumption (Darley & others, 1979). In homes, as elsewhere, immediate consequences most effectively influence behavior. Al Gore (1992, p. 348) suggests how tax policies might harness the power of consequences:

> There is an economic rule of thumb: whatever we tax, we tend to get less of; whatever we subsidize, we tend to get more of. Currently, we tax work and we subsidize the depletion of natural resources—and both policies have contributed to high unemployment and the waste of natural resources. What if we lowered the tax on work and simultaneously raised it on the burning of fossil fuels?

We can also use operant conditioning on ourselves, by reinforcing our most desired behaviors and extinguishing those undesired. To take charge of your own behavior, psychologists suggest these step-by-step procedures:

1. State your goal—say, to stop smoking, eat less, or study or exercise more—in measurable terms, and make it public. You might, for example, aim to boost your study time by an hour a day. Announce your goal to friends.

2. Record how often you engage in the behavior you wish to promote and note how this behavior is being reinforced. You might log your current study time, noting under what conditions you do and don't study. (When I began writing textbooks, I logged my time and was astonished to discover how much time I was wasting.)
3. Begin systematically to reinforce the desired behavior. To increase your study time, allow yourself a snack (or some other reinforcing activity) only after specified periods of study. Agree with your friends that you will join them for weekend activities only if you have met your weekly studying goal.
4. As your new behaviors become more habitual, gradually reduce the incentives while giving yourself a mental pat on the back.

## Contrasting Conditioning Techniques

*"O! This learning, what a thing it is."*
William Shakespeare
*Taming of the Shrew*, 1597

The last three decades of research have changed psychologists' views of both classical and operant conditioning (summarized in Table 8–1). Learning, like so much else, depends on both nature and nurture. Biological predispositions make learning some associations easier than learning others. Animals exhibit more sophisticated cognitive processes than once seemed likely. And rewarding people to do what they already enjoy may undermine their interest.

**Table 8–1 Comparison of Classical and Operant Conditioning**

| | Classical Conditioning | Operant Conditioning |
|---|---|---|
| *Acquisition* | Associating events; CS announces UCS. | Associating response with a subsequent consequence (reinforcer or punisher). |
| *Extinction* | CR decreases when CS is repeatedly presented alone. | Responding decreases when reinforcement stops. |
| *Cognitive processes* | Subjects develop expectation that the CS signals the arrival of the UCS. | Subjects develop expectation that a response will be reinforced or punished; they also exhibit latent learning. |
| *Biological predispositions* | Natural predispositions constrain what stimuli and responses can easily be associated. | Organisms best learn behaviors similar to their natural behaviors; unnatural behaviors instinctively drift back toward natural ones. |

## Summing Up

Through operant conditioning, organisms learn to produce behaviors that are followed by reinforcement and to suppress behaviors that are followed by punishment.

**Skinner's Experiments** When placed in a Skinner box, rats or pigeons can be shaped to display successively closer approximations of a desired behavior. Researchers have also studied the effects of primary and secondary reinforcers, and of immediate and delayed reinforcers. Partial reinforcement schedules (fixed-ratio, variable-ratio, fixed-interval, and variable-interval) produce slower acquisition of the target behavior than does continuous reinforcement, but they also create more resistance to extinction. Punishment is most effective when it is strong, immediate, and consistent. However, it can have undesirable side effects.

**Updating Skinner's Understanding** Skinner's emphasis on external control of behavior made him an influential but controversial figure. Many psychologists criticized Skinner (as they did Pavlov) for underestimating the importance of cognitive and biological constraints. For example, research on latent learning and overjustification further indicates the importance of cognition in learning.

**Skinner's Legacy** Skinner stimulated vigorous intellectual debate regarding the nature of human freedom and strategies and ethics of managing people. Nevertheless, his operant principles are being applied in schools, businesses, and homes. For example, computer-assisted instruction can embody the operant ideal of individualized shaping and immediate positive reinforcement.

## Learning by Observation

*Learning occurs not only through conditioning but also from our observations of others. Lord Chesterfield (1694–1773) had the idea: "We are, in truth, more than half what we are by imitation."*

From drooling dogs, running rats, and pecking pigeons we have learned much about the basic processes of learning. But conditioning principles alone do not tell us the whole story. Among higher animals, especially humans, learning need not occur through direct experience. **Observational learning**, in which we observe and imitate others' behaviors, also plays a big part.

The process of observing and imitating a specific behavior is often called **modeling**. By observing and imitating models we learn all kinds of social behaviors. By 9 months of age, infants will imitate novel play behaviors, and by age 14 months will imitate acts modeled on television (Meltzoff, 1988a,b,c). To persuade children to smoke, expose them to parents and older youth who smoke. To encourage children to read, read to them and surround them with books and people who read them. To increase the odds of your children practicing your religion, worship and attend other religious activities with them.

*"Children need models more than they need critics."*
Joseph Joubert
*Pensées*, 1842

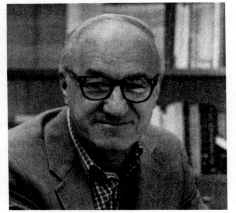

### Bandura's Experiments

Picture this scene from a famous experiment devised by Albert Bandura, the pioneering researcher of observational learning (Bandura & others, 1961). A nursery school child is at work on a picture. An adult in another part of the room is working with some Tinker Toys. The adult then gets up and for nearly 10 minutes pounds, kicks, and throws a large inflated Bobo doll around the room, while yelling such remarks as, "Sock him in the nose. . . . Hit him down. . . . Kick him."

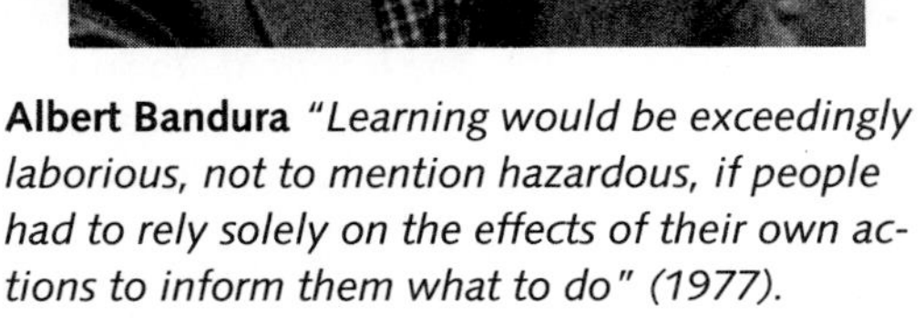

**Albert Bandura** *"Learning would be exceedingly laborious, not to mention hazardous, if people had to rely solely on the effects of their own actions to inform them what to do" (1977).*

**Learning From Observation** *This 14-month-old boy in Andrew Meltzoff's laboratory is imitating behavior he has seen on TV. In the top photo the infant leans forward and carefully watches the adult pull apart a novel toy. In the middle photo he has been given the toy. In the bottom photo he pulls the toy apart, imitating what he has seen the adult do.*

After observing this outburst, the child is taken to another room where there are many appealing toys. Soon the experimenter interrupts the child's play and explains that she has decided to save these good toys "for the other children." She now takes the frustrated child to an adjacent room containing a few toys, including a Bobo doll. Left alone, what does the child do?

Compared with children not exposed to the adult model, children who observed the aggressive outburst were much more likely to lash out at the doll. Apparently, observing the adult model beating up the doll lowered their inhibitions. But something more than lowered inhibitions is at work, for the children also imitated the very acts and used the identical words they had observed.

## Applications of Observational Learning

The bad news from such studies is that antisocial models—in one's family, neighborhood, or on TV—may have antisocial effects (pages 634–640). This helps us understand how abusive parents might have aggressive children and why men who batter their wives often had wife-battering fathers. The lessons we learn as children are not easily unlearned as adults, and they are sometimes visited on future generations.

The good news is that **prosocial** (positive, helpful) models can have prosocial effects. People who exemplify nonviolent, helpful behavior can prompt similar behavior in others. Mahatma Gandhi and Martin Luther King, Jr., both drew on the power of modeling, making nonviolent action a powerful force for social change. Parents are powerful models. European Christians who risked their lives to rescue Jews from the Nazis and civil rights activists of a generation ago usually had a close relationship with at least one parent who modeled a strong moral or humanitarian concern (London, 1970; Oliner & Oliner, 1988).

Models are most effective when their actions and words are consistent. Sometimes, however, models say one thing and do another. Many parents seem to operate according to the principle "Do as I *say*, not as I do." Experiments suggest that children learn to do both (Rice & Grusec, 1975; Rushton, 1975). When exposed to a hypocrite, they tend to imitate the hypocrisy by doing what the model did and saying what the model said.

What determines whether we will imitate a model? Bandura believes part of the answer is reinforcements and punishments—those received by the model as well as by the imitator. We look and we learn. By looking, we learn to anticipate a behavior's consequences in situations like those we are observing. By watching TV programs, children may "learn" that physical intimidation is an effective way to control others, that free and easy sex brings pleasure without the misery of unwanted pregnancy or disease, or that men are supposed to be tough and women gentle. We are especially likely to imitate those we respect and admire, those we perceive as similar to ourselves, and those we perceive as successful.

**A Model Grandma** *This boy is learning to cook by observing his grandmother. As the sixteenth-century proverb stated, "Example is better than precept."*

Although our knowledge of learning principles comes from the work of thousands of investigators, this chapter has focused on the ideas of a few pioneers—Pavlov, Watson, Skinner, and Bandura. They illustrate the impact that can result from single-minded devotion to a few well-defined problems and ideas. These researchers defined the issues and impressed on us the importance of learning. As their legacy demonstrates, intellectual history is often made by people who, at the risk of overstatement, pursue ideas to their limits.

## Summing Up

Another important type of learning, especially among humans, is what Albert Bandura and others call *observational learning*. In experiments, children tend to imitate both what a model does and says, whether the behavior is prosocial or antisocial. Such experiments have stimulated research on social modeling, in the home, on television, and within peer groups.

## Terms and Concepts to Remember

**learning** A relatively permanent change in an organism's behavior due to experience.

**associative learning** Learning that certain events occur together. The events may be two stimuli (as in classical conditioning) or a response and a rewarding or punishing stimulus (as in operant conditioning).

**behaviorism** The view that (1) psychology should be an objective science that (2) studies only overt behavior without reference to mental processes. Most research psychologists today agree with (1) but not (2).

### Classical Conditioning

**classical conditioning** A type of learning in which an organism comes to associate events. A neutral stimulus that signals an unconditioned stimulus (UCS) begins to produce a response that anticipates and prepares for the unconditioned stimulus. (Also known as *Pavlovian conditioning*.)

**unconditioned response (UCR)** In classical conditioning, the unlearned, naturally occurring response to the unconditioned stimulus, such as salivation when food is in the mouth.

**unconditioned stimulus (UCS)** In classical conditioning, a stimulus that unconditionally—naturally and automatically—triggers a response.

**conditioned response (CR)** In classical conditioning, the learned response to a previously neutral conditioned stimulus (CS).

**conditioned stimulus (CS)** In classical conditioning, an originally neutral stimulus that, after association with an unconditioned stimulus (UCS), comes to trigger a conditioned response.

**acquisition** The initial stage of learning, during which a response is established and gradually strengthened. In classical conditioning, the phase in which a stimulus comes to evoke a conditioned response. In operant conditioning, the strengthening of a reinforced response.

**extinction** The diminishing of a response when, in classical conditioning, an unconditioned stimulus (UCS) does not follow a conditioned stimulus (CS); or when, in operant conditioning, a response is no longer reinforced.

**spontaneous recovery** The reappearance, after a rest period, of an extinguished conditioned response.

**generalization** The tendency, once a response has been conditioned, for stimuli similar to the conditioned stimulus to evoke similar responses.

**discrimination** In classical conditioning, the ability to distinguish between a conditioned stimulus and similar stimuli that do not signal an unconditioned stimulus. In operant conditioning, responding differently to stimuli that signal that behavior will be reinforced or will not be reinforced.

### Operant Conditioning

**operant conditioning** A type of learning in which behavior is strengthened if followed by reinforcement or diminished if followed by punishment.

**respondent behavior** Behavior that occurs as an automatic response to some stimulus; Skinner's term for behavior learned through classical conditioning.

**operant behavior** Behavior that operates on the environment, producing consequences.

**Skinner box** A chamber containing a bar or key that an animal can manipulate to obtain a food or water reinforcer, and devices to record the animal's rate of bar pressing or key pecking. Used in operant conditioning research.

**shaping** An operant conditioning procedure in which reinforcers guide behavior toward closer and closer approximations of a desired goal.

**reinforcer** In operant conditioning, any event that *strengthens* the behavior it follows.

**primary reinforcer** An innately reinforcing stimulus, such as one that satisfies a biological need.

**secondary reinforcer** A conditioned reinforcer; a stimulus that gains its reinforcing power by association with a primary reinforcer.

**continuous reinforcement** Reinforcing the desired response every time it occurs.

**partial reinforcement** Reinforcing a response only part of the time; results in slower acquisition of response but much greater resistance to extinction than does continuous reinforcement.

**fixed-ratio schedule** In operant conditioning, a schedule of reinforcement that reinforces a response only after a specified number of responses.

**variable-ratio schedule** In operant conditioning, a schedule of reinforcement that reinforces a response after an unpredictable number of responses.

**fixed-interval schedule** In operant conditioning, a schedule of reinforcement that reinforces a response only after a specified time has elapsed.

**variable-interval schedule** In operant conditioning, a schedule of reinforcement that reinforces a response at unpredictable time intervals.

**punishment** An aversive event that *decreases* the behavior that it follows.

**cognitive map** A mental representation of the layout of one's environment. For example, after exploring a maze, rats act as if they learned a cognitive map of it.

**latent learning** Learning that occurs but is not apparent until there is an incentive to demonstrate it.

**overjustification effect** The effect of promising a reward for doing what one already likes to do. The person may now see the reward, rather than intrinsic interest, as the motivation for performing the task.

### Learning by Observation

**observational learning** Learning by observing and imitating the behavior of others.

**modeling** The process by which a behavior is observed and imitated.

**prosocial behavior** Positive, constructive, helpful behavior. The opposite of antisocial behavior.

## Critical Thinking Exercise

Now that you have read and reviewed Chapter 8, take your learning a step further by testing your critical thinking skills on the following pattern recognition exercise.

> Psychologists believe that children learn to control their bladders during sleep through classical conditioning, a type of learning in which an organism comes to associate different events. Normally, a wet bed or diaper causes a child to awaken. Through repeated pairings, bladder tension becomes associated with the sensation of wetness and children wake up when they sense that the bladder is full. Imagine that you are baby-sitting a 6-year-old bed wetter who has not yet learned the connection between bladder tension and wetness. In desperation, the child's parents consult a behavioral psychologist who has developed a classical conditioning technique for controlling bed-wetting that utilizes a special sheet containing fine electric wires. When a sleeping child wets the bed, the urine (which conducts electricity) immediately completes an electrical circuit and causes a loud bell to ring, awakening the child. Over time, bladder tension becomes associated with the bell and the child is conditioned to wake up before actually wetting the bed. Although the parents have read a pamphlet that explains the basic principles underlying the conditioning technique, they seek your help in understanding exactly *why* it works.

1. Can you identify the component parts of classical conditioning for children who learn to wake up before they wet the bed *without* special training?

   Unconditioned stimulus

   Unconditioned response

   Conditioned stimulus

   Conditioned response

2. Can you identify the components of classical conditioning for children who are conditioned to wake up with the special sheet and bell?

   Unconditioned stimulus

Unconditioned response
Conditioned stimulus
Conditioned response

3. Does the classical conditioning explanation of how children learn on their own to wake up before wetting the bed make sense? Can you explain this learning using principles of operant conditioning?

Check your progress on becoming a critical thinker by comparing your answers to the sample answers found in Appendix B.

## For Further Reading

**Pryor, K.** (1984). *Don't shoot the dog!: How to improve yourself and others through behavioral training.* New York: Simon & Schuster (Bantam Books paperback, 1985).

*A practical guide to applying reinforcement principles to various everyday problems, from training animals, managing employees, and dealing with messy roommates, to reforming your own bad habits.*

**Skinner, B. F.** (1948). *Walden two.* New York: Macmillan.

*A controversial novel by the noted behavioral psychologist, presenting his view of a utopian world guided by an intelligent application of the principles of operant learning.*

**Williams, R. L., & Long, J. D.** (1991). *Manage your life* (4th ed.). Boston: Houghton Mifflin.

*This book suggests how learning principles can be applied to managing one's own health, social relations, and academic and vocational pursuits.*

# CHAPTER 9



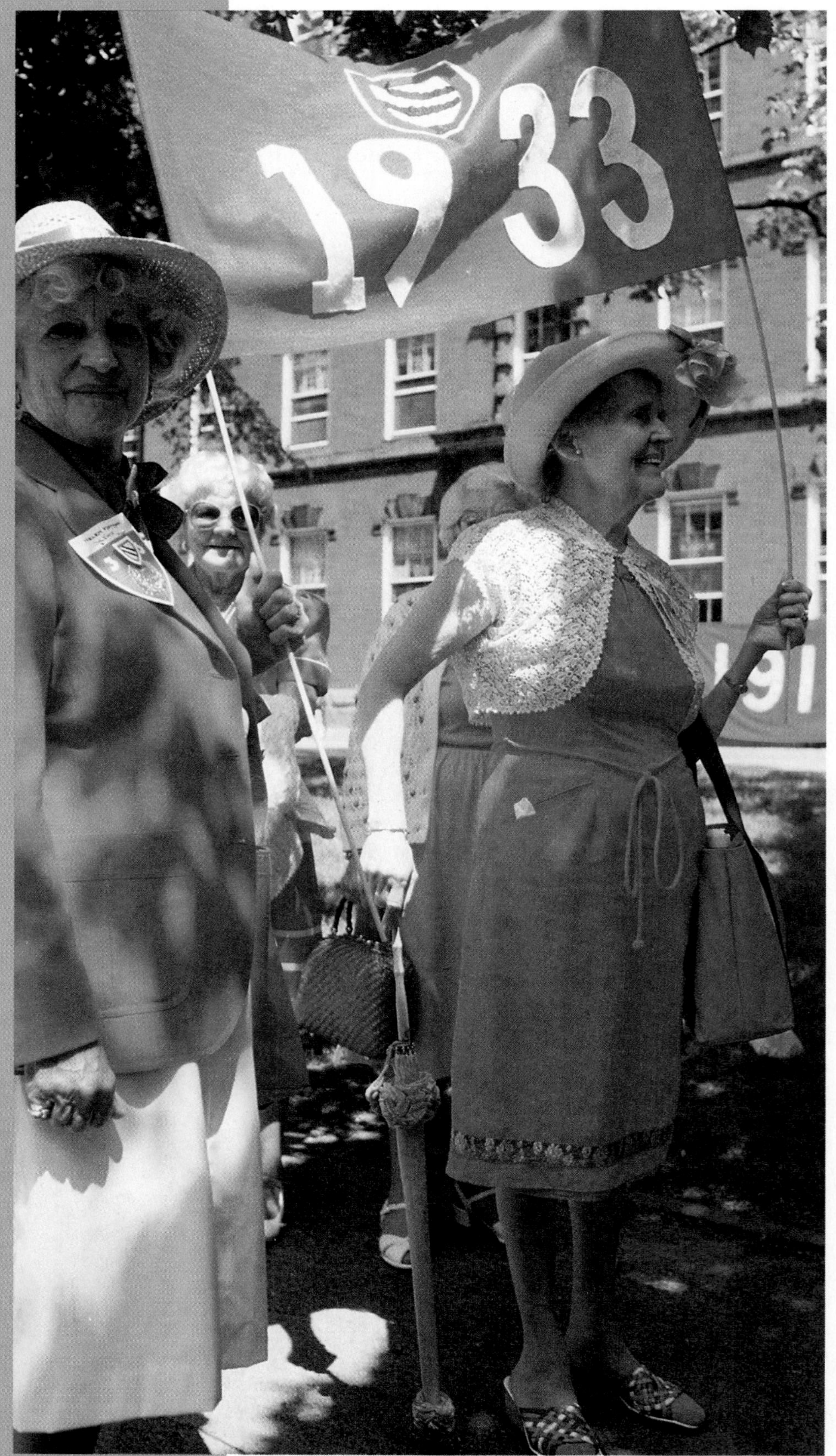

# Memory

Imagine your life without memory. There would be no savoring the remembrances of joyful moments, no guilt or misery over painful recollections. Each moment would be a fresh experience. But each person would be a stranger, every language foreign, each task—dressing, cooking, biking—a novel challenge.

Your memory is your mind's storehouse, the reservoir of your accumulated learning. To Cicero, memory was "the treasury and guardian of all things." To a psychologist, memory is any indication that learning has persisted over time.

## The Phenomenon of Memory

*The range of human memory is evident in some fascinating cases that stimulate our wonderings: How does the memory system work? What types of memory does it contain?*

Conversing with John, a former graduate student, you are impressed by his wit, his intelligence (he might explain his master's thesis), and his skill at tasks such as typing. It might be some time before you notice that John suffers a tragic defect, caused by a brain injury suffered in a motorcycle accident. John cannot form new memories. Although he remembers his life before the accident, John otherwise lives in an eternal present. Each morning when his rehabilitation therapist greets him she must reintroduce herself. She must listen patiently as over and over he retells anecdotes from his preaccident life. Each time the need arises, he inquires, "Where is the bathroom?" and is told anew.

**Memory Lost and Found** *Larry Treadgold, an engineer, invented a paging system that serves as a kind of artificial memory for his son Adrian. Brain-injured in an auto accident, the young man can speak, understand, and retain information for as long as he pays attention. But as soon as he is distracted, the information fades away. The paging system allows a central computer to take over memory functions, reminding him, for example, to "take your 8 A.M. medications, call 123–4567 to confirm." If he fails to do so, the computer continues to re-page him or contacts an emergency number.*

At the other extreme are some special people who would be medal winners in a memory Olympics. One woman, whom psychologist Ulric Neisser (1982) calls MZ, would have been the envy of every student. Until suffering a severe illness at age 29, MZ could recall anything her teachers wrote on the board and whole sections from her textbooks. When she worked as a biology technician, her employer began each day by giving her detailed instructions on the exact order in which to mount some 150 insects, which MZ then did without writing anything down.

The gold medalist of our memory Olympics would probably be a Russian journalist, Shereshevskii, or S, as psychologist Alexander Luria (1968) called him. S's memory not only allowed him merely to listen while other reporters were scribbling notes, it also earned him a place in virtually every modern book on memory. You and I can repeat back a string of about seven

Drawing by Miller; © 1987 The New Yorker Magazine, Inc.

*Which is more important—your experiences or your memories of them?*

**THE FAR SIDE**

*More facts of nature: All forest animals, to this very day, remember exactly where they were and what they were doing when they heard that Bambi's mother had been shot.*

THE FAR SIDE © 1993 FARWORKS INC./Dist. by UNIVERSAL PRESS SYNDICATE. Reprinted with permission. All rights reserved.

digits—almost surely no more than nine. S could repeat up to 70 digits or words, provided they were read about 3 seconds apart in an otherwise silent room. Moreover, he could recall them backward as easily as forward. His accuracy was unerring, even when asked to recall a list as much as 15 years later, after having memorized hundreds of other lists. "Yes, yes," he might recall. "This was a series you gave me once when we were in your apartment. . . . You were sitting at the table and I in the rocking chair. . . . You were wearing a gray suit and you looked at me like this. . . ."

Do these memory feats make your own memory seem feeble? If so, consider your capacity for remembering countless voices, sounds, and songs; tastes, smells, and textures; faces, places, and happenings. Imagine viewing more than 2500 slides of faces and places, for only 10 seconds each, and later seeing 280 of these slides one at a time, paired with a previously unseen slide. If you are like the subjects in an experiment by Ralph Haber (1970), you would recognize 90 percent of those you saw before.

Or consider the vividness of your memories of unique and highly emotional moments in your past—perhaps a car accident, your first romantic kiss, your first day as an immigrant in a new country, or where you were when you heard some tragic news. One such memory of mine is of my only hit in an entire season of Little League baseball. Most Americans over 45 feel sure of exactly what they were doing when they heard the news of President Kennedy's assassination (Brown & Kulik, 1982). Few San Francisco Bay Area residents will hesitate in recalling exactly where they were when the 1989 earthquake struck. This clarity for our memories of surprising, significant events leads some psychologists to call them **flashbulb memories**, because it's as if the brain commands, "Print this!"

How do we accomplish such memory feats? How can we remember things we have not thought about for years, yet forget the name of someone we met a minute ago? How are memories stored in our brains? Why can even our flashbulb memories sometimes prove dead wrong? (People who hours after the space shuttle *Challenger* explosion recalled where they had heard the news were sometimes wildly inaccurate when again recalling their whereabouts 1 to 3 years later [McCloskey & others, 1988; Neisser & Harsch, 1992].) Does what we know about memory give us clues to how we can improve our memories? These will be our questions as we review a century of research on memory.

## Forming Memories: An Example

History is sometimes determined by what people can remember about events. On June 17, 1972, police caught five men trying to tap the telephones of the Democratic National Committee in the Washington, D.C., Watergate Office Building. In 1973, when President Nixon's legal counselor, John Dean, testified before a U.S. Senate committee investigating White House involvement in what came to be called "the Watergate scandal," his recall of conversations with the President was so impressive that some writers called him "the human tape recorder." Ironically, it was later revealed that a secret taping system had actually recorded the conversations that Dean recounted, providing a rare opportunity to compare an eyewitness's recollections with the actual event. Dean's recollection of the essentials proved correct. The highest-ranking members of the White House staff went to prison for doing what John Dean said they did, and President Nixon was forced to resign.

However, when Ulric Neisser (1981) compared the details in the tapes to the testimony, he discovered that John Dean was far from a human tape recorder. For example, Dean recalled that entering a September 15 meeting with President Nixon and his chief-of-staff, Robert Haldeman,

> the President asked me to sit down. Both men appeared to be in very good spirits and my reception was very warm and cordial. The President then told me that Bob—referring to Haldeman—had kept him posted on my handling of the Watergate case. The President told me I had done a good job and he appreciated how difficult a task it had been and the President was pleased that the case had stopped with [his reelection committee's attorney] Liddy.

But almost every detail Dean recalled was wrong. The tape of the meeting revealed that the President did not ask Dean to sit down. He did not say Dean had done a good job. He did not say anything about Liddy or the indictments.

Dean's memory was better for a March 15 conversation during which he delivered a well-prepared report to the President on the unraveling of the White House cover-up. The tape caught Dean actually saying, "We have a cancer within, close to the presidency, that is growing. It is growing daily . . . because (1) we are being blackmailed, (2) people are going to start perjuring themselves. . . ." In his later congressional testimony, Dean *recalled* "telling the President that there was a cancer growing on the presidency and . . . that it was important that this cancer be removed immediately because it was growing more deadly every day."

How could John Dean have been so right in his basic understanding of the Watergate discussions, yet, except for the March 15 conversation, so wrong in recalling the details of most conversations? Why are you likely later in this chapter to misrecall a sentence such as, "The angry rioter threw the rock at the window"? To understand Dean's memory (and our own), we need a model of memory.

**A Human Tape Recorder** *John Dean is shown here testifying before the Senate Watergate Committee. When his testimony was compared to the White House tapes, Dean's memory was found to be accurate for the substance of most conversations but not for the details.*

## Memory as Information Processing

A helpful model of human memory is that of a computerlike information-processing system. To remember any event requires that we *get information into our brain* (**encoding**), *retain it* (**storage**), and later *get it back out* (**retrieval**). Consider how a computer encodes, stores, and retrieves information. First, it translates input (keystrokes) into an electronic language, much as the brain encodes sensory information into a neural language. The computer permanently stores vast amounts of information on a disk. From this information storehouse it can retrieve a file or document into a working memory, which also can receive new information from the keyboard. Part of this working memory is visible on the screen.

Similarly, we store vast amounts of information in **long-term memory**. From our memory storehouse we can retrieve information into an active working memory, part of which is displayed on our mental screen as **short-term memory**. And, just as a computer's screen-saver program blanks the screen after a period of inactivity, activated human memories rapidly decay unless kept active.

Like orchestra conductors, we can't focus on everything at once. So we shine the flashlight beam of attention on certain incoming stimuli, often novel or changing stimuli. As Figure 9–1 (page 290) suggests, we also retrieve experiences from long-term memory (Cowan, 1988).

Figure 9–1

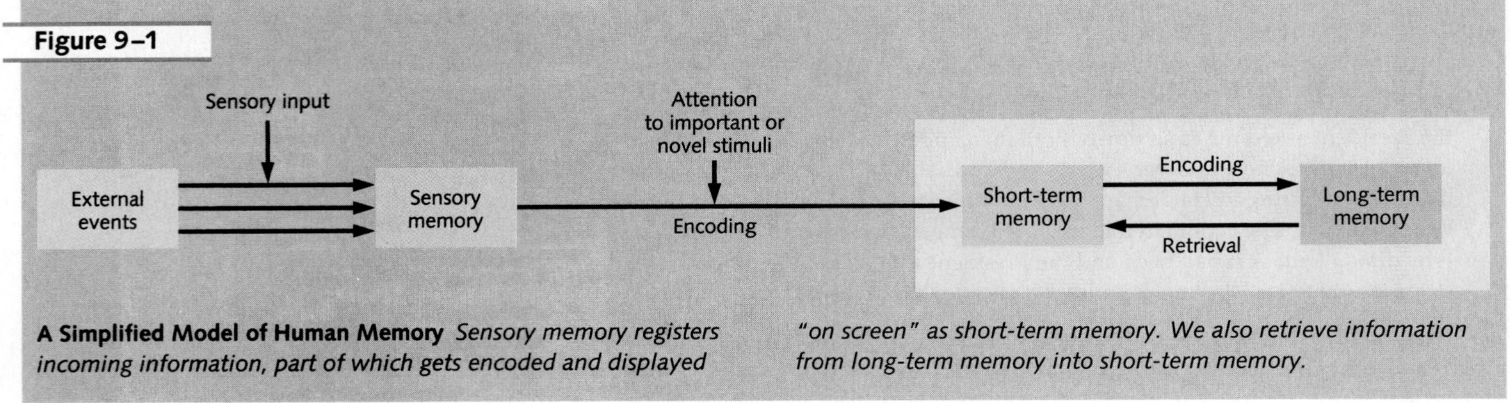


**A Simplified Model of Human Memory** *Sensory memory registers incoming information, part of which gets encoded and displayed "on screen" as short-term memory. We also retrieve information from long-term memory into short-term memory.*

## Summing Up

Memory is the persistence of learning over time. The computer is one convenient model for thinking about human memory. Both systems must encode, store, and retrieve information. Both feature long-term storage, from which we can activate information into a working memory, part of which is displayed on screen. On-screen memory is similar to our short-term memory; unless used or rehearsed, it quickly disappears.

# Encoding: Getting Information In

*How does sensory information, once registered, get encoded and transferred into the memory system? What types of information do we absorb incidentally? What types require intentional effort? Is the failure to encode information an important factor in forgetting?*

Some encoding occurs automatically, freeing your attention to simultaneously process information that requires effort. Thus, your memory for the route you walked to class yesterday you handled by **automatic processing**. Your learning this chapter's concepts requires **effortful processing**.

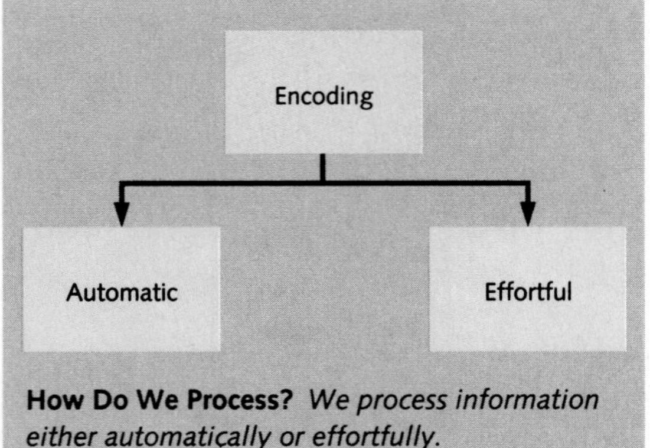


**How Do We Process?** *We process information either automatically or effortfully.*

## How We Encode

### Automatic Processing

With little or no effort, you encode an enormous amount of information about *space*, *time*, and *frequency*: During an exam, you may recall the place on the textbook page where the forgotten material appears. To guess where you left your coat, you can recreate a sequence of the day's events. You may realize that "this is the third time I've run into you this afternoon." Memories like these form almost automatically. In fact, not only does automatic processing occur effortlessly, it is difficult to shut off. When you hear or read a word in your native language, it is virtually impossible not to register its meaning automatically.

Some types of automatic processing we learn. For example, learning to read reversed sentences at first requires effort:

.citamotua emoceb nac gnissecorp luftroffE

**As Easy as Pie** *Riding a bicycle, rolling out pie dough, executing a dive—all of these complex motor skills require practice. As they are executed again and again, however, they take less and less effort and gradually become automatic. We can carry them out while thinking about other things.*

After practice, effortful processing becomes more automatic, much as reading from right to left becomes easy for students of Hebrew (Kolers, 1975).

Automatic processing occurs with little or no effort, without our awareness, and without interfering with our thinking about other things. (Here, then, is yet another example of our brain's capacity for parallel processing of multiple information streams.) If such processing indeed requires no special attention, then asking people to pay special attention to information they encode automatically, such as judging the frequency of words presented during an experiment, should be of little benefit. That is just what Lynn Hasher and Rose Zacks (1979, 1984) report is often the case. Although memory for such material may be modestly boosted by effort (Naveh-Benjamin, 1990), our encoding is mostly automatic: We cannot switch it on and off at will.

## Effortful Processing

We encode and retain vast amounts of information automatically, without any intentional effort. Other types of information we remember only with effort and attention. With novel information such as names, **rehearsal**, or conscious repetition, boosts memory. This was shown long ago by the pioneering researcher of verbal memory, German philosopher Hermann Ebbinghaus (1850–1909). Ebbinghaus did for the study of memory what Ivan Pavlov did for the study of conditioning. Impatient with philosophical speculations about memory, Ebbinghaus wanted to study it scientifically. To do so, he decided to study his own learning and forgetting of novel verbal materials.

Where could Ebbinghaus find verbal material that was not familiar? His solution was to form a list of all possible nonsense syllables created by sandwiching a vowel between two consonants. Then, for a particular experiment, he would randomly select a sample of the syllables. To get a feel for how Ebbinghaus tested himself, rapidly read aloud, eight times over, the following list. Then recall the items (from Baddeley, 1982):

JIH, BAZ, FUB, YOX, SUJ, XIR, DAX, LEQ, VUM, PID, KEL, WAV, TUV, ZOF, GEK, HIW.

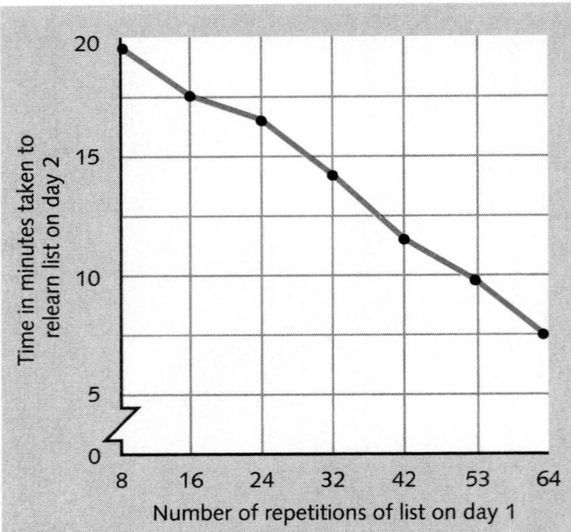


**Figure 9–2**

**Ebbinghaus's Retention Curve** *Ebbinghaus found that the more times he practiced a list of nonsense syllables on day 1, the fewer repetitions he required to relearn it on day 2. Said simply, the more time we spend learning novel information, the more we retain. (From Baddeley, 1982.)*

After learning such a list, Ebbinghaus could recall few of the syllables the following day. But were they entirely forgotten? As Figure 9–2 portrays, the more frequently he repeated the list aloud on day 1, the fewer repetitions he required to relearn the list on day 2. Here, then, was a simple beginning principle: *The amount remembered depends on the time spent learning*. Even after we learn material, additional rehearsal (*overlearning*) increases retention. Thus, John Dean almost perfectly recalled his "cancer on the presidency" remarks, which he had written out and rehearsed several times before uttering them to President Nixon.

The moral is that for novel verbal information, practice—effortful processing—does indeed make perfect. And that helps us understand some other interesting phenomena:

- The *next-in-line effect*: When people go around a circle reading words or saying their names, their poorest memories are for what was said by the person just before them (Bond & others, 1991; Brenner, 1973). When we are next in line, we focus on our own performance and often fail to process the last person's words.
- Information presented in the seconds just before sleep seldom is remembered (Wyatt & Bootzin, 1994). When our consciousness fades before we've processed the information, all is lost.
- Taped information played during sleep is registered by the ears but is not remembered (Wood & others, 1992). Without opportunity for rehearsal, "sleep learning" doesn't occur.

We also retain information better when rehearsal is distributed over time (as when learning classmates' names), a phenomenon called the **spacing effect** (Dempster, 1988). Harry Bahrick and Lynda Hall (1991) noted the effect of spaced rehearsal in a study of adults' memory of high school algebra. Those who took algebra only once forgot most of what they learned over the next half century. Others—after doing no better in high school—rehearsed their algebra knowledge while taking higher level math courses. For the rest of their lives these people remembered most of their high school algebra, especially if their college math was spaced over several semesters rather than massed into 1 year.

In a 9-year experiment, Bahrick and three of his family members (1993) practiced foreign language word translations for a given number of times, at intervals ranging from 14 to 56 days. Their consistent finding: The longer the space between practice sessions, the better their retention, up to 5 years later. Reflecting on the spacing effect, Bahrick saw a practical implication: Restudying material for comprehensive final exams, capstone review courses, and senior examinations will enhance lifelong retention. Spreading out learning—say, over a semester or a year, rather than over shorter terms—should also help. In the first century, the Roman philosopher Seneca urged spaced study rather than cramming: "The mind is slow in unlearning what it has been long in learning."

That makes adaptive sense, note John Anderson and Lael Schooler (1991). In our environments, events that are spaced out *are* more likely to recur. Compared with a name we've heard or read five times in one month, the name we've read once a month for five months is a name we're more likely to read again. (They confirmed this by looking at such things as word frequencies in 730 consecutive *New York Times* headlines.) In this and other ways, our memory system, like so much else about us, is optimally designed to support our functioning and survival.

A phenomenon you have surely experienced further illustrates the benefits of rehearsal. Experimenters have shown people a list of items (words, names, dates) and then immediately asked them to recall the items in any order. As people struggle to recall the list, they often demonstrate the **serial position effect**: They remember the last and first items better than they do those in the middle (Figure 9–3). Perhaps because they are still in short-term memory, the last items are briefly recalled especially quickly and well. But after a delay—after attention has shifted from the last items—recall is best for the first items. As an everyday parallel, imagine that as you are being introduced to several people, you repeat (rehearse) all their names from the beginning as you meet each person. By the end, you will have spent more time rehearsing the earlier names than the later names; thus, the next day you will probably recall the earlier names better. Also, learning some names may interfere with your learning more.

Rehearsal will not encode all information equally well. Sometimes merely repeating information, such as the new phone number we are about to dial, is not enough to store it for later recall (Craik & Watkins, 1973; Greene, 1987). How, then, do we process information into long-term memory? Processing our sensory input is like sorting through the day's mail: Some items we instantly discard. Others we process more thoughtfully: We open, read, and retain them. Our memory system processes information not just by repetitive rehearsal, but by encoding its significant features.

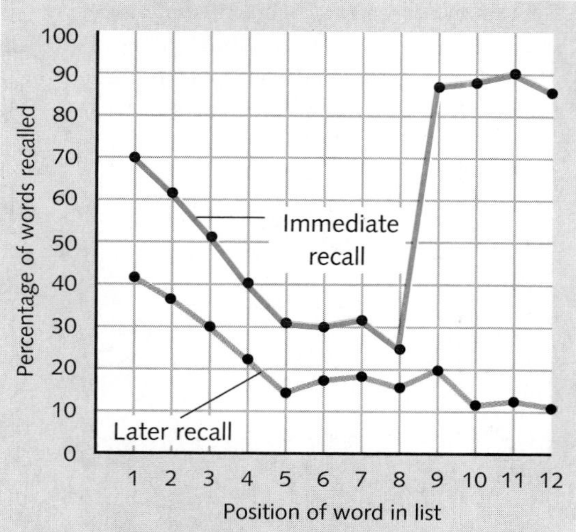


**Figure 9–3**

**The Serial Position Effect** *After being presented with a list of words, people immediately recall the last and first items most accurately. But later they recall only the first items best—even if they had repeated the last items for a few moments to keep them "on screen." (From Craik & Watkins, 1973.)*

## What We Encode

We process information in three key ways—by encoding its meaning, by visualizing it, and by mentally organizing it. To some extent we do so automatically. But in each case there are effortful strategies for enhancing memory.

### Encoding Meaning

Do you recall (from page 289) the sentence about the rioter? Can you complete the sentence: "The angry rioter threw . . ."?

When processing verbal information for storage, we usually encode its meaning. For example, we associate it with what we already know or imagine. Whether we hear "eye-screem" as "ice cream" or "I scream" depends on how the context and our experience guide us to interpret the sounds.

Perhaps, then, like the subjects in an experiment by William Brewer (1977), you recalled the rioter sentence as the meaning you encoded when you read it (for example, "The angry rioter threw the rock through the window") and not as written ("The angry rioter threw the rock *at* the window"). As such recall indicates, we tend not to remember things exactly as they were. Rather, we remember what we encoded. Studying for an exam, you may remember your lecture notes rather than the lecture itself. Likewise, as we hear or read about a situation, our minds construct a model of it. Gordon Bower and Daniel Morrow (1990) liken our minds to theater directors who, given a raw script, imagine a finished stage production. Asked later to recall what we heard or read, we recall not the literal text but the mental model we constructed from it. This helps us understand John Dean's misrecollections of precisely what President Nixon said and did, and Dean's better recall of the *meaning* that he encoded from his conversations with the President.

*How many Fs are in the following sentence? FINISHED FILES ARE THE RESULTS OF YEARS OF SCIENTIFIC STUDY COMBINED WITH THE EXPERIENCE OF YEARS. (See page 297.)*

Does **semantic encoding** (of meaning) yield better memory of verbal information than **acoustic encoding** (of sound) or **visual encoding** (of an image)? To find out, Fergus Craik and Endel Tulving (1975) flashed a word at people. Then they asked a question that required the people to process the words either (1) visually (the appearance of the letters), (2) acoustically (the sound of the words), or (3) semantically (the meaning of the words). To experience the task yourself, rapidly answer the following questions:

| Sample Questions to Elicit Processing | Word Flashed | Yes | No |
|---|---|---|---|
| 1. Is the word in capital letters? | chair | ____ | ____ |
| 2. Does the word rhyme with train? | BRAIN | ____ | ____ |
| 3. Would the word fit in this sentence: The girl put the _______ on the table. | gun | ____ | ____ |

Which type of processing would best prepare you to recognize the words at a later time? In Craik and Tulving's experiment, the deeper, semantic encoding—question 3—yielded much better memory than the "shallow processing" elicited by question 2 and especially question 1 (Figure 9–4).

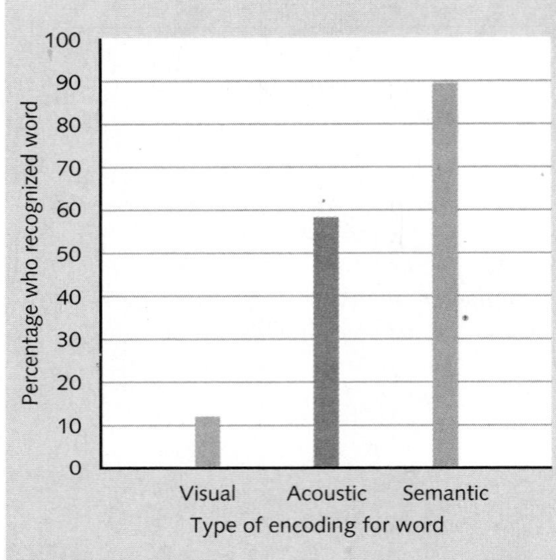


**Figure 9–4**

**Levels of Processing** *Processing a word deeply—by its meaning (semantic encoding)—produces better recognition of it than does processing its visual or acoustic features. (From Craik & Tulving, 1975.)*

To experience the importance of meaning for verbal memory, put yourself in the place of the students whom John Bransford and Marcia Johnson (1972) asked to remember the following recorded passage:

> The procedure is actually quite simple. First you arrange things into different groups. Of course, one pile may be sufficient depending on how much there is to do. . . . After the procedure is completed one arranges the materials into different groups again. Then they can be put into their appropriate places. Eventually they will be used once more and the whole cycle will then have to be repeated. However, that is part of life.

When the students heard the paragraph you have just read, without a meaningful context, they remembered little of it. When told that the paragraph was about washing clothes (something meaningful to them), they remembered much more of it—as you probably could now after rereading it.

Such research suggests the futility of trying to remember words we do not understand and the benefits of rephrasing into meaningful terms what we read and hear. From his experiments on himself, Ebbinghaus estimated that, compared with learning nonsense material, learning meaningful material required but one-tenth the effort. Further, as memory researcher Wayne Wickelgren (1977, p. 346) noted, "The time you spend thinking about material you are reading and relating it to previously stored material is about the most useful thing you can do in learning any new subject matter."

We have excellent recall for information we relate to ourselves. If asked how well certain adjectives describe another person, people will often forget them; if asked to rate how well the adjectives describe themselves, they remember the words well—a phenomenon called the *self-reference effect* (Kuiper & Rogers, 1979). Thus, students profit from taking time to find personal meaning in what they are studying. Information deemed "relevant to me" is more likely to be processed deeply and to be accessible in memory.

## Encoding Imagery

*"A thing when heard, remember, strikes less keen on the spectator's mind than when 'tis seen."*

Horace
*Ars Poetica*, 8 B.C.

We struggle to memorize formulas, definitions, and dates, yet we can easily picture where we were yesterday, who was with us, where we sat, and what we wore. Your earliest memories—probably of something that happened at around age 3 or 4—almost surely involve visual **imagery**, or mental pictures.

In a variety of experiments, researchers have documented the benefits of mental images.

- We recall our experiences with mental snapshots of their best or worst moments. Thus, the duration of a pleasure or pain, a joy or frustration, often colors our memories less than does our retained image of the best or worst moments (Fredrickson & Kahneman, 1993).
- People who form the most vivid visual images of strangers also remember them best (Swann & Miller, 1982).
- We remember words that lend themselves to picture images better than we remember abstract, low-imagery words. (When I quiz you later, which three of these words will you most likely recall: *typewriter, void, cigarette, inherent, fire, process*?) Similarly, you probably still recall the sentence about the rock-throwing rioter, not only because of the meaning you encoded but also because the sentence lent itself to a visual image. As the example suggests, and as some memory experts believe, memory for concrete nouns is aided by encoding them *both* semantically and visually (Marschark & others, 1987; Paivio, 1986). Two codes are better than one.

The imagery principle—that people have excellent memory for pictures and picture-evoking words—applies to teaching, preaching, and writing. Abstract ideas become memorable when carried by visual images. The statistics of the nuclear age are forgettable; their visual representation is more memorable.

Imagery is at the heart of many memory aids. **Mnemonic** (nih-MON-ik) devices (so named after the Greek word for memory) were developed by ancient Greek scholars and orators as aids to remembering lengthy passages and speeches. Using the "method of loci," they imagined themselves moving through a familiar series of locations, associating each place with a visual representation of the to-be-remembered topic. Then, when speaking, the orator would mentally revisit each location and retrieve the associated image.

A variation on this method uses vivid stories to organize words to be memorized. Gordon Bower and Michael Clark (1969) used lists of unrelated nouns, asking one group simply to study the lists and another group to invent stories using the nouns. (A sample made-up story: "A LUMBERJACK DARTed out of a forest, SKATEd around a HEDGE past a COLONY of DUCKs. He tripped on some FURNITURE, tearing his STOCKING while hastening toward the PILLOW where his MISTRESS lay.") After working through 12 lists of 10 words each, the group that merely studied each list struggled to recall 13 percent of the words; the group that invented vivid stories recalled an astounding 93 percent.

Other mnemonic devices involve both acoustic and visual codes. For example, the "peg-word" system requires that you first memorize a jingle:

One is a bun; two is a shoe;
Three is a tree; four is a door;
Five is a hive; six is sticks;
Seven is heaven; eight is a gate;
Nine is swine; ten is a hen.

Without much effort, you will soon be able to count by peg-words instead of numbers: bun, shoe, tree . . . and then to visually associate the peg-words with to-be-remembered items. Now you are ready to challenge anyone to give you a grocery list to remember. Carrots? Imagine them stuck into a

*"You simply associate each number with a word, such as 'table' and 3,476,029."*

© 1994 by Sidney Harris.

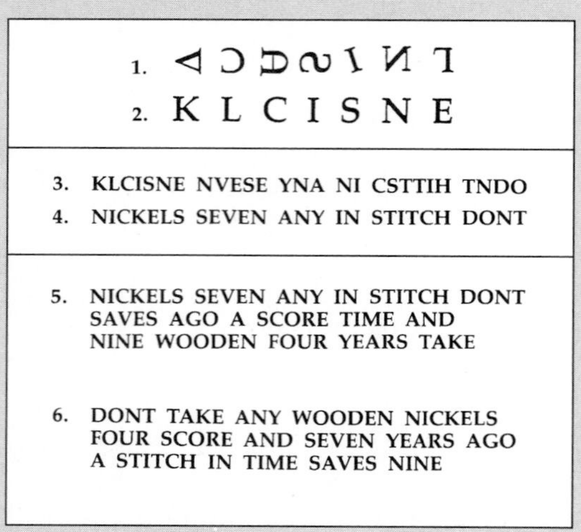

1. [illegible]
2. K L C I S N E

3. KLCISNE NVESE YNA NI CSTTIH TNDO
4. NICKELS SEVEN ANY IN STITCH DONT

5. NICKELS SEVEN ANY IN STITCH DONT
SAVES AGO A SCORE TIME AND
NINE WOODEN FOUR YEARS TAKE

6. DONT TAKE ANY WOODEN NICKELS
FOUR SCORE AND SEVEN YEARS AGO
A STITCH IN TIME SAVES NINE

**Figure 9–5**

**Effects of Chunking on Memory** *When we organize information into meaningful units, such as letters, words, and phrases, we recall it more easily. (From Hintzman, 1978.)*

bun. Milk? Fill the shoe with it. Paper towels? Drape them over the tree branch. Think "bun, shoe, tree" and you see their associated images: carrots, milk, paper towels. With few errors (Bugelski & others, 1968), you will be able to recall the items in any order and to name any given item. Such mnemonic systems are often the secret behind the feats of memory experts who repeat long lists of names and objects.

### Organizing Information for Encoding

Meaning and imagery enhance memory partly by helping us organize information. When the laundry paragraph became meaningful, its sentences formed a sequence. Mnemonic devices help organize material for later retrieval. To experience the importance of organization, glance for a few seconds at row 1 of Figure 9–5, then look away and try to reproduce what you saw. It's nearly impossible. But you can easily reproduce the second row, which is no less complex. Similarly, row 4 is much easier to remember than row 3, although both contain the same letters. And the sixth cluster is more easily remembered than the fifth, although both contain the same words.

**Chunking** As this demonstrates, we organize easily remembered information into meaningful units, or chunks. **Chunking** information into meaningful units occurs so naturally that we take it for granted. Consider your ability to reproduce perfectly the 150 or so line segments that make up the sixth cluster of phrases. Surely it would astonish an illiterate person or someone unfamiliar with the English alphabet.

You or I might feel similar admiration for the ability of someone literate in Chinese to glance at the ideographs in Figure 9–6 and then to reproduce all the strokes; or for chess masters who, after a 5-second look at the board during a game, can recall the exact positions of most of the pieces (Chase & Simon, 1973); or for varsity basketball players who, given a 4-second glance at a basketball play, can recall the positions of the players (Allard & Burnett, 1985). Like the experienced chess masters and athletes, we all remember information best when we can organize it into personally meaningful arrangements.

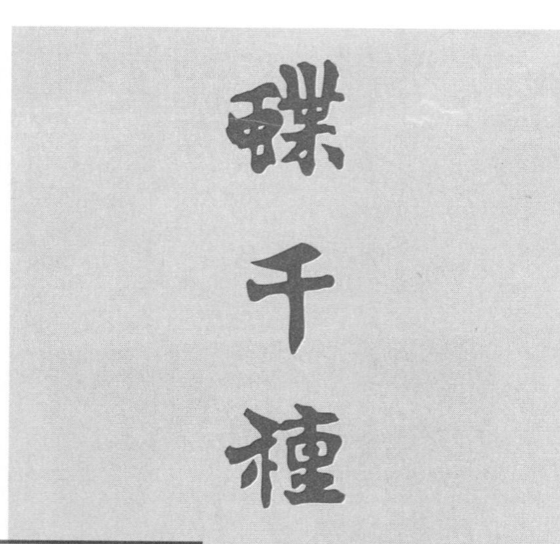

**Figure 9–6**

**An Example of Chunking—for Those Who Read Chinese** *After looking at these ideographs, can you reproduce them exactly? If so, you are almost certainly literate in Chinese.*

Chunking also aids our recall of unfamiliar material. One mnemonic technique organizes it into a more familiar form by creating words (called acronyms) or sentences from the first letters of words to be remembered. Should you ever need to recall the names of the five Great Lakes, just remember HOMES (*H*uron, *O*ntario, *M*ichigan, *E*rie, *S*uperior). Want to remember the colors of the rainbow in order of wavelength? Think of ROY G. BIV (*r*ed, *o*range, *y*ellow, *g*reen, *b*lue, *i*ndigo, *v*iolet).

With chunking, you can increase your recall of digits, too. An impossible string of 16 numbers—1-4-9-2-1-7-7-6-1-8-1-2-1-9-4-1—becomes easy when chunked into 1492, 1776, 1812, 1941. After more than 200 hours of practice in the laboratory of Anders Ericsson and William Chase (1982), two Carnegie-Mellon University students even managed to increase their memory span from the typical 7 digits to more than 80. In another testing session, Dario Donatelli heard the researcher read one digit per second in a monotonous voice: "15185937655021578416658506120948856867727314181 86105462974801294974965928." Motionless while learning the numbers, Donatelli then sprang alive. He whispered numbers, rubbed his chin, tapped his feet, counted on his fingers, and ran his hands through his hair. "Okay," he announced almost 2 minutes later. "The first set is 1518. Then 5937. . . ." He repeated all 73 digits, in groups of 3 and 4.

How did he do it? By increasing the capacity of his short-term memory? No. When asked to remember letters, Donatelli fell back to about a seven-

Figure 9–7

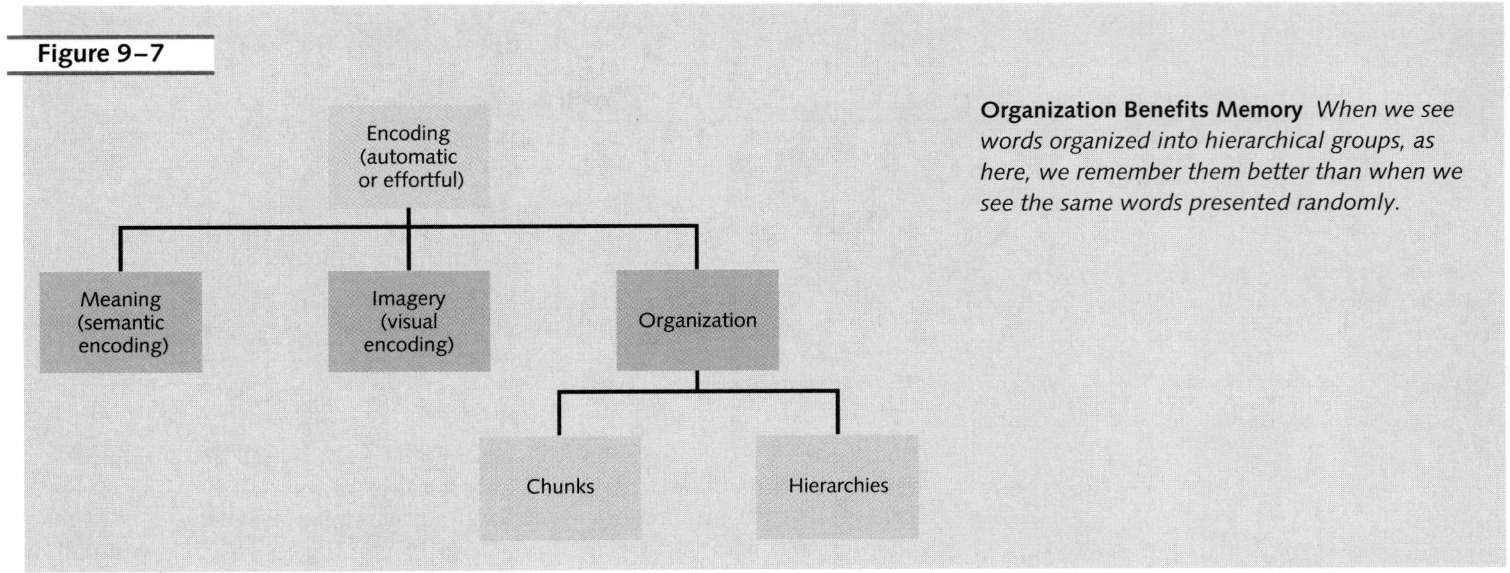


**Organization Benefits Memory** *When we see words organized into hierarchical groups, as here, we remember them better than when we see the same words presented randomly.*

item capacity. Rather, he had developed a sophisticated strategy for number chunking. "First set was a 3-mile time," reported Donatelli, an All-American cross-country runner. "Second set was a 10-mile time. Then a mile. Half-mile. Two-mile time. An age. . . . Two mile. Age. Age. Age. Two-mile. . . ." (Wells, 1983).

**Hierarchies** For Donatelli to reach his peak—106 digits—he retrieved the chunks of numbers by clustering them as a hierarchy (Waldrop, 1987). First came "three groups of four," he might think, and so forth. When people develop expertise in an area, they process information not only in chunks but also in hierarchies composed of a few broad concepts divided and subdivided into lesser concepts and facts. By organizing their knowledge in such ways, experts can retrieve information efficiently. This chapter therefore aims not only to teach you the elementary facts of memory but also to help you organize these facts around broad principles, such as encoding; subprinciples, such as automatic and effortful processing; and still more specific concepts, such as meaning, imagery, and organization (Figure 9–7).

Gordon Bower and his colleagues (1969) demonstrated the benefits of hierarchical organization by presenting words either randomly or grouped into categories. When the words were hierarchically organized, recall was two to three times better. Such results show the benefits of organizing what you study—of giving special attention to chapter outlines, headings, topic sentences, and summary paragraphs. If you can master a chapter's concepts with their overall organization, the odds are that your recall will be good at test time. Taking lecture and text notes in outline format—a type of hierarchical organization—may also prove effective.

*Answer to question on page 294: Partly because your initial processing of the letters was primarily acoustic rather than visual, you probably missed some of the six* Fs*, especially those that sound like a* V *rather than an* F.

## Forgetting as Encoding Failure

Amidst all the applause for memory—all the efforts to understand it, all the books on how to improve it—have any voices been heard in praise of forgetting? William James (1890, p. 680) was such a voice: "If we remembered everything, we should on most occasions be as ill off as if we remembered nothing." To discard the clutter of useless or out-of-date informa-

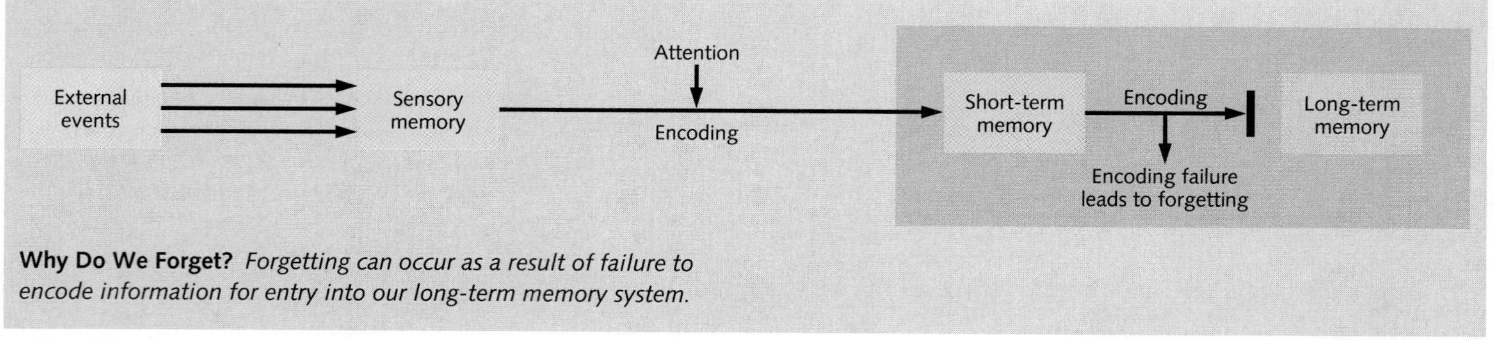


**Why Do We Forget?** *Forgetting can occur as a result of failure to encode information for entry into our long-term memory system.*

tion—where we parked the car yesterday, a friend's old phone number, restaurant orders already cooked and served—is surely a blessing (Bjork, 1978). The Russian memory whiz S, whom we met at the beginning of the chapter, was haunted by his junk heap of memories, which continually dominated his consciousness. He had more difficulty than others do in thinking abstractly—generalizing, organizing, evaluating. A good memory is helpful, but so is the ability to forget.

What causes forgetting? One answer is that we failed to encode the information. Thus, it never entered the memory system. The English novelist-critic C. S. Lewis (1967, p. 107) vividly described why we remember "next to nothing":

> Each of us finds that in his own life every moment of time is completely filled. He is bombarded every second by sensations, emotions, thoughts, which he cannot attend to for multitude, and nine-tenths of which he must simply ignore. . . . The past . . . was a roaring cataract of billions upon billions of such moments: any one of them too complex to grasp in its entirety, and the aggregate beyond all imagination. . . . At every tick of the clock, in every inhabited part of the world, an unimaginable richness and variety of "history" falls off the world into total oblivion.

Indeed, much of what we sense we never notice. Consider something you've looked at countless times: What letters accompany the number 5 on your telephone? If you live in North America, Britain, or Australia, you have probably also looked at thousands of pennies in your lifetime. You can surely recall the features (color and size) you use to distinguish coins. But can you recall what the side with the head looks like? If not, let's make the memory test easier: If you are familiar with United States coins, can you *recognize* the real thing in Figure 9–8? Raymond Nickerson and Marilyn Adams (1979) found that most people cannot. Likewise, few British people can draw from memory the one-pence coin they have seen thousands of times (Richardson, 1993). The details of a penny are not very meaningful—nor are they essential for distinguishing pennies from other coins—and few of us have made the effort to encode them. As we noted earlier, we encode some information automatically; other types of information require effortful processing. Without effort, many memories never form.

## Summing Up

Some types of information, notably concerning space, time, and frequency, we encode mostly automatically. Other types of information, including much of our processing of meaning, imagery, and organization, requires ef-

Figure 9–8

**Test Your Memory** *Which one of these pennies is the real thing? (If you live outside the United States, what does your country's penny look like?) (From Nickerson & Adams, 1979.) (See page 300.)*

fort. Mnemonic devices depend on the memorability of visual images and of information that is organized into chunks. Organizing information into chunks and hierarchies also aids memory.

One explanation of forgetting is that we fail to encode information for entry into our memory system. Without effortful processing, much of what we sense we never notice or process.

## Storage: Retaining Information

*At the heart of memory is storage. Our sensory memory, short-term memory, and long-term memory retain information for varying time periods. What is the capacity and duration of each? How and where does the brain physically store memories?*

If you experience something that you later recall, you must, somehow, have stored and retrieved it. What is stored in long-term memory lies dormant, waiting to be reawakened by a cue. What is our memory storage capacity? Let's start with the first memory store noted in Figure 9–1, our fleeting sensory memory.

### Sensory Memory Storage

Consider what one intriguing memory experiment revealed about our **sensory memory**—the initial recording of sensory information in the memory system. As part of his doctoral research, George Sperling (1960) showed people three rows of three letters each for only 1/20th of a second (Figure 9–9). It was harder than reading by lightning flashes. After the nine letters disappeared from the screen, the subjects could recall only about half of them.

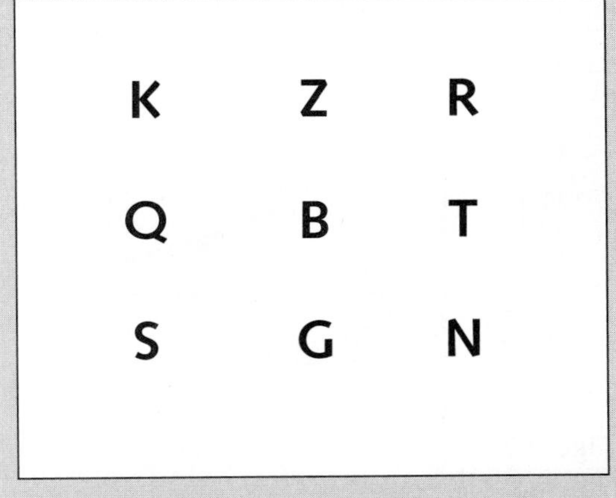


Figure 9–9

**Momentary Photographic Memory** *When George Sperling flashed a group of letters similar to this for 1/20th of a second, people could recall only about half of the letters. But when signaled to recall a particular row immediately after the letters had disappeared, they could do so with near-perfect accuracy.*

*How many of the six quiz words on page 295 can you now recall? Of these, how many are high-imagery words? How many are low-imagery?*

Why? Was it because they had insufficient time to glimpse them? No, Sperling cleverly demonstrated that even at faster than lightning-flash speed, people actually *can* see and recall all the letters, but only momentarily. Rather than ask them to recall all nine letters at once, Sperling would sound a high, medium, or low tone immediately *after* flashing the nine letters. This cue directed the subject to report only the letters of the top, middle, or bottom row, respectively. Now the subjects rarely missed a letter, showing that all nine letters were momentarily available for recall.

Sperling's experiment revealed that we have a fleeting photographic memory called **iconic memory**. For an instant, the eyes register an exact representation of a scene and we can recall any part of it in amazing detail. But only for a few tenths of a second. If Sperling delayed the tone signal by as much as a second, the iconic memory was gone and the subjects once again recalled only about half the letters. The visual screen clears quickly, as it must, lest new images be superimposed over old ones. The auditory sensory image, called **echoic memory**, also dies quickly, reflecting the quickly decaying activation of the auditory cortex (Cowan, 1988; Lu & others, 1992). But a partially interpreted auditory echo disappears more slowly. The last few words spoken seem to linger for 3 or 4 seconds. Sometimes, just as you ask, "What did you say?" you can hear in your mind the echo of what was said.

*Answer to question on page 299: The first penny (a) is the real penny.*

## Short-Term Memory Storage

Among the vast amounts of information registered by our sensory memory, we illuminate some with our attentional flashlight. We also retrieve information from long-term storage for "on screen" display. But unless we work with that information, it quickly disappears. During your finger's trip from the phone book to the phone, your memory of a telephone number will disappear unless you work to maintain it in consciousness.

To find out how quickly it will disappear, Lloyd Peterson and Margaret Peterson (1959) asked people to remember three consonants, such as *CHJ*. To prevent rehearsal of the letters by the working memory, they asked the subjects to begin immediately counting aloud backward by threes from some number. With the help of a friend, you can demonstrate the result shown in Figure 9–10. After 3 seconds people recalled the letters only about half the time; after 12 seconds they seldom recalled them at all. Without active processing, short-term memories have a limited life.

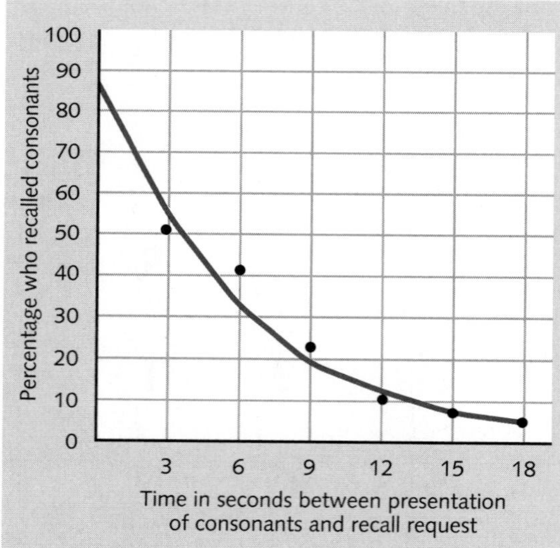


**Figure 9–10**

**Short-Term Memory Decay** *Unless rehearsed, verbal information may be quickly forgotten. (From Peterson & Peterson, 1959.)*

The short-term memory store also has limited capacity. It typically stores but seven or so chunks of information (give or take two), a recall capacity that has been enshrined in psychology as "the Magical Number Seven, plus or minus two" (Miller, 1956). Actually, people's short-term memory spans—the amount of information they can immediately recall correctly 50 percent of the time—vary. Short-term recall is slightly better for random digits (such as those of a phone number) than for random letters, which sometimes have similar sounds. It is slightly better for information we hear rather than see. Adults, especially younger adults, have greater memory spans than children (Chi, 1976; Salthouse, 1992). Still, the basic principle holds true: At any given moment, we can process only a very limited amount of information.

## Long-Term Memory Storage

In Arthur Conan Doyle's *A Study in Scarlet*, Sherlock Holmes offers a popular theory of memory capacity:

> I consider that a man's brain originally is like a little empty attic, and you have to stock it with such furniture as you choose. . . . It is a mistake to think that that little room has elastic walls and can distend to any extent. Depend upon it, there comes a time when for every addition of knowledge you forget something that you knew before.

Contrary to Sherlock Holmes's belief, our capacity for storing long-term memories is essentially limitless. By one careful estimate, the average adult has about a billion bits of information in memory. Allowing for all the brain must do to encode, store, retrieve, and manipulate this information, its storage capacity is probably a thousand to a million times greater (Landauer, 1986). So our brains are *not* like attics, which once filled can store more only by discarding old items.

The point is vividly illustrated by those whose efforts have enabled phenomenal memory feats. Rajan Mahadevan, a Florida State University graduate student from India, would be the current gold medalist of memorists. At last report, he had correctly recited the first 99,000 digits of pi. Moreover, in answer to questions from researcher Charles Thompson and his colleagues (1993), Rajan can give, say, the 9382nd digit. Or give him any string of 10 digits and, after a few moments of mental search for the string, he'll pick up the series from there, firing numbers like a machine gun. He also can repeat 50 random digits—backwards. It's no genetic gift, he says; anyone could learn to do it. But given the genetic influence on so many human traits, and the memorizing of Shakespeare's complete works by Rajan's father, one wonders.

**Clark's Nutcracker** *Among animals, one contender for champion memorist would be a mere birdbrain—the Clark's Nutcracker—which during winter and early spring can locate up to 6000 caches of buried pine seeds (Shettleworth, 1993).*

How precise and durable are our stored memories? Ebbinghaus (1885) learned lists of nonsense syllables and measured how much he retained when relearning each list, from 20 minutes to 30 days later. His famous "forgetting curve" (Figure 9–11) indicates that much of what we learn we may quickly forget. Many later experiments allow us to state the forgetting curve as one of psychology's laws: The course of forgetting is initially rapid, then levels off with time (Wixted & Ebbesen, 1991).

Harry Bahrick (1984) confirmed Ebbinghaus's finding with more meaningful material. He examined the forgetting curve for Spanish learned

**Figure 9–11**

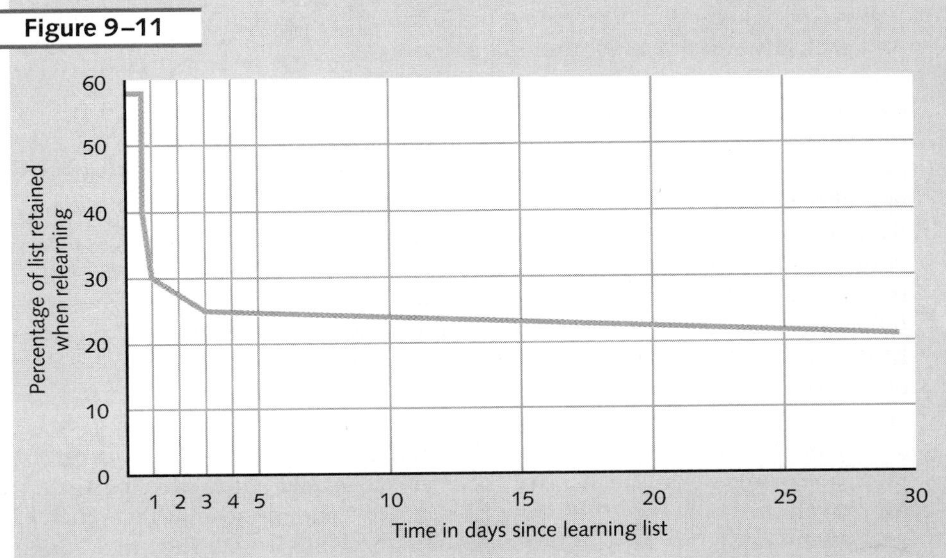


**Ebbinghaus's Forgetting Curve** *After learning lists of nonsense syllables, Ebbinghaus studied how much he retained up to 30 days later. He found that memory for novel information fades quickly, then levels out. (Adapted from Ebbinghaus, 1885.)*

**Figure 9–12**

**The Forgetting Curve for Spanish Vocabulary** *Compared with people just completing a Spanish course, those 3 years out of the course remembered much less. Compared with the 3-year group, however, those who studied Spanish even longer ago did not forget much more. (Adapted from Bahrick, 1984b.)*

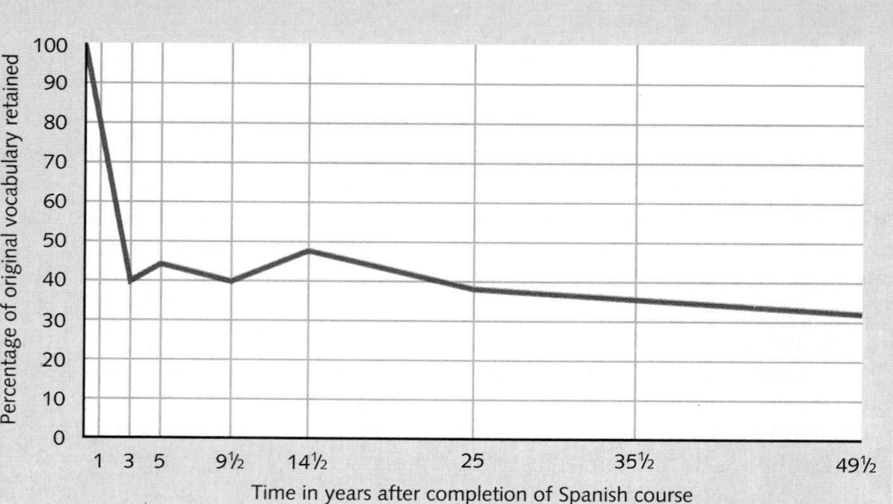


in school. By using the cross-sectional method (page 136), he compared the knowledge of Spanish among people who had just taken Spanish with the Spanish knowledge of those who had studied it up to 50 years before. Compared with those just completing a high school or college Spanish course, those who had been out of school for 3 years had forgotten much of what they had learned (Figure 9–12). However, after roughly 3 years, forgetting leveled off; what people remembered then, they still remembered 25 years later, even if they had not used their Spanish at all.

Is the forgotten Spanish gone—lost from storage—or merely inaccessible? If we could somehow uncover them, would we find our past experiences intact, like long-lost books in a dusty attic? Sigmund Freud thought so. If only we could recover and resolve the painful repressed memories of our childhoods, he thought, emotional healing would follow. When "age-regressed" under hypnosis, some people do offer detailed reports of childhood experiences. But as we noted in Chapter 7, such reports are unreliable and typically contain fabricated material.

## Memory's Physical Storage

For a time, it was thought that brain stimulation during surgery provided evidence that our past is "in there," in complete detail, just waiting to be relived. As you may recall from page 60, to predict possible side effects of surgery, brain surgeon Wilder Penfield helped map the brain's motor cortex by electrically stimulating wide-awake patients. Occasionally, Penfield's patients would report hearing things, such as "a mother calling her little boy." Penfield (1969) assumed he was activating long-lost experiences etched permanently on the brain.

Scrutinizing these famous reports, memory researchers Elizabeth Loftus and Geoffrey Loftus (1980) discovered that these flashbacks were extremely rare, occurring in only a handful of Penfield's 1100 stimulated patients. Moreover, the content of these few recollections suggested that the experiences were not being relived but were being invented. As if they had been dreaming, people would recall being in locations they had never visited.

Although the brain's storage capacity may be essentially unlimited, Penfield's evidence did *not* suggest that we store most information with the exactness of a tape recorder. Rather, say memory researchers, forgetting occurs as new experiences interfere with our retrieval (pages 314–315) and as the physical memory trace gradually decays.

But what exactly is the "memory trace"? Since 1980, new clues to the physical basis of long-term memory have surfaced rapidly. While cognitive psychologists study our memory "software," neuroscientists are gaining new insights into our memory "hardware"—how and where we physically store information in our brains.

For several decades, neuroscientists have searched the brain for physical evidence of memory. The search has at times been exasperating. One psychologist, Karl Lashley (1950), trained rats to solve a maze, then cut out pieces of the rats' cortexes and tested their memory of the maze. Eventually, he hoped to locate where memory of the maze was stored. Alas, no matter what part of the cortex he removed, the rats retained at least a partial memory of how to solve the maze. Lashley's conclusion: Memories do not reside in single, specific spots.

Are memories instead rooted in the brain's ongoing electrical activity? If so, then temporarily shutting down that activity should eliminate them, much as a power failure eliminates the settings on an electronic clock. To test this, Ralph Gerard (1953) trained hamsters to turn right or left to get food. Then he lowered their body temperature until the brain's electrical activity ceased. When the hamsters were revived and their brains were active again, would they remember which way to turn? Yes. Their long-term memories survived the electrical blackout.

### Synaptic Changes

Other neuroscientists are analyzing memory on a finer scale, by exploring changes within and between single neurons. Memories begin as impulses whizzing through brain circuits, which somehow cause permanent neural changes. Where does the neural change occur that makes memories permanent? The available clues point to the synapses—the sites where nerve cells communicate with one another through their neurotransmitter messengers (Alkon & others, 1991). Chapter 3 notes how experience modifies the brain's neural networks. Given increased activity in a particular pathway, neural interconnections form or strengthen.

Eric Kandel and James Schwartz (1982) observed actual changes in the sending neurons. Their subjects were among the simplest of animals, the California sea snail, *Aplysia*. Its mere 20,000 or so nerve cells are unusually large and accessible, enabling the researchers to observe synaptic changes during learning. Chapter 8 noted how the sea snail can be classically conditioned (with electric shock) to reflexively withdraw its gills when squirted with water, much as a shell-shocked soldier jumps at the sound of a snapping twig. By observing sea snails' neural connections before and after conditioning, the researchers pinpointed changes. When learning occurs, the snail releases more of the neurotransmitter serotonin at certain synapses, and these synapses become more efficient at transmitting signals.

Increased synaptic efficiency makes for more efficient neural circuits. In experiments, rapidly stimulating certain memory-circuit connections has increased their sensitivity for hours or even weeks to come. (The sending neuron now needs less prompting to release its neurotransmitter, and receptor sites may increase.) This prolonged strengthening of potential neural firing, called **long-term potentiation (LTP)**, looks like a neural basis for learning and remembering associations. Drugs that block LTP interfere

**What's Next?** *In the early stages of Alzheimer's disease, a loss of brain tissue that secretes important neurotransmitters results in considerable mental impairment. Although certain kinds of memory abilities are lost, patients can still read, making daily life a little easier. Discovering the neural and chemical mechanisms of memory may enable treatment.*

with learning (Lynch & Staubli, 1991). Mutant mice engineered to lack an enzyme needed for LTP can't learn their way out of a maze (Silva & others, 1992). Voila! says neuroscientist Gary Lynch (1992), long-term potentiation "sounds like memory."

Passing an electric current through the brain won't disrupt old memories after long-term potentiation has occurred. But very recent experiences will be wiped out. Such is the experience both of laboratory animals and of depressed people given electroconvulsive therapy (page 567). A blow to the head can do the same. When football players who have been dazed or momentarily knocked unconscious are interviewed a few minutes later, they typically cannot recall the name of the play during which the incident occurred (Yarnell & Lynch, 1970). Likewise, a boxer knocked out in round 2 may have no memory of round 1. (They are like sleepers who can't remember what they heard just before losing consciousness.) The information in short-term memory before the blow just didn't have time to consolidate into long-term memory. Drugs that block neurotransmitters also disrupt information storage (Squire, 1987). For example, alcohol impairs memory formation by disrupting serotonin's messenger activity (Weingartner & others, 1983). The morning after a night of heavy drinking, a person may have trouble remembering the previous evening.

The naturally stimulating hormones that humans and animals produce when excited or stressed have an opposite effect: They boost learning and retention. When a rat receives an arousing hormone and then a mild foot shock, it forms an indelible memory—like the one it forms when an intense foot shock naturally triggers release of the same hormone (Gold, 1987, 1992; Martinez & others, 1991). By making more glucose energy available to fuel brain activity, the hormone surge signals the brain that something important has happened.

Emotion-triggered hormonal changes help explain why we long remember exciting or shocking events, such as our first kiss, a political assassination, or an earthquake. People who were most emotionally upset by hearing the news of the *Challenger* explosion were most likely 3 years later to remember where they were (Bohannon & Symons, 1992). Understandably, then, people who actually *experienced* the San Francisco Bay earthquake had perfect recall a year and a half later of where they were and what they were doing (as they recorded a day or two later). Others' memories for the circumstances under which they *heard* about the quake were prone to errors (Neisser & others, 1991; Palmer & others, 1991). (A second reason for the durability of dramatic experiences is our reliving and rehearsing them.)

## Storing Implicit and Explicit Memories

After a memory-to-be enters the cortex through the senses, it winds its way into the depths of the brain. Where it goes depends on the type of information, as strikingly illustrated in the special cases of amnesic patients similar to John, whom we met at the beginning of this chapter.

Neurologist Oliver Sacks (1985, pp. 26–27) describes another such patient. Jimmie, a brain-damaged man, had no memories—thus, no sense of elapsed time—beyond 1945. Asked to name the President, he replied, "FDR's dead. Truman's at the helm."

When Jimmie gave his age as 19, Sacks thrust a mirror at him: "Look in the mirror and tell me what you see. Is that a 19-year-old looking out from the mirror?"

Jimmie turned ashen, gripped the chair, cursed, then became frantic: "What's going on? What's happened to me? Is this a nightmare? Am I crazy? Is this a joke?" When his attention was diverted to some children playing baseball, his panic ended, the dreadful mirror swiftly forgotten.

Flipping through a *National Geographic*, Sacks showed Jimmie a photo. "What is this?" he asked.

"It's the moon," Jimmie replied.

"No, it's not," Sacks answered. "It's a picture of the earth taken from the moon."

"Doc, you're kidding? Someone would've had to get a camera up there!"

"Naturally."

"Hell! You're joking—how the hell would you do that?" Jimmie's wonder was that of a bright young man from 40 years ago reacting with amazement to his travel back to the future.

Careful testing of these unique people reveals something even stranger: Although incapable of recalling new facts or anything they have recently done, Jimmie and other similarly amnesic people can learn. They can be classically conditioned, and with practice they can learn to read mirror-image writing or do a jigsaw puzzle (Schacter, 1992; Squire, 1987). They do all these things with absolutely no memory of having learned them. Or consider what happens when such patients have learned to solve a Tower of Hanoi puzzle, which requires moving rings from one pole to another until they are stacked in order of size. Amnesia victims will deny having seen the puzzle before, insist it is silly for them to try, and then, like a practiced expert, proceed to solve it. They are in some ways like the brain-damaged people who cannot consciously recognize faces, but whose physiological responses to familiar faces reveal an implicit (unconscious) recognition.

These curious findings make it hard to argue that memory is a single, unified system. Whatever has destroyed the amnesics' conscious recall has not destroyed their unconscious capacity for learning. They can learn *how* to do something—**implicit memory** (*nondeclarative memory*)—without knowing and declaring *that* they know—**explicit memory** (*declarative memory*). Having read a story once, they will read it faster a second time through, although they cannot recall having seen the story before. Having played golf on a new course, they will forget it completely, yet their game will improve with experience on the course. If repeatedly shown the word *perfume*, they wouldn't recall having seen it. But if asked the first word that comes to mind in response to the letters *per*, they surprise themselves by readily displaying their learning. Strangely, they retain their past but do not explicitly recall it (Figure 9–13).

*The two-track memory system reinforces an important principle introduced in Chapter 5's description of parallel processing: Mental feats such as vision, thinking, and memory may seem to be single abilities, but they are not. Rather, we split information into different components for separate and simultaneous processing.*

**Figure 9–13**

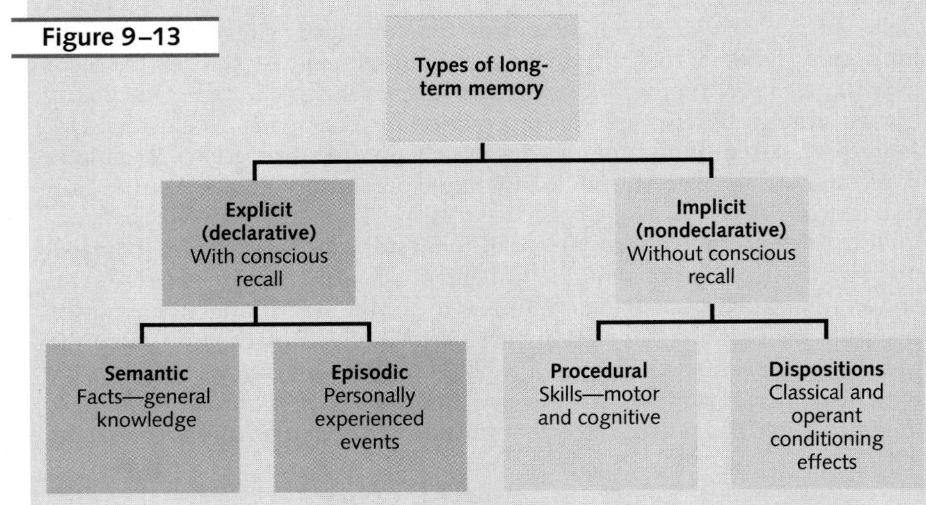


**Memory Subsystems** *Explicit and implicit memories are processed and stored separately. Thus, one may lose explicit memory (becoming amnesic), yet display implicit memory for what can't be consciously recalled.*

Our explicit and implicit memories involve separate brain systems. Brain scans and autopsies reveal that amnesic patients usually have suffered damage to the **hippocampus**, a limbic system structure that plays a vital role in the gradual processing of our explicit memories for names, images, and events into long-term memory (Figure 9–14). When people recall words (using explicit memory) the hippocampus lights up on a PET scan (Squire & Ojemann, 1992). Chickadees and other birds can store food in hundreds of places and return to these unmarked caches months later, but not if their hippocampus has been removed (Sherry & Vaccarino, 1989). Among older adults, recall for new words and pictures is impaired if the hippocampus has shrunk (Golomb & others, 1993, 1994).

**Figure 9–14**

**The Hippocampus** *Explicit memories for facts and episodes are processed in the hippocampus, marked yellow in the drawing (a) and red in the MRI scan (b).*

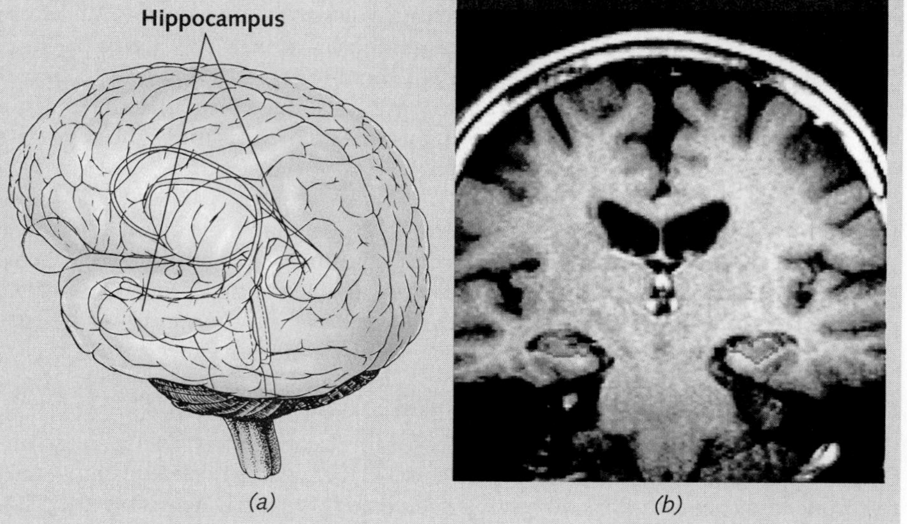

Hippocampus

(a)

(b)

When monkeys lose their hippocampus to surgery, they also lose most of their recall for things learned during the preceding month (Squire & Zola-Morgan, 1991). Older memories remain intact, suggesting that the hippocampus is not the permanent storehouse, but a way station that feeds new information to other brain circuits for permanent storage. Our neural library stores different types of information in specific neural clusters. One retired woman suffered injury to a brain network that left her unable to name animals, though she could still name plants and objects (Hart & Gordon, 1992).

Your hippocampus is an essential temporary storage site for your explicit memories, but you could lose it and still lay down memories for skills and conditioned associations. Hoping to locate such implicit memories, psychologist Richard Thompson and his fellow sleuths David Krupa and Judith Thompson studied how a rabbit's brain learns to associate a tone with an impending air puff in the eye (and thus to blink in anticipation of the puff). First, they discovered that the pathway connecting the brain's reception of the tone with the blink response runs through a part of the cerebellum (at the back of the head) to the brainstem. If they cut the pathway, the learned response was lost. That was like cutting the cords to your stereo speakers, which would confirm the cord's part of the electronic path but might still leave you wondering where the music is stored. Their next step was to administer a drug during eye-blink training with rabbits that could temporarily deaden different parts of the neural pathway. This pinpointed the implicit memory—in the cerebellum. The rejuvenated rabbits failed to display the learned response only when the cerebellum was deactivated during training (Krupa & others, 1993).

This dual explicit-implicit memory system helps explain infantile amnesia. Behaviorally, the reactions and skills we learned during infancy reach far into our future. Yet as adults we recall nothing (explicitly) of our first 3 years. Our conscious minds are blank, not only because we index so much of our explicit memory by words that nonspeaking children have not learned, but also because the hippocampus is one of the last brain structures to mature.

### Summing Up

**Sensory Memory Storage** Information first enters the memory system through the senses. We register and briefly store visual images via iconic memory, and sounds via echoic memory.

**Short-Term Memory Storage** Our short-term memory span for information just presented is very limited—a seconds-long retention of up to about seven or eight items, depending on the information and how it is presented.

**Long-Term Memory Storage** Our capacity for storing information permanently is essentially unlimited.

**Memory's Physical Storage** How and where we store information is uncertain. The search for the physical basis of memory has recently focused on the synapses and their neurotransmitters and on the long-term potentiation of brain circuits, such as those running through the hippocampus. Studies of brain-damaged patients reveal two types of memory—explicit (declarative) memories processed by the hippocampus, and implicit (nondeclarative) memories processed by more ancient brain regions.

## Retrieval: Getting Information Out

*To remember an event requires not only getting it in (encoding) and retaining it (storage), but getting it out. Retrieval is aided by cues associated with the event, including those in the context where we encoded it. Memory retrieval is, however, partly memory construction—a fact that raises questions about the accuracy of certain eyewitness memories.*

To most people, memory is **recall**, the ability to retrieve information not in conscious awareness. To a psychologist, memory is any sign that something learned has been retained. So *recognizing* or more quickly *relearning* information also indicates memory.

**Remembering Things Past** *Even if Madonna and Paul Newman had not become famous, their high school classmates would most likely still recognize their yearbook photos.*

*Multiple-choice questions test our:*
*(a) recall.*
*(b) recognition.*
*(c) relearning.*
*Fill-in-the-blank questions test our ________.*
*(See page 311.)*

Long after you cannot recall most of the people in your high school graduating class, you may still recognize their yearbook pictures from a photographic lineup and pick their names out from a list of names. Harry Bahrick and his colleagues (1975) reported that people who graduated 25 years earlier could not *recall* many of their old classmates, but they could *recognize* 90 percent of their pictures and names.

Relearning speed can reveal memory. If you once learned something and then forgot it, you probably will relearn it more quickly than when you learned it originally. When you study for a final exam or resurrect a language used in early childhood, the relearning is easier. Tests of **recognition** and of time spent **relearning** reveal that we remember more than we can recall.

The speed and vastness of our recognition memory dwarfs any librarian's ability to call up information. "Is your friend wearing a new or old outfit?" "Old." "Is this seconds-long movie clip from a film you've ever seen?" "Yes." "Have you ever before seen this person—this minor variation on the same old human features (two eyes, one nose, and so on)?" "No." Before the mouth can form our answer to any of millions of such questions, the mind knows, and knows that it knows.

## Retrieval Cues

To retrieve a fact from a library, you need a way to access it. In recognition tests, retrieval cues (such as photographs) provide reminders of information (classmates' names) we could not otherwise recall. Retrieval cues also are guides to where to look. If you want to know what the pyramid on the back of a dollar bill signifies, you might look in *Collier's Encyclopedia* under "dollar," "currency," or "money." But your efforts would be futile. To get the information you want, you would have to look under "Great Seal of the United States" (Hayes, 1981). Like information stored in encyclopedias, memories are inaccessible unless we have cues for retrieving them. The more and better learned the retrieval cues, the more accessible the memory.

You can think of a memory as held in storage by a web of associations (J. R. Anderson, 1983). To retrieve a specific memory, you first need to identify one of the strands that leads to it, a process called **priming** (Bower, 1986). Philosopher-psychologist William James referred to priming as the "wakening of associations." Often our associations are activated, or primed, without our awareness. Hearing or seeing the word *rabbit* can unconsciously prime people to spell the spoken word *hair* as *h-a-r-e*. As Figure 9–15 indicates, *rabbit* primes associations with *hare* even though we may not recall having heard *rabbit*. (Recall from Chapter 5 that even subliminal stimuli can sometimes prime responses to later stimuli.)

**Figure 9–15**

**Priming— Another Type of Implicit Memory** *The spreading of associations can unconsciously activate related associations. After seeing or hearing* rabbit, *we are later more likely to spell the spoken word* hair *as* h-a-r-e. *(Adapted from Bower, 1986.)*

Can we remember better if we activate retrieval cues within our web of associations? Definitely. Mnemonic devices provide us with handy retrieval cues: ROY G. BIV; HOMES; bun, shoe, tree. We can also expose ourselves to cues that prime our memories for earlier experiences. The best retrieval cues come from the associations formed at the time we encode a memory. Before the Watergate hearings, John Dean refreshed his memory "by going through every single newspaper article outlining what had happened and then placing myself in what I had done in a given sequence in time" (Neisser, 1981). This helped activate associations that were specific to the encoded memory (a phenomenon that Endel Tulving and Donald Thomson [1973] called *encoding specificity*).

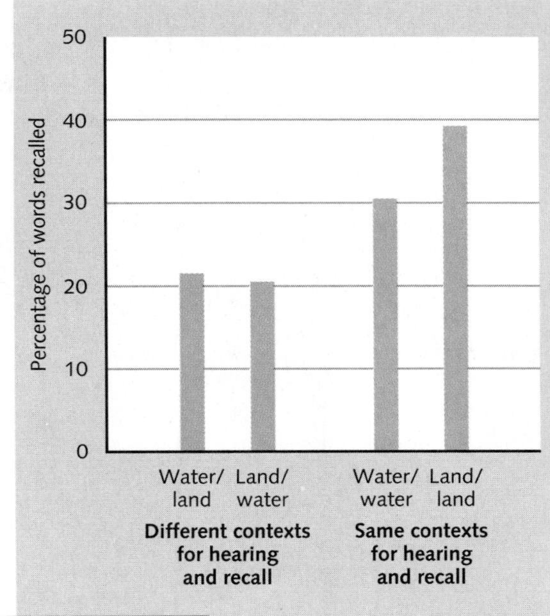


**Figure 9–16**

**The Effects of Context on Memory** *Words heard underwater are best recalled underwater; words heard on land are best recalled on land. (Adapted from Godden & Baddeley, 1975.)*

### Context Effects

It does help to put yourself back in the context where you experienced something. Duncan Godden and Alan Baddeley (1975) discovered this by having scuba divers listen to a list of words in two different settings, either 10 feet underwater or sitting on the beach. As Figure 9–16 illustrates, the divers recalled more words when they were retested in the same place.

You have probably experienced similar context effects. Returning to where you once lived or to the school you once attended may flood you with retrieval cues and memories. Taking an exam in the same room where you are taught may help a little. In several experiments, Carolyn Rovee-Collier (1993) found that a familiar context activates memories even in 3-month-olds. After learning that kicking would move a crib mobile (via a connecting ribbon from the ankle), the infants used this learning by kicking more when again tested in the same crib with the same bumper (Figure 9–17).

Sometimes, being in a context similar to one we've been in before may trigger the experience of **déjà vu**—that eerie sense that "I've been in this exact situation before." People who pose the question as, "How could I recognize a situation that I'm experiencing for the first time?" may suppose that something paranormal is occurring. Could it be reincarnation ("I must have experienced this in a previous life") or precognition ("I viewed this scene in my mind before experiencing it")? If we pose the question differ-

**Figure 9–17**

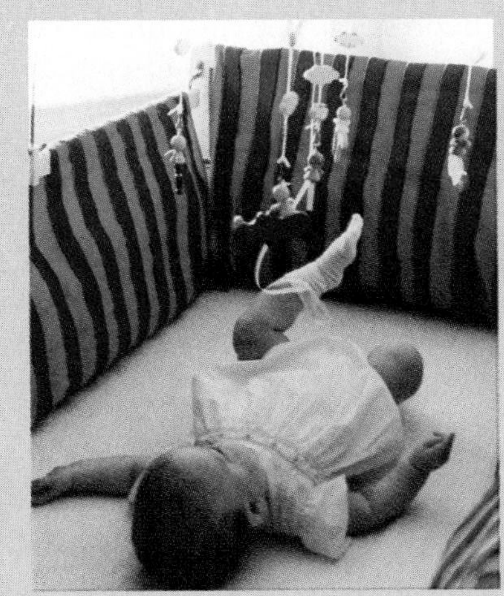

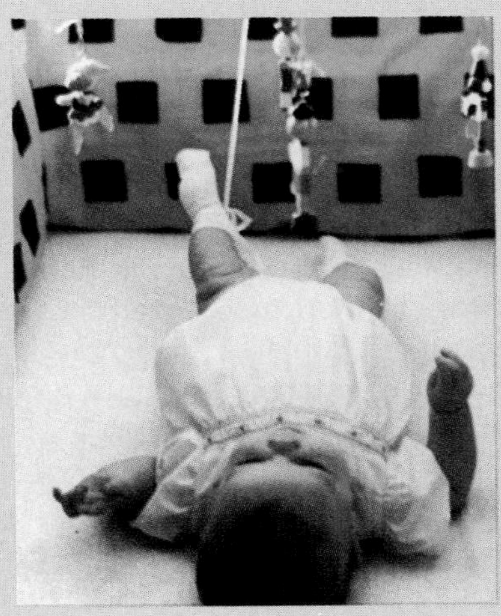

**Infants Learned to Move a Mobile by Kicking** *Later, this learning was reactivated most strongly when retesting the infants in the same rather than a different context. (From Butler & Rovee-Collier, 1989.)*

ently ("Why do I feel as if I recognize this situation?"), we can see how our memory system might produce the déjà vu feeling (Alcock, 1981). If we have previously been in a similar situation, although we can't recall what it was, the current situation may be loaded with cues that unconsciously help us to retrieve the earlier experience. Thus, if in such a context you see a stranger who looks and walks like one of your friends, the similarity may give rise to an eerie feeling of recognition. Because the feeling conflicts with your knowing that the person is a stranger, you may think, "I've seen that person in this situation before."

### Moods and Memories

Associated words, events, and contexts are not the only retrieval cues. Events in the past may have aroused a specific emotion, which later can prime us to recall its associated events. Cognitive psychologist Gordon Bower (1983) explains: "A specific emotional state is like a specific room in a library into which the subject places memory records, and he can most easily retrieve those records by returning to that same room or emotional state." The things we learn in one state—be it joyful or sad, drunk or sober—are sometimes more easily recalled when we are again in the same state, a subtle phenomenon called *state-dependent memory*. What is learned when drunk, high, or depressed is not recalled well in *any* state (drugs and depression interfere with encoding), but it's recalled slightly better when again drunk, high, or depressed. Someone who hides money when drunk may forget the location, until drunk again.

**CALLAHAN**

*"I wonder if you'd mind giving me directions. I've never been sober in this part of town before."*
Distributed by Levin Represents.

More reliable and striking is a mood's effect on emotionally tinged memories (Ellis & Ashbrook, 1989; Matt & others, 1992). We seem to associate good or bad events with their accompanying emotions. Thus, the emotions become retrieval cues; when again feeling good or bad, we more easily recall associated good or bad times. If people are put in a buoyant mood—whether under hypnosis or just by the day's events (a World Cup soccer victory for the German subjects of one study)—they recall the world through rose-colored glasses (Forgas & others, 1984; Schwarz & others, 1987). They judge themselves to be competent and effective, other people to be benevolent, life in general to be wonderful. Put in a bad mood by negative events, the very same people suddenly recall and predict everything more negatively.

So it shouldn't surprise us that in some studies *currently* depressed people recall their parents as having been rejecting, punitive, and guilt-promoting, whereas *formerly* depressed people describe their parents much as do those who have never suffered depression (Lewinsohn & Rosenbaum, 1987; Lewis, 1992). Our memories are somewhat **mood-congruent**. Being depressed sours memories by priming negative associations, which we use to explain our current mood. No wonder Robert Bornstein and others (1991) report that adolescents' ratings of parental warmth give little clue to how the same adolescents will rate their parents 6 weeks later. When teenagers are down, their world, including their parents, seems inhuman; as their mood brightens, their parents metamorphose from devils into angels. You and I may nod our heads knowingly. Yet, in a good or bad mood, we persist in attributing our changing judgments and memories to reality.

*"When a feeling was there, they felt as if it would never go; when it was gone, they felt as if it had never been; when it returned, they felt as if it had never gone."*

George MacDonald
*What's Mine's Mine*, 1886

Moods also influence how we *interpret* other people's behavior. In a bad mood, we read someone's look as a glare; in a good mood we encode the same look as interest. How we perceive the world depends on our mood. Passions exaggerate.

Finally, our moods affect how attentive we are to new information. Sad people are often preoccupied—less attentive to new information and more focused on their aches and woes (Salovey & Birnbaum, 1989; Wood & others, 1990). In some respects, that's healthy. There is sense in suffering. A negative mood signals that all's not well, motivating people to ruminate and reassess. But very happy moods can also trigger distracting thoughts, impairing memory for the task at hand (Seibert & Ellis, 1991).

Your mood's effect on encoding and retrieval helps explain why moods persist. When happy, you recall happy events, which helps prolong the good mood. When depressed, you recall depressing events, which in turn feeds depressing interpretations of current events. As we will see in Chapter 15, this process maintains depression's vicious cycle.

*Answers to questions on page 308: Multiple-choice questions test recognition. Fill-in-the-blank questions test recall.*

## Memory Construction

Picture yourself having the following pleasant experience:

> You decide to go to your favorite restaurant for dinner. You enter the restaurant and are seated at a table with a white tablecloth. You study the menu. You tell the waiter that you want prime rib, medium rare, a baked potato with sour cream, and a salad with blue cheese dressing. You also order some red wine from the wine list. A few minutes later the waiter returns with your salad. Later he brings the rest of the meal, which you enjoy, except that the prime rib is a bit overdone.

Were I immediately to quiz you on this paragraph (from Hyde, 1983), you could surely retrieve considerable detail. For example, without looking back, answer the following questions:

1. What kind of salad dressing did you order?
2. Was the tablecloth red checked?
3. What did you order to drink?
4. Did the waiter give you a menu?

You were probably able to recall exactly what you ordered, and maybe even the color of the tablecloth. Does retrieval therefore consist merely of "reading" the information stored in our brain's library? We do have an enormous capacity for storing and reproducing the incidental details of our daily experience. But as we have seen, we often construct our memories as we encode them, and we may also alter our memories as we withdraw them from the memory bank. Like a scientist who infers a dinosaur's appearance from its remains, we infer our past from stored information plus what we now assume. Did the waiter give you a menu? Not in the paragraph given. Nevertheless, many people answer yes. By filtering information and filling in missing pieces, their schemas for restaurants direct their memory construction.

In many dozens of experiments, involving more than 20,000 people, Elizabeth Loftus has shown how eyewitnesses similarly reconstruct their memories when questioned. In one experiment with John Palmer, Loftus showed a film of a traffic accident and then quizzed the viewers about what they saw (Loftus & Palmer, 1974). Those asked, "How fast were the cars going when they *smashed* into each other?" gave higher speed estimates than those asked, "How fast were the cars going when they *hit* each other?" A week later, the researchers asked the viewers if they recalled seeing any broken glass. Compared to those who had been asked the question with *hit*, those asked the question with *smashed* were more than twice as likely to recall broken glass (Figure 9–18). In fact, there was no broken glass.

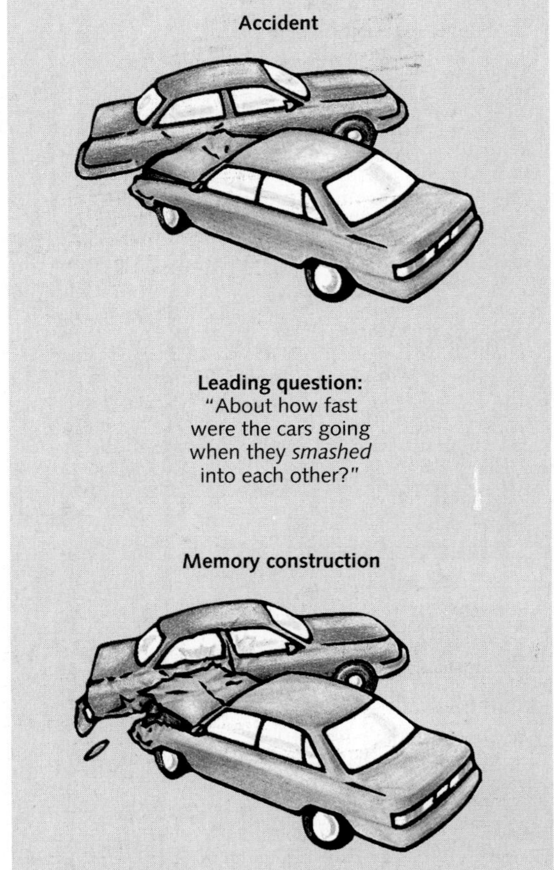
Accident
Leading question:
"About how fast were the cars going when they *smashed* into each other?"
Memory construction

**Figure 9–18**

**Memory Construction** *When people who saw the film of a car accident were asked a leading question, they recalled a more serious accident than they had witnessed. (From Loftus, 1979.)*

In many follow-up experiments around the world, people have witnessed an event, received or not received misleading information about it, and then taken a memory test. The repeated result is a **misinformation effect**: After exposure to subtle misinformation, many people misremember. They have misrecalled a yield sign as a stop sign, hammers as screwdrivers, Coke cans as peanut cans, *Vogue* magazine as *Mademoiselle*, "Dr. Henderson" as "Dr. Davidson," breakfast cereal as eggs, and a clean-shaven man as a man with a mustache (Loftus & others, 1992). As a memory fades with time following an event, the injection of misinformation becomes easier (Loftus, 1992).

So unwitting is the misinformation effect that people later find it nearly impossible to discriminate between their memories of real and suggested events (Schooler & others, 1986). This difficulty was strikingly true among those who 3 years later misrecalled their whereabouts on hearing of the space shuttle *Challenger's* explosion (Neisser & Harsch, 1992). When shown their own handwritten accounts from the day after, many were surprised. Some were so sure of their made-up memories that they insisted their original version must have been flawed.

*"Memory is insubstantial. Things keep replacing it. Your batch of snapshots will both fix and ruin your memory. . . . You can't remember anything from your trip except the wretched collection of snapshots."*

Annie Dillard
"To Fashion a Text," 1988

As people recount an experience, they fill in their memory gaps with plausible guesses and assumptions. After more retellings, they often recall these guessed details, now absorbed into their memories, as if they actually observed them (Roediger & others, 1993). Others' vivid retellings may also implant false memories. The psychologist Jean Piaget was startled as an adult to learn that his vivid, detailed memory of his nursemaid's thwarting his kidnapping was utterly false. Piaget apparently constructed the memory from the many retellings of the story he had heard (later confessed by the nursemaid to have been false).

*The moral*: Memory is reconstruction as well as reproduction. You therefore can't be sure whether a memory is real by how real it feels. Unreal memories feel like real memories. In experiments on eyewitness testimony, researchers have repeatedly found that the most confident eyewitnesses are the most persuasive, but they often are not the most accurate. Eyewitnesses, whether right or wrong, express roughly similar self-assurance (Bothwell & others, 1987; Cutler & Penrod, 1989; Wells & Murray, 1984). Confidence also gives little clue to accuracy in studies of "earwitness" identifications of a previously heard voice among a lineup of voices (Yarmey, 1991).

Memory construction helps explain why John Dean's recollections of the Watergate conversations were a mixture of real and imagined events. It explains why "hypnotically refreshed" memories of crimes so easily incorporate errors, some of which originate with the hypnotist's leading questions. ("Did you hear loud noises?") And it explains why dating partners who fall in love *over*estimate their first impressions of one another, while those who break up *under*estimate their earlier liking (McFarland & Ross, 1987).

*"Memory is a great betrayer."*

Anaïs Nin
*The Diary of Anaïs Nin*, 1974

Recognizing that the misinformation effect can occur as police and attorneys ask questions framed by their own understandings of an event, Ronald Fisher, Edward Geiselman, and their colleagues (1987, 1989) train police interviewers to ask less suggestive, more effective questions. To activate retrieval cues, the detective first asks witnesses to visualize the scene—the weather, time of day, lighting, sounds, smells, positions of objects, and their mood. Then the witness tells in detail, and without interruption, every point recalled, no matter how trivial. Only then does the detective ask evocative follow-up questions: "Was there anything unusual about the person's appearance or clothing?" Using this "cognitive interview" technique, Fisher and Geiselman report that accurate recall increases by some 50 percent.

### Children's Eyewitness Recall

If memories can be sincere, yet so sincerely wrong, might children's recollections of sexual abuse err? Who is most often victimized—abused children whose recollections are disbelieved, or those falsely accused whose reputations are ruined? Both sides in this emotional debate agree that

- child sexual abuse occurs and can leave a person scarred—more vulnerable to low self-image, sexual promiscuity, anxiety, and depression (Briere & Runtz, 1993; Trickett & Putnam, 1993).
- some innocent people, occasionally those caught in a child custody conflict, suffer the injustice of false accusations.
- some perpetrators hide their guilt by casting doubt on their truth-telling accusers.

At issue is the credibility of children's reports. By asking leading questions, can interviewers plant false memories of a story they expect to hear? Are children credible eyewitnesses in cases of murder, assault, and robbery? Research—most of it conducted in just the last decade—suggests that the truth lies between the two extremes (Brooks & Siegal, 1991; Ceci & Bruck, 1993a,b; Doris, 1991). Children are not, as some believe, as reliable and resistant to suggestion as are adults. In 15 of 18 studies, preschoolers were more suggestible than were older children or adults. In one study of nearly 2000 people who had watched a film clip while visiting a San Francisco science museum, younger children were especially susceptible to the misinformation effect (Loftus & others, 1992). But children also do not, as others believe, routinely confuse reality with fantasy. If questioned about their experiences in words they understand, they often freely recall what happened and who did it. Children are especially credible when their disclosure is made in a first interview with a neutral person who asks non-leading questions, when involved adults have not talked with them prior to the interview, and when their story is consistent over time.

Studies of children's recollections of physical examinations illustrate both reasonable accuracy and occasional lapses. Lynne Baker-Ward and her colleagues (1993) tested children's memories with general questions ("Tell me what the doctor did to check you") and specific questions ("Did the doctor shine a light in your eyes?"). Three to 6 weeks after the exam, 3-year-olds recalled about 60 percent and 7-year-olds about 90 percent of what the doctor did. Asked about things that didn't happen ("Did the doctor cut your hair?" "Did the nurse sit on top of you?"), 3-year-olds gave wrong answers nearly 30 percent of the time; 7-year-olds erred only about 15 percent of the time.

As a father of a young child, Stephen Ceci (1993) thinks "it would be truly awful to ever lose sight of the enormity of child abuse." Yet his Cornell University studies of children's memories have sensitized him to children's suggestibility. In one study, 3-year-olds were asked to show on anatomically correct dolls where a pediatrician had touched them. Fifty-five percent of the children who had not received genital examinations showed either genital or anal touching.

In another study, a child chose a card from a deck of possible happenings and an adult then read from the card. For example, "Think real hard, and tell me if this ever happened to you. Can you remember going to the hospital with the mousetrap on your finger?" After 10 weekly interviews, repeatedly asking children to think about several real and fictitious events, a new adult asked the same question. The stunning result: 58 percent of preschoolers produced false (often vivid) stories regarding one or more events they had never experienced. Here is one from a boy who initially had denied the mousetrap incident:

> My brother Colin was trying to get Blowtorch [an action figure] from me, and I wouldn't let him take it from me, so he pushed me into the wood pile where the mousetrap was. And then my finger got caught in it. And then we went to the hospital, and my mommy, daddy, and Colin drove me there, to the hospital in our van, because it was far away. And the doctor put a bandage on this finger.

*"[The] research leads me to worry about the possibility of false allegations. It is not a tribute to one's scientific integrity to walk down the middle of the road if the data are more to one side."*

Stephen Ceci (1993)

Given such detailed stories, professional psychologists who specialize in interviewing children were often fooled. They could not reliably separate real from false memories. Nor could the children themselves. One child, reminded that his parents had several times told him that the mousetrap incident never happened—he had only imagined it—protested, "But it really did happen. I remember it!"

## Forgetting as Retrieval Failure

We have seen that forgetting occurs when we fail to encode information and when our stored memories decay. Forgotten events are like books you can't find in your library—some because you never acquired them, others because you discarded them from storage.

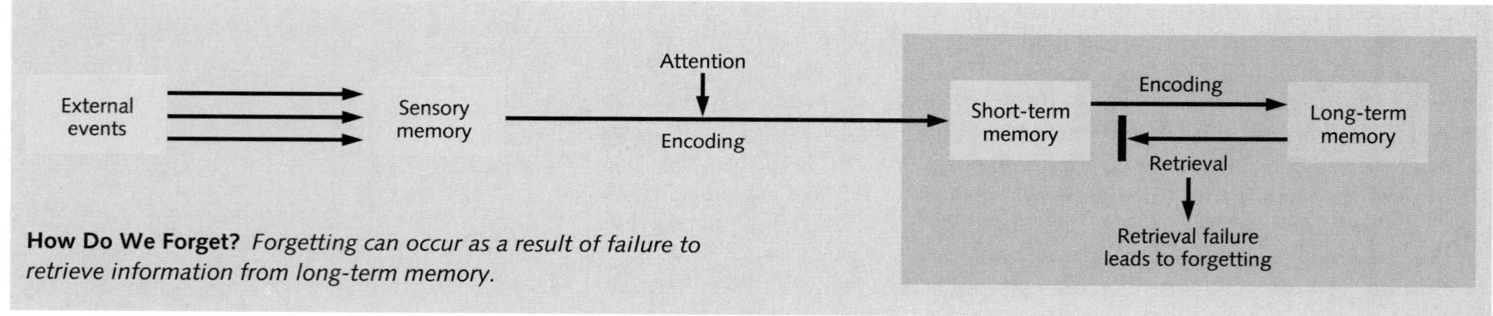


**How Do We Forget?** *Forgetting can occur as a result of failure to retrieve information from long-term memory.*

There is a third possibility: Even if the book is stored and available, it may be inaccessible. Perhaps you don't have the information needed to look it up and retrieve it. Information sometimes gets into our brain and, though we know it is there, we cannot get it out. A person's name may lie poised on the tip of the tongue, waiting to be retrieved. When people who cannot recall information get retrieval cues ("It begins with an *m*"), they often remember what they could not recall. Retrieval problems lie behind the occasional memory failures of older adults. (As Chapter 4 noted, older people tend to recall less than younger adults do, but they usually remember as well if given reminders or a recognition test.)

### Interference

Pro*active means forward-acting.*

Learning some items may interfere with retrieving others, especially when the items are similar. If someone gives you a phone number to remember, you may be able to recall it later. But if two more people give you their numbers, each successive number will be more difficult to recall. Such **proactive interference** occurs when something you learned earlier disrupts recall of something you experienced later. As you collect more and more information, your mental attic never fills, but it certainly gets cluttered.

For example, after buying a new combination lock or receiving a new phone number, the old one may interfere. Benton Underwood (1957) explored this phenomenon. He found that people who learn different lists of words on successive days have more and more difficulty remembering each new list the next day. This proactive interference explains why Ebbinghaus, after memorizing countless lists of nonsense syllables during his career, could remember only about one-fourth of a new list of syllables on the day after he learned it—far fewer than you as a novice could remember after learning a single list.

**Retroactive interference** occurs when new information makes it harder to recall something you learned earlier. For example, the learning of new students' names typically interferes with a professor's recall of names learned in previous classes. Table 9–1 illustrates both types of interference.

Retro*active means backward-acting.*

**Table 9–1 Proactive and Retroactive Interference**

| Time 1 | Time 2 | Time 3 | Interference |
|---|---|---|---|
| Study French | Study Spanish | Recall Spanish | French proactively interferes |
| Study French | Study Spanish | Recall French | Spanish retroactively interferes |

You can minimize retroactive interference by reducing the number of interfering events—say, by going to sleep shortly after learning new information. This is what John Jenkins and Karl Dallenbach (1924) found in a classic experiment. Day after day, two people each learned some nonsense syllables, then tried to recall them after up to 8 hours of being awake or asleep at night. As Figure 9–19 shows, forgetting occurred more rapidly

**Figure 9–19**

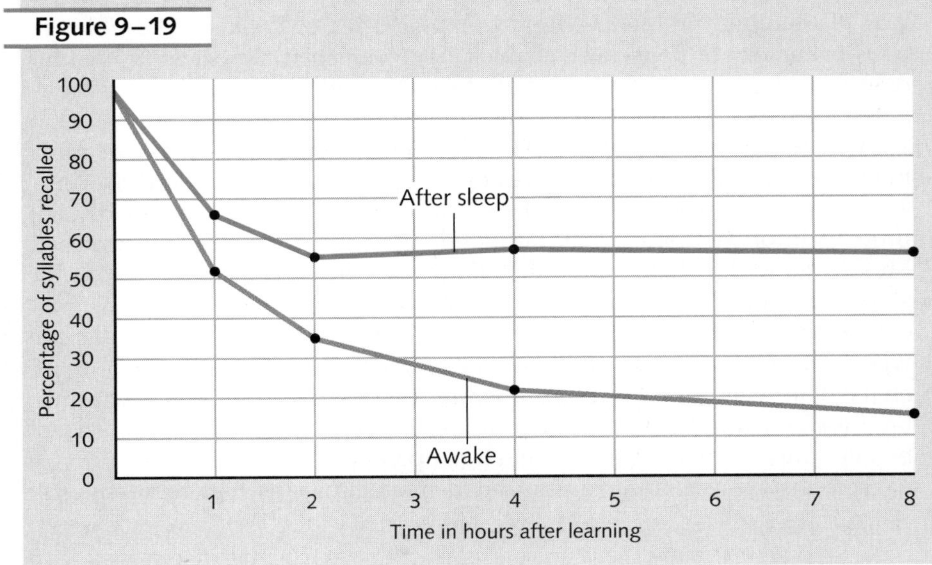


**Retroactive Interference** *More forgetting occurred when a person stayed awake and experienced other new material. (From Jenkins & Dallenbach, 1924.)*

after being awake and involved with other activities. The investigators surmised that "forgetting is not so much a matter of the decay of old impressions and associations as it is a matter of interference, inhibition, or obliteration of the old by the new" (p. 612). Later experiments confirm that the hour before a night's sleep (but not the minute before sleep) is a good time to commit information to memory (Fowler & others, 1973).

Although interference is an important cause of forgetting, we should not overstate the point. Sometimes old information facilitates our learning of new information. Knowledge of Latin may aid one's learning of French—a phenomenon called "positive transfer." It's when the old and new information compete with each other that interference occurs.

## Motivated Forgetting

The huge cookie jar in our kitchen was jammed with freshly baked chocolate chip cookies. Still more spread across the cooling racks on the counter. Twenty-four hours later, not a crumb was left. Who had taken them? My wife, three children, and I were the only people in the house during that time. So while memories were still fresh, I immediately undertook a little memory test. Andy acknowledged wolfing down as many as 20. Peter admitted eating 15. Laura guessed that she had stuffed her then-6-year-old body with 15 cookies. My wife, Carol, recalled eating 6, and I remembered consuming 15 and taking 18 more to the office. Collectively, our memories sheepishly accepted responsibility for 89 cookies. Still, we had not come close; 160 cookies had been baked.

In experiments that parallel the cookie-memory phenomenon, Michael Ross and his colleagues (1981) found that people unknowingly revise their own histories. After Ross persuaded a group of people that frequent toothbrushing is desirable, they (more than other people) recalled having frequently brushed their teeth in the last 2 weeks. Having taken a highly touted study skills course, students later inflated their estimates of self-improvement. By *de*flating their evaluations of their previous study habits they convinced themselves that they had really benefitted (Conway & Ross, 1984). To remember our past is often to revise it. By recalling events in a desired manner we protect and enhance our self-images.

*"[It is] necessary to remember that events happened in the desired manner. And if it is necessary to rearrange one's memories . . . then it is necessary to forget that one has done so. The trick of doing this can be learned like any other mental technique. . . . It is called doublethink."*

George Orwell
*Nineteen Eighty-Four*, 1948

Why do our memories fail us? Why did my family and I not encode, store, and retrieve almost half the instances of our cookie-eating? As noted earlier, we encode information about frequency fairly automatically. So was it a storage problem? Might our memories of cookies, like Ebbinghaus's memory of nonsense syllables, have vanished almost as fast as the cookies themselves? Or might the information still be intact but irretrievable because it would be embarrassing to remember?

With his concept of **repression**, Sigmund Freud proposed that with more painful information our memory systems are indeed self-censoring. To protect our self-concepts and to minimize anxiety, we supposedly repress painful memories. But the submerged memory still lingers, said Freud, and with patience and effort may be retrieved during therapy or by some later cue. One reported case involved a woman with an intense, unexplained fear of running water. An aunt solved the mystery one day by whispering, "I have never told." The words cued the woman's memory of an incident when, as a disobedient young child, she wandered away from a family picnic and became trapped under a waterfall—until being rescued by her aunt, who promised not to tell her parents (Kihlstrom, 1990).

Stories such as this have persuaded most clinicians that repression of painful memories can indeed occur. There are also anecdotes of stressed battlefield survivors who, for a time afterward, cannot remember their horror-filled experience. But not all memory researchers are convinced. After analyzing case reports of temporary battlefield amnesia, David Holmes (1994) reports that most "recovered memories" were unconfirmed and occurred during hypnosis, with drugs, or with role-playing suggested by the therapist. Physiological causes of memory loss, such as concussions, were not ruled out. In laboratory experiments, people have not been more likely to forget unpleasant experiences than pleasant ones. And in real life, most people remember horrible experiences all too well (see "Thinking Critically About Repressed Memories of Abuse"). Holocaust survivors and those who suffer other traumatic stresses seldom forget. "The things we remember best," noted Baltasar Gracian in 1647, "are those better forgotten."

*"Warning. Despite 70 years of research, there is no objective evidence to support the concept of repression."*

David A. Holmes (1994)

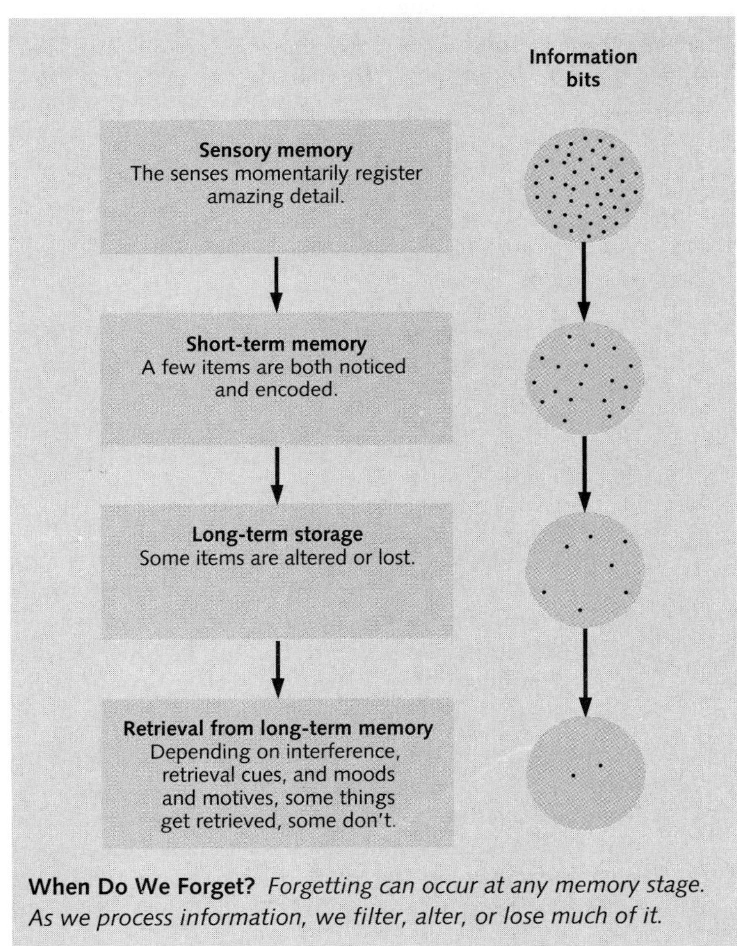


**When Do We Forget?** *Forgetting can occur at any memory stage. As we process information, we filter, alter, or lose much of it.*

The closest laboratory counterpart to repression (and an alternative explanation of it) is the phenomenon of state-dependent memory (page 310): What we learn in one emotional or physiological state we sometimes are unable to retrieve in a radically different state. Thus, what we experience when embarrassed or horror-stricken may be forgotten when relaxed.

## *Thinking Critically About* Repressed Memories of Abuse

*Serious questions lie at the heart of an intense controversy over reports of repressed and recovered memories of childhood sexual abuse. Without disputing the all-too-common reality and horror of such abuse, critics use principles of memory construction to question the reality of repressed memories.*

In 1974, 4-year-old Rachel (not her real name) and two others were molested by Rachel's uncle. Rachel told her mother, who informed the mother of one of the others, who proceeded to stab and kill the uncle. Seventeen years later, psychologist Linda Meyer Williams (in press) tracked down Rachel and 128 other women who were recorded as having experienced child sex abuse (sexual intercourse or fondling). When asked whether she had ever been sexually abused as a child or whether any family members had ever gotten into trouble for their sexual behavior, Rachel calmly said no, then added: "Oh wait a minute. . . . My uncle sexually assaulted someone. . . . I never met my uncle (my mother's brother), he died before I was born. You see, he molested a little boy. When the little boy's mother found out that her son was molested, she took a butcher knife and stabbed my uncle in the heart, killing him."

Rachel was but one of 49 victims—38 percent of those interviewed—who did not spontaneously recall the specific reported incident of their own abuse (although most did recall other traumatic sexual experiences). Elsewhere, scores of alleged victims have come forward claiming to have *recovered* memories of abuse. Ellen Bass and Laura Davis (1988), authors of the popular incest-recovery manual *The Courage to Heal*, have even offered a long list of incest survivor characteristics, including feelings of shame, powerlessness, unworthiness, vulnerability, perfectionism, and deficient goals and motivation. If you have some of these feelings, don't be surprised if you have no memory of sexual abuse, some therapists have said, because "denial" and "repression" are common. "If you are unable to remember any specific instances . . . but still have a feeling that something abusive happened to you, it probably did," say Bass and Davis (pp. 21–22). "If you think you were abused and your life shows the symptoms, then you were."

Believing this, some therapists have reasoned with patients that "people who've been abused often have your symptoms, so you probably were abused. Let's see if, aided by hypnosis or drugs, or helped to dig back and visualize your trauma, you can recover it." In one recent survey of British and American doctoral-level therapists, 7 in 10 said they had used such techniques to help clients recover suspected repressed memories of childhood sexual abuse (Poole & others, 1994).

Often, the patient then does form an image of a threatening person. With further visualization, the image grows more vivid, leaving the patient stunned, angry, and ready to confront or sue the equally stunned and devastated parent or other relative, who, as the therapist has predicted, vigorously denies the accusation. One woman in her 32nd therapy session recalled that her father had abused her at age 15 months. After such aided recall, actress Roseanne Barr Arnold (1991) claimed to recall sexual abuse beginning in infancy.

Persuading adult women that their fathers were incestuous is understandably tearing families apart, thousands of which have sought advice from the "False Memory Syndrome Foundation," established in 1992. Without questioning the professionalism of most therapists, the skeptics say that the uncorroborated accusations suggested by some therapists are a 1990s reenactment of the Salem witch trials. The trouble with working from symptoms to cause, notes Carol Tavris (1993), is that the symptom list is "general enough to include everybody at least sometimes. Nobody doesn't fit it." Moreover, people feel unworthy, ashamed, and perfectionistic for so many reasons that the symptoms hardly prove any one cause.

Psychologists committed to protecting abused children and those committed to protecting wrongly accused adults agree on the following:

- Incest happens, more often than we once supposed. Although there is no characteristic "survivor syndrome" (Kendell-Tackett & others, 1993), sexual abuse can leave its victims predisposed to problems ranging from sexual dysfunction to depression. Some victims have formed a "Protect the Children Foundation."
- Forgetting happens. Like Rachel, notes Elizabeth Loftus (in press), many of the women interviewed by Linda Meyer Williams were very young when abused or may not have understood the meaning of their experience—circumstances under which forgetting is "utterly common." Forgetting of isolated past events, both negative and positive, is an ordinary part of everyday life.
- Recovered memories are commonplace. Cued by a remark or an experience, we recover memories of long-forgotten events, both pleasant and unpleasant. The debate concerns whether the unconscious mind sometimes forcibly represses painful experiences and, if so, whether these can be retrieved by certain therapist-aided techniques.
- Memories "recovered" under hypnosis or drugs are unreliable. (Recall from Chapter 7 the ease with which "regressed" hypnotized subjects incorporate suggestions into their memories, even memories of "past lives.")
- Memories of things happening before age 3 are also unreliable, because people don't reliably recall happenings of any sort from their first 3 years—a phenomenon called *infantile amnesia*.

- Memories, whether real or false, can be emotionally upsetting. If a false memory of abuse becomes a real part of one's history, the client as well as the family may suffer. But then real traumas, too, can cause lasting suffering.
- Although repression has not been confirmed experimentally, most clinicians continue to believe that repression (or at least not thinking about a painful experience) happens.

Without knowing a person's initial experience (as we do in memory experiments) it is difficult to assess the person's memory. Nevertheless, to many memory researchers, the idea that people literally record, then repress, then recover painful experiences is scientifically naive. There just isn't evidence, notes David Holmes (1990, 1994), that an event can be repressed for years, and then accurately reproduced. With rare exceptions, most negative emotional events are actually remembered well (Christianson, 1992). In one study of 5- to 10-year-old children who had witnessed a parent's murder, not one repressed the memory; to the contrary, the unforgettable experience haunted them, like a flashbulb memory (Malmquist, 1986). Holocaust survivors remember all too well the Nazi atrocities (Helmreich, 1992, 1994). And in most child abuse cases that are substantiated with corroborating photos, diaries, testimony, or admitted guilt, victims never forget their horrific experiences. The family secret may be undisclosed, but it is not forgotten.

Moreover, 20 years of research on the misinformation effect reveals how easily and unwittingly people can fabricate false memories. Elizabeth Loftus and James Coan (in press) have demonstrated this by experimentally implanting false childhood memories. They had a trusted family member recall for a teenager three real childhood experiences and a false one—a vivid account of the child's being lost for an extended time in a shopping mall at age 5 until being rescued by an elderly person. Two days later, one subject, Chris, said, "That day I was so scared that I would never see my family again." Two days after that he began to visualize the flannel shirt, bald head, and glasses of the old man who supposedly had found him. Told the story was made up, Chris was incredulous: "I thought I remembered being lost . . . and looking around for the guys. I do remember that, and then crying, and Mom coming up and saying, 'Where were you? Don't you . . . ever do that again.'" Such is the memory construction process by which people can recall being abducted by UFOs, victimized by a satanic cult, or molested in a crib.

Loftus knows firsthand the phenomenon she studies. At a recent family reunion, an uncle told her that at 14, she found her mother's drowned body. Shocked, she denied it. But the uncle was adamant, and over the next few days she began to wonder if *she* had a repressed memory. "Maybe that's why I'm so obsessed with this topic." As the now-upset Loftus pondered her uncle's suggestion, she "recovered" an image of her mother lying in the pool, face down, and of herself finding the body. "I started putting everything into place. Maybe that's why I'm such a workaholic. Maybe that's why I'm so emotional when I think about her even though she died in 1959."

Then her brother called and said there was a mistake. The uncle had double-checked his story. Loftus had not found the body after all (Monaghan, 1992).

But then again, after being molested by a male baby-sitter at age 6 (and not forgetting), Loftus also knows firsthand the reality of sexual abuse. And that makes her wary of those whom she sees as trivializing real abuse by suggesting and probing for uncorroborated traumatic experiences, then accepting them uncritically as fact. The enemies of the truly victimized are not only those who prey and those who deny, she says, but those whose writings and allegations "are bound to lead to an increased likelihood that society in general will disbelieve the genuine cases of childhood sexual abuse that truly deserve our sustained attention" (Loftus, 1993).

TODAY'S SPECIAL GUEST
BRUNDAGE MORNALD, OF BATTLE CREEK, MONTANA
UNDER HYPNOSIS, MR. MORNALD RECOVERED LONG-BURIED MEMORIES OF A PERFECTLY NORMAL, HAPPY CHILDHOOD.


Drawing by Lorenz;© 1993 The New Yorker Magazine, Inc.

**Elizabeth Loftus (1944– )** *"People in general and jurors in particular have a lot of misconceptions about the way memory works" (quoted by Monaghan, 1992).*

## Summing Up

**Retrieval Cues** To be remembered, information that is "in there" must be retrieved, with the aid of associations (cues) that prime the memory. Retrieval is sometimes aided by returning to the original context. Mood affects memory, too. While in a good or bad mood, we often retrieve memories congruent with that mood.

**Memory Construction** Memories are not stored as exact copies, and they certainly are not retrieved as such. Rather, we construct our memories, using both stored and new information. Thus, when eyewitnesses are subtly exposed to misinformation after an event, they often believe they saw the misleading details as part of the event.

**Forgetting as Retrieval Failure** Forgetting that is related to retrieval failures may be caused by proactive or retroactive interference or even by motivated forgetting.

## Improving Memory

*To recap the chapter, let's consider how we might apply memory principles. What can we do in everyday situations to better remember a person's name, or even the material of this chapter?*

Now and then we are dismayed at our forgetfulness—at our embarrassing inability to recall someone's name, at forgetting to bring up a point in conversation, at forgetting to bring along something important, at finding ourselves standing in a room unable to recall why we are there (Herrmann, 1982). What can we do to minimize such lapses? Much as biology benefits medicine and botany benefits agriculture, so can the psychology of memory benefit education. Sprinkled throughout this chapter and summarized here for easy reference are concrete suggestions for improving memory. The PRTR—*P*review, *R*ead, *T*hink critically, *R*eview—study technique introduced in the Introduction incorporates several of these strategies.

***Study repeatedly to boost long-term recall.*** Overlearn. To learn a name, say it to yourself after being introduced; wait a few seconds and say it again; wait longer and say it again. To provide many separate study sessions, make use of life's little intervals—riding on the bus, walking across campus, waiting for class to start.

***Spend more time rehearsing or actively thinking about the material.*** Speed-reading (skimming) complex material—with minimal rehearsal—yields little retention. Rehearsal and critical reflection help more. It pays to study actively!

***Make the material personally meaningful.*** To build a network of retrieval cues, take thorough text and class notes in your own words. Mindlessly repeating information is relatively ineffective. Better to form images, understand and organize information, relate the material to what you already know or have experienced, and put it in your own words. Without such cues, you may be stuck when a question uses phrasing different from the rote forms you memorized. To increase retrieval cues, form as many associations as possible.

*"Knit each new thing on to some acquisition already there."*

William James
*Principles of Psychology*, 1890

***To remember a list of unfamiliar items, use mnemonic devices.*** Associate items with peg-words. Make up a story that incorporates vivid images of the items. Chunk information into acronyms.

***Refresh your memory by activating retrieval cues.*** Mentally recreate the situation and the mood in which the original learning occurred. Return to the same location. Jog your memory by allowing one thought to cue the next.

***Recall events while they are fresh, before you encounter possible misinformation.*** If you are an eyewitness to an important event, record your memory before allowing others to suggest what may have occurred.

***Minimize interference.*** Study right before sleeping. Don't study in close proximity topics that are likely to interfere with each other, such as Spanish and French.

***Test your own knowledge, both to rehearse it and to help determine what you do not yet know.*** If you must later *recall* information, do not be lulled into overconfidence by your ability to *recognize* it. Test your recall. Outline sections on a blank page. Define concepts before reading their end-of-chapter definitions. Take practice tests; the study guides that accompany many texts, including this one, can help.

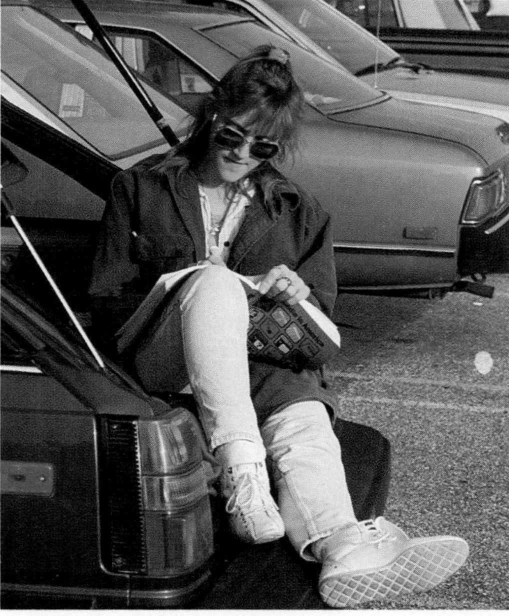

**Thinking and Memory** *Most of what we know is not the result of efforts to memorize. We learn because we're curious and because we spend time thinking about our experiences. Actively thinking as we read often yields the best retention.*

Without self-testing, one can easily suffer overconfidence, as John Shaughnessy and Eugene Zechmeister (1992) found in an experiment with two groups of students. Group 1 repeatedly reread dozens of factual statements, then judged the likelihood that they would remember each fact, and then were tested on their recall. Students in this group felt fairly confident of their knowledge, even on the questions they later missed. Students in group 2 read the statements, but then spent the rest of the time responding to practice tests requiring them to retrieve the facts. Compared with the "reread" group, group 2 students did just as well on the final recall test. What is more, this practice-test group could better discriminate what they did and did not know. Thus, self-testing enhances recall and can help you to know what you know—and thus to focus your study time on what you don't yet know. As former British Prime Minister Benjamin Disraeli once said, "To be conscious that you are ignorant is a great step to knowledge."

## Summing Up

The psychology of memory suggests concrete strategies for improving memory. These include spaced study; active rehearsal; encoding of well-organized, vivid, meaningful associations; mnemonic techniques; the return to contexts and moods that are rich with associations; minimizing interference; and self-testing and rehearsal.

## Terms and Concepts to Remember

### The Phenomenon of Memory

**flashbulb memory** A clear memory of an emotionally significant moment or event.

**encoding** The processing of information into the memory system, for example by extracting meaning.

**storage** The maintenance of encoded information over time.

**retrieval** The process of getting information out of memory storage.

**long-term memory** The relatively permanent and limitless storehouse of the memory system.

**short-term memory** Activated memory that holds a few items briefly, such as the seven digits of a phone number while dialing, before the information is stored or forgotten.

## Encoding: Getting Information In

**automatic processing** Unconscious encoding of incidental information, such as space, time, and frequency, and of well-learned information, such as word meanings.

**effortful processing** Encoding that requires attention and conscious effort.

**rehearsal** The conscious repetition of information, either to maintain it in consciousness or to encode it for storage.

**spacing effect** The tendency for distributed study or practice to yield better long-term retention than is achieved through massed study or practice.

**serial position effect** Our tendency to recall best the last and first items in a list.

**semantic encoding** The encoding of meaning, including the meaning of words.

**acoustic encoding** The encoding of sound, especially the sound of words.

**visual encoding** The encoding of picture images.

**imagery** Mental pictures. A powerful aid to effortful processing, especially when combined with semantic encoding.

**mnemonics** [nih-MON-iks] Memory aids, especially those techniques that use vivid imagery and organizational devices.

**chunking** Organizing items into familiar, manageable units; often done automatically.

## Storage: Retaining Information

**sensory memory** The immediate, initial recording of sensory information in the memory system.

**iconic memory** A momentary sensory memory of visual stimuli; a photographic or picture-image memory lasting no more than a second or so.

**echoic memory** A momentary sensory memory of auditory stimuli; if attention is elsewhere, sounds and words can still be recalled within 3 or 4 seconds.

**long-term potentiation (LTP)** An increase in a synapse's firing potential after brief, rapid stimulation. Believed to be a neural basis for learning and memory.

**implicit memory** Retention without conscious recollection (of skills, preferences, and dispositions). (Also called *nondeclarative memory*.)

**explicit memory** Memory of facts and experiences that one can consciously know and "declare." (Also called *declarative memory*.)

**hippocampus** A neural center that is located in the limbic system and that helps process explicit memories for storage.

## Retrieval: Getting Information Out

**recall** A measure of memory in which the person must retrieve information learned earlier, as on a fill-in-the-blank test.

**recognition** A measure of memory in which the person need only identify items previously learned, as on a multiple-choice test.

**relearning** A memory measure that assesses the amount of time saved when relearning previously learned information.

**priming** The implicit (unconscious) activation of particular associations in memory.

**déjà vu** (From French, literally meaning "already seen.") That eerie sense that "I've experienced this before." Cues from the current situation may subconsciously trigger retrieval of an earlier experience.

**mood-congruent memory** The tendency to recall experiences that are consistent with one's current good or bad mood.

**misinformation effect** After witnessing an event and receiving misleading information about it, incorporating the "misinformation" into one's memory of the event.

**proactive interference** The disruptive effect of prior learning on the recall of new information.

**retroactive interference** The disruptive effect of new learning on the recall of old information.

**repression** In psychoanalytic theory, the basic defense mechanism that banishes anxiety–arousing thoughts, feelings, and memories from consciousness.

## Critical Thinking Exercise

Now that you have read and reviewed Chapter 9, take your learning a step further by testing your critical thinking skills on the following practical problem solving exercise.

Danny just happened to be driving into the parking lot of a convenience store the night the attendant was killed in a holdup. He caught a quick glimpse of a fleeing man who seemed to be carrying a handgun. When the police arrived at the scene, Danny couldn't say much about the gunman's appearance. Nevertheless, they took him to headquarters and showed him hundreds of mug book photographs. After many frustrating hours, during which Danny was repeatedly shown a photo of a man named Raymond but was unable to identify anyone conclusively, the investigator handed him Raymond's photo and said, "We know this man visited the convenience store the night of the crime. Did you see him running from the store?" When Danny said he wasn't sure, he was allowed to leave and asked to think more carefully about what he had seen that night.

Three weeks later, Danny was asked to pick the killer from a five-man lineup that included Raymond. Although he remembered feeling uncertain of the identity of the man when he was first questioned, Danny was surprised at how easily and confidently he picked Raymond from the lineup now.

1. What's going on in this situation? What problem are the police trying to solve?
2. Why couldn't Danny identify the gunman right after he witnessed him fleeing from the store?
3. What is wrong with the police's questioning procedures?

Check your progress on becoming a critical thinker by comparing your answers to the sample answers found in Appendix B.

## For Further Reading

**Baddeley, A.** (1990). *Human memory.* Boston: Allyn and Bacon.

*One of the world's leading researchers offers a new and comprehensive review of memory research.*

**Brown, A. S.** (1987). *Maximizing memory power: Using recall to your advantage in business.* New York: Wiley.

*A practical guide to applying memory principles in everyday work.*

**Higbee, K. L.** (1988). *Your memory: How it works and how to improve it* (2nd ed.). Englewood Cliffs, NJ: Prentice-Hall.

*A practical guide that shows how to use memory principles to remember names, faces, and appointments, and to cope with aging.*

**Loftus, E., & Ketcham, K.** (1991). *Witness for the defense: The accused, the eyewitness, and the expert who puts memory on trial.* New York: St. Martin's Press.

*Memory researcher and frequent expert witness Elizabeth Loftus shows how the imperfections of human memory can produce persuasive but flawed eyewitness reports, by adults and especially by children.*

**Loftus, E. F., & Ketcham, K.** (1994). *The myth of repressed memory.* New York: St. Martin's Press.

*Challenges, with research findings and dramatic cases, the concept of repressed and recovered memories. Loftus and Ketcham argue that lives have been ruined by the idea that people involuntarily banish painful memories into the unconscious, from which they may later be recovered, sometimes aided by a therapist.*

**Rose, S.** (1993). *The making of memory: From molecules to mind.* New York: Anchor Books.

*Winner of England's Science Book Prize, this book offers a firsthand account of cutting-edge neuroscience—of why and how scientists do what they do, and what they have learned about how the brain makes memories.*

CHAPTER

# 10

## Thinking

Concepts

Solving Problems

Obstacles to Problem Solving

Making Decisions and Forming Judgments

Using and Misusing Heuristics

Overconfidence

Framing Decisions

Belief Bias

The Belief Perseverance Phenomenon

Artificial Intelligence

## Language

Language Structure

Language Development

Acquiring Language

Explaining Language Development

Animal Language

The Case of the Honeybee

The Case of the Apes

## Thinking and Language

Linguistic Influences on Thinking

Thinking Without Language

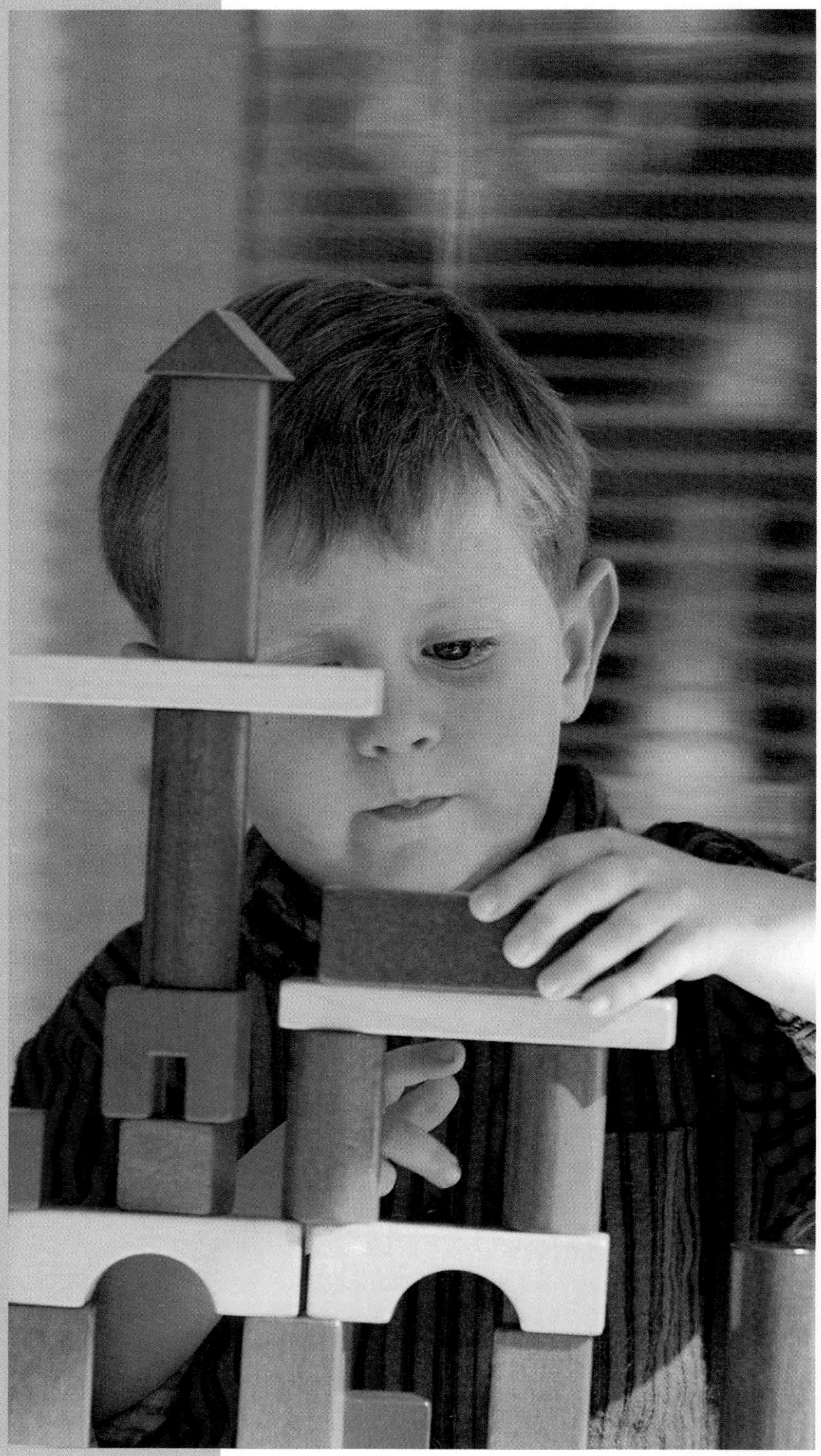

# Thinking and Language

Throughout history, we humans have deplored the depths of our foolishness and celebrated the heights of our wisdom. In a moment of humility the psalmist wondered, "What is man that thou art mindful of him?" but in the next breath rhapsodized that human beings were "little less than God." The poet T. S. Eliot was struck by "the hollow men . . . Headpiece filled with straw." But Shakespeare's Hamlet extolled the human species as "noble in reason! . . . infinite in faculties! . . . in apprehension how like a god!" In the preceding chapters, we, too, have sometimes marveled at our capabilities, sometimes at our propensity to err.

We have studied the human brain—a mere 3 pounds of tissue containing circuitry more complex than the planet's telephone networks. We have marveled at the competence of newborn infants. We have appreciated the human sensory system, which disassembles visual stimuli into millions of nerve impulses, distributes them for parallel processing, and then reassembles them into clear and colorful perceived images. We have acknowledged the seemingly limitless capacity of human memory and the ease with which we process information, consciously and unconsciously. Little wonder, then, that our species has the genius to invent the camera, the car, and the computer; to unlock the atom and crack the genetic code; to travel into space and probe the oceans' depths.

At the same time, we have seen that our species is kin to the other animals, influenced by principles that produce learning in rats and pigeons. We have noted that we assimilate reality into our preconceptions and succumb to perceptual illusions. We have seen how easily we deceive ourselves about hypnotic regression, pseudopsychic claims, and constructed memories. Little wonder, then, that we sometimes imagine we can read minds and travel outside our bodies; that we form distorted images of other ethnic, age, and gender groups; that we are subject to the same biological impulses as "lesser" creatures.

In this chapter, we encounter further instances of these two images of the human condition—the rational and the irrational. We will see how we form concepts, solve problems, and make judgments. We will look at our flair for language and ask whether our species alone is capable of language. In the end, we will reflect on how deserving we are of our name, *Homo sapiens*—wise human.

## Thinking

*To think is to form concepts that organize our world, to overcome obstacles as we solve problems, and to make efficient decisions and judgments. As we do so, what strategies do we typically use? What biases put us at risk for error? And what are the relative advantages of artificial intelligence and human intelligence?*

Previous chapters explained how we receive, perceive, store, and retrieve information. Now we consider how our cognitive system uses this information. Thinking, or **cognition**, is the mental activity associated with processing, understanding, and communicating information. *Cognitive psychologists* study these mental activities, including the logical and sometimes illogical ways in which we create concepts, solve problems, make decisions, and form judgments. We begin this chapter with the building blocks of thinking.

### Concepts

To think about the countless events, objects, and people in our world, we simplify things. We group them into **concepts** in mental groupings of similar objects, events, and people. The concept *chair* sums up a variety of items—a baby's high chair, a wing chair, the chairs around a dining room table, and folding chairs. Most share common features: They have legs and a back and can be sat on.

*"Attention everyone! I'd like to introduce the newest member of our family."*

Drawing by Kaufman; © 1977 The New Yorker Magazine, Inc.

Imagine life without concepts. We would need a different name for every object and idea. We could not ask a child to "throw the ball" because there would be no concept of ball. Instead of saying, "He was angry," we would have to describe facial expression, vocal intensity, gestures, and words. Concepts such as *ball* and *angry* provide much information with a minimum of cognitive effort. That is why concepts are the basic building blocks of thought.

To simplify things further, we organize concepts into hierarchies. The earliest naturalists simplified and ordered the overwhelming complexity of some 5 million living species by clustering them into two basic categories—the plant kingdom and the animal kingdom. Then they divided these basic categories into smaller and smaller subcategories—vertebrates, bony fish, and Atlantic salmon, for instance, in order of increasing specificity.

Classifying the world into hierarchies of concepts makes for cognitive efficiency. Using basic physical concepts, physicists speedily classify and solve physics problems. Cab drivers organize their cities into geographical sectors, which subdivide into neighborhoods and again into blocks. Chess masters conceptually organize chess games in ways that help them see the significance of various game positions (Bransford & others, 1986; Chi & others, 1988).

We form some concepts by definition. Told the rule that a triangle has three sides, we thereafter classify all three-sided geometric forms as triangles. By definition, a bird is an animal that has wings and feathers and hatches from an egg. More often, we form our concepts by developing **prototypes**—a best example of a particular category (Rosch, 1978). The more closely objects match our prototype of a concept, the more readily we recognize them as examples of the concept. A robin and a goose both satisfy our rule for *bird*. Yet people agree more quickly with the statement "A robin is a bird" than with the statement "A goose is a bird." For most of us, the robin is the birdier bird; it more closely resembles our bird prototype.

**A Bird and a . . . ?** *If asked to imagine a bird, most people quickly come up with a mental picture that is something like this robin. It takes them a bit longer to conceptualize a penguin as a bird because it doesn't match their prototype of a small, feathered, flying creature.*

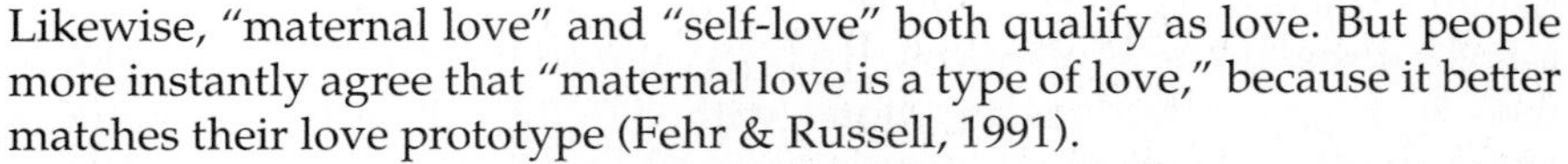

Likewise, "maternal love" and "self-love" both qualify as love. But people more instantly agree that "maternal love is a type of love," because it better matches their love prototype (Fehr & Russell, 1991).

If something fails to match our prototype, we may have trouble classifying it. Thus, we might be slow to recognize nonflying penguins and kiwis as birds. When our symptoms don't fit one of our disease prototypes, we are slow to perceive an illness (Bishop, 1991). People whose heart attack symptoms don't match their prototype of a heart attack are often slow to seek help.

## Solving Problems

One tribute to our rationality is our ability to form and use concepts. Another is our skill at solving problems—at coping with novel situations for which we have no well-established response. Some problems we solve through trial and error. Thomas Edison tried thousands of light bulb filaments before stumbling upon one that worked. For other problems, we may follow an **algorithm**, a step-by-step procedure that guarantees a solution. Told to find another word using all the letters in CINERAMA, we could try each letter in each position, but generating and examining the 20,160 resulting combinations would take too long. Because step-by-step algorithms can be laborious (well-suited to computers), we often solve problems with simple rule-of-thumb strategies, called **heuristics**. Thus, in rearranging the letters of CINERAMA, we might exclude letter combinations such as two *a*'s together or words starting with two consonants, such as *mc* or *nm*. By using rule-of-thumb heuristics and then applying trial and error, you may hit upon the answer (page 328).

*To search for horseradish in a supermarket you could search every aisle (an algorithm) or check the mustard, spice, and gourmet sections (heuristics).*

Sometimes we are unaware of using any problem-solving strategy; the answer just comes to us. We can all recall occasions when we puzzled over a problem for some time. Then, suddenly, the pieces fell together and we perceived the solution. This facility for sudden flashes of inspiration we call **insight**. Ten-year-old Johnny Appleton displayed insight in solving a problem that had stymied construction workers: how to rescue a young robin that had fallen into a narrow 30-inch-deep hole in a cement block wall. Johnny's solution: to slowly pour in sand, giving the bird enough time to keep its feet on top of the constantly rising sand (Ruchlis, 1990).

**Chimpanzee Inventiveness** *After learning that he could see himself on TV, Austin apparently wanted to see his throat better. So he picked up a flashlight and shined it in his throat, facing the camera. (Adapted from Rumbaugh & Savage-Rumbaugh, 1986.)*

We humans aren't the only creatures which display insight. German psychologist Wolfgang Köhler (1925) observed apparent insight while studying chimpanzees placed on an island off the coast of Africa. In one experiment with a caged chimp named Sultan, Köhler placed a piece of fruit and a long stick well beyond reach, and a short stick inside the cage. Spying the short stick, Sultan grabbed it and tried to reach the fruit with it. But the stick, by design, was too short. After several unsuccessful attempts, the chimp dropped the stick and paused to survey the situation. Then suddenly, as if thinking, "Aha!" Sultan jumped up, seized the short stick again, and this time used it to pull in the longer stick—which he then used to reach the fruit. Sultan's actions displayed animal cognition, claimed Köhler, and showed that there is more to learning than conditioning.

Thanks to problem solving shaped by reinforcements, forest-dwelling chimpanzees have become natural tool users (Boesch-Achermann & Boesch, 1993). They can select appropriate branches or stones to use as hammers in cracking nuts. They can also break off a reed or a stick, strip the twigs and leaves, carry it to a termite mound, fish for termites by twisting it just so, and then carefully remove it without scraping off many termites. One anthropologist, trying to mimic the chimpanzee's deft termite fishing, failed miserably. Tool use has been observed in 32 African chimpanzee populations, each of which has developed its own variations of tool use. Such group differences, along with differing dialects and hunting styles, are the chimpanzee equivalent of cultural diversity (Gibbons, 1992).

In human experience, insight provides a sense of satisfaction. After solving a difficult problem or discovering how to resolve a conflict, we feel happy. The joy of a joke may similarly lie in our capacity for insight—our sudden comprehension of an unexpected ending or a double meaning. We find double meaning in the story of Professor Smith, who complained to his colleagues that student interruptions had become a problem: "The minute I get up to speak, some fool begins to talk."

*Answer to CINERAMA anagram on page 327: AMERICAN.*

## Obstacles to Problem Solving

Inventive as we can be in solving problems, two cognitive tendencies—*confirmation bias* and *fixation*—often interfere.

**Confirmation Bias** A major obstacle to problem solving is our eagerness to search for information that confirms our ideas, a phenomenon known as **confirmation bias**. In an experiment with British university students, P. C. Wason (1960) demonstrated our reluctance to seek information that might disprove our beliefs. Wason gave students the three-number sequence, 2-4-6, and asked them to guess the rule he had used to devise the series. (The rule was simple: any three ascending numbers.) Before submitting their answers, the students generated their own sets of three numbers, and each time Wason told them whether or not their sets conformed to his rule. Once they had done enough testing to feel *certain* they had the rule, they were to announce it.

The result? Seldom right but never in doubt: Most people convinced themselves of a wrong rule. Typically, they formed a wrong idea ("Maybe it's counting by twos") and then searched only for confirming evidence (by testing 6-8-10, 100-102-104, and so forth). Such experiments reveal that we seek evidence that will verify our ideas more eagerly than we seek evidence that might refute them (Klayman & Ha, 1987; Skov & Sherman, 1986). Business managers, for example, are more likely to follow the successful careers of those they've hired than to track the achievements of those they've rejected, which helps them confirm their perceived hiring ability.

*"The human understanding, when any proposition has been once laid down . . . forces everything else to add fresh support and confirmation."*

Francis Bacon
*Novum Organum*, 1620

**Fixation** Try your hand at some brainteasers drawn from classic experiments.

> Arrange the six matches shown in Figure 10–1 so they form four equilateral triangles.
>
> Suppose that you have a 21-cup jug, a 127-cup jug, and a 3-cup jug. Using these three jugs to draw and discard as much water as you like, how will you measure out exactly 100 cups of water? Solve the other problems presented in Figure 10–2, too.
>
> How can you use the box of matches, thumbtacks, and candle shown in Figure 10–3 to mount the candle on a bulletin board? (After trying all these problems, read on.)

A major obstacle to problem solving is **fixation**—the inability to see a problem from a fresh perspective. Once we incorrectly represent the problem, it's hard to restructure how we approach it. If your attempts to solve the match-stick problem were fixated on two-dimensional solutions, then the three-dimensional solution shown in Figure 10–4 (page 330) will have eluded you.

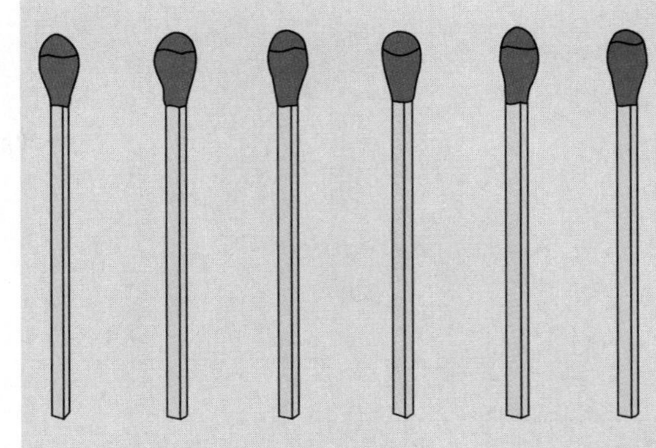

**Figure 10–1**

**The Matchstick Problem** *How would you arrange six matches to form four equilateral triangles? (From "Problem Solving" by M. Scheerer. Copyright © 1963 by Scientific American, Inc. All rights reserved.)*

**Figure 10–2**

| Problem | Given jugs of these sizes: *A* | *B* | *C* | Measure out this much water: |
|---|---|---|---|---|
| 1 | 21 | 127 | 3 | 100 |
| 2 | 14 | 46 | 5 | 22 |
| 3 | 18 | 43 | 10 | 5 |
| 4 | 7 | 42 | 6 | 23 |
| 5 | 20 | 57 | 4 | 29 |
| 6 | 23 | 49 | 3 | 20 |
| 7 | 15 | 39 | 3 | 18 |

**The Three-Jugs Problems** *Using jugs A, B, and C with the capacities shown in the table, how would you measure out the volumes indicated in the right-hand column? (From Luchins, 1946.)*

**Figure 10–3**

**The Candle-Mounting Problem** *Using these materials, how would you mount the candle on a bulletin board? (From Duncker, 1945.)*

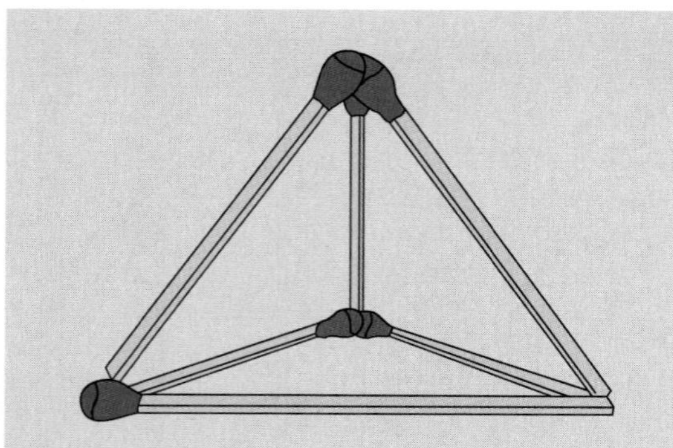

**Figure 10–4**

**Solution to the Matchstick Problem** *To solve this problem, you must break the fixation of limiting your considerations to two-dimensional solutions. (From "Problem Solving" by M. Scheerer. Copyright © 1963 by Scientific American, Inc. All rights reserved.)*

We become fixated on certain solutions for good reason: Solutions that worked in the past often work on new problems. Consider one more brain-teaser:

Given the sequence *O-T-T-F-?-?-?*, what are the final three letters?

Most people have difficulty recognizing that the three final letters are *F*(ive), *S*(ix), and *S*(even). But solving this problem may make the next one easier:

Given the sequence *J-F-M-A-?-?-?*, what are the final three letters? (If this one proved difficult, too, ask yourself what month it is.)

Although past success can help solve present problems, it may also interfere with our finding new solutions. This tendency to repeat solutions that have worked in the past is a type of fixation called **mental set**. Mental set is like perceptual set (pages 205–207), except it affects problem solving rather than perception. You probably ran into mental set in the water jug problems. For the first jug problem, you probably developed the following formula:

$$B - A - 2C = \text{desired amount of water}$$

This same formula works for all seven problems. Once you developed this mental set, you probably solved the later problems faster. But did this mental set cause you to miss the much simpler solutions for problems 6 and 7? (See Figure 10–5.)

**Figure 10–5**

**Solution to the Three-Jugs Problems** *(a) All seven problems can be solved by the equation shown in (a): B – A – 2C = desired volume. (b) But simpler solutions exist for problems 6 and 7, such as A – C for problem 6. Did your mental set cause you to miss it? (From Luchins, 1946.)*

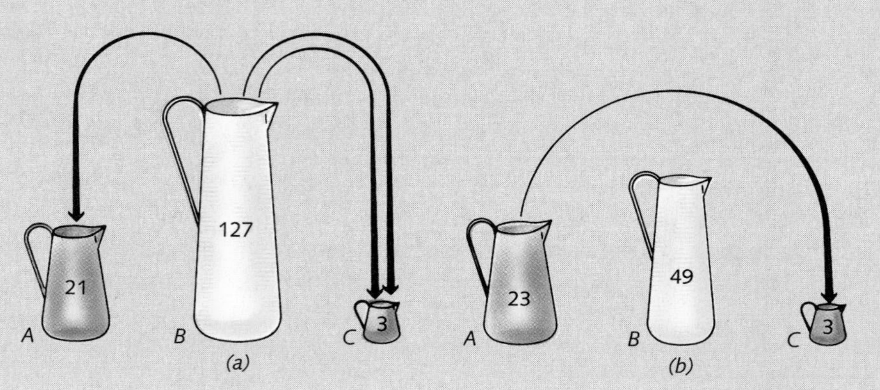


Flexible, rational thinking becomes even more difficult in times of stress and tension (Janis, 1989). During international crises, for example, views of an enemy become fixed in simplified good-versus-bad terms. During personal crises, too, thinking often becomes rigid. During the Korean War, a paratrooper readying for a mission was given the last parachute—a left-handed one. "It's the same as the others," explained the ordnance sergeant, "but the rip cord hangs on the left side of the harness." At 8000 feet, the soldiers jumped one by one, and all went well—except for this one man who fell straight to his death. Investigators discovered that under the stress of the jump the man had become fixated on the familiar way to open a chute.

The right side of his uniform, where normally he found the rip cord, was completely torn off. Even his chest flesh had been gouged by his bloody right hand. Inches to the left was the rip cord, apparently untouched (Csikszentmihalyi, 1990).

Another type of fixation goes by the awkward but appropriate label **functional fixedness**. This is our tendency to perceive the functions of objects as fixed and unchanging. A person may ransack the house for a screwdriver when a dime would have done the job. Perhaps you experienced functional fixedness when you tried to solve the candle-mounting problem. If you thought of the matchbox as having only the function of holding matches, you may have overlooked its use shown in Figure 10–6. Perceiving and relating familiar things in new ways is part of creativity.

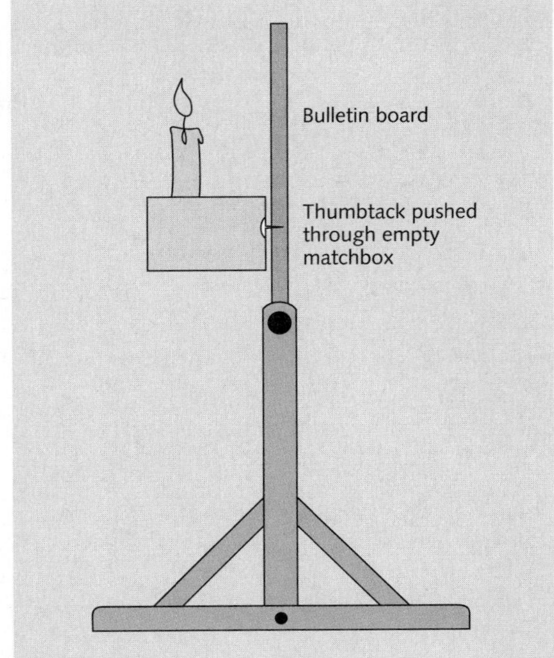


**Figure 10–6**

**Solution to the Candle-Mounting Problem**
*Solving this problem requires recognizing that a box need not always serve as a container. (From Duncker, 1945.)*

## Making Decisions and Forming Judgments

When making each day's hundreds of tiny judgments and decisions—Is it worth the bother to take an umbrella? Can I trust this person? Should I shoot the basketball or pass to the player who's hot?—we seldom take the time and effort to reason systematically. Usually, we follow our intuition. After interviewing policymakers in government, business, and education, social psychologist Irving Janis (1986) concluded that they "often do not use a reflective problem-solving approach. How do they usually arrive at their decisions? If you ask, they are likely to tell you . . . they do it mostly by the *seat of their pants*."

### Using and Misusing Heuristics

Those mental shortcuts we call heuristics often help us make reasonable seat-of-the-pants judgments. But the price we pay for their efficiency can sometimes be costly bad judgments. To gain an idea of how heuristics determine our intuitive judgments—and how they can lead smart people into dumb decisions—consider two heuristics identified by cognitive psychologists Amos Tversky and Daniel Kahneman (1974): *representativeness* and *availability*.

**The Representativeness Heuristic** To judge the likelihood of things in terms of how well they represent particular prototypes is to use the **representativeness heuristic**. To illustrate, consider:

> A stranger tells you about a person who is short, slim, and likes to read poetry, and then asks you to guess whether this person is more likely to be a professor of classics at an Ivy League university or a truck driver. Which would be the better guess? (Adapted from Nisbett & Ross, 1980.)

If you are like most people, you answered a professor because the description seems more *representative* of Ivy League scholars than of truck drivers. The representativeness heuristic enabled you to make a snap judgment. But it also led you to ignore other relevant information, such as the total number of classics professors versus truck drivers. When I help people think through this question, their own reasoning usually leads them to an answer that contradicts their immediate intuition. The typical conversation goes something like this:

**Question:** *First, let's figure out how many professors fit the description. How many Ivy League universities do you suppose there are?*

**Answer:** *Oh, about 10, I suppose.*

*"The information-processing shortcuts—called heuristics—which are normally both highly efficient and immensely time-saving in day-to-day situations, work systematically against us in the marketplace. . . . The tendency to underestimate or altogether ignore past probabilities in making a decision is undoubtedly the most significant problem of intuitive predictions."*

David Dreman
*Contrarian Investment Strategy: The Psychology of Stock Market Success*, 1979

**Question:** *How many classics professors would you guess there are at each?*

**Answer:** *Maybe four.*

**Question:** *Okay, that's 40 Ivy League classics professors. What fraction of these are short and slim?*

**Answer:** *Let's say half.*

**Question:** *And, of these 20, how many like to read poetry?*

**Answer:** *I'd say half—10 professors.*

**Question:** *Okay, now let's figure how many truck drivers fit the description. How many truck drivers do you suppose there are?*

**Answer:** *Maybe 400,000.*

**Question:** *What fraction are short and slim?*

**Answer:** *Not many—perhaps 1 in 8.*

**Question:** *Of these 50,000, what percentage like to read poetry?*

**Answer:** *Truck drivers who like poetry? Maybe 1 in 100—oh, oh, I can see where this is going—that leaves me with 500 short, slim, poetry-reading truck drivers.*

**Question:** *Yup. So, although the person I described may be much more representative of classics professors than of truck drivers, this person is still (even accepting your stereotypes) 50 times more likely to be a truck driver.*

The *conjunction fallacy* illustrates the power of the representativeness heuristic. Tversky and Kahneman (1983) told college students that "Bill is 34 years old. He is intelligent but unimaginative, compulsive, and generally lifeless. In school, he was strong in mathematics but weak in social studies and humanities." Based on this description, students judged there was little chance that "Bill plays jazz for a hobby." But 87 percent thought there was a better chance that "Bill is an accountant who plays jazz for a hobby" (because Bill seemed more representative of accountants). If you agree, think about it: Is there a better chance that Bill *both* plays jazz *and* is an accountant than that he plays jazz alone? (The conjunction of two events can't be more likely than either event alone, yet, even when alerted to the conjunction rule, people persist in making the logical error [Benassi & Knoth, 1993; Donovan & Epstein, 1993].)

*"In creating these problems, we didn't set out to fool people. All our problems fooled us, too."*

Amos Tversky (1985)

These examples illustrate people's illogical use of the representativeness heuristic. To judge the likelihood of something, we intuitively compare it to our mental representation of that category—of, say, what truck drivers or accountants are like. If the two match, then that fact usually overrides other considerations of statistics or logic.

**The Availability Heuristic** The **availability heuristic** operates when we base our judgments on the availability of information in our memories. If instances of an event are easily available—if they come to mind readily—we presume such events are common. The faster people can remember an instance of some event ("a broken promise"), the more they expect it to recur (MacLeod & Campbell, 1992). Usually, cognitively available events *are* more likely to recur—but not always. To see this, make a guess: Does the letter *k* appear more often as the first or third letter in English words?

Because words beginning with *k* come to mind more easily than words having *k* as their third letter, most people guess that *k* occurs more frequently as the first letter. Actually, *k* is three times more likely to appear as the third letter. So far in this chapter, words such as *know*, *kingdoms*, and *kin* are outnumbered 44 to 13 by words such as *make*, *likely*, *asked*, and *acknowledged*.

## *Thinking Critically About* Risks—When Statistics Clash With Heuristics

**Vivid Events Are More Available to Memory** *Photos of this July 1994 crash etched a sharper image in many minds than did the 16 million consecutive fatality-free flights on U.S. airlines during the preceding 27 months. Because such vivid happenings are more available to memory, they seem more common than they really are.*

"Most people reason dramatically, not quantitatively," said Oliver Wendell Holmes. With horrific television and magazine images of air crashes in mind, many people, petrified of air travel, prefer the safety of their own cars. Of those who do fly, 44 percent report feeling fearful (*Gallup Report*, 1989).

Ironically, the statistical reality is that, mile for mile, U.S. travelers during the 1980s were 26 times more likely to die in a car crash than on a commercial flight (National Safety Council, 1991). In the 27 months following March 22, 1992, major U.S. airlines carried more than 1 billion passengers on *16 million* flights without a single death (Tolchin, 1994). For most air travelers, the most dangerous part of the journey is the drive to the airport.

Still, when overall statistics vie with vivid images of helpless crash victims, many people find the memorable instances more persuasive. It's like judging the likelihood of shark attacks after watching *Jaws*: Regardless of statistics, memorable images have a way of heightening swimmers' feelings of risk. Or like judging, from seeing the faces of missing children on milk cartons, your child's risk of being abducted by a stranger—which the U.S. Justice Department reports actually happens to fewer than 1 in 100,000 children a year nationwide (Bonner, 1990). (Almost all child snatchings are family related.)

In 1988, a terrorist bomb that exploded Pan Am Flight 103 over Scotland caused many would-be international vacationers to stay home and brave the more dangerous highways. The same fearful public continues to drive without seatbelts, smoke billions of cigarettes a year, guzzle alcohol, and devour foods that put people at risk for the greatest of killers—heart disease. All because people's *perceptions* of risk are virtually unrelated to actual risk (Slovic, 1987)—a phenomenon due partly to our greater fear of things we cannot control and partly to our overestimating the likelihood of dreaded, publicized, and cognitively available events. Thus, the public dreads a catastrophic nuclear accident (which after Chernobyl we can readily visualize), yet accepts the less dramatic risks of coal-generated power, which quietly fuels acid rain and global warming.

*The moral*: Whether making travel plans or choosing foods, defining safety standards or evaluating environmental hazards, rational people will define risks based not on mentally available media images but on statistical reality.

The judgmental errors influenced by the availability heuristic are frequently harmless, but not always. Many important decisions involve judgments of risk. Whether we favor using nuclear power or burning coal to produce energy depends partly on our judgments of the risks to health and environment. Our efforts to prevent various deadly diseases depend on our judgments of the likelihood of their occurrence. Our choice to spend or not to spend money on state lotteries (which return in prizes only about half of each dollar bet) depends on our hunch of the odds of striking it rich. (Based on the roughly 10 million to 1 odds against a bet winning a state Lotto jackpot, our chances are not much better than the odds of being struck by lightning.)

Those who sell life and theft insurance sometimes exploit our tendency to believe that events are more likely if we can picture them readily (Cialdini & Carpenter, 1981). By having people imagine their families in mourning or their possessions stolen, salespeople may cause the images of these disasters to linger, making their occurrence seem more likely and the corresponding need for insurance more intense. In one experiment, Larry Gregory and his colleagues (1982) gave Arizona residents promotional information about cable TV; they asked others to picture themselves enjoying movies on cable instead of spending money on babysitters and gas. The latter group, having readily available images of themselves as subscribers, were more than twice as likely to subscribe.

The availability heuristic also affects our social judgments, as Ruth Hamill and her co-workers demonstrated (1980). They presented people with a single, vivid case of welfare abuse, in which a long-term welfare recipient had several unruly children fathered by different men. The statistical fact is that this case is exceptional: Most people who receive welfare do so for 4 years or less (Duncan & others, 1988). Yet when the statistical reality was pitted against the single vivid case, the memorable case had greater influence on people's opinions about welfare recipients.

*"The human understanding is most excited by that which strikes and enters the mind at once and suddenly, and by which the imagination is immediately filled and inflated. It then begins almost imperceptibly to conceive and suppose that everything is similar to the few objects which have taken possession of the mind."*

Francis Bacon
*Novum Organum*, 1620

In everyday life, too, a memorable picture sometimes overwhelms a thousand statistics. When a little girl named Jessica McClure fell into a Texas well, the attention of hundreds of millions of people worldwide was riveted on her 3-day rescue. During those 3 days, more than 100,000 invisible children—mere statistics on some world health ledger—died of preventable starvation, diarrhea, and disease (Gore, 1992).

## Overconfidence

Our use of intuitive heuristics when forming judgments, our eagerness to confirm the beliefs we already hold, and our facility for explaining away failures combine to create **overconfidence**, a tendency to overestimate the accuracy of our knowledge and judgments.

Kahneman and Tversky (1979) asked people to answer obscure factual questions with a wide enough range to surely include the actual answer. For example, "I feel 98 percent certain that the number of nuclear power plants operating in the world in 1980 was more than ______ but fewer than ______." Nearly one-third of the time, people's estimates, made with 98 percent confidence, failed to include the correct answer (189 nuclear power plants, in this instance). Although very sure of themselves, people were often wrong.

Similarly, people are more confident than correct when answering such questions as, "Is absinthe a liqueur or a precious stone?" On questions where people's answers are only 60 percent correct, they typically feel 75 percent confident. Even when people feel 100 percent certain of their answers to such questions, they err about 15 percent of the time (Fischhoff & others, 1977). (Absinthe is a licorice-flavored liqueur.)

*"What do you mean 'Your guess is as good as mine'? My guess is a hell of a lot better than your guess!"*

Drawing by Ross; © 1983 The New Yorker Magazine, Inc.

Overconfidence plagues decisions outside the laboratory, too. It was an overconfident Hitler who invaded Russia, an overconfident Lyndon Johnson who waged war with North Vietnam, an overconfident Saddam Hussein who marched into Kuwait. Stockbrokers and investment managers market their services with confidence that they can outperform the market average in picking stocks, despite overwhelming evidence to the contrary (Malkiel, 1985). A purchase of stock X, recommended by a broker who judges this to be the time to buy, is always balanced by a sale made by someone who judges this to be the time to sell. Despite their confidence, they can't both be right.

To check people's confidence in making social judgments, David Dunning and his colleagues (1990) asked Stanford University students to guess a stranger's answers to 20 two-choice questions. Topics included whether the person studied for exams alone or with others, kept neat or messy lecture notes, and would pocket $5 found in a restaurant or turn it in. Knowing the type of questions (but not the actual questions), the subjects were first given a chance to interview the target person about academic interests, hobbies, family background, aspirations, strengths and weaknesses, astrological sign, and anything else they thought might prove helpful. Then the target person answered the 20 questions while the interviewer predicted the target's answers.

The result? The interviewers were "markedly overconfident." Although they guessed right on 63 percent of their predictions, they felt, on average, 75 percent sure. When guessing their own roommates' responses to the 20 questions, subjects were somewhat more accurate—68 percent. But, again, their 78 percent confidence exceeded their accuracy. And the most confident people were the most *over*confident.

Roger Buehler and his colleagues (1994) were struck by how routinely planners exhibit overconfidence in estimating how quickly and inexpensively they can do a project. In 1957, planners predicted the Sydney Opera House would be completed in 1963 for $7 million. A reduced version actually opened in 1973 at a cost of $102 million. In 1969, Montreal Mayor Jean Drapeau proudly announced that a $120 million stadium with retractable roof would be built for the 1976 Olympics. The roof actually was finished in 1989 and by itself cost $120 million. (Even as I write this we are moving into a new kitchen that our architect estimated would take 1 month, our contractor estimated would take 3 months, and that actually took 5 months.) Buehler reports that students, too, are routinely overconfident of how quickly they can do assignments and write papers. Students typically expect to finish projects ahead of schedule. But projects generally get finished after about twice as many days as predicted. Although people know they have often underestimated completion times, they remain overly confident of any specific prediction at hand.

Overconfidence has adaptive value. Failing to appreciate one's potential for error when making military, economic, or political judgments can have devastating consequences, but so can *lack* of self-confidence. People who err on the side of overconfidence live more happily and find it easier to make tough decisions (Baumeister, 1989; Taylor, 1989). Moreover, when given prompt and clear feedback on the accuracy of their judgments—as weather forecasters are after each day's predictions—people soon learn to assess their accuracy more realistically (Fischhoff, 1982). The wisdom to know when we know a thing and when we do not is born of experience.

*"When you know a thing, to hold that you know it; and when you do not know a thing, to allow that you do not know it; this is knowledge."*

Confucius, 551–479 B.C.
*Analects*

### Framing Decisions

A further test of rationality is whether the same issue, presented in two different but logically equivalent ways, will elicit the same answer. For example, whether a surgeon tells someone that 10 percent die during a particular surgery or that 90 percent survive, the information is the same. But the effect is not. The risk seems greater to people who hear that 10 percent will die (Marteau, 1989). This impact of the way we present an issue is called **framing**.

Similarly, consumers respond more positively to ground beef described as "75 percent lean" rather than "25 percent fat" (Levin & Gaeth, 1988). A new medical treatment strikes people as more successful and recommendable if framed as having a "50 percent success rate" rather than a "50 percent failure rate". People are more bothered by student cheating if told that 65 percent of students had cheated than if told that 35 percent had not cheated (Levin & others, 1988). And 9 in 10 college students rate a condom as effective if it has a "95 percent success rate" in stopping the AIDS virus;

only 4 in 10 think it successful when given a "5 percent failure rate" (Linville & Others, 1992).

And consider how the framing effect influences economic and business decisions:

"This CD player costs less than players selling for twice as much."

Drawing by Weber; © 1989 The New Yorker Magazine, Inc.

- Merchants mark up their "regular prices" to appear to offer huge savings on "sale prices." A $100 coat marked down from $150 by Store X can seem like a better deal than the same coat priced regularly at $100 by Store Y (Urbany & others, 1988).
- Many people find taking a 7 percent pay cut in a period of inflation much more objectionable than receiving a 5 percent pay raise when inflation is 12 percent—though the effect is basically the same (Kahneman & others, 1986).
- If your dentist offers a 5 percent discount for immediate cash payment, you may not feel particularly unhappy paying the full fee 30 days later. But you probably would be irritated if the same fee were framed differently—say, if the basic fee were lowered 5 percent with an equivalent surcharge for late payment. Somehow, a 5 percent surcharge is more irritating than a forfeited 5 percent discount, although they add up to the same thing.

That people's judgments flip-flop so dramatically is startling. It suggests that our judgments and decisions may not be well reasoned, and that those who understand the power of framing can use it to influence important decisions—for example, by framing survey questions to support or reject a particular viewpoint. (Recall from Chapter 1 the potentially powerful effects of subtle wording differences.)

## Belief Bias

We have seen that part of psychology's new thinking about thinking emphasizes that we are prone to bias—from seeking confirmation for our hunches, from reliance on efficient but fallible heuristics, from overconfidence, and from the effects of framing. Through brute logic, can we escape the bias inflicted by our beliefs?

Logic helps, but we still find it easier to accept conclusions that agree with our opinions. Consider this logical argument:

Premise 1: Some communists are golfers.
Premise 2: All golfers are Marxists.
Conclusion: Some communists are Marxists.

In experiments, nearly everyone correctly recognized that the conclusion logically follows from the premises (Oakhill & others, 1989). But now consider this argument:

Premise 1: Some communists are golfers.
Premise 2: All golfers are capitalists.
Conclusion: Some communists are capitalists.

Many people had a harder time seeing that, given the premises, this conclusion is equally valid. Judge this next conclusion for yourself (adapted from Hunt, 1982):

Premise 1: People who believe in democracy believe in free speech.
Premise 2: Dictators do not believe in democracy.
Conclusion: Dictators do not believe in free speech.

If that conclusion seems logical, you are experiencing **belief bias**—the tendency for our beliefs to distort logical reasoning (Oakhill & others, 1990). Consider another set of statements *with identical form and logic* and note how much easier it feels to refute the conclusion:

Premise 1: Robins have feathers.
Premise 2: Chickens are not robins.
Conclusion: Chickens do not have feathers.

Thus, belief bias: We more easily see the illogic of conclusions that run counter to our beliefs ("Chickens do not have feathers") than those that agree with our beliefs ("Dictators do not believe in free speech").

*"God is love.*
*Love is blind.*
*Ray Charles is blind.*
*Ray Charles is God."*
Anonymous graffiti

### The Belief Perseverance Phenomenon

An additional source of irrationality is our tendency, called **belief perseverance**, to cling to our beliefs in the face of contrary evidence. Belief perseverance often fuels social conflict. Charles Lord and his colleagues (1979) revealed how this happens when they studied people with opposing views of capital punishment. People on both sides studied two supposedly new research findings, one supporting and the other refuting the claim that the death penalty deters crime. Each side was more impressed by the study that supported its beliefs, and each readily disputed the other study. Thus, showing the pro- and anti-capital-punishment groups the *same* mixed evidence actually *increased* their disagreement.

*"Once you have a belief, it influences how you perceive all other relevant information. Once you see a country as hostile, you are likely to interpret ambiguous actions on their part as signifying their hostility."*
Political scientist Robert Jervis (1985)

For those who wish to rein in the belief perseverance phenomenon, a simple remedy exists: *Consider the opposite.* When Lord and his colleagues (1984) repeated the capital-punishment study, they asked some of their subjects to be "as *objective* and *unbiased* as possible." The plea did nothing to reduce the biased evaluation of evidence. They asked another group, however, to consider the opposite—to ask themselves "whether you would have made the same high or low evaluations had exactly the same study produced results on the *other* side of the issue." Having imagined and pondered opposite findings, these people were much less biased in their evaluations of the evidence.

If ambiguous evidence gets interpreted as supporting a person's preexisting belief, would the belief be demolished by information that clearly discredits its basis? Not necessarily. Craig Anderson and Lee Ross discovered that it can be surprisingly difficult to change a false belief once a person has in mind ideas that support it. In one such study with Mark Lepper (1980), they asked subjects to consider whether risk-prone people or cautious people are better fire fighters. Then they told half the subjects about a risk-taker who was an excellent fire fighter and about a cautious person who was a poor fire fighter. From these cases, the subjects surmised that risk-prone people tend to be better fire fighters. "Risk-takers are braver," was a typical explanation. The researchers gave the other subjects two cases suggesting the opposite conclusion, that cautious people are better fire fighters. Subjects typically reasoned, "Cautious people think before they act. They're less likely to make foolish mistakes."

The researchers then discredited the basis for the beliefs by truthfully informing both groups that the cases were simply made up for the experiment. Did discrediting the evidence undermine the subjects' newly formed beliefs? Not by much, because the subjects held on to their explanations for *why* these new beliefs made sense. Although the evidence was gone, their theory survived.

**Belief Perseverance** *Do risk-prone or cautious people make better fire fighters? Once we've formed opinions on a question like this and developed reasons for our views, we tend to cling to our beliefs—even if presented with contradictory evidence.*

*"To begin with, it was only tentatively that I put forward the views I have developed . . . but in the course of time they have gained such a hold upon me that I can no longer think in any other way."*

Sigmund Freud
*Civilization and Its Discontents*, 1930

Paradoxically, the more we come to appreciate why our beliefs *might* be true, the more tightly we cling to them. Once people have explained to themselves why they believe a child is "gifted" or "learning disabled," or that presidential candidate X or Y will be more likely to preserve peace or start a war, or that women are naturally superior or inferior, they tend to ignore evidence that undermines that belief.

Belief perseverance applies even to our beliefs about ourselves. Lepper and Ross, with Richard Lau (1986), encountered it after showing California high school students either an effective or a confusing instructional film. Each film demonstrated how to solve some reasoning problems. Those shown the effective film did well on a later test, felt successful, and surmised that they were good at such problem solving. Those shown the useless film did poorly, felt like failures, and surmised that they weren't very competent on such problems. Even when the researchers then explained that the *film* was responsible for their success or failure and showed them the other film as evidence, the students persisted in seeing themselves as either good or incompetent at that type of reasoning problem.

*To prevent subjects from leaving the experiment feeling incompetent, the researchers more extensively debriefed and reassured them.*

And that, say the researchers, helps explain why early school failures can be so damaging. Even clearly demonstrating to children that their poor school performance "may well have been the consequence of an inept or biased teacher, a substandard school, or even prior social, cultural, or economic disadvantages" may fail to dent their feelings of incompetence. Once the belief that "I'm not very smart" forms, it tends to persist.

The belief perseverance phenomenon does not rule out people's changing their beliefs. It's just that once beliefs form and get justified, it takes more compelling evidence to change them than it did to create them.

*"I'm happy to say that my final judgment of a case is almost always consistent with my prejudgment of the case."*

Drawing by Fradon; © 1973 The New Yorker Magazine, Inc.

We have seen how our irrational thinking can plague our efforts to solve problems, make wise decisions, form valid judgments, and reason logically. From this we might conclude that our heads are indeed filled with straw. All in all, these and many other findings suggest "bleak implications for human rationality" (Nisbett & Borgida, 1975). Still, let us not forget that our cognition is effective and efficient: It enables our survival and our inventive genius.

One reason we function as well as we do is that in many real-life situations flawed reasoning *can* lead to correct conclusions (Funder, 1987). Physicians, for example, recognize the similarity between a patient's symptoms and those typical of a particular disease and then proceed to check out the hunch. In effect, their reasoning goes like this (Hunt, 1982):

Symptoms A, B, and C indicate disease X.

This patient has symptoms A, B, and C.

Therefore, I presume this patient has disease X.

The physician's conclusion is not necessarily logical. (Other diseases may also have symptoms A, B, and C.) Yet it is efficient and plausible, perhaps even probable. We reason, then, not so much by formal logic as by simplified, speedy heuristics, such as, "This situation reminds me of situations I have faced before, so what was true in those situations should be true here." Experts in fields other than medicine—even avid racetrack bettors who intuitively calculate the odds on horses (Ceci & Liker, 1986)—are similarly shrewd without necessarily knowing exactly how they reason.

Still, we should not underestimate the worth of sound reasoning. When we are deriving scientific hypotheses, playing chess, or debating political issues, it helps to have the powers of reason at our disposal. This is why many college courses, including this one, aim to enhance critical thinking. This is also why psychologists study obstacles to problem solving, and biases in reasoning. By learning about our irrational tendencies, we hope to raise some caution flags and to steer smart people away from dumb decisions.

## Artificial Intelligence

A tribute to human cognition comes from attempts to simulate human thinking on computers. **Artificial intelligence (AI)** is the science of designing computer systems to perform operations that mimic human thinking and do "intelligent" things. AI systems rely on massive stored information and rules for retrieving it. A hybrid of cognitive psychology and computer science, AI has two facets, one practical, the other theoretical.

The practical side of AI creates industrial robots that can "sense" their environment; "expert systems" that can carry out chemical analyses, offer tax planning advice, forecast weather, and help physicians diagnose their patients' diseases; and chess programs that can now challenge the world's top chess masters. The theoretical side of AI was pioneered by psychologist Herbert Simon, and it studies, by trying to design computer systems that mimic or rival human thought processes, how humans think. The goal is a "unified theory of cognition" embodied in a computer system that can process information, solve problems, learn from experience, and remember, much as humans do.

*Can* computers mimic our thinking powers? In those areas where humans seem to have the most difficulty—manipulating huge amounts of numerical data, retrieving detailed information from memory, making decisions using specified rules—the computer shines. Indeed, its proficiency makes the computer indispensable to banks, libraries, and the space program. But even the most sophisticated computers are dwarfed by the most ordinary of human mental abilities—recognizing a face, distinguishing a cat from a dog, knowing whether the word *line* refers to a rope or a fragment of poetry or a social come-on, and exercising common sense. Notes Donald Griffin (1984), "Human minds do more than process information; they think and feel. We experience beliefs, desires, fears, expectations, and many other subjective mental states."

*Discerning the difference between these two ads is much easier for a human than for a computer (from Schnitzer, 1984):*

1. *Car for sale. A classic! Lemon yellow coupe. Exterior is completely rustproof. Can be delivered upon request. No engine runs better. If the sun is out, you can remove the roof for the feel of the wind in your hair. Go ahead and kick the tires.*
2. *Car for sale. A classic lemon. Yellow coupe exterior is completely rust. Proof can be delivered upon request! No engine. Runs better if the sun is out. You can remove the roof. For the feel of the wind in your hair, go ahead and kick the tires.*

Compare computer operations with the brain's. Electricity races through the computer's microcircuits millions of times faster than neural impulses travel through our systems. Yet most computers process information serially—one step at a time, in sequence. Serial processing resembles a parade, where row after row passes by the reviewing stand, one at a time. By contrast, the human brain more closely resembles New York City's Grand Central Station at rush hour, processing millions of unrelated bits of information simultaneously. One part of the brain analyzes speech while other parts recognize pictures, detect smells, or plan action. As Chapter 5 explained, the visual system splits information about color, depth, movement, and form into separate channels, processes each channel simultaneously, and reassembles the information into a recognized image. Through this capacity for parallel processing, the brain outclasses the serial computer. Computer processing exceeds our thinking at tasks that use its unique strengths—vast memory and precise logic and retrieval. But computers have not duplicated the wide-ranging intelligence of a human mind, a mind that can *all at once* converse naturally, perceive the environment, use common sense, experience emotion, and consciously reflect on its own existence.

*"The things that distinguish us from monkeys—playing chess, for example—are easy for computers to do. But when it comes to doing things we share with the animal kingdom, computers are awful. In computing vision or movement, for example, no computer comes even close to matching the abilities of a fly."*

Brain researcher Christof Koch (1988)

As enthusiasm for traditional artificial intelligence moderates, excitement grows over **neural networks**—computer systems designed to mimic the brain's interconnected neural units (McClelland & Rumelhart, 1988). As the brain has billions of neurons, each connected to thousands of others, so each computer processing unit can be connected to many others. The computer's electronic "neural network" can be programmed to execute rules that mimic how the brain's neurons communicate—with positive (excitatory) or negative (inhibitory) messages that fire when the signal strength reaches a certain threshold. As in the brain, the "neural" connections are programmed to gain strength with experience. The computer system's complex interaction is mind-boggling, but the basic idea is that simple.

The most exciting feature of artificial neural networks is their capacity to learn from experience as some interconnections strengthen and others weaken. This feature, together with their capacity for parallel processing, enables neural network computers to learn to recognize particular shapes, sounds, and smells, which conventional computers find extremely difficult. The hoped-for payoffs are twofold. Neural network systems provide neuroscientists with new ways to test models of how living neural systems process sensations and memories. And they provide computer scientists with new insights into how to mimic the brain's thinking power. The dream is that someday we may better understand how our own brains function—*and* benefit from robots that can learn and from telephone systems that can understand and translate speech, allowing, for example, an English speaker and a Spanish speaker to converse without an interpreter (Waldrop, 1988). More and more, the brain provides a model of how computers of the future might work.

## Summing Up

Our cognitive system receives, perceives, and retrieves information, which we then use to think and communicate, sometimes wisely, sometimes foolishly. This chapter has so far explored how we form concepts, solve problems, and make judgments and decisions.

**Concepts** The building blocks of thinking, our concepts simplify and order the world by organizing it into a hierarchy of categories. Concepts often form around prototypes, or best examples of a category. Matching objects and ideas with prototypes is an efficient way of making snap judgments about what belongs to a specific concept.

**Solving Problems** When faced with a novel situation for which no well-learned response will do, we may use any of several strategies, such as trial and error, algorithms, and rule-of-thumb heuristics. Sometimes the solution comes in a flash of insight. We do, however, face obstacles to successful problem solving. The confirmation bias predisposes us to verify rather than challenge our hypotheses. And fixations, such as mental set and functional fixedness, may prevent our taking a needed fresh perspective on a problem.

**Making Decisions and Forming Judgments** Our use of heuristics, such as representativeness and availability, provide highly efficient but occasionally misleading guides for making quick decisions and forming intuitive judgments. Our tendencies to seek confirmation of our hypotheses and to use quick and easy heuristics can blind us to our vulnerability to error, a phenomenon known as overconfidence. And the way a question is posed, or framed, can significantly affect our responses.

**Belief Bias** People show a belief bias in their reasoning, accepting as more logical those conclusions that agree with their beliefs. We also exhibit belief perseverance, clinging to our ideas after their basis has been discredited because the explanation we accepted as valid lingers in our minds. Yet despite our capacity for error and our susceptibility to bias, human cognition is remarkably efficient and adaptive. As we gain expertise in a field, we grow adept at making quick, shrewd judgments.

**Artificial Intelligence** Experimental computers and robots are performing operations that mimic human thinking. The most notable AI successes focus computer capacities for memory and precise logic on specific tasks, such as playing chess or diagnosing illnesses. For now, the brain's capacity for processing unrelated information simultaneously and the wide range of its abilities dwarf those of the most sophisticated computer. But hopes grow that a new generation of computer neural networks, mimicking the brain's neural networks, will produce more humanlike capabilities.

## Language

*Language, the form taken by so much of our thinking, is built of various elements that emerge as a child matures. What are the elements of language? How and why do they develop? Are humans the only species capable of language?*

The most tangible indication of our thinking power is **language**—our spoken, written, or gestured words and the ways we combine them as we think and communicate. Humans have long and proudly proclaimed that language sets us above all other animals. "When we study human language," asserted linguist Noam Chomsky (1972), "we are approaching what some might call the 'human essence,' the qualities of mind that are, so far as we know, unique" to humans. To cognitive scientist Steven Pinker (1990), language is "the jewel in the crown of cognition." When the human vocal tract evolved the capacity to utter the commonest vowels (which chimps cannot), our capacity for language exploded. Complex vocalization boosted our ancestors' ability to communicate information, catapulting our species in a great leap forward (Diamond, 1989). Whether spoken, written, or signed, language enables us to communicate complex ideas from person to person and to transmit civilization's accumulated knowledge across generations.

**Language Transmits Culture** *The actual words and grammar may differ from culture to culture, but every society has a history that it transmits in story form to its children. Here, a group of Ivory Coast boys listen as an elder retells a tribal legend.*

### Language Structure

Consider how we might go about inventing a language. For a spoken language, we would need three building blocks. First, we would need a set of basic sounds, which linguists call **phonemes**. To say *bat* we utter the phoneme sounds *b*, *a*, and *t*. *Chat* has three phonemes—*ch*, *a*, and *t*. Languages have varying numbers of phonemes. English has about 40; other languages have anywhere from half to twice that many.

Changes in phonemes produce changes in meaning. Variations in the vowel sound between *b* and *t* can create 12 different meanings: *bait*, *bat*, *beat/beet*, *bet*, *bit*, *bite*, *boat*, *boot*, *bought*, *bout*, and *but* (Fromkin & Rodman, 1983). Generally, though, consonant phonemes carry more information than do vowel phonemes. The treth ef thes stetement shed be evedent frem thes bref demenstretien.

People who grow up learning one set of phonemes usually have difficulty pronouncing the phonemes of another language. The native English speaker may smile at the native German speaker's difficulties with the *th* sound, which often makes *this* sound like *dis*. But the German speaker can smile at the problems English speakers have rolling the German *r* or pronouncing the breathy *ch* in *Ich*, the German word for *I*.

*How many morphemes are in the word* cats? *(See page 345.)*

The second building block is the **morpheme**, the smallest unit of language that carries meaning. In English, a few morphemes are also phonemes—the personal pronoun *I* and the article *a*, for instance. But most are combinations of two or more phonemes. Some morphemes, like *bat*, are words, but others are only parts of words. Morphemes include prefixes and suffixes, such as the *pre* in *preview* or the *-ed* that shows past tense. *Undesirables* has four morphemes—*un, desir, able,* and *s*—each of which adds to the word's total meaning.

"Let me get this straight now. Is what you want to build a jean factory or a gene factory?"

From *The Wall Street Journal*—permission Cartoon Features Syndicate.

Finally, our new language must have a **grammar**, a system of rules (called *semantics* and *syntax*) that enables us to speak and understand. **Semantics** are the rules we use to derive meaning from morphemes, words, and even sentences. A semantic rule tells us that adding *ed* to *laugh* means that it happened in the past. **Syntax** refers to the rules we use to order words into sentences. One rule of English syntax says that adjectives usually come before nouns, so we say *white house*. Spanish adjectives usually come after nouns, so a Spanish speaker says *casa blanca*. The English rules of syntax allow the sentence *They are hunting dogs*. Given the context, semantics tells us whether it refers to dogs seeking animals or people seeking dogs.

*A cultural universal: In every language, the commonest words are the shortest. As a word is used more and more, it often gets shortened.* Television *becomes* TV *(Triandis, 1994).*

Note that language becomes more complex at each succeeding level. In English, the relatively small number of 40 or so phonemes can be combined to form more than 100,000 morphemes, which alone or in combination produce the 616,500 word forms in the *Oxford English Dictionary* (including 290,500 main entries, such as *meat* and 326,000 subentries such as *meat-eater*). We can then use these words to create an almost infinite number of sentences, most of which (like this one) are original. Like the brain that conceives it, language is complexity built of simplicity.

## Language Development

Make a quick guess: How many words did you learn in one average day during the years between your first birthday and your high school graduation?

*Although you probably know more than 80,000 words, you use only 150 words for about half of what you say.*

The average North American high school graduate knows some 80,000 words (Miller & Gildea, 1987). That averages (after age 1) to nearly 5000 words learned a year, or 13 a day! How you did it—how the 5000 words a year you learned could so far outnumber the roughly 200 words a year that your schoolteachers consciously taught you—is one of the great human wonders. Before children can add 2 + 2, they are creating their own original and grammatically appropriate sentences. Most parents would have trouble stating the rules of syntax. Yet their preschoolers comprehend and speak with a facility that puts to shame a college student struggling to learn a foreign language or a scientist struggling to simulate natural language on a computer. How does our astonishing facility for language unfold, and how can we explain it?

### Acquiring Language

Children's language development mirrors language structure—by moving from simplicity to complexity. By 4 months of age, babies can read lips and discriminate speech sounds. They prefer to look at a face that matches a sound, so we know they can recognize that *ah* comes from wide open lips and *ee* from a mouth with corners pulled back (Kuhl & Meltzoff, 1982). At about this age, babies enter a **babbling stage** in which they spontaneously utter a variety of sounds such as *ah-goo*. Babbling is not the imitation of adult speech, for it includes sounds from various languages, even sounds that do not occur in the household's language. From this early babbling, a listener could not identify an infant as being, say, French, Korean, or Ethiopian. Deaf infants babble (repeat syllablelike gestures), too, and they obviously are not imitating speech (Petitto & Marentette, 1991). It seems, then, that before nurture molds our speech, nature provides a whole range of possible phoneme sounds.

Babbling eventually comes to resemble the characteristic sounds and intonations of the household language. By about age 10 months, a trained ear can identify the language of the household by listening to an infant's babbling (de Boysson-Bardies & others, 1989). Phoneme sounds outside the infant's native tongue begin to disappear. And infants gradually lose their ability to discriminate sounds they never hear. Clever experiments by Janet Werker (1989) reveal that at 6 months infants can perceive phoneme differences from other languages, but by 12 months they cannot (Figure 10–7). Thus, by adulthood an English-speaker cannot discriminate certain Japanese phonemes nor can a Japanese adult with no training in English distinguish between the English *r* and *l* (Japanese has a consonant midway be-

**Figure 10–7**

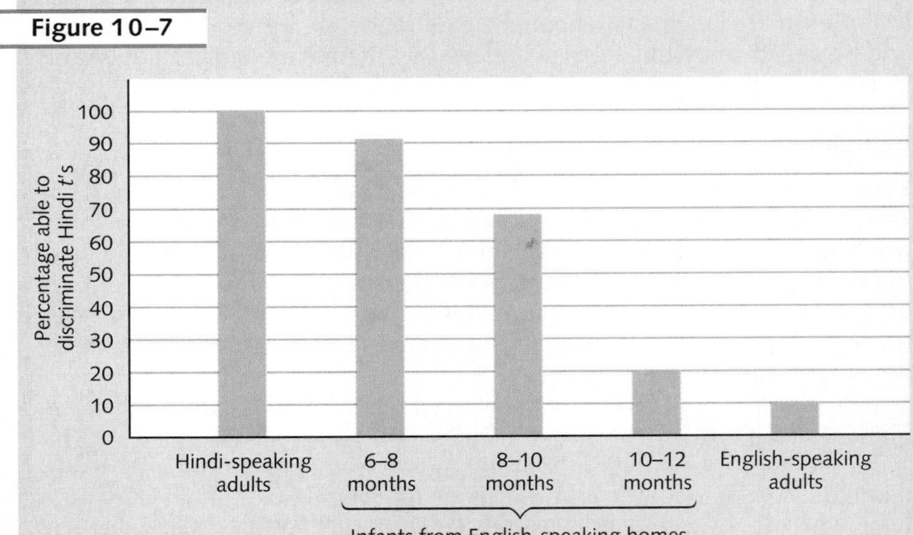


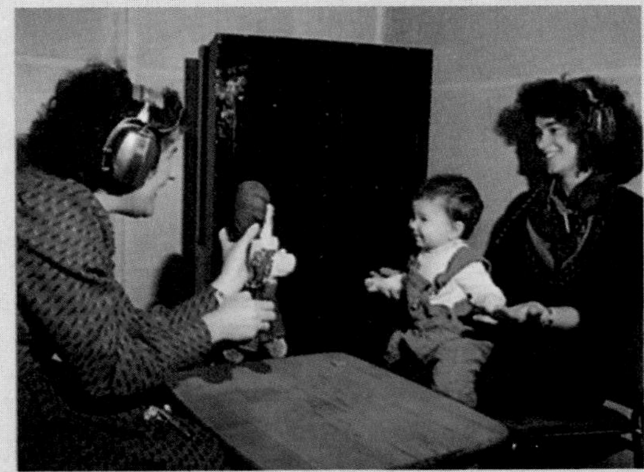

**Testing for Phoneme Perception** *We are all born with the ability to recognize speech sounds from all the world's languages. In Janet Werker's lab, an infant is reinforced with applause and by activating toy animals when he looks to the right after hearing a changed sound (as in* ba, ba, ba, ba, da, da*). Adult Hindi-speakers and young infants from English-speaking homes can easily discriminate two Hindi* t *sounds not spoken in English. By about age 1, however, English-speaking listeners rarely perceive the sound difference. (Adapted from Werker, 1989.)*

"Got idea. Talk better. Combine words. Make sentences."

© 1994 by Sidney Harris.

| Table 10–1 | Summary of Language Development |
|---|---|
| **Month (approximate)** | **Stage** |
| 4 | Babbles many speech sounds. |
| 10 | Babbling reveals household language. |
| 12 | One-word stage. |
| 24 | Two-word, telegraphic speech. |
| 24+ | Language develops rapidly into complete sentences. |

tween *r* and *l*). Japanese also has no *p* or *f*. Thus, *please* sounds very much like *freeze*, which may explain why Yoshihiro Hattori, a Japanese exchange student mistaken for a burglar, failed to understand a gun-toting Louisiana homeowner's order to *freeze* and was tragically shot to death.

Around the first birthday (the exact age varies from child to child), most children enter the **one-word stage**. Having already learned that sounds carry meanings, they begin to use sounds to communicate meaning. Their first words usually contain only one syllable—*ma* or *da*, for instance—and may be barely recognizable. But family members quickly learn to understand the infant's language, and gradually it conforms more and more to the family's language.

Most of the child's first words refer to things that move or can be played with—a dog or a ball, for example, rather than the table or crib that just sits there (Nelson, 1973). At this one-word stage, an inflected word may equal a sentence. "Doggy!" may mean "Look at the dog out there!"

Children typically use more and more single words during the second year and, by about their second birthday, enter the **two-word stage**, when they start uttering two-word sentences (Table 10–1). Language at this stage is characterized by **telegraphic speech**: Like telegrams (TERMS ACCEPTED. SEND MONEY.), it contains mostly nouns and verbs (*Want juice*). Also like telegrams, it follows rules of syntax; the words are in a sensible order. The English-speaking child typically says adjectives before nouns—*big doggy* rather than *doggy big*.

There seems to be no "three-word stage." Once children move out of the two-word stage, they quickly begin uttering longer phrases (Fromkin & Rodman, 1983). Although the sentences may still sound like a Western Union message, they continue to follow the rules of syntax (*Mommy get ball*). By early elementary school, the child understands complex sentences and begins to enjoy the humor conveyed by double meanings: "You never starve in the desert because of all the sand-which-is there."

### Explaining Language Development

Those who study language acquisition inevitably wonder how we do it. Attempts to answer this question have sparked a spirited intellectual controversy. The controversy parallels the debate we noted in Chapter 8 over the behaviorist view of the malleable organism versus the view that each organism comes biologically prepared to learn certain associations. The nature-nurture debate surfaces again and, here as elsewhere, appreciation for innate predisposition has grown.

Behaviorist B. F. Skinner (1957) believed we can explain language development with familiar learning principles, such as association (of the sights of things with the sounds of words); imitation (of the words and syntax modeled by others); and reinforcement (with success, smiles, and hugs when the child says something right). Thus, Skinner argued, babies learn to talk in many of the same ways that animals learn to peck keys and press bars. "Verbal behavior evidently came into existence when, through a critical step in the evolution of the human species, the vocal musculature became susceptible to operant conditioning," Skinner (1985) surmised.

Linguist Noam Chomsky (1959, 1987) thinks Skinner was naive. Surely, says Chomsky, a Martian scientist observing children in a single-language community would conclude that language is almost entirely inborn. It isn't, because children do learn the language used in their environment. But the rate at which they acquire words and grammar without being taught is too extraordinary to be explained solely by learning principles.

Children create all sorts of sentences they have never heard and, therefore, could not be imitating. They begin using morphemes in a predictable order. They begin adding *-ing* to words. Then they start using the prepositions *in* and *on*. Then come *a* and *the*, followed by *is* (Brown, 1973). Moreover, many of their errors result from overgeneralizing logical grammatical rules, such as adding -ed to make the past tense (from de Cuevas, 1990):

*Answer to question on page 342: Two—*cat *and* -s.

**Child:** *My teacher holded the baby rabbits and we petted them.*

**Mother:** *Did you say your teacher held the baby rabbits?*

**Child:** *Yes.*

**Mother:** *What did you say she did?*

**Child:** *She holded the baby rabbits and we petted them.*

**Mother:** *Did you say she held them tightly?*

**Child:** *No, she holded them loosely.*

Chomsky (1987) likens the behaviorist view of how language develops to filling a bottle with water. He views language development as "helping a flower to grow in its own way." It is, he believes, akin to sexual maturation—given adequate nurture, it just "happens to the child." Thanks to their inborn "universal grammar," children readily learn the grammar of whatever language they hear. Other worlds may have languages that, for us humans, are unlearnable, but our world does not. Chomsky maintains that our language acquisition capacity is like a box—a "language acquisition device"—in which grammar switches are thrown as children experience their language. Thus, English-speaking children learn to put the object of a sentence last ("She ate an apple"). Japanese-speaking children put the object before the verb ("She an apple ate"). We are born with the hardware and an operating system; experience writes the software.

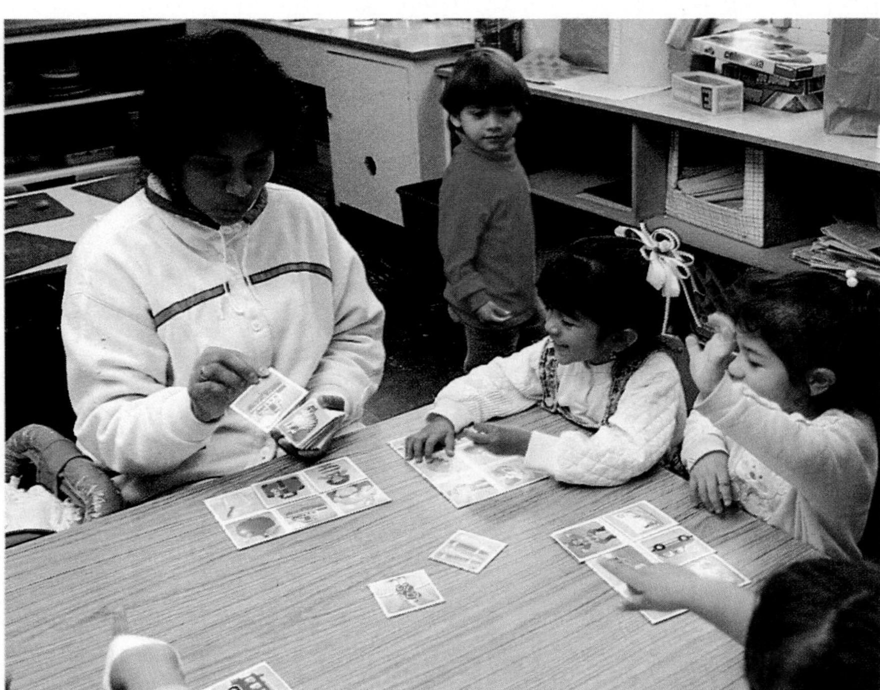

**The Game of Language Acquisition** *The first language of millions of children is not the dominant culture's language. This second language they learn when they reach school. For the children at this Berkeley, California, bilingual preschool, such learning flowers naturally with the aid of games and other kinds of play.*

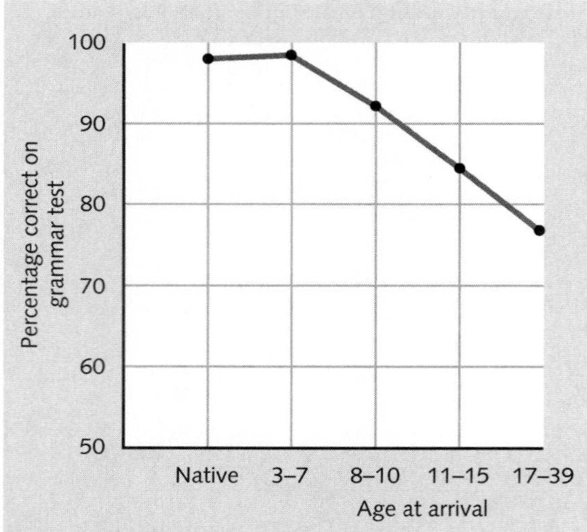


**Figure 10–8**

**Grammar Mastery** *Young children have a readiness to learn language. Ten years after coming to the United States, Asian immigrants took a grammar test. Those who arrived before age 8 understood grammar as well as native speakers. Those who arrived later did not. (From Johnson & Newport, 1989.)*

Cognitive scientists still debate how much of our language capacity is inborn (Shanks, 1993). With experience (but with no "inborn" linguistic rules), computer neural networks can learn to form past-tense verbs appropriately. They can learn, for example, to change words ending in *ow* to *ew*, as in *throw/threw*. To some scientists, this suggests the brain could be a blanker slate than Chomsky believes.

The scholars agree, however, that for language development, life's first years are critical. Those who learn a second language as adults usually speak it with the accent of their first language. Do they master the foreign grammar better? To find out, Jacqueline Johnson and Elissa Newport (1989) gave Korean and Chinese immigrants to the United States a grammar test, requiring them to identify each of 276 sentences ("Yesterday the hunter shoots a deer") as grammatically correct or incorrect. Some subjects had immigrated in early childhood, others as adults. Regardless of their age at immigration, the participants had each been in the United States for approximately 10 years. Nevertheless, as Figure 10–8 reveals, those who learned their second language early learned it best. Chomsky would say that once the grammar switches are thrown during a child's developing years, mastering another grammar becomes more difficult.

As a flower's growth is stunted without nourishment, so, too, are children linguistically stunted when isolated from language during the critical period for its acquisition. Consider Genie, who spent most of her early years tied to a chair without being spoken to. When discovered by Los Angeles authorities in 1970 at age 13, she was mute and uncomprehending (Curtiss, 1977, 1981). In the years that followed, Genie learned some individual words but not how to construct grammatically correct sentences. Today, she lives in a home for mentally impaired adults (Rymer, 1993).

The impact of early experience is also evident among the deaf. Hearing children of hearing-speaking parents, and deaf children of deaf-signing parents, have much in common. Both groups babble as infants—hearing children by repeating sounds, deaf children by repeating elementary sign gestures (Petitto & Marentette, 1991). Both groups develop vocabularies, at comparable rates (Meier, 1991). For both groups, late exposure to language (at age 2 or 3) unleashes their brain's idle language capacity, producing a rush of language. But consider the 90+ percent of deaf children born to hearing-nonsigning parents. These children typically do not experience language during their early years. Compared with deaf children exposed

*"Childhood is the time for language, no doubt about it. Young children, the younger the better, are good at it; it is child's play. It is a onetime gift to the species."*

Lewis Thomas
*The Fragile Species*, 1992

**No Means NO! No Matter How You Say It** *Deaf children of deaf-signing parents and hearing children of hearing parents have much in common. They develop language skills at about the same rate, and they are equally effective at opposing parental wishes and demanding their way.*

to sign language from birth, those who learn to sign as teens or adults are like immigrants who learn English after childhood. They can master the basic words and how to order them, but they never become as fluent as native signers in producing and comprehending subtle grammatical differences (Newport, 1990).

To summarize, children are biologically prepared to learn language as they interact with their caregivers. Skinner's emphasis on learning helps explain why infants acquire the language they hear and how they add new words to their vocabularies. Chomsky's emphasis on our built-in readiness to learn grammar rules helps explain why preschoolers acquire language so readily and use grammar so well. Once again, we see biology and experience working together.

Returning to our debate about humanity's thinking powers, let's pause to issue a report card. On decision making and judgment, our error-prone species might rate a *C+*. On problem solving, where humans are inventive yet vulnerable to fixation, we would probably receive better marks, perhaps a *B+*. On cognitive efficiency, our fallible but quick heuristics earn us an *A*. And when it comes to learning and using language, the awestruck experts would surely award the human species an *A+*.

## Animal Language

If in our use of language we humans are, as the psalmist rhapsodized, "little less than God," where do other animals fit in the scheme of things? Are they "little less than human"? In part, the answer lies in the extent to which animals share our capacity for language.

Without doubt, animals communicate. Vervet monkeys have different alarm cries for different predators: a barking call for a leopard, a coughing for an eagle, and a chuttering for a snake. Hearing the leopard alarm they climb the nearest tree. Hearing the eagle alarm they rush into the bushes. Hearing the snake chutter they stand up and scan the ground (Byrne, 1991). But do animals' communications make up a language?

### The Case of the Honeybee

More than 2000 years ago, the Greek philosopher Aristotle observed that once a lone honeybee discovers a source of nectar, other bees soon leave the hive and go straight to the newfound food source. Aristotle surmised that the original explorer must return to the hive and lead other bees back to the food. He was wrong. In 1901, a clever German researcher followed the explorer bee back to the hive and trapped it as it left to return to the food source. Although deprived of their guide, the new recruits still flew straight to the nectar.

How did the bees know where to go? Intrigued, Austrian biologist Karl von Frisch (1950) undertook experiments for which he later shared the Nobel prize. The experiments revealed that the explorer bee communicates with the other worker bees by means of an intricate dance. The direction and duration of the dance, Frisch discovered, informs other bees of the direction and distance of the food source (Figure 10–9). Using robotic honeybees that perform a credible song and dance act, experimenters have since discovered that it takes a combination of dance and sound to tell nestmate bees where to fly to find food (Kirchner & Towne, 1994).

Impressive as they are, the honeybees' song and dance hardly challenge the complexity, flexibility, and power of human language. The honeybee communicates, but not with the elements of language.

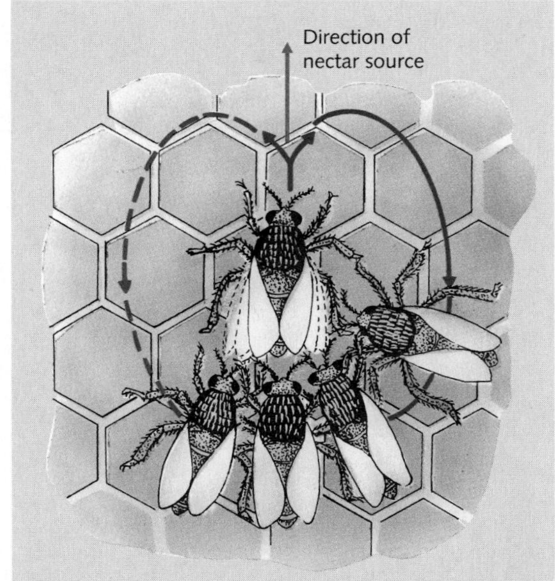


**Figure 10–9**

**The Dance of the Honeybee** *The straight-line part of the dance points in the direction of a nectar source relative to the sun, and its duration indicates the distance. The other bees, who cannot see the dance in the dark hive, huddle close to feel what is going on. (From von Frisch, 1974.)*

### The Case of the Apes

A greater challenge to humanity's claim to be the only language-using species has come from reports of apes that "talk" with people. Genetically speaking, our closest relatives are the chimpanzees, and the chimpanzees' closest relatives are not other apes, but us (Sagan & Druyan, 1992). Knowing that chimpanzees could not vocalize more than a few words, University of Nevada researchers Allen Gardner and Beatrice Gardner (1969) tried to teach sign language words to a chimp named Washoe, as though she were a deaf human child. After 4 years, Washoe could use 132 signs. By 1993, 27-year-old Washoe had a vocabulary of 240 signs (Geranios, 1993). The Gardners' announcement of the success of their efforts aroused enormous scientific and public interest. One *New York Times* reporter, having learned sign language from his deaf parents, visited Washoe and exclaimed, "Suddenly I realized I was conversing with a member of another species in my native tongue."

*Seeing a doll floating in her water, Washoe signed, "Baby in my drink."*

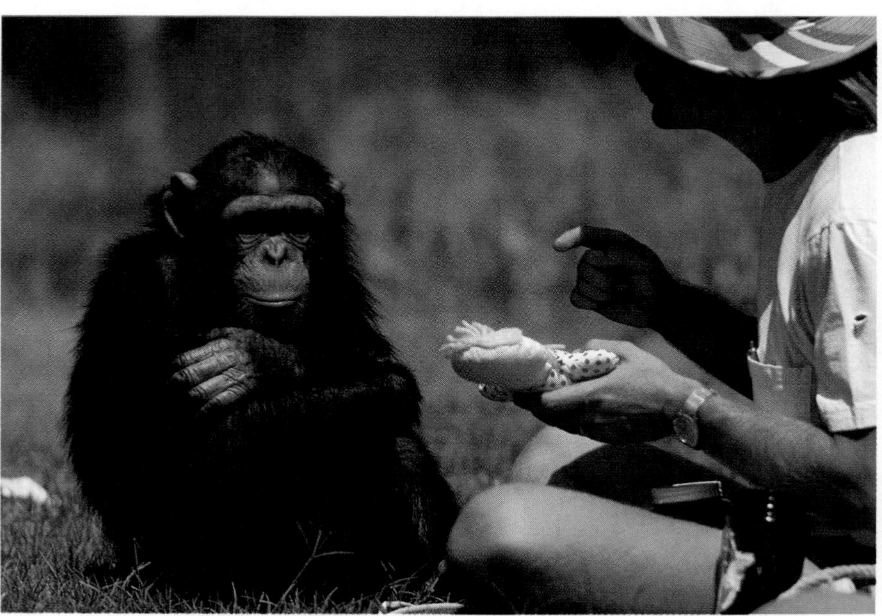

**But Is This Language?** *The ability of chimpanzees to express themselves in American Sign Languge (ASL) raises questions about the very nature of language. Here, the trainer is asking, "What is this?" The sign in response is "Baby." Does the response constitute language?*

During the 1970s, further evidence of "ape language" surfaced. Although apes usually signed just single words, they sometimes strung signs to form intelligible sentences. Washoe signed, "You me go out, please." Apes even appeared to combine words creatively. Washoe designated a swan as a "water bird." Koko, a gorilla trained by Francine Patterson (1978) in California, reportedly described a long-nosed Pinocchio doll as an "elephant baby." Lana, a chimpanzee that "talks" by punching buttons wired to a computer that translates her punchings into English, wanted her trainer's orange. She had no word for *orange*, but she did know her colors and the word for *apple*, so she improvised: "? Tim give apple which-is orange" (Rumbaugh, 1977).

**Another "Talking" Chimpanzee** *Lana has learned to speak by punching word symbols on a computer keyboard. When she presses a key, the symbol lights up.*

As ape language reports accumulated, it seemed that apes might indeed be "little less than human." Their vocabularies and sentences are simple, rather like those of a 2-year-old child. Yet the apes did seem to share what we humans have considered our unique ability.

**But Can Apes Really Talk?** By the late 1970s, the claims of "talking apes" raised a question: Were the chimps language champs or were the researchers chumps? The ape language researchers were making monkeys out of themselves, said the skeptics, who raised the following arguments:

- Apes gain their limited vocabularies only with great difficulty. They are hardly like speaking or signing children, who effortlessly soak up dozens of new words a week. Saying that apes can learn language because they can sign words is like saying humans can fly because they can jump.
- Chimps can make signs or push buttons in sequence to get a reward, but so can pigeons—by pecking a sequence of keys to get grain (Straub & others, 1979). No one says the pigeon is "talking."
- Apes can certainly use symbols meaningfully, but the evidence is far from convincing that they can equal even a 3-year-old's ability to order words with proper syntax. To the child, "you tickle" and "tickle you" communicate different ideas. A chimp might sign the phrases interchangeably.
- After training a chimp whom he named Nim Chimsky, Herbert Terrace (1979) concluded that much of chimpanzees' signing is nothing more than their imitating their trainers' signs.
- Presented with ambiguous information, people tend to see what they want or expect to see. (Recall the demonstrations of perceptual set in Chapter 6.) Interpreting chimpanzee signs as language may be little more than wishful thinking on the part of their trainers, claimed Terrace. (When Washoe signed "water bird," she perhaps was separately naming "water" and "bird.")

*"Although humans make sounds with their mouths and occasionally look at each other, there is no solid evidence that they actually communicate with each other."*

© 1979 by Sidney Harris/*American Scientist Magazine.*

In science as in politics, controversy stimulates progress. The provocative claim that "apes share our capacity for language" and the skeptical rejoinder that "apes no use language" (as Washoe might have put it) have moved psychologists toward a greater appreciation of apes' remarkable capabilities and of our own. Everyone agrees that humans alone possess language, if by the term we mean verbal or signed expression of complex grammar. If we mean, more simply, the ability to communicate through a meaningful sequence of symbols, then apes are indeed capable of language.

On reflection, one of chimpanzee Lana's trainers, Duane Rumbaugh (1985, 1987), believes it is too simplistic to ask, "Do the apes have a capacity for human language—or don't they?" Language "is very complex with many, many dimensions and facets. Our nearest living relatives have some, but not all, of those parts." So, rather than thinking of language, like pregnancy, as all or none, we might better view it as a continuum of skills, some of which apes possess.

*"[Our] egocentric view that [we are] unique from all other forms of animal life is being jarred to the core."*

Duane Rumbaugh and Sue Savage-Rumbaugh (1978)

Although chimpanzees do not have our facility for language, their thinking and communicating abilities continue to impress their trainers. After her second infant died, a depressed Washoe repeatedly asked "Baby?" and became withdrawn when told "Baby dead, baby gone, baby finished." Two weeks later, caretaker Roger Fouts (1992) had better news for Washoe: "I have baby for you." Washoe reacted to the signed news with instant excitement, her hair on end, swaggering and panting while signing over and again, "Baby, my baby." When Fouts then introduced the foster infant, Loulis, it took several hours for them to warm to each other, whereupon Washoe broke the ice by signing, "Come baby" and cuddling Loulis. In the months that followed, Loulis picked up 68 signs simply by observing Washoe and three other language-trained chimps.

Moreover, Washoe, Loulis, and the others now sign spontaneously, as when asking one another to *chase, tickle, hug, come,* or *groom.* People who sign can eavesdrop on these chimp-to-chimp conversations with near-perfect agreement about what the chimps are saying, 90 percent of which pertains to social interaction, reassurance, or play (Fouts & Bodamer, 1987). Moreover, the chimps are modestly bilingual; they can translate spoken English words into signs (Shaw, 1989–1990).

Lana's instructors have trained two other chimps, Sherman and Austin, to use computer keyboards to communicate with each other. The chimps ask one another for a specific food or even for a tool they can use to get food (Rumbaugh & Savage-Rumbaugh, 1986). Also impressive is the discovery by Savage-Rumbaugh and her colleagues (1993) that pygmy chimpanzees can learn to comprehend the semantic nuances of spoken English. Kanzi, one such chimp with the grammatical abilities of a 2½-year-old, behaves intelligently whether asked, "Can you show me the light?" or "Can you bring me the light [a flashlight]?" or "Can you turn the light on?" Kanzi also knows the spoken words *snake, bite,* and *dog*. Given stuffed animals and asked, for the first time, to "make the dog bite the snake," he put the snake to the dog's mouth. (See also Figure 10–10.) For chimps as for humans, early life is a critical time for learning language. If raised without early exposure to speech or word symbols, the chimps are unable as adults to gain language competence (Rumbaugh & Savage-Rumbaugh, 1994).

So, trained apes' language capabilities are modest by human standards. Yet their impressive cognitive powers seem indeed to make them "little less than human." If Kanzi "had a vocal tract, he would be talking," exclaims Duane Rumbaugh (1994). Realizing this, we see once again how animal research can increase our respect for the creatures studied. Believing that animals could not think, Descartes and other philosophers argued that they were living robots without moral rights. But some animals, including apes and dolphins, do show remarkable abilities to think, to feel family loyalty, even to display altruism. Working out the moral implications of all this is an unfinished task for our own thinking species.

**Figure 10–10**

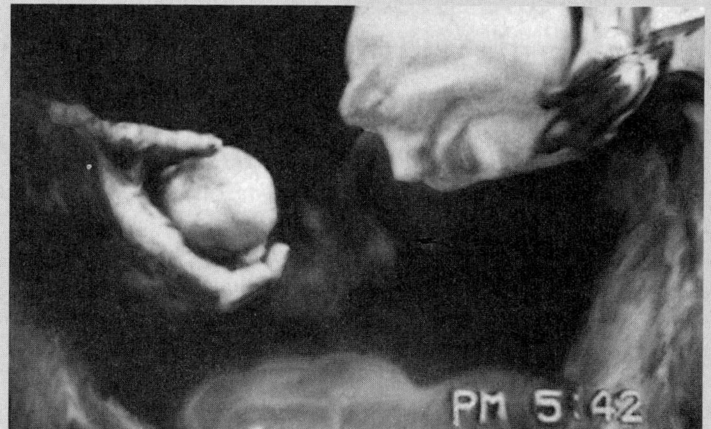


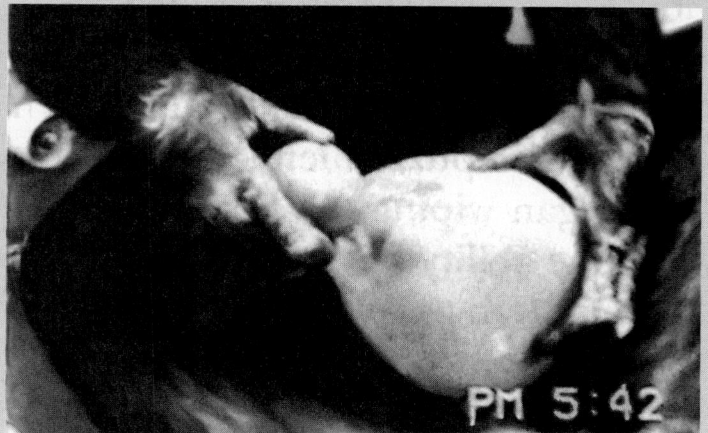


**Language?** *Asked to "feed your ball some tomato," Kanzi picked up a tomato and a pumpkin-faced spongeball, then placed the tomato to the ball's mouth. (From Savage-Rumbaugh & others, 1993.)*

## Summing Up

Language—our words and how we combine them to communicate meaning—facilitates and expresses our thoughts.

**Language Structure** Spoken language is built of basic speech sounds, called *phonemes;* elementary units of meaning, called *morphemes;* and the *semantics* (meaning) and *syntax* (rules for word order) that make up grammar.

**Language Development** Among the marvels of nature is a child's ability to acquire language. The ease with which children progress from the babbling stage through the one-word stage to the telegraphic speech of the two-word stage and beyond has sparked a lively debate concerning how they do it. Behaviorist Skinner explained that we learn language by the familiar principles of association, imitation, and reinforcement. Challenging this claim, linguist Noam Chomsky argued that children are biologically prepared to learn words and use grammar. For mastery of grammar, the learning that occurs during life's first few years is, however, critical.

**Animal Language** Another vigorously debated issue is whether language is uniquely human. Animals obviously communicate. Bees, for example, communicate the location of food through an intricate dance. And several teams of psychologists have taught various species of apes, including a number of chimpanzees, to communicate with humans by signing or by pushing buttons wired to a computer. Apes have developed considerable vocabularies. They string words together to express meaning and to make and follow requests. Skeptics point out important differences between apes' and humans' facilities with language, especially in their respective abilities to order words using proper syntax. Nevertheless, these studies reveal that apes have considerable cognitive ability.

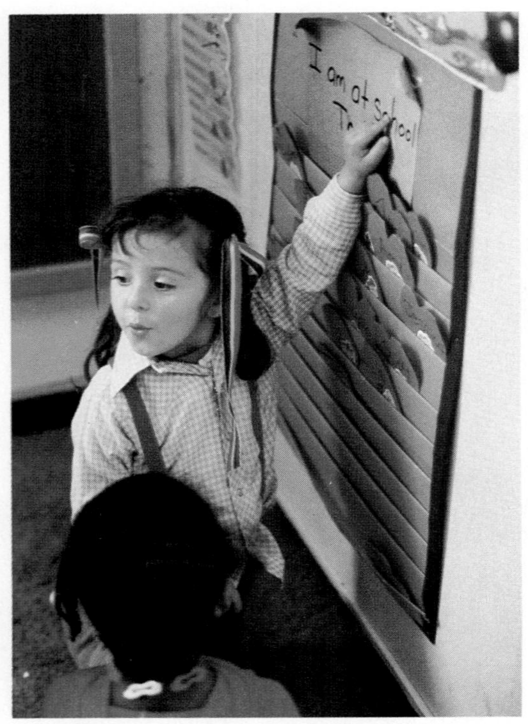

**It Pays to Increase Your Word Power** *This girl's efforts to increase her vocabulary will expand her capacity to think.*

*"All words are pegs to hang ideas on."*
Henry Ward Beecher
*Proverbs from Plymouth Pulpit*, 1887

*"To call forth a concept, a word is needed."*
Antoine Lavoisier
*Elements of Chemistry*, 1789

## Thinking and Language

*A world without language would be a world without the concepts and cultures we hang on language. Language influences what we think, perceive, and remember. Education therefore aims to increase our word (and thinking) power. Yet some thinking is rooted in images rather than words.*

Thinking and language intricately intertwine. Asking which comes first is one of psychology's chicken-and-egg questions. Do our ideas come first and wait for words to name them? Or are our thoughts conceived in words and unthinkable without them?

### Linguistic Influences on Thinking

Linguist Benjamin Lee Whorf contended that language determines the way we think. According to Whorf's (1956) **linguistic relativity** hypothesis, different languages impose different conceptions of reality: "Language itself shapes a man's basic ideas."

Whorf's idea seldom occurs to people who speak but one language. To them, language seems only a vehicle for thought. But to those who speak two dissimilar languages, such as English and Japanese, it seems obvious that one thinks differently in different languages (Brown, 1986). Unlike English, which has a rich vocabulary for self-focused emotions such as anger, Japanese has many words for interpersonal emotions such as sympathy (Markus & Kitayama, 1991). Many bilinguals report that they even have a different sense of self, depending on which language they are using (Matsumoto, 1994). After immigrating from Asia to North America, bilinguals may reveal different personalities when taking the same personality test in their two languages (Dinges & Hull, 1992). Learn a language and you learn about a culture. When a language becomes extinct—the likely fate of most of the world's 6000 remaining languages—the world loses the culture and thinking that hangs on that language.

Another example: In English, there is one word for *snow*. The Eskimo language has many. This, said Whorf, allows Eskimos to *perceive* differences in snow that would be unnoticed by people who speak another language. The language-thought link also occurs at the level of grammar—the Hopi Indians, for example, have no past tense for their verbs. Therefore, Whorf contended, the Hopi cannot so readily *think* about the past.

Critics of the language-determines-thought idea claim that words *reflect* rather than create the way we think. The Eskimos *need* words to describe sticky, powdery, and packed snow. We may lack the Eskimos' rich vocabulary for describing snow, but that does not mean we are incapable of perceiving these differences. My language lacks the dozen words with which the sea-hunting Makaw Indians could describe varying tides. But having grown up near them on Washington's coastal waters, I can understand what their words referred to. Likewise, a New Guinean without our words for shapes and colors nevertheless perceives them much as we do (Rosch, 1974).

Although it is too strong to say that language *determines* the *way* we think, our words certainly can *influence what* we think—what we perceive and remember and how we solve problems and make judgments (Hardin & Banaji, 1993). We therefore do well to choose our words carefully. When people refer to women as *girls*—as in "the girls at the office"—it perpetuates a view of women's having lower status, does it not? Or consider the generic use of the pronoun *he*. Does it make any difference whether I write "A child learns language as *he* interacts with *his* caregivers" or "Children learn language as *they* interact with *their* caregivers"? Some argue that it makes no difference because every reader knows that "the masculine gender shall be deemed and taken to include females" (as the British Parliament declared in 1850).

But is the generic *he* always taken to include females? Twenty studies have consistently found that it is not (Henley, 1989). For example, Janet Hyde (1984) asked children to finish stories for which she gave them a first line such as, "When a kid goes to school, ______ often feels excited on the first day." When Hyde used *he* in the blank, the children's stories were nearly always about males. *He* or *she* in the blank resulted in female characters about one-third of the time. Studies with adolescents and adults in North America and New Zealand have found similar effects of the generic *he* (Hamilton, 1988; Martyna, 1978; Ng, 1990). Sentences about "the artist and his work" tend to conjure up images of a man. Told "The average American believes he watches too much TV," a typical subject in one study pictured "a fat guy sitting on a couch with a remote control" (Gastil, 1990).

Consider, too, that people use generic pronouns selectively, as in "the doctor . . . he" and "the secretary . . . she" (MacKay, 1983). If *he* and *his* were truly gender-free, we shouldn't skip a beat when hearing that "a nurse must answer his calls" or that "man, like other mammals, nurses his young." That we are startled indicates that the *his* carries a gender connotation that clashes with our idea of *nurse*.

The power of language to influence thought makes vocabulary building a crucial part of education. To expand language is to expand the ability to think. David Premack (1983) reported that even among chimpanzees, language training enhances the ability to think abstractly and to reason by analogy. Shown a cylinder half filled with water, a chimp not trained in language had difficulty recognizing that half an apple was more like the half-filled cylinder than was three-fourths of an apple. Language-trained chimps could more readily grasp the analogy. In young children, too, thinking develops hand in hand with language (Gopnik & Meltzoff, 1986). What is true for chimpanzees and preschoolers is true for everyone: *It pays to increase your word power*. That is why most textbooks, including this one, introduce new words—to teach new ideas and new ways of thinking.

Increased word power also helps explain what McGill University researcher Wallace Lambert (1992; Lambert & others, 1993) calls the "bilingual advantage." Bilingual children in Canada, Switzerland, Israel, South Africa, and Singapore outperform monolinguals on intelligence tests. Knowing this, Lambert helped devise a Canadian program that enables English-speaking children to be immersed in French. For most of their first 3 school years they are taught by a French-speaking teacher; not until the fifth and sixth grades do they receive half their instruction in English. Not surprisingly, the children attain a natural French fluency unrivaled by other methods of language teaching. Moreover, compared with similarly capable children in control conditions, they do so without detriment to their English fluency, and with increased aptitude scores, math scores, and appreciation for French Canadian culture.

Increasing their word power through sign language has also had great benefits for deaf people, who for thousands of years were viewed as incompetent to inherit property, marry, be educated, or have challenging work (Sacks, 1990). Since the spread of signed instruction, the deaf have shown that, when exposed to signing as preschoolers and then schooled in their

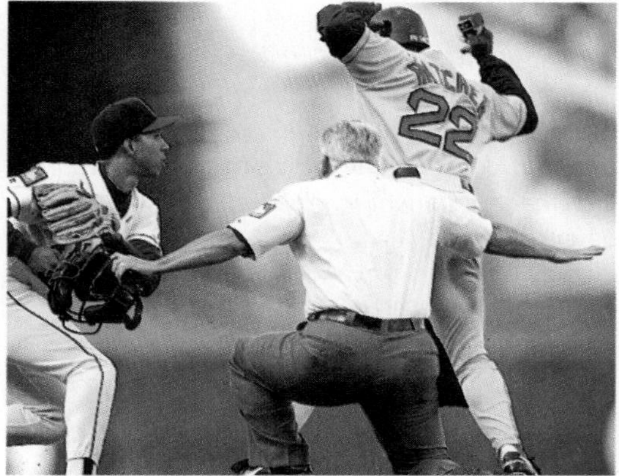

**A Safe Sign** *We have outfielder William Hoy to thank for baseball sign languge. The first deaf player to join the major leagues in 1892, he invented hand signals for "Strike!" "Safe!" (shown here) and "Yerr Out!" (Pollard, 1992). Such gestures worked so well that referees in all sports now use invented signs, and fans are fluent in sports sign language.*

language, they become fully literate. Deaf children with native sign fluency (as children of deaf parents) outperform other deaf children on measures of intelligence and academic achievement (Isham & Kamin, 1993). For both the deaf and the hearing, language transforms experience. Language connects us to past and future. Language fuels our imagination. Language links us to one another.

## Thinking Without Language

When you are alone, do you talk to yourself? Is "thinking" simply conversing with yourself? Without a doubt, words convey ideas. But are there not times when ideas precede words? To turn on the cold water in your bathroom, in which direction do you turn the handle?

To answer this question, you probably thought not in words but with a mental picture. Indeed, we often think in images. Artists think in images. So do composers, poets, mathematicians, athletes, and scientists. Albert Einstein reported that he achieved some of his greatest insights through visual images and only later put them into words.

Liu Chi Kung placed second in the 1958 Tchaikovsky competition—the piano Olympics—and was imprisoned a year later during China's cultural revolution. Soon after his release, after 7 years without touching a piano, he was back on tour and critics judged his musicianship better than ever. How did he do it without practice? "I did practice," said Liu, "every day. I rehearsed every piece I had ever played, note by note, in my mind" (Garfield, 1986).

Many successful athletes prepare for contests by imagining themselves performing their events (Suinn, 1986; Whelan & others, 1991). Golf great Jack Nicklaus has said that he would "watch a movie" in his head before each shot. The U.S. Olympic Ski Team and the New England Patriots football team have been given mental imagery training (Nicholi, 1987). Georgia Nigro (1984) demonstrated the wisdom of mental practice in a laboratory test. She had subjects make 24 actual dart throws at a target, then had half

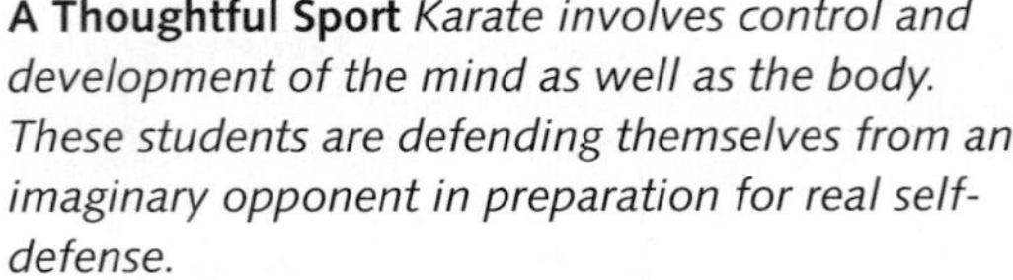
**A Thoughtful Sport** *Karate involves control and development of the mind as well as the body. These students are defending themselves from an imaginary opponent in preparation for real self-defense.*

the subjects throw 24 darts mentally, and, finally, had all the subjects again make 24 throws. Only those who had mentally practiced showed any improvement. A National Research Council committee of psychologists investigated claims of performance-enhancement techniques for the U.S. Army and concluded that most techniques (including ESP and "neurolinguistic programming") were of no value (Druckman & Swets, 1988). Based on experiments such as Nigro's, however, they deemed the mental practice of motor skills useful.

What, then, should we say about the relationship between thinking and language? We have seen that language influences thinking. But if thinking did not also affect language, there would never be any new words. New words express new ideas. The basketball term *slam dunk* was coined after the act itself had become fairly common. So, let us simply say that *thinking affects our language, which then affects our thought.*

Psychological research on thinking and language mirrors the mixed reviews given our species in literature and religion. The human mind is simultaneously capable of striking intellectual failures and of vast intellectual power. In an age when misjudgments can have disastrous consequences, we do well to appreciate our capacity for error. Yet our heuristics often serve us well, and they certainly are efficient. Moreover, our ingenuity at problem solving and our extraordinary power of language surely, among the animals, rank humankind as almost "infinite in faculties."

## Summing Up

We consider thinking and language in the same chapter, for they are hard to separate.

**Linguistic Influences on Thinking** There is no disputing that words convey ideas and that different languages can embody different ways of thinking. Although the linguistic relativity hypothesis suggests that language *determines* thought, it is more accurate to say that language *influences* thought. Studies of the effects of the generic pronoun *he* and the ability of vocabulary enrichment to enhance thinking reveal the influence of words.

**Thinking Without Language** Some ideas, such as the ability to perceive and remember different colors, do not depend on language. We sometimes think in images rather than in words, and we invent new words to describe new ideas. So we might say that our thinking affects our language, which then affects our thought.

## Terms and Concepts to Remember

### Thinking

**cognition** The mental activity associated with processing, understanding, and communicating information.

**concept** A mental grouping of similar objects, events, or people.

**prototype** The best example of a category; matching new items to the prototype provides a quick and easy method for including items in a category (as when comparing feathered creatures to a prototypical bird, such as a robin).

**algorithm** A methodical, logical rule or procedure that guarantees solving a particular problem. May be contrasted with the usually speedier but also more error-prone use of *heuristics*.

**heuristic** A rule-of-thumb strategy that often allows us to make judgments and solve problems efficiently; usually speedier but also more error-prone than *algorithms*.

**insight** A sudden and often novel realization of the solution to a problem; it contrasts with strategy-based solutions.

**confirmation bias** A tendency to search for information that confirms one's preconceptions.

**fixation** The inability to see a problem from a new perspective; an impediment to problem solving.

**mental set** A tendency to approach a problem in a particular way, especially a way that has been successful in the past but may or may not be helpful in solving a new problem.

**functional fixedness** The tendency to think of things only in terms of their usual functions; an impediment to problem solving.

**representativeness heuristic** A rule of thumb for judging the likelihood of things in terms of how well they seem to represent, or match, particular prototypes; may lead one to ignore other relevant information.

**availability heuristic** A rule of thumb for estimating the likelihood of events based on their availability in memory; if instances come readily to mind (perhaps because of their vividness), we presume such events are likely.

**overconfidence** The tendency to be more confident than correct—to overestimate the accuracy of one's beliefs and judgments.

**framing** The way an issue is posed; how an issue is framed can significantly affect decisions and judgments.

**belief bias** The tendency for one's preexisting beliefs to distort logical reasoning, sometimes by making invalid conclusions seem valid, or valid conclusions seem invalid.

**belief perseverance** Clinging to one's initial conceptions after the basis on which they were formed has been discredited.

**artificial intelligence (AI)** The science of designing and programming computer systems to do intelligent things and to simulate human thought processes such as intuitive reasoning, learning, and understanding language. Includes practical applications (chess playing, industrial robots, expert systems) and efforts to model human thinking inspired by our current understanding of how the brain works.

**neural networks** Computer circuits that mimic the brain's interconnected neural cells, performing tasks such as learning to recognize visual patterns and smells.

## Language

**language** Our spoken, written, or gestured words and the ways we combine them to communicate meaning.

**phonemes** In a spoken language, the smallest distinctive sound units.

**morphemes** In a language, the smallest units that carry meaning; may be words or parts of words (such as a prefix).

**grammar** A system of rules in a language that enables us to communicate with and understand others.

**semantics** Meaning (or the study of meaning), as derived from morphemes, words, and sentences.

**syntax** Rules for combining words into grammatically sensible sentences.

**babbling stage** Beginning at 3 to 4 months, the stage of speech development in which the infant spontaneously utters various sounds at first unrelated to the household language.

**one-word stage** The stage in speech development, from about age 1 to 2, during which a child speaks mostly in single words.

**two-word stage** Beginning about age 2, the stage in speech development during which a child speaks mostly two-word statements.

**telegraphic speech** Early speech stage in which the child speaks like a telegram—"go car"—using mostly nouns and verbs and omitting "auxiliary" words.

## Thinking and Language

**linguistic relativity** Whorf's hypothesis that language determines the way we think.

## Critical Thinking Exercise

Now that you have read and reviewed Chapter 10, take your learning a step further by testing your critical thinking skills on the following perspective taking exercise.

Attempts to explain language development have sparked a spirited intellectual controversy. At the heart of this controversy is the nature-nurture debate. Behaviorist B. F. Skinner believed that we can explain how babies acquire language entirely with principles of learning, such as the *association* of objects with the sounds of words, the *imitation* of language modeled by others, and the *reinforcement* of correct use of words and syntax by parents and teachers. Linguist Noam Chomsky, who favors the nurture position, believes that much of our language capacity is inborn. According to this perspective, just as "learning" to walk is programmed according to a timetable of biological maturation, so children are prewired to begin to babble and talk.

In this exercise, review each of the following examples of language use by children and decide whether it *best* supports the position of B. F. Skinner or Noam Chomsky. Then explain your reasoning.

1. While Marie and her mother are looking at a book together, Marie's mother shows her a picture of an animal and says "cow." Marie says "cow," and her mother praises her for her correct utterance. Two pages later, Marie spontaneously points to a picture and correctly identifies it as a *cow*.
   *Position supported:*
   *Explanation:*
2. When his day-care teacher asks 1-year-old Jack what he did last Saturday, he responds with "We goed to the zoo." His teacher smiles, marveling at the fact that all children Jack's age make this type of grammatical error.
   *Position supported:*
   *Explanation:*
3. Nicole, who is deaf and was not exposed to sign language until age 3, lacks the manual language skills of deaf children born to deaf-signing parents.
   *Position supported:*
   *Explanation:*
4. Twelve-year-old Malcolm, who emigrated to the United States when he was 4, understands English grammar much better than 20-year-old Maya, who was first exposed to English when she was 12.
   *Position supported*
   *Explanation:*

Check your progress on becoming a critical thinker by comparing your answers to the sample answers found in Appendix B.

## For Further Reading

**Gilovich, T.** (1991). *How we know what isn't so: The fallibility of human reasoning in everyday life*. New York: Free Press.

*A provocative analysis of pitfalls in everyday reasoning and ways of avoiding them.*

**Halpern, D. F.** (1989). *Thought and knowledge: An introduction to critical thinking* (2nd ed.). Hillsdale, NJ: Erlbaum.

*A marvelous book that shows how the findings of psychological research can help us think more rationally and critically.*

**Janis, I. L.** (1988). *Crucial decisions: Leadership in policymaking and crisis management*. New York: Free Press.

*Analyzes reasons for poor, ill-fated decisions and suggests four steps to reduce errors and produce better decisions.*

**Zechmeister, E. B., & Johnson, J. E.** (1992). *Critical thinking: A functional approach*. Pacific Grove, CA: Brooks/Cole.

*A delightful and useful review of principles of flawed versus accurate thinking and ways of applying them by thinking smart in everyday situations.*

# CHAPTER 11

## Assessing Intelligence

**The Origins of Intelligence Tests**

**Modern Tests of Mental Abilities**

**Principles of Test Construction**

Standardization

Reliability

Validity

## What Is Intelligence?

**Is Intelligence Culturally Defined?**

**Is Intelligence One General Ability or Several Specific Abilities?**

The Factor Analysis Approach

Contemporary Theories of Multiple Intelligences

**Is Intelligence Speedy Information Processing?**

**Is Intelligence Neurologically Measurable?**

Brain Size and Intelligence

Brain Function and Intelligence

## The Dynamics of Intelligence

**Stability or Change?**

**Extremes of Intelligence**

The Challenged

The Gifted

**Creativity and Intelligence**

## Genetic and Environmental Influences on Intelligence

**Genetic Influences**

Twin Studies

Adoption Studies

Heritability

**Environmental Influences**

**Group Differences in Intelligence Test Scores**

**The Question of Bias**

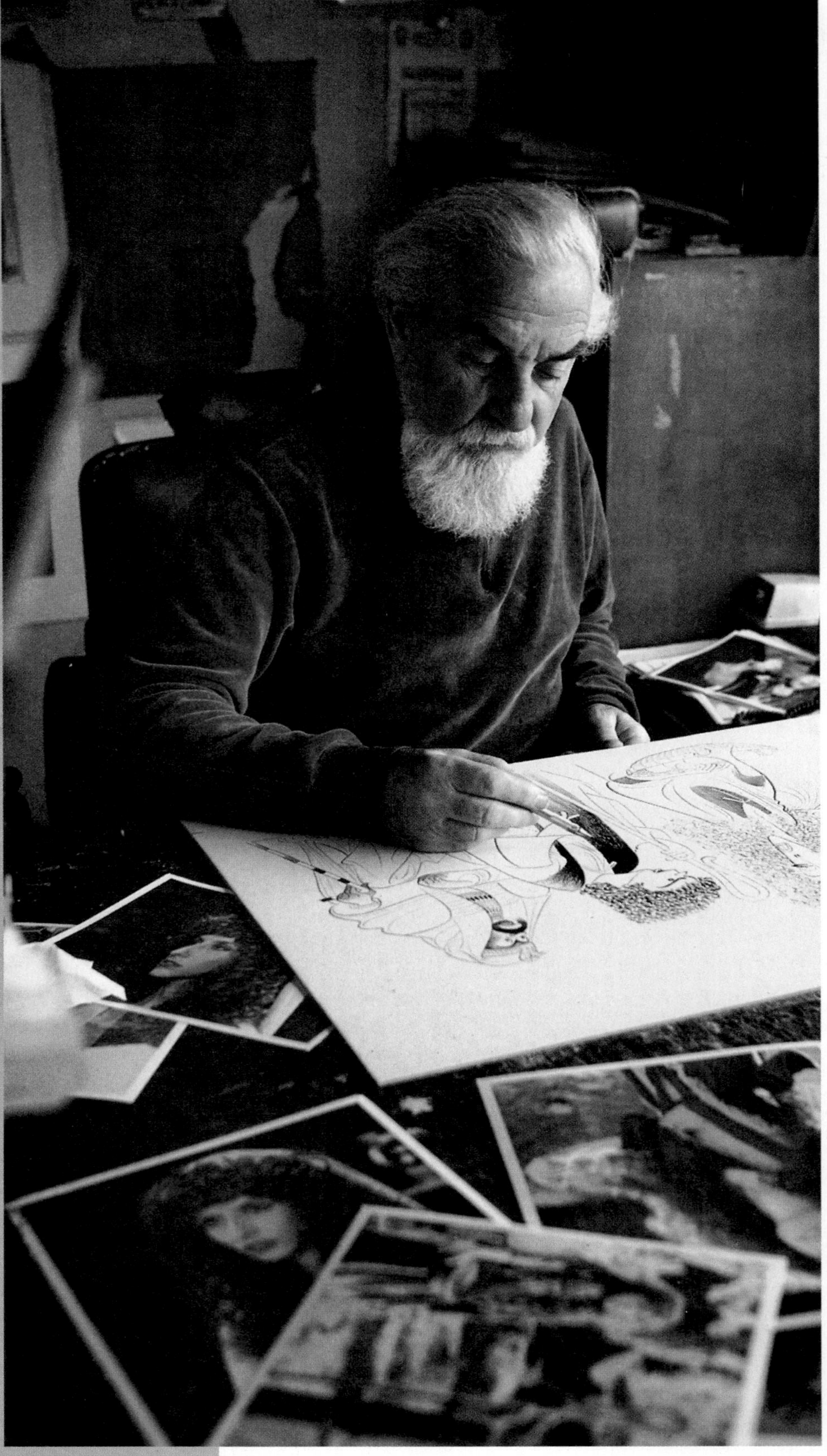

# Intelligence

*Rolanda, an energetic kindergartner, acts bored and restless in class. Concerned that Rolanda might have some mental impairment, her teacher asks the school psychologist to evaluate her. The psychologist's testing reveals that Rolanda is actually an extraordinarily capable girl who can read like a third-grader and add numbers like a second-grader. Little wonder that Rolanda acts bored; she needs activities better suited to her intellectual abilities.*

*Maria and Jennifer have been close friends throughout high school. Both have grade averages near the top of the class, and both hope to major in premedical studies at the same college. Early in their senior year, they spend a morning taking a college aptitude test. Maria does very well, and the school she and Jennifer have chosen admits her. Jennifer does less well and, despite her excellent high school record, is rejected. "How awful!" they moan. "After 3 years of making A's in the same classes, a 150-minute test separates us!"*

*After testing Larry and six other African-American children, California school officials assigned them to special education classes for those with mental retardation. Their parents and the San Francisco Bay Area Black Psychology Association were unconvinced by the psychologists' judgments. They suspected the tests were biased. In 1979, Federal District Court Judge Robert Peckham agreed. Intelligence tests, he ruled, are "racially and culturally biased, have a discriminatory impact on black children, and have not been validated for the purpose of [putting] black children into educationally dead-end, isolated, and stigmatizing classes" (Opton, 1979). In 1986, Judge Peckham reiterated his complete prohibition against using IQ tests in California "as part of an assessment . . . placing black pupils in special education" (Landers, 1986).*

Of all psychology's controversies, the most heated has been provoked by the idea that in each person there exists a general mental capacity (intelligence) and that we can measure and quantify this capacity as a number (an IQ score). School boards, courts, and scientists debate the usefulness and fairness of **intelligence tests**—tests for assessing a person's mental abilities and comparing them with others', using numerical scores. Should we use such tests to rank people and admit them to a particular college or to hire them for a particular job? If so, how might we assess intelligence? What *is* intelligence? To what extent does it result from nature (heredity) rather than nurture (environment)? What do test score differences among individuals and groups really mean? Is intelligence testing a positive way to guide people toward suitable opportunities? Or is it a potent, discriminatory weapon camouflaged as science? This chapter aims to help you gain a deeper understanding of these hotly debated issues.

## Assessing Intelligence

*"People are trapped in history," wrote James Baldwin in* Notes of a Native Son, *"and history is trapped in them." Recognizing that our concept of intelligence is a product of the history of intelligence testing, we begin with a look at why psychologists created intelligence tests and how they have used them. Then we consider why a good test must satisfy three criteria: standardization, reliability, and validity.*

To understand intelligence as a psychological concept, it helps first to know the origins and purposes of intelligence testing. The story of the testing movement once again illustrates an important lesson: Although science strives for objectivity, scientists are affected by their own attitudes.

### The Origins of Intelligence Tests

Some societies concern themselves less with promoting individual opportunity than with promoting the collective welfare of the family, community, and society. Other societies emphasize the individual over the group. A pioneer of this individualist tradition, Plato wrote more than 2000 years ago in *The Republic* that "no two persons are born exactly alike; but each differs from the other in natural endowments, one being suited for one occupation and the other for another." As heirs to Plato's individualism, people in Western societies ponder how and why individuals differ. About a century ago, Western attempts to assess individual differences in mental ability began in earnest.

**Francis Galton** *"I have no patience with the hypothesis occasionally expressed, and often implied, especially in tales written to teach children to be good, that babies are born pretty much alike, and that the sole agencies in creating differences between boy and boy, and man and man, are steady application and moral effort. It is in the most unqualified manner that I object to pretensions of natural equality" (1892).*

#### Francis Galton: Quantifying Superiority

In the history of the testing movement, no one measured and ranked people with greater enthusiasm than the English scientist Sir Francis Galton (1822–1911). Galton's fascination with quantification led him to invent methods for measuring boredom, even-temperedness, the beauty of British women, the effects of prayer, and much more.

When his cousin Charles Darwin proposed that nature selects successful traits through the "survival of the fittest," Galton concluded that he could scientifically apply the principle. Why not measure human traits, he reasoned, and then selectively breed superior people? Those with the greatest "natural ability" could be encouraged to mate with each other, and those not so well endowed could be discouraged or prevented from reproducing. To promote his plan for human betterment, Galton founded the "eugenics" movement (from the Greek word *eugenes*, which means "well-born").

Galton assumed that human traits are inherited. He supported this assumption by noting that social prominence, like height, tends to run in families. Not surprisingly, Galton himself was an eminent child of a well-known upper-class family, and he married a "suitable" woman (though, ironically, his marriage was childless). Furthermore, although he popularized the phrase "nature and nurture," he was oblivious to the advantages enjoyed by the upper class in Victorian England (Fancher, 1979). A British male, he instead believed in the *natural* superiority of white men.

Committed to quantifying human superiority, Galton set about trying to measure innate mental capacity. In his 1869 book, *Hereditary Genius*, he toyed with the idea of assessing intelligence by measuring head size, and over the next few years he developed various measures of what he presumed were the biological underpinnings of genius. Galton put his ideas to the test at London's 1884 International Exposition. Over 10,000 exposition visitors paid to receive his assessment of their "intellectual strengths," based on such things as reaction time, sensory acuity, muscular power, and body proportions.

How did the tests turn out? Did "superior" individuals (eminent adults and excellent students) outscore those supposedly not so bright? Did they, for instance, process information more swiftly on the tests of reaction time? They did not. Nor did the various measures correlate with one another. Nor did men consistently outscore women.

Although Galton failed in his efforts to invent simple measures of general mental ability, he was an innovative researcher who created some statistical techniques that we still use. Galton was also the first proponent of an idea that survives to this day—that we can quantitatively measure people's mental abilities.

### Alfred Binet: Predicting School Achievement

The modern intelligence-testing movement began when the pioneering French psychologist Alfred Binet (1857–1911) successfully applied Galton's idea of measuring intellectual abilities. When the French government passed a law requiring that all children attend school, teachers soon faced a distressing range of individual differences. Some children seemed incapable of benefitting from the regular school curriculum and in need of special classes. But how could the schools objectively identify children with special needs?

**Alfred Binet** *"The scale, properly speaking, does not permit the measure of intelligence, because intellectual qualities . . . cannot be measured as linear surfaces are measured" (Binet & Simon, 1905).*

The government was justifiably reluctant to trust teachers' subjective judgments of children's learning potential. Academic slowness might merely reflect inadequate prior education. Also, teachers might prejudge children on the basis of their social backgrounds. To minimize bias, France's minister of public education in 1904 commissioned Binet and others to study the problem. In response, Binet and his collaborator, Théodore Simon, decided to develop an objective test to identify children who were likely to have difficulty in the regular classes.

Binet and Simon began by assuming that all children follow the same course of intellectual development but that some develop more rapidly. "Dull" children, they presumed, were merely "retarded" in their development. On tests, therefore, a dull child should perform as does a typical younger child, and a "bright" child as does a typical older child.

Binet and Simon's task was to measure what came to be called a child's **mental age**, the chronological age that typically corresponds to a given level of performance. The average 9-year-old, then, has a mental age of 9. But many 9-year-olds have mental ages below or above 9. Children below average, such as 9-year-olds who perform as typical 7-year-olds do, would struggle with normal schoolwork for their age.

To measure mental age, Binet and Simon theorized that mental aptitude, like athletic aptitude, is a general capacity that shows up in various ways. They then developed varied reasoning and problem-solving questions that might predict school achievement. By testing "bright" and "backward" Parisian schoolchildren on these questions, Binet and Simon succeeded: They found items that did predict how well the children handled schoolwork.

Note that Binet and Simon made no assumptions concerning *why* a particular child was slow, average, or precocious. Binet personally leaned toward an environmental explanation. To raise the capacities of low-scoring children, he recommended "mental orthopedics" that would train them to develop their attention span and self-discipline. He refused to speculate about what the test was actually measuring, but he insisted that it did not

*"The IQ test was invented to predict academic performance, nothing else. If we wanted something that would predict life success, we'd have to invent another test completely."*

Social psychologist Robert Zajonc (1984b)

measure inborn intelligence as a meterstick measures height. Rather, it had a single practical purpose: to identify French schoolchildren needing special attention. Binet hoped his test would be used to improve children's education, but he also feared it would be used to label children and limit their opportunities (Gould, 1981).

### Lewis Terman: The Innate IQ

What Binet viewed as merely a practical guide for identifying slow learners who needed special help was soon seen by others to be what Galton sought: a numerical measure of inherited intelligence. After Binet's death in 1911, Stanford University professor Lewis Terman (1877–1956) decided to use Binet's test. He soon found, however, that the Paris-developed age norms worked poorly with California schoolchildren. So Terman revised the test. He adapted some of Binet's original items, added others, established new age norms, and extended the upper end of the test's range from teenagers to "superior adults." Terman gave his revision the name it retains today—the **Stanford-Binet**.

For such tests, German psychologist William Stern derived the famous **intelligence quotient**, or **IQ**. The IQ was simply a person's mental age divided by chronological age and multiplied by 100 to get rid of the decimal point:

$$\text{IQ} = \frac{\text{mental age}}{\text{chronological age}} \times 100$$

Thus, an average child, whose mental and chronological ages are the same, has an IQ of 100. But an 8-year-old who answers questions as would a typical 10-year-old has an IQ of 125.

*"You did very well on your IQ test. You're a man of 49 with the intelligence of a man of 53."*

© 1982 by Sidney Harris; *American Scientist* magazine.

Most current intelligence tests, including the Stanford-Binet, no longer compute an IQ. The original IQ formula works fairly well for children but not for adults. Consider: Should a 40-year-old who does as well on the test as an average 20-year-old be assigned an IQ of only 50? Obviously, something is out of whack. Today's intelligence tests therefore produce a mental ability score based on the test-taker's performance relative to the average performance of others the same age. As on the original Stanford-Binet, current tests define this score so that 100 is average, with about two-thirds of all people scoring between 85 and 115. Although there is no longer any intelligence *quotient*, the term "IQ" still lingers in everyday vocabulary as a shorthand expression for "intelligence test score."

Terman shared Galton's belief that intelligence was measurable, and he promoted the widespread use of intelligence testing. His motive was to "take account of the inequalities of children in original endowment" by assessing their "vocational fitness." In sympathy with the eugenics movement, Terman (1916, pp. 91–92) lamented what he believed was the "dullness" and "unusually prolific breeding" of certain ethnic groups. He envisioned that the use of intelligence tests would "ultimately result in curtailing the reproduction of feeble-mindedness and in the elimination of an enormous amount of crime, pauperism, and industrial inefficiency" (p. 7).

**Lewis Terman** *"The children of successful and cultured parents test higher than children from wretched and ignorant homes for the simple reason that their heredity is better" (1916, p. 115).*

With Terman's help, the U.S. government developed new tests to evaluate 1.7 million World War I army recruits and newly arriving immigrants. To some psychologists, the results indicated the inferiority of people not sharing their Anglo-Saxon heritage. Following his 1913 study of immigrants arriving at Ellis Island, psychologist Henry Goddard claimed that 83 percent of the Jewish immigrants, 80 percent of the Hungarians, 79 percent of the Italians, and 87 percent of the Russians were "feeble-minded" (Eysenck & Kamin, 1981). Such findings were part of the cultural climate that led to the 1924 immigration law, which reduced immigration quotas for southern and eastern Europe to less than a fifth of those for northern and western Europe.

That adaptations of his tests were being used to draw such conclusions would surely have horrified Binet. Indeed, such sweeping judgments eventually became an embarrassment to most of those who championed testing. Terman, for instance, came to appreciate that test scores reflect not only people's innate mental abilities but also their education and their familiarity with the culture assumed by the test. Nevertheless, abuses of the early intelligence tests serve to remind us that science can be value-laden. Influenced by his ideology, Terman (1916, pp. 91–92) had expected "enormously significant racial differences in intelligence." Influenced by Marxist ideology, the Russian Communist party was suspicious of biological explanations for behavior and instead favored environmental approaches, including Pavlov's work on conditioning (Sigmon, 1993). Behind the screen of scientific objectivity, ideology sometimes hides.

*"Science must be understood as a social phenomenon, a gutsy, human enterprise, not the work of robots programmed to collect pure information."*

Stephen Jay Gould (1981)

## Modern Tests of Mental Abilities

By this point in your life, you've faced dozens of different tests of your mental abilities: elementary school tests of basic reading and math skills, course examinations, intelligence tests, driver's license examinations, and college entrance examinations, to mention just a few. Psychologists classify such tests as either **aptitude tests**, intended to *predict* your ability to learn a new skill, or **achievement tests**, intended to *reflect* what you have learned. Thus, a college entrance exam, which seeks to predict your ability to do college work, is an aptitude test. Exams covering what you have learned in this course are achievement tests.

The actual differences between aptitude tests and achievement tests are not so clear-cut. Your achieved vocabulary influences your score on most aptitude tests. Similarly, your aptitudes for learning and test-taking influence your grades on tests of your course achievement. Most tests, whether labeled aptitude or achievement, assess both ability and its development. Distinguishing aptitude and achievement is a practical matter: We use aptitude tests to predict future performance and achievement tests to assess current performance.

To get a better feel for modern intelligence-related tests and some of the differences among them, let's look at two widely used tests. We can then refer to these examples as we consider what makes an effective test and how people might use and abuse test scores.

### The Most Widely Used Intelligence Test: The WAIS-R

Among the supposedly feeble-minded Eastern European immigrants of the early 1900s was a 6-year-old Romanian boy, David Wechsler. Ironically, three decades later *psychologist* David Wechsler created today's most widely used intelligence test, now known as the **Wechsler Adult Intelligence Scale—Revised (WAIS-R)**. Later he developed a similar test for school-age children called the Wechsler Intelligence Scale for Children (WISC), and still later a test for preschool children. The WAIS-R consists of 11 subtests, as illustrated in Figure 11–1 (page 364). It yields not only an overall intelligence score, as does the Stanford-Binet, but also separate "verbal" and "performance" (nonverbal) scores. Striking differences between the two scores alert the examiner to possible learning problems. For example, a verbal score much lower than the same person's performance score might indicate a reading or language disability. The tests also provide clues to cognitive strengths that a teacher or an employer might build upon.

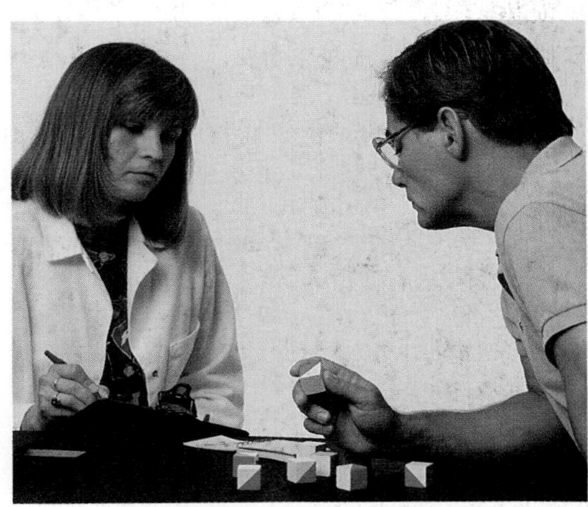

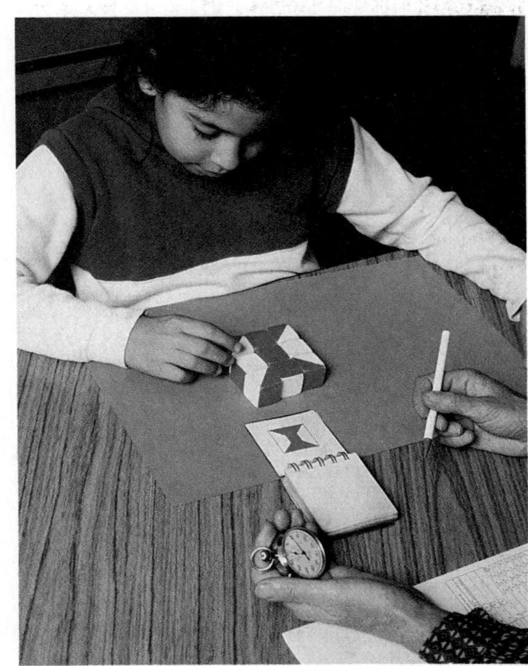

**Matching Patterns** *As psychometrists time their work, this man and girl concentrate on solving Block Design puzzles which test the ability to analyze patterns. Wechsler's individually administered intelligence test comes in forms suited for adults (WAIS-R) and children (WISC-R).*

**Figure 11–1**

VERBAL

**General Information**
What day of the year is Independence Day?

**Similarities**
In what way are *wool* and *cotton* alike?

**Arithmetic Reasoning**
If eggs cost 60 cents a dozen, what does 1 egg cost?

**Vocabulary**
Tell me the meaning of corrupt.

**Comprehension**
Why do people buy fire insurance?

**Digit Span**
Listen carefully, and when I am through, say the numbers right after me.

7 3 4 1 8 6

Now I am going to say some more numbers, but I want you to say them backward.

3 8 4 1 6

PERFORMANCE

**Picture Completion**
I am going to show you a picture with an important part missing. Tell me what is missing.

'85

| SUN | MON | TUE | WED | THU | FRI | SAT |
|---|---|---|---|---|---|---|
| 1 | 2 | 3 | 4 | 5 | 6 | 7 |
| 8 | 9 | 10 | 11 | 12 | 13 | 14 |
| 15 | 16 | 17 | 18 | 19 | 20 | 21 |
| 22 | 23 | 24 | 25 | 26 | 27 | 28 |
| 29 | 30 | | | | | |

**Picture Arrangement**
The pictures below tell a story. Put them in the right order to tell the story.

**Block Design**
Using the four blocks, make one just like this.

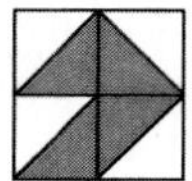

**Object Assembly**
If these pieces are put together correctly, they will make something. Go ahead and put them together as quickly as you can.

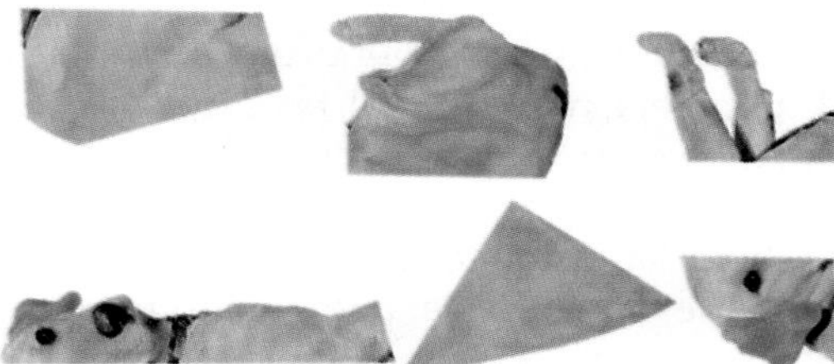

**Digit-Symbol Substitution**

Code

| △ | ○ | ▱ | × | 8 |
|---|---|---|---|---|
| 1 | 2 | 3 | 4 | 5 |

Test

| △ | 8 | × | ○ | △ | ▱ | 8 | × | △ | 8 |
|---|---|---|---|---|---|---|---|---|---|
| | | | | | | | | | |

**Sample Subtest Items From the Wechsler Adult Intelligence Scale—Revised (WAIS-R) Subtests** *(From Thorndike & Hagen, 1977.)*

## College Aptitude Tests: The SAT

Large-scale group testing is now efficiently accomplished through multiple-choice tests, such as the Scholastic Assessment Test (SAT), which is taken annually by 1 million Americans seeking college admission. (Most other countries, including Canada, have no such exam for college admission; instead, they evaluate an applicant's prior academic record, which reflects both aptitude and motivation.) Like the original Binet test, the SAT attempts to predict academic performance. Unlike the Stanford-Binet and Wechsler tests, however, the SAT yields no overall intelligence score. Rather, it separately assesses verbal and mathematical aptitudes.

As you can see from the sample items in Figure 11–2, the SAT is a good example of an aptitude test that also assumes some prior achievement. More than half of its 60 mathematical questions, for example, presume a basic knowledge of either algebra or geometry. The American College Testing (ACT) exam, also taken annually by a million college-bound high

**Figure 11–2**

VERBAL

Choose the word or phrase that is most nearly *opposite* in meaning to the word in capital letters.

WILT: (A) prevent (B) drain (C) expose (D) revive (E) stick

(93 percent correctly answered D)

GARNER: (A) disfigure (B) hedge (C) connect (D) forget (E) disperse

(26 percent correctly answered E)

Each question below consists of a related pair of words or phrases, followed by five lettered pairs of words or phrases. Select the lettered pair that best expresses a relationship similar to that expressed in the original pair.

PAINTING: CANVAS (A) drawing: lottery (B) fishing: pond (C) writing: paper (D) shading: crayon (E) sculpting: design

(92 percent correctly answered C)

SCOFF: DERISION (A) soothe: mollification (B) slander: repression (C) swear: precision (D) stimulate: appearance (E) startle: speediness

(21 percent correctly answered A)

MATHEMATICAL

If $x^3 + y = x^3 + 5$, then $y =$

(A) $-5$ (B) $-\sqrt[3]{5}$ (C) $\sqrt[3]{5}$ (D) 5 (E) $5^3$

(93 percent correctly answered D)

In a race, if Bob's running speed was 4/5 Alice's and Chris's speed was 3/4 Bob's, then Alice's speed was how many times the average (arithmetic mean) of the other two runners' speeds?

(A) 3/5 (B) 7/10 (C) 40/31 (D) 10/7 (E) 5/3

(10 percent correctly answered D)

FOR THE NEW (1994) MATH TEST:

Martin and Alice buy newspapers for \$0.20 each and sell them for \$0.25 each. If, at the end of one week, Martin made a profit of \$12.60 and Alice made a profit of \$18.75, how many more papers did Alice sell than Martin?

(Fill in answer at right.)

[Correct answer: 123]

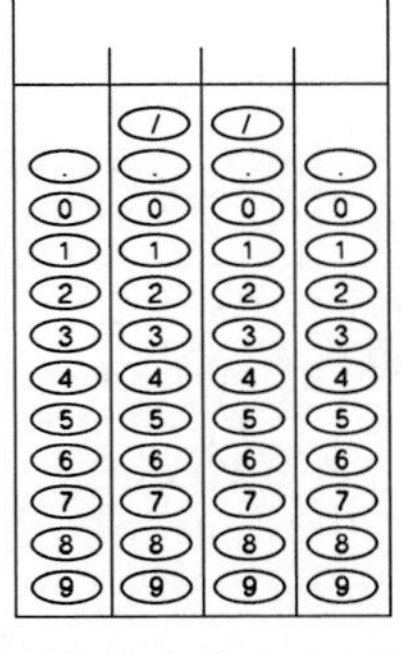

**Sample Items From the Scholastic Assessment Test (SAT)** *Since 1994, the test has included questions that require students to generate their own answers. (From College Entrance Examination Board, 1983, 1990.)*

school students, is even more of an achievement test. On the ACT, the average high school student today would probably outscore Aristotle and other geniuses of the distant past because the test measures students' "educational development" in English usage, mathematics, reading, and science reasoning.

## Principles of Test Construction

To be widely accepted, psychological tests must meet three criteria: They must be *standardized*, *reliable*, and *valid*. The Stanford-Binet, Wechsler tests, and SAT meet these requirements.

### Standardization

Knowing how many questions you got right on an intelligence test would tell us almost nothing. To evaluate your performance, we need a basis for comparing it with others' performance. To enable meaningful comparisons, test-makers first give the test to a representative sample of people. When other individuals take the test, we can then compare their scores with the standards defined by this group. This process of defining meaningful scores relative to a pretested group is called **standardization**.

Recall that Terman and his colleagues recognized that a scale standardized on Parisians did not provide a satisfactory standard for evaluating Americans. So they revised the test and standardized the new version by testing 2300 native-born, white Americans of differing socioeconomic levels. Ironically, they then evaluated nonwhite American and immigrant groups based on this standard (Van Leeuwen, 1982).

Standardized test results typically form a *normal distribution*, a bell-shaped pattern of scores that forms the **normal curve** (Figure 11–3). Whether we are measuring people's heights, weights, or mental aptitudes, most values tend to cluster around the average. On an intelligence test, we call this average value 100. As we move out from the average (toward either extreme) we find fewer and fewer values. Within each age group, the Stanford-Binet and the Wechsler tests assign any person a score according to how much that person's performance deviates above or below the average. As Figure 11–3 shows, a raw score higher than all but 2 percent of all scores earns an intelligence score of 130. A raw score that is comparably *below* 98 percent of all the scores earns an intelligence score of 70.

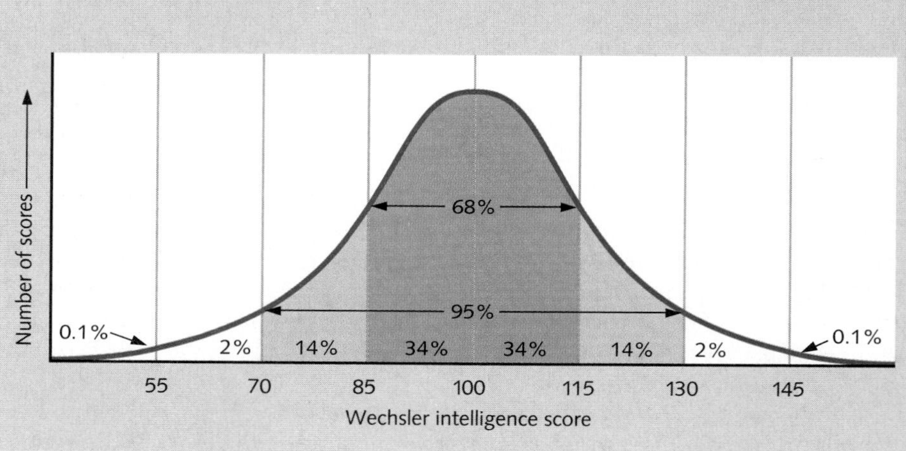


**Figure 11–3**

**The Normal Curve** *Scores on aptitude tests tend to form a normal, or bell-shaped, curve. For example, the Wechsler scale calls the average score 100. It defines other scores to make about 68 percent of them fall within 15 points above or below 100. About 95 percent fall within 30 points above and below 100.*

Initially, researchers standardized the SAT using a group of 10,654 students who took the test in April 1941 (Carroll, 1982). They arbitrarily assigned the average performance of these students on each portion of the SAT (verbal and mathematical) a score of 500 (rather than the 100 used on most intelligence tests). The points above and below the average that included 68 percent of all the raw scores were assigned SAT scores of 600 and 400, respectively (Figure 11–4). All the students in the SAT standardization sample were college-bound and thus were a select group, especially back in 1941. So this sample differs from the broader population samples used in standardizing the Stanford-Binet and Wechsler tests. A person who scores 500 on each part of the SAT would probably score well above 100 on an intelligence test.

If you took the SAT before 1995—some 50 years after those first 10,654 students set the standard—the questions you answered differed from theirs. However, the items on the test you took had been statistically equated to those on all previous versions of the test. (To equate the difficulty of past, present, and future items, each year's test-takers respond to

Figure 11–4

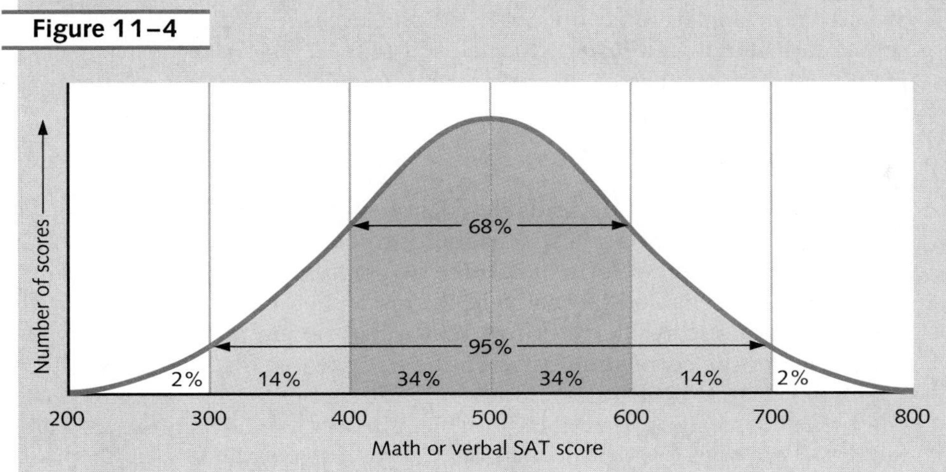


**Distribution of SAT Scores** *When the SAT test was standardized in 1941, the average score for each part was assigned a value of 500. The other SAT scores were defined to make 68 percent of them fall within about 100 points above and below 500. A score of 115 on the WAIS is therefore at the same relative position as a score of 600 on the SAT. Yet the two scores are not equivalent, because the academic ability of the groups on which the tests were standardized was not the same.*

some items being developed for use in future tests.) Thus, your performance was measured with the 1941 standards.

*This is about to change. In 1995 the SAT will be restandardized ("recentered") to make 500 today's average.*

Because of this comparability, the SAT has become a sort of educational barometer. Between 1963 and 1980, scores dropped steadily (Figure 11–5). In 1981, only those scoring in the upper 30 percent did better than the average test-taker in 1963. How can we explain this decline? Does it expose, as many believe, a failure of American public education?

Let's look at history. During the 1960s, the number of aspiring college students taking the test grew to include a broader range of people, including those with relatively modest academic achievements (Astin & Garber, 1982). With more and more people taking the test, SAT averages began to drop. If *all* high school seniors (not just college-bound seniors) were to take the test, the SAT average would drop to about 375 verbal and 415 math (Murray & Herrnstein, 1992).

But what might explain the sharper decline during the 1970s, when the number of students taking the SAT had stabilized? The displacement of reading by the spread of television? A combination of grade inflation, nonacademic electives, simplified textbooks, and reduced homework (Murray & Herrnstein, 1992; Turnbull, 1986)? Decreased adult influence and attention associated with increased family size during the 1950s? All these factors seem to have contributed to the continuing score decline.

Unlike the SAT, the Stanford-Binet and the Wechsler scales are periodically restandardized to keep the average score near 100. If you took the revised WAIS-R today, your performance would be compared with a standardization sample who took the test between 1976 and 1980, not to David Wechsler's initial 1930s sample. When we compare the performance of the most recent standardization sample with that of the 1930s sample, do you suppose we find rising or declining test performance? Amazingly—given the decline in SAT scores—intelligence test performance has *improved* (Flynn, 1987). A raw score that would earn you a 100 today would have earned you a 114 in the 1930s! Such rising performance has occurred across the industrialized world.

What an intriguing puzzle: Are aptitudes decreasing, as some have inferred from the decline in SAT scores, or are they rising, as the WAIS-R data suggest? First, remember that the SAT decline is due partly to the greater academic diversity of the students who began taking the test during the

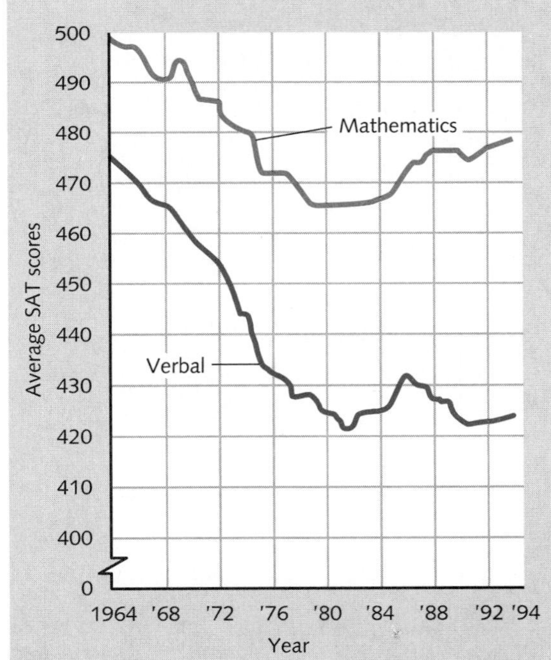


Figure 11–5

**Decline in SAT Scores** *Between 1963 and 1980, average SAT scores dropped significantly, with fluctuating scores in recent years. (Data from The College Board.)*

1960s. The WAIS has always been standardized on a more diverse and broadly representative group. Such people (people in general) have become more literate and better educated since the 1930s. These facts help explain why performance on the more complex SAT dropped while performance rose on the basic skills tested by the WAIS-R.

### Reliability

A good test must yield dependably consistent scores; in a word, it must have **reliability**. To check a test's reliability, researchers retest people using the same test or another form of it. If the two scores generally agree, or *correlate*, the test is reliable. Alternatively, the researcher may split a test in half and see whether scores derived from odd and even questions agree.

The higher the correlation between the *test-retest* or the *split-half* scores, the higher the test's reliability. Recall from Chapter 1 that the lowest correlation, –1.0, represents perfect disagreement between two sets of scores—as the first score goes up, the second goes down. A correlation of zero represents no consistency. The highest correlation, +1.0, represents perfect consistency—as the first score goes up, so does the second. The tests we have considered so far—the Stanford-Binet, the WAIS-R and WISC, and the SAT and ACT—all have reliabilities of about +.9, which is very high. When retested, people's scores tend to match their first score closely.

### Validity

High reliability does not ensure a test's **validity**—the extent to which the test actually measures what it is supposed to measure or predicts what it is supposed to predict. If you use a shrunken tape measure to measure people's heights, your data would have high reliability (consistency) but low validity. How, then, can we determine whether a test is valid? For some tests, it is enough that they have **content validity**, which means the test taps the pertinent behavior. The road test for a driver's license has content validity because it samples the tasks a driver routinely faces. Your course exams have content validity if they assess your mastery of a representative sample of course material.

Other tests are evaluated in terms of how well they agree with some **criterion**, an independent measure of what the test aims to assess. For some tests, the criterion is future performance. For example, aptitude tests must have **predictive validity**, which means they predict future achievement.

Are general aptitude tests strongly predictive as well as highly reliable? As critics are fond of noting, the answer is plainly no. The predictive power of aptitude tests is fairly strong in the early grades, but later it weakens. Academic aptitude test scores are reasonably good predictors of achievement in elementary school, where the correlation between intelligence score and grades is about +.60 (Jensen, 1980). The SAT is less successful in predicting first-year college grades; here, the correlation is less than +.50 (Willingham & others, 1990). By the time we get to the Graduate Record Examination (GRE) (an aptitude test similar to the SAT but for those applying to graduate school), the correlation with graduate school grades is an even more modest +.30 (GRE, 1990).

Why does the predictive power of aptitude scores diminish as students move up the educational ladder? Consider a parallel situation: Among all football linemen, body weight correlates with success. A 270-pound player tends to overwhelm a 190-pound opponent. But within the narrow 250- to 290-pound range typically found at the professional level, the correlation between weight and success becomes negligible (Figure 11–6). The narrower the *range* of weights, the lower the predictive power of body weight becomes.

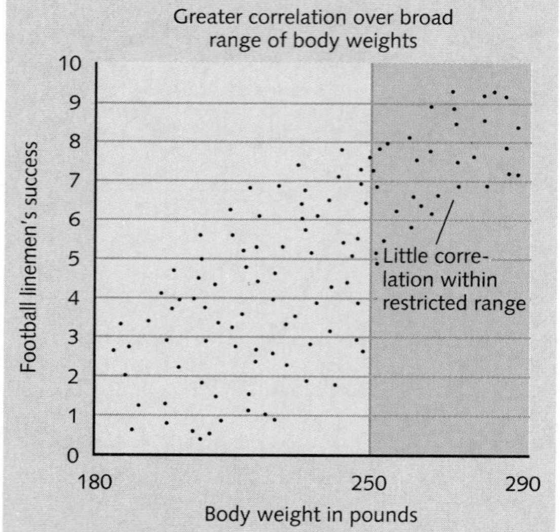

Greater correlation over broad range of body weights

Little correlation within restricted range

Football linemen's success

Body weight in pounds

**Figure 11–6**

**Diminishing Predictive Power** *Let's imagine a correlation between football linemen's body weight and their success on the field. Note how insignificant the relationship becomes when we narrow the range of weights to 250 to 290 pounds. As the range of data under consideration narrows, its predictive power diminishes.*

## *Thinking Critically About* Test Preparation Courses

*"I'm studying for my IQ test."*

© 1992 by Sidney Harris.

Suppose that after taking the SAT, the Law School Aptitude Test (LSAT), the Medical College Admission Test (MCAT), or the Graduate Record Examination (GRE), you were disappointed by your score. By enrolling in one of the widely advertised test-preparation courses, could you count on increasing your score when retaking the test? Or is your score on the test likely to be stable?

Being familiar with a test and knowing how to pace yourself on it does help. But this much you can get from taking the sample test that is available to anyone. Beyond this, does it pay to sign up for a crash test-preparation course? These courses help people brush up on their academic knowledge, especially in mathematics. They may also provide a few useful tips about how to take the test. For instance, on the first questions in a section, which 80 percent or more people get right, the most obvious answer is usually correct; on the final questions, which more than 75 percent typically get wrong, the "obvious" answer is often wrong.

Despite the test-relevant teaching and the test-taking clues that SAT-preparation courses provide, and contrary to advertised claims, three separate research reviews have concluded that the courses increased math and verbal scores by an average of only about 15 points each on the 200- to 800-point scale (DerSimonian & Laird, 1983; Kulik & others, 1984; Messick & Jungeblut, 1981). This small boost is greatest on test items that have complex and possibly confusing formats (Powers, 1986). So, for the SAT at least, the best advice is to take rigorous academic courses, brush up on algebra and geometry, and familiarize yourself with the test. Having done that, you needn't feel intimidated by those who have also taken a test-preparation course.

A similar narrowing of range explains why the GRE is only a modest predictor of graduate school grades. If a graduate school takes in only students whose aptitude scores fall within a narrow range it should not surprise us that their aptitude scores will not closely predict their grades. This will be true even if the test has excellent predictive validity with a more diverse sample of students. So, when we validate a test using a wide range of people but then use it with a restricted range of people, it loses much of its predictive validity. A narrowed range of grades—as in graduate school departments that award mostly *A*s and *B*s—similarly reduces predictive validity.

## Summing Up

Among the most controversial issues in psychology is the debate over intelligence testing: whether tests can measure and quantify a person's abilities and how widely the results can be used fairly.

**The Origins of Intelligence Tests** More than a century ago in Great Britain, Francis Galton sought to measure individual mental abilities. Although Galton failed to develop simple, quantifiable measures of mental ability, Alfred Binet developed questions that helped predict children's future progress in the Paris school system. Like Galton, Lewis Terman of Stanford University believed intelligence was inherited. And like Binet, Terman believed his test (the Stanford-Binet) could help guide people toward appropriate opportunities. During the early part of this century, intelligence tests were sometimes used in ways that, in hindsight, even their designers regretted—to "document" a presumed innate inferiority of certain ethnic and immigrant groups.

**Modern Tests of Mental Abilities** Tests are commonly classified as either aptitude tests (designed to predict learning ability, as are the Wechsler and SAT) or achievement tests (designed to assess current competence).

**Principles of Test Construction** A good test must be *standardized*, so that any person's performance can be meaningfully compared to others'; *reliable*, so it yields dependably consistent scores; and *valid*, so it measures what it is supposed to measure. Test scores usually fall into a bell-shaped distribution, the normal curve. The average score is assigned an arbitrary number (such as 100 on an intelligence test). Aptitude tests tend to be highly reliable, but they are weak predictors of success in life. Their predictive validity for academic success is fairly strong in the early grades, however. Test validity weakens for predicting grades in college and even more so in graduate school, as the range of student abilities becomes more restricted.

## What Is Intelligence?

*Intelligence is one of psychology's slippery concepts. Although psychologists generally agree that intelligence is a concept, not a concrete thing, they debate the issues surrounding this topic: Should we consider intelligence as culturally defined or culture free? As one aptitude or many? As linked to cognitive speed? As neurologically assessable?*

So far in this chapter we have used the term *intelligence* as though we all agree on what it means. We don't. Psychologists debate whether we should define intelligence as an inherent cognitive capacity, an achieved level of intellectual performance, or an ascribed quality that, like beauty, is in the eye of the beholder. Reading all the conflicting ideas about intelligence can leave you feeling as Alice in Wonderland felt after reading "Jabberwocky": "Somehow it seems to fill my head with ideas—only I don't exactly know what they are."

Intelligence experts agree on this much: Intelligence is not a "thing." When we refer to someone's "IQ" as if it were a fixed and objectively real trait like height, we commit a reasoning error called *reification*—viewing an abstract, immaterial concept as if it were a real, concrete thing. To reify is to invent a concept, give it a name, and then convince ourselves that such a thing objectively exists in the world. When someone says, "She has an IQ of 120," they are reifying IQ; they are imagining IQ to be a thing one *has*, rather than a score once obtained on a particular test.

Intelligence is a concept intended to explain why some people perform better than others on cognitive tasks. In the *Handbook of Human Intelligence*,

Robert Sternberg and William Salter (1982, p. 3) reported that most experts view **intelligence** as a person's capacity for "goal-directed adaptive behavior." Intelligent behavior reflects a capacity to adapt, by learning from experience, solving problems, and reasoning clearly.

Despite this general agreement about the concept, four controversies remain.

1. Should we consider intelligence as whatever abilities are adaptive in one's culture, or as a culture-free ability to solve problems?
2. Is intelligence a single overall ability or several specific abilities?
3. Is intelligence linked with cognitive speed—literal quick-wittedness?
4. With the tools of modern neuroscience, can we now fulfill Galton's dream of measuring intelligence as the brain's information-processing speed?

*"I've never gotten the hang of hunting. Luckily, we're invited out a lot."*

Drawing by Weber; © 1988 The New Yorker Magazine, Inc.

## Is Intelligence Culturally Defined?

According to one view, intelligent behavior varies with the situation. For Binet and the later intelligence testers, intelligence meant children's adapting successfully to academic demands. For islanders in the South Pacific, it might mean the ability to excel at fishing and navigating. For a manager or salesperson in our society, it might mean social skills. For an inner city resident, it might mean street smarts.

**A Common Challenge** *While their crafts look as different as their clothing and setting, these boys have much in common: they are working to perfect skills their societies deem important—to become "intelligent" in their culture's terms.*

Those who view intelligence as people's successful adaptation to their environment are skeptical about the prospects for a *culture-free* test of intelligence—a test uninfluenced by one's culture. They believe that those who hope for such a test fail to understand that *intelligence* is whatever abilities your culture deems important. It might make sense to talk about a *culture-free* measure of height, but not of intelligence. As intelligence researcher Howard Gardner noted, basketball superstar Larry Bird may not have been considered exceptionally intelligent when in school, but in a society of keen-eyed hunters and spear-throwing warriors he would be the gifted one.

Other researchers view intelligence as basic cognitive abilities that help people solve problems in *any* environment (Baron, 1985). The abstract and

*In Zambia, notes intelligence researcher Robert Serpell (1994), most boys find nonverbal intelligence tests using unfamiliar block design problems (as in Figure 11–1) difficult. Yet they show considerable nonverbal aptitude when designing their own wire cars, complete with axles, steering wheel, and hinged doors.*

novel questions asked on intelligence tests evaluate our abilities to solve various problems effectively, regardless of our cultural backgrounds. The assumption is that people who on the WAIS-R can recite a string of eight digits in reverse order, or who can find the missing element in a picture, probably will have an edge at solving all sorts of other problems, from taking tests in school to navigating the sea to growing corn. (As we will see, the support for this assumption is modest. There is a slight tendency for people who do well on academic aptitude tests also to do well on practical and vocational tasks outside of school.)

## Is Intelligence One General Ability or Several Specific Abilities?

We all know some people talented in mathematics, others in creative writing, and still others in art, music, or dance. We may therefore wonder whether people's mental abilities are too diverse to justify labeling them with the single word *intelligence* or quantifying them with a number from some single scale. Should we think of intelligence not as one general ability but as a collection of specific abilities?

### The Factor Analysis Approach

Virtually everyone agrees: There *are* specific mental abilities. Recall that the WAIS distinguishes verbal and performance intelligence, and that the SAT distinguishes verbal and mathematical skills. In your own experience, you may know a talented artist who is dumbfounded by the simplest mathematical problems, or a brilliant math student who has little aptitude for literary discussion. To find out whether there might be a general ability factor that runs throughout our specific mental abilities, psychologists study how various abilities relate to one another.

A statistical method called **factor analysis** allows researchers to identify clusters of test items that measure a common ability. For example, people who do well on vocabulary items often do well on paragraph comprehension. This cluster helps define a verbal intelligence factor. Psychologists have identified several such clusters, including a spatial ability factor and a reasoning ability factor.

Charles Spearman (1863–1945), who helped develop factor analysis, believed there is also a **general intelligence**, or *g*, factor that underlies the specific factors. People often have special abilities that stand out, Spearman allowed. But those who score high on one factor, such as verbal intelligence, typically score higher than average on other factors, such as spatial or reasoning ability. So there is at least a small tendency for different abilities to come in the same package. Spearman believed that this commonality, the *g* factor, underlies all of our intelligent behavior, from excelling in school to navigating the sea.

This idea of a general mental capacity expressed by a single intelligence score was controversial in Spearman's day, and it remains so in our own. Opposing Spearman, L. L. Thurstone (1887–1955) gave 56 different tests to people. By analyzing the results mathematically, he identified eight clusters of "primary mental abilities," such as word fluency, memory, and reasoning. Thurstone did not rank his subjects on a single scale of general aptitude. But when other investigators studied the profiles of his subjects, they detected a small tendency for those who excelled in one of the eight clusters to score well on the others. So, they concluded, there was still some evidence of a *g* factor.

We might, then, liken mental abilities to physical abilities. Athleticism is not one thing but many. The ability to run fast is distinct from brute strength, which is distinct from the eye-hand coordination required to throw a ball on target. A champion weightlifter rarely has the potential to be a skilled ice skater. Yet there remains some tendency for good things to come packaged together—for running speed and throwing accuracy to correlate, thanks to general athletic ability. Likewise, intelligence involves several distinct abilities, which cluster together in the same individual often enough to define a small general intelligence factor.

### Contemporary Theories of Multiple Intelligences

Psychologist Howard Gardner (1983, 1993) supports Thurstone's idea that intelligence comes in different packages. He notes that brain damage may diminish one type of ability but not others. Gardner also studied reports of people with exceptional abilities, including those who excel in only one. People with **savant syndrome**, for example, score at the low end on intelligence tests but have an island of brilliance—some incredible ability, as in computation, drawing, or musical memory (Figure 11–7). These people may have virtually no language ability, yet may be able to compute numbers as quickly and accurately as an electronic calculator, or identify almost instantly the day of the week that corresponds to any given date in history.

Using such evidence, Gardner argues that we do not have *an* intelligence, but instead have *multiple* intelligences, each independent of the others. In addition to the verbal and mathematical aptitudes assessed by the standard tests, he identifies distinct aptitudes for musical accomplishment, for spatially analyzing the visual world, for mastering movement skills (as in dance), and for insightfully understanding ourselves and others. According to Gardner, the computer programmer, the poet, the street-smart adolescent who becomes a crafty executive, and the point guard on the basketball team exhibit different kinds of intelligence.

**Figure 11–7**

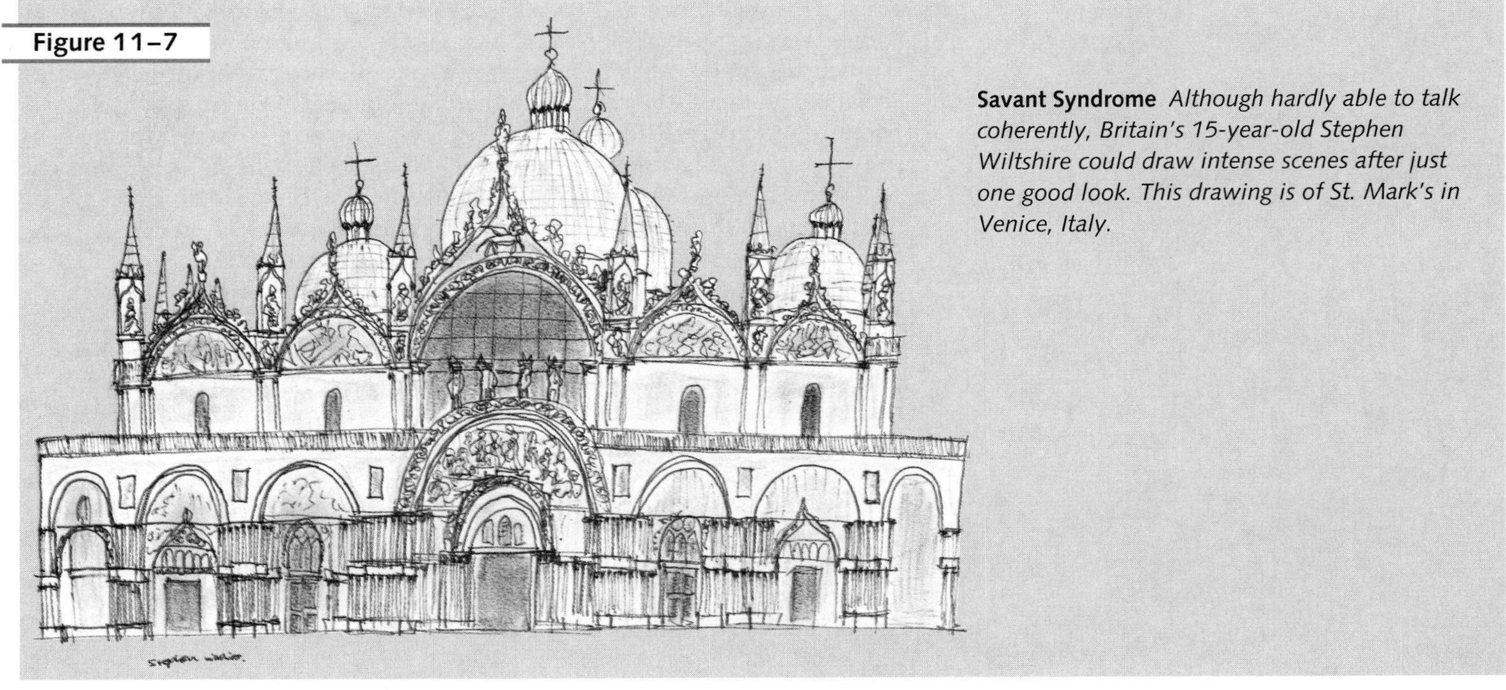

**Savant Syndrome** *Although hardly able to talk coherently, Britain's 15-year-old Stephen Wiltshire could draw intense scenes after just one good look. This drawing is of St. Mark's in Venice, Italy.*

Wouldn't it be wonderful if the world were so just, responds intelligence researcher Sandra Scarr (1989), that being weak in any area would be compensated by genius in some other area? Alas, the world is not just, for there remains some tendency for different skills to correlate. For example, people with mental disadvantages often have lesser physical abilities as well; thus, we hold Special Olympics to give them a chance to enjoy fair competition.

Moreover, Gardner's critics question, does it really make sense to lump all sorts of abilities under the concept of intelligence? Are not some, such as verbal and reasoning skills, really more crucial than others? Intelligence is *mental* ability, they say. Abilities that we can manage without, as in music and athletics, are better considered *talents* than intelligences. If people lack physical talent, do we consider them as lacking an *intelligence*?

Robert Sternberg and Richard Wagner (1987, 1993) agree with Gardner's idea of multiple intelligences but distinguish more simply among three intelligences: the *academic* problem-solving skills assessed by intelligence tests (presenting well-defined problems having a single right answer), the *practical* intelligence often required for everyday tasks (often ill-defined with multiple solutions), and the *creative* intelligence demonstrated in reacting to novel situations. Intelligence tests predict school grades reasonably well but predict vocational success less well. Managerial success, for example, depends less on the academic abilities assessed by an intelligence test score (assuming the score is average or above) than on a shrewd ability to manage oneself, one's tasks, and other people. Business executives who score high on Sternberg and Wagner's test of practical managerial intelligence (by knowing how to write effective memos, how to motivate people, when to delegate tasks and responsibilities, how to read people, and how to promote their own careers) earn higher salaries and receive better performance ratings than do those who score low. People who demonstrate keen practical intelligence may or may not have distinguished themselves in school. Likewise, Stephen Ceci and Jeffrey Liker (1986) report that racetrack fans' expertise in handicapping horses—a practical but complex cognitive task—is unrelated to their intelligence scores.

*"You're wise, but you lack tree smarts."*

Drawing by Reilly; © 1988 The New Yorker Magazine, Inc.

Nancy Cantor and John Kihlstrom (1987) similarly distinguish between academic intelligence and social intelligence—the know-how involved in comprehending social situations and managing oneself successfully. Seymour Epstein and Petra Meier (1989) agree. If academic aptitude signifies social competence, they ask, why then are high-aptitude people "not, by a wide margin, more effective . . . in achieving better marriages, in successfully raising their children, and in achieving better mental and physical well-being?" Consistent with this distinction between academic and social intelligence is the repeated finding that college grades only modestly predict later work achievement (Bretz, 1989; Dye & Reck, 1989).

In defense of the *g* factor, other researchers point to studies in which intelligence scores *do* predict both occupational status and job performance (Gottfredson, 1985; Jensen, 1993; Schmidt & Hunter, 1993). Intelligence matters most in mentally demanding jobs. Meteorology more than meter reading requires intelligence to excel. Moreover, most researchers agree that (a) getting into certain vocations requires crossing a certain threshold of intelligence, and (b) once admitted to a vocation, those who become highly successful have other traits as well—they are conscientious, knowledgeable, and energetic.

So it seems that the academic aptitude tapped by intelligence tests is indeed central to our lives. Yet personal competence in everyday living requires much that traditional intelligence tests do not measure.

## Is Intelligence Speedy Information Processing?

A different approach to intelligence has emerged. It asks whether on simple cognitive tasks intelligent people are literally more quick-witted.

As a pioneer of this new approach, Robert Sternberg wasted no time getting his career under way (Dorsey, 1987). His first studies of intelligence began when he gave intelligence tests to his seventh-grade classmates and did a science project on achievement testing. His senior yearbook quoted him as saying, "Intelligence is the most misunderstood personality trait." A decade and more later, he was still searching out the roots of intelligence.

To find out what goes on in people's heads, Sternberg had subjects signal as soon as they understood the question portions of multiple-choice analogies, such as, "Lawyer is to client as doctor is to ________." Then he showed them possible answers, such as (a) patient or (b) medicine, and measured how speedily they responded. Those scoring as highly intelligent spend *more* time analyzing the questions, but they then recognize the correct answer faster. Sternberg (1984, 1985) and fellow researcher James Pellegrino (1985) noted that their research findings put a qualification on the common-sense maxim that "smart is fast." High scorers are quick-witted *after* they comprehend a problem.

Examining a more elementary level of cognitive processing, Earl Hunt (1983) and his colleagues found that verbal intelligence scores are predictable from the speed with which people retrieve information from memory. Those who recognize quickly that *SINK* and *wink* are different words, or that *A* and *a* share the same name, tend to score high in verbal ability. Extremely precocious 12- to 14-year-old college students are especially quick in responding to such tasks (Jensen, 1989).

## Is Intelligence Neurologically Measurable?

Using today's neuroscience tools, might we link differences in people's intelligence-test performance to dissimilarities in their brains? Joseph Matarazzo (1992), the 1990 American Psychological Association president, thinks so; he expects that by early in the next century there will be neurological tests of intelligence.

Does this have a familiar ring? A century after Francis Galton's futile attempts to gauge intelligence in terms of head size, reaction times, and sensory abilities, his urge to reduce intelligence to simple brain measures still lives. Today's efforts ask whether intelligence scores correlate with brain anatomy or brain functioning.

### Brain Size and Intelligence

Even before Galton, the phrenologist Franz Gall realized that human intelligence surpasses animal intelligence because the human cortex is more developed. He therefore wondered whether intelligence differences among humans might similarly be due to differing brain structures, detectable in skull protrusions. Although his efforts to gauge mental abilities failed, as did Galton's, 25 modern studies do reveal a slight +.15 correlation between head size (relative to body size) and intelligence score (Jensen & Johnson, 1994).

*Other studies reveal slight positive correlations between height and intelligence, and near-sightedness and intelligence (Brody, 1992).*

Maybe the correlation is so near zero (and was therefore undetectable in the nineteenth century analyses) because head size is a weak proxy for brain size. There is, after all, more inside the skull than cortical tissue. Newer studies that directly measure brain volume using MRI scans reveal "significant, but modest" correlations near +.35 between brain size (ad-

**FOR BETTER OR WORSE**

FOR BETTER OR WORSE © Lynn Johnston Prod., Inc. Reprinted with permission of UNIVERSAL PRESS SYNDICATE. All rights reserved.

justed for body size) and IQ score (Andreasen & others, 1993; Willerman & others, 1991).

Efforts to link brain structure with cognition continue. One ongoing project is giving tests of abilities and personality to cancer patients with poor prognoses, and then collecting their brains for study after their deaths (Witelson & McCulloch, 1991). Should intelligence correlate with brain size, the cause could be differing genes, nutrition, environmental stimulation, some combination of these, or who knows what else. Recall from earlier chapters that experience alters the brain. Rats raised in a stimulating rather than deprived environment develop thicker, heavier cortexes. And learning leaves detectable traces in our brain's neural connections.

### Brain Function and Intelligence

Even if the modest correlations between brain anatomy and intelligence prove reliable, they hardly explain intelligence differences. Searching for other explanations, neuroscientists are studying the brain's functioning. R. J. Haier (1993) and Randolph Parks and his colleagues (1988) have done PET scans while people with high or low abilities perform cognitive tasks. High performers' brains are *less* active (they require less glucose energy). This link between ability on a task and neurological efficiency holds true whether one compares more versus less intelligent people, or those who have had more versus less opportunity to master the task.

Other researchers have wondered whether the greater reaction speeds of highly intelligent people reflect greater neurological speed. To their delight, repeated studies have found that the brain waves of highly intelligent people register a simple stimulus (such as a flash of light or a tone beep) more quickly and with greater complexity (Deary & Caryl, 1993; Hendrickson, 1982; Reed & Jensen, 1992). The evoked brain response also tends to be slightly faster when people with high intelligence scores perform a simple task, such as pushing a button when an X appears on a screen (McGarry-Roberts & others, 1992).

Neural processing speed on a simple task seems far removed from the untimed responses to complex intelligence test items, such as "In what way are *wool* and *cotton* alike?" As yet, notes intelligence expert Nathan Brody (1992), we have no firm understanding of *why* speedy reactions on simple tasks should predict intelligence test performance. Philip Vernon (1983) speculates, though, that "faster cognitive processing may allow more information to be acquired." Perhaps people who more quickly process information accumulate more information—about wool, cotton, and millions of other things.

The neurological approach to understanding intelligence (and so many other things in psychology) is currently in its heyday. Will this new research achieve Galton's aim of reducing what we now call the *g* factor to simple measures of underlying brain activity? Or are these efforts totally wrongheaded because what we call intelligence is not a single general trait but several culturally adaptive skills? The controversies surrounding the nature of intelligence are a long way from resolution.

## Summing Up

It is misleading to reify concepts such as "intelligence" and "giftedness"—to regard these abstract concepts as if they were real, concrete things. To most psychologists, intelligence is the capacity for goal-directed and adaptive behavior.

**Is Intelligence Culturally Defined?** Some psychologists argue that intelligent behavior (say, a person's ability to adapt successfully to the demands of school or work) is culturally relative; others contend that intelligence is a culture-free ability to solve all sorts of problems.

**Is Intelligence One General Ability or Several Specific Abilities?** Psychologists agree that people have specific abilities, such as verbal and mathematical aptitudes. However, they debate whether a general intelligence (*g*) factor runs through them all. Factor analysis and studies of special conditions, such as the savant syndrome, have identified clusters of mental aptitudes.

**Is Intelligence Speedy Information Processing?** Recently, psychologists have linked people's intelligence to their basic capacities for processing information. Some psychologists are studying the components that make up problem-solving skill. There does seem to be at least a modest tendency for highly intelligent people to have quick-witted reactions.

**Is Intelligence Neurologically Measurable?** Galton's efforts to gauge intelligence in terms of simple brain measures have been reborn in today's efforts to correlate intelligence scores with brain anatomy and functioning. Several studies report a very slight correlation between head size (adjusted for body size) and intelligence test score, and a slightly greater (though still modest) correlation between brain size and intelligence test score. Other studies suggest that the brains of highly skilled people require less glucose energy while performing certain cognitive tasks, and that the brain waves of highly intelligent people more quickly register simple stimuli such as a flash of light. Time will tell whether these new neurological approaches to intelligence will bear important fruit. If they do, researchers will surely debate the extent to which nature and nurture affect the brain's structure and functioning.

# The Dynamics of Intelligence

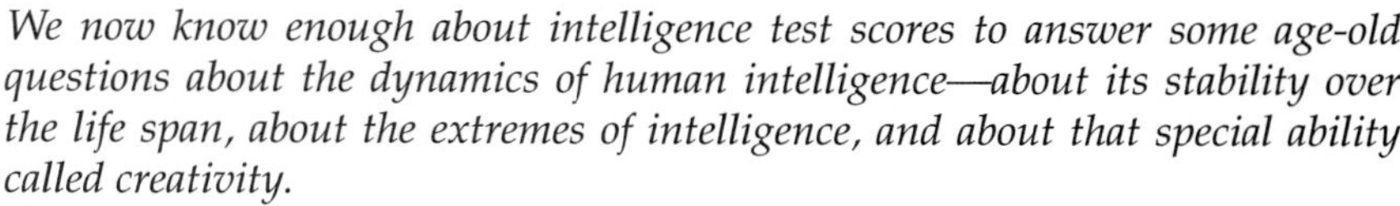

*We now know enough about intelligence test scores to answer some age-old questions about the dynamics of human intelligence—about its stability over the life span, about the extremes of intelligence, and about that special ability called creativity.*

## Stability or Change?

If we retested people periodically throughout their lives, would their intelligence scores be stable? Chapter 4 explored the stability of intelligence in later life. What about the stability of intelligence scores early in life?

The search for indicators of infants' later intelligence has left few stones unturned. Unable to talk with infants, developmental researchers have assessed what they can observe—everything from birth weight, to whether the third toe was longer than the second toe, to age of sitting up alone. None of these measures provides any useful prediction of intelligence scores at much later ages (Bell & Waldrop, 1989; Broman, 1989). Perhaps, as developmental psychologist Nancy Bayley (1949) reflected, "we have not yet found the right tests." She speculated that we might someday find "some infant behaviors which are characteristic of underlying intellectual functions" and which will predict later intelligence.

**How Smart Is This Baby?** *Infants' preference for novel stimuli is a moderate predictor of future intelligence. This researcher in Joseph Fagan's laboratory briefly shows an infant a previously seen picture alongside a new picture, recording how many seconds the child looks at each.*

Such a test may have been found. Two dozen studies by Joseph Fagan, Marc Bornstein, John Columbo, and others reveal that 2- to 6-month-old babies who quickly grow bored with a picture—who, given a choice, prefer to look at a new one—score higher on intelligence tests several years later (McCall & Carriger, 1993). Although the prediction is crude, the tests can help identify children likely to be extremely below or above average.

So, can everyday observations or intelligence test scores now predict preschoolers' future performance and educational needs? The question is especially interesting to new parents wondering about their baby's intelligence and to educators wanting an early identification of children with special needs. Those anxious about comparing their baby with others can relax. Except for extremely retarded or very precocious children, casual observation and intelligence tests before age 3 predict children's future aptitudes only minimally (Humphreys & Davey, 1988). For example, children who are early talkers—talking in sentences typical of 3-year-olds by age 20 months—are *not* especially likely to be reading by age 4½ (Crain-Thoreson & Dale, 1992). (A better predictor of early reading is having parents who have read lots of stories to you.)

*Albert Einstein was slow in learning to talk (Quasha, 1980).*

By age 3, however, children's performances on intelligence tests begin to predict their adolescent and adult scores. Moreover, high-scoring adolescents tend to have been early readers. One study surveyed the parents of 187 seventh- and eighth-graders who had taken the SAT as part of a seven-state talent search and had scored considerably higher than most high school seniors. If their parents' memories can be trusted, more than half of this precocious group of adolescents began reading by age 4 and more than 80 percent were reading by age 5 (Van Tassel-Baska, 1983). Not surprisingly, then, intelligence tests given in kindergarten begin to predict school achievement (Tramontana & others, 1988).

*"My dear Adele, I am 4 years old and I can read any English book. I can say all the Latin Substantives and Adjectives and active verbs besides 52 lines of Latin poetry."*

Francis Galton
Letter to his sister, 1827

After about age 7, intelligence test scores, though certainly not fixed, become even more stable (Bloom, 1964). Thus, the consistency of scores over time increases with the age of the child. The remarkable stability of aptitude scores by late adolescence is seen in an Educational Testing Service study of 23,000 students who took the SAT and then later took its more advanced counterpart, the GRE, which is taken by many college seniors (Angoff, 1988). On either test, verbal scores correlate only modestly with math scores—revealing that these two aptitudes are distinct. Yet scores on the SAT verbal test correlated +.86 with GRE verbal scores 4 to 5 years later. An equally astonishing +.86 correlation occurred between the two math tests. In view of the time lapse and differing educational experiences of these 23,000 students, the stability of their aptitude scores is remarkable—surely beyond what any of us would have predicted.

*Ironically, SAT and GRE scores correlate better with each other than either does with its intended criterion, school achievement. Thus, their reliability far exceeds their predictive validity. If either test was much affected by coaching, luck, or how one feels on the test day (as so many people believe), such reliability would be impossible.*

## Extremes of Intelligence

One way to glimpse the validity and significance of any test is to compare people who score at the two extremes of the normal curve. The two groups should differ noticeably, and they do.

### The Challenged

At one extreme are people whose intelligence test scores fall below 70. To be labeled as having **mental retardation**, a child must have both a low test score *and* difficulty adapting to the normal demands of living independently. Only about 1 percent of the population meets both criteria, with males outnumbering females by 50 percent (American Psychiatric Association, 1994). As Table 11–1 indicates, most such mentally challenged individuals can, with support, live in mainstream society.

**Table 11–1 Degrees of Mental Retardation**

| Level | Typical Intelligence Scores | Percentage of the Retarded | Adaptation to Demands of Life |
|---|---|---|---|
| Mild | 50–70 | 85 | May learn academic skills up to sixth-grade level. Adults may, with assistance, achieve self-supporting social and vocational skills. |
| Moderate | 35–49 | 10 | May progress to second-grade level academically. Adults may contribute to their own support by labor in sheltered workshops. |
| Severe | 20–34 | 3–4 | May learn to talk and to perform simple work tasks under close supervision but are generally unable to profit from vocational training. |
| Profound | Below 20 | 1–2 | Require constant aid and supervision. |

*Source:* Adapted from the American Psychiatric Association (1994).

Mental retardation sometimes results from known physical causes. **Down syndrome**, a disorder attributed to an extra chromosome in the person's genetic makeup, is one such cause (although most people with Down syndrome are not severely retarded).

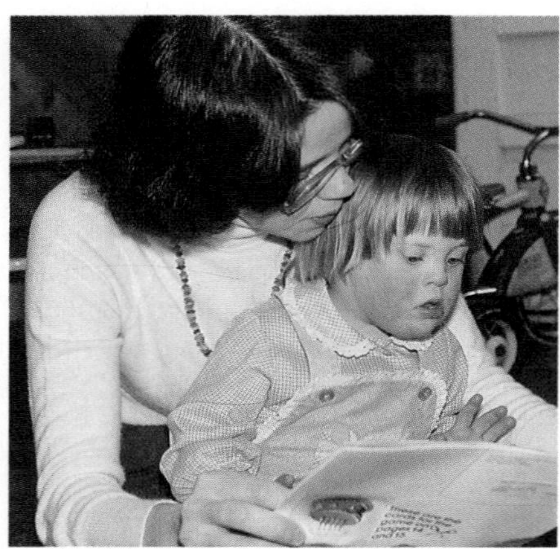

**A Child With Down Syndrome** *In the past, children with this condition were often institutionalized. We now know that with a supportive and stimulating family environment and special education, many Down syndrome children can achieve IQs in the mildly retarded range and are capable of learning to take care of themselves and holding a job.*

During the last two centuries the pendulum of opinion about how best to care for the mentally challenged has made a complete swing. Until the mid-nineteenth century, they were cared for at home. Those with the most severe disabilities often died, but people with milder forms of retardation found a place in a farm-based society. Then, residential schools for slow learners were established. By the twentieth century, many of these institutions had become warehouses providing residents no privacy, little attention, and no hope. Parents often were told to separate themselves permanently from a retarded child before they became attached.

Now, in the last half of this century, the pendulum has swung back to normalization—allowing mentally impaired people to live in their own communities as normally as their functioning permits. We educate mildly retarded children in less restrictive environments and we integrate, or *mainstream*, many into regular classrooms. Most grow up with their own families until moving into a protected living arrangement, such as a group home. The hope, and often the reality, is a happier and more dignified life.

### The Gifted

In one famous project begun in 1921, Lewis Terman studied more than 1500 California schoolchildren with IQ scores over 135. Contrary to the popular myth that intellectually gifted children are frequently maladjusted because they are "in a different world" from their nongifted peers, Terman's high-scoring children were unusually healthy, well adjusted, and academically successful. When restudied over the next six decades (Goleman, 1980), most of these people had attained high levels of education. Their vocational success varied, yet the group included many doctors, lawyers, professors, scientists, and writers. Terman's whiz kids remind one of Jean Piaget, who by age 7 was devoting his free time to studying birds, fossils, and machines; who by age 15 began publishing scientific articles on mollusks; and who later went on to become this century's most famous developmental psychologist (Hunt, 1993).

Critics nevertheless question many of the assumptions of currently popular "gifted child" programs, such as the belief that only some 3 to 5 percent of children are gifted (the other 95 percent being ungifted) and that it pays to identify and label these special few—to segregate them from the "nongifted" and give them academic enrichment not available to the masses. This is one example of "tracking" students in separate classes with others who share their level of aptitude score. Many research studies conclude that students tracked by aptitude have academic achievement scores

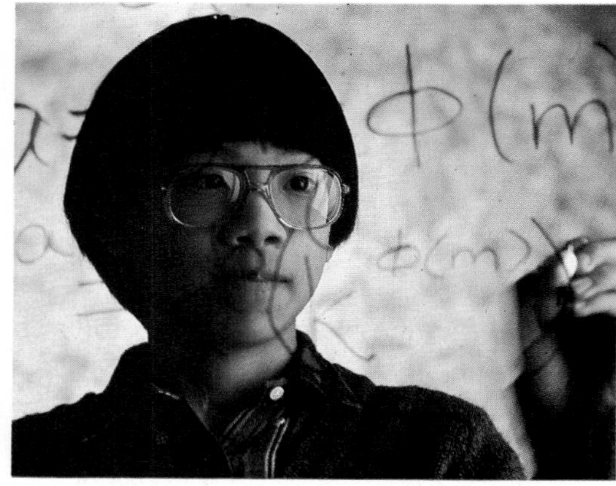

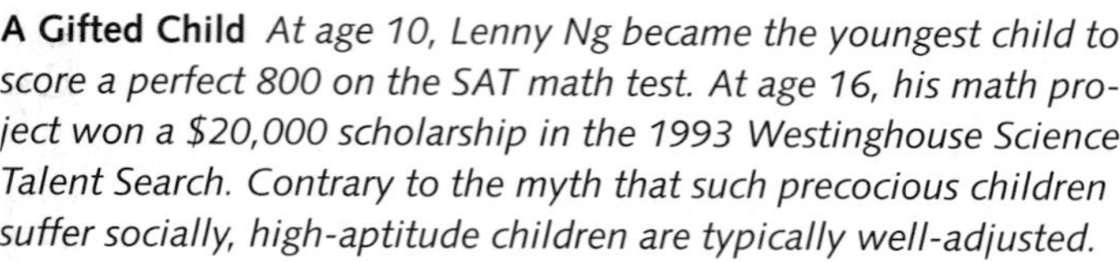

**A Gifted Child** *At age 10, Lenny Ng became the youngest child to score a perfect 800 on the SAT math test. At age 16, his math project won a $20,000 scholarship in the 1993 Westinghouse Science Talent Search. Contrary to the myth that such precocious children suffer socially, high-aptitude children are typically well-adjusted.*

hardly higher than similar untracked students. Moreover, ability tracking tends to lower students' self-esteem and sometimes creates self-fulfilling prophecies (Lipsey & Wilson, 1993; Slavin & Braddock, 1993).

A report of the Carnegie Council on Adolescent Development (1989) therefore condemned academic tracking as "one of the most divisive and damaging school practices in existence." Denying "low-ability" students opportunities for enriched education serves to widen the achievement gap between the two groups and to increase their social isolation from one another, one reason why there is no tracking in the elementary schools of Japan and China (Stevenson & Lee, 1990). Because minority and low-income youth are more often placed in lower academic groups, tracking can also promote segregation and prejudice—hardly healthy preparation for working and living in a multicultural society.

*"Alpha children wear grey. They work much harder than we do, because they're so frightfully clever. I'm really awfully glad I'm a Beta, because I don't work so hard. And then we are much better than the Gammas and Deltas. Gammas are stupid."*

Aldous Huxley
*Brave New World*, 1932

Sorting children into gifted and nongifted groups often presumes that giftedness is a single trait—measured by an intelligence test—rather than one of many potentials. Newspaper and magazine articles advise parents on how to spot "the signs of giftedness" in their children, as if giftedness were an objective quality, like blue eyes, that a child either has or lacks. This reifies giftedness—by creating the concept and then presuming that it has a concrete reality. It ignores the fact that we, not nature, are deciding the criteria of giftedness.

Critics and proponents of gifted education agree on this much, however: Children have differing gifts. Some are especially good at math, others at verbal reasoning, others at art, still others at social leadership. It is a maxim of biology that nature prefers diversity. By packaging different gifts in different bodies, nature enhances a group's welfare and the odds that some will survive environmental challenges. Educating children as if all were alike is as naive as assuming that giftedness is something you either have or don't have. One needn't hang value-laden labels on children to affirm their special talents and to challenge all at the frontiers of their own abilities and understandings.

## Creativity and Intelligence

**Creativity** is the ability to produce ideas that are both novel and valuable. The outlets for creativity vary by culture. Samoan culture encourages creativity in dance, Balinese culture in music, the African Ashanti culture in wood carvings (Lubart, 1990). In each, creativity means expressing familiar themes in novel ways.

Results from tests of intelligence and creativity suggest that a certain level of aptitude is necessary but not sufficient for creativity. In general, people with high intelligence scores do well on creativity tests. ("How many uses can you think of for a brick?") But beyond a certain level—a score of about 120—the correlation between intelligence scores and creativity disappears. Exceptionally creative architects, mathematicians, scientists, and engineers usually score no higher on intelligence tests than do their less creative peers (MacKinnon & Hall, 1972). So there is clearly more to creativity than intelligence scores.

*On his way home from picking up a Nobel prize in Stockholm, physicist Richard Feynman stopped in Queens, New York, to look at his high school record. "My grades were not as good as I remembered," he reported, "and my IQ was [a good, though unexceptional] 124" (Faber, 1987).*

Studies of creative people suggest five other components of creativity (Sternberg, 1988; Sternberg & Lubart, 1991, 1992). The first is *expertise*—a well-developed base of knowledge. "Chance favors only the prepared mind," observed Louis Pasteur. To a point, intelligence helps because it fills the brain with the mental elements of creativity—ideas, images, phrases. The more mental building blocks we have to work with, through our accumulated learning, the more chances we have to combine them in novel ways.

*Everyone held up their crackers as David threw the cheese log into the ceiling fan.*

Reprinted with permission of Paul Soderblom.

The second is *imaginative thinking skills*—an ability to see things in new ways, to recognize patterns, to make connections. To be creative you must first master the basic elements of a problem, then redefine or explore the problem in a new way. Copernicus first developed expertise regarding the solar system's sun and planets and then defined the system as revolving around the sun, not the earth. In its more extreme forms, imaginative thinking makes people vulnerable to losing touch with reality. Studies comparing the thinking styles of creative and psychotic people reveal that creativity is, as has long been supposed, sometimes akin to madness (Eysenck, 1993).

Creativity's third ingredient is a *venturesome personality*— one that tolerates ambiguity and risk, perseveres in overcoming obstacles, and seeks new experiences rather than following the pack. Inventors, for example, have a knack for persisting after failures, as Thomas Edison did in trying countless substances for his light-bulb filament.

The fourth component is what psychologist Teresa Amabile calls the *intrinsic motivation* principle of creativity: "People will be most creative when they feel motivated primarily by the interest, enjoyment, satisfaction, and challenge of the work itself—rather than by external pressures" (Amabile & Hennessey, 1992). Creative people focus not so much on extrinsic motivators—meeting deadlines, impressing people, or making money—as on the intrinsic pleasure and challenge of their work.

The final component is a *creative environment* that sparks, supports, and refines creative ideas. After studying the careers of 2026 prominent scientists and inventors, Dean Keith Simonton (1992) noted that the most eminent among them were not lone geniuses. Rather they were mentored, challenged, and supported by their relationships with colleagues.

Amabile's (1983, 1987) experiments show that creative environments also free people from concern about social approval. In one experiment, she asked college students to make paper collages, telling half beforehand that experts would evaluate their work. Those unaware that their work would be evaluated produced collages that judges later rated as more creative. Unworried about being evaluated, they felt freer to be creative.

*More on intrinsic motivation in the next chapter.*

At work, managers who wish to foster innovation should keep the intrinsic motivation principle in mind, notes Amabile (1988). They should set employees to work on activities that naturally interest them. And they can emulate managers who have successfully nurtured creativity—by providing their subordinates with time, freedom, and support to attain set goals. So it is at the 3M company, which has encouraged researchers to spend 15 percent of their time pursuing creative projects that don't have immediate payoff and where the Eleventh Commandment is "Thou shalt not kill a new product idea." From this creativity-nurturing environment has come such products as the removable Post-it notes found in most offices today (Kreitner, 1992).

## Summing Up

**Stability or Change?** The stability of intelligence test scores increases with age, with practical predictive value beginning by age 3 and scores becoming fairly stable by age 7. Among infants, those who become quickly bored with a picture, preferring to look at a new one, tend to score well on later intelligence tests.

**Extremes of Intelligence** Comparing those who score extremely low (the "challenged," or mentally retarded) with those who score extremely high (the "gifted") magnifies a test's apparent validity.

**Creativity and Intelligence** Intelligence correlates weakly with creativity. Increases in intelligence beyond a necessary threshold level are not linked with increased creativity.

## Genetic and Environmental Influences on Intelligence

*Studies of twins and adopted children, and of children raised in enriched or neglectful environments, indicate that genes and environment both contribute to individual differences. What, then, explains group differences in intelligence scores? And do such differences mean that tests are biased? These are among psychology's most controversial issues.*

Having considered the nature and dynamics of intelligence, we cannot resist asking: What determines intelligence—genes or environment? As Francis Galton recognized, intelligence seems to run in families. Moreover, we have seen that intelligence seems modestly predictable from infants' boredom with familiar pictures or from the complexity and speed of a person's brain wave responses to a flash of light. But why? Are intellectual abilities inherited? Or are they molded by one's environment? To understand why these questions stir up stormy debate, consider how people with differing views sometimes use nature and nurture to further their social agenda.

If, on the one hand, we mainly inherit our differing mental abilities, and if success reflects those abilities, then people's socioeconomic standing will correspond to their inborn differences. Thus, those on top may believe their innate mental superiority justifies their social positions. They may even remind us that it was Thomas Jefferson, not God, who insisted that all people are created equal.

If, on the other hand, mental abilities are primarily nurtured by the environments that raise and school us, then children from disadvantaged environments will often lead disadvantaged lives. In this case, people's socioeconomic standings will result from unequal opportunities, a situation that many regard as basically unjust. Setting aside such political implications as best we can, let's examine the evidence.

*"I am, somehow, less interested in the weight and convolutions of Einstein's brain than in the near certainty that people of equal talent have lived and died in cotton fields and sweatshops."*

Stephen Jay Gould
*The Panda's Thumb*, 1980

### Genetic Influences

Virtually everyone now acknowledges that both genes and the environment influence intelligence. This has motivated a search for specific genes (likely many) associated with high intelligence scores. Some genetic markers assessed from blood samples do seem to occur more often in high-scoring children (Plomin & others, 1994). Other researchers continue exploring the old nature-nurture issue: How, and how much, do genes and environment influence intelligence?

#### Twin Studies

Do people who share the same genes also share comparable mental abilities? As you can see from Figure 11–8 (page 384), which summarizes many studies, the answer is clearly yes.

Figure 11–8

**Intelligence: Nature and Nurture** *The most genetically similar people have the most similar intelligence scores. But the correlations also reveal an effect of environment: Identical twins reared apart test somewhat less alike than those reared together. Remember: 1.0 indicates a perfect correlation; zero indicates no correlation at all. (From Bouchard, 1982.)*

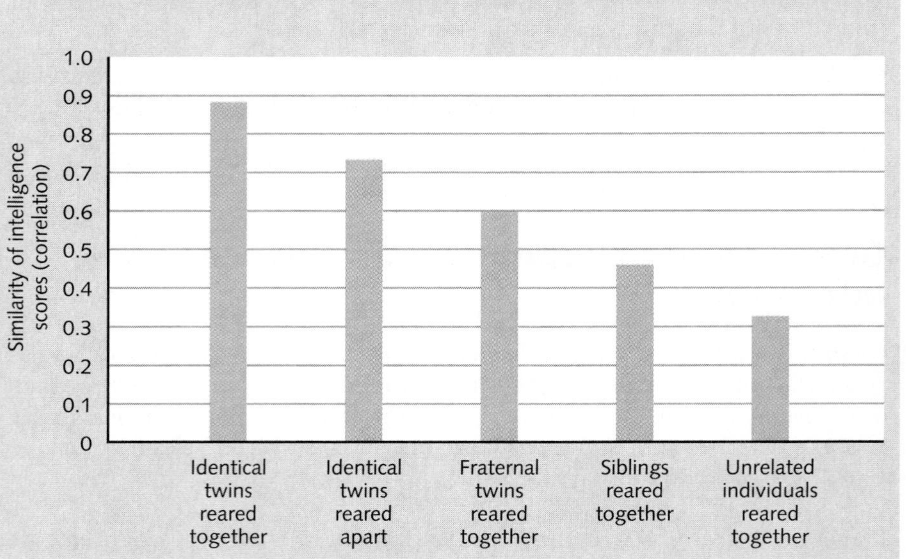


For example, the intelligence scores of identical twins reared together are more similar than those of fraternal twins. What shall we make of these results? Let's eavesdrop on an imaginary conversation between two psychologists—one who believes that heredity powerfully influences intelligence test performance, and one who does not.

**Hereditarian:** *Intelligence scores of genetically identical twins are almost as similar as those of the same person taking the test twice. Fraternal twins, who share only half their genes, are much less similar in intelligence scores.*

**Environmentalist:** *Ah, but the identical twins are similar because they were treated similarly. Look at the data again and you'll see that fraternal twins, who are genetically no more alike than any other siblings, nevertheless score more alike. John Loehlin and Robert Nichols (1976) studied hundreds of twins and found that identical twins are more likely than fraternal twins to be dressed alike, to sleep in the same room, to have the same friends and teachers, and so forth. So their greater similarity in test scores may be environmental.*

**Hereditarian:** *But Loehlin and Nichols also found that identical twins whose parents do not dress or treat them alike are virtual carbon copies of one another in intelligence scores. Much the same is true for identical twins who have been reared separately (Bouchard, 1993). They're more alike than fraternal twins reared together! Having the same genes has more effect than having the same environment.*

**Environmentalist:** *After analyzing the older studies of separated identical twins, Leon Kamin (1974) reported that the separated twins often were selectively placed in similar positive environments. Storks don't deliver these babies at random, you know. Moreover, as new data accumulate, behavior geneticists are dropping their estimates of the extent to which variation in intelligence scores can be attributed to heredity—from earlier estimates of around 80 percent to newer estimates of between 50 percent (Loehlin, 1989; Plomin & Rende, 1991) and 60 percent (Bouchard & Segal, 1988). Studies of the genetic determinants of behavior tell us as much about the importance of environment as about the importance of genes.*

### Adoption Studies

Psychologists struggling to disentangle the effects of genes and environment have searched for information in studies of adopted children in addition to twin studies. Several researchers have asked whether adopted children, thanks to their shared environment, share similar aptitudes. During childhood, the intelligence test scores of adoptive siblings correlate modestly. But with age, the effect of common rearing wanes; by adulthood, the correlation is roughly zero (McGue & others, 1993).

Researchers have also asked whether adopted children have intelligence test scores more like those of their biological parents, from whom they receive their genes, or of their adoptive parents, who provide their home environment. As Figure 11–9 illustrates, adopted children's scores more closely resemble those of their biological parents than those of their adoptive parents. Moreover, the older the children are, the more they score like their *biological* parents (Fulker & others, 1988; Loehlin & others, 1989). It matters whether one is adopted into an impoverished or an enriched environment (Turkheimer, 1991). Yet being reared "together in the same adoptive home does not make you intellectually similar to your brothers and sisters," notes Sandra Scarr (1989); "being genetically related by half of your genes does."

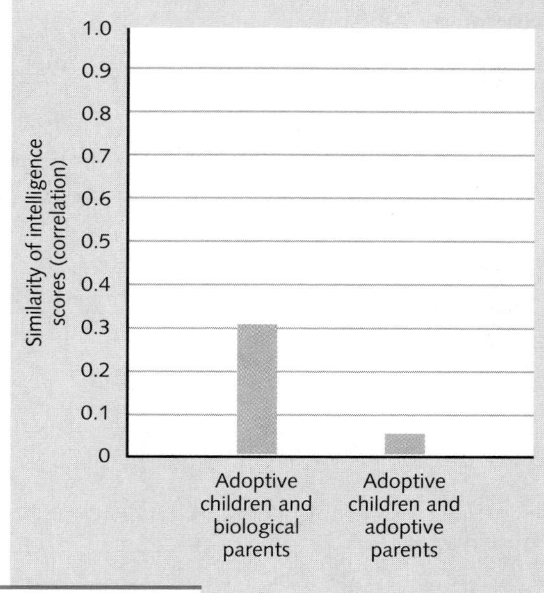


**Figure 11–9**

**The Correlations of Intelligence Test Scores Between 245 Adopted Colorado Children and Their Adoptive and Biological Parents** *By age 7, the adopted children had intelligence test scores more like those of their biological parents. (From Fulker & others, 1988.)*

### Heritability

To say that the **heritability** of intelligence—the variation in intelligence test scores attributable to genetic factors—is roughly 50 to 60 percent does *not* mean that your genes are responsible for 50 to 60 percent of your intelligence and your environment for the rest. (Likewise, saying that the heritability of height is 90 percent does not mean that a 60-inch-tall woman can credit her genes for 54 inches and her environment for the other 6 inches.) Rather, it means that we can attribute to heredity 50 to 60 percent *of the variation in intelligence within a group of people*. This point is so often misunderstood that I repeat: We can never say what percentage of an *individual's* intelligence is inherited. Heritability refers instead to the extent to which *differences among people* are attributable to genes.

Even this conclusion must be qualified. First, heritability can vary from study to study. To see why, imagine two researchers separately investigating how genes and life experience influence intelligence. One researcher gives intelligence tests to two groups of adopted children: One group is the biological offspring of retarded parents, the other of Nobel prize winners. Her conclusion: Differences in the children's intelligence are mostly attributable to the intelligence they inherited from their biological parents, not to their home environments. Meanwhile, another researcher compares the biological offspring of parents with average intelligence scores to the offspring of parents with slightly above-average scores. Half of each group of children are in loving homes, the other half in an impoverished orphanage. This researcher finds a bigger effect of environment. Meeting at a convention, the first researcher reports that in her study intelligence differences were primarily genetic; the second researcher reports that in his study they were primarily environmental. Who is right?

They both are—for the specific groups they studied. Let's generalize the point: Compare people with very different heredities from basically similar environments, and heritability—differences due to genes—will be high. Compare people with not-so-different heredities in drastically different environments (impoverished and enriched), and heritability will be low. If everyone had the same heredity, heritability would be zero. If everyone had exactly the same environment, heritability would be 100 percent. Ironically, then, a society marked by equality of opportunity *should* have higher heritability of traits and abilities than one marked by extreme advantages or disadvantages.

As a second qualification to statements about heritability, remember that genes and environment intertwine. Given the differences among children who grow up in the same families, researchers infer that our most important experiences are personal. Yet our genetically unique traits affect our experience: Others react to us in ways that encourage our natural gifts. Our traits also lead us to select congenial environments. Students with a natural aptitude for mathematics are more likely to select math courses in high school, and later to score well on the SAT math test—thanks *both* to their natural math aptitude *and* to their math experience. Thus, our genes shape the experiences that shape us.

## Environmental Influences

We have seen that our genes make a difference. Even if we were all raised in the same intellectually stimulating environment, we still would not have the same aptitudes. But we have also seen that heredity doesn't tell the whole story. Within the limits dictated by our genes, our life experiences matter. Under normal circumstances, the environment that siblings share doesn't much influence their aptitudes, but it significantly influences their scholastic achievement (Thompson & others, 1991).

Human environments are rarely so impoverished as the dark and barren cages inhabited by deprived rats that develop thinner-than-normal brain cortexes. Yet severe life experiences also leave marks on humans, as psychologist J. McVicker Hunt (1982) observed in a destitute Iranian orphanage in Tehran, where the typical child could not sit up unassisted at age 2 or walk at age 4. What care the infants received was not in response to their crying, cooing, or other behaviors. The infants were therefore not developing any sense of personal control over their environment, and so were becoming passive "glum lumps." Extreme deprivation was bludgeoning native intelligence.

Aware of the benefits of responsive caregiving, Hunt began a program of "tutored human enrichment." For instance, he trained caregivers to play vocal games with the infants. First, they imitated the babies' babbling. Then they led the babies in vocal follow-the-leader by shifting from one familiar sound to another. Then they began to teach sounds from the Persian language.

The results were dramatic. All 11 infants who received these language-fostering experiences could name more than 50 objects and body parts by 22 months. So charming had the infants become that most were adopted—an unprecedented success for the orphanage.

Hunt's findings testify to the importance of environment. Severe disadvantage takes a toll on children (Ramey & Ramey, 1992). But do such findings indicate a way to "give your child a superior intellect"? Some popular books claim that with intensive preschool training this is possible, but many experts are doubtful (Phillips & Stipek, 1993). Sandra Scarr (1984) agrees that neglectful upbringing can have grave long-term consequences. However, she also believes that "as long as an infant has normal human contact and normal exposure to sights, sounds, human speech, and so forth, the baby will thrive." As for future intelligence, "Parents who are very concerned about providing special educational lessons for their babies are wasting their time." Parents of children with high intelligence test

*"There is a large body of evidence indicating that there is little if anything to be gained by exposing middle-class children to early education."*

Developmental psychologist Edward F. Zigler (1987)

scores may have been more likely to hang crib mobiles, take the children to the theater, or whatever. But do such experiences have any effect? We don't know, says Scarr (1986). Parents supply their children with both genes and environments. So even if the environments of children with high intelligence test scores are noticeably different from those with low scores, we can't be sure how much difference their environments make.

Hunt would probably agree with Scarr that extra instruction has little effect on the intellectual development of children from stimulating environments. But he was optimistic when it came to children from disadvantaged environments. Indeed, his 1961 book, *Intelligence and Experience*, helped launch Project Head Start in 1965.

Head Start is a U.S. government–funded preschool program serving 700,000 children, most of whom come from families below the poverty level (Kramer, 1993). It aims to enhance children's chances for success in school and beyond by boosting their cognitive and social skills. Psychologist Edward Zigler, the program's first director, recalls that the program began with the hope that early childhood was a critical period during which intervention would have "indelible effects on the child" (Holden, 1990).

Does it? Researchers have studied Head Start and other preschool programs by comparing equivalent groups of children who do versus don't experience the intervention. Their findings indicate that high-quality programs for disadvantaged children produce at least short-term cognitive gains, even on intelligence tests (Haskins, 1989). Quality programs also increase school readiness, decreasing the likelihood of a child's repeating a grade or being placed in special education. On a less encouraging note, the benefits dissipate over time, reminding us that life experiences *after* Head Start matter, too.

Are there *any* long-term benefits? If Head Start doesn't make children fundamentally smarter, does it steer them onto a pathway toward success? Although the scientific jury is still out, studies of model programs give hope that ultimate graduation and employment rates can be increased. Zigler (1990; Zigler & Muenchow, 1992), for one, believes it is now "abundantly clear that high-quality preschool programs do indeed generate long-term effects." They improve attitudes toward learning, and they reduce school dropouts and criminality. Although other researchers are less sure, all look forward to the results of an intensive new Comprehensive Child Development Program under way at 24 centers.

The effect of education on aptitude doesn't end with the preschool years.

**Getting a Head Start** *To increase readiness for schoolwork and expand children's notions of where school might lead them, Project Head Start offers educational activities. Here children in a classroom learn about colors and those on a field trip learn what fire fighters do.*

As we noted earlier, intelligence test scores have risen during this century along with average years of schooling completed. Moreover, individuals obtain diminished IQ scores if they start schooling late, attend intermittently, or drop out early. Not only does intelligence affect school performance, concludes Stephen Ceci (1991), schooling affects intelligence.

## Group Differences in Intelligence Test Scores

Scholars could debate the issue of hereditary versus environmental determinants of intelligence dispassionately if there were no aptitude score differences among various groups. But there are.

- On the SAT, males in 1993 scored 45 points higher than females on the math test and a nominal 8 points higher on the verbal test. (For more on gender and aptitude, see Chapter 19.)
- Japanese children score slightly higher than American children on nonverbal items from the WISC-R (Lynn, 1982, 1983) and significantly higher on math achievement tests (Flynn, 1991; Stevenson 1992). During the 1980s, Asian-Americans constituted less than 3 percent of the U.S. population and won about 25 percent of the Westinghouse Science Talent Search awards (Goleman, 1990).
- Black Americans average about 15 points lower than white Americans on intelligence tests and a comparable 100 points lower on the SAT verbal and math aptitude tests (Jacobson, 1986; Jensen, 1993; Loehlin & others, 1975). Similar score differences exist between privileged and disadvantaged groups around the world—between European and native Maori New Zealanders; between Israeli Jews and Israeli Arabs; between Israeli Jews of Middle-Eastern descent and those of European descent; and between a stigmatized Japanese minority, the Burakumin, and other ethnic Japanese (Steele, 1990a; Zeidner, 1990).

Bear in mind that *group* differences don't tell us about specific *individuals*. Women outlive men by an average of 6 years, but knowing an individual's sex doesn't tell us how long that person is going to live. Similarly, knowing your race tells us very little about your likely performance on a mental aptitude test.

Nevertheless, argues sociologist Linda Gottfredson (1986), "Ignoring or denying the importance of group IQ differences does nothing to blunt their impact on society." We can all wish it were otherwise, but the fact is that the racial test score gap persists and that high-scoring people are more likely to attain high levels of education and pay than are low-scoring people. The hard truth: Using academic aptitude tests to select people for scholarships, school admissions, athletic eligibility, or jobs tends to exclude certain ethnic minorities. Racial-group gaps in test scores therefore raise a potent issue: Do they reflect racial gaps in inherent mental aptitude?

*Might test scores predict job attainment partly because such scores are used to admit people to educational opportunities?*

Let's start with a basic question: If heredity contributes to individual differences in intelligence, does it also contribute to group differences? It's possible, and a few psychologists speculate that differing climates and survival challenges could have produced an evolution of racial differences in reproductive strategies, aggressiveness, and intelligence (Lynn, 1991; Rushton, 1990). But one can accept genetic influences on individual differences while questioning genetic influences on group differences. Consider the following hypothetical case. Suppose that we were to study math aptitude in an American school and in a Japanese school. Suppose further that we were somehow able to determine that the differences among the children *within* each school were entirely due to heredity. If we then found that the Japanese children had higher scores than the American children, could we also attribute the differences *between* the two groups to heredity?

The answer to this question is plainly no, and geneticist Richard Lewontin (1976) shows why. If a mixture of seeds is sown in poor soil, the differing heights of the resulting plants will be the result of genetic differences among them. If seeds from the same mixture are sown in fertile soil, the differing heights of these plants will again be the result of genetic differences. But, as Figure 11–10 illustrates, the average height difference *between* the two groups of plants will be due to environmental soil differences. Thus, even if the heritability of a trait is extremely high *within* a particular group, differences in that trait *between* groups may nevertheless have environmental causes.

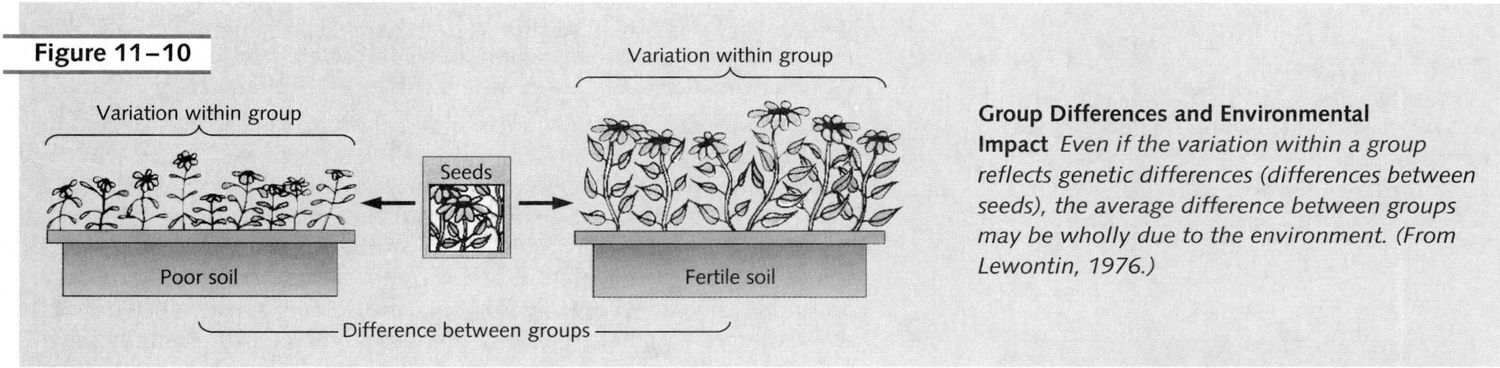


**Group Differences and Environmental Impact** *Even if the variation within a group reflects genetic differences (differences between seeds), the average difference between groups may be wholly due to the environment. (From Lewontin, 1976.)*

This point is so important, and so widely misunderstood, that it demands repeating. Consider: If each identical twin were exactly as tall as his or her co-twin, heritability would be 100 percent. Imagine that we then separated some young twins and gave only half of them a nutritious diet, and that the well-nourished twins all grew to be exactly 3 inches taller than their counterparts—an environmental effect comparable to that actually observed in Britain and America, where adolescents are several inches taller than their counterparts were half a century ago (Angoff, 1987; Lynn, 1987). What would the heritability of height be now for our well-nourished twins? Still 100 percent, because the variation in height within the group would remain entirely predictable from the heights of their malnourished identical siblings. So even perfect heritability within groups would not eliminate the possibility of a strong environmental impact on the group differences.

This is reflected in the belief of most expert psychologists that racial gaps in test scores are in large measure environmental (Snyderman & Rothman, 1987). To see why, let's consider the evidence:

*Recall that intelligence test score differences of 15 points can occur over generations of the same national group—clearly not a genetic effect. This suggests that a similar difference between two racial groups might also not be genetic.*

1. The impact of environment is evident in the mathematical achievement of Asian and American children. When psychologist Harold Stevenson and his co-workers (1986, 1990, 1992) studied a full range of schools in five comparable metropolitan areas—including Sendai in Japan, Taipei in Taiwan, and Minneapolis in the United States—they found that by fifth grade the Asian children scored significantly

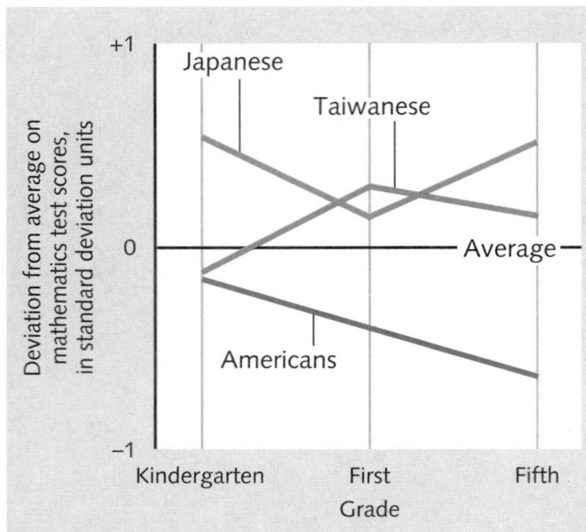


**Figure 11–11**

**Children's Mathematics Performance in Minneapolis (USA), Sendai (Japan), and Taipei (Taiwan)** *With time in school, math test scores by Minneapolis children fell further and further below the three-city average. (Adapted from Stevenson & others, 1986.)*

**The Culture of Scholarship** *The children of Indochinese refugee families studied by Nathan Caplan, Marcella Choy, and James Whitmore (1992) typically excel in school. On weekday nights after dinner, the family clears the table and begins homework. Family cooperation is valued and older siblings help younger ones.*

higher than the American children (Figure 11–11). In their first study, the best of the 20 American fifth-grade classes fell below the lowest of the Japanese classes. Among the top 100 students, 1 was American; among the lowest 100, 67 were American. (Although American students ranked lowest, American mothers were the most satisfied with their child's achievement and American students ranked first in self-rated math proficiency.)

Compared with elementary-school students in Minneapolis, those in Sendai and Taipei are nurtured in a more fertile academic soil. They attend school 30 percent more days per year, spend much more of their school day studying math, do much more homework, labor under great parental pressure and support, and more strongly believe that any student can be good at math if he or she works hard enough. These differences extend to high school, where U.S. students average 4 hours of homework per week and Japanese students average 19 hours (Juster & Stafford, 1991). Similarly, the current academic success rate of Asian-Americans is generally attributed not to heredity but to the values their culture places on hard work, family cohesiveness, and educational achievement as an escape from limits imposed by discrimination (Caplan & others, 1992).

2. The average European-American has grown up and been educated in a culture different from that of the average African-American. One attempt at equalizing educational opportunities—desegregation—had only slight effects on the school achievements of African-American children during its first 30 years. However, the benefits have been notable where desegregation began by first grade and extended over a number of years (Cook, 1984). As educational opportunities moved toward more equality between 1979 and 1993, the black-white difference in combined SAT scores (verbal + math) shrank by 48 points. Motivate children with rewards for correct answers on intelligence tests and the racial difference shrinks even more (Bradley-Johnson & others, 1984). Stanford psychologist Claude Steele (1990a, 1992) knows, both from experience and from a mountain of research, the barriers that limit African-American students' achievements. Those barriers, he reports, are not primarily lack of ability but self-perceptions shaped by a society that does not encourage these students to identify with schooling. Create "learning environments that affirm the potential, value, and prospects of black students," he notes, and their academic self-esteem and their grades and graduation rates also rise. Martin Luther King, Jr., anticipated this (Gardner, 1988). After hearing an address on education titled, "First, Teach Them to Read," he leaned over to a friend and said, "First, teach them to believe in themselves."

3. Further evidence of environmental impact on intelligence test scores comes from adoption studies. Consider: If black children were reared in privileged white middle-class homes, would their average intelligence score be closer to the average middle-class score? Sandra Scarr and Richard Weinberg (1976) studied 99 such children in Minneapolis. The average intelligence score of these children was 110, which is comparable to the average score of white children adopted into similarly advantaged families. Follow-up tests a decade later revealed "persisting beneficial effects of being reared in the culture of the school and tests" (Weinberg & others, 1990).

4. Recall that infants' preferences for novel stimuli help predict their future intelligence scores. There are, however, no known racial differences on this infant intelligence measure. White and black infants do equally well (Fagan, 1992).
5. Scarr and her colleagues (1977) also found that having more or less African ancestry bears no relation to scores on cognitive tests within the African-American population. If racial group differences in intelligence scores are due to racial differences per se, then people of uniform racial heritage should exhibit the racial difference more strongly. But in this study they didn't. Moreover, German children whose mothers were German and whose fathers were American servicemen stationed in Germany after World War II had nearly identical, average intelligence scores, regardless of whether their fathers were black or white (Mackenzie, 1984).
6. At different times in history, different ethnic groups have experienced golden ages, periods of remarkable achievement. Twenty-five hundred years ago it was the Greeks and the Egyptians, then the Romans; in the eighth and ninth centuries genius seemed to reside in the Arab world; 500 years ago it was the Aztec Indians and the peoples of northern Europe. Cultures rise and fall over centuries; genes do not. That fact makes it difficult to attribute a natural superiority to any race.

*"Do not obtain your slaves from Britain, because they are so stupid and so utterly incapable of being taught."*

Cicero, 106–43 B.C.

Despite all the evidence supporting environmental explanations, suppose that genetic differences *do* contribute to race and gender differences in test scores. Would it, should it, matter? Not to individuals, for whom what matters is their own potential. Not to potential employers, for knowing a person's race or gender does not reveal the individual applicant's potential. And not to social policy, for the impact of environmental disadvantages and cultural differences would unquestionably remain significant.

Finally, we must remember that *intelligence test scores reflect only one aspect of personal competence*. Other attributes—motivation, character, social skills, artistic talent, athletic ability, sensitivity, emotional maturity—matter. The competence that intelligence tests sample is important but far from all-inclusive. The spatial ability of the carpenter differs from the logical ability of the computer programmer, which differs from the verbal ability of the poet. Differences are not deficits. Because there are many ways of being successful, our personal and cultural differences—regardless of their origins—are valuable variations on the human theme of adaptability. Like ice cream, human traits and gifts come in many flavors.

*"Almost all the joyful things of life are outside the measure of IQ tests."*

Madeleine L'Engle
*A Circle of Quiet*, 1972

## The Question of Bias

Are intelligence tests biased? How we answer depends on what we mean by *bias*. One meaning is that the tests detect not only innate differences in intelligence but also differences caused by cultural experiences. In this sense, everyone agrees that intelligence tests are biased. No one claims that heritability is 100 percent responsible for any test score. An intelligence test measures a person's developed abilities at a particular time. These abilities necessarily reflect that person's experiences *and* environment. If people's experiences and backgrounds are unequal, the test's results will reflect those inequalities.

You may have read examples of intelligence test items that make middle-class assumptions (for example, that a cup goes with a saucer, or, as in one of the sample test items from the WAIS [Figure 11–1, page 364], that people buy fire insurance to protect the value of their homes and possessions). Do such items bias the test against those who do not use saucers and whose meager possessions hardly warrant the cost of fire insurance? Could such questions explain the racial differences in test performance? If so, are tests a discriminatory vehicle, consigning potentially capable children to dead-end classes and jobs (as the judge argued in the case of Larry and the six other children noted at this chapter's beginning)?

The defenders of aptitude testing respond that racial group differences occur on nonverbal items, such as counting digits backward, as well as on verbal items, such as vocabulary knowledge (Jensen, 1983). Moreover, they say that to blame the test for a group's lower scores is like blaming a messenger for bad news. Why blame the tests for exposing unequal experiences and opportunities? If, because of malnutrition, people were to suffer stunted growth, would one blame the measuring stick that reveals it? If unequal past experiences predict unequal future achievements, a valid aptitude test will detect such inequalities.

Another meaning of *bias* hinges on whether a test is less valid for some groups than for others. If the SAT accurately predicts the college achievement of one race but not that of another, then the test would be biased. The near-consensus among psychologists, as summarized by the National Research Council's Committee on Ability Testing, is that the major aptitude tests are *not* biased in this meaning of the term (Rowe & others, 1994; Wigdor & Garner, 1982). The predictive validity of the SAT or of a standard intelligence test is roughly the same for blacks and whites and for rich and poor. If an IQ score of 95 predicts C grades, the rough prediction usually applies to all ethnic and economic groups. Likewise, the question, "Name three parks in Manhattan" would put Texans at a disadvantage compared with New Yorkers. Like many aptitude test items, the question assumes a certain cultural background (Helms, 1992). But on a test for selecting Manhattan cab drivers, such a question might nevertheless be a valid predictor of job success—for both Texans and New Yorkers (Angoff, 1988).

So, it is possible for aptitude tests to be biased in one sense and not in another. Imagine a college—perhaps your own—where courses and teachers share a particular vocabulary and set of assumptions that make it difficult for people from a foreign culture to excel there. Test scores that predict success in such a school will be influenced by a person's cultural background. The test would therefore be culturally biased, because it mirrors the school's cultural bias. Yet the test might be an equally valid predictor of performance for all who take it, and in this sense be unbiased.

Are tests discriminatory? Again, the answer can be yes or no. In one sense, yes, their purpose is to discriminate—to distinguish among individuals. In another sense, their purpose is to reduce discrimination by reducing reliance on the subjective criteria that once were more crucial for school and job placement—criteria such as who you know, what you look like, or how much the interviewer happens to like "your kind of person." Banning aptitude tests would force the people who decide on admissions and jobs to rely more on other considerations, such as their personal opinions. Civil service tests, for example, discriminate among individuals, but they were devised to do so more fairly and objectively, by reducing the political, racial, and ethnic discrimination that preceded their use. So perhaps our aim should be to realize the benefits that Alfred Binet foresaw for intelligence tests—to enable schools to recognize who might best benefit from early intervention—while being alert to Binet's fear that test scores may be misinterpreted as literal measures of a person's worth and fixed potential.

## Summing Up

Because of its political and racial overtones, the debate over the nature and nurture of intelligence is an ongoing controversy.

**Genetic Influences** Studies of twins, family members, and adopted children together point to a significant hereditary contribution to intelligence scores. Heritability, the proportion of person-to-person variation attributable to genes, can vary depending on the range of populations and environments studied.

**Environmental Influences** These same studies, plus others that compare children reared in extremely impoverished or enriched environments or in different cultures, indicate that life experiences also significantly influence intelligence test performance.

**Group Differences in Intelligence Test Scores** Like individuals, groups vary in intelligence test scores. Hereditary variation *within* a group need not signify a hereditary explanation of *between*-group differences. In the case of the racial gaps in test scores, the evidence suggests that environmental differences are largely, perhaps entirely, responsible.

**The Question of Bias** Aptitude tests aim to predict how well a test-taker will perform in a given situation. So they are necessarily "biased" in the sense that they are sensitive to performance differences caused by cultural experience. But "bias" can also mean what psychologists commonly mean by the term—that a biased test predicts less accurately for one group than for another. In this sense of the term, most experts do not consider the major aptitude tests to be significantly biased.

## Terms and Concepts to Remember

**intelligence test** A method for assessing an individual's mental aptitudes and comparing them to those of others, using numerical scores.

### Assessing Intelligence

**mental age** A measure of intelligence test performance devised by Binet; the chronological age that most typically corresponds to a given level of performance. Thus, a child who does as well as the average 8-year-old is said to have a mental age of 8.

**Stanford-Binet** The widely used American revision (by Terman at Stanford University) of Binet's original intelligence test.

**intelligence quotient (IQ)** Defined originally as the ratio of mental age (ma) to chronological age (ca) multiplied by 100 (thus, $IQ = ma/ca \times 100$). On contemporary intelligence tests, the average performance for a given age is assigned a score of 100.

**aptitude tests** Tests designed to predict a person's future performance; aptitude is the capacity to learn.

**achievement tests** Tests designed to assess what a person has learned.

**Wechsler Adult Intelligence Scale (WAIS)** The current revision (WAIS-R) is the most widely used intelligence test; contains verbal and performance (nonverbal) subtests.

**standardization** Defining meaningful scores by comparison with the performance of a pretested "standardization group."

**normal curve** The symmetrical bell-shaped curve that describes the distribution of many physical and psychological attributes. Most scores fall near the average, and fewer and fewer scores lie near the extremes.

**reliability** The extent to which a test yields consistent results, as assessed by the consistency of scores on two halves of the test, on alternate forms of the test, or on retesting.

**validity** The extent to which a test measures or predicts what it is supposed to. (See also *content validity* and *predictive validity*.)

**content validity** The extent to which a test samples the behavior that is of interest (such as a driving test that samples driving tasks).

**criterion** The behavior (such as college grades) that a test (such as the SAT) is designed to predict; thus, the measure used in defining whether the test has predictive validity.

**predictive validity** The success with which a test predicts the behavior it is designed to predict; it is assessed by computing the correlation between test scores and the criterion behavior.

### What Is Intelligence?

**intelligence** The capacity for goal-directed and adaptive behavior. Involves the abilities to profit from experience, solve problems, reason, and successfully meet challenges and achieve goals.

**factor analysis** A statistical procedure that identifies clusters of related items (called *factors*) on a test; used to identify different dimensions of performance that underlie one's total score.

**general intelligence (*g*)** A general underlying intelligence factor believed by Spearman and others to be measured by every task on an intelligence test.

**savant syndrome** A condition in which a person otherwise limited in mental ability has an amazing specific skill, such as in computation or drawing.

### The Dynamics of Intelligence

**mental retardation** A condition of limited mental ability, as indicated by an intelligence score below 70, that produces difficulty in adapting to the demands of life; varies from mild to profound.

**Down syndrome** A condition of retardation and associated physical disorders caused by an extra chromosome in one's genetic makeup.

**creativity** The ability to produce novel and valuable ideas.

### Genetic and Environmental Influences on Intelligence

**heritability** The proportion of variation among individuals that we can attribute to genes. The heritability of a trait may vary, depending on the range of populations and environments studied.

## Critical Thinking Exercise

Now that you have read and reviewed Chapter 11, take your learning a step further by testing your critical thinking skills on the following creative problem solving exercise.

Carlton, who owns a publishing company that employs copy editors, personnel managers, and acquisitions editors, is fascinated by individual differences in intelligence. He believes that in each person there exists a measurable general mental capacity that forms the basis for all cognitive skills. Over the years, Carlton has made a study of the job performance of the people he hires. All applicants are required to take an intelligence test of his own invention: They are given a lengthy passage full of spelling, grammar, and punctuation errors, which they are expected to correct. To calculate the applicant's intelligence score, the number of proofreading errors missed is subtracted from the number of errors corrected. Over lunch with a friend one day, Carlton confides that he has had mixed results in predicting employee success. Whether people become successful employees or not seems to depend more on the type of job they are assigned than on their pre-employment test score.

1. What does Carlton mean by "intelligence"? What does his test actually measure?
2. Why doesn't Carlton's test measure what he wants it to measure?
3. What would be a more sensible way for Carlton to test potential employees?

Check your progress on becoming a critical thinker by comparing your answers to the sample answers found in Appendix B.

## For Further Reading

**Brody, N.** (1992). *Intelligence,* 2nd ed. San Diego: Academic Press.

*A balanced, scholarly, state-of-the-art review of human intelligence—its structure, origins, and consequences.*

**Fancher, R. E.** (1985). *The intelligence men.* New York: Norton.

*An account of past and current controversies about the nature of intelligence and the people who set out to measure it.*

**Gould, S. J.** (1981). *The mismeasure of man.* New York: Norton.

*Offers a provocative, engaging, and sharply critical look at the history of the intelligence-testing movement and its abuses.*

**Locurto, C.** (1991). *Sense and nonsense about IQ: The case for uniqueness.* New York: Praeger.

*Can intelligence be increased by smarter schooling and childrearing? Locurto critiques extreme hereditarianism and environmentalism answers.*

**Stevenson, H. W.** (1992). *Cultural lessons: A new look at the education of American children.* New York: Simon & Schuster.

*The leading researcher of Asian versus American academic achievements and values reflects on the implications of his studies.*

CHAPTER **12**

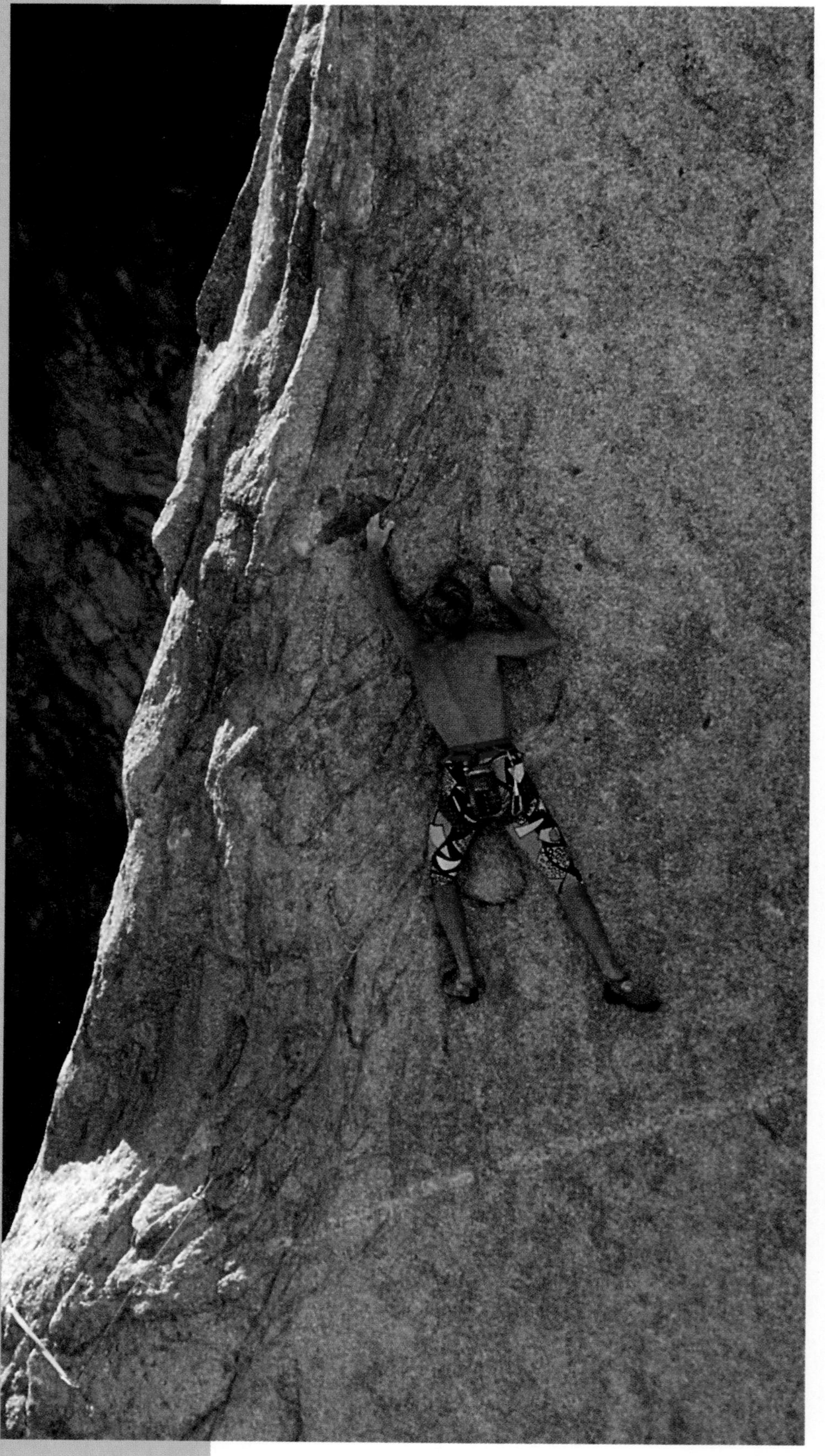

**Motivational Theories**

- Instinct Theory
- Drive-Reduction Theory
- Arousal Theory
- Incentive Theory
- A Hierarchy of Motives

**Hunger**

- The Physiology of Hunger
  - Body Chemistry
  - The Brain and Set Point
- The Psychology of Hunger
  - Culture and Hunger
  - External Incentives and Hunger
  - Eating Disorders

**Sexual Motivation**

- Describing Sexual Behavior
- The Physiology of Sex
  - The Sexual Response Cycle
  - Hormones and Sexual Behavior
- The Psychology of Sex
  - External Stimuli
  - Imaginative Stimuli
- Sexual Dysfunctions and Therapy
- Sexual Orientation
  - Understanding Sexual Orientation
- Sex and Human Values

**Achievement Motivation**

- Identifying Achievement Motivation
- Sources of Achievement Motivation
- Intrinsic Motivation and Achievement
- Motivating People
  - Cultivate Intrinsic Motivation
  - Attend to People's Motives
  - Set Specific, Challenging Goals
  - Choose an Appropriate Leadership Style

**The Need to Belong**

# Motivation

In everyday conversation, the question "What motivated you to do that?" is a way of asking "What *caused* your behavior? *Why* did you act that way?" To psychologists, a **motivation** is a need or desire that serves to *energize* behavior and to *direct* it toward a goal. Like intelligence, motivation is a hypothetical concept. We infer motivation from behaviors we observe. Consider motivation in these situations:

- David Mandel (1983), a former Nazi concentration camp inmate, recalls how a starving "father and son would fight over a piece of bread. Like dogs." One father, whose 20-year-old son stole his bread from under his pillow while he slept, went into a deep depression, asking over and again how his son could do such a thing. The next day the father died. "Hunger does something to you that's hard to describe. I can't believe it myself today, so how can I expect anyone else to understand it?"
- In the Old Testament's *Song of Solomon* love poems, a man and a woman express their intense sexual passion for one another. "I am sick with love," she declares. "O that his left hand were under my head, and that his right hand embraced me!" He, in turn, pronounces her "delectable." "You are stately as a palm tree, and your breasts are like its clusters. I say I will climb the palm tree and lay hold of its branches."
- In Texas, a school truant officer discovers Alfredo Gonzales, age 14, picking fruit and sends him off to the first day of school in his life. Although placed at the lowest skill level and paddled for asking questions in Spanish—he knows no English—Alfredo decides "I could do better." Indeed, today he is a highly educated college administrator who works to motivate youth to wake up, as he did, to "their own potential and to gain a desire to achieve it."
- Separated from friends or family—isolated in prison, alone at a new school, living in a foreign land—most people feel keenly their lost connections with important others. Wrenched from the only family she has ever known, 2½-year-old Jessica DeBoer sobs en route to her biological parents' home hundreds of miles away. As social animals, we all have something of Jessica within us—a sense of who we belong to, of who is "us."

In this chapter, we will explore motivation by focusing on these four motives—hunger, sex, achievement, and belonging. Although other identifiable motives exist (including thirst, curiosity, and a need for approval), a close look at these four reveals the interplay between nature (the physiological "push") and nurture (the cognitive and cultural "pulls").

## Motivational Theories

*Before considering hunger, sex, achievement, and belonging, let's step back and see how psychologists have understood motivation. Four perspectives have been influential: instinct theory (now replaced by an evolutionary perspective), drive reduction theory (emphasizing the inner pushes), arousal theory (emphasizing the urge for an optimum level of stimulation), and incentive theory (emphasizing the external pulls).*

**Same Motive; Different Wiring** *The more complex the nervous system, the more adaptable the organism. Both the weaver bird and the woman satisfy their need for shelter in ways that reflect their inherited capacities. The bird's behavior pattern is fixed; it can build only this kind of nest. The woman's behavior is flexible; she can learn whatever skills she needs to build a house.*

### Instinct Theory

Early in this century, as the influence of Charles Darwin's evolutionary theory grew, it became fashionable to classify all sorts of behaviors as instincts. If people criticized themselves, it was because of their "self-abasement instinct." If they boasted, it reflected their "self-assertion instinct." After scanning 500 books, one sociologist compiled a list of 5759 supposed human instincts! Before long, the instinct-naming fad collapsed under its own weight. For rather than *explaining* human behaviors, the early instinct theorists were simply *naming* them. It was like "explaining" a bright child's low grades by labeling the child an "underachiever." To name a behavior is *not* to explain it.

To qualify as an **instinct**, a complex behavior must have a fixed pattern throughout a species and be unlearned (Tinbergen, 1951). Such behaviors are common in other species (recall imprinting in birds and the return of salmon to their birthplace). Human behavior, too, exhibits certain innate tendencies, including simple fixed patterns such as an infant's rooting and sucking. Most psychologists, though, view human behavior as directed by physiological needs *and* psychological wants.

Although instinct theory failed to explain human motives, the underlying assumption that genes predispose species-typical behavior is as strong as ever. We saw this in Chapter 8's discussion of our biological predisposition to learn certain aversions. And we will see this in later discussions (Chapters 18 and 19) of how evolution might influence our helping behavior, our attraction to certain other people, and our gender differences, especially in sexual behavior.

### Drive-Reduction Theory

When the instinct theory of motivation collapsed, it was replaced by **drive-reduction theory**—the idea that a physiological need creates an aroused psychological state that *drives* the organism to reduce the need by, say, eating or drinking. With few exceptions, when a physiological need increases, so does a psychological drive.

The physiological aim of drive reduction is **homeostasis**—the maintenance of a steady internal state. An example of homeostasis (literally "staying the same") is the body's temperature-regulation system, which works much as a thermostat works to keep room temperature constant. Both systems operate through feedback loops: Sensors feed room temperature to a control device. If room temperature cools, the control device switches on the furnace. Likewise, if body temperature cools, blood vessels constrict to conserve warmth, and we feel driven to put on more clothes or seek a warmer environment. Similarly, if the water level in our cells drops, sensors detect our need for water and we feel thirsty.

## Arousal Theory

Rather than reduce a physiological need or minimize tension, some motivated behaviors *increase* arousal. Monkeys will monkey around trying to figure out how to unlock a latch that opens nothing, or how to open a window that allows them to see outside their room (Butler, 1954). The motivation to explore drives the 9-month-old infant who investigates every accessible corner of the house. It drives the scientists whose work this text discusses. And it drives the voyagers who first ventured across and beneath the oceans. Asked why he wanted to climb Mount Everest, George Mallory answered, "Because it is there." Those who, like Mallory, enjoy high arousal are most likely to enjoy intense music, novel foods, and risky behaviors (Zuckerman, 1979).

**Driven by Curiosity** *Baby monkeys and small people are fascinated by things they've never handled before. Their drive to explore the relatively unfamiliar is one of several motives that do not fill any obvious physiological need.*

Recall, too, the experiments on sensory restriction described in Chapter 5. The peace and quiet of sensory monotony sensitized the subjects to any available stimulation. Despite having all our biological needs satisfied, we feel driven to experience stimulation. Without it, we feel bored and look for a way to increase arousal to some optimum level. With too much stimulation, we feel stressed and look for a way to decrease arousal.

## Incentive Theory

Not only are we *pushed* by our "need" to reduce drives and achieve optimum arousal, we also are *pulled* by **incentives**—positive or negative stimuli that lure or repel us. This is one way our individual learning histories influence our motives. Depending on our learning, the aroma of fresh roasted peanuts (or toasted ants), the sight of someone we find attractive, and the threat of disapproval can all motivate our behavior. Our internal needs energize and direct our behavior, but so do these external incentives. When there is both a need and an incentive, we feel driven. The food-deprived person who smells bread baking feels a hunger for it. For each motive, we can therefore ask, "How is it pushed by our inborn physiological needs and pulled by incentives in the environment?"

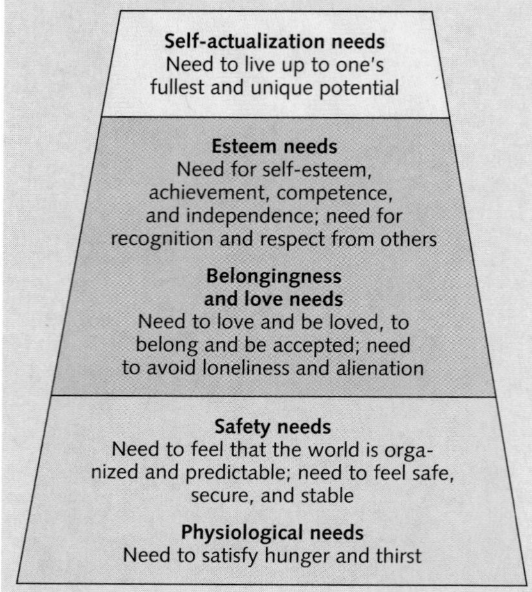

Self-actualization needs
Need to live up to one's fullest and unique potential

Esteem needs
Need for self-esteem, achievement, competence, and independence; need for recognition and respect from others

Belongingness and love needs
Need to love and be loved, to belong and be accepted; need to avoid loneliness and alienation

Safety needs
Need to feel that the world is organized and predictable; need to feel safe, secure, and stable

Physiological needs
Need to satisfy hunger and thirst

**Figure 12–1**

**Maslow's Hierarchy of Needs** *Once our lower-level needs are met, we are prompted to satisfy our higher-level needs. (From Maslow, 1970.)*

## A Hierarchy of Motives

Some needs take priority over others. At this moment, with your needs for air and water satisfied, other motives—such as your desire to achieve—energize and direct your behavior. Let your need for water go unsatisfied and your thirst will preoccupy you. But if you were deprived of air, your thirst would disappear.

These examples illustrate how the particular needs that motivate our behavior depend on which needs are unmet. Abraham Maslow (1970) proposed one such **hierarchy of needs** (Figure 12–1). At its base are our physiological needs, such as for food, water, and shelter. Only if these needs are met are we prompted to meet our need for safety, and then to meet the uniquely human needs to give and receive love and to enjoy self-esteem. Beyond this, said Maslow (1971), lies the highest of human needs: to actualize one's full potential. (More on self-esteem and self-actualization in Chapter 14, Personality.)

Maslow's hierarchy is somewhat arbitrary. Moreover, the order of such needs is not universally fixed. People have starved themselves to make a political statement. Nevertheless, the simple idea that, until they are satisfied, some motives are more compelling than others, provides a framework for thinking about motivation. Let's now consider the four representative motives, beginning at the basic, physiological level with hunger and working up through sexual motivation to higher-level motives, such as the needs to achieve and belong. At each level, we will see how psychological factors interact with what is physiologically given.

## Summing Up

Motivation is the energizing and directing of behavior, the force behind our yearning for food, our longing for sexual intimacy, our desire to achieve, our need to belong.

**Instinct Theory** Under Darwin's influence, early theorists viewed behavior as controlled by biological forces, such as instincts. But when it became clear that people were naming, not explaining, various behaviors by calling them instincts, psychologists turned to a drive-reduction theory of motivation.

**Drive-Reduction Theory** Most physiological needs create aroused psychological states that drive us to reduce or satisfy needs. The aim of drive reduction is internal stability, or homeostasis. Thus, drive reduction motivates survival behaviors, such as eating and drinking.

**Arousal Theory** Rather than reducing a physiological need or tension state, some motivated behaviors increase arousal. Curiosity-driven behaviors, for example, suggest that too little as well as too much stimulation can motivate people to seek an optimum level of arousal.

**Incentive Theory** Not only are we pushed by our internal drives, we are pulled by external incentives. Depending on our personal and cultural experiences, some stimuli (for example, certain foods or erotic images) will arouse our desires.

**A Hierarchy of Motives** Maslow's hierarchy of needs expresses the idea that, until satisfied, some motives are more compelling than others.

## Hunger

*Hunger, like so much of our experience, reflects the interplay of our physiology and our learning. Blood sugar levels are monitored by the brain's hypothalamus, which regulates hunger and body weight. But there's more to hunger than the hypothalamus, for some people are especially responsive to external food cues, and others suffer eating disorders.*

A vivid demonstration of the supremacy of physiological needs followed reports of starvation in World War II prison camps and occupied areas. To learn more about the results of semistarvation, scientist Ancel Keys and his colleagues (1950) solicited volunteers for an experiment. From among the more than 100 conscientious objectors to the war who applied, they selected 36 men. First, they fed the men just enough to maintain their initial weight. Then, for 6 months, they cut this food level in half.

The effects soon became visible. Without thinking about it, the men began conserving energy; they appeared listless and apathetic. Their body weights dropped rapidly, eventually stabilizing at about 25 percent below their starting weights. The psychological effects were even more dramatic. Consistent with Maslow's idea of a need hierarchy, the men became obsessed with food. They talked food. They daydreamed food. They collected recipes, read cookbooks, and feasted their eyes on delectable forbidden foods. Meanwhile, they lost their former interests in sex and social activities. They became preoccupied with their unfulfilled basic needs. As one subject reported, "If we see a show, the most interesting part of it is contained in scenes where people are eating. I couldn't laugh at the funniest picture in the world, and love scenes are completely dull."

*"Nobody wants to kiss when they are hungry."*
Dorothea Dix, 1801–1887

**GARFIELD**

GARFIELD © 1986 PAWS, INC. Dist. by UNIVERSAL PRESS SYNDICATE. Reprinted with permission. All rights reserved.

### The Physiology of Hunger

The hunger Keys's semistarved subjects felt was the response of a homeostatic system designed to maintain normal body weight and an adequate supply of nutrients. But precisely what is it that triggers hunger? Is it the pangs of an empty stomach? So it feels. And so it seemed after A. L. Washburn, working with Walter Cannon (Cannon & Washburn, 1912), intentionally swallowed a balloon. When inflated in his stomach, the balloon transmitted his stomach contractions to a recording device (Figure 12–2). While his stomach was being monitored, Washburn pressed a key each time he felt hungry. The result: Washburn was having stomach contractions whenever he felt hungry. (Some diet aids reduce this empty stomach feeling by filling the stomach with indigestible fibers that swell as they absorb water.)

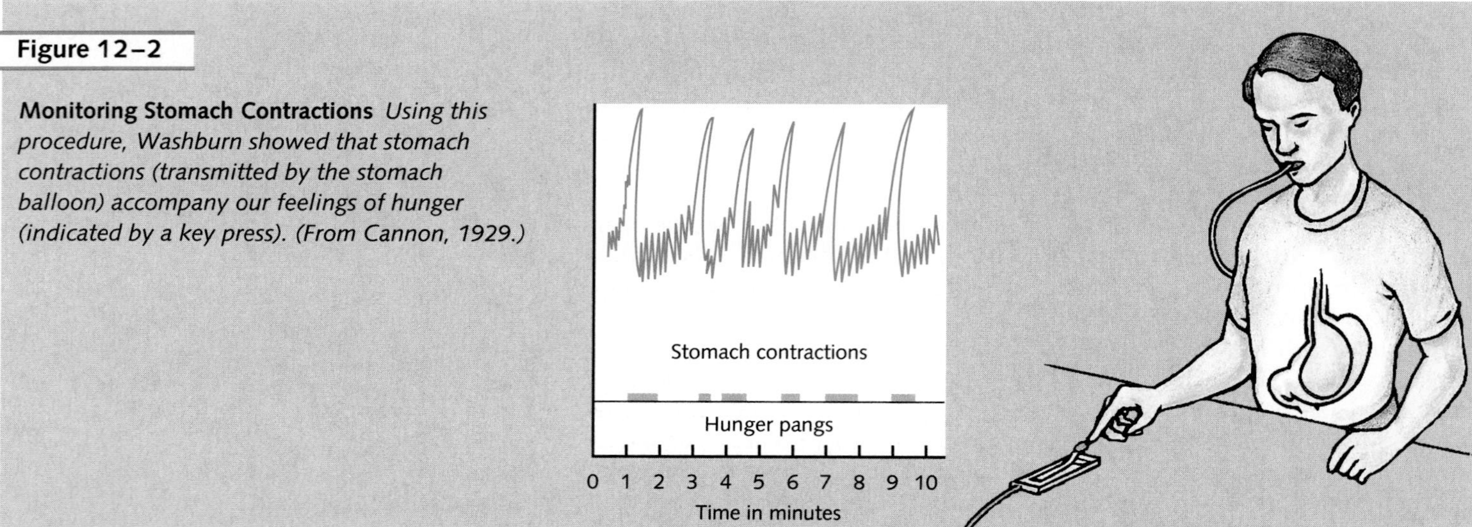


**Figure 12–2**

**Monitoring Stomach Contractions** *Using this procedure, Washburn showed that stomach contractions (transmitted by the stomach balloon) accompany our feelings of hunger (indicated by a key press). (From Cannon, 1929.)*

Alas, there is more to hunger than the pangs of an empty stomach. Researchers discovered this a quarter-century later when they removed some rats' stomachs and attached their esophagi to their small intestines (Tsang, 1938). Without stomach pangs, did hunger persist? Did the rats continue to eat regularly? Indeed they did. Hunger persists similarly in humans whose ulcerated or cancerous stomachs have been removed. In fact, one can feel hungry even on a full stomach. Animals that fill their stomachs by eating low-calorie food will eat more than animals that consume a less filling, high-calorie diet (McHugh & Moran, 1978). If the pangs of an empty stomach are not the only source of our hunger, what else is involved?

## Body Chemistry

Changes in body chemistry also affect hunger. People and other animals automatically regulate their caloric intake to maintain a stable body weight. This suggests that the body is somehow, somewhere keeping tabs on its available resources. One such resource is the blood sugar **glucose**. Increases in the hormone *insulin* diminish blood glucose, partly by converting it to stored fat, thus causing hunger to increase.

Body chemistry also influences taste preferences. When feeling tense or depressed, do you crave sweet or starchy carbohydrate-laden foods? Carbohydrates help boost levels of the neurotransmitter serotonin, which has calming effects. Given the drug fenfluramine, which similarly increases serotonin, carbohydrate cravers lose their cravings. This suggests that stress-related cravings might be treatable by providing food substitutes that mimic biochemical effects (Hall, 1987).

## The Brain and Set Point

Low blood glucose is a source of hunger. But you do not consciously feel your blood chemistry. Rather, the brain automatically monitors information on your body's internal state. Signals from the stomach, the intestines, and the liver (indicating whether glucose is being deposited or withdrawn) all signal the brain to motivate eating or not. But where in the brain are these messages integrated? During the 1940s and 1950s, researchers located hunger controls within the hypothalamus, a small but complex neural traffic intersection buried deep in the brain (Figure 12–3).

Actually, there are two distinct hypothalamic centers that help control eating. Activity along the sides of the hypothalamus, known as the *lateral hypothalamus*, or *LH*, brings on hunger. When electrically stimulated there, a well-fed animal will begin to eat; when the area is destroyed, even a starving animal has no interest in food. Activity in the lower middle of the hypothalamus, known as the *ventromedial hypothalamus*, or *VMH*, depresses hunger. Stimulate this area and an animal will stop eating; destroy it and the animal's stomach and intestines will process food more rapidly, causing it to eat more often and to become grossly fat (Duggan & Booth, 1986; Hoebel & Teitelbaum, 1966).

How do these complementary areas of the hypothalamus work? One theory is that they influence how much glucose is converted to fat and how much is left available to fuel immediate activity (thus minimizing hunger). After VMH lesions, rats produce more fat and release less fat as energy, rather like a miser who runs a bit of extra money to the bank and resists taking any out. Thus, the rat eats to keep enough calories in the blood to meet its energy requirements (Pinel, 1993).

An older theory is that manipulating these two areas of the hypothalamus alters the body's "weight thermostat," which predisposes us to keep our body at a particular weight level, called its **set point** (Keesey & Corbett, 1983). When semistarved rats fall below their normal weight, biological pressures act to restore the lost weight: Hunger increases and energy expenditure decreases. If body weight rises—as happens when rats are force-fed—hunger decreases and energy expenditure increases. Even VMH-lesioned rats will stop overeating, once fat enough. This stable weight toward which semistarved and overstuffed rats return is their set point.

Some researchers believe that slow, sustained changes in body weight can, however, alter one's set point. Other researchers now doubt that the body has a precise set point that drives hunger. Hunger, they say, is determined by too many factors, including learned incentives, for that to be true. Body weight settles around a level at which all these factors reach an equilibrium.

Despite the day-to-day variations in our eating, our bodies are astonishingly good at regulating our weight, much better than we could be through conscious efforts to control food intake precisely. Over the next 40 years you will eat about 20 tons of food. If during those years you increase your daily intake by just .01 ounce more than required for your energy needs, you will gain 24 pounds (Martin & others, 1991). With astonishing precision, our bodies automatically balance energy intake and expenditure.

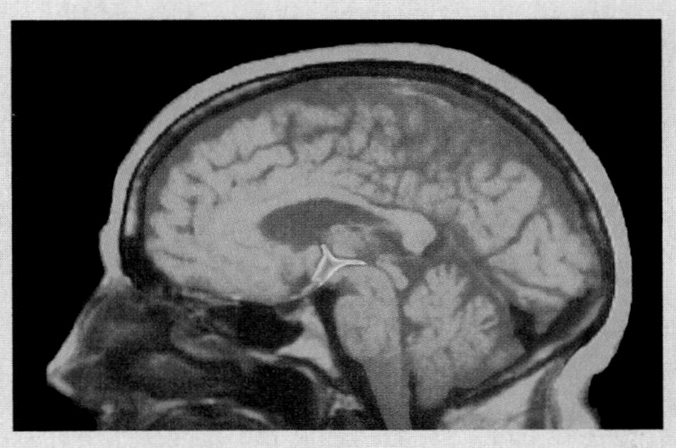

**Figure 12–3**

**The Hypothalamus** *As we saw in Chapter 2, the hypothalamus performs various body maintenance functions, including control of hunger. Blood vessels supply the hypothalamus, enabling it to respond to our current blood chemistry as well as to incoming neural information about the body's state.*

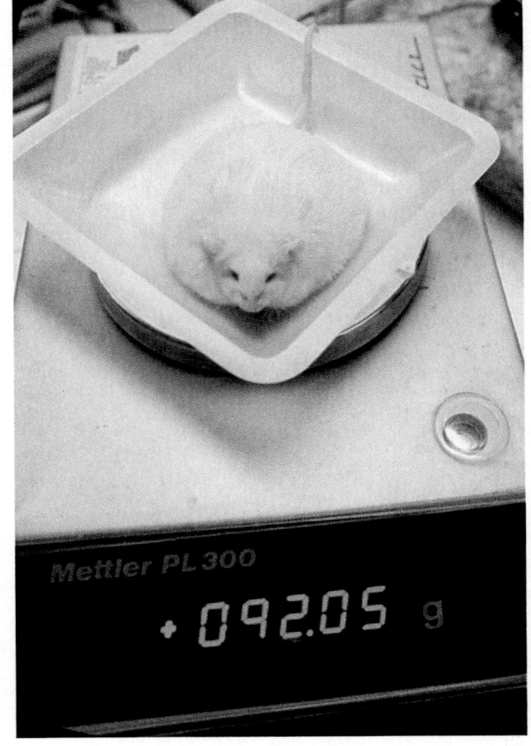


**Evidence for the Brain's Control of Eating** *A bilateral lesion of the ventromedial area of the hypothalamus (VMH) caused this rat's weight to triple. At 92.05 grams, it weighs about three times more than normal.*

Our bodies regulate weight much as rats' bodies do—through the control of food intake and energy output. If our body weight rises above our set point, we tend not to feel so hungry; if our weight drops below, we tend to eat more. To maintain its set-point weight, the body also adjusts its **metabolic rate**—its resting rate of energy expenditure. By the end of their 24 weeks of semistarvation, the subjects in the World War II experiment had stabilized at three-quarters of their normal weight—while eating half what they previously did. The stabilization resulted from reduced energy expenditure, achieved partly by physical lethargy and partly by a 29 percent drop in their resting metabolic rate.

## The Psychology of Hunger

Our eagerness to eat is both pushed by our physiological state—our body chemistry and hypothalamic activity—and pulled by our learned responses to external stimuli.

Psychologists have studied how we eat and what we like to eat. As hunger diminishes, eating behavior changes. Eliot Stellar (1985) discovered this after outfitting people with a special dental retainer engineered to record each chew and swallow. The device answers questions about human eating that you may never have thought to ask. During a meal of sandwich snacks, how often does the average person swallow? Every 14 seconds. How many chews on average per swallow? 19. How fast do people chew? 1.8 chews per second. As the meal progresses and both hunger and food tastiness decrease, people chew more. Ironically, the better a food tastes, the *less* time people leave it in their mouths.

### Culture and Hunger

Our preferences for sweet and salty tastes are genetic and universal. Other tastes are conditioned, as when people given highly salted foods develop a liking for excess salt (Beauchamp, 1987) or when people develop an

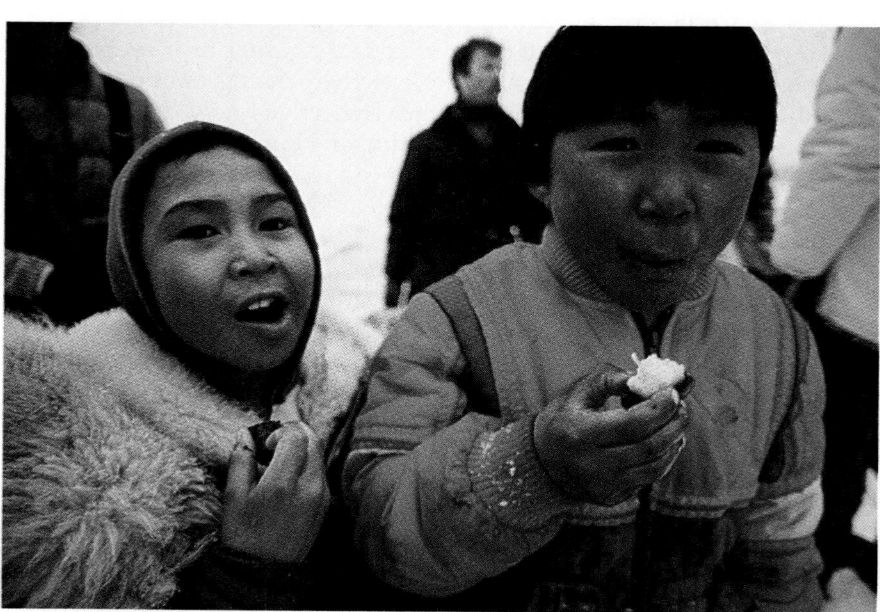

**An Acquired Taste** *For Alaskan Eskimos, but not for most other North Americans, whale blubber is a tasty treat. People everywhere learn to enjoy the fatty, bitter, or irritating foods that are prescribed by their culture.*

aversion to a food eaten before becoming violently ill. (The frequency of children's illnesses provides many chances for them to learn food aversions.)

Culture affects taste, too. Bedouins enjoy eating the eye of a camel, which most North Americans would find repulsive. Similarly, most North Americans shun dog, rat, and horse meat, all of which are prized elsewhere, but welcome beef, which Hindus wouldn't think of eating. Such preferences vary with exposure (Pliner & Pelchat, 1991; Rozin, 1976). We humans have a natural dislike of many things unfamiliar, including novel foods (especially novel animal-based rather than vegetarian foods). This "neophobia" surely was adaptive for our ancestors, serving to protect them from potentially toxic substances. In experiments, people have tried novel fruit drinks or ethnic foods. With repeated exposure, their appreciation for the new taste typically increases; moreover, exposure to one set of novel foods increases willingness to try another (Pliner 1982; Pliner & others, 1993).

**PEANUTS**

Drawing by Charles Schulz; © 1989 United Feature Syndicate, Inc. Reprinted by permission of UFS, Inc.

### External Incentives and Hunger

Like Pavlov's dogs, people learn to salivate in anticipation of appealing foods. Some people are especially responsive to appealing foods. When food is abundant, such people tend to gain the most weight.

Consider the 9- to 15-year-old girls studied by Judith Rodin and Joyce Slochower (1976) at an 8-week summer camp. During the first week of camp, some girls could not resist munching readily visible M&Ms even after a full meal. These girls were typical of a category the researchers called *externals*—people whose eating is triggered more by the presence of food than by internal factors. In the 7 weeks that followed, the "external" girls gained the most weight.

In a delicious demonstration of how internal and external factors interact, Rodin (1984) invited other research subjects to her laboratory for lunch after they went 18 hours without food. While blood samples were being taken, a large, juicy steak was wheeled in, crackling as it finished grilling. As the hungry subjects sat watching, hearing, and smelling the soon-to-be-eaten steak, Rodin monitored their rising blood insulin levels and their accompanying feelings of hunger. When stimulated by the sight, sound, and aroma of the steak, "externals" had the greatest insulin increase and accompanying hunger response. This illustrates how certain individuals' psychological experience of an external incentive (the steak) can affect their internal physiological state.

### Eating Disorders

Psychological influences on eating behavior are strikingly evident in those for whom normal homeostatic pressures are overwhelmed by a motive for thinness. Consider two eating disorder cases.

> Mary is a 5′ 3″ 15-year-old who, having reached 100 pounds, decided she needed to lose weight to enhance her attractiveness. After gradually reducing her food intake to a few vegetables a day and then adding a vigorous exercise program, she now weighs a mere 80 pounds. Yet she still feels "fat" and plans to continue dieting. Mary has been having difficulty sleeping, has at times been depressed, and no longer has regular menstrual periods. She is socially inactive and seldom dates, but she is very successful academically. Mary does not regard herself as ill or needing treatment.

Alice is a 5′ 9″, 160-pound 17-year-old who says she has always been a little chubby. For the last 5 years, she has often eaten in binges, followed by vomiting. She will eat a quart of ice cream or an entire pie and then, to control her weight, make herself vomit in secret. Alice wants to date, but she doesn't because she is ashamed of her looks. She has at times taken diet pills to try to lose weight.

Mary is diagnosed as having **anorexia nervosa**—a disorder in which a person becomes significantly underweight (typically, 15 percent or more) yet feels fat and fears becoming obese. Even when emaciated, the person continues to limit food intake. The disorder usually develops in adolescence, 9 times out of 10 in females.

Alice's condition, which is more common, is **bulimia nervosa**—a disorder marked by repeated binge-purge episodes of overeating followed by vomiting or laxative use. Bulimia patients eat as some alcoholics drink—in spurts, sometimes under the influence of friends who also are binging (Crandall, 1988). Most binge-purge eaters are women in their late teens or twenties. Like those with anorexia, they are preoccupied with food, are fearful of becoming overweight, and are depressed or anxious (Hinz & Williamson, 1987). The depression and shame are felt most keenly during and following binges. About half of those with anorexia also display the binge-purge-depression symptoms of bulimia. But unlike anorexia, bulimia is marked by weight fluctuations within or above normal ranges. This makes the condition easy to hide.

Researchers report that the families of bulimia patients have a higher-than-usual incidence of alcoholism, obesity, and depression. Anorexia patients often come from middle- and upper-class families that are competitive, high-achieving, and protective (Pate & others, 1992; Yates, 1989, 1990). They set high standards, fret about falling short of expectations, and are intensely concerned with how others perceive them (Heatherton & Baumeister, 1991; Striegel-Moore & others, 1993). To switch off painful self-awareness, they may focus on the immediate sensations of binge eating.

Genetics also may influence susceptibility to eating disorders. When one twin has bulimia, the chances of the other twin's sharing the disorder are much greater if they are identical rather than fraternal twins (Fichter & Noegel, 1990). People with eating disorders may also have abnormal supplies of certain neurotransmitters that put them at risk for anxiety or depression (Fava & others, 1989).

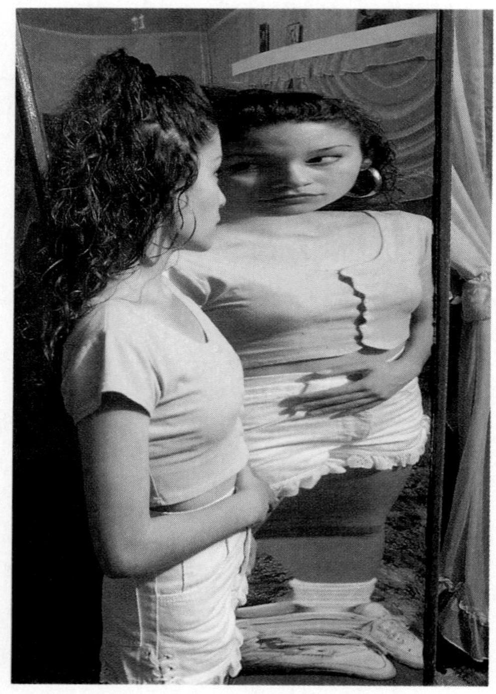

**A Cultural Obsession** *Millions of women in today's developed nations fear that they look like this distorted image. The rise of the cultural ideal of a "fat-free" female body has been accompanied by an explosion of eating disorders among young women.*

There is, however, a cultural explanation for the fact that anorexia and bulimia occur mostly in women and mostly in weight-conscious cultures. Mothers of girls with eating disorders are themselves often focused on their own weight and on their daughter's weight and appearance (Pike & Rodin, 1991). Anorexia nervosa always begins as a weight-loss diet, and the self-induced vomiting of bulimics nearly always begins after a dieter has broken diet restrictions and gorged. Although ideals of beauty have varied over the centuries, women in every era have struggled to make their bodies conform to the ideal of their day. Thus, the sickness of today's eating disorders lies not just within the victims but also within their weight-obsessed culture—a culture that says, in countless ways, "Fat is bad," that motivates millions of women to be "always dieting," and that encourages eating binges by pressuring women to live in a constant state of semistarvation. "You can't be too rich or too thin," declared the Duchess of Windsor. As obesity researchers Susan Wooley and Orland Wooley (1983) noted, "An increasingly stringent cultural standard of thinness for women has been accompanied by a steadily increasing incidence of serious eating disorders in women."

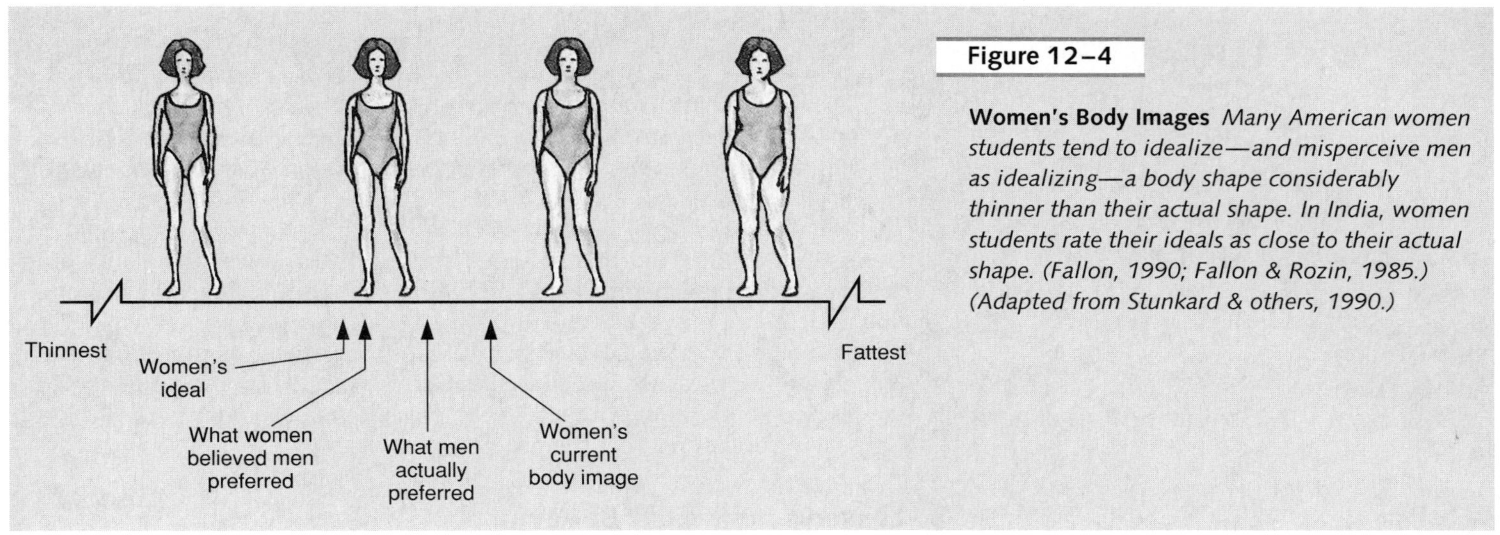


**Figure 12–4**

**Women's Body Images** *Many American women students tend to idealize—and misperceive men as idealizing—a body shape considerably thinner than their actual shape. In India, women students rate their ideals as close to their actual shape. (Fallon, 1990; Fallon & Rozin, 1985.) (Adapted from Stunkard & others, 1990.)*

Consistent with this explanation, the extremely thin women pictured in fashion magazines and advertisements distort women's perceptions of what men find attractive. In one study of nearly 500 University of Pennsylvania students, April Fallon and Paul Rozin (1985) found that women's ideal body weight was less than their current weight. Moreover, the weight they thought men preferred was less than the weight men actually preferred (Figure 12–4). The researchers found no such discrepancies in the men's self-ratings. Men more often judged their current weight, their ideal weight, and the weight they thought women preferred as all quite similar. Women's greater self-dissatisfaction stems from their perceiving their cheeks, waist, and hips as looking larger than they do (Thompson, 1986). Women with low self-esteem are particularly likely to have a negative body image and are especially vulnerable to eating disorders (Mintz & Betz, 1986; Strauman & others, 1991; Striegel-Moore & others, 1986).

*The Barbie fashion doll's proportions: 36–18–33 (*Life*, 1991).*

## Summing Up

**The Physiology of Hunger** Hunger's inner push primarily originates not from the stomach's contractions but from variations in body chemistry. For example, we are likely to feel hungry when our glucose levels are low. This information is monitored by the hypothalamus, which regulates the body's weight as it influences our feelings of hunger and satiety. To maintain weight, the body also adjusts its metabolic rate of energy expenditure.

**The Psychology of Hunger** Our preferences for certain tastes are partly genetic and universal, but also partly learned in a cultural context. Especially in "external" people, the sight and smell of food can trigger hunger and eating, partly by stimulating a rise in insulin level. The impact of psychological factors, such as challenging family settings and weight-obsessed societal pressures, on eating behavior is dramatic in people with anorexia nervosa, who keep themselves on near-starvation rations, and those with bulimia nervosa, who binge and purge in secret.

# Sexual Motivation

*The psychology of sexual motivation seeks to describe, explain, and treat sexually motivated behaviors. As with hunger, sex is a physiologically based motive that is steered by learning and by one's values. New evidence suggests that sexual orientation is subject to genetic influences via prenatal hormones and the hypothalamus.*

*"I lose my respect for the man who can make the mystery of sex the subject of a coarse jest, yet, when you speak earnestly and seriously on the subject, is silent."*

Henry David Thoreau
*Journal*, 1852

Sex is part of life. Had this not been so for all your ancestors, you would not be reading this book. Sexual motivation is nature's clever way of making people procreate, thus enabling our species' survival. When two people feel attracted, they hardly stop to think of themselves as guided by their genes. As the pleasure we take in eating is nature's inventive method of getting our body nourishment, so the pleasure of sex is our genes' way of preserving and spreading themselves.

## Describing Sexual Behavior

Before looking at what energizes and directs sexual arousal, let's consider the behavior patterns that a theory of sexual motivation must explain.

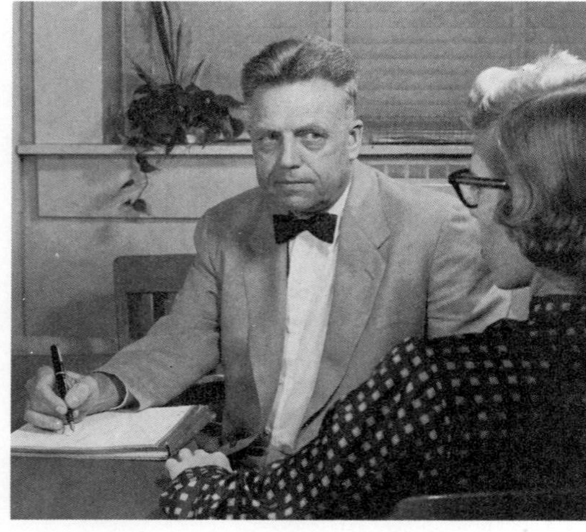

**Alfred Kinsey** *The eminent biologist, shown here conducting one of his interviews, did not begin with sexually explicit questions. Rather, he first helped people feel at ease by asking nonthreatening questions about family background, health, and education.*

Unable to answer his students' questions about people's sexual practices, Indiana University biologist Alfred Kinsey and his colleagues (1948, 1953) set out to find some answers. Kinsey's confidential interviews with 18,000 people—85 percent conducted by himself or his associate Wardell Pomeroy—asked more than 350 rapid fire questions. Social scientists were quick to point out what Kinsey readily acknowledged—that his nonrandom sample contained an overrepresentation of well-educated, white, urban residents of Indiana, Illinois, and several Eastern states. Nevertheless, his statistics-laden volumes became best-sellers. Here readers learned the surprising news that most of the men and nearly half the women reported having had premarital sexual intercourse; that a majority of women and virtually all men reported masturbating; and that women who reported masturbating to orgasm before marriage seldom had difficulties experiencing orgasm after marriage. One could also find evidence that sexual behavior is enormously varied. Kinsey found some men and women who said they had never had an orgasm, and others who said they had four or more a day. For those who evaluate themselves by comparisons with others, Kinsey's findings—and others showing wide variations in "normal" sexual behavior around the world—are reassuring. Given the range of sex drives and the variety of sexual behaviors, our own sexual interests probably fall well within the range of "normal."

Because we do not know whether Kinsey's sample accurately represented the nation's sexual practices in the 1940s, let alone those of today, it can be misleading to report his precise findings. Moreover, Kinsey and Pomeroy's questioning encouraged (some say, demanded) admission of sexual activity. They never asked subjects *whether* they had engaged in a particular activity, they asked them *when* they had first engaged in it (thus making it easier for people to divulge their behavior). But Pomeroy (1972, pp. 113, 124, 127) reported that he and Kinsey "went on the broad assumption that everybody had done everything." If Kinsey or Pomeroy doubted a subject's denial, they might respond, "Yes, I know you have never done that, but how old were you the *first* time you did it?" or even "Look, I don't give a damn what you've done, but if you don't tell me the straight of it, it's better that we stop this history right here. Now, how old were you the first time this or that happened?"

By today's standards of random sampling and nonleading questioning,

Kinsey's tactics, and thus his results, are suspect. Yet his surveys were surely less misleading than some of the haphazard sexual surveys that have been reported more recently in the popular press. Recall from Chapter 1 that when popular "sex reports" begin with a biased sample of people (such as subscribers to selected magazines) and receive replies from only 3 percent of this nonrandom sample, there is good reason to doubt the generality of their findings.

Better information is now becoming available. In the United States, for example, three new surveys of randomly sampled adults counter the media image of rampant marital infidelity—an image reinforced by media psychologist Joyce Brothers' (1990) pronouncement that two-thirds of married men and half of married women have affairs. Actually, in a recent Gallup survey 9 in 10 married adults claimed to have had sex only with their spouse during their present marriage (Greeley, 1991). When the National Opinion Research Center added an anonymous, self-administered, return envelope sex questionnaire to their annual survey, they found that during the past year only "1.5 percent of married people [had] a sex partner other than their spouse" (Smith, 1990). Similar results come from a recent government-funded national sex survey (Leigh & others, 1993). Faithful attractions greatly outnumber fatal attractions. And disapproval of extramarital sex, at 91 percent, runs as high as ever among adult Americans (Smith, 1994).

Eager to understand why the AIDS virus has spread more among some groups than others, researchers undertook new sex surveys at the beginning of this decade. The World Health Organization, for example, is conducting the first-ever global survey of human sexuality, based on interviews with some 2000 people in each of 20 countries. Researchers hope that results from such surveys will help us better understand the behaviors that spread AIDS and other sexually transmitted diseases.

## The Physiology of Sex

Like hunger, sexual arousal depends on the interplay of internal and external stimuli. To understand sexual motivation, we must consider both.

### The Sexual Response Cycle

The headlines created by Kinsey's 1940s surveys reappeared after some 1960s studies in which scientists recorded the physiological responses of volunteers who masturbated or had intercourse. With the help of 382 female and 312 male volunteers—a somewhat atypical sample, consisting only of people able and willing to display arousal and orgasm while being observed in a laboratory—gynecologist-obstetrician William Masters and his collaborator Virginia Johnson (1966) monitored or filmed more than 10,000 sexual "cycles."

Their description of the **sexual response cycle** identified four stages, similar in men and women. During the initial *excitement phase*, the genital areas become engorged with blood, causing the man's penis to become partially erect and the woman's clitoris to swell and the inner lips covering her vagina to open up. Her vagina also expands and secretes lubricant, and her breasts and nipples may enlarge.

In the *plateau phase*, excitement peaks as breathing, pulse, and blood pressure rates continue to increase. The penis becomes fully engorged and some fluid (frequently containing enough live sperm to enable conception) may appear at the tip of the penis. Vaginal secretion continues to increase, the clitoris retracts, and orgasm feels imminent.

Masters and Johnson observed muscle contractions all over the body during *orgasm*; these were accompanied by further increases in breathing, pulse, and blood pressure rates. A woman's arousal and orgasm facilitates conception by helping propel semen from the penis, positioning the uterus to receive sperm, and drawing the sperm further inward (Sarnoff & Sarnoff, 1989). In the excitement of the moment, men and women are hardly aware of all this but are more aware of their rhythmic genital contractions that create a pleasurable feeling of sexual release. The feeling apparently is much the same for both sexes. In one study, a panel of experts could not reliably distinguish between descriptions of orgasm written by men and those written by women (Vance & Wagner, 1976).

After orgasm, the body gradually returns to its unaroused state as the engorged genital blood vessels release their accumulated blood—relatively quickly if orgasm has occurred, relatively slowly otherwise. (It's like the nasal tickle that goes away rapidly if you have sneezed, slowly otherwise.) During this *resolution phase*, the male enters a **refractory period**, lasting from a few minutes to a day or more, during which he is incapable of another orgasm. A female does not have so lengthy a refractory period, which may make it possible for her to have another orgasm if restimulated during or soon after resolution.

### Hormones and Sexual Behavior

Sex hormones have two effects: They direct the development of male and female sex characteristics, and (especially in nonhuman animals) they activate sexual behavior. In most mammals, nature neatly synchronizes sex with fertility. The female becomes sexually receptive ("in heat") when production of the female hormone **estrogen** peaks at ovulation. (In experiments, researchers simulate this by injecting female animals with estrogen.) Male hormone levels are more constant, and researchers cannot so easily manipulate the sexual behavior of male animals by hormone treatments (Feder, 1984). Nevertheless, castrated male rats—having lost their testes, which manufacture the male sex hormone testosterone—gradually lose much of their interest in receptive females, and they gradually regain it if injected with testosterone.

Hormones don't so neatly control human sexual behavior. Natural daily and monthly hormone fluctuations do not greatly affect sexual desire. Women's sexual desire is only slightly higher at ovulation (Harvey, 1987; Meuwissen & Over, 1992). Women's sexuality also differs from that of other mammalian females in being more responsive to testosterone than to estrogen (Kaplan, 1979; Morris & others, 1987).

In men, normal fluctuations in testosterone levels, from man to man and hour to hour, have little effect on sexual drive (Byrne, 1982). Indeed, hormone fluctuations are partly a response to sexual stimulation. When James Dabbs and his colleagues (1987) had male collegians converse separately with a male and with a female student, the men's testosterone levels rose with the social arousal, but especially after talking with the female. Like the effect of the crackling steak on insulin level, sexual arousal can be a cause as well as a consequence of increased testosterone levels.

Although normal short-term hormonal changes have little effect on desire, large hormone shifts have a bigger effect over the life span. A person's interest in dating and sexual stimulation usually increases with the pubertal surge in sex hormones. If the hormonal surge is precluded—as happened with prepubertal boys who were castrated during the 1700s and 1800s to preserve their soprano voices for Italian opera—the normal development of sex characteristics and sexual desire does not occur (Peschel &

Peschel, 1987). Among adult men who suffer castration, sex drive typically falls along with declining testosterone levels (Hucker & Bain, 1990). Likewise, male sex offenders lose much of their sexual urge when voluntarily taking Depo-Provera, a drug that reduces testosterone levels to that of a prepubertal boy (Money & others, 1983). And in later life, the typical frequency of intercourse declines as sex hormone levels decline.

Hormones influence sexual arousal via the hypothalamus, which both monitors variations in blood hormone levels and activates the appropriate neural circuits. In rats, destroying a key area of the hypothalamus may end sexual activity; stimulating this area, either electrically or by directly inserting minute quantities of hormones, may activate sexual behavior.

To summarize, we might compare human sex hormones, especially testosterone, to the fuel in a car. Lacking fuel, the car will not run. But if the fuel level is minimally adequate, adding more fuel to the gas tank won't change how the car runs. The analogy is imperfect, because the interaction between hormones and sexual motivation is two-way. However, the analogy correctly suggests that biology is a necessary but not sufficient explanation of human sexual behavior. The hormonal fuel is essential, but so are the psychological stimuli that turn on the engine and shift it into high gear.

*"Fill'er up with testosterone."*

Drawing by Mankoff; © 1993 The New Yorker Magazine, Inc.

## The Psychology of Sex

Hunger and sex are different sorts of motives. Hunger responds to a *need*. If we do not eat, we die. Sex is not in this sense a need. If we do not have sex, we may feel like dying, but we do not die. There are nevertheless similarities between hunger and sexual motivation. Both depend on internal physiological factors. And both are influenced by external stimuli.

*"Ours is a society which stimulates interest in sex by constant titillation. . . . Cinema, television, and all the formidable array of our marketing technology project our very effective forms of titillation and our prejudices about man as a sexy animal into every corner of every hovel in the world."*

Germaine Greer (1984)

### External Stimuli

In many species, the members of one sex are aroused automatically by odors emitted by the other sex. Are humans, also? Despite the millions of dollars spent on advertising scents that supposedly attract sexual interest, attempts to detect *unlearned* human sexual responses to particular odors have not been very successful (Morris & Udry, 1978). The only unlearned stimulus for human sexual arousal appears to be touch—the pleasurable genital caresses that are part of foreplay worldwide (Byrne, 1982).

Many studies confirm that men become aroused when they see, hear, or read erotic material. More surprising to many people (because sexually explicit materials are sold mostly to men) is that most women—at least the less inhibited women who volunteer to participate in such studies—report nearly as much arousal to the same stimuli (Stockton & Murnen, 1992).

In one such study, psychologist Julia Heiman (1975) attached instruments that detected arousal (changes in penis circumference or in vaginal color) to sexually experienced university volunteers. Then the students listened to either a sexually explicit erotic tape, a romantic tape (of a couple expressing love without physical contact), a combined erotic-romantic tape, or a neutral control tape. Which do you suppose the men were most aroused by? And the women? Both the men and the women found the tape of explicit sex most arousing, especially when a woman initiated the sex and the depiction centered on her responses.

People may find such arousal either pleasing or disturbing. (Those who find it disturbing often limit their exposure to such materials, just as those wishing to control hunger limit their exposure to tempting cues.) Some sexually explicit materials can have adverse effects. First, depictions of women being sexually coerced—and enjoying it—tend to increase viewers' acceptance of the false idea that women enjoy rape, and they tend to increase male viewers' willingness to hurt women (see pages 637–638). Second, images of sexually attractive women and men may lead people to devalue their partners and relationships. After male collegians view TV or magazine depictions of sexually attractive women, they often find an average woman, or their own girlfriends or wives, less attractive (Gutierres & others, 1985; Kenrick & Gutierres, 1980; Weaver & others, 1984). Viewing X-rated sex films similarly tends to diminish people's satisfaction with their sexual partners (Zillmann, 1989). Some sex researchers fear that reading or viewing erotica may create expectations that few men and women can hope to live up to.

Figure 12–5

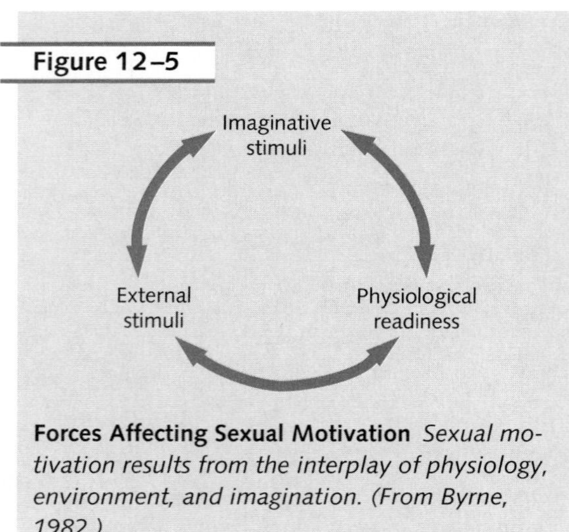


**Forces Affecting Sexual Motivation** *Sexual motivation results from the interplay of physiology, environment, and imagination. (From Byrne, 1982.)*

### Imaginative Stimuli

Sexual motivation arises from the interplay of physiology and environment. But the stimuli inside our heads—our imaginations—also influence sexual arousal and desire (Figure 12–5). The brain, it has been said, is our most significant sex organ. People who, because of a spinal cord injury, have no genital sensation, can still feel sexual desire (Willmuth, 1987). Consider, too, the erotic potential of dreams. As noted in Chapter 7, genital arousal accompanies all types of dreams, even though most dreams have no sexual content. But in nearly all men and some 40 percent of women (Wells, 1986), dreams sometimes do contain sexual imagery that leads to orgasm. In men, these nocturnal emissions ("wet dreams") are more likely when orgasm has not occurred recently.

Wide-awake people become sexually aroused not only by memories of prior sexual activities but also by fantasies. Fantasies need not correspond to actual behavior. In one survey of masturbation-related fantasies (Hunt, 1974), 19 percent of women and 10 percent of men reported imagining someone forcing them to have sex. Fantasy is not reality, however. To paraphrase Susan Brownmiller (1975), for women there's a big difference between fantasizing that Fabio just won't take no for an answer and having a hostile stranger actually force himself on you. (See page 638 for a discussion of the "rape myth.")

*"There is no difference between being raped and being run over by a truck except that afterward men ask if you enjoyed it."*

Marge Piercy
"Rape Poem," 1976

## Sexual Dysfunctions and Therapy

Masters and Johnson sought not only to describe the human sexual response cycle but also to understand and treat the inability to complete it. **Sexual dysfunctions** are problems that consistently impair sexual functioning. Some involve sexual motivation, especially lack of sexual energy and arousability. Men, for example, may experience *premature ejaculation* (before they or their partners wish) or *impotence* (the inability to have or maintain an erection). Women more often than men experience low sexual desire or *orgasmic dysfunction* (infrequently or never experiencing orgasm).

What causes such problems? The idea that personality disorders are to blame has been largely discounted. Men who experience premature ejaculation are similar, even in their sexual arousal patterns, to men who do not; they simply ejaculate at lower levels of sexual arousal—something that often occurs with young men who have had long periods of sexual abstinence (Spiess & others, 1984).

When Barbara Andersen (1983) reviewed research on the diagnosis and treatment of orgasmic dysfunction in women, she too could find no associated personality traits. Furthermore, she reported that treating orgasmic dysfunction through traditional psychotherapy (as though it were a disorder of personality) has been unsuccessful. She did, however, report a nearly 100 percent success rate with a behavioral treatment that trains women to enjoy their bodies and to give themselves orgasms, with a vibrator if necessary. Some of these women can then generalize their new sexual responsiveness to interactions with their mates (LoPiccolo & Stock, 1986; Wakefield, 1987). Success has also been reported in training men to control their premature ejaculations by repeatedly stimulating the penis and then stopping stimulation (or even firmly squeezing the head of the penis) when the urge to ejaculate arises.

## Sexual Orientation

To motivate is to energize and direct behavior. So far, we have considered the energizing of sexual motivation but not its direction. We express the direction of our sexual interest in our **sexual orientation**—our enduring sexual attraction toward members of a particular gender. Cultures vary in their attitudes toward homosexuality. Yet as far as we know, all cultures in all times have been predominantly heterosexual (Bullough, 1990). Whether a culture condemns and punishes homosexuality or views it as an acceptable alternative, homosexuality survives and heterosexuality prevails.

Most homosexual people report that they first became aware of same-gender sexual feelings during or shortly after puberty, but that they did not think of themselves as gay or lesbian until nearer to or after age 20 (Garnets & Kimmel, 1990). How many people are exclusively homosexual? Until recently, the popular press assumed a homosexuality rate of 10 percent. But in both Europe and the United States, a dozen national surveys have recently explored sexual orientation, using methods that protect the respondent's anonymity. Their results agree in suggesting that a more accurate figure is about 3 or 4 percent of men and 1 percent of women (Johnson & others, 1992; National Center for Health Statistics, 1991; Rogers & Turner, 1991). Less than 1 percent of people report being actively bisexual. But more adults report having had an isolated homosexual experience. And most people have an occasional homosexual fantasy.

*"It has been maintained for years that we each use only about 10 percent of our brain capacity; that the condom failure rate is 10 percent; and until just last year, that 10 percent of Americans are homosexual. Such statistics are partly artifacts, I suspect, of our decimal system; in a base 12 system, we'd no doubt show a similar affinity for statistics that were multiples of 8.333 percent."*

John Allen Paulos
"Counting on Dyscalculia," 1993

Although health experts find it helpful to know sexual statistics, numbers don't decide issues of human rights. Similarly, it's helpful in manufacturing school desks to know that about 10 percent of people are left-handed. But whether left-handers are 3 percent or 10 percent of the population doesn't answer the moral question of whether lefties should enjoy equal rights. Whether a minority is 3 percent of the population (as with Asian-Americans) or nearer 10 percent (as with African-Americans and Hispanics) is irrelevant to issues of justice.

What does it feel like to be homosexual in a heterosexual culture? One way for heterosexual people to understand is to imagine how they would feel if they were to be ostracized or fired for openly admitting or displaying their feelings toward someone of the other sex; if they were to overhear people making crude jokes about heterosexual people; if most movies, TV shows, and advertisements portrayed (or implied) homosexuality; and if their family members were pleading with them to change their heterosexual lifestyle and to enter into a homosexual marriage.

Facing such reactions, homosexual people often struggle with their sexual orientation. At first, they may try to ignore or deny their desires, hoping they will go away; but they don't. Then they may try to change, through psychotherapy, will power, or prayer. But the feelings typically persist, as do those of heterosexual people—who are similarly incapable of becoming homosexual. Eventually, homosexuals may accept their orientation—by electing celibacy (as do some heterosexuals); by engaging in promiscuous sex (a choice more commonly made by men than by women); or by entering into a committed, long-term love relationship (a choice more often made by women than by men) (Peplau, 1982; Weinberg & Williams, 1974).

*Did you choose your sexual orientation?*

Most psychologists today view sexual orientation as neither willfully chosen nor willfully changed. Sexual orientation in some ways is like handedness: Most people are one way, some the other. A very few are truly ambidextrous. Regardless, the way one is endures. Nor is sexual orientation linked with psychological disorder or sexual crime, such as being a child molester. Some homosexuals do abuse children, but most child molesters are heterosexual males (Gonsiorek, 1982). These facts led the American Psychiatric Association in 1973 to drop homosexuality from its list of "mental illnesses."

### Understanding Sexual Orientation

If our sexual orientation is indeed something we do not choose and cannot change, then where do these preferences come from? How do we move toward either a heterosexual or a homosexual orientation?[1] See if you can anticipate the consensus that has emerged from hundreds of research studies by responding yes or no to the following questions:

1. Is homosexuality linked with problems in a child's relationships with parents, such as with a domineering mother and an ineffectual father, or a possessive mother and a hostile father?
2. Does homosexuality involve a fear or hatred of people of the other gender, leading individuals to direct their sexual desires toward members of their own sex?
3. Is sexual orientation linked with levels of sex hormones currently in the blood?
4. As children, were many homosexuals molested, seduced, or otherwise sexually victimized by an adult homosexual?

**Erick Has Two Moms** *Maria Christina Vlassidis (left) and Marie Tatro (center) tell playmates of their son Erick, 8, that they are both his moms. Both women, who are lesbians, attend school conferences and are equally active in supporting other aspects of his life.*

Contrary to widely held ideas about homosexuality, the answer to all these questions is no (Storms, 1983). Consider the findings of lengthy Kinsey Institute interviews with nearly 1000 homosexuals and 500 heterosexuals (Bell & others, 1981; Hammersmith, 1982). The investigators assessed nearly every imaginable psychological cause of homosexuality—parental relationships, childhood sexual experiences, peer relationships, dating experiences, even number of brothers and sisters. Their findings: Apart from homosexuals' somewhat greater nonconformity, the reported backgrounds of homosexuals and heterosexuals were similar. Homosexuals were no more likely to have been smothered by maternal love, neglected by their father, or sexually abused.

So, what determines sexual orientation? One theory proposes that people develop same-sex erotic attachments if segregated by gender at the time their sex drive matures (Storms, 1981). But even in a tribal culture in which homosexual behavior is expected of all boys before marriage, heterosexuality prevails (Money, 1987). (As this illustrates, homosexual *behav-*

[1] Note that the scientific question is not "What causes homosexuality?" (or "What causes heterosexuality?") but "What causes differing sexual orientation?" In pursuit of answers, psychological science compares the backgrounds and physiology of people whose sexual orientations *differ*.

*ior* does not always indicate a homosexual *orientation*.) Another theory proposes the opposite: that people develop romantic attachments to those who *differ* from, and thus are more fascinating than, the peers they associated with while growing up (Bell, 1982).

New research indicates that sexual orientation may be at least partly physiological. Researcher Simon LeVay (1991) discovered this while studying sections of the hypothalamus taken from deceased heterosexual and homosexual people. As a gay scientist, LeVay wanted to do "something connected with my gay identity," but he knew he had to avoid biasing the results. So he did the study "blind," without knowing which donors were gay. After 9 months peering through his microscope at a cell cluster he thought might be important, LeVay sat down one morning and broke the codes. His discovery: The cell cluster was reliably larger in heterosexual men than in women and homosexual men. As the brain difference became apparent, "I was almost in a state of shock. . . . I took a walk by myself on the cliffs over the ocean. I sat for half an hour just thinking what this might mean" (LeVay, 1994).

It should not surprise us that brains differ with sexual orientation. Remember our maxim: Although we find it convenient to talk separately of psychological and biological explanations, *everything psychological is simultaneously biological*. The critical question is, when did the brain difference begin? At conception? In the womb? During childhood or adolescence? Did experience produce the difference? Or did genes or prenatal hormones?

LeVay does not view this little neural center as a sexual orientation center; rather, he sees it as an important part of the neural pathway engaged in sexual behavior. Moreover, he acknowledges that it's possible that sexual behavior patterns influence the brain's anatomy. (In fish, birds, and humans, brain structures are known to vary with experience.) But he believes it more likely that brain anatomy influences sexual orientation. Laura Allen and Roger Gorski (1992) offered a similar conclusion after discovering that a section of the fibers connecting right and left hemispheres is one-third larger in homosexual men than in heterosexual men.

The evidence suggests that genetic influence plays a role. One recent analysis studied the twin brothers of homosexual men. Among their identical twin brothers, 52 percent were homosexual, as were 22 percent of fraternal twin brothers (Bailey & Pillard, 1991). In a follow-up study of homosexual women, a similar 48 percent of their identical twins were homosexual, as were 16 percent of their fraternal twins (Bailey & others, 1993). With half the identical twin pairs differing, we know that genes aren't the whole story. Still, this is the sort of pattern we expect to see when genes are having an *influence*.

The genetic influence theory recently received a boost from research showing that gay men have a higher-than-normal number of male homosexual relatives—almost all on their mother's side of the family. This prompted Dean Hamer and his colleagues (1993) to analyze the X chromosomes (which boys inherit only from their mother) of 40 pairs of gay brothers. Their discovery: 33 pairs shared a piece of the chromosome, hinting at the possible location of an unidentified gene related to homosexuality.

The elevated rate of homosexual orientation even in fraternal twins might also result from their sharing the same prenatal environment. In animals and some exceptional human cases, sexual orientation has been altered by abnormal prenatal hormone conditions. Female sheep, for example, will show homosexual behavior if their pregnant mothers are injected with testosterone during a critical gestation period (Money, 1987). With humans, a critical period for the brain's neural-hormonal control system may

*"Were it not for delicately balanced combinations of genetic, neurological, hormonal, and environmental factors, largely occurring prior to birth, each and every one of us would be homosexual."*

Lee Ellis and M. Ashley Ames (1987)

*"Biological theories of sexual orientation are far more promising than any current alternatives."*

J. Michael Bailey and Richard C. Pillard (1994)

exist between the middle of the second and fifth months after conception (Ellis & Ames, 1987; Gladue, 1990). It seems that exposure to the hormone levels typically experienced by female fetuses during this time may predispose the person (whether female or male) to be attracted to males in later life. Cognitive tests reveal differences between homosexual and heterosexual men that are consistent with the hypothesis that homosexuals were exposed to atypical prenatal hormones (McCormick & Witelson, 1991).

Because the physiological evidence is preliminary and controversial, some scientists remain skeptical. Rather than specifying sexual orientation, perhaps biological factors predispose a temperament that influences sexuality "in the context of individual learning and experience" (Byne & Parsons, 1993). Nevertheless, the consistency of the genetic, prenatal, and brain findings has swung the pendulum toward a physiological explanation. If these influences prove critical (perhaps especially in certain environmental contexts), it would explain why sexual orientation is so difficult to change.

Still, some people wonder: Should the cause of sexual orientation matter? Maybe it shouldn't, but people's assumptions matter. Those who believe, as do most homosexual people, that sexual orientation is a biological given—an enduring identity, not a choice—express more accepting attitudes toward homosexual persons (Furnham & Taylor, 1990; Whitley, 1990). Others respond that diabetes, alcoholism, and schizophrenia are also biologically influenced—but are not considered desirable or normal (Krauthammer, 1993). Nevertheless, in American surveys, agreement that homosexuality is "something that people are born with" doubled from 16 to 31 percent between 1983 and 1993. Over roughly the same time period, support for equal job rights for homosexuals increased from 59 to 80 percent (Moore, 1993). (Disapproval of homosexual behavior remains strong, however—NORC, 1993.)

To gay and lesbian activists, the new biological research is a double-edged sword (Diamond, 1993). If sexual orientation, like skin color and sex, is genetically influenced, that offers a further rationale for civil rights protection. Moreover, it may alleviate parents' concerns about their children's having gay teachers and role models. It does, however, raise the haunting possibility that genetic markers of sexual orientation could someday be identified through fetal testing, and the fetus aborted. This new research on sexual orientation may be raising as many questions as answers.

**A Sharing of Love** *For most adults, a sexual relationship fulfills not only a biological motive, but a social need for intimacy.*

## Sex and Human Values

Recognizing that values are both personal and cultural, most sex researchers and educators strive to keep their writings on sexuality value-free.

But can the study of sexual behavior and what motivates it really be free of values? Those who think not say that the very words we use to describe behavior often reflect our personal values. When sex researchers label sexually restrained individuals as "erotophobic" and as having "high sex guilt," they express their own values. Whether we label sexual acts we do not practice as "perversions," "deviations," or part of an "alternative sexual life-style" depends on our attitudes toward the behaviors. Labels both describe and evaluate.

When information about sex is separated from the context of human values, some students may get the idea that sexual intercourse is merely recreational activity. Diana Baumrind (1982), a University of California child-

## *Thinking Critically About* Trial Marriages—Do They Reduce Divorce?

Changing sexual values are evident in changing norms regarding cohabitation. In 1958, the University of Illinois fired a professor who suggested, through the student newspaper, the desirability of young people testing their love relationship before venturing into marriage. When Barnard College sophomore Linda Leclair in 1968 moved in with her boyfriend, a Columbia University junior, a student-faculty committee debated several months before deciding that Leclair could remain a student. But they denied her the use of the cafeteria, snack bar, and recreation room.

Today, most universities look the other way. Cohabitation has become commonplace. The number of cohabiting unmarried couples in the United States tripled during the 1970s and doubled again during the 1980s (Bureau of the Census, 1993). Similar trends have occurred since 1960 in Australia, Scandinavia, and throughout much of Western Europe.

Many see premarital cohabitation as a trial marriage that serves to weed out unsuccessful unions before marriage occurs. In a 1989 survey of nearly 300,000 first-year American college students, 51 percent agreed that "a couple should live together before marriage" (Astin & others, 1989). Might those who are sexually experienced and thoroughly familiar with the living habits of their partner indeed be less likely to stumble into an ill-fated marriage? Does test-driving life together before committing reduce the risk of divorce?

It seems not. Eight recent studies concur that, compared with couples who don't cohabit with their spouses-to-be, those who do have *higher* divorce rates. A U.S. survey of 13,000 adults found that couples who lived together before marriage were one-third more likely to separate or divorce within a decade (Bumpass & Sweet, 1989). A 1990 Gallup survey of still-married Americans also found that 21 percent of those who had not cohabited before marrying, and 40 percent of those who had, said they might divorce (Greeley, 1991). A Canadian national survey of 5300 women found that those who cohabited were 54 percent more likely to divorce within 15 years (Balakrishan & others, 1987). And a Swedish study of 4300 women found cohabitation linked with an 80 percent greater risk of divorce (Bennett & others, 1988).

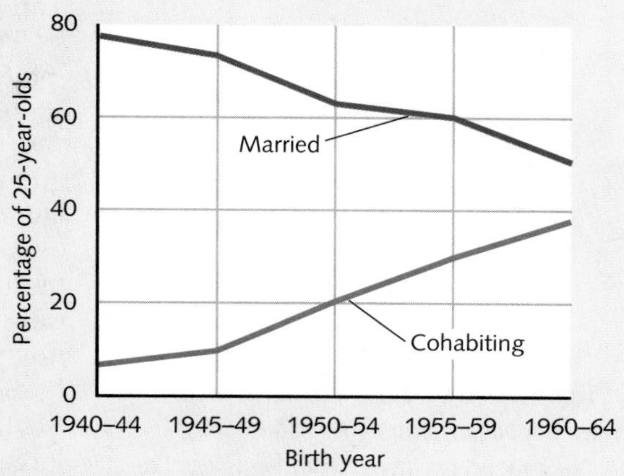


**U.S. Rates of Cohabitation and Marriage by Age 25** *From the U.S. National Survey of Families and Households. (From Bumpass & Sweet, 1989.)*

Can you imagine why? (Remember: A *correlation* between cohabitation and divorce risk need not imply that cohabitation is a *cause* of future divorce.) William Axinn and Arland Thornton (1992) report data that support two explanations.

First, cohabitation attracts people who are more open to terminating unsatisfying relationships. The very idea of cohabitation presumes that intimate relationships need not be permanent. It sees love as conditional rather than committed. If either partner becomes dissatisfied, he or she can seek bliss elsewhere. People who cohabit therefore bring a more individualistic ethic to marriage, are more likely to see close relationships as temporary and fragile, and are more accepting of divorce.

Second, the experience of cohabitation increases acceptance of divorce. Over time, those who cohabit tend to become more approving of dissolving an unfulfilling union. This divorce-accepting attitude increases the odds of later divorce.

rearing expert, suspects that adolescents interpret sex education that pretends to be "value-free" as meaning that adults are neutral about adolescent sexual activity. She feels that such an implication is unfortunate, because "promiscuous recreational sex poses certain psychological, social, health, and moral problems that must be faced realistically."

Nevertheless, researchers have found that teenagers who have had formal sex education are no more likely to engage in premarital sex than those who have not (Furstenberg & others, 1985; Zelnik & Kim, 1982). Moreover, we enrich our lives by knowing ourselves, by realizing that others share our feelings, by understanding what is likely to please or displease our loved one. Witness the crumbling of falsehoods about homosexuality. Witness the growing realization that some types of sexually explicit material can lead people to devalue or hurt others.

Perhaps we can agree that the knowledge provided by sex research is preferable to ignorance, yet also agree that researchers' values should be stated openly, enabling us to debate them and to reflect on our own values. We might also remember that scientific research on sexual motivation does not aim to define the personal meaning of sex in our lives. One can know every available fact about sex—that the initial spasms of male and female orgasm come at 0.8-second intervals, that the female nipples expand 10 millimeters at the peak of sexual arousal, that systolic blood pressure rises some 60 points and the respiration rate to 40 breaths per minute—but fail to understand the human significance of sexual intimacy.

*"The relationship between women and men should be characterized not by patronizing behavior or exploitation, but by love, partnership, and trustworthiness. . . . Sexuality should express and reinforce a loving relationship lived by equal partners."*

*Towards a Global Ethic*
1993 Parliament of the World's Religions

Surely one significance of sexual intimacy is its expression of our deeply social nature. Sex is a socially significant act. Men and women can achieve orgasm alone, yet most people find greater satisfaction while embracing their loved one. Although the yearning for closeness was not part of our description of sexual motivation, sex is a life-uniting and love-renewing experience.

## Summing Up

**Describing Sexual Behavior** Sexual behaviors vary across both place and time. The range of "normal" sexual interests and behaviors remains broad.

**The Physiology of Sex** Physiologically, the human sexual response cycle normally follows a pattern of excitement, plateau, orgasm, and resolution, followed in males by a refractory period, during which renewed arousal and orgasm are not possible. Sex hormones in combination with the hypothalamus help our bodies develop and function as either male or female. In nonhuman animals, hormones also help stimulate sexual activity. In humans, they influence sexual behavior more loosely, especially once sufficient hormone levels are present.

**The Psychology of Sex** External stimuli can trigger sexual arousal in both men and women. Sexually explicit materials may also lead people to perceive their partners as comparatively less appealing and to devalue their relationships. In combination with the internal hormonal push and the external pull of sexual stimuli, fantasies (imagined stimuli) influence sexual arousal.

**Sexual Dysfunctions and Therapy** Sexual dysfunctions, such as premature ejaculation and orgasmic dysfunction, are being successfully treated by new methods, which assume that people learn and can modify their sexual responses.

**Sexual Orientation** One's heterosexual or homosexual orientation seems neither willfully chosen nor willfully changed. Preliminary new evidence links sexual orientation with genetic influences, prenatal hormones, and the size of certain brain structures.

**Sex and Human Values** Sex research and education are not value-free. Some say that sex-related values should therefore be openly acknowledged, recognizing the emotional significance of sexual expression.

## Achievement Motivation

*With their basic needs met, humans to varying degrees also feel motivated to display competence and to reach goals. Who has the greatest need to achieve? Why? And how can effective leaders motivate higher levels of achievement?*

The biological perspective on motivation—the idea that physiological needs drive us to satisfy those needs—provides only a partial explanation of what energizes and directs our behavior. Hunger and sex have both social and physiological components. Moreover, there are motives that, unlike hunger and sex, seem not to satisfy any physical need. Millionaires may be motivated to make ever more money, movie stars to become ever more famous, politicians to achieve ever more power, daredevils to seek ever greater thrills. Such motives seem not to diminish when they are fed. The more we achieve, the more we may need to achieve.

**The Image of Achievement** *Her Emmy-Award–winning talk show and the millions of dollars she has earned have not dampened Oprah Winfrey's achievement motivation. She constantly seeks new ways to actualize her great energy and talent. "I've been blessed—but I create the blessings," she says.*

*What is your greatest achievement to date? What is your greatest future ambition—to attain fame? Fortune? Creative accomplishment? Security? Love? Power? Wisdom? Spiritual wholeness?*

### Identifying Achievement Motivation

Think of someone you know who strives to succeed by excelling at any task where evaluation is possible. Now think of someone who is less disciplined and driven. Psychologist Henry Murray (1938) defined the first person's high need for achievement, or **achievement motivation**, as a desire for significant accomplishment, for mastering skills or ideas, for control, and for rapidly attaining a high standard.

To study this motive, we first need a way to measure it. But how? Recall from the semistarvation studies that people driven by hunger begin to fantasize about food. Our sexual orientation is similarly reflected in our sexual fantasies. Do these examples suggest a way to assess a person's need to achieve?

Murray and investigators David McClelland and John Atkinson presumed that people's fantasies would reflect their achievement concerns. So they asked subjects to invent stories about ambiguous pictures. If, when shown the daydreaming boy in Figure 12–6, a subject commented that the boy was preoccupied with his pursuit of a goal, that he imagined himself performing a heroic act, or that he was feeling pride in some success, the story was scored as indicating achievement concerns. McClelland and Atkinson regarded people whose stories consistently included such themes as having a high need for achievement.

Would you expect people whose stories express high achievement to prefer tasks that are easy, moderately challenging, or very difficult? People whose stories suggest low achievement motivation tend to choose either very easy or very difficult tasks, where failure is either unlikely or not embarrassing (Geen, 1984). Those whose stories express a high need for achievement motivation tend to prefer moderately difficult tasks, where success is attainable yet attributable to their skill and effort. In a ring toss game, for instance, they often stand at an intermediate distance from the stake; this enables some successes, yet provides a suitable challenge. People with a strong need to achieve also are more likely to persist on a task when things get difficult (Cooper, 1983). By contrast, high school underachievers are less persistent in completing college degrees, holding on to jobs, and maintaining their marriages (McCall, 1994).

As you might expect from their persistence and eagerness for realistic challenge, people with high achievement motivation do achieve more. One study followed the lives of 1528 California children whose intelligence scores were in the top 1 percent. When researchers 40 years later compared men whose lives were most and least successful, they found the difference

**Figure 12–6**

**What Is This Boy Daydreaming About?** *By analyzing responses to ambiguous photos like this, motivation researchers seek clues to people's levels of achievement motivation.*

was not in intelligence but in motivation. Those most successful were more ambitious, energetic, and persistent. As children, they had more active hobbies. As adults, they participated in more groups and favored participating in sports over passively watching (Goleman, 1980). Another study of outstanding athletes, scholars, and artists found that all were highly motivated and self-disciplined, willing to dedicate hours every day to the pursuit of their goals (Bloom, 1985). These superstar achievers were distinguished not so much by their extraordinary natural talent as by their extraordinary daily discipline.

When achievement motivation increases, so does achievement. By training the businessmen of a village in India to think, talk, and act like achievement-motivated people, McClelland (1978) and his colleagues were able to boost the villagers' business successes. Compared with other businessmen from a comparable nearby town, those trained in achievement motivation started more new businesses and employed over twice as many new people during the ensuing 2 years.

## Sources of Achievement Motivation

Why, despite similar potentials, does one person become more motivated to achieve than another? Highly motivated children often have parents who encourage their independence from an early age and praise and reward them for their successes (Teevan & McGhee, 1972). Such parents encourage their children to dress and feed themselves and to do well in school, and they express delight when their children achieve. Theorists speculate that the high achievement motivation displayed by such children has *emotional* roots, as children learn to associate achievement with positive emotions. There may also be *cognitive* roots, as children learn to attribute their achievements to their own competence and effort and to develop higher expectations (Dweck & Elliott, 1983).

*"They can because they think they can."*

Virgil
*Aeneid*, 19 B.C.

*Remember the two people you chose, one who consistently strives to succeed, the other who is less concerned with achievement? Is either a first-born (or only) child?*

These parental influences also help explain a fascinating finding—that birth order correlates with achievement. First-born and only children do slightly better in school and on intelligence tests and are more likely to achieve admission to prestigious colleges than are their later-born brothers and sisters (Falbo & Polit, 1986). In China, which has many one-child families, only children academically outperform those with siblings (Falbo & Poston, 1993). These findings may partly reflect the generally higher socioeconomic status of small families, which have fewer later-born children (Blake, 1989). However, in separate studies of eminent people from two-children families, 64 percent of "distinguished Americans" were first-born, as were 61 percent of Rhodes scholars, 66 percent of National Merit scholars, 64 percent of those in *Who's Who*, and 21 of the 23 astronauts chosen for the first U.S. space program. Among the *Who's Who* designates and National Merit scholars who came from three-children families, 52 percent of both groups were first-born (Altus, 1966).

It is fun to speculate about differences between the experiences of first-born and later-born children. One difference might be the greater parental attention given the first-born during their years as solo children. Perhaps parents have invested more in a first-born child. They may take more pictures of their first child and provide that child with more encouragement and higher expectations. But the later-born often have noteworthy social strengths. They tend to be more socially relaxed and popular. Having less power than one's older siblings—less size, strength, verbal ability, and experience—apparently fosters more effective social skills (Miller & Maruyama, 1976).

Moreover, throughout history later-born scientists have been more supportive of new ideas. Copernicus, who proposed that the earth orbits around the sun, was the second of four children; Tycho Brahe, who defended the traditional view that the sun and stars revolved around the earth, was an only child. Charles Darwin, the fifth of six children, found his new ideas supported by most later-born scientists but rejected by his first-born peers (see Figure 12–7). In fact, science historian Frank Sulloway (1990) reports that 23 of 28 such scientific revolutions were led by later-borns. Among the 2784 scientists who participated in these controversies, 34 percent of the first-borns and 64 percent of the later-borns were supportive of the new ideas. The same was true of the Protestant Reformation, which later-born religious leaders more often supported. First-borns, it seems, identify more closely with the views of their parents and of tradition.

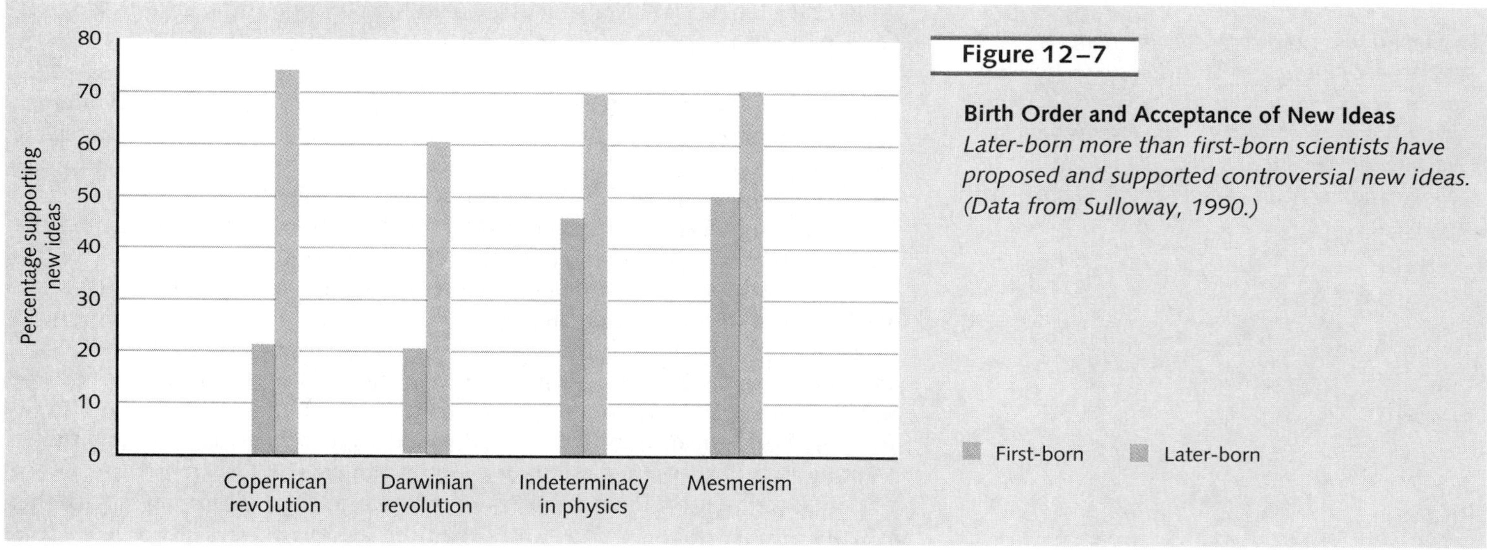


**Figure 12–7**

**Birth Order and Acceptance of New Ideas** *Later-born more than first-born scientists have proposed and supported controversial new ideas. (Data from Sulloway, 1990.)*

Of course, sometimes tradition is right. In cases such as phrenology (discerning traits by the shape of one's skull) and mesmerism (healing by restoring proper "magnetism" to one's body), the first-borns were less deceived by new, false ideas. Thus, there are benefits linked with both first and later birth orders: First-borns tend to be more conscientious and conventional, later-borns to be freewheeling and creative.

## Intrinsic Motivation and Achievement

In the classroom, at the workplace, and on the athletic field, two types of achievement motivation operate. **Intrinsic motivation** is the desire to be effective and to perform a behavior for its own sake. **Extrinsic motivation** is seeking external rewards and avoiding punishments.

To sense the difference between extrinsic and intrinsic motivation, you might reflect on your own current experience. Are you feeling pressured to get this reading finished before a deadline? Worried about your course grade? Eager for rewards that depend on your doing well? If your answers are yes, then you are extrinsically motivated (as, to some extent, almost all

**Reverend Jesse Jackson** *The civil rights leader's high level of intrinsic motivation drove him to seek new and more difficult challenges. A phrase from his speech at the 1983 civil rights march on Washington sums it up: "If my mind can conceive it and my heart can believe it, I know I can achieve it."*

students are). Are you also finding the course material interesting? Does learning it enable you to feel more competent? If there were no grade at stake, might you be curious enough to want to learn the material for its own sake? If your answers are yes, intrinsic motivation also fuels your efforts.

In sports, as in other activities, excessive external pressures and incentives can undermine intrinsic enjoyment. One researcher, Dean Ryan (1980), studied football players. He found that those on athletic scholarships (who were, in a sense, playing for pay) enjoyed their play less than did the nonscholarship players. Apparently, pay and pressure turn play into work. However, rewards can increase intrinsic motivation if their effect is to inform the players of their athletic competence (as with a "most improved player" award).

So, should coaches emphasize extrinsic pressures, rewards, and competition? It depends on the goal, report motivation researchers Edward Deci and Richard Ryan (1985, 1992). For some, as for professional football coach Vince Lombardi, "Winning isn't everything; it's the only thing." If so, it may pay to control the players with pressures and rewards for winning. But what if the goal is—as it should be for most programs of physical education, fitness, and amateur sports—the promotion of an enduring interest and participation in physical activity? Then, say Deci and Ryan, "External pressures, competitive emphasis, and evaluative feedback are in contradiction to this goal." Thus, if Little League coaches want their players to continue playing baseball after Little League, they should focus not on the urgency of winning but on the joy of playing one's best.

Researchers in the psychology of religion have also explored intrinsic versus extrinsic motivation (Bergin, 1991; Gorsuch, 1988). Some religiously active people score high on tests of extrinsic religious motivation, by reporting their religion is a means to other ends. (They might agree, for example, that "a primary reason for my interest in religion is that my church is a congenial social activity.") Others score high on *intrinsic* religious motivation, by reporting their religion is an end in itself. ("My religious beliefs are what really lie behind my whole approach to life.") Compared with the extrinsically religious, intrinsically religious people tend to score lower on tests of prejudice and anxiety. They also tend to live with a greater sense of control over their lives and a clearer sense of purpose (Wulff, 1991).

## Motivating People

The growing field of **industrial/organizational psychology** includes studies of how managers might best:

- match people with jobs, by identifying motivated, well-suited personnel.
- make jobs suit people, by creating work environments that boost morale and output.
- evaluate performance and create incentives for excellence.
- promote teamwork and group achievement.

What every leader (manager, coach, or teacher) wants to know is "How can I manage in ways that enhance people's motivation, productivity, satisfaction?" (Satisfied workers aren't always more productive, but they are less likely to be absent or to quit.) Four factors known to improve a leader's effectiveness are cultivating intrinsic motivation, attending to people's motives, setting goals, and choosing an appropriate leadership style.

### Cultivate Intrinsic Motivation

If intrinsic motivation stimulates achievement, especially in situations where people work independently (as students, executives, and scientists often do), then how might we encourage it? The consistent answers, from hundreds of studies: First, provide tasks that challenge and trigger curiosity (Malone & Lepper, 1986). Second, avoid snuffing out people's sense of self-determination with an overuse of controlling extrinsic rewards (Deci & Ryan, 1987).

Note that we can use extrinsic rewards in two ways: to *control* ("If you clean up your room, you can have some ice cream") or to *inform* someone of successes ("That was outstanding—we congratulate you"). Attempts to *control* people's behaviors through rewards and surveillance may be successful as long as these controls are present. But if taken away, interest in the activity often drops. Ironically, teachers who try hardest to boost their students' achievement on competency tests tend to be most controlling, thus undermining their students' intrinsic interest. (Recall from Chapter 8, Learning, the principle that unnecessary or excessive rewards can undermine intrinsic interest by overjustifying an activity.)

On the other hand, rewards that *inform* people they are doing well can boost their feelings of competence and intrinsic motivation. In one experiment, Thane Pittman and his colleagues (1980) asked college students to work on puzzles. Those given informative compliments ("Compared with most of my subjects, you're doing really well") usually continued playing with the puzzles when left alone. Those given either no praise or a controlling form of praise ("If you keep it up, I'll be able to use your data") were less likely to continue. So, depending on whether we use rewards to control or inform, they can either raise or lower intrinsic motivation.

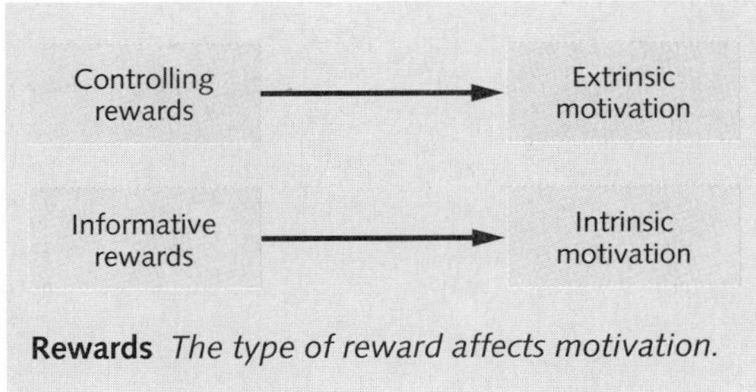


**Rewards** *The type of reward affects motivation.*

There is an important practical principle here. Because the controlling use of rewards undermines intrinsic motivation (and creativity—see page 382), parents, teachers, and managers should take care not to be overcontrolling. It is important to expect, support, challenge, and inform, but if you want to encourage internally motivated, self-directed achievements, do not overly control.

### Attend to People's Motives

Effective managerial styles vary with the people managed. To motivate people, Martin Maehr and Larry Braskamp (1986; Braskamp, 1987) advise managers to assess their people's motives and adjust their managerial style accordingly. Challenge employees who value *accomplishment* to try new things and to exhibit excellence. Give those who value *recognition* the attention they desire. Place those who value *affiliation* in a unit that has a family feeling and shares decision making. Motivate those who value *power* with competition and opportunities for triumphant success. Different strokes for different folks, but for each a way to motivate.

What workers value—and the management style to which they respond best—also varies from culture to culture. In cultures where work is less intrinsically valued than in, say, Japan, personal relationships are often a key to motivating workers (England & Misumi, 1986). As we noted in the Chapter 3 discussion of culture and child-rearing, human societies differ in whether they socialize children primarily toward social harmony and loyalty or toward thinking and achieving for themselves. The greater individualism of Europe and North America surfaced in surveys among 116,000 IBM employees in 40 countries. Individualism—for example, people's valuing their private lives outside of the company and wanting to adopt their own approach to their job—was highest in the United States, Australia, Britain, and Canada, somewhat lower in Scandinavia, and much lower in Asia and South America (Hofstede, 1980). Such cultural differences have implications for multicultural business ventures. A study for the Dutch Ministry of Economic Affairs, for example, found that Norwegian and Swedish businesspeople shared the same cluster of values important to the Dutch. As a result, Scandinavian management styles have worked better in The Netherlands than have those of American managers (Hofstede, 1980).

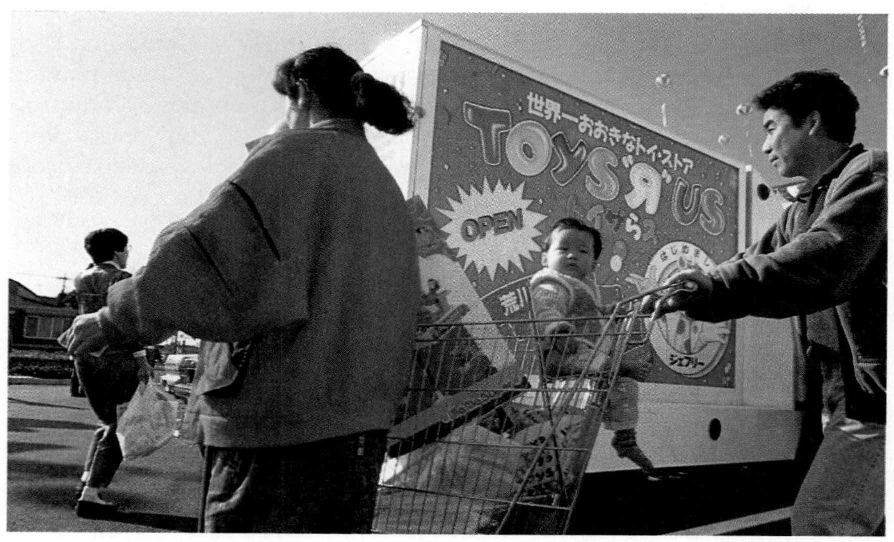


**Toys "R" Everywhere** *Hiring Japanese top executives who know their own culture and listening to what they have to say has enabled Toys "R" Us and other Western firms to succeed in Japanese markets. Here ladened shoppers leave the flagship store—one of 10 planned for Japan.*

## Set Specific, Challenging Goals

In study after study, specific, challenging goals have motivated higher achievement, especially when combined with progress reports (Locke & Latham, 1990; Mento & others, 1987; Tubbs, 1986). Clear objectives, such as those you might set in planning your course work, serve to direct attention, promote effort, and stimulate creative strategies. So, to motivate high productivity, effective leaders work with people to define explicit goals, elicit commitments, and provide feedback on progress.

*"Good leaders don't ask more than their constituents can give, but they often ask—and get—more than their constituents intended to give or thought it was possible to give."*

John W. Gardner
*Excellence*, 1984

## Choose an Appropriate Leadership Style

Whether a directive or a democratic leadership style works best depends on the situation and the leader. The best leadership style for leading a discussion is not the best style for leading troops on a charge (Fiedler, 1981). Moreover, different leaders are suited to different styles. Some excel at **task**

**leadership**—setting standards, organizing work, and focusing attention on goals. Being goal-oriented, task leaders are good at keeping a group centered on its mission. Typically, they have a directive style, which can work well if the leader is bright enough to give good orders (Fiedler, 1987).

Other managers excel at **social leadership**—mediating conflicts and building the sort of team spirit that makes for high performance (Evans & Dion, 1991). Social leaders often have a democratic style: They delegate authority and welcome the participation of team members. Many experiments show that social leadership is good for morale. Subordinates usually feel more satisfied and motivated when they can participate in decision making (Burger, 1987; Spector, 1986). Women more often excel at social leadership, men at task leadership (Eagly & Karau, 1991).

Because effective leadership styles vary with the situation and the person, the once-popular "great person" theory of leadership—that all great leaders share certain traits—fell out of favor. However, Peter Smith and Monir Tayeb (1989) report from recent studies in India, Taiwan, and Iran that effective managers in coal mines, banks, and government offices often exhibit a high degree of *both* task and social leadership. As achievement-minded people, they care about how work is progressing, yet they are sensitive to their subordinates' needs. Effective leaders of laboratory groups, work teams, and large corporations also tend to exude a self-confident

Drawing by Anthony; © 1988 The New Yorker Magazine, Inc.

"charisma" (House & Singh, 1987; Shamir & others, 1993). Their charisma involves a *vision* of some goal, an ability to *communicate* it clearly and simply, and enough optimism and faith in their group to *inspire* others to follow. Such leadership motivates others to identify with and commit themselves to the group's mission.

Whether managers favor a participative/democratic approach depends not only on their personality but also on their assumptions about human motivation. Douglas McGregor (1960) identified two contrasting views. **Theory X** managers assume that workers are basically lazy, error-prone, and extrinsically motivated by money. Thus, they need simple tasks, close monitoring, and incentives to work harder. **Theory Y** managers make opposite assumptions—that people are intrinsically motivated to work for reasons beyond money—for example, to promote self-esteem, enjoy satisfying relations with others, and fulfill their potential. Thus, given enough freedom and challenge, employees will strive to demonstrate their competence and creativity. Theory Y managers are more likely to give employees control over work procedures, to welcome employee participation in decision making, and to have creative and satisfied subordinates (Deci & others, 1989).

Theory Y is one guiding force behind the contemporary move by many businesses to increase employee participation in making decisions, a management style common in Sweden and Japan (Naylor, 1990; Sundstrom & others, 1990). Ironically, a major influence on the "Japanese-style participative management" now increasingly popular in North America was MIT social psychologist Kurt Lewin. Lewin and his students demonstrated the effects of worker participation on productivity in laboratory and factory experiments. Shortly before World War II, Lewin visited Japan and explained his findings to industrial and academic leaders (Nisbett & Ross, 1991).

Back in the United States, some companies quietly began implementing Lewin's participative management. One of these pioneer companies was Michigan's Herman Miller, Inc., now the world's second-largest manufacturer of office furniture and one of America's 10 most admired companies in *Fortune* magazine's survey of 8000 executives (Davenport, 1989). Its retired chair, Max DePree (1987), believes that workers want to be effective and productive, to feel they are making a meaningful contribution, to have control over their own destinies, and to be appreciated. When workers share in corporate profits and become part owners, they become invested in their company's success. When workers participate in decision making and know that they and their managers are mutually accountable, a shared commitment to corporate and personal goals replaces labor-versus-management hostility. When workers feel respected, cared about, and involved, they find work more satisfying. And, thanks to their productivity, their company benefits. Between 1974 and 1994 Herman Miller's annual sales grew from $40 million to nearly $1 billion.

**Participative Management** *General Motors' new Saturn plant in Tennessee has 10-member "teams" of employees. Each work team helps decide such things as new hires for their team and how to run their own area. Part of their salary depends on resulting car quality and company profits.*

## Summing Up

Some human behaviors are energized and directed without satisfying any obvious physiological need. Achieving personal goals, for example, may be motivated by a person's need for competence and self-determination.

**Identifying Achievement Motivation** People with a high need to achieve tend to prefer moderately challenging tasks and to persist in accomplishing them.

**Sources of Achievement Motivation** Many achievement-oriented children have parents and teachers who encourage and affirm independent achievement rather than overly controlling them with rewards and threats. First-born children tend to be higher achievers, but later-borns tend to have greater social skills and to be more accepting of new ideas.

**Intrinsic Motivation and Achievement** Intrinsic motivation is the desire to be effective and to perform a behavior for its own sake. Extrinsic motivation is seeking external rewards and avoiding punishments.

**Motivating People** Industrial/organizational psychologists explore how best to create a motivated, productive, and satisfied workforce. Rewards may increase intrinsic motivation if used not to control people but to boost their sense of competence or to inform them of improvement. It also helps to adjust one's managerial style in response to workers' motives; to set specific, challenging goals; and to combine goal-oriented task leadership with group-oriented social leadership.

## The Need to Belong

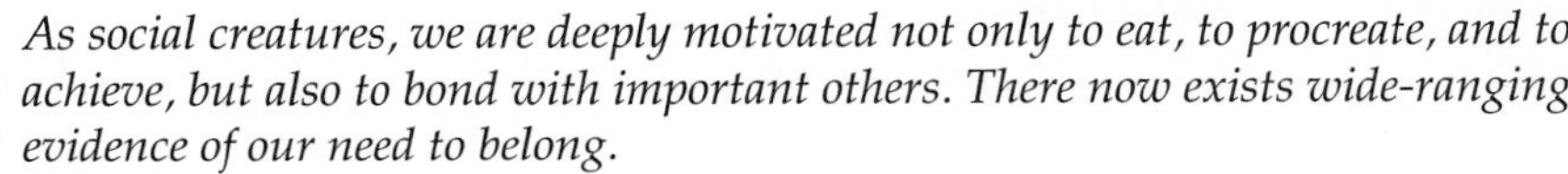

*As social creatures, we are deeply motivated not only to eat, to procreate, and to achieve, but also to bond with important others. There now exists wide-ranging evidence of our need to belong.*

We humans feel motivated to eat, to have sex, and to achieve. But being what Aristotle called "the social animal," we also have a **need to belong**, to feel connected with certain others in enduring, close relationships. Roy Baumeister and Mark Leary (1994) offer examples of this basic human motive.

### Aiding Survival

Social bonds boosted our ancestors' survival rate. For both children and adults, bonding was adaptive. By keeping children close to their caregivers, attachments served as a powerful survival impulse. As adults, those who formed attachments were more likely to come together to reproduce and to stay together to nurture their offspring to maturity.

Cooperation in groups also enhanced survival. In solo combat, our ancestors were not the toughest predators. But as hunters they learned that six hands were better than two. Those who foraged in groups also gained protection from predators and enemies. If those who felt a need to belong survived and reproduced most successfully, their genes would in time predominate. The inevitable result: an innately social creature. People in every society on earth belong to groups (and, as Chapter 19 explains, prefer and favor "us" over "them").

### Wanting to Belong

The need to belong colors our thoughts and emotions. People spend much time thinking about their actual and hoped-for relationships. When relationships form, we often feel joy. Falling in mutual love, people have been known to get cheek-aches from their irrepressible grin. Asked, "What is necessary for your happiness?" or "What is it that makes your life meaningful?" most people mention—before anything else—satisfying close relationships with family, friends, or romantic partners (Berscheid, 1985). As C. S. Lewis said, "The sun looks down on nothing half so good as a household laughing together over a meal." Happiness hits close to home.

### Increasing Social Acceptance

Much of our social behavior aims to increase our belonging—our social acceptance and inclusion. To avoid rejection, we generally conform to group standards and seek to make favorable impressions. (More on this in Chapter 18, Social Psychology.) To win friendship and esteem, we monitor our behavior, hoping to create the right impressions. Seeking love and belonging, we spend billions on clothes, cosmetics, and diet and fitness aids—all motivated by our quest for acceptance.

Like sexual motivation, which feeds both love and exploitation, the need to belong feeds both deep attachments and menacing threats. Out of our need to define a "we" comes loving families, faithful friendships, and team spirit, but also teen gangs, ethnic hostilities, and fanatic nationalism. So it goes with basic motives, which have multiple and strong effects on how we think, feel, and act. It therefore "seems safe to conclude," say Baumeister and Leary, "that human beings are fundamentally and pervasively motivated by a need to belong."

### Maintaining Relationships

People resist breaking social bonds. For most of us, familiarity breeds liking, not contempt. Thrown together at school, at summer camp, on a cross-country bus tour, people resist the group's dissolution. Hoping to maintain the relationships, they promise to call, to write, to come back for reunions. Parting, they feel distress. At the end of a mere vacation cruise, people may hug their waiter or cry when saying goodbye forever to their cabin attendant. Attachments can even keep people in abusive relationships; the fear of being alone may seem worse than the pain of emotional or physical abuse.

When something threatens or dissolves our social ties, negative emotions overwhelm us. Exile, imprisonment, and solitary confinement are progressively more severe forms of punishment. Recently bereaved people often feel that life is empty and pointless. Children reared in institutions without a sense of belonging to anyone, or locked away at home under extreme neglect, become pathetic creatures—withdrawn, frightened, speechless. Adults who are denied others' acceptance and inclusion may feel depressed. Anxiety, jealousy, loneliness, and guilt all involve threatened disruptions of our need to belong. People suffer even when bad relationships break. In one 16-nation survey, separated and divorced people were half as likely as married people to declare themselves "very happy" (Inglehart, 1990). After such separations, feelings of loneliness and anger are commonplace.

### Fortifying Health

Do you have close friends—people with whom you freely disclose your ups and downs? As we will see in Chapter 17, Stress and Health, people who feel supported by close relationships live with better health and at lower risk for psychological disorder and premature death than do those who lack social support. Married people, for example, are less at risk for depression, suicide, and early death than are unattached people.

In this chapter we have seen that identifiable physiological mechanisms drive some motives, such as hunger (though external incentives and learned tastes matter, too). Other motives, such as achievement, are more obviously driven by psychological factors, such as an intrinsic quest for mastery and the external rewards of recognition. What unifies all such motives is their common effect: the energizing and directing of behavior. Without motivation—without hunger, thirst, sex, curiosity, a drive to achieve, an urge to belong—life would be dull and aimless. Motivation adds purpose—and zing—to life.

## Summing Up

Although motivated to individual achievement, no one is an island; we are all, as John Donne noted in 1624, part of the human continent. Our need to belong—to feel connected and identified with others—boosted our ancestors' chances for survival and is therefore part of our human nature. We experience our need to belong when suffering the breaking of social bonds, when feeling the gloom of loneliness or the joy of love, and when seeking social acceptance.

## Terms and Concepts to Remember

**motivation** A need or desire that energizes and directs behavior.

### Motivational Theories

**instinct** A complex behavior that is rigidly patterned throughout a species and is unlearned.

**drive-reduction theory** The idea that a physiological need creates an aroused tension state (a drive) that motivates an organism to satisfy the need.

**homeostasis** A tendency to maintain a balanced or constant internal state; the regulation of any aspect of body chemistry, such as blood glucose, around a particular level.

**incentives** Positive or negative environmental stimuli that motivate behavior.

**hierarchy of needs** Maslow's pyramid of human needs, beginning at the base with physiological needs that must first be satisfied before higher level safety needs and then psychological needs become active.

### Hunger

**glucose** The form of sugar that circulates in the blood and provides the major source of energy for body tissues. When its level is low, we feel hunger.

**set point** The point at which an individual's "weight thermostat" is supposedly set. When the body falls below this weight, an increase in hunger and a lowered metabolic rate may act to restore the lost weight.

**metabolic rate** The body's base rate of energy expenditure.

**anorexia nervosa** An eating disorder in which a normal-weight person (usually an adolescent female) diets and becomes significantly (15 percent or more) underweight, yet, still feeling fat, continues to starve.

**bulimia nervosa** An eating disorder characterized by private, "binge-purge" episodes of overeating, usually of highly caloric foods, followed by vomiting or laxative use.

### Sexual Motivation

**sexual response cycle** The four stages of sexual responding described by Masters and Johnson—excitement, plateau, orgasm, and resolution.

**refractory period** A resting period after orgasm, during which a man cannot achieve another orgasm.

**estrogen** A sex hormone, secreted in greater amounts by females than by males. In nonhuman female mammals, estrogen levels peak during ovulation, promoting sexual receptivity.

**sexual dysfunction** A problem that consistently impairs sexual arousal or functioning.

**sexual orientation** An enduring sexual attraction toward members of either one's own gender (homosexual orientation) or the other gender (heterosexual orientation).

### Achievement Motivation

**achievement motivation** A desire for significant accomplishment: for mastery of things, people, or ideas; for attaining a high standard.

**intrinsic motivation** A desire to perform a behavior for its own sake and to be effective.

**extrinsic motivation** A desire to perform a behavior due to promised rewards or threats of punishment.

**industrial/organizational psychology** A subfield of psychology that studies and advises on workplace behavior. Industrial/organizational (I/O) psychologists help organizations select and train employees, boost morale and productivity, and design products and assess responses to them.

**task leadership** Goal-oriented leadership that sets standards, organizes work, and focuses attention on goals.

**social leadership** Group-oriented leadership that builds teamwork, mediates conflict, and offers support.

**Theory X** Assumes that workers are basically lazy, error-prone, and extrinsically motivated by money and, thus, should be directed from above.

**Theory Y** Assumes that, given challenge and freedom, workers are motivated to achieve self-esteem and to demonstrate their competence and creativity.

### The Need to Belong

**need to belong** A motivation to form and maintain enduring, close personal relationships.

## Critical Thinking Exercise

Now that you have read and reviewed Chapter 12, take your learning a step further by testing your critical thinking skills on the following pattern recognition exercise.

Rochelle has always felt very competitive with other people, especially her older and only sibling, Doreen. Doreen is less competitive and more motivated by the desire to perform to the best of her ability than by comparing herself with others. Rochelle has always received lower grades in school than Doreen, who receives consistently high scores. Rochelle claims this is because she intentionally selects more difficult classes and instructors than her sister. Doreen responds that she picks instructors who are challenging yet fair, while her sister picks either impossibly difficult or ridiculously easy instructors.

Rochelle has often followed in her older sister's footsteps as Doreen developed new interests. For example, Doreen recently took up the guitar. On her own initiative, she began taking lessons and diligently practicing for an hour each day. Her proud parents frequently praised her for her discipline and musical progress. Not to be outdone, Rochelle decided to start playing the guitar as well. After a week or two, however, her interest in practicing began to wane. To increase their daughter's motivation, Rochelle's parents announced that for 1 month they would reward both daughters' efforts by giving them one dollar for each hour they practiced. The additional incentive seemed effective for Rochelle, who increased practice time to nearly match Doreen's. Much to her parents' surprise, however, Doreen's interest level and practice time actually decreased when the monetary incentive was provided. At the end of the month the puzzled parents withdrew the reward for practicing. Three weeks later neither Rochelle nor Doreen seemed very interested in playing the guitar.

1. What principles of motivation might help explain why Rochelle and Doreen differ in the level of their school performance?
2. What principles of motivation might help explain why the monetary reward for practicing influenced Rochelle and Doreen differently?
3. What advice would you offer to Doreen's and Rochelle's parents if they wished to renew their daughters' interest in playing the guitar?

Check your progress on becoming a critical thinker by comparing your answers to the sample answers found in Appendix B.

## For Further Information

*You can find further information in this text regarding industrial/organizational psychology on the following pages:*



## For Further Reading

### Hunger

**Logue, A. W.** (1993). *The psychology of eating and drinking,* 2nd ed. New York: Freeman.

*Why do some foods taste better to you than others? Why do people develop problems related to eating and drinking? Logue provides authoritative and readable answers to these and other questions about hunger and thirst.*

### Sexuality

**Hyde, J. S.** (1990). *Understanding human sexuality* (4th ed.). New York: McGraw-Hill.

*A comprehensive overview of every aspect of human sexuality, including sexual orientation and sexual disorders.*

**Reinisch, J. M.** (1990). *The Kinsey Institute's new report on sex.* New York: St. Martin's.

*Informative answers to people's most frequently asked questions about sexuality.*

### Achievement

**Mook, D. G.** (1987). *Motivation: The organization of action.* New York: Norton.

*Provides a lucid and up-to-date overview of the major topics in motivation.*

**Steers, R. M., & Porter, L. W.** (1987). *Motivation and work behavior.* New York: McGraw-Hill.

*Reviews research on maximizing worker motivation and minimizing absenteeism and turnover.*

# CHAPTER 13

# Emotion

Feelings—powerful, spontaneous, sometimes unforgettable. Where do feelings come from? Of all the species, we humans seem the most emotional (Hebb, 1980). More often than any other creature, we express fear, anger, sadness, joy, and love. No one needs to tell you that emotions add color to your life, that in times of stress they can disrupt your life or save it. But what are the ingredients of emotion?

Imagine that, while walking home along a deserted street late at night, you hear the rumble of an engine and realize that someone on a motorcycle is stalking you. Your heart begins to race, your pace quickens, you wonder about the cyclist's intent, and you feel scared. As this illustrates, **emotions** are a mix of (1) physiological arousal (heart pounding), (2) expressive behavior (quickened pace), and (3) conscious experience (interpreting the person's intent and feeling fearful). The puzzle is how these three pieces fit together: Did you first notice your heart racing, your speeded-up walking, and *then* feel afraid? Or did your sense of fear come first, stirring your heart and legs to respond? Before trying to answer these questions, let's study the individual pieces of the emotion puzzle—its physiology, expression, and conscious experience.

*Not only emotion, but most psychological phenomena (vision, sleep, memory, sex, and so forth) can be approached these three ways—physiologically, behaviorally, and cognitively.*

## The Physiology of Emotion

*Emotions involve physiological arousal. Does this arousal differ with specific emotions? And can a person's arousal accurately detect whether the person is telling a lie or the truth?*

### Arousal

When emotionally aroused, you are physically aroused. Some physical responses are so obvious that you easily notice them. As you hear the motorcycle's rumble behind you, your muscles tense, your stomach develops butterflies, your mouth becomes dry.

Your body also mobilizes for action in less noticeable ways. To provide energy, your liver pours extra sugar into your bloodstream. To help burn the sugar, your respiration rate increases to supply needed oxygen. Your digestion slows, diverting blood from your internal organs to your muscles. Your pupils dilate, letting in more light. To cool your stirred-up body, you perspire more. If you were wounded, your blood would clot more quickly. Think of this after your next crisis: Without any conscious effort, your body's response to danger was wonderfully coordinated and adaptive—preparing you to fight or flee.

**Figure 13–1**

| Sympathetic (arousing) | | Parasympathetic (calming) |
|---|---|---|
| Pupils dilate | EYES | Pupils contract |
| Decreases | SALIVATION | Increases |
| Perspires | SKIN | Dries |
| Increases | RESPIRATION | Decreases |
| Accelerates | HEART | Slows |
| Inhibits | DIGESTION | Activates |
| Secrete stress hormones | ADRENAL GLANDS | Decrease secretion of stress hormones |

**Emotional Arousal** *Physiological arousal is controlled by our autonomic nervous system. The sympathetic division activates. The parasympathetic calms.*

*One explanation of sudden death caused by a voodoo "curse" is that the terrified person's parasympathetic nervous system, which calms the body, overreacts to the extreme arousal by slowing the heart to a stop (Seligman, 1974).*

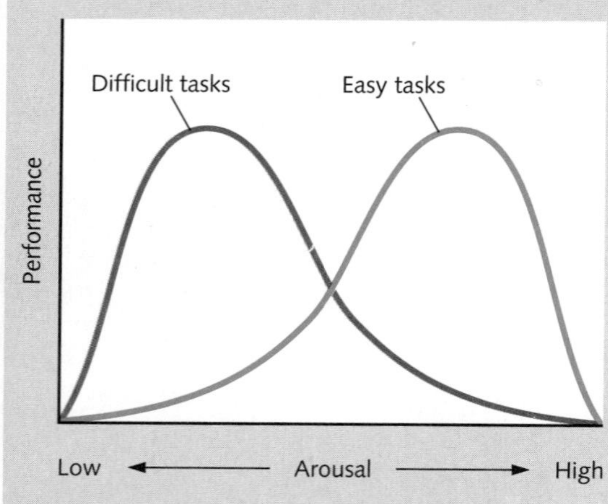


**Figure 13–2**

**Arousal and Performance** *Performance peaks at lower levels of arousal for difficult tasks, and at higher levels for easy or well-learned tasks.*

As we learned in Chapter 2 (page 49), our *autonomic nervous system* controls our arousal. Its sympathetic division (Figure 13–1) activates arousal by directing the adrenal glands atop the kidneys to release the stress hormones epinephrine (adrenaline) and norepinephrine (noradrenaline). The surge in epinephrine and norepinephrine increases heart rate, blood pressure, and blood sugar levels. When the crisis passes, the parasympathetic neural centers become active, calming the body. Even after the parasympathetic division inhibits further release of stress hormones, those already in the bloodstream linger awhile, so arousal diminishes gradually.

Prolonged arousal, produced by sustained stress, taxes the body (more on this in Chapter 17, Stress and Health). Yet in many situations arousal is adaptive. Too little arousal (say, sleepiness) can be as disruptive as extremely high levels of arousal. When you're taking an exam, it pays to be moderately aroused—alert but not trembling with nervousness.

Although performance is usually best when arousal is moderate, the level of arousal for optimal performance varies for different tasks. With easy or well-learned tasks, peak performance comes with relatively high arousal, which enhances the dominant, usually correct, response. With more difficult or unrehearsed tasks, the optimal arousal is somewhat less (Figure 13–2). Thus, runners, who are performing a well-learned task, usually achieve their peak performances when highly aroused by competition. Basketball players shooting free throws—a less routine skill—may perform slightly less well if a packed fieldhouse makes them hyperaroused (Sokoll & Mynatt, 1984). Likewise, students who feel great anxiety during exams perform more poorly than equally able but more confident students. Training anxious students how to relax before an exam often enables them to perform better (Hembree, 1988).

## Physiological States Accompanying Specific Emotions

Imagine conducting an experiment exploring physiological indicators of arousal. In each of four rooms, you have someone watching a movie: In the first is a horror show; in the second, an anger-provoking film; in the third, a sexually arousing film; in the fourth, an utterly boring film. From the control center you monitor each person's physiological responses. By examining the perspiration, breathing, and heart rates of the viewers, could you tell who was frightened, who was angry, who was sexually aroused, and who was bored?

With training, you could probably pick out the bored viewer from the other three. Discerning physiological differences among fear, anger, and sexual arousal is much harder (Zillmann, 1986). Fear and anger accelerate the heart rate more than happiness does (Levenson, 1992). Still, apart from the breathing disruption caused by laughter, experts even have difficulty distinguishing viewers' physiological responses to sad versus funny movies (Averill, 1969).

*"No one ever told me that grief felt so much like fear. I am not afraid, but the sensation is like being afraid. The same fluttering in the stomach, the same restlessness, the yawning. I keep on swallowing."*

C. S. Lewis
*A Grief Observed*, 1961

Fear, anger, sexual arousal, and sadness certainly *feel* different (and, as we will see, cognitively they *are* different). A terrified person may feel a clutching, sinking sensation in the chest and a knot in the stomach. An angry person may feel "hot under the collar" and will probably experience a pressing, inner tension. The sexually stimulated person will experience a genital response. The sad person may be choked up and have an empty, drained feeling (Epstein, 1984). Moreover, frightened, angered, and saddened people often *look* different—"paralyzed with fear," "ready to explode," or "down in the dumps." Knowing this, can we pinpoint some distinct physiological indicators of each emotion?

Fear and rage are accompanied by differing finger temperatures and hormone secretions (Ax, 1953; Levenson, 1992). Different emotions also arise through different brain circuits (Kalin, 1993; Panksepp, 1982). As we saw on page 58, stimulate one area of a cat's limbic system and it will pull back in terror at the sight of a mouse. Stimulate another limbic area and the cat will look enraged—pupils dilated, fur and tail erect, claws out, hissing furiously. As people experience negative emotions, such as disgust, the right hemisphere becomes more electrically active. The left hemisphere activates when processing positive emotions (Davidson & others, 1990, 1992). For some infants and adults, the left frontal lobe shows more activity than the right. These individuals are typically more cheerful and less readily threatened or depressed than those with more active right frontal lobes. "It may be that those people with more left front activity are better able to turn off upsetting feelings," speculates researcher Richard Davidson (1991).

*In 1966, a young man named Charles Whitman killed his wife and mother and then climbed to the top of a tower at the University of Texas and shot 38 people. An autopsy later revealed a tumor in his limbic system.*

So, although emotions as varied as fear and anger involve a similar general autonomic arousal (thanks to the sympathetic nervous system), there are real, if subtle, physiological differences that help explain why we experience them so differently. Moreover, the physical accompaniments of emotion appear innate and universal—the same in a Sumatran village as in North America (Levenson & others, 1991).

## Summing Up

**Arousal** Emotions are psychological responses that involve physiological arousal controlled by the autonomic nervous system. Our performance on a task is usually best when arousal is moderate, though this varies with the difficulty of the task.

## *Thinking Critically About* Lie Detection

Given the physical indicators of emotion, might we, like Pinocchio, give some telltale sign whenever we lie? The *lie detector*, or **polygraph**, was once used mainly in law enforcement and national security work. But by the mid-1980s, 2 million Americans annually were reportedly being tested, usually by corporations trying to screen applicants for honesty or to uncover employee theft (Holden, 1986a).

Just what does the polygraph do? It does not literally detect lies. Rather, it measures several of the physiological responses that accompany emotion, such as changes in breathing, pulse rate, blood pressure, and perspiration. While you try to relax, the examiner measures your physiological responses as you answer questions. Some of these, called control questions, are designed to make anyone a little nervous. If asked, "In the last 20 years, have you ever taken something that didn't belong to you?" many people will tell a white lie and say no, causing arousal that the polygraph would detect. If your physiological reactions to the critical questions ("Did you ever steal anything from your previous employer?") are weaker than to the control questions, the examiner infers you are telling the truth. The assumption is that only a thief becomes agitated when denying a theft.

But there is a problem: An innocent person might also respond with heightened tension to the accusations implied by the relevant questions. When a Yakima, Washington, woman was accused by her ex-husband's new wife of sexually abusing her 4-year-old son, the mother gladly accepted a police offer of a polygraph test "to prove her innocence." Asked, "Did you take Tommy's penis in your mouth?" the accused mother understandably reacted with greater perspiration and blood pressure than when asked "Have you ever told a lie to get out of trouble?" (Physiologically, the fear of being disbelieved looks a lot like the fear of being caught lying.) This revealed her guilt, explained the police sergeant-turned-polygrapher to the jury. (Fortunately for the mother, her attorney managed to locate a scientific expert who persuaded the jury that, by itself, this was not credible evidence of guilt.) Many rape victims similarly "fail" lie detector tests when reacting emotionally while telling the truth about their assailant (Lykken, 1992).

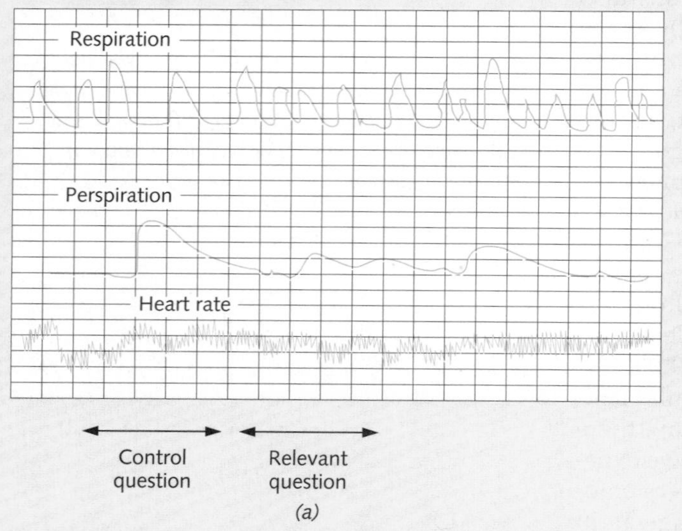


(a)

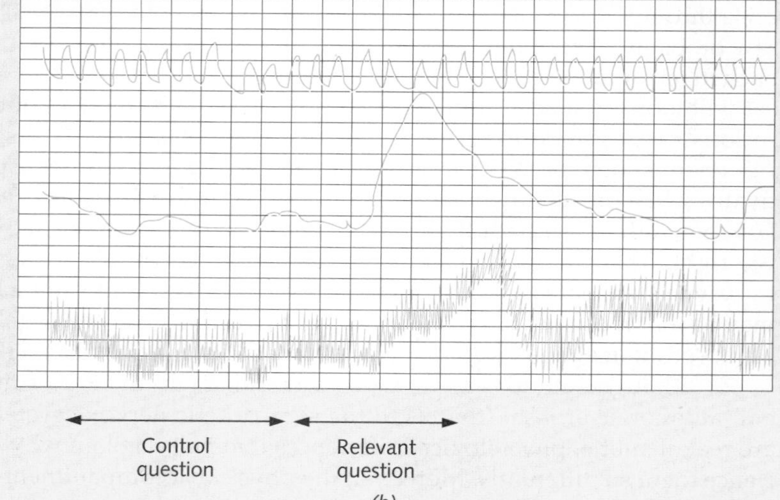


(b)

**Physiological Responses to a Lie Detector Test.** *(a) This is the record of a witness who supported an accused murderer's alibi. She reacted more strongly when answering no to a control question, "Up to age 18, did you ever deceive anyone?" than when answering yes to the relevant question, "Was [the accused] at another location at the time of the murder?" As a result, the examiner concluded she was telling the truth. (b) This is the record of an accused murderer judged to be lying when he pleaded self-defense. He reacted less strongly in answering no to the control question, "Up to age 18, did you ever physically harm anyone?" than when answering yes to the relevant question, "Did [the deceased] threaten to harm you in any way?" (From Raskin, 1982.)*

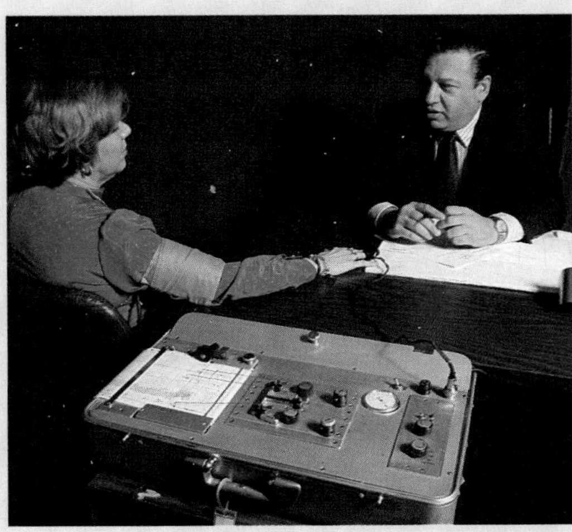

**Who's Lying?** *Can polygraph tests like this identify liars, or are its promoters putting something over on a gullible public? To learn more about this disputed issue, read on.*

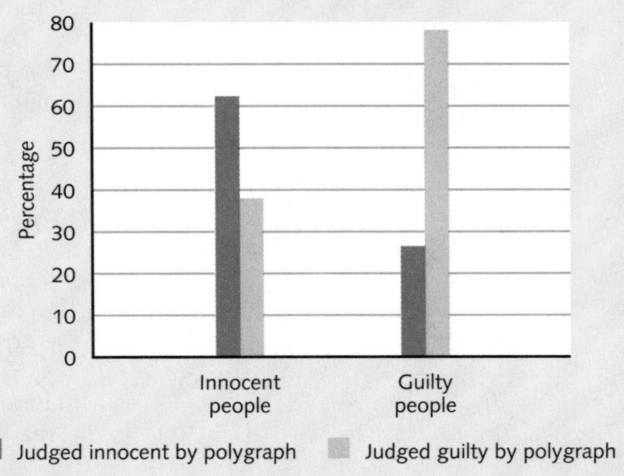


**Figure 13–3**

**How Often Do Lie Detectors Lie?** *Benjamin Kleinmuntz and Julian Szucko (1984) had polygraph experts study the polygraph data of 50 theft suspects who later confessed to being guilty and 50 suspects whose innocence was later established by someone's confession. Had the polygraph experts been the judges, more than one-third of the innocent would have been declared guilty, and almost one-fourth of the guilty would have been declared innocent.*

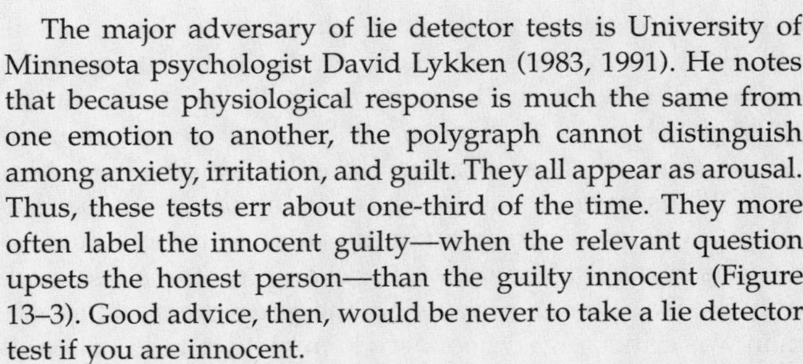

The major adversary of lie detector tests is University of Minnesota psychologist David Lykken (1983, 1991). He notes that because physiological response is much the same from one emotion to another, the polygraph cannot distinguish among anxiety, irritation, and guilt. They all appear as arousal. Thus, these tests err about one-third of the time. They more often label the innocent guilty—when the relevant question upsets the honest person—than the guilty innocent (Figure 13–3). Good advice, then, would be never to take a lie detector test if you are innocent.

Though more accurate than a 50–50 coin toss, polygraph tests have been deemed too inaccurate for about half of U.S. state courts (Patrick & Iacono, 1991). The Congressional Office of Technology Assessment (U.S. Congress, 1983, p. 4) warned that "the available research evidence does not establish the scientific validity of the polygraph test for personnel security screening." The American Psychological Association (1986) similarly has voiced great reservations about the use of polygraph tests to detect deception, as has the British Psychological Society (1986).

The polygraph functions more appropriately as a tool in criminal investigation. Police sometimes use the polygraph to induce confessions by criminals whom they scare into thinking that any lies will be transparent. A more honest approach uses the *guilty knowledge test*, which assesses a suspect's physiological responses to details of a crime known only to the police and the guilty person. If a camera and money were stolen, the polygraph examiner could see whether the suspect reacts strongly to such details as the specific brand name of the camera and the dollar amounts. Presumably, only a guilty person would. Given enough such specific probes, an innocent person will seldom be wrongly accused. Brain wave responses associated with lying hold promise of further increasing the accuracy of the guilty knowledge test (Bashore & Rapp, 1993).

Nevertheless, critics and advocates alike disapprove of commercial use of the polygraph. The truth is that lie detectors can lie. The U.S. Congress recognized this when it passed the Employee Polygraph Protection Act of 1988, prohibiting most nongovernmental polygraph testing.

**Physiological States Accompanying Specific Emotions** The physical arousal that occurs with one emotion is, in most ways, indistinguishable from arousal that occurs with another. However, scientists have discovered subtle differences in the brain pathways and hormones associated with different emotions.

The polygraph measures several physiological indicators of emotion. The polygraph detects lies better than chance, but not nearly well enough to justify its widespread use in business and government.

## Expressing Emotion

*Emotions are revealed not only in our bodily arousal but also in our expressive behavior. Does nonverbal language vary with culture, or is it universal? Do our expressions influence our experienced emotions?*

There is another, simpler method of deciphering people's emotions: We "read" their bodies, listen to their voices, and look at their faces.

### Nonverbal Communication

All of us communicate nonverbally as well as verbally. If irritated, we may tense our bodies, press our lips together, and turn away. With a gaze, an averted glance, or a stare we can communicate intimacy, submission, or dominance (Kleinke, 1986). Among couples passionately in love, eye-gazing is typically prolonged and mutual (Rubin, 1970). Would intimate gazes stir such feelings between strangers? To find out, Joan Kellerman, James Lewis, and James Laird (1989) asked unacquainted male-female pairs to gaze intently for 2 minutes either at one another's hands or into one another's eyes. After separating, the eye-gazers reported feeling a greater tingle of attraction and affection.

Most of us are good enough at reading nonverbal cues to decipher the emotions in an old silent film. We are especially good at detecting nonverbal threats. In a crowd of faces, a single angry face will "pop out" faster than a single happy one (Hansen & Hansen, 1988). Some of us are more sensitive to these cues than others are. Robert Rosenthal, Judith Hall, and their colleagues (1979) discovered this by showing hundreds of people brief film clips of portions of a person's emotionally expressive face or body, sometimes with a garbled voice added. For example, after a 2-second scene revealing only the face of an upset woman, the researchers would ask whether the woman was criticizing someone for being late or talking about her divorce. Rosenthal and Hall reported that some people are much better emotion detectors than others are, and that women are better at it than men. By exposing different parts of emotion-laden faces, Robert Kestenbaum (1992) discovered that we read fear and anger mostly from the eyes, happiness from the mouth.

*"Your face, my thane, is a book where men may read strange matters."*

William Shakespeare's Lady Macbeth to her husband

Armed with high-tech equipment, psychologists are now linking various emotions with specific facial muscles (Figure 13–4). Hard-to-control facial muscles reveal signs of emotions you may be trying to conceal. Lifting just the inner part of your eyebrows, which few people do consciously, reveals distress or worry. Eyebrows raised and pulled together signal fear. A feigned smile, such as one we make for a photographer, often continues for more than 4 or 5 seconds, by which time most authentic expressions have faded. Feigned smiles also get switched on more abruptly and off more abruptly than a genuine smile (Bugental, 1986).

**Figure 13–4**

(a)

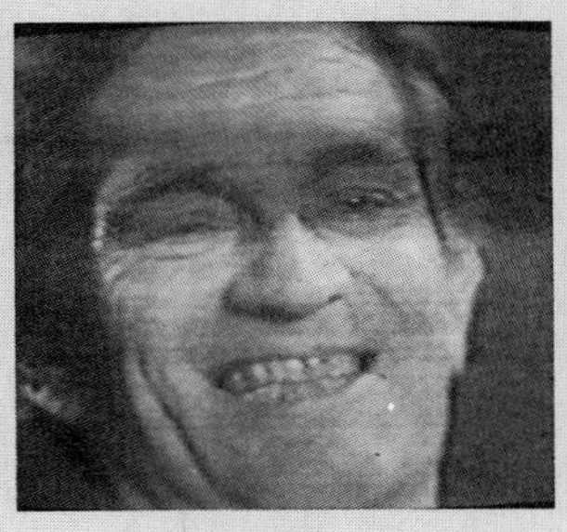
(b)

(c)

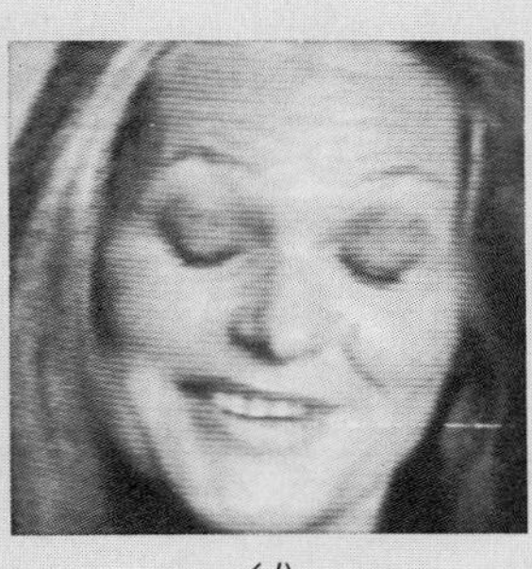
(d)

**Smiles as Indicators of Emotions** *Paul Ekman's system for classifying a particular smile consists of a specific code for each of the 80 facial muscles used to create it. Notice how different these smiles are. (a) A smile that masks anger (the woman has just been told she is being dismissed). (b) An overly polite smile (the man is telling a patient to enjoy her hospital stay). (c) A smile softening verbal criticism ("I'd appreciate it if you wouldn't come to rehearsal drunk"). And (d) a reluctant, compliant smile ("I guess I don't have any choice, so OK" ).*

Unless trained in recognizing such subtle signals, most people find it difficult to detect deceiving expressions. For example, Paul Ekman and Maureen O'Sullivan (1991) videotaped university students for a minute each as they watched either a nature film or an upsetting gruesome film. Regardless of which film they watched, the subjects were asked to talk and act as if they were watching and enjoying the nature film. Telltale signs of lying, such as a raised voice pitch, enabled the researchers to classify correctly 86 percent of the subjects as lying or truth-telling. But could the rest of us do as well, using only our intuition? Not likely. Ekman and O'Sullivan challenged 39 college students, 67 psychiatrists, 110 court judges, 126 police officers, and 90 federal polygraphers to spot the liars. All five groups' guesses were near chance (50 percent). Only a sixth group of experienced crowd-scanners—Secret Service agents—beat chance, though still with only 64 percent correct.

When people aren't seeking to deceive us, we do much better. In fact, our brains are rather amazing emotion-detectors. Elisha Babad, Frank Bernieri, and Robert Rosenthal (1991) discovered just *how* amazing after videotaping teachers talking to unseen school children. A mere 10-second clip of either the teacher's voice or face provided enough clues for both child and adult viewers to determine whether the teacher liked and admired the child he or she was addressing. Although teachers may think they can conceal their feelings and stay objective, their students can sense what their expressions and gestures reveal.

Subtle facial indicators of emotion may someday enable a new behavioral approach to lie detection. For example, given mild emotional stimuli, electrodes attached to your facial muscles can now detect your hidden reactions (Tassinary & Cacioppo, 1992). Your face may not look any different, but voltage changes on the skin reveal underlying micromuscular smiles or frowns.

The growing awareness that we communicate through the body's silent language has led to studies of how job applicants and interviewers communicate (or miscommunicate) nonverbally. Popular guidebooks and articles offer advice on how to interpret nonverbal signals when negotiating a business deal, selling a product, or flirting with someone. It pays to be able to read feelings that "leak through" via subtle facial expressions, body

**A Silent Language of Emotion** *The art of nonverbal communication reached a pinnacle early in the century as silent films became widely available. For a nickle, enraptured audiences could watch performers mime a wide range of unmistakable emotions. Here Chester Conklin woos a woman on horseback while Louise Fazenda fumes.*

movements, and postures. Fidgeting, for example, may reveal anxiety or boredom. More specific interpretations of postures and gestures are risky. Different expressions may convey the same emotion: Either a cold stare or the avoidance of eye contact may signify hostility. And a given expression can convey very different emotions: Folded arms, for example, can signify irritation or relaxation.

Such gestures, facial expressions, and tones of voice are all absent in computer-based communication. Experienced electronic mail users sometimes insert sideways "smiles," such as ;-) for a knowing wink and :-( for a frown. But e-mail letters and group discussions otherwise lack nonverbal cues to status, personality, and emotion. Thus, when first meeting an e-mail pen pal face to face, people are often surprised at the personality they encounter.

## Culture and Emotional Expression

The meaning of gestures varies with the culture. Some years ago, psychologist Otto Klineberg (1938) observed that in Chinese literature people clapped their hands to express worry or disappointment, laughed a great "ho-ho" to express anger, and stuck out their tongues to show surprise. Similarly, the North American "thumbs up" and "A-OK" signs would be interpreted as insults in certain other cultures. (When President Nixon made the latter sign in Brazil he didn't realize he was saying "Let's have sex.") Just how important cultural definitions of gestures can be was demonstrated in 1968, when North Korea photographed supposedly happy officers from a captured U.S. Navy spy ship. In the photo, three of the men made the obscene middle-finger gesture; they had explained to their captors it was a "Hawaiian good luck sign" (Fleming & Scott, 1991).

Do facial expressions also have different meanings in different cultures? To find out, two investigative teams—one led by Paul Ekman and Wallace Friesen (1975, 1987, 1994), the other by Carroll Izard (1977, 1994)—showed photographs of different facial expressions to people in different parts of the world and asked them to guess the emotion. You can try this yourself. Match the six emotions with the six faces of Figure 13–5.

**Figure 13–5**

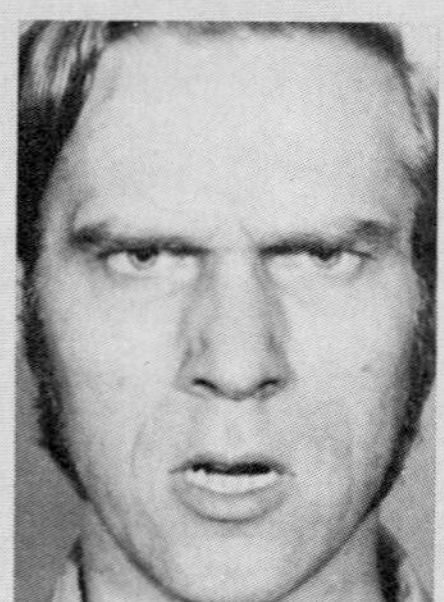
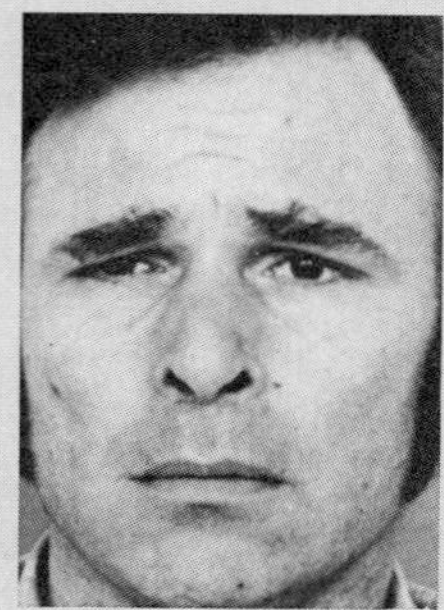
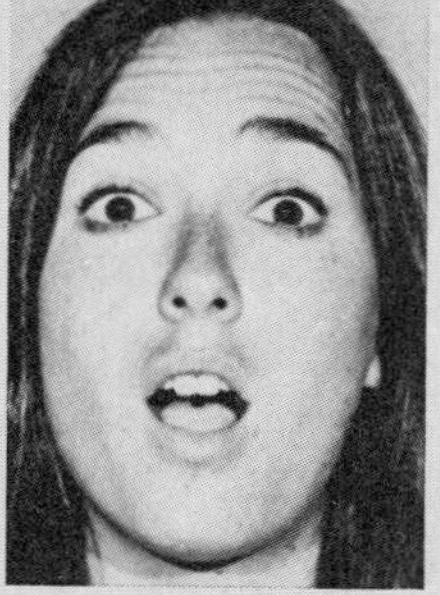
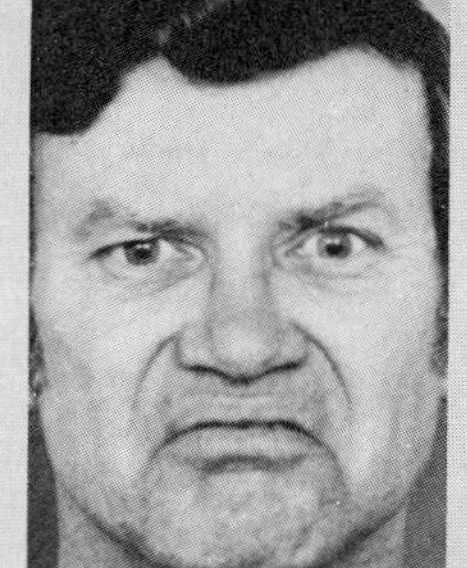
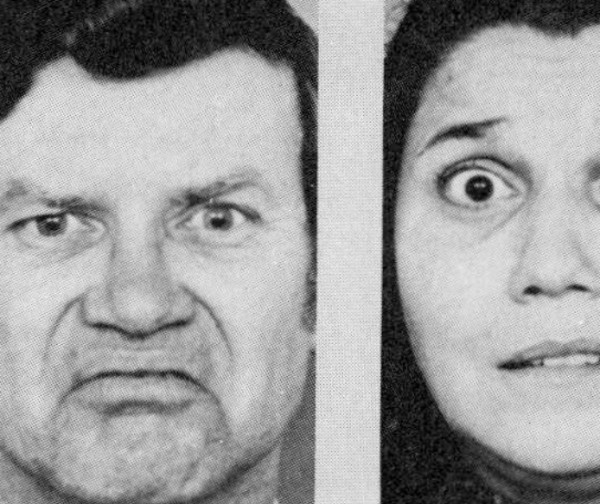

**Culture-Specific or Culturally Universal Expressions?** *As people of differing cultures and races, do our faces speak differing languages? Which face expresses disgust? Anger? Fear? Happiness? Sadness? Surprise? The answers are on page 443.*

You probably did pretty well. How do you suppose people from Brazil or Japan did when judging these pictures? About the same as North Americans, it turns out. A smile's a smile the world around. Ditto for the other basic expressions. Despite some differences, cultures and languages also share many similarities in how they categorize emotions—as anger, fear, and so on (Russell, 1991). The physiological symptoms of emotion also cross cultures (Levenson & others, 1992; Mesquita & Frijda, 1992).

Do people from different cultures make and interpret facial expressions similarly because they experience similar influences, such as American movies and CNN? Apparently not. Ekman and his team asked isolated people in New Guinea to display various emotions in response to such statements as, "Pretend your child has died." When the researchers showed videotapes of the New Guineans' facial reactions to North American collegians, the students could easily read them. Children's facial expressions—even those of blind children who have never seen a face—are also universal (Eibl-Eibesfeldt, 1971). The world over, children cry when distressed, shake their heads when defiant, and smile when happy.

*While weightless, astronauts' fluids move toward their upper body and their faces become puffy. This makes nonverbal communication more difficult, increasing the risks of misunderstanding, especially among multinational crews (Gelman, 1989).*

The discovery that the facial muscles speak a universal language would have come as no surprise to Charles Darwin. He speculated that in prehistoric times, before our ancestors communicated in words, their ability to convey threats, greetings, and submission with facial expressions helped them survive. That shared heritage, he believed, is why all humans express the basic emotions by similar facial expressions. A sneer, for example, retains elements of an animal's teeth-baring snarl. Smiles, too, are a form of social communication, not just emotional reflexes. Bowlers don't smile when they score a strike—they smile when they turn to face their companions (Jones & others, 1991; Kraut & Johnston, 1979).

Although cultures share a universal facial language, they differ in how, and how much, they express emotion. In cultures that encourage individuality, as in Western Europe, Australia, New Zealand, and North America, emotional displays often are intense and prolonged. People focus on their own goals and attitudes and express themselves accordingly. Watching a film of someone's hand being cut, Americans grimace (whether alone or with other viewers). In the presence of others, Japanese viewers hide their emotions (Triandis, 1994). In Asian and other cultures that emphasize social connections and interdependence, displays of emotions such as sympathy, respect, and shame are more common than in the West. Moreover, Asians rarely and briefly display self-aggrandizing or negative emotions that might disrupt communal feeling within close-knit groups (Markus & Kitayama, 1991; Matsumoto & others, 1988).

## The Effects of Facial Expressions

Expressions not only communicate emotion, they also amplify and regulate it. In his 1872 book, *The Expression of the Emotions in Man and Animals*, Darwin contended that "the free expression by outward signs of an emotion intensifies it. . . . He who gives way to violent gestures will increase his rage."

Was Darwin right? I was driving in my car one day when the song "Put On a Happy Face" came on the radio. How phony, I thought. But I tested Darwin's hypothesis anyway, as you can, too. Fake a big grin. Now scowl. Can you feel the difference?

The subjects in dozens of experiments have felt a difference. For example, when James Laird and his colleagues (1974, 1984, 1989) subtly induced students to make a frowning expression—by asking them to "contract these muscles" and "pull your brows together" (supposedly to help the re-

**Figure 13–6**

**How to Make People Frown Without Telling Them to Frown** *Randy Larsen, Margaret Kasimatis, and Kurt Frey's (1992) solution: Attach two golf tees above the eyebrows and ask the subjects to make the tee tips touch. With "sad face" muscles activated, subjects felt sadder while viewing scenes of war, sickness, and starvation.*

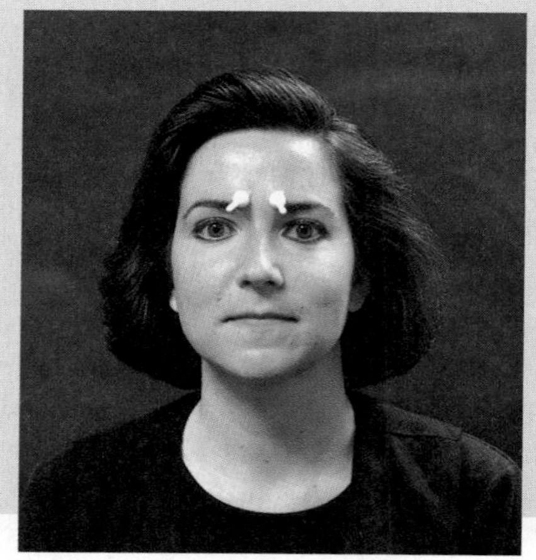

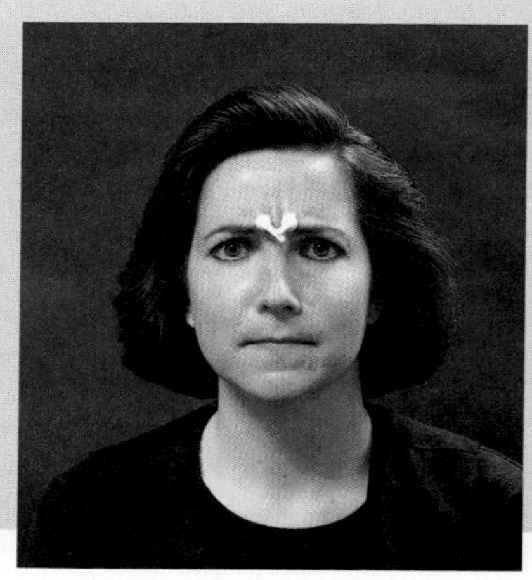

searchers attach facial electrodes). The results? The students reported feeling a little angry. Students similarly induced to smile felt happier, found cartoons more humorous, and recalled happier memories than did the frowners. People instructed to express other basic emotions also experienced them. For example, they reported feeling more fear than anger, disgust, or sadness when made to construct an expression of fear: "Raise your eyebrows. And open your eyes wide. Move your whole head back, so that your chin is tucked in a little bit, and let your mouth relax and hang open a little" (Duclos & others, 1989). Going through the motions awakens the emotions.

*"Refuse to express a passion and it dies. . . . If we wish to conquer undesirable emotional tendencies in ourselves, we must . . . go through the outward movements of those contrary dispositions which we prefer to cultivate."*

William James
*Principles of Psychology*, 1890

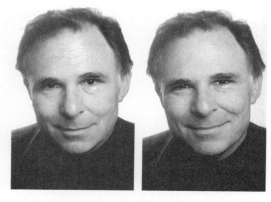

The effect is subtle, yet detectable in the absence of competing emotions. Consider these findings:

- If subtly manipulated into furrowing their brows (see Figure 13–6), people feel sadder while looking at sad photos.
- Saying the phonemes *e* and *ah*, which activate smiling muscles, puts people—believe it or not—in a better mood than saying the German *ü*, which activates muscles associated with negative emotions (Zajonc & others, 1989).
- Just activating one of the smiling muscles by holding a pen in the teeth (rather than with the lips, which activates a frowning muscle) is enough to make cartoons seem more amusing (Strack & others, 1988). A heartier smile, made not just with the mouth but with raised cheeks as well, works even better (Ekman & others, 1990). Smile warmly on the outside and you feel better on the inside. Scowl and the whole world seems to scowl back.

Why might this be so? Paul Ekman and his colleagues (1983) designed an experiment to find out. Their subjects were professional actors trained in the Stanislavsky method, in which they physically (and psychologically) "become" the characters they are playing. The actors would assume an expression and then hold it for 10 seconds while the researchers measured changes in their heart rates and finger temperatures. When they made a fearful expression, their heart rate increased some 8 beats per minute and finger temperature was steady. When making an angry expression, both heart rate and finger temperature increased as though the actor were indeed "hot-headed." Our facial expressions, it seems, send signals to our autonomic nervous system, which then responds accordingly.

**Which Smile Makes Paul Ekman Feel Happy?** *The smile on the right, which engages the face muscles of a natural smile.*

This experiment shows how facial feedback affects our emotions, and it provides further evidence that different emotions accompany subtly different body states. Sara Snodgrass and her associates (1986) observed the same phenomenon with walking behavior. You can duplicate her subjects' experience: Walk for a few minutes while taking short, shuffling steps, keeping your eyes downcast. Now walk around taking long strides, with your arms swinging and your eyes looking straight ahead. Can you feel your mood shift?

If assuming an emotional expression triggers a feeling, then imitating others' expressions should help us feel what they are feeling. Again, the laboratory evidence is supportive. Kathleen Burns Vaughn and John Lanzetta (1981) asked some students but not others to make a pained expression whenever an electric shock was apparently delivered to someone they were watching. With each apparent shock, the grimacing observers perspired more and had a faster heart rate than the other observers. So one small way to become more empathic—to feel what others feel—is to let your own face mimic the other person's expression. Acting as another acts helps us feel what another feels.

*Answers to the question in Figure 13–5: From left to right: happiness, anger, sadness, surprise, disgust, fear.*

## Summing Up

**Nonverbal Communication** Much of our communication is through the body's silent language. Psychologists have studied people's abilities to detect emotion, even from thin slices of behavior.

**Culture and Emotional Expression** Is nonverbal language universal? Although some gestures are culturally determined, facial expressions, such as those of happiness and fear, are common the world over. In communal cultures that value interdependence, intense displays of potentially disruptive emotions are infrequent.

**The Effects of Facial Expressions** Expressions not only communicate emotion, they also amplify the felt emotion and signal the body to respond accordingly.

## Experiencing Emotion

*The ingredients of emotion include not only physiological arousal and expressive behavior but also our conscious experience. Among the basic emotions, we will consider three: fear, anger, and happiness. What influences each?*

Our feelings are "obscure and confused," noted Benjamin Constant de Rebecque in 1816. To cut through the obscurity, psychologists have asked people to report their experience of different emotions. Estonians, Poles, Greeks, Chinese, and Canadians all seem to place emotions along two dimensions—pleasant versus unpleasant, and intensely aroused versus sleepy (Russell & others, 1989). On the intensity scale, for example, terrified is more frightened than afraid, enraged is angrier than angry, delighted is happier than happy. To these two dimensions, we might add a third: duration. Among Americans and Japanese, at least, the emotions of joy and sadness typically endure longer than anger and guilt, which outlast fear and disgust (Matsumoto & others, 1988).

**Figure 13–7**

**Infants' Naturally Occurring Emotions** *To identify the emotions present from birth, Carroll Izard analyzed the facial expressions of very young infants. Shown here are (a) joy (mouth forming smile, cheeks lifted, twinkle in eye); (b) anger (brows drawn together and downward, eyes fixed, mouth squarish); (c) interest (brows raised or knitted, mouth softly rounded, lips may be pursed); (d) disgust (nose wrinkled, upper lip raised, tongue pushed outward); (e) surprise (brows raised, eyes widened, mouth rounded in oval shape); (f) sadness (brow's inner corners raised, mouth corners drawn down); and (g) fear (brows level, drawn in and up, eyelids lifted, mouth corners retracted).*

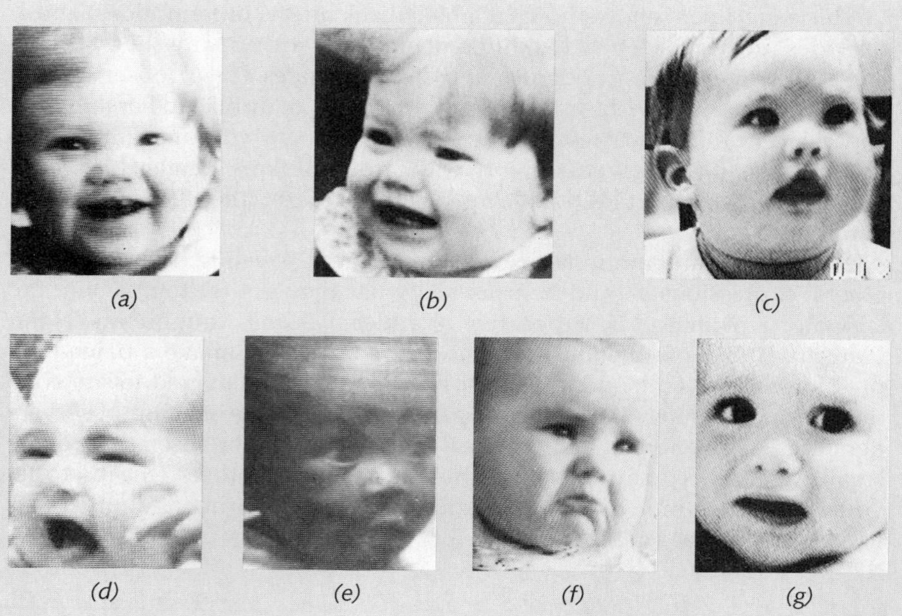


Other psychologists have sought to identify emotions that are physiologically, facially, and experientially distinct. Carroll Izard (1977) believes there are 10 such basic emotions (joy, interest-excitement, surprise, sadness, anger, disgust, contempt, fear, shame, and guilt), most of which are present in infancy (Figure 13–7). Other emotions, he says, are combinations of these. Love, for instance, is a mixture of joy and interest-excitement.

Let's now examine three important emotions: fear, anger, and happiness. What functions do these emotions serve? And what influences our experience of them?

## Fear

Fear can be a poisonous emotion. It can torment us, rob us of sleep, and preoccupy our thinking. People can be literally scared to death. Fear can also be contagious. In 1903, someone yelled "Fire!" as a fire broke out in Chicago's Iroquois Theater. Eddie Foy, the comedian on stage at the time, tried to reassure the crowd by calling out, "Don't get excited. There's no danger. Take it easy!" Alas, the crowd panicked. During the 10 minutes it took the fire department to arrive and quickly extinguish the flames, more than 500 people perished, most of them trampled or smothered in a stampede. Bodies were piled 7 or 8 feet deep in the stairways, and many of the faces bore heel marks (Brown, 1965).

*"He who fears all snares falls into none."*
Publilius Syrus
*Sententiae,* 43 B.C.

More often, fear is an adaptive response. Fear prepares our bodies to flee danger. Fear of real or imagined enemies binds people together as families, tribes, and nations. Fear of injury protects us from harm. Fear of punishment or retaliation constrains us from harming one another.

People can be afraid of almost anything—"afraid of truth, afraid of fortune, afraid of death, and afraid of each other," observed Ralph Waldo Emerson. Why so many fears? Psychologists note that we can learn to fear almost anything. Recall from Chapter 8 that dogs learn to fear neutral stimuli associated with shock, that infants come to fear furry objects associated with frightening noises, and that adults can become terrified of incidental stimuli linked with traumatic experiences such as rape. As infants become mobile they experience falls and near-falls—and become increasingly afraid of heights (Campos & others, 1992). Through such conditioning, the short list of naturally painful and frightening events can multiply into a long list of human fears—fear of driving or flying, fear of mice or cockroaches, fear of closed or open spaces, fear of failure, fear of another race or nation.

Learning by observation extends the list. Susan Mineka (1985) wondered why nearly all monkeys reared in the wild fear snakes, yet lab-reared monkeys do not. Surely, most wild monkeys do not actually suffer snake bites. Might they learn their fear through observation? To find out, Mineka experimented with six wild-reared monkeys (all strongly fearful of snakes) and their lab-reared offspring (virtually none of which feared snakes). After repeatedly observing their parents or peers refusing to reach for food in the presence of a snake, the younger monkeys developed a similar strong fear of snakes. When retested 3 months later, their learned fear persisted. This suggests that our fears reflect not only our own past traumas but also the fears of our parents and friends.

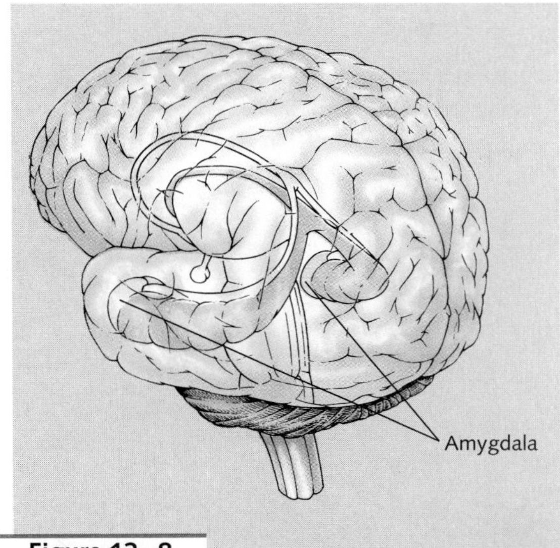


**Figure 13–8**

**The Amygdala–a Neural Key to Fear Learning**

Moreover, we may be biologically prepared to learn some fears more quickly than others. Monkeys learn to fear snakes even by watching videotapes of monkeys reacting fearfully to a snake; but they *don't* learn to fear flowers when video-splicing transposes the seemingly feared stimulus into a flower (Cook & Mineka, 1991). We humans quickly learn to fear snakes, spiders, and cliffs—fears that probably helped our ancestors survive. We are less predisposed to fear cars, electricity, bombs, and environmental warming, which in modern society are far more dangerous (Lumsden & Wilson, 1983; McNally, 1987). Stone Age fears leave us unprepared for high-tech dangers.

A key to fear-learning lies in the amygdala, a limbic system neural center deep in the brain (Figure 13–8). New experiments show the amygdala's role in associating various emotions, including fear, to certain situations (Barinaga, 1992b). Rabbits learn to react with fear to a tone that predicts an impending small shock—unless their amygdala is damaged. If rats have their amygdala deactivated by a drug that blocks the strengthening of neural connections, they, too, show no fear-learning. Not only does the amygdala link situations with fear responses, its output is wired to all the parts of the brain that produce the bodily symptoms of extreme fear, such as diarrhea and shortness of breath.

Of course, some people's fears are greater than others'. For a few people, intense fears of specific objects or situations disrupt their ability to cope. Furthermore, some people are very fearful of threatening or embarrassing situations. To be ever-attentive to potential threats is to be chronically anxious (Mineka & Sutton, 1992).

*Chapters 15 and 16 discuss how such* phobias *develop and are treated.*

Others—courageous heroes and remorseless criminals—are less fearful. Astronauts and adventurers who have "the right stuff"—who can keep their wits and can function coolly and effectively in moments of severe stress—seem to thrive on risk. So, too, do con artists and killers who charm their intended victims without a hint of nervousness, and who in laboratory tests exhibit little fear of a tone that predictably precedes a painful electric shock. Experience helps shape such fearfulness or fearlessness, but so do our genes. (Recall from Chapter 3 that genes influence our temperament—our emotional reactivity.) Even among identical twins reared separately, one twin's level of fearfulness is similar to the other's (Lykken, 1982).

## Anger

Anger is said by the sages to be "a short madness" (Horace, 65–8 B.C.) that "carries the mind away" (Virgil, 70–19 B.C.) and can be "many times more hurtful than the injury that caused it" (Thomas Fuller, 1654–1734). But other sages say "noble anger" (William Shakespeare, 1564–1616) "makes any coward brave" (Cato, 234–149 B.C.) and "brings back . . . strength" (Virgil).

*One problem with chronic hostility is its link with heart disease (page 582).*

What makes us angry? To find out, James Averill (1983) asked many people to recall or keep careful records of their experiences with anger. Most reported becoming at least mildly angry several times a week; some became angry several times a day. Often the anger was a response to friends' or loved ones' perceived misdeeds. Anger was especially common when another person's act seemed willful, unjustified, and avoidable. But blameless annoyances—foul odors, high temperatures, aches and pains—also have the power to make us angry (Berkowitz, 1990).

*"Anger will never disappear so long as thoughts of resentment are cherished in the mind."*

Buddha, 500 B.C.

What do people do with their anger? And what *should* they do with it? When anger fuels physically or verbally aggressive acts that we later regret, it is maladaptive. But Averill's subjects recalled that when they were angry they often reacted assertively rather than hurtfully. Their anger frequently led them to talk things over with the offending person, thereby lessening the aggravation. Such controlled expressions of anger are more adaptive than either hostile outbursts or internalizing the angry feelings.

Popular books and articles on aggression sometimes advise that even hostile outbursts can be better than keeping anger pent up. When irritated, should we go ahead and curse, tell a person off, or retaliate? Was Ann Landers (1969) right that "youngsters should be taught to vent their anger"?

Such advice is typical of individualized cultures, but it would seldom be heard in cultures where people's identity is more group-centered. People who keenly sense their interdependence see anger as a threat to group harmony (Markus & Kitayama, 1991). In Tahiti, for instance, people learn to be considerate and gentle. From infancy on in Japan, expressions of anger are less common than in Western cultures.

The "vent your anger" advice presumes that emotional expression provides emotional release, or **catharsis**. The catharsis hypothesis maintains that we reduce anger by releasing it through aggressive action or fantasy. Experimenters report that this sometimes occurs. When people retaliate against someone who has provoked them, they may indeed calm down—*if* their counterattack is directly against the provoker, *if* their retaliation seems justifiable, and *if* their target is not intimidating (Geen & Quanty, 1977; Hokanson & Edelman, 1966). In short, expressing anger can be *temporarily* calming *if* it does not leave us feeling guilty or anxious.

But expressing anger can also breed more anger. For one thing, it may provoke retaliation, thus escalating a minor conflict into a major confrontation. For another, expressing anger can magnify anger. (Recall Darwin's suggestion that violent gestures increase anger.) Ebbe Ebbesen and his colleagues (1975) saw this when they interviewed 100 frustrated engineers and technicians just laid off by an aerospace company. Some were asked questions that released hostility, such as, "What instances can you think of where the company has not been fair with you?" When these people later filled out a questionnaire that assessed their attitudes toward the company, did this opportunity to "drain off" their hostility reduce it? Quite the contrary. Compared with those who had not vented their anger, those who had let it all out exhibited more hostility.

Thus, although "blowing off steam" may temporarily calm an angry person, it may also amplify underlying hostility. When angry outbursts do calm us, they may be reinforcing and therefore habit forming. If basketball coaches can drain off some of their tension by berating referees, then the next time they feel tense with irritation they may be more likely to explode again. Similarly, the next time you are angry you are likely to do whatever has relieved your anger in the past.

What's the best way to handle anger? Experts offer two suggestions. First, bring down the physiological arousal of anger by waiting. "It is true of the body as of arrows," notes Carol Tavris (1982), "what goes up must come down. Any emotional arousal will simmer down if you just wait long enough." Second, deal with anger in a way that involves neither being chronically angry over every little annoyance nor passively sulking, which is merely rehearsing your reasons for anger. Don't be like those who, stifling their feelings over a series of provocations, finally overreact to a single incident (Baumeister & others, 1990). Vent the anger by exercising, playing an instrument, or confiding your feelings to a friend or a diary.

As we noted earlier, anger can benefit relationships when it expresses a grievance in ways that promote reconciliation rather than retaliation. Civility means not only keeping silent about trivial irritations but also communicating important ones clearly and assertively. A nonaccusing statement of feeling—perhaps letting one's partner know that "I get irritated when you leave your dirty dishes for me to clean up"—can help resolve the conflicts that cause anger.

**A Cool Culture** *Caregivers who turn abusive against other family members are rare in Micronesia. This photo of community life on Pulap Island suggests one reason why. Family life takes place in the open in the South Pacific, so relatives and neighbors can witness angry outbursts and step in before the emotion gets out of hand and turns into child, spouse, or elder abuse.*

## Happiness

"How to gain, how to keep, how to recover happiness is in fact for most men at all times the secret motive for all they do," observed William James (1902, p. 76). Understandably so, for one's state of happiness or unhappiness colors everything else. People who are happy perceive the world as safer (Johnson & Tversky, 1983), make decisions more easily (Isen & Means, 1983), rate job applicants more favorably (Baron, 1987), and report greater satisfaction with their whole lives (Schwarz & Clore, 1983). When your mood is gloomy, life as a whole seems depressing. Let your mood brighten, and suddenly your relationships, your self-image, and your hopes for the future all seem more promising.

Moreover—and this is one of psychology's most consistent findings—when we feel happy we are more willing to help others. In study after study, a mood-boosting experience (such as finding money, succeeding on a challenging task, or recalling a happy event) made people more likely to give money, pick up someone's dropped papers, volunteer time, and so forth. It's called the **feel-good, do-good phenomenon** (Salovey, 1990).

Despite the significance of happiness, psychology has more often focused on negative emotions. From 1974 to 1991, *Psychological Abstracts* (a sort of *Reader's Guide* to the psychological literature) included 5199 articles on anger, 27,244 on anxiety, and 29,216 on depression (Diener, 1993). But for every 17 articles on these topics, only one dealt with the positive emotions of joy (614), life satisfaction (1207), or happiness (1664). There is, of course, good reason to focus on negative emotions, which can make our lives miserable and drive us to seek help. But researchers are becoming increasingly interested in positive emotions as well. During the 1980s, annual research output on positive well-being nearly quadrupled (Myers, 1993).

*"Everything important has been said before."*
Philosopher Alfred North Whitehead, 1861–1947

On this subject, as on so many others, whatever psychological research reveals will have been anticipated by someone. The sages of the ages have given us any number of contradictory maxims: that happiness comes from living a virtuous life, but also that it comes from getting away with evil;

that it comes from knowing the truth, and from preserving illusions; that it comes from restraint, and from purging ourselves of pent-up rage and misery. They also have told us that happiness comes from living for the present, and living for the future; from making others happy, and from enjoying our enemies' misery; from being with others, and from living in peaceful solitude (Tatarkiewicz, 1976). The list goes on, but the implication is clear: The scientist's task is to ask which of these competing ideas fit reality. To sift the actual predictors of happiness from the merely plausible hunches requires research.

In their research on happiness, psychologists have studied influences upon both our temporary moods and our long-term life satisfaction. Studying people's reports of daily moods confirms that stressful events—an argument, a sick child, a car problem—trigger bad moods. No surprise there. But by the next day, the gloom nearly always lifts (Affleck & others, 1994; Bolger & others, 1989; Stone & Neale, 1984). If anything, people tend to rebound from bad days to a *better*-than-usual good mood the following day. (When in a bad mood, can you usually depend on rebounding within a day or two? Are your times of elation similarly hard to sustain?)

*"Weeping may tarry for the night, but joy comes with the morning."*

Psalms 30:5

Apart from prolonged grief over the loss of a loved one or lingering anxiety after a personal trauma, such as child abuse, rape, or the terrors of war, even tragedy is not permanently depressing. The finding is surprising but reliable. People who become blind or paralyzed usually recover near-normal levels of day-to-day happiness. For example, able-bodied University of Illinois students described themselves as happy 50 percent of the time, unhappy 22 percent of the time, and neutral 29 percent of the time. To within 1 percentage point, students with disabilities rated their emotions identically (Chwalisz & others, 1988). Moreover, students perceive their friends with disabilities as just as happy as their other friends (Allman, 1989).

*"If I couldn't know the joy of dancing, I could know the ecstasy of creating."*

Christy Brown
*My Left Foot*, 1954

The effect of dramatically positive events is similarly temporary. Once their rush of euphoria wears off, state lottery winners typically find their overall happiness unchanged (Brickman & others, 1978). Other research confirms that there is much more to well-being than being well-off. Many people (including most new collegians, as Figure 13–9 hints) believe they would be happier if they had more money. They probably would be—temporarily. But in the long run, increased affluence hardly affects happiness. People with lots of money are not much happier than those with only enough money to afford life's necessities. Within a given country there is a slight tendency for the wealthy to be happier than the poor. And people in wealthier countries report feeling only slightly more satisfied with their

**Figure 13–9**

**Are Today's Collegians Materialistic?** *From 1970 through most of the 1980s, annual surveys of more than 200,000 entering American college students revealed an increasing desire for wealth. (From Astin & others, 1993; Dey & others, 1991.)*

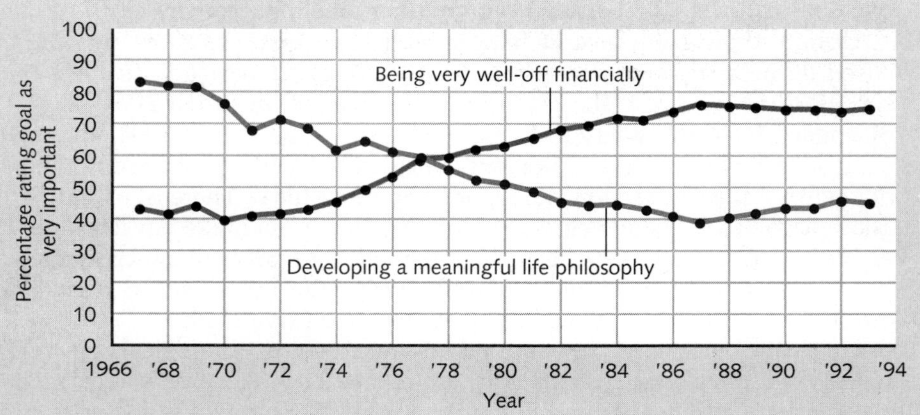

lives than do those in poorer countries. Interviews with more than 160,000 Europeans since the mid-1970s reveal that the Danes, Swiss, Irish, and Dutch have been much more likely than the French, Greeks, Italians, and former West Germans to report themselves happy and satisfied with life. But these national differences do not closely mirror differences in standards of living (Inglehart, 1990). During the 1980s, the wealthy West Germans, for example, had double the incomes of the Irish; nevertheless, year after year, the Irish reported more satisfaction with their lives. Wealth is like health: Its utter absence breeds misery, yet having it is no guarantee of happiness.

Although most people agree that money can't buy happiness, they do believe that a *little* more money would make them a *little* more secure, comfortable, and happy. So, over time, does our happiness grow little by little with our paychecks? The U.S. experience illustrates the answer: It does not. During the last three decades, the average U.S. citizen's buying power doubled. The 1957 per-person income, inflated to 1990 dollars, was approximately $7500; by 1993 it was almost $16,000. Did this increased wealth—enabling twice as many cars per capita, and color TVs, VCRs, home computers, microwave ovens, and answering machines galore—also buy more happiness? As Figure 13–10 shows, the average American is now twice as rich but no happier. In 1957, 35 percent said they were "very happy," as did slightly fewer—32 percent—in 1993. Indeed, judging by the doubled divorce rate, tripled teen-suicide rate, and mushrooming depression (page 515), Americans are more often miserable. Thus, despite popular materialism, an affluent society's economic growth does not necessarily improve its morale or social well-being.

Two psychological principles explain why more money buys no more than a temporary surge of happiness, and why our emotions seem attached to elastic bands that pull us back from highs or lows. In its own way, each principle suggests that happiness is relative.

*"No happiness lasts for long."*

Seneca
*Agamemnon*, A.D. 60

**Figure 13–10**

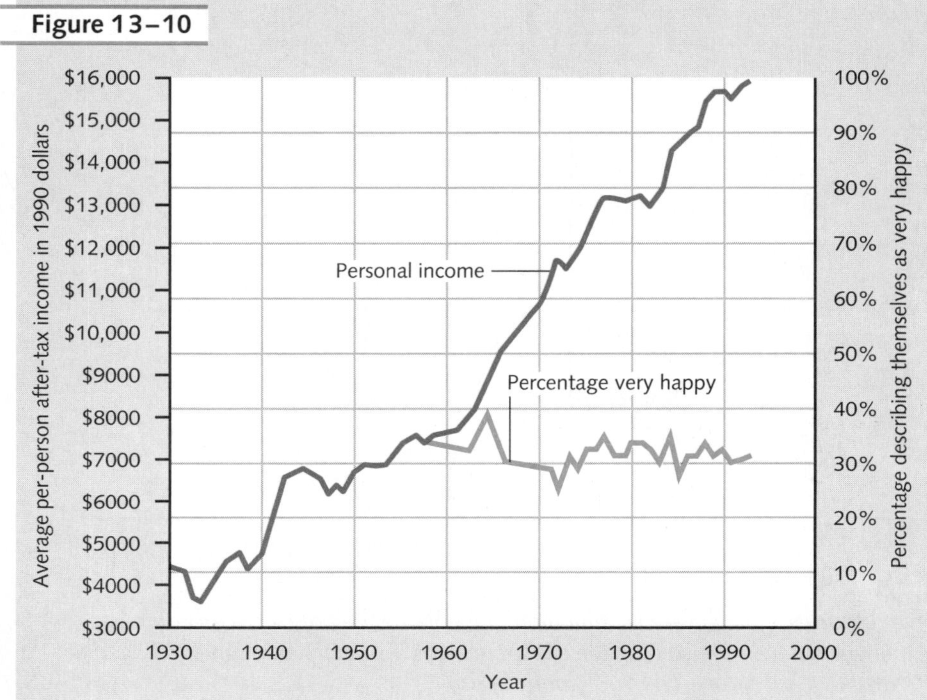


**Does Money Buy Happiness?** *It surely helps us to avoid certain types of pain. Yet, though buying power has doubled since the 1950s, the average American's reported happiness has remained almost unchanged. (Happiness data from Niemi & others, 1989, and T. Smith, 1994; income data from* Historical Statistics of the U.S. *and* Economic Indicators.*)*

## Close-Up

# Opponent-Process Theory of Emotion

The adaptation-level phenomenon helps explain why, in the long run, our emotional ups and downs tend to balance. University of Pennsylvania psychologist Richard Solomon (1980) believes that emotions balance in the short run as well, and he has developed a theory to explain why. Solomon was intrigued by the emotional price tag that so often follows pleasure, and the emotional dividends that can compensate for past suffering. For the pleasure of a drug high, one pays the price of discomfort when the drug wears off. For the pain of hard exercise or a hot sauna bath, one afterward receives the dividend of a pleasurable feeling of well-being.

Solomon proposes, with support from laboratory studies of human and animal emotions, that *every emotion triggers an opposing emotion.* He calls this the *opponent-process theory* of emotion. Imagine that you are about to take your first parachute jump. Solomon would say that the primary emotion you experience before the jump—fear—triggers an opposing emotion—elation—as you land. Once the opposing emotion activates, perhaps to keep the initial emotion under control, you experience a diminishing of the initial emotion's intensity. This happens because you experience the primary emotion minus the opposing emotion. As the primary emotion subsides, the opposing emotion lingers a while (Figure 13–11[*a*]). After parachutists survive their first free-fall, which for many is a terrifying experience, the fear switches off and they feel elated. For some women, the pain of labor and childbirth may enhance a euphoric feeling afterward.

Repetitions of the emotion-arousing event strengthen the opposing emotion. Thus, the primary emotional experience, such as the pleasure derived from drug use or the fear aroused by parachuting, diminishes. This helps explain drug tolerance; with repetition, the initial high lessens.

With repetition, the afterreaction, such as the pain of drug withdrawal remains strong or becomes stronger (Figure 13–11[*b*]). This helps explain both drug hangovers (the opponent feelings that knock down the initial pleasure and linger afterward) and drug addiction (the craving for more of the drug to switch off the pain of withdrawal).

As Solomon wisely notes, opponent-process theory and the research that supports it are good news for puritans and bad news for hedonists: Those who seek pleasure pay for it later, and with repetition even their pleasure will lose much of its intensity. With every kick comes a kickback. But those who suffer will receive their reward. With most pain comes a gain. "Take what you want," says an old Spanish saying. "Take it, and pay for it."

Looking over the whole of psychology, we can see a deep principle emerging: Human nature is a battlefield of opposing tendencies. Our sympathetic and parasympathetic nervous systems, our neural balance between excitation and inhibition, our endorphin responses to pain, our opponent neural processes that create color and negative afterimages, our regulation of hunger and satiety, and our experiences of pleasure and misery—all involve carefully negotiated truces between opposing forces.

**Figure 13–11**

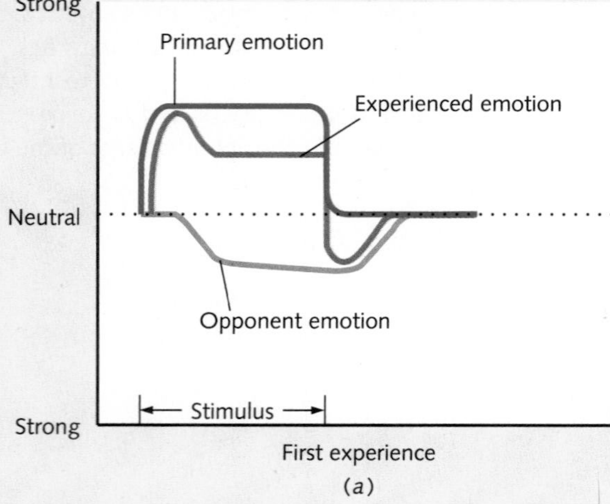


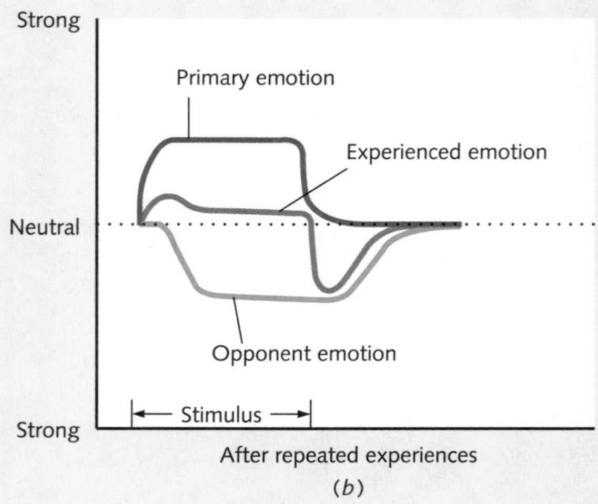


**Opponent Processes in Emotion** *(a) A primary emotional response to a stimulus triggers an opposing emotion. What we experience is the primary emotion minus the opposing emotion. (b) With repeated stimulation, the opponent emotion becomes stronger, weakening the experience of the primary emotion and lingering on. (From Solomon, 1980.)*

### The Adaptation-Level Principle: Happiness Is Relative to Our Prior Experience

The **adaptation-level phenomenon** describes our tendency to judge various stimuli relative to what we have previously experienced. We adjust our "neutral" levels—the points at which sounds seem neither loud nor soft, temperatures neither hot nor cold, events neither pleasant nor unpleasant—based on our experience. We then notice and react to variations up or down from these levels. Adaptation researcher Allen Parducci (in press) recalls a striking example: "On the Micronesian island of Ponope, which is almost on the equator, I was told of a bitter night back in 1915 when the temperature dropped to a record-breaking 69 degrees!"

Thus, if our income, grade-point average, or social prestige increases, we feel an initial surge of pleasure. We then adapt to this new level of achievement, come to see it as normal, and require something even better to give us another surge of happiness. From my childhood, I can recall the thrill of watching my family's first 12-inch, black-and-white television set. Now, if the color goes out on our 25-inch TV, I feel deprived. Having adapted upward, I perceive as negative what I once experienced as positive. Yesterday's luxury has become today's necessity. *The moral*: Satisfaction and dissatisfaction, success and failure—all are relative to our recent experience.

*"Continued pleasures wear off. . . . Pleasure is always contingent upon change and disappears with continuous satisfaction."*

Nico Frijda (1988)

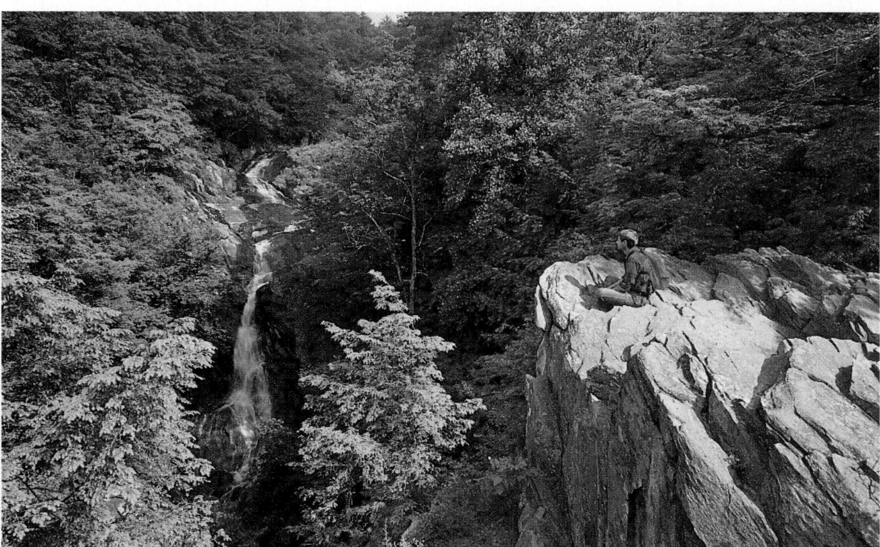

**The Pursuit of Happiness** *For some people happiness is a walk in the woods, a sunny view of a waterfall, or some other experience of the tranquility and beauty of unspoiled places. Such settings may free us from stress that triggers bad moods or may put us in touch with a place in ourselves that is beyond unhappiness.*

It follows that we will never create a permanent social paradise on earth (Campbell, 1975). If you woke up tomorrow to your utopia—perhaps a world with no bills, no ills, all *A*s, someone who loves you unreservedly—you would soon recalibrate your adaptation level. Before long you would again sometimes feel gratified (when achievements surpass expectations), sometimes deprived (when they fall below), and sometimes neutral. That helps explain why, despite the realities of triumph and tragedy, million-dollar lottery winners and paraplegics report similar levels of happiness. It also explains why material wants can be insatiable—why many a child "needs" just one more Nintendo game. Or why Imelda Marcos, surrounded by poverty while living in splendor as wife of the Philippines' president, bought 1060 pairs of shoes, more than she could ever wear. When the victor belongs to the spoils and the possessor is possessed by possessions, adaptation level has run amuck.

*"I have also learned why people work so hard to succeed: It is because they envy the things their neighbors have. But it is useless. It is like chasing the wind. . . . It is better to have only a little, with peace of mind, than be busy all the time with both hands, trying to catch the wind."*

Ecclesiastes 4:4

*"I've got the bowl, the big yard, I know I should be happy."*

Drawing by M. Twohy; © 1992 The New Yorker Magazine, Inc.

Seeking happiness through material achievement requires an ever-increasing abundance of things. At the end of his *Chronicles of Narnia,* writer C. S. Lewis depicts heaven as a place where good things *do* continually increase, where life is a never-ending story "in which every chapter is better than the one before." Here on earth the unavoidable ups and downs of real life preclude a perpetual high.

## The Relative Deprivation Principle: Happiness Is Relative to Others' Attainments

Happiness is relative not only to our past experience, but also to our comparisons with others. We are always comparing ourselves to others. And whether we feel good or bad depends on who those others are.

An example: To explain the frustration expressed by U.S. Air Corps soldiers during World War II, researchers formulated the concept of **relative deprivation**—the sense that we are worse off than others with whom we compare ourselves. Despite a relatively rapid promotion rate for the group, many soldiers were frustrated about their own promotion rates (Merton & Kitt, 1950). Apparently, seeing so many others being promoted inflated the soldiers' expectations. And when expectations soar above attainments, the result is frustration. When the Oakland Athletics signed outfielder Jose Canseco to a $4.7 million annual salary, his fellow outfielder Rickey Henderson became openly dissatisfied with his $3 million salary and refused to show up on time for spring training (King, 1991).

*"Our poverty became a reality. Not because of our having less, but by our neighbors having more."*
Will Campbell
*Brother to a Dragonfly*, 1977

Such comparisons help us understand why the middle- and upper-income people in a given country tend to be slightly more satisfied with life than the relatively poor, with whom the better-off can compare themselves (Diener, 1984). Nevertheless, once a person reaches a moderate income level, further increases do little to increase happiness. Why? Because as people climb the ladder of success they mostly compare themselves with those who are at or above their current level (Gruder, 1977; Suls & Tesch, 1978). For Rickey Henderson, Jose Canseco was the standard of comparison. For many American physicians, earning an average $170,000, the higher salaries of professional athletes and corporate CEOs become a point of comparison (Associated Press, 1993). As Bertrand Russell (1930, pp. 68–69) observed, "Napoleon envied Caesar, Caesar envied Alexander, and Alexander, I daresay, envied Hercules, who never existed. You cannot, therefore, get away from envy by means of success alone, for there will always be in history or legend some person even more successful than you are."

*"I wish I came in first more often."*
Michael Jordan
*Newsweek,* February 17, 1992

By "counting our blessings" when we compare ourselves with those less fortunate, we can, however, increase our satisfaction. As comparing ourselves with those better-off creates envy, so comparing ourselves with those less well-off boosts contentment. Marshall Dermer and his colleagues (1979) demonstrated this by asking University of Wisconsin-Milwaukee women to study others' deprivation and suffering. After viewing vivid depictions of how grim life was in Milwaukee in 1900, or after imagining and then writing about various personal tragedies, such as being burned and disfigured, the women expressed greater satisfaction with their own lives. Similarly, when mildly depressed people read about someone who is even more depressed, they feel somewhat better (Gibbons, 1986).

*The effect of comparison with others helps us understand why students of a given level of academic ability tend to have a higher academic self-concept if they attend a school where most other students are not exceptionally able (Marsh & Parker, 1984). If you were near the top of your class in high school, you might feel inferior upon entering a college where everyone was near the top of their class.*

## Predictors of Happiness

If, as the adaptation-level phenomenon implies, our emotions tend to balance around normal, then why do some people seem so filled with joy and others so gloomy day after day? What makes one person normally happy and another less so? Reviews of research (Diener, 1984; Myers, 1993) indicate there are several predictors of happiness (Table 13–1). Remember, though, that knowing that two variables correlate does not tell us whether one causes the other. For example, many studies indicate that religiously active people tend to report greater happiness and life satisfaction. Is happiness conducive to faith? Or does faith enhance happiness?

Whether at work or leisure, most of us derive greatest enjoyment from engaging, challenging activities. Mihaly Csikszentmihalyi (1990; pronounced chick-SENT-me-hi) and his colleagues discovered this after interrupting volunteers several times a day with an electronic paging device. When beeped, the people would note what they were doing and how they were feeling. Usually, they felt happier if mentally engaged by work or active leisure than if passively vegetating. Ironically, the less expensive (and usually more involving) a leisure activity is, the more absorbed and happier people are while doing it. People are happier gardening than sitting on a power boat. They're happier when talking to friends than when watching TV. Indeed, happy are those whose work and leisure absorb them, enabling them unself-consciously to "flow" in focused activity.

**When Downward Comparisons Lead Upward**
*Comparing ourselves with those worse off can sometimes prompt us not only to count our blessings but to share them. Self-made millionaire Eugene Lang (center) did just that during an address to the graduating class of the public grade school he had attended in Harlem. After reflecting on their poverty, he suddenly offered to pay the college costs of any who graduated from high school. (With his active support during the next 4 years, most did graduate from high school and over half went on to college.)*

**Table 13–1 Happiness Is . . .**

| Researchers Have Found That Happy People Tend to | However, Happiness Seems Only Minimally Related to Other Factors, Such as |
|---|---|
| Have high self-esteem | Age |
| Be optimistic and outgoing | Race |
| Have close friendships, or a satisfying marriage | Gender (women are more often depressed, but also more often joyful) |
| Have a meaningful religious faith | Educational level |
| Sleep well | Parenthood (having or not having children) |
| Exercise | |

*Source:* Summarized from Diener (1984) and Myers (1993).

## Summing Up

Among various human emotions, we looked closely at how we experience three: fear, anger, and happiness.

**Fear** Fear is an adaptive emotion, but it can be traumatic. Although we seem biologically predisposed to acquire some fears, what we learn through experience best explains the variety of human fears.

**Anger** Anger is most often aroused by events that are not only frustrating or insulting but also interpreted as willful, unjustified, and avoidable. Other negative emotions, such as depression, can also feed anger. Although blowing off steam may be temporarily calming, it does not, in the long run, reduce anger. Expressing anger can actually arouse more anger.

**Happiness** A good mood boosts people's perceptions of the world and their willingness to help others. The moods triggered by the day's good or bad events seldom last beyond that day. Even significant good events, such as a substantial raise in income, seldom increase happiness for long. We can explain the relativity of happiness with the adaptation-level phenomenon and relative-deprivation principle. Nevertheless, some people are usually happier than others, and researchers have identified factors that predict such happiness.

## Theories of Emotion

*We have seen that emotions arise from the interplay of physiological arousal, expressive behavior, and conscious experiences. But there are two controversies over this interplay. The first is an old debate: Does your heart pound because you are afraid, or are you afraid because you feel your heart pounding? The second concerns the link between our thinking and feeling: Does cognition always precede emotion?*

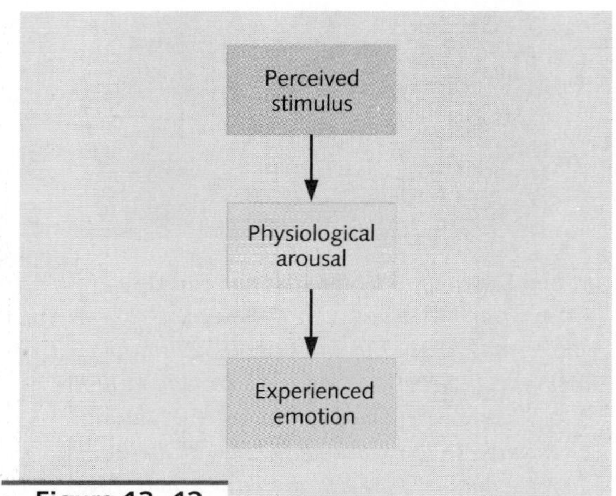


**Figure 13–12**

**The James-Lange Theory of Emotion** *To experience an emotion is to be aware of our physiological reactions.*

### The James-Lange and Cannon-Bard Theories

Common sense tells most of us that we cry because we are sad, lash out because we are angry, tremble because we are afraid. However, to pioneering psychologist William James the common-sense view of emotion was 180 degrees out of line. According to James, "We feel sorry because we cry, angry because we strike, afraid because we tremble" (1890, p. 1066). After you evade an oncoming car in your lane, you may *then* notice your racing heart and feel shaken with fright. Your feeling of fear follows your body's response (Figure 13–12).

James's idea, which was also proposed by Danish physiologist Carl Lange and is therefore called the **James-Lange theory**, struck American physiologist Walter Cannon as implausible. For one thing, Cannon thought the body's responses were not distinct enough to evoke the different emotions. Does a racing heart signal fear, anger, or love? For another, changes in heart rate, perspiration, and body temperature seemed to occur too slowly to trigger sudden emotion. Cannon, and later another physiologist, Philip Bard, concluded that physiological arousal and the emotional experience occur simultaneously: The emotion-arousing stimulus is routed simultaneously to the cortex, causing the subjective awareness of emotion, and to the sympathetic nervous system, causing the body's arousal. Thus, this **Cannon-Bard theory** implies that your heart begins pounding as you experience fear but that one does not cause the other (Figure 13–13).

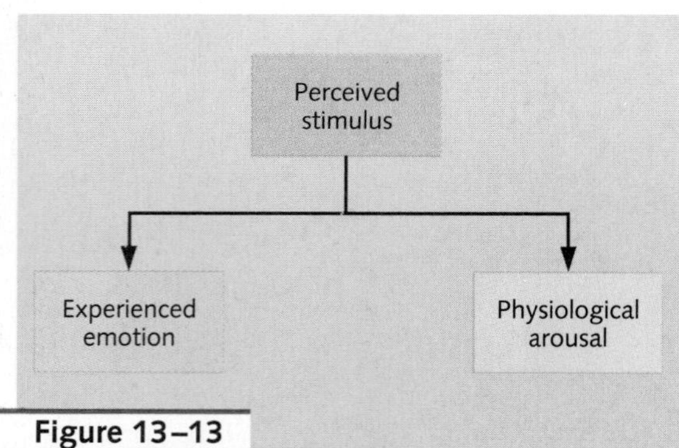


**Figure 13–13**

**The Cannon-Bard Theory of Emotion** *Emotions occur independent of physiology.*

As long as the evidence suggested that the arousal of one emotion is much the same as another, the James-Lange assumption that we experience our emotions through differing body states seemed improbable. With new evidence showing subtle physiological distinctions among the emotions, the James-Lange theory became more plausible. As James struggled with his own feelings of depression and grief, he came to believe that we can control emotions by going "through the outward motions" of whatever emotion one wants to experience. "To feel cheerful," he advised, "sit up cheerfully, look around cheerfully, and act as if cheerfulness were already there." The new findings concerning emotional effects of facial expressions (page 438) are precisely what James might have predicted.

Let's check your understanding of the James-Lange and Cannon-Bard theories. Imagine that your brain could not sense your heart pounding or your stomach churning. According to each theory, how would this affect your experienced emotions?

Cannon and Bard would have expected you to experience emotions normally, because they believed emotions occur separately from (though simultaneously with) the body's arousal. James and Lange would have expected greatly diminished emotions because they believed that to experience emotion you must first perceive your body responses.

The condition you imagined actually exists in people with severed spinal cords. Psychologist George Hohmann (1966) interviewed 25 soldiers who received such injuries in World War II. He asked them to recall emotion-arousing incidents that occurred before and after their spinal injuries. Those with injuries in the lower part of the spine, who had lost sensation only in their legs, reported little change in their emotions. Those who could feel nothing below the neck reported a considerable decrease in emotional intensity (as James and Lange would have expected). These soldiers said they might act much the same as before in emotion-arousing situations, but as one confessed about his anger, "It just doesn't have the heat to it that it used to. It's a mental kind of anger." On the other hand, emotions expressed mostly in body areas above the neck are felt more intensely by those with spinal cord injury. Virtually all the men Hohmann interviewed reported increases in weeping, lumps in the throat, and getting choked up when saying good-bye, worshipping, or watching a touching movie.

Although such evidence breathed new life into the James-Lange theory, most researchers agree with Cannon and Bard that our experienced emotions also involve cognition (Averill, 1993). Whether we fear the man behind us on the dark street depends entirely on whether we interpret his actions as hostile or friendly. So with James and Lange we can say that our arousal is an important ingredient of emotion. And with Cannon and Bard we can say that there is more to the experience of emotion than reading our physiology.

*"Whenever I feel afraid*
*I hold my head erect*
*And whistle a happy tune."*

Richard Rodgers and Oscar Hammerstein
*The King and I*

## Cognition and Emotion

Now, the second and newer controversy: Put simply, what is the connection between what we *think* and how we *feel*? Which is the chicken and which the egg? Do emotions always grow from thoughts? Is the heart always subject to our mind's appraisal of a situation?

We know that our emotions affect our thinking. When we *feel* like singing "Oh, what a beautiful morning!" we *see* the world and the people around us as wonderful; if the following day we feel crabby, we perceive the same world and the same people as less than wonderful.

Can we experience emotion apart from thinking? This issue has practical implications for self-improvement. Can we change our emotions by changing our thinking?

### Schachter's Two-Factor Theory of Emotion

Most psychologists today believe that our cognitions—our perceptions, memories, and interpretations—are an essential ingredient of emotion. One such theorist is Stanley Schachter, whose **two-factor theory** proposes that emotions have two ingredients: physical arousal and a cognitive label (Figure 13–14). Like James and Lange, Schachter presumes that our experience of emotion grows from our awareness of our body's arousal. But he also believes, like Cannon and Bard, that emotions are physiologically similar. Thus, he argues, an emotional experience requires a conscious interpretation of the arousal.

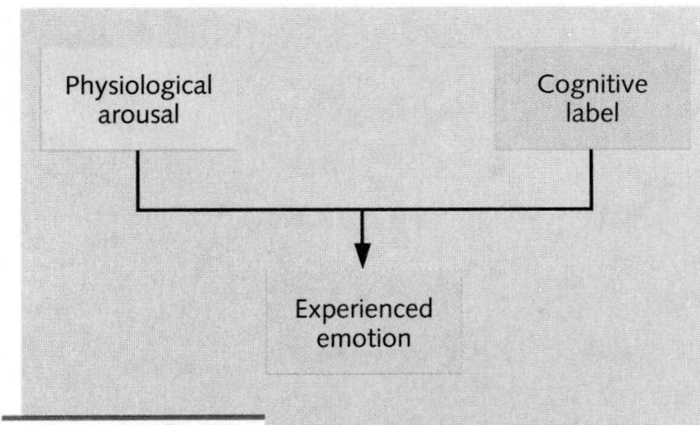


**Figure 13–14**

**Summary of Schachter's Two-Factor Theory of Emotion** *To experience emotion, we must be aroused and must cognitively label the arousal.*

It is often hard to disentangle our arousal response to an event from our interpretation of the event. Imagine that after an invigorating run you arrive home to find a message that you got the longed-for job. With arousal lingering from the run, would you feel more elated than if you received this news after awakening from a nap?

To find out, Schachter and Jerome Singer (1962) aroused college men with injections of the stimulating hormone, epinephrine. Picture yourself as one of their subjects: After receiving the injection, you go to a waiting room, where you find yourself with another person (actually an accomplice of the experimenters) who is acting either euphoric or irritated. As you observe this person, you begin to feel your heart race, your body flush, and your breathing becoming more rapid. If told to expect these effects from the injection, what would you feel? Schachter and Singer's subjects felt little emotion—because they attributed their arousal to the drug. But if told the injection would produce no effects, what would you feel? Perhaps you would react, as another group of subjects did, by "catching" the apparent emotion of the person you are with—becoming happy if the accomplice is acting euphoric, and testy if the accomplice is acting irritated.

This discovery—that a stirred-up state can be experienced as one emotion or another very different one, depending on how we interpret and label it—has been replicated in dozens of experiments. Although emotional arousal is not as undifferentiated as Schachter believed, arousal can intensify just about any emotion (Reisenzein, 1983; Sinclair & others, 1994). Insult people who have just been aroused by pedaling an exercise bike or watching a rock concert film and they will find it easy to misattribute their arousal to the provocation. Their feelings of anger will be greater than those of similarly provoked people who were not previously aroused. Arousal from emotions as diverse as anger, fear, and sexual excitement can spill from one emotion to another (Zillmann, 1986). In anger-provoking situations, sexually aroused people react with more hostility. Similarly, the arousal that lingers after an intense argument or a frightening experience may intensify sexual passion (Palace & Gorzalka, 1990).

### Must Cognition Precede Emotion?

So, to experience an emotion, must we first label our arousal? Robert Zajonc (pronounced ZI-yence) (1980, 1984a) contends the answer is no. He argues that our emotional reactions are sometimes quicker than our interpretations of a situation; we therefore feel some emotions *before* we think. For example, in earlier chapters, we noted that when people repeatedly view stimuli flashed too briefly for them to perceive and recall, they nevertheless come to prefer these stimuli. Without being consciously aware of having seen the stimuli, they rather like them. (Can you recall liking something or someone immediately without at first knowing why?)

Research on neurological processes supports the idea that we can experience emotion before cognition. Some neural pathways involved in emotion bypass the cortical areas involved in thinking. One such pathway runs from the eye via the thalamus to one of the brain's emotional control centers, the amygdala (LeDoux, 1986). This enables a quick, automatic emotional response, which may then be modified after the cortex has further interpreted a threat (Figure 13–15). In the forest, we jump at a nearby rustling sound, leaving the cortex to decide later whether it was made by a predator or just the wind. Such evidence convinces Zajonc that *some* of our emo-

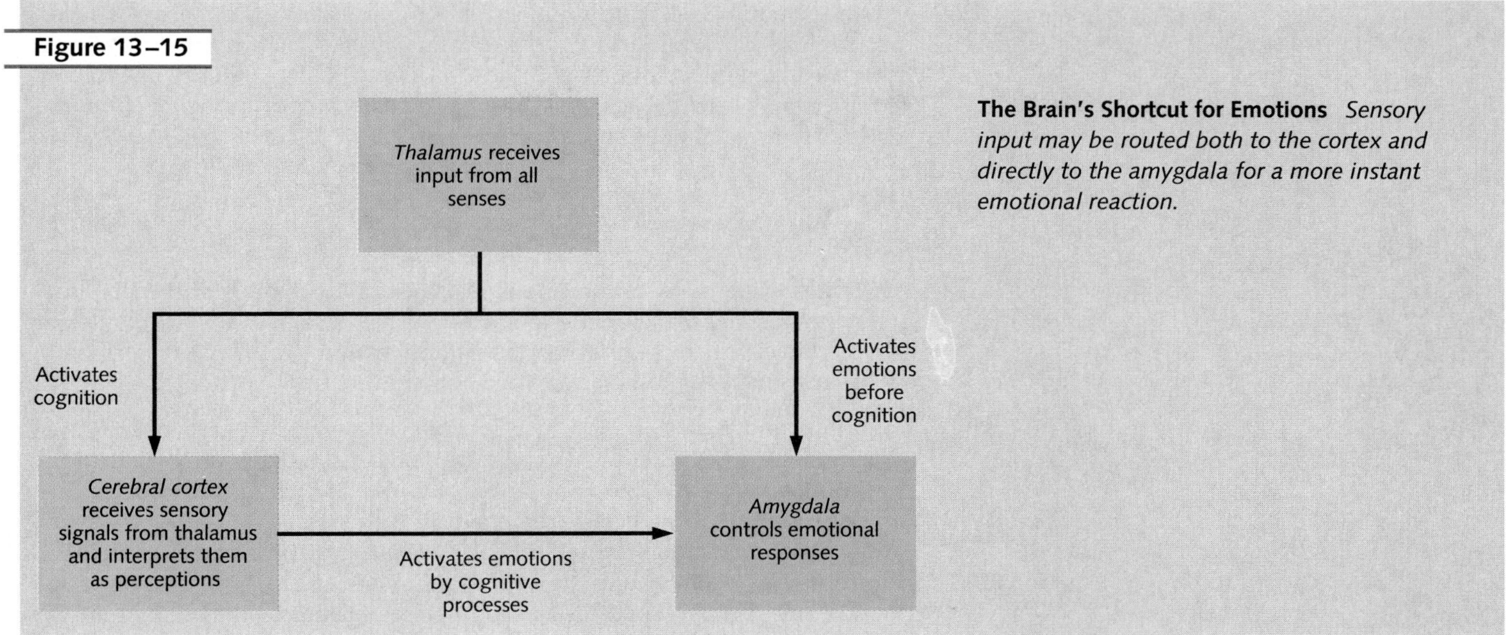
Thalamus receives input from all senses
Activates cognition
Activates emotions before cognition
Cerebral cortex receives sensory signals from thalamus and interprets them as perceptions
Activates emotions by cognitive processes
Amygdala controls emotional responses

**Figure 13–15**

**The Brain's Shortcut for Emotions** *Sensory input may be routed both to the cortex and directly to the amygdala for a more instant emotional reaction.*

tional reactions involve no deliberate thinking. Cognition, he believes, is not necessary for emotion. The heart is not always subject to the mind.

Emotion researcher Richard Lazarus (1984, 1991) disagrees. He concedes that our brains process and react to vast amounts of information without our conscious awareness, and he willingly grants that some emotional responses do not require *conscious* thinking. Nevertheless, he says, even instantaneously felt emotions require some sort of quick cognitive appraisal of the situation; otherwise, how do we *know* what we are reacting to? The appraisal may be effortless and we may not be conscious of it, but it is still a function of the mind (Figure 13–16). Emotions arise when we appraise an event as beneficial or harmful to our well-being.

Complex emotions, such as guilt, happiness, and love, most clearly arise from our interpretations and expectations. Highly emotional people are intense partly because of their interpretations. They *personalize* events as being somehow directed at them and *generalize* their experiences by blowing single incidents out of proportion (Larsen & others, 1987). How we explain good and bad events affects both our emotions and our motivation. Whether we attribute a low grade to an unfair exam, bad luck, or our own inability or laziness determines whether we feel irritated or depressed (Weiner, 1985). Attributing failure to our own inability erodes motivation. If I just don't have it, why try? Attributing failure to unfairness, we instead feel angry.

For us, the important conclusion concerns what Lazarus and Zajonc agree on: Some emotional responses—especially simple likes, dislikes, and fears—involve no conscious thinking. We may fear the spider, even if we "know" it is harmless. After conditioning, Little Albert was afraid of furry objects. Such responses are hard to alter by changing our thinking.

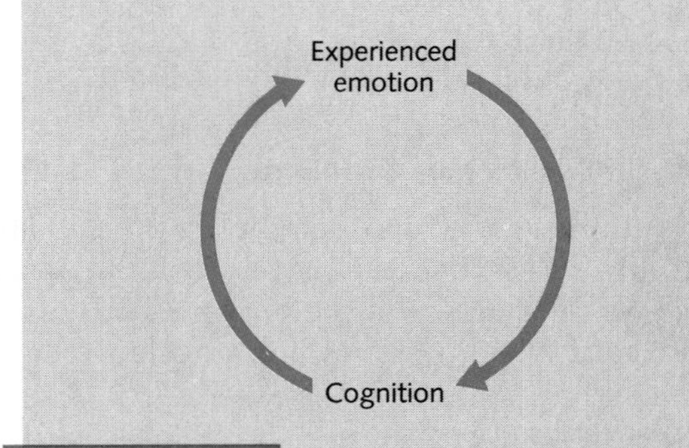
Experienced emotion
Cognition

**Figure 13–16**

**Emotion and Cognition Feed Each Other** *But which is the chicken and which the egg? Lazarus believes that, although emotions influence thinking, our cognitive appraisal of a situation always precedes emotion. Zajonc contends that some of our emotional reactions precede cognitive processing.*

Other emotions—including moods such as depression and complex feelings such as hatred and love—are greatly affected by our interpretations, memories, and expectations. For these emotions, as we will see in Chapter 16 (Therapy), learning to *think* more positively about ourselves and the world around us makes us *feel* better.

## Summing Up

**The James-Lange and Cannon-Bard Theories** One of the oldest theoretical controversies regarding emotion is whether we feel emotion *after* we notice our physiological responses (as James and Lange proposed) or *when* our bodies respond (as Cannon and Bard believed).

**Cognition and Emotion** A more recent controversy among emotion researchers concerns whether we can experience human emotions apart from cognition. Can we feel before we think? Stanley Schachter's two-factor theory of emotion contends that the cognitive labels we put on our states of arousal are an essential ingredient of emotion. Richard Lazarus agrees that cognition is essential: Many important emotions arise from our interpretations or inferences. Robert Zajonc, however, believes that some simple emotional responses occur instantly, not only outside of conscious awareness but before any cognitive processing occurs. The issue has practical implications: To the degree that emotions are rooted in thinking, we can hope to change them by changing our thinking.

## Terms and Concepts to Remember

**emotion** A response of the whole organism, involving (1) physical arousal, (2) expressive behaviors, and (3) conscious experience.

### The Physiology of Emotion

**polygraph** A machine, commonly used in attempts to detect lies, that measures several of the physiological responses accompanying emotion (such as perspiration, heart rate, blood pressure, and breathing changes).

### Experiencing Emotion

**catharsis** Emotional release. In psychology, the catharsis hypothesis maintains that "releasing" aggressive energy (through action or fantasy) relieves aggressive urges.

**feel-good, do-good phenomenon** People's tendency to be helpful when already in a good mood.

**adaptation-level phenomenon** Our tendency to form judgments (of sounds, of lights, of income) relative to a "neutral" level defined by our prior experience.

**relative deprivation** The perception that one is worse off relative to those with whom one compares oneself.

### Theories of Emotion

**James-Lange theory** The theory that our experience of emotion is our awareness of our physiological responses to emotion-arousing stimuli.

**Cannon-Bard theory** The theory that an emotion-arousing stimulus simultaneously triggers (1) physiological responses and (2) the subjective experience of emotion.

**two-factor theory** Schachter's theory that to experience emotion one must (1) be physically aroused and (2) cognitively label the arousal.

## Critical Thinking Exercise

Now that you have read and reviewed Chapter 13, take your learning a step further by testing your critical thinking skills on the following scientific problem solving exercise.

Subjects in a recent study were shown an erotic movie while they were in each of three phases of recovery from aerobic exercise. Subjects first pedaled an exercise bicycle intensely enough to produce significant physical arousal. During each of the three recovery phases, the subjects were asked (1) whether they still felt physically aroused from the exercise, and (2) how sexually excited by the film they felt. The subjects' actual physical arousal (heart rate) was measured throughout the experiment. During the first two phases of recovery, all of the subjects still showed signs of actual physical arousal, although by the second phases, they said they no longer felt physically aroused from the exercise. By the third phase, the subjects no longer showed signs of physical arousal from the exercise. The subjects reported feeling significantly more sexually excited by the film during the second phase of exercise recovery than they did during the first and third phases.

1. How well would the James-Lange theory explain the results of this experiment? What variations in reported feelings of sexual excitement would this theory have predicted in the three phases of exercise recovery?
2. How well would the Cannon-Bard theory explain the results of this experiment? What variations in reported feelings of sexual excitement would this theory have predicted in the three phases of exercise recovery?
3. How well would Schachter's two-factor theory explain the results of this experiment? What variations in reported feelings of sexual excitement would this theory have predicted in the three phases of exercise recovery?

Check your progress on becoming a critical thinker by comparing your answers to the sample answers found in Appendix B.

## For Further Reading

**Carlson, J. G., & Hatfield, E.** (1991). *Psychology of emotions.* Fort Worth, TX: Holt, Rinehart, and Winston.

*A delightfully down-to-earth account of the physiology and psychology of emotion, from anger to depression to joy.*

**Darwin, C.** (1872/1965). *The expression of the emotions in man and animals.* Chicago: University of Chicago Press.

*The classic description of emotional expressions and their adaptive functions.*

**Ekman, P.** (1985). *Telling lies: Clues to deceit in the marketplace, politics, and marriage.* New York: Norton.

*A fascinating book about how our faces and gestures communicate emotion and betray actual feelings.*

**Myers, D. G.** (1993). *The pursuit of happiness.* New York: Avon Books.

*A look at the things that do and don't predict happiness, and how you can use this knowledge to enhance your own well-being.*

**Tavris, C.** (1989). *Anger: The misunderstood emotion* (revised edition). New York: Simon & Schuster.

*A provocative, beautifully written summary of research that points to the dangers of unrestrained expression of anger.*

# CHAPTER 14



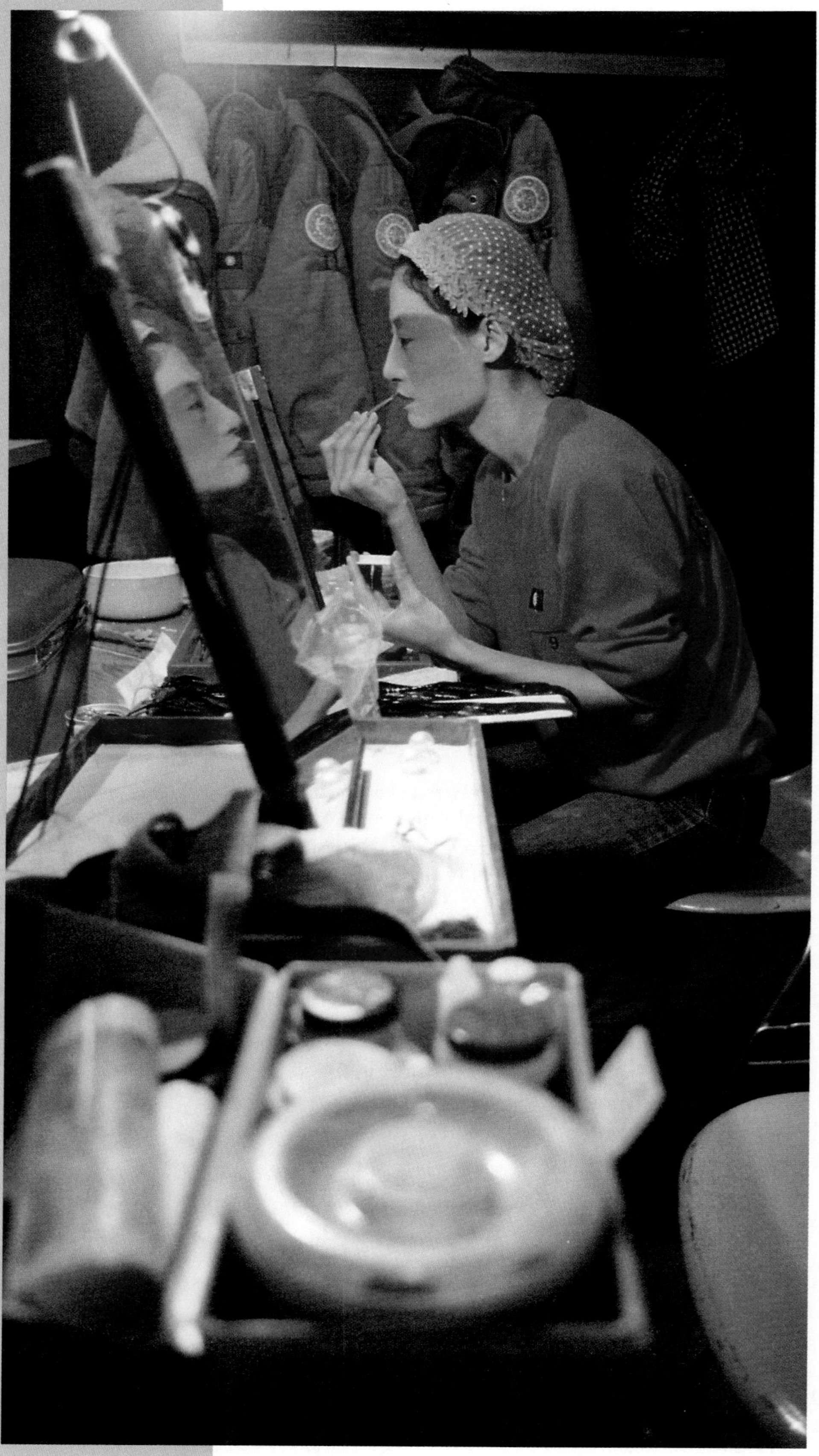

# Personality

Novelist William Faulkner was a master at creating characters with vivid personalities.[1] One of his creations, Ike McCaslin, appears at various ages in more than a dozen novels and short stories. Ike is highly principled, and consistently so. At age 10 he feels a deep reverence for the wilderness and its creatures. At 21 he forfeits a "tainted" inheritance. In his late seventies he counsels his nephew to use his land responsibly. Ike the adult is an extension of Ike the child.

Another Faulkner character, Jason Compson, is a selfish, whining 4-year-old in the opening section of *The Sound and the Fury*, and a selfish, screaming 34-year-old as the novel closes. As head of the Compson household, he verbally abuses family members and household servants. Lying, threatening, conniving, he is a self-centered child who becomes a self-centered adult.

*"There is no man who is not, at each moment, what he has been and what he will be."*
Oscar Wilde, 1854–1900

Faulkner's characters, as they appear and reappear throughout his fiction, exhibit the distinctiveness and consistency that define personality. The preceding chapters have emphasized how we are similar—how we develop, perceive, learn, remember, think, and feel. This chapter emphasizes our individuality. Your individual **personality** is your characteristic pattern of thinking, feeling, and acting. If your behavior pattern is unusually distinctive and consistent—if, say, you are strikingly outgoing, whether at a party or in a classroom—people are likely to say that you have a "strong" personality.

Actually, much of this book deals with personality. We have considered biological influences on personality, personality development across the life span, and personality-related aspects of learning, motivation, and emotion. In later chapters we will study disorders of personality, personality's influence on health, and social influences on personality.

In this chapter we explore and evaluate four major perspectives on personality:

Sigmund Freud's *psychoanalytic* theory proposes that childhood sexuality and unconscious motivations influence personality.

*Trait* researchers identify specific dimensions of our personality.

The *humanistic* approach focuses on our inner capacities for growth and self-fulfillment.

*Social-cognitive* psychologists emphasize how we shape and are shaped by our environment.

[1] Faulkner scholar Nancy Nicodemus assisted with these examples.

## The Psychoanalytic Perspective

*Love him or hate him, Sigmund Freud has influenced Western culture. To recognize his influence, we need to understand Freud's ideas concerning the unconscious, psychosexual stages, and mechanisms for defending against anxiety.*

**Sigmund Freud (1856–1939)** *"I was the only worker in a new field."*

Well before entering the University of Vienna in 1873, the youthful Sigmund Freud showed signs of the independence and brilliance that often mark people of eminence. He had a prodigious memory. He so loved serious reading that he once ran up a bookstore debt beyond his means, feeding his insatiable interest in plays, poetry, and philosophy. As a teen he often took his evening meal in his tiny bedroom, to lose no time from his studies.

After medical school, Freud began a private practice, specializing in nervous disorders. Before long, however, he faced patients whose disorders made no neurological sense. A patient might have lost all feeling in her hand—yet there is no sensory nerve that when damaged would numb the entire hand and nothing else. Noting that hypnosis could also produce such symptoms, Freud wondered whether they might be psychologically rather than physiologically caused. His wonderings set his mind running in a direction that was destined to change human self-understanding.

Freud wrote about his views, which evolved as he treated patients and analyzed himself, in 24 volumes published between 1888 and 1939. Following his first solo book, *The Interpretation of Dreams* (1900), his ideas gradually began to attract many followers—and intense criticism. For now, let us reserve judgment on Freud's theory and try to see things as he did. It is impossible to summarize 24 volumes in these few pages, but we can highlight Freud's psychoanalytic theory—the first comprehensive theory of personality.

### Exploring the Unconscious

To explore the possible psychological roots of nervous disorders, Freud spent several months in Paris studying with a neurologist who was using hypnosis to treat patients suffering from these disorders. On returning to Vienna, Freud began to hypnotize his patients, encouraging them while hypnotized to talk freely about themselves and the circumstances surrounding the onset of their symptoms. Often the patients responded openly, at times becoming quite agitated during the hypnotic experience. Sometimes their symptoms then diminished or even disappeared.

While experimenting with hypnosis, Freud "discovered" the unconscious. Piecing together his patients' accounts of their lives, he decided that the loss of feeling in one's hand might be caused by the fear of touching one's genitals; that blindness or deafness might be caused by not wanting to see or hear something that aroused intense anxiety. In time, Freud began to see patients with a variety of symptoms. Given patients' uneven capacity for hypnosis, he turned to **free association**—in which he merely told the patient to relax and say whatever came to mind, no matter how embarrassing or trivial. Freud believed that free association produced a chain of thought leading into the patient's unconscious, thereby retrieving and releasing painful unconscious memories, often from childhood. Freud called the process **psychoanalysis**.

Underlying Freud's psychoanalytic conception of personality was his belief that the mind is like an iceberg—mostly hidden. Our conscious

**Freud's Consulting Room** *Freud's office was rich with antiquities from around the world, including art work related to his ideas about unconscious motives. His famous couch, piled high with pillows, placed patients in a comfortable reclining position facing away from him to help them focus inward.*

awareness is the part of the iceberg that floats above the surface. Below the surface is the much larger, **unconscious** region containing thoughts, wishes, feelings, and memories, of which we are largely unaware. Some of these thoughts we store temporarily in a **preconscious** area, from which we can retrieve them at will into conscious awareness. Of greater interest to Freud was the mass of unacceptable passions and thoughts that we *repress*, or forcibly block from our consciousness because they would be so painful to acknowledge. Freud believed that, although we are not consciously aware of them, these troublesome feelings and ideas powerfully influence us. In his view, our unacknowledged impulses express themselves in disguised forms—the work we choose, the beliefs we hold, our daily habits, our troubling symptoms. In such ways, the unconscious seeps into our thoughts and actions.

*"Two passengers leaned against the ship's rail and stared at the sea. 'There sure is a lot of water in the ocean,' said one. 'Yes,' answered his friend, 'we've only seen the top of it.'"*

Psychologist George A. Miller (1962)

Freud believed he glimpsed the unconscious not only in people's free associations, beliefs, habits, and symptoms but also in their dreams and slips of the tongue and pen. Slips while reading, writing, and speaking suggested to Freud that what we say and do may reflect the workings of our unconscious minds. Consider his example of a financially stressed patient who, not wanting any large pills, said, "Please do not give me any bills, because I cannot swallow them." For Freud, something more than random error explains the new apartment occupant who misspoke "It suits my needs" as "It seats my nudes." Jokes, too, he viewed as a way to express repressed sexual and aggressive tendencies. For Freud the determinist, nothing was ever accidental.

Dreams, he contended, are a major outlet for people's unconscious wishes. The remembered content of dreams (their *manifest content*—see page 228) he believed to be a censored expression of those wishes (the dream's *latent content*). For Freud, dreams were the "royal road to the unconscious." By analyzing people's dreams, Freud believed he could reveal the nature of their inner conflicts and release their inner tensions.

*"Good morning, beheaded—uh, I mean beloved."*

Drawing by Fradon; © 1983 The New Yorker Magazine, Inc.

## Personality Structure

For Freud, human personality—including its emotions and strivings—arises from a conflict between our aggressive, pleasure-seeking biological impulses and the social restraints against them. In his view, personality results from our efforts to resolve this basic conflict—to express these impulses in ways that bring satisfaction without also bringing guilt or punishment.

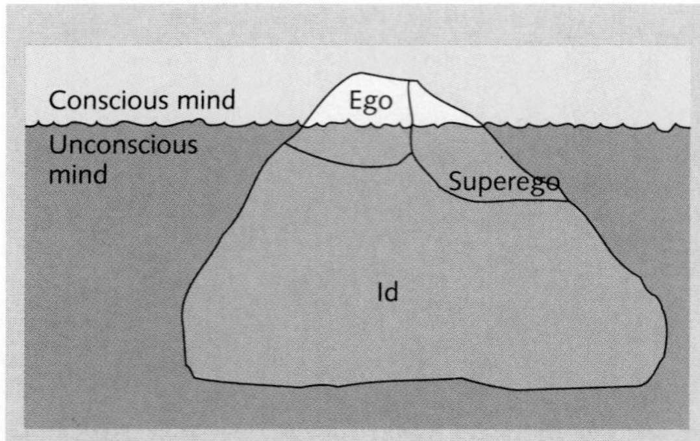


**Figure 14–1**

**Freud's Idea of the Mind's Structure** *Consciousness is like an iceberg's visible tip. Note that the id is totally unconscious, but ego and superego operate both consciously and unconsciously. (Adapted from Freud, 1933, page 111.)*

Freud theorized that the conflict centers on three interacting systems, id, ego, and superego. Like intelligence and memory, these are abstract psychological concepts (Figure 14–1). They are, said Freud, "useful aids to understanding" the mind's dynamics.

The **id** is a reservoir of unconscious psychic energy that constantly strives to satisfy basic drives to survive, reproduce, and aggress. The id operates on the **pleasure principle**: If unconstrained by reality, it seeks immediate gratification. Think of newborn infants, who, governed by the id, cry out for satisfaction the moment they feel a need, caring nothing for the outside world's conditions and demands.

As the **ego** develops, the young child learns to cope with the real world. The ego operates on the **reality principle**, which seeks to gratify the id's impulses in realistic ways that will bring long-term pleasure rather than pain or destruction. Imagine what would happen if, lacking an ego, we expressed our unrestrained sexual or aggressive impulses whenever we felt them. The ego, which contains our partly conscious perceptions, thoughts, judgments, and memories, is the personality "executive." It decides on our actions as it intervenes among the impulsive demands of the id, the restraining demands of the superego, and the real-life demands of the external world.

Beginning around age 4 or 5, a child's ego recognizes the demands of the newly emerging **superego**. The superego is a voice of conscience that forces the ego to consider not only the real but the ideal. Its sole focus is on how one *ought* to behave. The superego develops as we internalize the morals and values of parents and culture, thereby providing both our sense of right and wrong and our ideals. It strives for perfection and judges our actions, producing positive feelings of pride or negative feelings of guilt. Someone with an exceptionally strong superego may be continually upright yet, ironically, guilt-ridden; another with a weak superego may be wantonly self-indulgent and remorseless. Because the superego's demands often oppose the id's, the ego struggles to reconcile the two. The chaste student who is sexually attracted to someone satisfies both id and superego by, say, joining a volunteer organization to work with the desired person.

*"Fifty is plenty."*

*"Hundred and fifty."*

Drawing by Woodman; © 1987 The New Yorker Magazine, Inc.

### Personality Development

Analysis of his patients' histories convinced Freud that personality forms during life's first few years. Again and again his patients' symptoms seemed rooted in unresolved conflicts from early childhood. He concluded that children pass through a series of **psychosexual stages** during which the id's pleasure-seeking energies focus on distinct pleasure-sensitive areas of the body called *erogenous zones* (Table 14–1).

During the **oral stage**, which lasts throughout the first 18 months, the infant's sensual pleasures focus on sucking, biting, and chewing.

During the **anal stage**, from about 18 months to 3 years, the sphincter muscles become sensitive and controllable, and bowel and bladder retention and elimination become a source of gratification.

During the **phallic stage**, from roughly ages 3 to 6 years, the pleasure zone shifts to the genitals. Freud believed that during this stage boys seek genital stimulation and develop both unconscious sexual desires for their mother and jealousy and hatred for their father, whom they consider a rival. Boys also were said to feel guilt and a lurking fear that their father would punish them, such as by castration. Freud called this collection of feelings the **Oedipus complex** after the Greek legend of Oedipus, who unknowingly killed his father and married his mother. Although some psychoanalysts believed that girls experience a parallel *Electra complex*, Freud

**Table 14–1 Freud's Psychosexual Stages**

| Stage | Focus |
|---|---|
| *Oral* (0–18 months) | Pleasure centers on the mouth—sucking, biting, chewing |
| *Anal* (18–36 months) | Pleasure focuses on bowel/bladder elimination; coping with demands for control |
| *Phallic* (3–6 years) | Pleasure zone is the genitals; coping with incestuous sexual feelings |
| *Latency* (6 to puberty) | Repressed sexual feelings |
| *Genital* (puberty on) | Maturation of sexual interests |

(1931, page 229) said no: "It is only in the male child that we find the fateful combination of love for the one parent and simultaneous hatred for the other as a rival."

Children eventually cope with these threatening feelings, said Freud, by repressing them and by identifying with (trying to become like) the rival parent. It's as if something inside the child decides, "If you can't beat 'em (the parent of the same sex), join 'em." Through this **identification** process children's superegos gain strength as they incorporate many of their parents' values. Freud believed that identification with the same-sex parent provides our **gender identity**—our sense of being male or female.

With their sexual feelings repressed and redirected, children enter a **latency stage**. Freud maintained that during latency, extending from around age 6 to puberty, sexuality is dormant and children play mostly with peers of the same sex.

At puberty, latency gives way to the final stage, the **genital stage**, as youths begin to experience sexual feelings toward others.

In Freud's view, maladaptive behavior in the adult results from conflicts unresolved during earlier psychosexual stages. At any point in the oral, anal, or phallic stage, strong conflict can lock, or **fixate**, the person's pleasure-seeking energies in that stage. Thus, people who were either orally overindulged or deprived (perhaps by abrupt, early weaning) might fixate at the oral stage. Orally fixated adults are said to exhibit either passive dependence (like that of a nursing infant) or an exaggerated denial of this dependence—perhaps by acting tough and uttering biting sarcasm. They might also continue to seek oral gratification through excessive smoking and eating. Those who never quite resolve the anal conflict, between the desire to eliminate at will and the demands of toilet training, may be either messy and disorganized (*anal expulsive*) or highly controlled and compulsively neat (*anal retentive*). In such ways, believed Freud, the twig of personality is bent at an early age.

## Defense Mechanisms

To live in social groups, we cannot act out our sexual and aggressive impulses willy-nilly. We must control them. When the ego fears losing control of the inner war between the demands of the id and the superego, the result is anxiety. Anxiety, said Freud, is the price we pay for civilization.

Unlike specific fears, the dark cloud of anxiety is unfocused. Anxiety is therefore hard to cope with, as when we feel unsettled but are not sure why. Freud proposed that the ego protects itself against anxiety with ego **defense mechanisms**. Defense mechanisms reduce or redirect anxiety in various ways, but always by distorting reality. Some examples:

**Repression** banishes anxiety-arousing thoughts and feelings from consciousness. According to Freud, repression underlies the other defense mechanisms, all of which disguise threatening impulses and keep them from reaching consciousness. Freud believed that repression explains why we do not remember our childhood lust for our parent of the other sex. However, he also believed that repression is often incomplete, with the repressed urges seeping out in dream symbols and slips of the tongue.

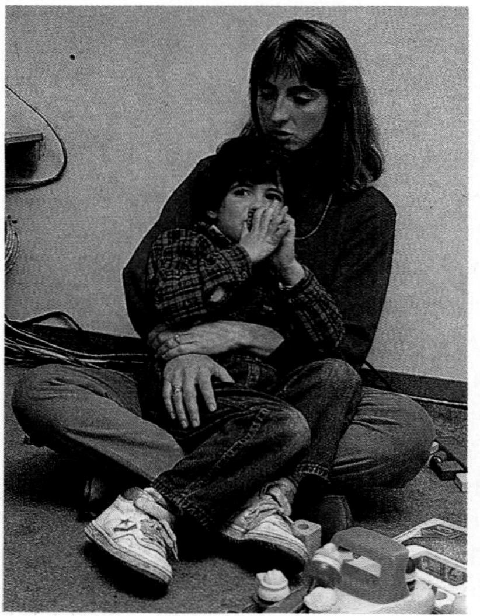

**Regression** *Faced with a mild stress, children and monkeys will regress, retreating to the comfort of earlier behaviors.*

We also cope with anxiety through **regression**—retreating to an earlier, more infantile stage of development where some of our psychic energies still fixate. Thus, when facing the anxious first days of school, a child may regress to the oral comfort of thumb sucking. Juvenile monkeys, when anxious, retreat to infantile clinging to their mothers or to one another (Suomi, 1987). Even homesick new college students may long for the security and comfort of home.

In **reaction formation**, the ego unconsciously makes unacceptable impulses look like their opposites. En route to consciousness, the unacceptable proposition "I hate him" becomes "I love him." Timidity becomes daring. Feelings of inadequacy become bravado. According to the principle behind this defense mechanism, vehement social crusaders, such as those who urgently campaign against gay rights, may be motivated by the very sexual desires against which they crusade.

*"The lady doth protest too much, methinks."*
William Shakespeare
*Hamlet*, 1600

**Projection** disguises threatening impulses by attributing them to others. Thus, "He hates me" may be a projection of the actual feeling "I hate him" or "I hate myself." An El Salvadoran saying captures the idea: "The thief thinks everyone else is a thief." According to Freudian theory, racial prejudice, too, may be the result of projecting one's own unacceptable impulses or characteristics onto members of another group. (As you can imagine, reaction formation and projection have sometimes provided a handy way to ridicule other people's motives.)

The familiar mechanism of **rationalization** lets us unconsciously generate self-justifying explanations so we can hide from ourselves the real reasons for our actions. Thus, habitual drinkers may say they drink with their friends "just to be sociable." Students who fail to study may rationalize, "All work and no play makes Jack [or Jill] a dull person."

**Displacement** diverts one's sexual or aggressive impulses toward an object more psychologically acceptable than the one that aroused them. Children who can't express anger against their parents may displace their anger onto the family pet. Students upset over an exam may snap at a roommate.

**Sublimation** is the transformation of unacceptable impulses into socially valued motivations. Sublimation is therefore socially adaptive and may even be a wellspring for great cultural and artistic achievements. Freud suggested that Leonardo da Vinci's paintings of Madonnas were a sublimation of his longing for intimacy with his mother, who was separated from him at an early age.

Note again that all these defense mechanisms function indirectly and unconsciously. They reduce anxiety by disguising our threatening impulses. We never say, "I'm feeling anxious; I'd better project my sexual or hostile feelings onto someone else." Defense mechanisms would not work if we recognized them. As the body unconsciously defends itself against disease, so also, believed Freud, does the ego unconsciously defend itself against anxiety.

**Alfred Adler** *"The individual feels at home in life and feels his existence to be worthwhile just so far as he is useful to others and is overcoming feelings of inferiority" (Problems of Neurosis, 1964).*

### Freud's Descendants and Dissenters

Although Freud was known to change his mind, he was deeply committed to his ideas and principles, even in the face of harsh criticism. His controversial writings soon attracted followers, mostly young, ambitious physicians who formed an inner circle around their strong-minded leader. From time to time sparks flew, and one member or another would leave or be outcast. Even the ideas of the outcasts, however, reflected Freud's influence.

These pioneering psychoanalysts and others, whom we now call neo-Freudians, accepted Freud's basic ideas: the personality structures of id, ego, and superego; the importance of the unconscious; the shaping of personality in childhood; and the dynamics of anxiety and the defense mechanisms. But they veered away from Freud in two important ways. First, they placed more emphasis on the role of the conscious mind in interpreting experience and coping with the environment. What's more, they doubted that sex and aggression were all-consuming motivations. Instead, they placed more emphasis on loftier motives and on social interaction, as the following examples illustrate.

**Karen Horney** *"The view that women are infantile and emotional creatures, and as such, incapable of responsibility and independence is the work of the masculine tendency to lower women's self-respect" (Feminine Psychology, 1932).*

Alfred Adler and Karen Horney agreed with Freud that childhood is important. But they believed that childhood *social*, not sexual, tensions are crucial for personality formation. Adler, who himself struggled to overcome childhood illnesses and accidents, said that much of our behavior is driven by an effort to conquer childhood feelings of inferiority, feelings that trigger strivings for superiority and power. (It was Adler who proposed the still-popular idea of the "inferiority complex.") Horney said that childhood anxiety, caused by the dependent child's sense of helplessness, triggers the desire for love and security. In countering Freud's assumptions that women have weak superegos and suffer "penis envy," Horney sought to balance the bias she detected in this masculine view of psychology.

*"The female . . . acknowledges the fact of her castration, and with it, too, the superiority of the male and her own inferiority; but she rebels against this unwelcome state of affairs."*

Sigmund Freud
*Female Sexuality*, 1931

Unlike other neo-Freudians, Carl Jung—Freud's disciple-turned-dissenter—placed less emphasis on social factors and agreed with Freud

**Carl Jung** *"We can keep from a child all knowledge of earlier myths, but we cannot take from him the need for mythology" (Symbols of Transformation, 1912).*

that the unconscious exerts a powerful influence. But to Jung (pronounced Yoong), the unconscious contains more than a person's repressed thoughts and feelings. There is also a **collective unconscious,** he believed, a common reservoir of images derived from our early ancestors' universal experiences. Jung said that the collective unconscious explains why, for many people, spiritual concerns are deeply rooted and why people in different cultures share certain myths and images, such as that of mother as a symbol of nurturance.

## Assessing the Unconscious

Those who study personality or provide therapy need ways to evaluate personality characteristics. Different personality theories imply different methods of assessment.

Freud's theory maintains that the significant influences on our personalities arise from the unconscious, which contains residues from early childhood experiences. Psychoanalysts therefore dismiss objective assessment tools, such as agree-disagree or true-false questionnaires, as merely tapping the conscious surface. Their tool of choice would be a sort of psychological x-ray—a test that can see through our surface pretensions and reveal our hidden conflicts and impulses.

**Projective tests** aim to provide such a view by providing people with an ambiguous stimulus and then asking them to describe it or tell a story about it. The stimulus has no inherent meaning, so any meaning people read into it presumably reflects their interests and conflicts. Henry Murray (1933) demonstrated a possible basis for such a test at a house party hosted by his 11-year-old daughter. Murray got the children to play a frightening game called "Murder." When shown some photographs after the game, the children perceived the photos as more malicious than they had before the game.

These children, it seemed to Murray, had *projected* their inner feelings into the pictures. A few years later, Murray introduced the **Thematic Apperception Test (TAT)**—ambiguous pictures about which people make up stories. As you may recall from page 419, one use of the TAT has been to assess achievement motivation. Shown a daydreaming boy, those who imagine him fantasizing an achievement are presumed to be projecting their own concerns.

There are now a variety of projective tests. These tests ask subjects to draw a person, to complete sentences ("My mother. . . ."), or to provide the first word that comes to mind after the examiner says a test word. Most widely used is the famous **Rorschach inkblot test,** introduced in 1921 by Swiss psychiatrist Hermann Rorschach. The test assumes that what we see in its 10 inkblots reflects our inner feelings and conflicts. If we see fierce animals or weapons, the examiner may infer we have aggressive tendencies.

Is this a reasonable assumption? If so, can a psychologist use the Rorschach to understand one's personality and diagnose an emotional disorder? Recall from Chapter 11's discussion of intelligence tests that the two primary criteria of a good test are reliability (consistent results) and validity (predicting what it's supposed to). On those criteria, how good is the Rorschach?

*"If a professional psychologist is 'evaluating' you in a situation in which you are at risk and asks you for responses to ink blots . . . walk out of that psychologist's office."*

Robyn Dawes
*House of Cards: Psychology and Psychotherapy Based on Myth,* 1994

Most researchers have considered it not very good (Peterson, 1978). There has been no one accepted system for scoring and interpreting the test. So unless two raters were trained in the same scoring system, their agreement on the results of any given test would be minimal. Nor has the test been very successful at predicting behavior or at discriminating between groups (for example, identifying who is suicidal and who is not).

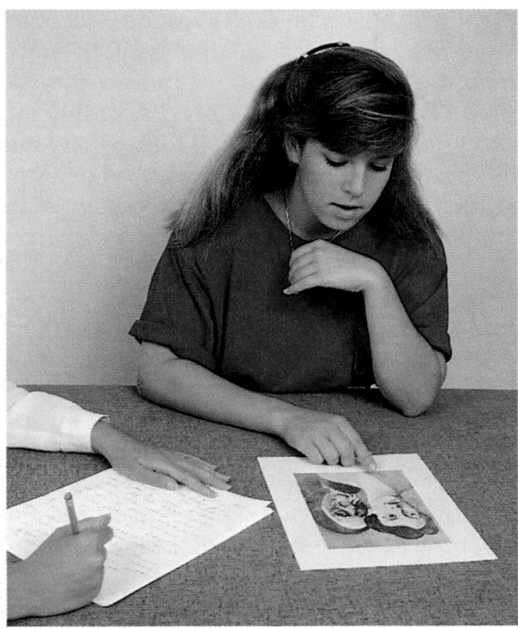

**The TAT** *This psychologist presumes that the hopes, fears, and interests expressed in this girl's descriptions of a series of ambiguous pictures in the Thematic Apperception Test (TAT) are projections of her inner feelings.*

**The Rorschach Test** *In this projective test, people say what a series of symmetrical inkblots look like. In psychoanalytic terms, tests like this are useful because the interpretation of ambiguous stimuli reveals unconscious aspects of the test-taker's personality.*

Although not as popular as it once was, the Rorschach remains one of the most widely used psychological instruments (Lubin & others, 1984; Piotrowski & Keller, 1989). Some clinicians continue to be confident of the test's validity—not as a device that by itself can provide a diagnosis, but as a source of suggestive leads that supplement other information. Other clinicians believe the test is still an icebreaker and a revealing interview technique. A new research-based, computer-aided scoring and interpretation tool is improving agreement among raters and enhancing the test's validity (Exner, 1986; Shontz & Green, 1992). This scoring system, however, assumes the blots actually do look like certain things—the opposite of the test's rationale (Dawes, 1994). Moreover, Freud himself would probably have been uncomfortable with trying to assign each patient a test score and more interested in the therapist–patient interactions that take place during the test.

*"The forward thrust of the antlers shows a determined personality, yet the small sun indicates a lack of self-confidence. . . ."*

© 1983 by Sidney Harris; *American Scientist Magazine.*

## Evaluating the Psychoanalytic Perspective

Knowing what you do about Freud's ideas, listen now to his critics. Bear in mind that we critique Freud from the perspective of the late twentieth century, a perspective that is itself subject to revision. Freud died in 1939 without the benefit of all that we have since learned about human development, thinking, and emotion and without today's research tools. To criticize Freud's theories by comparing them with current concepts is like comparing Henry Ford's Model T with today's Escort.

### Freud's Ideas in Light of Modern Research

Recent theories and research contradict many of Freud's specific ideas. Research indicates that human development is lifelong, not fixed in childhood. Developmental psychologists also question Freud's idea that conscience and gender identity form as the child resolves the Oedipus complex at age 5 or 6. Children gain their gender identity earlier. They become strongly masculine or feminine even without a same-sex parent present (Frieze & others, 1978). Freud's ideas about childhood sexuality arose from his rejection of stories of childhood sexual abuse told by his female patients—stories he thought were an expression of their own childhood sexual wishes and conflicts. Today we take reports of sexual abuse seriously. Freud's ideas about the natural superiority of men are widely discounted and considered sexist.

As we saw in Chapter 7, new ideas about why we dream dispute Freud's belief that dreams disguise and fulfill wishes. Even slips of the tongue can be explained as competition between similar verbal choices in our memory network. Researchers find little support for Freud's idea that people protect themselves against painful self-knowledge by projecting their own unrecognized negative impulses onto others (Holmes, 1978, 1981). And Jerome Kagan (1989b) notes that history has been equally unkind to another of Freud's ideas—that sexual repression causes psychological disorder. From Freud's time to ours, sexual repression has diminished, but psychological disorders have not.

Finally, as explained in Chapter 9, some memory researchers doubt that repression—a cornerstone of Freud's theory—ever occurs. The skeptical researchers are actually beginning to sound like those skeptical of ESP. "After a hundred years of research," observed parapsychology critic Mark Hansel (1980), there is no objective evidence of ESP. "Despite seventy years of research, there is no objective evidence to support the concept of repression," argues David Holmes (1994).

History has been kinder to Freud's "iceberg" view of the mind, at least in part. We now know that we indeed have limited access to all that goes on in our minds (Erdelyi, 1985, 1988; Kihlstrom, 1990; Lewicki & others, 1992). However, the "iceberg" notion held by today's research psychologists differs from Freud's—so much so, argues Anthony Greenwald (1992), that it is about time to abandon Freud's view of the unconscious. As we saw in earlier chapters, many researchers think of the unconscious not as seething passions and repressive censoring but as information processing that occurs without our awareness. To them, the unconscious involves the schemas that automatically control our perceptions and interpretations; the processing of stimuli to which we have not consciously attended; the right-hemisphere activity that enables the split-brain patient's left hand to carry out an instruction the patient cannot verbalize; the parallel processing of different aspects of vision and thinking; the implicit memories that operate without conscious recall; the conditioned emotions that activate instantly. This understanding of unconscious information processing is more like the pre-Freudian view of an unconscious underground stream of thought from which spontaneous creative ideas surface.

Recent history has supported Freud's idea that we defend ourselves against anxiety. Again, however, the contemporary idea differs from Freud's. Sheldon Solomon, Jeff Greenberg, and Tom Pyszczynski (1991) believe that one source of anxiety is "the terror resulting from our awareness of vulnerability and death." Experiments testing their *terror-management theory* show that thinking about one's mortality—by writing a short essay on dying and its associated emotions—provokes enough anxiety to intensify prejudices. Anxiety motivates not only contempt for others but also esteem for oneself. To feel self-esteem is to feel more loved, protected, and secure in a threatening world. Experiments that temporarily raise people's self-esteem (through flattering evaluations of their personality) also reduce their anxiety and their denial of vulnerability to death.

### Freud's Ideas as Scientific Theory

Psychologists also criticize Freud's theory for its scientific shortcomings. Recall from Chapter 1 that good scientific theories explain observations and offer testable hypotheses. Freud's theory, say the critics, rests on few objective observations and offers few hypotheses to verify or reject. (For Freud, his own recollections and interpretations of patients' free associations, dreams, and slips were evidence enough.)

The most serious problem with Freud's theory, according to critics, is that it offers after-the-fact explanations of any characteristic (of one person's smoking, another's fear of horses, another's sexual orientation) yet fails to *predict* such behavior and traits. If you feel angry at your mother's death, you illustrate the theory because "your unresolved childhood dependency needs are threatened." If you do not feel angry, you again illustrate the theory because "you are repressing your anger." That, said Calvin Hall and Gardner Lindzey (1978, p. 68), "is like betting on a horse after the race has been run." After-the-fact interpretation is perfectly appropriate for historical and literary scholarship, which helps explain Freud's currently greater influence on literary criticism than on psychological research. But in science a good theory makes testable predictions.

*"We are arguing like a man who should say, 'If there were an invisible cat in that chair, the chair would look empty; but the chair does look empty; therefore there is an invisible cat in it.'"*

C. S. Lewis
*Four Loves*, 1958

Such criticisms of Freud's specific concepts and after-the-fact interpretations have led some modern critics to scorn his theory. Peter Medawar (1982, pp. 71–72) compared it to "a dinosaur . . . one of the saddest and strangest of all landmarks in the history of twentieth-century thought." Perhaps we can evaluate Freud less harshly, for three reasons:

1. To criticize Freudian theory for not making testable predictions is like criticizing baseball for not being an aerobic exercise. Is it fair to fault something for not being what it was never intended to be? Freud never claimed that psychoanalysis was predictive science. He merely claimed that, looking back, psychoanalysts could find meaning in our state of mind (Rieff, 1979).
2. Some of Freud's ideas are enduring. It was Freud who drew our attention to the unconscious and the irrational, to anxiety and our struggle to cope with it, to the importance of human sexuality, and to the tension between our biological impulses and our social well-being. It was Freud who challenged our self-righteousness, punctured our pretensions, and reminded us of our potential for evil. Few dispute that Freud's ideas were creative, courageous, and comprehensive.
3. Correctly or incorrectly, Freud influenced our view of human nature. Rightly or wrongly, some ideas that many of us assume to be true—that childhood experiences mold personality, that many behaviors

PEANUTS reprinted by permission of UFS, Inc.

have disguised motives, that dreams have symbolic meaning—are Freud's legacy, which lives on in our thinking. His early 1900s concepts penetrate our 1990s language. Without realizing their source we may speak of ego, repression, projection, complex (as in "inferiority complex"), sibling rivalry, and fixation. As Peter Drucker (1982) remarked, "[Many] psychologists have no use for Freud, and I have some grave doubts about him, but he is the only one who created vision and insight and changed our view of ourselves and of the world." For that, Sigmund Freud continues to rank as one of modern history's towering intellectual figures.

## Summing Up

Like intelligence, personality is an abstract concept that cannot be seen, touched, or directly measured. To psychologists, personality is one's relatively distinctive and consistent pattern of thinking, feeling, and acting. We have first considered Freud's psychoanalytic perspective.

**Exploring the Unconscious** Sigmund Freud's treatment of emotional disorders led him to believe that they sprang from unconscious dynamics, which he sought to analyze through his own and his patients' free associations and dreams. Freud saw personality as composed of pleasure-seeking psychic impulses (the id), a reality-oriented executive (the ego), and an internalized set of ideals (the superego).

Freud believed that children develop through psychosexual stages, which he labeled the oral, anal, phallic, latency, and genital stages. He suggested that people's later personalities are influenced by how they resolve conflicts associated with these stages and whether they remain fixated at any stage.

Tensions between demands of the id and superego cause anxiety. The ego copes with defense mechanisms, of which repression is the most basic. Neo-Freudians Alfred Adler and Karen Horney accepted many of Freud's ideas, as did Carl Jung. But they also argued that we have more positive motives than sex and aggression and that the ego's conscious control is greater than Freud supposed.

**Assessing the Unconscious** Psychoanalytic assessment aims to reveal these unconscious aspects of personality. Although some critics question the reliability and validity of projective tests, such as the Rorschach inkblots, many clinicians continue to use the Rorschach.

**Evaluating the Psychoanalytic Perspective** Critics say many of Freud's specific ideas are implausible, unvalidated, or contradicted by new research, and that his theory offers only after-the-fact explanations. Nevertheless, Freud drew psychology's attention to the unconscious, to the struggle to cope with anxiety and sexuality, and to the conflict between biological impulses and social restraints. His cultural impact has been enormous.

## The Trait Perspective

*Rather than explaining hidden personality dynamics, trait researchers describe basic personality dimensions. What are some basic dimensions and how can we assess a person's standing on them?*

Psychoanalytic theory explains personality in terms of the dynamics that underlie behavior. It peers beneath the surface in search of hidden motives. In 1919, Gordon Allport, a curious 22-year-old psychology student, interviewed Freud in Vienna and discovered just how preoccupied the founder of psychoanalysis was with finding hidden motives.

> Soon after I had entered the famous red burlap room with pictures of dreams on the wall, he summoned me to his inner office. He did not speak to me but sat in expectant silence, for me to state my mission. I was not prepared for silence and had to think fast to find a suitable conversational gambit. I told him of an episode on the tram car on my way to his office. A small boy about 4 years of age had displayed a conspicuous dirt phobia. He kept saying to his mother, "I don't want to sit there . . . don't let that dirty man sit beside me." To him everything was *schmutzig* (filthy). His mother was a well-starched *Hausfrau*, so dominant and purposive looking that I thought the cause and effect apparent.
>
> When I finished my story Freud fixed his kindly therapeutic eyes upon me and said, "And was that little boy you?" Flabbergasted and feeling a bit guilty, I contrived to change the subject. While Freud's misunderstanding of my motivation was amusing, it also started a deep train of thought (1967, pp. 7–8).

That train of thought ultimately led Allport to do what Freud did not do—to describe personality in terms of fundamental **traits**—people's characteristic behaviors and conscious motives (such as the professional curiosity that actually motivated Allport to see Freud). Meeting Freud, said Allport, "taught me that [psychoanalysis], for all its merits, may plunge too deep, and that psychologists would do well to give full recognition to manifest motives before probing the unconscious." Allport therefore defined personality in terms of identifiable behavior patterns. He was less concerned with *explaining* and more with *describing* individual traits.

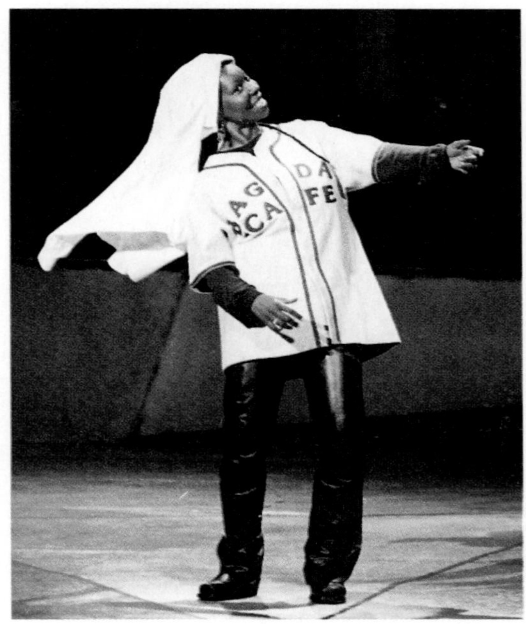

**Whoopie Whoops It Up!** *On stage, Whoopie Goldberg seems as outgoing and enthusiastic as her name implies. While few of us carry such apt names, trait terms can describe our temperaments and typical behaviors.*

How do psychologists describe and classify personalities? An analogy may help. Imagine that you want to describe and classify apples. Someone might correctly say that every apple is unique. Still, you might find it useful to begin by classifying apples as distinct *types*—Delicious, Granny Smith, McIntosh, and so forth. That is how the ancient Greeks described personality—by classifying people according to four types. Depending on which of one's bodily "humors," or fluids, they believed to predominate, they declared people either melancholic (depressed), sanguine (cheerful), phlegmatic (unemotional), or choleric (irritable).

We now have other ideas of basic personality types. Based on children's physiological and psychological reactivity, Jerome Kagan (1989b) classifies children's temperaments as either shy-inhibited or fearless-uninhibited types. Some health psychologists find it useful to classify people as intense, *Type A*, or as laid back, *Type B*, personalities (pages 581–582).

Psychologist William Sheldon (1954) classified people by body type. Santa Claus typifies the plump *endomorph*: relaxed and jolly. Superman typifies the muscular *mesomorph*: bold and physically active. Sherlock Holmes typifies the thin *ectomorph*: high strung and solitary. Are different body types actually associated with different personalities? When researchers assess people's body types and personalities separately, there is a linkage, but it is modest. The stereotypes of the chubby, happy-go-lucky person and of the muscular, confident person turn out to be just that—stereotypes that exaggerate a kernel of truth (Tucker, 1983).

More popular today, especially in business and career counseling, is an effort to classify people according to Carl Jung's personality types, based on their responses to 126 questions written by Isabel Briggs Myers (1987) and her mother, Kathleen Briggs. The *Myers-Briggs Type Indicator* is quite simple. It offers its 2 million annual takers choices, such as "Do you usually value sentiment more than logic, or value logic more than sentiment?" Then it counts their preferences, labels them as indicating, say, a "feeling" or "thinking" type, and describes each type in complimentary terms. Feeling types, for example, are told they are sensitive to values and "sympathetic, appreciative, and tactful"; thinking types are told they "prefer an objective standard of truth" and are "good at analyzing." Most people therefore readily embrace their announced type profile, which mirrors their declared preferences. They may also accept it as a basis for being matched with work partners and tasks that supposedly suit their temperaments. A recent National Research Council report, however, notes that the test's use has outrun research on its value as a predictor of job performance, and that "the popularity of this instrument in the absence of proven scientific worth is troublesome" (Druckman & Bjork, 1991, p. 101).

## Exploring Traits

If classifying people as one or another distinct personality type fails to fully capture their individuality, how else could we describe their personalities? To return to our apple analogy, we might describe an apple along several trait dimensions—as relatively large or small, red or yellow, sweet or sour. By placing people on several trait dimensions simultaneously, psychologists can describe countless individual personality variations. (Remember from Chapter 5 that variations on just three color dimensions—hue, saturation, and brightness—create many thousands of colors.)

What trait dimensions describe personality? Allport and his associate H. S. Odbert (1936) literally counted all the words in an unabridged dictionary with which one could describe people. The list numbered almost 18,000! How, then, could psychologists condense the list to a manageable number of basic traits?

One way has been to propose traits, such as anxiety, that some theory regards as basic. A newer technique is *factor analysis*, the statistical procedure described in Chapter 11 to identify clusters of test items that tap basic components of intelligence (such as spatial ability, reasoning ability, or verbal skill). Imagine that people who describe themselves as outgoing also tend to say they like excitement and practical jokes, and that they do not like quiet reading. Such a statistically correlated cluster of behaviors reflects a basic trait, or factor—in this case, a trait called *extraversion*.

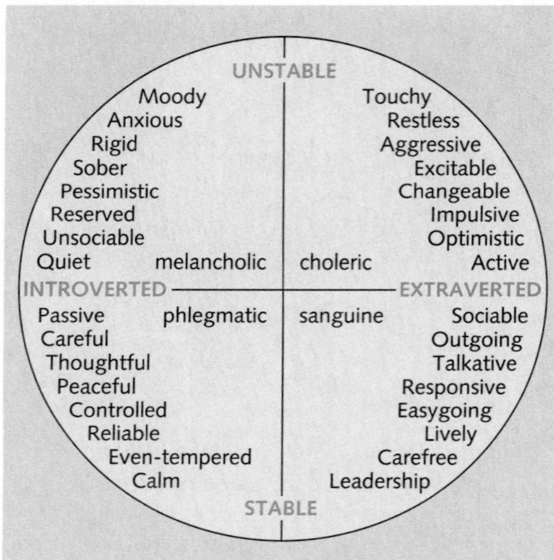


**Figure 14–2**

**Two Personality Factors** *As mapmakers can tell us a lot by using two axes (north-south and east-west), so can the Eysencks by using two primary personality factors—extraversion-introversion and stability-instability. Varying combinations define other, more specific traits. Note that the four basic combinations of the two factors resemble the personality types proposed by the ancient Greeks, which are noted in the center of the chart. (From Eysenck & Eysenck, 1963.)*

British psychologists Hans Eysenck and Sybil Eysenck believe that we can reduce many of our normal individual variations to two or three genetically influenced dimensions, including *extraversion-introversion* and *emotional stability-instability* (Figure 14–2). Their *Eysenck Personality Questionnaire* has been given to people in 35 countries around the world, from China to Uganda to Russia. When people's answers are analyzed, the extraversion and emotionality factors inevitably emerge as basic personality dimensions (Eysenck, 1990, 1992). Extraverts, they contend, seek stimulation because their normal levels of brain arousal are relatively low. Emotionally stable people react calmly because their autonomic nervous systems are not so reactive as those of unstable people.

Many other trait theorists, too, view personality traits as biologically rooted. As noted earlier in this chapter, Jerome Kagan attributes differences in children's shyness and inhibition to their autonomic nervous system reactivity. Twin and adoption studies of genetic influences on personality traits (pages 108–111) further remind us that behavior patterns form as a person's genetic endowment interacts with a particular environment.

**Table 14–2 The "Big Five" Personality Factors**

| Trait Dimension | Description |
|---|---|
| Emotional stability | Calm versus anxious<br>Secure versus insecure<br>Self-satisfied versus self-pitying |
| Extraversion | Sociable versus retiring<br>Fun-loving versus sober<br>Affectionate versus reserved |
| Openness | Imaginative versus practical<br>Preference for variety versus preference for routine<br>Independent versus conforming |
| Agreeableness | Soft-hearted versus ruthless<br>Trusting versus suspicious<br>Helpful versus uncooperative |
| Conscientiousness | Organized versus disorganized<br>Careful versus careless<br>Disciplined versus impulsive |

*Source*: Adapted from "Clinical assessment can benefit from recent advances in personality psychology" by R. McCrae & P. T. Costa, Jr., 1986, *American Psychologist, 41*, p. 1002.

Most researchers believe that the Eysencks' dimensions are important but that they don't tell the whole story of someone's personality. They offer a slightly expanded set of factors—dubbed the *Big Five* (Goldberg, 1993; John, 1990; Noller & others, 1987). If a test specifies where you are on the five dimensions of Table 14–2, it has said much of what there is to say about your personality. In different languages and cultures, people notice and name slightly varying traits (Church & Katigbak, 1989; Yang & Bond, 1990). Yet around the world, people describe others in terms roughly consistent with the Big Five—how agreeable they are, how extraverted they are, and so forth. The Big Five may not be the last word: Other theorists wonder whether we should add dimensions such as self-consciousness and masculinity/femininity. And even a comprehensive personality description doesn't *explain* how personality develops (McAdams, 1992.) But it's currently our best approximation of the basic trait dimensions. If you could ask five questions about the personality of a stranger—say, a blind date you were soon to meet—querying where the person is on these five dimensions would be most revealing.

## Assessing Traits

Assessment techniques derived from trait concepts aim simply to profile a person's behavior patterns, not to reveal the hidden personality dynamics (which is the intent of projective tests). Many trait scales provide quick assessments of a single trait, such as extraversion, anxiety, or self-esteem. Such measures are commonly used in studies of personality and behavior. Alternatively, psychologists can assess several traits at once by administering **personality inventories**—longer questionnaires on which people respond to items covering a wide range of feelings and behaviors.

The personality inventory that psychologists have most extensively researched and widely used is the **Minnesota Multiphasic Personality Inventory (MMPI)**. Although it assesses psychological disorders rather than "normal" personality traits, the MMPI illustrates a good way to develop a personality inventory. One of its creators, Starke Hathaway (1960), compared his effort to that of Alfred Binet. Binet, as you may recall, developed the first intelligence test by selecting items that discriminated children who were and were not progressing normally in French schools. The MMPI items, too, were **empirically derived**. That is, from a large pool of items Hathaway and his colleagues selected those that discriminated particular groups.

They initially gave hundreds of true-false statements ("No one seems to understand me"; "I get all the sympathy I should"; "I like poetry") to groups of psychologically disordered patients and to "normal" people. They retained any statement—no matter how silly it sounded—on which the patient group's answer differed from that of the normal group. "Nothing in the newspaper interests me except the comics" may seem senseless, but it just so happened that depressed people were more likely to answer "true." (Nevertheless, pundits have had fun spoofing the MMPI with their own mock items, such as: "Weeping brings tears to my eyes"; "As a child I often suffered from bubonic plague"; "I think oatmeal is erotic"; "Frantic screams make me nervous"; "I stay in the bathtub until I look like a raisin" [Frankel & others, 1983].)

Today's new MMPI-2, renormed on a full cross-section of Americans and containing revised items, still contains 10 clinical scales (see Figure 14–3). It also retains several validity scales, including the so-called lie scale that assesses the extent to which a person is faking a good impression (by responding "false" to statements such as "I get angry sometimes"). And it

**Figure 14–3**

**Minnesota Multiphasic Personality Inventory (MMPI-2) Test Profile** *High scores suggest a psychological disorder. This graph plots the scores of Ed, a depressed and anxious young man, before and after psychotherapy. Scores are converted to a "T-scale," such that an average score is called 50 and about two-thirds of people fall between 40 and 60. (Adapted from Butcher, 1990.)*

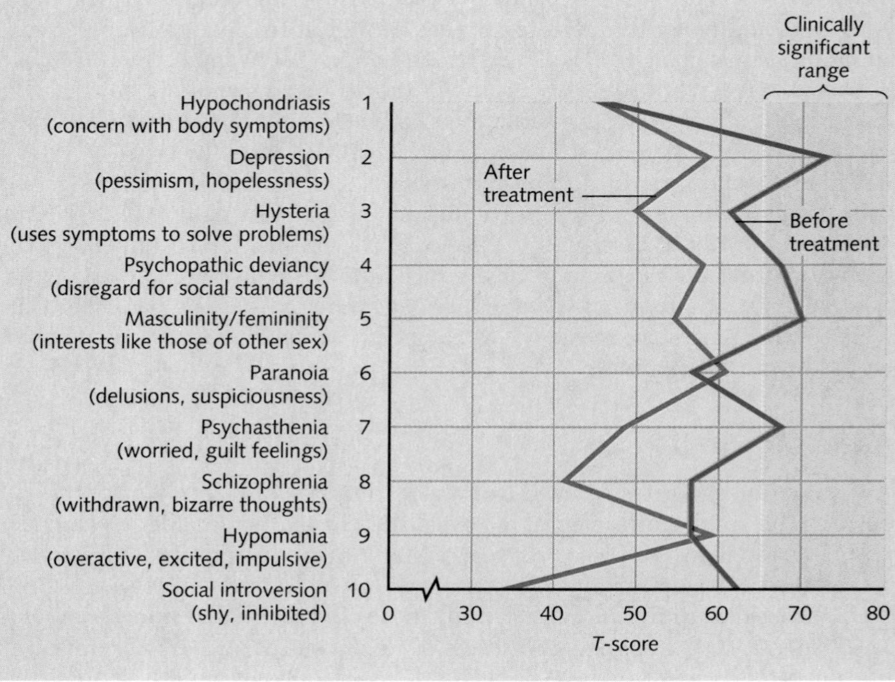

has 15 content scales assessing, for instance, work attitudes, family problems, and anger. Scores are converted to a "*T*-scale," such that an average score is called 50 and about two-thirds of people fall between 40 and 60.

In contrast to the subjectivity of projective tests, personality inventories are scored objectively—so objectively that a computer can administer and score them. (The computer can also provide descriptions of people who previously responded similarly.) Objectivity does not, however, guarantee validity. Sophisticated test-takers can fake a good impression if taking the MMPI for employment purposes (by answering in socially desirable ways, except on those items for which nearly anyone would admit to being imperfect). Moreover, the ease of computerized testing tempts untrained administrators—including many personnel officers, educational admissions officers, and physicians—to use the test in ways for which it has not been validated (Matarazzo, 1983). Nevertheless, for better or worse, the objectivity of the MMPI contributes to its rising popularity (Piotrowski & Keller, 1989) and to its translation into more than 100 languages.

Although self-report personality tests are the most widely used method of assessing traits, psychologist David Funder (1991) believes that peer reports provide more trustworthy information. Friends who have observed you repeatedly in everyday situations provide the acid test for judging, say, how extraverted you are. Self-reports and peer reports tend to agree (Borkenau & Liebler, 1993). But when they disagree, Funder would put his money on peer reports. If everyone who knows you agrees you are outgoing, then, regardless of what you think, you *are* outgoing.

## Evaluating the Trait Perspective

Are our personality traits stable and enduring? Or does our behavior depend on where we are and whom we're with? William Faulkner strove to mirror reality in fiction by creating characters, like the self-centered Jason Compson, whose personal traits were consistent across various times and places. The Italian playwright Luigi Pirandello had a different view. For him, personality was ever-changing, tailored to the particular role or situation. In one of Pirandello's plays Lamberto Laudisi describes himself to Signora Sirelli: "I am really what you take me to be; though, my dear madam, that does not prevent me from also being really what your husband, my sister, my niece, and Signora Cini take me to be—because they also are absolutely right!" To which she responds, "In other words you are a different person for each of us."

*"There is as much difference between us and ourselves, as between us and others."*
Michel de Montaigne
*Essays*, 1588

Who best represents human personality, Faulkner's consistent Jason Compson or Pirandello's inconsistent Laudisi? Most of us agree that this is not an either/or question: Our behavior is influenced by the interaction of our inner disposition with our environment. Still, the question lingers: Which is *more* important? Are we *more* as Faulkner or as Pirandello imagined us to be? Forced to choose, most people would probably side with Faulkner. Until the late 1960s, most psychologists would have, too. Isn't it obvious that some people are dependably conscientious and others unreliable, some cheerful and others dour, some outgoing and others shy?

*Roughly speaking, the temporary, external influences on behavior are the focus of social psychology, and the enduring, inner influences are the focus of personality psychology. In actuality, behavior always depends on the interaction of persons with situations.*

Remember, to be a genuine personality trait a characteristic must persist over time *and* across situations. If friendliness is a trait, friendly people must act friendly at different times and places. Do they? In Chapter 4, we considered research that has followed lives through time. We noted that some scholars are impressed with personality change (especially those who study infants); others are struck by personality stability during adulthood.

*"Mr. Coughlin over there was the founder of one of the first motorcycle gangs."*

Drawing by Miller; © 1984 The New Yorker Magazine, Inc.

If people's personalities are assessed in young adulthood and then assessed again several decades later, their characteristics persist. Faulkner would not have been surprised.

The consistency of specific behaviors from one situation to the next is another matter. As Walter Mischel (1968, 1984) points out, people do not act with predictable consistency. In one of the first studies to reveal this, Hugh Hartshorne and Mark May (1928b) gave thousands of children opportunities to lie, cheat, and steal while at home, at play, and in the classroom. Were some children consistently honest, others dishonest? Generally not. "Most children will deceive in certain situations and not in others," the researchers reported. A child's "lying, cheating, and stealing as measured by the test situations used in these studies are only very loosely related" (p. 411). More than a half-century later, Mischel's studies of college students' conscientiousness revealed a similar finding. There was virtually no relation between a student's being conscientious on one occasion (say, showing up for class on time) and being similarly conscientious on another occasion (say, turning in assignments on time). Pirandello would not have been surprised.

Mischel also points out that people's scores on personality tests only mildly predict their behaviors. For example, people's scores on an extraversion test do not neatly predict how sociable they actually will be on any given occasion. If we remember such results, says Mischel, we will be more cautious about labeling and pigeonholing individuals. We will be more restrained when asked to predict whether someone is likely to violate parole, commit suicide, or be an effective employee. Years in advance, science can tell us the phase of the moon for any given date, but we're a long way from being able to predict how you will feel and act tomorrow.

In defense of traits, Seymour Epstein (1983a,b) maintains that trying to predict a specific act on the basis of a personality test is like trying to predict your answer to a single test question on the basis of an intelligence test. Your answer to any given question is unpredictable because it depends on so many variables (your reading of the question, your understanding of the topic, your concentration level at the moment, luck). Your *average* accuracy over many questions on several tests is more predictable. Similarly, says Epstein, people's *average* outgoingness, happiness, or carelessness over *many* situations is predictable. When rating someone's shyness or agreeableness, this consistency enables people who know someone well to agree (Kenrick & Funder, 1988). As our best friends can verify, we *do* have personality traits. Moreover, our traits are socially significant. They influence our health, our thinking, and our job performance (Deary & Matthews, 1993; Jackson & Rothstein, 1993).

In unfamiliar, formal situations—perhaps when eating in a strange home—our traits may remain hidden as we attend carefully to social cues. In familiar, informal situations—just hanging out with friends—we feel less constrained, allowing our traits to emerge (Buss, 1989). In such situations, our expressive styles are impressively consistent. Thus, we often form lasting impressions within a few moments of meeting someone and noting the person's animation, manner of speaking, and gestures. Nalini Ambady and Robert Rosenthal (1992, 1993) videotaped 13 Harvard University graduate students teaching undergraduate courses. Observers then viewed three thin slices of each teacher's behavior—mere 10-second clips from the beginning, middle, and end of a class—and rated each teacher's level of confidence, activeness, warmth, and so forth. These behavior ratings, based on 30 *seconds* of teaching from an entire semester, predicted amazingly well the teacher's average student ratings at the semester's end.

Observing even thinner slices—three 2-second clips—yielded ratings that still correlated as high as +.72 with the student evaluations. Some people's first impressions, derived from expressive behavior, predicted other people's lasting impressions!

Mere glimpses of someone's behavior can be revealing because of the potency of traits such as expressiveness. Some people are naturally expressive (and therefore talented at pantomime and charades); others are more expressionless. To evaluate people's voluntary control over their expressiveness, Bella DePaulo and her colleagues (1992) asked people to *act* as expressive or inhibited as possible while stating opinions. Their remarkable findings: Inexpressive people, even when feigning expressiveness, were less expressive than expressive people acting naturally. Similarly, expressive people, even when trying to act inhibited, were less inhibited than inexpressive people acting naturally. It's hard to be someone you're not, or not to be what you are.

The irrepressibility of expressiveness explains why we can size up someone's outgoingness within seconds. Imagine yourself as a subject in an experiment by Maurice Levesque and David Kenny (1993). They seated groups of four university women around a table and asked each woman merely to state her name, year, hometown, and college residence. Judging from just these few seconds of verbal and nonverbal behavior, the women were then to guess each other's talkativeness. (Do you think you would be able to guess someone's talkativeness based on a mere glimpse of their behavior?) When later correlated with how talkative each woman actually was during a series of one-on-one videotaped conversations, the snap judgments proved reasonably accurate. As this experiment demonstrated, thin slices of behavior can be revealing when we judge an expressive trait such as outgoingness.

To sum up, we can say that at any moment the immediate situation powerfully influences a person's behavior, especially when the situation makes clear demands. We can better predict drivers' behavior at traffic lights from knowing the color of the lights than from knowing their personalities. Thus, professors may perceive a student as subdued (based on classroom behavior), but friends may perceive her as rather wild (based on party behavior). However, averaging people's behavior across many occasions reveals that they do have distinct personality traits. Moreover, individual differences in some traits such as expressiveness can be quickly perceived.

## Summing Up

**Exploring Traits** Rather than explain the hidden aspects of personality, trait researchers describe the predispositions that underlie our actions. For example, through factor analysis, researchers have isolated five important dimensions of personality. Genetic predispositions influence most such traits.

**Assessing Traits** To assess traits, psychologists have devised self-report inventories, such as the empirically derived MMPI-2. Peer reports may provide even more trustworthy clues to a person's behavioral traits.

**Evaluating the Trait Perspective** Critics of traits question the consistency with which they are expressed. Although people's traits persist over time, human behavior varies widely from situation to situation. Despite these variations, a person's *average* behavior across different situations is more consistent.

# The Humanistic Perspective

*Led by Abraham Maslow and Carl Rogers, humanistic psychologists have emphasized the growth potential of healthy people. By what methods have they studied personality and hoped to foster personal growth?*

By 1960, some personality psychologists became discontented with Freud's negativity and with trait psychology's objectivity. In contrast to Freud's study of the base motives of "sick" people, these *humanistic psychologists* focused on the strivings of "healthy" people for self-determination and self-realization. In contrast to trait psychologists' profiles, they viewed whole persons as beyond encapsulation as so many test scores. Two pioneering theorists illustrate these emphases on human potential and seeing the world through the person's (not the experimenter's) eyes: Abraham Maslow (1908–1970) and Carl Rogers (1902–1987).

## Exploring the Self

### Abraham Maslow's Self-Actualizing Person

Maslow proposed that we are motivated by a hierarchy of needs (page 400). If our physiological needs are met, we become concerned with personal safety; if we achieve a sense of security, we then seek to love, to be loved, and to love ourselves. Given self-esteem, we ultimately seek **self-actualization**, the process of fulfilling our potential.

**Abraham Maslow** *"Any theory of motivation that is worthy of attention must deal with the highest capacities of the healthy and strong person as well as with the defensive maneuvers of crippled spirits" (Motivation and Personality, 1970).*

Unlike many theorists before him, Maslow (1970) developed his ideas by studying healthy, creative people rather than troubled clinical cases. He based his description of self-actualization on a study of people who seemed notable for their rich and productive lives—Abraham Lincoln, Thomas Jefferson, and Eleanor Roosevelt among them. These people shared certain characteristics. Maslow reported they were self-aware and self-accepting, open and spontaneous, loving and caring, and not paralyzed by others' opinions. Secure in their sense of who they were, their interests were problem-centered rather than self-centered. Often they focused their energies on a particular task, which they regarded as their mission in life. Most enjoyed a few deep relationships rather than many superficial ones. Many had been moved by spiritual or personal *peak experiences* that surpassed ordinary consciousness.

These are mature adult qualities, said Maslow, ones found in those who have learned enough about life to be compassionate, to have outgrown their mixed feelings toward their parents, to have found their calling, to have "acquired enough courage to be unpopular, to be unashamed about being openly virtuous, etc." Maslow's work with college students led him to speculate that those likely to become self-actualizing adults were likable, caring, "privately affectionate to those of their elders who deserve it," and "secretly uneasy about the cruelty, meanness, and mob spirit so often found in young people."

### Carl Rogers's Person-Centered Perspective

Fellow humanistic psychologist Carl Rogers agreed with much of Maslow's thinking. Rogers believed that people are basically good and are endowed with actualizing tendencies. Each of us is like an acorn, primed for growth and fulfillment, unless thwarted by an environment that inhibits growth. Rogers (1980) surmised that a growth-promoting climate required three conditions—genuineness, acceptance, and empathy.

According to Rogers, people nurture our growth by being *genuine*—by being open with their own feelings, dropping their facades, and being transparent and self-disclosing.

People also nurture growth by being *accepting*—by offering us what Rogers called **unconditional positive regard**. This is an attitude of grace, an attitude that values us even knowing our failings. Have you ever experienced the relief of having dropped your pretenses, confessed your worst feelings, and discovered that you were still accepted? We sometimes enjoy this gratifying experience in a good marriage, a close family, or an intimate friendship in which we no longer feel a need to explain ourselves and are free to be spontaneous without fear of losing the other's esteem.

*Rogers believed that genuineness, acceptance, and empathy nurture growth not only in the relationship between therapist and client but also between parent and child, leader and group, teacher and student, administrator and staff member—in fact, between any two human beings.*

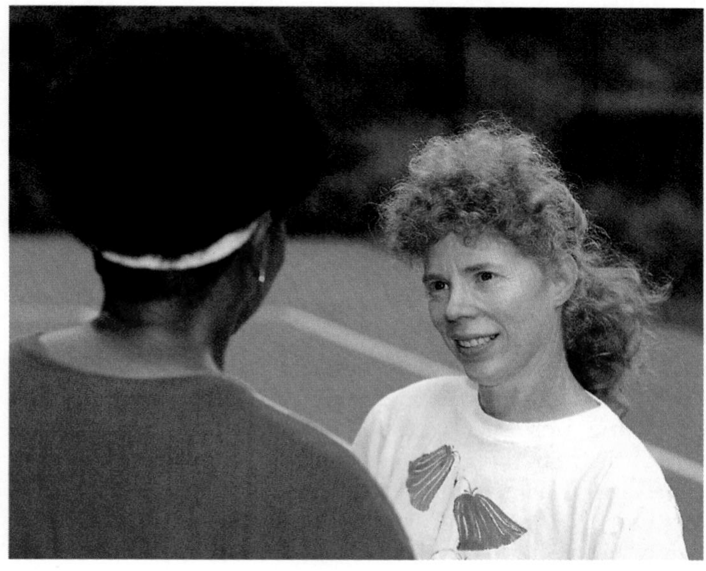

**The Picture of Empathy** *Being open and sharing confidences is easier when the listener shows* real *understanding. Within such relationships people can relax and fully express their true selves.*

Finally, people nurture growth by being *empathic*—by nonjudgmentally reflecting our feelings and meanings. "Rarely do we listen with real understanding, true empathy," said Rogers. "Yet listening, of this very special kind, is one of the most potent forces for change that I know."

Genuineness, acceptance, and empathy are the water, sun, and nutrients that enable people to grow like vigorous oak trees, according to Rogers. For "as persons are accepted and prized, they tend to develop a more caring attitude toward themselves" (Rogers 1980, p. 116). As persons are empathically heard, "it becomes possible for them to listen more accurately to the flow of inner experiencings." Rogers would have been pleased by a finding published shortly after his death: Preschool children whose parents exhibit such attitudes usually become creative adolescents (Harrington & others, 1987).

For Maslow, and even more for Rogers, a central feature of personality is one's **self-concept**—all the thoughts and feelings we have in response to the question, "Who am I?" If our self-concept is positive, we tend to act and perceive the world positively. If it is negative—if in our own eyes we fall far short of our "ideal self"—said Rogers, we feel dissatisfied and unhappy. A worthwhile goal for parents, teachers, and friends is, therefore, to help others know, accept, and be true to themselves.

*College of Positive Self-Image 7. University of Low Self-Esteem 0.*

Reprinted by permission: Tribune Media Services.

## Assessing the Self

Humanistic psychologists sometimes assess personality with questionnaires that evaluate people's self-concepts. One questionnaire, inspired by Carl Rogers, asks people to describe themselves both as they ideally would like to be and as they actually are. When the ideal and the actual self are nearly alike, said Rogers, the self-concept is positive. Thus, to assess his clients' personal growth during therapy he looked for successively closer ratings of actual and ideal self.

Other humanistic psychologists believe that any standardized assessment of personality is depersonalizing, that even a questionnaire detaches the psychologist from the living human. Rather than forcing the person to respond to narrow categories, these humanistic psychologists believe that interviews and intimate conversation enable a better understanding of each person's unique experiences.

### Research on the Self

Psychology's concern with people's sense of self dates back at least to William James, who devoted more than 100 pages to the topic in his 1890 *Principles of Psychology*. By 1943, Gordon Allport lamented that the self had become "lost to view." Although humanistic psychology's emphasis on the self did not instigate much scientific research, it did help renew the concept of self and keep it alive. Now, a century after James, the self is one of Western psychology's most vigorously researched topics. Every year new studies galore appear on self-esteem, self-disclosure, self-awareness, self-schemas, self-monitoring, and so forth. During 1993, *Psychological Abstracts*, the reader's guide to psychology's research, offered 5396 article and book summaries in which the word *self* appeared—quadruple the number in 1970. One example of the new thinking about self is the concept of *possible selves* put forth by Hazel Markus and her colleagues (Markus & Nurius, 1986; Inglehart & others, 1989). Your possible selves include your visions of the self you dream of becoming—the rich self, the thin self, the loved and admired self. They also include the self you fear becoming—the unemployed self, the alcoholic self, the academically failed self. Such possible selves motivate us by laying out specific goals to pursue and the energy to

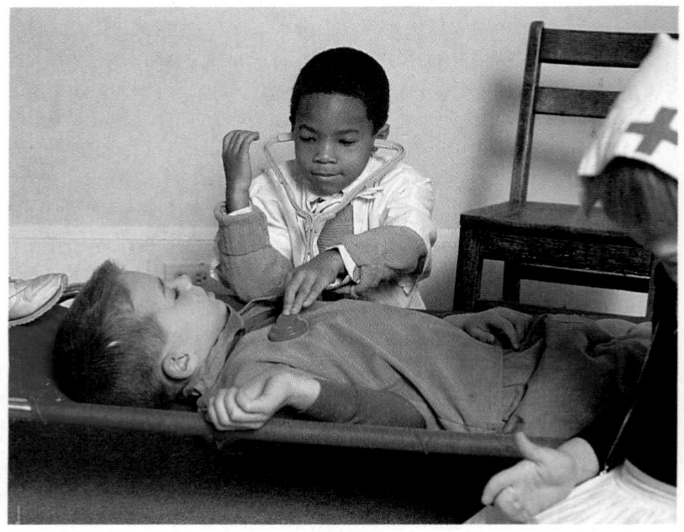

**Possible Selves** *By giving them a chance to try out many possible selves, pretend games offer children important opportunities to grow emotionally, socially, and cognitively. Although this young boy may not grow up to be a physician, playing adult roles will certainly bear fruit in terms of an expanded vision of what he might become.*

work toward them. Olympian Carl Lewis concentrated on the achievements of Olympic hero Jesse Owens to give form to his aspirations. Similarly, University of Michigan students in a combined undergraduate/medical school program earn higher grades if they undergo the program with a clear vision of themselves as successful doctors. Those who dream most, achieve most.

*What possible future selves do you envision? To what extent do these imagined selves motivate you now?*

Underlying this research is an assumption (shared by humanistic psychologists) that the self, as organizer of our thoughts, feelings, and actions, is a pivotal center of personality (Markus & Wurf, 1987). We even remember information better if we encode it in terms of ourselves. Asked whether specific words such as *friendly* describe them, people later recall those words better than if asked whether the words describe someone else (Higgins & Bargh, 1987).

How we *feel* about ourselves is also important. Research studies reveal the benefits of positive self-esteem and the hazards of pride.

**The Benefits of Self-Esteem** High **self-esteem**—a feeling of self-worth—pays dividends. People who feel good about themselves (who strongly agree with self-affirming questionnaire statements) have fewer ulcers and fewer sleepless nights, succumb less easily to pressures to conform, are less likely to use drugs, are more persistent at difficult tasks, and are just plain happier (Brockner & Hulton, 1978; Brown, 1991).

Low self-esteem people don't necessarily see themselves as worthless or wicked, but they do lack good things to say about themselves. Such low self-esteem exacts costs. More often than not, unhappiness and despair coexist with low self-esteem. People who feel they are falling short of their hopes are vulnerable to depression. Those whose self-image falls short of what they think they *ought* to be are vulnerable to anxiety (Higgins, 1987).

These correlational links between low self-esteem and life problems have other possible interpretations. Maybe life problems cause low self-esteem. Maybe self-esteem reflects reality. However, an *effect* of low self-esteem appears in experiments. Temporarily deflate people's self-image (say, by telling them they did poorly on an aptitude test or by disparaging their personality) and they will be more likely to disparage other people or to express heightened racial prejudice. People who are negative about themselves also tend to be thin-skinned and judgmental (Baumeister, 1993; Baumgardner & others, 1989; Pelham, 1993). Although some "love their neighbors as themselves," others loathe their neighbors as themselves. In experiments, those made to feel insecure often become excessively critical, as if to impress others with their own brilliance (Amabile, 1983). Such findings are consistent with Maslow's and Rogers's presumptions that a healthy self-image pays dividends. Accept yourself and you'll find it easier to accept others.

**The Pervasiveness of Self-Serving Bias** Carl Rogers (1958) once objected to the religious doctrine that humanity's problems arise from excessive self-love, or pride. He noted that most people he had known "despise themselves, regard themselves as worthless and unlovable." Mark Twain had the idea: "No man, deep down in the privacy of his heart, has any considerable respect for himself."

Actually, most of us have a good reputation with ourselves. In studies of self-esteem, even low-scoring people respond in the midrange of possible scores (Baumeister & others, 1989). (A "low" self-esteem person responds to statements such as "I have good ideas" with qualifying adjectives such as *somewhat* or *sometimes*.) Moreover, one of psychology's most provocative

*"To love oneself is the beginning of a life-long romance."*

Oscar Wilde
*An Ideal Husband*, 1895

yet firmly established recent conclusions concerns our potent **self-serving bias**—our readiness to perceive ourselves favorably (Brown, 1991; Myers, 1993). Consider:

***People accept more responsibility for good deeds than for bad, and for successes than for failures.*** Athletes often privately credit their victories to their own prowess and their losses to bad breaks, lousy officiating, or the other team's exceptional performance. After receiving poor exam grades, most students in a half dozen studies criticized the exam, not themselves. Most university students think the Scholastic Assessment Test underestimates their actual ability, although the higher scores they *think* they deserved would have predicted their later grades *less* accurately (Shepperd, 1993). On insurance forms, drivers have explained accidents in such words as: "An invisible car came out of nowhere, struck my car, and vanished." "As I reached an intersection, a hedge sprang up, obscuring my vision, and I did not see the other car." "A pedestrian hit me and went under my car." The question "What have I done to deserve this?" is one we ask of our troubles, not our successes—those we assume we deserve.

*"It is only our bad temper that we put down to being tired or worried or hungry. We put our good temper down to ourselves."*

C. S. Lewis, 1898–1963

***Most people see themselves as better than average.*** This is true for nearly any subjective and socially desirable dimension. In national surveys, most business executives say they are more ethical than their average counterpart. In several studies, 90 percent of business managers and more than 90 percent of college professors rated their performance as superior to their average peer. In Australia, 86 percent of people rate their job performance as above average, and only 1 percent as below average. And in the United States, most high school seniors rate themselves in the top 10 percent of their agemates in their ability to get along with others. Although the phenomenon is less striking in Asia, where modesty is valued, self-serving biases have been observed worldwide: among Dutch, Australian, and Chinese students; Japanese drivers; Indian Hindus; and French people of all walks of life. The world, it seems, is Garrison Keillor's Lake Wobegon writ large—a place where "all the women are strong, all the men are good-looking, and all the children are above average."

*"The [self-]portraits that we actually believe, when we are given freedom to voice them, are dramatically more positive than reality can sustain."*

Shelley Taylor
*Positive Illusions*, 1989

**PEANUTS**

PEANUTS reprinted by permission of UFS, Inc.

Self-serving bias flies in the face of today's pop psychology. "All of us have inferiority complexes," insists John Powell (1989, p. 15). "Those who seem not to have such a complex are only pretending." But additional streams of evidence remove any doubts: We remember and justify our past actions in self-enhancing ways. We exhibit an inflated confidence in the accuracy of our beliefs and judgments. We overestimate how desirably *we* would act in situations where most people behave less than admirably. We are quicker to believe flattering descriptions of ourselves than unflattering ones, and we are impressed with psychological tests that make us look good. We shore up our self-image by overestimating how much others support our opinions and share our foibles and by *under*estimating the commonality of our strengths. We exhibit group pride—a tendency to see our group (our school, our country, our race) as superior.

Moreover, pride does often go before a fall. Self-serving perceptions underlie conflicts ranging from other-blaming marital discord to self-promoting ethnic snobbery. It was "Aryan pride" that fueled Nazi atrocities. It was national self-righteousness that led both the Americans and Soviets during the arms race to say, "Your weapons threaten us, ours are only for defense." No wonder religion and literature so often warn against the perils of excessive pride.

Still, people object to the idea of self-serving bias. They think of those who do seem to despise themselves, who feel worthless and unlovable. If self-serving bias prevails, why do so many people disparage themselves? For at least two reasons. Sometimes people's self-directed put-downs are subtly strategic: They elicit reassuring strokes. Saying "No one likes me" may at least elicit "But not everyone has met you!" At other times, such as before a game or an exam, self-disparaging comments prepare us for possible failure. The coach who extols the superior strength of the upcoming opponent makes a loss understandable, a victory noteworthy.

Even so, it's true: All of us some of the time, and some of us much of the time, *do* feel inferior—especially when we compare ourselves with those who are a step or two higher on the ladder of status, grades, looks, income, or agility. The deeper and more frequently we have such feelings, the more unhappy, even depressed, we are. But for most people—the 98 percent who at anytime are *not* suffering depression (Diener, 1993; Gotlib, 1992)—thinking has a natural positive bias.

*"If you compare yourself with others, you may become vain and bitter; for always there will be greater and lesser persons than yourself."*

"Desiderata"
Found in Old St. Paul's Church, London, 1692

We can therefore affirm what humanistic psychologists rightly emphasize: For the individual, self-affirming thinking is generally adaptive. To a point, even our positive illusions are beneficial. They maintain our self-confidence, protect against anxiety and depression, and sustain our sense of well-being. "Life is the art of being well-deceived," observed the English essayist William Hazlitt.

Recognizing both the perils of self-righteousness and the dividends of positive self-esteem, psychologists Roy Baumeister (1989), Jonathan Brown (1991), and Shelley Taylor (1989) all suggest that humans function best with modest self-enhancing illusions. We are like the new Japanese and European magnetic levitation trains, says Brown: We function optimally when riding high, just off the rails—not so high that we gyrate and crash, yet not so in touch that we grind to a halt.

## Evaluating the Humanistic Perspective

One thing said of Freud can also be said of the humanistic psychologists: Their impact has been pervasive. Their ideas have influenced counseling, education, child-rearing, and management. They have also influenced—sometimes in ways they did not intend—much of today's popular psychology.

It is through popular psychology that many of us absorb some of what Maslow and Rogers so effectively taught—that a positive self-concept is the key to happiness and success, that acceptance and empathy help nurture positive feelings about oneself, and that people are basically good and capable of self-improvement. The National Opinion Research Center (1985) reported that by a 4 to 1 margin, Americans believe "human nature is basically good" rather than "fundamentally perverse and corrupt." Humanistic psychologists can also take satisfaction in the dramatic difference between today's response to one of the MMPI statements and the response given 50 years ago. Among those in the 1930s normal standardization sample, only 9 percent agreed that "I am an important person"; in the mid-1980s, more than half of the new sample agreed with the statement (Holden, 1986b). Responding to a 1989 Gallup Poll, 85 percent of Americans rated "having a good self-image or self-respect" as *very* important; 0 percent rated it unimportant. And 89 percent of people responding to a 1992 *Newsweek* Gallup Poll rated self-esteem as very important for "motivating a person to work hard and succeed." Humanistic psychology's message has been heard.

Perhaps one reason humanistic psychology's message has been so well received is that its emphasis on the individual self reflects and reinforces Western cultural values (see Chapter 19). As self-reliant individualism has grown, with increased priority given to personal identity and aspirations, the popular media have celebrated the rugged individual. Movie plots feature rugged heroes who, true to themselves, buck social convention or coercion. Popular songs proclaim that "I Did it My Way" and "I Gotta Be Me" and remind us that to love yourself is "The Greatest Love of All" (Schoeneman, 1994).

*"We do pretty well when you stop to think that people are basically good."*

Drawing by Fradon; © 1979 The New Yorker Magazine, Inc.

The prominence of the humanistic perspective set off a backlash of criticism. First, said the critics, its concepts are vague and subjective. Consider the description of self-actualizing people as open, spontaneous, loving, self-accepting, and productive. Is this really a scientific description? Or is it merely a description of Maslow's personal values and ideals? What Maslow did, noted M. Brewster Smith (1978), was to offer impressions of his own personal heroes. Imagine another theorist who began with a different set of heroes—perhaps Napoleon, Alexander the Great, and John D. Rockefeller, Sr. This theorist would likely describe self-actualizing people as "undeterred by the needs of others," "motivated to achieve," and "obsessed with power."

Second, some critics object to the idea that, as Carl Rogers put it, "The only question which matters is, 'Am I living in a way which is deeply satisfying to me, and which truly expresses me?'" (quoted by Wallach & Wallach, 1985). They fear that the individualism encouraged by humanistic psychology—trusting and acting on one's feelings, being true to oneself, fulfilling oneself—promotes self-indulgence, selfishness, and an erosion of moral restraints (Campbell & Specht, 1985; Wallach & Wallach, 1983). Indeed it is those who focus not on themselves but beyond themselves who are most likely to experience social support, to enjoy life, and to cope effectively with stress (Crandall, 1984).

Humanistic psychologists rebut such objections. They counter that belligerence, hostility, and insensitivity are often traceable to a poor self-concept. Moreover, they argue, a secure, nondefensive self-acceptance is actually the first step toward loving others.

Finally, the humanistic psychologists have been accused of failing to appreciate the reality of our human capacity for evil. Faced with assaults on the environment, overpopulation, and threats of nuclear war, apathy can develop from either of two rationalizations. One is a naïve optimism that denies the threat ("People are basically good; everything will work out"). The other is a dark despair ("It's hopeless; why try?"). Action requires enough realism to fuel concern and enough optimism to provide hope. Humanistic psychology, say the critics, encourages the needed hope but not the equally necessary realism about evil.

However, even within humanistic psychology there is debate over whether people are basically good. Carl Rogers clearly thought so. Although aware of the "incredible amount" of cruel, destructive behavior in today's world, he stated, "I do not find that this evil is inherent in human nature." Given growth-promoting conditions, "I have never known an individual to choose the cruel or destructive path" (Rogers, 1981). Evil, in his view, arose not from human nature but from toxic cultural influences, including "the constricting, destructive influence of our educational system, the injustice of our distribution of wealth, [and] our cultivated prejudices against individuals who are different."

Fellow humanistic psychologist Rollo May dissented from Rogers's optimism. Of course the cultural context matters, he said. But "Who makes up the culture except persons like you and me? The culture is evil as well as good because we, the human beings who constitute it, are evil as well as good." May agreed with critics who see people joining the humanistic movement seeking "a community of like-minded persons who also are playing possum to the evils about us." Accepting human evil requires "the age-old religious truths of mercy and forgiveness," he said, "and it leaves no place for self-righteousness" (May, 1982).

## Summing Up

Humanistic psychologists have sought to turn psychology's attention from baser motives and environmental conditioning to the growth potential of healthy people, as seen through the individual's own experiences.

**Exploring the Self** Abraham Maslow believed that if basic human needs are fulfilled, people will strive to actualize their highest potential. To describe self-actualization, he studied some exemplary personalities and summarized his impressions of their qualities. To nurture growth in others, Carl Rogers advised being genuine, accepting, and empathic. In such a climate, people can develop a deeper self-awareness and a more realistic and positive self-concept. Research on the self documents the importance of high self-esteem and the potency of self-serving bias.

**Assessing the Self** Humanistic psychologists assess personality through questionnaires on which people report their self-concept and by seeking to understand others' subjective personal experiences in therapy.

**Evaluating the Humanistic Perspective** Humanistic psychology's critics complain that its concepts are vague and subjective, its values individualistic and self-centered, and its assumptions naïvely optimistic. Nevertheless, humanistic psychology helped to renew psychology's interest in the self.

## The Social-Cognitive Perspective

*Social-cognitive psychologists apply principles of learning, thinking, and social context. How might such principles work together to influence behavior in particular situations?*

Our fourth major perspective on personality derives from psychological principles of learning, cognition, and social behavior. Called the *social-cognitive perspective* by psychologist Albert Bandura (1986), its proponents emphasize the importance of external events. Like learning theorists, they believe that we learn many of our behaviors either by conditioning or by observing others and modeling our behavior after them. They emphasize the importance of mental processes: What we think about our situations affects our behavior. So instead of focusing solely on how our environment controls us (behaviorism), social-cognitive theorists focus on how we and our environment interact: How do we interpret and respond to external events? How do our schemas, our memories, and our expectations influence our behavior patterns?

### Exploring Behavior in Situations

#### Reciprocal Influences

Bandura (1986) calls the process of interacting with our environment **reciprocal determinism**. "Behavior, internal personal factors, and environmental influences," he says, "all operate as interlocking determinants of each other" (Figure 14–4). For example, children's TV-viewing habits (past behavior) influence their viewing preferences (internal personal factor), which influence how television (environmental factor) affects their current behavior. The influences are mutual.

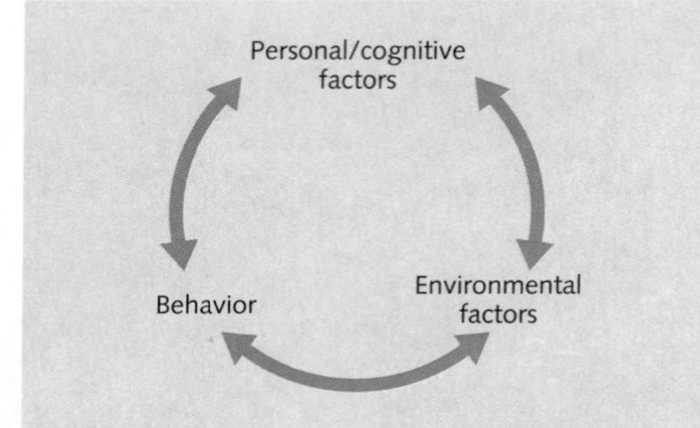


**Figure 14–4**

**Reciprocal Determinism** *The social-cognitive perspective proposes that our personalities are shaped by the interaction of our situations, our thoughts and feelings, and our behaviors.*

Consider three specific ways in which persons and environments interact:

1. ***Different people choose different environments.*** The college you attend, the reading you do, the television you watch, the music you listen to, the friends you associate with—all are part of an environment you have chosen, based partly on your dispositions. You choose it and it shapes you.
2. ***Our personalities shape how we interpret and react to events.*** Anxious people, for example, are more likely to be attuned to potentially threatening events than are nonanxious people (Eysenck & others, 1987). Thus, anxious people perceive the world as more threatening, and they react accordingly.
3. ***Our personalities help create situations to which we react.*** Many experiments reveal that how we view and treat our families, roommates, and friends influences how they in turn treat us. If we expect someone to be angry with us, we may give the person a cold shoulder, touching off the very behavior we expect.

In such ways, we are both the products and the architects of our environments. If all this has a familiar ring, it may be because it parallels and reinforces a pervasive theme in psychology and in this book: Behavior emerges from the interplay of external and internal influences. Boiling water turns an egg hard and a potato soft. A threatening environment turns one person into a hero, another into a scoundrel. *At every moment,* our behavior is determined by our experiences *and* our genes, our environments *and* our personalities.

**Chill or Thrill** *Bungee jumping is not an environment for timid people, but for a thrill-seeker it's just right. Our individual personalities are expressed in the situations we choose and how we react to our experiences.*

## Personal Control

One important aspect of personality is our sense of **personal control**—whether we learn to see ourselves as controlling, or as controlled by, our environments. Studies of people's sense of personal control demonstrate that behavior is affected by whether people perceive the control of their lives as internal (in themselves) or external (at the mercy of the outside world).

Psychologists have two basic ways to study the effect of personal control (or any personality factor). One: *Correlate* people's feelings of control with their behaviors and achievements. Two: *Experiment*, by raising or lowering people's sense of control and noting the effects.

**Locus of Control** Consider your own feelings of control. Do you feel that your life is beyond your control? That the world is run by a few powerful people? That getting a good job depends mainly on being in the right place at the right time? Or do you more strongly believe that what happens to you is your own doing? That the average person can influence government decisions? That being a success is a matter of hard work, not luck?

Hundreds of studies have compared people who perceive what psychologist Julian Rotter calls an **external locus of control** (that chance or outside forces determine their fate) with those who perceive an **internal locus of control** (that to a great extent they control their own destinies). In study after study, internals achieve more in school, act more independently, and feel less depressed than do externals (Benassi & others, 1988; Findley & Cooper, 1983; Lefcourt, 1982). Moreover, they are better able to delay gratification and cope with various stresses, including marital problems (Miller & others, 1986).

**Learned Helplessness Versus Personal Control** Helpless, oppressed people often perceive control to be external, and this perception may deepen their feelings of resignation. This is precisely what researcher Martin Seligman (1975, 1991) and others found in experiments with both animals and people. When dogs were strapped in a harness and given repeated shocks, with no opportunity to avoid them, they learned a sense of helplessness. When later placed in another situation where they *could* escape the punishment by merely leaping a hurdle, they cowered without hope. Faced with repeated traumatic events over which they have no control, people, too, come to feel helpless, hopeless, and depressed. This passive resignation is called **learned helplessness** (Figure 14–5). In contrast, animals that escape the shocks in the first situation learn personal control and easily escape shocks in the new situation.

**Figure 14–5**

**Learned Helplessness** *When animals and people experience no control over repeated bad events, they often learn helplessness.*

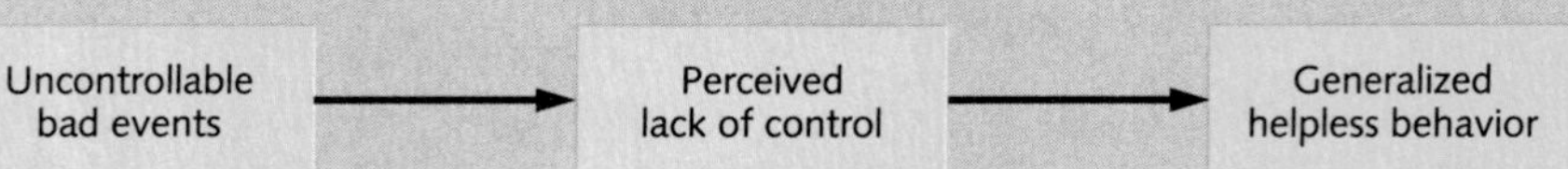


In concentration camps, in prisons, even in factories, colleges, and well-meaning nursing homes, people given little control experience a similar lowering of morale and increased stress. In a new place, part of the culture shock is a sense of lowered control when we become unsure of how people in the unfamiliar environment will respond (Triandis, 1994). Increasing control—allowing prisoners to move chairs and control room lights and the TV, workers to participate in decision making, nursing home patients to make choices about their environment—noticeably improves health and morale (Miller & Monge, 1986; Ruback & others, 1986; Wener & others, 1987). In one famous study of nursing home patients, 93 percent of those encouraged to exert more control became more alert, active, and happy (Rodin, 1986). As researcher Ellen Langer (1983, p. 291) concluded, "Perceived control is basic to human functioning." She recommended that "for the young and old alike," we create environments that enhance a sense of control and personal efficacy.

**Control Affects Well-Being** *Nursing home residents who can arrange their own possessions, control other aspects of their daily lives, and pursue their own interests are more vigorous and happy than those who do not have these opportunities.*

To those who worry that the behavioral sciences might undermine traditional values, the verdict of these studies is reassuring: People thrive under conditions of democracy, personal freedom, and empowerment. Small wonder that the citizens of stable democracies report higher levels of happiness (Inglehart, 1990). Shortly before the democratic revolution in the former East Germany, psychologists Gabriele Oettingen and Martin Seligman (1990) compared the telltale body language of working-class men in East and West Berlin bars. Compared with their counterparts on the other side of the Wall, the empowered West Berliners much more often laughed, sat upright rather than slumped, and had upward rather than downward turned mouths. To paraphrase the Roman philosopher Seneca, happy are those who choose their own business.

**Optimism** One measure of how helpless or effective you feel is where you stand on the trait dimension of optimism/pessimism. How do you characteristically explain negative and positive events? Perhaps you have known students who blame poor grades on their lack of ability ("I can't do this") or on situations beyond their control ("bad" teachers, textbooks, or exam questions). Such students are more likely to persist in getting low grades than are students who adopt the more hopeful attitude that effort, good study habits, and self-discipline can make a difference (Noel & others, 1987; Peterson & Barrett, 1987). Similarly, Martin Seligman and Peter Schulman (1986) compared new life insurance representatives who were more or less optimistic in their outlooks. Those who put an optimistic spin on setbacks—by seeing them as flukes or as suggesting a new approach rather than viewing them as signs of incompetence—sold more policies during their first year and were half as likely to quit. Seligman's finding came to life for him when Bob Dell, one of the optimistic recruits who began selling for Metropolitan Life after taking Seligman's optimism test, later dialed him up and sold him a policy.

If positive thinking in the face of adversity pays dividends, so, too, can a realistic dash of pessimism. Anxiety over contemplated failure can actually fuel energetic efforts to avoid the dreaded fate (Cantor & Norem, 1989; Goodhart, 1986; Showers, 1992). Overconfident students often perform less well than their equally able peers who, fearing they are going to bomb on the upcoming exam, proceed to study furiously and get fabulous grades. Success requires enough optimism to provide hope, but also enough pessimism to prevent complacency.

*"O God, give us grace to accept with serenity the things that cannot be changed, courage to change the things which should be changed, and the wisdom to distinguish the one from the other."*

Reinhold Niebuhr
"The Serenity Prayer," 1943

Health, too, benefits from a basic optimism. As we will see in Chapter 17, a depressed hopelessness dampens the body's disease-fighting immune system. In repeated studies, optimists have been found to outlive pessimists or to live with fewer illnessses.

Excessive optimism can, however, blind us to real risks. Neil Weinstein (1980, 1982) has shown how our natural positive-thinking bias can promote "an unrealistic optimism about future life events." Most college students perceive themselves as less likely than their average classmate to develop drinking problems, drop out of school, or have a heart attack by age 40. Most late adolescents see themselves as much less vulnerable than their peers to the AIDS virus (Abrams, 1991).

Given such illusory optimism, people may fail to take sensible precautions. Most young Americans know that half of U.S. marriages end in divorce, but they are confident that *theirs* will not (Lehman & Nisbett, 1985). Most cigarette smokers smoke hazardous high-tar brands, but only 17 percent believe their brand to have a more hazardous tar level than most others (Segerstrom and others, 1993). Sexually active undergraduate women perceive themselves, compared with other women at their university, as much *less* vulnerable to unwanted pregnancy, especially if they do *not* consistently use effective contraception (Burger & Burns, 1988). Those who optimistically shun seat belts, deny the effects of smoking, and venture into ill-fated relationships remind us that, like pride, blind optimism may go before a fall.

## Assessing Behavior in Situations

Social-cognitive researchers explore the effect of differing situations on people's behavior patterns and attitudes. They study, for example, how viewing aggressive or nonaggressive models affects behavior. They assess the impact of dehumanizing situations on people's attitudes. And they examine the consistency of people's personalities in varying circumstances.

## Thinking Critically About

## Pseudo-Assessment—How to Be a "Successful" Astrologer or Palm Reader

How should we evaluate alternative ways of assessing personality? Does the alignment of the stars and planets at the time of one's birth give a clue? Is one's handwriting revealing? Do our palms expose deep secrets? While astronomers scoff at the naiveté of astrology, psychologists ask a different question: Does it work? Are birth dates correlated with character traits? Given someone's birth date, can astrologers surpass chance when asked to identify the person from a short lineup of different personality descriptions? Can people pick out their own horoscopes from a lineup of horoscopes? The consistent answers have been: no, no, no, and no (British Psychological Society, 1993; Carlson, 1985). Graphologists, who make predictions from handwriting samples, have similarly been found to do no better than chance when trying to guess people's occupations, based on several pages of their handwriting (Beyerstein & Beyerstein, 1992; Dean & others, 1992).

How, then, do astrologers and the like persuade millions of people to buy their advice? Ray Hyman (1981), palm reader turned research psychologist, helps us to see why people get suckered, by revealing the methods of astrologers, palm readers, and crystal-ball gazers.

Their first technique, the "stock spiel," builds on the observation that each of us is in some ways like no one else and in other ways like everyone. That some things are true of us all enables the "seer" to offer statements that seem impressively accurate: "I sense that you're nursing a grudge against someone; you really ought to let that go." "You worry about things more than you let on, even to your best friends." "You are adaptable to social situations and your interests are wide-ranging."

Such generally true statements can be combined into a personality description. Imagine that you take a personality test and then receive the following character sketch:

> You have a strong need for other people to like and to admire you. You have a tendency to be critical of yourself. . . . You pride yourself on being an independent thinker and do not accept other opinions without satisfactory proof. You have found it unwise to be too frank in revealing yourself to others. At times you are extraverted, affable, sociable; at other times you are introverted, wary, and reserved. Some of your aspirations tend to be pretty unrealistic (Forer, 1949).

In experiments, college students have received stock assessments like this one. When they think the bogus feedback was prepared just for them and when it is generally favorable, they nearly always rate the description as either "good" or "excellent." Peter Glick and his coworkers (1989) found that even skeptics of astrology, when given a flattering description attributed to an astrologer, begin to think that "maybe there's something to this astrology business after all."

French psychologist Michael Gauguelin placed an ad in a Paris newspaper offering a free personal horoscope. Ninety-four percent of those receiving the horoscope later praised the description as accurate. Actually, all had received the horoscope of France's Dr. Petiot, a notorious mass murderer (Kurtz, 1983).

This acceptance is called the Barnum effect, named in honor of master showman P. T. Barnum's dictum, "There's a sucker born every minute." So powerful is the Barnum effect that, given a choice between this stock spiel and an individualized personality description actually based on a real test, most people choose the phony description as being more accurate. Astrologers and palm readers sprinkle their assessments with stock statements (as in the description quoted, which was drawn from statements in a newsstand astrology book).

An ambitious example that predates social-cognitive theory is the U.S. Army's World War II strategy for assessing candidates for spy missions. Rather than use paper-and-pencil tests, army psychologists subjected the candidates to simulated undercover conditions. They tested their ability to handle stress, solve problems, maintain leadership, and withstand intense interrogation without blowing their covers. Although time-consuming and expensive, the assessment of behavior in a realistic situation helped predict later success on real spy missions (OSS Assessment Staff, 1948).

Business, military, and educational organizations are continuing this strategy in their evaluations of several hundred thousand persons each year in some 2000 assessment centers (Bray & Byham, 1991). AT&T observes prospective managers doing simulated managerial work. Many colleges assess potential faculty members' teaching abilities by observing

SPECIAL BULLETIN! THIS JUST IN! THE FAULT IS NOT IN OURSELVES, BUT IN OUR STARS.
HEY! DID YOU HEAR THAT!
WE'RE OFF THE HOOK!


Drawing by Bruce Eric Kaplan; © 1992 The New Yorker Magazine, Inc.

Even some popular psychological labels are made plausible by Barnum statements. Mary Beth Logue and her colleagues (1992) report that adult children of alcoholics rate descriptions of their supposed traits ("You are sensitive to the difficulties of others"; "You sometimes project a front, hiding your true feelings"; etc.) as accurate. But people who are not children of alcoholics similarly rate the statements as descriptive of themselves.

Another technique is to "read" the person's clothing, physical features, nonverbal gestures, and reactions to what you are saying. Imagine yourself as the character reader who was visited by a young woman in her late twenties or early thirties. Hyman describes the woman as "wearing expensive jewelry, a wedding band, and a black dress of cheap material. The observant reader noted that she was wearing shoes which were advertised for people with foot trouble." Do these clues suggest anything?

Drawing on these observations, the character reader proceeded to amaze his client with his insights. He assumed that the woman had come to see him, as did most of his female customers, because of a love or financial problem. The black dress and the wedding band led him to reason that her husband had died recently. The expensive jewelry suggested that she had been financially comfortable during marriage, but the cheap dress suggested that her husband's death had left her impoverished. The therapeutic shoes signified that she was now standing on her feet more than she was used to, implying that she had been working to support herself since her husband's death.

If you are not as shrewd as this character reader (who correctly guessed that the woman was wondering if she should remarry in hope of ending her economic hardship), no matter, says Hyman. Just tell people what they want to hear. Memorize some Barnum statements from astrology and fortune-telling manuals and use them liberally. Tell people it is their responsibility to cooperate by relating your message to their specific experiences. Later they will recall that you predicted the specifics. Phrase statements as questions, and when you detect a positive response assert the statement strongly. Be a good listener, and later, in different words, reveal to people what they earlier revealed to you.

Better yet, beware of fortune-tellers, who, by exploiting people with these techniques, become fortune-takers.

them teach. The army assesses its soldiers by observing them during military exercises.

These procedures exploit the principle that the best means of predicting people's future behavior is not a personality test or an interviewer's intuition. Rather, it is their past behavior patterns in similar situations (Mischel, 1981). As long as the situation and the person remain much the same, the best predictor of future job performance is past job performance; the best predictor of future grades is past grades; the best predictor of future aggressiveness is past aggressiveness; the best predictor of drug use in young adulthood is high school drug use. If you can't check the person's past behavior, the next-best thing is to create an assessment situation that simulates the task demands so you can see how the person handles them.

## Evaluating the Social-Cognitive Perspective

The social-cognitive perspective on personality sensitizes researchers to how situations affect, and are affected by, individuals. More than the other perspectives, we can also credit it with building from psychological research on learning and cognition.

One criticism is that the theory works *too* well, after the fact. In hindsight, we can explain anything as a product of cognition and the social environment. Another criticism is that the theory focuses so much on the situation that it fails to appreciate the person's inner traits. Where is the *person* in this view of personality, ask the dissenters (Carlson, 1984). And where are human emotions? True, the situation guides our behavior. But in many instances our unconscious motives, our emotions, and our pervasive traits shine through, say the critics. Percy Ray Pridgen and Charles Gill faced the same situation: They jointly won a $90 million lottery jackpot (Harriston, 1993). Upon learning the winning numbers, Pridgen began trembling uncontrollably, then huddled with a friend behind a bathroom door while confirming the win, then sobbed. Gill told his wife, and then went to sleep.

And that brings us back to where we began our review of these personality theories: Each of the perspectives summarized in Table 14–3 can teach us something. The psychoanalytic perspective draws our attention to the unconscious and irrational aspects of human existence. The trait perspective systematically describes and classifies important personality components. The humanistic perspective reminds us of the pivotal importance of our sense of self and of our healthy potential. The social-cognitive perspective applies psychology's basic concepts of learning and thinking and teaches us that we always act in the context of situations that we help to create.

Seldom in life does a single perspective on any issue give us the complete picture. Human personality reveals its different aspects when we view it from different perspectives. Each perspective enlarges our vision of the whole person.

*"Nature is always more subtle, more intricate, more elegant than what we are able to imagine."*

Carl Sagan
"Science—Who Cares?," 1991

**Table 14–3 The Four Perspectives on Personality**

| Perspective | Behavior Springs From | Assessment Techniques | Evaluation |
|---|---|---|---|
| *Psychoanalytic* | Unconscious conflicts between pleasure-seeking impulses and social restraints | Projective tests aimed at revealing unconscious motivations | A speculative, hard-to-confirm theory with enormous cultural impact |
| *Trait* | Expressing biologically influenced dispositions, such as extraversion or introversion | (a) Personality inventories that assess the strength of different traits (b) Peer ratings of behavior patterns | A descriptive approach criticized as sometimes underestimating the variability of behavior from situation to situation |
| *Humanistic* | Processing conscious feelings about oneself in light of one's experiences | (a) Questionnaire assessments of self-concept (b) Empathic understandings of people's unique experiences | A humane theory that reinvigorated contemporary interest in the self; criticized as subjective and sometimes naïvely self-centered and optimistic |
| *Social-cognitive* | Reciprocal influences between people and their situations, colored by perceptions of control | (a) Questionnaire assessments of people's feelings of control (b) Observations of people's behavior in particular situations | An interactive theory that integrates research on learning, cognition, and social behavior; criticized as underestimating the importance of the unconscious, of emotions, and of enduring traits |

## Summing Up

**Exploring Behavior in Situations** The social-cognitive perspective applies principles of learning, cognition, and social behavior to personality, with particular emphasis on the ways in which our personalities influence and are influenced by our interaction with the environment. It assumes reciprocal determinism—that personal-cognitive factors combine with the environment to influence people's behavior. By studying variations among people in their perceived locus of control and in their experiences of learned helplessness, researchers have found that a sense of personal control helps people to cope with life.

**Assessing Behavior in Situations** Social-cognitive researchers observe how people's behaviors and beliefs both affect and are affected by their situations. They have found that the best way to predict someone's behavior in a given situation is to observe that person's behavior pattern in similar situations.

**Evaluating the Social-Cognitive Perspective** Although faulted for slighting the importance of unconscious dynamics and inner traits, the social-cognitive perspective builds on psychology's well-established concepts of learning and cognition and reminds us of the power of social situations.

## Terms and Concepts to Remember

**personality** An individual's characteristic pattern of thinking, feeling, and acting.

### The Psychoanalytic Perspective

**free association** In psychoanalysis, a method of exploring the unconscious in which the person relaxes and says whatever comes to mind, no matter how trivial or embarrassing.

**psychoanalysis** The technique of treating psychological disorders by seeking to expose and interpret unconscious tensions. Freud's psychoanalytic theory of personality sought to explain what he observed during psychoanalysis.

**unconscious** According to Freud, a reservoir of mostly unacceptable thoughts, wishes, feelings, and memories. According to contemporary research psychologists, information processing of which we are unaware.

**preconscious** Information that is not conscious, but is retrievable into conscious awareness.

**id** A reservoir of unconscious psychic energy that, according to Freud, strives to satisfy basic sexual and aggressive drives.

**pleasure principle** The id's demand for immediate gratification.

**ego** The largely conscious, "executive" part of personality that, according to Freud, mediates among the demands of the id, superego, and reality.

**reality principle** The ego's tendency to satisfy the id's desires in ways that will realistically bring pleasure rather than pain.

**superego** The part of personality that, according to Freud, represents internalized ideals and provides standards for judgment (the conscience) and for future aspirations.

**psychosexual stages** The childhood stages of development (oral, anal, phallic, latency, genital) during which, according to Freud, the id's pleasure-seeking energies focus on distinct erogenous zones.

**oral stage** The first of Freud's psychosexual stages, from birth to about 18 months, during which sensual pleasure centers on the mouth via sucking, biting, and chewing.

**anal stage** The second of Freud's psychosexual stages, from about 18 months to 3 years, during which pleasure focuses on bowel and bladder elimination, retention, and control.

**phallic stage** The third of Freud's psychosexual stages, from about ages 3 to 6, during which the pleasure zone is the genitals and sexual feelings arise toward the parent of the other sex.

**Oedipus** [ED-uh-puss] **complex** According to Freud, a child's sexual desires toward the parent of the other sex and feelings of jealousy and hatred for the rival parent of the same sex.

**identification** The process by which, according to Freud, children incorporate their parents' values into their developing superegos.

**gender identity** One's sense of being male or female.

**latency stage** The fourth of Freud's psychosexual stages, from about age 6 to puberty, during which sexual impulses are repressed.

**genital stage** The last of Freud's psychosexual stages, beginning in puberty, during which sexuality matures and the person seeks pleasure through sexual contact with others.

**fixation** According to Freud, a lingering focus of pleasure-seeking energies at an earlier psychosexual stage, where conflicts were unresolved.

**defense mechanisms** In psychoanalytic theory, the ego's protective methods of reducing anxiety by unconsciously distorting reality.

**repression** In psychoanalytic theory, the basic defense mechanism that banishes anxiety-arousing thoughts, feelings, and memories from consciousness.

**regression** In psychoanalytic theory, an individual's retreat, when faced with anxiety, to a more infantile psychosexual stage where some psychic energy remains fixated.

**reaction formation** In psychoanalytic theory, a defense mechanism by which the ego unconsciously switches unacceptable impulses into their opposites. Thus, people may express feelings that are the opposite of their anxiety-arousing unconscious feelings.

**projection** In psychoanalytic theory, the defense mechanism by which people disguise their own threatening impulses by attributing them to others.

**rationalization** In psychoanalytic theory, a defense mechanism that offers self-justifying explanations in place of the real, more threatening, unconscious reasons for one's actions.

**displacement** In psychoanalytic theory, the defense mechanism that shifts sexual or aggressive impulses toward a more acceptable or less threatening object or person, as when redirecting anger toward a safer outlet.

**sublimation** In psychoanalytic theory, the defense mechanism by which people rechannel their unacceptable impulses into socially approved activities.

**collective unconscious** Carl Jung's concept of a shared, inherited reservoir of memory traces from our species' history.

**projective tests** Personality tests, such as the Rorschach and TAT, that provide ambiguous stimuli designed to trigger projection of one's inner dynamics.

**Thematic Apperception Test (TAT)** A projective test in which people express their inner feelings and interests through the stories they make up about ambiguous scenes.

**Rorschach inkblot test** The most widely used projective test, a set of 10 inkblots, designed by Hermann Rorschach; seeks to identify people's inner feelings by analyzing their interpretation.

### The Trait Perspective

**trait** A characteristic pattern of behavior or conscious motive; assessed by self-report inventories and peer reports.

**personality inventory** A questionnaire (often with true-false or agree-disagree items) on which people respond to items designed to gauge a wide range of feelings and behaviors; used to assess selected personality traits.

**Minnesota Multiphasic Personality Inventory-2 (MMPI-2)** The most widely researched and clinically used of all personality tests. Originally developed to identify emotionally troubled people (still considered its most appropriate use), this test is now used for many other screening purposes.

**empirically derived test** A test (such as the MMPI) developed by testing a pool of items and then selecting those that discriminate groups of interest.

### The Humanistic Perspective

**self-actualization** According to Maslow, the ultimate psychological need that arises after basic physical and psychological needs are met and self-esteem is achieved; the motivation to fulfill one's potential.

**unconditional positive regard** According to Rogers, an attitude of total acceptance toward another person.

**self-concept** All our thoughts and feelings about ourselves, in answer to the question, "Who am I?"

**self-esteem** One's feelings of high or low self-worth.

**self-serving bias** A readiness to perceive oneself favorably.

### The Social-Cognitive Perspective

**reciprocal determinism** The interacting influences between personality and environmental factors.

**personal control** Our sense of controlling our environments rather than feeling helpless.

**external locus of control** The perception that chance or outside forces beyond one's personal control determine one's fate.

**internal locus of control** The perception that one controls one's own fate.

**learned helplessness** The hopelessness and passive resignation learned when an animal or human is unable to avoid repeated aversive events.

## Critical Thinking Exercise

Now that you have read and reviewed Chapter 14, take your learning a step further by testing your critical thinking skills on the following perspective taking exercise.

Darren is a first-year college student who has a biting, sarcastic manner. He has a pessimistic outlook on life and feels that the world is run by a few powerful people. When he received a poor grade on a recent exam, Darren blamed the instructor and claimed the test was unfair. He stopped attending lectures, gave up studying for the course, and will probably drop it. He is experiencing similar difficulties in his other courses.

Darren always dreamed of doing well in college. Now he is despondent over his failure and believes his professors hate him. Most of all, he is concerned that if he fails in school his parents will no longer love him.

1. How might Darren's problems be explained from the psychoanalytic perspective?
2. How might Darren's problems be explained by a trait theorist?
3. How might Darren's problems be explained by a humanistic theorist?
4. How might Darren's problems be explained by a social-cognitive theorist?
5. Which perspective most closely represents your own belief about Darren's problems? Why?

Check your progress on becoming a critical thinker by comparing your answers to the sample answers found in Appendix B.

## For Further Reading

**Freud, S.** (1933). *Introductory lectures on psychoanalysis.* In J. Strachey (Ed. & trans.), *The standard edition of the complete psychological works of Sigmund Freud.* London: Hogarth, 1963.

*One of Freud's most popular works, introducing his ideas about human motivation, dream interpretation, slips of the tongue, and psychoanalytic therapy.*

**Rogers, C. R.** (1961). *On becoming a person.* Boston: Houghton Mifflin.

*A warm and readable introduction to Carl Rogers's view of the person and of how to nurture personal growth.*

**Seligman, M.** (1991). *Learned optimism.* New York: Knopf.

*A leading researcher describes his research on learned helplessness and optimism, showing why optimism is important and how to acquire it.*

**Storr, A.** (1989) *Freud.* New York: Oxford.

*A concise overview and evaluation of Freud—the man and his ideas.*

**Taylor, S. E.** (1989). *Positive illusions.* New York: Basic Books.

*The ancient wisdom to "know thyself" notwithstanding, mental health may instead reflect the art of being well deceived. Or so social psychologist Taylor suggests in this captivating summary of research on the benefits of positive, if self-serving, thinking.*

# CHAPTER 15



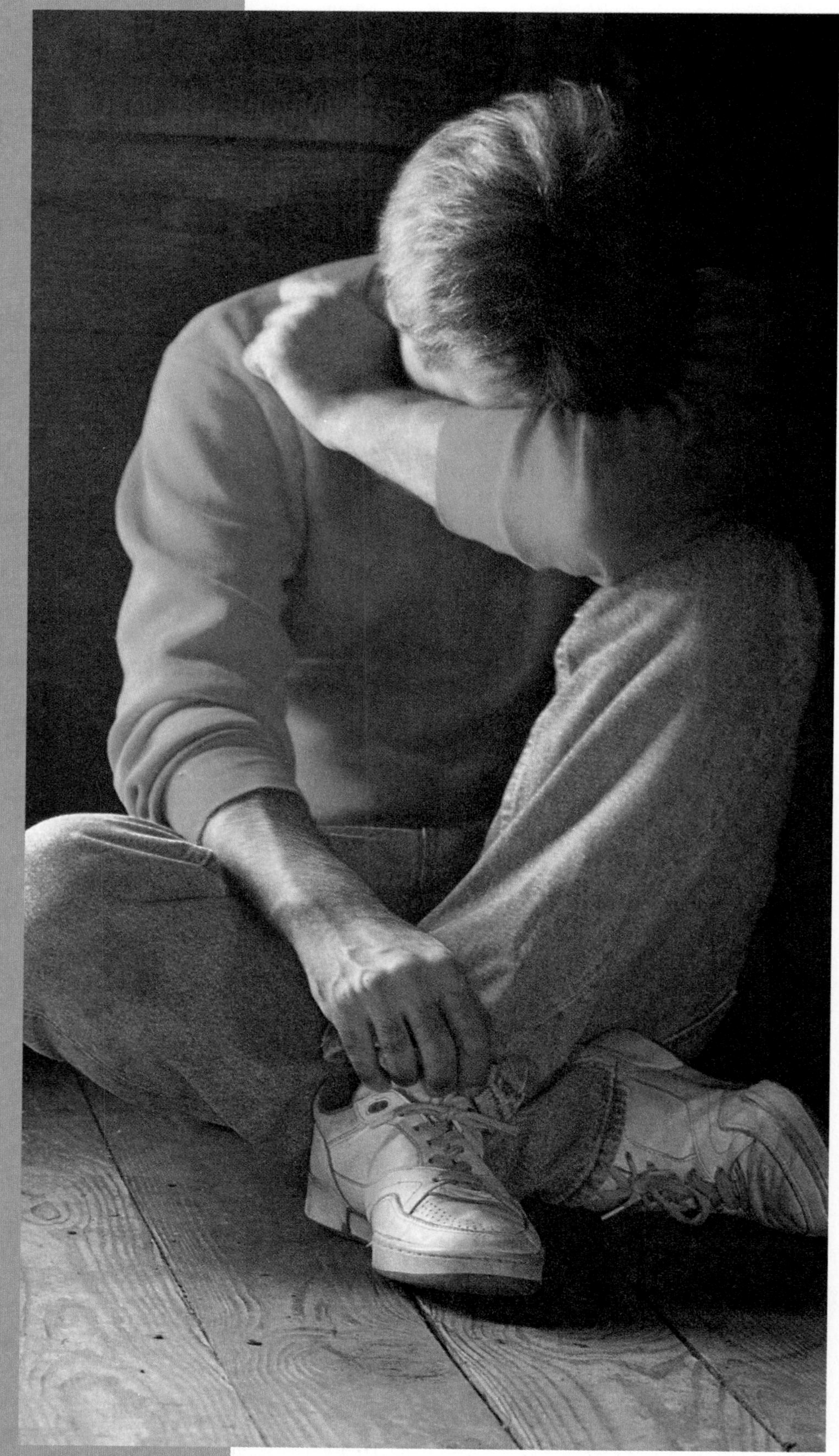

# Psychological Disorders

People are fascinated by the exceptional, the unusual, and the abnormal. "The sun shines and warms and lights us and we have no curiosity to know why this is so," observed Ralph Waldo Emerson, "but we ask the reason of all evil, of pain, and hunger, and mosquitoes and silly people."

Why this fascination with disturbed people? Perhaps in them we often see something of ourselves. At various moments, all of us feel, think, or act as disturbed people do much of the time. We, too, get anxious, depressed, withdrawn, suspicious, deluded, or antisocial, although less intensely and enduringly. Studying psychological disorders may therefore at times evoke an eerie sense of self-recognition that illuminates our own personality dynamics. "To study the abnormal is the best way of understanding the normal," proposed William James.

Another reason for our curiosity is that so many of us have felt, either personally or through friends or family members, the bewilderment and pain of a psychological disorder. In all likelihood, you or someone you care about has been disabled by unexplained physical symptoms, overwhelmed by irrational fears, or paralyzed by the feeling that life is not worth living. Each year there are nearly 1.7 million inpatient admissions to U.S. mental hospitals and psychiatric units (Rosenstein & others, 1989). Some 2.4 million others, often troubled but not disabled, seek help as outpatients from mental health organizations and clinics. Many more—15 percent of Americans, according to one government study—are judged to need such help (Robins & Regier, 1991). Such problems are not peculiar to the United States. No known culture is free of the two terrible maladies this chapter examines in depth—depression and schizophrenia (Draguns, 1990a,b). Thanks in part to brain dysfunctions, some 400 million people worldwide suffer psychological disorders, reports the World Health Organization's mental health director (Sartorius, 1994). As members of the human family, few of us go through life unacquainted with the reality of psychological disturbance.

*"We are all mad at some time or another."*

Battista Mantuanus
*Eclogues*, 1500

## Perspectives on Psychological Disorders

*Where should we draw the line between normality and disorder? Should we think of psychological disorders as genuine illnesses or as socially defined categories? How are disorders classified and labeled?*

Most people would agree that someone who is too depressed to get out of bed for weeks at a time suffers a psychological disorder. But what about those who, having experienced a loss, are unable to resume their usual social activities? Where should we draw the line between normality and abnormality? How should we *define* psychological disorders? Equally important, how should we *understand* disorders—as sicknesses that need to be diagnosed and cured, or as natural responses to a troubling environment? Finally, how might we *classify* disordered personalities? Can we do so in a way that allows us to help disturbed people and not merely stigmatize them with labels?

## Defining Psychological Disorders

James Oliver Huberty had been hearing voices. He "talked with God," his wife reported. Although he had never been to Vietnam, he strode into a San Ysidro, California, McDonald's restaurant one summer day in 1984 screaming, "I've killed a thousand in Vietnam and I'll kill a thousand more." In the next few minutes, before police gunned him down, Huberty murdered 21 people.

At the end of World War II, James Forrestal, the first U.S. secretary of defense, became convinced that Israeli secret agents were following him. His suspiciousness struck his physicians as bizarre. They diagnosed him as mentally ill and confined him to an upper floor of Walter Reed Army Hospital. From there he plunged to his death. Although Forrestal had problems, it was later discovered that he was, in fact, being followed by Israeli agents, who feared he might secretly negotiate with representatives of Arab nations (Sagan, 1979b). As Woody Allen once said, even paranoids can have enemies.

Both the voices that Huberty heard and the degree of anxiety and depression that Forrestal experienced were deviations from the normal. These were "*ab*normal" (atypical) perceptions. Being different from most other people in one's culture is *part* of what it takes to define a psychological disorder. As the reclusive poet Emily Dickinson observed in 1862,

> Assent—and you are sane—
> Demur—you're straightaway dangerous—
> and handled with a Chain.

But there is more to a disorder than being atypical. Olympic gold medalists are abnormal in their physical abilities, and they are heroes. To be considered disordered, other people must find the atypical behavior *disturbing*. Certainly the atypical behavior of a James Oliver Huberty is disturbing.

Standards of acceptability for behaviors vary. In some cultures, people routinely behave in ways (such as going about naked) that in other cultures would be grounds for arrest. In at least one cultural context—wartime—even mass killing may be viewed as heroic. One person's homicidal "terrorist" is another person's "freedom fighter." Standards of acceptability also vary over time. Sexologists William Acton, writing in the late 1800s, and William Masters and Virginia Johnson, writing in the late 1900s, all knew that some women have orgasms during intercourse while others don't (Wakefield, 1992). For Acton, orgasm was the disorder (resulting from overstimulation); for Masters and Johnson, lack of orgasm was the disorder (resulting from inadequate stimulation). Two decades ago, the American Psychiatric Association dropped homosexuality as a disorder (because it was no longer believed connected with psychological problems). Later it added tobacco dependence (because it deemed smoking both addictive and self-destructive).

Atypical and disturbing behaviors are more likely to be considered disordered when judged as harmful. Indeed, many clinicians define disorders as behaviors that are *maladaptive*—as when a smoker's nicotine depen-

**A Benign Obsession** *Although British street cleaner Snowy Farr's eccentric behavior may indeed be* atypical, *clinicians would not label it disordered because it is neither particularly* disturbing *nor* maladaptive.

dence produces physical damage. Accordingly, even typical behaviors, such as the occasional despondency that many college students feel, may signal a psychological disorder if they become disabling. For those who define disorder, maladaptiveness is a key; the behaviors must be distressing or disabling or put one at greatly increased risk of suffering or death.

Finally, abnormal behavior is most likely to be considered disordered when others find it rationally *unjustifiable*. Doctors attributed Forrestal's suspicions to his imagination—and declared him disordered. Had he managed to convince others of his suspicions, he might have been helped, not merely labeled. James Oliver Huberty claimed to hear voices and to talk with God, and we presume he was deranged. But Shirley MacLaine can wear a crystal on her neck and say, "See the outer bubble of white light watching you. It is part of you," and she is not considered disordered because enough people take her seriously (Friedrich, 1987). If someone is depressed following a loved one's death, that is justifiable. And if hearing the voice of a deceased relative is an expected event in one's culture, clinicians from outside that culture should be culturally sensitive.

*"If a man is in a minority of one, we lock him up."*
Oliver Wendell Holmes, 1841–1935

So, mental health workers label behavior **psychologically disordered** when they judge it *atypical*, *disturbing*, *maladaptive*, and *unjustifiable*. Huberty's behavior met these criteria, so we have few doubts in judging him a disordered man.

## Understanding Psychological Disorders

Imagine yourself living hundreds or thousands of years ago. How might you have accounted for the behavior of a James Oliver Huberty? To explain puzzling behavior, our ancestors often presumed that strange forces—the movements of the stars, godlike powers, or evil spirits—were at work. "The devil made him do it," you might have said. The cure might have been to get rid of the evil force—by exorcising the demon or even by chipping a hole in the skull to allow the evil spirit to escape (Figure 15–1). Until the last two centuries, "mad" people were sometimes caged in zoolike conditions or given "therapies" appropriate to a demon. Disordered people have been beaten, burned, and castrated. They have had teeth pulled, lengths of intestines removed, and the clitoris cauterized. They have had their own blood removed and replaced with transfusions of animal blood (Farina, 1982).

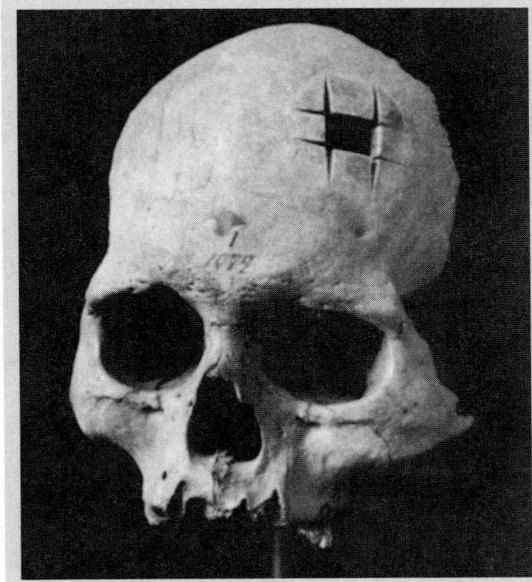

**Figure 15–1**

**An Ancient Cure** *The hole chipped in this ancient skull found in Peru may have been designed to open the cranium to allow evil spirits to escape. One wonders whether the patient survived the cure.*

### The Medical Perspective

In response to such brutal treatment, reformers such as Philippe Pinel (1745–1826) in France insisted that madness was not demon possession but a sickness in response to severe stresses and inhumane conditions. For Pinel and other reformers, treatment meant boosting patients' morale by unchaining them, talking with them, and replacing brutality with gentleness, isolation with activity, and filth with fresh air and sun.

When it was later discovered that an infectious brain disease, syphilis, produced a particular psychological disorder, people also came to believe in physical causes for disorders and to search for medical treatments. Today, this medical perspective is familiar to us in the medical terminology of the mental *health* movement: A mental *illness* (also called a psycho*pathology*) needs to be *diagnosed* on the basis of its *symptoms* and *cured* through *therapy*, which may include *treatment* in a psychiatric *hospital*. In the 1800s, the assumption of this **medical model**—that psychological disorders are sicknesses—provided the impetus for much-needed reform. The "sick" were unchained and hospitals replaced asylums.

The medical perspective gains credibility from recent discoveries. Genetically influenced abnormalities in brain biochemistry contribute to two of the most troubling disorders, depression and schizophrenia, both of which are often treated medically. As we will see, psychological factors, such as traumatic stress, also play a role.

### Social-Cultural Perspectives

Equating psychological disorders with sickness does, however, have its critics, among them psychiatrist Thomas Szasz. Szasz believes that mental "illnesses" are socially, not medically, defined. When, for many years, Soviet psychiatrists diagnosed dissident citizens as "psychotic," they were using medical metaphors to disguise their contempt for these people's political ideas. Szasz (1984, 1987) concludes that in North America, too, mental health practitioners have too much authority in today's society. When they demean people with the label "mentally ill," their patients may begin to view themselves as "sick" and therefore give up taking responsibility for coping with their problems. As we noted earlier (page 249), many critics respond similarly to the idea that alcohol abuse, overeating, gambling, and sexual promiscuity are addictive diseases—purely uncontrollable compulsions that require sympathy and treatment. Labels, as we will see, can be self-fulfilling fables.

*"Who in the rainbow can draw the line where the violet tint ends and the orange tint begins? Distinctly we see the difference of the colors, but where exactly does the one first blendingly enter into the other? So with sanity and insanity?"*

Herman Melville
*Billy Budd, Sailor*, 1924

Psychologists who reject the "sickness" idea typically contend that *all* behavior, whether called normal or disordered, arises from the interaction of nature (genetic and physiological factors) and nurture (past and present experiences). To presume that a person is "mentally ill" attributes the condition solely to an internal problem—to a "sickness" that must be found and cured. Maybe there *is* no deep, internal problem. Maybe there is instead a growth-blocking difficulty in the person's environment, in the person's current interpretations of events, or in the person's bad habits and poor social skills.

*"It's no measure of health to be well adjusted to a profoundly sick society."*

Krishnamurti, 1895–1986

When Native Americans were banished from their ancestral lands, forced onto reservations to live in poverty and unemployment, and deprived of personal control, the result was a rate of alcoholism more than five times that of other Americans (May, 1986). Because only some Native Americans become alcoholic, the medical model would attribute such alcoholism to individual "sickness." A psychological perspective would emphasize the interaction between an individual's vulnerability and a hope-eroding environment.

Evidence of environmental effects comes from links between disorder and culture. As noted earlier in this chapter, some major disorders such as depression and schizophrenia are universal. From Asia to Africa and across the Americas, the core symptoms of schizophrenia include irrationality and incoherent speech (Draguns, 1990b; Brislin, 1993). Other disorders are culture-bound (Beardsley, 1994; Carson & others, 1988). Different cultures have different stresses and produce different ways of coping. Anorexia nervosa and bulimia, for example, are disorders mostly of Western cultures (page 406). *Susto*, marked by severe anxiety, restlessness, and fear of black magic, is a disorder found in Latin America. *Taijin-kyofusho*, which combines social anxiety with easy blushing and fear of eye contact, appears in Japan. Such disorders may share an underlying dynamic (anxiety), yet culturally differ in surface symptom (eating problem or type of fear).

Most mental health workers today assume that disorders are indeed influenced by genetic predispositions and physiological states. And by inner psychological dynamics. And by social circumstances. To get the whole picture, we need an interdisciplinary "bio-psycho-social" perspective.

## Close-Up

## The Insanity Defense on Trial

The definition of psychological disorders does not include the term *insanity*. That is because *sane* and *insane* are *legal*, not psychological, terms. They are also either/or categories. You can be a little depressed or greatly depressed; you cannot be a little insane.

The British created the insanity defense in 1843 after a deluded Scotsman, Daniel M'Naghten, tried to shoot the prime minister (who he thought was persecuting him) and killed the prime minister's secretary by mistake. A furor erupted after M'Naghten was acquitted as insane and sent to a mental hospital rather than to prison. When the M'Naghten verdict was upheld, an insanity rule emerged. It limited the insanity defense to cases where persons were judged not to have known what they were doing or not to have known that it was wrong. Shakespeare's Hamlet anticipated the defense. If I wrong someone when not myself, he explains, "then Hamlet does it not, Hamlet denies it. Who does it then? His madness."

By the time John Hinckley, Jr., came to trial in 1982 for shooting then-President Ronald Reagan and his press secretary, the insanity defense had been broadened. The prosecution had to prove that Hinckley was sane. This meant his having "a substantial capacity" not merely to "know" his act was wrong but to "appreciate" its wrongfulness and to act accordingly.

**Is This Man Sane?** *A posed self-portrait of John W. Hinckley, Jr., former President Reagan's would-be assassin.*

The prosecution was unable to prove sanity to the jurors' satisfaction. So Hinckley, like M'Naghten, was sent to a mental hospital. (If lawbreakers are "bad" they go to prison for punishment; if "mad" they go to a hospital for treatment.) As in the first insanity case, the public was outraged. One newspaper headlined "Hinckley Insane, Public Mad." The outrage was partly because Hinckley, like others declared not guilty by reason of insanity, will be released when declared sane and no longer dangerous—conceivably earlier, though quite possibly later, than he would have been released from a prison.

Some news commentators complained that the heinousness of a crime had become the very basis for evading responsibility for it, "like the person who kills his parents and demands mercy because he is an orphan." Are "sick crimes" necessarily the products of sick minds that need treatment, not punishment? Was there a serious point to the joke that "Anyone crazy enough to want to kill the President must be crazy"? Was Jeffrey Dahmer, who in 1991 admitted murdering 15 men and eating parts of their bodies, necessarily insane? Are the genuinely bad truly mad? If so, said one commentator, then modern society has become like Aldous Huxley's nightmarish *Brave New World*, in which the correct response when someone commits a crime is, "I did not know he was ill."

In defense of the insanity plea, psychologists note that, actually, such a plea is entered in only about 1 percent of felony cases (Callahan & others, 1991). Even then, it is unsuccessful three times out of four. When the insanity plea is successful, the judge and prosecution usually concur that the deranged person was not responsible. Thus, the most important issues that involve psychology and law are not the rare disputes over insanity. They are instead the far more frequent cases concerning child custody (judging who will be the better parent), involuntary commitment to mental hospitals, and predictions about a criminal's future behavior made at the time of sentencing or parole. (When psychiatrists and psychologists use their clinical judgment to predict violence, they are more often wrong than right [Faust & Ziskin, 1988].)

In Canada, and now in three-fourths of the United States, the insanity defense survives in a restricted format that shifts the burden of proving insanity to the defense (Ogloff & others, 1993). Now defendants must show that they did not understand the wrongfulness of their acts.

Some states have instituted a verdict of "guilty but mentally ill." This verdict recognizes a need for treatment but holds people responsible and sends them to prison if they are judged recovered before their sentence is over (Rosenfeld, 1987). Jurors find the verdict a viable option. In mock trials, defendants who otherwise would have been judged either innocent or not guilty by reason of insanity are often judged guilty but mentally ill (Savitsky & Lindblom, 1986).

## Classifying Psychological Disorders

In biology and the other sciences, classification creates order. To classify an animal as a mammal says a great deal—that it is warm-blooded, has hair or fur, and nourishes its young with milk. In psychiatry and psychology, too, classification orders and describes clusters of symptoms. To classify a person's disorder as "schizophrenia" suggests that the person talks incoherently, hallucinates or has delusions (bizarre beliefs), shows either little emotion or inappropriate emotion, or is socially withdrawn. Thus, the diagnostic term provides a handy shorthand for describing a complex disorder.

*"I'm always like this, and my family was wondering if you could prescribe a mild depressant."*

© 1992 by Sidney Harris.

In psychiatry and psychology, diagnostic classification ideally aims to describe a disorder, to predict its future course, to imply appropriate treatment, and to stimulate research into its causes. Indeed, to study a disorder we must first name and describe it. The current authoritative scheme for classifying psychological disorders is the American Psychiatric Association's *Diagnostic and Statistical Manual of Mental Disorders (Fourth Edition)*, nicknamed **DSM-IV**. This 1994 volume and accompanying case illustrations provide the basis for much of the material in this chapter. DSM-IV was developed in coordination with the tenth edition of the World Health Organization's *International Classification of Diseases* (ICD-10).

DSM-IV assumes the medical model. The very idea of "diagnosing" people's problems in terms of their "symptoms" presumes a mental "illness." Some practitioners are not enthralled with this medical terminology, but most find DSM-IV a helpful and practical tool. And a financially necessary one: Most North American health insurance companies require a DSM-IV diagnosis before they will pay for therapy.

The DSM describes disorders and their prevalence without presuming to explain their causes. Thus, the once-popular term *neurosis* is no longer a diagnostic category—because neurosis was Freud's idea of the process by which unconscious conflicts create anxiety. DSM-IV does mention **neurotic disorders**—psychological disorders that, although distressing, still allow one to think rationally and function socially. But even this term is so vague that psychologists now use it minimally, usually as a contrast to the more bizarre and debilitating **psychotic disorders**, marked by irrationality.

Instead of emphasizing the old neurotic/psychotic distinction, DSM-IV groups some 230 psychological disorders and conditions into 17 major categories of "mental disorder." There are diagnoses for almost every conceivable complaint. In fact, some critics fault DSM for bringing "almost any kind of behavior within the compass of psychiatry" (Eysenck & others, 1983)—from irrational fear of humiliation and embarrassment (social phobia) to persistently breaking rules at home or school (conduct disorder).

For the DSM-IV categories to be valid, they must first be reliable. If one psychiatrist or psychologist diagnoses someone as having, say, a "catatonic schizophrenia disorder," what are the chances that another mental health worker will independently give the same diagnosis? With the DSM-IV's diagnostic guidelines, the chances are good. The guidelines work by asking clinicians a series of objective questions about observable behaviors, such as, "Is the person afraid to leave home?" In one study, 16 psychologists used this structured-interview procedure to diagnose 75 psychiatric patients as suffering either (1) depression, (2) generalized anxiety, or (3) some other disorder (Riskind & others, 1987). Without knowing the first psychologist's diagnosis, another psychologist viewed a videotape of each interview and offered a second opinion. For 83 percent of the patients, the two opinions agreed.

Let us now consider a few of the most prevalent and perplexing disorders, remembering that the people we will meet are not sideshow curiosities but real people—troubled people whose loved ones are troubled for them.

## Summing Up

Psychological disorders fascinate us, partly because most of us will at some time experience or witness them close at hand.

**Defining Psychological Disorders** Between normality and abnormality there is not a gulf, but a fine and somewhat arbitrary line. Where we draw the line depends on how atypical, disturbing, maladaptive, and unjustifiable a person's behavior is.

**Understanding Psychological Disorders** The medical model's assumption that psychological disorders are mental illnesses has displaced earlier views that demons and evil spirits were to blame. However, critics question the medical model's labeling of psychological disorders as sicknesses. They argue that the disorders are socially defined and that some disorders are found only in certain cultures. Most mental health workers today believe that disorders are influenced by genetic predisposition, physiological states, psychological dynamics, and social circumstances.

**Classifying Psychological Disorders** Many psychiatrists and psychologists believe that a system for naming and describing psychological disorders facilitates treatment and research. The current edition of the *Diagnostic and Statistical Manual of Mental Disorders* (DSM-IV) provides an authoritative classification scheme.

# Anxiety Disorders

*Anxiety becomes disabling when people are unexplainably and uncontrollably tense (general anxiety disorder), irrationally fearful of something (phobic disorder), or troubled by repetitive thoughts and actions (obsessive-compulsive disorder). What do these disorders look like in real people? What causes them?*

Anxiety is part of our everyday experience. When speaking in front of a class, when peering down from a ledge, when waiting for a big game to begin, any one of us might feel anxious. And, at one time or another, most of us feel enough anxiety that we fail to make eye contact or we avoid talking to someone—"shyness" we call it. Fortunately for most of us, our occasional uneasiness is not intense and persistent. If it becomes so, we may have one of the three important **anxiety disorders**: **generalized anxiety disorder**, in which a person feels unexplainably tense and uneasy; **phobic disorder**, in which a person feels irrationally afraid of a specific object or situation; and **obsessive-compulsive disorder**, in which a person is troubled by repetitive thoughts or actions.

## Generalized Anxiety Disorder

Tom, a 27-year-old electrician, seeks help, complaining of dizziness, sweating palms, heart palpitations, and ringing in his ears. He feels edgy and sometimes finds himself shaking. With reasonable success he hides his symptoms from his family and coworkers. Nevertheless, he has had few social contacts since the symptoms began 2 years ago. Worse, he occasionally has to leave work. His family doctor and neurologist can find no physical problem, and a diet for those with low blood sugar has not helped.

Tom's unfocused, out-of-control, threatened feelings suggest a generalized anxiety disorder. The symptoms of this disorder are commonplace; their persistence is not. The sufferers are continually tense and jittery, worried about bad things that might happen, and experience all the symptoms of autonomic nervous system arousal (racing heart, clammy hands, stomach butterflies, sleeplessness). The tension and apprehension may leak out through furrowed brows, twitching eyelids, or fidgeting.

One of the worst characteristics of a generalized anxiety disorder is that the person cannot identify, and therefore cannot avoid, its cause. To use Freud's term, the anxiety is "free-floating." As some 1 in 75 people know, for no apparent reason the anxiety may at times suddenly escalate into a terrifying **panic attack**—a minutes-long episode of intense fear that something horrible is about to happen to them. Heart palpitations, shortness of breath, choking sensations, trembling, or dizziness typically accompany the panic. The experience is unpredictable and so frightening that the sufferer often comes to fear the fear itself and to avoid situations where panic has struck.

## Phobic Disorders

Phobic anxiety focuses on some specific object, activity, or situation. (See Figure 15–2 for a ranking of some common fears.) Phobias—irrational fears—are a common psychological disorder that people often accept and

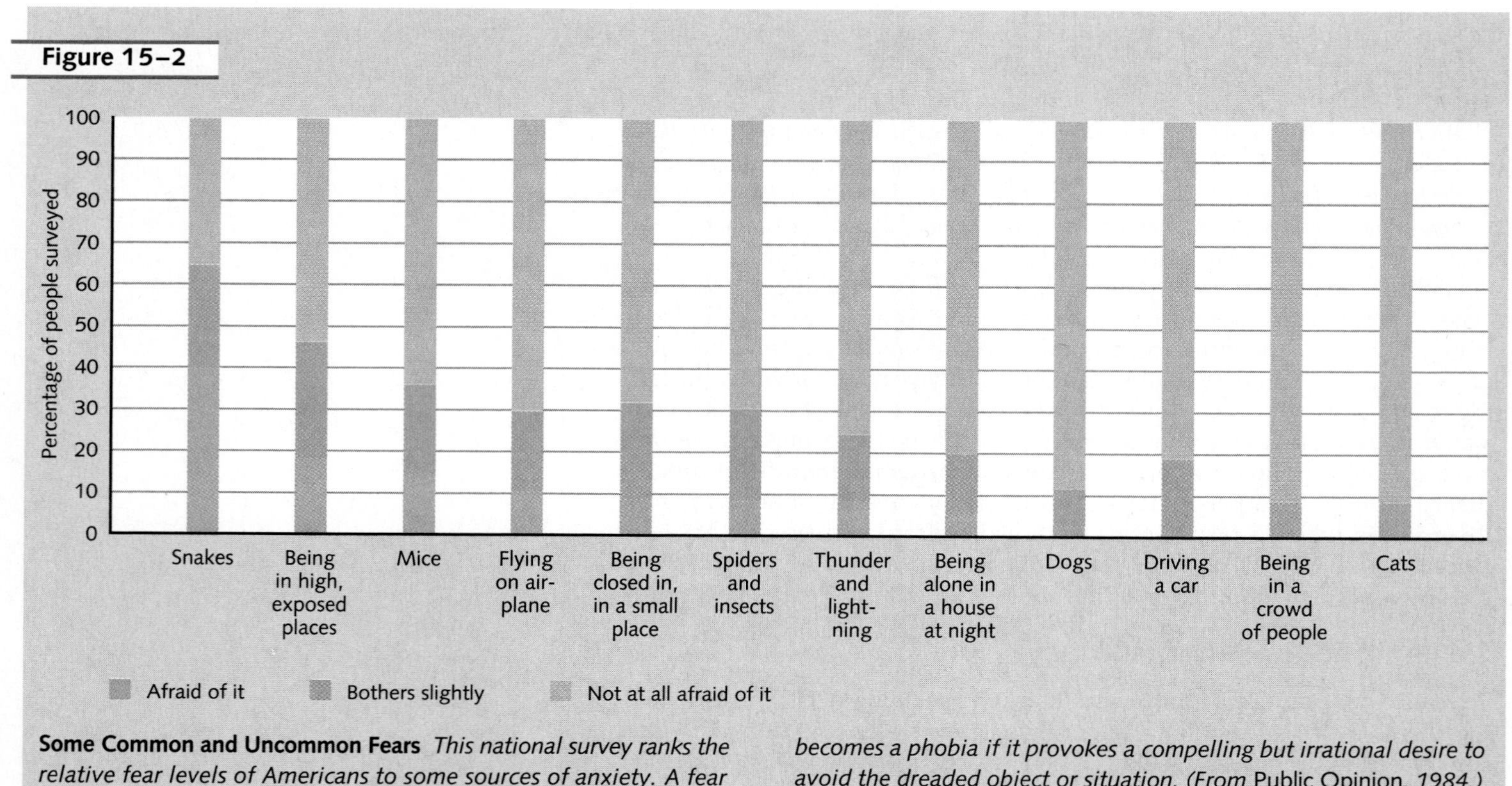


**Some Common and Uncommon Fears** *This national survey ranks the relative fear levels of Americans to some sources of anxiety. A fear becomes a phobia if it provokes a compelling but irrational desire to avoid the dreaded object or situation. (From* Public Opinion, *1984.)*

live with. Some phobic disorders are incapacitating, however. Marilyn, a 28-year-old homemaker, so fears thunderstorms that she feels anxious as soon as a weather forecaster mentions possible storms later in the week. If her husband is away and a storm is forecast, she sometimes stays with a close relative. During a storm, she hides from windows and buries her head to avoid seeing the lightning. She is otherwise healthy and happy.

Other people with phobic disorders suffer from irrational fears of specific animals or of airplanes or elevators or even public places such as department stores. Sometimes it is possible to avoid the fear-arousing stimulus: One can hide during thunderstorms or avoid air travel. With other phobias, such as an intense fear of being scrutinized by others (*social phobia*) or of being in open or public places (*agoraphobia*), avoiding fear-arousing situations may dictate never leaving home. Compared with the other disorders discussed in this chapter, phobias have an earlier onset—often by the early teens (Burke & others, 1990).

## Obsessive-Compulsive Disorder

As with the generalized anxiety and phobic disorders, we can see aspects of ourselves in the obsessive-compulsive disorder. We may at times be obsessed with senseless or offensive thoughts that will not go away. Or we may engage in compulsive, rigid behavior—rechecking a locked door, stepping over cracks in the sidewalk, or lining up our books and pencils "just so" before studying.

Obsessive thoughts and compulsive behaviors cross the fine line between normality and disorder when they become so persistent that they interfere with the way we live or when they cause distress. Checking to see that the door is locked is normal; checking the door 10 times is not. Hand washing is normal; hand washing so often that one's skin becomes raw is not. (Table 15–1 offers more examples.) At some time during their lives, often during their late teens or twenties, 2 to 3 percent cross that line from normal preoccupations and fussiness to debilitating disorder (Karno & others, 1988). The thoughts become so haunting, the rituals so senselessly time-consuming, that effective functioning becomes impossible.

*"He always times '60 Minutes.'"*

Drawing by Richter; © 1983 The New Yorker Magazine, Inc.

**Table 15–1 Common Obsessions and Compulsions***

| | Percentage Reporting Symptom |
|---|---|
| *Obsessions (repetitive thoughts)* | |
| Concern with dirt, germs, or toxins | 40 |
| Something terrible happening (fire, death, illness) | 24 |
| Symmetry, order, or exactness | 17 |
| *Compulsions (repetitive behaviors)* | |
| Excessive hand washing, bathing, tooth brushing, or grooming | 85 |
| Repeating rituals (in/out of a door, up/down from a chair) | 51 |
| Checking doors, locks, appliances, car brake, homework | 46 |

*Seventy children and adolescents suffering obsessive-compulsive disorder reported their symptoms.
*Source:* Adapted from Rapoport, 1989.

One such person was billionaire Howard Hughes. Hughes would compulsively dictate the same phrases over and over again. Under stress, he developed an obsessive fear of germs. He became reclusive and insisted that his assistants carry out elaborate hand-washing rituals and wear white gloves when handling documents he would later touch. He ordered tape around doors and windows and forbade his staff to touch or even look at him. "Everybody carries germs around with them," he explained. "I want to live longer than my parents, so I avoid germs" (Fowler, 1986).

During the late 1980s researchers explored the causes of obsessive-compulsive disorder and new treatments for it. Coincident with this publicity, mental health workers were more and more likely to diagnose their patients as having the disorder. To psychiatric researcher Andrew Stoll and his colleagues (1992), this suggests that clinicians "more readily consider and diagnose a condition for which an innovative or effective treatment is available."

## Explaining Anxiety Disorders

In seeking to understand anxiety disorders, psychologists have emphasized three familiar perspectives—psychoanalytic, learning, and biological.

### The Psychoanalytic Perspective

Psychoanalytic theory assumes that, beginning in childhood, intolerable impulses, ideas, and feelings get repressed. This submerged mental energy nevertheless influences our actions and emotions, sometimes producing feelings of anxiety, depression, or other maladaptive symptoms that mystify even the sufferer.

One of Freud's classic cases concerned a 5-year-old boy known as Little Hans, whose phobia of horses prevented (in those days before cars) his going outdoors. Freud's controversial speculation was that Little Hans's fear of horses expressed his underlying fear of his father, whom Hans viewed as a rival for his mother's affections.

Alternatively, the forbidden impulses may break through as thinly disguised thoughts, which may provoke acts aimed at suppressing the associated anxiety. The result: obsessions and compulsions. Repetitive hand washing, for instance, supposedly helps suppress anxiety over one's "dirty" urges.

### The Learning Perspective

Learning researchers link general anxiety with learned helplessness (page 490). In the laboratory, researchers can create chronically anxious, ulcer-prone rats by giving them unpredictable electric shocks (Schwartz, 1984). Like the rape victim who reported feeling anxious when entering her old neighborhood (page 267), the animals are apprehensive in their lab environment. For many victims of post-traumatic stress disorder (page 579), anxiety swells with any reminder of their trauma. Such experiences might help explain why anxious people are hyperattentive to possible threats (Mineka & Sutton, 1992).

When experimental shocks become predictable—when preceded by a particular conditioned stimulus—the animals' fear focuses on *that* stimulus and they relax in its absence. So it can happen with human fears. Recently, my car was struck by another whose driver missed a stop sign. For months afterward, I felt a twinge of unease with the approach of any car from a side street. Perhaps Marilyn's phobia was similarly conditioned during a terrifying or painful experience associated with a thunderstorm.

Conditioned fears may remain long after we have forgotten the experiences that produced them (Jacobs & Nadel, 1985). Moreover, some fears arise from stimulus generalization. A person who fears heights after a fall may be afraid of airplanes without ever having flown. Fearing panic attacks, a person may just stay inside (Antony & others, 1992). Someone might also learn fear through observational learning—by observing others' fears. As we saw in Chapter 13, wild monkeys transmit their fear of snakes to their offspring; similarly, human parents transmit their fears to their children. Avoiding or escaping the feared situation reduces anxiety, thus reinforcing the phobic behavior. Compulsive behaviors similarly reduce anxiety. If washing your hands relieves your feelings of unease, you will likely wash your hands again when the feelings return.

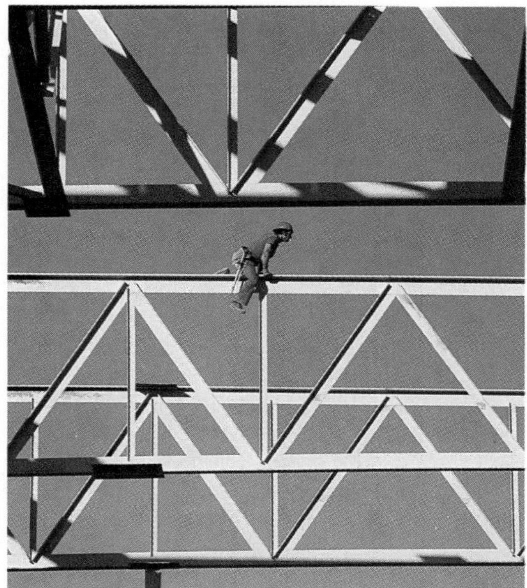

**An Emotional High** *Although we humans seem biologically predisposed to fear heights—certainly an adaptive response—this construction worker seems fearless. The biological perspective helps us understand why most people would be terrified in this situation.*

### The Biological Perspective

Other researchers explain our anxiety-proneness in evolutionary, genetic, and physiological terms.

As we noted on page 445, we humans seem biologically prepared to develop fears of heights, storms, snakes, and insects—dangers our ancestors faced. Compulsive acts typically exaggerate behaviors that contributed to our species' survival. Grooming gone wild becomes hair pulling. Washing up becomes ritual hand washing. Checking territorial boundaries becomes checking and rechecking a door known to be locked (Rapoport, 1989).

Some people more than others seem genetically predisposed to particular fears and high anxiety. Identical twins often develop similar phobias, in some cases even when raised separately (Carey, 1990; Eckert & others, 1981). One pair of 35-year-old identical female twins independently developed claustrophobia. They also become so fearful of water that each would gingerly wade backward into the ocean, only up to the knees. Among monkeys, fearfulness runs in families. Individual monkeys react more strongly to stress if their close relatives are anxiously reactive (Suomi, 1986). Among humans, the risk of anxiety disorder rises when the afflicted relative is an identical twin (Kendler & others, 1992).

The biology of general anxiety disorder, panic, and even obsessions and compulsions is measurable as an overarousal of brain areas involved in impulse control and habitual behaviors. PET scans of persons with obsessive-compulsive disorder reveal unusually high activity in an area of the frontal lobes just above the eyes (Figure 15–3) and in a more primitive area deep in the brain (Rauch & Jenike, 1993; Resnick, 1992). Some antidepressant drugs control obsessive-compulsive behavior by dampening this activity through affecting the availability of the neurotransmitter serotonin.

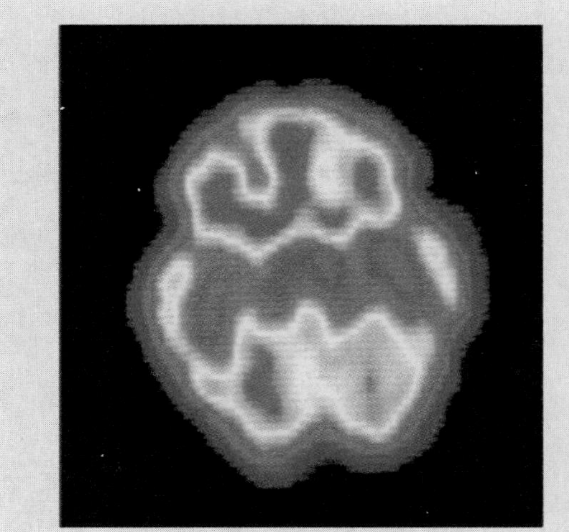

**Figure 15–3**

**A PET Scan of the Brain of a Person With Obsessive-Compulsive Disorder** *The scan reveals a normally high metabolic activity (red areas) in the frontal lobes, seen at the top of the photo. This is visible in a region of the left hemisphere's frontal lobe involved in directing attention.*

## Summing Up

Anxiety is part of our everyday experience. It is classified as a psychological disorder only when it becomes distressing or persistent or is characterized by maladaptive behaviors intended to reduce it. There are three types of anxiety disorders.

**Generalized Anxiety Disorders** Those who suffer a generalized anxiety disorder may for no clear reason feel uncontrollably tense and uneasy, an anxiety that can escalate into a panic attack.

**Phobic Disorder** Those with phobic disorder may be irrationally afraid of a specific object or situation.

**Obsessive-Compulsive Disorder** Persistent and repetitive thoughts and actions characterize the obsessive-compulsive disorder.

**Explaining Anxiety Disorders** The psychoanalytic perspective views anxiety disorders as the discharging of repressed impulses. The learning perspective sees them as a product of learned helplessness or fear conditioning. The biological perspective considers possible evolutionary, genetic, and physiological influences.

## Somatoform Disorders

*Somatoform disorders have a somatic (bodily) symptom. In what forms might such symptoms appear?*

Ellen becomes dizzy and nauseated in the late afternoon—shortly before she expects her husband home. Her doctor and a neurologist cannot identify a physical cause. They suspect the symptoms have an unconscious psychological origin, possibly triggered by her mixed feelings about her husband. In **somatoform disorders**, such as Ellen's, the distressing symptoms take a somatic (bodily) form, without apparent physical causes. One person may have a variety of complaints—vomiting, dizziness, blurred vision, difficulty in swallowing. Another may experience severe and prolonged pain.

In China, where people less often express the emotional aspects of distress, bodily complaints are common (Draguns, 1990a). Because psychological explanations of anxiety and depression are socially less approved, the Chinese appear more sensitive to, and more willing to report, the bodily symptoms of their distress. Mr. Wu, a 36-year-old technician in Hunan, illustrates one of China's most common psychological disorders (Spitzer & others, 1989). He finds work difficult because of his insomnia, fatigue, weakness, and headaches. Chinese herbs and Western medicines provide no relief. To his Chinese clinician, he seems not so much depressed as exhausted. Similar, generalized bodily complaints have often been observed in African cultures (Binitie, 1975).

Even to people in the West, somatic symptoms are familiar. To a lesser extent, we have all experienced inexplicable physical symptoms under stress. It is little comfort to be told that the problem is "all in your head." Although the symptoms may be psychological in origin, they are nevertheless genuinely felt.

*"He was a dreadful hypochondriac."*

Punch/Rothco

One type of somatoform disorder, more common in Freud's day than ours, is **conversion disorder**, so called because anxiety was presumed to be converted into a physical symptom. (As we noted in Chapter 14, Freud's effort to treat and understand psychological disorders stemmed from his puzzlement over ailments that had no physiological basis.) A patient with a conversion disorder might lose sensation in a way that makes no neurological sense. Yet the physical symptoms would be real; one could stick pins in the affected area and get no response. Others experience unexplained paralysis, blindness, or an inability to swallow, and they are strangely indifferent to their problems.

As you can imagine, somatoform disorders send people not to a psychologist or psychiatrist but to a physician. This is especially true of those who experience **hypochondriasis**. In this relatively common somatoform disorder, people interpret normal sensations (a stomach cramp today, a headache tomorrow) as symptoms of a dreaded disease. Sympathy or temporary relief from everyday demands may reinforce such complaints. No amount of reassurance by any physician convinces the patient not to worry. So the patient moves on to another physician, seeking and receiving more medical attention but failing to confront the disorder's psychological root.

### Summing Up

The somatoform disorders involve a somatic (bodily) symptom—a physiologically unexplained but genuinely felt ailment. The incidence of bodily symptoms of psychological stress varies among cultures. Freud was particularly fascinated by conversion disorders, in which anxiety seemed converted to a symptom that had no physiological basis. Today, hypochondriasis (interpreting one's normal sensations as symptoms of a dreaded disease) is a more common somatoform disorder.

## Dissociative Disorders

*Most controversial of all presumed disorders are those in which conscious awareness is said to become dissociated (separated) from previous memories, thoughts, and feelings. What are these disorders, and why are they controversial?*

Among the most intriguing disorders are the rare **dissociative disorders**, in which a person appears to experience a sudden loss of memory or change in identity. When a situation becomes too stressful, people may dissociate themselves from it. Their conscious awareness becomes separated from painful memories, thoughts, and feelings. (Note that this presumes the existence of repressed memories, which as Chapter 9 explained, have recently been questioned.)

Certain symptoms of dissociation are not so rare. Now and then, many people may have a sense of being unreal, of being separated from one's body, of watching oneself as in a movie. Facing trauma, such detachment may actually protect a person from being overwhelmed by emotion. Only when such experiences are severe and prolonged do they suggest a dissociative disorder.

### Amnesia

**Amnesia**, the failure to recall events, can be caused by head injuries or alcoholic intoxication. But dissociative amnesia, some psychologists believe, usually begins as a response to intolerable psychological stress. One 18-year-old victim was rescued from his sailboat by the Coast Guard and brought to a hospital. He knew he had gone sailing with friends and that he was a college student, but said he could not recall what had happened to his friends. Moreover, he kept forgetting he was in a hospital; each reminder surprised him. Later, aided by a drug that relaxed him, he formed a memory: A ferocious storm had washed his companions overboard.

As this case illustrates, the forgetfulness of amnesia is selective: The young man supposedly forgot what was intolerably painful. Those with amnesia may be somewhat disoriented and may forget who they are, but they will remember how to drive, count, and talk. Typically, the amnesia vanishes as abruptly as it began and rarely recurs.

## Fugue

Like amnesia, **fugue** (pronounced fewg, meaning "flight") involves presumed forgetting, but it also involves fleeing one's home and identity for days, months, or years. Gene Smith, a mid-level manager, had been passed over for promotion, faulted by his supervisor, and rejected by his 18-year-old son, who during a violent argument called him a "failure." Two days later, Smith disappeared. A month later and 200 miles away, police brought a man who said he was "Burt Tate" to the emergency room. Tate had been hurt in a fight at a diner, where he had been working as a short-order cook since drifting into town a month earlier. He claimed not to recall where he had lived or worked before that. He admitted that was strange but did not seem upset by it. After a missing-person check, Mrs. Smith confirmed that Burt Tate was Gene Smith. Though noticeably anxious when faced with his wife, he denied recognizing her. When "awakening" from a fugue state, people such as Gene Smith remember their old identities but typically deny remembering what occurred during the fugue. Skeptics wonder if such patients may be feigning memory loss for strategic reasons.

## Multiple Personality

Even more mysterious and controversial is the massive dissociation of self from ordinary consciousness in those with **multiple personality disorder**, also called dissociative identity disorder. These people have two or more distinct personalities. The first is usually restrained and dull, the second more impulsive and uninhibited. The person may be prim and proper one moment and loud and flirtatious the next. Each personality has its own voice and mannerisms, and the original one typically denies awareness of the other(s).

Although people diagnosed as having multiple personality disorder are usually not violent, there have been cases in which the person reportedly became dissociated into a "good" and a "bad" or aggressive personality—a modest version of the Dr. Jekyll/Mr. Hyde split immortalized in Robert Louis Stevenson's story. Freud would say that, rid of the original "good" personality's awareness, the wanton second personality is free to discharge forbidden impulses. One unusual case that for a time seemed to support this interpretation involved Kenneth Bianchi, who was convicted of the "Hillside Strangler" rapes and murders of 10 California women. During a hypnosis session with Bianchi, psychologist John Watkins (1984) "called forth" a hidden personality:

**The "Hillside Strangler"** *Kenneth Bianchi is shown here at his trial.*

**Watkins:** *I've talked a bit to Ken, but I think that perhaps there might be another part of Ken that I haven't talked to, another part that maybe feels somewhat differently from the part that I've talked to. . . . Would you talk with me, Part, by saying, "I'm here"?*

Bianchi answered "Yes" and engaged in the following interchange:

**Watkins:** *Part, are you the same thing as Ken, or are you different in any way?*

**Bianchi:** *I'm not him.*

**Watkins:** *You're not him? Who are you? Do you have a name?*

**Bianchi:** *Steve. You can call me Steve.*

When speaking as Steve, Bianchi stated that he hated Ken because Ken was nice and that he (Steve), aided by a cousin, had murdered women. He also claimed that Ken knew nothing about his existence and that Ken was innocent of the murders.

Was Bianchi's second personality a ruse, simply a way of disavowing responsibility for his actions? (Bianchi, who was later convicted, was a practiced liar who had read about multiple personality in psychology books.) Even normal people sometimes act as if they had a multiple personality, as when displaying a goofy, loud-mouthed self while hanging out with friends, and a subdued, respectful self around grandparents. Exploring our capacity for personality shifts, Nicholas Spanos (1986) asked college students to pretend they were accused murderers being examined by a psychiatrist. When given the same hypnotic treatment Bianchi received, most spontaneously expressed a second personality.

This discovery made Spanos wonder: Is multiple personality simply a more extreme version of our normal human capacity to shift moods and to vary the "selves" we present in different situations? Are clinicians who discover multiple personalities merely triggering fantasy-prone people's enactment of a role? If so, can such people then convince themselves of the authenticity of their own role enactments? Are they like actors, who commonly report "losing themselves" in their roles? (Recall from Chapter 7 that Spanos also raises these questions about the hypnotic state. Given that most multiple personality patients are highly hypnotizable, whatever explains one condition—dissociation or role playing—may help explain the other.)

*"Pretense may become reality."*

Chinese proverb

Those who accept multiple personality as a genuine disorder find support in the distinct brain and body states associated with differing personalities (Putnam, 1991). Even handedness sometimes switches with personality (Henninger, 1992). In one study, ophthalmologists detected shifting visual acuity and eye-muscle balance as patients switched personalities. Such changes did not occur among control subjects trying to simulate multiple personality (Miller & others, 1991).

Skeptics nevertheless find it suspicious that the disorder has just recently become rather popular, with an estimated 7000 diagnosed cases in North America alone (Shulruff, 1990). That means that the number of cases reported just since 1980 is 35 times greater than the 200 cases reported until that year (Humphrey & Dennett, 1989). This is just what one might expect now that the role of multiple personality has been well publicized in books and films, such as *The Three Faces of Eve* and *Sybil*. Moreover, most clinicians have never encountered a multiple personality, and the disorder is almost nonexistent outside North America, although in other cultures some people are said to be "possessed" by an alien spirit (Aldridge-Morris, 1989; Kluft, 1991). In Britain, the diagnosis is rare, and in India and Japan it is essentially nonexistent. In North America, not only has the number of such diagnoses exploded, from only two reported cases per decade from 1930 to 1960, but so has the average number of personalities displayed—from 3 to 12 per patient (Goff & Sims, 1993).

To skeptics, that sounds like a cultural phenomenon—a disorder created by therapists in a particular social context (Merskey, 1992). Skeptics note how some therapists go fishing for it: "Have you ever felt like another part of you does things you can't control? Does this part of you have a name? Can I talk to the angry part of you?" Once patients permit a therapist to "talk to the part of you that says those angry things" they have begun acting out the fantasy. Moreover, say skeptics, "It is no coincidence" that multiple personality studies began among hypnosis practitioners (Goff, 1993).

With the dissociative disorders, as with the anxiety and somatoform disorders, the psychoanalytic and learning perspectives view the symptoms as ways of dealing with anxiety. Psychoanalysts see them as defenses against the anxiety caused by the eruption of unacceptable impulses. Learning theorists see them as behaviors reinforced by anxiety reduction.

Others view dissociative disorders as hypnoticlike states into which people lapse as a protective response to traumatic childhood experiences. People diagnosed as having multiple personality disorder increasingly are women, most of whom reportedly suffered physical, sexual, or emotional abuse as children (Coon & others, 1988; Goff & Sims, 1993; Kluft, 1991). Perhaps, then, multiple personalities are the desperate efforts of the traumatized to flee inward. Maladaptive as they may be, are such psychological disorders expressions of our human struggle to cope with and survive the stresses of life?

*"Though this be madness, yet there is method in 't."*
William Shakespeare
*Hamlet*, 1600

## Summing Up

Under stress, a person's conscious awareness may become dissociated (separated) from previous memories, thoughts, and feelings.

**Amnesia** Dissociative amnesia can be caused by head injuries or alcoholic intoxication. It usually involves selective forgetting in response to stress.

**Fugue** Fugue involves not only forgetting one's identity but also fleeing one's home.

**Multiple Personality** Most mysterious of all dissociative disorders are cases of multiple personality. The afflicted person is said to have two or more distinct personalities, with the original typically unaware of the other(s). Skeptics question whether this disorder may be a cultural phenomenon, finding it suspicious that the disorder has just recently become popular.

# Mood Disorders

*In the Western world, more and more youth and younger adults have been suffering depression. What forms does depression take? What might explain depression and its rising incidence?*

The emotional extremes of **mood disorders** come in two principal forms: (1) **major depressive disorder**, in which the person experiences prolonged hopelessness and lethargy until eventually rebounding to normality; and (2) **bipolar disorder** (often called manic depressive disorder), in which the person alternates between depression and *mania*, an overexcited, hyperactive state.

## Major Depressive Disorder

*For some people, recurring depression during winter's dark months constitutes a* seasonal affective disorder.

Perhaps you know what depression feels like. If you are like most college students, at some time during this year—more likely the dark months of winter than the bright days of summer—you will probably experience a few of the symptoms of depression (Beck & Young, 1978). You may feel deeply discouraged about the future, dissatisfied with your life, or isolated from others. You may lack the energy to get things done or even to force yourself out of bed; be unable to concentrate, eat, or sleep normally; or even wonder if you would be better off dead. Perhaps academic success came easily to you in high school, and now you find that disappointing grades jeopardize your goals. Maybe conflicting parental and peer pressures seem intolerable. Perhaps social difficulties, such as loneliness or the breakup of a romance, have plunged you into despair. And maybe your brooding has at times only worsened your self-torment.

If so, you are not alone. Depression is a "common cold" of psychological disorders—an expression that effectively states its pervasiveness, but not its seriousness. Although phobias are more common, depression is the number one reason why people seek mental health services.

The line between life's normal "downs" and major depression is difficult to define. Joy, contentment, sadness, and despair are different points on a continuum, points at which any of us may be found at any given moment. Depression can be an appropriate response to profoundly sad events, such as a significant loss or bereavement. To feel bad in reaction to painful events is to be in touch with reality. In such times, depression is like a car's low-oil-pressure light—a signal that warns us to stop and take protective measures. Depression is a sort of psychic hibernation: It slows us down, avoids attracting predators, and evokes support. To grind to a halt and ruminate, as depressed people do, is to reassess one's life when feeling threatened. Biologically speaking, the purpose of life is not happiness but survival and reproduction. From this perspective, there is sense to suffering (Neese, 1991).

Major depression occurs when signs of depression (poor appetite, insomnia, lethargy, feelings of worthlessness, or loss of interest in family, friends, and activities) last 2 weeks or more without any notable cause. The difference between a blue mood after bad news and a mood disorder is like the difference between gasping for breath after exercising and being chronically short of breath.

*"My life had come to a sudden stop. I was able to breathe, to eat, to drink, to sleep. I could not, indeed, help doing so; but there was no real life in me."*

Leo Tolstoy
*My Confession*, 1887

## Bipolar Disorder

With or without therapy, depressive episodes usually end. Depressed people typically rebound—usually by returning to their previous behavior patterns. However, some people rebound to or from the opposite emotional extreme—a euphoric, hyperactive, wildly optimistic state of **mania**. If depression is living in slow motion, mania is fast forward. Alternating between depression and mania signals *bipolar disorder*. During the manic phase of a bipolar disorder, the person is typically overtalkative, overactive, elated (though easily irritated if crossed), has little need for sleep, and shows fewer sexual inhibitions. Speech is loud, flighty, and hard to interrupt.

One of mania's maladaptive symptoms is grandiose optimism and self-esteem, which may lead to reckless spending and investment sprees. Although people in a manic state find advice irritating, they need protection from their own poor judgment. In milder forms, however, the energy and free-flowing thinking of mania can fuel creativity. Bipolar disorder is especially common among poets, artists, and playwrights (DeAngelis, 1989; Jamison, 1993). Handel composed his nearly 4-hour-long *Messiah* during 3 weeks of intense, creative energy.

*"All the people in history, literature, art, whom I most admire: Mozart, Shakespeare, Homer, El Greco, St. John, Chekhov, Gregory of Nyssa, Dostoevsky, Emily Brontë: not one of them would qualify for a mental-health certificate."*

Madeleine L'Engle
*A Circle of Quiet*, 1972

It is as true of emotions as all else: What goes up comes down. Before long, the mood either returns to normal or plunges into a brief depression.

## Close-Up Suicide

*"But life, being weary of these worldly bars,*
*Never lacks power to dismiss itself."*

William Shakespeare
*Julius Caesar*, 1599

Each year some three-quarters of a million wearied, despairing people worldwide will say no to life by electing a permanent solution to what may be a temporary problem (Retterstøl, 1993). In retrospect, their families and friends may recall signs they now believe should have forewarned them—the suicidal talk, the giving away of possessions, or the withdrawal and preoccupation with death. Most have been depressed. One-third of those who kill themselves have tried suicide before.

Few of those who talk suicide or think suicidal thoughts (a number that includes one-third of all adolescents and college students) actually attempt suicide, and few of these succeed in killing themselves (Centers for Disease Control, 1989; Westefeld & Furr, 1987). Still, most individuals who do commit suicide have talked of it. And any who do talk suicide are at least sending a signal of their desperate or despondent feelings.

To find out who commits suicide, researchers have compared the suicide rates of different groups.

- ***National differences*** The suicide rates of England, Italy, and Spain are little more than those of Canada, Australia, and the United States; Austrian, Danish, and Swiss suicide rates are nearly double (Bureau of the Census, 1993).
- ***Racial differences*** In the United States, whites are twice as likely as blacks to kill themselves (Figure 15–4).

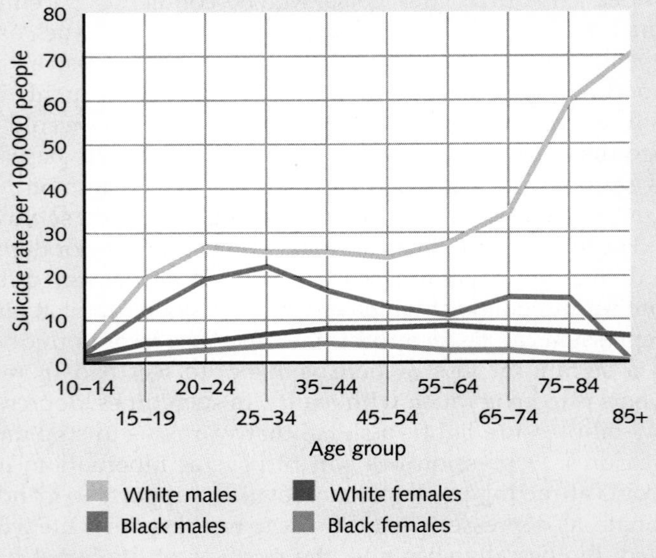


**Figure 15–4**

**Suicide Rate by Gender and Age** *In the United States, suicide rates are higher among whites than blacks, and higher among males than among females. (From Bureau of the Census, 1993.)*

- ***Group differences*** Suicide rates are much higher among the rich, the nonreligious, and those who are single, widowed, or divorced (Hoyer & Lund, 1993; Stack, 1992; Stengel, 1981).

Though equally maladaptive as major depression, bipolar disorder is much less common, occurring in about 1 percent of the population. Unlike major depression, it afflicts as many men as women.

## Explaining Mood Disorders

Because depression profoundly affects many people, it has been the subject of thousands of studies. Psychologists are working to develop a theory of mood disorders that will suggest ways to treat or prevent them. Researcher Peter Lewinsohn and his colleagues (1985) summarized the facts that any theory of depression must explain. Among them are the following:

- ***Many behavioral and cognitive changes accompany depression.*** Depressed people are inactive and unmotivated. They also are sensitive to negative happenings, expect negative outcomes, and are more likely to recall negative information. When the depression lifts, these behavioral and cognitive accompaniments disappear.

- *Gender differences* Women are much more likely than men to attempt suicide. Depending on the country, however, men are two to four times more likely to succeed. (Men are more likely to use foolproof methods, such as putting a bullet into the brain, the method of choice in 6 of 10 U.S. suicides.)
- *Age differences* Due partly to improved reporting (Gist & Welch, 1989), the known suicide rate among 15- to 19-year-olds has more than doubled since 1950. It now nearly equals the traditionally higher suicide rate among adults (Figure 15–5).

People who commit suicide often do so not while in the depths of depression, when energy and initiative are lacking, but when they begin to rebound and become capable of following through. Teenage suicides may follow a traumatic event, such as a romantic breakup or a guilt-provoking antisocial act; they are often linked with drug and alcohol abuse (Fowler & others, 1986; Kolata, 1986). Compared with people who suffer no disorder, alcoholics are roughly 100 times more likely to commit suicide, as some 3 percent of them do (Murphy & Wetzel, 1990). Even among those who have attempted suicide, alcoholics are five times more likely than nonalcoholics eventually to kill themselves (Beck & Steer, 1989). Among the elderly, suicide is sometimes chosen as an alternative to future suffering. In people of all ages, suicide is not necessarily an act of hostility or revenge, as many people think, but may be a way of switching off unendurable pain (Shneidman, 1987).

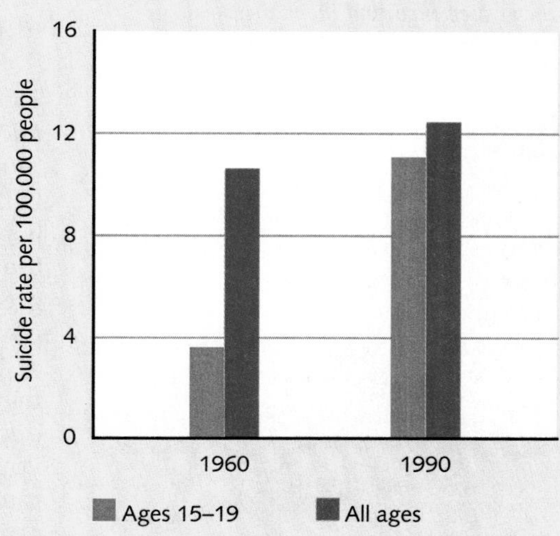


**Figure 15–5**

**Increasing Rates of Teen Suicide** *Teen suicide has soared since 1960. (From National Center for Health Statistics.) In both the United States and Australia, the teen suicide surge is almost entirely among males (Hassan & Carr, 1989).*

Social suggestion may trigger the final act. Following highly publicized suicides and TV programs featuring suicide, known suicides increase. So do fatal auto "accidents" and private airplane crashes (page 620).

- ***Depression is widespread.*** Its commonality suggests that its causes, too, must be common.
- ***Compared with men, women are twice as vulnerable to major depression, even more so if they have been depressed before.*** (In general, women are most vulnerable to passive disorders—things internal, such as depression, anxiety, and inhibited sexual desire. Men's disorders are more active—alcohol abuse, antisocial conduct, lack of impulse control [see Table 15–2, page 532].) Curiously, the gender difference in depression rates does *not* exist among college students or bereaved persons (Goodman & Koenig, 1992; Nolen-Hoeksema, 1990).
- ***Most depressive episodes last less than 3 months.*** Although therapy can speed recovery, most people suffering major depression return to normal without professional help. Depression comes and, a few weeks or months later, it goes.

*About 50 percent of those who recover from depression will suffer another episode within 2 years. Recovery is more likely to be enduring the longer patients stay well, the fewer their previous episodes, the less stress they experience, and the more social support they have (Belsher & Costello, 1988).*

- ***Stressful events related to work, marriage, and close relationships often precede depression.*** A family member's death, a wage cut, or a physical assault increase one's risk of depression (Shrout & others, 1989). National samples of Israelis, whose tiny nation is a living stress laboratory, revealed greater feelings of depression after the outbreak of the 1982 Israel-Lebanon war (Hobfoll & others, 1989).

To these to-be-explained facts we can add one more: With each new generation, the rate of depression is increasing and the disorder is striking earlier (now often in the late teens). It's true in Canada and the United States—and in Germany, Italy, France, Lebanon, New Zealand, Taiwan, and Puerto Rico (Cross-National Collaborative Group, 1992). In North America, the odds of today's young adults having suffered depression are more than three times greater than for their grandparents (despite the grandparents' having had many more years at risk). In one National Institute of Mental Health study of 18,244 Americans, only 1 percent of those born before 1905 had suffered major depression by age 75. Of those born since 1955, 6 percent had been depressed by age 25. The increase appears genuine, *not* primarily a result of younger adults' greater willingness to admit depression. The increasing rate of depression helps explain a dramatic rise in the proportion of psychiatric patients with mood disorder. In a survey of North American psychiatric teaching hospitals, mood disorder diagnoses rose from 10 percent of patients in 1972 to 44 percent in 1990 (Stoll & others, 1993).

As you might expect, researchers understand and interpret these facts in ways that reflect their different perspectives.

**They Know the Pain of Depression** *Actress Patty Duke spent years suffering from bipolar disorder before she was finally treated. Now she spends her free time educating others about mental illness in thanks "for having been saved from that pit." CBS correspondent Mike Wallace became debilitated by severe depression during a tough libel trial. "Depression is palpable," he says. "You begin to feel like a fake and a fraud. You second-guess everything about everything."*

### The Psychoanalytic Perspective

Psychoanalytic theory applies to depression Freud's ideas about the importance of early childhood experiences and unconscious impulses. It suggests that depression occurs when significant losses evoke feelings associated with losses experienced in childhood. Loss of a romantic relationship or a job might evoke feelings associated with the loss of the intimate relationship with one's mother. Unresolved anger toward one's parents is also a factor, Freud believed. Some losses, such as a loved one's death, may evoke the anger once felt toward parents who were similarly "abandoning" or "rejecting." This anger is unacceptable to the superego, so the emotion turns inward against the self. Combined with the sense of loss, this internalized anger is said to produce depression.

### The Biological Perspective

Most of the mental health research dollars of late have funded explorations of physiological influences on mood disorders. Depression is a whole-body disorder, involving genetic predispositions, biochemical imbalances, melancholy mood, and negative thoughts.

**Genetic Influences** We have long known that mood disorders run in families. The risk of major depression and bipolar disorder increases if you have a parent or sibling who became depressed before age 30 (Pauls & others, 1992; Weissman & others, 1986). If one identical twin is diagnosed as suffering major depressive disorder, the chances are about 1 in 2 that at some time the other twin will be, too. If one identical twin has bipolar disorder, the chances are 7 in 10 that the other twin will at some point be diagnosed similarly. (Led by James Watson, Nobel laureate for discovering DNA, a collaborative search for the genes that put people at risk for bipolar disorder is now under way. Stay tuned.) Among fraternal twins, the corresponding odds are just under 1 in 5 (Tsuang & Faraone, 1990). Moreover, adopted people who suffer a mood disorder often have close biological relatives who suffer mood disorders, become alcoholic, or commit suicide (Wender & others, 1986).

**The Depressed Brain** Genes act by directing biochemical events that, down the line, influence behavior. One biochemical key is the neurotransmitters, those messenger molecules that shuttle signals between nerve cells. Norepinephrine, a neurotransmitter that increases arousal and boosts mood, is overabundant during mania and scarce during depression. A second neurotransmitter, serotonin, appears scarce during depression. Drugs that alleviate mania reduce norepinephrine; drugs that relieve depression tend to increase norepinephrine or serotonin supplies by blocking either their uptake (as Prozac does with serotonin) or chemical breakdown.

Using the new scanning machines, researchers are also spotting neurological signs of depression. In recent studies, the brains of depressed people have been found to be less active, indicating a slowed-down state (Figure 15–6). The left frontal lobe, which serves functions related to positive emotions, is especially likely to be relatively inactive (Davidson, 1992). MRI scans have even shown the frontal lobes to be 7 percent smaller in severely depressed patients (Coffey & others, 1993).

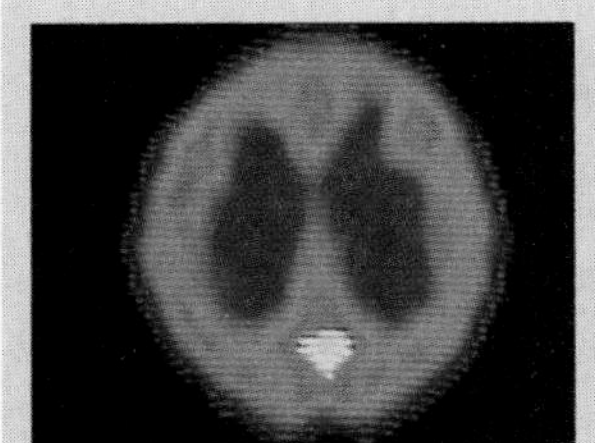

*Depressed state (17-May-83)*

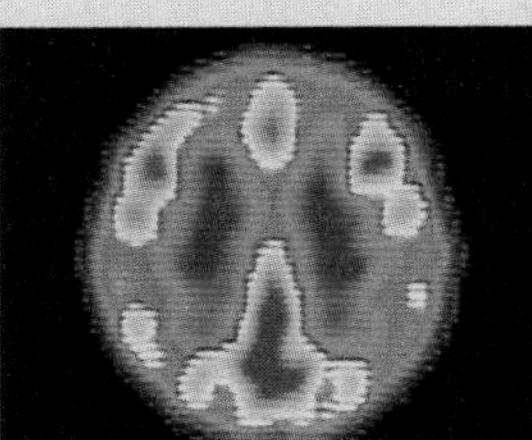

*Manic state (18-May-83)*

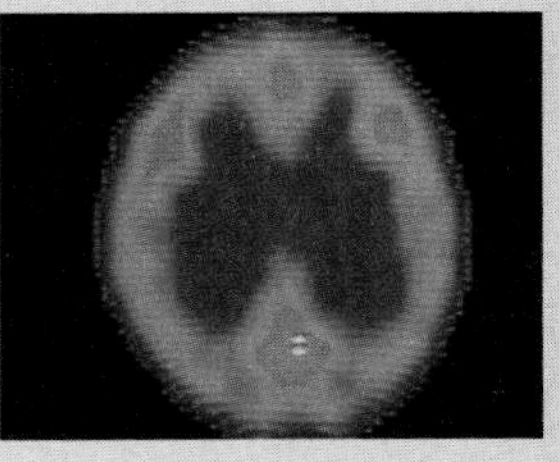

*Depressed state (27-May-83)*

**Figure 15–6**

**The Ups and Downs of Bipolar Disorder** *Brain energy consumption rises and falls with the patient's emotional switches. (PET scans courtesy of Drs. Lewis Baxter and Michael E. Phelps, UCLA School of Medicine.)*

## The Social-Cognitive Perspective

Biological factors do not operate in a social vacuum. As Figure 15–7 suggests, they accompany psychological reactions to experience. The mind's negative thoughts somehow influence biochemical events that in a vicious cycle amplify depressing thoughts.

Recent research reveals how *self-defeating beliefs* feed the vicious cycle. Depressed people view life through dark glasses. Their intensely negative assumptions about themselves, their situations, and their futures lead them to magnify bad experiences and minimize good ones. As one occasionally depressed young woman put it:

> My thoughts become negative and pessimistic. As I look into the past, I become convinced that everything that I've ever done is worthless. Any happy period seems like an illusion. My accomplishments appear as genuine as the false facade of a Western movie. I become convinced that the real me is worthless and inadequate. I can't move forward with my work because I become frozen with doubt (Burns, 1980, pp. 28–29).

Self-defeating beliefs may arise from *learned helplessness*. As we saw in Chapter 14, both dogs and humans act depressed, passive, and withdrawn

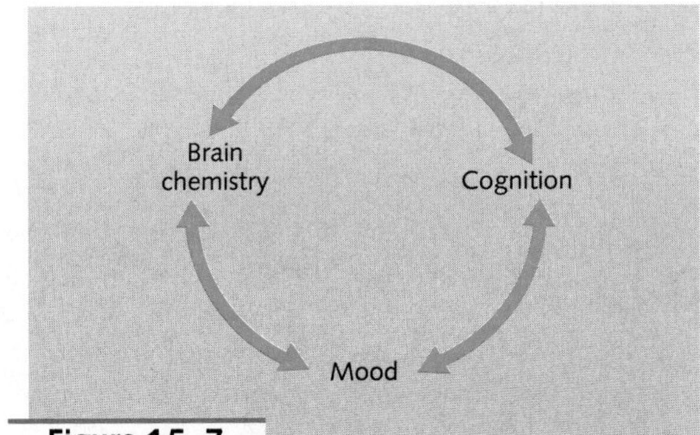


**Figure 15–7**

**Depression—An Ailing Mind in an Ailing Body** *Altering any component of the chemistry-cognition-mood circuit can alter the others.*

after experiencing uncontrollable painful events. Women more often than men have been abused or made to feel helpless, which helps explain why women have been twice as vulnerable to depression as have men (Nolen-Hoeksema, 1990, and see page 517). (Another explanation is that men more often repress their depressed feelings or drown them in alcohol.)

**Maladaptive Explanations Feed Depression** Why do life's unavoidable failures lead some people, but not others, to become depressed? The difference lies partly with people's *attributions* of blame. We have some choice of whom or what to blame for our failures. If you fail a test and blame yourself, you may feel stupid and depressed. If you externalize the blame—perhaps attributing your failure to an unfair test—you are more likely to feel angry.

*"I have learned to accept my mistakes by referring them to a personal history which was not of my making."*

B. F. Skinner (1983)

Depressed people tend to explain bad events in terms that are *stable* ("It's going to last forever"), *global* ("It's going to affect everything I do"), and *internal* ("It's all my fault"). Lyn Abramson, Gerald Metalsky, and Lauren Alloy (1989) theorize that the result of these pessimistic, overgeneralized, self-blaming attributions is a depressing sense of hopelessness.

Drawing by Charles Schulz; © 1956 United Feature Syndicate, Inc.

Martin Seligman (1991) argues that depression is now common among young Americans because of epidemic hopelessness, which stems from the rise of individualism and the decline of commitment to religion and family. When facing failure or rejection, contends Seligman, the self-focused individual takes on personal responsibility for problems and has nothing to fall back on for hope. In non-Western cultures, where close-knit relationships and cooperation are the norm, major depression is less common and less tied to guilt and self-blame over perceived failure. In Japan, for example, depressed people instead tend to report feeling shame over letting down their family or co-workers (Draguns, 1990a).

**Negative Moods Feed Negative Thoughts and Actions** There is, however, a chicken-and-egg problem with the social-cognitive explanation of depression. Self-defeating beliefs, self-blame, and negative attributions surely do support depression. But do they *cause* depression, any more than a speedometer's reading 70 mph causes a car's speed? Peter Barnett and Ian Gotlib (1988) note that such cognitions are better *indicators* than predictors of depression. Depressing thoughts *coincide* with a depressed mood. But before or after being depressed, people's thoughts are less negative. Perhaps this is because, as we noted in our discussion of state-dependent memory (page 310), a depressed mood triggers negative thoughts. If you temporarily put people in a bad or sad mood, their memories, judgments, and expectations are suddenly more pessimistic.

Joseph Forgas and his associates (1984) provided a striking demonstration of the mood effect. Subjects put in a good or bad mood via hypnosis watched a videotape of themselves talking with someone the day before. The happy subjects detected in themselves more instances of positive behavior than of negative; the unhappy subjects more often saw themselves behaving negatively (Figure 15–8). Thus, even when viewing themselves on videotape, people judge themselves more negatively when feeling depressed.

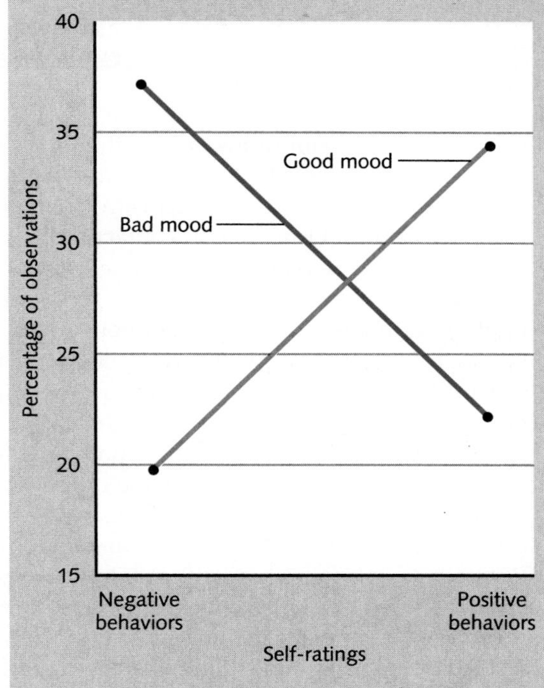


**Figure 15–8**

**The Mood Effect** *A happy or depressed mood strongly influences people's rating of their own behavior. In this experiment, those in a hypnotically induced good mood detected many more positive than negative behaviors. The reverse was true for those in a bad mood. (From Forgas & others, 1984.)*

**Depression's Vicious Cycle** "A recipe for severe depression is preexisting pessimism encountering failure," notes Martin Seligman (1991, p. 78). Depression is often brought on by stressful experiences—losing a job, getting divorced or rejected, physical trauma—anything that disrupts your sense of who you are and why you are a worthy human being (Hamilton & others, 1993; Kendler & others, 1993). Such brooding after failure can be adaptive; insights gained during times of depressed inactivity may later enable better strategies for interacting with the world. But depression-prone people respond to bad events in an especially self-focused, self-blaming way (Pyszczynski & others, 1991; Wood & others, 1990a,b). Their self-esteem fluctuates more rapidly up with boosts and down with threats (Butler & others, 1994). When down, their brooding amplifies negative feelings, which in turn trigger depression's other cognitive and behavioral symptoms.

None of us is immune to the emotions, diminished self-esteem, and negative thinking brought on by rejection or defeat. As Edward Hirt and his colleagues (1992) demonstrated, even small losses can temporarily sour our thinking. They studied some Indiana University basketball fans who seemed to regard the team as an extension of themselves. After the fans were depressed by watching their team lose, or elated by a victory, the researchers asked them to predict the team's future performance, and their own. After a loss, people offered bleaker assessments not only of the team's future, but also of their own likely performance at throwing darts, solving anagrams, and getting a date. When things aren't going our way, it may seem as though they never will.

New evidence suggests there is two-way traffic between depressed mood and negative thinking. Depression causes self-focused negative thinking, and a self-focused, self-blaming style of explaining events puts one at risk for depression when bad events strike. If you tend to see bad grades, social rejection, and work problems as inevitable and your own fault, and if you ruminate about such things, then when bad events happen you will experience a bad case of the blues. In research demonstrating this effect, Susan Nolen-Hoeksema and Jannay Morrow (1991) happened to assess Stanford University students' moods and ruminations 2 weeks before the 1989 earthquake devastated much of their area. Those identified as prone to brood over negative events showed more symptoms of depression both 10 days and 7 weeks after the earthquake. If you have an optimistic way of interpreting events, a failure or stress is unlikely to provoke depression (Seligman, 1991). Even if you do get depressed, you are more likely to recover quickly (Metalsky & others, 1993; Needles & Abramson, 1990).

Another source of depression's vicious cycle is its social consequences. Being withdrawn, self-focused, and complaining elicits rejection (Gotlib & Hammen, 1992; Segrin & Dillard, 1992). In one study, researchers Stephen Strack and James Coyne (1983) noted that "depressed persons induced hostility, depression, and anxiety in others and got rejected. Their guesses that they were not accepted were not a matter of cognitive distortion." Weary of

*"Man never reasons so much and becomes so introspective as when he suffers, since he is anxious to get at the cause of his sufferings."*

Luigi Pirandello
*Six Characters in Search of an Author*, 1922

## Close-Up Loneliness

Loneliness—the painful awareness that one's social relationships are deficient—is both a contributor to depression and its own problem. The deficiency stems from a mismatch between one's actual and desired social contacts. One person may feel lonely when isolated and another may feel lonely in a crowd.

Aloneness often breeds loneliness. People who are alone—unmarried, unattached, and often young—are more likely to feel lonely (Figure 15–9). Dutch psychologist Jenny de Jong-Gierveld (1987) speculates that the current emphasis on individual fulfillment and the downgrading of stable relationships and commitment to others are "loneliness-provoking factors."

People commonly experience one or more of four types of loneliness (Beck & Young, 1978). To be lonely is to feel *excluded* from a group you would like to belong to; to feel *unloved* and uncared about by those around you; to feel *constricted* and unable to share your private concerns with anyone; or to feel *alienated*, or different from, those in your community.

Like depressed people, lonely people tend to blame themselves, attributing their deficient social relationships to their own inadequacies (Snodgrass, 1987). There may be a basis for this self-blame: Chronically lonely people tend to be shy, self-conscious, and lacking in self-esteem, and to be perceived as less socially competent and attractive (Check & Melchior, 1990; Lau & Gruen, 1992; Vaux, 1988). They often find it hard to introduce themselves, make phone calls, and participate in groups (Rook, 1984; Spitzberg & Hurt, 1987). In addition, their belief in their social unworthiness restricts their noticing and remembering positive feedback and from taking steps that would reduce their loneliness (Frankel & Prentice-Dunn, 1990). Thus, factors that work to create and maintain the cycle of depression can also produce a cycle of loneliness.

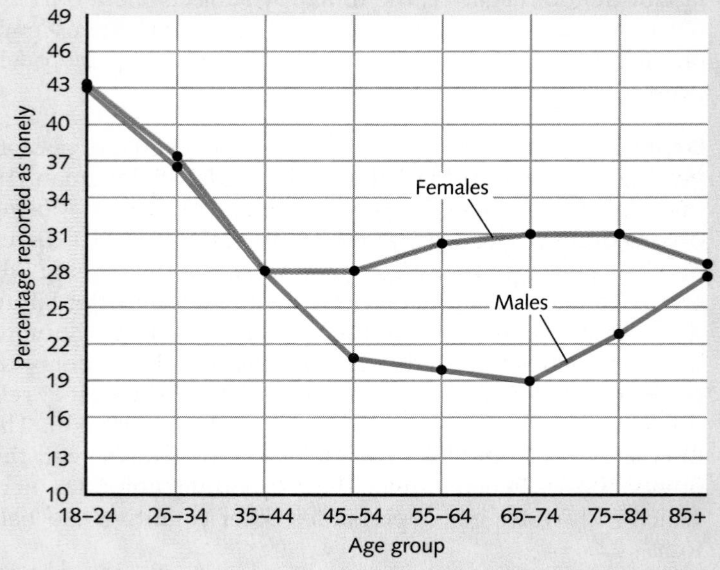


**Figure 15–9**

**Age Differences in Loneliness** *A statistical digest of 14 data sets involving 25,000 people reveals that loneliness is most common among young adults. (From Perlman, 1991.)*

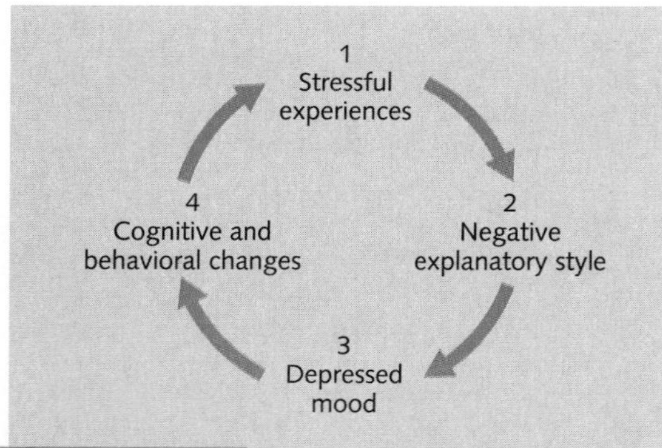


**Figure 15–10**

**The Vicious Cycle of Depression** *This cycle can be broken at any point. The next chapter describes some therapeutic techniques. (Adapted from Lewinsohn & others, 1985.)*

the depressed person's fatigue, hopeless attitude, and lethargy, a spouse may threaten to leave or a boss may begin to question the person's competence. Indeed, depressed people are at high risk for divorce and job loss, thus compounding their depression. Misery may love another's company, but company does not love another's misery.

We can now assemble the pieces of the depression puzzle (Figure 15–10): (1) Stressful events interpreted through (2) a pessimistic explanatory style create (3) a hopeless, depressed state that (4) hampers the way the person thinks and acts. This, in turn, fuels (1) more negative experiences. On the brighter side, one can break the cycle of depression at any of these points—by moving to a different environment, by reversing one's self-blame and negative attributions, by turning one's attention outward, or by engaging in more pleasant activities and more competent behavior.

The several points at which the cycle can be broken enable several different therapeutic methods (Chapter 16). Even without therapy, depression will usually end on its own. Winston Churchill called depression a "black dog" that periodically hounded him. Poet Emily Dickinson was so afraid of bursting into tears in public that she spent much of her adult life in seclusion (Patterson, 1951). Abraham Lincoln was so withdrawn and brooding as a young man that his friends feared he might take his own life (Kline, 1974). As each of these lives reminds us, people can and do struggle through depression. Most regain their capacity to love, to work, and even to succeed at the highest levels.

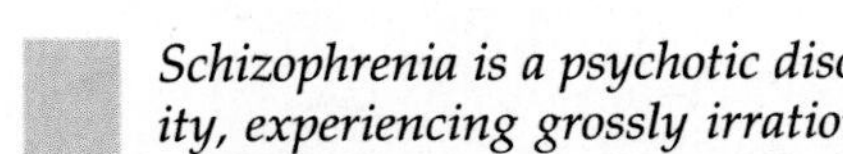


**Major Depressive Disorder** In major depression, the person—without apparent reason—descends for weeks or months into deep unhappiness, lethargy, and feelings of worthlessness before rebounding to normality.

**Bipolar Disorder** In the less common bipolar disorder, the person alternates between the hopelessness and lethargy of depression and the hyperactive, wildly optimistic, impulsive phase of mania.

**Explaining Mood Disorders** Current research on depression is vigorously exploring two sets of influences. The first focuses on genetic predispositions and neurotransmitter abnormalities. The second views the cycle of depression from a social-cognitive perspective, in light of cyclic self-defeating beliefs, learned helplessness, negative attributions, and aversive experiences.

## Schizophrenia Disorders

*Schizophrenia is a psychotic disorder in which a person loses contact with reality, experiencing grossly irrational ideas or distorted perceptions. What forms does schizophrenia take? And what are its possible causes?*

If depression is the common cold of psychological disorders, chronic schizophrenia is the cancer. About 1 in 100 people will develop schizophrenia, joining the millions who have suffered one of humanity's most dreaded disorders. It typically strikes during adolescence or young adulthood. It knows no national boundaries and it affects males and females about equally.

### Symptoms of Schizophrenia

Literally translated, **schizophrenia** means "split mind." It refers not to a multiple-personality split but rather to a split from reality that shows itself in disorganized thinking, disturbed perceptions, and inappropriate emotions and actions.

#### Disorganized Thinking

Imagine trying to communicate with Sylvia Frumkin, a young woman whose thoughts spill out in no logical order. Her biographer, Susan Sheehan (1982, p. 25), observed her saying aloud to no one in particular,

> "This morning, when I was at Hillside [Hospital], I was making a movie. I was surrounded by movie stars. The X-ray technician was Peter Lawford. The security guard was Don Knotts. That Indian doctor in Building 40 was Lou Costello. I'm Mary Poppins. Is this room painted blue to get me upset? My grandmother died four weeks after my eighteenth birthday." Miss Frumkin laughed.

As this strange monologue illustrates, the schizophrenia patient's thinking is fragmented, bizarre, and distorted by false beliefs, called **delusions** ("I'm Mary Poppins"). Jumping from one idea to another may occur even within sentences, creating a sort of "word salad." One young man begged for "a little more allegro in the treatment," and suggested that "liberationary movement with a view to the widening of the horizon" will "ergo extort some wit in lectures."

Many psychologists believe disorganized thoughts result from a breakdown in selective attention. Recall from Chapter 6 that we normally have a remarkable capacity for selective attention—for, say, giving our undivided attention to one voice at a party while filtering out competing sensory stimuli. Schizophrenia sufferers have impaired attention (Gjerde, 1983). Thus, an irrelevant stimulus or an extraneous part of the preceding thought easily distracts them. As one former schizophrenia patient recalled, "What had happened to me . . . was a breakdown in the filter, and a hodge-podge of unrelated stimuli were distracting me from things which should have had my undivided attention" (MacDonald, 1960, p. 218).

### Disturbed Perceptions

The schizophrenia victim experiences an altered world. Minute stimuli, such as the grooves on a brick or the inflections of a voice, may distract attention from the whole scene or from the speaker's meaning. Worse, the person may perceive things that are not there.

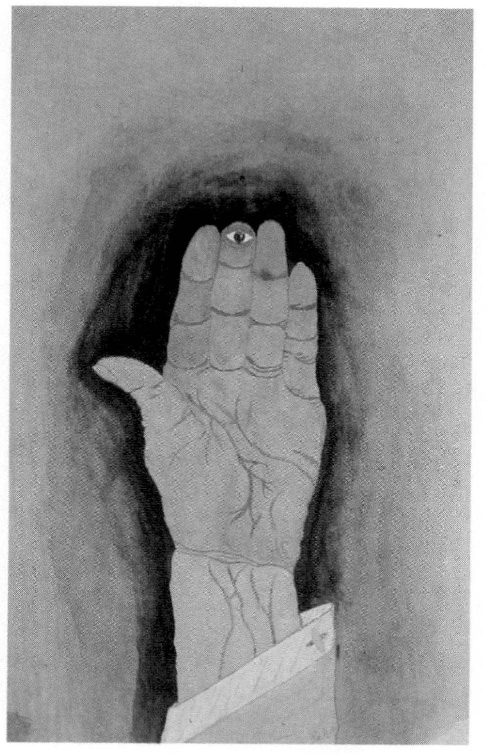

**Art by People Diagnosed With Schizophrenia** *Commenting on the kind of artwork shown here, poet John Ashbery wrote: "The lure of the work is strong, but so is the terror of the unanswerable riddles it proposes."*

Such *hallucinations* (sensory experiences without sensory stimulation) are usually auditory. The person may hear voices that seem to come from outside the head and that make insulting statements or give orders. The voices may tell the patient that she is bad or that he must burn himself with a cigarette lighter or even commit murder. Less commonly, people see, feel, taste, or smell things that are nonexistent. Such hallucinations have been compared to dreams breaking into waking consciousness. When the unreal seems real, the resulting perceptions are at best bizarre and at worst terrifying.

### Inappropriate Emotions and Actions

The emotions of schizophrenia are often utterly inappropriate. Sylvia Frumkin's emotions seemed split off from reality. She laughed after recalling her grandmother's death. On occasion, she became angry for no apparent reason or cried when others laughed. Other victims of schizophrenia sometimes lapse into *flat affect*, a zombielike state of apparent apathy.

Motor behavior also may be inappropriate. The person may perform senseless, compulsive acts, such as continually rocking or rubbing an arm. Those who exhibit *catatonia* may remain motionless for hours on end and then become agitated.

As you can imagine, disorganized thinking, disturbed perceptions, and inappropriate emotions and actions disrupt social relationships. During their most severe periods, schizophrenia sufferers live in a private inner world, preoccupied with illogical ideas and unreal images. Although some people suffer from schizophrenia only intermittently, others remain socially withdrawn and isolated throughout much of their lives. Rarely is schizophrenia a one-time episode that is "cured," never to return.

## Types of Schizophrenia

We have described schizophrenia as if it were a single disorder. Actually, it is a cluster of disorders that have common features but also some distinguishing symptoms. Schizophrenia patients with *positive symptoms* are disorganized and deluded in their talk or prone to inappropriate laughter, tears, or rage. Schizophrenia patients with *negative symptoms* have toneless voices, expressionless faces, or mute and rigid bodies. Because schizophrenia is more than one disorder, there could be more than one cause.

Sometimes, as in the case of Sylvia Frumkin, schizophrenia develops gradually, emerging from a long history of social inadequacy (which partially explains why those predisposed to schizophrenia often end up in the lower socioeconomic levels, or even as homeless people). Other times it appears suddenly, seemingly as a reaction to stress. There is a rule that holds true around the world (World Health Organization, 1979): When the schizophrenia is a slow-developing process (called *chronic*, or *process*, schizophrenia), recovery is doubtful. When, in reaction to particular life stresses, a previously well-adjusted person develops schizophrenia rapidly (*acute*, or *reactive*, schizophrenia), recovery is much more likely. Those with chronic schizophrenia often exhibit the negative symptoms of withdrawal. The outlook is better for those exhibiting positive symptoms, who more often have a reactive condition that responds to drug therapy (Fenton & McGlashan, 1991, 1994; Fowles, 1992).

## Understanding Schizophrenia

Schizophrenia is not only the most dreaded psychological disorder but also one of the most heavily researched. At the 1993 International Congress on Schizophrenia, more than 70 percent of the new research studies explored the biology of schizophrenia (Iacono & Grove, 1993). Important new discoveries link schizophrenia with brain abnormalities and genetic predispositions.

### Brain Abnormalities

The idea that imbalances in brain chemistry might underlie schizophrenia has long intrigued scientists. Strange behaviors, they knew, could have strange chemical causes. The saying "mad as a hatter" refers to the psychological deterioration of British hatmakers whose brains, it was later discovered, were slowly poisoned as they moistened the brims of mercury-laden felt hats with their lips (Smith, 1983). As we saw on page 245, scientists are beginning to understand the mechanism by which chemicals such as LSD produce hallucinations. These discoveries hint that schizophrenia might have a biochemical key.

One such key to schizophrenia involves the neurotransmitter dopamine. When researchers examined patients' brains after death, they found an excess of receptors for dopamine—in fact, a sixfold excess for the so-called D4 dopamine receptor (Seeman & others, 1993; Wong & others, 1986). Such a high level may intensify brain signals, the researchers speculate, creating schizophrenia's positive symptoms. As we might therefore expect, drugs that block dopamine receptors often lessen schizophrenia symptoms. Drugs that increase dopamine levels, such as amphetamines and cocaine, sometimes intensify schizophrenia symptoms (Swerdlow & Koob, 1987). Such dopamine overactivity may be what makes schizophrenia victims overreact to irrelevant external and internal stimuli.

Modern brain-scanning techniques reveal that many chronic schizophrenia patients have abnormal brain tissue. Some have abnormally low brain activity in the frontal lobes (Pettegrew & others, 1993; Resnick, 1992). Others, most often men, have enlarged, fluid-filled areas and a corresponding shrinkage of cerebral tissue (Gur & others, 1991; Van Horn & McManus, 1992). The greater the shrinkage, the worse the thought disorder often is (Shenton & others, 1992). It remains for future research, however, to link specific brain abnormalities to specific schizophrenia symptoms (Heinrichs, 1993).

Naturally, scientists wonder what causes these brain abnormalities. One possibility is a prenatal problem, such as a midpregnancy viral infection that might impair development of the fetal brain (Waddington, 1993). Can you imagine some ways to test this fetal virus idea? Scientists exploring this possibility have asked the following questions:

- ***Are people at increased risk of schizophrenia if, during the middle of their fetal development, their country experienced a flu epidemic?*** The repeated answer is yes (Mednick & others, 1994; Murray & others, 1992).
- ***Are those born during the winter and spring months—after the fall-winter flu season—also at increased risk?*** The answer is yes, at 5 to 15 percent increased risk (Pulver & others, 1992; Torrey & others, 1977, 1993; Wright & Murray, 1993).
- ***In the southern hemisphere, where the seasons are the reverse of the northern hemisphere, are the months of excess schizophrenia births similarly reversed?*** Again, the answer is yes. In Australia, for example, people born between August and October are at greater risk—unless they migrated from the northern hemisphere, in which case their risk is greater if born between January and March (McGrath & others, 1994).
- ***As infectious disease rates have declined, has there been a correlated decline in the later incidence of schizophrenia?*** Once again, the answer is yes (Eagles, 1991).

Although schizophrenia has other causes as well (as genetics research makes plain), these converging lines of evidence suggest that prenatal viral infections do play a contributing role.

### Genetic Factors

Might people also inherit a predisposition to certain brain abnormalities? The evidence strongly suggests that some do. The 1 in 100 odds of any person's being diagnosed with schizophrenia become 1 in 10 among those who have an afflicted sibling or parent, and close to 1 in 2 among those who have an afflicted identical twin (Figure 15–11). Although there are only a dozen such known cases, it appears that an identical twin of a schizophrenia victim retains that 1 in 2 chance whether they are reared together or apart.

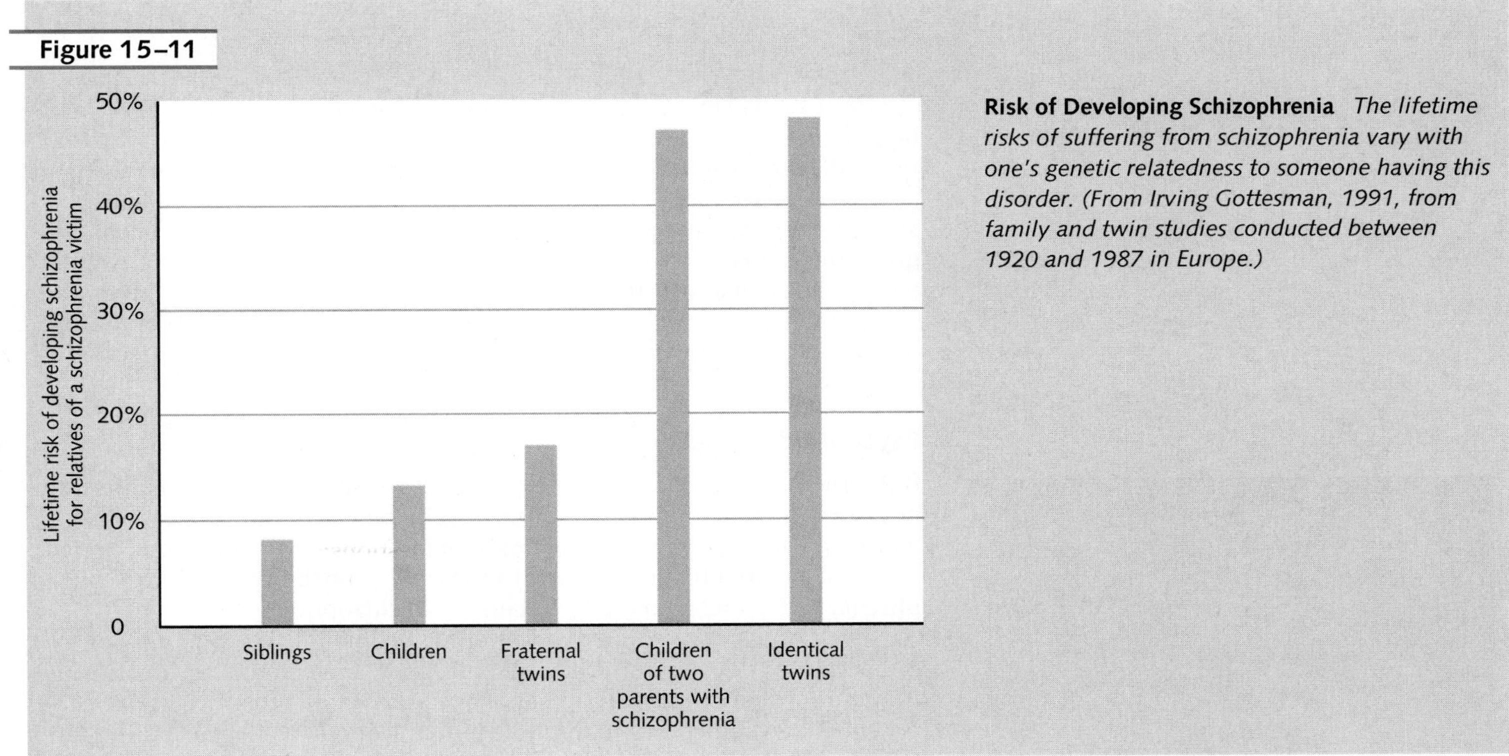


**Risk of Developing Schizophrenia** *The lifetime risks of suffering from schizophrenia vary with one's genetic relatedness to someone having this disorder. (From Irving Gottesman, 1991, from family and twin studies conducted between 1920 and 1987 in Europe.)*

Adoption studies confirm a genetic link (Gottesman, 1991). Children adopted by someone who develops schizophrenia are unlikely to "catch" the disorder. Rather, adopted children have an elevated risk if a biological parent is diagnosed with schizophrenia.

The genetic contribution to schizophrenia is beyond question. But the genetic role is not so straightforward as the inheritance of eye color. After all, about half the twins who share identical genes with a schizophrenia victim do *not* develop the disorder. Thus, behavior geneticists Susan Nicol and Irving Gottesman (1983) concluded that some people "have a genetic predisposition to the disorder but that this predisposition by itself is not sufficient for the development of schizophrenia."

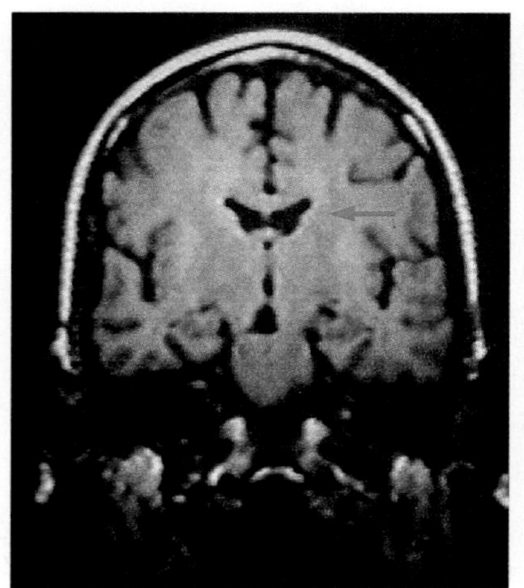

No schizophrenia

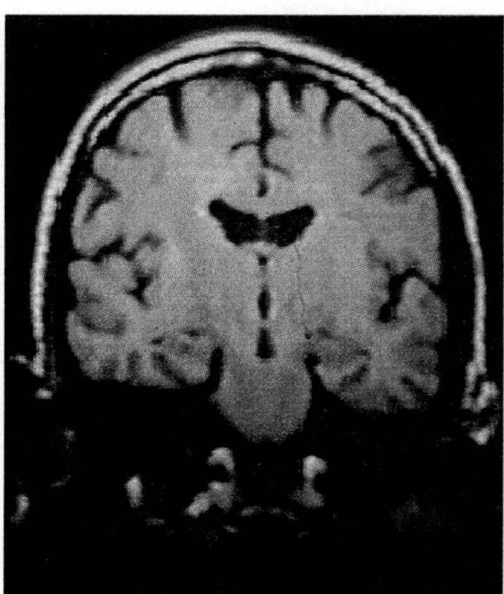

Schizophrenia

**Schizophrenia in Twins** *When twins differ, only the one afflicted with schizophrenia typically has enlarged, fluid-filled cranial cavities (Suddath & others, 1990). The difference between the twins implies some nongenetic factor, such as a virus, is also at work.*

Given the genetic influences upon disorders such as schizophrenia and bipolar disorder, might scientists develop genetic tests that reveal who is at risk? (We do know, for example, that genes influence the excess of one type of dopamine receptor—Anderson, 1994.) If so, might it be possible to prescribe treatments that prevent the disorder? Although hopes for such tests grow, the patterns of inheritance seem too complex to hope that a single gene abnormality will prove predictive (Gottesman, 1993). But given the explosion in gene and brain research technologies, scientists are optimistic that schizophrenia will be much better understood before this "decade of the brain" is over.

## Psychological Factors

If, by themselves, genetically predisposed physiological abnormalities do not cause schizophrenia, neither do psychological factors alone. As Nicol and Gottesman report, "No environmental causes have been discovered that will invariably, or even with moderate probability, produce schizophrenia in persons who are not related to a schizophrenic."

Nevertheless, if genes predispose some people to *react* to particular experiences by developing schizophrenia, then there must be identifiable triggering experiences. Researchers have asked: Can stress trigger schizophrenia? Can difficulties in family communications be a contributing factor?

**The Genain Quadruplets** *The odds of any four people picked at random all being diagnosed with schizophrenia are 1 in 100 million. But Nora, Iris, Myra, and Hester Genain have the disease. Two of the sisters have more severe forms of the disorder than the others, suggesting the influence of environmental as well as biological factors.*

The answer to each question is a strong maybe. The psychological triggers of schizophrenia have proved elusive, partly because they may vary with the type of schizophrenia and whether it is a slow-developing, chronic schizophrenia, or a sudden, acute reaction to stress. It is true that young people with schizophrenia tend to have unusually disturbed communications with their parents. But is this a cause or a result of their disorder? It is true that stressful experiences, biochemical abnormalities, and schizophrenia's symptoms often occur together. But the traffic between brain biochemistry and psychological experiences runs both ways, so cause and effect are difficult to sort out. It is true that schizophrenic withdrawal often occurs in adolescence or early adulthood, coinciding with the stresses of having to become independent, assert oneself, and achieve social success and intimacy. So is schizophrenia the maladaptive coping reaction of biologically vulnerable people?

Hoping to identify the psychological causes of schizophrenia, several in-

## *Close-Up* Experiencing Schizophrenia

*These recollections by a recovered schizophrenia patient illustrate the symptoms often experienced by those who suffer the positive symptoms of schizophrenia. Note the hallucinations and the delusions of persecution and grandeur.*

One night I was invited to listen to a talk by a worker in the foreign service. I was suspicious of him and thought he thought I was a Communist spy. I didn't say anything. I just leaned over and stared at him.

I thought the Government was spying on my room with a telescope in a building across the street. I thought people were loading down my food in the cafeteria with salt. In criminology class I thought the professor and the other students were laughing about me. I thought they were directing the poisoning of my food in the cafeteria. When I went to the cafeteria my hand shook as the waitress poured what I thought was poisonous coffee into my cup. I thought everyone in the cafeteria knew I was going to die. They all thought it was too bad but I was so evil it was necessary.

On a Saturday I drank lemonade to try to neutralize the poison. Then I would take showers to try to sweat the poison out. I was so nervous I could hardly think. I thought I might only have hours left to live. I thought of taking a bus home to my parents. But no, I thought, it was too late for that.

One day when my strange behavior landed me in a jail cell, the walls began to buzz like bees. I felt there were thousands of bees in the walls buzzing. The buzzing went on and on. There was no relief. It was maddening. Finally, I felt my father's hand rest on my head and I felt peace. Then voices, like the roar of a crowd came. I felt like Jesus; I was being crucified. Night settled in. It was dark. I just continued to huddle under the blanket, feeling weak, laid bare and defenseless in a cruel world I could no longer understand.

When someone asks me to explain schizophrenia I tell them, you know how sometimes in your dreams you are in them yourself and some of them feel like real nightmares? My schizophrenia was like I was walking through a dream. But everything around me was real. At times, today's world seems so boring and I wonder if I would like to step back into the schizophrenic dream, but then I remember all the scary and horrifying experiences. (Excerpted with permission from S. Emmons and C. Geiser, *Adventures in Schizophrenia*, unpublished manuscript.)

vestigators are now following the development of "high-risk" children, such as those born to a parent with schizophrenia (Asarnow, 1988; Cannon & Mednick, 1991; King, 1990). By comparing the experiences of high- and low-risk children who do and do not develop schizophrenia, they are seeking the early warning signs of schizophrenia. So far, these warning signs seem to include

- a mother whose schizophrenia was severe and long-lasting;
- birth complications and low birth weight;
- separation from parents;
- short attention span and poor muscle coordination;
- disruptive or withdrawn behavior.

Most of us can relate more easily to the ups and downs of mood disorders than to the strange thoughts, perceptions, and behaviors of schizophrenia. Sometimes our thoughts do jump around, but we do not talk nonsensically. Occasionally we feel unjustly suspicious of someone, but we do not fear that the world is plotting against us. Often our perceptions err, but rarely do we see or hear things that are not there. We have felt regret after laughing at someone's misfortune, but we rarely giggle in response to bad news. At times we just want to be alone, but we do not live in social isolation. However, millions of people around the world do talk strangely, suffer delusions, hear nonexistent voices, see things that are not there, laugh or cry at inappropriate times, or withdraw into their private imaginary worlds. Because this is true, the quest to solve the cruel puzzle of schizophrenia continues.

## Summing Up

Schizophrenia typically strikes during adolescence. It affects men and women about equally, and it seems to occur in all cultures.

**Symptoms of Schizophrenia** Schizophrenia shows itself in disorganized thinking (nonsensical talk and delusions, which may stem from a breakdown of selective attention); disturbed perceptions (including hallucinations); and inappropriate emotions and actions. It is rarely a one-time episode.

**Types of Schizophrenia** Schizophrenia is a set of disorders that emerge either gradually from a long history of social inadequacy (in which case the outlook is dim) or suddenly in reaction to stress (in which case the prospects for recovery are brighter).

**Understanding Schizophrenia** As they have for depression, researchers have linked certain forms of schizophrenia with brain abnormalities, such as enlarged, fluid-filled cerebral cavities or increased receptors for the neurotransmitter dopamine. Twin and adoption studies also point to a genetic predisposition that, in conjunction with environmental factors, may bring about a schizophrenia disorder.

## Personality Disorders

*Some maladaptive behavior patterns impair people's social functioning without anxiety, depression, or delusions. For society the most troubling of these is the antisocial personality disorder.*

*Does a full moon trigger "madness" in some people? James Rotton and I. W. Kelly (1985) examined data from 37 studies that related lunar phase to crime, homicides, crisis calls, and mental hospital admissions. Their conclusion: There is virtually no evidence of "moon madness." Nor does lunar phase correlate with suicides, assaults, emergency room visits, or traffic disasters (Byrnes & Kelly, 1992; Kelly & others, 1990; Martin & others, 1992).*

**Personality disorders**—inflexible and enduring patterns of behavior that impair one's social functioning—sometimes coexist with one of the other psychological disorders, but they need not involve anxiety, depression, or loss of contact with reality. A person with a *histrionic personality disorder* displays a shallow, attention-getting emotionality. Histrionic individuals go to great lengths to gain others' praise and reassurance. Those with *narcissistic personality disorder* exaggerate their own importance, aided by success fantasies. They find criticism hard to accept, often reacting with rage or shame. Those with *borderline personality disorder* have an unstable identity, unstable relationships, and unstable emotions. If personality is one's enduring pattern of thinking, feeling, and acting, then a markedly unstable sense of self defines a "borderline personality."

The most frequent of these disorders, and the most troubling to society, is the **antisocial personality** disorder. The person (formerly called a *sociopath* or a *psychopath*) is typically a male whose lack of conscience becomes plain before age 15, as he begins to lie, steal, fight, or display unrestrained sexual behavior. About half of such children become antisocial adults—unable to keep a job, irresponsible as a spouse and parent, and assaultive or otherwise criminal (Farrington, 1991). When the antisocial personality combines a keen intelligence with amorality, the result may be a charming and clever con artist—or worse.

Despite their antisocial behavior, most criminals do not fit the description of antisocial personality disorder. Most criminals show responsible concern for their friends and family members; antisocial personalities feel little and fear little. In extreme cases, the results can be tragic. Henry Lee Lucas reported that at age 13 he strangled a woman who refused to have sex with him. He at one time confessed to having bludgeoned, suffocated, stabbed, shot, or mutilated some 360 women, men, and children during his 32 years of crime. During the last 6 years of his reign of terror, Lucas teamed with Elwood Toole, who reportedly slaughtered about 50 people whom he "didn't think was worth living anyhow." It ended when Lucas confessed to stabbing and dismembering his 15-year-old common-law wife, who was Toole's niece.

The antisocial personality expresses little regret over violating others' rights. "Once I've done a crime, I just forget it," said Lucas. Toole was equally matter-of-fact: "I think of killing like smoking a cigarette, like another habit" (Darrach & Norris, 1984).

As with mood disorders and schizophrenia, the antisocial personality disorder is woven of biological as well as psychological strands. Although there is no single gene that codes for a complex behavior such as crime, twin and adoption studies reveal that biological relatives of certain individuals are at increased risk for criminality (DiLalla & Gottesman, 1991; Brennan & Mednick, 1993). Their genetic vulnerability surfaces as minimal arousal under stress, which makes for a rather fearless approach to life. When they await aversive events, such as electric shocks or loud noises, they show little autonomic nervous system arousal (Hare, 1975). Even as youngsters, before committing any crime, they react with lower levels of stress hormones than do others their age (Figure 15–12). If channeled in more productive directions, such fearlessness may lead to courageous heroism or adventurism. Lacking a sense of social responsibility, the same disposition produces a cool con artist or killer (Lykken, 1982).

Perhaps a biologically-based fearlessness, as well as early environment, helps explain the reunion of long-separated sisters Joyce Lott, 27, and Mary Jones, 29—in a South Carolina prison where both were sent on drug charges. After a newspaper story about their reunion, their long-lost half-brother Frank Strickland called. He explained it would be a while before he could come see them—because he, too, was in jail, on drug, burglary, and larceny charges (Shepherd & others, 1990).

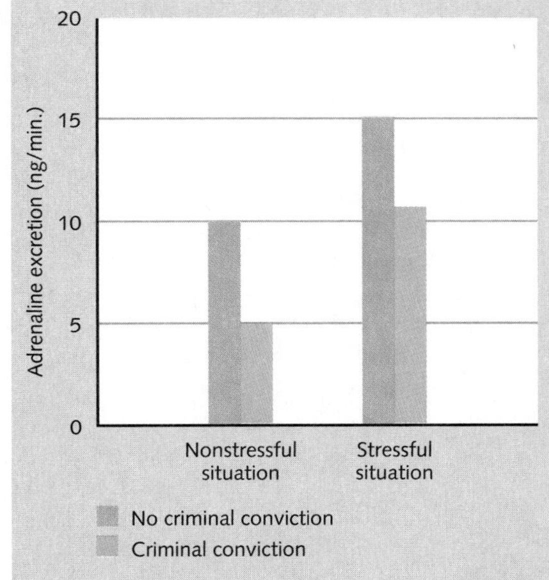


**Figure 15–12**

**Arousability and Risk of Crime** *Levels of the stress hormone adrenaline were measured in two groups of 13-year-old Swedish boys. In both stressful and nonstressful situations, those who were later convicted of a crime (as 18- to 26-year-olds) showed relatively low reactivity. (From Magnusson, 1990.)*

## Summing Up

Personality disorders are enduring, maladaptive patterns of behavior that impair social functioning. For society, the most troubling of these is the remorseless and fearless antisocial personality.

## The Commonality of Psychological Disorders

*How prevalent are the different psychological disorders? Does risk of specific disorder vary with one's ethnicity or gender?*

How prevalent are the various disorders discussed in this chapter? Who is most vulnerable to them? At what times of life? To answer such questions, the National Institute of Mental Health (NIMH) undertook during the 1980s a short census of psychological disorders in America. In five different regions of the country researchers conducted lengthy, structured interviews with a representative sample of people—all told, nearly 20,000 people—and then projected their findings to the entire U.S. population. After asking hundreds of questions that probed for symptoms—"Has there ever been a period of 2 weeks or more when you felt like you wanted to die?"—the researchers estimated both the current and the lifetime prevalence of various disorders.

How many people suffer, or have suffered, a psychological disorder? More than most of us suppose. Reporting on the NIMH study, Lee Robins and Darrel Regier (1991, p. 329) note that "one or more of the psychiatric disorders described in this volume had been experienced at some time in their lives by 32% of American adults, and 20% had an active disorder." These surprisingly high rates reflect the inclusion of institutionalized as well as community samples, and surely also reflect how well many people manage to hide disorders such as a phobia, alcohol abuse, or depression. Table 15–2 shows the relative prevalence of most of the disorders we have considered among three ethnic groups and among men and women. As you can see, despite differences in their rates of various psychological disorders, all these groups are vulnerable.

**Table 15–2** **Percentage of Americans Who Have Ever Experienced Psychological Disorders**

| | Ethnicity | | | Gender | | |
|---|---|---|---|---|---|---|
| | White | Black | Hispanic | Men | Women | Totals |
| Alcohol abuse or dependence | 13.6% | 13.8% | 16.7% | 23.8% | 4.6% | 13.8% |
| Generalized anxiety | 3.4 | 6.1 | 3.7 | 2.4 | 5.0 | 3.8 |
| Phobic disorder | 9.7 | 23.4 | 12.2 | 10.4 | 17.7 | 14.3 |
| Obsessive-compulsive disorder | 2.6 | 2.3 | 1.8 | 2.0 | 3.0 | 2.6 |
| Mood disorder | 8.0 | 6.3 | 7.8 | 5.2 | 10.2 | 7.8 |
| Schizophrenic disorders | 1.4 | 2.1 | 0.8 | 1.2 | 1.7 | 1.5 |
| Antisocial personality | 2.6 | 2.3 | 3.4 | 4.5 | 0.8 | 2.6 |

*Source:* Data from Robins & Regier, 1991. Similar gender differences, though with somewhat higher rates of disorder, come from the U.S. National Comorbidity Survey (Kessler & others, 1994).

The incidence of serious psychological disorders is doubly high among those below the poverty line (Centers for Disease Control, 1992). Like so many other correlations, the poverty-disorder association raises a chicken-and-egg question: Does poverty cause disorders? Or do disorders cause poverty? It's both, though the answer varies with the disorder. Schizophrenia understandably leads to poverty. Yet the stresses and demoralization of poverty can also precipitate disorders, especially depression in women and antisocial personality and substance abuse in men (Dohrenwend & others, 1992).

Those who experience a psychological disorder usually do so by early adulthood. "Over 75% of our sample with any disorder had experienced its first symptoms by age 24," report Robins and Regier (1991, p. 331). The symptoms of antisocial personality and of phobic disorder appear earliest, by a median age of 8 and 10, respectively. Symptoms of alcohol abuse, obsessive-compulsive disorder, bipolar disorder, and schizophrenia appear at a median age near 20. Major depression often hits somewhat later, at a median age of 25. Such findings make clear the need for research and treatment to help the growing number of people, especially youth and young adults, who suffer the bewilderment and pain of a psychological disorder.

### Summing Up

A 1980s National Institute of Mental Health survey of nearly 20,000 institutionalized and community residents revealed that 1 in 3 American adults has experienced a psychological disorder, and that 1 in 5 does so currently. The three most common disorders are phobic disorder and mood disorder (with women outnumbering men 2 to 1) and alcohol abuse or dependence (with men outnumbering women 5 to 1).

## Labeling People: The Power of Preconceptions

*Why do clinicians label patients with different diagnoses? Why do some psychologists criticize such labeling?*

As noted earlier, the practice of attaching diagnostic labels to people is controversial. Most clinicians believe that classification helps in describing, treating, and researching the causes of psychological disorders. Critics, however, say that these labels are at best arbitrary and at worst value judgments that, thanks to the medical model, masquerade as science. It is better, they say, to study the roots of specific symptoms, such as delusions or hallucinations, than to study catchall categories, such as schizophrenia (Persons, 1986). Moreover, once we label a person, we view that person differently (Farina, 1982). Labels create preconceptions that can bias our perceptions and interpretations.

In the most controversial demonstration of the biasing power of diagnostic labels, David Rosenhan (1973) and seven of his friends and Stanford University colleagues went to mental hospital admissions offices, complaining of "hearing voices" that were saying "empty," "hollow," and "thud." Apart from this complaint and giving false names and occupations, they truthfully answered all the questions. All eight were diagnosed as psychotic, seven of them as suffering schizophrenia.

That these normal people were misdiagnosed is not surprising. As one psychiatrist noted, if someone swallowed blood, went to an emergency room, and spat it up, would we fault the doctor for diagnosing a bleeding ulcer? What followed was more startling. After admission, the "patients" exhibited no further symptoms. Yet the clinicians were able to "discover" the causes of their disorders after analyzing their (quite normal) life histories. One person was said to be reacting to mixed emotions about his parents. Furthermore, before being released (an average of 19 days later), the "patients'" normal behaviors, such as taking notes, were often misinterpreted as symptoms.

*"One of the unpardonable sins, in the eyes of most people, is for a man to go about unlabelled. The world regards such a person as the police do an unmuzzled dog, not under proper control."*

T. H. Huxley
*Evolution and Ethics*, 1893

Other studies confirm that labels affect how we perceive one another. Ellen Langer and her colleagues (1974, 1980) had people rate an interviewee they thought was either normal (a job applicant) or out of the ordinary (a psychiatric or cancer patient). All subjects saw the identical videotape. Those who watched unlabeled interviewees perceived them as normal; those who watched supposed patients perceived them as "different from most people." Therapists (who thought they were evaluating a psychiatric patient) perceived the interviewee as "frightened of his own aggressive impulses," a "passive, dependent type," and so forth. A label can serve a useful purpose. But as Rosenhan discovered, it can also have "a life and an influence of its own."

Labels can also stigmatize people in others' eyes. U.S. Senator Thomas Eagleton experienced this in 1972, when he was dumped as the Democratic party's vice-presidential candidate after it was discovered he had been treated for depression with electroshock therapy. The same stigma surfaced when a female associate of psychologist Stewart Page (1977) called 180 people in Toronto who were advertising furnished rooms for rent. When she merely asked if the room was still available, the answer was nearly always yes. When she said she was about to be released from a mental hospital, the answer three times out of four was no (as it was when she said she was calling for her brother who was about to be released from jail). When some of those who answered no were called by a second person who simply asked if the room was still available, the advertiser nearly always revealed that it was. Surveys in Western Europe have uncovered similar attitudes toward those labeled mentally ill.

If people form their impressions of psychological disorder from the media, such findings are hardly surprising. Television researcher George Gerbner (1985) reports that 1 in 5 prime-time and daytime programs depicts a psychologically disordered person, and 7 in 10 such programs portray this character as violent or criminal. Movies, too, stereotype mental patients, sometimes as homicidal (Anthony Hopkins in *Silence of the Lambs*), or as "zoo specimens" (Woody Allen in *Zelig*) (Hyler & others, 1991; Wahl, 1992). A few schizophrenia-prone people do commit crimes, and some disordered people are amoral and antisocial (Monahan, 1992; Phillips & others, 1988; Silverton, 1988). However, at least 9 in 10 disordered people are *not* dangerous; instead, they are anxious, depressed, or withdrawn.

Labels not only bias perceptions, they can also change reality. When teachers are told certain students are "gifted," when students expect someone to be "hostile," or when interviewers check to see whether someone is "extraverted," they may act in ways that elicit the very behavior expected (Snyder, 1984). Someone who was led to think you are nasty may treat you coldly, provoking you to respond as a nasty person would. Labels can serve as self-fulfilling prophecies.

But let us also remember the benefits of diagnostic labels. As Robert Spitzer (1975), a chief author of the current diagnostic system explains:

> There is a purpose to psychiatric diagnosis. It is to enable mental health professionals to (a) communicate with each other about the subject matter of their concern, (b) comprehend the pathological processes involved in psychiatric illness, and (c) control psychiatric outcomes.

We need not dismiss psychological labels in order to be encouraged by the many successful people—including Leonardo da Vinci, Isaac Newton, and Leo Tolstoy—who pursued brilliant careers while enduring psychological difficulties. The bewilderment, fear, and sorrow caused by psychological disorders are real. But, as the next chapter shows, hope is also real.

## Summing Up

Diagnostic labels facilitate mental health professionals' communications and research. Critics point out that we pay a price for these benefits. Labels also create preconceptions that bias our perceptions of people's past and present behavior and unfairly stigmatize them.

## Terms and Concepts to Remember

### Perspectives on Psychological Disorders

**psychological disorder** A condition in which behavior is judged atypical, disturbing, maladaptive, and unjustifiable.

**medical model** The concept that diseases have physical causes that can be diagnosed, treated, and, in most cases, cured. When applied to psychological disorders, the medical model assumes that these "mental" illnesses can be diagnosed on the basis of their symptoms and cured through therapy, which may include treatment in a psychiatric hospital.

**DSM-IV** The American Psychiatric Association's *Diagnostic and Statistical Manual of Mental Disorders (Fourth Edition)*, a widely used system for classifying psychological disorders.

**neurotic disorders** Former term for psychological disorders that are usually distressing but allow one to think rationally and function socially. Freud saw the neurotic disorders as ways of dealing with anxiety.

**psychotic disorders** Psychological disorders in which a person loses contact with reality, experiencing irrational ideas and distorted perceptions.

### Anxiety Disorders

**anxiety disorders** Psychological disorders characterized by distressing, persistent anxiety or maladaptive behaviors that reduce anxiety. See *generalized anxiety disorder*, *obsessive-compulsive disorder*, *panic attack*, and *phobic disorder*.

**generalized anxiety disorder** An anxiety disorder in which a person is continually tense, apprehensive, and in a state of autonomic nervous system arousal.

**phobic disorder** An anxiety disorder marked by a persistent, irrational fear of a specific object or situation.

**obsessive-compulsive disorder** An anxiety disorder characterized by unwanted repetitive thoughts (obsessions) and/or actions (compulsions).

**panic attack** An anxiety disorder marked by a minutes-long episode of intense dread in which a person experiences terror and accompanying chest pain, choking, or other frightening sensations.

### Somatoform Disorders

**somatoform disorders** Psychological disorders in which the symptoms take a somatic (bodily) form without apparent physical cause. See *conversion disorder* and *hypochondriasis*.

**conversion disorder** A rare somatoform disorder in which a person experiences very specific genuine physical symptoms for which no physiological basis can be found.

**hypochondriasis** A somatoform disorder in which a person misinterprets normal physical sensations as symptoms of a disease.

### Dissociative Disorders

**dissociative disorders** Disorders in which conscious awareness becomes separated (dissociated) from previous memories, thoughts, and feelings. See *amnesia*, *fugue*, and *multiple personality*.

**amnesia** Loss of memory. Psychogenic amnesia, a dissociative disorder, is selective memory loss often brought on by extreme stress.

**fugue** [fewg] A dissociative disorder in which flight from one's home and identity accompanies amnesia.

**multiple personality disorder** A rare dissociative disorder in which a person exhibits two or more distinct and alternating personalities.

### Mood Disorders

**mood disorders** Psychological disorders characterized by emotional extremes. See *bipolar disorder*, *major depressive disorder*, and *mania*.

**major depressive disorder** A mood disorder in which a person, for no apparent reason, experiences 2 or more weeks of depressed moods, feelings of worthlessness, and diminished interest or pleasure in most activities.

**bipolar disorder** A mood disorder in which the person alternates between the hopelessness and lethargy of depression and the overexcited state of mania.

**mania** A mood disorder marked by a hyperactive, wildly optimistic state.

### Schizophrenia Disorders

**schizophrenia** A group of severe psychotic disorders characterized by disorganized and deluded thinking, disturbed perceptions, and inappropriate emotions and actions.

**delusions** False beliefs, often of persecution or grandeur, that may accompany psychotic disorders.

### Personality Disorders

**personality disorders** Psychological disorders characterized by inflexible and enduring behavior patterns that impair social functioning.

**antisocial personality** A personality disorder in which the person (usually a man) exhibits a lack of conscience for wrongdoing, even toward friends and family members. May be aggressive and ruthless or a clever con artist.

## Critical Thinking Exercise

Now that you have read and reviewed Chapter 15, take your learning a step further by testing your critical thinking skills on the following perspective taking exercise.

> Since her divorce three months ago, 65-year-old Phyllis has constantly felt tired, has had difficulty sleeping and eating, and has lost all interest in her family, friends, and usual activities. Once proud of her accomplishments and optimistic about her future, Phyllis now believes that everything she has ever done, or will do, is worthless. Although her husband was far from a perfect partner, Phyllis is convinced that the divorce really was her fault. Her once-close friends, weary of Phyllis's self-absorbed and hopeless attitude, have stopped calling her. The family physician referred Phyllis to a psychiatrist, who prescribed an antidepressant. The drug seemed to help somewhat, but Phyllis, worried that she would become addicted, stopped taking it regularly. Phyllis's son-in-law is concerned about her dejected attitude. Her daughter, however, insists that there is no cause for alarm. She says that her mother is simply growing old—that the listlessness is reminiscent of her maternal grandmother's behavior at the same age.

1. Should Phyllis's daughter be more concerned about her mother's behavior, or is she correct in attributing it to aging? Explain your reasoning.
2. How might Phyllis's behavior be classified by a clinical psychologist?
3. How might Phyllis's behavior be explained according to (a) the psychoanalytic, (b) the biological, and (c) the social-cognitive perspectives?
4. Which diagnostic perspective most closely represents your own belief about Phyllis's condition? Why?

Check your progress on becoming a critical thinker by comparing your answers to the sample answers found in Appendix B.

## For Further Information

*You can find further information in this text regarding psychological disorders on the following pages:*

## For Further Reading

*Diagnostic and statistical manual of mental disorders* (4th ed., 1994). Washington, DC: American Psychiatric Association.

*Provides the most widely accepted definitions and descriptions of the categories of psychological disorder, including those described in this chapter.*

**Duke, P.** (1992). *The brilliant madness: Living with manic depressive illness.* New York: Bantam.

*Oscar winner Patty Duke recalls her bipolar disorder with the drunken rages, impulsive spending, and promiscuous sex that occurred before her diagnosis. Alternating chapters by a medical writer offer information about the disorder, its causes, and its treatment.*

**Gottesman, I. I.** (1991). *Schizophrenia genesis: The origins of madness.* New York: Freeman.

*A leading expert reviews the genetic and environmental roots of schizophrenia and provides first-person accounts of the disorder by patients and their families.*

**Greist, J. H., & Jefferson, J. W.** (1992). *Depression and its treatment* (rev. ed.). Washington, DC: American Psychiatric Press.

*For those wondering about depression, this manual answers common questions, such as: What is depression? Am I depressed? How is depression treated? How effective is psychotherapy? Drugs? ECT?*

**Jamison, K. R.** (1993). *Touched with fire: Manic-depressive illness and the artistic temperament.* New York: Free Press.

*Explores the links between bipolar disorder and creativity. Of interest to those interested in the creative/artistic process.*

**Styron, W.** (1990). *Darkness visible: A memoir of madness.* New York: Random House.

*A famous writer's poignant description of his descent into depression. Highly recommended for the family members of depressed people—indeed, for anyone wishing to understand depression's anguish and despair.*

**Torrey, E. F.** (1988). *Surviving schizophrenia: A family manual* (rev. ed.). New York: Harper/Collins.

*A comprehensive and caring guide to coping with schizophrenia, written for laypeople.*

# CHAPTER 16



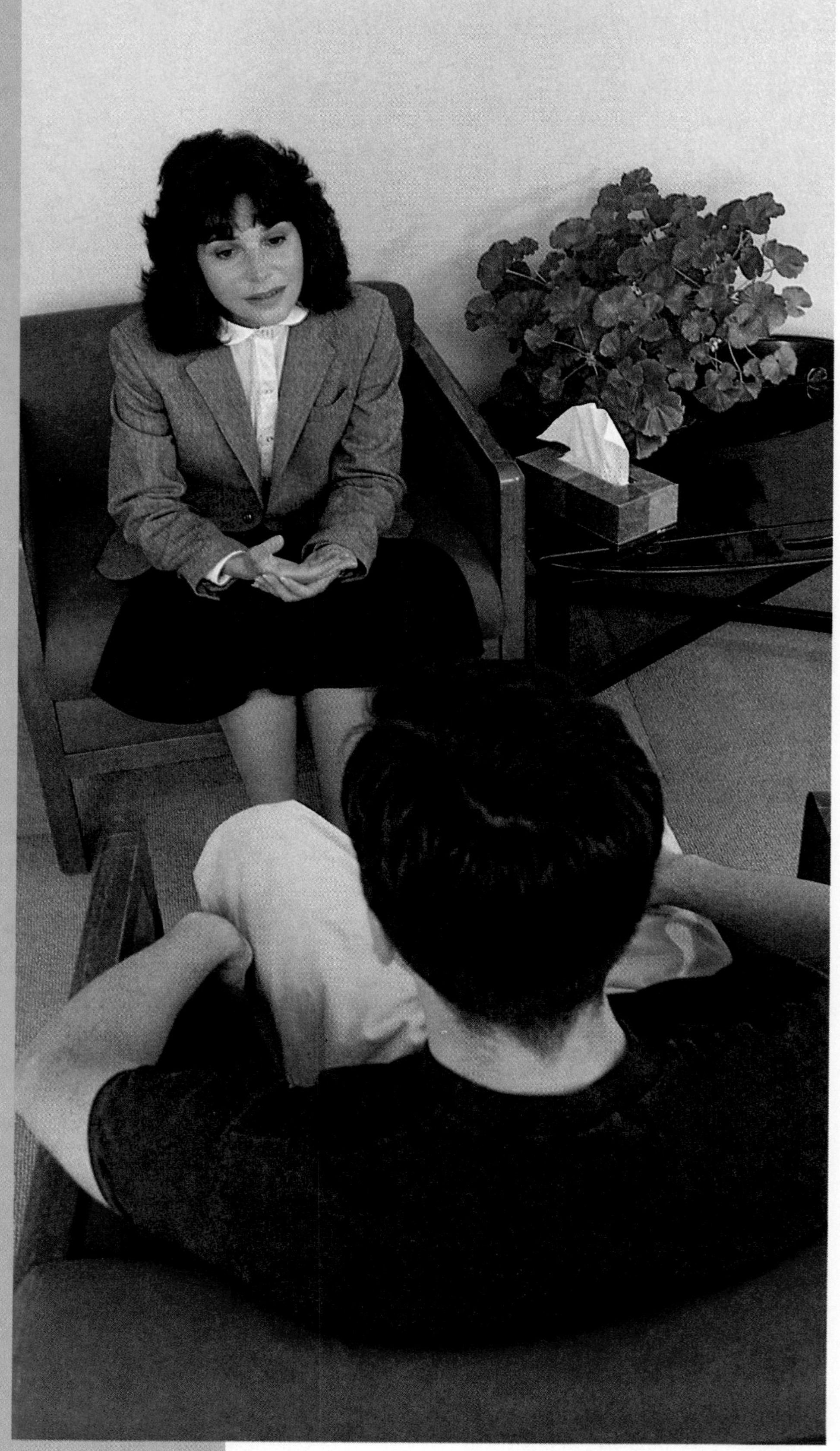

# Therapy

The history of treating psychological disorders reveals how mystifying and intractable these problems are. We can now state with certainty the chemical composition of Jupiter's atmosphere. But in understanding and treating what is much closer to home—the psychological disorders described in Chapter 15—we are only beginning to make real progress. Consider: In the 2200 years since Eratosthenes correctly estimated the earth's circumference, we have charted the heavens, explored the solar system, reconstructed the basic history of life on earth, cracked the genetic code, and eliminated or found cures for all sorts of diseases. Meanwhile, we have treated psychological disorders with a bewildering variety of methods, harsh and gentle: by cutting holes in the head and by giving warm baths and massages; by restraining, bleeding, or "beating the devil" out of people; by placing them in sunny, serene environments; by administering drugs and electric shocks; and by talking—talking about childhood experiences, about current feelings, about maladaptive thoughts and behaviors.

The transition from brutal to gentler treatments occurred thanks to the efforts of reformers such as Philippe Pinel in France and Dorothea Dix in the United States, Canada, and Scotland. Both advocated the construction of mental hospitals offering more humane methods of treatment. As we will see, the introduction of therapeutic drugs and community-based treatment programs has, however, largely emptied mental health hospitals since the mid-1950s.

**The History of Treatment** *William Hogarth's (1697–1764) engraving (left) of St. Mary of Bethlehem hospital in London (commonly called Bedlam) depicts the treatment of mental disorders in the eighteenth century. Visitors paid to gawk at the patients as if they were gawking at zoo animals. The chair above was designed by Benjamin Rush (1746–1813) "for the benefit of maniacal patients." Rush, a founder of the movement for more humane treatment of the mentally ill, believed that they required restraint to regain their sensibilities.*

**Dorothea Dix (1802–1887)** *"I . . . call your attention," she said, "to the state of the Insane Persons confined within this Commonwealth, in cages."*

Today's favored treatment depends on the therapist's viewpoint. Those who believe that psychological disorders are learned tend to favor psychological therapies. Those who view disorders as biologically rooted are likely to advocate medication as well. Those who believe that disorders are responses to social conditions will, in addition, want to reform the "sick" environment.

We can classify therapies into two main categories: The *psychological therapies* involve structured interaction (usually verbal) between a trained professional and a client with a problem. The *biomedical therapies* directly affect the nervous system.

## The Psychological Therapies

*What are the aims and methods of each major type of psychotherapy? And how does each apply the personality theory that underlies it?*

Psychological therapy, or **psychotherapy**, is "a planned, emotionally charged, confiding interaction between a trained, socially sanctioned healer and a sufferer" (Frank, 1982). From among the 250 or more types of psychotherapy (Parloff, 1987), we will consider the most influential techniques. These derive from psychology's major personality theories: psychoanalytic, humanistic, behavioral, and cognitive. We will also consider the use of these techniques in group therapies.

Although each technique is distinctive, common threads run through them. Therapists who view disorders as an interplay of bio–psycho–social influences may welcome a combination of treatments. Indeed, half of all psychotherapists describe themselves as taking an **eclectic approach**—as using a blend of therapies (Beitman & others, 1989; Smith, 1982). Depending on the client and the problem, an eclectic therapist will use a variety of techniques.

### Psychoanalysis

Although most of today's therapists do not practice as Sigmund Freud did, his psychoanalytic techniques survive. **Psychoanalysis** is part of our modern vocabulary, and its assumptions influence many other therapies.

#### Aims

As we noted when considering Freud's theory in Chapters 14 and 15, psychoanalysis assumes that many psychological problems are fueled by childhood's residue of supposedly repressed impulses and conflicts. Psychoanalysts try to bring these repressed feelings into conscious awareness where the patient can deal with them. By gaining insight into the origins of the disorder—by fulfilling the ancient imperative to "know thyself" in a deep way—the patient "works through" the buried feelings. The theory presumes that healthier, less anxious living becomes possible when patients release the energy previously devoted to id-ego-superego conflicts.

#### Methods

Psychoanalysis is historical reconstruction. It unearths the past in hopes of unmasking the present. But how?

When Freud discarded hypnosis as unreliable, he turned to *free association*. Imagine yourself as a patient using the free association technique. The analyst invites you to relax, perhaps by lying on a couch. He or she will probably sit out of your line of vision, helping you focus attention on your internal thoughts and feelings. Beginning with a childhood memory, a dream, or a recent experience, you say aloud whatever comes to your mind from moment to moment. It sounds easy, but soon you notice how often you edit your thoughts as you speak, omitting material that seems trivial, irrelevant, or shameful. Even in the safe presence of the analyst, you may pause momentarily before uttering an embarrassing thought. You may make a joking remark or change the subject to something less threatening. Sometimes your mind may go blank or you may find yourself unable to remember important details.

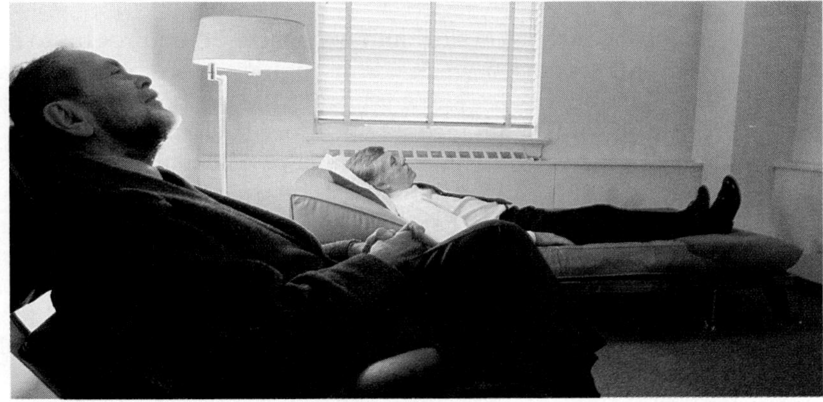

**Classical Psychoanalysis** *The placement of the analyst's chair out of view is thought to minimize distraction and make it easy for the patient—relaxed on a couch—to verbalize whatever comes to mind.*

To the psychoanalyst, these blocks in the flow of your free associations are **resistances**. They hint that anxiety lurks and that you are repressing sensitive material. The analyst will want to explore these sensitive areas by making you aware of your resistances and by helping you interpret their underlying meaning. The analyst's **interpretations**—suggestions of underlying wishes, feelings, and conflicts—aim to provide rational, nonpsychotic people with *insight*. If offered at the right moment, the analyst's interpretation—of, say, your not wanting to talk about your mother—may illuminate what you are avoiding. You may then discover what your resistances mean and how they fit with other pieces of your psychological puzzle.

Freud believed that another clue to repressed impulses is our dreams' *latent content* (page 228). Thus, after inviting you to report a dream, the analyst may suggest its hidden meaning, thereby adding yet another piece to your developing self-portrait.

Drawing by Miller; © 1983 The New Yorker Magazine, Inc.

During many such sessions you will probably disclose more of yourself to your analyst than you have ever revealed to anyone. Because psychoanalytic theory emphasizes the formative power of childhood experiences, much of what you reveal will pertain to your earliest memories. You will also probably find yourself experiencing strong positive or negative feelings for your analyst. Such feelings may express the dependency or mingled love and anger that you earlier experienced toward family members or other important people in your life. When this happens, Freud would say you are actually "transferring" your strongest feelings from those other relationships to the analyst. Analysts and other therapists believe that this **transference** exposes long-repressed feelings, giving you a belated chance to work through them with your analyst's help. By examining your feelings toward the analyst you may also gain insight into your current relationships.

Note how much of psychoanalysis and psychodynamic therapy is built on the assumption that repressed memories exist. That assumption, as we noted in Chapter 9, is now being challenged. This challenge to an assumption that is basic to so much of professional and popular psychology is provoking a new and intense debate.

Critics also say that psychoanalysts' interpretations are hard to refute. If, in response to the analyst's suggested interpretation, you say, "Yes! I see now," your acceptance confirms the analyst's interpretation. If you emphatically say, "No! That doesn't ring true," your denial may be taken to reveal more resistance, which would also confirm the interpretation. Psychoanalysts acknowledge that it's hard to prove or disprove their interpretations. But they insist that interpretations often are a great help to patients.

*Woody Allen, after awakening from suspended animation in* Sleeper: *"I haven't seen my analyst in 200 years. He was a strict Freudian. If I'd been going all this time, I'd probably almost be cured by now."*

Traditional psychoanalysis is slow and expensive. It requires up to several years of several sessions a week with a highly trained and well-paid analyst. (Three times a week for just 2 years at $100 per hour equals about $30,000.) Only those with a high income can afford such treatment.

Although there are relatively few traditional psychoanalysts, psychoanalytic assumptions influence many therapists, especially those who make "psychodynamic" assumptions. Psychodynamic therapists try to understand patients' current symptoms by exploring their childhood experiences. They probe for repressed, emotion-laden information. They seek to help people gain insight into the unconscious roots of problems and work through newly resurrected feelings. Although influenced by psychoanalysis, these therapists may talk to people face to face (rather than out of the line of vision), once a week (rather than several times weekly), and for only a few weeks or months (rather than several years).

**Face-to-Face Therapy** *In this type of therapy session the couch has disappeared. But the influence of psychoanalytic theory probably has not, especially if the therapist probes for the origin of the patient's symptoms by analyzing repressed information from the past.*

No brief therapy excerpt can exemplify the lengthy process of probing the past. But we can illustrate psychoanalysts' goal of enabling insight via their interpretations. In the following interaction, therapist David Malan responds to all that he has heard from a depressed patient by suggesting insights into her problems. Note how Malan interprets the woman's earlier remarks and suggests that her relationship with him reveals a characteristic pattern of behavior (1978, pp. 133–134)

**Malan:** *I get the feeling that you're the sort of person who needs to keep active. If you don't keep active, then something goes wrong. Is that true?*

**Patient:** *Yes.*

**Malan:** *I get a second feeling about you and that is that you must, underneath all this, have an awful lot of very strong and upsetting feelings. Somehow they're there but you aren't really quite in touch with them. Isn't this right? I feel you've been like that as long as you can remember.*

**Patient:** *For quite a few years, whenever I really sat down and thought about it I got depressed, so I tried not to think about it.*

**Malan:** *You see, you've established a pattern, haven't you? You're even like that here with me, because in spite of the fact that you're in some trouble and you feel that the bottom is falling out of your world, the way you're telling me this is just as if there wasn't anything wrong.*

## Humanistic Therapies

As we noted in Chapter 14, the humanistic perspective emphasizes people's inherent potential for self-fulfillment. Not surprisingly, then, humanistic therapists aim to boost self-fulfillment by helping people grow in self-awareness and self-acceptance. Unlike psychoanalytic therapists, humanistic therapists tend to focus on

- the present instead of the past;
- awareness of feelings as they occur rather than achieving insights into the childhood origins of the feelings;
- conscious rather than unconscious thoughts;
- taking immediate responsibility for one's feelings and actions rather than uncovering hidden determinants;
- promoting growth and fulfillment instead of curing illness.

### Person-Centered Therapy

The most widely used humanistic technique is Carl Rogers's (1961, 1980) **person-centered therapy**. Person-centered therapists focus on the client's conscious self-perceptions rather than on their own interpretations as therapists. The therapist listens, without judgment or interpretation, and refrains from directing the client toward certain insights. This strategy has earned person-centered therapy the label *nondirective* therapy.

Believing that most people already possess the resources for growth, Rogers encouraged therapists to exhibit *genuineness*, *acceptance*, and *empathy*. When therapists drop their facades and genuinely express their true feelings, when they enable their clients to feel unconditionally accepted, and when they empathically sense and reflect their clients' feelings, the clients may increase in self-understanding and self-acceptance. Rogers (1980, p. 10) explained:

> Hearing has consequences. When I truly hear a person and the meanings that are important to him at that moment, hearing not simply his words, but him, and when I let him know that I have heard his own private personal meanings, many things happen. There is first of all a grateful look. He feels released. He wants to tell me more about his world. He surges forth in a new sense of freedom. He becomes more open to the process of change.

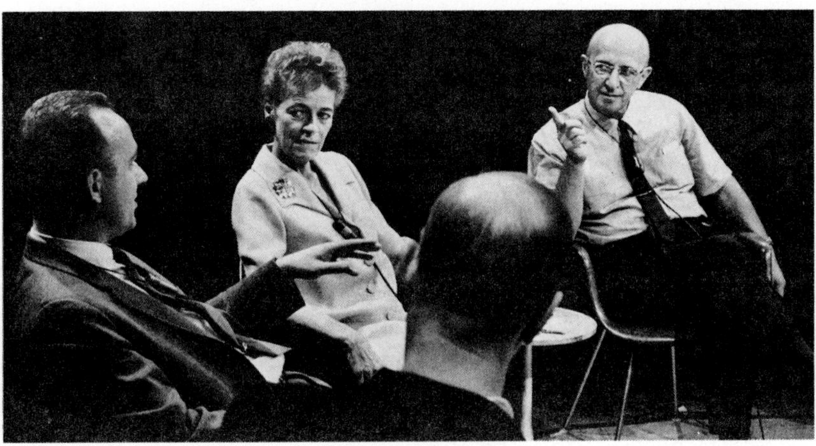

**Active Listening** *The late Carl Rogers (right) empathizes with a client during a group therapy session.*

> I have often noticed that the more deeply I hear the meanings of the person, the more there is that happens. Almost always, when a person realizes he has been deeply heard, his eyes moisten. I think in some real sense he is weeping for joy. It is as though he were saying, "Thank God, somebody heard me. Someone knows what it's like to be me."

"Hearing" refers to Rogers's technique of **active listening**—echoing, restating, and seeking clarification of what the person expresses—verbally or nonverbally—and acknowledging the expressed feelings. Active listening is now an accepted part of therapeutic counseling practices in many schools, colleges, and clinics. The counselor listens attentively and interrupts only to restate and confirm the client's feelings, to accept what the client is expressing, or to seek clarification. In fact, active listening is so easily described (though not so easily practiced) that computer scientist Joseph Weizenbaum developed a delightful computer program named ELIZA that simulates a Rogerian counselor. A few moments ago I (DGM) sat before a computer terminal and had the following "conversation" with ELIZA:

*"We have two ears and one mouth that we may listen the more and talk the less."*

Zeno, 335–263 B.C.
*Diogenes Laertius*

**ELIZA:** *How do you do. Please state your problem.*

**DGM:** *Hi, I guess I am feeling just a little nervous.*

**ELIZA:** *How long have you been feeling a little nervous?*

**DGM:** *I suppose that when I am writing I am always a little anxious.*

**ELIZA:** *Can you think of a specific example?*

**DGM:** *Well, I'm wondering whether students will find this stuff as interesting as I do.*

**ELIZA:** *Why do you believe it isn't normal to be wondering whether students will find this stuff as interesting as you do?*

**DGM:** *Maybe it is normal. I guess every author must feel the same. . . .*

**ELIZA:** *What are your feelings now?*

**DGM:** *Glad that you are willing to listen.*

**ELIZA:** *Why would you confide in someone who is willing to listen?*

**DGM:** *Sometimes it just helps to talk things over.*

**ELIZA:** *What does that suggest to you?*

**DGM:** *Perhaps that I should share my feelings more openly.*

**ELIZA:** *Your feelings more openly.*

**DGM:** *Yes.*

**ELIZA:** *I understand, please go on.*

**DGM:** *Do you understand?*

**ELIZA:** *Oh, I do understand at times.*

Although ELIZA is infinitely patient and nonjudgmental, she does not understand. She is nothing more than what Weizenbaum programmed—a parody of a nonjudgmental, person-centered therapist. Real interaction requires what the computer lacks—a sensitivity to meaning and nonverbal cues and an ability to clarify by reflecting meanings in *different* words. Compare ELIZA's conversation with me with the interaction between Carl Rogers and a 28-year-old male client:

**Client:** *I just ain't no good to nobody, never was, and never will be.*

**Rogers:** *Feeling that now, hm? That you're just no good to yourself, no good to anybody. Never will be any good to anybody. Just that you're completely worthless, huh?—Those really are lousy feelings. Just feel that you're no good at all, hm?*

**Client:** *Yeah. (Muttering in low, discouraged voice) That's what this guy I went to town with just the other day told me.*

**Rogers:** *This guy that you went to town with really told you that you were no good? Is that what you're saying? Did I get that right?*

**Client:** *M-hm.*

**Rogers:** *I guess the meaning of that if I get it right is that here's somebody that—meant something to you and what does he think of you? Why, he's told you that he thinks you're no good at all. And that just really knocks the props out from under you. (Client weeps quietly.) It just brings the tears. (Silence of 20 seconds)*

**Client:** *(Rather defiantly) I don't care though.*

**Rogers:** *You tell yourself you don't care at all, but somehow I guess some part of you cares because some part of you weeps over it* (Meador & Rogers, 1984, p. 167).

*"You say, 'Off with her head,' but what I'm hearing is, 'I feel neglected.'"*

As this brief excerpt illustrates, the person-centered counselor seeks to provide a psychological mirror that helps clients see themselves more clearly. But can a therapist be a perfect mirror, without selecting and interpreting what is reflected? Rogers conceded that one cannot be *totally* nondirective. Nevertheless, he believed that the therapist's most important contribution is to accept and understand the client. Given a nonjudgmental, grace-filled environment that provides *unconditional positive regard*, people may accept even their worst traits and feel valued and whole.

### Gestalt Therapy

Another influential humanistic therapy, developed by Fritz Perls (1969), joins the psychoanalytic emphasis on bringing unconscious feelings and conflicts into awareness with the humanistic emphasis on getting in touch with oneself and taking responsibility for oneself in the present. Perls's **Gestalt therapy** aims to make people whole by breaking through their defenses and helping them sense and express their moment-to-moment feelings. "All therapy that has to be done can only be done in the now," said Perls (1970). "Nothing exists except in the now."

Eavesdropping on a Gestalt therapy session, we might hear the therapist using any one of several techniques for getting people to express their real feelings and to "own responsibility" for them. One way is to train people to speak in the first person (Passons, 1975, p. 79):

**Client:** *When you go skiing you feel healthy and vigorous. You have this sense of excitement.*

**Therapist:** *Sue, try saying the same thing only substituting the word "I" for "you."*

**Client:** *Why?*

**Therapist:** *Because I believe you're saying something about yourself except you're not sounding that way.*

**Client:** *When I'm skiing I feel healthy and excited.*

**Therapist:** *Do you hear the difference?*

**Client:** *Yes. The second one is what I really meant.*

To encourage people to take responsibility for their feelings, the Gestalt therapist might get them to change their verbs—to say, "I want" instead of "I need," "I choose to" instead of "I have to," and "I won't" instead of "I can't" (Passons, 1975, p. 82):

**Client:** *Every day I just sit there and feel like a stooge. I just can't speak up in that class.*

**Therapist:** *You say you can't.*

**Client:** *That's right. I've tried and I know I should, I mean I know the stuff, that's not the problem. I just can't get the words out.*

**Therapist:** *Try saying "I won't talk" instead of "I can't talk."*

**Client:** *I won't talk in that class.*

**Therapist:** *Let yourself feel how you are refusing to talk.*

**Client:** *I guess I am holding myself back a little.*

**Therapist:** *What are your objections to speaking up?*

**Client:** *Well, everyone else in there seems to be talking just to talk. I don't like doing that.*

Gestalt therapists also capitalize on the power of actions to affect thoughts and feelings (see Chapter 18, Social Psychology). The therapist may ask people to role-play different aspects of their relationships or to act out suppressed feelings. Gestalt therapists encourage people to be true to themselves by becoming more aware and expressive of their feelings.

## Behavior Therapies

All the therapies we have considered so far assume that, for nonpsychotic people at least, psychological problems diminish as self-awareness grows. The psychoanalyst expects problems to subside as people gain insight into their unresolved and unconscious tensions. So does the humanistic therapist, as people "get in touch with their feelings." Behavior therapists, however, doubt that self-awareness is the key. They assume that the problem behaviors *are* the problems. You can, for example, become aware of why you are highly anxious during exams and still be anxious. Instead of trying to alleviate distressing behaviors by resolving a presumed underlying problem, **behavior therapy** applies well-established learning principles to eliminate the unwanted behavior. To treat phobias or sexual dysfunctions, behavior therapists do not delve deep below the surface looking for inner causes. Rather, they try to replace problem thoughts and maladaptive behaviors with more constructive ways of thinking and acting.

### Classical Conditioning Techniques

One cluster of behavior therapies derives from principles developed in Pavlov's conditioning experiments (pages 259–263). As Pavlov and others showed, we learn various behaviors and emotions through classical conditioning. So, are maladaptive symptoms conditioned responses? If, say, a claustrophobic fear of elevators is a learned response to the stimulus of being in an enclosed space, then might one unlearn the fear by applying extinction principles? Or by counterconditioning the fear response? **Counterconditioning** pairs the trigger stimulus with a new response that is incompatible with fear. For example, if we repeatedly pair the enclosed space of the elevator with a relaxed response, the fear response may be displaced. Two such counterconditioning techniques are *systematic desensitization* and *aversive conditioning*.

**Systematic Desensitization** Picture this scene reported in 1924 by Mary Cover Jones, an associate of the behaviorist John B. Watson: Three-year-old Peter is petrified of rabbits and other furry objects. (Unlike Little Albert's laboratory-conditioned fear of white rats, described in Chapter 8, Peter's fears arose during the course of his life at home and is more intense.) Jones aims to replace Peter's fear of rabbits with a conditioned response that is incompatible with fear. Her strategy is to associate the fear-evoking rabbit with the pleasurable, relaxed response associated with eating.

As the hungry child begins eating his midafternoon snack, Jones introduces a caged rabbit on the other side of the huge room. Peter hardly notices as he eagerly munches his crackers and milk. On succeeding days, she gradually moves the rabbit closer and closer. Within 2 months, Peter tolerates the rabbit in his lap and strokes it while he eats. Moreover, his fear of other furry objects subsides as well, having been "countered" or replaced by a relaxed state that cannot coexist with fear (Fisher, 1984; Jones, 1924).

Unfortunately for those who might have been helped by her counterconditioning procedures, Jones's story of Peter and the rabbit did not immediately become part of psychology's lore. It was not until more than 30 years later that psychiatrist Joseph Wolpe (1958, 1982) refined her technique into what has become the most widely used method of behavior therapy: **systematic desensitization**. Wolpe assumed, as did Jones, that you cannot simultaneously be anxious and relaxed. Therefore, if you can repeatedly relax when facing anxiety-provoking stimuli, you can gradually eliminate your anxiety. The trick is to proceed gradually.

Let's see how this might work with a common phobia. Imagine yourself afraid of public speaking. A behavior therapist might first ask your help in constructing a hierarchy of anxiety-triggering speaking situations. Your anxiety hierarchy could range from mildly anxiety-provoking situations, such as speaking up in a small group of friends, to panic-provoking situations, such as having to address a large audience.

The therapist would then train you to relax. Using *progressive relaxation*, you learn to relax one muscle group after another, until you achieve a drowsy state of complete relaxation and comfort. Then, with your eyes closed, the therapist asks you to imagine a mildly anxiety-arousing situation: You are having coffee with a group of friends and are deciding whether to speak up. If imagining the scene causes you to feel any anxiety, you signal your tension by raising your finger, and the therapist instructs you to switch off the mental image and go back to deep relaxation.

This imagined scene is repeatedly paired with relaxation until you can feel no trace of anxiety while imagining it. The therapist progresses up your anxiety hierarchy, using the relaxed state to desensitize you to each imagined situation. After several therapy sessions, you practice the imagined behaviors in actual situations, beginning with relatively easy tasks and gradually moving to more anxiety-filled ones (Figure 16–1). Conquering your anxiety in an actual situation, not just in your imagination, raises your self-confidence (Foa & Kozak, 1986; Williams, 1987). Eventually, you may even become a confident public speaker.

Therapists sometimes combine systematic desensitization with other techniques. With phobias, they may have someone model appropriate behavior in a fear-arousing situation. If you were afraid of snakes, you would first observe someone handling a snake. Then you would be coaxed in gradual steps to approach, touch, and handle it yourself (Bandura & others, 1969). By applying this principle of observational learning, therapists have helped people overcome disruptive fears of snakes, spiders, and dogs.

**THE FAR SIDE**

*Professor Gallagher and his controversial technique of simultaneously confronting the fear of heights, snakes and the dark.*

The Far Side © 1986 FARWORKS, INC./Distributed by Universal Press Syndicate. Reprinted with permission. All rights reserved.

Figure 16–1

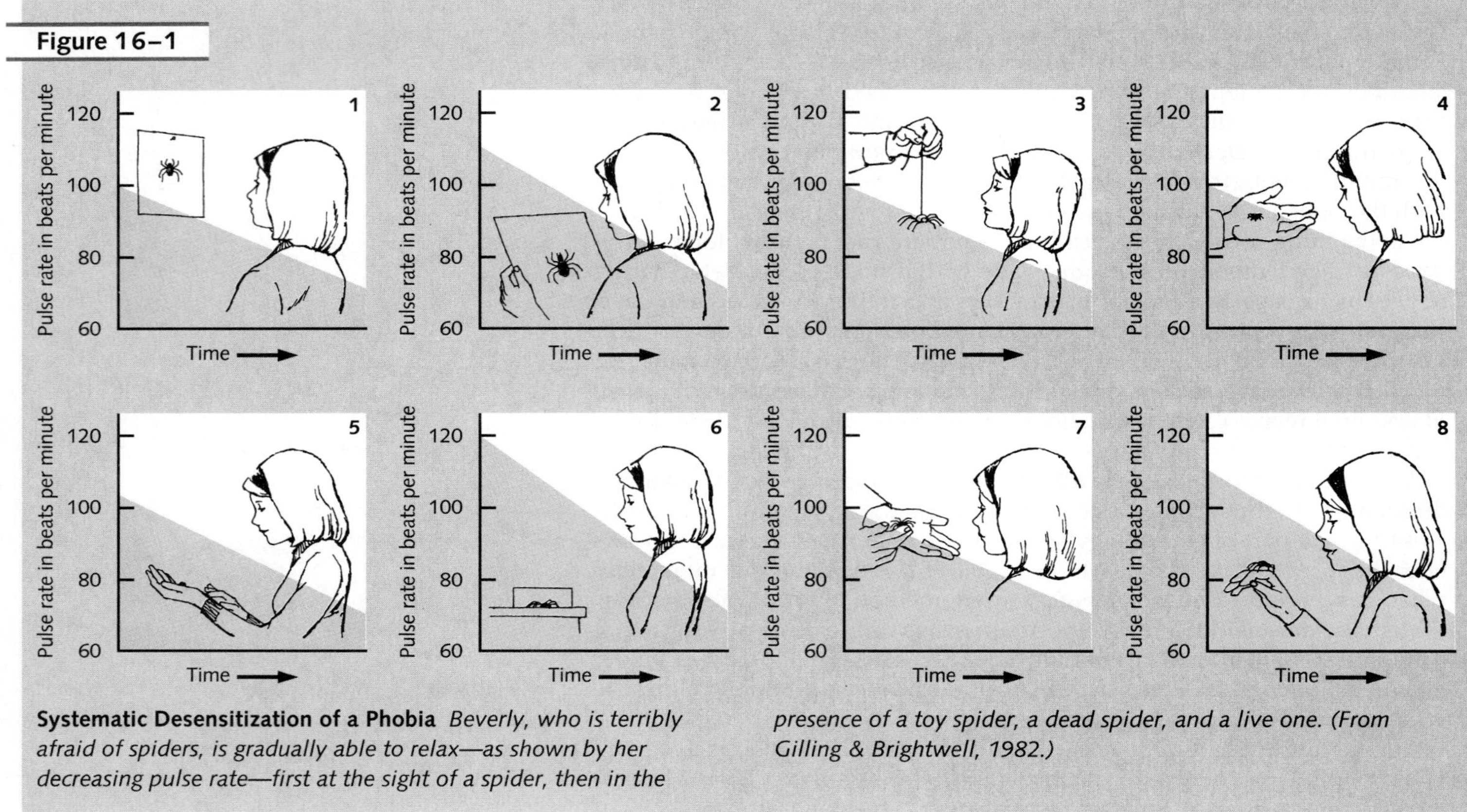


**Systematic Desensitization of a Phobia** *Beverly, who is terribly afraid of spiders, is gradually able to relax—as shown by her decreasing pulse rate—first at the sight of a spider, then in the presence of a toy spider, a dead spider, and a live one. (From Gilling & Brightwell, 1982.)*

Notice that the systematic desensitization and modeling procedures make no attempt to help you achieve insight into your fear's underlying cause. If you are afraid of heights, the therapist will not spend much time probing when you first experienced this fear or what may have caused it. Nor do behavior therapists worry that eliminating your fear of heights will leave an underlying problem that may now be expressed as, say, a fear of elevators. On the contrary, they find that overcoming maladaptive behaviors helps people feel better about themselves.

**Aversive Conditioning** In systematically desensitizing a patient, the therapist seeks to substitute a positive (relaxed) response for a negative (fearful) response to a harmless stimulus. In **aversive conditioning**, the therapist tries to replace a positive response to a harmful stimulus with a negative (aversive) response. Thus, aversive conditioning is the reverse of systematic desensitization.

The procedure is simple: It associates unwanted behavior with unpleasant feelings. In treating an alcoholic, aversion therapists offer appealing drinks laced with a drug that produces severe nausea. By linking the drinking of alcohol with violent nausea, the therapist seeks to transform the alcoholic's reaction to alcohol from positive to negative (see Figure 16–2, and recall the taste aversion experiments with rats and coyotes in Chapter 8). Similarly, by giving child molesters electric shocks as they view photos of nude children, aversion therapists aim to eliminate the molesters' sexual response to children. And by giving withdrawn and self-abusing autistic children harmless "aversives," such as a spray of cold water in the face, therapists hope to suppress self-injury while reinforcing more appropriate behavior. Because this therapy involves an unpleasant experience, it is practiced sparingly and only with the appropriate consent.

Does aversive conditioning work? In the short run it may. But, as we saw in Chapter 8, the problem is that cognition influences conditioning. People know that outside the therapist's office they can drink without fear of nausea or engage in sexually deviant behavior without fear of shock. The person's ability to discriminate between the aversive conditioning situation and all other situations can limit the treatment's effectiveness.

Aversive conditioning of alcoholics has, nevertheless, enjoyed renewed popularity. For example, Arthur Wiens and Carol Menustik (1983) studied 685 alcoholic patients who completed an aversion therapy program at a Portland, Oregon, hospital. One year later, after returning for several booster treatments of alcohol-sickness pairings, 63 percent were still successfully abstaining. Three years later, 33 percent remained abstinent.

A milder form of aversive conditioning, developed by learning theorist O. H. Mowrer, exists for chronic bedwetters. The child sleeps on a liquid-sensitive pad connected to an alarm. Moisture on the pad triggers the alarm, awakening the child. With repetition, this association of urinary relaxation with awakening stops the bedwetting. In three out of four cases the treatment is effective and the success provides a boost to the child's self-image (Christophersen & Edwards, 1992).

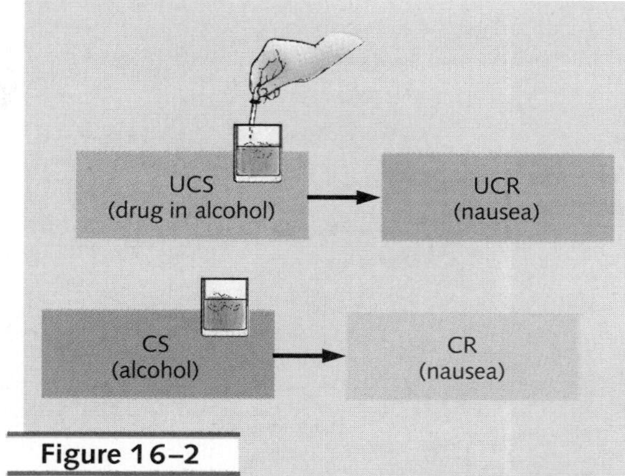


**Figure 16–2**

**Aversion Therapy for Alcoholics** *After repeatedly imbibing an alcoholic drink mixed with a drug that produces severe nausea, some patients develop at least a temporary conditioned aversion to alcohol.*

*What might a psychoanalyst say about this therapy for bedwetting? How might a behavior therapist reply?*

### Operant Conditioning

As we saw in Chapter 8, voluntary behaviors are strongly influenced by their consequences. This simple fact enables behavior therapists to reinforce desired behaviors and to withhold reinforcement for undesired behaviors. Using operant conditioning to solve specific behavior problems has raised hopes for some cases thought to be hopeless. Retarded children have been taught to care for themselves. Socially withdrawn autistic children have learned to interact. People with schizophrenia have been helped to behave more rationally on the hospital ward.

In extreme cases, the treatment must be intensive. For 19 withdrawn, uncommunicative, 3-year-old autistic children in one study, it involved a 2-year, 40-hour-a-week shaping program by their parents (Lovaas, 1987). But the combination of positive reinforcement of desired behaviors and the ignoring or punishing of aggressive and self-abusive behaviors worked wonders. By first grade, 9 of the 19 children were functioning successfully in school and exhibiting normal intelligence. Only 1 of 40 comparable children who did not undergo this treatment showed similar improvement.

The rewards used to modify behavior vary. With some people the reinforcing power of attention or praise is sufficient. Others require more concrete rewards, such as food. In institutional settings, therapists may create a **token economy**. When people display appropriate behavior, such as getting out of bed, washing, dressing, eating, talking coherently, cleaning up their rooms, or playing cooperatively, they receive a token or plastic coin. Later, they can exchange their accumulated tokens for various rewards, such as candy, television watching, trips to town, or better living quarters. Therapists use tokens to shape behavior in the step-by-step manner described on page 269. Token economies have been successfully applied in various settings (classrooms, hospitals, homes for the delinquent) and with various populations (disturbed children, the mentally retarded, schizophrenia patients).

Critics of such "behavior modification" express two concerns. One concern is practical: What happens when the reinforcers stop, as when the person leaves the institution? Might the person have become so dependent on the extrinsic rewards that the appropriate behaviors quickly disappear? If so, how can behavior therapists make the appropriate behaviors durable? First, they may wean patients from the tokens by shifting them toward rewards, such as social approval, more typical of life outside the institution. They may also train patients to behave in ways that are intrinsically rewarding. For example, as a withdrawn person becomes more socially competent, the intrinsic satisfactions of social interaction may help maintain the behavior.

The second concern is ethical: Is it right for one human to control another's behavior? Those who set up token economies typically deprive people of something they desire and then decide which behaviors they will reinforce. To critics, the whole behavior modification process has a totalitarian taint. Advocates reply that control already exists; rewards and punishers are already maintaining destructive behavior patterns. So why not reinforce adaptive behavior instead? They argue that treatment with positive rewards is more humane than being institutionalized or punished, and that the right to effective treatment and to an improved life justifies temporary deprivation.

## Cognitive Therapies

We have seen how behavior therapists treat specific fears and problem behaviors. But how do they deal with major depression or general anxiety? One can reinforce healthier behaviors and train people to avoid "high risk" situations. Still, when anxiety has no focus, making a hierarchy of anxiety-triggering situations is difficult. The cognitive revolution that has so changed psychology during the last 3 decades has influenced how therapists treat these less clearly defined psychological problems.

The **cognitive therapies** assume that our thinking colors our feelings (Figure 16–3). As we noted in Chapter 15, self-blaming and overgeneralized explanations of bad events are an integral part of the vicious cycle of depression. The depressed person interprets a suggestion as criticism, disagreement as dislike, praise as flattery, friendliness as pity. Ruminating on such thoughts sustains the bad mood. (That explains why distracting oneself, perhaps by getting absorbed in a task, can alleviate a bad mood—

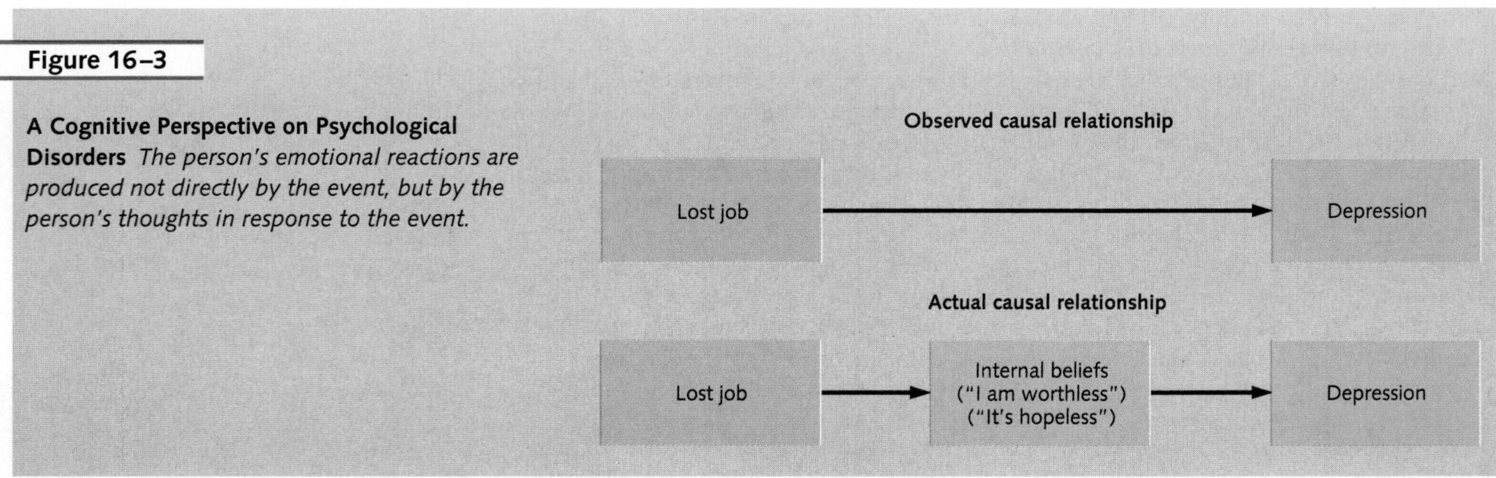


**Figure 16–3**

**A Cognitive Perspective on Psychological Disorders** *The person's emotional reactions are produced not directly by the event, but by the person's thoughts in response to the event.*

Erber & Tesser, 1992; Lyubomirsky & Nolen-Hoeksema, 1994.) If depressing thinking patterns are learned, then surely they can be replaced (Brewin, 1989). Thus, cognitive therapists try in various ways to teach people new, more constructive ways of thinking.

### Rational-Emotive Therapy

According to Albert Ellis (1962, 1987, 1993), the creator of **rational-emotive therapy** (also called *rational-emotive behavior therapy*), many problems arise from irrational thinking. For example, he describes a disturbed woman and suggests how therapy might challenge her illogical, self-defeating assumptions (1984, p. 198):

> [She] does not merely believe it is *undesirable* if her love partner is rejecting. She tends to believe, also, that (1) it is *awful*; (2) she *cannot stand* it; (3) she *should not*, must not be rejected; (4) she will *never* be accepted by any desirable partner; (5) she is a *worthless person* because one lover has rejected her; and (6) she *deserves to be damned* for being so worthless. Such common covert hypotheses are nonsensical. . . . They can be easily elicited and demolished by any scientist worth his or her salt; and the rational-emotive therapist is exactly that: an exposing and nonsense-annihilating scientist.

Does this sound like the opposite of the warm, caring, reflective acceptance of feelings expressed by Carl Rogers? It very nearly is. Ellis intends to "make mincemeat" of people's illogical ideas—that we must be loved by everyone, that we must be thoroughly competent and successful at everything, that it is a disaster when things do not go as we wish. Change people's thinking by revealing the "absurdity" of their self-defeating ideas, he believes, and you will change their self-defeating feelings and actions. Let's eavesdrop as tart-tongued Ellis exhibits his confrontational style with a 25-year-old female client who suffers feelings of guilt, unworthiness, and depression (1989, p. 219):

**Ellis:** *The same crap! It's always the same crap. Now if you would look at the crap—instead of "Oh, how stupid I am! He hates me! I think I'll kill myself!"—then you'd get better right away.*

**Client:** *You've been listening! (laughs)*

**Ellis:** *Listening to what?*

**Client:** *(laughs) Those wild statements in my mind, like that, that I make.*

**Ellis:** *That's right! Because I know that you have to make those statements—because I have a good theory. And according to my theory, people couldn't get upset unless they made those nutty statements to themselves. . . . Even if I loved you madly, the next person you talk to is likely to hate you. So I like brown eyes and he likes blue eyes, or something. So you're then dead! Because you really think: "I've got to be accepted! I've got to act intelligently!" Well, why?*

**Client:** *(very soberly and reflectively) True.*

**Ellis:** *You see?*

**Client:** *Yes.*

**Ellis:** *Now, if you will learn that lesson, then you've had a very valuable session. Because you don't have to upset yourself. As I said before: If I thought you were the worst [expletive] who ever existed, well that's my* opinion. *And I'm entitled to it. But does it make you a turd?*

**Client:** *(reflective silence)*

**Ellis:** *Does it?*

**Client:** *No.*

**Ellis:** *What makes you a turd?*

**Client:** *Thinking that you are.*

**Ellis:** *That's right! Your belief that you are. That's the only thing that could ever do it. And you never have to believe that. See? You control your thinking. I control my thinking—my belief about you. But you don't have to be affected by that. You always control what you think.*

### Cognitive Therapy for Depression

Like Ellis, cognitive therapist Aaron Beck was originally trained in Freudian techniques. As Beck analyzed his depressed patients' dreams, he found recurring negative themes of loss, rejection, and abandonment that extended into their waking thoughts. So in his form of cognitive therapy, Beck and his colleagues (1979) seek to reverse clients' catastrophizing beliefs about themselves, their situations, and their futures. Beck shares with Ellis the goal of getting depressed people to take off the dark glasses through which they view life. But his technique is a kinder, gentler questioning that aims to help people discover their irrationalities (Beck & others, 1979, pp. 145–146):

**Patient:** *I agree with the descriptions of me but I guess I don't agree that the way I think makes me depressed.*

**Beck:** *How do you understand it?*

**Patient:** *I get depressed when things go wrong. Like when I fail a test.*

**Beck:** *How can failing a test make you depressed?*

**Patient:** *Well, if I fail I'll never get into law school.*

**Beck:** *So failing the test means a lot to you. But if failing a test could drive people into clinical depression, wouldn't you expect everyone who failed the test to have a depression? . . . Did everyone who failed get depressed enough to require treatment?*

**Patient:** *No, but it depends on how important the test was to the person.*

**Beck:** *Right, and who decides the importance?*

**Patient:** *I do.*

**Beck:** *And so, what we have to examine is your way of viewing the test (or the way that you think about the test) and how it affects your chances of getting into law school. Do you agree?*

**Patient:** *Right.*

**Beck:** *Do you agree that the way you interpret the results of the test will affect you? You might feel depressed, you might have trouble sleeping, not feel like eating, and you might even wonder if you should drop out of the course.*

**Patient:** *I have been thinking that I wasn't going to make it. Yes, I agree.*

**Beck:** *Now what did failing mean?*

**Patient:** *(tearful) That I couldn't get into law school.*

CATHY © Cathy Guisewite. Reprinted with permission of UNIVERSAL PRESS SYNDICATE. All rights reserved.

**Beck:** *And what does that mean to you?*

**Patient:** *That I'm just not smart enough.*

**Beck:** *Anything else?*

**Patient:** *That I can never be happy.*

**Beck:** *And how do these* thoughts *make you feel?*

**Patient:** *Very unhappy.*

**Beck:** *So it is the meaning of failing a test that makes you very unhappy. In fact, believing that you can never be happy is a powerful factor in producing unhappiness. So, you get yourself into a trap—by definition, failure to get into law school equals "I can never be happy."*

A newer variety of cognitive therapy builds on the finding that depressed people do not exhibit the self-serving bias common in nondepressed people (page 520). Instead, they often attribute their failures to themselves and attribute their successes to external circumstances. Thus, Adele Rabin and her colleagues (1986) explained to 235 depressed adults the advantages of interpreting events as nondepressed people do. She then trained them to reform their habitually negative patterns of thinking and labeling. For example, she gave the patients homework assignments that required them to record each day's positive events and to write down how they contributed to each. Compared with depressed people who remained on a waiting list, those who went through the positive thinking exercises became much less depressed (Figure 16–4). Changed thinking after cognitive therapy also reduces the risk of relapse (Hollon & others, 1992).

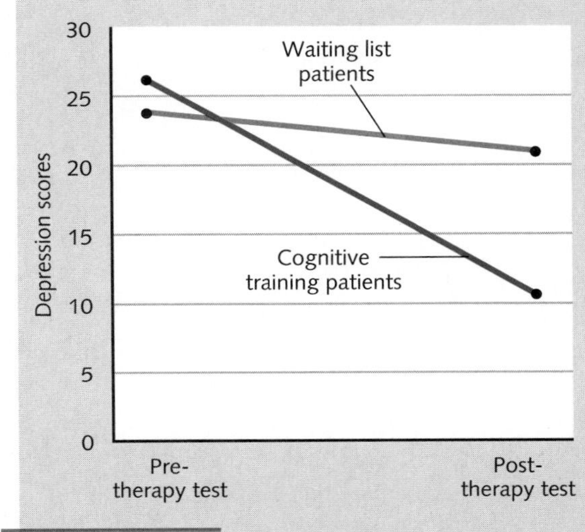


**Figure 16–4**

**Cognitive Therapy for Depression** *After undergoing a program that trained them to think more like nondepressed people—by noticing and taking personal credit for good events and by not taking blame for or overgeneralizing from bad events—patients' depression dropped dramatically. (From Rabin and others, 1986.)*

The more people change their negative thinking styles, the more their depression lifts (Seligman, 1989). Cognitive therapists often combine the reversal of self-defeating thinking with efforts to modify behavior. *Cognitive behavior therapy* aims to make people aware of their irrational negative thinking, to replace it with new ways of thinking and talking, *and* to practice the more positive approach in everyday settings. Cognitive behavior therapy has been found effective for treating anxiety disorders such as panic attacks (Zinbarg & others, 1992).

For example: Because we often think in words, getting people to change what they say to themselves is an effective way to change their thinking. Perhaps you can identify with the anxious students who before an exam make matters worse with self-defeating thoughts: "This exam is probably going to be impossible. All these other students seem so relaxed and self-confident. I wish I were better prepared. Anyhow, I'm so nervous I'll forget everything." To change such negative patterns, Donald Meichenbaum (1977, 1985) trains people to restructure the way they think in stressful situations. Sometimes it may be enough simply to say more positive things to oneself: "Relax. The exam may be hard, but it will be hard for everyone else, too. I studied harder than most people. Besides, I don't need a perfect score to get a good grade."

## Group Therapies

Except for traditional psychoanalysis, the therapies we have considered may also occur in therapist-led small groups. Although it does not provide the same degree of therapist involvement with each client, group therapy saves therapists' time and clients' money. More important, the social context allows people both to discover that others have problems similar to their own and to try out new ways of behaving. As you have perhaps experienced, receiving honest feedback—being reassured that you look poised even though you feel anxious and self-conscious, for example—can be very helpful. And it can be a relief to find that you are not alone—to learn that others, despite their seeming composure, share your problems and your feelings of loneliness, inadequacy, or anger. Such has been the experience of a wide range of people, from cancer patients to dieters to recovering alcoholics (Yalom, 1985).

One popular form of group experience for those not seriously disturbed began as sensitivity training groups (T-groups, for short) in which teachers, executives, and others practiced relating to one another more sensitively and openly. Leaders encouraged groups of 12 to 20 people to be less inhibited and defensive, to "talk straight," and to listen empathically. Before long, Carl Rogers (1970) and others were offering *encounter groups*—groups that confronted emotion-laden experiences openly and honestly.

Although encounter groups are not as popular today as they were during the 1970s, they set the stage for the emergence of countless *self-help* and *support groups*—for substance abusers, divorced people, gamblers, the bereaved, and those simply seeking personal growth. In an individualistic age, with more and more people living or feeling alone, support also reflects a longing for community and connectedness. The grandparent of self-help groups, Alcoholics Anonymous (AA), has 60,000 chapters in 112 countries. Its famous 12-step strategy, emulated by many other self-help groups, asks members to admit their powerlessness, to seek help from a higher power and from one another, and (the twelfth step) to take the message to others in need of it.

**Family Therapy** *This type of therapy often acts as a preventive mental health strategy. The therapist helps family members understand how the ways they relate to each other create problems. The treatment emphasis is not on changing the individuals but rather on changing their relationships and interactions.*

One special type of group interaction, **family therapy**, assumes that no person is an island. We live and grow in relation to others, especially our families. We struggle to differentiate ourselves from our families but we also need to connect with them emotionally. Some of our problem behaviors arise from the tension between these two tendencies, which often creates family stress. Thus, patients often come to therapists seeking help with relational problems.

Unlike most psychotherapy, which focuses on what happens inside the person's own skin, family therapists work with family groups to heal relationships and to mobilize family resources. Their aim is to help family members discover the role they play within their family's social system. A child's rebellion, for example, affects and is affected by other family tensions. Family therapists also attempt—usually with some success, research suggests (Hazelrigg & others, 1987; Shadish, 1992)—to open up communication within the family or to help family members discover new ways of preventing or resolving conflicts.

## Summing Up

Treatment for psychological disorders encompasses both the psychological therapies, involving structured interactions, and the biomedical therapies, which alter neural functions. The major psychotherapies derive from the familiar psychoanalytic, humanistic, behavioral, and cognitive perspectives on psychology.

**Psychoanalysis** Psychoanalysts try to help people gain insight into the unconscious origins of their disorders and to work through the accompanying feelings. To do so, an analyst draws on techniques such as free association and the interpretation of patients' dreams, resistances, and their transference to the therapist of long-repressed feelings. Like psychoanalytic theory, psychoanalysis is criticized for after-the-fact interpretations and for being time-consuming and costly. Although traditional psychoanalysis is not practiced widely, its influence can be seen in the work of therapists who explore childhood experiences, who assume that defense mechanisms repress emotion-laden information, and who seek to help their (nonpsychotic) clients achieve insight into the root of their problems.

**Humanistic Therapies** Unlike psychoanalysts, humanistic therapists focus on clients' current conscious feelings and on their taking responsibility for their own growth. Carl Rogers, in his person-centered therapy, used active listening to express genuineness, acceptance, and empathy. With Gestalt therapy, Fritz Perls sought to break down people's defenses and to make them accept responsibility for their feelings.

**Behavior Therapies** Behavior therapists worry less about promoting self-awareness and more about directly modifying problem behaviors. Thus, they may countercondition behaviors through systematic desensitization or aversive conditioning. Or they may apply operant conditioning principles with behavior modification techniques, such as token economies.

**Cognitive Therapies** The newer cognitive therapies, such as Albert Ellis's rational-emotive therapy and Aaron Beck's cognitive therapy for depression, aim to change self-defeating thinking by training people to look at themselves in new, more positive ways.

**Group Therapies** Many therapeutic techniques can also be applied in a group context. One special form is family therapy, which treats the family as an interactive system from which problems may arise.

## Evaluating Psychotherapies

*Does psychotherapy work? More specifically, do particular therapies work for particular problems? How might psychology's critical thinking methods provide answers?*

Advice columnist Ann Landers frequently advises her troubled letter writers to get professional help. One response urged the writer "not to give up. Hang in there until you find [a psychotherapist] who fills the bill. It's worth the effort." She advised the same day's second letter writer, "There are many excellent mental health facilities in your city. I urge you to make an appointment at once" (Farina & Fisher, 1982). Many people share Ann Landers's confidence in psychotherapy's effectiveness. The National Institute of Mental Health estimates that 15 percent of Americans seek help for psychological and addictive disorders each year (Figure 16–5).

Before 1950, the main mental health providers were psychiatrists. Since then the demand has outgrown the psychiatric profession, and most psychotherapy is now done by clinical and counseling psychologists; clinical social workers; pastoral, marital, abuse, and school counselors; and psychiatric nurses. Much of it is done through *community mental health* programs, which provide outpatient therapy, crisis phone lines, and halfway houses for those making the transition from hospitalization to independent living. Is the faith that Ann Landers and millions of other Americans have placed in these therapists justified?

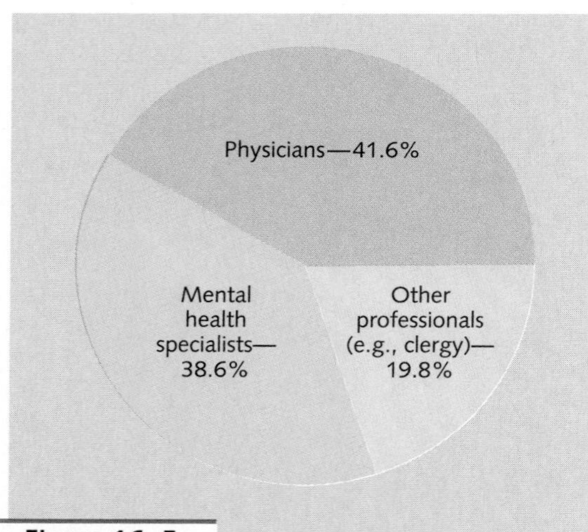


**Figure 16–5**

**To Whom Do People Turn?** *The National Institute of Mental Health reports that 19 million Americans a year seek out human service professionals. About 2 in 5 turn to their physician. Another 2 in 5 seek out a mental health worker, such as a psychologist or psychiatrist. (Data from Regier & others, 1993.)*

### Is Psychotherapy Effective?

The question, though simply put, is not simply answered. For one thing, measuring therapy's effectiveness is not like taking your body's temperature. If you and I were to undergo psychotherapy, how would we gauge its effectiveness? By how we feel about our progress? How our therapist feels about it? How our friends and family feel about it? How our behavior has changed?

#### Clients' Perceptions

If clients' testimonials were the only yardstick, we could strongly affirm the effectiveness of psychotherapy. Three out of four clients report themselves satisfied, and one in two say they are "very satisfied" (Lebow, 1982). We have their word for it—and who should know better?

We should not dismiss these testimonials lightly. People enter therapy because they are suffering, and most leave feeling better about themselves. But there are several reasons why client testimonials do not persuade psychotherapy's skeptics:

***People often enter therapy in crisis.*** When, with the normal ebb and flow of events, the crisis passes, people may attribute their improvement to the therapy.

***Clients may need to believe the therapy was worth the effort.*** To admit investing time and money in something ineffective is like admitting to having one's car serviced repeatedly by a mechanic who never fixed it. Self-justification is a powerful human motive.

***Clients generally like their therapists and speak kindly of them.*** Even if the clients' problems remain, say the therapy critics, "they work hard to find something positive to say. The therapist had been very understanding, the client had gained a new perspective, he learned to communicate better, his mind was eased, anything at all so as not to have to say treatment was a failure" (Zilbergeld, 1983, p. 117).

Such testimonials can be misleading. As earlier chapters document, we are prone to selective and biased recall and to making judgments that confirm our beliefs. Consider a massive experiment with over 500 Massachusetts boys, aged 5 to 13 years, many of whom seemed bound for delinquency. By the toss of a coin, half the boys were assigned to a 5-year treatment program. Counselors visited them twice a month. They were involved in community programs such as the Boy Scouts. And, as the need arose, they received academic tutoring, medical attention, and family assistance. Some 30 years after the end of the program, Joan McCord (1978, 1979) located 97 percent of the participants. To assess the treatment's impact she sent them questionnaires and checked public records from courts, mental hospitals, and other sources.

Assessing the treatment program with client testimonials yielded encouraging results. Many of the men offered glowing reports. Some noted that had it not been for their counselors, "I would probably be in jail"; "My life would have gone the other way"; or "I think I would have ended up in a life of crime." The court records offered apparent support for these testimonials. Even among the "difficult" boys in the program, 66 percent had no official juvenile crime record.

But recall that psychology's most powerful weapon for sorting reality from wishful thinking is the *control group*. For every boy who was counseled there was a similar boy in a control group who was not. McCord tracked down these untreated people and found that among the predelinquent boys in the control group, *70 percent* had no juvenile record. Moreover, on some measures, such as a record of having committed a second crime, alcoholic tendencies, death rate, and job satisfaction, the untreated men exhibited slightly *fewer* problems.

The glowing testimonials of those treated had been deceiving. Perhaps, McCord speculated, the intervention had created a dependency. Or maybe it generated such high expectations that the boys later experienced greater frustration. Or perhaps it led the boys to view themselves as requiring help.

*Although many suicide-prone people have turned to suicide-prevention centers for help, such centers have not been found to affect community suicide rates (Dew & others, 1987).*

### Clinicians' Perceptions

If clinicians' perceptions accurately reflected their own therapeutic effectiveness, we would have even more reason to celebrate. Case studies of successful treatment abound. Furthermore, every therapist treasures compliments from clients as they say goodbye or later express their gratitude. The problem is that clients justify entering psychotherapy by emphasizing their woes, justify leaving therapy by emphasizing their well-being, and stay in touch only if satisfied. Therapists are aware of failures, but they are mostly the failures of *other* therapists—those whose clients, having experienced only temporary relief, are now seeking a new therapist for their recurring problems. Thus, the same person with the same recurring difficulty—the same old weight problem, depression, or marital difficulty—may represent "success" stories in several therapists' files.

### Outcome Research

How, then, can we objectively measure the effectiveness of psychotherapy? What types of people and problems are best helped, and by what type of psychotherapy? The questions have both academic and personal relevance.

If you or someone you care about feels anxious or depressed, or suffers some psychological disorder, how likely is it that psychotherapy will help?

In hopes of better assessing psychotherapy's effectiveness, psychologists have turned to controlled research studies. Similar research in the 1800s transformed medicine from concocted treatments (bleeding, purging, infusions of plant and metal substances) into a science. The transformation occurred when skeptical physicians began to realize that many patients got better on their own, that most of the fashionable treatments were doing no good, and that sorting sense from nonsense required closely following illnesses—with and without a particular treatment. Typhoid fever patients, for example, often improved after a treatment such as bleeding. That convinced most physicians that the treatment worked. It was not until a control group was given mere bed rest—and 70 percent were observed to improve after 5 weeks of fever—that physicians were shocked to learn that their treatments were, at best, worthless (Thomas, 1992).

In psychology, the opening volley in what became a spirited debate over such research was fired by British psychologist Hans Eysenck (1952). He summarized studies showing that after undergoing psychotherapy, two-thirds of those suffering nonpsychotic disorders improve markedly. To this day, no one disputes that optimistic estimate.

So why are we still debating psychotherapy's effectiveness? Because Eysenck also reported similar improvement among *untreated* persons, such as those who were on waiting lists. With or without psychotherapy, he said, roughly two-thirds improved noticeably. Time was a great healer.

*"Fortunately, [psycho]analysis is not the only way to resolve inner conflicts. Life itself still remains a very effective therapist."*

Karen Horney
*Our Inner Conflicts*, 1945

The avalanche of criticism prompted by Eysenck's conclusions revealed shortcomings in his analyses. Also, Eysenck could find only 24 studies of psychotherapy outcomes to analyze in 1952. Today, there are hundreds. The best of these studies randomly assign people on a waiting list to alternative treatments or to no treatment. Afterward, researchers evaluate everyone, using tests and the reports of friends and family or of psychologists who don't know whether therapy was given. The results of such studies are then digested by a technique called **meta-analysis**, a procedure for statistically combining the results of many different studies as if they had come from one huge study with thousands of participants.

In the first reported meta-analysis of psychotherapy outcome studies, Mary Lee Smith and her colleagues (1980) combined the results of 475 investigations. For psychotherapists, the welcome result was that "the evidence overwhelmingly supports the efficacy of psychotherapy" (p. 183). Figure 16–6 depicts their finding—that the average therapy client ends up better off than 80 percent of the untreated individuals on waiting lists. The claim is more modest than it first appears—by definition, about 50 percent of untreated people also are better off than the average untreated person. Nevertheless, Smith and her collaborators concluded that "psychotherapy benefits people of all ages as reliably as schooling educates them, medicine cures them, or business turns a profit" (p. 183).

Newer research summaries confirm this optimism (Lipsey & Wilson, 1993). The most ambitious of the new psychotherapy studies is a National Institute of Mental Health evaluation of three depression treatments: cognitive therapy, interpersonal therapy (which focuses on social relations), and a standard drug therapy. Twenty-eight experienced therapists at research sites in Norman, Oklahoma; Washington, DC; and Pittsburgh, Pennsylvania, were trained in one of the three methods and randomly assigned their share of the 239 depressed patients who participated. Patients in all three groups improved more than did those who were in a control condition and received merely an inert medication and supportive

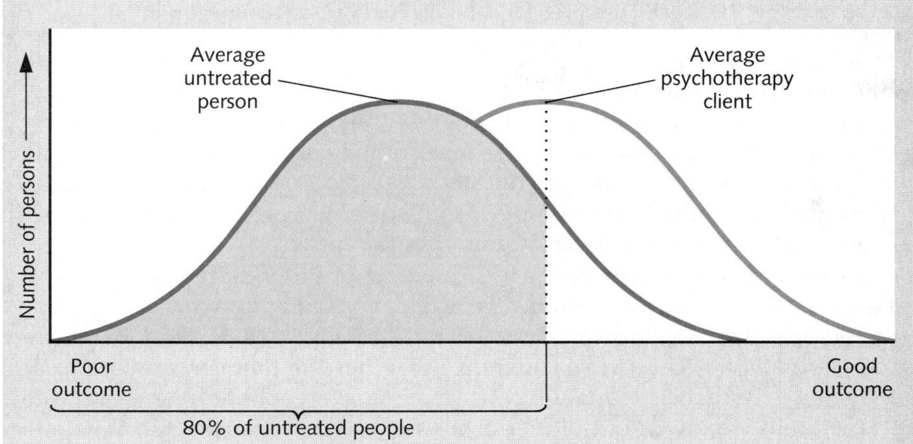


**Figure 16–6**

**Treatment Versus No Treatment** *These two normal distribution curves based on data from 475 studies show the improvement of untreated people and psychotherapy clients. The outcome for the average therapy client surpassed that for 80 percent of the untreated people. (Adapted from Smith & others, 1980.)*

attention, encouragement, and advice. Among patients who completed a full 16-week treatment program, the depression had lifted for slightly more than half of those in each treatment group—but only for 29 percent of those in the control group (Elkin & others, 1989). This verdict echoes the results of the earlier outcome studies: *Those not undergoing therapy improved, but those undergoing therapy improved more.*

Often, however, the improvement was not permanent. Only 1 in 4 patients undergoing psychotherapy and 1 in 6 undergoing drug therapy both recovered and experienced no relapse within 18 months (Shea & others, 1992). So, extravagant expectations that psychotherapy will transform your life and personality seem unwarranted. Still, Eysenck's pessimism also seems unwarranted. *On the average,* psychotherapy is somewhat effective—and is also cost-effective compared with the greater costs of medical care for psychologically-related ailments (Turkington, 1987). The annual cost of psychological disorders and substance abuse is staggering—in the United States, $273 billion annually in crime, accidents, and lost productivity, says the Alcohol, Drug Abuse, and Mental Health Administration (1990). Thus, as an investment in prenatal and well-baby care *reduces* long-term costs, so will an investment in almost any effective treatment for psychological problems. Anything that boosts employees' psychological well-being will reduce medical costs, improve work efficiency, and diminish absenteeism. Studies by health insurers show that mental health treatment can more than pay for itself with reduced medical costs (American Psychological Association, 1991).

But note that "on the average" refers to no one therapy in particular. It is like saying, "Surgery is somewhat effective," or like reassuring lung-cancer patients that "on the average" medical treatment of health problems is effective. What people want to know is not the effectiveness of therapy in general but the effectiveness of particular treatments for their particular problems.

In general, therapy is most effective when the problem is clear-cut and specific (Singer, 1981). Those who suffer phobias, who are unassertive, or who are frustrated by sexual performance problems can hope for improvement. Those who suffer chronic schizophrenia or who wish to change their whole personality are unlikely to benefit from psychotherapy alone (Zilbergeld, 1983).

## The Relative Effectiveness of Different Therapies

People considering therapy also want to know *which* psychotherapy will be most effective for their problem. The meta-analysis conducted by Mary Lee Smith and her colleagues (1977, 1980) allowed a comparison of the effectiveness of different therapies. What do you suppose they found? Did one therapeutic technique get the best results? Did people benefit more from group or individual therapy? From sustained or short-term therapy? From therapy with experienced or novice therapists?

Despite claims of superiority by advocates of different types of therapy, Smith's comparison of therapies revealed no clear winner. No one type of therapy proved consistently superior. Moreover—and more astonishing—it made no discernible difference whether the therapy was group or individual, whether many or few sessions were offered, or how well trained and experienced the therapist was. It seemed as though the dodo bird in *Alice in Wonderland* was right: "Everyone has won and all must have prizes."

Some therapies are, however, well suited to particular disorders. With specific behavior problems such as phobias, compulsions, or sexual dysfunctions, behavioral conditioning therapies achieve especially favorable results (Bowers & Clum, 1988; Giles, 1983). With depression, the cognitive therapies prove most successful (Dobson, 1989; Shapiro & Shapiro, 1982). Just as physicians offer particular treatments for specific problems rather than treating every complaint with the same drug or surgical procedure, so psychotherapists increasingly offer particular treatments for specific problems (Stiles & others, 1986).

## Commonalities Among Psychotherapies

*"I utilize the best from Freud, the best from Jung, and the best from my Uncle Marty, a very smart fellow."*

© 1994 by Sidney Harris—"Stress Test," Rutgers University Press.

Some clinicians suggest a reason why no one therapeutic method proves generally superior or inferior to another. Despite their differences, each therapy's effectiveness may derive from underlying commonalities. Jerome Frank (1982), Marvin Goldfried (Goldfried & Padawer, 1982), and Hans Strupp (1986) studied common ingredients of various therapies and suggested that they all offer at least three benefits: hope for demoralized people; a new perspective on oneself and the world; and an empathic, trusting, caring relationship. These "nonspecific" factors aren't all that therapy offers (Barker & others, 1988; Jones & others, 1988), but they are important aspects. They are part of what the growing numbers of self-help and support groups offer their members. And they have been part of what traditional healers offer (Jackson, 1992). Healers—special people to whom others disclose their suffering—have for centuries listened to understand and to empathize, reassure, advise, console, interpret, or explain.

### Hope for Demoralized People

People who seek therapy typically feel anxious, depressed, devoid of self-esteem, and incapable of turning things around. What any therapy offers is the expectation that, with commitment from the patient, things can and will get better. Apart from the particular therapeutic technique, this belief may itself promote improved morale, new feelings of self-efficacy, and diminished symptoms (Prioleau & others, 1983). This benefit of a person's belief in a treatment is the *placebo effect*. As we saw in Chapter 1, a placebo is an inert treatment often used as a control treatment in drug experiments. The placebo has no effect apart from a person's belief in it. In psychotherapy experiments, the placebo treatment may be listening to inspirational tapes, attending group discussions, or taking a fake pill.

The finding that placebo-treated people improve more than do untreated people, although not as much as do those receiving actual psychotherapy, suggests that one reason therapies help is that they offer hope. Said differently, therapy outcomes vary with the client's attitude—the client's motivation, confidence, and commitment. Each therapy, in its individual way, may harness the client's own healing powers. And that, says psychiatrist Jerome Frank, helps us understand why all sorts of treatments—including some folk healing rites known to be powerless apart from the patient's belief—may in their own time and place produce cures. Until the 1800s, most medicines and the healers who prescribed them owed their good reputations to natural recoveries—and to placebo effects. (In the next chapter we will explore the power and the limits of this mind-over-body factor.)

### A New Perspective

Every therapy offers people a plausible explanation of their symptoms and an alternative way of looking at themselves or responding to their worlds. Therapy also offers new experiences that help people change their views of themselves and their behaviors. Armed with a believable fresh perspective, they may approach life with a new attitude.

### An Empathic, Trusting, Caring Relationship

To say that all therapies are about equally effective is not to say all *therapists* are equally effective. Regardless of their therapeutic technique, effective therapists are empathic people who seek to understand another's experience; whose care and concern the client feels; and whose respectful listening, reassurance, and advice earn the client's trust and respect. Indeed, some believe that warmth and empathy are hallmarks of healers everywhere, whether psychiatrists, witch doctors, or shamans (Torrey, 1986).

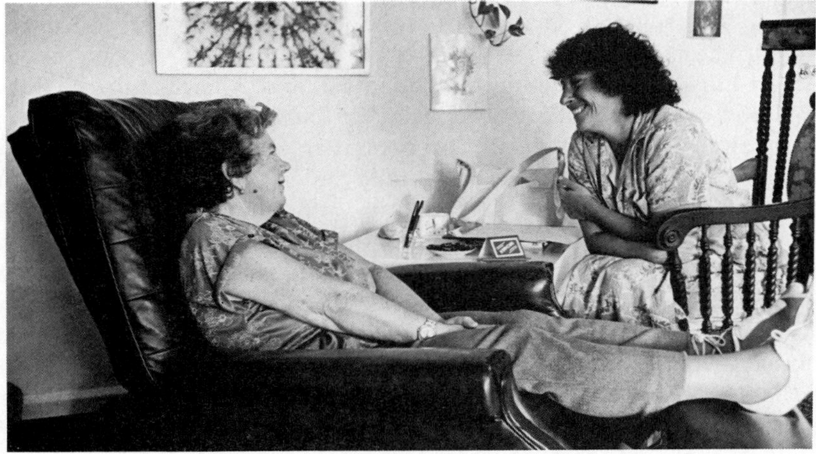

**A Caring Relationship** *Effective therapists form a bond of trust with their patients.*

The notion that all therapies offer *hope* through the *fresh perspective* offered by a *caring person* gains support from a meta-analysis of 39 studies. Each study compared treatment offered by professional therapists with treatment offered by laypeople. These laypeople included friendly professors, people with a few hours' training in empathic listening skills, and college students supervised by a professional clinician. The result? The "paraprofessionals," as we call these briefly trained people, typically proved as effective as the professionals (Christensen & Jacobson, 1994). Most of the problems they treated were mild. In these studies, however, trained paraprofessionals were—believe it or not—as effective as professionals, even when dealing with more disturbed adults, such as those diagnosed as seriously depressed.

To recap, people who seek help usually improve. So do many of those who do not undergo psychotherapy, and that is a tribute to our human resourcefulness and to our capacity to care for one another. Nevertheless, though it appears not to matter much which type of therapy is practiced, how long it lasts, or how experienced the therapist is, those who receive some psychotherapy usually improve more than those who do not. Mature, articulate people with specific emotional or behavior problems often improve the most.

Part of what all therapies offer is hope, a fresh way of looking at life, and an empathic, caring relationship. That may explain why the empathy and friendly counsel of paraprofessionals so often are as helpful as professional psychotherapy. And that may also explain why people who feel supported by close relationships—who enjoy the fellowship and friendship of caring people—are less likely to need or seek therapy (Frank, 1982; O'Connor & Brown, 1984).

## Culture and Values in Psychotherapy

All therapies offer hope, and nearly all therapists attempt to enhance their clients' sensitivity, openness, personal responsibility, and sense of purpose (Jensen & Bergin, 1988). But on certain matters of cultural diversity they may differ from one another and from their clients (Kelly, 1990). In Canada and the United States, for example, about 1 in 25 people—but (depending on the survey) one-fourth to one-half of psychiatrists and clinical psychologists—declare themselves atheist or agnostic (Gallup, 1993; Jensen, 1991; Lukoff & others, 1992). That raises an issue: What values prevail in psychotherapy? What values *should* prevail?

Albert Ellis, the rational-emotive therapist, and Allen Bergin, co-editor of the *Handbook of Psychotherapy and Behavior Change*, illustrate how sharply values can differ. Ellis (1980) assumes that "no one and nothing is supreme," that "self-gratification" should be encouraged, and that "unequivocal love, commitment, service, and . . . fidelity to any interpersonal commitment, especially marriage, leads to harmful consequences." Bergin (1980) assumes the opposite—that "because God is supreme, humility and the acceptance of divine authority are virtues," that "self-control and committed love and self-sacrifice are to be encouraged," and that "infidelity to any interpersonal commitment, especially marriage, leads to harmful consequences." Bergin and Ellis disagree more radically than most therapists regarding what values are healthiest. In so doing, however, they illustrate what they agree on: that psychotherapists' personal beliefs and values influence their therapy, and that therapists should divulge their values more openly.

Value differences may become significant when a therapist from one culture meets a client from another. In North America, Europe, and Australia, for example, most therapists reflect their culture's individualism (by giving priority to personal desires and identity). Clients who are immigrants from

## Close-Up: A Consumer's Guide to Psychotherapists

When should a person consider seeking a mental health professional? Life for everyone is marked by a mix of serenity and stress, blessing and bereavement, good moods and bad. It is only when troubling thoughts and emotions interfere with normal living that we should consider talking to a professional. The American Psychological Association notes that among the common trouble signals are these:

- Feelings of hopelessness
- Deep and lasting depression
- Self-destructive behavior such as alcohol and drug abuse
- Disruptive fears
- Sudden mood shifts
- Thoughts of suicide
- Compulsive rituals such as handwashing
- Sexual difficulties

If you are looking for a therapist, you may wish to shop around by having a preliminary consultation with two or three therapists. You can describe your problem and learn each therapist's treatment approach. You can ask questions about the therapists' values, credentials, and fees. And, you can assess your feelings about each.

| Type | Description |
|---|---|
| Psychiatrists | Physicians who specialize in the treatment of psychological disorders. Not all psychiatrists have had extensive training in psychotherapy, but as M.D.s they can prescribe medications. Thus, they tend to see those with the most serious problems. Many have a private practice. |
| Clinical psychologists | Most are psychologists with Ph.D.s and expertise in research, assessment, and therapy, usually supplemented by a supervised internship. About half work in agencies and institutions, half in private practice. |
| Clinical or psychiatric social workers | A 2-year Master of Social Work graduate program plus postgraduate supervision prepares some social workers to offer psychotherapy, mostly to people with everyday personal and family problems. About half have earned the National Association of Social Workers' designation of clinical social worker. |
| Counselors | Marriage and family counselors specialize in problems arising from family relations. Pastoral counselors, some certified by the American Association of Pastoral Counselors, provide counseling to countless people. Abuse counselors work with substance abusers, spouse and child abusers, and their victims. |

Asian countries, which expect people to be mindful of others' expectations, may therefore have difficulty with therapies that require them to think independently. Such differences help explain the reluctance of some minority populations to use mental health services (Sue, 1990). Recognizing that therapists and clients may differ in values, in communication styles, and in language, many therapy training programs are now providing training in cultural sensitivity and recruiting members of underrepresented culture groups.

## Summing Up

Because the positive testimonials of clients and therapists cannot prove that therapy is actually effective, psychologists have conducted hundreds of studies of psychotherapy's outcomes. Meta-analyses of these studies reveal that (1) people who remain untreated often improve; (2) those who receive psychotherapy are more likely to improve, regardless of what kind of therapy they receive and for how long; (3) mature, articulate people with specific behavior problems often receive the greatest benefits from therapy;

but (4) placebo treatments or the sympathy and friendly counsel of paraprofessionals also tend to produce more improvement than occurs with untreated people.

Different types of psychotherapy offer certain commonalities, such as new hope and a fresh perspective. Therapists do, however, differ in the values that influence their aims.

## The Biomedical Therapies

*Psychotherapy is one way to treat psychological disorders. The other is physically changing the brain's functioning—by altering its electrochemical transmissions with drugs, by overloading its circuits with electroconvulsive shock, or by disconnecting its circuits through psychosurgery.*

### Drug Therapies

By far the most widely used biomedical treatments today are the drug therapies. When introduced in the 1950s, drug therapy greatly reduced the need for psychosurgery or hospitalization. Discoveries in **psychopharmacology** (the study of drug effects on mind and behavior) revolutionized the treatment of severely disordered people, liberating hundreds of thousands from confinement in mental hospitals. Thanks to drug therapy—and to political and legal efforts to minimize involuntary hospitalization and to return hospitalized people to their communities—the resident population of state and county mental hospitals in the United States today is but 20 percent of what it was 40 years ago (Figure 16–7).

For those still unable to care for themselves, however, release from hospitals has meant not liberation but homelessness. If home is the place where, as Robert Frost said, when you go there, they have to take you in,

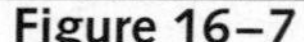
Figure 16–7

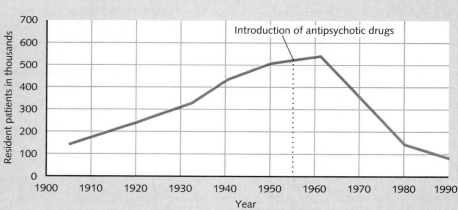

**The Emptying of U.S. Mental Hospitals** *After the widespread introduction of antipsychotic drugs, starting in about 1955, the number of residents in state and county mental hospitals declined sharply. But in the rush to deinstitutionalize the mentally ill, many people who are ill-equipped to care for themselves were left homeless on city streets. (Data from the National Institute of Mental Health and Bureau of the Census, 1993.)*

then some 200,000 disordered Americans have no place to call home (Leshner, 1992). Studies suggest that about one-third of the homeless suffer disabling psychological disorders (Fischer & Breakey, 1991; Levine & Rog, 1990; McCarty & others, 1991). And that doesn't include alcohol or drug abuse, which also plague about 1 in 3 homeless people. Unlike the homeless on yesterday's skid rows in major cities, 3 percent of whom were female, 25 percent of today's homeless are female.

*"The mentally ill were out of the hospital, but in many cases they were simply out on the streets, less agitated but lost, still disabled but now uncared for."*

Lewis Thomas
*Late Night Thoughts on Listening to Mahler's Ninth Symphony*, 1983

With almost any new treatment, including drug therapy, there is a first wave of enthusiasm as many people apparently improve. But that enthusiasm often diminishes after researchers subtract the rate of (1) normal recovery among untreated persons and (2) recovery due to the placebo effect, which arises from the positive expectations of patients and staff alike. So, to evaluate the effectiveness of any new drug, researchers use the double-blind technique. Half the patients receive the drug, the other half a similar-appearing placebo. Neither the staff nor the patients know who gets which. In double-blind studies, several types of drugs have proved useful in treating psychological disorders.

## Antipsychotic Drugs

The revolution in drug therapy for psychological disorders began when it was accidentally discovered that certain drugs, used for other medical purposes, also calmed psychotic patients. These antipsychotic drugs, such as chlorpromazine (sold as Thorazine), provide most help to people experiencing the positive symptoms of auditory hallucinations and paranoia, by dampening their responsiveness to irrelevant stimuli (Lenzenweger & others, 1989). Schizophrenia patients with the negative symptoms of apathy and withdrawal often do not respond well to these antipsychotic drugs. A newer drug, clozapine (marketed as Clozaril), does sometimes enable "awakenings" in such people. It also sometimes helps those with positive symptoms who haven't responded to other drugs. Although clozapine has a toxic effect on white blood cells in 1 or 2 percent of cases—thus necessitating regular blood tests—it is currently regarded as the most effective schizophrenia treatment. In 1994 the patent expired on this very expensive drug, permitting competitive pricing that now makes clozapine affordable to more people. Researchers are testing possible cousin drugs that would offer the same benefits without the blood problem.

**Herself Renewed** *Thanks to clozapine, Daphne Moss went "from hating the sunshine in the morning to loving it." No longer suffering from the paranoid delusion that her parents were witches, Moss began teaching school and living independently.*

The molecules of antipsychotic drugs are similar enough to molecules of the neurotransmitter dopamine to occupy its receptor sites and block its activity (Pickar & others, 1984). (Clozapine also blocks serotonin activity.) This finding—that most antipsychotic drugs block dopamine receptors—reinforces the idea that, as psychopharmacologist Soloman Snyder (1984) put it, "Dopamine systems in the brain are closely related to whatever is fundamentally abnormal in schizophrenic brains—either an excess of dopamine formation or perhaps a supersensitivity of dopamine receptors."

Antipsychotics such as Thorazine are powerful drugs that can produce sluggishness, tremors, and twitches similar to those of Parkinson's disease (Kaplan & Saddock, 1989). (Clozapine, thankfully, has few such side effects.) What is an effective dose for some people may be an overdose for others. Asians, for example, seem to require lower doses than Caucasians (Holden, 1991). By carefully monitoring the dosage and its effects, therapist and patient tread the fine line between relieving the symptoms and causing extremely unpleasant side effects. In this way, and with the help of supportive people, hundreds of thousands of schizophrenia patients who had been consigned to the back wards of mental hospitals have returned to jobs and to near-normal lives.

### Antianxiety Drugs

Among the most heavily prescribed and abused drugs are the antianxiety agents, such as Valium and Librium. Like alcohol, these drugs depress central nervous system activity. Because they reduce tension and anxiety without causing excessive sleepiness, they have been prescribed even for minor emotional stresses. Used in combination with other therapy, however, an antianxiety drug sometimes helps a person learn to cope successfully with frightening situations and fear-triggering stimuli.

The criticism sometimes made of the behavior therapies—that they reduce symptoms without resolving underlying problems—is also made of antianxiety drugs. Unlike the behavior therapies, they may even be used as a continuing treatment. Routinely "popping a Valium" at the first sign of tension can produce psychological dependence on the drug. When heavy users stop taking the drug, they may experience increased anxiety and insomnia, driving them back to the drug for relief.

### Antidepressant Drugs

As the antianxiety drugs calm anxious people down, the antidepressants sometimes lift depressed people up. Most of these drugs increase the availability of the neurotransmitters norepinephrine or serotonin, which appear to be scarce during depression. For example, the popular antidepressant fluoxetine (marketed as Prozac) blocks the reabsorption and removal of serotonin from synapses (Figure 16–8). (Prozac, and its cousins Zoloft and Paxil, are therefore called serotonin-reuptake-inhibitor drugs.) Other anti-

*1993 worldwide sales (Sleek, 1994):*
*Prozac—$1 billion*
*Zoloft —$460 million*
*Paxil —$225 million*

**Figure 16–8**

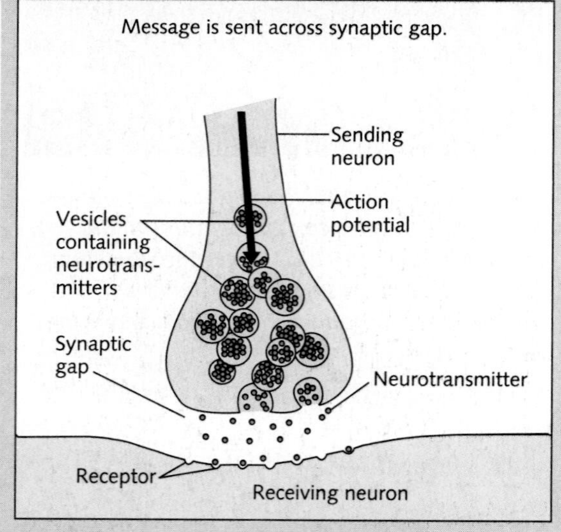

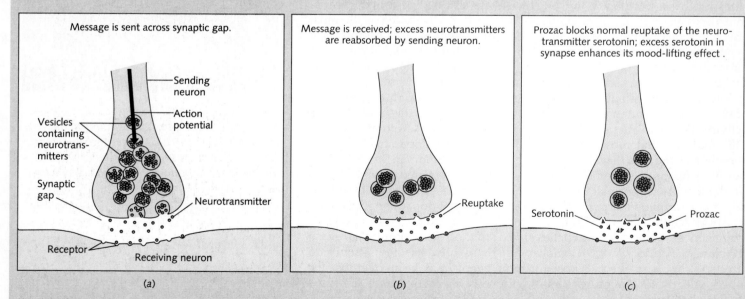


Message is sent across synaptic gap.

**Biology of Antidepressants** *After neurotransmitters carry a message across a synapse (a), the sending nerve cell normally reabsorbs excess neurotransmitters (a process called reuptake) (b). Prozac blocks reuptake of the neurotransmitter serotonin. The extra serotonin molecules therefore remain in the synapse, enhancing their mood-lifting effects (c).*

depressants work by blocking the reabsorption of both norepinephrine and serotonin or by inhibiting an enzyme that breaks down neurotransmitters such as serotonin. These drugs, however, have more potential side effects, such as dry mouth, weight gain, or dizzy spells.

Patients who begin taking antidepressants do not wake up the next day singing "Oh, what a beautiful morning!" Although the influence of antidepressants on neurotransmission occurs within hours, their full psychological effect often requires 3 or 4 weeks, sometimes aided by cognitive therapy to help the patient reverse a now-habitual negative thinking style. Moreover, the effect of these drugs—beyond that of natural recovery and the placebo effect—is often modest (Greenberg & others, 1992).

For those suffering the manic-depressive mood swings of a bipolar disorder, the simple salt **lithium** can be an effective mood stabilizer. An Australian physician, John Cade, discovered this in the 1940s when he administered lithium to a severely manic patient. Although his reason for doing so was misguided—he thought lithium had calmed excitable guinea pigs when actually it made them sick—Cade found that in less than a week the patient became perfectly well (Snyder, 1986). With continued lithium use, the emotional highs and lows typically level. After suffering mood swings for years, many people find relief with a daily dose of this cheap salt.

## Electroconvulsive Therapy

A more controversial brain manipulation occurs through shock treatment, or **electroconvulsive therapy (ECT)**. When ECT was first introduced in 1938, the wide-awake patient was strapped to a table and jolted with roughly 100 volts of electricity to the brain, producing racking convulsions and brief unconsciousness. ECT therefore gained a barbaric image that lingers to the present. Today, however, patients first receive a general anesthetic so they are not conscious, and a muscle relaxant to prevent injury from convulsions. Then a psychiatrist electrically shocks the unconscious patient's brain for 1 twenty-fifth of a second. Within 30 minutes the patient awakens and remembers nothing of the treatment or of the hours preceding it.

*The medical use of electricity is an ancient practice. Physicians treated the Roman Emperor Claudius (10 B.C.–A.D. 54) for headaches by pressing electric eels to his temples.*

Psychiatrists usually limit ECT to severely depressed patients. (It is usually ineffective in treating other psychological disorders.) After three such treatments a week for 2 to 4 weeks, 80 percent or more of depressed people improve markedly and without discernible brain damage (Bergsholm & others, 1989; Coffey, 1993). "A miracle had happened in 2 weeks," reported noted research psychologist Norman Endler (1982) after ECT alleviated his deep depression. A 1985 panel of the National Institutes of Health, as well as newer research reviews, report that for many others, too, ECT is an effective treatment for severe depression that has not responded to drug therapy (Consensus Conference, 1985; Parker & others, 1992). Thus, reports the American Psychiatric Association (1990), ECT has regained respectability as a "major treatment" for depression.

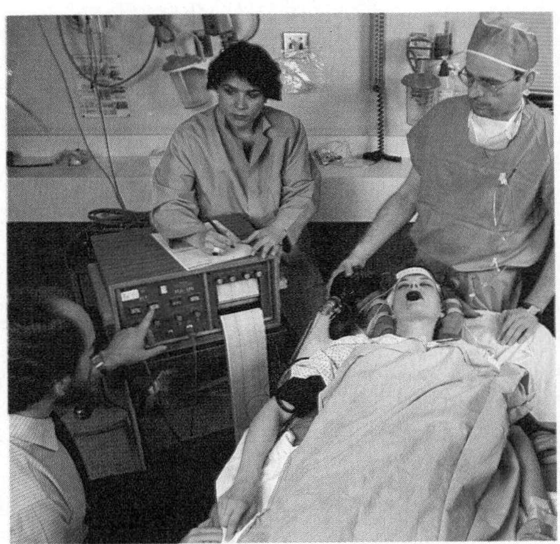

**Electroconvulsive Therapy** *Although ECT is controversial, it is the preferred treatment for depression that does not respond to drug therapy.*

How does ECT work? After more than 50 years, no one knows for sure (Kapur & Mann, 1993). Perhaps electrical shock increases the release of norepinephrine, a neurotransmitter that elevates arousal and mood and seems in short supply during depression. Or perhaps the shock-induced seizures cause the brain to react by calming neural centers where overactivity produces depression.

Although ECT is credited with saving many from suicide, its Frankensteinlike image continues. No matter how impressive the results, the idea of electrically shocking people into convulsions still strikes many as barbaric, especially given our ignorance about why ECT works. Moreover, ECT-treated patients, like other formerly depressed patients, are vulnerable to relapse. Nevertheless, electroconvulsive therapy is, in the minds of many psychiatrists and patients, a lesser evil than depression's misery, anguish, and risk of suicide.

## Psychosurgery

Because its effects are irreversible, **psychosurgery**—surgery that removes or destroys brain tissue to change behavior—is the most drastic and the least-used biomedical intervention. In the 1930s, Portuguese physician Egas Moniz developed what became the best known psychosurgical operation: the **lobotomy**. Moniz found that cutting the nerves connecting the frontal lobes with the emotion-controlling centers of the inner brain calmed uncontrollably emotional and violent patients. After shocking the patient into a coma, a neurosurgeon would hammer an icepicklike instrument through each eye socket into the brain, then wiggle it to sever connections running up to the front lobes. If a bit crude, the whole procedure was at least easy and cheap, taking only about 10 minutes. During the 1940s and 1950s, tens of thousands of severely disturbed people were "lobotomized," and Moniz was honored with a Nobel prize (Valenstein, 1986).

Although the intention was simply to disconnect emotion from thought, the effect was often more drastic: The lobotomy produced a permanently lethargic, immature, impulsive personality. During the 1950s, after some 35,000 people had been lobotomized in the United States alone, calming drugs became available and psychosurgery was largely abandoned. Today, lobotomies are almost never performed. Other psychosurgery is used only in extreme cases. For example, if a patient suffers uncontrollable seizures, surgeons can deactivate the specific nerve clusters that cause or transmit the convulsions. Because such beneficial operations are irreversible, however, neurosurgeons perform them only as a last resort.

The effectiveness of the biomedical therapies reminds us of a fundamental lesson: We find it convenient to talk of separate psychological and biological influences, but everything psychological *is* biological. Every thought and feeling depends on the functioning brain. Every creative idea, every moment of joy or anger, every period of depression emerges from the electrochemical activity of the living brain.

Body

Mind

**Mind-Body Interaction.** *The biomedical therapies assume that mind and body are a unit: Affect one and you will affect the other.*

## Summing Up

**Drug Therapies** The most widely used biomedical therapies are the antipsychotic, antianxiety, and antidepressant drugs.

**Electroconvulsive Therapy** Although controversial, ECT is an effective treatment for many severely depressed people who do not respond to drug therapy.

**Psychosurgery** Neurosurgeons rarely perform brain surgery to alleviate specific problems, because the effects of radical psychosurgical procedures such as lobotomy are irreversible and potentially drastic.

## Preventing Psychological Disorders

*There is an alternative perspective on alleviating disorder: Rather than treat the "sick" person, change the "sick" social contexts that breed disorder.*

Psychotherapies and biomedical therapies tend to locate the cause of psychological disorders within the disordered person. We infer that people who act cruelly must be cruel and that people who act "crazy" must be "sick." We attach labels to such people, thereby distinguishing them from "normal" folks. It follows, then, that we try to treat "abnormal" people by giving them insight into their problems, by changing their thinking, or by controlling them with drugs.

There is an alternative viewpoint: We could interpret many psychological disorders as understandable responses to a disturbing and stressful society. According to this view, it is not just the person who needs treatment, but also the person's social context. Better to prevent a problem by reforming a sick situation than to wait for a problem to arise and then treat it.

A story about the rescue of a drowning person from a rushing river illustrates the need for prevention. Having successfully administered first aid, the rescuer spots another struggling person and pulls her out, too. After a half dozen repetitions, the rescuer suddenly turns and starts running away while the river sweeps yet another floundering person into view. "Aren't you going to rescue that fellow?" asks a bystander. "Heck no," the rescuer replies. "I'm going upstream to find out what's pushing all these people in."

Preventive mental health is upstream work. It seeks to prevent psychological casualties by identifying and alleviating the conditions that cause them. George Albee (1986) believes there is abundant evidence that poverty, meaningless work, constant criticism, unemployment, racism, and sexism undermine people's sense of competence, personal control, and self-esteem. Such stresses increase their risk of depression, alcoholism, and suicide.

Albee contends that those who care about preventing psychological casualties should therefore support programs that alleviate poverty, discrimination, and other demoralizing situations. We eliminated smallpox not by treating the afflicted but by inoculating the unafflicted. We conquered yellow fever by controlling mosquitos. Prevention of psychological problems means empowering those who have learned an attitude of helplessness, changing environments that breed loneliness, renewing the disintegrating family, and bolstering parents' and teachers' skills at nurturing children's self-esteem. Indeed, "Everything aimed at improving the human condition, at making life more fulfilling and meaningful, may be considered part of primary prevention of mental or emotional disturbance" (Kessler & Albee, 1975, p. 557).

Albee reminds us again of one of this book's themes: A human being is an integrated bio-psycho-social system. For years we have trusted our bodies to physicians and our minds to psychiatrists and psychologists. That neat separation no longer seems valid. Chemical imbalances can produce schizophrenia and depression. And anger, depression, and stress, as the next chapter shows, can threaten our physical health. "*Mens sana in corpore sano*," says an ancient Latin adage: A healthy mind in a healthy body.

*"Mental disorders arise from physical ones, and likewise physical disorders arise from mental ones."*

*The Mahabharata*, c. A.D. 200

## Summing Up

Advocates of preventive mental health argue that many psychological disorders could be prevented. Their aim is to change oppressive, esteem-destroying environments into more benevolent, nurturing environments that foster individual growth and self-confidence.

## Terms and Concepts to Remember

### The Psychological Therapies

**psychotherapy** An emotionally charged, confiding interaction between a trained therapist and someone who suffers a psychological difficulty.

**eclectic approach** An approach to psychotherapy that takes advantage of techniques from the various forms of therapy, depending on the client's problems.

**psychoanalysis** Sigmund Freud's therapeutic technique, in which the patient's free associations, resistances, dreams, and transferences—and the therapist's interpretations of them—release previously repressed feelings, allowing the patient to gain self-insight.

**resistance** In psychoanalysis, the blocking from consciousness of anxiety-laden material.

**interpretation** In psychoanalysis, the analyst's assisting the patient to note and understand resistances and other significant behaviors in order to promote insight.

**transference** In psychoanalysis, the patient's transfer to the analyst of emotions linked with other relationships (such as love or hatred for a parent).

**person-centered therapy** A humanistic therapy, developed by Carl Rogers, in which the therapist uses techniques such as active listening within a genuine, accepting, empathic environment to facilitate clients' growth.

**active listening** Empathic listening in which the listener echoes, restates, and clarifies. A feature of Rogers's person-centered therapy.

**Gestalt therapy** Developed by Fritz Perls to combine the psychoanalytic emphasis on bringing unconscious feelings to awareness and the humanistic emphasis on getting "in touch with oneself"; aims to help people become more aware of and able to express their feelings, and to take responsibility for their feelings and actions.

**behavior therapy** Therapy that applies learning principles to the elimination of unwanted behaviors.

**counterconditioning** A behavior therapy procedure that conditions new responses to stimuli that trigger unwanted behaviors; based on classical conditioning. See also *systematic desensitization* and *aversive conditioning*.

**systematic desensitization** A type of counterconditioning that associates a pleasant relaxed state with gradually increasing anxiety-triggering stimuli. Commonly used to treat phobias.

**aversive conditioning** A type of counterconditioning that associates an unpleasant state (such as nausea) with an unwanted behavior (such as drinking alcohol).

**token economy** An operant conditioning procedure that rewards desired behavior. A patient exchanges a token of some sort, earned for exhibiting the desired behavior, for various privileges or treats.

**cognitive therapy** Therapy that teaches people new, more adaptive ways of thinking and acting; based on the assumption that thoughts intervene between events and our emotional reactions.

**rational-emotive therapy** A confrontational cognitive therapy, developed by Albert Ellis, that vigorously challenges people's illogical, self-defeating attitudes and assumptions. Also recently called *rational-emotive behavior therapy* by Ellis, emphasizing a behavioral "homework" component.

**family therapy** Therapy that treats the family as a system. Views an individual's unwanted behaviors as influenced by or directed at other family members; encourages family members toward positive relationships and improved communication.

### Evaluating Therapies

**meta-analysis** A procedure for statistically combining the results of many different research studies.

### The Biomedical Therapies

**psychopharmacology** The study of the effects of drugs on mind and behavior.

**lithium** A chemical that provides an effective drug therapy for the mood swings of bipolar (manic-depressive) disorders.

**electroconvulsive therapy (ECT)** Shock treatment. A biomedical therapy for severely depressed patients in which a brief electric current is sent through the brain of an anesthetized patient.

**psychosurgery** Surgery that removes or destroys brain tissue in an effort to change behavior.

**lobotomy** A now-rare psychosurgical procedure once used to calm uncontrollably emotional or violent patients. In this procedure the nerves that connect the frontal lobes to the emotion-controlling centers of the inner brain are cut.

## Critical Thinking Exercise

Now that you have read and reviewed Chapter 16, take your learning a step further by testing your critical thinking skills on the following practical problem solving exercise.

Deborah is very satisfied with the large amount of time and money she has invested in psychotherapy. When she began therapy, her life was in crisis and she was desperate for help in overcoming her depressed, pessimistic attitude. After shopping around, she finally found an understanding cognitive therapist who made her feel she could get her life back on track. After 3 months of psychotherapy, Deborah is once again enjoying her life and attributes her recovery to the psychotherapy.

Vincent is a middle-aged manager of an auto parts store. He is under a lot of pressure at work, has a very negative attitude about life, and "blows up" frequently at minor family annoyances. Although he admits that he is depressed and complains to his family a lot, he doesn't feel there is anything wrong with him. His family disagrees and is concerned that he is increasingly showing signs of psychologically disordered behavior. At their insistence, Vincent reluctantly agrees to see a psychotherapist. He picks a name at random from the phone book and grudgingly endures several weeks of "overpriced gibberish" to appease his family. Despite the good efforts of the psychotherapist, who attempts to countercondition Vincent's maladaptive behaviors, Vincent shows no improvement following psychotherapy.

1. Assuming their initial problems were equally serious, what could account for Deborah's and Vincent's very different experiences with psychotherapy?
2. Deborah now swears by cognitive therapy, while Vincent is very critical of behavior therapy. Are their recommendations acceptable as scientific evidence regarding the effectiveness of psychotherapy? Why or why not?

Check your progress on becoming a critical thinker by comparing your answers to the sample answers found in Appendix B.

## For Further Reading

**Burns, D. D.** (1989). *The feeling good handbook.* New York: William Morrow.

*Cognitive therapist David Burns suggests practical strategies for overcoming depression, conquering anxiety and fears, and building better relationships.*

**Corsini, R. J.** (1991). *Five therapists and one client.* Itasca, IL: Peacock.

*Therapists taking five distinct approaches describe their assumptions and techniques and show how they might work in therapy with the same fictitious client.*

**Dawes, R. M.** (1994). *House of cards: Psychology and psychotherapy built on myth.* New York: Free Press.

*A critical analysis of therapists' beliefs and powers. Provocative and controversial, but informed by research and logic.*

**Endler, N. S.** (1982). *Holiday of darkness.* New York: Wiley.

*A psychologist's account of his own struggle with depression. Discusses various attempts at treatment, including electroconvulsive therapy.*

**Engler, J., & Goleman, D.** (1992). *The consumer's guide to psychotherapy.* New York: Simon & Schuster.

*A 700-page handbook to help people decide whether they need therapy, how to find the right therapist, and how to evaluate their therapist and therapy.*

**Garfield, S. L., & Bergin, A. E.** (Eds.). (1994). *Handbook of psychotherapy and behavior change* (4th ed.). New York: Wiley.

*An authoritative source of research information. Contains expertly written chapters on every major therapeutic approach and on scientific issues regarding psychotherapy.*

# CHAPTER 17

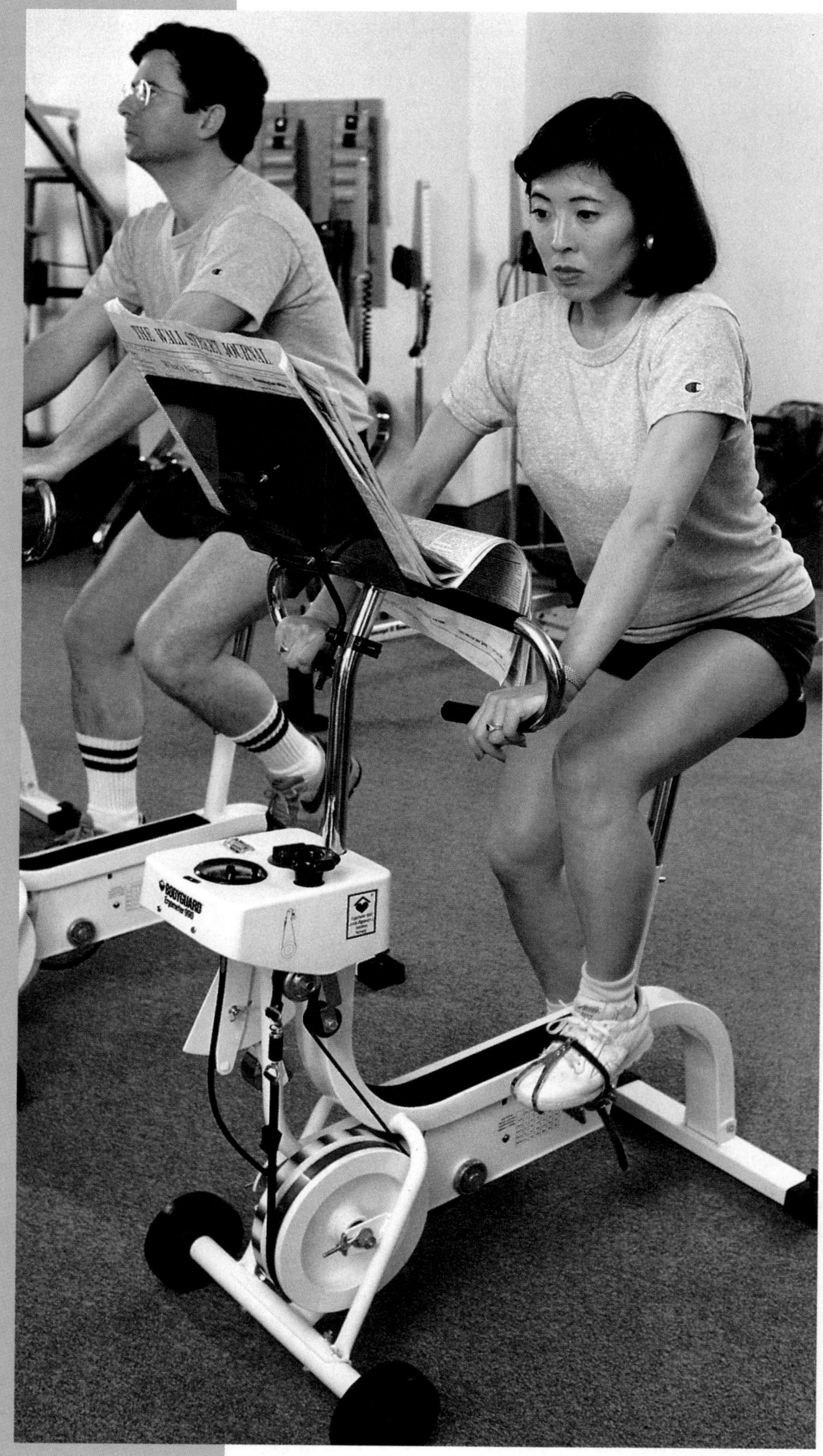

## Stress and Illness

**Stress and Stressors**
- The Stress Response System
- Stressful Life Events
- Perceived Control

**Stress, Personality, and Heart Disease**

**Stress and Resistance to Disease**
- Stress and the Immune System
- Stress and Cancer
- Conditioning the Immune System

## Reactions to Illness

**Am I Sick?**
- Noticing Symptoms
- Explaining Symptoms

**Do I Need Treatment?**

## Promoting Health

**Coping With Stress**
- Aerobic Exercise
- Biofeedback
- Relaxation
- Social Support

**Modifying Illness-Related Behaviors**
- Smoking
- Nutrition
- Obesity and Weight Control

# Stress and Health

No one needs to be told that psychological states cause physical reactions. Nervous about an important exam, we feel stomach butterflies. Anxious over a public speaking assignment, we frequent the bathroom. Smoldering over a conflict with a family member, we develop a splitting headache. If such stress endures, it may also bring on (in those physiologically predisposed) skin rashes, asthma attacks, or ulcers.

Many people are less aware of how behavior kills. Our behaviors influence whether we will become victims of one of today's four leading causes of serious illness and death: heart disease, cancer, stroke, and chronic lung disease (Figure 17–1). The National Academy of Sciences' Institute of Medicine (1982) has traced half the mortality from the 10 leading causes of death to people's behavior—to cigarette smoking, alcohol abuse, unprotected sex, ignoring doctors' orders, insufficient exercise, use of illicit drugs, and poor nutrition. If we could understand and modify these behavioral sources of illness, we might lessen people's suffering and increase their life expectancy and quality of life. To pursue these goals, psychologists and physicians created the interdisciplinary field of **behavioral medicine**, integrating behavioral and medical knowledge.

**Health psychology** provides psychology's contribution to behavioral medicine. Its numbers include many of the 3500 psychologists now on the faculties of Canadian and U.S. medical schools (Michaelson, 1993). Health psychologists ask: How do our perceptions of a situation determine the stress we feel? How do our emotions and personality influence our risk of disease? How do people decide they are sick, and when do they seek treatment? What attitudes and behaviors help prevent illness and promote health and well-being? How can we reduce or control stress?

**Figure 17–1**

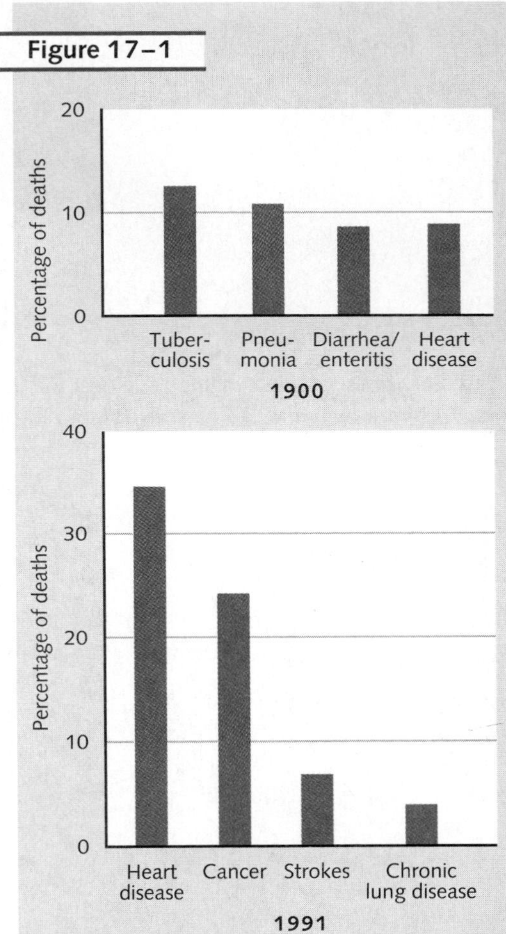


**The Four Leading Causes of Death in the United States in 1900 and 1991** *With the conquering of the major infectious diseases, diseases that are influenced by behavior have now emerged as the major causes of death. (From National Center for Health Statistics.) The story is much the same in Canada, Australia, New Zealand, and most European countries (World Health Statistics Annual).*

## Stress and Illness

*What is stress? To what extent, and by what mechanisms, does stress contribute to heart disease, infectious diseases, and cancer? What types of people are most at risk for stress-related ailments?*

Walking along the path toward her Rocky Mountain campsite, Karen hears a rustle at her feet. As she glimpses a rattlesnake, her body mobilizes for fight or flight: Her muscles tense, her adrenaline flows, her heart pounds. Flee she does, racing to the security of camp. Once there, Karen's muscles gradually relax and her heart rate and breathing ease.

Karl leaves his suburban apartment one morning and, delayed by road construction, arrives at the parking lot of the commuter train station just in time to see the 8:05 pull away. Catching the next train, he arrives in the city late and elbows his way through crowds of rush-hour pedestrians. Once at his bank office, he apologizes to his first client, who wonders where Karl has been and why his quarterly investment report is not ready. Karl does his best to mollify the client. Afterward, he notices signs of his pent-up emotion—his tense muscles, clenched teeth, and churning stomach.

*Worldwide, reports the World Health Organization, nearly a quarter of health care contacts are prompted by psychological problems (Sartorius, 1994).*

Karen's response to stress saved her life; Karl's, if chronic, could increase his risk of heart disease, high blood pressure, and other stress-linked health problems. Moreover, feeling under pressure, he might sleep and exercise less and smoke and drink more, further endangering his long-term health.

**The Faces of Stress** *Challenging positive events, such as graduating into the working world can be stressful. But most stresses arise from negative events that threaten our well-being, such as a child's sudden death from a stray bullet.*

## Stress and Stressors

Stress is a slippery concept. People sometimes use the word *stress* to describe threats or challenges ("Karl was under a lot of stress"), other times to describe our responses ("When Karen saw the rattler she experienced acute stress"). Most psychologists would define Karl's missed train as a "stressor," Karen's physical and emotional responses as a "stress reaction," and the process by which they both related to their environments as **stress**. Thus, stress is not just a stimulus or a response. It is the process by which we appraise and cope with environmental threats and challenges (Figure 17–2).

**Figure 17–2**

**The Stress Process** *How we react to stressors depends on who we are and how we appraise and cope with them. For example, criticism that an easygoing optimist perceives as a challenge may seem a dire threat to a temperamental pessimist.*

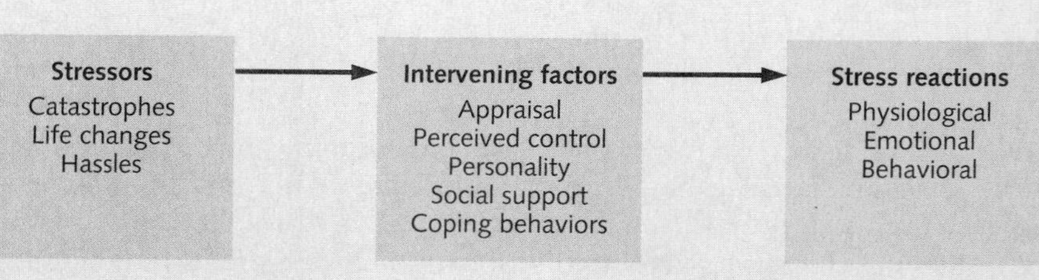

When perceived as challenges, stressors can have positive effects by arousing and motivating us to conquer problems. Championship athletes, successful entertainers, and great teachers and leaders all thrive and excel when aroused by a challenge. But more often stressors threaten our resources—our status and security on the job, our loved ones' health or well-being, our deeply held beliefs, our self-image (Hobfoll, 1989). And when such stress is severe or prolonged, it may also harm.

### The Stress Response System

Although medical interest in stress dates back to Hippocrates (460–377 B.C.), it was not until the 1920s that physiologist Walter Cannon (1929) confirmed that the stress response is part of a unified mind–body system. He observed that extreme cold, lack of oxygen, and emotion-arousing incidents all trigger an outpouring of epinephrine (adrenaline) and norepinephrine (noradrenaline). These stress hormones enter the bloodstream from sympathetic nerve endings in the inner part of the adrenal glands. As we saw in Chapter 13's discussion of emotional arousal, this is but one part of the sympathetic nervous system's response. When alerted by any of a number of brain pathways, the sympathetic nervous system increases heart rate and respiration, diverts blood to skeletal muscles, and releases fat from the body's stores—all to prepare the body for what Cannon called "fight or flight." All in all, this stress response struck Cannon as wonderfully adaptive. Physiologists have also identified a second stress response system (Figure 17–3). On orders from the cerebral cortex (via the hypothalamus and pituitary gland), the outer (cortex) part of the adrenal gland secretes the stress hormone cortisol.

Canadian scientist Hans Selye's (1936, 1976) 40 years of research on stress extended Cannon's findings and helped make stress a major concept in both psychology and medicine. The story of how Selye arrived at his concept of the stress response is one worth remembering in times of intelectual discouragement. Hoping to discover a new sex hormone, Selye injected rats with ovarian hormone extract. He detected three effects: enlargement of the adrenal cortex, shrinkage of the thymus gland (which contains disease-fighting white blood cells), and bleeding ulcers. Because no known hormone had ever produced such symptoms, Selye was elated. "At the age of 28, I seemed to be already on the track of a new hormone."

Before long, Selye's elation became disappointment. When he injected the rats with other fluids, he observed the same adrenal enlargement, thymus shrinkage, and bleeding ulcers. Alas, Selye concluded, the effects were *not* due to a new hormone:

> All my dreams of discovering a new hormone were shattered. All the time and all the materials that went into this long study were wasted. . . . I became so depressed that for a few days I could not do any work at all. I just sat in my laboratory, brooding. . . . The ensuing period of introverted contemplation turned out to be the decisive factor in my whole career; it pointed the way for all my subsequent work. . . . As I repetitiously continued to go over my ill-fated experiments and their possible interpretation, it suddenly struck me that one could look at them from an entirely different angle. If there was such a thing as a single nonspecific reaction of the body to damage of any kind, . . . the general medical implications of the syndrome would be enormous! (1976, pp. 24–26).

To verify his hunch, Selye studied animals' reactions to various other stressors, such as electric shock, surgical trauma, and immobilizing restraint. He discovered that the body's adaptive response to stress was so

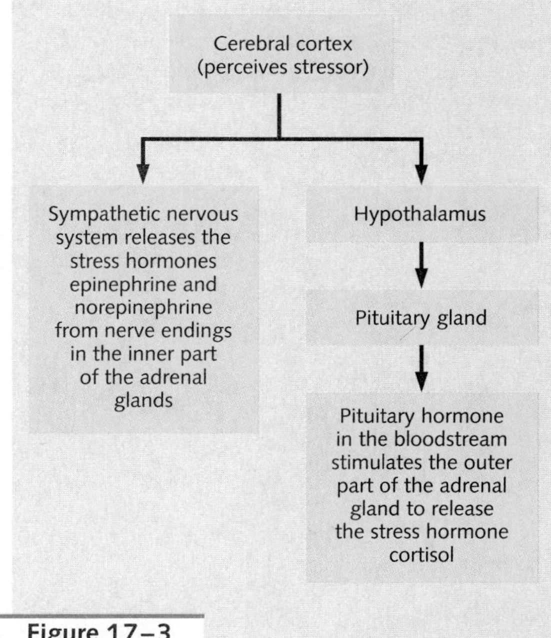


**Figure 17–3**

**Dual-Response System** *The adrenal glands (atop the kidneys) release stress hormones on orders received through a dual-track system.*

general—like a single burglar alarm that sounds no matter what intrudes—that he called it the **general adaptation syndrome (GAS)**.

Selye saw the GAS as having three phases (Figure 17–4). Let's say you suffer a physical or emotional trauma. In Phase 1, you experience an *alarm reaction* due to the sudden activation of your sympathetic nervous system. Your heart rate zooms, blood is diverted to your skeletal muscles, and you feel the faintness of shock. With your resources mobilized you are now ready to fight the challenge during Phase 2, *resistance*. Your temperature, blood pressure, and respiration remain high, and there is a sudden outpouring of hormones. If persistent, the stress may eventually deplete your body's reserves during Phase 3, *exhaustion*. With exhaustion, you are more vulnerable to illness or even, in extreme cases, collapse and death.

Newer research reveals subtle differences in the body's reactions to different stressors. Nevertheless, few medical experts today quarrel with Selye's basic point: Prolonged stress can produce physical deterioration. This leads to the practical concerns of today's health psychologists: What causes stress? What are the effects of stress? And how can we alleviate those effects?

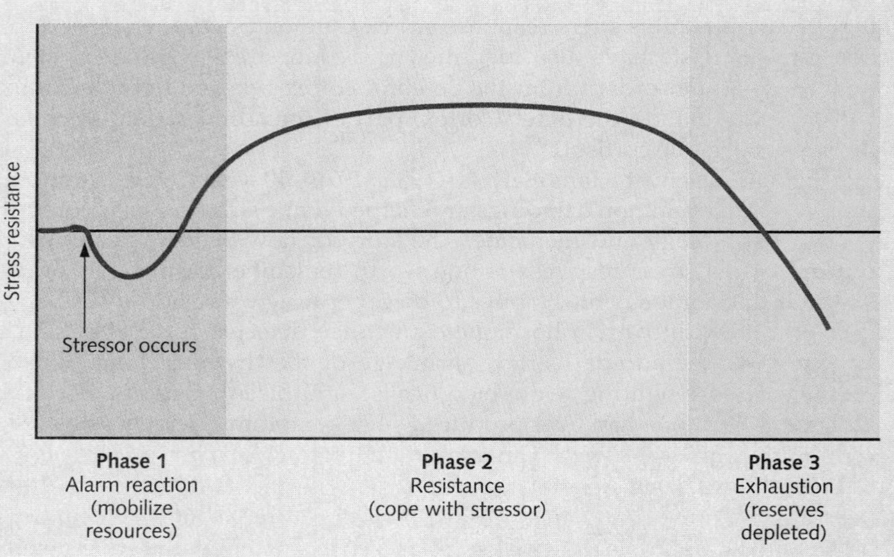


Figure 17–4

**Selye's General Adaptation Syndrome** *After a traumatic stress, the body enters an alarm phase of temporary shock. From this it rebounds, as stress resistance rises. If the stress is prolonged, wear and tear may lead to exhaustion.*

### Stressful Life Events

How stressed we feel depends on how we appraise events. One person alone in a house dismisses its creaking sounds and experiences no stress; someone else suspects an intruder and becomes alarmed. One person regards a new job as a welcome challenge; someone else appraises it as risking failure. Research has focused on our responses to three types of stressors: catastrophes, significant life changes, and daily hassles.

**Catastrophes** Catastrophes are unpredictable, large-scale events such as war and natural disasters that nearly everyone appraises as threatening. Although people often provide one another with aid and comfort after such events, the health consequences can be significant. Three examples:

- Paul Adams and Gerald Adams (1984) documented the effect of catastrophic events on health by studying the aftermath of the 1980 Mount Saint Helens eruption and ash fall. Compared with the same period during the previous year, and well after the ash had settled, emergency room visits in the nearby town of Othello, Washington, rose 34 percent during the 7 months following the eruption (Figure 17–5).
- In the year following the crash of a 747 jumbo jet at Lockerbie, Scotland, police officers—after being pressed into recovering human remains and patrolling the disaster zone—suffered a 38 percent increase in short-term illnesses (Paton, 1992).
- In the Republic of Belarus, where the worst fallout rained down from the nearby Chernobyl nuclear disaster, those who have left their native homes and friends and those who have stayed to live in a threatening environment have all suffered severe stress. Stress-related ailments such as hypertension and heart disease have reportedly tripled (Kolominsky & Parkhomenko, 1993).

Do community disasters usually produce effects this great? After digesting data from 52 such studies of catastrophic floods, hurricanes, and fires, Anthony Rubonis and Leonard Bickman (1991) found the typical effect more modest but nonetheless genuine. In disaster's wake, rates of psychological disorders, such as depression and anxiety, rose an average 17 percent. The nuclear accident at Three Mile Island produced similar stress symptoms in area residents (Baum & Fleming, 1993). Refugees fleeing their homeland also suffer increased rates of psychological disorder. Their stress

**Figure 17–5**

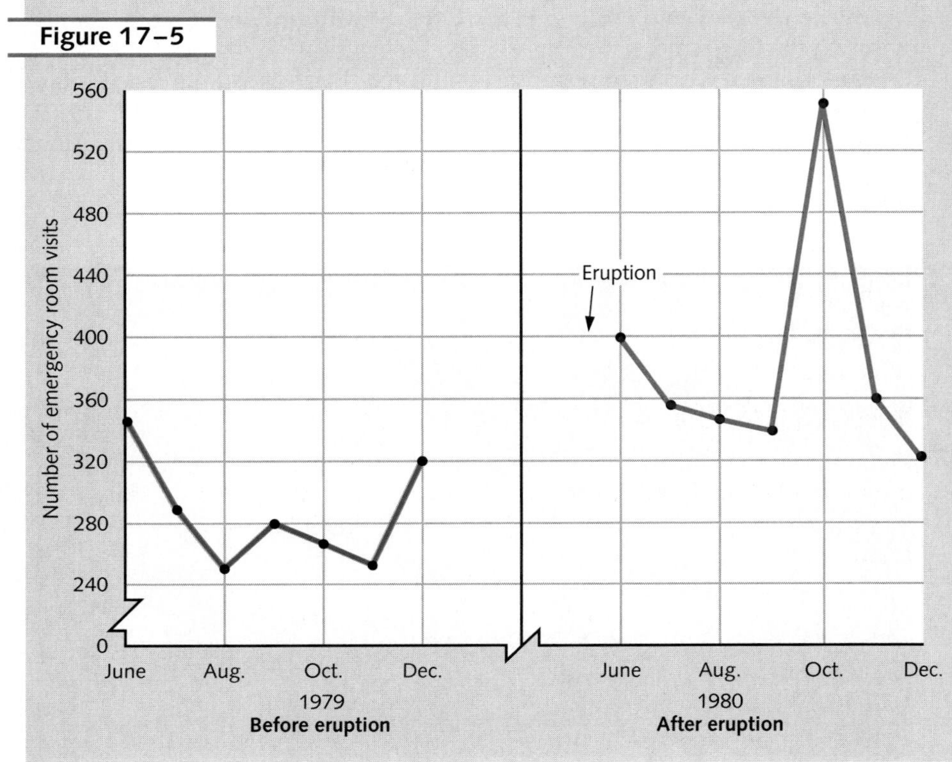


**Consequences of a Catastrophic Event** *During the 7 months following the May 18, 1980, eruption of Mount Saint Helens, emergency room visits in nearby Othello, Washington, rose 34 percent compared with the same 7-month period during the previous year. (From Adams & Adams, 1984.)*

stems from the trauma of uprooting and family separation and from the challenges of adjusting to a foreign culture, with its differing language, ethnicity, climate, and social norms (Williams & Berry, 1991). In all these cases, the health consequences often come only after prolonged stress.

**Significant Life Changes** The second type of life event stressor is personal life changes—the death of a loved one, the loss of a job, a marriage or divorce. Some psychologists study the health effects of life changes by following people over time to see if such events precede illnesses. Others compare the life changes recalled by those who have or have not suffered a specific health problem, such as a heart attack. A review of these studies commissioned by the National Academy of Sciences revealed that people recently widowed, fired, or divorced are more vulnerable to disease (Dohrenwend & others, 1982). A Finnish study of 96,000 widowed people confirmed the phenomenon: Their risk of death doubled in the week following their partner's death (Kaprio & others, 1987). Experiencing a cluster of crises puts one even more at risk.

Why, then, do some people feel stressed after a major life change while others do not? Because what matters more than the situation itself is our appraisal of it. Retirement may be viewed by one person as a time to relax and enjoy, by another person as a threat to identity and income. Having an abortion creates stress for women who morally oppose abortion and who lack their partner's or parents' support. Yet most women who appraise abortion differently do not experience severe distress after abortion (Adler & others, 1990; Major & others, 1990; Russo, 1992). The events of our lives flow through a psychological filter.

**Daily Hassles** As a famous Peanuts book says, "*Happiness is* . . . an *A* on your spelling test . . . finding someone you like at the front door . . . an invitation to a party . . . your first kiss in the rain." As we noted in Chapter 13, our happiness stems less from enduring good fortune than from our response to daily events—a longed-for date, a gratifying letter, your team's winning the big game.

The principle works for negative events, too. Everyday annoyances may be the most significant sources of stress (Kohn & Macdonald, 1992; Lazarus, 1990). These daily hassles include rush-hour traffic, aggravating

**No End in Sight** *"It's not the large things that send a man to the madhouse . . . no, it's the continuing series of small tragedies . . . not the death of his love but the shoelace that snaps with no time left" (Charles Bukowski, cited by Lazarus in Wallis, 1983).*

## Close-Up

## The Wounds of War—Post-Traumatic Stress Disorder

During the fighting in Vietnam, Jack's platoon was repeatedly under fire. In one ambush, his closest friend was killed while standing a few feet away. Jack himself killed a young Vietcong soldier by bludgeoning him with a rifle butt. Years later, images of these events intrude as flashbacks and nightmares. He still jumps at the sound of a cap gun or the backfire of a car. When annoyed by family or friends, he lashes out in ways he seldom did before Vietnam. To calm his continuing anxiety, he drinks more than he should.

Such has been the experience of combat veterans and sexual assault victims. Traumatic stress—experiencing or witnessing severely threatening events with a sense of fear, helplessness, or horror—can produce a *post-traumatic stress disorder*, symptoms of which include haunting memories and nightmares, social withdrawal, and anxiety or depression (Goodman & others, 1993; Kaylor & others, 1987; Wilson & others, 1988). After witnessing atrocities or living in life-threatening circumstances, children of the world's war zones and violent neighborhoods show similar symptoms (Garbarino, 1991, 1992). Their sense of basic trust erodes; many experience fearful wariness, troubled sleep, nightmares, and a sense of hopelessness about their future.

To pin down the frequency of post-traumatic stress disorder, the Centers for Disease Control (1988) compared 7000 Vietnam combat veterans with 7000 noncombat veterans who served during the same years. Combat stress more than doubled a veteran's risk of suffering alcohol abuse, depression, or anxiety.

Studies of Israeli and American soldiers reveal that the more terrifying and prolonged the battle experience, the greater the psychological casualties (King & King, 1991; Solomon, 1990). Among Vietnam veterans, the roughly 15 percent rate of post-traumatic stress symptoms was halved among those who never saw combat and tripled among those who experienced heavy combat. For example, more than a decade after the war, one study located 2095 identical twins among Vietnam-era veterans (Goldberg & others, 1990). Compared with co-twins who served noncombat roles in Vietnam, those who experienced heavy combat were 5.4 times more likely to be suffering post-traumatic stress disorder.

Researchers have also found that psychological disorders and suicide attempts were most common among vets who felt responsible for a trauma, because they had either killed someone or failed to prevent a death (Fontana & others, 1992). Many still experience nightmares, have trouble sleeping and concentrating, and find themselves easily startled. This is especially so for those exposed to savage mutilation, torture, or the sight of a friend's death. Much as they might wish to avoid or supress the memory, it intrudes.

Despite such symptoms, most combat-stressed veterans live productive lives. So have most American Jews who survived the Holocaust trauma—starvation, beatings, lost freedom, and the murders of loved ones—although they, too, often suffered lingering post-traumatic stress symptoms. In fact, compared with other American Jews of the same age, these survivors have been *less* likely to have seen a psychotherapist (18 percent versus 31 percent) and *more* likely to have had stable marriages (83 percent versus 62 percent). Moreover, virtually none have committed criminal acts. Researcher William Helmreich (1992, p. 276) reflects on their successes:

> The story of the survivors is one of courage and strength, of people who are living proof of the indomitable will of human beings to survive and of their tremendous capacity for hope. It is not a story of remarkable people. It is a story of just how remarkable people can be.

housemates, long lines at the bank or store, too many things to do, and getting caught in the rain without an umbrella. Although some people can simply shrug them off, others are "driven up the wall" by such inconveniences. Thus, 6 in 10 people say they feel "great stress" at least once a week (Harris, 1987).

Over time, these little stressors can add up and take a toll on health and well-being. Hypertension (high blood pressure) is common among the residents of urban ghettos, who endure the daily stresses that accompany poverty, unemployment, single parenting, crime, and overcrowding. There is a correspondingly low rate of heart attacks among those who live the relatively peaceful monastic life (Henry & Stephens, 1977).

Persistent on-the-job hassles can lead to a condition of mental, physical, and emotional exhaustion called **burnout** (Maslach, 1982). Teachers, nurses, social workers, and police officers—indeed, anyone facing persistent work hassles—may become worn down by the never-ending stress of their job. The result may be a sharp drop in performance caused by the fatigue of physical exhaustion, the depression of emotional exhaustion, and the cynicism of mental exhaustion.

## Perceived Control

Catastrophes, important life changes, and daily hassles and conflicts are especially stressful when we appraise them as both negative *and* uncontrollable. If two rats receive simultaneous shocks, but one of them can turn a wheel to stop the shocks, the helpless rat becomes more susceptible to ulcers and lowered immunity to disease (Laudenslager & Reite, 1984) (Figure 17–6).

So it goes in humans: Perceiving a loss of control, we are vulnerable to ill health. As we noted in Chapter 14, elderly nursing home patients who have little perceived control over their activities tend to decline faster and die sooner than do those given more control over their activities (Rodin, 1986). Given control over their work environments—by being able to adjust office furnishings and control interruptions and distractions—workers, too, experience less stress (O'Neill, 1993).

Another factor that influences our stress vulnerability is optimism. Psychologists Michael Scheier and Charles Carver (1992) report that optimists—people who agree with statements such as, "In uncertain times, I usually expect the best"—cope better with stressful events and enjoy better health. During the last month of a semester, students previously identified as optimistic report less fatigue and fewer coughs, aches, and pains. Optimists also respond to stress with smaller increases in blood pressure, and they recover faster from heart bypass surgery.

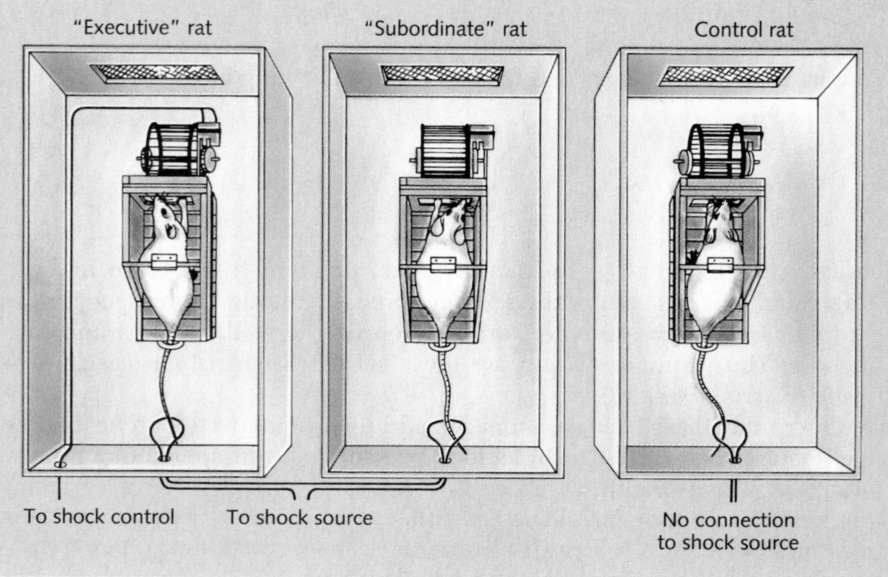


**Figure 17–6**

**Health Consequences of a Loss of Control**
*The "executive" rat at the left can switch off the tail shock by turning the wheel. Because it has control over the shock, it is no more likely to develop ulcers than is the unshocked control rat on the right. The "subordinate" rat in the center receives the same shocks as the executive rat. But because the subordinate rat has no control over the shocks, it is more likely to develop ulcers. (Adapted from Weiss, 1977.)*

Why do perceived loss of control and pessimism predict health problems? Animal studies show—and human studies confirm—that losing control provokes an outpouring of stress hormones. When rats cannot control shock or when humans feel unable to control their environment, cortisol levels rise and immune responses drop (Rodin, 1986). Captive animals therefore experience more stress and are more vulnerable to disease than are wild animals (Roberts, 1988). The crowding that occurs in high-density neighborhoods, prisons, and college dorms is another source of diminished feelings of control—and of increased levels of stress hormones and blood pressure (Fleming & others, 1987; Ostfeld & others, 1987).

## Stress, Personality, and Heart Disease

Although infrequent before this century, **coronary heart disease**—the narrowing of the vessels that nourish the heart muscle—had become North America's leading cause of death by the 1950s. In the United States alone, more than 700,000 people die annually from heart disease. Why this dramatic increase in coronary deaths? Eliminating some causes of death, such as diphtheria, enables people to live longer. Because everyone dies, that necessarily boosts the frequency of other death-causing ailments, such as heart attacks. But changing longevity does not explain why heart disease also is claiming more younger adults (Chesney, 1984).

Many factors increase the risk of heart disease—smoking, obesity, family history of the disease, high-fat diet, physical inactivity, elevated blood pressure, and elevated cholesterol level. But even when all these factors are considered, a large number of instances of heart disease remain unexplained. Many inactive, overweight smokers are free of the disease and many active, slender nonsmokers suffer heart attacks.

So what else might be involved? In 1956, cardiologists Meyer Friedman, Ray Rosenman, and their colleagues stumbled upon an idea (Friedman & Ulmer, 1984). While studying the eating behavior of white, San Francisco Junior League women and their husbands, Friedman and Rosenman discovered that the women consumed as much cholesterol and fat as their husbands did, yet they were far less susceptible to heart disease. Was it because of their female sex hormones? No, the researchers surmised, because African-American women with the same sex hormones but facing more stress are as prone to heart disease as their husbands are.

The Junior League president thought she knew the answer. "If you really want to know what is going to give our husbands heart attacks, I'll tell you. It's stress," she said sadly, "the stress they have to face in their businesses, day in, day out. Why, when my husband comes home at night, it takes at least one martini just to unclench his jaws."

To test the idea that stress increases heart disease, Friedman and Rosenman measured the blood cholesterol level and clotting speed of 40 tax accountants. From January through March, both of these coronary warning indicators were completely normal. Then, as the accountants began scrambling to finish their clients' tax returns before the April 15 filing deadline, their cholesterol and clotting measures rose to dangerous levels. In May and June, with the deadline past, the measures returned to normal. The researchers' hunch had paid off: Stress predicted heart attack risk.

The stage was set for what was to become Friedman and Rosenman's classic 9-year study of more than 3000 healthy men aged 35 to 59. At the start of the study, they interviewed each man for 15 minutes about his work and eating habits. During the interview, they noted the man's manner of talking and other behavioral patterns. Those who seemed the most reactive, competitive, hard-driving, impatient, time-conscious, supermotivated, verbally aggressive, and easily angered they called **Type A**. A roughly equal number who were more easygoing they called **Type B**. Which group do you suppose turned out to be the most coronary-prone?

*In both India and America, Type A bus drivers are literally hard-driving; they brake, pass, and honk their horns more often than their more easygoing Type B colleagues (Evans & others, 1987).*

By the time the study was complete, 257 of the men had suffered heart attacks, 69 percent of whom were Type A. Thus, compared with the Type B men, the Type As were more than twice as vulnerable. Moreover, not one of the "pure" Type Bs—the most mellow and laid-back of their group—had suffered a heart attack.

As often happens in science, this exciting discovery provoked enormous public interest. But after the honeymoon period, in which the finding seemed definitive and revolutionary, other researchers began asking, Is the finding reliable? If so, what is the toxic component of the Type A profile—the time-consciousness? The competitiveness? The anger?

*"At ten-thirty, you have an appointment to get even with Ward Ingram. At twelve, you're going to get even with Holus Wentworth at lunch. At three, you're getting even with the Pro-Tech Company at their annual meeting. And at five you're going to get even with Fred Benton over drinks."*

Drawing by Fradon; ©1985 The New Yorker Magazine, Inc.

Type A people may be more prone to heart disease because first, such individuals smoke more, sleep less, and drink more caffeinated drinks, all of which are associated with coronary risk (Hicks & others, 1982, 1983a,b). Second, their temperament may contribute directly to heart disease. In relaxed situations, the arousal of Type As and Type Bs is no different. But when harassed, given a challenge, or threatened with a loss of control, Type A individuals are more physiologically reactive. Their hormonal secretions, pulse rate, and blood pressure soar, whereas those of Type Bs remain moderate (Lyness, 1993). For example, when Redford Williams (1989) asked Duke University men to do simple math problems (with a prize for the fastest), the Type A students' stress hormone levels rose to more than double those of their Type B classmates. These hormones accelerate the buildup of plaques (scarlike masses formed by cholesterol deposits) on the artery walls, producing atherosclerosis, or "hardening" of the arteries. Atherosclerosis also makes reactive people vulnerable to high blood pressure, a risk factor for strokes and heart attacks (Schneiderman & others, 1989).

These findings suggest that reactive Type A individuals are more often "combat ready." When harassed or challenged, their active sympathetic nervous system redistributes blood flow to the muscles and away from the internal organs—including the liver, which removes cholesterol and fat from the blood. Thus, their blood may contain excess cholesterol and fat that is later deposited around the heart. Further stress—sometimes conflicts triggered by their own abrasiveness—may then trigger the altered heart rhythms that, in those with weakened hearts, can cause sudden death (Kamarck & Jennings, 1991). In such ways, the hearts and minds of people interact.

Newer research reveals that the Type A's toxic core is not a fast-paced life but is negative emotions—especially the anger associated with an aggressively reactive temperament (Matthews, 1988; Williams, 1993). The effect of an anger-prone personality appears most noticeably in studies in which interviewers assess verbal assertiveness and emotional intensity. (If you pause in the middle of a sentence, an intense, anger-prone person may jump in and finish it for you.) Among young and middle-aged adults, those who react with anger over little things are the most coronary-prone. One study followed Duke University law students over 25 years. Those inclined to be hostile and cynical were five times more likely than their gentler, trusting classmates to die by middle age (Williams, 1989). As Charles Spielberger and Perry London (1982) put it, rage "seems to lash back and strike us in the heart muscle."

*"The fire you kindle for your enemy often burns you more than him."*

Chinese proverb

Anger isn't the only toxic emotion. Depression, too, can be lethal. Centers for Disease Control researchers studied adults who were feeling a sense of hopelessness or at least mild depression. Compared with those without such feelings, these downhearted people were more vulnerable to heart disease in the ensuing 12 years. This was true even after controlling for differences in age, sex, smoking, and other factors linked to heart ailments (Anda & others, 1993). The depression that follows a spouse's death also increases one's risk of having a heart attack or stroke (National Academy of Sciences, 1984).

## Stress and Resistance to Disease

Not so long ago, the term *psychosomatic* described psychologically caused physical symptoms. To laypeople, the term implied that the symptoms were unreal—they were "merely" psychosomatic. To avoid such connotations and to describe better the genuine physiological effects of psychological states, most experts today refer instead to **psychophysiological** ("mind–body") **illnesses**. These illnesses, which include certain forms of hypertension, ulcers, and headaches, are stress-related. In people with reactive temperaments, chronic stress produces various changes. In one person, prolonged resentment, anger, or anxiety may stimulate an excess of digestive acids that eats away parts of the lining of the stomach or small intestine, creating ulcers. Another person under stress may retain excess sodium and fluids, which, together with constriction of the arteries' muscle walls, contributes to increased blood pressure (Light & others, 1983).

### Stress and the Immune System

Evidence that psychophysiological ailments are real comes from hundreds of new experiments that reveal the nervous and endocrine systems' influence on the immune system. The immune system is a complex surveillance system that defends the body by isolating and destroying bacteria, viruses, and other foreign substances. It includes two types of white blood cells, called **lymphocytes**. B lymphocytes form in the *b*one marrow and release antibodies that fight bacterial infections. T lymphocytes form in the *t*hymus and other lymphatic tissue and attack cancer cells, viruses, and foreign substances—even "good" ones, such as transplanted organs. Another agent of the immune system is the *macrophage* ("big eater"), which identifies, pursues, and ingests harmful invaders. Age, nutrition, genetics, body temperature, and stress all influence the immune system's activity.

The immune system can err in two directions. Responding too strongly, it may attack the body's own tissues, causing arthritis or an allergic reaction. Or it may underreact, allowing, say, a dormant herpes virus to erupt or cancer cells to multiply.

The immune system is not a headless horseman. Rather, it exchanges information with the brain and the hormone-secreting endocrine system. The brain regulates the secretion of stress hormones, which in turn suppress the disease-fighting lymphocytes. Thus, when animals are physically restrained, given unavoidable electric shocks, or subjected to noise or crowding, they become more susceptible to disease (Jemmott & Locke, 1984). One study monitored immune responses in 43 monkeys over 6 months (Cohen & others, 1992). Twenty-one were stressed by being housed with new roommates—three or four new monkeys—each month. (To empathize with

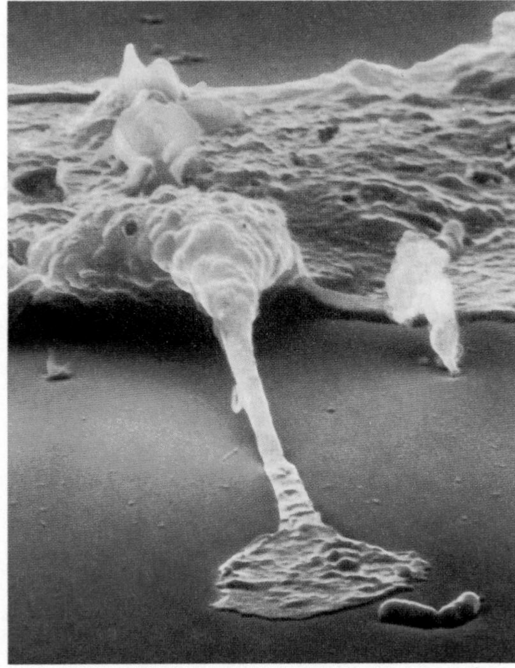

**The Immune System in Action** *A large macrophage (at top) is about to trap and ingest a tiny bacterium (lower right). Macrophages constantly patrol the body in a search for invaders, such as this* Escherichia coli *bacterium, and for debris, such as worn-out red blood cells.*

the monkeys, recall the stress of leaving home to attend school or summer camp, and imagine having to repeat this experience weekly.) Compared with monkeys left in stable groups, the socially disrupted monkeys developed suppressed immune systems.

Does stress similarly depress the immune system of humans? Consider:

- Accumulating evidence shows that stress lowers the body's resistance to upper respiratory infections as well as to herpes (Cohen & Williamson, 1991).
- In three separate Skylab missions, the immune systems of the astronauts showed reduced effectiveness immediately after the stress of reentry and splashdown (Kimzey, 1975; Kimzey & others, 1976).
- Marital spats are not good for health. As 90 healthy newlywed couples spent a half hour discussing problem areas in their marriage, some became angrier than others—and suffered more immune system suppression during the next day (Kiecolt-Glaser & others, 1993).
- Other studies show that students' disease-fighting mechanisms are weaker during high-stress times, such as exam weeks, and on days when they are upset (Jemmott & Magloire, 1988; Stone & others, 1987). In one experiment, a stressful experience increased the severity of symptoms experienced by volunteers who were knowingly infected with a cold virus (Dixon, 1986). In another, 47 percent of subjects living stress-filled lives developed colds after a virus was dropped in their noses, but only 27 percent of those living relatively free of stress caught colds (Cohen & others, 1991, 1993).
- The National Academy of Sciences (1984) reports that the grief and depression that follow the death of a spouse decrease immune defenses (which helps explain the increase in disease among those recently widowed). In fact, depression of any sort tends to suppress the immune system (Herbert & Cohen, 1993; Weisse, 1992). Thus, in one study of leukemia patients preparing to undergo bone marrow transplants, 12 of 13 depressed patients died within a year. Among the many more who were not depressed, 39 percent were still alive after 2 years (Colon & others, 1991).

### Stress and Cancer

Stress and negative emotions such as depression also have been linked to cancer. To explore a possible connection between stress and cancer, experimenters have given rodents tumor cells or cancer-producing substances. Those rodents also exposed to uncontrollable stress, such as inescapable shocks, are more prone to cancer (Sklar & Anisman, 1981). With their immune systems weakened by stress, their tumors develop sooner and grow larger.

Several investigators report that people, too, are at increased risk for cancer a year or so after experiencing depression, helplessness, or bereavement. For example, cancer occurs more often than usual among those widowed, divorced, or separated. One study of the husbands of women with terminal breast cancer pinpointed a possible reason: During the first 2 months after their wives' deaths, the bereaved men's lymphocyte responses dropped (Schleifer & others, 1979).

Another study gave a personality test to 2018 middle-aged men employed by the Western Electric Company in 1958. During the next 20 years, 7 percent of those not depressed and 12 percent of those somewhat depressed died of cancer (Persky & others, 1987). A large Swedish study revealed that people with a history of workplace stress had 5.5 times greater risk of colon cancer than those who reported no such problems (Courtney & others, 1993). In both these studies, the cancer difference was not attributable to differences in age, smoking, drinking, or physical characteristics.

What is more, ever-nice cancer patients who bottle up their negative emotions have less chance of survival than do those who verbalize their feelings (O'Leary, 1990; Temoshok, 1992). A UCLA survey of 649 cancer specialists, who had treated more than 100,000 cancer patients, supported the idea that patients' attitudes matter. Four in five of these physicians rated "a positive approach to the challenge of the illness" and a "strong will to live" as important contributors to longevity (Cousins, 1989).

*"A cheerful heart is a good medicine, but a downcast spirit dries up the bones."*

Proverbs 17:22

In the first weeks after receiving their diagnosis, cancer patients and those carrying the AIDS virus are understandably anxious and depressed (Andersen, 1989; Antoni & others, 1991). Might promoting their fighting spirit aid their survival? Can hope boost the body by alleviating negative emotions that suppress the cancer-fighting immune system?

With cancer patients, several studies offer hope. Mastectomy patients who display a determination to conquer their breast cancer survive longer than do those who are stoic or feel hopeless (Hall & Goldstein, 1986; Pettingale & others, 1985). And a study of 86 women undergoing breast cancer therapy at Stanford University Medical School found that those who participated in weekly group therapy survived an average of 37 months, double the 19-month average survival rate among the nonparticipants (Spiegel & others, 1989). The investigator, psychiatrist David Spiegel (1993), was stunned. He expected the support groups to alleviate cancer-related emotional distress, but he was intending to show that more positive emotions would *not* influence the course of cancer. At least half a dozen research teams are now repeating his study. If Spiegel's finding proves reliable, it will surely reinforce efforts to train physicians to communicate with patients in ways that minimize resignation and sustain hope.

**Supporting Survival** *This "Sharing Group" is part of California's Wellness Community program, which promotes stress reduction and optimism as possible boosts for its cancer-patient participants.*

One danger in publicizing reports on attitudes and cancer is that they may lead some patients to blame themselves for their cancer—"If only I had been more expressive, relaxed, and hopeful." A corollary danger is a "wellness macho" among the healthy, who credit their health to their healthy character and lay a guilt trip on the ill: "She has cancer? Tough darts. That's what you get for holding your feelings in and being so nice." Dying thus becomes "the ultimate failure."

*"I didn't give myself cancer."*

Mayor Barbara Boggs Sigmund, 1939–1990
Princeton, New Jersey

## Thinking Critically About Handedness and Health—The Case of the Disappearing Southpaws

While studying handedness, psychologist Stanley Coren (1993) stumbled upon a rather stunning fact of life: With age, the percentage of left-handers declines dramatically. In his initial sample of 5147 people, he found that left-handers were 14.6 percent of 10-year-olds, 4.6 percent of 50-year-olds, and less than 1 percent of those over age 80 (Figure 17–7). Other researchers around the world have confirmed Coren's finding: Left-handers disappear with age.

One cannot resist asking, Why? Intrigued, Coren and fellow sleuth Diane Halpern (1991; Halpern & Coren, 1988, 1991, 1993) set out in search of an answer. (If you were they, what explanations might have come to mind?)

**Figure 17–7**

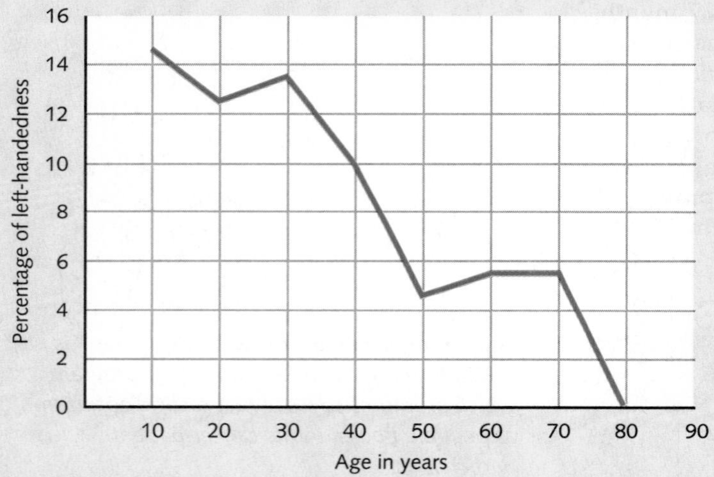


**The Disappearing Southpaws** *The percentage of left-handers decreases sharply in samples of older people. (Adapted from Coren, 1993.)*

Perhaps, Coren and Halpern first thought, childhood coercion causes natural lefties to become right-handed as they age. (Many older people can recall having their left hands slapped, tied down, or even balled into a fist with surgical tape when they tried to use it.) If today's parents and teachers are more accepting of left-handedness than were those earlier in this century, the result might be more young left-handers.

If indeed the vanishing southpaws are a historical rather than an age-driven phenomenon, then left-handedness should be increasing along with its acceptance. But no—North American and European studies suggest that during this century left-handers have increased only from about 6 percent of the population to 10 percent (Porac & others, 1980). This small increase hardly explains the much greater percentage of left-handers among the very young. Examining handedness in art works over centuries, Coren and his colleagues again were amazed by the stability of left-handedness. In art works dated from 15,400 to 3000 B.C., 10 percent of the people were depicted as left-handed. In modern art works, 11 percent were left-handers.

If childhood coercion doesn't explain the disappearance of left-handers, might the world's being designed for right-handers make it easier for lefties to learn *gradually* to use their right hands? But again, no—preschoolers who switch handedness complete the process before adolescence. Handedness rarely switches after age 8 or 9, and even before then it occurs only for specific coerced actions (such as eating or writing). So simple learning just doesn't explain the slow and gradual disappearance of left-handers.

"Truth is arrived at by the painstaking process of eliminating the untrue," said Sherlock Holmes. "When you have eliminated the impossible, whatever remains, *however improbable*, must be the truth." But what else remains? Coren and Halpern then dared to think the unthinkable: that left-handers die younger. "That can't be true," skeptical colleagues replied

*When organic causes of illness are unknown, it is tempting to invent psychological explanations. Before the germ that causes tuberculosis was discovered, personality explanations of TB were popular (Sontag, 1978).*

In noting the link between emotions and cancer, we must remember that stress does not *create* cancer cells. Rather, it affects their growth by weakening the body's natural defenses against a few proliferating, malignant cells. Although a relaxed, hopeful state may enhance these defenses, we must be aware of the thin line that divides science from wishful thinking. The physiological processes at work in advanced cancer or AIDS are *not* likely to be derailed by avoiding stress or by a relaxed but determined spirit (Kessler & others, 1991).

when Coren first voiced the idea. "If true, surely someone would have noticed by now. Besides, my paternal grandmother was left-handed and lived to 91. And what about lefties Benjamin Franklin (who lived to 84), Charlie Chaplin (88), and Pablo Picasso (92)?"

As we have seen many times, vivid anecdotes ("I know a person who . . .") are no substitute for conclusions based on large and representative samples. Examples do not prove a generality, nor do counter-examples of short-lived left-handers, such as Babe Ruth (53), Marilyn Monroe (36), and Alexander the Great (33). So, to explore their morbid idea, Coren and Halpern first reflected on the lefties' known health risks. Left-handers are more likely to have experienced birth stress, such as prematurity or the need for assisted respiration. They also endure more headaches, have more accidents (probably because of right-handed equipment), use more tobacco and alcohol, and suffer more immune system problems (including allergies such as asthma, eczema, and hay fever).

These handedness differences aren't huge (individual differences are much greater). But might they, like sex differences in health risks, add up to differing life spans? When Coren and Halpern studied a random sample of recently deceased people of all ages they felt they were on to something. On average, right-handers lived 8 or 9 years longer. When Coren, Halpern, and other researchers excluded children, by comparing left- and right-handed former baseball and cricket players, they found the life-span difference reduced but still apparent (Aggleton & others, 1993; Rogerson, 1994).

This stunning finding triggered an avalanche of publicity and some follow-up research that produced no life-expectancy advantage for right-handers (Harris, 1993). One National Institute of Aging research team followed 3800 East Boston adults for 6 years and found that, at any age, left-handers were *not* more likely to die (Salive & others, 1993). Coren (1993) is not convinced. He responds that 6 years is not long enough to catch a statistically significant handedness effect in a sample this small.

The unfinished case of the disappearing southpaws illustrates the very heart of science. Science dares to ask researchable questions, even those with unsettling implications. It welcomes new ideas, but it also subjects them to skeptical scrutiny. In the court of scientific judgment, researchers must state their case and expose themselves to counterexamination from opposing views. The process is imperfect. During heated debate, scientists sometimes forget their own ideals. Yet, over time, science has a way of unmasking error and taking us closer to truth. As it does so, explaining the absence of old left-handers, perhaps it will also point the way to safer, more comfortable environments for left-handed people.

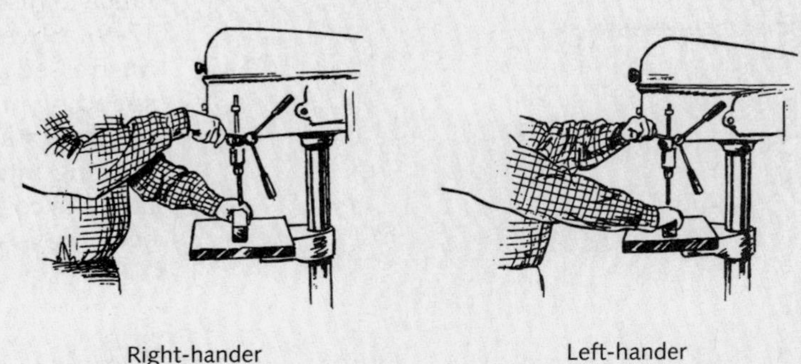


**The Southpaw's Hazardous Life** *In the book* The Left-Hander Syndrome, *Stanley Coren illustrates risks posed by a world made for right-handers. When left-handers use a drill press, their left arm may obscure their view.*

We must also remember that our emotional reactivity is partly inherited (recall pages 97–98). As theologian Reinhold Niebuhr recognized in his "serenity prayer," we do well to accept those things about ourselves that we cannot change, to change those things that we can, and to seek wisdom to discern the difference. By studying the interplay among emotions, the brain, and the immune system, health psychologists seek the wisdom needed to distinguish between pseudoscientific hocus-pocus and the genuine effects of emotions on health.

## Conditioning the Immune System

A hay fever sufferer sees the flower on the restaurant table and, not realizing it is plastic, begins to sneeze. Such experiences hint that stress is not the only psychological influence on the body's ailments. Simple classical conditioning may be an added influence. This raises an intriguing question: If conditioning affects the body's overt physiological responses, might it affect the immune system as well?

Psychologist Robert Ader together with immunologist Nicholas Cohen (1985) discovered that the answer is yes. Ader came upon this discovery while researching taste aversion in rats. He paired the rats' drinking of saccharin-sweetened water with injections of a drug that happened to suppress immune functioning. After repeated pairings, sweetened water alone triggered immune suppression as if the drug had been given (Figure 17–8). Such conditioned immune suppression can triple an animal's likelihood of growing a tumor when fed a carcinogen (Blom & others, 1994).

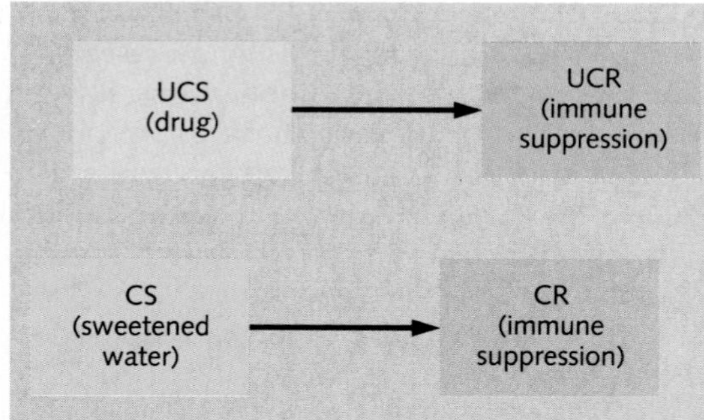


**Figure 17–8**

**The Conditioning of Immune Suppression** *After Ader and Cohen associated sweetened water with a drug that causes immune suppression in rats, the inert substance alone triggered the immune response.*

Many questions about the role of the immune system and how to harness its healing potential remain unanswered. If it is possible to condition the immune system's suppression, should it not also be possible to condition its enhancement? Might this be one way in which placebos—treatments that have no biochemical effect—promote healing? Can a placebo sometimes elicit the same healthful state produced by an actual drug? Research now under way may soon answer such questions.

For now, we can view the toll that stress sometimes takes on our resistance to disease as a price we pay for the adaptive benefits of stress (Figure 17–9). Stress invigorates our lives by arousing and motivating us. An unstressed life would hardly be challenging or productive. Moreover, spending our resources in fighting or fleeing an external threat aids our immediate survival. But it does so at the cost of diminished resources for fighting internal threats to our body's health. When the stress is momentary, the cost is negligible. When uncontrollable aggravations persist, however, the cost may become considerable.

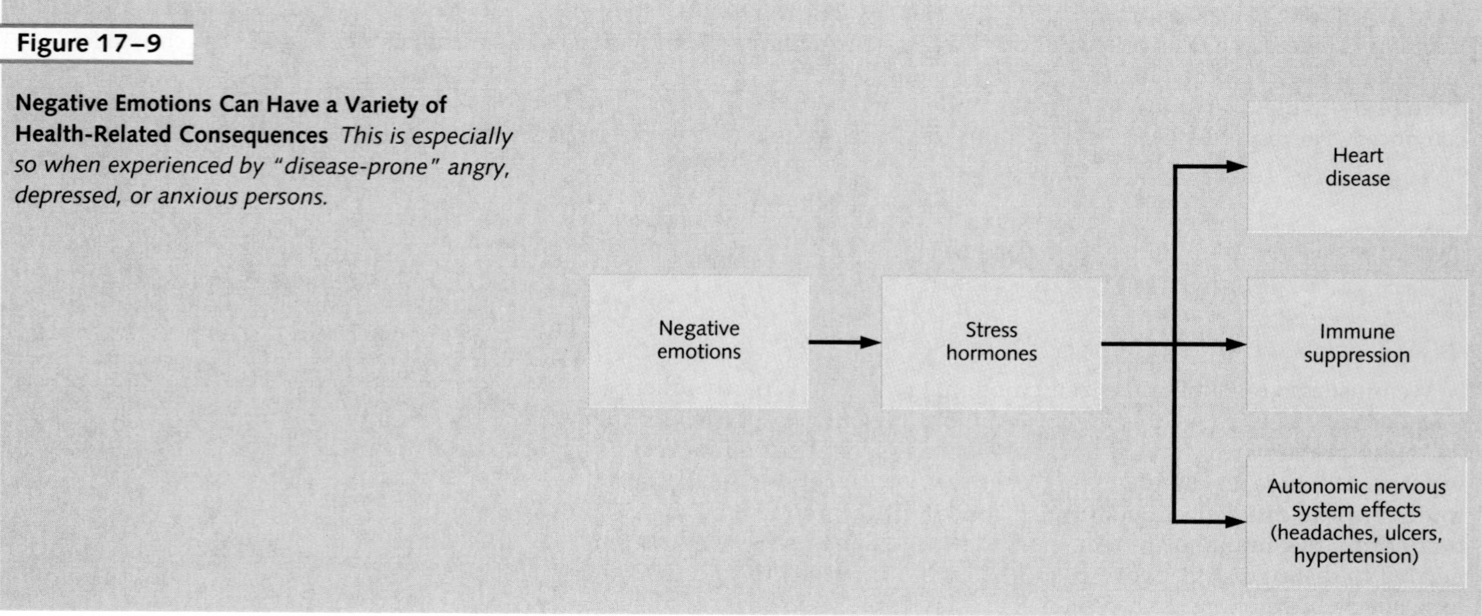


**Figure 17–9**

**Negative Emotions Can Have a Variety of Health-Related Consequences** *This is especially so when experienced by "disease-prone" angry, depressed, or anxious persons.*

On the up side, we can celebrate the self-healing powers of people who maintain a sense of control and a positive approach to life. Facing surmountable challenges and striving for realistic goals may at first be fatiguing. But in the long run, self-confidence, stability, and future stress resistance come not from avoiding challenges but from conquering them (Aspinwall & Taylor, 1992; Friedman, 1991).

All this new behavioral medicine research provides yet another reminder of one of contemporary psychology's overriding themes. Mind and body continuously interact. Everything psychological is simultaneously biological. And because psychological states are biological events, they influence other parts of our biological system. As the Indian sage Santi Parva recognized more than 4000 years ago, "Mental disorders arise from physical causes, and likewise physical disorders arise from mental causes."

## Summing Up

People's behaviors and stress responses are major influences on health and disease. Health psychology contributes to the interdisciplinary field of behavioral medicine, which provides new avenues for the prevention and treatment of illness. Among health psychology's concerns are the effects of stress, the seeking and following of medical treatment, and the promotion of healthier living.

**Stress and Stressors** Walter Cannon viewed stress, the process by which we appraise and respond to events that challenge or threaten us, as a "fight or flight" system. Hans Selye saw it as a three-stage, general adaptation syndrome (alarm/resistance/exhaustion). Modern research on stress assesses the health consequences of catastrophic events, significant life changes, and daily hassles. Events are stressful when perceived as both negative and uncontrollable.

**Stress, Personality, and Heart Disease** Coronary heart disease, North America's number one cause of death, has been linked with the competitive, hard-driving, impatient, and (especially) anger-prone Type A personality. Under stress, the body of a reactive, hostile person secretes more of the hormones that accelerate the buildup of plaques on the heart's artery walls.

**Stress and Resistance to Disease** Stress can suppress the immune system, making a person more vulnerable to infections and malignancy. New experiments show that conditioning also influences the immune system's responses.

## Reactions to Illness

*Given our myriad body sensations, how do we define some as indicating sickness? And what influences whether we seek treatment?*

Health psychologists study not only the links between stress and illness but also how we cope with illness. In the perfect world suggested by Figure 17–10 (page 590), people would behave rationally when deciding whether to seek medical treatment. First, they would notice and realistically evaluate the seriousness of their aches and pains. Second, they would seek medical care when needed. But most people do not do this. Let's see why.

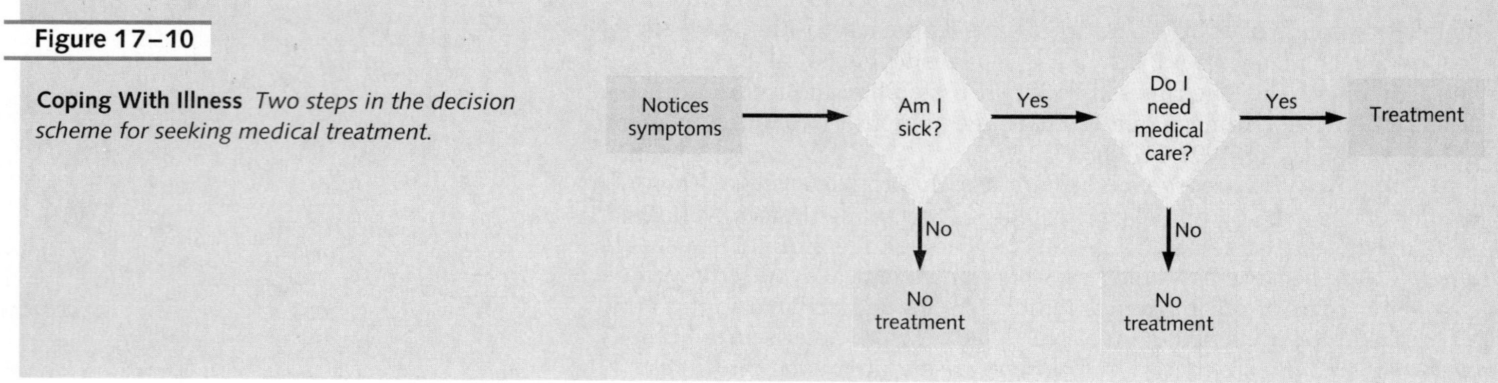


Figure 17–10

**Coping With Illness** *Two steps in the decision scheme for seeking medical treatment.*

## Am I Sick?

Chances are you have recently experienced one or more of college students' typical physical complaints: headache, stomachache, nasal congestion, sore muscles, ringing in the ears, excess perspiration, cold hands, racing heart, dizziness, stiff joints, and diarrhea or constipation (Pennebaker, 1982). Such symptoms require your interpretation. Are they meaningless? Or are you coming down with the flu or a cold? Hardly a week goes by without our playing doctor by self-diagnosing the significance of some symptom.

With more serious aches and pains, the questions become more specific—and more critical. Is your stubbed toe bruised or broken? Is your abdominal pain caused by indigestion or a ruptured appendix? Is the chest pain a muscle spasm or a heart attack? Is the small lump a meaningless cyst or a tumor? What factors influence whether we notice and how we explain such symptoms?

### Noticing Symptoms

Noticing and interpreting our body's signals is like noticing and interpreting how our car is running. Unless the signals are loud and clear, we often miss them. Most of us cannot tell whether our car needs an oil change merely by listening to its engine. Similarly, most of us are not astute judges of our heart rate, blood-sugar level, or blood pressure. People guess their blood pressure based on how they feel, which often is unrelated to their actual blood pressure (Baumann & Leventhal, 1985). Furthermore, the early signs of many illnesses, including cancer and heart disease, are subtle and easy to miss. Half or more of heart attack victims die before seeking and receiving medical help (Friedman & DiMatteo, 1989).

### Explaining Symptoms

Once we notice symptoms, we interpret them according to familiar disease schemas. In medical schools, this can have amusing results. As part of their training, medical students learn the symptoms associated with various diseases. Because they also experience various symptoms, they sometimes attribute their symptoms to recently learned disease schemas. ("Maybe this wheeze is the beginning of pneumonia.") By now, you may have discovered, psychology students are prone to this same effect as they read about psychological disorders.

The commonness and ambiguity of mild symptoms opens the door to social suggestion. On April 13, 1989, 2000 spectators assembled in the Santa

Monica Civic Auditorium in California to enjoy music performances by 600 secondary school students. Shortly after the program began, the nervous students began complaining to one another of headaches, dizziness, stomachaches, and nausea. Eventually 247 became ill, forcing the auditorium's evacuation and a fire department treatment operation on the lawn outside. Later investigation revealed nothing—no diagnosable illnesses and no environmental problems. The symptoms subsided quickly and were not shared by the audience. The instant epidemic, it seemed, was socially constructed (Small & others, 1991).

Might people also socially construct an everyday ailment? Might people form the idea that their everyday symptoms match those of an ailment they've heard about, and then use it to explain such symptoms? That, researchers Pamela Kato and Diane Ruble (1992) maintain, helps explain why many women believe they are more depressed, tense, and irritable during the 2 or 3 days before menstruation. As we saw in Chapter 10, people tend to notice and remember instances that confirm their beliefs and not to notice instances that contradict them. Thus, a woman who feels tense the day before her period is due may attribute the tension to her being premenstrual—the so-called premenstrual syndrome (PMS). But if the woman feels similarly tense a week later or does not feel tense the day her next period is about to start, she may be less likely to notice and remember these disconfirming instances.

Many researchers now believe that some women do indeed experience not only menstrual discomfort but also premenstrual tension (Hurt & others, 1992; Richardson, 1990). Thus, the American Psychiatric Association included a severe form of PMS (called premenstrual dysphoric disorder) in DSM-IV. They did so despite objections from the American Psychological Association and from the Psychiatric Association's Committee on Women, which maintain that women's menstrual cycle problems should not be pathologized as a psychiatric disorder (DeAngelis, 1993).

Although many women *recall* feeling out of sorts just before their last period, their own day-to-day self-reports often reveal little emotional fluctuation across the menstrual cycle (Figure 17–11). In one study, those who reported severe premenstrual symptoms differed only slightly from other women in actual day-to-day reports throughout their menstrual cycles (Gallant & others, 1992). And contrary to the presumptions of some employers, women's physical and mental skills do not fluctuate noticeably with their menstrual cycles. Leta Hollingworth discovered this in her 1914 doctoral dissertation (using women's daily reports rather than their recollections), and many others since then have confirmed her finding (Rosenberg, 1984; Sommer, 1992).

Moreover, PMS complaints vary with culture but not with any known biological differences among women. For most PMS patients, inactive placebos provide as much relief as actual drugs. All this is just what one would expect from a socially constructed disorder, say critics (Richardson, 1993; Rodin, 1992; Usher, 1992). With so many everyday symptoms on PMS checklists—lethargy, sadness, irritability, headaches, insomnia (or sleepiness), disinterest in sex (or heightened interest in sex)—"who wouldn't have 'PMS'?" asks Carol Tavris (1992).

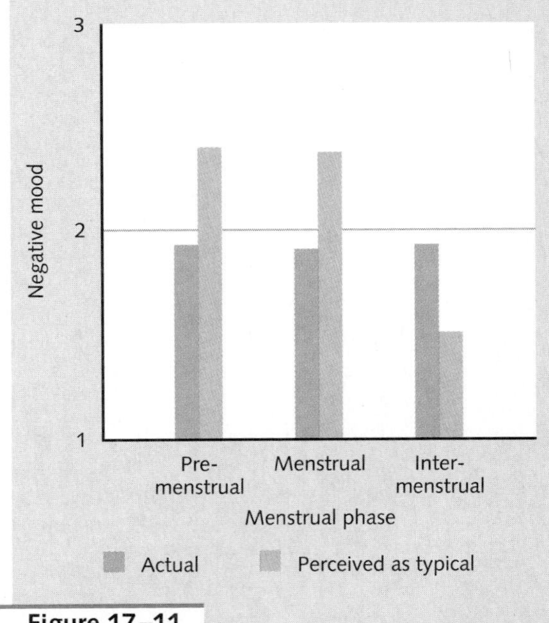


**Figure 17–11**

**Menstruation, Actual Mood, and Perceived Mood** *Cathy McFarland and her colleagues (1989) found that Ontario women's daily mood reports did not vary across their menstrual cycle. Yet they perceived that their moods were generally worse just before and after menstruation and better at other times of the cycle.*

## Do I Need Treatment?

Once people notice a symptom and interpret it as possibly serious, several factors influence their decision to seek medical care. People more often seek treatment if they believe their symptoms have a physical rather than a psychological cause (Bishop, 1987). However, they may delay seeking help if they feel embarrassed, if they think the likely benefits of medical attention won't justify the cost and inconvenience, or if they want to avoid a possibly devastating diagnosis.

The U.S. National Center for Health Statistics reports a gender difference in decisions to seek medical treatment: Women report more symptoms, use more prescription and nonprescription drugs, and visit physicians 40 percent more often. Are women more often sick? In fact, men may be more disease-prone. Among other problems, men have higher rates of hypertension, ulcers, and cancer, as well as shorter life expectancies. So why are women more likely to see a doctor? Perhaps women are more attentive to their internal states. Perhaps they are less reluctant to admit "weakness" and seek help (Bishop, 1984). Or perhaps women not employed full-time simply feel freer to make time for a doctor's appointment (Marcus & Siegel, 1982).

### Summing Up

Our body provides us with a variety of ambiguous signals. If they catch our attention, we often interpret them according to familiar disease schemas. If the symptoms fit one of our disease schemas, we must decide whether anticipated costs and benefits warrant our seeking diagnosis and treatment.

## Promoting Health

*Health promotion involves not only treating illness but also implementing strategies that help prevent illness or enhance wellness. What tactics can people use to reduce stress-related ailments? What influences health-destructive behaviors such as smoking? And how effective are programs that aim to help people stop smoking or lose weight?*

Traditionally, people have sought out medical doctors for the diagnosis and treatment of disease. That, say the advocates of behavioral medicine, is like ignoring your car's maintenance and going to a mechanic only when the car breaks down. Now that we realize that our attitudes and behaviors affect our health, attention is focusing more and more on health maintenance—on ways of coping with stress, preventing illness, and promoting well-being.

### Coping With Stress

Coping with stress can mean confronting or escaping the problem and taking steps to prevent its recurrence. Coping can involve fight or flight, repelling the challenge or avoiding it, solving the problem or mentally distancing oneself from it. Yet stressors are an unavoidable part of life. This fact, coupled with the growing awareness that recurring stress correlates with heart disease, lowered immunity, and other bodily ailments, gives us a clear message. If the stress cannot be eliminated by changing or ignoring the situation, we had best learn to manage it. Stress management includes aerobic exercise, biofeedback, relaxation, and social support networks.

*"Is there anyone here who specializes in stress management?"*
Drawing by Koren; ©1993 The New Yorker Magazine, Inc.

### Aerobic Exercise

Many studies suggest that **aerobic exercise**—sustained exercise that increases heart and lung fitness—can reduce stress, depression, and anxiety. People who regularly exercise cope with stressful events better, exhibit more self-confidence, and are less often depressed than those who exercise less (Brown, 1991; Hogan, 1989). But when stated the other way around—stressed and depressed people exercise less—cause and effect become unclear.

Experiments resolve the ambiguity by randomly assigning stressed, depressed, or anxious people either to aerobic exercise treatments or to other treatments. In one such experiment, Lisa McCann and David Holmes (1984) assigned one third of a group of mildly depressed female college students to a program of aerobic exercise and another third to a treatment of relaxation exercises; the remaining third, a control group, received no treatment. As Figure 17–12 shows, 10 weeks later the women in the aerobic exercise program reported the greatest decrease in depression. Many of them had, quite literally, run away from their troubles.

More than 100 other studies confirm that exercise reduces depression and anxiety (Petruzzello & others, 1991; Scott & Pepperell, 1992). Repeated surveys, some by government health agencies, reveal that Canadians and Americans are more self-confident, self-disciplined, and psychologically resilient if physically fit (Stephens, 1988). Even a 10-minute walk stimulates 2 hours of increased well-being by raising energy levels and lowering tension (Thayer, 1987, 1993).

Other research reveals that exercise also benefits health. One 16-year study of 17,000 middle-aged Harvard alumni found that those who exercised regularly were likely to live longer (Paffenbarger & others, 1986). A study of 15,000 Control Data Corporation employees found that those who exercised had 25 percent fewer hospital days than those who didn't (Anderson & Jose, 1987). And a digest of data from 43 studies revealed that, compared with inactive adults, people who exercise suffer half as many heart attacks (Powell & others, 1987). The "movement movement" is reaping dividends. So off your duffs, couch potatoes!

Researchers are now wondering *why* aerobic exercise alleviates the effects of stress and negative emotions. They know that exercise strengthens the heart and lowers both blood pressure and the blood pressure reaction to stress (Perkins & others, 1986; Roviario & others, 1984). Perhaps exercise

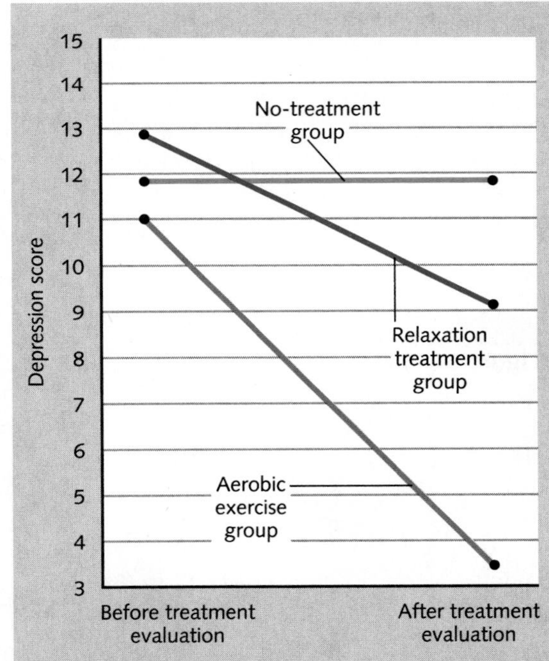


**Figure 17–12**

**Aerobic Exercise and Depression** *Mildly depressed college women who participated in an aerobic exercise program showed markedly reduced depression compared with those who did relaxation exercises or received no treatment. (From McCann & Holmes, 1984.)*

also orders up chemicals from our body's internal pharmacy by increasing production of mood-boosting neurotransmitters such as norepinephrine, serotonin, and the endorphins. Perhaps the emotional benefits of exercise are a side effect of increased body warmth or of the muscle relaxation and sounder sleep that occur afterward. Or perhaps a sense of accomplishment and an improved physique enhance one's emotional state. Such possibilities help explain why exercise relieves stress and boosts well-being (Martinsen, 1987).

### Biofeedback

When a few psychologists started experimenting with ways to train people to bring their heart rate and blood pressure under conscious control, many of their colleagues thought them foolish. These functions are, after all, controlled by the autonomic ("involuntary") nervous system. Then, in the late 1960s, ingenious experiments by respected psychologists began to make the doubters wonder. Neal Miller, for one, found that rats could modify their heartbeat if given pleasurable brain stimulation when their heartbeat increased or decreased. Later research revealed that some paralyzed humans (who cannot use their skeletal muscles) could also learn to control their blood pressure (Miller & Brucker, 1979).

Miller was experimenting with **biofeedback**, a system of recording, amplifying, and feeding back information about subtle physiological responses. Biofeedback instruments have been likened to a mirror (Norris, 1986). The instruments no more control one's body than a mirror combs one's hair. Rather, by reflecting the results of a person's own efforts, they allow the person to assess which techniques are most effective in controlling a particular physiological response.

In the example in Figure 17–13, a sensor records tension in the forehead muscle of a headache sufferer. A computer processes this physiological information and instantly feeds it back to the person in some easily understood image. As a person relaxes the forehead muscle, a pointer on a screen

**Figure 17–13**

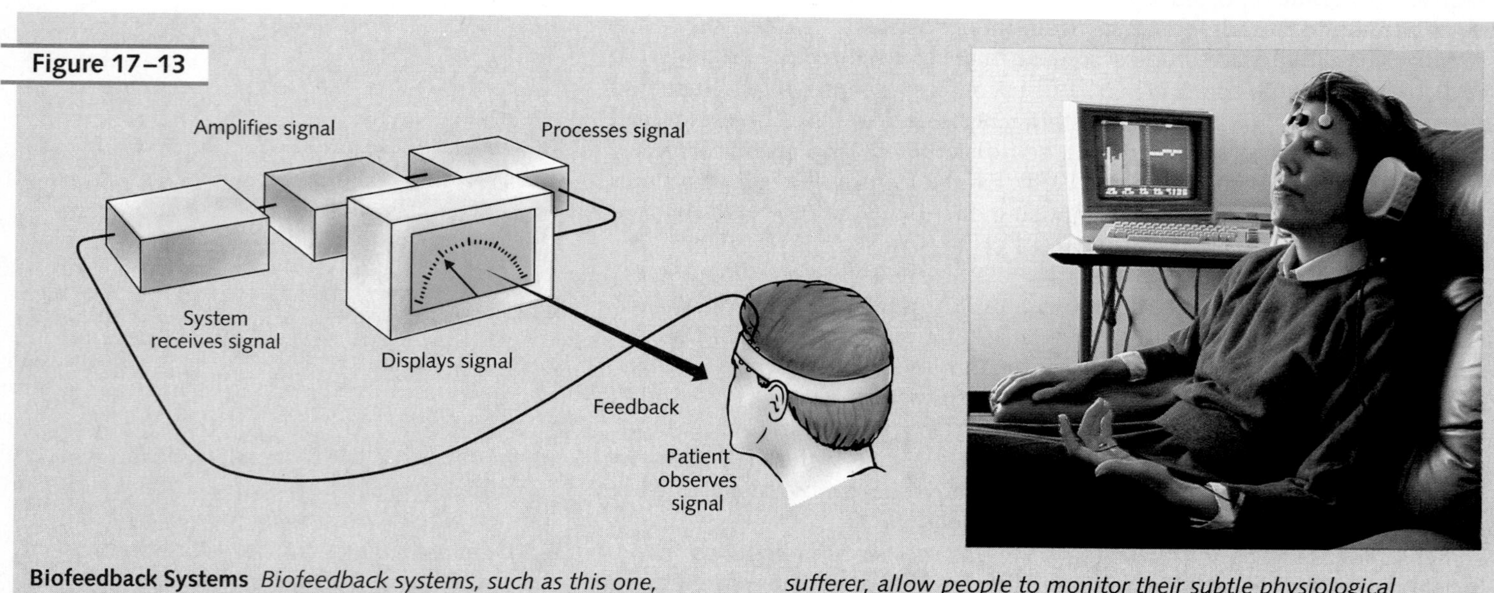


**Biofeedback Systems** *Biofeedback systems, such as this one, which records tension in the forehead muscle of a headache sufferer, allow people to monitor their subtle physiological responses.*

may go lower or a light may grow brighter. The patient's task is to learn to control the pointer or the light and thereby learn to control the tension in the forehead muscle and the accompanying headaches.

Initially, biofeedback researchers and practitioners reported that people could learn to increase their production of alpha brain waves, warm their hands, and lower their blood pressure—all signs of a more relaxed state. These reports triggered both excitement and some 4000 studies, including more than 400 in Russia (Sokhadze & Shtark, 1991). A decade later, when researchers stepped back to assess the results, they decided the initial claims for biofeedback were overblown and oversold (Miller, 1985). Biofeedback does enable some people to influence their finger temperature and forehead-muscle tension, and it can help somewhat in reducing the intensity of migraine headaches and chronic pain (King & Montgomery, 1980; Qualls & Sheehan, 1981; Turk & others, 1979). But other, simpler methods of relaxation, which require no expensive equipment, produce many of the same benefits.

## Relaxation

If relaxation is an important part of biofeedback, then might relaxation exercises alone be a natural antidote to stress? Cardiologist Herbert Benson (1976 to 1992) became intrigued with this possibility when he found that experienced meditators could decrease their blood pressure, heart rate, and oxygen consumption and raise their fingertip temperature. You can experience the essence of this *relaxation response*, as Benson calls it, right now: Assume a comfortable position, breathe deeply, and relax your muscles from foot to face. Now, concentrate on a single word or a phrase—perhaps, as for 80 percent of Benson's patients, a favorite prayer. Close your eyes and let other thoughts drift away when they intrude as you repeat this phrase continually for 10 to 20 minutes. Simply by setting aside a quiet time or two each day, many people report enjoying greater tranquility and a spiritual sense of closeness to a power beyond themselves. Stress worsens pain, infertility, and insomnia, and it also suppresses the immune system. Meditative relaxation counteracts all these effects, reports Benson. One astonishing study assigned 73 residents of homes for the elderly either to daily meditation or to none. After 3 years, one-fourth of the nonmeditators had died, while all the meditators were still alive (Alexander & others, 1989).

*Meditation—a modern phenomenon with a long history: "Sit down alone and in silence. Lower your head, shut your eyes, breathe out gently, and imagine yourself looking into your own heart. . . . As you breathe out, say 'Lord Jesus Christ, have mercy on me.'. . . Try to put all other thoughts aside. Be calm, be patient and repeat the process very frequently."*

Gregory of Sinai, died 1346

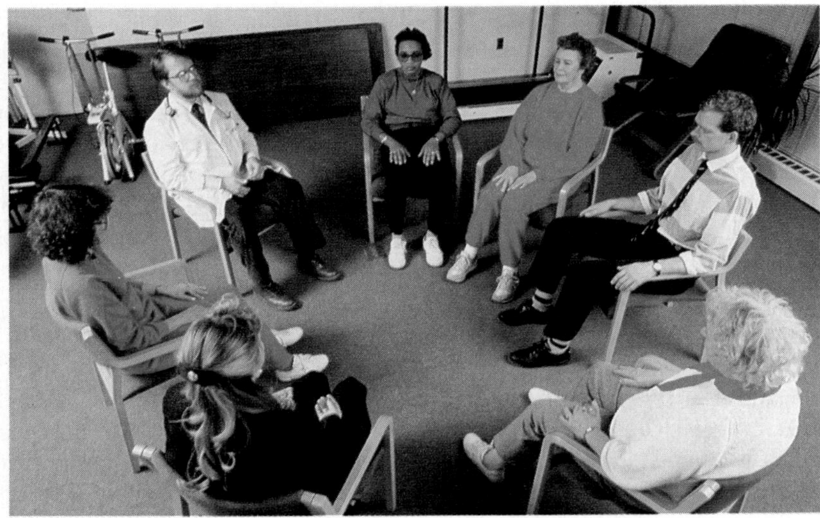

**Learning the "Relaxation Response"** *Relaxation training is a component of many stress-reduction programs. At Boston's Deaconess Hospital, hypertension patients learn meditation techniques that counteract stress.*

If Type A heart attack victims could be taught to relax, might their risk of another attack be reduced? To find out, Meyer Friedman and his colleagues randomly assigned hundreds of middle-aged heart attack survivors in San Francisco to one of two groups. The first group received standard advice from cardiologists concerning medications, diet, and exercise habits. The second group received similar advice plus continuing support and counseling on how to slow down and relax—by walking, talking, and eating more slowly; smiling at others and laughing at themselves; admitting mistakes; taking time to enjoy life; and renewing their religious faith. As Figure 17–14 indicates, during the ensuing 3 years the second group experienced half as many repeat heart attacks as the first group. This, wrote the exuberant Friedman, is an unprecedented, spectacular reduction in heart attack recurrence. A smaller-scale British study similarly divided heart attack-prone people into control and life-style modification groups (Eysenck & Grossarth-Maticek, 1991). During the next 13 years, it also found a 50 percent reduction in death rate among those trained to alter their thinking and life-style.

**Figure 17–14**

**Recurrent Heart Attacks and Life-Style Modification** *The San Francisco Recurrent Coronary Prevention Project offered heart attack survivors counseling from a cardiologist. Those who were also guided in modifying their Type A life-style suffered fewer repeat heart attacks. (From Friedman & Ulmer, 1984.)*

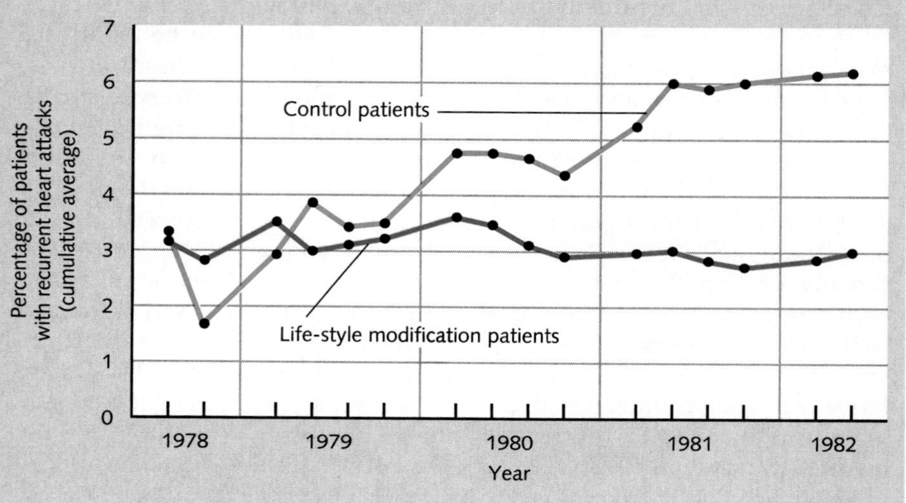


It remains for other researchers to do the painstaking work of identifying which of Friedman's dozens of stress-reduction drills are beneficial. Even while Friedman was collecting his data, other investigators were studying specific stress buffers. For example, laughter seems to work in ways similar to exercise—it arouses us, massages muscles, and then leaves us feeling relaxed (Robinson, 1983). This may help explain findings that stressful life events are less disturbing to good-humored people (Lefcourt & Davidson-Katz, 1991; Nezu & others, 1988). Although it would probably be an overstatement to suggest that "laughter is the best medicine," there is reason to suspect that those who laugh, last.

*"There ain't much fun in medicine, but there's a heck of a lot of medicine in fun."*

Humorist Josh Billings, 1818–1885

## Social Support

Linda and Emily had much in common. When interviewed for a study conducted by UCLA social psychologist Shelley Taylor (1989), both Los Angeles women had married, raised three children, suffered comparable breast tumors, and recovered from surgery and 6 months of chemotherapy.

But there was a difference. Linda, a widow in her early fifties, was living alone, her children scattered in Atlanta, Boston, and Europe. "She had become odd in ways that people sometimes do when they are isolated," reported Taylor. "Having no one with whom to share her thoughts on a daily basis, she unloaded them somewhat inappropriately with strangers, including our interviewer."

Interviewing Emily was difficult in a different way. Phone calls interrupted. Her children, all living nearby, were in and out of the house, dropping things off with a quick kiss. Her husband called from his office for a brief chat. Two dogs roamed the house, greeting visitors enthusiastically. All in all, Emily "seemed a serene and contented person, basking in the warmth of her family."

Three years later the researchers tried to reinterview the women. Linda, they learned, had died 2 years before. Emily was still lovingly supported by her family and friends and was as happy and healthy as ever.

Because no two cancers are identical, we can't be certain that different situations led to Linda's and Emily's fates. But they do illustrate a conclusion drawn from several large studies: Social support—feeling liked, affirmed, and encouraged by intimate friends and family—promotes happiness and health.

*Humans aren't the only source of stress-buffering comfort. After stressful events, Medicare patients who have a dog or other companionable pet are less likely to visit their doctor (Siegel, 1990).*

If this result seems obvious, imagine why close relationships could contribute to *illness*. Relationships are often fraught with stress, especially in crowded living conditions lacking privacy (Evans & others, 1989). "Hell is others," wrote Jean-Paul Sartre. Peter Warr and Roy Payne (1982) at the University of Sheffield asked a representative sample of British adults what, if anything, had emotionally strained them the day before. "Family" was their most frequent answer. Even when well-meaning, family intrusions can be stressful. And stress, as we have seen, contributes to heart disease, hypertension, and a suppressed immune system.

On balance, however, close relationships more often contribute to health and happiness. Asked what prompted yesterday's times of pleasure, the same British sample, by an even larger margin, again answered "family." For most of us, family relationships provide not only our greatest heartaches, but also our greatest comfort and joy.

Moreover, seven massive investigations, each following thousands of people for several years, reveal that close relationships affect health. Compared with those having few social ties, people are less likely to die prematurely if supported by close relationships with friends, family, or fellow members of church, work, or other support groups (Cohen & others, 1988; House & others, 1988; Nelson, 1988). Some recent examples:

*"Woe to one who is alone and falls and does not have another to help."*

Ecclesiastes 4:10

- Recall the study that followed leukemia patients preparing to undergo bone marrow transplants. Two years later, only 20 percent of those who said they had little social support from their family or friends were still alive. Among those who felt strong emotional support, the 2-year survival rate was 54 percent (Colon & others, 1991).
- A study of 1234 heart attack patients found a near-double rate of a recurring attack within 6 months among those living alone (Case & others, 1992).
- A study of 1965 heart disease patients revealed a 5-year survival rate of 82 percent among those married or having a confidant, but only 50 percent among those not (Williams & others, 1992).

There are several possible reasons for the link between health and social support. Perhaps people with strong social ties eat better and exercise more because their partners guide and goad them into adhering to treatment regimens. Perhaps they smoke and drink less, which would help explain the repeated finding that religiously active people enjoy better health (Idler & Kasl, 1992; Levin & Vanderpool, 1987). Perhaps such relationships help us evaluate and overcome stressful events, such as social rejection. Perhaps they help bolster our self-esteem. When we are wounded by someone's dislike or by the loss of a job, a friend's advice, assistance, and reassurance may be good medicine (Cutrona, 1986; Rook, 1987). Given lots of social support, spouses of cancer patients exhibit stronger immune functioning (Baron & others, 1990).

*"I get by with a little help from my friends."*
John Lennon and Paul McCartney
*Sgt. Pepper's Lonely Hearts Club Band*, 1967

**Friendships Are Good Medicine** *Several long-term studies of thousands of people have found that individuals with close supportive relationships are less likely than socially isolated people to die prematurely.*

Close relationships also provide the opportunity to confide painful feelings. In one study, health psychologists James Pennebaker and Robin O'Heeron (1984) contacted the surviving spouses of people who had committed suicide or died in car accidents. Those who bore their grief alone had more health problems than those who openly expressed it. Talking about our troubles can be "open-heart therapy."

In a simulated confessional, Pennebaker asked volunteers to share with a hidden experimenter some upsetting events that had been preying on their minds. He asked some of the volunteers to describe a trivial event before they divulged the troubling one. Physiological measures revealed that their bodies remained tense the whole time they talked about the trivial event; they relaxed only when they later confided the cause of their turmoil. Even writing about personal traumas in a diary can help. When volunteers in other experiments did this, they had fewer health problems during the ensuing 4 to 6 months (Pennebaker, 1990). As one subject explained, "Although I have not talked with anyone about what I wrote, I was finally able to deal with it, work through the pain instead of trying to block it out. Now it doesn't hurt to think about it."

Suppressed traumas sometimes eat away at us and affect our physical health. Consider:

- When Pennebaker surveyed more than 700 undergraduate women, he found that about 1 in 12 reported a traumatic sexual experience in childhood. Compared with women who had experienced nonsexual traumas, such as parental death or divorce, the sexually abused women—especially those who had kept their secret to themselves—reported more headaches and stomach ailments.
- After the 1989 San Francisco Bay Area earthquake, residents talked nonstop about the upheaval for about 2 weeks. Then the talking died down as people tired of hearing others' opinions and feelings. ("Thank you for not sharing your earthquake experience," read one popular T-shirt.) But for another month people kept thinking about the quake. During this inhibition phase—when people kept ruminating but with less disclosure of their anxieties and feelings—hostility, nightmares, and health problems peaked (Pennebaker & Harber, 1993).
- Pennebaker and his colleagues (1989) also invited 33 Holocaust survivors to spend 2 hours recalling their experiences. Many did so in intimate detail never before disclosed. Most watched and showed family and friends a videotape of their recollections in the weeks following. Again, those who were most self-disclosing had the most improved health 14 months later. Although talking about a stressful event can temporarily arouse people, it calms them in the long run (Mendolia & Kleck, 1993). Confiding is good for the soul.

Sustained emotional reactions to stressful events can be debilitating. However, the level of stress experienced depends on the person and the environment. Nothing is stressful until we appraise it as such. Thus, our personalities and interpretations influence how we react emotionally when stressful things happen. Moreover, the toxic impact of stressful events can be buffered by a relaxed, healthy life-style and by the comfort and aid provided by supportive friends and family (Figure 17–15).

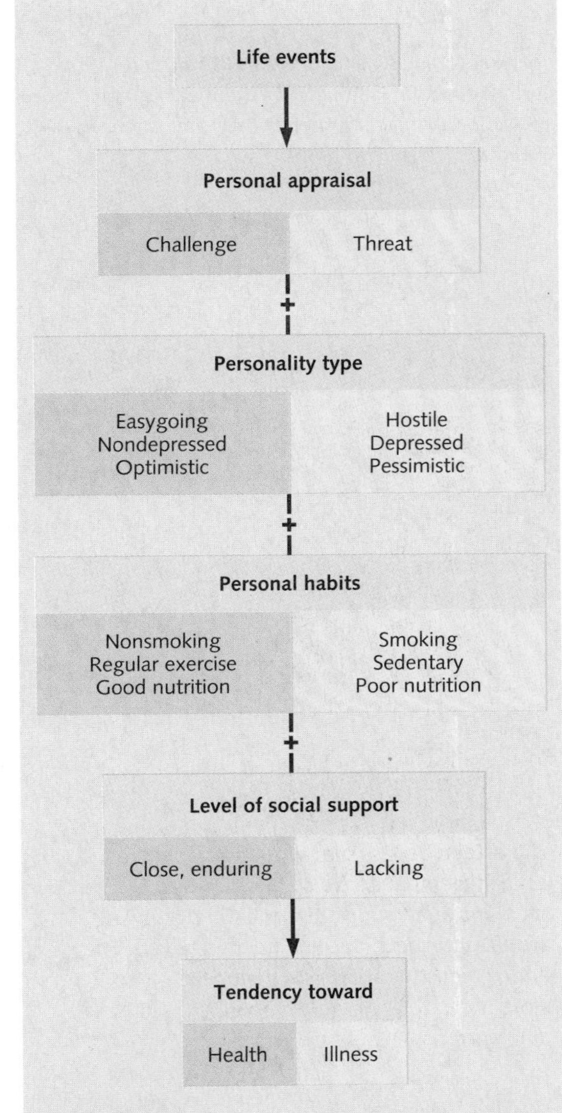


**Figure 17–15**

**Coping With Stress** *Life events can be debilitating or not. It all depends on how we appraise them and whether the stresses are buffered by a stress-resistant disposition, healthy habits, and enduring social support.*

## Modifying Illness-Related Behaviors

Researchers are only beginning to compute the cost-effectiveness of various health-promotion programs (Kaplan, 1984; Taylor, 1987). But most are optimistic that creating programs to prevent disease by modifying people's personal habits will cost far less than it now costs to treat their diseases. With Canada now spending 9 percent and the United States 12 percent of their gross domestic product on health care—with expenditures of nearly $1 trillion annually (not counting lost workdays)—even modestly successful health-promotion programs could save more money than they cost (Fein, 1992).

In the United States, where businesses pay half the nation's health care costs, two-thirds of organizations with more than 50 employees now offer some sort of health-promoting program, most of which began during the 1980s (Gebhardt & Crump, 1990; Roberts & Harris, 1989). Such programs commonly provide health assessments and support fitness training, quitting smoking, and stress management. The workplace is an ideal location for the promotion of health and vitality because most employees are there regularly. In addition, employers can actively encourage healthy behaviors by providing social support, arranging for competition among work groups, and awarding bonuses or days off for sticking to an exercise or smoking cessation regimen (Cataldo & Coates, 1986).

Are such programs effective? Several careful evaluations reveal that they can be. At Prudential Insurance Company, for example, a fitness program reduced sick days by 20 percent and major medical costs by 46 percent. Thus, the company saved $1.93 for every dollar it spent operating the program (Bowne & others, 1984). Control Data Corporation also found that its StayWell health program improved employee health and the company's balance sheet. Compared with other Control Data sites, sites that implemented the program reported decreases in smoking by 20 percent, in the number of overweight employees by 25 percent, and in the number of nonexercising employees by 32 percent—with corresponding reductions in health care claims and sick leave (Jose & Anderson, 1991). Other studies reveal decreases in seeking expensive medical care for minor illnesses, acute asthma, and arthritis (Sobel, 1993).

How might such programs modify health-related behaviors such as smoking and eating habits? Let's see.

### Smoking

Imagine the headline: A jumbo jet crashes, killing all 400 passengers—one of the worst airplane crashes in history. No, worse, imagine *three* jumbo jets colliding in midair, taking nearly 1200 lives. Then, worse yet, imagine that happening every day. Now you've reached the daily number of deaths attributable to smoking. And that is just in the United States, where the tobacco industry each year kills 420,000 of its best customers. These customers in turn kill nearly 40,000 people per year who die of passive smoking—inhaling smokers' toxic fumes.

*The United States spends three times more per person on health care than does Great Britain (partly because the average income of a U.S. doctor is nearly four times that of a British doctor). In the United States, average life expectancy is 75; in Britain it is also 75 (Fein, 1992; Roemer, 1992;* Information Please Almanac*).*

*Smokers repay society for the health, disability, and fire risk costs of their habit by dying earlier, saving Social Security and retirement pension payments (Manning & others, 1989).*

In the whole industrialized world, smoking causes 20 percent of all deaths—about 2 million people a year or 14 loaded jumbo jets daily—making it the largest preventable cause of death (Peto & others, 1992). Thus, the elimination of smoking would do more to increase life expectancy than would any other preventive measure. Smoking's destructiveness has prompted psychologists to study why people start smoking, why they keep smoking, and how we might prevent smoking or help people to quit.

**When and Why Do People Start Smoking?** Smoking usually begins during early adolescence and is especially common among those who get low grades, who feel less competent and in control of their future, and whose friends, parents, and siblings smoke (Chassin & others, 1987; Schulenberg, 1994). If you are still a nonsmoker, the odds are overwhelming that you will forever remain so.

We can understand adolescents' vulnerability to the allure of smoking with the help of social-cognitive theory, which explains how we learn behaviors through the models we imitate and the social rewards we receive (pages 281–282, 488). Many teens perceive teenage smokers as tough, precocious, and sociable (Barton & others, 1982). Self-conscious adolescents, who think the world is watching their every move, may begin smoking to imitate those cool models, to receive the social reward of being accepted by them, and to project a mature image (Covington & Omelich, 1988). Teens who start smoking typically also have friends who model smoking, suggest its pleasures, and offer cigarettes (Eiser, 1985; Evans & others, 1988). Among teens whose parents and best friends are *non*smokers the smoking rate is close to zero (Moss & others, 1992).

**Nic-a-teen** *Aware that virtually all smokers start as teenagers, cigarette companies often target their ads at a young audience. By portraying tough, appealing, socially adept smokers, they entice teens to imitate such models.*

**Why Do People Continue Smoking?** Three in four smokers have tried to stop (Niemi & others, 1989). However, once addicted to nicotine it is hard to quit, because tobacco products are as addictive as heroin and cocaine. As with other addictions, the smoker becomes *dependent*; each year fewer than 1 in 10 smokers who want to quit do so. The smoker also develops *tolerance*, eventually needing larger and larger doses to get the same benefit. Those who initially are most sensitive to nicotine—and most likely to feel sick or dizzy on first smoking—tend to develop tolerance quickly and to become most strongly addicted (Pomerleau & others, 1993). A final reason smokers do not stop is that quitting causes *withdrawal* symptoms. The craving, insomnia, anxiety, and irritability that accompany nicotine withdrawal are aversive states that a cigarette relieves (Figure 17–16). Cigarettes provide nicotine with the same rushed delivery method as crack cocaine, and after an hour or a day without smoking, the habitual smoker finds a cigarette powerfully reinforcing. Given low-nicotine cigarettes, the smoker will smoke more of them to maintain a roughly constant level of nicotine in the blood.

Smoking reinforces by both terminating the aversive craving and offering a pleasurable lift. Nicotine triggers the release of epinephrine and norepinephrine, which in turn diminish appetite and boost alertness and mental efficiency. More important, nicotine also stimulates the central nervous system to release neurotransmitters that calm anxiety and reduce pain sensitivity. For example, nicotine, like cocaine, increases dopamine—cocaine does so by blocking its reuptake, nicotine by stimulating its release (Nowak, 1994). Anxious or depressed people therefore often find it especially hard to forgo smoking's rewards (Mansnerus, 1992). These rewards of smoking, combined with the relief smoking provides from the unpleasantness of withdrawal, keep people smoking even when they wish they could stop—indeed, even when they know they are committing slow-motion suicide.

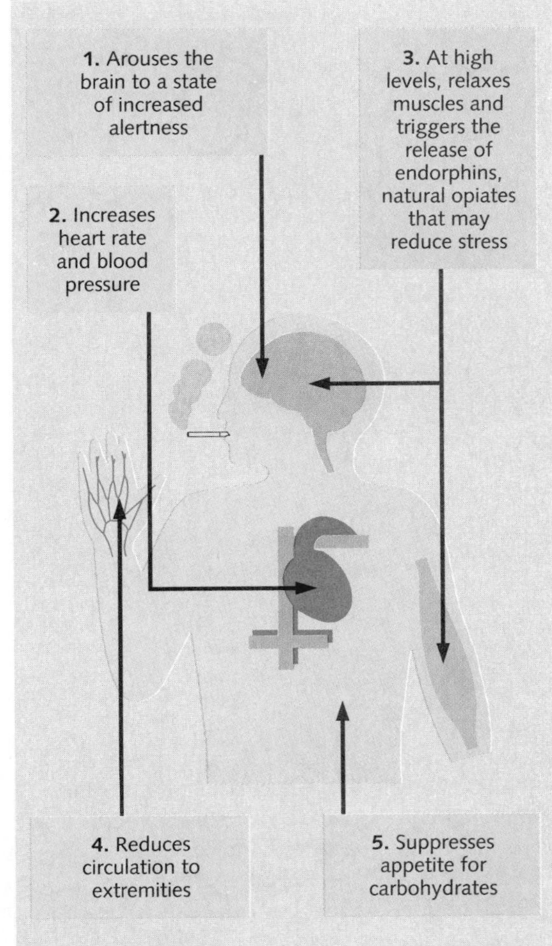
1. Arouses the brain to a state of increased alertness
2. Increases heart rate and blood pressure
3. At high levels, relaxes muscles and triggers the release of endorphins, natural opiates that may reduce stress
4. Reduces circulation to extremities
5. Suppresses appetite for carbohydrates

**Figure 17–16**

**Where There's Smoke . . . : The Physiological Effects of Nicotine** *Nicotine reaches the brain within 7 seconds, twice as fast as intravenous heroin. Within minutes, the amount in the blood soars. Nicotine stimulates neurons by mimicking the action of the neurotransmitter acetylcholine and produces the effects shown above.*

**How Effective Are Programs to Stop Smoking?** Efforts to help people stop smoking include public health warnings, counseling, drug treatments, hypnosis, aversive conditioning (for example, having people sicken themselves by rapidly smoking cigarette after cigarette), operant conditioning, cognitive therapy, and support groups. These treatments are often effective in the short run. But the bad news is that all but one-fifth of the participants eventually succumb to the habit again (Schelling, 1992). With a pack of cigarettes seldom more than 5 minutes away, a single moment of weakness is enough to break the resolve. (If one could buy cigarettes only by mail order, allowing time for renewed resolve, efforts to quit would succeed far more often.)

Better news comes from a Centers for Disease Control report that half of Americans who have ever smoked have quit. More than 90 percent did so on their own, often after repeated attempts. Because so many people have stopped or not started smoking, the percentage of Americans who smoke is down to 26 percent, barely more than half the rate of 30 years ago. Time was when public places were aswirl with tobacco smoke. Among high school dropouts and those of lower socioeconomic levels, smoking rates remain higher. But among college students and graduates, smoking has become gauche rather than cool; nearly 9 in 10 are nonsmokers. The drop has been most pronounced in the male smoking rate, which now barely exceeds women's smoking rate. Thanks in part to such trends, the death rate due to coronary heart disease has declined by about 30 percent since the mid-1960s. For the tobacco industry the news is not all bad. Despite the declining cigarette sales among educated people in Western countries and the new restrictions on cigarette advertising and smoking, per-person cigarette consumption worldwide is near an all-time high. With per-person consumption rates at about one-tenth that of those found in many Western industrialized societies, countries like Kenya and Zimbabwe are developing markets. In other countries such as Russia, where smoking is not discouraged, and in the Third World, where smoking is on the increase, British and American tobacco companies are more than making up for declining domestic production (Shenon, 1994). In so doing, they are putting hundreds of millions of unsuspecting people at risk for ill health and premature death.

**How Can We Prevent Smoking?** It is vastly easier never to begin smoking than to stop once addicted. Drawing on social psychological analyses of why youngsters start smoking, several research teams have devised strategies for averting the behavior patterns that lead to smoking (Evans & others, 1984; Murray & others, 1984). In one such study, a research team led by Alfred McAlister (1980) had high school students "inoculate" seventh-graders against peer pressure to smoke. The older peers taught the youngsters to respond to ads implying that liberated women smoke by saying, "She's not really liberated if she is hooked on tobacco." They also role-played calling someone a "chicken" for not trying a cigarette and responding with statements like, "I'd be a real chicken if I smoked just to impress you." After several sessions during the seventh and eighth grades, these students were only half as likely to begin smoking as were those in a control group at a neighboring junior high school, even though the parents of both sets of students had the same smoking rate (Figure 17–17).

**Figure 17–17**

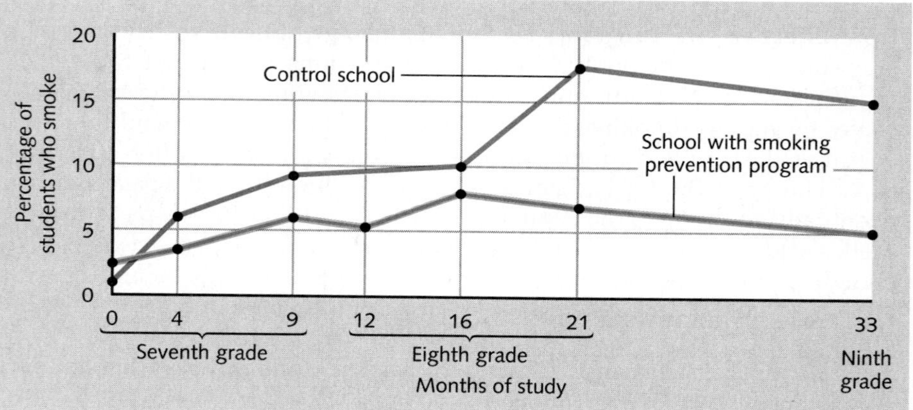


**Results of a Smoking "Inoculation" Program** *After participating in a smoking prevention program that prepared them to cope with smoking ads and peer pressure, junior high school students were much less likely to begin smoking than were students at a matched control school. (Data from McAlister & others, 1980.)*

This experiment and others like it have generated curricular programs that teachers can implement easily and inexpensively. According to a National Cancer Institute panel, the key ingredients of such programs are information about the effects of smoking; information about peer, parent, and media influences; and training in refusal skills, through modeling and role playing. The informational ingredients can also be offered through the mass media, which Australia has effectively used to discourage smoking across educational levels (Macaskill & others, 1992). To be permanently effective, such programs may require follow-up booster sessions in later years (Murray & others, 1989). Nevertheless, the plummeting rate of smoking suggests that smoking prevention programs are succeeding.

There is one other way to discourage smoking: Make it more immediately costly. Recall from Chapter 8, Learning, that the most effective rewards and punishments are immediate. When the delayed rewards of exercise compete with the immediate discomfort of doing so, the immediate consequences often win out. Likewise, we can *know* that in the long run smoking is often suicidal, yet continue to smoke. If we could only raise the immediate costs, consumption would surely decline.

Consider one such cost: the tax paid per pack. The 1993 taxes varied considerably, from $3.68 per pack in Denmark and $3.01 per pack in Canada to $0.56 per pack in the United States and $0.24 per pack in the Philippines. Raising taxes (and therefore prices) cuts consumption—by about 4 percent for each 10 percent rise, reports the Centers for Disease Control (Brown & others, 1993). The effect is even greater among teenagers—the age when 90 percent of smokers start their habit. To raise revenues, cut government health expenditures, and increase worker productivity, Canada raised its average tax more than sevenfold since 1980, and smoking declined there dramatically (Figure 17–18). When a pack of cigarettes costs more than five Canadian dollars—as it did until a recent tax revolt in Canada—many younger people will choose not to start a pack-a-day habit.

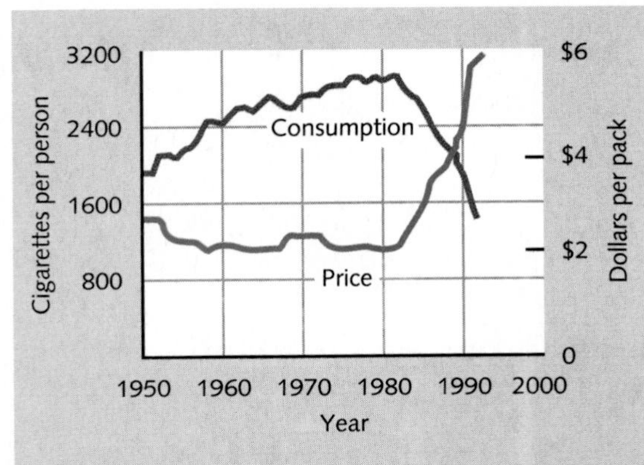


**Figure 17–18**

**Canadian Cigarette Consumption and Price, 1950–1992** *(In 1992 Canadian dollars.)(NSRA of Canada, in Brown & others, 1993.)*

### Nutrition

Is the way you feel and act affected by what you eat? The discovery that specific neurotransmitters affect emotion and behavior has fueled speculation: Might eating foods that provide the biochemical building blocks for those neurotransmitters affect mood and behavior? For example, the body synthesizes the neurotransmitter serotonin from the amino acid tryptophan. Several studies have found that high-carbohydrate foods (such as bread, potatoes, and pasta) increase the relative amount of tryptophan reaching the brain. That, in turn, raises the level of serotonin, which makes us feel relaxed, sleepy, and less sensitive to pain (Spring, 1988). And that helps explain why people in a bad mood, including those on nicotine withdrawal, often snack on carbohydrate-rich foods for a mood lift (Christensen, in press). When we instead desire food for thought, a high-protein meal improves concentration and alertness. Deprived of adequate protein, malnourished young children may suffer enduring cognitive deficits (Lozoff, 1989).

Other nutritional issues are now the subject of vigorous research and debate. Are children and prisoners hyped by a diet high in sugar and calmed by one that is low in sugar? Researchers now doubt this folk wisdom (Spring & others, 1987). They have, however, found that well-nourished children are more active and happy at play (Espinoza & others, 1992). What are the links between diet and high blood pressure? Hypertensive people tend to have higher than normal salt intake and lower than normal calcium intake (Feinleib & others, 1984; McCarron & others, 1984). Does skipping breakfast matter? Three studies by Bonnie Spring and her colleagues (1992) suggest it does. Those who eat a balanced breakfast are, by late morning, more alert and less fatigued.

### Obesity and Weight Control

People wonder: Why do some people gain while others who eat the same amount remain slim? Why do so few overweight people win the battle of the bulge? And what hope is there for the one-quarter of Americans who, according to the National Center for Health Statistics, are overweight?

First, the good news about fat. Fat is an ideal form of stored energy that provides the body with a high-caloric fuel reserve to carry it through periods when food is scarce—a common occurrence in the feast-or-famine existence of our prehistoric ancestors. Eating three or more meals every day is a relatively recent phenomenon and a luxury hundreds of millions of people

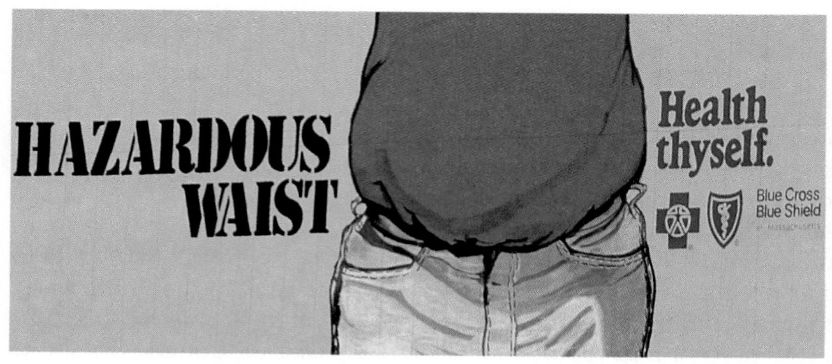


still do not enjoy. In circumstances of alternating feast and famine, overeating and storing the excess as fat is adaptive; it prepares the body to withstand famine. This may explain why in most developing societies today, as in Europe in earlier centuries—in fact, wherever people face famine—obesity is a sign of affluence and status (Furnham & Baguma, 1994).

The bad news is that in those parts of the world where food and sweets are now abundantly available, the adaptive tendency to store fat has become maladaptive. Being slightly overweight poses no health risks. But the National Institutes of Health reports that genuine obesity increases the risk of diabetes, high blood pressure and heart disease, gallstones, arthritis, and certain types of cancer. This is more true for apple-shaped people who carry their weight in pot bellies than for pear-shaped people with ample hips and thighs (Greenwood, 1989).

Obesity is not just a threat to physical health. Being perceived as obese can affect how you are treated and how you feel about yourself. People often stereotype the obese as slow, lazy, and sloppy (Ryckman & others, 1989). The obese—sometimes victims of ridicule and job discrimination—know it. In studies of patients who were especially unhappy with their weight—those who had lost an average of 100 pounds after intestinal bypass surgery—4 in 5 said their children had asked them not to attend school functions. Nine in 10 said they would rather have a leg amputated than be obese again (Rand & Macgregor, 1990, 1991). Another study followed 370 obese 16- to 24-year-olds (Gortmaker & others, 1993). When restudied 7 years later, two-thirds of the women were still obese—and were less likely to be married and were making less money than a comparison group of some 5000 other women. Even after correcting for aptitude test scores, race, and parental income, the obese women's incomes were $7000 a year below average.

Many people think fat people are gluttons. They see obesity as a matter of choice or as a reflection of a personality problem (a maladjusted way of reducing anxiety, dealing with guilt, or gratifying an "oral fixation"). If being obese signifies either a lack of self-discipline or a personality problem, then who would want to hire, date, or associate with such people? And if obese people believe such things about themselves, how could they feel anything but unworthy and undesirable?

Research on the physiology of obesity challenges these ideas. Consider the arithmetic of weight gain: People get fat by consuming more calories than they expend, and the energy equivalent of a pound of fat is 3500 calories. Dieters have therefore been told that they will lose a pound for every 3500-calorie reduction in their diet. Surprise: This conclusion turns out to be false. To see why, consider the physiology of fat.

**Fat Cells** The immediate determinants of body fat are the size and number of fat cells. A typical adult has about 30 billion of these miniature fuel tanks, half of which lie near the skin's surface. A fat cell can vary from relatively empty, like a deflated balloon, to overly full. In the obese, fat cells may swell to two or three times their normal size and then divide. Once the number of fat cells increases—due to genetic predisposition, early childhood eating patterns, or adult overeating—it never decreases. On a diet, fat cells may shrink, but they do not disappear (Sjöstrum, 1980).

The unyielding nature of our fat cells is but one way in which, once we become fat, our bodies maintain fat. Another way is that fat tissue has a low metabolic (energy expenditure) rate. Compared with other tissue, fat takes less food energy to maintain. Thus, once we become fat, we require less food to maintain our weight than we did to attain it.

**Body Chemistry** For the would-be dieter there are more reasons why being fat works to keep a person fat. In Chapter 12, we noted that insulin, a short-term hunger trigger, is secreted in response to tempting food stimuli. The insulin response is greatest in people who are most responsive to external food cues, especially dieters (Herman & others, 1983). For a dieter, a waitress's appetizing description of a dessert evokes a bigger physiological response, felt as a stronger craving.

**Set Points and Metabolism** Many scientists believe there is another reason why most obese people find it so difficult to lose weight permanently. Their bodies' weight "thermostats" are set to maintain body weight within a higher than average range. When weight drops below the set point range, hunger increases and metabolism decreases.

As many a dieter can testify, the drop in resting metabolic rate can be particularly frustrating. After the rapid weight losses that occur during the initial 3 weeks or so of a rigorous diet, further weight loss comes slowly. In one experiment (Bray, 1969), obese patients whose daily food intake was reduced from 3500 to 450 calories lost only 6 percent of their weight—partly because their metabolic rates dropped about 15 percent (Figure 17–19).

**Figure 17–19**

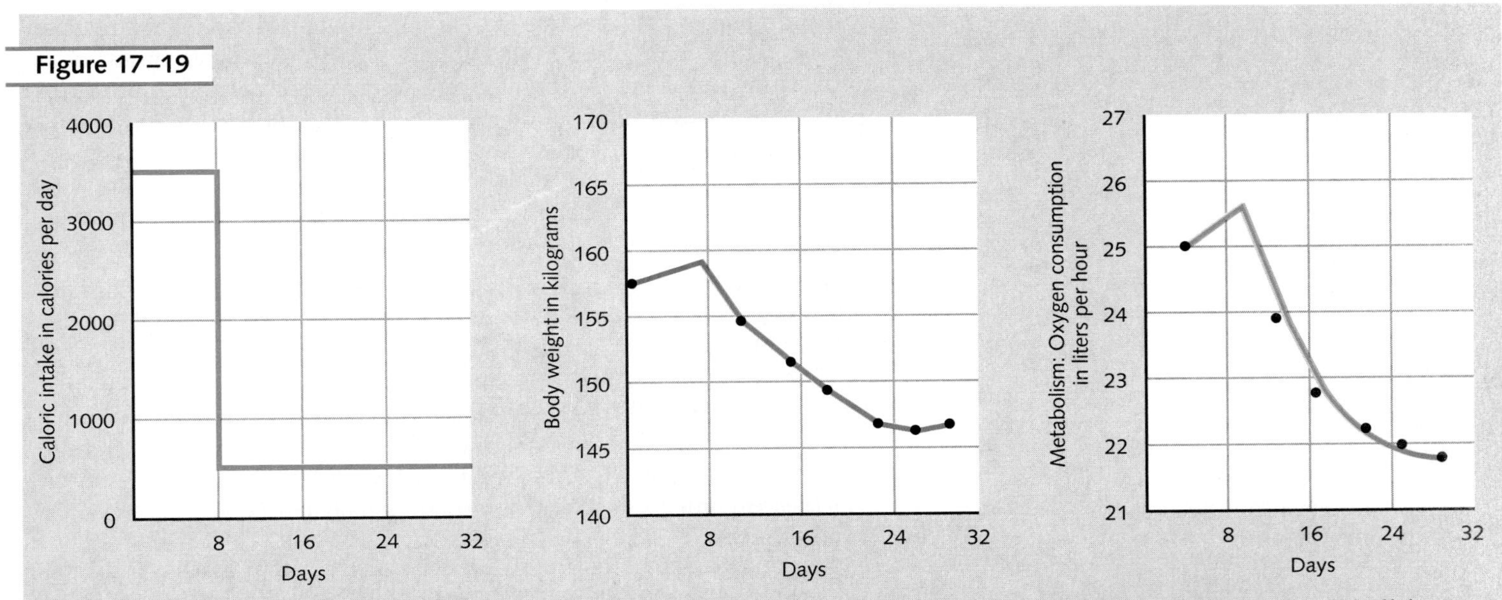


**The Effects of a Severe Diet on Obese Patients' Body Weight and Metabolism** *After 7 days on a 3500-calorie diet, six obese patients were given only 450 calories a day for the next 24 days. Body weight declined only 6 percent and then leveled off, because metabolism dropped about 15 percent. (From Bray, 1969.)*

**The Lean Look** *Contemporary clothing ads and films present an ideal of thinness that most women cannot attain. The message is so pervasive in our culture that even those of flawless appearance are often worried about their bodily "imperfections."*

Thus, the body adapts to starvation by burning off fewer calories, and to extra calories by burning off more. That is why reducing your food intake by 3500 calories may not reduce your weight by 1 pound. And that is why when a diet ends and the body is still conserving energy, amounts of food that only maintained weight before the diet may now increase it.

Individual differences in resting metabolism explain why—contrary to the stereotype of the overweight glutton—it is possible for two people of the same height, age, and activity level to maintain the same weight, even if one of them eats much more than the other does. Or why it is possible for a person to eat less than another similarly active person, yet weigh more (Rose & Williams, 1961). This appears true despite findings that people—obese people, especially—tend to overestimate their physical activity and underestimate their caloric intake (Brownell & Wadden, 1992; Lichtman & others, 1992).

**The Genetic Factor** Studies of adoptees and twins reveal a genetic influence on body weight. Consider:

- Despite shared family meals, the body weights of adoptive siblings are uncorrelated with one another and with their adoptive parents. Rather, people's weights resemble those of their biological parents, and they do so equally in adoptive and nonadoptive families (Grilo & Pogue-Geile, 1991).
- Brought together in a laboratory and fed an extra 1000 calories a day for 14 weeks, some identical twin pairs gained considerable weight and others didn't (C. Bouchard & others, 1990). If one of a twin pair gained extra fat, the other twin responded similarly.
- Identical twins have closely similar weights, even when reared apart (Stunkard & others, 1990). Being overweight is therefore *not* simply a matter of scarfing too many hot fudge sundaes. And losing weight is not simply a matter of mind over platter.

Genes aren't the whole story, however. Gender and culture play a role in obesity, as they do in eating disorders. Weight resemblance between identical twin women is somewhat less than among identical twin men. And diet or exercise rather than genes must explain why obesity is six times more common among lower-class than among upper-class women, more common among Americans than among Europeans, and more common among Americans today than in 1900. (Compared with their counterparts in the early 1900s, people are eating a higher fat diet and expending fewer calories.) Ironically, the growing pudginess of Americans coincides with an increasing idealization of the thin and fit look. Consider:

- American models of a generation ago weighed 8 percent less than the average woman; today they weigh 23 percent less—which makes them thinner than 95 percent of women (Wolf, 1991).
- In 1950, department-store mannequins looked nearly like real women. Since then, they have lost about 3 inches around their hips, which now average only 31 inches—quite unlike today's average young adult woman's 37 inches. In fact, women with as little body fat as these mannequins likely would not menstruate (University of California, 1993).
- While the average North American woman weighs more than her counterpart of 40 years ago, today's average Miss America contestant weighs about 15 pounds less.
- Most of today's models and actresses have hardly more than half the 22 to 26 percent body fat of a normal woman (Brownell, 1991).

**Losing Weight** Perhaps you shake your head in sympathy with obese people: "Slim chance they (or we) have of becoming and staying thin. If they lose weight on a diet, their metabolism slows and their hungry fat cells cry out, 'Feed me!'" Indeed, the condition of a dieter's body reduced to average weight is much like that of a semistarved body. Held under normal set point, each body "thinks" it is starving. Having lost weight, formerly obese people look normal, but their fat cells may be abnormally small, their metabolism slows, and, like the semistarved subjects we met in Chapter 12, their minds are obsessed with food.

All this explains why most people who succeed on a weight loss program eventually gain it nearly all back (Garner & Wooley, 1991; Wing & Jeffery, 1979). One study followed 207 obese patients who had lost large amounts of weight during a 2-month hospital fast (Johnson & Drenick, 1977). Half gained back all the lost weight within 3 years, and virtually all were again obese within 9 years. Programs that modify life-style and ongoing eating behavior have better carryover to postdiet weight management. Yet participants in these programs, too, typically regain much of their lost weight (Figure 17–20). When cultural ideals of slimness collide with hunger, hunger usually wins. Commercial weight loss programs can justifiably proclaim that they help people lose weight, *temporarily*. For most people, however, the only long-term result is a thinner wallet.

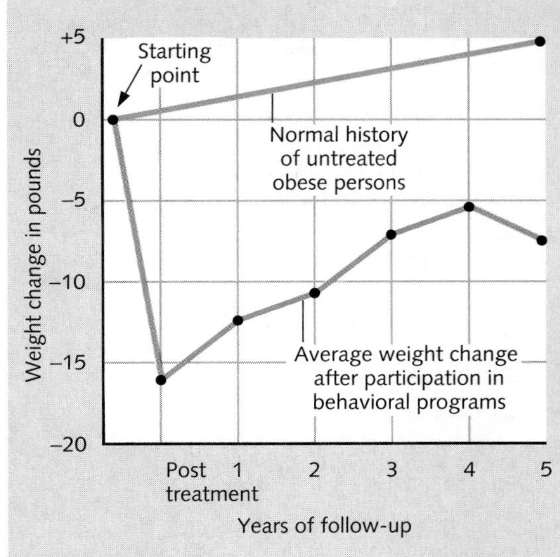


**Figure 17–20**

**Weight Change and Weight Loss Programs** *Behavior management weight loss programs promote weight loss, but most lost weight is regained. (From Brownell & Jeffery, 1987.)*

Nonetheless, the battle of the bulge rages as intensely as ever. It is especially intense in North America, where weight concern and dieting are a greater preoccupation than in, say, Australia or Third World countries (Rothblum, 1990; Tiggemann & Rothblum, 1988). Americans spend about $30 billion a year trying to lose weight (Brownell, 1991). In a 1991 poll, 32 percent of men and 44 percent of women said they were trying to lose weight (Castro, 1991). The gender difference is even larger for teenagers: 15 percent of boys and 44 percent of girls are trying to lose weight (Centers for Disease Control, 1991). With fat cells, blood chemistry, set points, metabolism, and genetic factors all tirelessly conspiring to make losing weight a big problem, what advice can we offer to those who wish to shed excess pounds?

*Janet Polivy and Peter Herman (1987) believe that widespread, chronic dieting among basically normal-weight girls and women represents the seeds of eating disorder on a massive scale.*

We should first advise assessing the costs. Maintaining weight loss will be difficult. Some researchers believe that the more weight fluctuates from going on and off a diet, the more quickly the body switches on its energy-saving metabolic slowdown with each new diet. Kelly Brownell and his associates (1986) confirmed this effect of yo-yo dieting by making rats obese, putting them on a diet, and then repeating the cycle of weight gain and loss. On the first diet, the rats lost their excess weight in 21 days and took 46 days to regain it. The second time, eating precisely the same amount of food, they took 46 days to lose the weight and 24 days to regain it.

Weight management is unlike love: 'Tis *not* better to have gained and lost than never to have gained at all. It's as if the body learns from previous diets how to defend its set-point weight, thereby protecting itself from what it interprets as the threat of starvation. Moreover, people whose weight fluctuates are at greater risk of heart disease (Garner & Wooley, 1991; Lissner & others, 1991). So rather than following the principle of "If at first you don't succeed, try, try again," a dieter's motto should be, "Get it right the first time" (or, if your weight poses no health risks, simply accept your body type). Begin a diet only if you feel motivated and self-disciplined enough to restrict your eating permanently. For most people, permanent weight loss requires making a career of staying thin—a lifelong change in eating habits combined with gradually increased exercise. In fact, sustained exercise can be a weapon against the body's normal metabolic slowdown when dieting. One of the few predictors of successful long-term weight loss is exercise during and after dieting (Brownell & Wadden, 1991, 1992) [see Close-Up: Helpful Hints for Dieters].

Although preserving weight loss is a constant challenge, Stanley Schachter (1982) is not as pessimistic as most obesity researchers are about the likelihood of doing it successfully. He recognizes the overwhelming rate of failure among people in structured weight loss programs. But he also notes that these are a special group of people, probably people who have been unable to help themselves. Moreover, the failure rates recorded for these programs are based on single attempts at weight loss. Perhaps when people try repeatedly to lose weight, more of them do eventually succeed, despite the negative effects of repeated dieting. When Schachter interviewed a haphazard sample of people, he found that one-fourth of them had at one time been significantly overweight and had tried to slim down. Of these, 6 out of 10 had *succeeded*: They weighed at least 10 percent less than their maximum prediet weight (an average loss of 35 pounds) and were no longer obese.

Two other studies reveal less encouraging results: Fewer than a third of formerly overweight people were no longer overweight (Jeffrey & Wing, 1983; Rzewnicki & Forgays, 1987). But the findings do hint that prospects for losing weight may be somewhat brighter than the dismal conclusions we draw from following patients who undergo a single weight loss program. If all this has a familiar ring, recall that stop-smoking programs tend to be (1) effective in the short run and (2) ineffective in the long run, but that (3) many people are former smokers.

There is, however, another option for overweight people, the one chosen by 13 percent of the people Schachter interviewed—simply to accept one's weight. We all do well to note what researchers have *not* identified as causes of obesity: guilt, hostility, oral fixation, or any similar personality maladjustment. Nor is obesity simply a matter of a lack of willpower. If dieters are more likely to binge when under stress or after breaking their diets, this may be largely a consequence of their constant dieting. "Fat is not a four-letter word," proclaims the National Association to Aid Fat Acceptance. Although this motto disregards the health risks linked with significant obesity, it does convey a valid point: It is surely better to accept oneself as a little chubby than to diet and binge, suffer the health risks of fluctuating weight, and feel continually out of control and guilty. America loved Oprah Winfrey before she lost 67 pounds, it loved her after she put most of them back on, it loved her when she shed most of them again, and it will love her still, chubby or not.

While working to clarify the precise relation among diet, behavior, and health, health psychologists continue their efforts to persuade people to adopt healthier life-styles. Doing so is quite a challenge, however. Happy people tend to see themselves as relatively invulnerable to health problems, especially those that might arise from their own actions (Salovey & Birnbaum, 1989; Weinstein, 1987). They also typically believe their own life-style is healthier than other people's—that they drink less alcohol, consume less fat and cholesterol, and get more exercise. Often they are fooling themselves. Furthermore, many individuals who admit to behaviors known to increase health risks will deny that the behaviors actually make them personally more vulnerable to illness or injury. Unlike people told they have normal blood pressure, those told they have high blood pressure tend to dismiss its seriousness (Croyle & Ditto, 1990). Smokers may delude themselves by saying that their exercising counteracts the negative effects of smoking.

## Close-Up Helpful Hints for Dieters

***Minimize exposure to tempting food cues.*** Keep tempting foods out of the house or out of sight, and go to the supermarket only on a full stomach.

***Take steps to boost your metabolism.*** Inactive people are often overweight (Figure 17–21). Sustained exercise, such as brisk walking, running, and swimming, not only empties fat cells, builds muscle, and makes you feel better, it can also temporarily speed up metabolism (Kolata, 1987; Thompson & others, 1982).

***Modify both your metabolic rate and your hunger by changing the food you eat.*** Findings suggest that complex carbohydrates (pasta, grains, potatoes) increase metabolism and are less readily converted to body fat than are the same calories eaten as fats (Rodin, 1979, 1985). Complex carbohydrates and fructose (in fruits) stimulate less of the hunger-producing insulin jump than does refined sugar (sucrose).

***Don't starve all day and eat one big meal at night.*** This eating pattern, common among overweight people, slows metabolism.

***Beware of the binge.*** Among people who consciously restrain their eating, drinking alcohol or feeling anxious or depressed can unleash the urge to eat (Herman & Polivy, 1980). Once the diet is broken, the person often thinks "what the heck" and then binges (Polivy & Herman, 1985, 1987): A lapse becomes a full collapse. Remember, most people occasionally lapse. Remind yourself that you've succeeded before and continue with your plan.

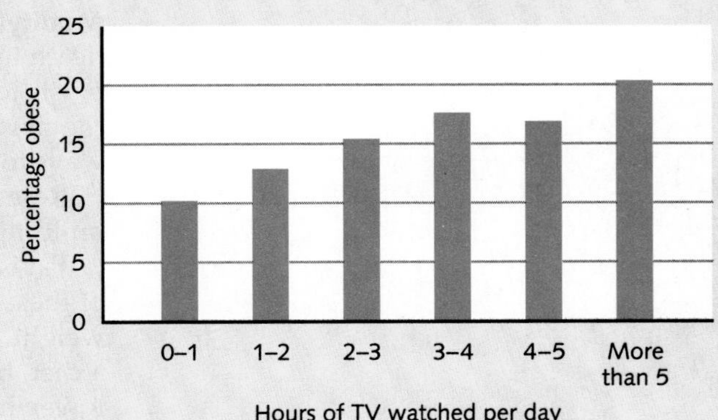


**Figure 17–21**

**Couch Potatoes Beware: A Correlational Study of TV Watching and Obesity** *In one study of 6671 12- to 17-year-olds, obesity was more common among those who watched the most television. Of course, overweight people may avoid activity, preferring to sit and watch TV. But the association between TV watching and obesity remained when many other factors were controlled, suggesting that the inactivity of TV watching contributes to obesity. (From Dietz & Gortmaker, 1985.)*

***Set realistic goals.*** Targeting an ambitiously low weight usually dooms a dieter to eventual defeat, but setting a realistic objective—such as walking several times a week—can promote effort and persistence.

Because of people's optimistic denials of health risks, the first hurdle that health promotion programs must surmount is to get people to realize their vulnerability to stress- and behavior-related health problems. Only then will people make an effort to control stress, stop smoking, moderate their drinking, eat wisely, exercise regularly, and even buckle their seat belts.

## Summing Up

Preventing illness and promoting health through stress management and behavior change is far better than attempting to treat problems after they occur.

**Coping With Stress** Among the components of stress management programs are training in aerobic exercise, biofeedback, and relaxation. Although the degree of mind control over the body that can be gained through biofeedback has fallen short of early expectations, it sometimes helps people control tension headaches and high blood pressure. Simple relaxation exercises offer some of the same benefits. Counseling Type A heart attack survivors to slow down and relax has helped them lower their rate of recurring attacks. Social support also helps people cope, partly by buffering the impact of stress.

**Modifying Illness-Related Behaviors** The largest preventable cause of death in North America is cigarette smoking, a fact that motivates psychologists to study the social influences that cause adolescents to start smoking, the negative and positive reinforcers that maintain the habit, and possible ways to stop and prevent smoking.

Researchers are now exploring how certain foods, by providing the building blocks for specific neurotransmitters, affect mood and behavior.

Fat is a concentrated fuel reserve stored in fat cells. The number and size of these cells determine one's body fat. Obese people find it difficult to lose weight permanently because the number of fat cells is not reduced by a diet, because the energy expenditure necessary for tissue maintenance is lower in fat than in other tissues, and because the overall metabolic rate decreases when body weight drops below the set point. Those who nevertheless wish to diet should minimize exposure to food cues, boost energy expenditure through exercise, and make a lifelong change in eating patterns.

## Terms and Concepts to Remember

**behavioral medicine** An interdisciplinary field that integrates and applies behavioral and medical knowledge to health and disease.

**health psychology** A subfield of psychology that provides psychology's contribution to behavioral medicine.

### Stress and Illness

**stress** The process by which we perceive and respond to certain events, called *stressors*, that we appraise as threatening or challenging.

**general adaptation syndrome (GAS)** Selye's concept of the body's adaptive response to stress as composed of three stages—alarm, resistance, exhaustion.

**burnout** Physical, emotional, and mental exhaustion brought on by persistent job-related stress.

**coronary heart disease** The clogging of the vessels that nourish the heart muscle; the leading cause of death in the United States.

**Type A** Friedman and Rosenman's term for competitive, hard-driving, impatient, verbally aggressive, and anger-prone people.

**Type B** Friedman and Rosenman's term for easygoing, relaxed people.

**psychophysiological illness** Literally, "mind–body" illness; any stress-related physical illness, such as hypertension, ulcers, and headaches. Note: This is distinct from *hypochondriasis*—misinterpreting normal physical sensations as symptoms of a disease.

**lymphocytes** The two types of white blood cells that are part of the body's immune system: B lymphocytes form in the *b*one marrow and release antibodies that fight bacterial infections; T lymphocytes form in the *t*hymus and, among other duties, attack cancer cells, viruses, and foreign substances.

### Promoting Health

**aerobic exercise** Sustained exercise that increases heart and lung fitness; may also alleviate depression and anxiety.

**biofeedback** A system for electronically recording, amplifying, and feeding back information regarding a subtle physiological state, such as blood pressure or muscle tension.

## Critical Thinking Exercise

Now that you have read and reviewed Chapter 17, take your learning a step further by testing your critical thinking skills on the following practical problem solving exercise.

Janet and Sheila have been good friends since meeting in their introductory psychology class freshman year. Although they are about the same height and age, their weights differ. Janet, whose parents are both obese, has always been between 0 and 25 percent above normal. Acquaintances assume she is lazy and gluttonous, but Janet's friends know that she is neither. Sheila's weight is normal, as are her parents'.

As a final project in their health psychology class, Janet and Sheila decided to make themselves the subjects of an experiment. For a month, they ate the same total number of calories per day, spread across several small, healthy meals that were low in fat and included whole grains, fruits, and vegetables. They also added a brisk, 30-minute walk to their daily routines. At the end of the month, Janet and Sheila weighed themselves for the first time since the experiment began. Although Janet was pleased to find that she had lost some weight, Sheila had lost more. When they presented their findings to the class, several students speculated that perhaps Janet simply hadn't employed the willpower that Sheila had, and that was why Sheila lost more weight.

1. What factors in Janet's background might have contributed to her obesity?
2. What factors in Sheila's background might have contributed to her being of normal weight?
3. Why did Sheila lose more weight than Janet even though they consumed the same number of calories, the same types of food, and did the same amount of exercise?

Check your progress on becoming a critical thinker by comparing your answers to the sample answers found in Appendix B.

## For Further Reading

**Benson, H., & Stuart, E.** (1992). *The wellness book: The comprehensive guide to maintaining health and treating stress-related illness*. New York: Carol Publishing.

*A complete resource for those who want to learn how to apply behavioral medicine to managing stress, eating well, and staying fit.*

**Friedman, H. S.** (1991). *The self-healing personality: Why some people achieve health and others succumb to illness*. New York: Holt.

*Health psychologist Howard Friedman offers a lucid, state-of-the-art analysis of how our genes, habits, and emotions make us disease-prone or health-prone.*

**Goleman, D., & Gurin, J.** (Eds.) (1993). *Mind/body medicine: How to use your mind for better health*. Yonkers, NY: Consumer Reports Books.

*Accessible chapters by leading researchers explain the mind's influence on health, disease, and comfort. Discusses heart disease, cancer, pain, diabetes, skin problems, arthritis, asthma, and infertility.*

**Pennebaker, J.** (1990). *Opening up: The healing power of confiding in others*. New York: William Morrow.

*Researcher James Pennebaker explains why disclosing oneself to others is good for the body as well as the soul.*

**Polivy, J., & Herman, C. P.** (1983; paperback, 1985). *Breaking the diet habit: The natural weight alternative*. New York: Basic Books.

*Two psychologists who are obesity researchers question the practice of dieting and instead recommend realizing one's "natural weight" with an "undiet" that meets needs and discourages eating when hunger is satisfied.*

**Rodin, J.** (1992). *Body traps*. New York: William Morrow.

*A leading obesity researcher examines our obsession with weight and appearance—how we form our body image, how it affects our self-esteem, and how we can free ourselves from dieting-related "body traps" that provoke needless anguish and shame.*

# CHAPTER 18

# Social Psychology

"We cannot live for ourselves alone," remarked the novelist Herman Melville, for "our lives are connected by a thousand invisible threads." **Social psychologists** explore these connections by scientifically studying how we *think about*, *influence*, and *relate* to one another.

## Social Thinking

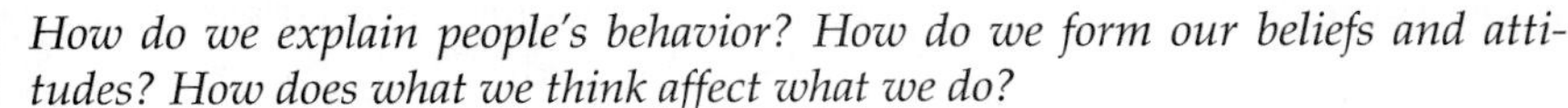

*How do we explain people's behavior? How do we form our beliefs and attitudes? How does what we think affect what we do?*

Especially when the unexpected occurs, we analyze and discuss why people act as they do. Does her warmth reflect romantic interest in me, or is that how she relates to everyone? Does his absenteeism signify laziness or an oppressive work atmosphere?

### Attributing Behavior to Persons or to Situations

After studying how people explain others' behavior, Fritz Heider (1958) proposed an **attribution theory**. Heider noted that people usually attribute others' behavior either to their internal dispositions or to their external situations. A teacher, for example, may wonder whether a child's hostility reflects an aggressive personality (*a dispositional attribution*) or whether the child is reacting to stress or abuse (*a situational attribution*).

In class, we notice that Julie doesn't say much; over coffee, Jack talks nonstop. Attributing their behaviors to their personal dispositions, we decide that Julie is shy and Jack is outgoing. Because people do have enduring personality traits, such attributions are sometimes valid. However, we often overestimate the influence of personality and underestimate the situation. In class, Jack may be as quiet as Julie. Catch Julie at a party and you may hardly recognize your quiet classmate. Underestimating situational influences is known as the **fundamental attribution error**.

An experiment by David Napolitan and George Goethals (1979) illustrates the phenomenon. They had Williams College students talk, one at a time, with a young woman who acted either aloof and critical or warm and friendly. Beforehand, they told half the students the woman's behavior would be spontaneous. They told the other half the truth—that she had been instructed to *act* friendly (or unfriendly). What effect do you suppose this information had?

None. The students disregarded the information. If the woman acted friendly, they inferred she really was a warm person. If she acted unfriendly, they inferred she really was a cold person. In other words, they attributed her behavior to her personal disposition *even when told that her behavior was situational*—that she was merely acting that way for purposes of the experiment.

Knowing about the fundamental attribution error is helpful, yet committing it is almost irresistible. In a high school play I attended recently, a talented 16-year-old girl convincingly played the part of a bitter old woman—so convincingly that, although I reminded myself of the fundamental attribution error, I still assumed that the young actress was typecast because she was well-suited for the part. Meeting her later at a cast party, I discovered she actually has a very pleasant disposition. I then remembered that several months earlier I had seen her play the part of a charming 10-year-old in *The Sound of Music*. Leonard Nimoy of *Star Trek* fame would not have been surprised by my error. He titled one of his books *I Am Not Spock*.

You, too, have surely committed the fundamental attribution error. In judging, say, whether your psychology instructor is shy or outgoing, you perhaps inferred from your class experience that he or she has an outgoing personality. But you know your instructor only from the classroom, a situation that demands outgoing behavior. Catch the instructor in a different situation and you might be surprised (as some of my students are when confronting me in a pick-up basketball game). Outside of their assigned roles, professors seem less professorial, presidents less presidential, servants less servile.

The instructor, on the other hand, observes his or her own behavior in many different situations—in the classroom, in meetings, at home—and so might say, "Me, outgoing? It all depends on the situation. In class or with good friends, yes, I'm outgoing. But at conventions I'm really rather shy."

*Recall from Chapter 14 that personality psychologists study the enduring, inner determinants of behavior that help to explain why different people act differently in a given situation. Social psychologists study the social influences that help explain why the same person will act differently in different situations.*

So, when explaining *our own* behavior, we are sensitive to how our behavior changes with the situations we encounter. When explaining *others'* behavior, particularly after observing them in only one type of situation, we often commit the fundamental attribution error. We disregard the situation and leap to unwarranted conclusions about their personality traits. We do so partly because we have learned to focus our attention more on the person than on the situational context. To use the language of perception, the person is a "figure" that stands out from the situational "ground." Meanwhile, the person's own attention focuses more on the situation to which he or she is reacting. Reverse the perspectives of actor and observer—by having each view a videotape replay of the situation from the other's perspective—and this reverses the attributions (Lassiter & Irvine, 1986; Storms, 1973). By seeing the world from the actor's perspective, the observers better appreciate the situation. Given an observer's point of view, the actors better appreciate their own initiative and personal style.

### The Effects of Attribution

In everyday life we often struggle to explain others' actions. To what should we attribute them? A jury must decide whether a shooting was malicious or in self-defense. An unhappy wife and husband each ponder why the other behaves so selfishly. An interviewer must judge whether the applicant's geniality is genuine. When making such judgments, our attributions—either to the person or to the situation—have important consequences (Fincham & Bradbury, 1993; Fletcher & others, 1990). Happily married couples attribute their spouse's tart-tongued remark to a temporary situation ("She must have had a bad day at work"). Unhappily married persons attribute the same remark to a mean disposition ("Why did I marry such a hostile person?").

Or consider the political effects of attribution: How do you explain poverty or unemployment? Researchers in Britain, India, Australia, and the United States (Furnham, 1982; Pandey & others, 1982; Wagstaff, 1982; Zucker & Weiner, 1993) report that political conservatives tend to attribute such social problems to the personal dispositions of the poor and unemployed themselves: "People generally get what they deserve. Those who don't work are often freeloaders. People who take initiative can still get ahead." Political liberals are more likely to blame past and present situations: "If you or I had to live with the same poor education, lack of opportunity, and discrimination, would we be any better off?"

And how do you explain homelessness? Some people—45 percent in one survey (Lee & others, 1990)—attribute homelessness to society's failure to provide adequate jobs and housing. Others—33 percent—blame the homeless themselves. President Reagan (1988), for example, believed that many homeless people "make it their own choice" not to seek shelter. Clearly, there are political implications to whether we attribute people's behavior to social conditions or to their own choices and shortcomings.

In evaluating employees, managers must also make attributions. They are likely to attribute the poor performance of workers to personal factors, such as low ability or lack of motivation. Workers who are doing poorly on a job recognize situational influences: inadequate supplies, poor working conditions, difficult co-workers, impossible demands (Rice, 1985).

The practical point to remember: Our attributions—to individuals' dispositions or to their situations—have real consequences.

*"Otis, shout at that man to pull himself together."*

Drawing by Handelsman; © 1980 The New Yorker Magazine, Inc.

## Attitudes and Actions

Social psychology's single most important concept has been that of *attitudes*. **Attitudes** are beliefs and feelings that predispose our reactions to objects, people, and events. If we *believe* that someone is mean, we may *feel* dislike for the person and *act* unfriendly. "Change the way people think," said South African civil rights martyr Steve Biko, "and things will never be the same."

### Do Our Attitudes Guide Our Actions?

Although most persuasive appeals assume that changed attitudes can indeed change behavior, dozens of studies during the 1960s challenged this idea (Wicker, 1971). Moreover, studies of people's attitudes and behaviors regarding cheating, the church, and racial minorities revealed that folks often talk and act a different game. "Thinking is easy," said the German poet Goethe (1749–1832), "acting difficult, and to put one's thoughts into action, the most difficult thing in the world."

But the seeming hypocrisy did startle social psychologists, most of whom shared Biko's belief that there is a close connection between thought and action, character and conduct, private words and public deeds. So they conducted many follow-up studies during the 1970s and 1980s (Kraus, 1991). These studies reveal that our attitudes *will* guide our actions if:

***Outside influences on what we say and do are minimal.*** Social pressures may blur the underlying connection between our attitudes and actions by affecting either what we say or what we do (Figure 18–1). In 1990, 4 weeks before a congressional election, President Bush and political leaders from both parties asked members of the U.S. House of Representatives to pass a compromise deficit-reducing budget. Privately, most members of Congress agreed that the painful cuts and tax increases were essential to the nation's health: Among those retiring or unopposed for

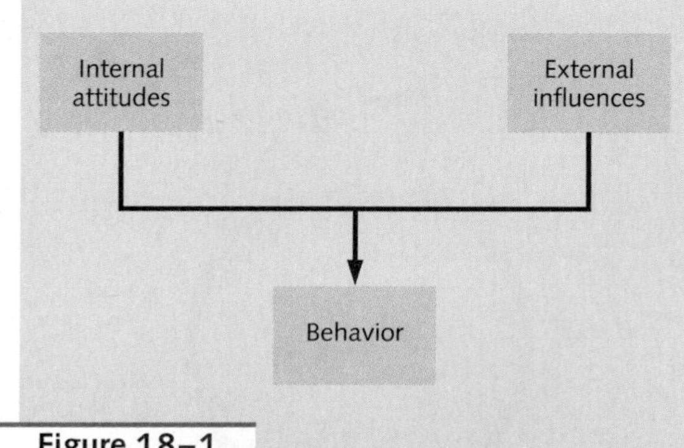


**Figure 18–1**

**Attitudes, External Influences, and Actions** *Our behavior is affected by our inner attitudes and by external social influences.*

reelection and thus facing little external pressure, 86 percent voted for the bill. For others, voting their privately held attitudes was more difficult. Among the 36 representatives who were about to face angry voters in close races back home, there were no profiles in courage: All 36 voted against it.

***The attitude is specifically relevant to the behavior.*** People readily profess *general* attitudes that are inconsistent with their behavior. They proclaim love while yelling at their mate, cherish honesty while cheating on their income tax returns, and value good health while smoking and not exercising. Attitudes about the specific act do, however, guide action. Attitudes toward exercise predict exercising behavior.

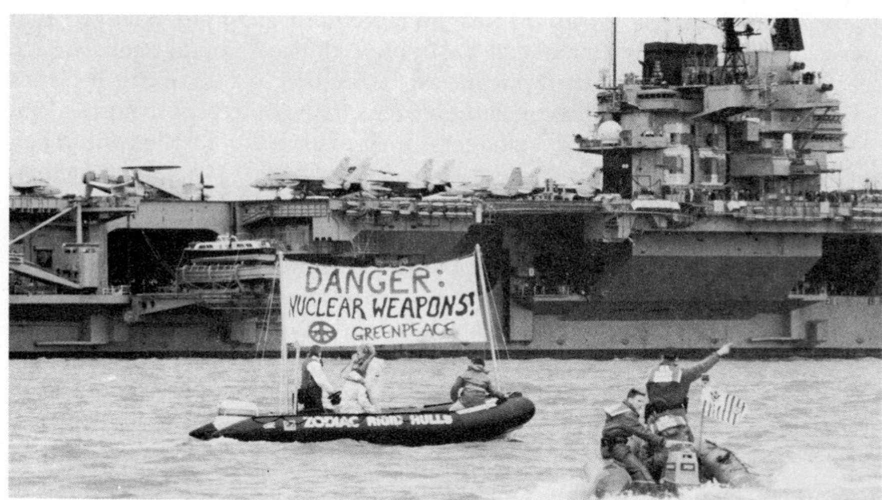


**When Attitudes Drive Action** *If we know what we believe and if our beliefs are relevant to our behavior, attitudes can inspire remarkable actions. Strong in their beliefs and steadfast in their intentions, these Greenpeace activists engage in perilous activities.*

***We are keenly aware of our attitudes.*** When we mindlessly follow habit or social expectations, our attitudes lie dormant. If something makes us self-conscious or reminds us of how we feel, we are truer to our convictions. For example, Martha Powell and Russell Fazio (1984) had people rate their attitudes about gun control and about the Equal Rights Amendment. They found that repeating an attitude makes it come to mind more quickly. And attitudes that come quickly to mind are more likely to guide our behavior (Fazio, 1990). When we know what we believe and are conscious of its implications for our actions, we are true to ourselves.

## Do Our Actions Affect Our Attitudes?

So, under certain circumstances—when other influences are minimal, when the attitude is specific to the behavior, and when mindful of their attitudes—people will stand up for what they believe. Attitudes will affect behavior. Now consider a more surprising principle: People also come to believe in what they have stood up for. Many streams of evidence confirm that *attitudes follow behavior*. Here are two.

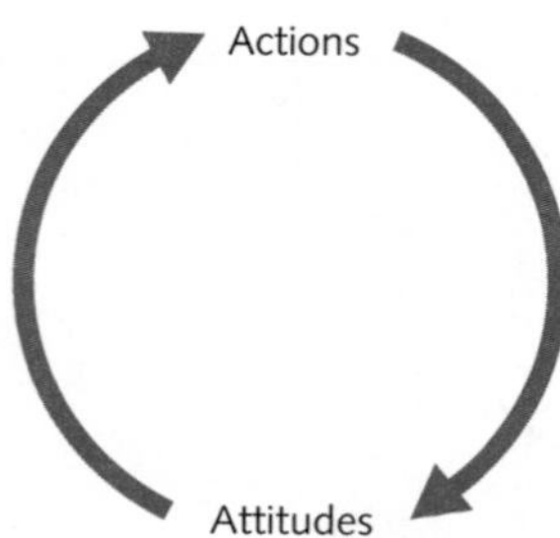


**The Foot-in-the-Door Phenomenon** During the Korean War, many captured American soldiers were imprisoned in war camps run by Chinese communists. Without using brutality, the captors secured their prisoners' collaboration in activities ranging from running errands and accepting favors to making radio appeals and false confessions to informing on fellow prisoners and divulging military information. When the war ended, 21 prisoners chose to stay with the communists. Many others returned home "brainwashed"—convinced that communism was a good thing for Asia.

A key ingredient of the Chinese "thought-control" program was their effective use of the **foot-in-the-door phenomenon**—a tendency for people who agree to a small request to comply later with a larger one. The Chinese harnessed this phenomenon by gradually escalating their demands on the prisoners, beginning with harmless requests (Schein, 1956). Having "trained" the prisoners to speak or write trivial statements, the communists then asked them to copy or create something more important, noting, perhaps, the flaws of capitalism. The prisoners then participated in group discussions, wrote self-criticisms, or uttered public confessions. Once they did so, perhaps to gain privileges, the prisoners then often adjusted their beliefs toward consistency with their public acts.

Research studies show that the foot-in-the-door tactic also helps boost charitable contributions, blood donations, and product sales. In one experiment, researchers posing as safety-drive volunteers asked Californians to permit the installation of a large, poorly lettered "Drive Carefully" sign in their front yards. Only 17 percent consented. Others were first approached with a small request: Would they display a 3-inch "Be a Safe Driver" sign? Nearly all readily agreed. When reapproached 2 weeks later to allow the large, ugly sign in their front yards, 76 percent consented (Freedman & Fraser, 1966).

The moral is simple, says Robert Cialdini (1993): To get people to agree to something big, "Start small and build." And be wary of those who would exploit you with the tactic. This chicken-and-egg spiral of actions feeding attitudes feeding actions enables behavior to escalate. A trifling act makes the next act easier. Succumb to a temptation and you will find the next temptation harder to resist.

Dozens of experiments have simulated part of the war prisoners' experience, by coaxing people into acting against their attitudes or violating their moral standards. The nearly inevitable result: Most subjects begin to rationalize their behavior by persuading themselves that they were justified in saying or doing what they did. If induced to speak or write on behalf of a point of view they have doubts about, they begin to believe their own words. Saying becomes believing. Similarly, subjects induced to harm an innocent victim—by making cutting comments or by delivering electric shocks—typically begin to disparage their victim.

*"If the King destroys a man, that's proof to the King it must have been a bad man."*

Thomas Cromwell in Robert Bolt's *A Man for All Seasons*, 1960

Fortunately, the attitudes-follow-behavior principle works as well for good deeds as for bad. In the years immediately following the introduction of school desegregation and the passage of the Civil Rights Act of 1964, white Americans expressed diminishing racial prejudice. And as Americans in different regions came to act more alike—thanks to more uniform national standards against discrimination—they began to think more alike. Experiments confirm that moral action has positive effects on the actor, and that doing favors for another person often leads to greater liking of the person. We love people for the good we do them as well as for the good they do us. Evil acts shape the self, but so do moral acts.

**Role Playing Affects Attitudes** In psychology, as in the theater, a **role** refers to a cluster of prescribed actions—the behaviors we expect of those who occupy a particular social position. When you adopt a new role—when you become a college student, marry, or begin a new job—you strive

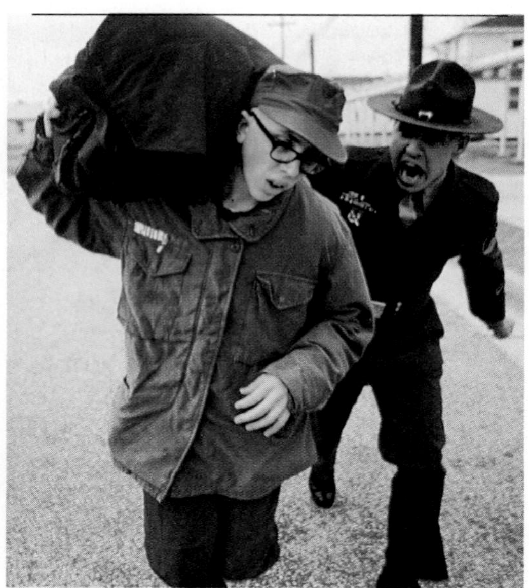

**Social Roles Are Powerful** *Initially both the obedient recruit and the abusive sergeant may have consciously adopted the behavior expected of them. But in time they may become the characters they are playing.*

to follow the social prescriptions. At first, the behaviors may feel phony, because you are *acting* the role. The first weeks in the military feel artificial—as if one is pretending to be a soldier. The first weeks of a marriage may feel like "playing house." Before long, however, your behavior no longer feels forced. What began as play-acting in the theater of life becomes *you*.

Researchers have confirmed this effect by assessing people's attitudes before and after they adopt a new role. Sometimes this occurs in laboratory situations, sometimes in everyday situations, such as before and after taking a job. In one laboratory study, college students volunteered to spend time in a simulated prison devised by psychologist Philip Zimbardo (1972). Some he randomly designated as guards; he gave them uniforms, billy clubs, and whistles and instructed them to enforce certain rules. The remainder became prisoners; they were locked in barren cells and forced to wear humiliating outfits. After a day or two of self-consciously "playing" their roles, the simulation became real—too real. Most of the guards developed disparaging attitudes and some devised cruel and degrading routines. One by one the prisoners either broke down, rebelled, or passively resigned, causing Zimbardo to call the study off after only 6 days.

Meanwhile, in real life, the military junta then in power in Greece was training another group of men to become torturers (Staub, 1989). The men's indoctrination into their roles occurred in small steps. First, the trainee stood guard outside the interrogation cells—the "foot in the door." Next, he stood guard inside. Only then was he ready to become actively involved in the questioning and torture. As the nineteenth-century writer Nathaniel Hawthorne noted, "No man, for any considerable period, can wear one face to himself and another to the multitude without finally getting bewildered as to which may be true." Behavior affects attitudes. What we do, we gradually become.

**Why Do Our Actions Affect Our Attitudes?** Without doubt, then, actions can affect attitudes, sometimes turning prisoners into collaborators, doubters into believers, or mere acquaintances into friends. But why? One explanation is that we feel motivated to justify our actions. When aware that our thoughts and actions don't coincide, we experience tension, called *cognitive dissonance*. To relieve this tension, according to the **cognitive dissonance theory** proposed by Leon Festinger, people often bring their attitudes into line with their actions. It's as if people rationalize, "If I chose to do it (or say it), I must believe in it." The less coerced and more responsible we feel for a troubling act, the more dissonance we feel. The more dissonance we feel, the more motivated we are to find consistency, such as by changing our attitudes to help justify the act.

Dozens of experiments have confirmed cognitive dissonance by making people feel responsible for behavior which has foreseeable consequences. As a subject in one of these experiments, you might agree for a measly $2 to help a researcher by writing an essay that supports something you don't believe in (perhaps a tuition increase). Feeling responsible for the statements (which are inconsistent with your prior attitudes), you likely would feel dissonance, especially if you thought an administrator would be reading your essay. How would you reduce the uncomfortable dissonance? One way would be to start believing your phony words. Let your pretense become your reality.

The attitudes-follow-behavior principle has some heartening implications. Although we cannot directly control all our feelings, we can influence them by altering our behavior. If we are unloving, we can become more loving by behaving as if we were so—by doing thoughtful things, expressing affection, giving affirmation. If we are down in the dumps, we can do as cognitive therapists advise and talk in more positive, self-accepting ways with fewer self put-downs. *The moral*: We can act ourselves into a way of thinking about as easily as we can think ourselves into a way of acting.

*"Sit all day in a moping posture, sigh, and reply to everything with a dismal voice, and your melancholy lingers. . . . If we wish to conquer undesirable emotional tendencies in ourselves, we must . . . go through the outward movements of those contrary dispositions which we prefer to cultivate."*

William James
*Principles of Psychology*, 1890

## Summing Up

Social psychology is the study of how people think about, influence, and relate to one another.

**Attributing Behavior to Persons or to Situations** We generally explain people's behavior by attributing it either to internal dispositions or to external situations. In accounting for others' actions, we often underestimate the influence of the situation, thus committing the fundamental attribution error. When we explain our own behavior, however, we more often point to the situation and not to ourselves.

**Attitudes and Actions** Attitudes predict behavior only under certain conditions, as when other influences are minimized, when the attitude is specific to the behavior, and when people are aware of their attitudes. Studies of the foot-in-the-door phenomenon and of role playing reveal that our actions can also modify our attitudes, especially when we feel responsible for those actions. Cognitive dissonance theorists explain that behavior shapes attitudes because people feel discomfort when their actions go against their feelings and beliefs; they reduce the discomfort by bringing their attitudes more into line with what they have done.

# Social Influence

*What invisible social threads pull us? How strong are they? How do they operate?*

Social psychology's great lesson—the enormous power of social influence on our attitudes, beliefs, decisions, and actions—can be seen in our conformity, compliance, and group behavior. Suicides, bomb threats, airplane hijackings, and UFO sightings all have a curious tendency to come in waves. Armed with principles of social influence, advertisers and salespeople aim to sway our decisions to buy, to donate, to vote. Isolated with others who share their grievances, dissenters may gradually become rebels and rebels may become terrorists. Let's examine these potent social forces.

## Conformity and Obedience

How powerful are the social strings that pull us? How do they operate? To find out, social psychologists often create laboratory simulations of everyday social situations. In the miniature social world of the experiment, researchers hold constant all the factors that might influence our behavior, except for one or two. These they vary, to pinpoint how changes in them affect us.

### Suggestibility

Behavior is contagious. One person giggles, coughs, or yawns, and others in the group are soon doing the same. A cluster of people stands gazing up-

*"The person we have to thank is Arthur here. He's the one with the infectious grin."*

Drawing by Handelsman; © 1984 The New Yorker Magazine, Inc.

ward, and passersby pause to do likewise. Laughter, even canned laughter, can be infectious. Bartenders and street musicians know to "seed" their tip cups with money to suggest that others have given.

Muzafer Sherif (1937) designed a simple social situation to study people's suggestibility. Shown a stationary point of light in a dark room, people misperceive it as moving. Some might see it as moving about 8 inches, others just an inch or two. When such people then participate together, hearing one another's estimates of how far the light moved, their estimates gradually converge. And when later retested individually, they still maintain their revised judgments.

In real life, the effects of suggestibility are sometimes devastating. Sociologist David Phillips and his colleagues (1985, 1989) found that known suicides increase following a highly publicized suicide (Figure 18–2). So do fatal auto accidents and private airplane crashes (some of which disguise suicides)—and they do so only in areas where the suicide is publicized. Following film star Marilyn Monroe's suicide on August 6, 1962, the number of August suicides in the United States exceeded the usual count by 200. In Germany and the United States, suicide increases have also followed fictional suicides on soap operas and on dramas dealing with suicide (Gould & Shaffer, 1986; Hafner & Schmidtke, 1989; Phillips, 1982). Such copycat suicides help explain the clusters of teenage suicides that occasionally occur in some communities.

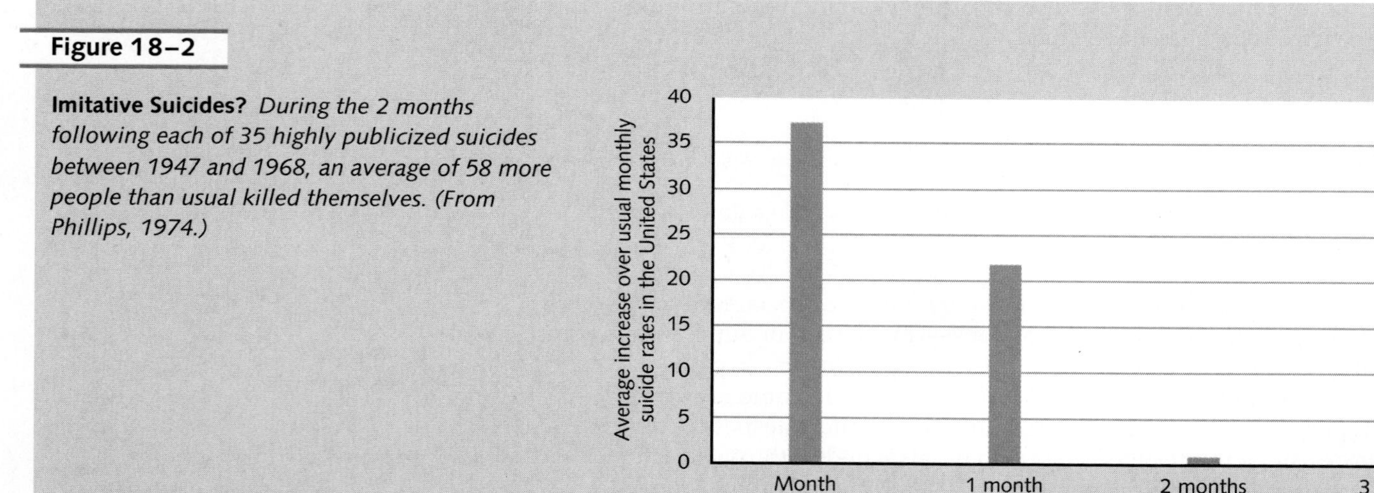


**Figure 18–2**

**Imitative Suicides?** *During the 2 months following each of 35 highly publicized suicides between 1947 and 1968, an average of 58 more people than usual killed themselves. (From Phillips, 1974.)*

## Group Pressure and Conformity

Suggestibility is a subtle type of **conformity**—adjusting our behavior or thinking to bring it into line with some group standard. Faced with the "moving" light, Sherif's subjects were unsure of the truth, so it is easy to understand why they adjusted their responses toward one another. But what would happen if people could easily judge the truth for themselves? Would they conform to a clearly incorrect group standard? Solomon Asch (1955) guessed not. To test his hunch, Asch devised a simple test.

Figure 18–3

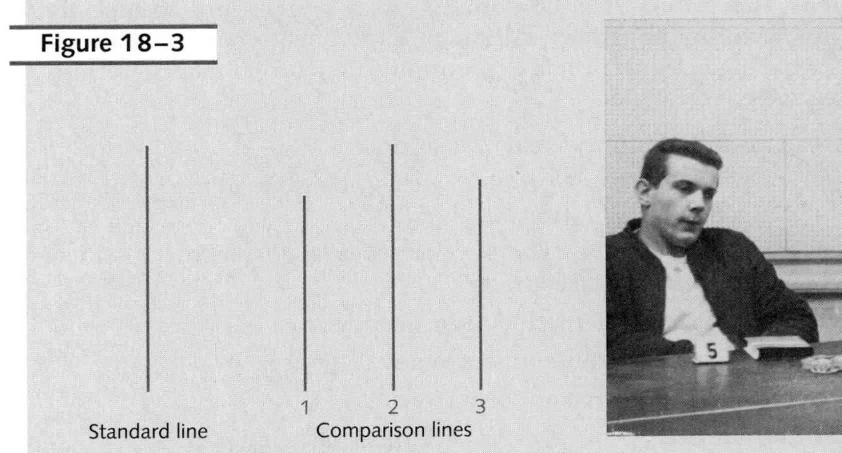

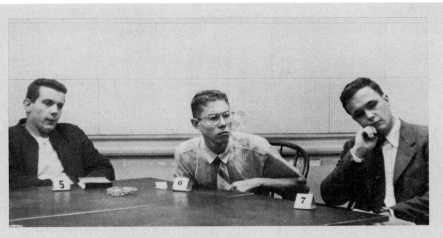

**Asch's Conformity Experiments** *Which of the three comparison lines is equal to the standard line? What do you suppose most people would say after hearing four others say, "Line 3"? In this photo from one of Asch's experiments, the subject (center) shows the severe discomfort that comes from disagreeing with the responses of other group members.*

As one of his subjects, you arrive at the experiment location in time to take a seat at the end of a row where four people are already seated. The experimenter asks which of three comparison lines is identical to a standard line (Figure 18–3). You see clearly that the answer is line 2 and await your turn to say so after the others. Your boredom with this experiment begins to show when the next set of lines proves equally easy.

Now comes the third trial, and the correct answer seems just as clear-cut, but the first person gives what strikes you as a wrong answer: "line 3." When the second person and then the third give the same wrong answer, you sit straight up and squint. When the fourth person agrees with the first three, you feel your heart begin to pound. The experimenter then looks to you for your answer. Torn between the unanimity of your four fellow subjects and the evidence of your own eyes, you feel tense and much less sure of yourself than you were moments ago. You hesitate before answering, wondering whether you should suffer the discomfort of being viewed as an oddball. What answer do you give?

In the experiments conducted by Asch and others after him, thousands of college students have experienced this conflict. Answering such questions alone, they erred less than 1 percent of the time. But it was a different story when several others—confederates working for the experimenter—answered incorrectly. Asch reports that his "intelligent and well-meaning" college subjects were then "willing to call white black" more than one-third of the time by going along with the group.

Do social examples similarly influence our everyday perceptions? To find out, Steven Fein and his colleagues (1993) had college students view the third Bush–Clinton Presidential Debate and then rate the candidates' performances. One group of 30 students included 10 confederates who cheered Bush and jeered Clinton. Another group included 10 confederates who cheered Clinton and jeered Bush. A third group had no confederates. As Figure 18–4 illustrates, the effect on students' perceptions were dramatic.

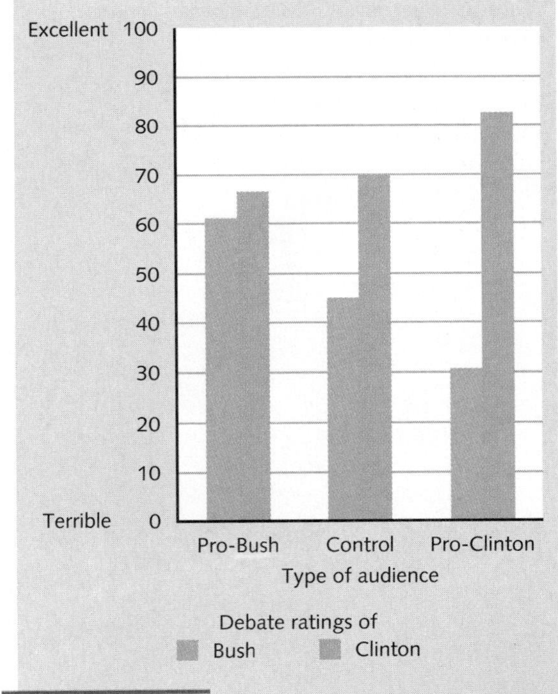


Figure 18–4

**Social Influences on Debate Perceptions** *All viewers (even the pro-Bush group) rated Clinton's performance more favorably when some in the audience cheered him and jeered Bush. (Adapted from Fein & others, 1993.)*

**Conditions That Strengthen Conformity** Asch's procedure became the model for later investigations. Although experiments have not always found such a high degree of blind conformity, they reveal that conformity increases when:

we are made to feel incompetent or insecure.

the group has at least three people. (Further increases in the group size yield not much more conformity.)

the group is unanimous. (The support of a single fellow dissident greatly increases our social courage.)

we admire the group's status and attractiveness.

we have made no prior commitment to any response.

others in the group observe our behavior.

our culture strongly encourages respect for social standards.

Thus, we might predict the behavior of Joe, an eager but insecure new member of a prestigious fraternity: Noting that the 40 other members appear unanimous in their plans for an upcoming fund-raiser, Joe is unlikely to voice his dissent.

**Reasons for Conforming** Why do we clap when others clap, eat as others eat, believe what others believe, even see what others see? Frequently, it is to avoid rejection or to gain social approval. In such cases, we are responding to what social psychologists call **normative social influence**. We are sensitive to social **norms**—understood rules for accepted and expected behavior—because the price we pay for being different may be severe. Marco Lokar knows. During the 1991 Persian Gulf War, Lokar, an Italian, was the only Seton Hall University basketball player who chose not to display an American flag on his uniform. As the team traveled about, the fans' abusive responses to his nonconforming behavior became unbearable, so he quit the team and returned to Italy.

*"'The way to get along,' I was told when I entered Congress, 'is to go along.'"*

John F. Kennedy
*Profiles in Courage*, 1956

But there is another reason we may conform: The group may provide valuable information. When we accept others' opinions about reality, we are responding to **informational social influence**. As a subject in Sherif's experiment—feeling very unsure about how far the light had moved—would it not have seemed reasonable to be open to others' judgments?

As these reasons for conformity suggest, we perceive social influence as negative or positive according to the situation and our own unique attitudes and experiences. When influence supports what we approve, we applaud those who are "open-minded" and "sensitive" enough to be "responsive." When influence supports what we disapprove, we scorn the "submissive conformity" of those who comply with others' wishes. As we will see in Chapter 19, cultures vary in the value they place on independence versus responsiveness to others. Western Europeans and those in most English-speaking countries tend to prize individualism more than conformity and obedience. In experiments conducted in 14 countries, conformity rates have been lower in individualistic cultures than in more group-centered cultures (Bond & Smith, 1994).

### Obedience

Social psychologist Stanley Milgram (1974) knew that people often comply with social pressures. But how would they respond to outright commands? To find out, he undertook what have become social psychology's most famous and controversial experiments. Imagine yourself as one of the nearly 1000 participants in Milgram's 20 experiments.

Responding to an advertisement, you come to Yale University's psychology department to participate in an experiment. Professor Milgram's assistant explains that the study concerns the effect of punishment on learning. You and another subject draw slips out of a hat to see who will be the "teacher" (which your slip says) and who will be the "learner." The learner is then led to an adjoining room and strapped into a chair that is wired through the wall to an electric shock machine. You sit down in front of the machine, which has switches labeled with voltages. Your task: to teach and then test the learner on a list of word pairs. You are to punish the learner for wrong answers by delivering brief electric shocks, beginning with a switch labeled "15 Volts—Slight Shock." After each error by the learner, you are to move up to the next higher voltage. With each flick of a switch, lights flash, relay switches click on, and an electric buzzing fills the air.

**Stanley Milgram (1933–1984)** *The late social psychologist's obedience experiments now "belong to the self-understanding of literate people in our age" (Sabini, 1986).*

If you comply with the experimenter's instructions, you hear the learner grunt when you flick the third, fourth, and fifth switches. After you activate the eighth switch (labeled "120 Volts"), the learner shouts that the shocks are painful. After the tenth switch ("150 Volts—Strong Shock"), he cries, "Experimenter, get me out of here! I won't be in the experiment anymore! I refuse to go on!" You draw back when you hear these pleas, but the experimenter prods you: "Please continue—the experiment requires that you continue." If you still resist, he insists, "It is absolutely essential that you continue," or "You have no other choice, you *must* go on."

If you obey, you hear the learner's protests escalate to shrieks of agony as you continue to raise the shock level with each succeeding error. After the 330-volt level, the learner refuses to answer and soon falls silent. Still, the experimenter pushes you toward the final, 450-volt switch, ordering you to ask the questions and, if a correct answer is not given, to administer the next shock level.

How far do you think you would follow the experimenter's commands? When Milgram surveyed people before conducting the experiment, most declared they would stop playing such a sadistic role soon after the learner first indicates pain and certainly before he shrieks in agony. This also was the prediction made by each of 40 psychiatrists whom Milgram asked to guess the outcome. When Milgram actually conducted the experiment with men aged 20 to 50, he was astonished to find that 63 percent complied fully—right up to the last switch.

Did the "teachers" figure out the hoax—that no shock was being delivered? Did they guess that the learner was a confederate who only pretended to feel the shocks? Did they realize that the experiment was really testing their willingness to comply with commands to inflict punishment? No, the teachers typically displayed genuine agony: They sweated, trembled, laughed nervously, and bit their lips. In defense of his use of deception, Milgram pointed out that, after the subjects learned of the deception and actual research purposes, virtually none regretted participating. When 40 of the subjects who had agonized most were later interviewed by a psychiatrist, none appeared to be suffering emotional aftereffects.

Perhaps the subjects obeyed because the learners' protests were not convincing. To preclude this possibility, Milgram repeated the experiment, with 40 new teachers. This time his confederate mentioned a "slight heart condition" while being strapped into the chair and then complained and screamed more intensely as the shocks became more punishing. Still, 65 percent of the new teachers complied fully (Figure 18–5, page 624).

In later experiments, Milgram discovered that subtle details of a situation powerfully influence people. When he varied the social conditions, the proportion of fully compliant subjects varied from 0 to 93 percent. Obedience was highest when:

the person giving the orders was close at hand and perceived to be a legitimate authority figure.

the authority figure was supported by a prestigious institution. (Milgram got somewhat less compliance when he dissociated his experiments from Yale University.)

the victim was depersonalized or at a distance, even in another room. (Similarly, in combat with an enemy they can see, many soldiers either do not fire their rifles or do not aim them properly. Such refusals to kill are rare among those who operate the more distant weapons of artillery or aircraft [Padgett, 1989].)

there were no role models for defiance; that is, no other subjects were seen disobeying the experimenter.

Figure 18–5

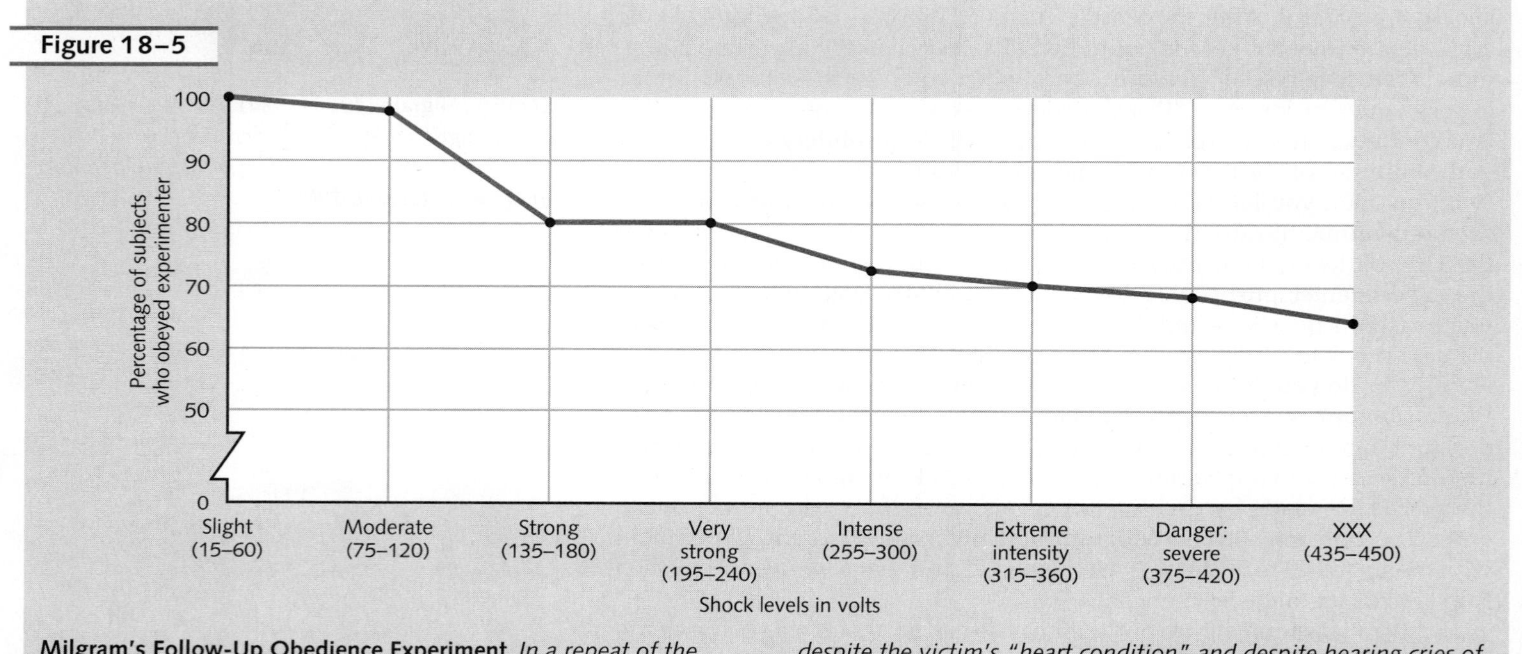


**Milgram's Follow-Up Obedience Experiment** *In a repeat of the earlier experiment, 65 percent of the adult male subjects fully obeyed the experimenter's commands to continue. This was despite the victim's "heart condition" and despite hearing cries of protest after 150 volts and agonized protests after 330 volts. (Data from Milgram, 1974.)*

The power of legitimate, close-at-hand authorities is dramatically apparent in stories of those who complied with orders to carry out the Holocaust, and those who didn't. In the summer of 1942 nearly 500 middle-aged German reserve police officers were dispatched to Jozefow, Poland, in German-occupied territory. On July 13, the group's visibly upset commander informed his recruits, mostly family men, that they had been ordered to round up the village's Jews, who were said to be aiding the enemy. Able-bodied men were to be sent to work camps and all the rest were to be shot on the spot. Given a chance to refuse participation in the executions, only about a dozen immediately refused. Within 17 hours, the remaining 485 officers killed 1500 helpless women, children, and elderly by shooting them in the back of the head as they lay face down, gruesomely spraying their skulls and brains. Faced with the pleadings of the personalized victims, and seeing the gruesome results, some 20 percent of the officers did eventually dissent, managing either to miss their victims or to wander away and hide until the slaughter was over (Browning, 1992). But, as in Milgram's experiments, the disobedient were the minority.

Meanwhile, in the French village of Le Chambon, French Jews destined for deportation to Germany were being sheltered by villagers who openly defied orders to cooperate with the "New Order." The villagers' ancestors had themselves been persecuted and their pastors had been teaching them to "resist whenever our adversaries will demand of us obedience contrary to the orders of the Gospel" (Rochat, 1993). Ordered by police to give a list of sheltered Jews, the head pastor modeled defiance: "I don't know of Jews, I only know of human beings." Without realizing how long and terrible the war would be, or how much punishment and poverty they would suffer, the resisters made an initial commitment to resist. Supported by their beliefs, their role models, their interaction with one another, and their own initial acts, they remained defiant to the war's end.

**Standing Up for Democracy** *Some individuals—roughly one in three in Milgram's experiments—resist social coercion, as did this unarmed man in Beijing, by single-handedly challenging an advancing line of tanks the day after the 1989 Tiananmen Square uprising was crushed.*

### Lessons From the Conformity and Obedience Studies

What do these experiments teach us about ourselves? How does guessing the movement of a light, judging the length of a line, or flicking a shock switch relate to everyday social behavior? Recall from Chapter 1 that psychological experiments aim not to recreate the literal behaviors of everyday life but to capture and explore the underlying processes that shape those behaviors. Sherif, Asch, and Milgram devised experiments in which the subjects had to choose between holding to their own standards and being responsive to others, a dilemma we all face frequently.

In Milgram's experiments, subjects were also torn between what they should respond to—the pleas of the victim or the orders of the experimenter. Their moral sense warned them not to harm another, but it also prompted them to obey the experimenter and to be a good subject. With kindness and obedience on a collision course, obedience usually won.

These experiments demonstrate that social influences can be strong enough to make people conform to falsehoods or capitulate to cruelty. "The most fundamental lesson of our study," Milgram noted, is that "ordinary people, simply doing their jobs, and without any particular hostility on their part, can become agents in a terrible destructive process" (1974, p. 6). Milgram entrapped his subjects not by asking them first to zap someone with enough electricity to stand their hair on end. Rather, he exploited the foot-in-the-door effect, beginning with a little tickle of electricity and escalating step by step. In the subjects' minds, the little action became justified, making the next act tolerable. In Jozefow, in Le Chambon, and in Milgram's experiments, those who resisted often did so early. With the first acts of compliance or resistance, attitudes began to follow and justify behavior.

*"Drive off the cliff, James, I want to commit suicide."*

Drawing by Mel Yauk.

So it happens when people succumb, gradually, to evil. In any society, great evils sometimes grow out of people's compliance with little evils. The Nazi leaders suspected that most German civil servants would resist shooting or gassing Jews directly, but they found them surprisingly willing to handle the paperwork of the Holocaust (Silver & Geller, 1978). Likewise, when Milgram asked 40 men to administer the learning test while someone else did the shocking, 93 percent complied. Contrary to our images of devilish villains, evil doesn't require monstrous evil characters; it's enough to have ordinary people corrupted by an evil situation.

*"I was only following orders."*

Adolf Eichmann, director of Nazi deportation of Jews to concentration camps

## *Thinking Critically About* Social Influence

Many social influences are so subtle that we don't notice them. Or if we do we think ourselves immune. "Yes, TV affects others," most people say, "but not me." Peer examples don't intimidate us. Role models don't sway us. Ads don't persuade us. For we are not slaves to fads, fashions, and opinions; we are true to ourselves.

Or so we think. The reality, as social influence research has a thousand times demonstrated, is that the influence others have on us, and we on them, is real, though often unnoticed. The extent to which influences go unnoticed, even by those looking for them, appears in studies of "facilitated communication" with autistic children. *Autism*, a pervasive disorder that appears during the preschool years, is marked by apparent indifference to others, minimal intelligible speech, and restricted interests and activities. Hoping to break down the walls that isolate such children, a facilitator holds or steadies the arm of an autistic child, who uses one finger to type words on a keyboard.

The technique is said to have produced breathtaking results with thousands of children, who suddenly begin typing intelligible words (sometimes elaborate sentences) which supposedly report their experiences and feelings. In several dozen cases where a person other than the parent was a facilitator, children have typed accusations of sexual abuse by their parents.

These spectacular findings and serious accusations led some people to question who was doing the communicating and the accusing—the child or the facilitator? To find out, Douglas Wheeler and his colleagues (1993) had 12 autistic children view pictures of everyday objects (a shoe, a book, a comb) and then type what they saw. When their facilitators saw the same picture, the children often typed the correct answer. When the facilitators saw a different picture, or no picture, the children were *never* correct (Figure 18–6).

Seventeen other experiments have produced similar results, some by not allowing the facilitator to see the keyboard (Green & Shane, 1993). Facilitated communication proponents reply (as have ESP proponents) that the pressure of the testing situation obliterates the delicate phenomenon. But to the researchers, the more logical conclusion is the one reluctantly drawn by some of the shocked facilitators: The communication comes not from the child but from the facilitator. The results stunned the well-meaning facilitators. Until the controlled experiment they had no awareness of their influence on the child's movements. In this situation, as in so many others, human influence is subtle, unnoticed, even disbelieved, yet very real.

**Figure 18–6**

**Testing Facilitated Communication** *The child responds after the facilitator and child see the same or different pictures. (Adapted from Wheeler & others, 1993.)*

## Group Influence

How do groups affect our behavior? To find out, social psychologists study the various influences that operate in the simplest of groups—one person in the presence of another—and those that operate in more complex groups, such as families, teams, and committees.

### Individual Behavior in the Presence of Others

Appropriately, social psychology's first experiments focused on the simplest of all questions about social behavior: How are we influenced by the mere presence of others—by people watching us or joining us as we engage in various activities?

**Social Facilitation** Having noticed that cyclists' racing times were faster when they competed against each other than when competing with a clock, Norman Triplett (1898) guessed that the presence of others boosts performance. To test his hypothesis, Triplett had adolescents wind a fishing reel as rapidly as possible. He discovered that they wound faster in the presence of a **co-actor**, someone who works simultaneously on the same task. This stronger performance in the presence of others is known as **social facilitation**. For example, after a light turns green, drivers take about 15 percent less time to travel the first 100 yards when another car is beside them at the intersection than when they are alone (Towler, 1986). When dining with friends, people also eat more than when served the same large meal alone (Clendenen & Herman, 1994).

For a while, social facilitation seemed a universal principle, an effect that occurred in varying circumstances. Researchers were therefore mystified when they began to find the opposite effect: On tougher tasks (learning nonsense syllables or solving complex multiplication problems), people performed less well when there were observers or co-actors. Some 300 studies and 25,000 subjects later (Guerin, 1986), the mystery of why the presence of others sometimes helps and sometimes hurts task performance has been solved. The Sherlock Holmes in this scientific detective story was social psychologist Robert Zajonc (1965). Zajonc recalled an effect of arousal on performance (page 434): Arousal facilitates the most likely response—the correct one on an easy task, an incorrect one on a difficult task. If performing tasks in the presence of others causes people to become aroused, reasoned Zajonc, then easy tasks should become easier and difficult tasks should become harder.

Sure enough, when observed by others, people do become aroused (Geen & Gange, 1983; Moore & Baron, 1983). And with arousal, they do perform well-learned tasks more quickly and accurately and unmastered tasks less quickly and accurately. James Michaels and his associates (1982) found that expert pool players who made 71 percent of their shots when alone made 80 percent when four people came up to watch them. Poor shooters, who made 36 percent of their shots when alone, made only 25 percent when watched. The energizing effects of an enthusiastic audience likely contributes to the home advantage enjoyed by various sports teams. Studies of more than 80,000 college and professional athletic events in Canada, the United States, and England reveal that home teams win about 6 in 10 games (somewhat fewer for baseball and football, somewhat more for basketball and soccer).

*The moral*: What you do well, you are likely to do even better in front of an audience, especially a friendly audience; what you normally find difficult may seem impossible when others are watching.

Social facilitation also helps explain a funny effect of crowding: Comedy records that are mildly amusing to people in an uncrowded room seem funnier to people in a densely packed room (Aiello & others, 1983; Freedman & Perlick, 1979). As comedians and actors know, a "good house" is a full one. The arousal triggered by crowding amplifies other reactions, too. If sitting close, experimental subjects like a friendly person more, an unfriendly person less (Schiffenbauer & Schiavo, 1976; Storms & Thomas, 1977).

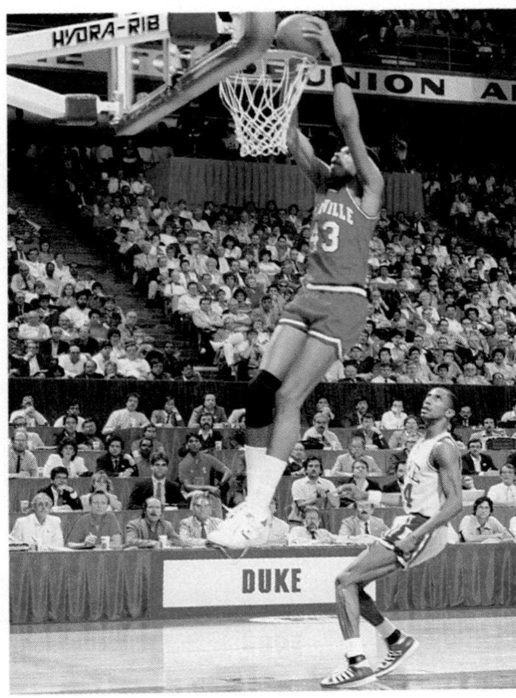


**Social Facilitation** *Skilled athletes often find they are "on" before an audience. What they do well, they do even better when people are watching.*

**Social Loafing** The social facilitation experiments test the effect of others' presence on *individual* effort in tasks ranging from winding fishing reels to shooting pool. But what happens in situations that require a *team* effort to achieve a common goal? In a team tug-of-war, for example, do you suppose the effort people would individually put forth would be more than, less than, or the same as the effort they would exert in a one-on-one tug-of-war?

To find out, Alan Ingham and his fellow researchers (1974) asked blindfolded University of Massachusetts students to "pull as hard as you can" on a rope. When Ingham fooled the students into believing three others were also pulling behind them, they exerted only 82 percent as much effort as when they knew they were pulling alone.

To describe the diminished effort by those submerged in a group, Bibb Latané and his colleagues (1981; Jackson & Williams, 1988) coined the term **social loafing**. In 78 experiments conducted in the United States, India, Thailand, Japan, China, and Taiwan, social loafing occurred on various tasks, though especially among men in individualistic cultures (Karau & Williams, 1993). For example, blindfolded subjects seated in a group have clapped or shouted as loud as they could while listening through headphones to the sound of loud clapping or shouting. When told they were doing it with the others, the subjects produced about one-third less noise than when they thought their individual efforts were identifiable.

Why? First, people acting as part of a group feel less accountable and therefore worry less about what others think. Second, they may view their contribution as dispensable (Harkins & Szymanski, 1989; Kerr & Bruun, 1983). As many leaders of organizations know, if group members share equally in the group's benefits regardless of how much they contribute, they may slack off and "free-ride" on the other group members' efforts.

**Deindividuation** So, the presence of others can arouse people (as in the social facilitation experiments) or can diminish their feelings of responsibility (as in the social loafing experiments). Sometimes the presence of others both arouses people *and* diminishes their sense of responsibility. The result can be uninhibited behavior ranging from a food fight in the dining hall or screaming at a basketball referee to vandalism or rioting. Abandoning normal restraints to the power of the group is termed **deindividuation**. To be deindividuated is to be less self-conscious and less restrained in a group situation.

Deindividuation often occurs when group participation makes people feel aroused and anonymous. In one experiment, New York University women dressed in depersonalizing Ku Klux Klan-style hoods delivered twice as much electric shock to a victim as did identifiable women (Zimbardo, 1970). (As in all such experiments, the "victim" did not actually receive the shocks.) Similarly, tribal warriors who depersonalize themselves with face paints or masks are more likely than those with exposed faces to kill, torture, or mutilate captured enemies (Watson, 1973). Whether in a mob, at a rock concert, at a dance, or at worship, to lose self-consciousness (to become deindividuated) is to become more responsive to the group experience.

## Effects of Group Interaction

We have examined the conditions under which the presence of others can make easy tasks easier and difficult tasks harder; tempt people to free-ride on the efforts of others and motivate them to cycle faster; enhance humor and fuel mob violence. Research shows how group interaction, too, can have both bad and good effects.

**Group Polarization** Educational researchers have noted that, over time, initial differences between groups of college students often grow. If the first-year students at College X tend to be more intellectually oriented than those at College Y, chances are their difference will be amplified by the time they are seniors. Similarly, if the political conservatism of students who join fraternities and sororities is greater than that of students who do not, the gap in the political attitudes of the two groups will probably widen as they progress through college (Wilson & others, 1975).

This enhancement of a group's prevailing tendencies—called **group polarization**—occurs when people within a group discuss attitudes that most of them favor or oppose. For example, one study discovered that when prejudiced high school students discussed racial issues, their attitudes became more prejudiced. When low-prejudice students discussed the same issues, they became more tolerant (Figure 18–7).

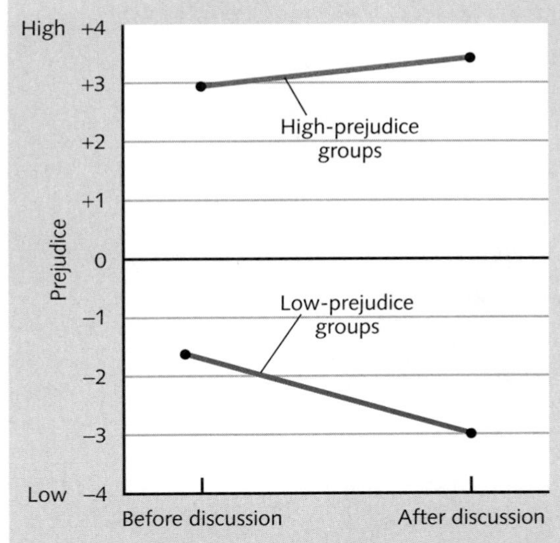


**Figure 18–7**

**Group Polarization** *If a group is like-minded, discussion strengthens its prevailing opinions. Talking over racial issues increased prejudice in a high-prejudice group of high school students and decreased it in a low-prejudice group. (Data from Myers & Bishop, 1970.)*

Group polarization can have beneficial results, as when it amplifies a sought-after spiritual awareness or strengthens the resolve of those in a self-help group. But it can also have dire consequences. From their analysis of terrorist organizations around the world, psychologists Clark McCauley and Mary Segal (1987) note that the terrorist mentality does not erupt suddenly. Rather, it arises among people who have come together because of a grievance and who become more and more extreme as they interact in isolation from moderating influences.

**Groupthink** Does group interaction ever distort important group decisions? Social psychologist Irving Janis thought so when he first read historian Arthur M. Schlesinger, Jr.'s, account of how President John F. Kennedy and his advisers blundered into an ill-fated plan to invade Cuba with 1400 CIA-trained Cuban exiles. When the invaders were easily captured and soon linked to the American government, Kennedy wondered aloud, "How could we have been so stupid?"

To find out, Janis (1982) studied the decision-making procedures that led to the fiasco. He discovered that the high morale of the recently elected President and his advisers fostered a sense that the plan would succeed. To preserve the good group feeling, dissenting views were suppressed or self-censored, especially after the President voiced his enthusiasm for the scheme. Since no one spoke sharply against the idea, everyone assumed there was consensus support for it. To describe this harmonious but unrealistic group thinking, Janis coined the term **groupthink**.

*"One's impulse to blow the whistle on this nonsense was simply undone by the circumstances of the discussion."*

Arthur M. Schlesinger, Jr. (1965, p. 255)

Janis and others then examined other historical fiascos—the failure to anticipate the Pearl Harbor attack, the escalation of the Vietnam war, the Watergate cover-up, the Chernobyl reactor accident (Reason, 1987), and the space shuttle *Challenger* explosion (Esser & Lindoerfer, 1989). They discovered that in these cases, too, groupthink was fed by overconfidence, conformity, self-justification, and group polarization. Buoyed by a string of successful space shuttle launches, the NASA management team approached the 1985 *Challenger* mission brimming with confidence but frustrated by launch delays. When the rocket booster's engineers opposed the launch because of dangers posed by freezing temperatures, group pressures to go ahead effectively silenced their warnings. Unless the engineers could *prove* that the rocket seals would not hold, the management group would not agree to another delay. Moreover, managers shielded the NASA executive who made the final "go" decision from information about the warnings. Wrongly assuming that support was unanimous, he launched the *Challenger* on its one-way flight to annihilation.

*"There was a serious flaw in the decision-making process."*

*Report of the Presidential Commission on the Space Shuttle Challenger Accident,* 1986

Despite such fiascos and tragedies, Janis also knew that, with some types of problems, two heads are better than one. So he also studied instances in which American presidents and their advisers collectively made good decisions. Examples were the Truman administration's formulation of the Marshall Plan for getting Europe back on its feet after World War II and the Kennedy administration's actions to keep the Soviets from installing missiles in Cuba. In such instances—and in the business world, too, Janis believed—groupthink is prevented by a leader who welcomes various opinions, invites experts' critiques of developing plans, or even assigns people to identify possible problems. As the suppression of dissent bends a group toward bad decisions, so open debate often shapes good decisions.

*"Truth springs from argument among friends."*
Philosopher David Hume, 1711–1776

In affirming the power of social influence, we must not overlook our power as individuals. As we noted in Chapter 14, *social control* (the power of the situation) and *personal control* (the power of the individual) interact. People aren't billiard balls. When feeling pressured, we may react by doing the opposite, thereby reasserting our sense of freedom (Brehm & Brehm, 1981). Moreover, many of the situations that influence us are ones we choose or help create. If we expect people to be uncooperative and hostile, we may treat them in ways that elicit such behavior. Thus, our expectations may be self-fulfilling. In one experiment, men talked more charmingly by phone to women they believed to be beautiful. This led the women to respond more warmly—confirming the men's idea that attractive people are likable (Snyder & others, 1977).

*"I thought I told you not to drink your milk."*
Drawing by Shanahan; © 1993 The New Yorker Magazine, Inc.

## Minority Influence

The power of committed individuals also appears in their influence over their groups. Social history is often made by a minority that sways the majority. Were this not so, women in Western democracies would still lack the right to vote, communism would be an obscure theory, Christianity would be a small Middle Eastern sect, and Rosa Parks's refusal to sit at the back of the bus would not have ignited the civil rights movement. Technological history, too, is often made by innovative minorities who overcome the majority's resistance to change. To many folks, the railroad was a nonsensical idea; some farmers feared that train noise would prevent hens from laying eggs. People derided Robert Fulton's steamboat as "Fulton's Folly." As Fulton later said, "Never did a single encouraging remark, a bright hope, a warm wish, cross my path." Much the same reaction greeted the printing press, the telegraph, the incandescent lamp, and the typewriter (Cantril & Bumstead, 1960).

To better understand how minorities can sway majorities, European social psychologists led by Serge Moscovici have investigated groups in which an individual or two consistently expresses a controversial attitude or an unusual perceptual judgment. They have repeatedly found that a minority that unswervingly holds to its position is far more successful in swaying the majority than is a minority that waffles. Holding consistently to a minority opinion will not make you popular, but it may make you influential. This is especially so if your self-confidence stimulates others to consider why you react as you do. Although people often follow the majority view publicly, they may privately develop sympathy for the minority view. Even when a minority's influence is not yet visible, it may be persuading some members of the majority to rethink their views (Wood & others, 1994). Thus, the combined powers of social thinking and social influence are enormous; but so are the powers of the committed individual.

We also do well to remember that explaining *why* an individual holds a particular belief says nothing about the belief's truth or falsity. To know why someone believes that running benefits health does not tell us whether running is, in fact, beneficial. To know why one person is a believer and another is an atheist does not tell us whether God exists. So let no one say to you and do not say to anyone, "Your convictions are silly. You believe them because of social influence." The second statement may be true, but it doesn't justify the first.

**Gandhi** *As the life of Mahatma Gandhi powerfully testifies, a consistent and persistent minority voice can sometimes sway the majority. The nonviolent appeals and fasts of the Hindu nationalist and spiritual leader were instrumental in winning India's independence from Britain.*

## Summing Up

**Conformity and Obedience** As suggestibility studies demonstrate, when we are unsure about our judgments, we are likely to adjust them toward the group standard. Solomon Asch found that under certain conditions people will conform to a group's judgment even when it is clearly incorrect. We may conform either to gain social approval (normative social influence) or because we welcome the information that others provide (informational social influence). In Milgram's famous experiments, people torn between obeying an experimenter and responding to another's pleas usually chose to obey orders, even though obedience supposedly meant harming the other person. Such is the potency of social influence.

**Group Influence** Experiments on social facilitation reveal that the presence of either observers or co-actors can arouse individuals, boosting their performance on easy tasks but hindering it on difficult ones. When people pool their efforts toward a group goal, social loafing may occur as individuals free-ride on others' efforts. When a group experience arouses people and makes them anonymous, they may become less self-aware and self-restrained, a psychological state known as deindividuation.

Within groups, discussions among like-minded members often produce group polarization, an enhancement of the group's prevailing attitudes. This is one cause of groupthink, the tendency for harmony-seeking groups to make unrealistic decisions after suppressing unwelcome information.

The power of the group is great, but so is the power of the person. Even a small minority sometimes sways a group, especially when it expresses its views consistently.

# Social Relations

*What makes us harm or help or fall in love? How can we transform the closed fists of aggression into the open arms of compassion?*

Having sampled how we *think* about and *influence* one another, we come finally to social psychology's third focus—how we *relate* to one another. We will ponder the bad and the good: aggression, helpfulness, and attraction.

## Aggression

In psychology, *aggression* has a more precise meaning than it does in everyday usage. The assertive, persistent salesperson is not aggressive. Nor is the dentist who makes you wince with pain. But the person who passes along a vicious rumor about you and the attacker who mugs you are aggressive. **Aggression** is any physical or verbal behavior intended to hurt or destroy, whether done out of hostility or as a calculated means to an end. Some of the 23,760 murders and 1,126,974 assaults recorded in the United States during 1992 were cool, calculated aggressive acts, but more were hostile outbursts.

*In the last 25 years in the United States, guns have caused 800,000 suicidal, homicidal, and accidental deaths. Compared with people of the same sex, race, age, and neighborhood, those who keep a gun in the home (often for protection) are 2.7 times more likely to be murdered—nearly always by a family member or close acquaintance (Kellermann & others, 1993).*

A rising tide of violence, especially violence by youth, plagues many countries. Most readers living outside the United States can, however, take comfort that their risk of being murdered is *much* lower—for example, one-fourth as much for Canadians and Australians, one-fifth as much for New Zealanders, and, on average, one-sixth as much for Europeans (United Nations, 1992). With 1.2 million people currently in jail or prison, Americans can also proclaim that "We're number one" among the industrialized nations in inmates—nearly 50 percent ahead of the incarceration rate in what was the number two nation, South Africa.

Why are some countries, and some individuals, so violence-prone? And why have violence rates increased in so many countries?

Time and again, we have seen that behavior emerges from the interaction of biology and experience. Research on aggression reinforces that theme. For a gun to fire, the trigger must be pulled; with some people, as with hair-trigger guns, it doesn't take much to trip an explosion. Let us look first at biological factors that influence our thresholds for aggressive behavior. Then we will examine the psychological factors that pull the trigger.

## The Biology of Aggression

According to one view, argued by Sigmund Freud and others, our species has a volcanic potential to erupt in aggression. Freud thought that, along with positive survival instincts, we harbor a self-destructive "death instinct" that we usually displace toward others as aggression or release in socially approved activities such as painting or sports.

Although aggression varies too widely from culture to culture and person to person to be considered an unlearned instinct, biology does influence aggression. Stimuli that influence aggressive behavior operate through our biological system. We can look for biological influences at three levels—genetic, neural, and biochemical. Our genes engineer our individual nervous systems, which operate electrochemically.

**Genetic Influences** Animals have been bred for aggressiveness—sometimes for sport, sometimes for research. Finnish psychologist Kirsti Lagerspetz (1979) took a group of normal mice and bred the most aggressive with one another and the least aggressive with one another. After repeating this selective breeding for another 25 generations, she had a group of vicious mice that would attack immediately when put together and a group of docile mice that, no matter what she did, refused to fight. Twin studies suggest that genes influence human aggression as well (Rushton & others, 1986). If one identical twin admits to "having a violent temper," the other twin will often independently admit the same. Fraternal twins are much more likely to respond differently.

**Neural Influences** Animal and human brains have neural systems that produce aggressive behavior when stimulated (Moyer, 1983). Consider:

> The domineering leader of a caged monkey colony has a radio-controlled electrode implanted in a brain area that, when stimulated, inhibits aggression. When researchers place the button that activates the electrode in the colony's cage, one small monkey learns to push it every time the boss becomes threatening.
>
> A mild-mannered woman has an electrode implanted in her brain's limbic system (in the amygdala) by neurosurgeons seeking to diagnose a disorder. Because the brain has no sensory receptors, she cannot feel stimulation. But at the flick of a switch she snarls, "Take my blood pressure. Take it now," and then stands up and begins to strike the doctor.

> Intensive evaluation of 15 death-row inmates reveals that all 15 have suffered severe head injury. Researcher Dorothy Lewis and her colleagues (1986) infer that many condemned criminals suffer unrecognized neurological disorders.

So, does the brain have a "violence center" that produces aggression when stimulated? Actually, no one spot in the brain controls aggression, because aggression is a complex behavior that occurs in particular contexts. Rather, the brain has neural systems that facilitate aggression, making it more likely, given provocation and no deterrents.

**Biochemical Influences** Hormones, alcohol, and other substances in the blood influence the neural systems that control aggression. A raging bull will become a gentle Ferdinand when castration reduces its testosterone level. The same is true of castrated mice. When injected with testosterone, the castrated mice again become aggressive. However, the traffic between hormones and behavior is two-way. Testosterone heightens dominance and aggressiveness, but dominating or defeating behavior also boosts testosterone levels (Gladue & others, 1989).

Although humans are less sensitive to hormonal changes, violent criminals tend to be muscular young males with lower than average intelligence scores and higher than average testosterone levels (Dabbs, 1992; Wilson & Herrnstein, 1985). Drugs that sharply reduce their testosterone levels subdue their aggressive tendencies. Among the normal range of teenage boys and adult men, high testosterone levels correlate with delinquency, hard drug use, and aggressive, bullying responses to provocation (Berman & others, 1993; Dabbs & Morris, 1990; Olweus & others, 1988).

For both biological and psychological reasons, alcohol unleashes aggressive responses to provocation (Bushman, 1993; Taylor & Chermack, 1993). (Just *thinking* you've imbibed alcohol has some effect; but so, too, does unknowingly ingesting alcohol slipped into a drink.) Police data and prison surveys reinforce conclusions from experiments on alcohol and aggression. Aggression-prone people are more likely to drink and to become violent when intoxicated (White & others, 1993). People who have been drinking commit about 50 percent of rapes and other violent crimes (Abbey & others, 1993; Reiss & Roth, 1993).

*"He that is naturally addicted to Anger, let him Abstain from Wine; for it is but adding Fire to Fire."*

Seneca
*De Ira*, A.D. 49

**Deindividuation + Competition + Alcohol = Aggression** *A 1985 riot at a soccer game in Brussels left 38 dead and 437 injured. Aroused by the competition and loaded with alcohol, English fans lost all restraint when provoked by Italian fans. They attacked the Italians, who retreated and were then crushed against a wall.*

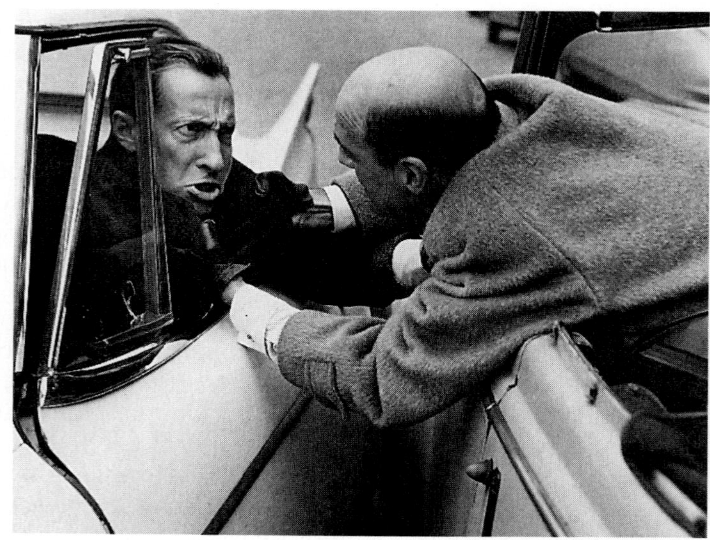

**A Classic Picture of Aggression** *An unpleasant experience—such as an accident—can trigger aggression and even physical violence, especially when the situation can be blamed on the other.*

### The Psychology of Aggression

Biological factors influence the ease with which the aggression trigger pulls. But what psychological factors do the pulling?

**Aversive Events** Although suffering sometimes builds character, it may also bring out the worst in us. Studies in which animals or humans experience unpleasant events reveal that those made miserable often make others miserable (Berkowitz, 1983, 1989).

Being blocked short of a goal also increases people's readiness to aggress. This phenomenon we know as the **frustration-aggression principle**: Frustration creates anger, which may in some people generate aggression, especially in the presence of an aggressive cue, such as a gun. Frustrations are instances of aversive events. Like frustration, physical pain, personal insults, foul odors, hot temperatures, cigarette smoke, and a host of other aversive stimuli can also evoke hostility (Figure 18–8).

Figure 18–8

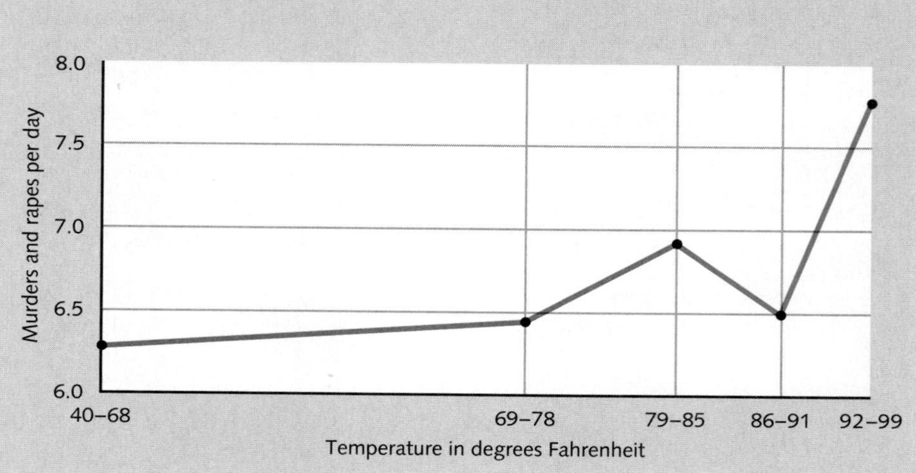


**Uncomfortably Hot Weather and Aggressive Reactions** *Violent crime and spouse abuse occur more in summer than in winter, in hot years than in cooler years, in hot cities than in cooler cities, and on hotter days than on colder days (Anderson 1989). For example, between 1980 and 1982 in Houston, murders and rapes were more common on days over 91° F. This finding is consistent with those from laboratory experiments in which people working in a hot room react to provocations with greater hostility. (From Anderson & Anderson, 1984.)*

**Learning to Express and Inhibit Aggression** Aggression may be a natural response to aversive events, but learning can alter natural reactions. Animals naturally eat when they are hungry. But if appropriately rewarded or punished, they can be taught either to overeat or to starve.

Aggressive reactions are more likely in situations where experience has taught us that aggression pays. Children whose aggression successfully intimidates other children may become more aggressive. Violent demonstrations that provide demonstrators with desired attention may recur.

Aggressive behavior can be learned through direct rewards. Animals that have fought successfully to get food or mates become increasingly ferocious. It can also be learned through observation. Children who grow up observing aggressive models often imitate the behaviors they see. Parents of delinquent youngsters typically discipline with beatings, thus modeling aggression as a method of dealing with problems (Patterson & others, 1982).

*"Why do we kill people who kill people to show that killing people is wrong?"*

National Coalition to Abolish the Death Penalty, 1992

Different cultures model, reinforce, and evoke differing tendencies toward violence. For example, crime rates are higher in countries marked by a great disparity between rich and poor (Triandis, 1994). Richard Nisbett (1993) showed how cultures can also differ within a country. He analyzed violence among whites in southern American towns settled by Scottish-Irish herders whose tradition emphasized "manly honor" and the use of arms to protect one's flock. To this day, their cultural descendants have triple the homicide rates of whites in New England towns settled by sober Puritan, Quaker, and Dutch farmer-artisans. They also are more supportive of physically punishing children, of warfare initiatives, and of uncontrolled gun ownership.

Social influence also appears in high violence rates among cultures and families that experience minimal father care (Triandis, 1994). For example, the U.S. Bureau of Justice Statistics reports that 70 percent of imprisoned juveniles did not grow up with two parents (Beck & others, 1988). (Because an absent parent is usually a father, most grew up with minimal father care.) The correlation between father absence and violence holds for all races, income levels, and locations (Prothrow-Stith, 1991; Staub, 1993). The correlation also appears over time. In the United States in 1960, barely over 1 in 10 children did not live with two parents, and only 16,000 juveniles were arrested for violent crime. In 1992, nearly 3 in 10 children did not live with two parents, and a similar-sized juvenile population produced 96,000 arrests for violent crime.

That many individuals lead gentle, even heroic, lives amid social stresses reminds us that individuals differ. The person matters. That people differ over time and place reminds us that environments differ. Situations matter. Aggressive behavior, like all behavior, arises from the interaction of persons and situations.

Once established, however, aggressive behavior patterns are difficult to change. To foster a kinder, gentler world we had best model and reward sensitivity and cooperation from an early age, perhaps by training parents how to discipline without modeling violence. Often, modeling violence—screaming and hitting—is precisely what exasperated parents do. Parent-training programs usually advise a more positive approach. They encourage parents to reinforce desirable behaviors and to frame statements positively ("When you finish loading the dishwasher you can go play," rather than "If you don't load the dishwasher there'll be no playing.") One "aggression-replacement program" that brought down re-arrest rates of juvenile offenders and gang members taught the youth and their parents communication skills, trained them in how to control anger, and raised their level of moral reasoning (Goldstein & Glick, in press).

*"The problem with television is that the people must sit and keep their eyes glued to a screen: the average American family hasn't time for it. Therefore the showmen are convinced that . . . television will never be a serious competitor of [radio] broadcasting."*

*The New York Times*, 1939

**Television Watching and Aggression** Parents are hardly the only aggression models. During their first 18 years, most children spend more time watching television than they spend in school. In urban homes across the world, including those of South America and Asia, television is now commonplace. In Beijing, for example, the percentage of homes with television skyrocketed from 32 percent in 1980 to 95 percent by the end of the decade (Lull, 1988). With more than 1 billion TV sets now in homes around the world, CNN reaching 150 countries, and MTV videos seen from Alaska to Bangladesh, television is creating a global pop culture (Lippman, 1992). One can watch American programs in Perth or Prague and hear Madonna and Pearl Jam from New Delhi to Newfoundland. Television does not reflect the world we live in. On evening dramas broadcast in the United States during the 1980s and early 1990s and often exported to the world, only one-third of the characters were women. Fewer than 3 percent were visibly old. One percent were Hispanic. Only 1 in 10 was married (Gerbner, 1993).

THE FAR SIDE

*In the days before television*

Drawing by Gary Larson: "The Far Side" cartoon is reprinted by permission of Chronicle Features, San Francisco.

In 1993, U.S. network programs offered about 3 violent acts per hour during prime time, and 18 per hour during children's Saturday morning programs (Gerbner & others, 1993). During the last 20 years the average child has viewed some 8000 TV murders and 100,000 other acts of violence before finishing elementary school (Huston & others, 1992). If one includes cable programming and video rentals, the violence numbers escalate. (Popular rental films like *Die Hard 1*, with its 264 deaths, are much more violent than major network programs.) This is life as rendered by a rather peculiar storyteller, one who reflects the culture's mythology but not its reality. In U.S. action-oriented crime shows (the shows most often exported to the world market), TV cops fire their guns in almost every episode; in Chicago, the average police officer fires a gun once every 27 years (Radecki, 1989).

Does viewing televised aggression influence some people to commit aggression? Was the judge who in 1993 tried two British 10-year-olds for their murder of a 2-year-old right to suspect that one possible influence was their exposure to "violent video films"? To answer such questions, researchers have conducted correlational and experimental studies (Hearold, 1986; Wood & others, 1991).

Correlational studies link young childrens' viewing of violence and their combativeness as teenagers and young adults (Eron, 1987; Turner & others, 1986). In the United States and Canada, a doubling of homicide rates between 1957 and 1974 coincided with the introduction and spread of television. Moreover, census regions that acquired television late showed the homicide jump correspondingly later. Among white South Africans, who were first introduced to television in 1975, a similar near-doubling of the homicide rate did not begin until after 1975 (Centerwall, 1989).

Critics respond that these correlational studies do not prove that viewing violence *causes* aggression (Freedman, 1988; McGuire, 1986). Maybe aggressive children prefer violent programs. Maybe children of neglectful or abusive parents are both more aggressive and more often left in front of the TV. Or maybe television simply reflects, rather than affects, violent trends.

*TV's greatest effect may stem from what it displaces. Children and adults who spend 4 hours a day watching television spend 4 fewer hours in active pursuits—talking, studying, playing, reading, or socializing with friends. What would you have done with your extra time if you had never watched television, and how might you therefore be different?*

To pin down causation, experimenters have randomly assigned some viewers to view violence and others to view entertaining nonviolence. Does viewing murder and mayhem make people react more cruelly when irritated? "The consensus among most of the research community," reported the National Institute of Mental Health (1982), "is that violence on television does lead to aggressive behavior by children and teenagers who watch the programs." "There is absolutely no doubt," concluded the 1993 American Psychological Association Commission on Violence and Youth, "that higher levels of viewing violence on television are correlated with increased acceptance of aggressive attitudes and increased aggressive behavior." Medical, pediatric, and public health societies have voiced similar conclusions. The violence effect stems from a combination of factors—from *arousal* by the violent excitement, from the strengthening of violence-related *ideas*, from the erosion of one's *inhibitions*, and from *imitation* (Geen & Thomas, 1986).

*"Thirty seconds worth of glorification of a soap bar sells soap. Twenty-five minutes worth of glorification of violence sells violence."*

U.S. Senator Paul Simon
Remarks to the Communitarian Network, 1993

Television's unreal world, in which acts of aggression greatly outnumber acts of affection, can also affect our thinking about the real world. Those who avidly watch prime-time crime regard the world as more dangerous (Gerbner & others, 1993; Heath & Petraitis, 1987; Singer & Singer, 1986). Prolonged exposure to violence also desensitizes viewers; they become more indifferent to it when later viewing a brawl, whether on TV or in real life (Rule & Ferguson, 1986). Indeed, suggest Edward Donnerstein and his co-researchers (1987), an evil psychologist could hardly imagine a better way to make people indifferent to brutality than to expose them to a graded series of scenes, from fights to killings to the mutilations in slasher movies.

Stayskal/Tampa Tribune.

**Sexual Aggression and the Media** Although there are no known rape-free cultures (Rozee, 1993), a woman's risk of rape has varied across cultures and times. Over the last 30 years, America's reported rape rate has quadrupled. Recent surveys of both women and men reveal that unreported rapes, most committed by dates or acquaintances, greatly outnumber those reported. In surveys among a nationwide sample of 6200 college students and 2200 Ohio working women, Mary Koss and her colleagues (1987, 1988, 1990, 1993) found that 27.5 percent of the women reported that a man had made them "have sex by using force or threatening to harm you"—an experience that met the legal definition of rape or attempted rape (although only one-fourth of them labeled it as such). Only 1 of 4 victims of stranger rape and 1 of 30 victims of acquaintance rape reported the incident to the police. In a 1990 survey of 4000 women, 1 in 8 reported experiencing rape, most while younger than 18 (National Victim Center, 1992).

*In other surveys, about half of women report some form of unwanted sexual coercion and most report experiencing verbal sexual harassment (Craig & others, 1989; Koss & Burkhart, 1989; Sandberg & others, 1985).*

What factors might explain the modern epidemic of sexual aggression? Alcohol consumption—often linked with aggression—has not increased. Might changes in the media contribute?

Coinciding with the increase in sexual aggression has been, thanks to the home video business, easier access to *R*-rated "slasher films" and *X*-rated films. Content analyses reveal that *X*-rated films mostly depict quick, casual sex between strangers, but that scenes of rape and sexual exploitation of women by men are also common (Cowan & others, 1988; NCTV, 1987; Yang & Linz, 1990).

Rape scenes often portray the victim at first fleeing and resisting her attacker, then becoming aroused and finally driven to ecstasy. Most men are not sexually aroused (as measured by a "penile plethysmograph") while viewing rape depictions. But convicted rapists are. So are normal men if they have been drinking or if, after being aroused by exercise, a woman's insults anger them (Barbaree & Marshall, 1991). In less graphic form, the same unrealistic script—she resists, he persists, she melts—is commonplace in TV scenes and in romance novels. The woman who first thwarts the insistent man ends up passionately kissing him. In *Gone with the Wind*, Scarlett O'Hara is carried to bed screaming and wakes up singing. Most rapists accept this "rape myth"—the idea that some women invite or enjoy rape and get "swept away" while being "taken" (Brinson, 1992).

Do such films and other similar materials influence sexual aggression?

When interviewed, Canadian and U.S. sex offenders (rapists, child molesters, and serial killers) do report a greater-than-usual appetite for sexually explicit and sexually violent materials—materials typically labeled as "pornography" (Marshall, 1989; Ressler & others, 1988). For example, the Los Angeles Police Department reports that pornography was "conspicuously present" or used in 62 percent of its extrafamilial child sexual abuse cases during the 1980s (Bennett, 1991). But are the sexual offenders merely, as sex researcher John Money (1988) suspects, using pornography "as an alibi to explain to themselves and their captors what otherwise is inexplicable"?

*Pornography means different things to different people. Following Webster's dictionary, some define pornography as erotic depictions intended to excite sexual arousal. Others define it as sexual materials that exploit, degrade, or subordinate women.*

Laboratory experiments reveal that repeated viewing of X-rated films (even if nonviolent) makes one's own partner seem less attractive (page 412), makes women's friendliness seem more sexual, and makes sexual aggression seem less serious (Harris, 1994). In one such experiment, Dolf Zillmann and Jennings Bryant (1984) showed undergraduates six brief, sexually explicit films a week for 6 weeks. A control group viewed nonerotic films during the same 6-week period. Three weeks later, both groups read a newspaper report about a man convicted but not yet sentenced for raping a hitchhiker. When asked to suggest an appropriate prison term, those who had viewed sexually explicit films recommended sentences half as long as the control group's.

*In follow-up studies, Zillmann (1989) found that after massive exposure to X-rated sexual films, men and women became more accepting of extramarital sex, of women's sexual submission to men, and of a man's seducing a 12-year-old girl. As people heavily exposed to televised crime perceive the world as more dangerous, so people heavily exposed to pornography see the world as more sexual.*

In search of possible media effects on men's willingness to aggress against women, experimenters examined, first, the effect of film viewing on men's acceptance of the rape myth. Neil Malamuth and James Check (1981) compared University of Manitoba men who were shown either two nonsexual movies or two movies depicting a man sexually overpowering a woman. A week later, when surveyed by a different experimenter, those who had seen the films with mild sexual violence were more accepting of violence against women and reported themselves a little more likely to rape if assured they could get away with it. Further experiments showed that viewing slasher movies, such as *The Texas Chainsaw Massacre*, can also lead viewers to trivialize rape.

Experiments have also explored the effect of violent versus nonviolent films on men's willingness to deliver supposed electric shocks to women who earlier provoked them. (Although such experiments cannot study actual sexual violence, they can assess a man's willingness to hurt a woman.) These experiments suggest that it's not eroticism but depictions of sexual *violence* (whether in *R*-rated slasher films or *X*-rated films) that most directly affect men's acceptance and performance of aggression against women. A 1986 conference of 21 social scientists, including many of the researchers who conducted these experiments, produced a consensus that "pornography that portrays sexual aggression as pleasurable for the victim increases the acceptance of the use of coercion in sexual relations." Contrary to much popular opinion, viewing such depictions does not provide an outlet for bottled-up impulses. Rather, "in laboratory studies measuring short-term effects, exposure to violent pornography increases punitive behavior toward women" (Surgeon General, 1986).

*Do you think Hillary Rodham Clinton and others are right or wrong to worry that the media model an "impulsive sexuality" that encourages uncommitted sex (a predictor of sexual violence) and father-absent families (a predictor of juvenile violence)?*

**TV Violence, Pornography, and Society** Significant behaviors such as violence usually have many determinants, making any single explanation an oversimplification. Asking what causes violence is therefore like asking what causes cancer. Those who study, say, the effects of asbestos exposure on cancer rates may remind us that asbestos is indeed a cancer cause, but only one among many. Likewise, report Neil Malamuth and his colleagues (1991), several factors can create a predisposition to sexual violence; they include not only the media but also child abuse, hostility, dominance motives, and disinhibition by alcohol (Figure 18–9). Still, if media depictions of violence can disinhibit and desensitize, if viewing sexual violence fosters attitudes and behaviors that degrade women, and if viewing pornography can lead viewers to trivialize rape and devalue their partners, then media violence is not a minor issue.

Figure 18–9

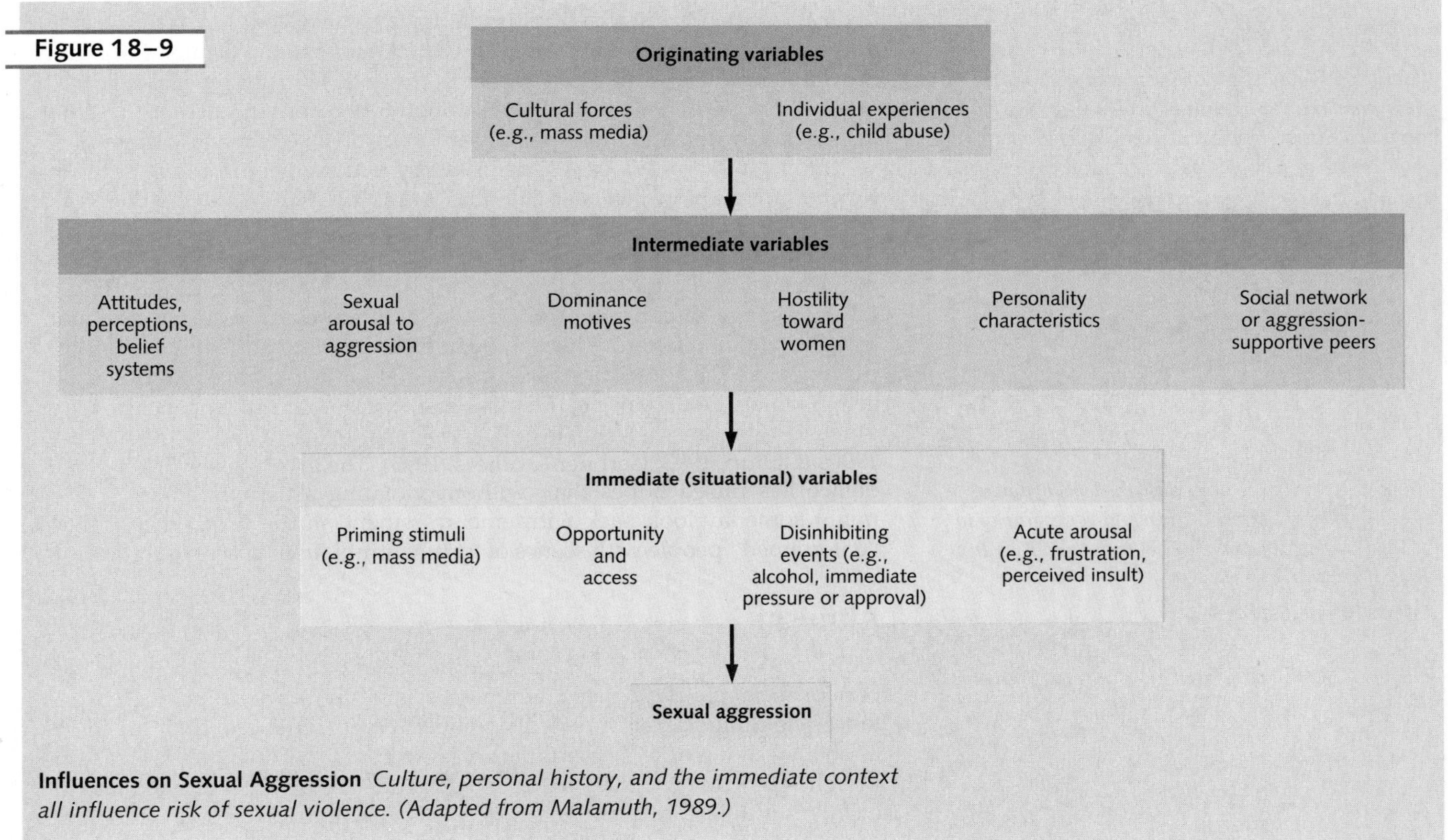


**Influences on Sexual Aggression** *Culture, personal history, and the immediate context all influence risk of sexual violence. (Adapted from Malamuth, 1989.)*

Social psychologists attribute the media's influence partly to the *social scripts* they provide. When we find ourselves in new situations, uncertain how to act, we rely on social scripts provided by our culture. After so many episodes of Ninja Turtles, followed by Clint Eastwood, Sylvester Stallone, and Arnold Schwarzenegger action films, youngsters may acquire a script—a mental tape for how to act—that gets played when they face real-life conflicts. Challenged, they may "act like a man" by intimidating or eliminating the threat. Likewise, after viewing 15 sexual innuendoes and acts per prime-time TV hour—nearly all involving short-term relationships—youths may acquire scripts they later enact in real-life relationships (Sapolsky & Tabarlet, 1991).

The American Psychological Association therefore advises parents to limit their children's TV watching and to watch programs and discuss the social scripts with their children. Some researchers advocate "media-awareness training." Doubting that the TV networks would ever "face the facts and change their programming," Leonard Eron and Rowell Huesmann (1984) taught Chicago-area children that TV portrays an unreal world, that aggression is less common and effective than TV makes it seem, and that violence is wrong. When restudied 2 years later, these children were less influenced by viewing violence than were untrained children.

To promote critical viewing skills, pornography researchers debrief, resensitize, and educate their subjects about pornography's images of women (Intons-Peterson & others, 1989; Linz & Donnerstein, 1989). When surveyed later, these subjects are *less* likely than most people to agree that "being roughed up is sexually stimulating to many women." "Our utopian and perhaps naive hope," say Edward Donnerstein, Daniel Linz, and Steven Penrod (1987, p. 196), "is that in the end the truth revealed through good science will prevail and the public will be convinced that these images not only demean those portrayed but also those who view them."

*"If we expect families to teach children not to solve their problems with guns and violence, we need cultural and media signals and public policies that demonize rather than glamorize and support violence."*

Children's Defense Fund, 1992

Might public consciousness be raised by making people aware of the information you have just been reading? In the 1940s, movies often depicted African-Americans as childlike, superstitious buffoons. Today, such images are offensive. In the 1960s and 1970s, entertainment from Beatles' music to movies such as *Easy Rider* glamorized drug use. No longer. Responding to a tidal change in cultural attitudes, the entertainment industry now portrays drugs as dangerous. Even gratuitous cigarette smoking has largely disappeared. It's something most health-conscious producers, writers, and actors choose not to model. Responding to growing public concern about violence and the media, television violence levels declined in the early 1990s (Gallup, 1993; Gerbner & others, 1993). The growing sensitivity to violence has raised hopes that, without violating artistic freedom, society might someday look back with embarrassment on the days when movies "entertained" people with scenes of torture, mutilation, and sexual coercion.

*"What we're trying to do is raise the level of awareness of violence against women and pornography to at least the level of awareness of racist and Ku Klux Klan literature."*

Gloria Steinem (1988)

## Altruism

**Altruism**—an unselfish regard for others' welfare—became a major concern of social psychologists after an especially vile act of sexual violence. A knife-wielding stalker repeatedly stabbed Kitty Genovese, then raped her as she lay dying outside her Queens, New York, apartment at 3:30 A.M. on March 13, 1964. "Oh, my God, he stabbed me!" Genovese screamed into the early-morning stillness. "Please help me!" Windows opened and lights went on as 38 of her neighbors heard her screams. Her attacker fled and then returned to stab her eight more times and rape her again. Not until he departed for good did anyone so much as call the police, at 3:50 A.M.

*"Probably no single incident has caused social psychologists to pay as much attention to an aspect of social behavior as Kitty Genovese's murder."*

R. Lance Shotland (1984)

### Bystander Intervention

Reflecting on the Genovese murder and other such tragedies, most commentators lamented the bystanders' "apathy" and "indifference." Rather than blaming them, social psychologists John Darley and Bibb Latané (1968b) attributed onlooker inaction to an important situational factor—the presence of others. Given the right circumstances, they suspected, most of us might behave similarly.

After staging emergencies under various conditions, Darley and Latané assembled their findings into a decision scheme: We will help only if the situation enables us first to *notice* the incident, then to *interpret* it as an emergency, and finally to *assume responsibility* for helping (Figure 18–10).

At each step, other bystanders turn people away from the path that leads to helping. In the laboratory and on the street, people in groups of strangers are more likely than solitary individuals to keep their eyes on what they are doing or where they are going. If they notice an unusual situ-

Figure 18–10

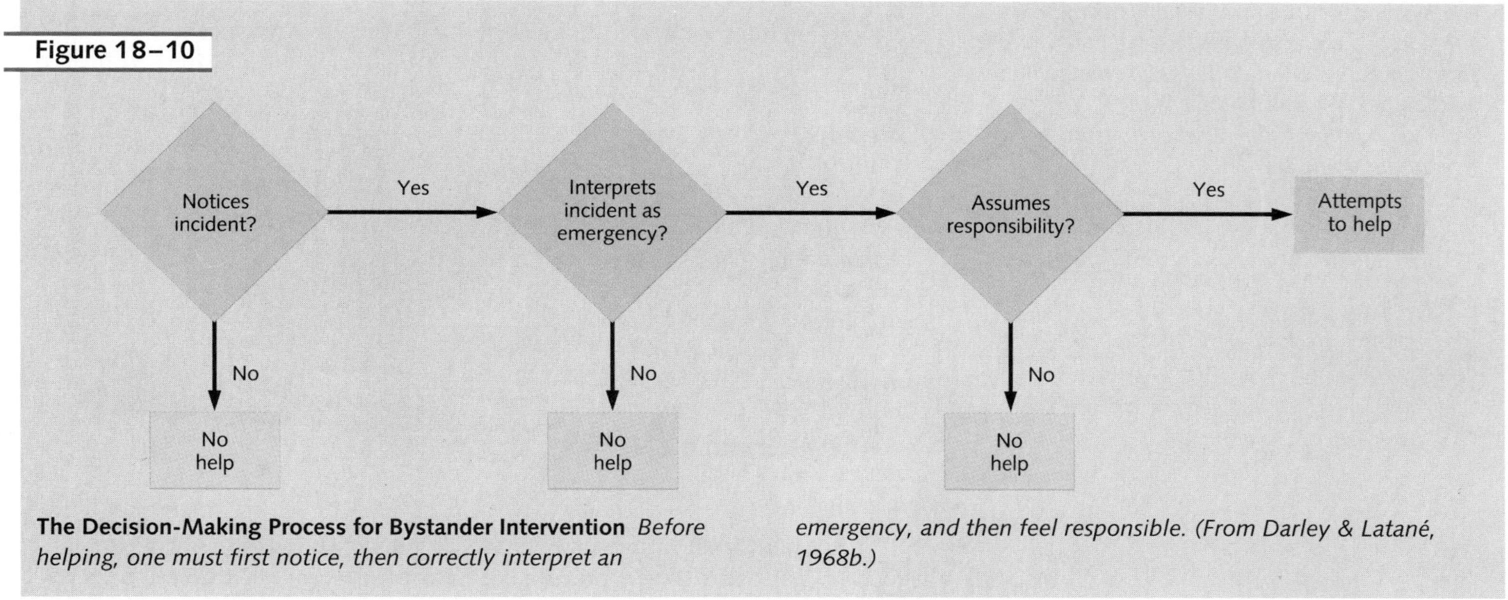


**The Decision-Making Process for Bystander Intervention** *Before helping, one must first notice, then correctly interpret an emergency, and then feel responsible. (From Darley & Latané, 1968b.)*

ation, they may infer from the blasé reactions of the other passersby that the situation is not an emergency. "The person lying on the sidewalk must be drunk," they think, and move on.

But sometimes, as with the Genovese murder, the emergency is unambiguous and people still fail to help. The witnesses looking out through their windows noticed the incident, correctly interpreted the emergency, yet failed to assume responsibility. To find out why, Darley and Latané (1968a) simulated a physical emergency in their laboratory. University students participated in a discussion over an intercom. Each student was in a separate cubicle, and only the person whose microphone was switched on could be heard. One of the students was an accomplice of the experimenters. When his turn came, he called for help and made sounds as though he were having an epileptic seizure.

How did the other students react? As Figure 18–11 shows, those who believed they were the only one who could hear the victim—and therefore thought they bore total responsibility for helping—usually went to his aid. Those who thought others could also hear were more likely to react as did Kitty Genovese's neighbors. When more people shared responsibility for helping, any single listener was less likely to help.

In hundreds of additional experiments, psychologists have studied the factors that influence bystanders' willingness to relay an emergency phone call, aid a stranded motorist, donate blood, pick up dropped books, contribute money, and give time. For example, Latané, James Dabbs (1975), and 145 collaborators took 1497 elevator rides in three cities and "accidentally" dropped coins or pencils in front of 4813 fellow passengers. The women coin-droppers were more likely to receive help than were the men—a gender difference often reported by other researchers (Eagly & Crowley, 1986). But the major finding was the **bystander effect**—any particular bystander was less likely to give aid with other bystanders present. When one other person was on the elevator, those who dropped the coins were helped 40 percent of the time. When there were six passengers, help came less than 20 percent of the time.

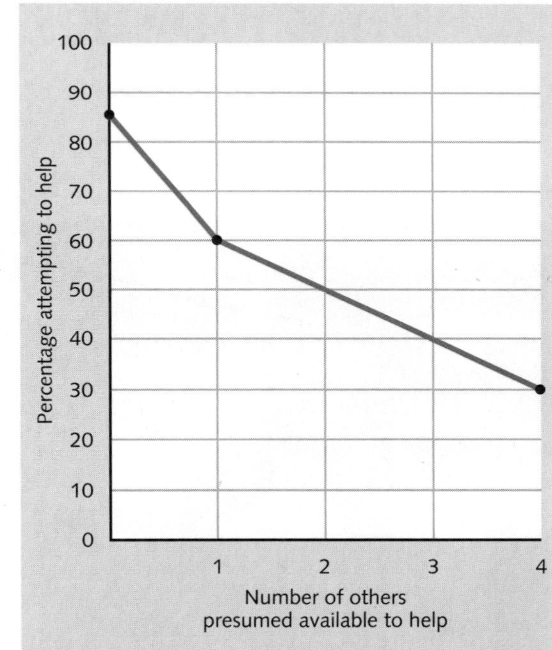


Figure 18–11

**Responses to a Simulated Physical Emergency** *When people thought they alone heard an epileptic seizure victim calling for help, they usually helped. But when they thought four others were hearing it too, fewer than a third responded. (From Darley & Latané, 1968a.)*

**The Bystander's Dilemma** *When passing someone slumped on a city sidewalk, we may wonder, "Is this person sick? If I offer help, what will the reaction be? What can I do anyway?" Yet sometimes we do offer help. What circumstances prompt our doing so?*

From their observations of behavior in tens of thousands of such "emergencies," altruism researchers have discerned some additional patterns. The odds of our helping someone are best when:

- we have just observed someone else being helpful.
- we are not in a hurry.
- the victim appears to need and deserve help.
- the victim is in some way similar to us.
- we are in a small town or rural area.
- we are feeling guilty.
- we are focused on others and not preoccupied.
- we are in a good mood.

This last result, that happy people are helpful people, is one of the most consistent findings in all psychology. No matter how people are cheered—whether by being made to feel successful and intelligent, by thinking happy thoughts, by finding money, or even by receiving a posthypnotic suggestion—they become more generous and more eager to help (Carlson & others, 1988).

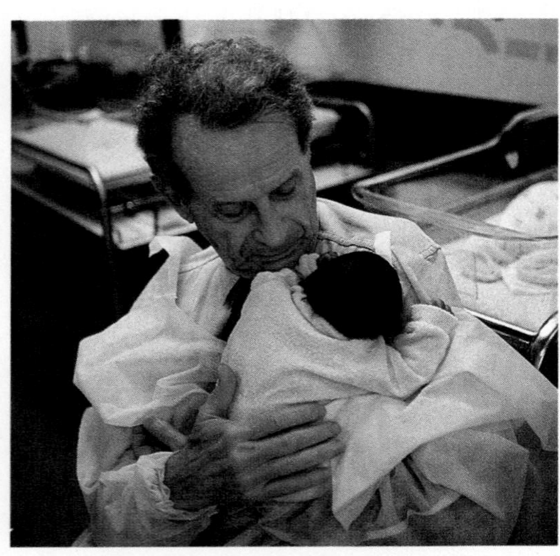

**Bonding With a Boarder Baby** *Volunteers are motivated to help if the rewards, whether psychological or social, are greater than the costs. This man finds satisfaction in comforting boarder babies, infants born to mothers who cannot care for them.*

### The Psychology of Helping

Why do we help? One widely held view is that self-interest underlies all human interactions: Our constant goal is to maximize rewards and minimize costs. Accountants call it cost–benefit analysis. Philosophers call it utilitarianism. Social psychologists call it **social exchange theory**. If you are pondering whether to donate blood, you may weigh the costs of doing so (time, discomfort, and anxiety) against the benefits (reduced guilt, social approval, good feelings). If the anticipated rewards of helping exceed the anticipated costs, you help.

Social exchange theory helps explain why we help those whose approval we seek or who can reciprocate favors in the future. But perhaps you are wondering, "Doesn't social exchange theory suggest that helping is not truly altruistic but is rather a disguised form of selfishness?" If we helped merely to feel good, the answer might be yes. But to gain pleasure from helping others is surely more a virtue than a vice. Moreover, from babyhood onward many people exhibit a natural **empathy** for others—

they feel distress when they see someone in distress and relief when suffering is alleviated (Batson, 1987).

Social expectations also influence helping. They prescribe how we ought to behave, often to our mutual benefit. Through socialization, we learn the *reciprocity norm*, the expectation that we should return help, not harm, to those who have helped us. In our relations with others of similar status, the reciprocity norm compels us to give (in favors, gifts, or social invitations) about as much as we receive. With young children and others who cannot give as much as they receive, we also learn a *social responsibility norm*—that we should help those who need our help, even if the costs outweigh the benefits.

Cultures vary in the strength of their social responsibility norms. Faced with a need that is not life-threatening, people in India feel a moral obligation to offer help, and they feel it more keenly than do Americans (Miller & others, 1990). In repeated Gallup surveys, people who each week attend church or synagogue services report volunteering more than twice as many hours in helping the poor and infirm than do those who rarely or never attend (Hodgkinson & Weitzman, 1992). They also give away three times as much money.

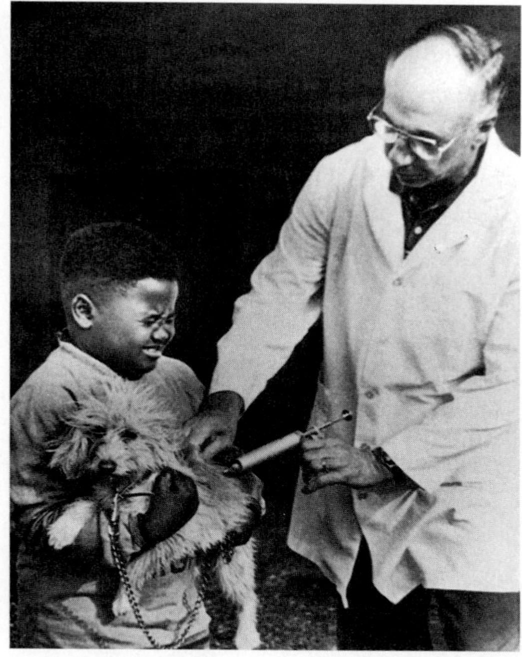

**Empathy: Feeling What Another Feels** *When we see someone in trouble, we sometimes feel their pain. This can motivate helping designed to relieve our own distress and the victim's suffering.*

**The Evolutionary Psychology of Helping** Culture matters, but don't all humans share inherent altruistic tendencies? **Evolutionary psychology**—the study of how natural selection influences behavior—suggests that our genes predispose psychological mechanisms that enhance their chance of surviving and spreading. When infants develop a fear of strangers about the time of mobility, their genes are promoting their own survival.

Although heroes who sacrifice their lives for another leave fewer descendants, evolutionary psychologists contend that some forms of altruism help perpetuate our genes. One example is being good to those who can later reciprocate our helpfulness—benefiting us both. A more obvious example is devotion to our children—the carriers of our genes. Natural selection favors parents who care deeply about their children's survival and welfare. People usually feel empathy toward other relatives, too, in proportion to their genetic closeness. In experiments, people also give more empathy and help to a stranger who looks, acts, and thinks like themselves—someone whose genetic similarities they detect, an evolutionary psychologist would say (Rushton, 1989).

*"A hen is only an egg's way of making another egg."*
Novelist Samuel Butler, 1835–1902

Nevertheless, for some heroic people, a sense of *human* kinship entails the risk of self-sacrifice. The Holocaust memorial in Jerusalem honors 8000 "Righteous Gentiles"—those whose identities are known among the many more Europeans who gave refuge to Jews during World War II. These people knew that if the Nazis learned of their subterfuge, they might suffer a common fate with their guests, as many did. For decades afterward, social scientists interviewed rescuers, searching for the patterns of personality and belief that predict why these heroes acted as so few did.

Where did these people gain the compassion to care and the courage to defy power and authority? Often, their initial commitment was merely to hide a family in the cellar for a short time. With their actions feeding their attitudes, they gradually became more committed to helping. Those who made the commitment to help often had caring parental models, close-knit families, and friendships with Jews who confronted them with the need for help (London, 1970; Oliner & Oliner, 1988). They also had religious or humanitarian convictions that led them to include people outside their group within their circle of moral concern (Staub, 1992). Long after the war, rescuers more than bystanders were caring in new ways—feeding the sick

*"We consider humankind our family."*
Parliament of the World's Religions
*Towards a Global Ethic*, 1993

and aged, supporting groups and causes, leading recreational activities, offering counsel. Their lives remind us that some attributes of character shine through differing situations.

## Attraction

Pause a moment and think about your relationships with two people—a close friend, and someone who has stirred in you feelings of romantic love. What factors lead to friendship and romance? What factors help us sustain these relationships?

We endlessly wonder how we can win others' affection and what makes our own affections flourish or fade. Do birds of a feather flock together, or do opposites attract? Does familiarity breed contempt or liking? Does absence make the heart grow fonder, or is out of sight out of mind? Social psychology suggests some answers.

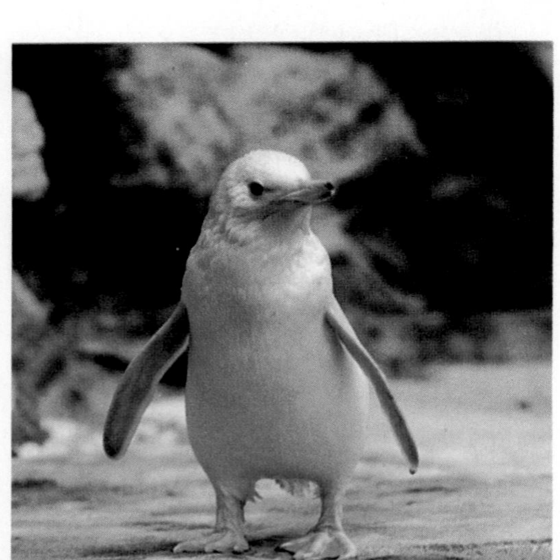

**Familiarity Breeds Acceptance** *When this rare white penguin was born in the Sydney, Australia, zoo, his tuxedoed peers ostracized him. To gain his acceptance, zookeepers thought they would need to dye him black. But after 3 weeks of contact, the other penguins came to accept him.*

### The Psychology of Attraction

What is the psychological chemistry that binds two people together in that special sort of friendship that helps one cope with all other relationships? Consider three ingredients of our liking for one another.

**Proximity** Before friendships become close, they must begin. Proximity—geographic nearness—is perhaps the most powerful predictor of friendship. Proximity provides opportunities for aggression, but much more often it instigates liking. Study after study reveals that people are most likely to like, and even to marry, those who live in the same neighborhood, who sit nearby in class, who work in the same office, who share the same parking lot. Look around.

Why is proximity so conducive to liking? Obviously, part of the answer is the greater availability of those we often meet. But there is more to it than that. For one thing, repeated exposure to novel stimuli—be they nonsense syllables, musical selections, geometric figures, Chinese characters, human faces, or the letters of our own name—increases our liking for them (Moreland & Zajonc, 1982; Nuttin, 1987). This phenomenon, which is now exploited by advertisers, we call the **mere exposure effect**. Within certain limits (Bornstein, 1989), familiarity breeds fondness. Richard Moreland and Scott Beach (1992) demonstrated this by having four equally attractive women silently attend a 200-student class for 0, 5, 10, or 15 class sessions.

**The Mere Exposure Effect** *The mere exposure effect applies even to ourselves. Because the human face is not perfectly symmetrical, the face we see in the mirror is not the same as the one our friends see. Most of us prefer the familiar mirror image, while our friends like the reverse (Mita & others, 1977). The Prime Minister Paul Keating whom Australians know is shown at left. The person Keating sees in the mirror each morning is shown at right, and that's the photo he would probably prefer.*

Shown slides of each woman at the end of the class, the students rated the ones they'd seen the most as most attractive. The phenomenon will come as no surprise to the young Taiwanese man who wrote over 700 letters to his girlfriend, urging her to get married. She did—to the mail carrier (Steinberg, 1993).

**Physical Attractiveness** Once proximity affords you contact, what most affects your first impressions: the person's sincerity? intelligence? personality? Hundreds of experiments reveal that it is likely something more superficial: appearance.

For people taught that "beauty is only skin deep" and that "appearances can be deceiving," the power of physical attractiveness is unnerving. In one early study, Elaine Hatfield and her co-workers (Walster & others, 1966) randomly matched new University of Minnesota students for a "Welcome Week" dance. Before the dance, all took a battery of personality and aptitude tests. On the night of the blind date, the couples danced and talked for more than 2 hours and then took a brief intermission to rate their dates. What determined whether they liked each other? So far as the researchers could determine, only one thing mattered: physical attractiveness (which had been rated by the researchers beforehand). Both the men and the women liked good-looking dates best. Although women are more likely than men to *say* that another's looks don't affect them, a man's looks do affect women's behavior (Feingold, 1990; Sprecher, 1989; Woll, 1986).

*"Personal beauty is a greater recommendation than any letter of introduction."*

Aristotle
*Apothegems*, 330 B.C.

*"Love comes in at the eye."*

William Butler Yeats
"A Drinking Song," 1909

People's physical attractiveness has wide-ranging effects. It predicts their dating frequency, their feelings of popularity, and others' initial impressions of their personalities. We perceive attractive people, even children and those of our own sex, to be happier, more sensitive, more successful, and more socially skilled, though not more honest or compassionate (Eagly & others, 1991; Feingold, 1992; Hatfield & Sprecher, 1986). Attractive and well-dressed people are more likely to make a favorable impression on potential employers (Cash & Janda, 1984; Solomon, 1987). To judge from their gazing times, even babies prefer attractive over unattractive faces (Langlois & others, 1987).

If looks matter so much, who dates and marries those less attractive? Although people might prefer someone superattractive, they tend not to approach those who are "out of their league." Thus, we often match up with people who are about as attractive as we are (Murstein, 1986). When partners are noticeably unequal in attractiveness, the less physically attractive person often has compensating assets, such as greater wealth, status, or social competence. This helps explain why beautiful young women sometimes marry older men whose social or financial status is higher than their own (Elder, 1969).

That looks are important may seem unfair and unenlightened. Two thousand years ago the Roman statesman Cicero felt the same way: "The final good and the supreme duty of the wise person is to resist appearance." Cicero might be reassured by two other findings about attractiveness.

First, people's attractiveness is surprisingly unrelated to their self-esteem (Major & others, 1984). One reason may be that, except after comparing themselves with superattractive people, few people view themselves as unattractive (Thornton & Moore, 1993). (Thanks, perhaps, to the mere exposure effect, most of us become accustomed to our faces.) Another reason is that strikingly attractive people are sometimes suspicious that praise may be simply a reaction to their looks. When less attractive people are praised for their work, they are more likely to accept it as sincere (Berscheid, 1981).

**Pretty Pair** *Couples tend to be matched in attractiveness. If unmatched, the less attractive member often has compensating assets.*

*"The thin, narrow-shouldered ectomorph who was yesterday's spinster librarian is today's high fashion model; the plump and buxom endomorph who was a Victorian romantic ideal today is eating cottage cheese and grapefruit, and weighing in every Tuesday at Weight Watchers."*

Phyllis Bronstein-Burrows (1981)

Cicero might also find comfort in knowing that attractiveness judgments are relative. They depend first on the accepted standards of beauty in one's place and time. Hoping to look attractive, people in different cultures have pierced their noses, lengthened their necks, bound their feet, dyed their skin and hair, eaten to achieve a full figure or liposuctioned fat to achieve a slim one, strapped on leather garments to prevent their breasts from growing or stuffed their breasts with silicone to make them bigger. (The standards by which judges crown "Miss Universe" hardly even apply to the whole planet.) In North America, the ultra-thin ideal of the Roaring Twenties gave way to the soft, voluptuous Marilyn Monroe ideal of the 1950s, to be replaced by the lean, athletic ideal of the 1990s.

**In the Eye of the Beholder** *Conceptions of attractiveness vary by culture and across time. What may be deemed attractive in one culture may seem strange or unattractive in another. And the current concept of beauty in Kenya, Morocco, and the United States may well change in the future.*

Some aspects of attractiveness, however, cross place and time. It comes as no surprise to evolutionary psychologists that men in 37 cultures, from Australia to Zambia, judge women as more attractive if they have a youthful appearance (Buss, 1989; Cunningham, 1986). Evolutionary psychologists say that men drawn to healthy, fertile-appearing women have stood a better chance of sending their genes into the future. From yesterday's Stone Age figurines to today's *Playboy* centerfolds and Miss America winners—and regardless of cultural variations in ideal weight—men feel most attracted to women whose waists are roughly a third narrower than their hips—a sign of youthful fertility (Singh, 1993). To women, men seem more attractive if they appear mature and dominant. This connotes, say the evolutionary psychologists, a capacity to support and protect (Buss, 1994).

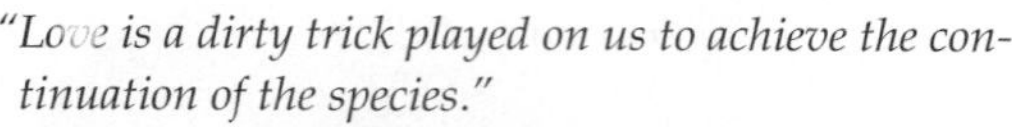

*"Love is a dirty trick played on us to achieve the continuation of the species."*

Novelist W. Somerset Maugham, 1874–1965

People also seem to prefer physical features—noses, legs, physiques—that are neither unusually large or small. In one clever demonstration of this, Judith Langlois and Lori Roggman (1990) digitized the faces of up to 32 college students and used a computer to average them. Students judged the averaged, composite faces as more attractive than 96 percent of the individual faces. To be truly average is to be beautiful.

Cultural differences and similarities aside, attractiveness also depends on our feelings about the person. In a Rodgers and Hammerstein musical, Prince Charming asks Cinderella, "Do I love you because you're beautiful, or are you beautiful because I love you?" Chances are it is both. As we discover someone's similarities to us, see them again and again, and come to like them, their physical imperfections grow less noticeable and their attractiveness grows more apparent (Beaman & Klentz, 1983; Gross & Crofton, 1977). As Shakespeare put it in *A Midsummer Night's Dream*, "Love looks not with the eyes, but with the mind." Until you get to know him, E.T. is as ugly as Darth Vader.

*"Love has ever in view the absolute loveliness of that which it beholds."*

George MacDonald
*Unspoken Sermons*, 1867

**Similarity** Let's say that proximity has brought you into contact with someone and that your appearance has made a favorable first impression. What now influences whether acquaintances develop into friends? For example, as you get to know someone better, is the chemistry better if you are opposites or if you are alike?

It makes a good story—extremely different types living in harmonious union: Rat, Mole, and Badger in *The Wind in the Willows*, Frog and Toad in Arnold Lobel's books. The stories delight us by expressing what we seldom experience, for we tend *not* to like dissimilar people (Rosenbaum, 1986). In real life, opposites retract. Birds that flock together usually *are* of a feather. Friends and couples are far more likely to share common attitudes, beliefs, and interests (and, for that matter, age, religion, race, education, intelligence, smoking behavior, and economic status) than are randomly paired people. Moreover, the greater their likeness, the more their liking will endure (Byrne, 1971). Journalist Walter Lippmann was right to suppose that love is best sustained "when the lovers love many things together, and not merely each other." Similarity breeds content.

*"Pardon me, but I can't help noticing that we share similar tastes in tropical-fruit-flavored chewing gum."*

Drawing by Maslin; © 1992 The New Yorker Magazine, Inc.

Proximity, attractiveness, and similarity are not the only determinants of attraction. We also like those who like us, especially when our self-image is low. When we believe someone likes us, we respond to them more warmly, which leads them to like us even more (Curtis & Miller, 1986). To be liked is powerfully rewarding.

Indeed, a simple reward theory of attraction—that we will like those whose behavior is rewarding to us and that we will continue relationships that offer more rewards than costs—can explain all the findings we have considered so far. When a person lives or works in close proximity with someone else, it costs less time and effort to develop the friendship and enjoy its benefits. Attractive people are aesthetically pleasing, and associating with them can be socially rewarding. Those with similar views reward us by validating our own.

### Romantic Love

Occasionally, people progress quickly from initial impressions to friendship to the more intense, complex, and mysterious state of romantic love. Elaine Hatfield (1988) distinguishes two types of love: temporary passionate love and a more enduring companionate love.

**Passionate Love** Noting that arousal is a key ingredient of **passionate love**, Hatfield suggests that the two-factor theory of emotion (page 455) can help us understand this intense positive absorption in another. The theory assumes that emotions have two ingredients—physical arousal plus cognitive appraisal—and that arousal from any source can enhance one emotion or another, depending on how we interpret and label the arousal.

In tests of this theory, college men have been aroused by fright, by running in place, by viewing erotic materials, or by listening to humorous or repulsive monologues. They are then introduced to an attractive woman and asked to rate her (or their girlfriend). Unlike unaroused men, those who are stirred up attribute some of their arousal to the woman or girlfriend and feel more attracted to her (Carducci & others, 1978; Dermer & Pyszczynski, 1978; White & Kight, 1984).

**HI & LOIS**

Reprinted with special permission of King Features Syndicate.

Outside the laboratory, Donald Dutton and Arthur Aron (1974, 1989) went to two bridges across British Columbia's rocky Capilano River. One was a swaying footbridge 230 feet above the rocks; the other was a low, solid bridge. An attractive young female accomplice intercepted men coming off each bridge, sought their help in filling out a short questionnaire, and then offered her phone number in case they wanted to hear more about her project. Far more of those who had just crossed the high bridge—which left their hearts pounding—accepted the number and later called the woman. To be revved up and to associate some of that arousal with a desirable person is to feel the pull of passion. As lovers who take a thrilling roller coaster ride together know, adrenaline makes the heart grow fonder.

**Companionate Love** Inevitably, the passion of romantic love subsides. The intense absorption in the other, the thrill of the romance, the giddy "floating on a cloud" feeling fades. *Just Married* becomes just married, the magic lost. Recognizing the short duration of passionate love, some societies have deemed such feelings an irrational reason for marrying. Better, such cultures say, to choose (or have someone choose for you) a partner with compatible backgrounds and interests.

*"When two people are under the influence of the most violent, most insane, most delusive, and most transient of passions, they are required to swear that they will remain in that excited, abnormal, and exhausting condition continuously until death do them part."*

George Bernard Shaw
*Man and Superman*, 1903

So, are the French correct in saying that "love makes the time pass and time makes love pass"? Or can friendship and commitment keep a relationship going after the passion cools? Hatfield notes that if love matures it becomes a steadier **companionate love**—a deep, affectionate attachment. There may be adaptive wisdom to this change from passion to affection. Passionate love often produces children, whose survival is aided by the parents' waning obsession with one another. Social psychologist Ellen Berscheid and her colleagues (1984) note that the failure to appreciate passionate love's limited half-life can doom a relationship: "If the inevitable odds against eternal passionate love in a relationship were better understood, more people might choose to be satisfied with the quieter feelings of satisfaction and contentment."

**Passionate Love to Companionate Love** *The quality of love changes as a relationship matures from passionate absorption to affectionate attachment.*

One key to a gratifying and enduring relationship is **equity**: Both partners receive in proportion to what they give. When equity exists—when both partners freely give and receive, when they share decision making—their chances for sustained and satisfying companionate love are good (Gray-Little & Burks, 1983; Van Yperen & Buunk, 1990). Mutually sharing self and possessions, giving and getting emotional support, promoting and caring about one another's welfare, are at the core of every type of loving relationship (Sternberg & Grajek, 1984). It's true for lovers, for parent and child, and for intimate friends.

*"When a match has equal partners then I fear not."*
Aeschylus
*Prometheus Bound*, 478 B.C.

Another vital ingredient of loving relationships is intimacy. A strong friendship or marriage permits **self-disclosure**, a revealing of intimate details about ourselves—our likes and dislikes, our dreams and worries, our proud and shameful moments. "When I am with my friend," noted the Roman statesman Seneca, "me thinks I am alone, and as much at liberty to speak anything as to think it." Self-disclosure grows as a relationship deepens. As one person reveals a little, the other reciprocates, the first person reveals more, and on and on, as friends or lovers move to deeper intimacy. Given self-disclosing intimacy plus mutually supportive equality, the odds favor enduring companionate love.

## Summing Up

**Aggression** Aggressive behavior, like all behavior, is a product of nature and nurture. Although psychologists dismiss the idea that aggression is instinctual, aggressiveness *is* genetically influenced. Moreover, certain areas of the brain, when stimulated, activate or inhibit aggression, and these neural areas are biochemically influenced.

A variety of psychological factors also influence aggression. Aversive events heighten people's hostility. Such stimuli are especially likely to trigger aggression in those rewarded for their own aggression or those who have learned aggression from role models or observed violent media portrayals of aggressive models. Such factors desensitize people to cruelty and prime them to behave aggressively when provoked.

**Altruism** In response to incidents of bystander nonintervention in emergencies, social psychologists undertook experiments that revealed a bystander effect: Any given bystander is less likely to help if others are present. The bystander effect is most likely to occur when the presence of others inhibits one's (1) noticing the event, (2) interpreting it as an emergency, or (3) assuming responsibility for helping. Many factors, including mood, also influence willingness to help someone in distress.

Both psychological and biological explanations have been offered for why we help others. Social exchange theory proposes that our social behaviors—even our helpful acts—maximize our benefits (which may include our own good feelings) and minimize our costs. Our desire to help is also affected by social norms, which prescribe reciprocating the help we receive and being socially responsible toward those in need. Evolutionary psychologists believe that a genetic predisposition to preserve our genes, through devotion to those with whom we share them, underlies altruism.

**Attraction** Three factors are known to influence our liking for one another. Proximity—geographical nearness—is conducive to attraction, partly because mere exposure to novel stimuli enhances liking. Physical attractiveness influences social opportunities and the way one is perceived. As acquaintanceship moves toward friendship, similarity of attitudes and interests greatly increases liking.

We can view passionate love as an aroused state that we cognitively label as love. The strong affection of companionate love, which often emerges as a relationship matures, is enhanced by an equitable relationship and by intimate self-disclosure.

## Terms and Concepts to Remember

**social psychology** The scientific study of how we think about, influence, and relate to one another.

### Social Thinking

**attribution theory** The theory that we tend to give a causal explanation for someone's behavior, often by crediting either the situation or the person's disposition.

**fundamental attribution error** The tendency for observers, when analyzing another's behavior, to underestimate the impact of the situation and to overestimate the impact of personal disposition.

**attitude** A belief and feeling that predisposes one to respond in a particular way to objects, people, and events.

**foot-in-the-door phenomenon** The tendency for people who have first agreed to a small request to comply later with a larger request.

**role** A set of expectations about a social position, defining how those in the position ought to behave.

**cognitive dissonance theory** The theory that we act to reduce the discomfort (dissonance) we feel when two of our thoughts (cognitions) are inconsistent—as when we respond to our having acted contrary to our attitudes by changing our attitude.

### Social Influence

**conformity** Adjusting one's behavior or thinking to coincide with a group standard.

**normative social influence** Influence resulting from a person's desire to gain approval or avoid disapproval.

**norms** Understood rules for accepted and expected behavior. Norms prescribe "proper" behavior.

**informational social influence** Influence resulting from one's willingness to accept others' opinions about reality.

**co-actors** People who are simultaneously at work on the same noncompetitive task.

**social facilitation** Improved performance of tasks in the presence of others; occurs with simple or well-learned tasks but not with tasks that are difficult or not yet mastered.

**social loafing** The tendency for people in a group to exert less effort when pooling their efforts toward attaining a common goal than when individually accountable.

**deindividuation** The loss of self-awareness and self-restraint occurring in group situations that foster arousal and anonymity.

**group polarization** The enhancement of a group's prevailing attitudes through discussion.

**groupthink** The mode of thinking that occurs when the desire for harmony in a decision-making group overrides a realistic appraisal of alternatives.

### Social Relations

**aggression** Any physical or verbal behavior intended to hurt or destroy.

**frustration-aggression principle** The principle that frustration—the blocking of an attempt to achieve some goal—creates anger, which can generate aggression.

**altruism** Unselfish regard for the welfare of others.

**bystander effect** The tendency for any given bystander to be less likely to give aid if other bystanders are present.

**social exchange theory** The theory that our social behavior is an exchange process, the aim of which is to maximize benefits and minimize costs.

**empathy** The ability to understand and feel what another feels, to put oneself in someone else's shoes.

**evolutionary psychology** The study of the evolution of behavior using the principles of natural selection; it assumes that natural selection favors genetically influenced behaviors that contribute to the preservation and spread of one's genes.

**mere exposure effect** The phenomenon that repeated exposure to novel stimuli increases liking of them.

**passionate love** An aroused state of intense positive absorption in another, usually present at the beginning of a love relationship.

**companionate love** The deep affectionate attachment we feel for those with whom our lives are intertwined.

**equity** A condition in which people receive from a relationship in proportion to what they give to it.

**self-disclosure** Revealing intimate aspects of oneself to others.

## Critical Thinking Exercise

Now that you have read and reviewed Chapter 18, take your learning a step further by testing your critical thinking skills on the following pattern recognition exercise.

In their first year of college Mary and Kathy quickly became friends, after discovering they had a great deal in common. They talked a lot about their feelings, including a shared dislike of prejudice. In their sophomore year, they pledged different sororities, with Kathy joining a sorority said to be both elitist and somewhat prejudiced against minority groups, including Mary's. Although this had concerned Kathy, she didn't notice any problem at first. As time passed, however, the comments of her sorority sisters became increasingly tinged with bigotry. Kathy gradually found herself sharing their views and even openly making a few contemptuous remarks about minority groups. Although she sometimes felt troubled by her behavior, Kathy had worked so hard to become a member of the sorority that she decided she must really have felt this way about minority groups all along.

Kathy and Mary did not see each other for several months, until their sororities met at an intramural softball game. Running to greet her friend, Mary was hurt by Kathy's cool, almost haughty manner toward her and other minority members of Mary's sorority. In the midst of her sorority sisters, Kathy seemed a different person altogether. Later that evening, Mary confided in her journal that she must have initially misjudged Kathy as sharing her beliefs and that Kathy had finally displayed her true personality as a very prejudiced person.

1. What social psychological principles might help explain why Mary and Kathy became friends?
2. Illustrate how the following social psychological principles might explain why Mary and Kathy grew apart: norms and roles, normative social influence, mere exposure effect, cognitive dissonance.

Check your progress on becoming a critical thinker by comparing your answers to the sample answers found in Appendix B.

## For Further Reading

**Cialdini, R. B.** (1993). *Influence: Science and practice* (3rd ed.). New York: Harper Collins.

*A delightful, captivating introduction to six "weapons of influence." Robert Cialdini brings to life the lessons from social-psychological research on persuasion, with riveting everyday examples of influence—from Tupperware parties to cult indoctrination programs.*

**Hunt, M.** (1993). *The compassionate beast: What science is discovering about the humane side of humankind*. New York: William Morrow.

*An intimate look at the new altruism researchers and their discoveries about why and when people help.*

**Janis, I. L.** (1982). *Groupthink: Psychological studies of policy decisions and fiascos*. Boston: Houghton Mifflin.

*A provocative, readable analysis of the group decision making that led to several historical fiascos, from the failure to anticipate the Pearl Harbor attack to the Watergate cover-up. Janis beautifully interweaves basic concepts in social psychology with recent American history, explains how groupthink occurs, and suggests ways to avoid it.*

**Milgram, S.** (1974). *Obedience to authority*. New York: Harper & Row.

*The full description of Milgram's controversial research on obedience, complete with reflections on the dilemmas of obedience and the ethics of such research.*

**Staub, E.** (1989). *The roots of evil: The psychological and cultural sources of genocide*. New York: Cambridge University Press.

*How can human beings kill, brutalize, and torture other human beings? By analyzing genocide during the Holocaust and in countries around the world, Staub exposes the roots and evolution of mass killing and cruelty.*

# CHAPTER 19



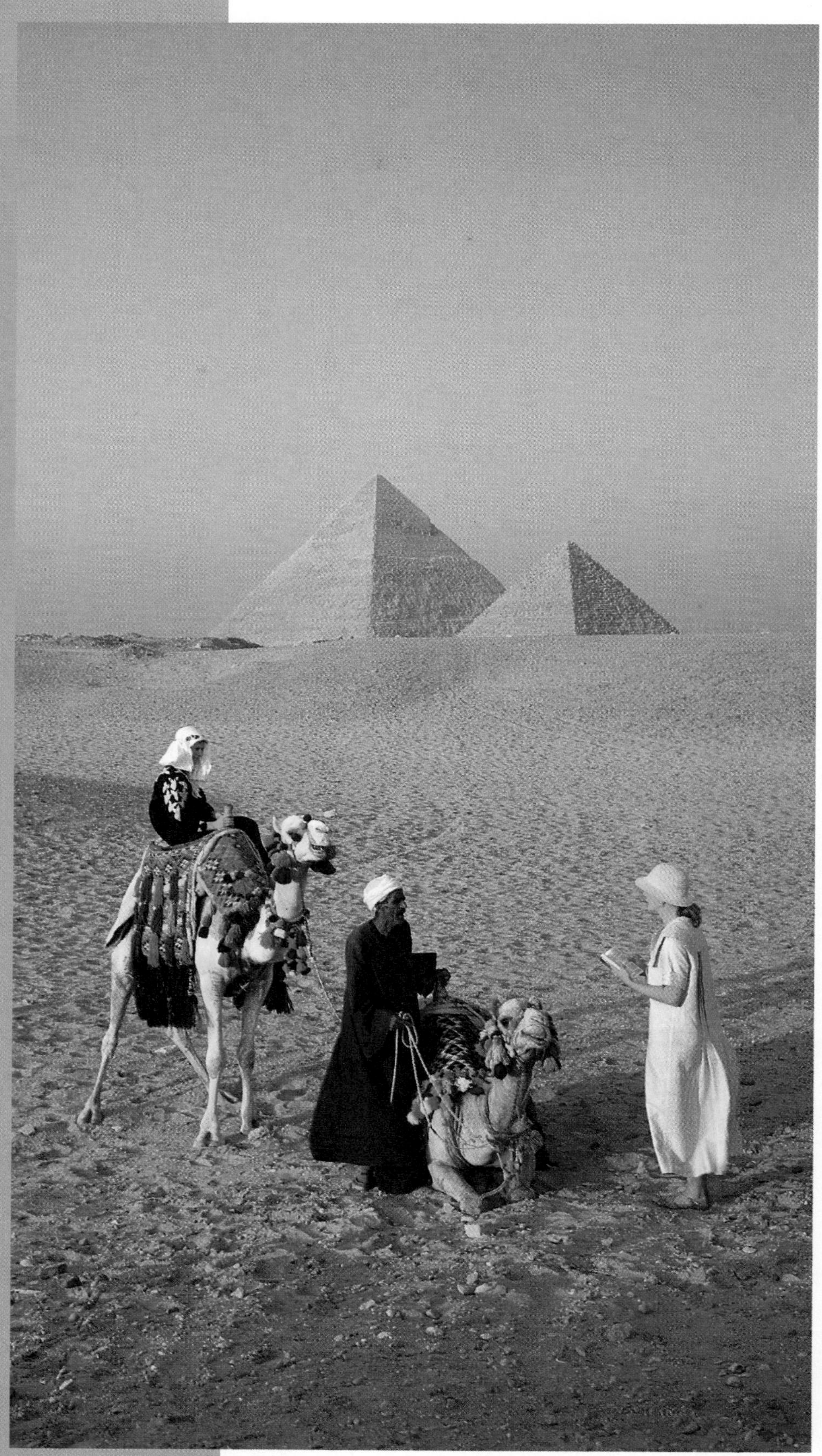

# Diversity and Community

*In previous chapters we have explored our individual diversity, and we have repeatedly considered our social diversity. We now cap our journey through psychology by focusing more closely on one of the great issues of our time: As people of varying cultures, ethnicities, and genders, how are we different and how are we alike? In a world torn asunder by differences, how can we value our social identity and our diversity while affirming our human kinship? In short, how can we realize the ideal of community incorporating diversity?*

*"Good news, Mr. Vanderfirth. We've traced your lineage back to a woman who lived in East Africa two hundred thousand years ago."*

Drawing by Mankoff; © 1991 The New Yorker Magazine, Inc.

Some 100,000 to 200,000 years ago, most anthropologists believe, we humans were all Africans. Feeling an urge to "be fruitful and multiply, and fill the earth," many of our ancestors moved out of Africa, displacing their humanlike cousins elsewhere, such as the Neanderthals in Europe (Simons, 1989; Stringer, 1990). In adapting to their new environments, our forebears developed differences that, measured on anthropological scales, are relatively recent and superficial. Those who went far north of the equator, for example, evolved lighter skins capable of synthesizing vitamin D in less direct sunlight. Still, historically, we all are Africans.

Whatever our differences, we are the leaves of one tree. We in the human family share not only a common biological heritage—cut us and we bleed—but also common behavioral tendencies. Our shared brain architecture predisposes us to sense the world, develop language, and feel hunger through identical mechanisms. Coming from opposite sides of the globe, we know how to read one another's smiles and frowns. Whether our last name is Wong, Nkomo, Gonzales, or Smith, we fear strangers beginning at about 8 months of age and as adults prefer the company of individuals whose attitudes and attributes are similar to our own. Regardless of our culture or gender, we regard female features that signify youth and health—and reproductive potential—as attractive. Whether we live in the Arctic or the tropics, we prefer sweet tastes to sour, we divide the color spectrum into similar colors, and we feel drawn to behaviors that produce and protect offspring. As members of one species, we affiliate, conform, reciprocate favors, punish offenses, organize hierarchies of status, and grieve a child's death. A visitor from outer space could drop in anywhere and find humans playing sports and games, dancing and feasting, singing and worshipping, laughing and crying, living in families, and forming groups. To be human is to be more alike than different. Taken together, such universal behavioral tendencies define human nature.

*"Whatever I do or think as a black can never be more than a variant of what all people do and think. . . . All races are composed of human beings."*

Shelby Steele
*The Content of Our Character*, 1990

These behavioral similarities arise from our biological similarity. Only 6 percent of human genetic variation is differences among races. Only 8 percent is differences among tribes or nations within a race. The rest—85+ per-

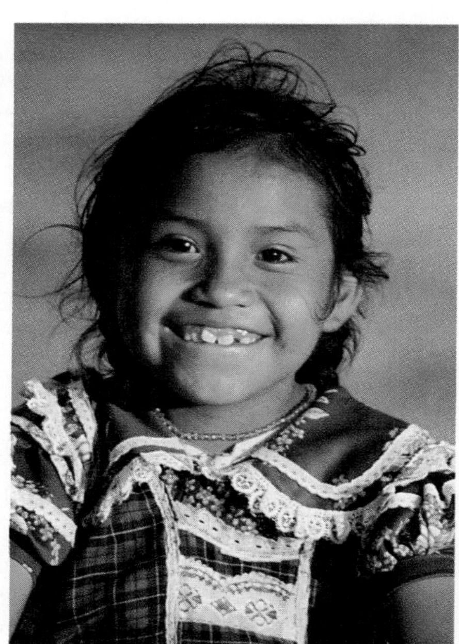

cent—is individual variation within local groups. The average genetic difference between two Icelandic villagers or between two Kenyans is much greater than the difference between the two groups. Thus, notes geneticist Richard Lewontin (1982), if after a worldwide catastrophe only Icelanders or Kenyans survived, the human species would suffer only "a trivial reduction" in its genetic diversity.

Among our similarities, the most important—the behavioral hallmark of our species—is our enormous capacity to learn and adapt. Ironically, this fundamental likeness enables human diversity. We all are driven to eat, but depending on our culturally learned tastes, we may have a yen for fish eyes, fried insects, or chicken legs. Go barefoot for a summer and you will develop toughened, calloused feet—a biologically disposed adaptation to friction. Meanwhile, your shoed neighbor will remain a tenderfoot. Is the difference between the two of you an effect of environment? Yes, of course. Is it also the product of a biological mechanism? Yes again. Our shared biology enables our adaptive diversity (Buss, 1991).

*"Everybody is very much alike, really. But fortunately, perhaps, they don't realize it."*

Miss Marple in Agatha Christie's *The Tuesday Club Murders*, 1933

As citizens in a multicultural world, we need to understand our similarities. We also need to understand our differences. At various points throughout this book we have examined our *individual differences* in traits such as temperament, intelligence, personality, disorder, and health. Depending on their experiences in particular environments, one person may become aggressive, another gentle; one may value freedom, another order and control; one may prize individuality, another the social ties that bind people together. We have also glimpsed a second dimension of diversity—our *group differences* in tendencies ranging from expressing anger to concern about weight. Here again, our shared biology enables our adaptive diversity: Where famine threatens, plump seems beautiful; where food is abundant, slender seems beautiful.

*To review cultural and gender similarities and differences mentioned in previous chapters, see pages 692–693.*

Having closely examined individual diversity, let us conclude our journey through psychology by focusing on our *social* diversity and how we respond to it. How do culture and gender shape our social identities and behaviors? What leads us to loathe or to love those who are different?

**A Universal Behavior** *You know the meaning of each facial expression, and each of these people would understand the same expression on your face.*

## Cultural Diversity

*Our shrinking planet, with its mixing cultures, increasingly presents us with its social diversity. Different cultures have different norms, or expectations, that guide behavior. One significant cultural difference arises from people's valuing of individual identity and self-reliance (as in Western cultures) or of group identity and collective solidarity (as in Asian and many Third World cultures). Within immigrant countries such as Australia, the United States, and Canada, ethnicity contributes to cultural diversity and identity.*

**Culture** is the behaviors, ideas, attitudes, and traditions shared by a large group of people and transmitted from one generation to the next (Brislin, 1988). If we all lived as homogeneous ethnic groups in separate regions of the world, as some people still do, cultural diversity would be less relevant. In Japan, where there are 120 million people, of whom 119 million are Japanese, internal cultural differences are minimal compared with those found in Los Angeles, where the public schools teach 82 different languages (Iyer, 1993). Riding along with a unified culture is like riding a bike with the wind: As it carries us along, we hardly notice it's there. When we try riding *against* it we feel its force. Face-to-face with a different culture, people become aware of the cultural winds. Visiting Europe, most North Americans are struck by the smallness of the cars, the left-handed use of the fork, the uninhibited attire on the beaches. Stationed in Saudi Arabia, European and American soldiers alike realized the liberality of their home cultures. Visiting North America, visitors from some cultures struggle to understand why people wear their dirty *street* shoes in the house, or why people find it fun to eat a picnic lunch out in the bush amid flies and ants.

Increasingly, cultural diversity surrounds us. More and more we live in a global village, connected to our fellow villagers by telecommunications, jumbo jets, and international trade. Cultural diversity exists within nations, too. As Middle Easterners and East Europeans know well, conflicts stem-

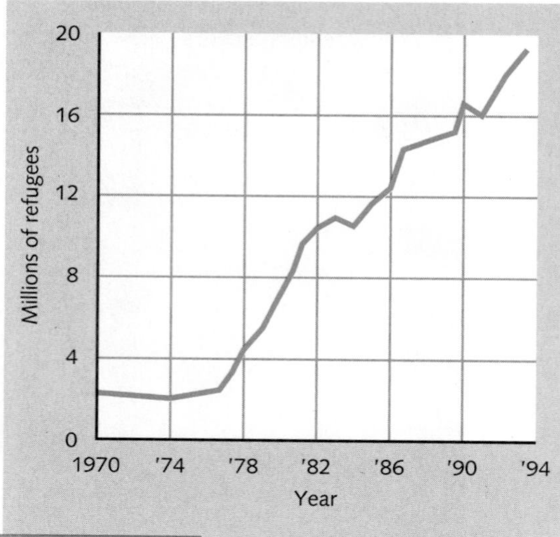


**Figure 19–1**

**World Refugees, 1970–1993** *United Nations data reveal an exploding refugee population. (Data from Brown & others, 1994.)*

ming from cultural differences are longstanding. Cultural conflicts have been described as "the AIDS of international politics—lying dormant for years, then flaring up to destroy countries" (*Economist*, 1991).

Migration and refugee evacuations are mixing cultures more than ever (Figure 19–1). "East is East and West is West, and never the twain shall meet," wrote nineteenth-century author Rudyard Kipling. But today, East and West, and North and South, meet all the time. Italy is home to many Albanians, Germany to Turks, England to Pakistanis and West Indians, and the result is both new friendship and surging hate crimes. For North Americans and Australians, too, one's country is more and more a mingling of cultures. One in six Canadians is an immigrant. In half of the 100 largest U.S. cities, ethnic minorities will together have become the majority by the end of this decade (Jones, 1990). As we work, play, and live with people from diverse cultural backgrounds, it helps to understand how our cultures influence us and to appreciate important ways in which cultures differ. In a world divided by wars, genuine peace requires respect for both differences and similarities.

## Cultural Norms

All cultural groups evolve norms—their rules for accepted and expected behavior. Muslims use only the right hand's fingers for eating. The Japanese have norms for taking shoes off, for giving and opening gifts, and for showing respect to one's social superiors. Sometimes social expectations seem oppressive. "Why should it matter how I dress?" However, norms also grease the social machinery. Prescribed, well-learned behaviors free us from self-preoccupation. When we know when to clap or bow, which fork to pick up first at the dinner party, and what sorts of gestures and compliments are appropriate, we can relax and enjoy one another without fear of embarrassment or insult. Likewise, having a well-understood norm for greeting people in one's culture—by shaking hands or kissing each cheek—precludes awkward moments deciding whether to lead with one's hand or cheek.

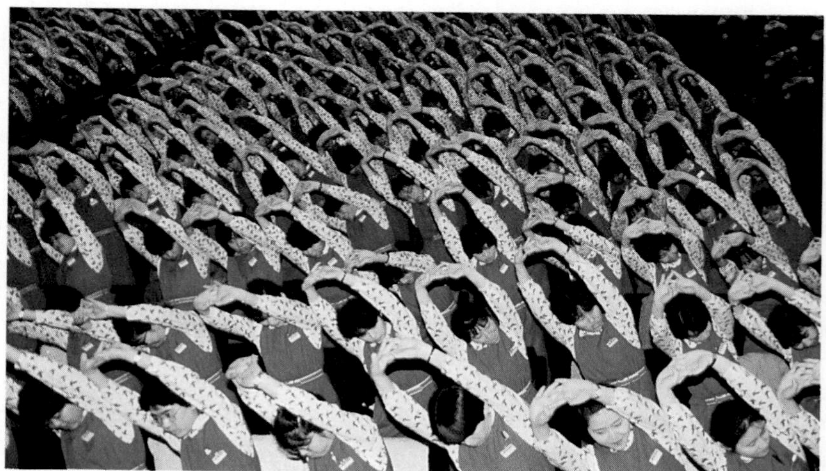

**An Exercise in Culture** *People in individualist Western cultures sometimes see the Japanese as straitjacketed by their culture's norms. But from the Japanese perspective the same tradition expresses a "serenity that comes to people who know exactly what to expect from each other" (Weisz & others, 1984).*

When cultures collide, their differing norms often bemuse or befuddle. If someone invades our **personal space**—the portable buffer zone we like to maintain around our bodies—we feel uncomfortable. Scandinavians, North Americans, and the British prefer more personal space than do Latin

**Culture Influences Personal Space** *Behavior that is seen as appropriate in one culture may violate the norms of another group. In Arab countries, such as Morocco, people typically require less personal space than do members of some European and North American groups.*

Americans, Arabs, and the French (Sommer, 1969). At a social gathering, a Mexican seeking a comfortable conversation distance may waltz around a room with a backpedaling American. (You can demonstrate this at a party by playing space invader as you talk with someone.) To the American, the Mexican may seem intrusive; to the Mexican, the American may seem cold and standoffish.

Cultures also vary in their expressiveness. People whose roots are in northern European culture often perceive people from Mediterranean cultures as warm and charming, but inefficient. The Mediterraneans, in turn, see the northern Europeans as efficient, but cold and preoccupied with punctuality (Triandis, 1981). When cultures mix, misunderstandings are commonplace. This was disastrously apparent after Iraqi representatives met U.S. Secretary of State James Baker in Geneva on January 9, 1991, in a last-minute effort to avert war. Baker clearly warned that the United States would attack Iraq if it did not leave Kuwait. But he said it so calmly that Saddam Hussein's half-brother reported, "The Americans will not attack. . . . They are calm. They are not angry." The Iraqi expressive style, by contrast, was expressive to the point of exaggeration: "If you attack you will face the mother of all battles!" Cross-cultural expert Harry Triandis (1994) speculates that had Baker communicated in a traditional (rather than Westernized) Iraqi style—by banging the table, looking ferocious, and snarling, "We are going to make hamburgers out of you," his message would have been read correctly.

Cultures vary in their pace of life, too. The British businessperson may feel frustrated by a Latin American client who arrives 30 minutes late for lunch. People from time-conscious Japan—where bank clocks keep exact time, pedestrians walk briskly, and postal clerks fill requests speedily—may find themselves growing impatient when visiting Indonesia, where clocks keep less exact time and the pace of life is slower (Levine, 1990). In adjusting to their host countries, U.S. Peace Corps volunteers reported that two of their greatest culture shocks, after the language difference, were the slower pace of life and the differing punctuality of the people (Spradley & Phillips, 1972).

Of course, cross-cultural communication can also suffer in translation, as in these signs for English-speaking tourists (Lederer, 1987; Triandis, 1994):

- ***In a Greek tailor shop:*** "Because of a big rush, we will execute customers in strict rotation."
- ***An Italian laundry:*** "Ladies, leave your clothes here and spend the afternoon having a good time."
- ***A Danish airline:*** "We take your bags and send them in all directions."
- ***A Moscow hotel room:*** "If this is your first visit to the USSR, you are welcome to it."
- ***A detour sign in Japan:*** "Stop: Drive Sideways."

## Individualism Versus Collectivism

Some animals, like wolves, are communal. Others, like tigers, are solitary. Although we humans are basically gregarious, our social styles vary from stressing personal control and individual achievement to emphasizing social intimacy and solidarity. Northern European norms nurture **individualism**. Individualists give priority to personal goals and define their identity mostly in terms of their personal attributes. Western literature—from the *Iliad* and *Odyssey* to *The Adventures of Huckleberry Finn*—celebrates self-reliant individuals who seek their own fulfillment rather than follow others' expectations, or (as in *Moby Dick*) focuses on the interior drives and obsessions of a few lead characters.

Other cultures—especially those native to Asia, Africa, and Central and South America—nurture **collectivism**. Collectivists give priority to the goals of their groups—often their family, clan, or work group—and define their identity accordingly. By their group identifications, collectivists gain a sense of belonging, a set of values, a network of caring individuals, an assurance of security. Eastern literature expresses these ideals by celebrating those who do their duty to others, despite temptations to self-indulgence. Classic Chinese novels focus not on what the characters do and feel as individuals but on "what the characters do in their roles" (Hsu, 1953).

*"We must delight in each other, make others' conditions our own, rejoyce together, mourn together, labor and suffer together, always having before our eyes our community as members of the same body."*

Puritan leader John Winthrop at Salem Harbor, just before his people set foot on American soil in 1630

**Celebrating Collectively** *Like athletes who take more pleasure in their team's victory than in their own performance, collectivists find satisfaction in advancing their groups' interests, even at the expense of personal needs.*

Although individualism varies from person to person, cross-cultural psychologists have mostly studied how it varies by culture, ranging from the extreme collectivism of rural Asia to the extreme individualism of the United States (Hofstede, 1980; Triandis, 1994). The extent to which a culture stresses individualism versus collectivism in turn affects its people's self-concepts, attitudes, and family relations.

### Culture and the Self

If someone were to rip away your social connections, making you a solitary refugee in a foreign land, how much of your identity would remain intact? The answer might depend in large part on whether your culture nurtures individualism or collectivism.

*"No mind can take the same interest in his neighbor's me as in his own. The neighbor's me falls together with all the rest of things in one foreign mass, against which his own me stands out in startling relief."*

William James
*Principles of Psychology*, 1890

For individualists, a great deal of their identity would remain intact—the very core of their being, their sense of "me," their awareness of their personal convictions and values. In many ways, Western psychology reflects the individualism of its cultures. In Chapter 4, we examined Western adolescents' struggle to separate from parents and define their personal identity. In Chapter 14, we focused on personality—the distinctiveness and consistency that make each of us in some ways unique. At each of these points, we assumed the importance of achieving individual identity, fulfillment, and self-acceptance—and if you are a product of Western culture, you probably did not question this assumption. Therapist Fritz Perls's "Gestalt credo" (1972, p. 70) stated these ideas explicitly: "I do my thing, and you do your thing. I am not in this world to live up to your expectations. And you are not in this world to live up to mine."

*"Good morning, folks, this is Captain Holwood from the flight deck. We'll be cruising at thirty-five thousand feet today, and I'll be finally taking control of my life, struggling to satisfy the needs of only one person—me!"*

Drawing by Koren, © 1990 The New Yorker Magazine, Inc.

For collectivists, being set adrift in a foreign land might entail a much greater loss of identity. Cut off from family, groups, and loyal friends, collectivists would lose connections that have defined who they are. In a collectivist culture, a social network provides one's bearings. What's important is not "me" but "we."

The contrast between these two types of cultures is apparent even in the way members are named. Individualist cultures give priority to personal identity, by putting the personal name first ("Laura Myers"). Collectivist cultures give priority to one's family identity ("Hui Harry"). Compared with American students, students in Japan and China are less likely to complete the sentence "I am . . ." with personal traits ("I am sincere," "I am confident") and are much more likely to declare their social identities ("I am a Keio University student," "I am the third son in my family") (Cousins, 1989; Triandis, 1989a,b). For Westerners, individual identity is primary; for Japanese, collective identity is more often primary.

Individualists easily move in and out of social groups. They feel relatively free to switch churches, leave one job for another, or even to leave their extended families and migrate to a new place. In contrast, collectivists may act shy in new groups. They have deeper, more stable attachments to their familiar groups and friends. Relationships are long term. Thus, loyalties run strong between employer and employees. And compared with American students, university students in Hong Kong talk with half as many people during a day, but for longer periods (Wheeler & others, 1989). Advised "To thine own self be true," collectivists more often respond, "Which self? My 'self-with-friend'? 'Self-at-work'? 'Self-with-parents'?" (Cross & others, 1992).

*No wonder, says Harry Triandis (1989b), that modern world colonization was led not by Asians, who were reluctant to cut social and family ties, but by the more individualist Europeans. And no wonder that countries colonized by Europeans willing to leave friends and family are today highly individualistic.*

Because they value communal solidarity, people in collectivist cultures place a premium on maintaining harmony and allowing others to save face. Direct confrontation and blunt honesty are rare, as are expressions of personal egotism. What people say reflects not just what they feel (their inner attitudes) but what they presume others feel (Kashima & others, 1992). Elders and superiors command respect. To preserve group spirit, people avoid touchy topics, defer to others' wishes, and display a polite, self-effacing humility (Kitayama & Markus, in press; Markus & Kitayama, 1991). Self-aggrandizing talk they may regard as childish immaturity. People remember those who have done them favors and make reciprocation a social art. The collectivist self is not independent but *inter*dependent (Table 19–1). Among collectivists, no person is an island.

**Table 19–1 Individualist and Collectivist Values**

| | Individualism | Collectivism |
|---|---|---|
| Concept of self | Independent (identity from individual traits) | Interdependent (identity from belonging) |
| Life task | Discover and express one's uniqueness | Maintain connections, fit in |
| What matters | Me—personal achievement and fulfillment; rights and liberties | We—group goals and solidarity; social responsibilities and relationships |
| Coping method | Change reality | Accommodate to reality |
| Morality | Defined by individuals (self-based) | Defined by social networks (duty-based) |
| Relationships | Many, often temporary or casual; confrontation acceptable | Few, close and enduring; harmony required |
| Attributions | Behavior reflects one's personality and attitudes | Behavior reflects social norms and roles |

*Source:* Adapted from Thomas Schoeneman (1994) and Harry Triandis (1994).

In terms of the self, individualism and collectivism each offers benefits—at a cost. People in competitive, individualist cultures have more personal freedom, take more pride in personal achievements, are less geographically bound to their families, and enjoy more privacy. Their less unified cultures offer a smorgasbord of life-styles and invite individuals to construct their own identities. But compared with collectivists, individualists are also lonelier; more alienated; more homicidal; more vulnerable to stress-related diseases, such as heart attacks; and more likely to divorce (Popenoe, 1993; Triandis & others, 1988). Collectivists demand less romance and personal fulfillment in marriage, which puts the marriage relationship under less pressure (Dion & Dion, 1993). In one survey, "keeping romance alive" was rated as important to a good marriage by 78 percent of American women and 29 percent of Japanese women (*American Enterprise*, 1992). In recent decades, Western individualism has increased and the priority placed on social obligations and family ties has decreased (Yankelovich, 1993). Reflecting on such findings, Martin Seligman (1988) notes that "rampant individualism carries with it two seeds of its own destruction. First, a society that exalts the individual to the extent ours now does will be ridden with depression. . . . Second, and perhaps most important, is meaninglessness [which occurs when there is no] attachment to something larger than you are."

## Close-Up: Tips for Crossing Cultures

When people from individualist and collectivist cultures interact, misunderstandings are common. Harry Triandis, Richard Brislin, and C. Harry Hui (1988) offer these tips for cultural voyagers:

**Individualists Interacting With Collectivists**

1. Pay attention to the other's group memberships and authorities; these define important norms, roles, and attitudes.
2. Persuade by getting the person's superiors to signal approval and by showing how the other's groups will benefit.
3. Emphasize harmony and cooperation. Help the other save face. Avoid confrontation. Criticize gently and in private, after praising.
4. Patiently cultivate long-term relationships. The other prefers doing business with old friends. Intimacy develops gradually.
5. If the other is East Asian, expect unjustified modesty and self-deprecation. Begin presentations more modestly than you normally would.
6. Let the other know your social position, so the other knows how to relate to you. Expect age to engender respect. Who you are matters more than what you've accomplished.
7. Regard the other's accompanying you and spending time with you as relationship-building, not as an invasion of your privacy.

**Collectivists Interacting With Individualists**

1. Pay less attention to the other's groups (when outside the group context) than to the other's personal beliefs and attitudes.
2. Expect the other to be less worried about what superiors think and more influenced by peers and spouse than in your culture.
3. Emphasize personal costs and benefits of what you propose. Be aware that lack of criticism may be interpreted as approval.
4. Feel free to get right to business, with few preliminaries. Expect relationships to be good natured but superficial and short term.
5. Feel free to present yourself in a positive light but without obvious boasting. It's okay to speak highly of your skills and accomplishments.
6. Expect the other to care less about status differences, such as your age or position. Avoid being bossy to those of lower status or servile toward those of higher status.
7. Do not expect to be accompanied at all times. Individualists are comfortable alone, and they show their confidence by leaving you on your own.

### Culture and Social Judgment

Our culture also affects our readiness to prejudge others. Individualists idealize *not* stereotyping people based on their group memberships. Because Jane is an individual, you shouldn't prejudge her attitudes and beliefs just from knowing her background and affiliations. Collectivists respond that in their culture it *helps* to know a person's group identifications: "If I know Yasumasa's family, work group, and schooling, I know a good deal about Yasumasa."

Individualists are strongly disposed to see causes residing in personal traits ("He is lazy; she needs to be in therapy"). Collectivists are somewhat less vulnerable to this fundamental attribution error (Zebrowitz-McArthur, 1988). When told of someone's actions, Hindus in India are less likely than are North Americans to offer dispositional explanations ("She is sociable") and more likely to propose situational explanations ("Her friends were with her") (Miller, 1984). Because group identifications are important in judging others, personal attributes, such as physical attractiveness, matter less to collectivists (Dion & others, 1990).

### Culture and Parent-Child Relations

Right from the start, Japanese and Chinese parents foster interdependence. Even after birth, mother and child continue to be joined—sleeping, bathing, and moving about together. The traditional Japanese mother car-

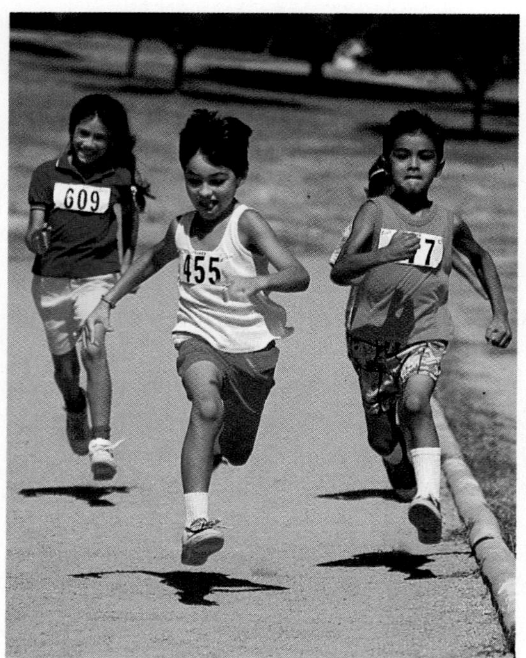


**Kids Are Competitive—in the West** *Children in Western cultures learn from an early age to be independent and competitive and take pride in their achievement.*

ries her child on her back for much of the first 2 years, a practice that may help explain why Japanese infants experience greater separation stress than do American infants (Markus & Kitayama, 1991).

In modern individualist cultures, parents want their children to become independent and "have good judgment." They express less concern for training in conformity and submissiveness—or, as a collectivist might say, for communal sensitivity and cooperation (Alwin, 1990). Schools teach children to clarify their own values so they can make good decisions for themselves. Thus, in Western restaurants, parents and children decide their own orders individually. In Western homes, adolescents open their own mail, refuse parental guidance in choosing their own boyfriends and girlfriends, and often seek the privacy of their own rooms. As adults they chart their own goals and separate from their parents, who already live apart from the grandparents. If a child fails, the embarrassed parents will nevertheless be able to discuss the child's problems openly.

All of this seems strange to Asian collectivists, whose parents more actively guide or decide their children's choices and whose schools are less bashful about teaching accepted cultural values (Hui, 1990). So close is the mutual identification of parent and child that the crushed parents of an errant child seldom discuss their feelings of shame.

## Ethnicity

The traditions and styles contributed by different ethnic and racial groups add another dimension to cultural diversity. When groups of people migrate, they do not leave their cultural values behind. Over time and generations, they will absorb many cultural norms from their new homeland. Yet, especially if connected to fellow immigrants, they also will retain much of their original ethnic identity and cultural heritage. This makes their new homeland a more culturally diverse place.

A culture, as we've seen, is a people's shared behaviors, ideas, attitudes, and traditions. **Ethnicity** is defined by the common ancestors and cultural heritage one shares with others. Culture and ethnicity are at times hard to disentangle, but they can be distinguished. A family living in New York, for example, may be ethnically Italian and culturally East Coast, urban Americans who therefore define themselves as Italian-Americans.

### Ethnicity and Race

In practice, race is socially as well as physically defined. For example, North Americans typically regard those whose ancestors are mostly white, but who retain features that reveal African ancestry, as "black." Brazilians regard anyone whose features reveal a partial Caucasian ancestry as "white." Thus, studies that purport to compare races often are comparing groups defined socially, not physiologically. Moreover, in nearly every trait studied, from blood proteins to intelligence test scores, individual differences within racial groups greatly exceed the differences between groups. Different "racial groups are much more alike than they are different," concludes Marvin Zuckerman (1990). For these reasons, it is difficult to draw conclusions about physiologically based racial differences.

Although we can't really compare groups that differ only on biological race, we *can* explore cultural differences between socially defined racial or ethnic groups. In adapting to the geographical and social circumstances of their past, ethnic groups have developed differing styles of communicating and relating. Between East and West, the norms of individualism or collectivism define one such difference. In the United States, the language, literature, music, foods, religion, and style of today's white culture incorporate African influences, just as today's black culture incorporates European influences. Mechal Sobel describes the American South, fed by African and European streams, as *The World They Made Together*. Nevertheless, notes social psychologist James Jones (1988), partly as a result of its African heritage and partly as an adaptation to the prevailing attitudes of the larger culture, African-American culture has evolved its own style. It tends to be present-oriented, expressive, spiritual, and emotion-driven. White culture is more often future-oriented, reserved, rationalistic, and achievement-driven. Jones argues that we are wiser to accept such diversity than to pretend the differences don't matter or don't exist. Differing cultures have something to offer each other. In some situations expressiveness is an advantage, and in others future-orientation is an advantage. The capacity for each enriches a multicultural society.

**James M. Jones** *"Color makes a difference. Gender makes a difference. Ethnicity makes a difference. Acting as if they don't will create more problems than it will solve" (1990).*

### Ethnic Self-Awareness

Self-concept is a mix of personal identity (self-esteem, outgoingness, appearance) and social identity (identification with certain people and groups). Which aspects we're aware of at any moment will depend not only on our culture but also on the immediate context. When invited by researchers to "tell us about yourself," children emphasize their distinctive attributes. Foreign-born children mention their birthplace, redheads their hair color, skinny or obese children their body weight, minority children their ethnicity (McGuire & others, 1978, 1979).

Surely you've noticed. You become conscious of your gender when alone among people of the other gender. You are more racially self-aware when among people of another race, but you may give no thought to it when everyone around you is of your race. Indeed, notes Jean Phinney (1990), in an ethnically homogeneous society, "ethnic identity is a virtually meaningless concept." The simple principle, say William McGuire and colleagues (1978), is that

> one is conscious of oneself insofar as, and in the ways that, one is different. . . . If I am a black woman in a group of white women, I tend to think of myself as black; if I move to a group of black men, my blackness loses salience and I become more conscious of being a woman.

Self-awareness of our distinctiveness explains why *any* minority group is conscious of itself in contrast with the majority. One way to appreciate the minority experience is to become a minority. One doesn't realize how American one is until, as an American Jew, one lives for a time in Israel, or until, as an African-American, one sojourns in Africa. Living for a year in Scotland, I was daily conscious of what I hardly noticed at home—the Americanness of my accent, clothing, and personal style. I also wondered how people were reacting to my obvious difference: Is she being extra polite because I am a foreigner? Is he snubbing me because he doesn't like Americans?

**Context Defines the Self** *At this moment, the American engineer may not have been aware of his maleness, but he probably was aware of his ethnicity. Had he been standing with a group of American women, the process would probably have reversed. In a given situation, we tend to be conscious of how we are distinct.*

In unfamiliar settings, those in the minority may enjoy one another's company. Canadians who have little in common back home in British Columbia will talk like old friends upon discovering one another at a sidewalk cafe in Prague. To the majority culture, the minority may seem peculiarly clannish or sensitive about their social identity. But that behavior only reflects that unpeculiar tendency for people to be conscious of their distinctiveness.

### Ethnic Identity and National Identity

In ethnically diverse cultures, how do people balance their racial and ethnic identities with their national identities? This was a tension noted by W. E. B. DuBois (1903, p. 17) in his *The Souls of Black Folk:* "The American Negro [longs] to merge his double self into a better and truer self. In this merging he wishes neither of the older selves to be lost. He would not Africanize America. . . . He would not bleach his Negro soul in a flood of white Americanism. . . . He simply wishes to make it possible for a man to be both a Negro and an American."

Nearly a century later, DuBois's longing was still expressed by presidential candidate Jesse Jackson in a "Meet the Press" (1984) interview with Marvin Kalb:

**Kalb:** *Are you a black man who happens to be an American running for the presidency, or are you an American who happens to be a black man running for the Presidency?*

**Jackson:** *Well, I'm both an American and a black at one and the same time. I'm both of these . . .*

**Kalb:** *What I'm trying to get at is . . . are your priorities deep inside yourself, to the degree that anyone can look inside himself, those of a black man who happens to be an American or the reverse?*

**Jackson:** *Well, I was born black in America, I was not born American in black! You're asking a funny kind of Catch-22 question.* My *interests are* national *interests.*

Jackson's response reflects what identity researcher Jean Phinney (1990) calls a "bicultural" identity, one that identifies both with the ethnic culture and the larger culture. Ethnically conscious Asians living in England may or may not also feel strongly British (Hutnik, 1985). French Canadians who identify with their ethnic roots may or may not also feel strongly Canadian (Driedger, 1975). Hispanic Americans who retain a strong sense of their "Cubanness" (or of their Mexican or Puerto Rican heritage) may or may not feel strongly American (Roger & others, 1991). With time, one's identification with a new culture often grows. Second-generation Chinese immigrants to Australia and the United States feel their Chinese identity somewhat less keenly, and their new national identity more strongly, than do immigrants who were born in China (Rosenthal & Feldman, 1992). Often, however, the *grand*children of immigrants feel more comfortable identifying with their ethnicity (Triandis, 1994).

Researchers have wondered, as did Marvin Kalb, whether pride in one's group competes with identification with the larger culture. Does a strong ethnic identification displace other social identities? Social psychologist John Turner (1987) notes that we evaluate ourselves partly in terms of our group memberships. Seeing our own group (our school, our employer, our family, our race, our nation) as praiseworthy helps us feel good about ourselves. A positive ethnic identity can therefore contribute to positive self-esteem. So can a positive social identity among those who have assimilated into the mainstream culture. "Marginal" people, who have neither an ethnic nor a mainstream identity (Table 19–2), often have low self-esteem. Bicultural people, who affirm both identities, typically have a strongly positive self-concept (Phinney, 1990). Often, they alternate between their two cultures, adapting their language and behavior to flow comfortably with whichever group they are with (LaFromboise & others, 1993).

**A Difficult Balancing Act** *These ethnically conscious French Canadians—supporting Bill 101 "to live French in Quebec"—may or may not also feel strongly Canadian. As countries become more ethnically diverse, people debate how we can build societies that are both pluralistic and unified.*

**Table 19–2 Ethnic and Cultural Identity**

| Identification With Majority Group | Identification With Ethnic Group: Strong | Identification With Ethnic Group: Weak |
|---|---|---|
| Strong | Bicultural | Assimilated |
| Weak | Separated | Marginal |

By forging national identities and unifying ideals, immigrant countries such as the United States, Canada, and Australia have avoided ethnic wars. In these countries, Irish and Italians, Swedes and Scots, Asians and Africans seldom kill in defense of their ethnic identities. When overemphasized, diversity becomes destructive tribalism. Nevertheless, even the immigrant nations struggle between separation and wholeness, between people's pride in their distinct heritage and unity as one nation, between acknowledging the reality of diversity and questing for shared values. These tensions, and the ideal of *community incorporating diversity* form the motto of the United States: *E pluribus unum*. Out of many, one.

*"We rededicate ourselves to the very idea of America. . . . An idea ennobled by the faith that our nation can summon from its myriad diversity the deepest measure of unity."*

President Bill Clinton
Inaugural Address, January 20, 1993

## Summing Up

As kindred descendants of common ancestors, we humans share all the behavior tendencies that together define our human nature. One such tendency, our capacity to learn and adapt, helps explain our individual diversity, explored in previous chapters, and our social diversity, explored here. Our shrinking world, with its increasingly multicultural countries, more and more confronts us with our diversity. Distinct cultures are defined by a group's shared behaviors and thinking transmitted from one generation to the next.

**Cultural Norms** Cultural rules for accepted and expected behavior vary in ways that befuddle people. Cultures differ, for example, in their requirements for personal space, their expressiveness, their pace of life, and the strength of their role expectations.

**Individualism Versus Collectivism** Individuals and cultures also vary in whether they emphasize individual self-reliance and self-control or collective solidarity. This cultural factor affects how people define their self-concepts, make judgments of others, and relate to their families. Industrialized cultures derived from northern Europe are predominantly individualist; those of Asia, Africa, and Central and South America are more collectivist.

**Ethnicity** Common ancestors and cultural heritage define one's ethnicity. Ethnic groups have developed differing cultural styles. For example, African-Americans tend to be more expressive than European-Americans. Nevertheless, individual differences within ethnic groups greatly exceed differences between the groups.

One's ethnic awareness varies with the situation. In general, we are conscious of our distinctiveness and oblivious to our commonalities. We become especially conscious of our nationality, our gender, or our ethnicity when we are the different ones. And though the phenomenon of ingroup bias leads people to favor the group with which they identify, people who manage to be bicultural typically enjoy a more positive self-esteem than do socially marginal people. As countries become more diverse, we struggle with how to be multicultural yet unified.

## Gender Diversity

*Like culture and ethnicity, gender contributes to our social diversity. As males and females, how are we similar? How and why do we differ?*

As we saw in Chapter 10, Thinking and Language, we humans have an urge to organize our complex worlds into simple categories. We categorize people as well as things. Among all the ways we classify people—as tall or short, fair-haired or dark, slim or muscular or rotund—two dimensions are especially potent. For people's self-concepts and identities, for selecting friends and mates, and for how others regard and treat them, height and hair color may matter, but ethnicity and sex matter much more. Among the dimensions of diversity, people first attune to another's ethnicity and, especially, to another's sex. When you were born, the first thing people wanted to know about you was, "Is it a boy or a girl?" When your sex was ambiguous—say, when not cued by a pink or blue outfit—people were unsure how to react.

As common ancestry and cultural heritage define our ethnicity, our biological sex helps define our **gender**—the characteristics by which people identify us as male or female. In considering how culture creates social diversity, let's look at the nature and nurture of gender. How different *are* males and females at different life stages? How does our culture's concept of gender affect how we see ourselves and how others see us?

### Gender Similarities and Differences

In many traits, the sexes are alike. Whether you are male or female had no bearing on when you sat up, teethed, or walked (Maccoby, 1980). Tell me your sex and you've given me no clues to your vocabulary, intelligence, happiness, or overall self-esteem. But there are some intriguing differences. Compared with the average man, the average woman has 70 percent more fat, possesses 40 percent less muscle, and is 5 inches shorter. Compared with women, men enter puberty 2 years later, are 20 times more likely to have color-deficient vision, and, depending on the country, die about 5 years sooner. Unlike women, half of men are balding by age 50. If it's any consolation, twice as many men can wiggle their ears.

*Even in physical traits, individual differences among men and among women far exceed the average differences between the sexes. Don Schollander's world-record-setting 4 minutes, 12 seconds in the 400-meter freestyle swim at the 1964 Olympics would have placed him sixth against the women racing in the 1992 Olympics and 5 seconds behind winner Dagmar Hase.*

In earlier chapters we also noted other gender differences. Women are more likely to dream equally of men and women, to become sexually rearoused immediately after orgasm, and to smell faint odors. Women are twice as vulnerable to anxiety disorders and depression, and perhaps 10 times more susceptible to eating disorders. Men are 3 times more likely to commit suicide, 5 times more likely to become alcoholic, and far more likely to be diagnosed as hyperactive as children and to display antisocial personalities as adults.

## Cognitive Abilities and Gender

In science, as in everyday life, differences, not similarities, excite interest. Compared with the anatomical and physiological similarities between men and women, our sex differences are relatively minor. Yet it is the differences we find exciting. Similarly, in the psychological domain, gender similarities dwarf gender differences, but the differences often capture our attention. To some, it is news that there is no gender gap in average verbal ability as assessed by tests of vocabulary, reading comprehension, and solving analogies (Hyde & Linn, 1988). Likewise, there is no noticeable gender gap in learning, memory, or creativity. But most people find differences more newsworthy. Girls are better spellers: At the end of high school, only 30 percent of males spell better than the average female (Lubinski & Benbow, 1992). Boys outnumber girls at the low extremes. Boys are more often slow to talk. In remedial reading classes, boys outnumber girls three to one (Finucci & Childs, 1981). In high school, underachieving boys outnumber girls by two to one (McCall & others, 1992).

*Gallup Poll (1993): "Not including purely physical differences, do you think men and women are basically similar or basically different?"*

| | *Respondents* | |
|---|---|---|
| | *Men* | *Women* |
| *Similar* | *43%* | *26%* |
| *Different* | *56%* | *73%* |

In math grades, the average girl typically equals or surpasses the average boy (ETS, 1992; Kimball, 1989). And on math tests given to more than 3 million representatively sampled people in 100 independent studies, males and females have obtained nearly identical average scores (Hyde & others, 1990). But again—despite much greater diversity within the genders than between them—group differences make the news. Although females have an edge in math computation, males in various cultures score higher in math problem solving (Benbow, 1988; Lummis & Stevenson, 1990). For example, male high school seniors average 45 points higher on the SAT math test (which literally means that they average 4 more correct answers on the 60-question test). Because U.S. National Merit Scholarships are based on SAT scores, only about 35 percent of these awards have gone to girls. In all 50 states, more boys than girls receive the awards (despite girls' generally higher grades).

The score differences are sharpest at the extremes. Among precocious 12-year-olds scoring above 700 on SAT math, boys outnumber girls 13 to 1 (Lubinski & Benbow, 1992). In other Western countries, virtually all math prodigies participating in the International Mathematics Olympiad have been males. Female math prodigies have, however, reached the top levels in non-Western countries such as China (Halpern, 1991). The average male edge seems most reliable at speedily rotating three-dimensional objects in one's mind (Halpern, 1986; Linn & Peterson, 1986; Sanders & Soares, 1986) (Figure 19–2). Such spatial ability helps when fitting suitcases into a car trunk, playing chess, or doing certain types of geometry problems.

*More often than others their age, whiz kids such as these also are left-handed, nearsighted, and allergic or asthmatic—traits that some brain scientists attribute to excess testosterone during prenatal development (Geschwind & Behan, 1984).*

**Figure 19–2**

Which two circles contain a configuration of blocks identical to the one in the circle at the left?

Standard

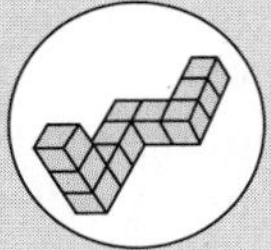

Responses

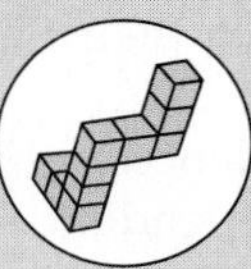

**The Mental Rotation Test** *This illustrates a test of spatial abilities. Which two responses show a different view of the standard? (See page 668 for the answer.) (From Zandenberg & Krause, 1978.)*

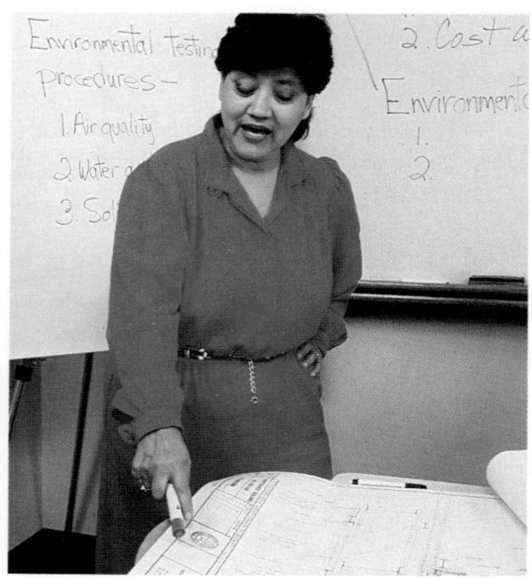


**Women's Work?** *Although few women currently hold jobs in engineering and other sciences, their numbers may increase as young girls are encouraged to develop their abilities in science and math and as business organizations change, reforming structures that have prevented women from succeeding.*

Do natural sex differences therefore explain why most mathematicians and more than 9 in 10 rated chess players and American architects are men? Before concluding yes, consider how social expectations shape boys' and girls' interests and abilities (Eccles & others, 1990). Traditionally, math and science were considered masculine subjects. For example, many parents would send their sons to computer camps and give their daughters more encouragement in English. As you might expect, the male edge in math problem solving grows with age, becoming detectable only after elementary school. But as more and more girls are encouraged to develop their abilities in math and science, the gender gap is narrowing. Among representative national samples of high school juniors taking the Preliminary Scholastic Aptitude Test (PSAT), the male edge nearly disappeared between 1960 and the mid-1980s (Linn & Hyde, 1991).

## Social Behavior and Gender

Research on the psychology of women and men evokes concern: Given people's fascination with differences, might studies of male-female differences exaggerate people's gender stereotypes? Reflecting the mood of the 1970s, sociologist Jessie Bernard (1976, p. 13) cautioned that scientific demonstrations of differences between the sexes often serve as "battle weapons against women." When one group has more status and power, the less powerful group's differences are often interpreted as deficiencies.

During the 1980s, scholars felt freer to search for and affirm gender diversity. Some argued, as did Alice Eagly (1986, 1993), that by reducing overblown gender stereotypes "gender-difference research has probably furthered the cause of gender equality." Others asserted that gender differences are not women's deficits. Although the findings confirm some stereotypes of women—as less aggressive, more empathic, more sensitive, and so forth—those are traits that some feminists celebrate and that most people prefer (Eagly, 1993; Swim, 1994). Thus, most people rate their feelings regarding "women" as more favorable than their feelings regarding "men" (Haddock & Zanna, 1994).

*"There should be no qualms about the forthright study of racial and gender differences; science is in desperate need of good studies that . . . inform us of what we need to do to help underrepresented people to succeed in this society. Unlike the ostrich, we cannot afford to hide our heads for fear of socially uncomfortable discoveries."*

Developmental psychologist Sandra Scarr (1988)

Let's consider gender comparisons in social connectedness, aggression, social dominance, and sexuality. Having *described* these gender differences, without assuming *why* they might exist, let's then step back to reflect on some possible explanations. Do gender differences reflect the evolution of the sexes or physiological differences between the sexes? Might they instead be socially constructed—a reflection, say, of the social roles that men and women often play? Might the answer vary depending on what aspect of gender we are considering?

**Social Connectedness** Individual men and women vary from gently nurturant to fiercely competitive. Yet diversity exists between as well as within the genders. After listening to women's reasoning and concerns, psychologists Nancy Chodorow (1978, 1989), Jean Baker Miller (1986), and Carol Gilligan and her colleagues (1982, 1990) concluded that women more than men give priority to relationships. Unlike boys, who define themselves in separation from their usual female caregiver, girls, they believe, more easily identify with their mothers and develop an identity based on their social connections.

Later experiences reinforce the sense of independent self among men and of interdependent self among women. Men's identity is more self-contained, women's more connected to others. Although men and women express similar self-esteem, men's self-esteem is more rooted in successful independence, women's in achieving positive relationships (Josephs & oth-

*Answer to the mental rotation test on page 667: The first and fourth alternatives.*

ers, 1992; Stake, 1992). Women use conversation to explore relationships, men use it to convey solutions (Tannen, 1990). Women emphasize caring and provide most of the care to the very young and the very old. Although 69 percent of people say they have a close relationship with their father, 90 percent say they're close to their mother (Hugick, 1989). Men, like empowered people generally, emphasize freedom and self-reliance. (That helps explain why at all ages men assign less importance to religion and pray less often than do women [Benson, 1992].)

Women also have closer relationships with each other. Study after study finds the bonds and feelings of support stronger among women than those among men (Rossi & Rossi, 1993). Women's ties, as mothers, daughters, sisters, and grandmothers bind families together. As friends, women are more intimate than men; they talk more often and more openly (Berndt, 1992; Dindia & Allen, 1992). And they more often talk to make connections and to share lives, not just to provide information. One study of nearly 3000 Swedes found that nearly all married men reported their closest relationship was with their wife. But as Figure 19–3 depicts, nearly one-fourth of the wives reported having an even closer relationship with someone else (a soul-sister friend) (Tornstam, 1992).

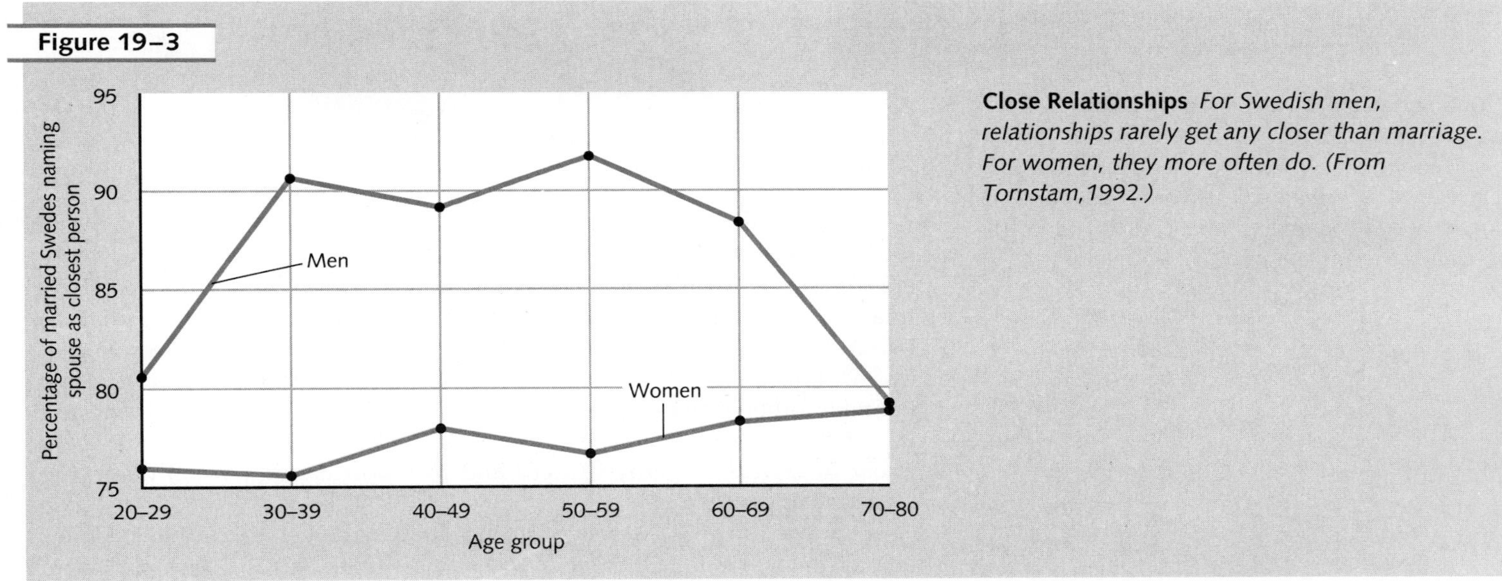


**Close Relationships** *For Swedish men, relationships rarely get any closer than marriage. For women, they more often do. (From Tornstam, 1992.)*

Partly because of their close relationships, women display more of what Gilligan calls "an ethic of care." Daughters more than sons take primary responsibility for aging parents (Aronson, 1992; Troll, 1987). In a 1989 Gallup poll, adult women were twice as likely as men to report talking daily with their parents. In the United States, polls continue to find that women more than men favor the Democratic party platform, which promotes programs for the disadvantaged. Although physical heroism is more common among men, women more often than men enter helping professions such as child care, teaching, and social work (Eagley & Crowley, 1986). Among the 221,000 first-year college students surveyed in 1993 (Astin & others, 1993), 54 percent of males but 72 percent of females said it was very important to "help others who are in difficulty."

*"It is obvious that the values of women differ very often from the values which have been made by the other sex."*

Virginia Woolf
*A Room of One's Own*, 1929

The greater connectedness of females surfaces early, in children's play. Boys typically play in large groups with an activity focus and little intimate discussion. Girls play in smaller groups, often with a single friend. Girls' play is less competitive than boys' and more imitative of social relationships (Lever, 1978). In play and in later achievement settings, females are more open and responsive to feedback than are males (Maccoby, 1990; Roberts, 1991). As teens, girls spend more time than do boys with friends and less time alone (Wong & Csikszentmihalyi, 1991).

**Different Ways to Play** *Although gender differences in play activities arise early and are found universally, the reasons are not clear. Would you give a young boy a tea set? Would you give a girl a sword? As you read on, think about your own gender concepts and your tolerance for diversity.*

When surveyed, women also are far more likely than men to describe themselves as having empathy. If you are empathic, you identify with others. You rejoice with those who rejoice and weep with those who weep. You imagine what it must feel like to live with that handicap, what it must be like to try so hard to impress people, what a thrill it must be to win that award. Physiological measures of empathy, such as one's heart rate while seeing another's distress, reveal a much smaller gender gap than reported in surveys (Eisenberg & Lennon, 1983). Nevertheless, females are more likely to *express* empathy—to cry and to report distress when observing someone in distress.

Moreover, studies consistently find females better at reading people's emotional cues (Hall, 1987). Shown, say, a silent, 2-second film clip of an upset woman's face, women are better than men at sensing whether she is criticizing someone for being late or talking about her divorce. Women's nonverbal sensitivity, perhaps a by-product of their roles, helps explain their greater emotional responsiveness in positive and negative situations (Grossman & Wood, 1993; Sprecher & Sedikides, 1993; Stoppard & Gruchy, 1993). It also helps explain why both men and women report their friendships with women to be more intimate, enjoyable, and nurturing (Rubin, 1985; Sapadin, 1988). When wanting understanding and someone with whom to share worries and hurts, both men and women usually turn to women.

Given the low value that Western societies place on caregiving (as reflected in the low pay of traditionally female helping occupations, such as preschool teacher or social worker), some psychologists wonder: Doesn't affirming women's connectedness reinforce what should be changed?

Shouldn't Western women get in step with their culture's individualism? Mightn't women better serve their own needs by being more self-reliant? Other psychologists argue that women's relational approach to life holds the promise of transforming power-oriented, individualist societies into more caring communities. With the growing problems of homelessness, child neglect, loneliness, and depression, one doesn't get the impression that too much caring is a massive social problem.

The renewed valuing of human connectedness is strikingly similar to the values that predominate in collectivist cultures. Together, the feminist and cross-cultural scholars are forging what Hazel Markus and Shinobu Kitayama (1991) call a new understanding of dependence: "Being dependent does not invariably mean being helpless, powerless, or without control. It often means being *inter*dependent." It means affecting others and being responsive to them, giving and receiving support, confiding and being confided in. It means seeing oneself not as a lone island but as mutually attached to important others.

**Aggression** In surveys, men admit to considerably more hostility and aggression than do women. In laboratory experiments that assess *physical* aggression, men indeed behave more aggressively, by administering what they think are higher levels of hurtful electric shock (Eagly, 1987; Hyde, 1986). In every society that keeps crime records, males commit far more physical violence (Kenrick, 1987). In the United States during 1992, the male-to-female arrest ratio was 9 to 1 for murder and 10 to 1 for robbery. In Canada it was 11 to 1 for murder and 13 to 1 for robbery. Murder rates vary from India to Africa to Britain to North America. But in all these regions, men are 20 times or so more likely to murder men than women are to murder women (Daly & Wilson, 1989). Throughout the world, hunting, fighting, and warring are also primarily men's activities.

**Social Dominance** Around the world, men are also perceived as more dominant. From Finland to France, Peru to Pakistan, Nigeria to New Zealand, people rate men as more dominant, aggressive, and achievement-driven, and women as more deferential, nurturant, and affiliative. These beliefs about men and women are highly similar across cultural groups worldwide, report John Williams and Deborah Best (1990). Imagine, suggest Williams and Best (p. 15), hearing about two people: One is "adventurous, autocratic, coarse, dominant, forceful, independent, and strong." The other is "affectionate, dependent, dreamy, emotional, submissive, and weak." If you find it easy to imagine the first person as a man, and the second as a woman, you are not alone. The world around, people perceive the first set of traits as more descriptive of men, the second set as more descriptive of women.

Indeed, in virtually every society, men *are* socially dominant. When groups are formed, leadership tends to go to males. As leaders, men tend to be directive, even autocratic, and women tend to be more democratic (Eagly & Johnson, 1990). When people interact, men are more likely to utter opinions, women to express support (Aries, 1987; Wood, 1987). In everyday behavior, men are more likely to act as powerful people do—to talk assertively, to interrupt, to initiate touching, to smile less, to stare (J. Hall, 1987; Major & others, 1990).

Such behaviors help maintain the inequities of social power. When political leaders are elected, they usually are men. When salaries are paid, those in traditionally male occupations receive more. When asked what pay they deserve, women often expect less than do similarly qualified men (Major, 1987).

*At last count, 96.2 percent of nations were headed by men, and 96.5 percent of the world's cabinet ministers were men (United Nations, 1991).*

Gender differences in dominance do appear to lessen with maturity, however, as middle-aged women become more assertive and men more empathic (Pratt & others, 1990; Todd & others, 1990). During courtship and early parenthood, social expectations have led both sexes to downplay traits that interfere with their roles. As long as men were expected to provide and protect, they curbed their dependence and tenderness (Gutmann, 1977). As long as women were expected to nurture, they curbed their impulses to be assertive and independent. As they have graduated from these early adult roles, men and women have become freer to develop and express their previously inhibited tendencies.

*"In the long years liker must they grow;*
*The man be more of woman, she of man."*
Alfred, Lord Tennyson
"The Princess," 1847

**Sexuality** "With few exceptions anywhere in the world," report cross-cultural psychologist Marshall Segall and his colleagues (1990, p. 244), "males are more likely than females to initiate sexual activity." Across 177 studies of some 130,000 people, men are much more accepting of casual sex and they report masturbating much more often (Oliver & Hyde, 1993). These large gender differences are much greater than, say, the gender differences in math ability or empathy. A few examples:

- In a Canadian survey of 2350 Adults Only video store customers, 80 percent were males (though half claimed to engage a partner in watching the movies) (Jenish, 1993).
- In a 1991 Gallup survey, almost two-thirds of 18- to 26-year-old men, but only one-third of their female contemporaries, welcomed still "more acceptance of sexual freedom."
- In a 1993 survey of new American college students 58 percent of men but only 33 percent of women agreed that "It is all right for two people who really like each other to have sex even if they've known each other for a very short time" (Astin & others, 1993).
- Such gender differences are true of both heterosexuals and homosexuals, who share a similar mating psychology. Like heterosexual men, gay men report more interest than lesbian women in uncommitted sex, more responsiveness to visual sexual stimuli, and more concern with their partner's physical attractiveness (Bailey & others, 1994).

Such attitudes carry over to behavior. Casual hit-and-run sex is most frequent among males with traditional masculine attitudes (Pleck & others, 1993). Russell Clark and Elaine Hatfield (1989) observed the striking gender difference in sexuality when in 1978 they sent some average-looking

**SALLY FORTH**

Reprinted with special permission of King Features Syndicate.

student research assistants strolling across the Florida State University quadrangle. Spotting an attractive person of the other sex, the researchers would approach and say, "I have been noticing you around campus and I find you to be very attractive. Would you go to bed with me tonight?" The women all declined, some with obvious irritation ("What's wrong with you, creep, leave me alone"). But 75 percent of the men readily agreed, often with comments such as "Why do we have to wait until tonight?" Somewhat astonished by their result, Clark and Hatfield repeated their study in 1982 and twice more during the late-eighties AIDS era (Clark 1990). Each time, virtually no women, but half or more of the men, agreed to go to bed with a stranger.

Men also have a lower threshold for perceiving someone's warmth as a sexual come-on. Here we find another practical consequence of how we attribute behavior (pages 613–614). In study after study, men more often than women attribute a woman's friendliness to sexual interest (Abbey, 1987; Johnson & others, 1991). Such misattribution of a woman's cordiality helps explain men's greater sexual assertiveness (Kenrick & Trost, 1987). The unfortunate results can range from sexual harassment to date rape (Kanekar & Nazareth, 1988; Muehlenhard, 1988; Shotland, 1989).

## Is Biology Destiny?

What explains our sex-related differences? Are they ordained by biology? By cultural shaping? By the interplay between biology and culture? Let's first consider some possible biological influences. Do men's and women's physical differences influence their social behavior? The "biosocial" view of gender says yes—perhaps via the social consequences of physical differences, but yes.

### Sex Hormones and Social Behavior

Males and females are variations on a single form. Eight weeks after conception, they are anatomically indistinguishable. (For example, both sexes have nipples, although only women will ever nurse.) Then, our genes activate our biological sex. *XY* sex chromosomes direct development of a male; *XX* chromosomes produce a female. After a male embryo's testes form internally, they begin to secrete testosterone, the principal male sex hormone. Testosterone triggers the development of external male sex organs. Otherwise, the embryo continues its course toward the development of female sex organs.

*Note to computer students: The sex variable has a default value of female.*

What, then, do you suppose happens when glandular malfunction or hormone injections expose a female embryo to excess testosterone? Genetically female infants are born with masculine-appearing genitals, which can be corrected surgically. Until puberty, such females typically act in more aggressive "tomboyish" ways than most girls, and they dress and play in ways more typical of boys than of girls (Berenbaum & Hines, 1992; Ehrhardt, 1987). Given a choice of toys, they (like boys) play with cars and blocks rather than with dolls and crayons.

Is their behavior due to the prenatal hormones? If so, may we conclude that biological sex differences produce behavioral gender differences? Experiments with many species, from rats to monkeys, confirm that female embryos given male hormones will later exhibit more masculine appearance and behavior (Hines & Green 1991). But these girls frequently look masculine and are known to be "different," so perhaps people also treat them more like boys. Early exposure to sex hormones thus affects us both directly (physically) and indirectly—by influencing experiences that shape us. Biological appearances have social consequences.

Researchers have studied the influence of sex hormones on spatial ability. Melissa Hines (1990) reports that girls whose glands overproduce testosterone have spatial abilities more like those of the average boy. Doreen Kimura (1989) reports that boys whose glands underproduce testosterone (and who therefore fail to undergo normal puberty) have spatial abilities more like those of the average girl. Moreover, there is some tendency—at best a small tendency, say skeptics (Benderly, 1989)—for women's spatial performance to vary with hormonal changes during the menstrual cycle.

Testosterone also influences aggression. In various animal species, one can increase aggressiveness by administering testosterone. In humans, violent male criminals average higher than normal testosterone levels (Dabbs & others, 1987). National Football League players have higher testosterone levels than ministers (Dabbs & others, 1990). Moreover, the gender difference in aggression appears early in life and across many species of mammals. In humans it wanes as men's testosterone levels decline during adulthood. No one of these findings is conclusive, but the convergence of evidence suggests that male aggressiveness has biological roots. As we saw in Chapter 18, it also has social roots.

*"There is little doubt that we would all be safer if the world's weapon systems were controlled by average women instead of by average men."*

Melvin Konner

*The Tangled Wing: Biological Constraints of the Human Spirit*, 1982

### Evolution and Sex Differences

Evolutionary psychologists attribute gender diversity partly to males' and females' differing reproductive strategies (Buss & Schmitt, 1993; Feingold, 1992; Kenrick, 1989). Natural selection favors organisms that send their genes into the future, producing offspring that survive to reproduce. Men, they suggest, are quicker to perceive friendliness as sexual interest and to initiate sexual relations because sperm are cheap. (Males will produce about 2000 new sperm during the time it takes to read this sentence.) Males who compete successfully with other males to fertilize the most females will be winners in the genetic sweepstakes—they will produce more offspring who carry their genes and their traits. Thus, nature's mating game favors male sexual initiative toward females and aggressive dominance in competing with other males.

*The average male will produce 18 trillion sperm over his lifetime and, if living in an industrialized nation, will father two children (Small, 1991).*

Female reproductive strategy differs radically, say the evolutionary psychologists. A female has relatively few eggs and invests enormous time and energy in carrying and nursing a single offspring. To avoid squandering their few reproductive chances, females cautiously select mates who will maximize their children's survival. They respond to signs of health and strength and, in our own species, to an ability to commit time and resources to protecting and nurturing their young. This helps explain the differing sexual values, mate preferences, and behaviors of women and men, suggests psychologist David Buss (1994a). Consider these findings:

- Studies in 37 cultures worldwide reveal similarities in what men find attractive in women (physical features suggesting fertility) and what women find attractive in men (wealth, power, ambition). (See Figure 19–4.)
- The older a man is, the greater the age difference he prefers when selecting a mate. From Europe to the Philippines, men in their twenties prefer, and marry, women near their age. Men in their sixties prefer, and marry, women about 10 years younger. Women of all ages prefer men just slightly older than themselves (Kenrick & Keefe, 1992). Evo-

Figure 19–4

**Worldwide Mating Preferences** *David Buss and an international team of collaborators surveyed the mating preferences of 10,047 people in 37 countries. Men everywhere preferred attractive physical features suggesting youth and health—and reproductive potential. Women everywhere preferred men with resources and social status. (From Buss, 1994b.)*

lutionary psychologists don't suggest that the world's men are *consciously* thinking about their reproductive chances when selecting a mate. Rather, natural selection predisposes their attraction to female features associated with reproductive success.

- Men feel jealous rage over their mate's having sex with someone else. Women often feel greater jealousy over their mate's becoming deeply emotionally attached to someone else. Evolutionary psychologists say this gender difference fits men's natural concern with their offspring's paternity and women's natural concern with resource provision (Buss, 1994a).

Critics question evolutionary psychology. Granted, evolution must have *some* influence on behavior. Perhaps men's being hunters during 99 percent of evolutionary history explains their spatial ability. But when it comes to complex social behaviors, such as fathers' investment in infant care or relations between the sexes, cultural diversity is enormous. Marriage patterns vary from monogamy (one spouse) to serial monogamy (a succession of spouses) to polygamy (several wives) to polyandry (several husbands) to spouse-swapping.

Furthermore, say critics, evolutionary explanations take place after the fact. Knowing the sexual double standard, we can imagine how natural selection might predispose men's promiscuous inclinations. But let's also explain the many men who are faithful to one woman. Of course! answer the evolutionists—the offspring of two invested parents who support each other have better survival chances.

Both sides agree, first, that our shared biology predisposes all humans to fear snakes and strangers, feel anger and love, understand smiles and frowns, and reciprocate favors and punish transgressions. Second, sex differences, which may have enhanced the survival of our ancestors when hunting animals and gathering roots, may no longer be adaptive. Evolutionary wisdom is wisdom about what worked in the past. Third, men and women are the products of their mammalian and human history, *and* of

*"The genes sing a prehistoric song that today should sometimes be resisted but which it would be foolish to ignore."*

Thomas J. Bouchard and others (1990)

their environments and cultural history. (Recall that where food is scarce, plump is beautiful.) Biology, psychology, and culture are all seamlessly interconnected. Today's evolutionary psychology affirms that nature's special gift to humans is our great capacity to learn and adapt. Therein lies a culture's power to create our concept of gender.

## The Social Construction of Gender

**Gender** *The social definition of male and female.*
**Gender identity** *One's sense of being male or female.*
**Gender-typing** *The acquisition of a masculine or feminine gender identity and role.*

What biology initiates, environment accentuates. Society assigns each of us—even those few whose biological sex is ambiguous at birth—to the social category of male or female. The inevitable result is our strong **gender identity** (our sense of being male or female). To varying extents, we also become **gender-typed**. That is, some boys more than others exhibit traditionally masculine traits and interests, and some girls more than others become distinctly feminine.

### Gender-Typing

Social learning theory assumes that children learn gender-linked behaviors by observing and imitating and by being rewarded or punished. "Susie, you're such a good mommy to your dolls"; "Big boys don't cry, Dick." The modeling and rewarding is not done by parents alone, because differences in the way parents rear boys and girls aren't enough to explain gender-typing (Lytton & Romney, 1991). Even when their families discourage traditional gender-typing, children organize themselves into "boy worlds" and "girl worlds," each guided by rules for what boys and girls do.

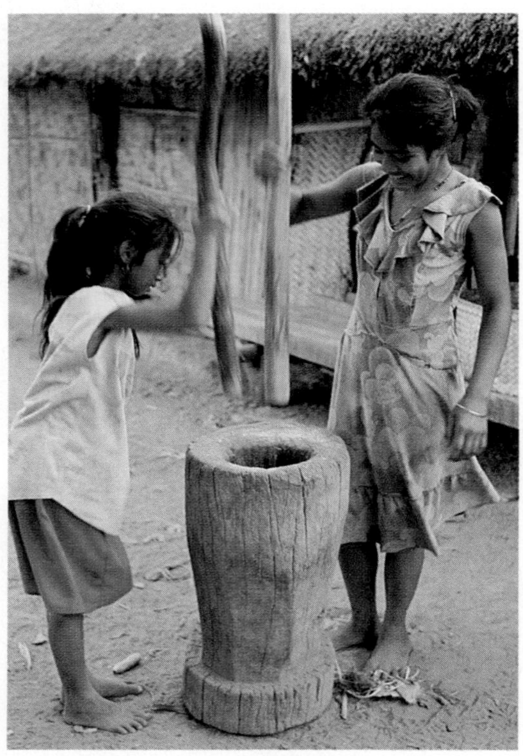

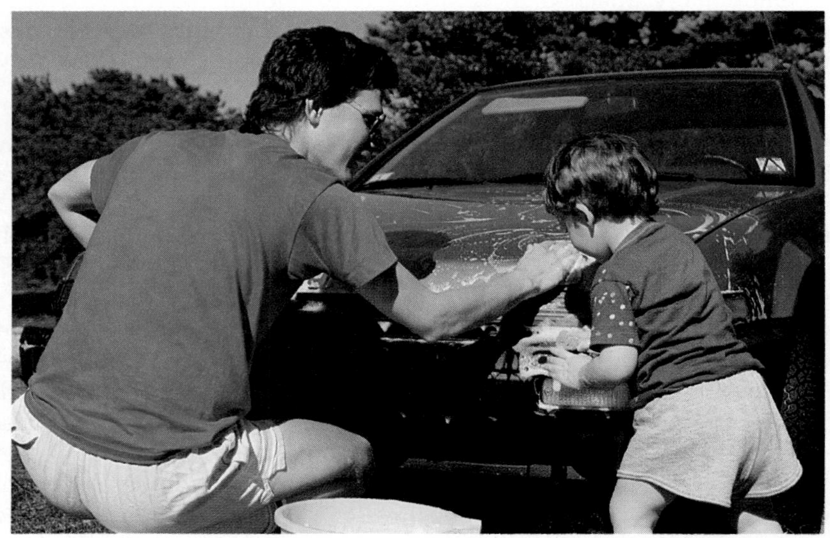

**Gender Typing: Learned Behavior** *Around the world, from North America to Indonesia, children learn gender-typed behaviors partly by observing them and partly by being rewarded or punished.*

**Gender schema theory** (Figure 19–5) combines social learning theory with cognition: Out of children's struggles to comprehend the world come concepts, or schemas, including a schema for their own gender (Bem, 1987, 1993). Gender becomes a lens (a schema) through which children view their experience. By age 3, language forces them to begin organizing their worlds on the basis of gender. English, for example, uses the pronouns *he* and *she*; other languages classify objects as masculine ("*le* train") or feminine ("*la* table"). Through language, dress, toys, and songs, social learning

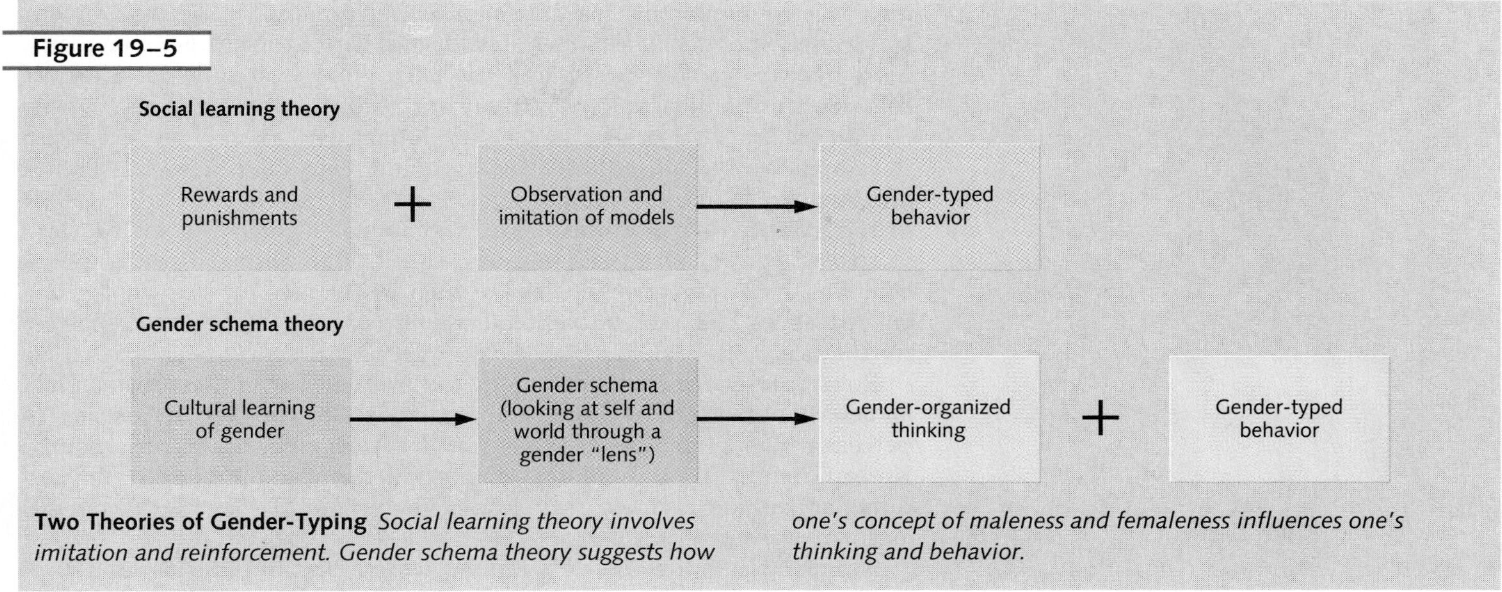


**Two Theories of Gender-Typing** *Social learning theory involves imitation and reinforcement. Gender schema theory suggests how one's concept of maleness and femaleness influences one's thinking and behavior.*

shapes gender schemas. Children then compare themselves to their concept of gender ("I am male—thus, masculine, strong, aggressive," or "I am female—therefore, feminine, sweet, and helpful") and adjust their behavior accordingly.

## Gender Roles

In becoming gender-typed we learn our culture's expectations for our gender role. Traditionally, men initiate dates, drive the car, and pick up the check; women cook the meals, buy the children's clothes, and do the laundry. Such formulas smooth social relations, saving awkward decisions about who does what. But they do so at the cost of limiting individual freedom. When deviating from social convention, as when a woman initiates a formal date with a man, we may feel anxious or be viewed as weird (Green & Sandos, 1983).

Experiments show that many people do act to fulfill gender expectations. For example, Mark Zanna and Susan Pack (1975) had college women write descriptions of themselves for a tall, unattached, male senior whom they anticipated meeting. Those expecting to meet a man who liked nontraditional women described themselves as relatively nontraditional. Those led to think he favored traditional gender roles described themselves as more traditionally feminine. They also performed less well on an aptitude test, solving 15 percent fewer problems. Gender expectations influence behavior.

Unlike biological differences, **gender roles**—expectations about the way men and women behave—vary across cultures and over time. Such variations illustrate the social construction of gender.

**Gender roles** *Expected behaviors for males and females.*

**Cultural Variations in Gender Roles** In some ways, cultures are alike. Around the world, men predominate in fighting wars and hunting, women in caring for infants. In many other ways, cultures differ. Different societies socialize children for varying gender roles. In nomadic societies of food-gathering people, there is little division of labor by sex. Thus, boys and girls receive much the same upbringing. In agricultural societies, women stay close to home, working in the fields and with the children; men roam more freely. Such societies typically socialize children into distinct gender roles (Segall & others, 1990; Van Leeuwen, 1978).

In industrialized societies, men and women who assume distinct roles develop skills and attitudes that help explain their differing social behaviors (Eagly & Wood, 1991). In the United States women have been 3 percent of top executives at Fortune 1000 corporations, 4 percent of the Marine Corps, 97 percent of nurses, and 99 percent of secretaries (Castro, 1990; Williams, 1989). Such roles enacted by men and women have psychological consequences. Leadership roles foster assertiveness; caregiving roles foster nurturance.

Roles vary enormously among the industrialized countries. Women fill 48 percent of managerial positions in Switzerland, 28 percent in Austria, 17 percent in the United States, 3 percent in Ghana, and 2 percent in South Korea (Triandis, 1994). In North America, medicine and dentistry are predominantly male occupations; in Russia, most medical doctors are women, as are most dentists in Denmark.

Socialization practices vary just as widely. In countries around the world, girls spend more time helping with housework and child care than boys do; boys spend more time in unsupervised play (Edwards, 1991). But the differences are greater in some cultures. In rural central India, for example, girls spend two-thirds of their time doing household work, including an hour and a half fetching water daily; boys spend two-thirds of their time in leisure (Sarawathi & Dutta, 1988). In Israel, Arab adolescents favor more distinct gender roles than do Jewish adolescents, thus anticipating the adult Arab world's more distinct norms for male and female behavior (Seginer & others, 1990). Similarly, compared with American 14-year-olds, Mexico City youth have more strongly gender-typed ideals (Figure 19–6).

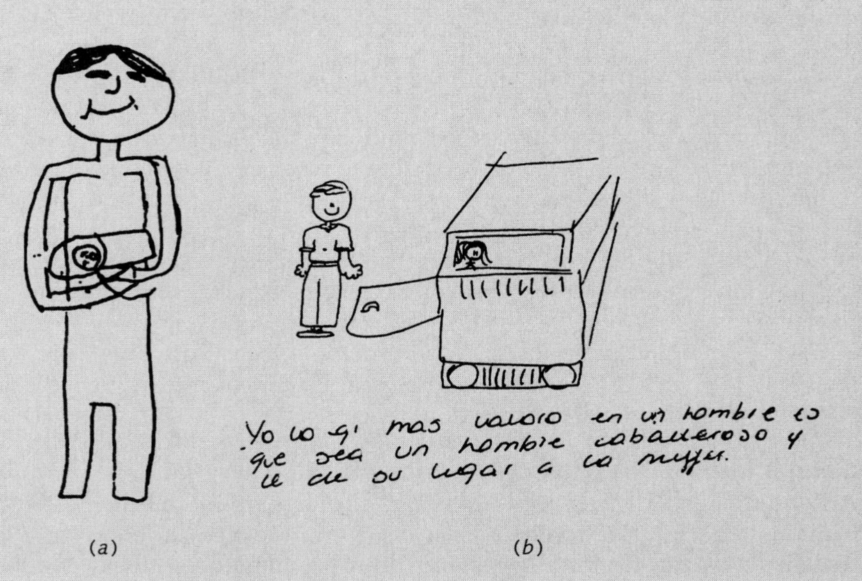


**Figure 19–6**

**Variation in Cultural Gender Ideals** *Drawing of an ideal man by (a) an American girl, and (b) a Mexican girl. (Translation: "What is most valued in a man is that he be a chivalrous man and that he give his place to the woman.") (From Stiles & others, 1990.)*

**Variations in Gender Roles Over Time** Gender roles vary over time as well as across cultures. In 1938, only 1 in 5 Americans approved of "a married woman earning money in business or industry if she has a husband capable of supporting her"; by 1988, 4 in 5 approved (Niemi & others, 1989). In the flick of an apron, the number of American college women hoping to be full-time homemakers plunged during the late 1960s and early 1970s (Figure 19–7).

The change is behavioral as well. The number of women earning education degrees fell sharply after 1970, while the number of women awarded business degrees rose sharply. Moreover, between 1960 and 1993, the proportion of American women in the work force increased from 1 in 3 to nearly 3 in 5. Over roughly the same period, these trends contributed to a 7-fold increase in the number of female doctors and a 24-fold increase in the numbers of female lawyers and engineers (Wallis, 1989).

A more subtle revolution has also been occurring in men's roles. Since 1965, British and American men have been devoting more and more time to family work (Gershuny, 1989; Verbrugge & Gruber-Baldini, 1993). Increasingly, men are found behind the vacuum cleaner and over the diaper-changing table. But cultural differences remain huge: In Japan, where women are taught to endure their roles without complaining, the average husband devotes 3 to 5 hours a week to domestic chores (one-ninth as much as his spouse); Swedish husbands clock 18 domestic hours per week (Juster & Stafford, 1991). However, even in countries that have promoted equality, gender distinctions persist. Whether in Russia, China, or Sweden, answers to "Who works in the child care nurseries?" "Who cooks dinner?" and "Who leads the country?" remain the same as in North America. "Everywhere," reports the United Nations' report on *The World's Women*, women do most household work. And "everywhere, cooking and dishwashing are the least shared household chores."

**Crossing the Gender Bar** *The election of both Barbara Boxer and Diane Feinstein to the U.S. Senate in 1992 was a first for California. The state had never had even one woman senator. Women are increasingly moving into political roles. As their numbers grow, will barriers to the White House fall? What do you think?*

**Should There Be Gender Roles?** Should distinct gender roles be preserved? Psychologist Sandra Bem (1985) answers no: "Human behaviors and personality attributes should no longer be linked with gender." If this requires imposing one's egalitarian values on one's children, then so be it, says Bem. If the children don't absorb ideology and values at home, they will absorb them elsewhere. To raise children who are less gender-typed, Bem suggests making gender irrelevant to cooking, dishwashing, and toys. Give boys and girls the same privileges and responsibilities. And teach them to recognize subtle sex stereotyping and discrimination.

Noting the strength and persistence of gender roles worldwide, some psychologists doubt they will ever disappear. Douglas Kenrick (1987) believes that, try as we might to reconstruct our gender concepts, "we cannot change the evolutionary history of our species, and some of the differences between us are undoubtedly a function of that history." True, the sexes share many traits and abilities in common. But each sex also bears special gifts. To distinguish between two wines, composers, or sexes can be to discern the virtues of each. Equality and freedom of individual choice, yes; sameness, no.

Others reply that biological differences are socially trivial. Human beings—both women *and* men—should be unshackled from all that constrains their being fully human—assertive *and* nurturant, self-confident *and* tender, independent *and* compassionate. Bem (1987) acknowledges that there may be "biologically based sex differences in behavior." But she believes that the social construction of gender greatly exaggerates them. Thus, she says, if under egalitarian social conditions,

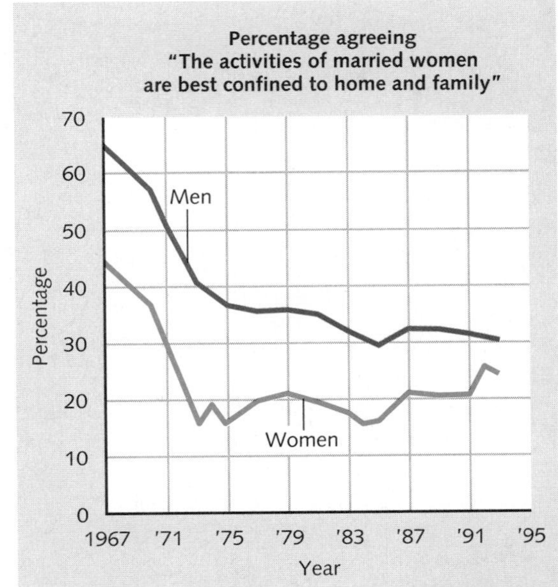


**Figure 19–7**

**Changing Attitudes About Gender Roles** *American college students' endorsement of the traditional view of women's role has declined dramatically. Men's and women's attitudes have also converged. (From Astin & others, 1993; Dey & others, 1991.)*

it turns out that more men than women become engineers or that more women than men decide to stay at home with their children, I'll live happily with those sex differences as well as with any others that emerge. But I am willing to bet that the sex differences that emerge under those conditions will not be nearly as large or as diverse as the ones that currently exist in our society.

So, what can we conclude about gender similarities and differences? First, gender similarities are impressive, especially during middle and late adulthood. Compared with the huge differences among individuals, differences between the sexes are small. Second, we can appreciate the detectable differences, without using them to judge individuals. It's like estimating someone's life expectancy: Knowing the person's gender is undeniably one clue (worldwide, women outlive men by about 5 years). But knowing whether the individual smokes, drinks heavily, eats a high-fat diet, and had parents who died young tells us much more. Because most of the cognitive and social differences are smaller than the life expectancy difference, it makes even less sense to judge people based on gender. Could you become a competent engineer? A child care worker? Knowing that you are a man or a woman tells us little; knowing you as an individual tells us much more.

The overlapping distributions of male and female qualities caused researcher Lauren Harris (1978) to caution against thinking of females and males as *opposite* sexes: "Neither in any physiological nor in any psychological sense are males and females 'contrary or antithetical in nature or tendency, diametrically opposed, or altogether different.'" Instead we might think of our own gender and the *other* gender as like the two halves of an oyster shell—similar but not identical, equally important, and fitting together because they grow together and change around each other.

*"This fundamental truth—that women are not just men who can have babies and men are not just women who spike footballs—gives marriage its vitality, its dynamics, its delights, and its divorce."*

Bill Cosby
*Love and Marriage*, 1989

## Summing Up

In considering how culture shapes social diversity we must also consider the nature and nurture of gender.

**Gender Similarities and Differences** The genders are in many ways alike, but their differences excite more interest. Although fewer girls than boys have reading and speech disorders, males and females don't differ noticeably in average verbal ability. Males do, however, retain a small edge in the ability to solve math problems and a more significant edge on some spatial tasks. Women and men, like Asians and North Americans, differ in their social connectedness. Boys define themselves apart from their caregivers and playmates, girls through their social ties. As adults, women typically become more caring, supportive, and empathic, and men more independent, self-reliant, and unexpressive. Research studies also reveal male-female differences in aggressiveness, social dominance, and sexual initiative.

**Is Biology Destiny?** Hormonal differences, stemming from evolved biological sex differences, help explain certain gender differences. But biology is not destiny. What biology initiates, culture accentuates.

**The Social Construction of Gender** Cultural socialization explains why some children become more gender-typed than others and why gender roles vary so sharply across cultures and over time.

## Responding to Diversity

*With diversity often comes discord and division. What causes prejudice and conflict? And what strategies might help us transform swords into plowshares and closed fists into open arms?*

As we noted in Chapter 18, similarity promotes attraction. If likeness leads to liking, do differences foster disliking? If so, how can people of differing cultures or sexes accept, embrace, and enjoy their diversity? In today's world, few questions are more important. Thus, noted Carl Sagan (1980),

> Human history can be viewed as a slowly dawning awareness that we are members of a larger group. Initially our loyalties were to ourselves and our immediate family, next, to bands of wandering hunter-gatherers, then to tribes, small settlements, city-states, nations. We have broadened the circle of those we love. . . . If we are to survive, our loyalties must be broadened further, to include the whole human community, the entire planet Earth.

**Love Your Mother!** *Earth day celebrations help us to see beyond our own small communities and to identify with the* global *community in all its unity and diversity.*

Together we all face the challenges of environmental pollution, global warming, resource depletion, and weapons proliferation. Yet seldom do we identify with our common humanity. Conscious of our diversity, we instead divide the world into "us"—our own nation, culture, creed, ethnic group, and gender—and "them." In a time when ethnic and national loyalties hinder our solving pressing global problems, we need to ask: How can we welcome diversity without accentuating divisiveness? How can we respect others' social identity without defining them (or ourselves) by the color of our skin, the place of our birth, or the accent of our voice?

*"Wholeness incorporating diversity is the transcendent goal of our time, the task for our generation worldwide."*

John W. Gardner (1993)
Founder of Common Cause

### Rejecting Diversity

How much prejudice persists? What causes it? And what replaces it with understanding and good will?

#### Prejudice

Prejudice means prejudgment. It is an unjustifiable and usually negative attitude toward a group—typically a different cultural, ethnic, or gender group. Like all attitudes, **prejudice** is a mixture of beliefs (often overgeneralized and called **stereotypes**), emotions (hostility, envy, or fear), and predispositions to action (to discriminate). To believe that overweight people are gluttonous, to feel antipathy for an overweight person, and to be hesitant to hire or date an overweight person is to be prejudiced.

Like other forms of prejudgment, prejudices are schemas that influence how we notice and interpret events. In one study, most whites perceived a white man shoving a black as "horsing around." The same shove by the black man to the white was more often seen as "violent" (Duncan, 1976). Our preconceived ideas about people bias our impressions of their behavior. Prejudgments color perceptions.

**Does Perception Change With Race?** *The Italian clothing manufacturer Benetton asked this question with altered photographs in their company magazine.*

Courtesy of *COLORS Magazine*.

How prejudiced are people? To find out, we can assess what they say and what they do. To judge by what Americans say, racial and gender attitudes have changed dramatically in the last half-century (Figure 19–8).

**Hooray for Us!** *For people with disabilities, prejudice and discrimination can be more devastating than physical limitations. The Special Olympics offers opportunities for acceptance and recognition that help heal such wounds.*

Figure 19–8

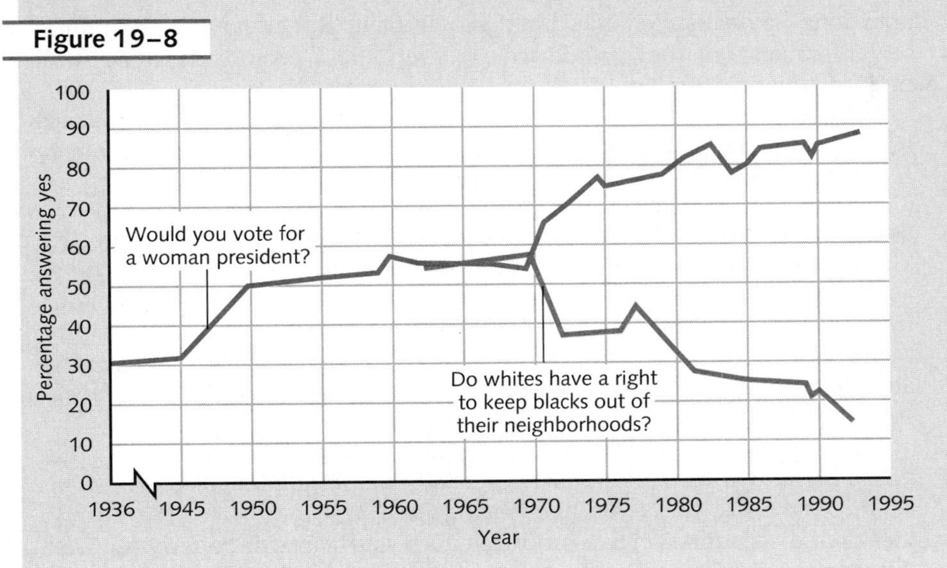


**Prejudice Over Time** *Americans today express much less racial and gender prejudice than they did 2 and 3 decades ago. (Niemi & others, 1989; T. Smith, 1994.)*

Nearly everyone agrees that children of all races should attend the same schools and that women and men should receive the same pay for the same job.

Despite these more accepting attitudes, prejudice persists. In socially intimate settings (dating, dancing, marrying), many people admit they would feel uncomfortable with someone of another race. This fact helps explain why, in a survey of students at 390 colleges and universities, 53 percent of African-American students felt excluded from school activities (Hurtado & others, 1994). (Similar feelings were reported by 24 percent of Asian-Americans, 16 percent of Mexican-Americans, and 6 percent of European-Americans.)

*Gallup Poll (1993): "In your view, does the increasing diversity that immigrants bring to this country mostly* improve *American culture or mostly* threaten *American culture?"*

| | |
|---|---|
| *Mostly improve* | 35% |
| *Mostly threaten* | 55% |
| *Other response* | 10% |

Since the late 1980s, prejudice has occasionally resurfaced in public settings as well. European and North American cities and campuses have experienced significant increases in "hate crimes" (slurs, vandalism, and physical violence) against immigrants, African-Americans, and homosexuals (Herek, 1989, 1990; Levine, 1990). Elsewhere, hate has raged openly—between Israel's Palestinians and Jews, Yugoslavia's Serbs and Muslims, Rwanda's Tutsi and Hutu.

Around the world, gender prejudice and discrimination persist, too. Worldwide, two-thirds of children without basic schooling are girls. Thus, there are some 350 million illiterate men and 600 million illiterate women (United Nations, 1991, 1993). In the Sudan, a woman may not leave the country without the permission of her husband, father, or brother (Beyer, 1990). In Saudi Arabia, women are forbidden to drive. In Western countries, we pay more to those (usually men) who take care of our garbage than to those (usually women) who take care of our children.

Nowhere are female infants left out on a hillside to die of exposure, as was the practice in ancient Greece. Yet even today boys are often valued more than their sisters. During the 1970s Bangladesh famine, preschool girls were more malnourished than boys, and in many developing countries death rates are higher for girls than boys (Bairagi, 1987). In South Korea, where testing often reveals the sex of an abortable fetus, male births exceed female births by 14 percent. In China, male births during 1992 exceeded female births by 18 percent. In five of China's provinces there are now 120 boys for every 100 girls (Kristof, 1993). Sex-selective neglect and abortions have resulted in China and India together having 76 million fewer females than they should have (Klasen, 1994). (You read that right: 76 million "missing women.")

Why does prejudice arise? Inequalities, social divisions, and emotional scapegoating are partly responsible. But so are the natural cognitive mechanisms by which we simplify our worlds.

**Social Inequalities** When some people have money, power, and prestige and others do not, the "haves" usually develop attitudes that justify things as they are. In the extreme case, slave owners perceived slaves as lazy, ignorant, and irresponsible—as having the very traits that "justified" enslaving them. More commonly, women are perceived as unassertive but sensitive and therefore suited for the tasks they often perform (Hoffman & Hurst, 1990). In short, prejudice rationalizes inequalities.

Discrimination also increases prejudice through the reactions it provokes in its victims, a phenomenon called the *self-fulfilling prophecy*. In his classic 1954 book, *The Nature of Prejudice*, Gordon Allport noted that being a victim of discrimination can produce either self-blame or anger. Both reactions may create new grounds for prejudice through the classic *blame-the-victim* dynamic. If the circumstances of ghetto life breed a higher crime rate, someone can then use the higher crime rate to justify continuing the discrimination that helped to create the ghetto.

> *"You cannot oppress people for over three centuries and then say it is all over and expect them to put on suits and ties and become decent attaché-carrying citizens and go to work on Wall Street."*
>
> Shelby Steele
> "The New Segregation," 1992

**Us and Them: Ingroup and Outgroup** The social definition of who you are—your ethnicity, gender, religion, academic major—also implies who you are not. Mentally drawing a circle that defines "us" excludes "them." Such group identifications typically promote an **ingroup bias**—a favoring of one's own group. Even an arbitrary us-them distinction—created by grouping people with the toss of a coin—leads people to show favoritism to their own group when dividing rewards (Tajfel, 1982; Wilder, 1981).

The urge to distinguish predator from prey and enemies from friends predisposes prejudice against strangers. To Greeks of the classical era, all non-Greeks were "barbarians." Most citizens in the coalition of countries fighting in the 1991 Persian Gulf War felt more pain over the few hundred dead Allied soldiers than over the reported 100,000 Iraqi dead. In Africa,

> *"All good people agree,*
> *And all good people say*
> *All nice people, like us, are We*
> *And everyone else is They.*
> *But if you cross over the sea*
> *Instead of over the way*
> *You may end by (think of it)*
> *looking on We*
> *As only a sort of They."*
>
> Rudyard Kipling
> "We and They," 1926

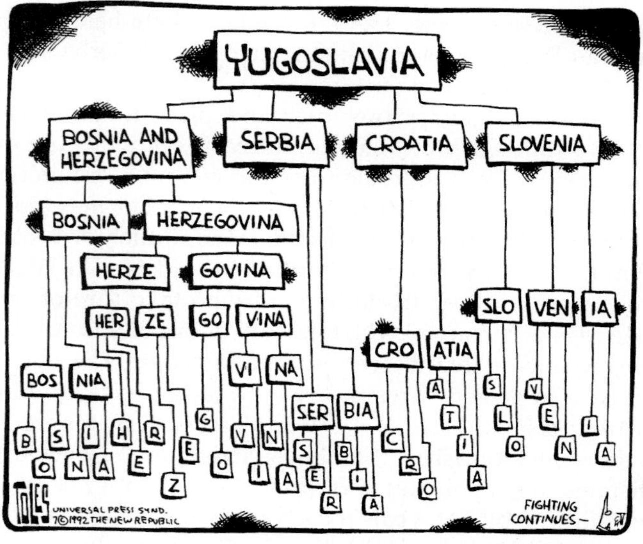


TOLES © 1992 *The Buffalo News.*
Reprinted with permission of UNIVERSAL PRESS SYNDICATE. All rights reserved.

where some 700 traditional societies cluster into fewer than 50 nations, people typically like and admire their own group and direct their hostility toward other groups (Segall & others, 1990). Most children believe their school is better than the other schools in town. Even chimpanzees have been seen to wipe clean the spot where they were touched by a chimp from another group (Goodall, 1986).

**Scapegoating** Prejudice springs not only from the divisions of society but also from the passions of the heart. Prejudice may express anger: When things go wrong, finding someone to blame can provide an outlet. Evidence for this **scapegoat theory** of prejudice comes from high prejudice levels among economically frustrated people and from experiments in which a temporary frustration intensifies prejudice. Nazi leader Hermann Rausching once explained the Nazis' need to scapegoat: "If the Jew did not exist, we should have to invent him" (quoted by Koltz, 1983). Passions produce prejudice.

*"If the Tiber reaches the walls, if the Nile does not rise to the fields, if the sky doesn't move or the earth does, if there is famine, if there is plague, the cry is at once: 'The Christians to the lion!'"*

Tertullian
*Apologeticus*, A.D. 197

In addition to providing a handy emotional outlet for anger, despised outgroups can also boost ingroup members' self-esteem. In experiments, students who experience failure or are made to feel insecure will often restore their self-esteem by disparaging a rival school or another person (Cialdini & Richardson, 1980; Crocker & others, 1987). To boost our own sense of status, it helps to have others to denigrate. For this reason, a rival's misfortune sometimes provides a twinge of pleasure. To a Chicago Cubs baseball fan, happiness is the Cubs winning—and the Chicago White Sox losing.

**Cognitive Roots of Prejudice** Prejudice springs from the divisions of society, the passions of the heart, and also from the mind's natural workings. Stereotyped beliefs are a by-product of how we cognitively simplify the world.

*Categorization* One way we simplify our world is to categorize things. A chemist classifies molecules as organic and inorganic. A mental health professional classifies people's psychological disorders by types. In categorizing people into groups we often stereotype them. Although we view ourselves as individuals, we overestimate the similarity of people within groups other than our own. "They"—the members of some other group—seem to look and act alike, but "we" are diverse (Bothwell & others, 1989). To us on the outside, the members of fraternity X are jocks and those in fraternity Y are intellectuals. Members of each fraternity see their own diversity. To those in one ethnic group, members of another often seem more alike in appearance, personality, and attitudes than they are.

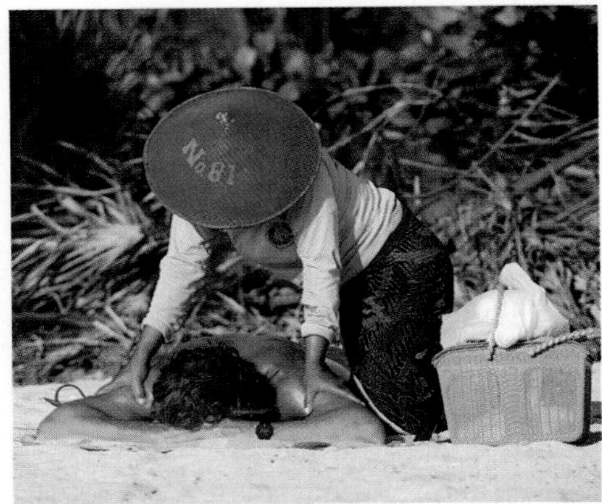


**Do People of Another Race Look Alike?** *Foreign sunbathers on Bali's beaches may think they do, or perhaps they're merely inattentive. Whatever the reason, Balinese masseuses wear identifying numbers on their hats, enabling visitors to recognize them easily.*

*Vivid cases* As noted in Chapter 10's discussion of the availability heuristic, we often judge the frequency of events by instances that readily come to mind. If asked whether blacks run faster than whites, many people may think of Leroy Burrell and Florence Griffith Joyner. From such vivid but exceptional cases they overgeneralize that "yes, blacks run faster."

In an experiment with University of Oregon students, Myron Rothbart and his colleagues (1978) showed how we overgeneralize from vivid, memorable cases. They divided the students into two groups and showed them information about 50 men. The first group's list included 10 men arrested for nonviolent crimes, such as forgery. The second group's list included 10 men arrested for violent crimes, such as assault. When both groups later recalled how many men on their list had committed any sort of crime, the second group overestimated how many there were. Vivid (violent) cases, being readily available to memory, influence our judgments of a group.

*The just-world phenomenon* We noted earlier that people often justify their prejudice by blaming its victims. Bystanders may also blame victims, by assuming the world is just and that people get what they deserve. In experiments, merely observing someone receive painful shocks has led many people to think less of the victim (Lerner, 1980). This **just-world phenomenon** reflects an idea we commonly teach our children—that good is rewarded and evil is punished. From this it is a short leap to assume that those who succeed must be good and those who suffer must be bad. Such reasoning enables the rich to see their own wealth, and the poor's misfortune, as justly deserved. As one German civilian is said to have remarked when visiting the Bergen-Belsen concentration camp shortly after World War II, "What terrible criminals these prisoners must have been to receive such treatment."

Drawing by Mankoff; © 1981 The New Yorker Magazine, Inc.

Hindsight bias is also at work here (Carli & Leonard, 1989). Have you ever heard people say that rape victims, abused spouses, or people with AIDS got what they deserved? An experiment by Ronnie Janoff-Bulman and her collaborators (1985) illustrates victim-blaming. When given an account of a date that ended with the woman's being raped, people perceived the woman as partly to blame. In hindsight, they thought, "She should have known better." (Victim-blaming also reassures people that it couldn't happen to them.) Others who were given the same account, without the rape, did not perceive the woman as inviting rape. Only when victimized was she faulted for her behavior.

## Conflict

We live in surprising times. With astonishing speed, democratic movements have swept away totalitarian rule in Eastern European countries. Hopes for a new world order have displaced the Cold War chill. Yet world spending for arms and armies continues to drain $2 billion per day from spending for housing, nutrition, education, and health. Knowing that, as the UNESCO motto declares, wars begin in human minds, psychologists have wondered what steps might reverse destructive spirals of conflict. How might the perceived threats of social diversity be replaced by a spirit of cooperation?

To a social psychologist, a **conflict** is a seeming incompatibility of actions, goals, or ideas. The elements of conflict are much the same at all levels, from nations in an arms race, to cultural disputes within a society, to individuals in marital strife. In each situation, people become enmeshed in a destructive social process that produces results no one wants. Among these destructive processes are social traps and distorted perceptions.

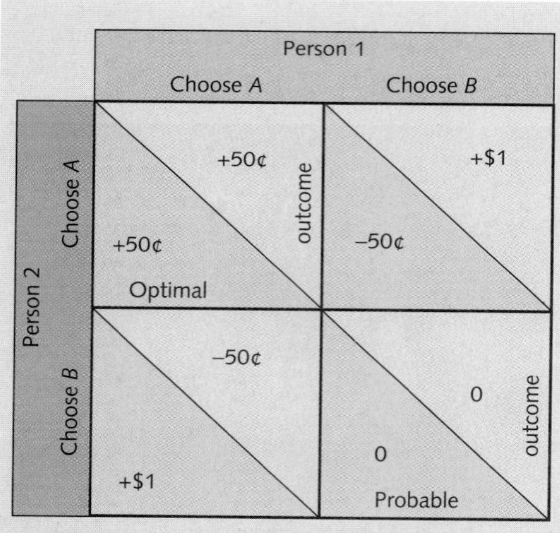


**Figure 19–9**

**Social Trap Game Matrix** *By pursuing our self-interest and not trusting others, we can end up losers. To illustrate this, imagine playing the game above. The pink triangles show the outcomes for person 1, which depend on the choices made by both persons. If you were person 1, would you choose A or B? (This game is called a "non-zero-sum game" because the outcomes need not add up to zero; both sides can win or both can lose.)*

**Social Traps** In some situations, we can enhance our collective well-being by pursuing our personal interests. As capitalist Adam Smith wrote in *The Wealth of Nations* (1776), "It is not from the benevolence of the butcher, the brewer, or the baker that we expect our dinner, but from their regard to their own interest." In other situations, the parties involved may become caught up in mutually harmful behavior as they pursue their own ends. Such situations are **social traps**.

Consider the simple game matrix in Figure 19–9, which is similar to those used in experiments with thousands of people. In this game, both sides can win or both can lose, depending on the players' individual choices. Pretend that you are person 1, and that you and person 2 will each receive the amount shown after you separately choose either *A* or *B*. (You might invite someone to look at the matrix with you and take the role of person 2.) Which do you choose—*A* or *B*?

As you ponder the game, you will discover that you and person 2 are caught in a dilemma. If you both choose *A* you both benefit, making 50 cents each. Neither of you benefits if you both choose *B*, for neither of you make anything. Nevertheless, on any single trial you serve your own interests if you choose *B*: You can't lose, and you might make $1. But the same is true for the other person. Hence, the social trap: As long as you both pursue your own immediate best interest and choose *B*, you will both end up with nothing—the typical result—when you could have made 50 cents.

Many real-life situations similarly pit people's individual interests against their communal well-being. Individual whalers reason that the few whales they take will not threaten the species and that if they didn't take them others would anyway. The result: A species of whales becomes endangered. The individual car owner and home owner reasons, "It would cost me comfort or money to buy a more fuel-efficient car and furnace. Besides, the fossil fuels I burn don't noticeably add to the greenhouse gases." When others reason similarly, the collective result threatens disaster—global warming. Political leaders reason that if an antagonist nation is arming, so must their own. Acquiring strong weapons, they believe, deters an enemy's attack by preserving their own capacity to retaliate. But as social psychologist George Levinger (1987) noted, "When multiplied by 2, a national policy of Peace Through Strength leads inevitably to an arms race." In each of these social traps, parties pursuing their self-interest become caught up in mutually destructive behavior.

Social traps challenge us to find ways of reconciling our right to pursue our personal well-being with our responsibility for the well-being of all. Psychologists are therefore exploring ways to convince people to cooperate for their mutual betterment—through agreed-upon *regulations*, through better *communication*, and through promoting *awareness* of our responsibilities toward community, nation, and the whole of humanity (Dawes, 1980; Linder, 1982; Sato, 1987). Under such conditions, people more often cooperate, whether playing laboratory games or playing the game of real life.

*"Every gun that is made, every warship launched, every rocket fired signifies, in the final sense, a theft from those who hunger and are not fed, those who are cold and are not clothed."*

President Dwight Eisenhower
Speech to the American Society of Newspaper Editors, 1953

**A Social Trap** *In the Atlantic waters off Newfoundland, those who fished knew that their individual catch was their livelihood and, by itself, hardly depleted the whole fish population. Such reasoning by everyone, including outsiders, depleted fish stocks. The result: Newfoundland's fishing fleet sits idle and an economy is in ruins during a 1990s fishing moratorium. This unemployed fisherman has been forced to use his boat for firewood.*

**Enemy Perceptions** Psychologists have noted a curious tendency for those in conflict to form diabolical images of each other. These distorted images are so similar that we call them *mirror-image perceptions*: As we see them—as untrustworthy and evil intentioned—so they see us. Thus, during the early 1980s, the U.S. government viewed the Communist support of guerrillas trying to overthrow the government of El Salvador as evidence of an "evil empire" at work. Meanwhile, the Soviets saw the U.S. support of guerrillas trying to overthrow the government of Nicaragua as the work of "imperialist warmongers." As enemies change, so do perceptions. In American minds and media, the "bloodthirsty, cruel, treacherous," Japanese of World War II later became our "intelligent, hardworking, self-disciplined, resourceful allies" (Gallup, 1972).

In Chapters 18 and 19, we have considered the psychological roots of biased perceptions. The *self-serving bias* leads each party to accept credit for good deeds and to shuck the blame for bad deeds. Although two nations admit to a buildup of military forces, the *fundamental attribution error* leads each to see the other's actions as arising from its aggressive disposition but to view its own buildup as necessary self-defense. Information about one another's actions is then filtered, interpreted, and remembered through preconceived *stereotypes*. Group interaction among like-minded policymakers may *polarize* these tendencies, leading to *groupthink* that sees one's own group as more moral, thereby justifying one's retaliation. In Soviet-U.S. relations, such biases resulted in the social perceptions that fueled the arms race: Both sides (1) wished for mutual arms reduction, but (2) wanted

*"Why do you see the speck that is in your brother's eye, but do not notice the log that is in your own eye?"*

Jesus
Luke 6:41–42

above all to avoid disarming while the other armed, and (3) perceived the other side as wanting above all to gain an arms advantage (Plous, 1993).

Another result of such perceptions is a vicious cycle of hostility. If John believes Mary is annoyed with him, he may snub her, causing her to act in ways that justify his perception. As with individuals, so with countries. Perceptions confirm themselves by influencing the other country to react in ways that seem to justify them. The self-fulfilling prophecy rides again.

## Accepting Diversity

*"Come, my friends,*
*'Tis not too late to seek*
*a newer world."*

Alfred, Lord Tennyson
"Ulysses," 1842

How, then, can we transform antagonisms fed by prejudice, social traps, and misperceptions into constructive attitudes that promote peace? Such transformations are most likely in situations characterized by cooperation, communication, and conciliation.

### Cooperation

Does it help to put two conflicting parties into close contact so they might get to know and like each other? It depends. When the contact is noncompetitive and between parties of equal status, such as fellow store clerks, it may help. Initially prejudiced coworkers of different races have, in such circumstances, usually learned to accept one another (Pettigrew, 1969). However, mere contact is sometimes not enough. In most desegregated junior high schools, whites and blacks resegregate themselves in the lunchrooms and on the school grounds (Schofield, 1986).

*"You cannot shake hands with a clenched fist."*
Indira Gandhi (1971)

Mere contact was not enough to defuse intense conflicts instigated by researcher Muzafer Sherif (1966). He placed 22 Oklahoma City boys in two separate areas of a Boy Scout camp. He then put the two groups through a series of competitive activities, with prizes going to the victors. Before long, each group became intensely proud of itself and hostile to the other group's "sneaky," "smart-alecky stinkers." Food wars broke out during meals. Cabins were ransacked. Fistfights had to be broken up by members of the camp staff. When Sherif brought the two groups together, they avoided one another, except to taunt and threaten.

Nevertheless, within a few days Sherif transformed these young enemies into jovial comrades by giving them **superordinate goals**—shared goals that overrode their differences and required their cooperation. A planned disruption of the camp water supply necessitated that all 22 boys work together to restore water. Renting a movie in those pre-VCR days required their pooled resources. A truck stalled until all the boys pulled and pushed together to get it moving. Having used isolation and competition to make strangers into enemies, Sherif used shared predicaments and goals to reconcile the enemies and make them friends. What reduced conflict was not contact itself, but *cooperative* contact.

Extending these findings, Samuel Gaertner and his coworkers (1989) report that cooperation has especially positive effects when it leads people to define a new, inclusive group that dissolves their former subgroups. Seat the members of two groups not on opposite sides, but alternately around the table. Give them a new, shared name. Have them work together. Such experiences change "us and them" into "we." People once perceived as in another group now are part of one's own group.

During the 1970s, several teams of educational researchers simultaneously wondered: If cooperative contacts between members of rival groups encourage positive attitudes, could we apply this principle in multicultural schools? Could we promote interracial friendships by replacing competitive classroom situations with cooperative ones? And could cooperative learning maintain or even enhance student achievement? Many experiments confirm that in all three cases, the answer is yes (Johnson & Johnson, 1989, 1994; Slavin, 1989). Members of interracial groups who work together on projects and play together on athletic teams typically come to feel friendly toward those of the other race. So do those who engage in cooperative classroom learning. So encouraging are these results that more than 25,000 teachers have introduced interracial cooperative learning into their classrooms (Kohn, 1987). Working with fellow students in all their diversity sets the stage, declared the Carnegie Council on Adolescent Development (1989), for "adult work life and for citizenship in a multicultural society."

**Superordinate Goals Override Differences** *Cooperative efforts to achieve shared goals are an effective way to break down social barriers.*

The power of cooperative activity to make friends of former enemies has led psychologists to urge increased international exchange and cooperation (Klineberg, 1984). As we engage in mutually beneficial trade, as we work to protect our common destiny on this fragile planet, and as we become more aware that our hopes and fears are shared, we will change misperceptions into a solidarity based on common interests.

### Communication

In the social trap game matrix we considered earlier, people usually are distrustful and pursue their individual interests as a defense against exploitation. But when allowed to discuss the dilemma and negotiate, cooperation increases (Jorgenson & Papciak, 1981).

When conflicts become intense, a third-party mediator—a marriage counselor, labor mediator, diplomat, community volunteer—may facilitate communication (Rubin & others, 1994). Mediators help each party to voice its viewpoint and to understand the other's. By helping each side think about one another's underlying needs and goals, the mediator aims to replace a competitive *win-lose* orientation with a cooperative *win-win* orientation that aims at a mutually beneficial resolution. A classic example concerns the two friends who, after quarreling over an orange, agreed to split it, whereupon one squeezed his half for juice while the other used the peel from her half to make a cake. If only the two had understood each other's motives, they could have hit on the win-win solution of one having all the juice, the other all the peel.

Such understanding and cooperative resolution is most needed, yet least likely, in times of anger or crisis (Bodenhausen & others, 1994; Tetlock, 1988). When conflicts intensify, images become more stereotyped, communication becomes more difficult, and judgments become more rigid. Iraq's President Saddam Hussein, America's friend while attacking Iran in the 1980s, became to George Bush "another Hitler" after attacking oil-producing Kuwait in 1990. To Hussein, Bush became "Satan in the White House."

Neutral third parties may also suggest proposals that would be dismissed if offered by either side. People often "reactively devalue" a concession offered by an adversary ("they must not value it"); the same concession may seem less like a token gesture when suggested by a third party. Lee Ross and Constance Stillinger (1991) showed how this works. They found that a nuclear disarmament proposal which Americans dismissed when attributed to the Soviet Union seemed more acceptable when attributed to a neutral third party.

### Conciliation

When tension and suspicion peak, cooperation and communication may become impossible. Each party is likely to threaten, coerce, or retaliate. In the weeks before the Persian Gulf War, President Bush threatened, in the full glare of publicity, to "kick Saddam's ass." Saddam Hussein communicated in kind, threatening to make Americans "swim in their own blood."

Under such conditions, is there an alternative to war or surrender? Social psychologist Charles Osgood (1962, 1980) advocates a strategy of "Graduated and Reciprocated Initiatives in Tension-Reduction," nicknamed **GRIT**. In applying GRIT, one side first announces its recognition of mutual interests and its intent to reduce tensions. It then initiates one or more small, conciliatory acts. Without weakening one's retaliatory capability, this modest beginning opens the door for reciprocation by the other party. Should the enemy respond with hostility, one reciprocates in kind. But so, too, with any conciliatory response. Thus, President Kennedy's gesture of stopping atmospheric nuclear tests began a series of reciprocated conciliatory acts that culminated in the atmospheric test-ban treaty.

*"To begin with, I would like to express my sincere thanks and deep appreciation for the opportunity to meet with you. While there are still profound differences between us, I think the very fact of my presence here today is a major breakthrough."*

Drawing by W. Miller; © 1983 The New Yorker Magazine, Inc.

In laboratory experiments, GRIT is the most effective strategy known for increasing trust and cooperation (Lindskold & others, 1978–1988). Even during intense personal conflict, when communication has been nonexistent, a small conciliatory gesture—a smile, a touch, a word of apology—may work wonders. Conciliations allow both parties to begin edging down the tension ladder to a safer rung where communication and mutual understanding can begin.

And how good that such can happen, for civilization advances not by cultural isolation—maintaining walls around ethnic enclaves—but by tapping the knowledge, the skills, and the arts that are each culture's legacy to the whole human race. Thomas Sowell (1991) notes that, thanks to cultural sharing, every modern society is enriched by a cultural mix. We have China to thank for paper and printing, and for the magnetic compass that opened the great explorations. We have Egypt to thank for trigonometry. We have the Islamic world and India's Hindus to thank for our Arabic numerals, which, except for numbering Superbowls and Kings and Queens, really are superior to the Roman numerals they replaced. While celebrating and claiming these cultural legacies, we can also welcome the enrichment of today's social diversity. We can view ourselves as individual instruments in a human orchestra. And we can therefore affirm our own culture's heritage while building bridges of communication, understanding, and cooperation across cultural traditions.

*"I am prepared this day to declare myself a citizen of the world, and to invite everyone everywhere to embrace this broader vision of our interdependent world, our common quest for justice, and ultimately for Peace on Earth."*

Father Theodore Hesburgh
*The Human Imperative*, 1974

## Summing Up

Although conscious of our cultural, ethnic, and gender diversity, we also face social and global challenges that require unified answers. What factors impede and promote our sense of human kinship?

**Rejecting Diversity** Although overt racial and gender animosity have declined, prejudice still surfaces in blatant and subtle ways. Prejudice often arises from social inequalities, social divisions, and emotional scapegoating. New research shows that stereotypes also are a cognitive by-product of our natural ways of simplifying our complex worlds. Conflicts between individuals and cultures often arise from malignant social processes. These include social traps, in which each party, by protecting and pursuing its self-interest, creates an outcome that no one wants. The spiral of conflict also feeds and is fed by distorted mirror-image perceptions, in which each party views itself as moral and the other as untrustworthy and evil-intentioned.

**Accepting Diversity** Enemies sometimes become friends, especially when the circumstances favor cooperation toward superordinate goals, understanding through communication, and reciprocated conciliatory gestures.

## Terms and Concepts to Remember

### Cultural Diversity

**culture** The enduring behaviors, ideas, attitudes, and traditions shared by a large group of people and transmitted from one generation to the next.

**personal space** The buffer zone we like to maintain around our bodies.

**individualism** Giving priority to one's own goals over group goals, and defining one's identity in terms of personal attributes rather than group identifications.

**collectivism** Giving priority to the goals of one's groups (often one's extended family or work group) and defining one's identity accordingly.

**ethnicity** That part of one's social identity defined by the ancestors, heritage, and traits one shares with others.

### Gender Diversity

**gender** In psychology, the characteristics, whether biologically or socially influenced, by which people define male and female.

**gender identity** One's sense of being male or female. Note: One's gender identity is distinct from one's sexual orientation (as heterosexual or homosexual) and from the strength of one's gender-typing.

**gender-typing** The acquisition of a masculine or feminine gender identity and role.

**gender schema theory** The theory that children learn from their cultures a concept of what it means to be male and female and that they adjust their behavior accordingly.

**gender role** A set of expected behaviors for males and for females.

### Responding to Diversity

**prejudice** An unjustifiable (and usually negative) attitude toward a group and its members. Prejudice generally involves stereotyped beliefs, negative feelings, and a predisposition to discriminatory action.

**stereotype** A generalized (often overgeneralized) belief about a group of people.

**ingroup bias** The tendency to favor one's own group.

**scapegoat theory** The theory that prejudice provides an outlet for anger by providing someone to blame.

**just-world phenomenon** The tendency of people to believe the world is just and that people therefore get what they deserve and deserve what they get.

**conflict** A perceived incompatibility of actions, goals, or ideas.

**social traps** Situations in which the conflicting parties, by each rationally pursuing their self-interest, become caught in mutually destructive behavior.

**superordinate goals** Shared goals that override differences among people and require their cooperation.

**GRIT** Graduated and Reciprocated Initiatives in Tension-Reduction—a strategy designed to decrease international tensions.

## Critical Thinking Exercise

Now that you have read and reviewed Chapter 19, take your learning a step further by testing your critical thinking skills on the following pattern recognition exercise (adapted from Zechmeister & Johnson, 1992).

Write down three characteristics or descriptions that you associate with each of the following groups of people.

| | | | |
|---|---|---|---|
| Physicians | ________ | ________ | ________ |
| Athletes | ________ | ________ | ________ |
| Artists | ________ | ________ | ________ |
| Vegetarians | ________ | ________ | ________ |
| College students | ________ | ________ | ________ |
| Lawyers | ________ | ________ | ________ |

With which of these groups do you most closely identify? With which do you least identify? The group with which you most closely identify can be considered one of your ingroups; the one that you feel most unlike is one of your outgroups.

1. Was it easier to come up with descriptions for your ingroup or for your outgroup? Why do you think this is so?
2. Are your descriptions of your ingroup and outgroup equally favorable? If not, why do you think this is so?
3. In the answer key you will find ingroup and outgroup descriptions made by a group of college students. Before looking at it, decide whether your ingroup or your outgroup descriptions are more likely to match those of the other college students. How would you explain this phenomenon?

Check your progress on becoming a critical thinker by comparing your answers to the sample answers found in Appendix B.

## For Further Information

*For further information in this text on culture and multicultural experience, see:*

Adolescence, pp. 117, 125–126
Aggression, p. 636
Aging, p. 129
Alcoholism, p. 502
Altruism, p. 643
Anger, p. 446
Attractiveness, p. 646
Behavioral effects of culture, p. 32
Bilingualism, p. 353
Child-rearing, pp. 105–106
Cognitive development, p. 120
Conformity, p. 622
Culture shock, p. 490
Deaf culture, pp. 171–173, 346
Depression, pp. 518, 520
Developmental similarities, pp. 106–107
Dieting, p. 607
Eating disorders, p. 406
Experiencing emotion, p. 443
Expressing emotion, pp. 440–441
Father care (Ch. 3 box), p. 100
Intelligence, pp. 371–372, 388–391
Life expectancy, p. 131
Management styles, p. 424
Math performance, pp. 390–391
Moral development, p. 122
Multiple personality, p. 513
Obesity, pp. 604, 606
Participative management, p. 426
Perception, p. 200

*For further information in this text on the psychology of women and men, see:*



## For Further Reading

**Buss, D. M.** (1994). *The evolution of desire: Strategies of human mating*. New York: Basic Books.

*What do women want? What do men want? Psychologist Buss suggests how motives forged by our common evolutionary past influence the attractions and sexual choices of women and of men worldwide.*

**Lonner, W. J., & Malpass, R.** (Eds.) (1994). *Psychology and culture*. Needham Heights, MA: Allyn & Bacon.

*In 43 crisp essays, leading contributors to cross-cultural psychology offer a smorgasbord of their most important findings.*

**Rubin, J. Z., Pruitt, D. G., & Kim, S. H.** (1994). *Social conflict: Escalation, stalemate, and settlement*. New York: Mc Graw-Hill.

*Why do conflicts escalate? What can be done to manage and resolve them? Three social psychologists distill what psychological science has learned about strategies for turning closed fists into open arms.*

**Tavris, C.** (1992). *The mismeasure of woman*. New York: Simon & Schuster.

*One of psychology's leading writers offers an engaging account of the stereotyping, and the reality, of women.*

**Triandis, H.** (1994). *Culture and social behavior*. New York: McGraw-Hill.

*A senior cross-cultural researcher draws on his research and experience in many cultures as he summarizes how we humans are alike and how we differ.*

**Unger, R., & Crawford, M.** (1992). *Women and gender*. New York: McGraw-Hill.

*A state-of-the-art research review and feminist perspective on how we become gendered, with special attention to women's experiences, achievements, and stresses across the life span.*

APPENDIX 

# Statistical Reasoning



Science fiction writer H. G. Wells predicted that "statistical thinking will one day be as necessary for efficient citizenship as the ability to read and write." That day has arrived. Today's statistics are tools that help us see and interpret what the unaided eye might miss.

## Describing Data

Researchers or not, we all make observations or gather data that we must organize and interpret. Let's see how we might effectively do this.

### Distributions

Laura is a college admissions officer. Attempting to predict which students succeed at her school, she sorts through their high school grades, aptitude scores, biographical statements, recommendation letters, and subsequent college grades. But there is too much information to remember. Moreover, she knows that impressions are swayed by remembered information, often the vivid or extreme instances. So she starts by laying out the basic data on a small random sample of students (Table A–1).

**Table A–1 Laura's Sample Data**

| Student | Precollege GPA | College GPA | SAT | Family Income | Student | Precollege GPA | College GPA | SAT | Family Income |
|---|---|---|---|---|---|---|---|---|---|
| Andrea | 2.1 | 1.6 | 950 | $15,000 | Mark | 3.6 | 4.0 | 1370 | $45,000 |
| Bubba | 2.9 | 2.8 | 720 | 20,000 | Nicole | 2.9 | 2.2 | 875 | 35,000 |
| Cindy | 3.7 | 3.6 | 1350 | 30,000 | Nobuyuki | 3.2 | 2.1 | 1180 | 25,000 |
| Dang Cho | 3.1 | 3.9 | 1100 | 20,000 | Ralph | 2.7 | 2.8 | 1065 | 35,000 |
| Ezekiel | 3.4 | 3.1 | 1100 | 40,000 | Renae | 3.9 | 3.3 | 1130 | 20,000 |
| Fiona | 2.9 | 2.6 | 775 | 20,000 | Rochelle | 2.3 | 2.5 | 725 | 30,000 |
| Hope | 2.0 | 2.4 | 800 | 45,000 | Rowland | 2.8 | 2.5 | 700 | 40,000 |
| Huong | 3.5 | 2.7 | 1010 | 70,000 | Tammy | 3.0 | 3.5 | 1270 | 20,000 |
| Gamal | 2.7 | 3.3 | 750 | 25,000 | Tiffany | 3.1 | 2.7 | 810 | 25,000 |
| Jae-Min | 3.9 | 3.5 | 1375 | 475,000 | Timothy | 3.5 | 2.9 | 900 | 90,000 |
| Kraig | 3.4 | 3.7 | 820 | 30,000 | Todd | 3.8 | 3.2 | 940 | 20,000 |
| Larry | 3.1 | 2.5 | 1105 | 15,000 | Wilbur | 2.6 | 2.1 | 750 | 30,000 |
| Malachi | 3.4 | 3.3 | 800 | 50,000 | Xandria | 3.5 | 3.3 | 1020 | 20,000 |
| Manuel | 3.3 | 3.3 | 1120 | 25,000 | Xin | 4.0 | 3.8 | 1400 | 45,000 |
| Maria | 3.5 | 3.6 | 900 | 710,000 | Yolanda | 3.1 | 2.8 | 900 | 30,000 |

**Figure A–1**

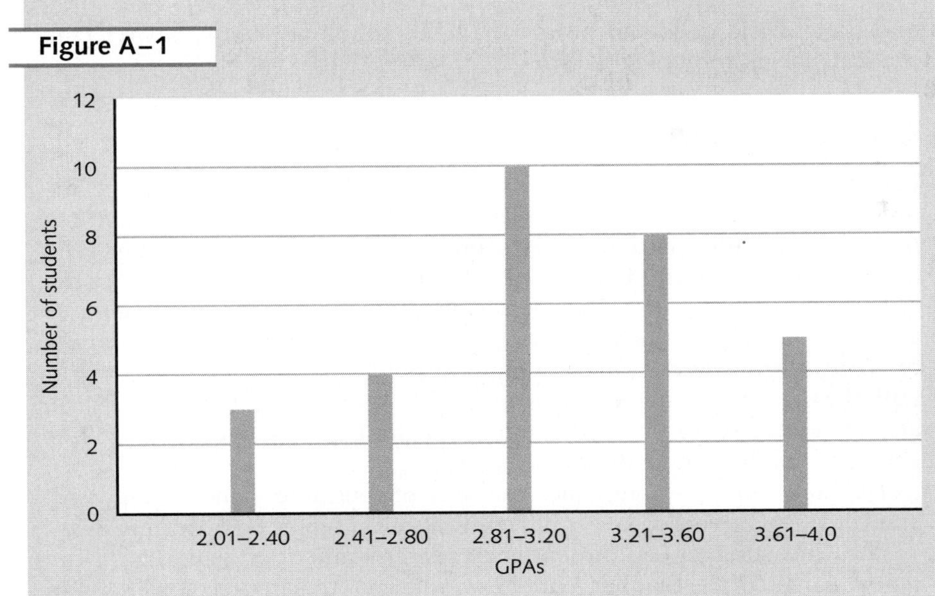


**Bar Graph** *High school GPAs of 30 students.*

She is first interested in how these students did in high school. She therefore displays the applicants' precollege grade point averages as a bar graph (Figure A–1). By showing the number of GPAs within a particular interval as a bar, Laura can see about where any particular student's GPA falls relative to the others. She can also express any student's ranking as a **percentile rank**, which states the percentage of scores that fall below a particular score. A student whose percentile rank is 99 has a GPA that exceeds those of 99 percent of all the students. (You can never have a percentile rank of 100. Your score can never exceed those of 100 percent of the people because you are one of them.)

A note of caution: Take care when reading statistical graphs. Depending on what people want to emphasize, they can design the graph to make the same difference look small or big.

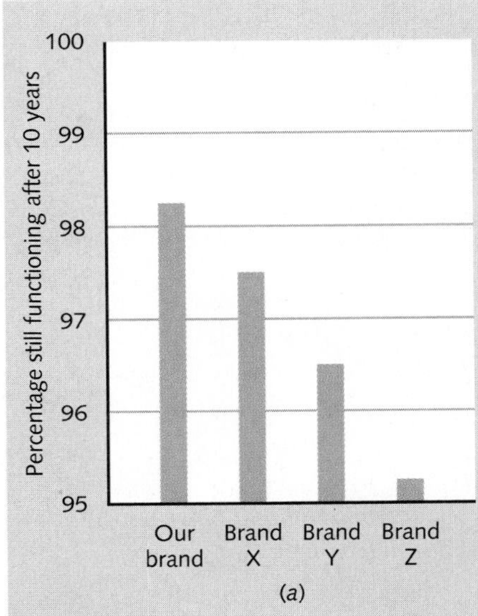


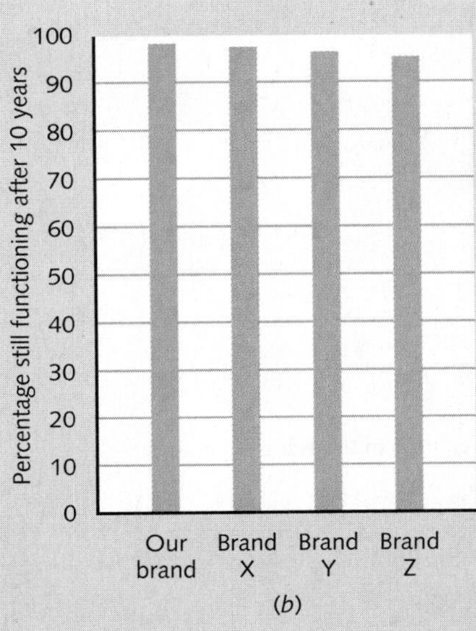


**Read the Scale Labels** *An American truck manufacturer offered graph (a)—with actual brand names included—to suggest the much greater durability of their trucks. Note, however, how the apparent difference shrinks as the vertical scale changes in graph (b).*

*The moral:* When looking at statistical graphs in books and magazines and on television ads and news broadcasts, think critically: Always read the scale labels and note their range.

## Central Tendencies

Laura wonders: What are typical precollege grades and family income levels among her college's students? That is, what is a representative or *central tendency?* For any distribution of scores there are three commonly used measures of the central tendency. The simplest is the **mode**, the most frequently occurring score. The most commonly reported is the **mean**, or arithmetic average—the total sum of all the scores divided by the number of scores. (From calculating your grade point average, you are familiar with the mean.) The **median** is the middle score—the 50th percentile; if you arrange all the scores in order from the highest to the lowest, half will be above the median and half will be below it.

*The moral:* Always note which measure of central tendency is reported, and consider: If it is a mean, could a few atypical scores be distorting it?

*"The poor are getting poorer, but with the rich getting richer it all averages out in the long run."*

Drawing by Mirachi; © 1988 The New Yorker Magazine, Inc.

Such measures of central tendency neatly summarize data. Laura can report, for example, that her student sample has a mean precollege GPA of 3.16. But consider what happens to the mean when a distribution is lopsided or *skewed* (rather than symmetrical). As Figure A–2 shows with the family income data, the mode, median, and mean tell different stories. This is because the mean is biased by a few extreme scores (in this case, the two families with very high income). To say her students have a mean family income of $70,000 is true but misleading. (Understanding this, you can see how a British newspaper could accurately run the headline "Income for 62% Is Below Average" [Waterhouse, 1993]. Because the bottom half of British income earners receive only a quarter of the national income cake, most British people, like most people everywhere, make less than the mean.)

Figure A–2

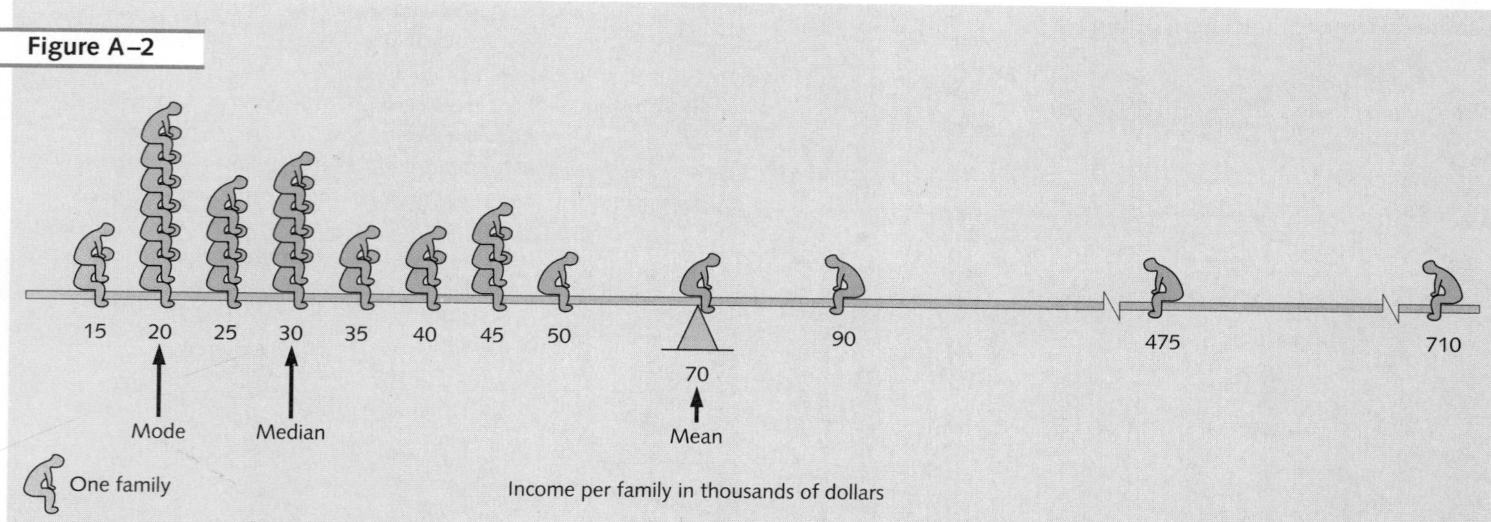


**A Skewed Distribution** *This graphic representation of the distribution of incomes illustrates the three measures of central tendency—mode, median, and mean. Note how just a few high incomes make the mean—the fulcrum point that balances the incomes above and below—deceptively high.*

## Variation

Knowing the value of an appropriate measure of central tendency can tell us a great deal. But it also helps to know how similar or diverse the scores are. Thus, Laura wonders: How much do my students vary from one another?

Averages derived from scores with low variability are more reliable than averages based on scores with high variability. If a basketball player scored between 13 and 17 points in each of her first 10 games in a season, we would be more confident that she would score near 15 points in her next game than if her scores had varied from 5 to 25 points.

The **range** of scores—the gap between the lowest and highest score—provides only a crude estimate of variation because just one extreme score in an otherwise uniform group will create a deceptively large range. The $695,000 income range in Laura's sample ($710,000–$15,000) is misleadingly large because all but the two high incomes range between $15,000 and $90,000.

The more standard measure of how much scores deviate from one another is the **standard deviation**. It better gauges whether scores are packed together or dispersed, because it uses information from each score. The standard deviation is important and not hard to compute: (1) calculate the difference, or deviation, between each score and the mean; (2) square these deviations; (3) find their average; and (4) find the square root of this average.

As an example, consider Peter, the punter on his college football team. To keep track of his progress, he records the distance of each of his punts. He does not trust his gut-level impression of how consistent his punting is. After his first football game, Peter therefore calculates the standard deviation for his four punts (Table A–2).

To grasp the meaning of this statistic, Peter would need to understand how scores tend to be distributed. In nature, large amounts of data—heights, weights, intelligence scores, grades, punt distances (though not incomes)—often form a roughly symmetrical, bell-shaped distribution. Most cases fall near the mean, and fewer cases fall near either extreme. This bell-shaped distribution is so typical that we call the curve it forms the **normal curve**.

As Figure A–3 shows, a useful property of the normal curve is that roughly 68 percent of the cases fall within 1 standard deviation on either side of the mean (in Peter's case, within 3.4 yards of his 40-yard average).

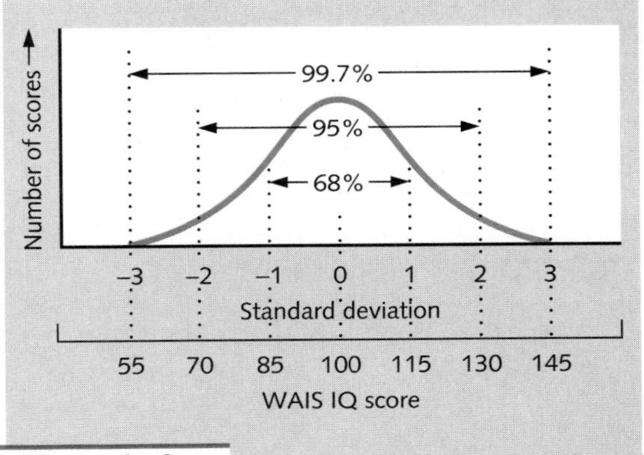


**Figure A–3**

**The Normal Curve** *Data often form a normal, or bell-shaped, curve in which 68 percent of the cases fall within 1 standard deviation of the mean and 95 percent fall within 2 standard deviations. For example, on an IQ test such as the WAIS, we assign the mean a value of 100 and 1 standard deviation we call 15 points; therefore 68 percent of the scores fall between 85 and 115, and 95 percent fall between 70 and 130.*

**Table A–2** **Standard Deviation**

| Punting Distance | Deviation From Mean (40 Yards) | Deviation Squared |
|---|---|---|
| 36 | −4 | 16 |
| 38 | −2 | 4 |
| 41 | +1 | 1 |
| 45 | +5 | 25 |
| **Mean = 160/4 = 40** | | **Sum of (deviations)² = 46** |

$$\text{Standard deviation} = \sqrt{\frac{\text{Sum of (deviations)}^2}{\text{Number of scores}}} = \sqrt{\frac{46}{4}} = 3.4 \text{ yards}$$

About 95 percent of cases fall within 2 standard deviations. Thus, Chapter 11, Intelligence, notes that about 68 percent of people taking an intelligence test will score within ±15 IQ points of 100. About 95 percent will score within ±30 points.

## Correlation

In this book we often ask how much two things relate: How closely related are the personality scores of identical twins? How well do intelligence test scores predict achievement? How often does stress lead to disease? To get a feel for whether one set of scores relates to a second set, we can display the data as a **scatterplot**. Figure A–4(*a*) depicts the actual relationship between SAT scores and college GPAs for Laura's 30 students. Each point on the graph represents these two numbers for one student. Figure A–4(*b*) is a scatterplot of the relationship between these students' precollege and college GPAs.

Figure A–4

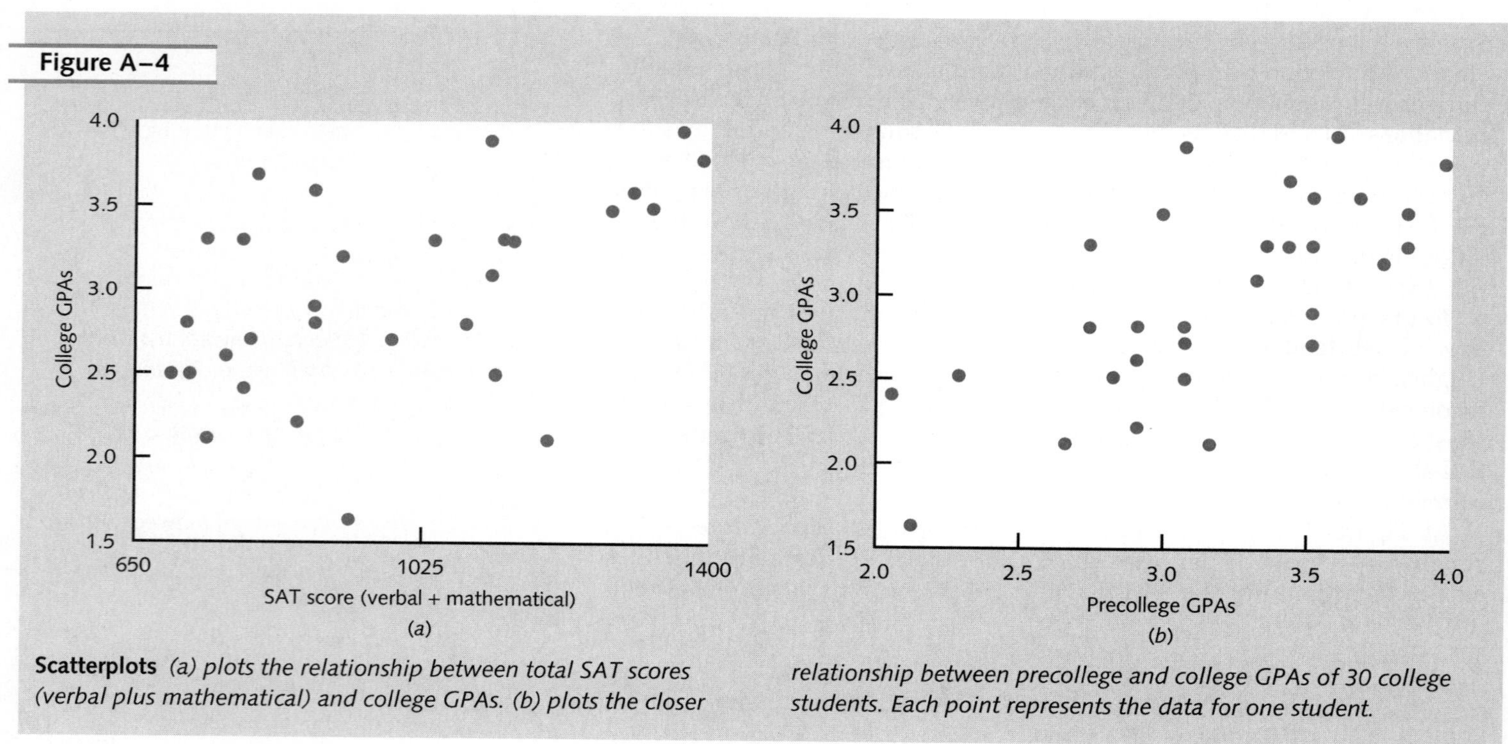


**Scatterplots** *(a) plots the relationship between total SAT scores (verbal plus mathematical) and college GPAs. (b) plots the closer relationship between precollege and college GPAs of 30 college students. Each point represents the data for one student.*

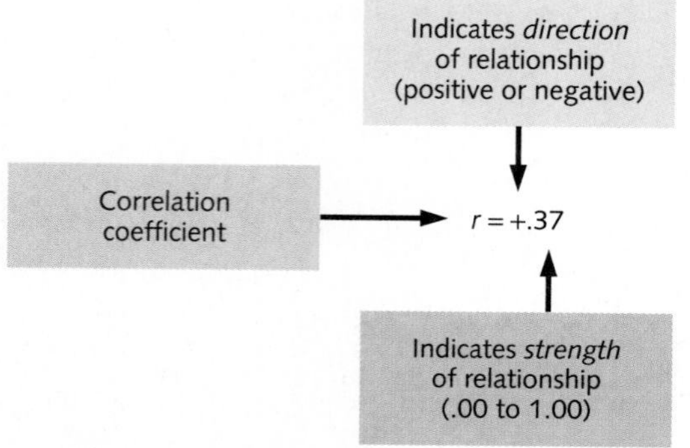


**How to Read a Correlation Coefficient**

The **correlation coefficient** is a statistical measure of how strongly related any two sets of scores are. It can range

from +1.00, which means that one set of scores increases in direct proportion to the other's increase

through 0.00, meaning that the scores are unrelated

to −1.00, which means that one set of scores goes up precisely as the other goes down.

(Note that a correlation's being negative has nothing to do with its strength or weakness; a negative correlation means two things relate inversely. A weak correlation, indicating little or no relationship, is one that has a coeffi-

Perfect positive correlation (+1.00)

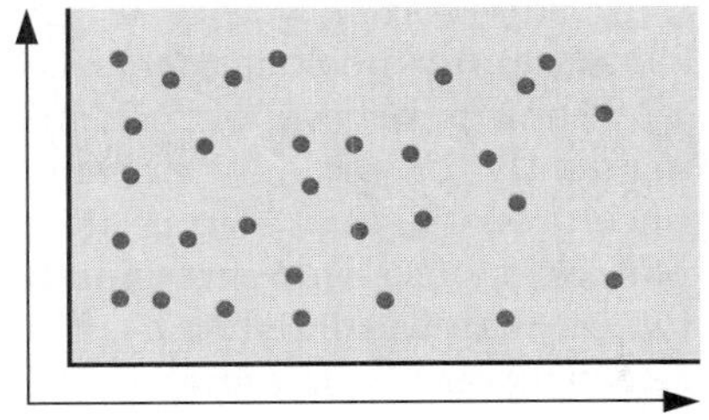
No relationship (0.00)

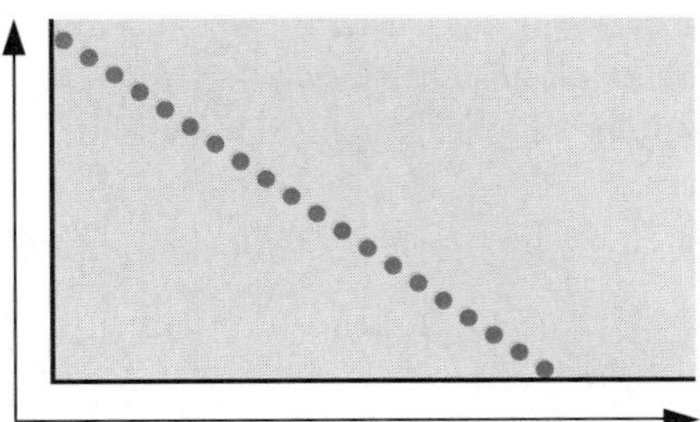
Perfect negative correlation (–1.00)

cient near zero.) Now look again at the scatterplots in Figure A–4. Do the correlations look positive or negative?

In each scatterplot in Figure A–4, the upward, oval-shaped slope of the cluster of points as one moves to the right shows that the two sets of scores tend to rise together. This means the correlations are positive: +.50 for the SAT–college GPA relationship shown in Figure A–4(*a*), and a stronger +.69 for the precollege GPA–college GPA relationship shown in Figure A–4(*b*). High SAT scores and, especially, high precollege grades predict high college grades. (The high school–college GPA relationship, incidentally, illustrates the common finding that the best predictor of people's future behavior is usually their behavior in similar situations in the past. The best predictor of future grades is past grades, which reflect both aptitude and motivation. Still, people do sometimes change.)

Statistics can help us see what the naked eye sometimes misses. To demonstrate this for yourself, try to discern what relationship, if any, exists between two sets of scores not yet organized into a scatterplot: Alessandra wonders whether men's heights correlate with their temperaments. She measures the heights of 20 men, has someone else independently assess their temperaments (from zero for extremely calm to 100 for highly reactive), and obtains the data in Table A–3.

With all the relevant data right in front of you, can you tell whether there is (1) a positive correlation between height and reactive temperament, (2) very little or no correlation, or (3) a negative correlation?

Comparing the columns in Table A–3, most people detect very little relationship between height and temperament. In fact, the correlation in this imaginary example is moderately positive, +.57, as you could see if you made a scatterplot of the data. If we fail to see a relationship when data are presented as systematically as in this table, how much less likely are we to notice them in everyday life? To see what is right in front of us, we sometimes need statistical illumination. People can easily see evidence of gender discrimination when given statistically summarized information about job level, seniority, performance, gender, and salary. But they often see no discrimination when the same information dribbles in, case by case (Twiss & others, 1989).

*The moral:* Although the correlation coefficient tells us nothing about cause and effect, it *can* help us see the world more clearly by revealing the actual extent to which two things relate.

Correlations not only make visible relationships that we might otherwise miss, they also restrain our "seeing" nonexistent relationships. As Chapter 1 explained, perceived correlation that does not really exist is an *illusory correlation*. When we *believe* there is a relationship between two things, we are likely to *notice* and *recall* instances that confirm our belief. If we believe that dreamt events are forecasts of actual events, we may notice and recall confirming instances more than disconfirming instances. The result is an illusory correlation.

**Table A–3 Height and Temperament of Twenty Men**

| Subject | Height in Inches | Temperament |
|---|---|---|
| 1 | 80 | 75 |
| 2 | 63 | 66 |
| 3 | 61 | 60 |
| 4 | 79 | 90 |
| 5 | 74 | 60 |
| 6 | 69 | 42 |
| 7 | 62 | 42 |
| 8 | 75 | 60 |
| 9 | 77 | 81 |
| 10 | 60 | 39 |
| 11 | 64 | 48 |
| 12 | 76 | 69 |
| 13 | 71 | 72 |
| 14 | 66 | 57 |
| 15 | 73 | 63 |
| 16 | 70 | 75 |
| 17 | 63 | 30 |
| 18 | 71 | 30 |
| 19 | 68 | 84 |
| 20 | 70 | 39 |

*"The real purpose of [the] scientific method is to make sure Nature hasn't misled you into thinking you know something that you actually don't."*

Robert Pirsig
*Zen and the Art of Motorcycle Maintenance*, 1974

Illusory correlations feed an *illusion of control*—that chance events are subject to our personal control. Gamblers, remembering their lucky rolls, may come to believe they can influence the roll of the dice by again throwing gently for low numbers and hard for high numbers. The illusion that uncontrollable events correlate with our actions is also fed by a statistical phenomenon called **regression toward the mean**. Average results are more typical than extreme results. Thus, after an unusual event, things tend to return toward their average level; extraordinary happenings tend to be followed by more ordinary ones.

Examples are abundant: Basketball players who make or miss all their shots in the first half of the game are likely to "regress" (fall back) to their more usual performance level during the second half. Students who score much lower or higher on an exam than they usually do are likely, when retested, to regress toward their average. Unusual ESP subjects who defy chance when first tested nearly always lose their "psychic powers" when retested (a phenomenon parapsychologists have called the "decline effect").

The point may seem obvious, yet we regularly miss it. Thus, we sometimes attribute what may be a normal statistical regression (the expected falling back to normal) to something we have done:

> After a sudden crime wave, the town council initiates a "stop crime" drive and the crime rate then returns to previous levels. The drive may therefore appear more successful than it was.
>
> Coaches who yell at their players after an unusually bad first half may feel rewarded for having done so when the team's performance improves (returns to normal) during the second half.
>
> Scientists who win a Nobel prize often have diminished accomplishments thereafter, leading some to wonder whether winning a Nobel hinders creativity.
>
> Some people also believe there is a "*Sports Illustrated* jinx"—that athletes whose peak performances get them on the cover of the magazine will then suffer a decline in their performance.

In each of these cases, it is possible that the effect is genuine. It is more likely, however, that these represent the natural tendency for behavior to regress from the unusual to the more usual.

Failure to recognize regression is the source of many superstitions and of some ineffective practices as well. When day-to-day behavior has a large element of chance fluctuation, we may notice that others' behavior improves (regresses toward average) after we criticize them for very bad performance, and that it worsens (regresses toward average) after we warmly praise them for an exceptionally fine performance. Ironically, then, regression toward the average can mislead us into feeling rewarded for having criticized others and into feeling punished for having praised them (Tversky & Kahneman, 1974).

*"Once you become sensitized to it, you see regression everywhere."*

Psychologist Daniel Kahneman (1985)

*The moral:* When a fluctuating behavior returns to normal, there is no need to invent fancy explanations for why it does. Regression toward the mean is probably at work.

## Statistical Inference

Data are "noisy." One group's average score (women's salaries) could conceivably differ from another's (men's salaries) not because of any real difference but merely due to chance fluctuation in the people sampled. So how confidently can we infer that an observed difference is reliable?

## When Is It Safe to Generalize From a Sample?

In deciding whether to generalize from our samples, three principles are worth keeping in mind. Let's look at each in turn.

**1. Representative Samples Are Better Than Biased Samples.** As Chapter 1 explained, the best basis for generalizing is not from the exceptional, memorable cases one finds at the extremes but from a representative sample of cases. No research involves a representative sample of the whole human population. Thus, it pays to keep in mind what population a study has sampled.

**2. Less-Variable Observations Are More Reliable Than Those That Are More Variable.** As we noted in the example of the basketball player whose scores were consistent, an average is more reliable when it comes from scores with low variability.

**3. More Cases Are Better Than Fewer.** I have seen it happen: An eager high school senior visits two college campuses, each for a day. At the first, the student randomly attends three classes and discovers each instructor to be witty and engaging. At the next campus, the three sampled instructors seem dull and uninspiring. Returning home, the student tells friends about the "great teachers" at the first school, and the "bores" at the second school. Again, we know it but we ignore it: Small samples provide less reliable estimates of the average than do large samples. The proportion of heads in samples of 10 coin tosses varies more than in samples of 100 tosses.

Said differently, *averages based on more cases are more reliable* (less variable) than averages based on only a few cases. Knowing this, answer a question posed by Christopher Jepson, David Krantz, and Richard Nisbett (1983) to University of Michigan introductory psychology students:

> The registrar's office at the University of Michigan has found that usually about 100 students in Arts and Sciences have a 4.00 GPA at the end of their first term at the University. However, only about 10–15 students graduate with a 4.00 GPA. What do you think is the most likely explanation for the fact that there are more 4.00 GPAs after one term than at graduation?

Most of the students came up with plausible causes for the drop in GPA, such as, "Students tend to work harder at the beginning of their college careers than toward the end." Fewer than a third recognized the statistical phenomenon clearly at work: Averages based on fewer courses are more variable, which guarantees a greater number of extremely low and high GPAs at the end of the first term.

*The moral:* Don't be overly impressed by a few anecdotes. Generalizations based on only a few cases are unreliable.

## When Is a Difference Significant?

We can have most confidence when generalizing from samples that (1) are representative of the population we wish to study, (2) give us consistent rather than highly variable data, and (3) are large rather than small. These principles extend to the inferences we make about differences between groups—as when we generalize from a gender difference in grades in our sample to the whole campus population.

Statistical tests help us decide by indicating the reliability of differences. You needn't understand how they are computed to understand the logic behind them: When *averages* from two samples are each *reliable* measures of their respective populations (as when each is based on many observations that have small variability), then the difference between the samples is likely to be reliable as well. When the *difference* between the averages for the two samples is *large*, we have even more confidence that the difference between them reflects a real difference in their populations.

In short, *when the sample averages are reliable and the difference between them is large*, we say the difference has **statistical significance**. This simply means that the difference probably reflects a real difference and is not due to chance variation between the samples. In judging statistical significance, psychologists are conservative. They are like judges who assume innocence unless guilt is proven, because they would rather risk setting a guilty person free than risk convicting an innocent person. For psychologists, proof beyond a reasonable doubt means not making much of a finding unless the odds of its occurring by chance are less than 5 percent (an arbitrary but agreed-upon criterion).

**PEANUTS**

PEANUTS reprinted by permission of UFS, Inc.

When reading about research, you should remember that, given large enough or homogeneous enough samples, a difference between them may be "statistically significant" yet have little practical significance. For example, when comparing the intelligence test scores among several hundred-thousand first-born and later-born individuals, there is a highly significant tendency for first-born individuals within a family to have higher average scores than their later-born siblings—but only by a single IQ point or two (Zajonc & Markus, 1975).

*The moral: Statistical significance* indicates the likelihood that a result will happen by chance. It does not indicate a result's importance.

## Summing Up

To be an educated person today is to be able to apply simple statistical principles to everyday reasoning. One needn't remember complicated formulas to think more clearly and critically about data.

From our consideration of how we can organize and describe data—by constructing distributions and computing measures of central tendency, variation, correlation, and statistical significance—we derived six practical morals for statistical reasoning:

1. When looking at statistical graphs in books and magazines and on TV ads and news broadcasts, think critically: Always read the scale labels and note their range.

2. Always note which measure of central tendency is reported, and consider: If it is a mean, could a few atypical scores be distorting it?
3. Although the correlation coefficient tells us nothing about cause and effect, it *can* help us see the world more clearly by revealing the actual extent to which two things relate.
4. When a fluctuating behavior returns to normal, there is no need to invent fancy explanations for why it does. Regression toward the mean is probably at work.
5. Don't be overly impressed by a few anecdotes. Generalizations based on only a few cases are unreliable.
6. Statistical significance indicates the likelihood that a result will happen by chance. It does not indicate a result's importance.

## Terms and Concepts to Remember

### Describing Data

**percentile rank** The percentage of the scores in a distribution that fall below a given score.

**mode** The most frequently occurring score in a distribution.

**mean** The arithmetic average of a distribution, obtained by adding the scores and then dividing by the number of scores.

**median** The middle score in a distribution; half the scores are above it and half are below it.

**range** The difference between the highest and lowest scores in a distribution.

**standard deviation** A measure of score variability; computed by (1) calculating the deviation of each score from the mean, (2) squaring those deviations, (3) finding their average, and (4) finding the square root of this average.

**normal curve** (or normal distribution) A symmetrical, bell-shaped curve that describes the distribution of many types of data; most scores fall near the mean (68 percent fall within 1 standard deviation of it) and fewer and fewer near the extremes.

**scatterplot** A graphed cluster of dots, each of which represents the values of two variables (such as a student's high school and college GPAs). The slope of the points suggests the degree and direction of the relationship between the two variables. (Also called a *scattergram* or *scatter diagram*.)

**correlation coefficient** A statistical measure of the extent to which two factors vary together and thus how well either factor predicts the other. Scores with a *positive correlation coefficient* go up and down together (as with high school and college GPAs). A *negative correlation coefficient* indicates that one score falls as the other rises (as in the relationship between self-esteem and depression).

**regression toward the mean** The tendency for extremes of unusual scores to fall back (regress) toward the average.

### Statistical Inference

**statistical significance** A statistical statement of how likely it is that an obtained result occurred by chance.

# Sample Answers to Critical Thinking Exercises

Most psychology courses have two major goals: (1) to help you acquire a basic understanding of psychology's knowledge base, and (2) to help you learn to think like a psychologist. The second goal—learning to think like a psychologist—involves critical thinking. Critical thinking can be regarded as a special set of "thinking skills that promote conscious, purposeful, and active involvement of the thinker with new ideas" (Halonen, 1994). Included among these skills are careful observation, asking questions, seeing connections among ideas, and the ability to analyze arguments and the evidence on which they are based.

The critical thinking exercises in this textbook have been designed to help you develop your ability to think critically as you learn about psychology.[1] Each exercise emphasizes one of six categories of critical thinking: *pattern recognition, practical problem solving, creative problem solving, scientific problem solving, psychological reasoning,* and *perspective taking.*

As the foundation for all other forms of critical thinking, *pattern recognition* is the ability to use psychological concepts to describe behavior patterns and events, especially when there are discrepancies between your expectations of what is normal in a certain situation and what actually occurs.

When events or behavior are unexpected, they may constitute a problem. *Practical problem solving* is the ability to use psychological concepts to develop a plan of action that will lead to the problem's solution.

*Creative problem solving* is the ability to make novel connections between previously unrelated ideas. This type of critical thinking often leads to new insights about behavior and mental phenomena.

Psychologists employ the scientific method to develop comprehensive and systematic explanations of behavior and mental phenomena. At the heart of this is *scientific problem solving,* which seeks to uncover relationships among the many factors, or variables, involved in producing behavior.

Psychological information is transmitted through persuasive arguments that state a relationship between some aspect of behavior, such as intelligence, and another factor, such as age. *Psychological reasoning* is thinking critically about such arguments, especially the evidence on which they are based.

The final category of critical thinking is *perspective taking,* which refers to the ability to recognize the ways in which each person's thinking is shaped by his or her values and past experiences.

You should now be ready to expand your critical thinking skills by completing the exercises prepared for each chapter of your textbook. For some chapters, the exercise presents a hypothetical situation that you will need to think through. For others, you will be asked to evaluate arguments that are derived from actual psychological research. And for still other chapters, your understanding of psychological concepts will be tested by asking you to apply them to a new situation. Carefully read the passage for each exercise and then answer the questions that follow.

Polish your critical thinking skills by applying them to each of your college courses, and to other aspects of life as well. Learn to think critically about advertising, political speeches, and the material presented in popular periodicals.

CHAPTER **1**

## Thinking Critically With Psychological Science

### Scientific Problem Solving

1. *Focal behavior:* Reading ability among first graders.
2. *Hypothesis*: Children who watch *Sesame Street* develop greater reading ability than children who watch cartoons.
3. *Independent variable*: Type of television program (educational versus cartoon).
4. *Dependent variable*: Reading test score.

[1] The model for these exercises comes from J. S. Halonen (1994), *Critical thinking companion for introductory psychology*. New York: Worth Publishers, Inc.

5. *Controlled variables*:
   (a) Television program content (educational versus non-educational) during the daily, 1-hour period of exposure.
   (b) Ages of subjects.
   (c) Reading ability measured over the same time period.
6. *Uncontrolled variables*:
   (a) Absence of random assignment leaves alternative explanations for reading improvement in the educational television group. As volunteers, the *Sesame Street* subjects may have been more highly motivated to have their children succeed in reading than the cartoon subjects, who were drafted.
   (b) Reading ability of subjects in the two groups was not measured *before* the experiment began. At the outset, the *Sesame Street* subjects may have had higher reading scores than the cartoon subjects.
   (c) Knowledge of the teacher's hypothesis (by both students and their parents) may have influenced the results so that the experimental group outperformed the control group.
   (d) Other daily activities, such as reading to parents or watching other television programs, might have differentially influenced the reading skills in the two groups.
7. *Valid test of hypothesis*? No. Since so many variables were not controlled, virtually nothing can be concluded from this study. A more valid test would have *randomly assigned* volunteers, who were *not informed* of the teacher's hypothesis and who had been pretested and matched for comparable reading ability to the two groups.

CHAPTER **2**

## Neuroscience and Behavior

### Pattern Recognition

| Lower Level Brain Structures | How the Structures Are Involved in Musical Performance |
|---|---|
| Medulla | This structure controls heartbeat, breathing, and other vital systems that keep the musician's body functioning while he or she plays. |
| Thalamus | By routing sensory information from the musician's eyes, ears, and fingertips to higher brain regions, this structure facilitates the musician's seeing, hearing, touching, decision making, and coordination. |
| Reticular formation | By helping to control arousal, this structure is crucial in maintaining the musician's attention to the task. |
| Hippocampus | This structure is involved in the formation of memories for musical theory, as well as of memories of how to play the musical instrument. |
| Cerebellum | This structure helps coordinate movements involved in playing the instrument. |

| Upper Level Brain Structures | How the Structures Are Involved in Musical Performance |
|---|---|
| Motor cortex | This area is involved in organizing the body movements necessary for playing the instrument. |
| Sensory cortex | This area is involved in processing incoming sensory information from the musician's fingertips. |
| Association areas | These areas are involved in the planning and decision making inherent in reading music and playing the instrument. |
| Corpus callosum | This area is involved in combining information processed by the left and right hemispheres so that the performance reflects the integrated activity of both sides of the brain. |

CHAPTER **3**

## The Developing Child

### Perspective Taking

1. *Eighteen-month-old child's experience of the world*: During Piaget's sensorimotor stage children understand the world through their senses and actions.
2. *Appropriate activities*: This age group would be most stimulated by a variety of visually interesting toys that foster stacking, banging, rolling, and fitting things together.
3. *Five-year-old-child's experience of the world*: During Piaget's preoperational stage, children understand the world through pretend play that typically is egocentric.
4. *Appropriate activities*: Preoperational children would enjoy activities that are based on pretend play. Dress-up and make-believe games of "go-to-work" and "school" would be appropriate.
5. *Eight-year-old child's experience of the world*: During Piaget's concrete operational stage, children reason logically about concrete events.
6. *Appropriate activities*: Arithmetic games, card games, and other activities based on logical thinking about concrete events would be appropriate activities for this age group.
7. *Twelve-year-old child's experience of the world*: Youngsters who are on the threshold of formal operational thinking reason abstractly about events in their lives.
8. *Appropriate activities*: Problem-solving activities, "whodunnit?" games and role-playing games based on hypothetical propositions and deductive reasoning would be stimulating activities for this age group.

CHAPTER 4

## Adolescence and Adulthood

### Psychological Reasoning

1. Mary's argument is that her father is suffering from Alzheimer's disease, which is causing his memory lapse occasionally and his thinking to be uncharacteristically slow.
2. The evidence for Mary's argument comes from her daily observations of her father's behavior and the memory "experiment" she conducted.
3. Mary's evidence in not trustworthy for at least three reasons. *First*, informal observations of this type are subjective and unreliable. Since she recently read an article on Alzheimer's disease, Mary may be looking too hard for symptoms of this disorder. Her expectations may bias her observations. *Second*, Mary is comparing her father's performance on the memory "experiment" only with her recollection of his former quick thinking and excellent memory. To be a valid test, Mary would need to have actual data on how her father would have performed on this test *before* he began to display the memory symptoms that are the basis for her concern. *Third*, even if Bentley's thinking ability has changed recently, the cause of the change has not been pinpointed. True experiments rule out the potential effects of other variables. It may be that Bentley's uncharacteristically poor performance is the result of his generally poor health, the medication he is taking for his muscle tremors (which is known to produce Alzheimer's-like symptoms), or his lack of physical and intellectual stimulation since retiring.

(By the way, the answer to Mary's brain teaser—an expanding alphabetical sequence—is *m*.)

CHAPTER 5

## Sensation

### Psychological Reasoning

1. Several assertions are made: (1) There is an unconscious component of the mind; (2) the unconscious mind is capable of perceiving stimuli that are below the threshold of conscious awareness; (3) subliminal stimuli have motivational power; and (4) subliminal suggestions can persuade a person to quit smoking.
2. The evidence is Carlos's expressed preference for a stimulus (the triangle) to which he had been repeatedly exposed. The evidence is not trustworthy for several reasons. For one, it assumes that Carlos had no initial preference for one geometric form over another. In the absence of some sort of preference pretest, there is no basis to conclude that the subliminal stimulus presentations directly caused his choice of the triangle. Second, the demonstration was based on *visual* stimuli, but the smoking cessation program is based on *auditory* suggestions. There is no evidence that the audio stimuli will be as persuasive as visual stimuli. Moreover, the triangle preference is a trivial choice—probably easier to influence than the drive for nicotine.
3. "Subliminal" merely means that a stimulus is *below* the intensity at which it can be detected half the time. Since Carlos was aware of flashes of light, he may actually have detected the triangle presentations at least part of the time. Thus, his preference for the triangle was not necessarily the result of *unconscious* thought processes, but simply the result of repeated exposure to a specific stimulus. For this reason, it is unnecessary to assume that subliminal visual (or audio) stimuli have an irresistible power to motivate or persuade.

CHAPTER 6

## Perception

### Practical Problem Solving

*Figure-ground*: This principle of grouping permits the air controller to distinguish the airplane from its background. Whenever an airplane (the figure) is recognized against the surroundings of the sky or radar screen (the ground), this principle is illustrated.

*Relative size*: This monocular cue allows the air controller to estimate the distance between airplanes that appear on the horizon or radar screen. When two airplanes that are known to be the same size appear, the one that produces the larger image is perceived as nearer.

*Continuity*: This grouping principle enables the air controller to perceive smooth, continuous patterns. This principle is illustrated whenever the air controller determines the particular angle, or trajectory, of an airplane from successively appearing blips on the radar screen and distinguishes this trajectory from that of other airplanes.

*Relative height*: This monocular cue provides the air controller with additional information about the distance of an airplane from the airport. The higher an airplane appears on the radar screen or in the sky, the greater its distance.

CHAPTER 7

## States of Consciousness

### Scientific Problem Solving

1. The research is not trustworthy for several reasons. First, Geraldo's belief in the power of hypnosis prevents him from being an objective and unbiased experimenter. His

expectations of what people will do when hypnotized could bias the outcome of his "experiment." Second, enrollment in a hypnosis course signifies belief in its effectiveness. So the beliefs of the "volunteers" could also affect the outcome. Finally, because there is no control group of fully conscious subjects who are given the same suggestions as the hypnotized volunteers, this is not a true experiment.

2. Geraldo's explanation for the subjects' childlike behavior is that hypnosis allows subjects to "relive" earlier experiences. Posthypnotic amnesia is explained as due to the power of hypnosis to erase memories from the brain.
3. The explanation does not prove that hypnosis involves a unique state of consciousness, nor does it rule out alternative explanations for the hypnotized subjects' behavior. Perhaps the behaviors attributed to age regression and posthypnotic amnesia could be induced in fully conscious subjects.
4. An alternative explanation is that hypnotic phenomena may be nothing more than the workings of normal consciousness. It is possible that the "hypnotized" people were merely acting the role of "good hypnotic subjects" as they confirmed the hypnotist's, and their own, beliefs about hypnotic behavior.
5. A more valid test of hypnosis would control for the possibility that the subjects' and the hypnotist's beliefs could influence the results. One way of doing so would be to pre-test volunteers by asking them whether they believe that hypnosis "works" and whether it involves a unique state of consciousness. "Believers" and "nonbelievers" would then undergo hypnosis. Another more valid test would compare the suggestibility of unhypnotized subjects with that of hypnotized subjects given the same "hypnotic suggestions."

CHAPTER **8**

## Learning

### Pattern Recognition

1. For children who learn to wake up without special training, the sensation of a wet bed or diaper functions as a UCS that elicits awakening, which is the UCR. Bladder tension (unless painful) is an initially neutral stimulus that becomes associated with the UCS. Over time, bladder tension becomes a CS and will cause the child to awaken before the bed or diaper is wet. This learned awakening is the CR.
2. For children who are trained with the special sheet and bell, the UCS is the bell that causes them to wake up; the UCR is waking up in response to the bell; the CS is bladder tension; and the CR is waking up in response to bladder tension.
3. Although the classical conditioning explanation for this example makes sense based on the evidence, an explanation based on operant conditioning is also possible. Although in very young children waking up is normally a reflexive act (and therefore subject to classical conditioning), in older children it might be considered a *voluntary* act and (therefore subject to operant conditioning). Children may learn to wake up because this behavior *operates* on the environment to produce rewarding stimuli, such as the pleasurable sensation of relieving one's bladder.

CHAPTER **9**

## Memory

### Practical Problem Solving

1. The police, who for whatever reason are convinced that Raymond committed the crime, are attempting to obtain solid evidence by jogging Danny's eyewitness memory.
2. Danny was probably initially unable to identify the gunman because the fleeting glimpse did not allow him to encode the details of his appearance. The confusion of the moment may also have prevented Danny from rehearsing his mental image of the perpetrator so that his memory quickly decayed. Moreover, seeing hundreds of mug book photographs so soon after the crime could have retroactively interfered with whatever real memory Danny had of the gunman's appearance. Finally, the mug book may not actually have contained the gunman's photograph.
3. The misleading questioning and repeated exposure to Raymond's photograph may have caused Danny to misremember the actual event and to reconstruct his memory of it to include Raymond's involvement. Seeing the line-up of men several weeks later, Danny may have been unable to discriminate his eyewitness memory from his memory of the mug book photographs. This would also account for Danny's new-found confidence in the accuracy of his memory.

CHAPTER **10**

## Thinking and Language

### Perspective Taking

1. *Position supported*: B. F. Skinner
   *Explanation*: Marie's utterances can be explained by three principles of learning: *imitation*, *association*, and *reinforcement*. The first time she said "cow," she may merely have been imitating her mother's utterance. The fact that she later spontaneously identified a cow indicates that she had formed an association between the picture and word, and had been reinforced (by her mother's praise) for demonstrating her new knowledge.

2. *Position supported*: Noam Chomsky
*Explanation*: Jack's grammatical error ("goed") is an example of overgeneralizing a grammatical rule (adding *-ed* to form the past tense of a regular verb). Because it is unlikely that Jack has ever heard his parents or teacher make this error, principles of learning cannot explain this utterance. Because all children make this type of error, the existence of a common underlying biological language acquisition device is implicated.
3. *Position supported*: B. F. Skinner
*Explanation*: Nicole's deficiency in signing demonstrates the impact of early experience in language development.
4. *Position supported*: Noam Chomsky
*Explanation*: Because Malcolm and Maya have presumably been exposed to English for the same number of years, principles of learning cannot explain the difference in their fluency. Chomsky would say that Maya was exposed to English too late in life for her inborn "language acquisition device" to fully benefit.

CHAPTER **11**

## Intelligence

### Creative Problem Solving

1. Carlton considers intelligence to be a measurable general mental capacity that forms the basis for all cognitive skills. His "intelligence test," however, only measures a collection of proofreading skills.
2. Although Carlton believes that intelligence is a single, *general* entity, he has created a test that taps a collection of *specific* abilities. Moreover, some of these abilities (such as spelling) may have little to do with intelligence. Carlton's problem is that he's confusing general intelligence with aptitude for an everyday task.
3. Carlton would be well advised to test potential employees on the actual skills they will be required to use in their jobs (or their aptitude for learning these skills). The first step would be to identify specific skills for *each job category* and then to devise separate, specialized tests. A test for potential managers, for example, might be based on *practical intelligence* skills such as how to motivate people, when to delegate tasks, and how to write effective memos. Those whose job it is to find new topics for publication might be tested for skills involving *creative intelligence*. His proofreading test might work quite well for potential copy editors.

CHAPTER **12**

## Motivation

### Pattern Recognition

1. Assuming that Rochelle and Doreen have roughly equal ability, there must be another explanation for the difference in their school performance. Doreen's high grades, her motivation to select moderately challenging classes where success is attainable yet attributable to her own efforts, and her desire to do *her* best rather than compare herself to others point to a high level of achievement motivation. Rochelle's preference for very easy or very difficult tasks is typical of people with a lower need for achievement. In such situations, failure is either unlikely or unembarrassing because it is attributable to the impossibility of the task rather than the individual's performance. Because birth order correlates with achievement, parental influences may help explain why first-born Doreen apparently has higher achievement motivation than Rochelle. It is possible that Doreen received more attention and encouragement from her parents than did later-born Rochelle.
2. Initially, practicing the guitar was its own reward for Doreen; extrinsic rewards were unnecessary. The monetary reward her parents later provided may have *overjustified* guitar playing, turning it into a form of work and lessening Doreen's intrinsic enjoyment and, thus, her motivation for practicing. Rochelle's primary motive for learning the guitar apparently involved competing with her sister. This is an example of extrinsic motivation rather than motivation to master a skill for its own sake. The monetary reward offered by her parents provided an additional extrinsic incentive, to which Rochelle responded by increasing her practice time. When Doreen began to lose interest in practicing and the monetary reward was withdrawn, the extrinsic basis for Rochelle's motivation was lost. As a result Rochelle lost interest in playing the guitar.
3. The parents would be wise to recognize the different levels of achievement motivation in their daughters and to individualize their treatment in order to capitalize on this difference. As an independent "self-starter," Doreen will probably respond more to rewards that are informative rather than controlling. Praise and encouragement rather than extrinsic rewards will be more effective in boosting Doreen's feelings of competence and intrinsic motivation. For Rochelle, the parents first need to clarify their goal. If they want to do everything in their power to improve Rochelle's proficiency on the guitar, they might capitalize on her competitiveness by placing her in group classes where comparisons with others are inevitable. If they want to cultivate intrinsic motivation, they would do well to encourage greater independence

in Rochelle by challenging her to reach her own potential as a musician and frequently praising her for her successes.

CHAPTER 13
## Emotion

### Scientific Problem Solving

1. The James-Lange theory proposes that the experience of emotion derives from our awareness of our physiological responses to emotion-arousing stimuli. It also equates different emotions with specific body states. Assuming that sexual excitement can be triggered by the physical changes induced by exercise, this theory would predict greater reported feelings of sexual excitement during the first two phases of exercise recovery, when the subjects were actually physically aroused, than during the third phase, when the subjects were no longer aroused. The fact that sexual excitement was low during the first phase of recovery, when physical arousal was high, seems to conflict with the theory.
2. The Cannon-Bard theory proposes that an emotion-arousing stimulus simultaneously triggers physical arousal and the subjective experience of emotion. Assuming that the film was an emotion-arousing stimulus, this theory would predict greater reported feelings of sexual excitement during all three phases of the experiment because subjects viewed the film in each phase. However, this explanation is inconsistent with the finding that subjects reported being sexually excited only during the second phase of the experiment. The theory offers no explanation of why the emotional experiences of subjects during phases one and two differed.
3. According to Schachter's two-factor theory, to experience an emotion one must be physically aroused and cognitively label that arousal as an emotion. Of the three theories, this one seems to explain the results of the experiment most fully. During the first phase, subjects were physically aroused, and a potential "emotional" explanation for their arousal (the film) was available. Because they *perceived* that they were still aroused from the exercise, however, subjects during this phase attributed their arousal to the exercise rather than to sexual excitement. By the third phase, the subjects had fully recovered from the exercise and lacked the physical arousal necessary to trigger the emotion-attribution process. In phase two, the subjects were physically aroused but did not subjectively perceive this arousal. According to the two-factor theory, this unexplained arousal was therefore attributed to sexual excitement from the film.

CHAPTER 14
## Personality

### Perspective Taking

1. A psychoanalyst might explain Darren's problems as being rooted in unresolved childhood conflicts. His sarcastic manner might indicate that he was orally overindulged as a child and is fixated in the oral stage of psychosexual development. A psychoanalyst might also say that Darren's ego is attempting to defend itself from anxiety by offering a self-justifying explanation for his poor performance on the exam ("the test was unfair") in place of the real, more threatening reason for failure ("I was unprepared").
2. A trait theorist would probably describe Darren's personality in terms of characteristic behaviors and motives. According to the "big five" personality factors, for example, Darren might be described as anxious and self-pitying (emotional stability), sober and reserved (extraversion), suspicious and undisciplined (agreeableness and conscientiousness, respectively).
3. A humanistic theorist might explain Darren's pessimism and sarcastic manner as the result of low self-esteem and perhaps not having his basic needs met as his personality was formed. Humanistic theorists might also suggest that Darren has a negative self-concept because his ideal self (a successful college student) differs from his actual self (an academic failure). His unwillingness to accept responsibility for his failure might be described as a self-serving bias.
4. A social-cognitive theorist would probably point to the reciprocal influences among Darren's past behavior, internal personal factors, and external experiences in shaping his personality. His anxiety and unwillingness to accept responsibility for failure suggest that he perceives the world as threatening, and himself as being controlled by his environment. Darren's hopeless attitude and external locus of control may have resulted from repeated experiences with undesirable events over which he had no control.

CHAPTER 15
## Psychological Disorders

### Perspective Taking

1. Phyllis's daughter should be more concerned; she may by wrongly attributing to old age what is really psychologically disordered behavior. Phyllis's behavior satisfies at least three of the criteria for such a label: it is atypical, disturbing, and maladaptive. Furthermore, although triggered by the stress of her divorce, her symptoms

have persisted too long and are too extreme to be considered a normal, justifiable response to a stressful event. Phyllis's daughter is also misinterpreting the biological evidence: The grandmother's similar symptoms and the effectiveness of antidepressant medication are further evidence for a psychological disorder.

2. A clinical psychologist would argue that Phyllis is showing classic symptoms of *major depressive disorder*, including poor appetite, insomnia, lethargy, feelings of worthlessness, and loss of interest in family and friends. He or she would also point out that these symptoms have persisted much longer than would normally be expected following a stressful event.

3. (a) Psychoanalysts would attribute Phyllis's behavior to early childhood experiences and unconscious impulses. They might seek evidence of troubling losses in childhood, for example, and then argue that the divorce evoked feelings associated with these losses.
(b) A biologically-oriented therapist would cite two pieces of evidence: (1) Since her mother seems to have suffered depression in late middle age, Phyllis may have a genetic predisposition to this condition; and (2) the fact that an antidepressant drug made her feel less depressed suggests Phyllis's depression may be caused by a biochemical imbalance.
(c) From the social-cognitive perspective, Phyllis's depression is fueled by a vicious cycle of overgeneralized, self-focused, negative thinking. She has explained a stressful experience (her divorce) in terms that are *stable* and *global* ("Everything I have ever done, or will do, is worthless") and *internal* ("The divorce is my fault"). The hopelessness resulting from these self-blaming attributions has elicited social rejection, hampered her behavior, and is likely to lead to further negative experiences.

CHAPTER **16**

## Therapy

### Practical Problem Solving

1. There are several possible reasons why psychotherapy was apparently effective for Deborah, but not for Vincent. One is that cognitive therapies, such as Deborah's, have proven most successful in treating depression. Behavior therapies, such as the counterconditioning Vincent experienced, have proven to be more effective in treating specific behavior problems, such as phobias, compulsions, or sexual dysfunctions. A second reason is that Deborah actively sought and entered therapy at a time of personal crisis, while Vincent felt that there was nothing unusual about his behavior or attitude. Deborah's depression may have lifted partly as a result of the passage of time and the lessening of the crisis. A third reason is that Deborah chose her therapist carefully, and she worked with someone who offered her hope that things would improve. Vincent picked his therapist randomly, maintained a skeptical attitude throughout therapy, and never admitted he needed help. Thus, Deborah's belief in her treatment could have created a powerful placebo effect that harnessed her own healing powers and led to improvement. Finally, Deborah invested considerably more time and money in her therapy than Vincent did. This would probably result in a stronger need to justify the therapy and, thus, a more favorable evaluation of its effectiveness.

2. Clients' perceptions of the effectiveness of psychotherapy are not acceptable as scientific evidence. One reason is that people who are suffering nonpsychotic disorders often improve whether or not they receive treatment. Psychotherapy clients who would have improved anyway might misattribute their improvement to therapy. Furthermore, people who go into therapy with the expectation that it will be effective may fall victim to the confirmation bias and remember only information that confirms their expectation.

CHAPTER **17**

## Stress and Health

### Practical Problem Solving

1. Since her parents are both obese, it is likely that Janet inherited a genetic predisposition toward obesity and possibly a lower metabolic rate than Sheila. Janet may also have a higher body weight set point than Sheila.

2. Because her parents are of normal weight, it is likely that Sheila herself is genetically predisposed to be of normal body weight. It is also likely that Sheila has a lower body weight set point and a higher metabolic rate than Janet.

3. The diet Janet and Sheila chose was effective, but more effective for Sheila due to her genetic background. Janet, like her parents, is overweight, so it is likely that her body has a higher percentage of fat than does Sheila's. Because fat tissue has a low metabolic rate (and therefore takes less food energy than other tissues to maintain), Janet's body probably requires fewer calories to maintain its weight than does Sheila's. There is no reason to believe that Janet cheated on her diet for lack of willpower. Those genetically predisposed to obesity can eat the same foods, do the same amount of exercising, and still not lose weight as easily as those of normal body weight.

CHAPTER 18

## Social Psychology

### Pattern Recognition

1. Several principles of social psychology help explain why Mary and Kathy became friends. Through the *mere exposure effect*, their proximity in the dormitory would have encouraged their friendship. Their similarity in attitudes, beliefs, interests, and education probably helped cement their fondness for each other.

2. The strongest factor in the disintegration of Mary and Kathy's friendship was probably the social influence of Kathy's sorority on her attitudes and behavior. Being a sorority sister created a *role* with specific *norms* that Kathy strived to adopt. This role included an expectation that she would harbor prejudiced attitudes toward minority groups. Although Kathy was initially troubled by these attitudes, she experienced *normative social influence* as her desire to win approval of her sorority sisters created pressure to conform to their expectations. Over time the hateful attitudes became more acceptable (through *mere exposure*), and Kathy found herself going along with the group—feeling more and more comfortable in her new role. Kathy probably also experienced *cognitive dissonance* when she first joined the sorority, as her beliefs and actions conflicted.

CHAPTER 19

## Diversity and Community

### Pattern Recognition

1. If, like many people, you found it more difficult to generate descriptions of outgroups, this may be the result of your relatively limited contact with members of such groups.

2. If your ingroup descriptions were more favorable than your outgroup descriptions, you may be expressing a tendency to favor one's own group, called the *ingroup bias*.

3. When 50 college students were asked to describe each of these groups, their top five descriptions were as follows:

   *Physicians*: (1) intelligent/smart; (2) caring/understanding/compassionate; (3) wealthy/rich; (4) busy/hardworking; (5) well-educated
   *Athletes*: (1) athletic/fit/strong; (2) driven/highly motivated/dedicated; (3) competitive; (4) agile/quick; (5) glorified/famous/popular and egotistical/ proud
   *Artists*: (1) creative; (2) bizarre/strange; (3) free-spirited/nonconforming/individualistic; (4) liberal/tolerant/ openminded; (5) talented/gifted
   *Vegetarians*: (1) healthy/health-conscious; (2) environmentally or ecologically conscious; (3) limited in diet/picky about food; (4) caring/sensitive; (5) liberal
   *College students*: (1) fun/wild/exciting; (2) stressed/pressured/fatigued; (3) intelligent/bright; (4) diligent/dedicated/studious; (5) poor/broke and openminded/tolerant/liberal
   *Lawyers*: (1) articulate/convincing/persuasive; (2) deceptive/dishonest; (3) wealthy/rich; (4) intelligent/smart; (5) strong-willed/powerful and ambitious/success-oriented

If your outgroup descriptions match better with the above than your ingroup descriptions, it may reflect the human tendency to form stereotyped beliefs in order to simplify the world. In categorizing people into groups, we see the members of the outgroup as all alike, whereas the members of the ingroup are viewed as much more diverse.

# Glossary

**absolute threshold** The minimum stimulation needed to detect a particular stimulus. (p. 153)

**accommodation** 1. Adapting one's current understandings (schemas) to incorporate new information. (p. 89) 2. The process by which the eye's lens changes shape to focus the image of near objects on the retina. (p. 159)

**acetylcholine** [ah-seat-el-KO-leen] **(ACh)** A neurotransmitter that, among its functions, triggers muscle contraction. (p. 46)

**achievement motivation** A desire for significant accomplishment: for mastery of things, people, or ideas; for attaining a high standard. (p. 419)

**achievement tests** Tests designed to assess what a person has learned. (p. 363)

**acoustic encoding** The encoding of sound, especially the sound of words. (p. 294)

**acquisition** The initial stage of learning, during which a response is established and gradually strengthened. In classical conditioning, the phase in which a stimulus comes to evoke a conditioned response. In operant conditioning, the strengthening of a reinforced response. (p. 261)

**action potential** A neural impulse; a brief electrical charge that travels down an axon. The action potential is generated by the movement of positively charged atoms in and out of channels in the axon's membrane. (p. 43)

**active listening** Empathic listening in which the listener echoes, restates, and clarifies. A feature of Rogers's person-centered therapy. (p. 544)

**adaptation-level phenomenon** Our tendency to form judgments (of sounds, of lights, of income) to be relative to a "neutral" level defined by our prior experience. (p. 451)

**adolescence** The transition period from childhood to adulthood, extending from puberty to independence. (p. 117)

**adrenal** [ah-DREEN-el] **glands** A pair of endocrine glands just above the kidneys. The adrenals secrete the hormones epinephrine (adrenaline) and norepinephrine (noradrenaline), which help to arouse the body in times of stress. (p. 52)

**aerobic exercise** Sustained exercise that increases heart and lung fitness; may also alleviate depression and anxiety. (p. 593)

**age regression** In hypnosis, the supposed reliving of earlier experiences, such as in early childhood; greatly susceptible to false recollections. (p. 235)

**aggression** Any physical or verbal behavior intended to hurt or destroy. (p. 631)

**algorithm** A methodical, logical rule or procedure that guarantees solving a particular problem. May be contrasted with the usually speedier but also more error-prone use of *heuristics.* (p. 327)

**alpha waves** The relatively slow brain waves of a relaxed, awake state. (p. 223)

**altruism** Unselfish regard for the welfare of others. (p. 640)

**Alzheimer's disease** A progressive and irreversible brain disorder characterized by gradual deterioration of memory, reasoning, language, and, finally, physical functioning. (p. 133)

**amnesia** Loss of memory. Psychogenic amnesia, a dissociative disorder, is selective memory loss often brought on by extreme stress. (p. 511)

**amphetamines** Drugs that stimulate neural activity, causing speeded-up body functions and associated energy and mood changes. (p. 243)

**amygdala** [ah-MIG-dah-la] Two almond-shaped neural centers in the limbic system that are linked to emotion. (p. 57)

**anal stage** The second of Freud's psychosexual stages, from about 18 months to 3 years, during which pleasure focuses on bowel and bladder elimination, retention, and control. (p. 464)

**anorexia nervosa** An eating disorder in which a normal-weight person (usually an adolescent female) diets and becomes significantly (15 percent or more) underweight, yet, still feeling fat, continues to starve. (p. 406)

**antisocial personality** A personality disorder in which the person (usually a man) exhibits a lack of conscience for wrongdoing, even toward friends and family members. May be aggressive and ruthless or a clever con artist. (p. 530)

**anxiety disorders** Psychological disorders characterized by distressing, persistent anxiety or maladaptive behaviors that reduce anxiety. See *generalized anxiety disorder, obsessive-compulsive disorder, panic attack,* and *phobic disorder*. (p. 505)

**aphasia** Impairment of language, usually caused by left hemisphere damage either to Broca's area (impairing speaking) or to Wernicke's area (impairing understanding). (p. 63)

**applied research** Scientific study that aims to solve practical problems. (p. 6)

**aptitude tests** Tests designed to predict a person's future performance; aptitude is the capacity to learn. (p. 363)

**artificial intelligence (AI)** The science of designing and programming computer systems to do intelligent things and to simulate human thought processes such as intuitive reasoning, learning, and understanding language. Includes practical applications (chess playing, industrial robots, expert systems) and efforts to model human thinking inspired by our current understanding of how the brain works. (p. 339)

**assimilation** Interpreting one's new experience in terms of one's existing schemas. (p. 88)

**association areas** Areas of the cerebral cortex that are not involved in primary motor or sensory functions; rather, they are involved in higher mental functions such as learning, remembering, thinking, and speaking. (p. 62)

**associative learning** Learning that certain events occur together. The events may be two stimuli (as in classical conditioning) or a response and a rewarding or punishing stimulus (as in operant conditioning). (p. 258)

**attachment** An emotional tie with another person; shown in young children by their seeking closeness to the caregiver and showing distress on separation. (p. 96)

**attitude** A belief and feeling that predisposes one to respond in a particular way to objects, people, and events. (p. 615)

**attribution theory** The theory that we tend to give a causal explanation for someone's behavior, often by crediting either the situation or the person's disposition. (p. 613)

**audition** The sense of hearing. (p. 168)

**automatic processing** Unconscious encoding of incidental information, such as space, time, and frequency, and of well-learned information, such as word meanings. (p. 290)

**autonomic** [aw-tuh-NAHM-ik] **nervous system** The part of the peripheral nervous system that controls the glands and the muscles of the internal organs (such as the heart). Its sympathetic division arouses; its parasympathetic division calms. (p. 48)

**availability heuristic** A rule of thumb for estimating the likelihood of events based on their availability in memory; if instances come readily to mind (perhaps because of their vividness), we presume such events are likely. (p. 332)

**aversive conditioning** A type of counterconditioning that associates an unpleasant state (such as nausea) with an unwanted behavior (such as drinking alcohol). (p. 548)

**axon** The extension of a neuron, ending in branching terminal fibers, through which messages are sent to other neurons or to muscles or glands. (p. 43)

**babbling stage** Beginning at 3 to 4 months, the stage of speech development in which the infant spontaneously utters various sounds at first unrelated to the household language. (p. 343)

**barbiturates** Drugs that depress the activity of the central nervous system, reducing anxiety but impairing memory and judgment. (p. 243)

**basic research** Pure science, that aims to increase the scientific knowledge base. (p. 6)

**basic trust** According to Erik Erikson, a sense that the world is predictable and trustworthy; said to be formed during infancy by appropriate experiences with responsive caregivers. (p. 99)

**behavior therapy** Therapy that applies learning principles to the elimination of unwanted behaviors. (p. 546)

**behavioral medicine** An interdisciplinary field that integrates and applies behavioral and medical knowledge to health and disease. (p. 573)

**behaviorism** The view that (1) psychology should be an objective science that (2) studies only overt behavior without reference to mental processes. Most research psychologists today agree with (1) but not (2). (p. 259)

**belief bias** The tendency for one's preexisting beliefs to distort logical reasoning, sometimes by making invalid conclusions seem valid, or valid conclusions seem invalid. (p. 337)

**belief perseverance** Clinging to one's initial conceptions after the basis on which they were formed has been discredited. (p. 337)

**binocular cues** Depth cues, such as retinal disparity and convergence, that depend on the use of two eyes. (p. 193)

**biofeedback** A system for electronically recording, amplifying, and feeding back information regarding a subtle physiological state, such as blood pressure or muscle tension. (p. 594)

**biological psychology** A branch of psychology concerned with the links between biology and behavior. (Some biological psychologists call themselves *behavioral neuroscientists, neuropsychologists, physiological psychologists*, or *biopsychologists*.) (p. 42)

**bipolar disorder** A mood disorder in which the person alternates between the hopelessness and lethargy of depression and the overexcited state of mania. (p. 514)

**blind spot** The point at which the optic nerve leaves the eye, creating a "blind" spot because no receptor cells are located there. (p. 160)

**brainstem** The oldest part and central core of the brain, beginning where the spinal cord swells as it enters the skull; it is responsible for automatic survival functions. (p. 55)

**Broca's area** An area of the left frontal lobe that directs the muscle movements involved in speech. (p. 63)

**bulimia nervosa** An eating disorder characterized by private, "binge-purge" episodes of overeating, usually of highly caloric foods, followed by vomiting or laxative use. (p. 406)

**burnout** Physical, emotional, and mental exhaustion brought on by persistent job-related stress. (p. 580)

**bystander effect** The tendency for any given bystander to be less likely to give aid if other bystanders are present. (p. 641)

**Cannon-Bard theory** The theory that an emotion-arousing stimulus simultaneously triggers (1) physiological responses and (2) the subjective experience of emotion. (p. 454)

**case study** An observation technique in which one person is studied in depth in the hopes of revealing universal principles. (p. 18)

**CAT (computerized axial tomograph) scan** A series of x-ray photographs taken from different angles and combined by computer into a composite three-dimensional representation of a slice through the body. (p. 54)

**catharsis** Emotional release. In psychology, the catharsis hypothesis maintains that "releasing" aggressive energy (through action or fantasy) relieves aggressive urges. (p. 446)

**central nervous system** The brain and spinal cord. (p. 48)

**cerebellum** [sehr-uh-BELL-um] The "little brain" attached to the rear of the brainstem; it helps coordinate voluntary movement and balance. (p. 57)

**cerebral** [seh-REE-bruhl] **cortex** The intricate fabric of interconnected neural cells that covers the cerebral hemispheres; the body's ultimate control and information-processing center. (p. 59)

**chromosomes** Threadlike structures made of DNA molecules that contain the genes. (p. 80)

**chunking** Organizing items into familiar, manageable units; often done automatically. (p. 296)

**circadian rhythm** [ser-KAY-dee-an] The biological clock; regular bodily rhythms (for example, of temperature and wakefulness) that occur on a 24-hour cycle. (p. 221)

**classical conditioning** A type of learning in which an organism comes to associate events. A neutral stimulus that signals an unconditioned stimulus (UCS) begins to produce a response that anticipates and prepares for the unconditioned stimulus. (Also known as *Pavlovian conditioning*.) (p. 259)

**clinical psychology** A branch of psychology involving the assessment and treatment of those who suffer psychological disorders. (p. 7)

**closure** The perceptual tendency to fill in gaps, thus enabling one to perceive disconnected parts as a whole object. (p. 192)

**co-actors** People who are simultaneously at work on the same noncompetitive task. (p. 627)

**cochlea** [KOHK-lee-uh] A coiled, bony, fluid-filled tube in the inner ear through which sound waves trigger nerve impulses. (p. 168)

**cognition** All the mental activities associated with thinking, knowing, remembering, and communicating. (p. 88)

**cognitive dissonance theory** The theory that we act to reduce the discomfort (dissonance) we feel when two of our thoughts (cognitions) are inconsistent—as when we respond to our having acted contrary to our attitudes by changing our attitude. (p. 618)

**cognitive map** A mental representation of the layout of one's environment. For example, after exploring a maze, rats act as if they learned a cognitive map of it. (p. 276)

**cognitive therapy** Therapy that teaches people new, more adaptive ways of thinking and acting; based on the assumption that thoughts intervene between events and our emotional reactions. (p. 550)

**collective unconscious** Carl Jung's concept of a shared, inherited reservoir of memory traces from our species' history. (p. 468)

**collectivism** Giving priority to the goals of one's groups (often one's extended family or work group) and defining one's identity accordingly. (p. 658)

**color constancy** Perceiving familiar objects as having consistent color, even if changing illumination alters the wavelengths reflected by the object. (p. 167)

**companionate love** The deep affectionate attachment we feel for those with whom our lives are intertwined. (p. 648)

**concept** A mental grouping of similar objects, events, or people. (p. 326)

**concrete operational stage** In Piaget's theory, the stage of cognitive development (from about 6 or 7 to 11 years of age) during which children gain the mental operations that enable them to think logically about concrete events. (p. 94)

**conditioned response (CR)** In classical conditioning, the learned response to a previously neutral conditioned stimulus (CS). (p. 260)

**conditioned stimulus (CS)** In classical conditioning, an originally neutral stimulus that, after association with an unconditioned stimulus (UCS), comes to trigger a conditioned response. (p. 260)

**conduction deafness** Hearing loss caused by damage to the mechanical system that conducts sound waves to the cochlea. (p. 171)

**cones** Receptor cells that are concentrated near the center of the retina and that function in daylight or in well-lit conditions. The cones detect fine detail and give rise to color sensations. (p. 160)

**confirmation bias** A tendency to search for information that confirms one's preconceptions. (p. 328)

**conflict** A perceived incompatibility of actions, goals, or ideas. (p. 686)

**conformity** Adjusting one's behavior or thinking to coincide with a group standard. (p. 620)

**connectedness** The perceptual tendency to perceive features, such as dots, as a single unit when uniform and linked. (p. 192)

**consciousness** Our awareness of ourselves and our environments. (p. 220)

**conservation** The principle (which Piaget believed to be a part of concrete operational reasoning) that properties such as mass, volume, and number remain the same despite changes in the forms of objects. (p. 93)

**content validity** The extent to which a test samples the behavior that is of interest (such as a driving test that samples driving tasks). (p. 368)

**continuity** The perceptual tendency to group stimuli into smooth, continuous patterns. (p. 192)

**continuous reinforcement** Reinforcing the desired response every time it occurs. (p. 272)

**control condition** The condition of an experiment that contrasts with the experimental treatment and serves as a comparison for evaluating the effect of the treatment. (p. 26)

**convergence** A binocular cue for perceiving depth; the extent to which the eyes converge inward when looking at an object. (p. 194)

**conversion disorder** A rare somatoform disorder in which a person experiences very specific genuine physical symptoms for which no physiological basis can be found. (p. 510)

**coronary heart disease** The clogging of the vessels that nourish the heart muscle; the leading cause of death in the United States. (p. 581)

**corpus callosum** [KOR-pus kah-LOW-sum] The largest bundle of neural fibers connecting and carrying messages between the two brain hemispheres. (p. 65)

**correlation** A statistical measure that indicates the extent to which two factors vary together and thus how well either factor predicts the other. (p. 21)

**correlation coefficient** A statistical measure of the extent to which two factors vary together and thus how well either factor predicts the other. Scores with a *positive correlation coefficient* go up and down together (as with high school and college GPAs). A *negative correlation coefficient* indicates that one score falls as the other rises (as in the relationship between self-esteem and depression). (p. A–4)

**counterconditioning** A behavior therapy procedure that conditions new responses to stimuli that trigger unwanted behaviors; based on classical conditioning. See also *systematic desensitization* and *aversive conditioning*. (p. 546)

**creativity** The ability to produce novel and valuable ideas. (p. 381)

**criterion** The behavior (such as college grades) that a test (such as the SAT) is designed to predict; thus, the measure used in defining whether the test has predictive validity. (p. 368)

**critical period** An optimal period shortly after birth when an organism's exposure to certain influences produces proper development. (p. 96)

**critical thinking** Thinking that does not blindly accept arguments and conclusions. Rather, it examines assumptions, discerns hidden values, evaluates evidence, and assesses conclusions. (p. 12)

**cross-sectional study** A study in which people of different ages are tested or observed at the same point in time. (p. 136)

**crystallized intelligence** One's accumulated knowledge and verbal skills; tends to increase with age. (p. 137)

**culture** The enduring behaviors, ideas, attitudes, and traditions shared by a large group of people and transmitted from one generation to the next. (p. 655)

**defense mechanisms** In psychoanalytic theory, the ego's protective methods of reducing anxiety by unconsciously distorting reality. (p. 466)

**deindividuation** The loss of self-awareness and self-restraint occurring in group situations that foster arousal and anonymity. (p. 628)

**déjà vu** (From French, literally meaning "already seen.") That eerie sense that "I've experienced this before." Cues from the current situation may subconsciously trigger retrieval of an earlier experience. (p. 309)

**delta waves** The large, slow brain waves associated with deep sleep. (p. 223)

**delusions** False beliefs, often of persecution or grandeur, that may accompany psychotic disorders. (p. 524)

**dendrite** The bushy, branching extensions of a neuron that receive messages and conduct impulses toward the cell body. (p. 43)

**dependent variable** The experimental factor—in psychology, the behavior or mental process—that is being measured; the variable that may change in response to manipulations of the independent variable. (p. 27)

**depressants** Drugs (such as alcohol, barbiturates, and opiates) that reduce neural activity and slow body functions. (p. 241)

**depth perception** The ability to see objects in three dimensions although the images that strike the retina are two-dimensional; allows us to judge distance. (p. 193)

**developmental psychology** A branch of psychology that studies physical, cognitive, and social change throughout the life span. (p. 77)

**difference threshold** The minimum difference that a subject can detect between two stimuli 50 percent of the time. We experience the difference threshold as a just noticeable difference (jnd). (p. 156)

**discrimination** In classical conditioning, the ability to distinguish between a conditioned stimulus and similar stimuli that do not signal an unconditioned stimulus. In operant conditioning, responding differently to stimuli that signal that behavior will be reinforced or will not be reinforced. (p. 263)

**displacement** In psychoanalytic theory, the defense mechanism that shifts sexual or aggressive impulses toward a more acceptable or less threatening object or person, as when redirecting anger toward a safer outlet. (p. 467)

**dissociation** A split in consciousness, which allows some thoughts and behaviors to occur simultaneously with others. (p. 236)

**dissociative disorders** Disorders in which conscious awareness becomes separated (dissociated) from previous memories, thoughts, and feelings. See *amnesia, fugue,* and *multiple personality*. (p. 511)

**DNA (deoxyribonucleic acid)** A complex molecule containing the genetic information that makes up the chromosomes. (p. 80)

**double-blind procedure** An experimental procedure in which both the subject and the research staff are ignorant (blind) about whether the subject has received the treatment or a placebo. Commonly used in drug evaluation studies. (p. 29)

**Down syndrome** A condition of retardation and associated physical disorders caused by an extra chromosome in one's genetic makeup. (p. 379)

**drive-reduction theory** The idea that a physiological need creates an aroused tension state (a drive) that motivates an organism to satisfy the need. (p. 398)

**DSM-IV** The American Psychiatric Association's *Diagnostic and Statistical Manual of Mental Disorders (Fourth Edition)*, a widely used system for classifying psychological disorders. (p. 504)

**dualism** The presumption that mind and body are two distinct entities that interact. (p. 252)

**echoic memory** A momentary sensory memory of auditory stimuli; if attention is elsewhere, sounds and words can still be recalled within 3 or 4 seconds. (p. 300)

**eclectic approach** An approach to psychotherapy that takes advantage of techniques from the various forms of therapy, depending on the client's problems. (p. 540)

**effortful processing** Encoding that requires attention and conscious effort. (p. 290)

**ego** The largely conscious, "executive" part of personality that, according to Freud, mediates among the demands of the id, superego, and reality. (p. 464)

**egocentrism** In Piaget's theory, the inability of the preoperational child to take another's point of view. (p. 92)

**electroconvulsive therapy (ECT)** Shock treatment. A biomedical therapy for severely depressed patients in which a brief electric current is sent through the brain of an anesthetized patient. (p. 567)

**electroencephalogram (EEG)** An amplified recording of the waves of electrical activity that sweep across the brain's surface. These waves are measured by placing electrodes on the scalp. (p. 54)

**embryo** The developing human organism from about 2 weeks after fertilization through the second month. (p. 81)

**emotion** A response of the whole organism, involving (1) physical arousal, (2) expressive behaviors, and (3) conscious experience. (p. 433)

**empathy** The ability to understand and feel what another feels, to put oneself in someone else's shoes. (p. 642)

**empirically derived test** A test (such as the MMPI) developed by testing a pool of items and then selecting those that discriminate groups of interest. (p. 476)

**encoding** The processing of information into the memory system, for example by extracting meaning. (p. 289)

**endocrine** [EN-duh-krin] **system** The body's "slow" chemical communication system; a set of glands that secrete hormones into the bloodstream. (p. 51)

**endorphins** [en-DOR-fins] "Morphine within"—natural, opiate-like neurotransmitters linked to pain control and to pleasure. (p. 46)

**equilibrium** The sense of body movement and position, including the sense of balance. (p. 181)

**equity** A condition in which people receive from a relationship in proportion to what they give to it. (p. 649)

**estrogen** A sex hormone, secreted in greater amounts by females than by males. In nonhuman female mammals, estrogen levels peak during ovulation, promoting sexual receptivity. (p. 410)

**ethnicity** That part of one's social identity defined by the ancestors, heritage, and traits one shares with others. (p. 662)

**evolutionary psychology** The study of the evolution of behavior using the principles of natural selection; it assumes that natural selection favors genetically influenced behaviors that contribute to the preservation and spread of one's genes. (p. 643)

**experiment** A research method in which the investigator manipulates one or more factors (independent variables) to observe their effect on some behavior or mental process (the dependent variable) while controlling other relevant factors by random assignment of subjects. (p. 25)

**experimental condition** The condition of an experiment that exposes subjects to the treatment, that is, to one version of the independent variable. (p. 26)

**explicit memory** Memory of facts and experiences that one can consciously know and "declare." (Also called *declarative memory*.) (p. 305)

**external locus of control** The perception that chance or outside forces beyond one's personal control determine one's fate. (p. 489)

**extinction** The diminishing of a response when, in classical conditioning, an unconditioned stimulus (UCS) does not follow a conditioned stimulus (CS); or when, in operant conditioning, a response is no longer reinforced. (p. 262)

**extrasensory perception (ESP)** The controversial claim that perception can occur apart from sensory input. Said to include *telepathy*, *clairvoyance*, and *precognition*. (p. 210)

**extrinsic motivation** A desire to perform a behavior due to promised rewards or threats of punishment. (p. 421)

**factor analysis** A statistical procedure that identifies clusters of related items (called *factors*) on a test; used to identify different dimensions of performance that underlie one's total score. (p. 372)

**false consensus effect** The tendency to overestimate the extent to which others share our beliefs and behaviors. (p. 19)

**family therapy** Therapy that treats the family as a system. Views an individual's unwanted behaviors as influenced by or directed at other family members; encourages family members toward positive relationships and improved communication. (p. 554)

**fantasy-prone personality** Someone who imagines and recalls experiences with lifelike vividness and who spends considerable time fantasizing. (p. 231)

**feature detectors** Nerve cells in the brain that respond to specific features of the stimulus, such as movement, angle, or shape. (p. 163)

**feel-good, do-good phenomenon** People's tendency to be helpful when already in a good mood. (p. 447)

**fetal alcohol syndrome (FAS)** Physical and cognitive abnormalities in children caused by a pregnant woman's heavy drinking. In severe cases, symptoms include noticeable facial misproportions. (p. 82)

**fetus** The developing human organism from 9 weeks after conception to birth. (p. 81)

**figure-ground** The organization of the visual field into objects (the *figures*) that stand out from their surroundings (the *ground*). (p. 192)

**fixation** 1. The inability to see a problem from a new perspective; an impediment to problem solving. (p. 329) 2. According to Freud, a lingering focus of pleasure-seeking energies at an earlier psychosexual stage, where conflicts were unresolved. (p. 465)

**fixed-interval schedule** In operant conditioning, a schedule of reinforcement that reinforces a response only after a specified time has elapsed. (p. 273)

**fixed-ratio schedule** In operant conditioning, a schedule of reinforcement that reinforces a response only after a specified number of responses. (p. 272)

**flashbulb memory** A clear memory of an emotionally significant moment or event. (p. 288)

**fluid intelligence** One's ability to reason speedily and abstractly; tends to decrease during late adulthood. (p. 137)

**foot-in-the-door phenomenon** The tendency for people who have first agreed to a small request to comply later with a larger request. (p. 617)

**formal operational stage** In Piaget's theory, the stage of cognitive development (normally beginning about age 12) during which people begin to think logically about abstract concepts. (p. 94)

**fovea** The central focal point in the retina, around which the eye's cones cluster. (p. 160)

**framing** The way an issue is posed; how an issue is framed can significantly affect decisions and judgments. (p. 335)

**fraternal twins** Twins who develop from separate zygotes. They are genetically no closer than brothers and sisters, but they share the fetal environment. (p. 108)

**free association** In psychoanalysis, a method of exploring the unconscious in which the person relaxes and says whatever comes to mind, no matter how trivial or embarrassing. (pp. 462, 541)

**frequency** The number of complete wavelengths that pass a point in a given time (for example, per second). (p. 168)

**frequency theory** In hearing, the theory that the rate of nerve impulses traveling up the auditory nerve matches the frequency of a tone, thus enabling us to sense its pitch. (p. 170)

**frontal lobes** The portion of the cerebral cortex lying just behind the forehead; involved in speaking and muscle movements and in making plans and judgments. (p. 60)

**frustration-aggression principle** The principle that frustration—the blocking of an attempt to achieve some goal—creates anger, which can generate aggression. (p. 634)

**fugue** [fewg] A dissociative disorder in which flight from one's home and identity accompanies amnesia. (p. 512)

**functional fixedness** The tendency to think of things only in terms of their usual functions; an impediment to problem solving. (p. 331)

**fundamental attribution error** The tendency for observers, when analyzing another's behavior, to underestimate the impact of the situation and to overestimate the impact of personal disposition. (p. 613)

**gate-control theory** Melzack and Wall's theory that the spinal cord contains a neurological "gate" that blocks or allows pain signals to pass on to the brain. The "gate" is opened by the activity of pain signals traveling up small nerve fibers and closed by activity in larger fibers or by information coming from the brain. (p. 175)

**gender** In psychology, the characteristics, whether biologically or socially influenced, by which people define male and female. (p. 666)

**gender identity** One's sense of being male or female. Note: One's gender identity is distinct from one's sexual orientation (as heterosexual or homosexual) and from the strength of one's gender-typing. (pp. 465, 676)

**gender role** A set of expected behaviors for males and for females. (p. 677)

**gender schema theory** The theory that children learn from their cultures a concept of what it means to be male and female and that they adjust their behavior accordingly. (p. 676)

**gender-typing** The acquisition of a masculine or feminine gender identity and role. (p. 676)

**general adaptation syndrome (GAS)** Selye's concept of the body's adaptive response to stress as composed of three stages—alarm, resistance, exhaustion. (p. 576)

**general intelligence (*g*)** A general underlying intelligence factor believed by Spearman and others to be measured by every task on an intelligence test. (p. 372)

**generalization** The tendency, once a response has been conditioned, for stimuli similar to the conditioned stimulus to evoke similar responses. (p. 262)

**generalized anxiety disorder** An anxiety disorder in which a person is continually tense, apprehensive, and in a state of autonomic nervous system arousal. (p. 505)

**genes** The biochemical units of heredity that make up the chromosomes; a segment of DNA capable of synthesizing a protein. (p. 78)

**genital stage** The last of Freud's psychosexual stages, beginning in puberty, during which sexuality matures and the person seeks pleasure through sexual contact with others. (p. 465)

**gestalt** An organized whole. Gestalt psychologists emphasize our tendency to integrate pieces of information into meaningful wholes. (p. 191)

**Gestalt therapy** Developed by Fritz Perls to combine the psychoanalytic emphasis on bringing unconscious feelings to awareness and the humanistic emphasis on getting "in touch with oneself"; aims to help people become more aware of and able to express their feelings, and to take responsibility for their feelings and actions. (p. 545)

**glucose** The form of sugar that circulates in the blood and provides the major source of energy for body tissues. When its level is low, we feel hunger. (p. 402)

**grammar** A system of rules in a language that enables us to communicate with and understand others. (p. 342)

**GRIT** Graduated and Reciprocated Initiatives in Tension-Reduction—a strategy designed to decrease international tensions. (p. 690)

**group polarization** The enhancement of a group's prevailing attitudes through discussion. (p. 629)

**grouping** The perceptual tendency to organize stimuli into coherent groups. (p. 192)

**groupthink** The mode of thinking that occurs when the desire for harmony in a decision-making group overrides a realistic appraisal of alternatives. (p. 629)

**habituation** Decreasing responsiveness with repeated stimulation. For example, as infants gain familiarity with repeated exposure to a visual stimulus, their interest wanes and they look away sooner. (p. 91)

**hallucinations** False sensory experiences, such as seeing something without any external visual stimulus. (p. 223)

**hallucinogens** Psychedelic ("mind-manifesting") drugs, such as LSD, that distort perceptions and evoke sensory images in the absence of sensory input. (p. 241)

**health psychology** A subfield of psychology that provides psychology's contribution to behavioral medicine. (p. 573)

**heritability** The proportion of variation among individuals that we can attribute to genes. The heritability of a trait may vary, depending on the range of populations and environments studied. (p. 385)

**heuristic** A rule-of-thumb strategy that often allows us to make judgments and solve problems efficiently; usually speedier but also more error-prone than *algorithms*. (p. 327)

**hidden observer** Hilgard's term describing a hypnotized subject's awareness of experiences, such as pain, that go unreported during hypnosis. (p. 239)

**hierarchy of needs** Maslow's pyramid of human needs, beginning at the base with physiological needs that must first be satisfied before higher level safety needs and then psychological needs become active. (p. 400)

**hindsight bias** The tendency to believe, *after* learning an outcome, that one would have foreseen it. (Also known as the *I-knew-it-all-along phenomenon*.) (p. 14)

**hippocampus** A neural center that is located in the limbic system and that helps process explicit memories for storage. (p. 306)

**homeostasis** A tendency to maintain a balanced or constant internal state; the regulation of any aspect of body chemistry, such as blood glucose, around a particular level. (p. 398)

**hormones** Chemical messengers, mostly those manufactured by the endocrine glands, that are produced in one tissue and affect another. (p. 51)

**hospice** An organization whose largely volunteer staff provides support for dying people and their families either in special facilities or in people's own homes. (p. 144)

**hue** The dimension of color that is determined by the wavelength of light; what we know as the color names *blue*, *green*, and so forth. (p. 158)

**hypnosis** An apparently heightened suggestibility in which some people narrow their focus of attention and claim to experience imaginary happenings as if they were real. (p. 232)

**hypochondriasis** A somatoform disorder in which a person misinterprets normal physical sensations as symptoms of a disease. (p. 510)

**hypothalamus** [hi-po-THAL-uh-muss] A neural structure lying below *(hypo)* the thalamus; it directs several maintenance activities (eating, drinking, body temperature), helps govern the endocrine system via the pituitary gland, and is linked to emotion. (p. 58)

**hypothesis** A testable prediction, often implied by a theory. (p. 17)

**iconic memory** A momentary sensory memory of visual stimuli; a photographic or picture-image memory lasting no more than a second or so. (p. 300)

**id** A reservoir of unconscious psychic energy that, according to Freud, strives to satisfy basic sexual and aggressive drives. (p. 464)

**identical twins** Twins who develop from a single zygote (fertilized egg) that splits in two, creating two genetic replicas. (p. 108)

**identification** The process by which, according to Freud, children incorporate their parents' values into their developing superegos. (p. 465)

**identity** One's sense of self; according to Erikson, the adolescent's task is to solidify a sense of self by testing and integrating various roles. (p. 123)

**illusory correlation** The perception of a relationship where none exists. (p. 22)

**imagery** Mental pictures. A powerful aid to effortful processing, especially when combined with semantic encoding. (p. 294)

**implicit memory** Retention without conscious recollection (of skills, preferences, and dispositions). (Also called *nondeclarative memory*.) (p. 305)

**imprinting** The process by which certain animals form attachments during a critical period very early in life. (p. 97)

**incentives** Positive or negative environmental stimuli that motivate behavior. (p. 399)

**independent variable** The experimental factor that is manipulated; the variable whose effect is being studied. (p. 27)

**individualism** Giving priority to one's own goals over group goals, and defining one's identity in terms of personal attributes rather than group identifications. (p. 658)

**industrial/organizational psychology** A subfield of psychology that studies and advises on workplace behavior. Industrial/organizational (I/O) psychologists help organizations select and train employees, boost morale and productivity, and design products and assess responses to them. (p. 422)

**informational social influence** Influence resulting from one's willingness to accept others' opinions about reality. (p. 622)

**ingroup bias** The tendency to favor one's own group. (p. 684)

**inner ear** The innermost part of the ear, containing the cochlea, semicircular canals, and vestibular sacs. (p. 168)

**insight** A sudden and often novel realization of the solution to a problem; it contrasts with strategy-based solutions. (p. 327)

**insomnia** A sleep disorder involving recurring problems in falling or staying asleep. (p. 226)

**instinct** A complex behavior that is rigidly patterned throughout a species and is unlearned. (p. 398)

**intelligence** The capacity for goal-directed and adaptive behavior. Involves the abilities to profit from experience, solve problems, reason, and successfully meet challenges and achieve goals. (p. 371)

**intelligence quotient (IQ)** Defined originally as the ratio of mental age to chronological age multiplied by 100 (thus, IQ = ma/ca × 100). On contemporary intelligence tests, the average performance for a given age is assigned a score of 100. (p. 362)

**intelligence test** A method for assessing an individual's mental aptitudes and comparing them to those of others, using numerical scores. (p. 359)

**intensity** The amount of energy in a light or sound wave, which we perceive as brightness or loudness, as determined by the wave's amplitude. (p. 158)

**internal locus of control** The perception that one controls one's own fate. (p. 489)

**interneurons** Central nervous system neurons that intervene directly between the sensory inputs and motor outputs. (p. 48)

**interposition** A monocular cue for perceiving distance; nearby objects partially block our view of more distant objects. (p. 195)

**interpretation** In psychoanalysis, the analyst's assisting the patient to note and understand resistances and other significant behaviors in order to promote insight. (p. 541)

**intimacy** In Erikson's theory, the ability to form close, loving relationships; a primary developmental task in late adolescence and early adulthood. (p. 125)

**intrinsic motivation** A desire to perform a behavior for its own sake and to be effective. (p. 421)

**iris** A ring of muscle tissue that forms the colored portion of the eye around the pupil and controls the size of the pupil opening. (p. 159)

**James-Lange theory** The theory that our experience of emotion is our awareness of our physiological responses to emotion-arousing stimuli. (p. 454)

**just noticeable difference (jnd)** See *difference threshold*. (p. 156)

**just-world phenomenon** The tendency of people to believe the world is just and that people therefore get what they deserve and deserve what they get. (p. 686)

**kinesthesis** [kin-ehs-THEE-sehs] The system for sensing the position and movement of individual body parts. (p. 181)

**language** Our spoken, written, or gestured words and the ways we combine them to communicate meaning. (p. 341)

**latency stage** The fourth of Freud's psychosexual stages, from about age 6 to puberty, during which sexual impulses are repressed. (p. 465)

**latent content** According to Freud, the underlying but censored meaning of a dream (as distinct from its manifest content). Freud believed that a dream's latent content functions as a safety valve. (p. 228)

**latent learning** Learning that occurs but is not apparent until there is an incentive to demonstrate it. (p. 276)

**learned helplessness** The hopelessness and passive resignation learned when an animal or human is unable to avoid repeated aversive events. (p. 490)

**learning** A relatively permanent change in an organism's behavior due to experience. (p. 257)

**lens** The transparent structure behind the pupil that changes shape to focus images on the retina. (p. 159)

**lesion** [LEE-zhuhn] Tissue destruction. A brain lesion is a naturally or experimentally caused destruction of brain tissue. (p. 54)

**limbic system** A doughnut-shaped system of neural structures at the border of the brainstem and cerebral hemispheres; associated with emotions such as fear and aggression and drives such as those for food and sex. (p. 57)

**linear perspective** A monocular cue for perceiving distance; we perceive the converging of what we know to be parallel lines as indicating increasing distance. (p. 196)

**linguistic relativity** Whorf's hypothesis that language determines the way we think. (p. 352)

**lithium** A chemical that provides an effective drug therapy for the mood swings of bipolar (manic-depressive) disorders. (p. 567)

**lobotomy** A now-rare psychosurgical procedure once used to calm uncontrollably emotional or violent patients. In this procedure the nerves that connect the frontal lobes to the emotion-controlling centers of the inner brain are cut. (p. 568)

**long-term memory** The relatively permanent and limitless storehouse of the memory system. (p. 289)

**long-term potentiation (LTP)** An increase in a synapse's firing potential after brief, rapid stimulation. Believed to be a neural basis for learning and memory. (p. 303)

**longitudinal study** Research in which the same people are restudied and retested over a long time period. (p. 136)

**LSD** (*lysergic acid diethylamide*) A powerful hallucinogenic drug; also known as *acid*. (p. 245)

**lymphocytes** The two types of white blood cells that are part of the body's immune system: B lymphocytes form in the *b*one marrow and release antibodies that fight bacterial infections; T lymphocytes form in the *t*hymus and, among other duties, attack cancer cells, viruses, and foreign substances. (p. 583)

**major depressive disorder** A mood disorder in which a person, for no apparent reason, experiences 2 or more weeks of depressed moods, feelings of worthlessness, and diminished interest or pleasure in most activities. (p. 514)

**mania** A mood disorder marked by a hyperactive, wildly optimistic state. (p. 514)

**manifest content** According to Freud, the remembered story line of a dream (as distinct from its latent content). (p. 228)

**maturation** Biological growth processes that enable orderly changes in behavior, relatively uninfluenced by experience. (p. 78)

**mean** The arithmetic average of a distribution, obtained by adding the scores and then dividing by the number of scores. (p. A–2)

**median** The middle score in a distribution; half the scores are above it and half are below it. (p. A–2)

**medical model** The concept that diseases have physical causes that can be diagnosed, treated, and, in most cases, cured. When applied to psychological disorders, the medical model assumes that these "mental" illnesses can be diagnosed on the basis of their symptoms and cured through therapy, which may include treatment in a psychiatric hospital. (p. 501)

**medulla** [muh-DUL-uh] The base of the brainstem; controls heartbeat and breathing. (p. 55)

**menarche** [meh-NAR-key] The first menstrual period. (p. 118)

**menopause** The time of natural cessation of menstruation; also refers to the biological changes experienced during a woman's years of declining ability to reproduce. (p. 130)

**mental age** A measure of intelligence test performance devised by Binet; the chronological age that most typically corresponds to a given level of performance. Thus, a child who does as well as the average 8-year-old is said to have a mental age of 8. (p. 361)

**mental retardation** A condition of limited mental ability, as indicated by an intelligence score below 70, that produces difficulty in adapting to the demands of life; varies from mild to profound. (p. 379)

**mental set** A tendency to approach a problem in a particular way, especially a way that has been successful in the past but may or may not be helpful in solving a new problem. (p. 330)

**mere exposure effect** The phenomenon that repeated exposure to novel stimuli increases liking of them. (p. 644)

**meta-analysis** A procedure for statistically combining the results of many different research studies. (p. 558)

**metabolic rate** The body's base rate of energy expenditure. (p. 404)

**middle ear** The chamber between the eardrum and cochlea containing three tiny bones (hammer, anvil, and stirrup) that concentrate the vibrations of the eardrum on the cochlea's oval window. (p. 168)

**Minnesota Multiphasic Personality Inventory-2 (MMPI-2)** The most widely researched and clinically used of all personality tests. Originally developed to identify emotionally troubled people (still considered its most appropriate use), this test is now used for many other screening purposes. (p. 476)

**misinformation effect** After witnessing an event and receiving misleading information about it, incorporating the "misinformation" into one's memory of the event. (p. 312)

**mnemonics** [nih-MON-iks] Memory aids, especially those techniques that use vivid imagery and organizational devices. (p. 295)

**mode** The most frequently occurring score in a distribution. (p. A–2)

**modeling** The process by which a behavior is observed and imitated. (p. 281)

**monism** The presumption that mind and body are different aspects of the same thing. (p. 252)

**monocular cues** Distance cues, such as aerial and linear perspective and overlap, available to either eye alone. (p. 193)

**mood-congruent memory** The tendency to recall experiences that are consistent with one's current good or bad mood. (p. 310)

**mood disorders** Psychological disorders characterized by emotional extremes. See *bipolar disorder, major depressive disorder,* and *mania*. (p. 514)

**morphemes** In a language, the smallest units that carry meaning; may be words or parts of words (such as a prefix). (p. 342)

**motivation** A need or desire that energizes and directs behavior. (p. 397)

**motor cortex** An area at the rear of the frontal lobes that controls voluntary movements. (p. 60)

**motor neurons** The neurons that carry outgoing information from the central nervous system to the muscles and glands. (p. 48)

**MRI (magnetic resonance imaging)** A technique that uses magnetic fields and radio waves to produce computer-generated images that distinguish among different types of soft tissue; allows us to see structures within the brain. (p. 54)

**multiple personality disorder** A rare dissociative disorder in which a person exhibits two or more distinct and alternating personalities. (p. 512)

**myelin** [MY-uh-lin] **sheath** A layer of fatty cells segmentally encasing the fibers of many neurons; makes possible vastly greater transmission speed of neural impulses. (p. 43)

**narcolepsy** A sleep disorder characterized by uncontrollable sleep attacks in which the sufferer lapses directly into REM sleep, often at inopportune times. (p. 226)

**naturalistic observation** Observing and recording behavior in naturally occurring situations without trying to manipulate and control the situation. (p. 21)

**nature-nurture issue** The long-standing controversy over the relative contributions that genes and experience make to the development of psychological traits and behaviors. (p. 4)

**near-death experience** An altered state of consciousness reported after a close brush with death (such as through cardiac arrest); often similar to drug-induced hallucinations. (p. 251)

**need to belong** A motivation to form and maintain enduring, close personal relationships. (p. 427)

**nerve deafness** Hearing loss caused by damage to the cochlea's receptor cells or to the auditory nerves. (p. 171)

**nerves** Neural "cables" containing many axons. These bundled axons, which are part of the peripheral nervous system, connect the central nervous system with muscles, glands, and sense organs. (p. 48)

**nervous system** The body's speedy, electrochemical communication system, consisting of all the nerve cells of the peripheral and central nervous systems. (p. 48)

**neural networks** 1. Interconnected neural cells. With experience, networks can learn, as feedback strengthens or inhibits connections that produce certain results. (p. 51) 2. Computer circuits that mimic the brain's interconnected neural cells, performing tasks such as learning to recognize visual patterns and smells. (p. 340)

**neuron** A nerve cell; the basic building block of the nervous system. (p. 42)

**neurotic disorders** Former term for psychological disorders that are usually distressing but allow one to think rationally and function socially. Freud saw the neurotic disorders as ways of dealing with anxiety. (p. 504)

**neurotransmitters** Chemical messengers that traverse the synaptic gaps between neurons. When released by the sending neuron, neurotransmitters travel across the synapse and bind to receptor sites on the receiving neuron, thereby influencing whether it will generate a neural impulse. (p. 45)

**night terrors** A sleep disorder characterized by high arousal and an appearance of being terrified; unlike nightmares, night terrors occur during Stage 4 sleep, within 2 or 3 hours of falling asleep, and are seldom remembered. (p. 227)

**normal curve** The symmetrical bell-shaped curve that describes the distribution of many physical and psychological attributes. Most scores fall near the average, and fewer and fewer scores lie near the extremes. (pp. 366, A–3)

**normative social influence** Influence resulting from a person's desire to gain approval or avoid disapproval. (p. 622)

**norms** Understood rules for accepted and expected behavior. Norms prescribe "proper" behavior. (p. 622)

**object permanence** The awareness that things continue to exist even when not perceived. (p. 90)

**observational learning** Learning by observing and imitating the behavior of others. (p. 281)

**obsessive-compulsive disorder** An anxiety disorder characterized by unwanted repetitive thoughts (obsessions) and/or actions (compulsions). (p. 505)

**occipital** [ahk-SIP-uh-tuhl] **lobes** The portion of the cerebral cortex lying at the back of the head; includes the visual areas, each of which receives visual information from the opposite visual field. (p. 60)

**Oedipus** [ed-uh-puss] **complex** According to Freud, a child's sexual desires toward the parent of the other sex and feelings of jealousy and hatred for the rival parent of the same sex. (p. 464)

**one-word stage** The stage in speech development, from about age 1 to 2, during which a child speaks mostly in single words. (p. 344)

**operant behavior** Behavior that operates on the environment, producing consequences. (p. 268)

**operant conditioning** A type of learning in which behavior is strengthened if followed by reinforcement or diminished if followed by punishment. (p. 268)

**operational definition** A statement of the procedures (operations) used to define research variables. (p. 27)

**opiates** Opium and its derivatives, such as morphine and heroin; they depress neural activity, temporarily lessening pain and anxiety. (p. 243)

**opponent-process theory** The theory that opposing retinal processes (red-green, yellow-blue, white-black) enable color vision. For example, some cells are stimulated by green and inhibited by red; others are stimulated by red and inhibited by green. (p. 166)

**optic nerve** The nerve that carries neural impulses from the eye to the brain. (p. 160)

**oral stage** The first of Freud's psychosexual stages, from birth to about 18 months, during which sensual pleasure centers on the mouth via sucking, biting, and chewing. (p. 464)

**overconfidence** The tendency to be more confident than correct—to overestimate the accuracy of one's beliefs and judgments. (p. 334)

**overjustification effect** The effect of promising a reward for doing what one already likes to do. The person may now see the reward, rather than intrinsic interest, as the motivation for performing the task. (p. 276)

**panic attack** An anxiety disorder marked by a minutes-long episode of intense dread in which a person experiences terror and accompanying chest pain, choking, or other frightening sensations. (p. 506)

**parallel processing** Information processing in which several aspects of a problem are processed simultaneously. The brain's natural mode of information processing for many functions, including vision; contrasts with the step-by-step (serial) processing of most computers and of conscious problem-solving. (p. 163)

**parapsychology** The study of paranormal phenomena including ESP and psychokinesis. (p. 211)

**parasympathetic nervous system** The division of the autonomic nervous system that calms the body, conserving its energy. (p. 49)

**parietal** [puh-RYE-uh-tuhl] **lobes** The portion of the cerebral cortex lying at the top of the head and toward the rear; includes the sensory cortex. (p. 60)

**partial reinforcement** Reinforcing a response only part of the time; results in slower acquisition of response but much greater resistance to extinction than does continuous reinforcement. (p. 272)

**passionate love** An aroused state of intense positive absorption in another, usually present at the beginning of a love relationship. (p. 647)

**percentile rank** The percentage of the scores in a distribution that fall below a given score. (p. A–1)

**perception** The process of organizing and interpreting sensory information, enabling us to recognize meaningful objects and events. (p. 151)

**perceptual adaptation** In vision, the ability to adjust to an artificially displaced or even inverted visual field. (p. 204)

**perceptual constancy** Perceiving objects as unchanging (having consistent lightness, color, shape, and size) even as illumination and retinal images change. (p. 198)

**perceptual set** A mental predisposition to perceive one thing and not another. (p. 205)

**peripheral nervous system** The neurons that connect the central nervous system to the rest of the body. It consists of the sensory neurons, which carry messages to the central nervous system from the body's sense receptors, and the motor neurons, which carry messages from the central nervous system to the muscles and glands. (p. 48)

**person-centered therapy** A humanistic therapy, developed by Carl Rogers, in which the therapist uses techniques such as active listening within a genuine, accepting, empathic environment to facilitate clients' growth. (p. 543)

**personal control** Our sense of controlling our environments rather than feeling helpless. (p. 489)

**personal space** The buffer zone we like to maintain around our bodies. (p. 656)

**personality** An individual's characteristic pattern of thinking, feeling, and acting. (p. 461)

**personality disorders** Psychological disorders characterized by inflexible and enduring behavior patterns that impair social functioning. (p. 530)

**personality inventory** A questionnaire (often with true-false or agree-disagree items) on which people respond to items designed to gauge a wide range of feelings and behaviors; used to assess selected personality traits. (p. 475)

**PET (positron emission tomograph) scan** A visual display of brain activity that detects where a radioactive form of glucose goes while the brain performs a given task. (p. 54)

**phallic stage** The third of Freud's psychosexual stages, from about ages 3 to 6, during which the pleasure zone is the genitals and sexual feelings arise toward the parent of the other sex. (p. 464)

**phi phenomenon** An illusion of movement created when two or more adjacent lights blink on and off in succession. (p. 198)

**phobic disorder** An anxiety disorder marked by a persistent, irrational fear of a specific object or situation. (p. 505)

**phonemes** In a spoken language, the smallest distinctive sound units. (p. 341)

**physical dependence** A physiological need for a drug, with unpleasant withdrawal symptoms when discontinued. (p. 240)

**pitch** A tone's highness or lowness; depends on frequency. (p. 168)

**pituitary gland** The endocrine system's most influential gland. Under the influence of the hypothalamus, the pituitary regulates growth and controls other endocrine glands. (p. 52)

**place theory** In hearing, the theory that links the pitch we hear with the place where the cochlea's membrane is stimulated. (p. 169)

**placebo** [pluh-SEE-bo] An inert substance or condition that may be administered instead of a presumed active agent, such as a drug, to see if it triggers the effects believed to characterize the active agent. (p. 29)

**plasticity** The brain's capacity for modification, as evident in brain reorganization following damage (especially in children) and in experiments on the effects of experience on brain development. (p. 86)

**pleasure principle** The id's demand for immediate gratification. (p. 464)

**polygraph** A machine, commonly used in attempts to detect lies, that measures several of the physiological responses accompanying emotion (such as perspiration, heart rate, blood pressure, and breathing changes). (p. 436)

**population** All the cases in a group, from which samples may be drawn for a study. (p. 19)

**posthypnotic amnesia** Supposed inability to recall what one experienced during hypnosis; induced by the hypnotist's suggestion. (p. 232)

**posthypnotic suggestion** A suggestion, made during a hypnosis session, to be carried out after the subject is no longer hypnotized; used by some clinicians to help control undesired symptoms and behaviors. (p. 236)

**preconscious** Information that is not conscious, but is retrievable into conscious awareness. (p. 463)

**predictive validity** The success with which a test predicts the behavior it is designed to predict; it is assessed by computing the correlation between test scores and the criterion behavior. (p. 368)

**prejudice** An unjustifiable (and usually negative) attitude toward a group and its members. Prejudice generally involves stereotyped beliefs, negative feelings, and a predisposition to discriminatory action. (p. 681)

**preoperational stage** In Piaget's theory, the stage (from about 2 to 6 or 7 years of age) during which a child learns to use language but does not yet comprehend the mental operations of concrete logic. (p. 93)

**primary reinforcer** An innately reinforcing stimulus, such as one that satisfies a biological need. (p. 271)

**primary sex characteristics** The body structures (ovaries and testes) that make sexual reproduction possible. (p. 118)

**priming** The implicit (unconscious) activation of particular associations in memory. (p. 308)

**proactive interference** The disruptive effect of prior learning on the recall of new information. (p. 314)

**projection** In psychoanalytic theory, the defense mechanism by which people disguise their own threatening impulses by attributing them to others. (p. 466)

**projective tests** Personality tests, such as the Rorschach and TAT, that provide ambiguous stimuli designed to trigger projection of one's inner feelings, interests, biases, and conflicts. (p. 468)

**prosocial behavior** Positive, constructive, helpful behavior. The opposite of antisocial behavior. (p. 282)

**prototype** The best example of a category; matching new items to the prototype provides a quick and easy method for including items in a category (as when comparing feathered creatures to a prototypical bird, such as a robin). (p. 326)

**proximity** The perceptual tendency to group together visual and auditory events that are near each other. (p. 192)

**psychiatry** A branch of medicine dealing with psychological disorders; practiced by physicians and sometimes involving medical (for example, drug) treatments as well as psychological therapy. (p. 7)

**psychoactive drug** A chemical substance that alters mood and perceptions. (p. 240)

**psychoanalysis** Freud's technique of treating psychological disorders by seeking to expose and interpret unconscious tensions. The patient's free associations, resistances, dreams, and transferences—and the therapist's interpretations of them—supposedly release previously repressed feelings, allowing the patient to gain self-insight. Freud's psychoanalytic theory of personality sought to explain what he observed during psychoanalysis. (pp. 462, 540)

**psychological dependence** A psychological need to use a drug, such as to relieve negative emotions. (p. 240)

**psychological disorder** A condition in which behavior is judged atypical, disturbing, maladaptive, and unjustifiable. (p. 500)

**psychology** The science of behavior and mental processes. (p. 2)

**psychopharmacology** The study of the effects of drugs on mind and behavior. (p. 564)

**psychophysics** The study of relationships between the physical characteristics of stimuli and our psychological experience of them. (p. 152)

**psychophysiological illness** Literally, "mind-body" illness; any stress-related physical illness, such as hypertension, ulcers, and headaches. Note: This is distinct from *hypochondriasis*—misinterpreting normal physical sensations as symptoms of a disease. (p. 583)

**psychosexual stages** The childhood stages of development (oral, anal, phallic, latency, genital) during which, according to Freud, the id's pleasure-seeking energies focus on distinct erogenous zones. (p. 464)

**psychosurgery** Surgery that removes or destroys brain tissue in an effort to change behavior. (p. 568)

**psychotherapy** An emotionally charged, confiding interaction between a trained therapist and someone who suffers a psychological difficulty. (p. 540)

**psychotic disorders** Psychological disorders in which a person loses contact with reality, experiencing irrational ideas and distorted perceptions. (p. 504)

**puberty** The time of sexual maturation, when one first becomes capable of reproducing. (p. 118)

**punishment** Any event that *decreases* the behavior that it follows. (p. 273)

**pupil** The adjustable opening in the center of the eye through which light enters. (p. 159)

**random assignment** Assigning subjects to experimental and control conditions by chance, thus minimizing preexisting differences between those assigned to the different groups. (p. 26)

**random sample** A sample that fairly represents a population because each member has an equal chance of inclusion. (p. 19)

**range** The difference between the highest and lowest scores in a distribution. (p. A–3)

**rational-emotive therapy** A confrontational cognitive therapy, developed by Albert Ellis, that vigorously challenges people's illogical, self-defeating attitudes and assumptions. Also recently called *rational-emotive behavior therapy* by Ellis, emphasizing a behavioral "homework" component. (p. 551)

**rationalization** In psychoanalytic theory, a defense mechanism that offers self-justifying explanations in place of the real, more threatening, unconscious reasons for one's actions. (p. 467)

**reaction formation** In psychoanalytic theory, a defense mechanism by which the ego unconsciously switches unacceptable impulses into their opposites. Thus, people may express feelings that are the opposite of their anxiety-arousing unconscious feelings. (p. 466)

**reality principle** The ego's tendency to satisfy the id's desires in ways that will realistically bring pleasure rather than pain. (p. 464)

**recall** A measure of memory in which the person must retrieve information learned earlier, as on a fill-in-the-blank test. (p. 307)

**reciprocal determinism** The interacting influences between personality and environmental factors. (p. 488)

**recognition** A measure of memory in which the person need only identify items previously learned, as on a multiple-choice test. (p. 308)

**reflex** A simple, automatic, inborn response to a sensory stimulus, such as the knee-jerk response. (p. 50)

**refractory period** A resting period after orgasm, during which a man cannot achieve another orgasm. (p. 410)

**regression** In psychoanalytic theory, an individual's retreat, when faced with anxiety, to a more infantile psychosexual stage where some psychic energy remains fixated. (p. 466)

**regression toward the mean** The tendency for extremes of unusual scores to fall back (regress) toward the average. (p. A–6)

**rehearsal** The conscious repetition of information, either to maintain it in consciousness or to encode it for storage. (p. 291)

**reinforcer** In operant conditioning, any event that *strengthens* the behavior it follows. (p. 270)

**relative brightness** A monocular cue for perceiving distance; dimmer objects appear more distant. (p. 196)

**relative clarity** A monocular cue for perceiving distance; hazier objects appear more distant. (p. 195)

**relative deprivation** The perception that one is worse off relative to those with whom one compares oneself. (p. 452)

**relative height** A monocular cue for perceiving distance; higher objects appear more distant. (p. 195)

**relative motion** A monocular cue for perceiving distance; when we move, objects at different distances change their relative positions in our visual image, with those closest moving most. (p. 195)

**relative size** A monocular cue for perceiving distance; when we assume two objects are the same size, the one that produces the smaller image appears more distant. (p. 194)

**relearning** A memory measure that assesses the amount of time saved when relearning previously learned information. (p. 308)

**reliability** The extent to which a test yields consistent results, as assessed by the consistency of scores on two halves of the test, on alternate forms of the test, or on retesting. (p. 368)

**REM rebound** The tendency for REM sleep to increase following REM sleep deprivation (created by repeated awakenings during REM sleep). (p. 230)

**REM sleep** Rapid eye movement sleep, a recurring sleep stage during which vivid dreams commonly occur. Also known as *paradoxical sleep* because the muscles are relaxed (except for minor twitches) but other body systems are active. (p. 222)

**replication** Repeating the essence of a research study, usually with different subjects in different situations, to see whether the basic finding generalizes to other subjects and circumstances. (p. 17)

**representativeness heuristic** A rule of thumb for judging the likelihood of things in terms of how well they seem to represent, or match, particular prototypes; may lead one to ignore other relevant information. (p. 331)

**repression** In psychoanalytic theory, the basic defense mechanism that banishes anxiety-arousing thoughts, feelings, and memories from consciousness. (pp. 316, 466)

**resistance** In psychoanalysis, the blocking from consciousness of anxiety-laden material. (p. 541)

**respondent behavior** Behavior that occurs as an automatic response to some stimulus; Skinner's term for behavior learned through classical conditioning. (p. 268)

**reticular formation** A nerve network in the brainstem that plays an important role in controlling arousal. (p. 56)

**retina** The light-sensitive inner surface of the eye, containing the receptor rods and cones plus layers of neurons that begin the processing of visual information. (p. 159)

**retinal disparity** A binocular cue for perceiving depth; the greater the disparity (difference) between the two images the retina receives of an object, the closer the object is to us. (p. 194)

**retrieval** The process of getting information out of memory storage. (p. 289)

**retroactive interference** The disruptive effect of new learning on the recall of old information. (p. 315)

**rods** Retinal receptors that detect black, white, and gray; necessary for peripheral and twilight vision, when cones don't respond. (p. 160)

**role** A set of expectations about a social position, defining how those in the position ought to behave. (p. 617)

**rooting reflex** A baby's tendency, when touched on the cheek, to open the mouth and search for the nipple. (p. 83)

**Rorschach inkblot test** The most widely used projective test, a set of 10 inkblots, designed by Hermann Rorschach; seeks to identify people's inner feelings by analyzing their interpretation. (p. 468)

**savant syndrome** A condition in which a person otherwise limited in mental ability has an amazing specific skill, such as in computation or drawing. (p. 373)

**scapegoat theory** The theory that prejudice provides an outlet for anger by providing someone to blame. (p. 685)

**scatterplot** A graphed cluster of dots, each of which represents the values of two variables (such as a student's high school and college GPAs). The slope of the points suggests the degree and direction of the relationship between the two variables. (Also called a *scattergram* or *scatter diagram*.) (p. A–4)

**schema** A concept or framework that organizes and interprets information. (p. 88)

**schizophrenia** A group of severe psychotic disorders characterized by disorganized and deluded thinking, disturbed perceptions, and inappropriate emotions and actions. (p. 523)

**secondary reinforcer** A conditioned reinforcer; a stimulus that gains its reinforcing power by association with a primary reinforcer. (p. 271)

**secondary sex characteristics** Nonreproductive sexual characteristics, such as female breasts and hips, male voice quality, and body hair. (p. 118)

**selective attention** The focusing of conscious awareness on a particular stimulus, as in the cocktail party effect. (p. 188)

**self-actualization** According to Maslow, the ultimate psychological need that arises after basic physical and psychological needs are met and self-esteem is achieved; the motivation to fulfill one's potential. (p. 480)

**self-concept** All our thoughts and feelings about ourselves, in answer to the question, "Who am I?" (p. 481)

**self-disclosure** Revealing intimate aspects of oneself to others. (p. 649)

**self-esteem** One's feelings of high or low self-worth. (p. 483)

**self-serving bias** A readiness to perceive oneself favorably. (p. 484)

**semantic encoding** The encoding of meaning, including the meaning of words. (p. 294)

**semantics** Meaning (or the study of meaning), as derived from morphemes, words, and sentences. (p. 342)

**sensation** The process by which our sense receptors and nervous system receive and represent stimulus energies from our environment. (p. 151)

**sensorimotor stage** In Piaget's theory, the stage (from birth to about 2 years of age) during which infants know the world mostly in terms of their sensory impressions and motor activities. (p. 89)

**sensory adaptation** Diminished sensitivity that is a consequence of constant stimulation. (p. 156)

**sensory cortex** The area at the front of the parietal lobes that registers and processes body sensations. (p. 61)

**sensory interaction** The principle that one sense may influence another, as when the smell of food influences its taste. (p. 178)

**sensory memory** The immediate, initial recording of sensory information in the memory system. (p. 299)

**sensory neurons** Neurons that carry incoming information from the sense receptors to the central nervous system. (p. 48)

**serial position effect** Our tendency to recall best the last and first items in a list. (p. 293)

**set point** The point at which an individual's "weight thermostat" is supposedly set. When the body falls below this weight, an increase in hunger and a lowered metabolic rate may act to restore the lost weight. (p. 403)

**sexual dysfunction** A problem that consistently impairs sexual arousal or functioning. (p. 412)

**sexual orientation** An enduring sexual attraction toward members of either one's own gender (homosexual orientation) or the other gender (heterosexual orientation). (p. 413)

**sexual response cycle** The four stages of sexual responding described by Masters and Johnson—excitement, plateau, orgasm, and resolution. (p. 409)

**shaping** An operant conditioning procedure in which reinforcers guide behavior toward closer and closer approximations of a desired goal. (p. 269)

**short-term memory** Activated memory that holds a few items briefly, such as the seven digits of a phone number while dialing, before the information is stored or forgotten. (p. 289)

**signal detection** The task of judging the presence of a faint stimulus ("signal"). Signal detection researchers assume there is no single absolute threshold, because the detection of a weak signal depends partly on a person's experience, expectation, motivation, and level of fatigue. (p. 153)

**similarity** The perceptual tendency to group together similar elements. (p. 192)

**skeletal nervous system** The division of the peripheral nervous system that controls the body's skeletal muscles. (p. 48)

**Skinner box** A chamber containing a bar or key that an animal can manipulate to obtain a food or water reinforcer, and devices to record the animal's rate of bar pressing or key pecking. Used in operant conditioning research. (p. 269)

**sleep apnea** A sleep disorder characterized by temporary cessations of breathing during sleep and consequent momentary reawakenings. (p. 227)

**social clock** The culturally preferred timing of social events such as marriage, parenthood, and retirement. (p. 139)

**social exchange theory** The theory that our social behavior is an exchange process, the aim of which is to maximize benefits and minimize costs. (p. 642)

**social facilitation** Improved performance of tasks in the presence of others; occurs with simple or well-learned tasks but not with tasks that are difficult or not yet mastered. (p. 627)

**social leadership** Group-oriented leadership that builds teamwork, mediates conflict, and offers support. (p. 425)

**social loafing** The tendency for people in a group to exert less effort when pooling their efforts toward attaining a common goal than when individually accountable. (p. 628)

**social psychology** The scientific study of how we think about, influence, and relate to one another. (p. 613)

**social traps** Situations in which the conflicting parties, by each rationally pursuing their self-interest, become caught in mutually destructive behavior. (p. 686)

**somatoform disorders** Psychological disorders in which the symptoms take a somatic (bodily) form without apparent physical cause. See *conversion disorder* and *hypochondriasis*. (p. 510)

**spacing effect** The tendency for distributed study or practice to yield better long-term retention than is achieved through massed study or practice. (p. 292)

**split brain** A condition in which the two hemispheres of the brain are isolated by cutting the connecting fibers (mainly those of the corpus callosum) between them. (p. 65)

**spontaneous recovery** The reappearance, after a rest period, of an extinguished conditioned response. (p. 262)

**standard deviation** A measure of score variability; computed by (1) calculating the deviation of each score from the mean, (2) squaring those deviations, (3) finding their average, and (4) finding the square root of this average. (p. A–3)

**standardization** Defining meaningful scores by comparison with the performance of a pretested "standardization group." (p. 365)

**Stanford-Binet** The widely used American revision (by Terman at Stanford University) of Binet's original intelligence test. (p. 362)

**statistical significance** A statistical statement of how likely it is that an obtained result occurred by chance. (p. A–8)

**stereotype** A generalized (often overgeneralized) belief about a group of people. (p. 682)

**stimulants** Drugs (such as caffeine, nicotine, and the more powerful amphetamines and cocaine) that excite neural activity and speed up body functions. (p. 241)

**storage** The maintenance of encoded information over time. (p. 289)

**stranger anxiety** The fear of strangers that infants commonly display, beginning by about 8 months of age. (p. 95)

**stress** The process by which we perceive and respond to certain events, called *stressors*, that we appraise as threatening or challenging. (p. 574)

**sublimation** In psychoanalytic theory, the defense mechanism by which people rechannel their unacceptable impulses into socially approved activities. (p. 467)

**subliminal** Below one's absolute threshold for conscious awareness. (p. 154)

**superego** The part of personality that, according to Freud, represents internalized ideals and provides standards for judgment (the conscience) and for future aspirations. (p. 464)

**superordinate goals** Shared goals that override differences among people and require their cooperation. (p. 688)

**survey** A technique for ascertaining the self-reported attitudes or behaviors of people, usually by questioning a representative, random sample of them. (p. 19)

**sympathetic nervous system** The division of the autonomic nervous system that arouses the body, mobilizing its energy in stressful situations. (p. 49)

**synapse** [SIN-aps] The junction between the axon tip of the sending neuron and the dendrite or cell body of the receiving neuron. The tiny gap at this junction is called the *synaptic gap* or cleft. (p. 45)

**syntax** Rules for combining words into grammatically sensible sentences. (p. 342)

**systematic desensitization** A type of counterconditioning that associates a pleasant relaxed state with gradually increasing anxiety-triggering stimuli. Commonly used to treat phobias. (p. 547)

**task leadership** Goal-oriented leadership that sets standards, organizes work, and focuses attention on goals. (p. 424)

**telegraphic speech** Early speech stage in which the child speaks like a telegram—"go car"—using mostly nouns and verbs and omitting "auxiliary" words. (p. 344)

**temperament** A person's characteristic emotional reactivity and intensity. (p. 97)

**temporal lobes** The portion of the cerebral cortex lying roughly above the ears; includes the auditory areas, each of which receives auditory information primarily from the opposite ear. (p. 60)

**teratogens** Agents, such as chemicals and viruses, that can reach the embryo or fetus during prenatal development and cause harm. (p. 82)

**testosterone** The most important of the male sex hormones. Both males and females have it, but the additional testosterone in males stimulates the growth of the male sex organs in the fetus and the development of the male sex characteristics during puberty. (p. 80)

**texture gradient** A monocular cue for perceiving distance; a gradual change to a less distinct texture suggests increasing distance. (p. 195)

**thalamus** [THAL-uh-muss] The brain's sensory switchboard, located on top of the brainstem; it directs messages to the sensory receiving areas in the cortex and transmits replies to the cerebellum and medulla. (p. 56)

**THC** The major active ingredient in marijuana; triggers a variety of effects, including mild hallucinations. (p. 245)

**Thematic Apperception Test (TAT)** A projective test in which people express their inner feelings and interests through the stories they make up about ambiguous scenes. (p. 468)

**theory** An explanation via an integrated set of principles that organizes and predicts observations. (p. 17)

**Theory X** Assumes that workers are basically lazy, error-prone, and extrinsically motivated by money and, thus, should be directed from above. (p. 425)

**Theory Y** Assumes that, given challenge and freedom, workers are motivated to achieve self-esteem and to demonstrate their competence and creativity. (p. 425)

**threshold** The level of stimulation required to trigger a neural impulse. (p. 44)

**token economy** An operant conditioning procedure that rewards desired behavior. A patient exchanges a token of some sort, earned for exhibiting the desired behavior, for various privileges or treats. (p. 549)

**tolerance** The diminishing of a drug's effect with regular use of the same dose, requiring the user to take larger and larger doses before experiencing the drug's effect. (p. 240)

**trait** A characteristic pattern of behavior or conscious motive; assessed by self-report inventories and peer reports. (p. 473)

**transduction** Conversion of one form of energy into another. In sensation, the transforming of stimulus energies into neural impulses. (p. 157)

**transference** In psychoanalysis, the patient's transfer to the analyst of emotions linked with other relationships (such as love or hatred for a parent). (p. 541)

**two-factor theory** Schachter's theory that to experience emotion one must (1) be physically aroused and (2) cognitively label the arousal. (p. 455)

**two-word stage** Beginning about age 2, the stage in speech development during which a child speaks mostly two-word statements. (p. 344)

**Type A** Friedman and Rosenman's term for competitive, hard-driving, impatient, verbally aggressive, and anger-prone people. (p. 582)

**Type B** Friedman and Rosenman's term for easygoing, relaxed people. (p. 582)

**unconditional positive regard** According to Rogers, an attitude of total acceptance toward another person. (p. 481)

**unconditioned response (UCR)** In classical conditioning, the unlearned, naturally occurring response to the unconditioned stimulus, such as salivation when food is in the mouth. (p. 260)

**unconditioned stimulus (UCS)** In classical conditioning, a stimulus that unconditionally—naturally and automatically—triggers a response. (p. 260)

**unconscious** According to Freud, a reservoir of mostly unacceptable thoughts, wishes, feelings, and memories. According to contemporary research psychologists, information processing of which we are unaware. (p. 463)

**validity** The extent to which a test measures or predicts what it is supposed to. (See also *content validity* and *predictive validity*.) (p. 368)

**variable-interval schedule** In operant conditioning, a schedule of reinforcement that reinforces a response at unpredictable time intervals. (p. 273)

**variable-ratio schedule** In operant conditioning, a schedule of reinforcement that reinforces a response after an unpredictable number of responses. (p. 273)

**visual capture** The tendency for vision to dominate the other senses; we perceive filmed voices as coming from the screen we see rather than from the projector behind us. (p. 191)

**visual cliff** A laboratory device for testing depth perception in infants and young animals. (p. 193)

**visual encoding** The encoding of picture images. (p. 294)

**wavelength** The distance from the peak of one light or sound wave to the peak of the next. Electromagnetic wavelengths vary from the long pulses of radio transmission to the short blips of cosmic rays. (p. 158)

**Weber's law** The principle that, to perceive their difference, two stimuli must differ by a constant minimum percentage (rather than a constant amount). (p. 156)

**Wechsler Adult Intelligence Scale (WAIS)** The current revision (WAIS-R) is the most widely used intelligence test; contains verbal and performance (nonverbal) subtests. (p. 363)

**Wernicke's area** An area of the left temporal lobe involved in language comprehension. (p. 63)

**withdrawal** The discomfort and distress that follow the discontinued use of addictive drugs. (p. 240)

***X* chromosome** The sex chromosome found in both men and women. Females have two *X* chromosomes; males have one. An *X* chromosome from each parent produces a female. (p. 80)

***Y* chromosome** The sex chromosome found only in males. When paired with an *X* sex chromosome from the mother, it produces a male child. (p. 80)

**Young-Helmholtz trichromatic (three-color) theory** The theory that the retina contains three different color receptors—one most sensitive to red, one to green, one to blue—which combined can produce the perception of any color. (p. 165)

**zygote** The fertilized egg; it enters a 2-week period of rapid cell division and develops into an embryo. (p. 81)

# References


**Aas, H., & Klepp, K-I.** (1992). Adolescents' alcohol use related to perceived norms. *Scandinavian Journal of Psychology, 33,* 315–325. (p. 250)

**Abbey, A.** (1987). Misperceptions of friendly behavior as sexual interest: A survey of naturally occurring incidents. *Psychology of Women Quarterly, 11,* 173–194. (p. 673)

**Abbey, A.** (1991). Acquaintance rape and alcohol consumption on college campuses: How are they linked? *Journal of American College Health, 39,* 165–169. (p. 241)

**Abbey, A., Ross, L. T., & McDuffie, D.** (1993). Alcohol's role in sexual assault. In R. R. Watson (Ed.), *Drug and alcohol abuse reviews. Vol. 5: Addictive behaviors in women.* Totowa, NJ: Humana Press. (p. 633)

**ABC News.** (1993). "Hello, tele-psychic," a "Primetime Live" program summarized by *Skeptical Briefs,* March, 1993, p. 8. (p. 210)

**Abrams, D.** (1991). AIDS: What young people believe and what they do. Paper presented at the British Association for the Advancement of Science conference. (p. 491)

**Abrams, D. B., & Wilson, G. T.** (1983). Alcohol, sexual arousal, and self-control. *Journal of Personality and Social Psychology, 45,* 188–198. (p. 242)

**Abramson, L. Y., Metalsky, G. I., & Alloy, L. B.** (1989). Hopelessness depression: A theory-based subtype. *Psychological Review, 96,* 358–372. (p. 520)

**Adams, P. R., & Adams, G. R.** (1984). Mount Saint Helens's ashfall: Evidence for a disaster stress reaction. *American Psychologist, 39,* 252–260. (p. 577)

**Adelmann, P. K., Antonucci, T. C., Crohan, S. F., & Coleman, L. M.** (1989). Empty nest, cohort, and employment in the well-being of midlife women. *Sex Roles, 20,* 173–189. (p. 141)

**Ader, R., & Cohen, N.** (1985). CNS-immune system interactions: Conditioning phenomena. *Behavioral and Brain Sciences, 8,* 379–394. (p. 588)

**Adler, N. E., David, H. P., Major, B. N., Roth, S. H., Russo, N. F., & Wyatt, G. E.** (1990). Psychological responses after abortion. *Science, 248,* 41–44. (p. 578)

**Adler, T.** (1989, March). FAA establishes unit to study human error. *APA Monitor,* p. 4. (p. 190)

***Advertising Age*** (1958, February 10). "Phone now," said CBC subliminally—but nobody did. p. 8. (p. 155)

**Affleck, G., Tennen, H., Urrows, S., & Higgins, P.** (1994). Person and contextual features of daily stress reactivity: Individual differences in relations of undesirable daily events with mood disturbance and chronic pain intensity. *Journal of Personality and Social Psychology, 66,* 329–340. (p. 448)

**Aggleton, J. P., Kentridge, R. W., & Neave, N. J.** (1993). Evidence for longevity differences between left handed and right handed men: An archival study of cricketers. *Journal of Epidemiology and Community Health, 47,* 206–209. (p. 587)

**Agnati, L. F., Bjelke, B., & Fuxe, K.** (1992). Volume transmission in the brain. *American Scientist, 80,* 362–373. (p. 52)

**Aiello, J. R., Thompson, D. D., & Brodzinsky, D. M.** (1983). How funny is crowding anyway? Effects of room size, group size, and the introduction of humor. *Basic and Applied Social Psychology, 4,* 193–207. (p. 627)

**Ainsworth, M. D. S.** (1973). The development of infant-mother attachment. In B. Caldwell & H. Ricciuti (Eds.), *Review of child development research* (Vol. 3). Chicago: University of Chicago Press. (p. 97)

**Ainsworth, M. D. S.** (1979). Infant-mother attachment. *American Psychologist, 34,* 932–937. (p. 98)

**Ainsworth, M. D. S.** (1989). Attachments beyond infancy. *American Psychologist, 44,* 709–716. (p. 97)

**Akin-Ogundeji, O.** (1991). Asserting psychology in Africa. *The Psychologist, 14,* 2–4. (p. 2)

**Albee, G. W.** (1986). Toward a just society: Lessons from observations on the primary prevention of psychopathology. *American Psychologist, 41,* 891–898. (p. 569)

**Alcock, J. E.** (1981). *Parapsychology: Science or magic?* Oxford: Pergamon. (p. 310)

**Alcock, J. E.** (1985, Spring). Parapsychology: The "spiritual" science. *Free Inquiry,* pp. 25–35. (p. 215)

**Alcohol, Drug Abuse, and Mental Health Administration.** (1990). *Economic costs of alcohol and drug abuse and mental illness: 1985.* Rockville, MD: National Clearinghouse for Alcohol and Drug Information. (p. 559)

**Aldrich, M. S.** (1989). Automobile accidents in patients with sleep disorders. *Sleep, 12,* 487–494. (p. 227)

**Aldridge-Morris, R.** (1989). *Multiple personality: An exercise in deception.* Hillsdale, NJ: Erlbaum. (p. 513)

**Alexander, C. N., Langer, E. J., Newman, R. I., Chandler, H. M., & Davies, J. L.** (1989). Transcendental meditation, mindfulness, and longevity: An experimental study with the elderly. *Journal of Personality and Social Psychology, 57,* 950–964. (p. 595)

**Alkon, D. L., Amaral, D. G., Baer, M. F., Black, J., Carew, T. J., Cohen, N. J., Disterhoft, J. F., Eichenbaum, H., Golski, S., Gorman, L. K., Lynch, G., McNaughton, B. L., Mishkin, M., Moyer, J. R., Jr., Olds, J. L., Olton, D. S., Otto, T., Squire, L. R., Staubli, U., Thompson, L. T., & Wible, C.** (1991). Learning and memory. *Brain Research Reviews, 16,* 193–220. (p. 303)

**Allard, F., & Burnett, N.** (1985). Skill in sport. *Canadian Journal of Psychology, 39,* 294–312. (p. 296)

**Allen, L. S., & Gorski, R. A.** (1992). Sexual orientation and the size of the anterior commissure in the human brain. *Proceedings of the National Academy of Sciences, 89,* 7199–7202. (p. 415)

**Allman, A. L.** (1989). Subjective well-being of students with and without disabilities. Paper presented at the Midwestern Psychological Association convention. (p. 448)

**Allport, G. W., & Odbert, H. S.** (1936). Trait-names: A psycholexical study. *Psychological Monographs, 47*(1). (p. 474)

**Altus, W. D.** (1966). Birth order and its sequelae. *Science, 151,* 44–49. (p. 420)

**Alwin, D. F.** (1990). Historical changes in parental orientations to children. In N. Mandell (Ed.), *Sociological studies of child development* (Vol. 3). Greenwich, CT: JAI Press. (p. 105)

**Amabile, T. M.** (1983). *The social psychology of creativity.* New York: Springer-Verlag. (pp. 382, 483)

**Amabile, T. M.** (1987). The motivation to be creative. In S. Isaksen (Ed.), *Frontiers in creativity: Beyond the basics.* Buffalo, NY: Bearly Limited. (p. 382)

**Amabile, T. M.** (1988). From individual creativity to organizational innovation. In K. Gronhaug & G. Kaufmann (Eds.), *Innovation: A crossdisciplinary perspective.* Oslo: Norwegian University Press. (p. 382)

**Amabile, T. M., & Hennessey, B. A.** (1992). The motivation for creativity in children. In A. K. Boggiano & T. S. Pittman (Eds.), *Achievement and motivation: A social-developmental perspective.* New York: Cambridge University Press. (p. 382)

**Amato, P. R., & Keith, B.** (1991). Parental divorce and the well-being of children: A meta-analysis. *Psychological Bulletin, 110,* 26–46. (p. 103)

**Ambady, N., & Rosenthal, R.** (1992). Thin slices of expressive behavior as predictors of interpersonal consequences: A meta-analysis. *Psychological Bulletin, 111,* 256–274. (p. 478)

**Ambady, N., & Rosenthal, R.** (1993). Half a minute: Predicting teacher evaluations from thin slices of nonverbal behavior and physical attractiveness. *Journal of Personality and Social Psychology, 64,* 431–441. (p. 478)

**American Enterprise.** (1992, January/February). Women, men, marriages & ministers. p. 106. (p. 660)

**American Psychiatric Association.** (1990). *The practice of ECT: Recommendations for treatment, training, and privileging.* Washington, DC: American Psychiatric Press. (p. 567)

**American Psychiatric Association.** (1994). *Diagnostic and statistical manual of mental disorders* (4th ed.). Washington, DC: American Psychiatric Press. (p. 379)

**American Psychological Association.** (1986). Council of Representatives statement cited by N. Abeles, Proceedings of the American Psychological Association, Incorporated, for the year 1985: Minutes of the annual meeting of the Council of Representatives August 22 and 25, 1985, Los Angeles, California, and January 31–February 2, 1986, Washington, DC. *American Psychologist, 41,* 633–663. (p. 437)

**American Psychological Association.** (1991). Medical cost offset. Washington, DC: American Psychological Association Practice Directorate. (p. 559)

**American Psychological Association.** (1992). Ethical principles of psychologists and code of conduct. *American Psychologist, 47,* 1597–1611. (p. 35)

**Anda, R., Williamson, D., Jones, D., Macera, C., Eaker, E., Glassman, A., & Marks, J.** (1993). Depressed affect, hopelessness, and the risk of ischemic heart disease in a cohort of U.S. adults. *Epidemiology, 4,* 285–294. (p. 583)

**Andersen, B. L.** (1983). Primary orgasmic dysfunction: Diagnostic considerations and review of treatment. *Psychological Bulletin, 93,* 105–136. (p. 412)

**Andersen, B. L.** (1989). Health psychology's contribution to addressing the cancer problem: Update on accomplishments. *Health Psychology,* 8, 683–703. (p. 585)

**Anderson, C. A., Lepper, M. R., & Ross, L.** (1980). Perseverance of social theories: The role of explanation in the persistence of discredited information. *Journal of Personality and Social Psychology, 39,* 1037–1049. (p. 337)

**Anderson, D. R., & Jose, W. S., II** (1987, December). Employee lifestyle and the bottom line: Results from the StayWell evaluation. *Fitness in Business,* pp. 86–91. (p. 593)

**Anderson, J. R.** (1983). Retrieval of information from long-term memory. *Science, 220,* 25–30. (p. 308)

**Anderson, J. R., & Schooler, L. J.** (1991). Reflections of the environment in memory. *Psychological Science, 2,* 396–408. (p. 292)

**Anderson, V. E.** (1994). Genes, behavior, and responsibility: Research perspectives. In M. S. Frankel & A. H. Teich (Eds.), *The genetic frontier: Ethics, law, and policy.* Washington, DC: American Association for the Advancement of Science. (p. 528)

**Andersson, B. E.** (1989). Effects of public daycare: A longitudinal study. *Child Development, 60,* 857–866. (p. 102)

**Andreasen, N. C., Flaum, M., Swayze, V., II, O'Leary, D. S., Alliger, R., Cohen, G., Ehrhardt, J., & Yuh, W. T. C.** (1993). Intelligence and brain structure in normal individuals. *American Journal of Psychiatry, 150,* 130–134. (p. 376)

**Angoff, W. H.** (1987). The nature-nurture debate, aptitudes, and group differences. Presidential address to American Psychological Association Division 5. (p. 388)

**Angoff, W. H.** (1988, Winter). A philosophical discussion: The issues of test and item bias. *ETS Developments,* pp. 10–11. (pp. 379, 392)

**Antaki, C.** (1989, May). A brief account of psychology in Nicaragua. *The Psychologist*, pp. 208–209. (p. 2)

**Antoni, M. H., LaPerriere, A., Schneiderman, N., & Fletcher, M. A.** (1991). Stress and immunity in individuals at risk for AIDS. *Stress Medicine, 7,* 35–44. (p. 585)

**Antony, M. M., Brown, T. A., & Barlow, D. H.** (1992). Current perspectives on panic and panic disorder. *Current Directions in Psychological Science, 1,* 79–82. (p. 509)

**Antrobus, J.** (1991). Dreaming: Cognitive processes during cortical activation and high afferent thresholds. *Psychological Review, 98,* 96–121. (p. 229)

**Arendt, H.** (1963). *Eichmann in Jerusalem: A report on the banality of evil.* New York: Viking Press. (p. 122)

**Aries, E.** (1987). Gender and communication. In P. Shaver & C. Henrick (Eds.), *Review of Personality and Social Psychology, 7,* 177–200. (p. 671)

**Arnold, R. B.** (1991, October 7). A star cries incest. *People,* pp. 84–88. (p. 318)

**Aronson, J.** (1992). Women's sense of responsibility for the care of old people: "But who else is going to do it?" *Gender & Society, 6,* 8–29. (p. 669)

**Asarnow, J. R.** (1988). Children at risk for schizophrenia: Converging lines of evidence. *Schizophrenia Bulletin, 14,* 613–621. (p. 529)

**Asch, S. E.** (1955). Opinions and social pressure. *Scientific American, 193,* 31–35. (p. 620)

**Aserinsky, E.** (1988, January 17). Personal communication. (p. 222)

**Aspinwall, L. G., & Taylor, S. E.** (1992). Modeling cognitive adaptation: A longitudinal investigation of the impact of individual differences and coping on college adjustment and performance. *Journal of Personality and Social Psychology, 63,* 989–1003. (p. 589)

**Associated Press.** (1993, June 17). `We deserve the money we make,' doctors say. *Grand Rapids Press,* p. A9. (p. 452)

**Astin, A., Korn, W. S., & Riggs, E. R.** (1993). *The American freshman: National norms for Fall 1993.* Los Angeles: Higher Education Research Institute, Graduate School of Education, UCLA. (pp. 15, 248, 448, 669, 672, 679)

**Astin, A. W., Green, K. C., & Korn, W. S.** (1987). The American freshman: Twenty year trends. (A report of the Cooperative Institutional Research Program sponsored by the American Council on Education.) Los Angeles, CA: Higher Education Research Institute, Graduate School of Education, UCLA. (p. 248)

**Astin, A. W., Korn, W. S., & Berz, E. R.** (1989). *The American freshman: National norms for Fall 1989.* Los Angeles: American Council on Education and UCLA. (p. 417)

**Astin, G. R., & Garber, H.** (1982). *The rise and fall of national test scores.* New York: Academic Press. (p. 367)

**Atkinson, R.** (1988). *The teenage world: Adolescent self-image in ten countries.* New York: Plenum Press. (p. 106)

**Atwell, R. H.** (1986, July 28). Drugs on campus: A perspective. *Higher Education & National Affairs,* p. 5. (p. 242)

**Averill, J. R.** (1969). Autonomic response patterns during sadness and mirth. *Psychophysiology, 5,* 399–414. (p. 435)

**Averill, J. R.** (1983). Studies on anger and aggression: Implications for theories of emotion. *American Psychologist, 38,* 1145–1160. (p. 446)

**Averill, J. R.** (1993). William James's other theory of emotion. In M. E. Donnelly (Ed.), *Reinterpreting the legacy of William James.* Washington, DC: American Psychological Association. (p. 455)

**Ax, A. F.** (1953). The physiological differentiation of fear and anger in humans. *Psychosomatic Medicine, 15,* 433–442. (p. 435)

**Axinn, W. G., & Thornton, A.** (1992). The relationship between cohabitation and divorce: Selectivity or causal influence? *Demography, 29,* 357–374. (p. 417)

**Baars, B. J., & McGovern, K.** (1994). Consciousness. In V. Ramachandran (Ed.), *Encyclopedia of human behavior.* Orlando, FL: Academic Press. (p. 188)

**Babad, E., Bernieri, F., & Rosenthal, R.** (1991). Students as judges of teachers' verbal and nonverbal behavior. *American Educational Research Journal, 28,* 211–234. (p. 439)

**Bachevalier, J., Landis, L. S., Walker, L. C., Brickson, M., Mishkin, M., Price, D.L., & Cork, L. C.** (1991). Aged monkeys exhibit behavioral deficits indicative of widespread cerebral dysfunction. *Neurobiology of Aging, 12,* 99–111. (p. 135)

**Bachevalier, J., & Mishkin, M.** (1992). Ontogenetic development and decline of memory functions in nonhuman primates. In I. Kostovic (Ed.), *Neurodevelopment, aging, and cognition.* Boston: Birkhauser. (p. 135)

**Bachman, J. G., Johnston, L. D., & O'Malley, P. M.** (1987). *Monitoring the future: Questionnaire responses from the nation's high school seniors, 1986.* Ann Arbor, MI: Institute for Social Research, University of Michigan. (p. 125)

**Backman, L., & Dixon, R. A.** (1992). Psychological compensation: A theoretical framework. *Psychological Bulletin, 112,* 259–283. (p. 172)

**Backus, J.** (1977). *The acoustical foundations of music* (2nd ed.). New York: Norton. (p. 170)

**Baddeley, A. D.** (1982). *Your memory: A user's guide.* New York: Macmillan. (pp. 291, 292)

**Badenhoop, M. S., & Johansen, M. K.** (1980). Do reentry women have special needs? *Psychology of Women Quarterly, 4,* 591–595. (p. 136)

**Bahrick, H. P.** (1984). Semantic memory content in permastore: 50 years of memory for Spanish learned in school. *Journal of Experimental Psychology: General, 111,* 1–29. (pp. 301, 302)

**Bahrick, H. P., Bahrick, L. E., Bahrick, A. S., & Bahrick, P. E.** (1993). Maintenance of foreign language vocabulary and the spacing effect. *Psychological Science, 4,* 316–321. (p. 292)

**Bahrick, H. P., Bahrick, P. O., & Wittlinger, R. P.** (1975). Fifty years of memory for names and faces: A cross-sectional approach. *Journal of Experimental Psychology: General, 104,* 54–75. (p. 308)

**Bahrick, H. P., & Hall, L. K.** (1991). Lifetime maintenance of high school mathematics content. *Journal of Experimental Psychology: General, 120,* 20–33. (p. 292)

**Bailey, J. M., Gaulin, S., Agyei, Y, & Gladue, B. A.** (1994). Effects of gender and sexual orientation on evolutionarily relevant aspects of human mating psychology. *Journal of Personality and Social Psychology, 66,* 1081–1093. (p. 672)

**Bailey, J. M., & Pillard, R.** (1991, December 17). Are some people born gay? *New York Times,* p. A21. (p. 415)

**Bailey, J. M., & Pillard, R. C.** (1991). A genetic study of male sexual orientation. *Archives of General Psychiatry, 48,* 1089–1096. (p. 415)

**Bailey, J. M., & Pillard, R. C.** (1994, January). The innateness of homosexuality. *Harvard Mental Health Letter,* pp. 4–6. (p. 416)

**Bailey, J. M., Pillard, R. C., Neale, M. C., & Agyei, Y.** (1993). Heritable factors influence sexual orientation in women. *Archives of General Psychiatry, 50,* 217–223. (p. 415)

**Baillargeon, R.** (1992). The object concept revisited. In C. Granrud (Ed.), *Visual perception and cognition in infancy. Carnegie-Mellon Symposia on Cognition* (Vol. 23). Hillsdale, NJ: Erlbaum. (p. 92)

**Bairagi, R.** (1987). Food crises and female children in rural Bangladesh. *Social Science, 72,* 48–51. (p. 683)

**Baker, E. L.** (1987). The state of the art of clinical hypnosis. *International Journal of Clinical and Experimental Hypnosis, 35,* 203–214. (p. 236)

**Baker-Ward, L., Gordon, B. N., Ornstein, P. A., Larus, D. M., & Clubb, P. A.** (1993). Young children's long-term retention of a pediatric examination. *Child Development, 64,* 1519–1533. (p. 313)

**Balakrishan, T. R., Rao, K. V., Lapierre-Adamcyk, E., & Krotki, K. J.** (1987). A hazard model analysis of the covariates of marriage dissolution in Canada. *Demography, 24,* 395–406. (p. 417)

**Baldwin, E.** (1993). The case for animal research in psychology. *Journal of Social Issues, 49*(1), 121–131. (p. 34)

**Ball, W., & Tronick, E.** (1971). Infant responses to impending collision: Optical and real. *Science, 171,* 818–820. (p. 193)

**Baltes, P. B.** (1993). The aging mind: Potential and limits. *The Gerontologist, 33,* 580–594. (p. 137)

**Bandura, A.** (1982). The psychology of chance encounters and life paths. *American Psychologist, 37,* 747–755. (p. 139)

**Bandura, A.** (1986). *Social foundations of thought and action: A social-cognitive theory.* Englewood Cliffs, NJ: Prentice-Hall. (p. 488)

**Bandura, A., Blanchard, E. B., & Ritter, B.** (1969). Relative efficacy of desensitization and modeling approaches for inducing behavioral, affective, and attitudinal changes. *Journal of Personality and Social Psychology, 13,* 173–199. (p. 547)

**Bandura, A., Ross, D., & Ross, S. A.** (1961). Transmission of aggression through imitation of aggressive models. *Journal of Abnormal and Social Psychology, 63,* 575–582. (p. 281)

**Barbaree, H. E., & Marshall, W. L.** (1991). The role of male sexual arousal in rape: Six models. *Journal of Consulting and Clinical Psychology, 59,* 621–630. (p. 637)

**Barinaga, M.** (1991). How long is the human life-span? *Science, 254,* 936–938. (p. 132)

**Barinaga, M.** (1992a). The brain remaps its own contours. *Science, 258,* 216–218. (p. 86)

**Barinaga, M.** (1992b). How scary things get that way. *Science, 258,* 887–888. (p. 445)

**Barker, S. L., Funk, S. C., & Houston, B. K.** (1988). Psychological treatment versus nonspecific factors: A meta-analysis of conditions that engender comparable expectations for improvement. *Clinical Psychology Review, 8,* 579–594. (p. 560)

**Barnett, P. A., & Gotlib, I. H.** (1988). Psychosocial functioning and depression: Distinguishing among antecedents, concomitants, and consequences. *Psychological Bulletin, 104,* 97–126. (p. 520)

**Barnier, A. J., & McConkey, K. M.** (1992). Reports of real and false memories: The relevance of hypnosis, hypnotizability, and context of memory test. *Journal of Abnormal Psychology, 101,* 521–527. (p. 235)

**Baron, J.** (1985). *Rationality and intelligence.* New York: Cambridge University Press. (p. 371)

**Baron, R. A.** (1987). Interviewer's mood and reaction to job applicants: The influence of affective states on applied social judgments. *Journal of Applied Social Psychology, 17,* 911–926. (p. 447)

**Baron, R. A.** (1988). Negative effects of destructive criticism: Impact on conflict, self-efficacy, and task performance. *Journal of Applied Psychology, 73,* 199–207. (p. 279)

**Baron, R. A.** (1990). Environmentally induced positive affect: Its impact on self-efficacy, task performance, negotiation, and conflict. *Journal of Applied Social Psychology, 20,* 368–384. (p. 180)

**Baron, R. S., Cutrona, C. E., Hicklin, D., Russell, D. W., & Lubaroff, D. M.** (1990). Social support and immune function among spouses of cancer patients. *Journal of Personality and Social Psychology, 59,* 344–352. (p. 598)

**Barton, J., Chassin, L., Presson, C. C., & Sherman, S. J.** (1982). Social image factors as motivators of smoking initiation in early and middle adolescence. *Child Development, 53,* 1499–1511. (p. 600)

**Bartoshuk, L. M.** (1993). The wisdom of the body: Using case studies to teach sensation and perception. Paper presented to the National Institute on the Teaching of Psychology, St. Petersburg Beach, FL. (p. 178)

**Baruch, G. K., & Barnett, R.** (1986). Role quality, multiple role involvement, and psychological well-being in midlife women. *Journal of Personality and Social Psychology, 51,* 578–585. (p. 142)

**Bashore, T. R., & Rapp, P. E.** (1993). Are there alternatives to traditional polygraph procedures? *Psychological Bulletin, 113,* 3–22. (p. 437)

**Bass, E., & Davis, L.** (1988). *The courage to heal.* New York: Harper & Row. (p. 318)

**Bass, L. E., & Kane-Williams, E.** (1993). Stereotype or reality: Another look at alcohol and drug use among African American children. U.S. Department of Health and Human Services, *Public Health Reports, 108* (Supplement 1), 78–84. (p. 250)

**Bat-Chava, Y.** (1993). Antecedents of self-esteem in deaf people: A meta-analytic review. *Rehabilitation Psychology, 38*(4), 221–234. (p. 173)

**Batson, C. D.** (1987). Prosocial motivation: Is it ever truly altruistic? In L. Berkowitz (Ed.), *Advances in experimental social psychology* (Vol. 20). Orlando, FL: Academic Press. (p. 643)

**Baum, A., & Fleming, I.** (1993). Implications of psychological research on stress and technological accidents. *American Psychologist, 48,* 665–672. (p. 577)

**Baumann, L. J., & Leventhal, H.** (1985). "I can tell when my blood pressure is up, can't I?" *Health Psychology, 4,* 203–218. (p. 590)

**Baumeister, R. F.** (1989). The optimal margin of illusion. *Journal of Social and Clinical Psychology, 8,* 176–189. (pp. 335, 485)

**Baumeister, R. F.** (1993). Understanding the inner nature of low self-esteem: Uncertain, fragile, protective, and conflicted. In R. F. Baumeister (Ed.), *Self-esteem: The puzzle of low self-regard.* New York: Plenum. (p. 483)

**Baumeister, R. F., & Leary, M. R.** (1994). The need to belong: Desire for interpersonal attachment as a fundamental human motivation. *Psychological Bulletin,* in press. (p. 427)

**Baumeister, R. F., Stillwell, A., & Wotman, S. R.** (1990). Victim and perpetrator accounts of interpersonal conflict: Autobiographical narratives about anger. *Journal of Personality and Social Psychology, 59,* 994–1005. (p. 447)

**Baumeister, R. F., & Tice, D. M.** (1986). How adolescence became the struggle for self: A historical transformation of psychological development. In J. Suls & A. G. Greenwald (Eds.), *Psychological perspectives on the self* (Vol. 3). Hillsdale, NJ: Erlbaum. (p. 117)

**Baumeister, R. F., Tice, D. M., & Hutton, D. G.** (1989). Self-presentational motivations and personality differences in self-esteem. *Journal of Personality, 57,* 547–579. (p. 483)

**Baumgardner, A. H.** (1990). To know oneself is to like oneself: Self-certainty and self-affect. *Journal of Personality and Social Psychology, 58,* 1062–1072. (p. 124)

**Baumgardner, A. H., Kaufman, C. M., & Levy, P. E.** (1989). Regulating affect interpersonally: When low esteem leads to greater enhancement. *Journal of Personality and Social Psychology, 56,* 907–921. (p. 483)

**Baumrind, D.** (1982). Adolescent sexuality: Comment on Williams' and Silka's comments on Baumrind. *American Psychologist, 37,* 1402–1403. (p. 416)

**Baumrind, D.** (1983). Rejoinder to Lewis's reinterpretation of parental firm control effects: Are authoritative families really harmonious? *Psychological Bulletin, 94,* 132–142. (pp. 104, 105)

**Baumrind, D.** (1991). Parenting styles and adolescent development. In J. Brooks-Gunn, R. Lerner, & A. C. Petersen (Eds.), *The encyclopedia of adolescence.* New York: Garland. (p. 104)

**Bayley, N.** (1949). Consistency and variability in the growth of intelligence from birth to eighteen years. *Journal of Genetic Psychology, 75,* 165–196. (p. 378)

**Beaman, A. L., & Klentz, B.** (1983). The supposed physical attractiveness bias against supporters of the women's movement: A meta-analysis. *Personality and Social Psychology Bulletin, 9,* 544–550. (p. 647)

**Beardsley, L. M.** (1994). Medical diagnosis and treatment across cultures. In W. J. Lonner & R. Malpass (Eds.), *Psychology and culture.* Boston: Allyn & Bacon. (p. 502)

**Beauchamp, G. K.** (1987). The human preference for excess salt. *American Scientist, 75,* 27–33. (p. 404)

**Beck, A. J., Kline, S. A., & Greenfeld, L. A.** (1988). Survey of youth in custody, 1987 (U.S. Department of Justice, Bureau of Justice Statistics Special Report). (p. 635)

**Beck, A. T., Rush, A. J., Shaw, B. F., & Emery, G.** (1979). *Cognitive therapy of depression.* New York: Guilford Press. (p. 552)

**Beck, A. T., & Steer, R. A.** (1989). Clinical predictors of eventual suicide: A 5– to 10–year prospective study of suicide attempters. *Journal of Affective Disorders, 17,* 203–209. (p. 517)

**Beck, A. T., & Young, J. E.** (1978, September). College blues. *Psychology Today,* pp. 80–92. (pp. 514, 522)

**Becklen, R., & Cervone, D.** (1983). Selective looking and the noticing of unexpected events. *Memory and Cognition, 11,* 601–608. (p. 188)

**Begg, I. M., Needham, D. R., & Bookbinder, M.** (1993). Do backward messages unconsciously affect listeners? No. *Canadian Journal of Experimental Psychology, 47,* 1–14. (p. 154)

**Beitman, B. D., Goldfried, M. R., & Norcross, J. C.** (1989). The movement toward integrating the psychotherapies: An overview. *American Journal of Psychiatry, 146,* 138–147. (p. 540)

**Bell, A. P.** (1982, November/December). Sexual preference: A postscript (SIECUS Report, 11, No. 2). *Church and Society,* pp. 34–37 (p. 415)

**Bell, A. P., Weinberg, M. S., & Hammersmith, S. K.** (1981). *Sexual preference: Its development in men and women.* Bloomington: Indiana University Press. (p. 414)

**Bell, R. Q., & Harper, L. V.** (1977). *Child effects on adults.* Hillsdale, NJ: Erlbaum. (p. 112)

**Bell, R. Q., & Waldrop, M. F.** (1989). Achievement and cognitive correlates of minor physical anomalies in early development. In M. G. Bornstein & N. A. Krasnegor (Eds.), *Stability and continuity in mental development: Behavioral and biological perspectives.* Hillsdale, NJ: Erlbaum. (p. 378)

**Beloff, J.** (1985, Spring). Science, religion and the paranormal. *Free Inquiry,* pp. 36–41 (p. 215)

**Belsher, G., & Costello, C. G.** (1988). Relapse after recovery from unipolar depression: A critical review. *Psychological Bulletin, 104,* 84–96. (p. 518)

**Belsky, J.** (1988). The "effects" of infant day care reconsidered. *Early Childhood Research Quarterly,* 3, 235–272. (p. 101)

**Belsky, J.** (1990). Parental and nonparental child care and children's socioemotional development: A decade in review. *Journal of Marriage and the Family, 52,* 885–903. (p. 101)

**Belsky, J., Lang, M., & Huston, T. L.** (1986). Sex typing and division of labor as determinants of marital change across the transition to parenthood. *Journal of Personality and Social Psychology, 50,* 517–522. (p. 141)

**Bem, D. J.** (1984). Quoted in *The Skeptical Inquirer, 8,* 194. (p. 212)

**Bem, D. J., & Honorton, C.** (1994). Does psi exist? Replicable evidence for an anomalous process of information transfer. *Psychological Bulletin, 115,* 4–18. (p. 214)

**Bem, S.** (1993). *The lenses of gender.* New Haven, CT: Yale University Press. (p. 676)

**Bem, S. L.** (1985). Androgyny and gender schema theory: A conceptual and empirical integration. *Nebraska Symposium on Motivation, 32,* 179–226. (p. 679)

**Bem, S. L.** (1987). Masculinity and femininity exist only in the mind of the perceiver. In J. M. Reinisch, L. A. Rosenblum, & S. A. Sanders (Eds.), *Masculinity/femininity: Basic perspectives.* New York: Oxford University Press. (pp. 676, 679)

**Benassi, V. A., & Knoth, R. L.** (1993). The intractable conjunction fallacy: Statistical sophistication, instructional set, and training. *Journal of Social Behavior and Personality, 8,* 83–96. (p. 332)

**Benassi, V. A., Sweeney, P. D., & Dufour, C. L.** (1988). Is there a relation between locus of control orientation and depression? *Journal of Abnormal Psychology, 97,* 357–367. (p. 489)

**Benbow, C. P.** (1988). Sex differences in mathematical reasoning ability in intellectually talented preadolescents: Their nature, effects, and possible causes. *Behavioral and Brain Sciences, 11,* 169–182. (p. 667)

**Benderly, B. L.** (1989, November). Don't believe everything you read: A case study of how the politics of sex-difference research turned a small finding into a major media flap. *Psychology Today,* pp. 67–69. (p. 674)

**Bennett, N. G., Blanc, A. K., & Bloom, D. E.** (1988). Commitment and the modern union: Assessing the link between premarital cohabitation and subsequent marital stability. *American Sociological Review, 53,* 127–138. (p. 417).

**Bennett, R.** (1991, February). Pornography and extrafamilial child sexual abuse: Examining the relationship. Unpublished manuscript, Los Angeles Police Department Sexually Exploited Child Unit. (p. 638)

**Benson, H., & Klipper, M. Z.** (1976). *The relaxation response.* New York: Morrow. (p. 595)

**Benson, H., & Proctor, W.** (1984). *Beyond the relaxation response: How to harness the healing power of your personal beliefs.* New York: Times Books. (p. 595)

**Benson, H., & Proctor, W.** (1987). *Your maximum mind.* New York: Times Books/Random House. (p. 595)

**Benson, P. L.** (1992, Spring). Patterns of religious development in adolescence and adulthood. *Psychologists Interested in Religious Issues Newsletter,* 2–9. (p. 669)

**Berenbaum, S. A., & Hines, M.** (1992). Early androgens are related to childhood sex-typed toy preferences. *Psychological Science, 3,* 203–206. (p. 673)

**Bergin, A. E.** (1980). Psychotherapy and religious values. *Journal of Consulting and Clinical Psychology, 48,* 95–105. (p. 562)

**Bergin, A. E.** (1991). Values and religious issues in psychotherapy and mental health. *American Psychologist, 46,* 394–403. (p. 422)

**Bergsholm, P., Larsen, J. L., Rosendahl, K., & Holsten, F.** (1989). Electroconvulsive therapy and cerebral computed tomography. *Acta Psychiatrica Scandinavia, 80,* 566–572. (p. 567)

**Berkowitz, L.** (1983). Aversively stimulated aggression: Some parallels and differences in research with animals and humans. *American Psychologist, 38,* 1135–1144. (p. 634)

**Berkowitz, L.** (1989). Frustration-aggression hypothesis: Examination and reformulation. *Psychological Bulletin, 106,* 59–73. (p. 634)

**Berkowitz, L.** (1990). On the formation and regulation of anger and aggression: A cognitive-neoassociationistic analysis. *American Psychologist, 45,* 494–503. (p. 446)

**Berman, M., Gladue, B., & Taylor, S.** (1993). The effects of hormones, Type A behavior pattern, and provocation on aggression in men. *Motivation and Emotion, 17,* 125–138. (p. 633)

**Bernard, J.** (1976). *Sex differences: An overview.* New York: MSS Modular Publications. (p. 668)

**Berndt, T. J.** (1992). Friendship and friends' influence in adolescence. *Current Directions in Psychological Science, 1,* 156–159. (p. 669)

**Berry, D. S., & McArthur, L. Z.** (1986). Perceiving character in faces: The impact of age-related craniofacial changes on social perception. *Psychological Bulletin, 100,* 3–18. (p. 263)

**Berscheid, E.** (1981). An overview of the psychological effects of physical attractiveness and some comments upon the psychological effects of knowledge of the effects of physical attractiveness. In G. W. Lucker, K. Ribbens, & J. A. McNamara (Eds.), *Psychological aspects of facial form* (Craniofacial growth series). Ann Arbor: Center for Human Growth and Development, University of Michigan. (p. 645)

**Berscheid, E.** (1985). Interpersonal attraction. In G. Lindzey & E. Aronson (Eds.), *The handbook of social psychology.* New York: Random House. (p. 428)

**Berscheid, E., Gangestad, S. W., & Kulakowski, D.** (1984). Emotion in close relationships: Implications for relationship counseling. In S. D. Brown & R. W. Lent (Eds.), *Handbook of counseling psychology.* New York: Wiley. (p. 648)

**Best, J. A., & Suedfeld, P.** (1982). Restricted environmental stimulation therapy and behavioral self-management in smoking cessation. *Journal of Applied Social Psychology, 12,* 408–419. (p. 182)

**Beyer, L.** (1990, Fall issue on women). Life behind the veil. *Time,* p. 37. (p. 683)

**Beyerstein, B., & Beyerstein, D.** (Eds.). (1992). *The write stuff: Evaluations of graphology.* Buffalo, NY: Prometheus Books. (p. 492)

**Bhatt, R. S., Wasserman, E. A., Reynolds, W. F., Jr., & Knauss, K. S.** (1988). Conceptual behavior in pigeons: Categorization of both familiar and novel examples from four classes of natural and artificial stimuli. *Journal of Experimental Psychology: Animal Behavior Processes, 14,* 219–234. (p. 269)

**Binet, A., & Simon, T.** (1905; reprinted 1916). New methods for the diagnosis of the intellectual level of subnormals. In A. Binet & T. Simon, *The development of intelligence in children.* Baltimore: Williams & Wilkins. (p. 361)

**Binitie, A.** (1975). A factor-analytical study of depression across cultures (African and European). *British Journal of Psychiatry, 127,* 559–563. (p. 510)

**Birren, J. E., & Fisher, L. M.** (1990). The elements of wisdom: Overview and integration. In R. J. Sternberg (Ed.), *Wisdom: Its nature, origins, and development.* New York: Cambridge University Press. (p. 137)

**Bishop, G. D.** (1984). Gender, role, and illness behavior in a military population. *Health Psychology, 3,* 519–534. (p. 592)

**Bishop, G. D.** (1987). Lay conceptions of physical symptoms. *Journal of Applied Social Psychology, 17,* 127–146. (p. 592)

**Bishop, G. D.** (1991). Understanding the understanding of illness: Lay disease representations. In J. A. Skelton & R. T. Croyle (Eds.), *Mental representation in health and illness.* New York: Springer-Verlag. (p. 327)

**Bjork, R. A.** (1978). The updating of human memory. In G. H. Bower (Ed.), *The psychology of learning and motivation* (Vol. 12). New York: Academic Press. (p. 298)

**Bjorklund, D. F., & Green, B. L.** (1992). The adaptive nature of cognitive immaturity. *American Psychologist, 47,* 46–54. (p. 94)

**Blackmore, S.** (1991, Fall). Near-death experiences: In or out of the body? *Skeptical Inquirer,* pp. 34–45. (p. 251)

**Blackmore, S.** (1993). *Dying to live.* Amherst, NY: Prometheus Books. (p. 251)

**Blake, J.** (1989). Number of siblings and educational attainment. *Science, 245,* 32–36. (p. 420)

**Blakemore, C., & Cooper, G. F.** (1970). Development of the brain depends on the visual environment. *Nature, 228,* 477–478. (p. 204)

**Block, J.** (1981). Some enduring and consequential structures of personality. In A. I. Rabin (Ed.), *Further explorations in personality.* New York: Wiley. (p. 146)

**Blom, J. M. C., Tamarkin, L., Shiber, J.R., & Nelson, R. J.** (1994). *Learned conditioned immunosuppression is associated with increased risk of chemically-induced tumors.* Unpublished manuscript, Department of Psychology, Johns Hopkins University. (p. 588)

**Bloom, B. J.** (1964). *Stability and change in human characteristics.* New York: Wiley. (p. 378)

**Bloom, B. S.** (Ed.). (1985). *Developing talent in young people.* New York: Ballantine. (p. 420)

**Bloom, F. E.** (1993, January/February). What's new in neurotransmitters. *BrainWork,* pp. 7–9. (p. 46)

**Bodenhausen, G. V., Sheppard, L. A., & Kramer, G. P.** (1994). Negative affect and social judgment: The differential impact of anger and sadness. *European Journal of Social Psychology, 24,* 45–62. (p. 690)

**Boesch-Achermann, H., & Boesch, C.** (1993). Tool use in wild chimpanzees: New light from dark forests. *Current Directions in Psychological Science, 2,* 18–21. (p. 328)

**Boggiano, A. K., Barrett, M., Weiher, A. W., McClelland, G. H., & Lusk, C. M.** (1987). Use of the maximal-operant principle to motivate children's intrinsic interest. *Journal of Personality and Social Psychology, 53,* 866–879. (p. 276)

**Boggiano, A. K., Harackiewicz, J. M., Bessette, M. M., & Main, D. S.** (1985). Increasing children's interest through performance-contingent reward. *Social Cognition, 3,* 400–411. (p. 277)

**Bohannon, J. N., & Symons, V. L.** (1992). Flashbulb memories: Confidence, consistency, and quantity. In E. Winograd & U. Neisser (Eds.), *Affect and accuracy in recall: Studies of "flashbulb" memories.* New York: Cambridge University Press. (p. 304)

**Bolger, N., DeLongis, A., Kessler, R. C., & Schilling, E. A.** (1989). Effects of daily stress on negative mood. *Journal of Personality and Social Psychology, 57,* 808–818. (p. 448)

**Bond, C. F., Jr., Pitre, U., & Van Leeuwen, M. D.** (1991). Encoding operations and the next-in-line effect. *Personality and Social Psychology Bulletin, 17,* 435–441. (p. 292)

**Bond, M. H.** (1988). Finding universal dimensions of individual variation in multi-cultural studies of values: The Rokeach and Chinese values surveys. *Journal of Personality and Social Psychology, 55,* 1009–1015. (p. 106)

**Bond, R., & Smith, P. B.** (1994). Culture and conformity: A meta-analysis of studies using the Asch-type perceptual judgment task. *British Psychological Society 1994 Proceedings,* p. 41. (p. 622)

**Bonner, E.** (1990, May 4). Missing-child study: Relative often to blame. *Chicago Tribune.* (p. 333)

**Boring, E. G.** (1930). A new ambiguous figure. *American Journal of Psychology, 42,* 444–445. (p. 205)

**Borkenau, P., & Liebler, A.** (1993). Convergence of stranger ratings of personality and intelligence with self-ratings, partner ratings, and measured intelligence. *Journal of Personality and Social Psychology, 65,* 546–553. (p. 477)

**Bornstein, M. H.** (1989). Stability in early mental development: From attention and information processing in infancy to language and cognition in childhood. In M. G. Bornstein & N. A. Krasnegor (Eds.), *Stability and continuity in mental development: Behavioral and biological perspectives.* Hillsdale, NJ: Erlbaum. (p. 96)

**Bornstein, M. H., Tal, J., Rahn, C., Galperin, C. Z., Pecheux, M-G., Lamour, M., Toda, S., Azuma, H., Ogino, M., & Tamis-LeMonda, C. S.** (1992). Functional analysis of the contents of maternal speech to infants of 5 and 13 months in four cultures: Argentina, France, Japan, and the United States. *Developmental Psychology, 28,* 593–603. (p. 106)

**Bornstein, M. H., Tamis-LeMonda, C. S., Tal, J., Ludemann, P., Toda, S., Rahn, C. W., Pecheux, M-G., Azuma, H., & Vardi, D.** (1992). Maternal responsiveness to infants in three societies: The United States, France, and Japan. *Child Development, 63,* 808–821. (p. 106)

**Bornstein, R. F.** (1989). Exposure and affect: Overview and meta-analysis of research, 1968–1987. *Psychological Bulletin, 106,* 265–289. (p. 644)

**Bornstein, R. F., Galley, D. J., Leone, D. R., & Kale, A. R.** (1991). The temporal stability of ratings of parents: Test-retest reliability and influence of parental contact. *Journal of Social Behavior and Personality, 6,* 641–649. (p. 310)

**Bornstein, R. F., & Pittman, T. S.** (Eds.). (1992). *Perception without awareness: Cognitive, clinical, and social perspectives.* New York: Guilford Press. (p. 155)

**Bothwell, R. K., Brigham, J. C., & Malpass, R. S.** (1989). Cross-racial identification. *Personality and Social Psychology Bulletin, 15,* 19–25. (p. 685)

**Bothwell, R. K., Deffenbacher, K. A., & Brigham, J. C.** (1987). Correlation of eyewitness accuracy and confidence: Optimality hypothesis revised. *Journal of Applied Psychology, 72,* 691–695. (p. 312)

**Bouchard, T.** (1990). Interview with T. M. Skovholt, Counseling implications of genetic research: A dialogue with Thomas Bouchard. *Journal of Counseling and Development, 68,* 633–636. (p. 112)

**Bouchard, T. J., Jr.** (1981, December 6). Interview on *Nova: Twins* [program broadcast by the Public Broadcasting Service]. (p. 109)

**Bouchard, T. J., Jr.** (1982). Twins—Nature's twice told tale. In *1983 Yearbook of science and the future.* Chicago: Encyclopaedia Britannica. (p. 384)

**Bouchard, T. J., Jr.** (1993). The genetic architecture of human intelligence. In P. A. Vernon (Ed.), *Biological approaches to the study of human intelligence.* Norwood, NJ: Ablex. (p. 384)

**Bouchard, T. J., Lykken, D. T., McGue, M., Segal, N. L., & Tellegen, A.** (1990). Sources of human psychological differences: The Minnesota study of twins reared apart. *Science, 250,* 223–228. (pp. 109, 675)

**Bouchard, T. J., Jr., & Segal, N. L.** (1988). Heredity, environment, and IQ. In *Instructor's Resource Manual* to accompany G. Lindzey, R. Thompson, & B. Spring, *Psychology* (3rd ed.). New York: Worth Publishers. (p. 384)

**Bower, G. H.** (1983). Affect and cognition. *Philosophical Transaction: Royal Society of London, Series B, 302,* 387–402. (p. 310)

**Bower, G. H.** (1986). Prime time in cognitive psychology. In P. Eelen (Ed.), *Cognitive research and behavior therapy: Beyond the conditioning paradigm.* Amsterdam: North Holland Publishers. (p. 308)

**Bower, G. H., & Clark, M. C.** (1969). Narrative stories as mediators for serial learning. *Psychonomic Science, 14,* 181–182. (p. 295)

**Bower, G. H., Clark, M. C., Lesgold, A. M., & Winzenz, D.** (1969). Hierarchical retrieval schemes in recall of categorized word lists. *Journal of Verbal Learning and Verbal Behavior, 8,* 323–343. (p. 297)

**Bower, G. H., & Morrow, D. G.** (1990). Mental models in narrative comprehension. *Science, 247,* 44–48. (p. 293)

**Bowers, K. S.** (1984). Hypnosis. In N. Endler & J. M. Hunt (Eds.), *Personality and behavioral disorders* (2nd ed.). New York: Wiley. (pp. 234, 236)

**Bowers, K. S.** (1987, July). Personal communication. (p. 235)

**Bowers, K. S.** (1990). Unconscious influences and hypnosis. In J. E. Singer (Ed.), *Repression and dissociation: Implications for personality theory, psychopathology, and health.* Chicago: University of Chicago Press. (p. 239)

**Bowers, K. S., & LeBaron, S.** (1986). Hypnosis and hypnotizability: Implications for clinical intervention. *Hospital and Community Psychiatry, 37,* 457–467. (p. 236)

**Bowers, T. G., & Clum, G. A.** (1988). Relative contribution of specific and nonspecific treatment effects: Meta-analysis of placebo-controlled behavior therapy research. *Psychological Bulletin, 103,* 315–323. (p. 560)

**Bowlby, J.** (1973). *Separation: Anxiety and anger.* New York: Basic Books. (p. 101)

**Bowlby, J.** (1979). *The making and breaking of affectional bonds.* London: Tavistock. (p. 96)

**Bowne, D. W., Russell, M. L., Morgan, M. A., Optenberg, S., & Clarke, A.** (1984). Reduced disability and health care costs in an industrial fitness program. *Journal of Occupational Medicine, 26,* 809–816. (p. 599)

**Boynton, R. M.** (1979). *Human color vision.* New York: Holt, Rinehart & Winston. (p. 165)

**Bradley-Johnson, S., Johnson, C. M., Shanahan, R. H., Rickert, V. L., & Tardona, D. R.** (1984). Effects of token reinforcement on WISC-R performance of black and white, low-socioeconomic second graders. *Behavioral Assessment, 6,* 365–373. (p. 390)

**Bradshaw, J.** (1990). *Homecoming: Reclaiming and championing your inner child.* New York: Bantam Books. (p. 112)

**Bransford, J., Sherwood, R., Vye, N., & Rieser, J.** (1986). Teaching thinking and problem solving. *American Psychologist, 41,* 1078–1089. (p. 326)

**Bransford, J. D., & Johnson, M. K.** (1972). Contextual prerequisites for understanding: Some investigations of comprehension and recall. *Journal of Verbal Learning and Verbal Behavior, 11,* 717–726. (p. 294)

**Braskamp, L. A.** (1987). Spectrum: Utility for educational selection and organizational development. Paper presented at the American Psychological Association convention. (p. 423)

**Bray, D. W., & Byham, W. C.** (1991, Winter). Assessment centers and their derivatives. *Journal of Continuing Higher Education,* pp. 8–11. (p. 492)

**Bray, G. A.** (1969). Effect of caloric restriction on energy expenditure in obese patients. *Lancet, 2,* 397–398. (pp. 605)

**Brehm, S., & Brehm, J. W.** (1981). *Psychological reactance: A theory of freedom and control.* New York: Academic Press. (p. 630)

**Breland, K., & Breland, M.** (1961). The misbehavior of organisms. *American Psychologist, 16,* 661–664. (p. 277)

**Brennan, P. A., & Mednick, S. A.** (1993). Genetic perspectives on crime. *Acta Psychiatrica Scandinavia, 370*(Suppl.), 19–26. (p. 531)

**Brenner, M.** (1973). The next-in-line effect. *Journal of Verbal Learning and Verbal Behavior, 12,* 320–323. (p. 292)

**Bretz, R. D.** (1989). College grade point average as a predictor of adult success: A meta-analytic review and some additional evidence. *Public Personnel Management, 18,* 11–22. (p. 374)

**Brewer, C.** (1990). Personal communication. (p. 113)

**Brewer, W. F.** (1977). Memory for the pragmatic implications of sentences. *Memory and Cognition, 5,* 673–678. (p. 293)

**Brewin, C. F.** (1989). Cognitive change processes in psychotherapy. *Psychological Review, 96,* 379–394. (p. 551)

**Brickman, P., Coates, D., & Janoff-Bulman, R. J.** (1978). Lottery winners and accident victims: Is happiness relative? *Journal of Personality and Social Psychology, 36,* 917–927. (p. 448)

**Briere, J., & Runtz, M.** (1993). Childhood sexual abuse: Long-term sequelae and implications for psychological assessment. *Journal of Interpersonal Violence, 8,* 312–330. (p. 313)

**Bril, B.** (1986). Motor development and cultural attitudes. In H. T. A. Whiting & M. G. Wade (Eds.), *Themes in motor development.* Dordrecht, Netherlands: Martinus Nijhoff. (p. 87)

**Brinson, S. L.** (1992). The use and opposition of rape myths in prime-time television dramas. *Sex Roles, 27,* 359–375. (p. 637)

**Brislin, R.** (1993). *Understanding culture's influence on behavior.* Fort Worth, TX: Harcourt Brace. (p. 502)

**Brislin, R. W.** (1988). Increasing awareness of class, ethnicity, culture, and race by expanding on students' own experiences. In I. S. Cohen (Ed.), *The G. Stanley Hall Lecture Series* (Vol. 8). Washington, DC: American Psychological Association. (p. 655)

**British Psychological Society.** (1986). Report of the working group on the use of the polygraph in criminal investigation and personnel screening. *The Psychologist: Bulletin of the British Psychological Society, 39,* 81–94. (p. 437)

**British Psychological Society** (1993). Ethical principles for conducting research with human participants. *The Psychologist: Bulletin of the British Psychological Society, 6,* 33–36. (p. 35)

**British Psychological Society.** (1993). *Graphology in personnel assessment.* Leicester, England: British Psychological Society. (p. 492)

**Broadbent, D. E.** (1978). The current state of noise research: Reply to Poulton. *Psychological Bulletin, 85,* 1052–1067. (p. 170)

**Brockner, J., & Hulton, A. J. B.** (1978). How to reverse the vicious cycle of low self-esteem: The importance of attentional focus. *Journal of Experimental Social Psychology, 14,* 564–578. (p. 483)

**Brody, N.** (1992). *Intelligence* (2nd ed.). San Diego: Academic Press. (pp. 375, 377)

**Brodzinsky, D. M., & Schechter, M. D.** (Eds.). (1990). *The psychology of adoption.* New York: Oxford University Press. (p. 111)

**Broman, S. H.** (1989). Infant physical status and later cognitive development. In M. G. Bornstein & N. A. Krasnegor (Eds.), *Stability and continuity in mental development: Behavioral and biological perspectives.* Hillsdale, NJ: Erlbaum. (p. 378)

**Bronstein-Burrows, P.** (1981). *Introductory psychology: A course in the psychology of both sexes.* Paper presented at the meeting of the American Psychological Association. (p. 646)

**Brooks, K., & Siegal, M.** (1991). Children as eyewitnesses: Memory, suggestibility, and credibility. *Australian Psychologist, 26,* 84–88. (p. 313)

**Brooks-Gunn, J.** (1989). Adolescents as daughters and as mothers: A developmental perspective. In I. Sigel & G. Brody (Eds.), *Family research.* Hillsdale, NJ: Erlbaum. (p. 118)

**Brooks-Gunn, J., & Furstenberg, F. F., Jr.** (1989). Adolescent sexual behavior. *American Psychologist, 44,* 249–257. (p. 126)

**Brothers, J.** (1990, February 18). Why wives have affairs. *Parade,* pp. 4–7. (p. 409)

**Brown, E. L., & Deffenbacher, K.** (1979). *Perception and the senses.* New York: Oxford University Press. (p. 171)

**Brown, J. D.** (1991). Accuracy and bias in self-knowledge. In C. R. Snyder & D. F. Forsyth (Eds.), *Handbook of social and clinical psychology: The health perspective.* New York: Pergamon Press. (pp. 483–485)

**Brown, J. D.** (1991). Staying fit and staying well: Physical fitness as a moderator of life stress. *Journal of Personality and Social Psychology, 60,* 555–561. (p. 593)

**Brown, L. R., Kane, H., & Ayres, E.** (1993). *Vital signs 1993: The trends that are shaping our future.* New York: Norton. (p. 603)

**Brown, L. R., Kane, H., & Roodman, D. M.** (1994). *Vital signs 1994: The trends that are shaping our future.* New York: Norton. (p. 656)

**Brown, R.** (1965). *Social psychology.* New York: Free Press. (p. 444)

**Brown, R.** (1973). *A first language: The early stages.* Cambridge, MA: Harvard University Press. (p. 345)

**Brown, R.** (1986). Linguistic relativity. In S. H. Hulse & B. F. Green, Jr. (Eds.), *One hundred years of psychological research in America.* Baltimore: Johns Hopkins University Press. (p. 352)

**Brown, R., & Kulik, J.** (1982). Flashbulb memories. In U. Neisser (Ed.), *Memory observed.* San Francisco: Freeman. (p. 288)

**Brownell, K. D.** (1991). Dieting and the search for the perfect body: Where physiology and culture collide. *Behavior Therapy, 22,* 1–12. (pp. 606–607)

**Brownell, K. D., Greenwood, M. R. C., Stellar, E., & Shrager, E. E.** (1986). The effects of repeated cycles of weight loss and regain in rats. *Physiology and Behavior, 38,* 459–464. (p. 607)

**Brownell, K. D., & Jeffry, R. W.** (1987). Improving long-term weight loss: Pushing the limits of treatment. *Behavior Therapy, 18,* 353–374. (p. 607)

**Brownell, K. D., & Wadden, T. A.** (1991). The heterogeneity of obesity: Fitting treatments to individuals. *Behavior Therapy, 22,* 153–177. (pp. 606, 608)

**Brownell, K. D., & Wadden, T. A.** (1992). Etiology and treatment of obesity: Understanding a serious, prevalent, and refractory disorder. *Journal of Consulting and Clinical Psychology, 60,* 505–517. (p. 608)

**Browning, C.** (1992). *Ordinary men: Reserve police battalion 101 and the final solution in Poland.* New York: HarperCollins. (p. 625)

**Brownmiller, S.** (1975). *Against our will: Men, women, and rape.* New York: Simon & Schuster. (p. 412)

**Bruner, J. S., & Potter, M. C.** (1964). Interference in visual recognition. *Science, 144,* 424–425. (p. 205)

**Buck, L., & Axel, R.** (1991). A novel multigene family may encode odorant receptors: A molecular basis for odor recognition. *Cell, 65,* 175–187. (p. 179)

**Buehler, R., Griffin, D., & Ross, M.** (1994). Exploring the "planning fallacy": Why people underestimate their task completion times. *Journal of Personality and Social Psychology,* in press. (p. 335)

**Bugelski, B. R., Kidd, E., & Segmen, J.** (1968). Image as a mediator in one-trial paired-associate learning. *Journal of Experimental Psychology, 76,* 69–73. (p. 296)

**Bugental, D. B.** (1986). Unmasking the "polite smile": Situational and personal determinants of managed affect in adult-child interaction. *Personality and Social Psychology Bulletin, 12,* 7–16. (p. 438)

**Bullough, V.** (1990). The Kinsey scale in historical perspective. In D. P. McWhirter, S. A. Sanders, & J. M. Reinisch (Eds.), *Homosexuality/heterosexuality: Concepts of sexual orientation.* New York: Oxford University Press. (p. 413)

**Bumpass, L. L., & Sweet, J. A.** (1989). National estimates of cohabitation. *Demography, 26,* 615–625. (p. 417)

**Buquet, R.** (1988). Le reve et les deficients visuels [Dreams and the visually-impaired]. *Psychanalyse-a-l'Universite, 13,* 319–327. (p. 227)

**Bureau of the Census.** (1993). *Statistical abstract of the United States 1993.* Washington, DC: U.S. Government Printing Office. (pp. 100, 126, 136, 248, 417, 516, 564)

**Burger, J. M.** (1987). Increased performance with increased personal control: A self-presentation interpretation. *Journal of Experimental Social Psychology, 23,* 350–360. (p. 425)

**Burger, J. M., & Burns, L.** (1988). The illusion of unique invulnerability and the use of effective contraception. *Personality and Social Psychology Bulletin, 14,* 264–270. (p. 491)

**Buri, J. R., Louiselle, P. A., Misukanis, T. M., & Mueller, R. A.** (1988). Effects of parental authoritarianism and authoritativeness on self-esteem. *Personality and Social Psychology Bulletin, 14,* 271–282. (p. 104)

**Burish, T. G., & Carey, M. P.** (1986). Conditioned aversive responses in cancer chemotherapy patients: Theoretical and developmental analysis. *Journal of Counseling and Clinical Psychology, 54,* 593–600. (p. 265)

**Burke, K. C., Burke, J. D., Regier, D. A., & Rae, D. S.** (1990). Age at onset of selected mental disorders in five community populations. *Archives of General Psychiatry, 47,* 511–518. (p. 507)

**Bushman, B. J.** (1993). Human aggression while under the influence of alcohol and other drugs: An integrative research review. *Current Directions in Psychological Science, 2,* 148–152. (p. 633)

**Busnel, M. C., Granier-Deferre, C., & Lecanuet, J. P.** (1992). Fetal audition. *New York Academy of Sciences, 662,* 118–134. (p. 82)

**Buss, A. H.** (1989). Personality as traits. *American Psychologist, 44,* 1378–1388. (p. 478)

**Buss, D.** (1994a). *The evolution of desire.* New York: Basic Books. (pp. 646, 674–675)

**Buss, D.** (1994b). The strategies of human mating. *American Scientist, 82,* 238–249. (pp. 646, 675)

**Buss, D. M.** (1989). Sex differences in human mate preferences: Evolutionary hypotheses tested in 37 cultures. *Behavioral and Brain Sciences, 12,* 1–49. (pp. 126, 646)

**Buss, D. M.** (1991). Evolutionary personality psychology. *Annual Review of Psychology, 42,* 459–491. (p. 654)

**Buss, D. M., & Schmitt, D. P.** (1993). Sexual strategies theory: An evolutionary perspective on human mating. *Psychological Review, 100,* 204–232. (p. 674)

**Butcher, J. N.** (1990). *The MMPI-2 in psychological treatment.* New York: Oxford University Press. (p. 476)

**Butler, A. C., Hokanson, J. E., & Flynn, H. A.** (1994). A comparison of self-esteem lability and low trait self-esteem as vulnerability factors for depression. *Journal of Personality and Social Psychology, 66,* 166–177. (p. 521)

**Butler, R. A.** (1954, February). Curiosity in monkeys. *Scientific American,* pp. 70–75. (p. 399)

**Butterworth, G.** (1992). Origins of self-perception in infancy. *Psychological Inquiry, 3,* 103–111. (p. 104)

**Byne, W., & Parsons, B.** (1993). Human sexual orientation: The biologic theories reappraised. *Archives of General Psychiatry, 50,* 228–239. (p. 416)

**Byrne, D.** (1971). *The attraction paradigm.* New York: Academic Press. (p. 647)

**Byrne, D.** (1982). Predicting human sexual behavior. In A. G. Kraut (Ed.), *The G. Stanley Hall Lecture Series* (Vol. 2). Washington, DC: American Psychological Association. (pp. 262, 410–412)

**Byrne, D., Kelley, K., & Fisher, W. A.** (1993). Unwanted teenage pregnancies: Incidence, interpretation, and intervention. *Applied and Preventive Psychology, 2,* 101–113. (p. 126)

**Byrne, R. W.** (1991, May/June). Brute intellect. *The Sciences,* pp. 42–47. (p. 347)

**Byrnes, G., & Kelly, I. W.** (1992). Crisis calls and lunar cycles: A twenty-year review. *Psychological Reports, 71,* 779–785. (p. 530)

**Cacioppo, J. T., Priester, J. R., & Berntson, G. G.** (1993). Rudimentary determinants of attitudes. II: Arm flexion and extension have differential effects on attitudes. *Journal of Personality and Social Psychology, 65,* 5–17. (p. 258)

**Callahan, L. A., Steadman, H. J., McGreevy, M. A., & Robbins, P. C.** (1991). The volume and characteristics of insanity defense pleas: An eight-state study. *Bulletin of the American Academy of Psychiatry and Law, 19,* 331–338. (p. 503)

**Cameron, P., & Biber, H.** (1973). Sexual thought throughout the life-span. *Gerontologist, 13,* 144–147. (p. 231)

**Campbell, B. A., & Coulter, X.** (1976). The ontogenesis of learning and memory. In M. R. Rosenzweig & E. L. Bennet (Eds.), *Neural mechanisms of learning and memory* (pp. 209–235). Cambridge, MA: MIT Press. (p. 85)

**Campbell, D. T.** (1975). On the conflicts between biological and social evolution and between psychology and moral tradition. *American Psychologist, 30,* 1103–1126. (p. 451)

**Campbell, D. T., & Specht, J. C.** (1985). Altruism: Biology, culture, and religion. *Journal of Social and Clinical Psychology, 3*(1), 33–42. (p. 486)

**Campbell, S.** (1986). *The Loch Ness monster: The evidence.* Willingborough, Northamptonshire, England: Acquarian Press. (p. 206)

**Camper, J.** (1990, February 7). Drop pompom squad, U. of I. rape study says. *Chicago Tribune,* p. 1. (p. 241)

**Campos, J. J., Bertenthal, B. I., & Kermoian, R.** (1992). Early experience and emotional development: The emergence of wariness and heights. *Psychological Science, 3,* 61–64. (pp. 193, 445)

**Cannon, T. D., & Mednick, S. A.** (1993). The schizophrenia high-risk project in Copenhagen: Three decades of progress. *Acta Psychiatrica Scandinavia, 370*(Suppl.), 33–47. (p. 529)

**Cannon, W. B., & Washburn, A.** (1912). An explanation of hunger. *American Journal of Physiology, 29,* 441–454. (p. 401)

**Cantor, N., & Kihlstrom, J. F.** (1987). *Personality and social intelligence.* Englewood Cliffs, NJ: Prentice-Hall. (p. 374)

**Cantor, N., & Norem, J. K.** (1989). Defensive pessimism and stress and coping. *Social Cognition, 7,* 92–112. (p. 491)

**Cantril, H., & Bumstead, C. H.** (1960). *Reflections on the human venture.* New York: New York University Press. (p. 630)

**Caplan, N., Choy, M. H., & Whitmore, J. K.** (1992, February). Indochinese refugee families and academic achievement. *Scientific American,* pp. 36–42. (pp. 111, 390)

**Carducci, B. J., Cosby, P. C., & Ward, D. D.** (1978). Sexual arousal and interpersonal evaluations. *Journal of Experimental Social Psychology, 14,* 449–457. (p. 647)

**Carey, G.** (1990). Genes, fears, phobias, and phobic disorders. *Journal of Counseling and Development, 68,* 628–632. (p. 509)

**Carli, L. L., & Leonard, J. B.** (1989). The effect of hindsight on victim derogation. *Journal of Social and Clinical Psychology, 8,* 331–343. (p. 686)

**Carlson, M., Charlin, V., & Miller, N.** (1988). Positive mood and helping behavior: A test of six hypotheses. *Journal of Personality and Social Psychology, 55,* 211–229. (p. 642)

**Carlson, R.** (1984). What's social about social psychology? Where's the person in personality research? *Journal of Personality and Social Psychology, 47,* 1304–1309. (p. 494)

**Carlson, S.** (1985). A double-blind test of astrology. *Nature, 318,* 419–425. (p. 492)

**Carnegie Council on Adolescent Development.** (1989, June). *Turning points: Preparing American youth for the 21st century* (Report of the Task Force on Education of Young Adolescents). New York: Carnegie Corporation. (p. 381, 689)

**Carr, T. H., Kontowicz, A., & Dagenbach, D.** (1987). Subthreshold priming and the cognitive unconscious. Invited paper presented to the Midwestern Psychological Association convention. (p. 155)

**Carroll, J. B.** (1982). The measurement of intelligence. In R. J. Sternberg (Ed.), *Handbook of human intelligence.* New York: Cambridge University Press. (p. 366)

**Carson, R. C., Butcher, J. N., & Coleman, J. C.** (1988). *Abnormal psychology and modern life* (8th ed.). Glenview, IL: Scott, Foresman. (p. 502)

**Case, R. B., Moss, A. J., Case, N., McDermott, M., & Eberly, S.** (1992). Living alone after myocardial infarction: Impact on prognosis. *Journal of the American Medical Association, 267,* 515–519. (p. 597)

**Cash, T., & Janda, L. H.** (1984, December). The eye of the beholder. *Psychology Today,* pp. 46–52. (p. 645)

**Caspi, A., & Herbener, E. S.** (1990). Continuity and change: Assortative marriage and the consistency of personality in adulthood. *Journal of Personality and Social Psychology, 58,* 250–258. (p. 146)

**Caspi, A., Elder, G. H., Jr., & Bem, D. J.** (1987). Moving against the world: Life-course patterns of explosive children. *Developmental Psychology, 23,* 308–313. (p. 146)

**Caspi, A., & Moffitt, T. E.** (1991). Individual differences are accentuated during periods of social change: The sample case of girls at puberty. *Journal of Personality and Social Psychology, 61,* 157–168. (p. 119)

**Castro, J.** (1990, Fall issue on women). Get set: Here they come. *Time,* pp. 50–52. (p. 678)

**Castro, J.** (1991, October 28). Vox pop. *Time,* p. 23. (p. 607)

**Cataldo, M. F., & Coates, T. J.** (1986). *Health and industry: A behavioral medicine perspective.* New York: Wiley. (p. 599)

**Cattell, R. B.** (1963). Theory of fluid and crystallized intelligence: A critical experiment. *Journal of Educational Psychology, 54,* 1–22. (p. 137)

**Ceci, S. J.** (1991). How much does schooling influence intellectual development and its cognitive components? A reassessment of the evidence. *Developmental Psychology, 27,* 703–722. (p. 388)

**Ceci, S. J.** (1993). Cognitive and social factors in children's testimony. Master lecture, American Psychological Association convention. (pp. 313, 314)

**Ceci, S. J., & Bruck, M.** (1993a). Child witnesses: Translating research into policy. *Social Policy Report* (Society for Research in Child Development), *7*(3), 1–30. (p. 313)

**Ceci, S. J., & Bruck, M.** (1993b). Suggestibility of the child witness: A historical review and synthesis. *Psychological Bulletin, 113,* 403–439. (p. 313)

**Ceci, S. J., & Liker, J. K.** (1986). A day at the races: A study of IQ, expertise, and cognitive complexity. *Journal of Experimental Psychology: General, 115,* 255–266. (pp. 338, 374)

**Centers for Disease Control.** (1983). Behavioral risk factor prevalence surveys—United States. Reported in *Behavior Today Newsletter,* October 29, 1984, p. 7. (p. 242)

**Centers for Disease Control.** (1989). Results from the national adolescent student health survey. *Morbidity and Mortality Weekly Report, 38*(9), 147–150. (p. 516)

**Centers for Disease Control.** (1989). Weekly report summarized in *Detroit Free Press,* November 25, p. A1. (p. 242)

**Centers for Disease Control.** (1991). Body-weight perceptions and selected weight-management goals and practices of high school students—United States, 1990. *Morbidity and Mortality Weekly Report, 40,* 741, 747–750. (p. 607)

**Centers for Disease Control.** (1992, January 3). Sexual behavior among high school students—United States, 1990. *Morbidity and Mortality Weekly Report, 40*(51, 52), 885–888. (p. 127)

**Centers for Disease Control.** (1992, September 16). Serious mental illness and disability in the adult household population: United States, 1989. *Advance Data* No. 218 from *Vital and Health Statistics,* National Center for Health Statistics. (p. 532)

**Centers for Disease Control.** (1992, November 20). HIV instruction and selected HIV-risk behaviors among high school students—United States, 1989–1991. *Morbidity and Mortality Weekly Report, 41*(46), 866–867. (p. 127)

**Centers for Disease Control Vietnam Experience Study.** (1988). Health status of Vietnam veterans. *Journal of the American Medical Association, 259,* 2701–2709. (p. 579)

**Centerwall, B. S.** (1989). Exposure to television as a risk factor for violence. *American Journal of Epidemiology, 129,* 643–652. (p. 636)

**Cerella, J.** (1985). Information processing rates in the elderly. *Psychological Bulletin, 98,* 67–83. (p. 133)

**Chase, M. H., & Morales, F. R.** (1983). Subthreshold excitatory activity and motorneuron discharge during REM periods of active sleep. *Science, 221,* 1195–1198. (p. 224)

**Chase, W. G., & Simon, H. A.** (1973). Perception in chess. *Cognitive Psychology, 4,* 55–81. (p. 296)

**Chassin, L., Presson, C. C., Sherman, S. J., & McGrew, J.** (1987). The changing smoking environment for middle and high school students: 1980–1983. *Journal of Behavioral Medicine, 10,* 581–593. (p. 600)

**Chaves, J. F.** (1989). Hypnotic control of clinical pain. In N. P. Spanos & J. F. Chaves (Eds.), *Hypnosis: The cognitive-behavioral perspective.* Buffalo, NY: Prometheus Books. (p. 236)

**Cheek, J. M., & Melchior, L. A.** (1990). Shyness, self-esteem, and self-consciousness. In H. Leitenberg (Ed.), *Handbook of social and evaluation anxiety.* New York: Plenum. (pp. 106, 522)

**Cherfas, J.** (1990). Two bomb attacks on scientists in the U.K. *Science, 248,* 1485. (p. 35)

**Cherlin, A. J., Furstenberg, F. F., Jr., Chase-Landale, P. L., Kiernan, K. E., Robins, P. K., Morrison, D. R., & Teitler, J. O.** (1991). Longitudinal studies of effects of divorce on children in Great Britain and the United States. *Science, 252,* 1386–1389. (p. 103)

**Chesney, M. A.** (1984). *Behavioral factors in coronary heart disease separating benign from malignant.* Paper presented at the meeting of the American Psychological Association. (p. 581)

**Chess, S., & Thomas, A.** (1987). *Know your child: An authoritative guide for today's parents.* New York: Basic Books. (p. 97)

**Chi, M. T. H.** (1976). Short-term memory limitations in children: Capacity or processing deficits. *Memory & Cognition, 4,* 559–572. (p. 300)

**Chi, M. T. H., Glaser, R., & Farr, M. J.** (Eds.). (1988). *The nature of expertise.* Hillsdale, NJ: Erlbaum. (p. 326)

**Chodorow, N. J.** (1978). *The reproduction of mothering: Psychoanalysis and the sociology of gender.* Berkeley: University of California Press. (p. 668)

**Chodorow, N. J.** (1989). *Feminism and psychoanalytic theory.* New Haven, CT: Yale University Press. (p. 668)

**Chomsky, N.** (1959). [Review of B. F. Skinner's *Verbal behavior.*] *Language, 35,* 26–58. (p. 344)

**Chomsky, N.** (1972). *Language and mind.* New York: Harcourt Brace Jovanovich. (p. 341)

**Chomsky, N.** (1987). Language in a psychological setting (Sophia Linguistic Working Papers in Linguistics, No. 22). Sophia University, Tokyo. (pp. 344–345)

**Christensen, A., & Jacobson, N. S.** (1994). Who (or what) can do psychotherapy: The status and challenge of nonprofessional therapies. *Psychological Science, 5,* 8–14. (p. 562)

**Christensen, L.** (in press). Food as a mood regulator. *International Journal of Eating Disorders.* (p. 603)

**Christianson, S. A.** (1992). Emotional stress and eyewitness memory: A critical review. *Psychological Bulletin, 112,* 284–309. (p. 319)

**Christophersen, E. R., & Edwards, K. J.** (1992). Treatment of elimination disorders: State of the art 1991. *Applied & Preventive Psychology, 1,* 15–22. (p. 549)

**Chugani, H. T., & Phelps, M. E.** (1986). Maturational changes in cerebral function in infants determined by $^{18}$FDG Positron Emission Tomography. *Science, 231,* 840–843. (p. 88)

**Church, A. T., & Katigbak, M. S.** (1989). Internal, external, and self-report structure of personality in non-Western culture: An investigation of cross-language and cross-cultural generalizability. *Journal of Personality and Social Psychology, 57,* 857–872. (p. 475)

**Chwalisz, K., Diener, E., & Gallagher, D.** (1988). Autonomic arousal feedback and emotional experience: Evidence from the spinal cord injured. *Journal of Personality and Social Psychology, 54,* 820–828. (p. 448)

**Cialdini, R. B.** (1993). *Influence: Science and practice* (3rd ed.). New York: HarperCollins. (p. 617)

**Cialdini, R. B., & Carpenter, K.** (1981). The availability heuristic: Does imagining make it so? In P. H. Reingen & A. G. Woodside (Eds.), *Buyer-seller interactions: Empirical issues and normative issues.* Chicago: American Marketing Association. (p. 333)

**Cialdini, R. B., & Richardson, K. D.** (1980). Two indirect tactics of image management: Basking and blasting. *Journal of Personality and Social Psychology, 39,* 406–415. (p. 685)

**Clark, R. D., III** (1990). The impact of AIDS on gender differences in willingness to engage in casual sex. *Journal of Applied Social Psychology, 20,* 771–782. (p. 673)

**Clark, R. D., III, & Hatfield, E.** (1989). Gender differences in willingness to engage in casual sex. *Journal of Psychology and Human Sexuality, 2,* 39–55. (p. 672)

**Clarke-Stewart, K. A.** (1991). A home is not a school: The effects of child care on children's development. *Journal of Social Issues, 47*(2), 105–123. (p. 101)

**Clendenen, V. I., & Herman, C. P.** (in press). Social facilitation of eating among friends and strangers. *Appetite.* (p. 627)

**Coe, W. C.** (1989a). Posthypnotic amnesia: Theory and research. In N. P. Spanos & J. F. Chaves (Eds.), *Hypnosis: The cognitive-behavioral perspective.* Buffalo, NY: Prometheus Books. (p. 233)

**Coe, W. C.** (1989b). Hypnosis: The role of sociopolitical factors in a paradigm clash. In N. P. Spanos & J. F. Chaves (Eds.), *Hypnosis: The cognitive-behavioral perspective.* Buffalo, NY: Prometheus Books. (p. 239)

**Coffey, C. E.** (Ed.). (1993). *Clinical science of electroconvulsive therapy.* Washington, DC: American Psychiatric Press. (p. 567)

**Coffey, C. E., Wilkinson, W. E., Weiner, R. D., Parashos, I. A., Djang, W. T., Webb, M. C., Figiel, G. S., & Spritzer, C. E.** (1993). Quantitative cerebral anatomy in depression: A controlled magnetic resonance imaging study. *Archives of General Psychiatry, 50,* 7–16. (p. 519)

**Cohen, S.** (1988). Psychosocial models of the role of social support in the etiology of physical disease. *Health Psychology, 7,* 269–297. (p. 597)

**Cohen, S., Evans, G. W., Stokols, D., & Krantz, D. S.** (1986). *Behavior, health, and environmental stress.* New York: Plenum. (p. 170)

**Cohen, S., Kaplan, J. R., Cunnick, J. E., Manuck, S. B., & Rabin, B. S.** (1992). Chronic social stress, affiliation, and cellular immune response in nonhuman primates. *Psychological Science, 3,* 301–304. (p. 583)

**Cohen, S., Tyrrell, D. A. J., & Smith, A. P.** (1991). Psychological stress and susceptibility to the common cold. *New England Journal of Medicine, 325,* 606–612. (p. 584)

**Cohen, S., Tyrrell, D. A. J., & Smith, A. P.** (1993). Negative life events, perceived stress, negative affect, and susceptibility to the common cold. *Journal of Personality and Social Psychology, 64,* 131–140. (p. 584)

**Cohen, S., & Williamson, G. M.** (1991). Stress and infectious disease in humans. *Psychological Bulletin, 109,* 5–24. (p. 584)

**Coile, D. C., & Miller, N. E.** (1984). How radical animal activists try to mislead humane people. *American Psychologist, 39,* 700–701. (p. 34)

**Coleman, J. C.** (1980). *The nature of adolescence.* London: Methuen. (p. 118)

**Coleman, P. D., & Flood, D. G.** (1986). Dendritic proliferation in the aging brain as a compensatory repair mechanism. In D. F. Swaab, E. Fliers, M. Mirmiram, W. A. Van Gool, & F. Van Haaren (Eds.), *Progress in brain research* (Vol. 20). New York: Elsevier. (p. 133)

**College Entrance Examination Board.** (1983, 1990). *Sample SAT questions from 10 SATs.* Princeton, NJ: Educational Testing Service. (p. 365)

**Colombo, J.** (1982). The critical period concept: Research, methodology, and theoretical issues. *Psychological Bulletin, 91,* 260–275. (p. 97)

**Colon, E. A., Callies, A. L., Popkin, M. K., & McGlave, P. B.** (1991). Depressed mood and other variables related to bone marrow transplantation survival in acute leukemia. *Psychosomatics, 32,* 420–425. (pp. 584, 597)

**Conley, J. J.** (1985). Longitudinal stability of personality traits: A multitrait-multimethod-multioccasion analysis. *Journal of Personality and Social Psychology, 49,* 1266–1282. (p. 146)

**Consensus Conference.** (1985). Electroconvulsive therapy. *Journal of the American Medical Association, 254,* 2103–2108. (p. 567)

**Conway, M., & Ross, M.** (1984). Getting what you want by revising what you had. *Journal of Personality and Social Psychology, 47,* 738–748. (p. 316)

**Cook, E. W., III, Hodes, R. L., & Lang, P. J.** (1986). Preparedness and phobia: Effects of stimulus content on human visceral conditioning. *Journal of Abnormal Psychology, 95,* 195–207. (p. 264)

**Cook, M., & Mineka, S.** (1991). Selective associations in the origins of phobic fears and their implications for behavior therapy. In P. Martin (Ed.), *Handbook of behavior therapy and psychological science: An integrative approach.* New York: Pergamon Press. (p. 445)

**Cook, S. W.** (1984). The 1954 social science statement and school desegregation—A reply to Gerard. *American Psychologist, 39,* 819–832. (p. 390)

**Coon, P. M., Bowman, E. S., & Milstein, V.** (1988). Multiple personality disorder: A clinical investigation of 50 cases. *Journal of Nervous and Mental Disease, 176,* 519–527. (p. 514)

**Cooper, G. D., Adams, H. B., & Scott, J. C.** (1988). Studies in REST: I. Reduced environmental stimulation therapy (REST) and reduced alcohol consumption. *Journal of Substance Abuse Treatment, 5,* 61–68. (p. 182)

**Cooper, W. H.** (1983). An achievement motivation nomological network. *Journal of Personality and Social Psychology, 44,* 841–861. (p. 419)

**Coopersmith, S.** (1967). *The antecedents of self-esteem.* San Francisco: Freeman. (p. 104)

**Corballis, M. C.** (1989). Laterality and human evolution. *Psychological Review, 96,* 492–505. (p. 68)

**Coren, S.** (1993). Failure to find statistical significance in left-handedness and pathology studies: A forgotten consideration. *Bulletin of the Psychonomic Society, 31,* 443–446. (p. 587)

**Coren, S.** (1993). *The left-hander syndrome: The causes and consequences of left-handedness.* New York: Vintage Books. (pp. 70, 586)

**Coren, S., & Halpern, D. F.** (1991). Left-handedness: A marker for decreased survival fitness. *Psychological Bulletin, 109,* 90–106. (p. 586)

**Corina, D. P., Vaid, J., & Bellugi, U.** (1992). The linguistic basis of left hemisphere specialization. *Science, 255,* 1258–1260. (p. 68)

**Costa, P. T., Jr., & McCrae, R. R.** (1989). Personality continuity and the changes of adult life. In M. Storandt & G. R. VandenBos (Eds.), *The adult years: Continuity and change.* Washington, DC: American Psychological Association. (p. 147)

**Costa, P. T., Jr., & McCrae, R. R.** (1993). "Set like plaster"? Evidence for the stability of adult personality. In T. Heatherton & J. Weinberger (Eds.), *Can personality change?* Washington, DC: American Psychological Association. (p. 146)

**Costa, P. T., Jr., Zonderman, A. B., McCrae, R. R., Cornoni-Huntley, J., Locke, B. Z., & Barbano, H. E.** (1987). Longitudinal analyses of psychological well-being in a national sample: Stability of mean levels. *Journal of Gerontology, 42,* 50–55. (p. 143)

**Courneya, K. S., & Carron, A. V.** (1992). The home advantage in sport competitions: A literature review. *Journal of Sport and Exercise Psychology, 14,* 13–27. (p. 615)

**Courtney, J. G., Longnecker, M. P., Theorell, T., & de Verdier, M. G.** (1993). Stressful life events and the risk of colorectal cancer. *Epidemiology, 4,* 407–414. (p. 585)

**Cousins, N.** (1989). *Head first: The biology of hope.* New York: Dutton. (p. 585)

**Cousins, S. D.** (1989). Culture and self-perception in Japan and the United States. *Journal of Personality and Social Psychology, 56,* 124–131. (p. 659)

**Covington, M. V., & Omelich, C. L.** (1988). I can resist anything but temptation: Adolescent expectations for smoking cigarettes. *Journal of Applied Social Psychology, 18,* 203–227. (p. 600)

**Cowan, G., Lee, C., Levy, D., & Snyder, D.** (1988). Dominance and inequality in X-rated videocassettes. *Psychology of Women Quarterly, 12,* 299–311. (p. 637)

**Cowan, N.** (1988). Evolving conceptions of memory storage, selective attention, and their mutual constraints within the human information-processing system. *Psychological Bulletin, 104,* 163–191. (pp. 289, 300)

**Cowart, B. J.** (1981). Development of taste perception in humans: Sensitivity and preference throughout the life span. *Psychological Bulletin, 90,* 43–73. (p. 178)

**Craig, M. E., Kalichman, S. C., & Follingstad, D. R.** (1989). Verbal coercive sexual behavior among college students. *Archives of Sexual Behavior, 18,* 421–434. (p. 637)

**Craik, F. I. M.** (1986). A functional account of age differences in memory. In F. Klix & H. Hagendorf (Eds.), *Human memory and cognitive capabilities.* Amsterdam: Elsevier. (p. 137)

**Craik, F. I. M., & Tulving, E.** (1975). Depth of processing and the retention of words in episodic memory. *Journal of Experimental Psychology: General, 104,* 268–294. (p. 294)

**Craik, F. I. M., & Watkins, M. J.** (1973). The role of rehearsal in short-term memory. *Journal of Verbal Learning and Verbal Behavior, 12,* 599–607. (p. 293)

**Crain-Thoreson, C., & Dale, P. S.** (1992). Do early talkers become early readers? Linguistic precocity, preschool language, and emergent literacy. *Developmental Psychology, 28,* 421–429. (p. 378)

**Crandall, C. S.** (1988). Social contagion of binge eating. *Journal of Personality and Social Psychology, 55,* 588–598. (p. 406)

**Crandall, J. E.** (1984). Social interest as a moderator of life stress. *Journal of Personality and Social Psychology, 47,* 164–174. (p. 486)

**Crocker, J., Thompson, L. L., McGraw, K. M., & Ingerman, C.** (1987). Downward comparison, prejudice, and evaluation of others: Effects of self-esteem and threat. *Journal of Personality and Social Psychology, 52,* 907–916. (p. 685)

**Crombie, A. C.** (1964, May). Early concepts of the senses and the mind. *Scientific American,* pp. 108–116. (p. 160)

**Crook, T. H., & West, R. L.** (1990). Name recall performance across the adult life-span. *British Journal of Psychology, 81,* 335–340. (pp. 133–134)

**Cross, S. E., Liao, M-H., & Josephs, R.** (1992). A cross-cultural test of the self-evaluation maintenance model. Paper presented at the American Psychological Association convention. (p. 659)

**Cross-National Collaborative Group.** (1992). The changing rate of major depression. *Journal of the American Medical Association, 268,* 3098–3105. (p. 518)

**Crowe, L. C., & George, W. H.** (1989). Alcohol and human sexuality: Review and integration. *Psychological Bulletin, 105,* 374–386. (p. 242)

**Crowell, J. A., & Waters, E.** (1994). Bowlby's theory grown up: The role of attachment in adult love relationships. *Psychological Inquiry, 5,* 1–22. (p. 96)

**Croyle, R. T., & Ditto, P. H.** (1990). Illness cognition and behavior: An experimental approach. *Journal of Behavioral Medicine, 13,* 31–52. (p. 608)

**Csikszentmihalyi, M.** (1990). *Flow: The psychology of optimal experience.* New York: Harper & Row. (pp. 331, 453)

**Csikszentmihalyi, M., & Larson, R.** (1984). *Being adolescent: Conflict and growth in the teenage years.* New York: Basic Books. (p. 143)

**Cunningham, M. R.** (1986). Measuring the physical in physical attractiveness: Quasi-experiments on the sociobiology of female facial beauty. *Journal of Personality and Social Psychology, 50,* 925–935. (p. 646)

**Curtis, R. C., & Miller, K.** (1986). Believing another likes or dislikes you: Behaviors making the beliefs come true. *Journal of Personality and Social Psychology, 51,* 284–290. (p. 647)

**Curtiss, S.** (1977). *Genie: A psycholinguistic study of a modern-day "wild child."* New York: Academic Press. (p. 346)

**Curtiss, S.** (1981). Dissociations between language and cognition: Cases and implications. *Journal of Autism and Developmental Disorders, 11,* 15–30. (p. 346)

**Cutler, B. L., & Penrod, S. D.** (1989). Forensically relevant moderators of the relation between eyewitness identification accuracy and confidence. *Journal of Applied Psychology, 74,* 650–652. (p. 312)

**Cutrona, C. E.** (1986). Behavioral manifestations of social support: A microanalytic investigation. *Journal of Personality and Social Psychology, 51,* 201–208. (p. 598)

**Dabbs, J. M., Jr.** (1992). Testosterone measurements in social and clinical psychology. *Journal of Social and Clinical Psychology, 11,* 302–321. (p. 633)

**Dabbs, J. M., Jr., Frady, R. L., Carr, T. S., & Besch, N. F.** (1987). Saliva testosterone and criminal violence in young adult prison inmates. *Psychosomatic Medicine, 49,* 174–182. (p. 624)

**Dabbs, J. M., Jr., & Morris, R.** (1990). Testosterone, social class, and antisocial behavior in a sample of 4,462 men. *Psychological Science, 1,* 209–211. (pp. 633, 674)

**Dabbs, J. M., Jr., Ruback, R. B., & Besch, N. F.** (1987). Male saliva testosterone following conversations with male and female partners. Paper presented at the American Psychological Association convention. (p. 410)

**Daly, M., & Wilson, M.** (1989). Killing the competition: Female/female and male/male homicide. *Human Nature, 1,* 81–107. (p. 671)

**Damon, W., & Hart, D.** (1982). The development of self-understanding from infancy through adolescence. *Child Development, 53,* 841–864. (p. 104)

**Damon, W., & Hart, D.** (1988). *Self-understanding in childhood and adolescence.* Cambridge, England: Cambridge University Press. (p. 104)

**Darley, J. M., & Latané, B.** (1968a). Bystander intervention in emergencies: Diffusion of responsibility. *Journal of Personality and Social Psychology, 8,* 377–383. (p. 640)

**Darley, J. M., & Latané, B.** (1968b, December). When will people help in a crisis? *Psychology Today,* pp. 54–57, 70–71. (p. 640)

**Darley, J. M., Seligman, C., & Becker, L. J.** (1979, April). The lesson of twin rivers: Feedback works. *Psychology Today,* pp. 16, 23–24. (p. 279)

**Darrach, B., & Norris, J.** (1984, August). An American tragedy. *Life,* pp. 58–74. (p. 531)

**Davenport, C.** (1989, January 30). America's most admired corporations. *Fortune,* pp. 68–94. (p. 426)

**Davey, G. C. L.** (1992). Classical conditioning and the acquisition of human fears and phobias: A review and synthesis of the literature. *Advances in Behavior Research and Therapy, 14,* 29–66. (p. 265)

**Davidson, R. J.** (1991, February 12). Quoted in D. Goleman, Feeling cheerful? Thank brain's left lobe. *New York Times,* pp. C1, C10. (p. 435)

**Davidson, R. J.** (1992). Emotion and affective style: Hemispheric substrates. *Psychological Science, 3,* 39–43. (pp. 435, 519)

**Davidson, R. J., Ekman, P., Saron, C. D., Senulis, J. A., & Friesen, W. V.** (1990). Approach-withdrawal and cerebral asymmetry: Emotional expression and brain physiology I. *Journal of Personality and Social Psychology, 58,* 330–341. (p. 435)

**Davies, D. R., Matthews, G., & Wong, C. S. K.** (1991). Aging and work. *International Review of Industrial and Organizational Psychology, 6,* 149–211. (p. 139)

**Dawes, R. M.** (1980). Social dilemmas. *Annual Review of Psychology, 31,* 169–193. (p. 687)

**Dawes, R. M.** (1994). *House of cards: Psychology and psychotherapy built on myth.* New York: Free Press. (p. 469)

**Dawson, N. V., Arkes, H. R., Siciliano, C., Blinkhorn, R., Lakshmanan, M., & Petrelli, M.** (1988). Hindsight bias: An impediment to accurate probability estimation in clinicopathologic conferences. *Medical Decision Making, 8,* 259–264. (p. 14)

**Dean, G. A., Kelly, I. W., Saklofske, D. H., & Furnham, A.** (1992). Graphology and human judgment. In B. Beyerstein & D. Beyerstein (Eds.), *The write stuff: Evaluations of graphology*. Buffalo, NY: Prometheus Books. (p. 492)

**DeAngelis, T.** (1988, October). Chinese psychologists focus on practical. *APA Monitor*, p. 8. (p. 2)

**DeAngelis, T.** (1989, January). Mania, depression, and genius. *APA Monitor*, pp. 1, 24. (p. 515)

**DeAngelis, T.** (1993, September). Controversial diagnosis is voted into latest DSM. *APA Monitor*, pp. 32–33. (p. 591)

**Deary, I. J., & Caryl, P. G.** (1993). Intelligence, EEG and evoked potentials. In P. A. Vernon (Ed.), *Biological approaches to the study of human intelligence*. Norwood, NJ: Ablex. (p. 376)

**Deary, I. J., & Matthews, G.** (1993). Personality traits are alive and well. *The Psychologist: Bulletin of the British Psychological Society, 6*, 299–311. (p. 478)

**de Boysson-Bardies, B., Halle, P., Sagart, L., & Durand, C.** (1989). A cross linguistic investigation of vowel formats in babbling. *Journal of Child Language, 16*, 1–17. (p. 343)

**DeCasper, A. J., & Fifer, W.** (1980). Of human bonding: Newborns prefer their mother's voices. *Science, 208*, 1174–1176. (p. 82)

**DeCasper, A. J., & Prescott, P. A.** (1984). Human newborns' perception of male voices: Preference, discrimination and reinforcing value. *Developmental Psychobiology, 17*, 481–491. (p. 82)

**DeCasper, A. J., & Spence, M. J.** (1986). Prenatal maternal speech influences newborns' perception of speech sounds. *Infant Behavior and Development, 9*, 133–150. (p. 82)

**Deci, E. L., Connell, J. P., & Ryan, R. M.** (1989). Self-determination in a work organization. *Journal of Applied Psychology, 74*, 580–590. (p. 426)

**Deci, E. L., & Ryan, R. M.** (1985). *Intrinsic motivation and self-determination in human behavior.* New York: Plenum Press. (p. 423)

**Deci, E. L., & Ryan, R. M.** (1987). The support of autonomy and the control of behavior. *Journal of Personality and Social Psychology, 53*, 1024–1037. (p. 423)

**Deci, E. L., & Ryan, R. M.** (1992). The initiation and regulation of intrinsically motivated learning and achievement. In A. K. Boggiano & T. S. Pittman (Eds.), *Achievement and motivation: A social-developmental perspective.* New York: Cambridge University Press. (p. 422)

**de Cuevas, J.** (1990, September-October). "No, she holded them loosely." *Harvard Magazine*, pp. 60–67. (p. 345)

**de Jong-Gierveld, J.** (1987). Developing and testing a model of loneliness. *Journal of Personality and Social Psychology, 53*, 119–128. (p. 522)

**Delgado, J. M. R.** (1969). *Physical control of the mind: Toward a psychocivilized society.* New York: Harper & Row. (p. 61)

**DeLoache, J. S.** (1987). Rapid change in the symbolic functioning of very young children. *Science, 238*, 1556–1557. (p. 93)

**Dement, W.** (1990). In the PBS film, *Sleep alert*. Quoted by *Behavior Today*, March 12, p. 8. (p. 225)

**Dement, W. C.** (1978). *Some must watch while some must sleep.* New York: Norton. (pp. 222–223, 225–226)

**Dement, W. C., & Wolpert, E. A.** (1958). The relation of eye movements, body mobility, and external stimuli to dream content. *Journal of Experimental Psychology, 55*, 543–553. (p. 228)

**Dempster, F. N.** (1988). The spacing effect: A case study in the failure to apply the results of psychological research. *American Psychologist, 43*, 627–634. (p. 292)

**Denton, K., & Krebs, D.** (1990). From the scene to the crime: The effect of alcohol and social context on moral judgment. *Journal of Personality and Social Psychology, 59*, 242–248. (p. 241)

**D'Eon, J. L.** (1989). Hypnosis in the control of labor pain. In N. P. Spanos & J. F. Chaves (Eds.), *Hypnosis: The cognitive-behavioral perspective.* Buffalo, NY: Prometheus Books. (p. 236)

**DePaulo, B. M., Blank, A. L., Swaim, G. W., & Hairfield, J. G.** (1992). Expressiveness and expressive control. *Personality and Social Psychology Bulletin, 18*, 276–285. (p. 479)

**De Pree, M.** (1987). *Leadership is an art.* East Lansing: Michigan State University Press. (p. 426)

**Deregowski, J. B.** (1989). Real space and represented space: Cross-cultural perspectives. *Behavioral and Brain Sciences, 12*, 51–119. (p. 200)

**Dermer, M., Cohen, S. J., Jacobsen, E., & Anderson, E. A.** (1979). Evaluative judgments of aspects of life as a function of vicarious exposure to hedonic extremes. *Journal of Personality and Social Psychology, 37*, 247–260. (p. 452)

**Dermer, M., & Pyszczynski, T. A.** (1978). Effects of erotica upon men's loving and liking responses for women they love. *Journal of Personality and Social Psychology, 36*, 1302–1309. (p. 647)

**DerSimonian, R., & Laird, N. M.** (1983). Evaluating the effect of coaching on SAT scores: A meta-analysis. *Harvard Educational Review, 53*, 1–15. (p. 369)

**Deutsch, J. A.** (1972, July). Brain reward: ESP and ecstasy. *Psychology Today*, pp. 46–48. (p. 59)

**Deutsch, M.** (1991). Egalitarianism in the laboratory and at work. In R. Vermunt & H. Steensma (Eds.), *Social justice in human relations.* New York: Plenum. (p. 279)

**DeValois, R. L., & DeValois, K. K.** (1975). Neural coding of color. In E. C. Carterette & M. P. Friedman (Eds.), *Handbook of perception: Vol. V. Seeing.* New York: Academic Press. (p. 166).

**Dew, M. A., Bromet, E. J., Brent, D., & Greenhouse, J. B.** (1987). A quantitative literature review of the effectiveness of suicide prevention centers. *Journal of Consulting and Clinical Psychology, 55*, 239–244. (p. 557)

**Dey, E. L., Astin, A. W., & Korn, W. S.** (1991). *The American freshman: Twenty-five year trends.* Los Angeles: Higher Education Research Institute, UCLA. (pp. 448, 679)

**Diaconis, P., & Mosteller, F.** (1989). Methods for studying coincidences. *Journal of the American Statistical Association, 84*, 853–861. (p. 23)

**Diamond, J.** (1986). Variation in human testis size. *Nature, 320*, 488–489. (p. 108)

**Diamond, J.** (1989, May). The great leap forward. *Discover*, pp. 50–60. (p. 341)

**Diamond, R.** (1993). Genetics and male sexual orientation [Letter to the editor]. *Science, 261*, p. 1258. (p. 416)

**Dickie, J. R.** (1987). Interrelationships within the mother-father-infant triad. In P. W. Berman & F. A. Pedersen (Eds.), *Men's transitions to parenthood: Longitudinal studies of early family experience.* Hillsdale, NJ: Erlbaum. (p. 100)

**Diener, E.** (1984). Subjective well-being. *Psychological Bulletin, 95,* 542–575. (pp. 452–453)

**Diener, E.** (1993). Most Americans are happy. Unpublished manuscript, University of Illinois. (pp. 447, 485)

**Diener, E., Emmons, R. A., & Sandvik, E.** (1986). The dual nature of happiness: Independence of positive and negative moods. Unpublished manuscript, University of Illinois. (p. 143)

**Dietz, W. H., Jr., & Gortmaker, S. L.** (1985). Do we fatten our children at the television set? Obesity and television viewing in children and adolescents. *Pediatrics, 75,* 807–812. (p. 609)

**DiLalla, L. F., & Gottesman, I. I.** (1991). Biological and genetic contributors to violence—Widom's untold tale. *Psychological Bulletin, 109,* 125–129. (p. 531)

**Dindia, K., & Allen, M.** (1992). Sex differences in self-disclosure: A meta-analysis. *Psychological Bulletin, 112,* 106–124. (p. 669)

**Dinges, N. G., & Hull, P.** (1992). Personality, culture, and international studies. In D. Lieberman (Ed.), *Revealing the world: An interdisciplinary reader for international studies.* Dubuque, IA: Kendall-Hunt. (p. 352)

**Dion, K. K., & Dion, K. L.** (1993). Individualistic and collectivistic perspectives on gender and the cultural context of love and intimacy. *Journal of Social Issues, 49,* 53–69. (p. 660)

**Dion, K. K., Pak, A. W-P., & Dion, K. L.** (1990). Stereotyping physical attractiveness: A sociocultural perspective. *Journal of Cross-Cultural Psychology, 21,* 378–398. (p. 661)

**Dixon, B.** (1986, April). Dangerous thoughts: How we think and feel can make us sick. *Science, 86,* pp. 63–66. (p. 584)

**Dobson, K. S.** (1989). A meta-analysis of the efficacy of cognitive therapy for depression. *Journal of Consulting and Clinical Psychology, 57,* 414–419. (p. 560)

**Dohrenwend, B., Pearlin, L., Clayton, P., Hamburg, B., Dohrenwend, B. P., Riley, M., & Rose, R.** (1982). Report on stress and life events. In G. R. Elliott & C. Eisdorfer (Eds.), *Stress and human health: Analysis and implications of research* (A study by the Institute of Medicine/National Academy of Sciences). New York: Springer. (p. 578)

**Dohrenwend, B. P., Levav, I., Shrout, P. E., Schwartz, S., Naveh, G., Link, B. G., Skodol, A. E., & Stueve, A.** (1992). Socioeconomic status and psychiatric disorders: The causation-selection issue. *Science, 255,* 946–952. (p. 532)

**Dolezal, H.** (1982). *Living in a world transformed.* New York: Academic Press. (p. 205)

**Domjan, M.** (1992). Adult learning and mate choice: Possibilities and experimental evidence. *American Zoologist, 32,* 48–61. (p. 261)

**Donaldson, M.** (1979, March). The mismatch between school and children's minds. *Human Nature,* pp. 60–67. (p. 93)

**Donnerstein, E., Linz, D., & Penrod, S.** (1987). *The question of pornography.* New York: Free Press. (pp. 637, 640)

**Donovan, S., & Epstein, S.** (1993). Resistance of the Linda problem to solution: Implications for the relative influence of natural and analytical thought processes. Paper presented to the American Psychological Society convention. (p. 332)

**Doris, J.** (Ed.) (1991). *The suggestibility of children's recollections: Implications for eyewitness testimony.* Washington, DC: American Psychological Association. (p. 313)

**Dorozyaski, A.** (1993, January/February). Maternal alcoholism: Grapes of wrath. *Psychology Today,* p. 18. (p. 82)

**Dorris, M.** (1989). *The broken cord.* New York: HarperCollins. (p. 82)

**Dorsey, G.** (1987, February 8). The love doctor. *Hartford Courant/Northeast,* pp. 12–21, 33–35. (p. 375)

**Doty, R. L., Shaman, P., Applebaum, S. L., Giberson, R., Siksorski, L., & Rosenberg, L.** (1984). Smell identification ability: Changes with age. *Science, 226,* 1441–1443. (p. 132)

**Draguns, J. G.** (1990a). Normal and abnormal behavior in cross-cultural perspective: Specifying the nature of their relationship. *Nebraska Symposium on Motivation 1989, 37,* 235–277. (pp. 499, 510, 520)

**Draguns, J. G.** (1990b). Applications of cross-cultural psychology in the field of mental health. In R. W. Brislin (Ed.), *Applied cross-cultural psychology.* Newbury Park, CA: Sage. (pp. 499, 502)

**Dreman, D. N.** (1982). *The new contrarian investment strategy.* New York: Random House. (p. 331)

**Driedger, L.** (1975). In search of cultural identity factors: A comparison of ethnic students. *Canadian Review of Sociology and Anthropology, 12,* 150–161. (p. 664)

**Drucker, P. F.** (1982, December). A conversation with Peter F. Drucker. *Psychology Today,* pp. 60–67. (p. 472)

**Druckman, D., & Bjork, R. A.** (1991). *In the mind's eye: Enhancing human performance.* Washington, DC: National Academy Press. (p. 474)

**Druckman, D., & Swets, J. A.** (Eds.). (1988). *Enhancing human performance: Issues, theories, and techniques.* Washington, DC: National Academy Press. (pp. 213, 355)

**DuBois, W. E. B.** (1903/1961). *The souls of black folk.* Greenwich, CT: Fawcett Books. (p. 664)

**Duclos, S. E., Laird, J. D., Sexter, M., Stern, L., & Van Lighten, O.** (1989). Emotion-specific effects of facial expressions and postures on emotional experience. *Journal of Personality and Social Psychology, 57,* 100–108. (p. 442)

**Duggan, J. P., & Booth, D. A.** (1986). Obesity, overeating, and rapid gastric emptying in rats with ventromedial hypothalamic lesions. *Science, 231,* 609–611. (p. 403)

**Duncan, B. L.** (1976). Differential social perception and attribution of intergroup violence: Testing the lower limits of stereotyping of blacks. *Journal of Personality and Social Psychology, 34,* 590–598. (p. 682)

**Duncan, G. J., Hill, M. S., & Hoffman, S. D.** (1988). Welfare dependence within and across generations. *Science, 239,* 467–471. (p. 334)

**Duncker, K.** (1945). On problem solving. *Psychological Monographs, 58* (Whole no. 270). (pp. 329–330)

**Dunn, J., & Plomin, R.** (1990). *Separate lives: Why siblings are so different.* New York: Basic Books. (pp. 110, 115)

**Dunnett, S. B.** (1989). Neural transplantation: Normal brain function and repair after damage. *The Psychologist, 1,* 4–8. (p. 134)

**Dunning, D., Griffin, D. W., Milojkovic, J. D., & Ross, L.** (1990). *Journal of Personality and Social Psychology, 58,* 568–581. (p. 334)

**Dutton, D. G., & Aron, A.** (1989). Romantic attraction and generalized liking for others who are sources of conflict-based arousal. *Canadian Journal of Behavioural Sciences, 21,* 246–257. (p. 648)

**Dweck, C. S., & Elliott, E. S.** (1983). Achievement motivation. In P. Mussen & E. M. Hetherington (Eds.), *Handbook of child psychology* (Vol. IV). New York: Wiley. (p. 420)

**Dye, D. A., & Reck, M.** (1989). College grade point average as a predictor of adult success: A reply. *Public Personnel Management, 18,* 235–241. (p. 374)

**Eagles, J. M.** (1991). Is schizophrenia disappearing? *British Journal of Psychiatry, 158,* 834–835. (p. 526)

**Eagly, A. H.** (1986). Some meta-analytic approaches to examining the validity of gender-difference research. In J. S. Hyde & M. C. Linn (Eds.), *The psychology of gender: Advances through meta-analysis.* Baltimore: John Hopkins University Press. (p. 668)

**Eagly, A. H.** (1987). *Sex differences in social behavior: A social-role interpretation.* Hillsdale, NJ: Erlbaum. (p. 671)

**Eagly, A. H.** (1993). The science and politics of comparing women and men. Invited address to the American Psychological Society convention. (p. 668)

**Eagly, A. H., Ashmore, R. D., Makhijani, M. G., & Kennedy, L. C.** (1991). What is beautiful is good, but . . .: A meta-analytic review of research on the physical attractiveness stereotype. *Psychological Bulletin, 110,* 109–128. (p. 645)

**Eagly, A. H., & Crowley, M.** (1986). Gender and helping behavior: A meta-analytic review of the social psychological literature. *Psychological Bulletin, 100,* 283–308. (pp. 641, 669)

**Eagly, A. H., & Johnson, B. T.** (1990). Gender and leadership style: A meta-analysis. *Psychological Bulletin, 108,* 233–256. (p. 671)

**Eagly, A. H., & Karau, S. J.** (1991). Gender and the emergence of leaders: A meta-analysis. *Journal of Personality and Social Psychology, 60,* 685–710. (p. 425)

**Eagly, A. H., & Wood, W.** (1991). Explaining sex differences in social behavior: A meta-analytic perspective. *Personality and Social Psychology Bulletin, 17,* 306–315. (p. 678)

**Ebbesen, E. B., Duncan, B., & Konecni, V. J.** (1975). Effects of content of verbal aggression on future verbal aggression: A field experiment. *Journal of Experimental Social Psychology, 11,* 192–204. (p. 446)

**Ebbinghaus, H.** (1885). *Über das Gedachtnis.* Leipzig: Duncker & Humblot. Cited in R. Klatzky (1980), *Human memory: Structures and processes.* San Francisco: Freeman. (p. 301)

**Eccles, J. S., Jacobs, J. E., & Harold, R. D.** (1990). Gender role stereotypes, expectancy effects, and parents' socialization of gender differences. *Journal of Social Issues, 46,* 183–201. (p. 668)

**Eckensberger, L. H.** (1994). Moral development and its measurement across cultures. In W. J. Lonner & R. Malpass (Eds.), *Psychology and culture.* Boston: Allyn and Bacon. (p. 122)

**Eckert, E. D., Heston, L. L., & Bouchard, T. J., Jr.** (1981). MZ twins reared apart: Preliminary findings of psychiatric disturbances and traits. In L. Gedda, P. Paris, & W. D. Nance (Eds.), *Twin research: Vol. 3. Pt. B. Intelligence, personality, and development.* New York: Alan Liss. (p. 509)

**Ecklund-Flores, L.** (1992). The infant as a model for the teaching of introductory psychology. Paper presented to the American Psychological Association annual convention. (p. 81)

***Economist*** (1991, July 6). War in Europe. p. 11. (p. 656)

**Edwards, C. P.** (1981). The comparative study of the development of moral judgment and reasoning. In R. H. Munroe, R. L. Munroe, & B. B. Whiting (Eds.), *Handbook of cross-cultural human development.* New York: Garland Press. (p. 122)

**Edwards, C. P.** (1982). Moral development in comparative cultural perspective. In D. A. Wagner & H. W. Stevenson (Eds.), *Cultural perspectives on child development.* San Francisco: Freeman. (p. 122)

**Edwards, C. P.** (1991). Behavioral sex differences in children of diverse cultures: The case of nurturance to infants. In M. Pereira & L. Fairbanks (Eds.), *Juveniles: Comparative socioecology.* Oxford: Oxford University Press. (p. 678)

**Ehrhardt, A. A.** (1987). A transactional perspective on the development of gender differences. In J. M. Reinisch, L. A. Rosenblum, & S. A. Sanders (Eds.), *Masculinity/femininity: Basic perspectives.* New York: Oxford University Press. (p. 673)

**Ehrlichman, H., & Halpern, J. N.** (1988). Affect and memory: Effects of pleasant and unpleasant odors on retrieval of happy and unhappy memories. *Journal of Personality and Social Psychology, 55,* 769–779. (p. 180)

**Eibl-Eibesfeldt, I.** (1971). *Love and hate: The natural history of behavior patterns.* New York: Holt, Rinehart & Winston. (p. 441)

**Eich, E.** (1990). Learning during sleep. In R. B. Bootzin, J. F. Kihlstrom, & D. L. Schacter (Eds.), *Sleep and cognition.* Washington, DC: American Psychological Association. (p. 228)

**Eich, J. E.** (1980). The cue-dependent nature of state-dependent retrieval. *Memory and Cognition, 8,* 157–173. (p. 241)

**Einstein, G. O., & McDaniel, M. A.** (1990). Normal aging and prospective memory. *Journal of Experimental Psychology: Learning, Memory, and Cognition, 16,* 717–726. (p. 135)

**Eisenberg, N., & Lennon, R.** (1983). Sex differences in empathy and related capacities. *Psychological Bulletin, 94,* 100–131. (p. 670)

**Eiser, J. R.** (1985). Smoking: The social learning of an addiction. *Journal of Social and Clinical Psychology, 3,* 446–457. (p. 600)

**Ekman, P.** (1994). Strong evidence for universals in facial expressions: A reply to Russell's mistaken critique. *Psychological Bulletin, 115,* 268–287. (p. 440)

**Ekman, P., Davidson, R. J., & Friesen, W. V.** (1990). The Duchenne smile: Emotional expression and brain physiology II. *Journal of Personality and Social Psychology, 58,* 342–353. (p. 442)

**Ekman, P., & Friesen, W. V.** (1975). *Unmasking the face.* Englewood Cliffs, NJ: Prentice-Hall. (p. 440)

**Ekman, P., Friesen, W. V., O'Sullivan, M., Chan, A., Diacoyanni-Tarlatzis, I., Heider, K., Krause, R., LeCompte, W. A., Pitcairn, T., Ricci-Bitti, P. E., Scherer, K., Tomita, M., & Tzavaras, A.** (1987). Universals and cultural differences in the judgments of facial expressions of emotion. *Journal of Personality and Social Psychology, 53,* 712–717. (p. 440)

**Ekman, P., Levenson, R. W., & Friesen, W. V.** (1983). Autonomic nervous system activity distinguishes among emotions. *Science, 221,* 1208–1210. (p. 442)

**Ekman, P., & O'Sullivan, M.** (1991). Who can catch a liar? *American Psychologist, 46,* 913–920. (p. 439)

**Elder, G. H., Jr.** (1969). Appearance and education in marriage mobility. *American Sociological Review, 34,* 519–533. (p. 645)

**Elkin, I., Shea, T., Watkins, J. T., Imber, S. D., Sotsky, S. M., Collins, J. F., Glass, D. R., Pilkonis, P. A., Leber, W. R., Docherty, J. P., Fiester, S. J., & Parloff, M. B.** (1989). National Institute of Mental Health treatment of depression collaborative research program. *Archives of General Psychiatry, 46,* 971–983. (p. 559)

**Elkind, D.** (1970). The origins of religion in the child. *Review of Religious Research, 12,* 35–42. (p. 120)

**Elkind, D.** (1978). *The child's reality: Three developmental themes.* Hillsdale, NJ: Erlbaum. (p. 120)

**Ellis, A.** (1962). *Reason and emotion in psychotherapy.* Secaucus, NJ: Citadel Press. (p. 551)

**Ellis, A.** (1980). Psychotherapy and atheistic values: A response to A. E. Bergin's "Psychotherapy and religious values." *Journal of Consulting and Clinical Psychology, 48* 635–639. (p. 562)

**Ellis, A.** (1984). Rational-emotive therapy. In R. J. Corsini (Ed.), *Current psychotherapies* (3rd ed.). Itasca, IL: Peacock. (p. 551)

**Ellis, A.** (1987). The impossibility of achieving consistently good mental health. *American Psychologist, 42,* 364–375. (p. 551)

**Ellis, A.** (1989). Rational-emotive therapy. In R. J. Corsini & D. Wedding (Eds.), *Current psychotherapies* (4th ed.). Itasca, IL: Peacock. (p. 551)

**Ellis, A.** (1993). Changing rational-emotive therapy (RET) to rational emotive behavior therapy (REBT). *The Behavior Therapist, 16,* 257–258. (p. 551)

**Ellis, A., & Becker, I. M.** (1982). *A guide to personal happiness.* North Hollywood, CA: Wilshire Book Co. (p. 266)

**Ellis, H. C., & Ashbrook, P. W.** (1989). The "state" of mood and memory research: A selective review. *Journal of Social Behavior and Personality, 4,* 1–21. (p. 310)

**Ellis, L., & Ames, M. A.** (1987). Neurohormonal functioning and sexual orientation: A theory of homosexuality-heterosexuality. *Psychological Bulletin, 101,* 233–258. (p. 416)

**Emde, R. N., Plomin, R., Robinson, J., Corley, R., DeFries, J., Fulker, D. W., Reznick, J. S., Campos, J., Kagan, J., & Zahn-Waxler, C.** (1992). Temperament, emotion, and cognition at fourteen months: The MacArthur Longitudinal Twin Study. *Child Development, 63,* 1437–1455. (p. 98)

**Empson, J. A. C., & Clarke, P. R. F.** (1970). Rapid eye movements and remembering. *Nature, 227,* 287–288. (p. 229)

**Endler, N. S.** (1982). *Holiday of darkness: A psychologist's personal journey out of his depression.* New York: Wiley. (p. 567)

**Engen, T.** (1987). Remembering odors and their names. *American Scientist, 75,* 497–503. (p. 180)

**England, G. W., & Misumi, J.** (1986). Work centrality in Japan and the United States. *Journal of Cross-Cultural Psychology, 17,* 396–416. (p. 424)

**Epstein, S.** (1983a). Aggregation and beyond: Some basic issues on the prediction of behavior. *Journal of Personality, 51,* 360–392. (p. 478)

**Epstein, S.** (1983b). The stability of behavior across time and situations. In R. Zucker, J. Aronoff, & A. I. Rabin (Eds.), *Personality and the prediction of behavior.* San Diego: Academic Press. (p. 478)

**Epstein, S.** (1984). Controversial issues in emotions. In P. Shaver (Ed.), *Review of Personality and Social Psychology.* Beverly Hills, CA: Sage. (p. 435)

**Epstein, S., & Meier, P.** (1989). Constructive thinking: A broad coping variable with specific components. *Journal of Personality and Social Psychology, 57,* 332–350. (p. 374)

**Erber, R., & Tesser, A.** (1992). Task effort and the regulation of mood: The absorption hypothesis. *Journal of Experimental Social Psychology, 28,* 339–359. (p. 551)

**Erdelyi, M. H.** (1985). *Psychoanalysis: Freud's cognitive psychology.* New York: Freeman. (p. 470)

**Erdelyi, M. H.** (1988). Repression, reconstruction, and defense: History and integration of the psychoanalytic and experimental frameworks. In J. Singer (Ed.), *Repression: Defense mechanism and cognitive style.* Chicago: University of Chicago Press. (p. 470)

**Ericsson, K. A., & Chase, W. G.** (1982). Exceptional memory. *American Scientist, 70,* 607–615. (p. 296)

**Erikson, E. H.** (1963). *Childhood and society.* New York: Norton. (p. 122)

**Eron, L. D.** (1987). The development of aggressive behavior from the perspective of a developing behaviorism. *American Psychologist, 42,* 435–442. (pp. 146, 636)

**Eron, L. D., & Huesmann, L. R.** (1984). The control of aggressive behavior by changes in attitudes, values and the conditions of learning. In R. J. Blanchard & C. Blanchard (Eds.), *Advances in the study of aggression* (Vol. 1). Orlando, FL: Academic Press. (pp. 147, 639–640)

**Espinoza, M. P., Sigman, M. D., Neumann, C. G., Bwibo, N. O., & McDonald, M. A.** (1992). Playground behaviors of school-age children in relation to nutrition, schooling, and family characteristics. *Developmental Psychology, 28,* 1188–1195. (p. 603)

**Esser, J. K., & Lindoerfer, J. S.** (1989). Groupthink and the space shuttle *Challenger* accident: Toward a quantitative case analysis. *Journal of Behavioral Decision Making, 2,* 167–177. (p. 629)

**ETS.** (1992). Three reports shed new light on gender differences in testing. *ETS Developments, 37*(3), 4–7. (p. 667)

**Evans, C. R., & Dion, K. L.** (1991). Group cohesion and performance: A meta-analysis. *Small Group Research, 22,* 175–186. (p. 425)

**Evans, G. W., Palsane, M. N., & Carrere, S.** (1987). Type A behavior and occupational stress: A cross-cultural study of blue-collar workers. *Journal of Personality and Social Psychology, 52,* 1002–1007. (p. 582)

**Evans, G. W., Palsane, M. N., Lepore, S. J., & Martin, J.** (1989). Residential density and psychological health: The mediating effects of social support. *Journal of Personality and Social Psychology, 57,* 994–999. (p. 597)

**Evans, R. I., Dratt, L. M., Raines, B. E., & Rosenberg, S. S.** (1988). Social influences on smoking initiation: Importance of distinguishing descriptive versus mediating process variables. *Journal of Applied Social Psychology, 18,* 925–943. (p. 600)

**Evans, R. I., Raines, B. E., & Hanselka, L.** (1984). Developing data-based communications in social psychological research: Adolescent smoking prevention. *Journal of Applied Social Psychology, 14,* 289–295. (p. 602)

**Exner, J. E., Jr.** (1986). *The Rorschach: A comprehensive system: Vol. 1. Basic foundations* (2nd ed.). New York: Wiley. (p. 469)

**Eyer, D. E.** (1992). *Mother-infant bonding: A scientific fiction.* New Haven, CT: Yale University Press. (p. 97)

**Eysenck, H. J.** (1952). The effects of psychotherapy: An evaluation. *Journal of Consulting Psychology, 16,* 319–324. (p. 558)

**Eysenck, H. J.** (1990, April 30). An improvement on personality inventory. *Current Contents: Social and Behavioral Sciences, 22*(18), 20. (p. 474)

**Eysenck, H. J.** (1992). Four ways five factors are *not* basic. *Personality and Individual Differences, 13,* 667–673. (p. 474)

**Eysenck, H. J.** (1993). Creativity and personality. *Psychological Inquiry, 4,* 147–178. (p. 382)

**Eysenck, H. J., & Grossarth-Maticek, R.** (1991). Creative novation behaviour therapy as a prophylactic treatment for cancer and coronary heart disease: Part II—Effects of treatment. *Behaviour Research and Therapy, 29,* 17–31. (p. 596)

**Eysenck, H. J., & Kamin, L.** (1981). *The intelligence controversy: H. J. Eysenck vs. Leon Kamin.* New York: Wiley. (p. 362)

**Eysenck, H. J., Wakefield, J. A., Jr., & Friedman, A. F.** (1983). Diagnosis and clinical assessment: The DSM-III. *Annual Review of Psychology, 34,* 167–193. (p. 504)

**Eysenck, M. W., MacLeod, C., & Mathews, A.** (1987). Cognitive functioning and anxiety. *Psychological Research, 49,* 189–195. (p. 488)

**Eysenck, S. B. G., & Eysenck, H. J.** (1963). The validity of questionnaire and rating assessments of extraversion and neuroticism, and their factorial stability. *British Journal of Psychology, 54,* 51–62. (p. 474)

**Faber, N.** (1987, July). Personal glimpse. *Reader's Digest,* p. 34. (p. 381)

**Fagan, J. F., III** (1992). Intelligence: A theoretical viewpoint. *Current Directions in Psychological Science, 1,* 82–86. (p. 391)

**Falbo, T., & Polit, D. F.** (1986). Quantitative review of the only child literature: Research evidence and theory development. *Psychological Bulletin, 100,* 176–189. (p. 420)

**Falbo, T., & Poston, D. L., Jr.** (1993). The academic, personality, and physical outcomes of only children in China. *Child Development, 64,* 18–35. (p. 420)

**Fallon, A. E., & Rozin, P.** (1985). Sex differences in perceptions of desirable body shape. *Journal of Abnormal Psychology, 94,* 102–105. (p. 407)

**Fancher, R. E.** (1979). *Pioneers of psychology.* New York: Norton. (p. 360)

**Farina, A.** (1982). The stigma of mental disorders. In A. G. Miller (Ed.), *In the eye of the beholder.* New York: Praeger. (pp. 501, 533)

**Farina, A., & Fisher, J. D.** (1982). Beliefs about mental disorders: Findings and implications. In G. Weary & H. L. Mirels (Eds.), *Integrations of clinical and social psychology.* New York: Oxford University Press. (p. 556)

**Farrell, P. A., Gates, W. K., Maksud, M. G., & Morgan, W. P.** (1982). Increases in plasma beta-endorphin/beta-lipotropin immunoreactivity after treadmill running in humans. *Journal of Applied Physiology, 52,* 1245–1249. (p. 46)

**Farrington, D. P.** (1991). Antisocial personality from childhood to adulthood. *The Psychologist: Bulletin of the British Psychological Society, 4,* 389–394. (p. 530)

**Faust, D., & Ziskin, J.** (1988). The expert witness in psychology and psychiatry. *Science, 241,* 31–35. (p. 503)

**Fava, M., Copeland, P. M., Schweiger, U., & Herzog, D. B.** (1989). Neurochemical abnormalities of anorexia nervosa and bulimia nervosa. *American Journal of Psychiatry, 146,* 963–971. (p. 406)

**Fazio, R. H.** (1990). Multiple processes by which attitudes guide behavior: The MODE model as an integrative framework. In M. P. Zanna (Ed.), *Advances in experimental social psychology* (Vol. 23). San Diego, CA: Academic Press. (p. 616)

**Feder, H. H.** (1984). Hormones and sexual behavior. *Annual Review of Psychology, 35,* 165–200. (p. 410)

**Feeney, D. M.** (1987). Human rights and animal welfare. *American Psychologist, 42,* 593–599. (p. 34)

**Feeney, J. A., & Noller, P.** (1990). Attachment style as a predictor of adult romantic relationships. *Journal of Personality and Social Psychology, 58,* 281–291. (p. 99)

**Fehr, B., & Russell, J. A.** (1991). The concept of love viewed from a prototype perspective. *Journal of Personality and Social Psychology, 60,* 425–438. (p. 327)

**Fein, R.** (1992, November). Health care reform. *Scientific American,* pp. 46–53. (p. 599)

**Fein, S., Goethals, G. R., Kassin, S. M., & Cross, J.** (1993). Social influence and presidential debates. Paper presented at the American Psychological Association convention. (p. 621)

**Feingold, A.** (1990). Gender differences in effects of physical attractiveness on romantic attraction: A comparison across five research paradigms. *Journal of Personality and Social Psychology, 59,* 981–993. (p. 645)

**Feingold, A.** (1992). Gender differences in mate selection preferences: A test of the parental investment model. *Psychological Bulletin, 112,* 125–139. (p. 674)

**Feingold, A.** (1992). Good-looking people are not what we think. *Psychological Bulletin, 111,* 304–341. (p. 645)

**Feinleib, M., Lenfant, C., & Miller, S. A.** (1984). Hypertension and calcium. *Science, 226,* 384–385. (p. 603)

**Fenton, W. S., & McGlashan, T. H.** (1991). Natural history of schizophrenia subtypes: II. Positive and negative symptoms and long-term course. *Archives of General Psychiatry, 48,* 978–986. (p. 525)

**Fenton, W. S., & McGlashan, T. H.** (1994). Antecedents, symptom progression, and long-term outcome of the deficit syndrome in schizophrenia. *American Journal of Psychiatry, 151,* 351–356. (p. 525)

**Fernandez, E., & Turk, D. C.** (1989). The utility of cognitive coping strategies for altering pain perception: A meta-analysis. *Pain, 38,* 123–135. (p. 177)

**Fichter, M. M., & Noegel, R.** (1990). Concordance for bulimia nervosa in twins. *International Journal of Eating Disorders, 9,* 255–263. (p. 406)

**Fiedler, F. E.** (1981). Leadership effectiveness. *American Behavioral Scientist, 24,* 619–632. (p. 424)

**Fiedler, F. E.** (1987, September). When to lead, when to stand back. *Psychology Today,* pp. 26–27. (p. 425)

**Field, T.** (1991). Quality infant daycare and grade school behavior and performance. *Child Development, 62,* 863–870. (p. 102)

**Field, T. M.** (1987, May). Baby research comes to age. *Psychology Today,* p. 46. (p. 83)

**Field, T. M., Schanberg, S. M., Scafidi, F., Bauer, C. R., Vega-Lahr, N., Garcia, R., Nystrom, J., & Kuhn, C. M.** (1986). Tactile/kinesthetic stimulation effects on preterm neonates. *Pediatrics, 77,* 654–658. (p. 85)

**Fincham, F. D., & Bradbury, T. N.** (1993). Marital satisfaction, depression, and attributions: A longitudinal analysis. *Journal of Personality and Social Psychology, 64,* 442–452. (p. 614)

**Findley, M. J., & Cooper, H. M.** (1983). Locus of control and academic achievement: A literature review. *Journal of Personality and Social Psychology, 44,* 419–427. (p. 489)

**Finn, S. E.** (1986). Stability of personality self-ratings over 30 years: Evidence for an age/cohort interaction. *Journal of Personality and Social Psychology, 50,* 813–818. (p. 146)

**Finucci, J. M., & Childs, B.** (1981). Are there really more dyslexic boys than girls? In A. Ansara, N. Geschwind, A. Galaburda, M. Albert, & N. Gartrell (Eds.), *Sex differences in dyslexia.* Towson, MD: The Orton Dyslexia Society. (p. 667)

**Fischer, P. J., & Breakey, W. R.** (1991). The epidemiology of alcohol, drug, and mental disorders among homeless persons. *American Psychologist, 46,* 1115–1128. (p. 565)

**Fischhoff, B.** (1982). Debiasing. In D. Kahneman, P. Slovic, & A. Tversky (Eds.), *Judgment under uncertainty: Heuristics and biases.* New York: Cambridge University Press. (p. 335)

**Fischhoff, B., Slovic, P., & Lichtenstein, S.** (1977). Knowing with certainty: The appropriateness of extreme confidence. *Journal of Experimental Psychology: Human Perception and Performance, 3,* 552–564. (p. 334)

**Fisher, H. E.** (1993, March/April). After all, maybe it's biology. *Psychology Today,* pp. 40–45. (p. 140)

**Fisher, H. T.** (1984). Little Albert and Little Peter. *Bulletin of the British Psychological Society, 37,* 269. (p. 547)

**Fisher, R. P., Geiselman, R. E., & Amador, M.** (1989). Field test of the cognitive interview: Enhancing the recollection of actual victims and witnesses of crime. *Journal of Applied Psychology, 74,* 722–727. (p. 312)

**Fisher, R. P., Geiselman, R. E., & Raymond, D. S.** (1987). Critical analysis of police interview techniques. *Journal of Police Science and Administration, 15,* 177–185. (p. 312)

**Fitzgerald, R. C.** (1970). Reactions to blindness: An exploratory study of adults with recent loss of sight. *Archives of General Psychiatry, 22,* 370–379. (p. 143)

**Fleming, I., Baum, A., & Weiss, L.** (1987). Social density and perceived control as mediator of crowding stress in high-density residential neighborhoods. *Journal of Personality and Social Psychology, 52,* 899–906. (p. 581)

**Fleming, J. H., & Scott, B. A.** (1991). The costs of confession: The Persian Gulf War POW tapes in historical and theoretical perspective. *Contemporary Social Psychology, 15,* 127–138. (p. 440)

**Fletcher, G. J. O., Fitness, J., & Blampied, N. M.** (1990). The link between attributions and happiness in close relationships: The roles of depression and explanatory style. *Journal of Social and Clinical Psychology, 9,* 243–255. (p. 614)

**Floderus-Myrhed, B., Pedersen, N., & Rasmuson, I.** (1980). Assessment of heritability for personality, based on a short form of the Eysenck Personality Inventory: A study of 12,898 twin pairs. *Behavior Genetics, 10,* 153–162. (p. 108)

**Flynn, J. R.** (1987). Massive IQ gains in 14 nations: What IQ tests really measure. *Psychological Bulletin, 101,* 171–191. (p. 367)

**Flynn, J. R.** (1991). *Asian Americans: Achievement beyond IQ.* Hillsdale, NJ: Erlbaum. (p. 388)

**Foa, E. B., & Kozak, M. J.** (1986). Emotional processing of fear: Exposure to corrective information. *Psychological Bulletin, 99,* 20–35. (p. 547)

**Fong, G. T., Frantz, D. H., & Nisbett, R. E.** (1986). The effects of statistical training on thinking about everyday problems. *Cognitive Psychology, 18,* 253–292. (p. 30)

**Fontana, A., Rosenheck, R., & Brett, E.** (1992). War zone traumas and posttraumatic stress disorder symptomatology. *Journal of Nervous and Mental Disease, 180,* 748–755. (p. 579)

**Forer, B. R.** (1949). The fallacy of personal validation: A classroom demonstration of gullibility. *Journal of Abnormal and Social Psychology, 44,* 118–123. (p. 492)

**Forgas, J. P., Bower, G. H., & Krantz, S. E.** (1984). The influence of mood on perceptions of social interactions. *Journal of Experimental Social Psychology, 20,* 497–513. (p. 310)

**Forge, A., Li, L., Corwin, J. T., & Nevill, G.** (1993). Ultrastructural evidence for hair cell regeneration in the mammalian inner ear. *Science, 259,* 1616–1619. (p. 172)

**Fouts, R. S.** (1992). Transmission of a human gestural language in a chimpanzee mother-infant relationship. *Friends of Washoe, 12/13,* 2–8. (p. 350)

**Fouts, R. S., & Bodamer, M.** (1987). Preliminary report to the National Geographic Society on: "Chimpanzee intrapersonal signing." *Friends of Washoe, 7*(1), 4–12. (p. 350)

**Fowler, M. J., Sullivan, M. J., & Ekstrand, B. R.** (1973). Sleep and memory. *Science, 179,* 302–304. (p. 316)

**Fowler, R. C., Rich, C. L., & Young, D.** (1986). San Diego suicide study: II. Substance abuse in young cases. *Archives of General Psychiatry, 43,* 962–965. (p. 517)

**Fowler, R. D.** (1986, May). Howard Hughes: A psychological autopsy. *Psychology Today,* pp. 22–33. (p. 508)

**Fowles, D. C.** (1992). Schizophrenia: Diathesis-stress revisited. *Annual Review of Psychology, 43,* 303–336. (p. 525)

**Fox, J. L.** (1984). The brain's dynamic way of keeping in touch. *Science, 225,* 820–821. (p. 62)

**Fozard, J. L., & Popkin, S. J.** (1978). Optimizing adult development: Ends and means of an applied psychology of aging. *American Psychologist, 33,* 975–989. (p. 132)

**Frank, J. D.** (1982). Therapeutic components shared by all psychotherapies. In J. H. Harvey & M. M. Parks (Eds.), *The Master Lecture Series: Vol. 1. Psychotherapy research and behavior change.* Washington, DC: American Psychological Association. (pp. 540, 560, 562)

**Frank, M. G., & Gilovich, T.** (1988). The dark side of self and social perception: Black uniforms and aggression in professional sports. *Journal of Personality and Social Psychology, 54,* 74–85. (p. 26)

**Frank, S. J.** (1988). Young adults' perceptions of their relationships with their parents: Individual differences in connectedness, competence, and emotional autonomy. *Developmental Psychology, 24,* 729–737. (p. 125)

**Frankel, A., & Prentice-Dunn, S.** (1990). Loneliness and the processing of self-relevant information. *Journal of Social and Clinical Psychology, 9,* 303–315. (p. 522)

**Frankel, A., Strange, D. R., & Schoonover, R.** (1983). CRAP: Consumer rated assessment procedure. In G. H. Scherr & R. Liebmann-Smith (Eds.), *The best of The Journal of Irreproducible Results.* New York: Workman Publishing. (p. 476)

**Frankenburg, W., Dodds, J., Archer, P., Shapiro, H., & Bresnick, B.** (1992). The Denver II: A major revision and restandardization of the Denver Developmental Screening Test. *Pediatrics, 89,* 91–97. (p. 87)

**Fredrickson, B. L., & Kahneman, D.** (1993). Duration neglect in retrospective evaluations of affective episodes. *Journal of Personality and Social Psychology, 65,* 45–55. (p. 295)

**Freedman, J. L.** (1978). *Happy people.* San Diego: Harcourt Brace Jovanovich. (p. 142)

**Freedman, J. L.** (1988). Television violence and aggression: What the evidence shows. In S. Oskamp (Ed.), *Television as a social issue.* Newbury Park, CA: Sage. (p. 636)

**Freedman, J. L., & Fraser, S. C.** (1966). Compliance without pressure: The foot-in-the-door technique. *Journal of Personality and Social Psychology, 4,* 195–202. (p. 617)

**Freedman, J. L., & Perlick, D.** (1979). Crowding, contagion, and laughter. *Journal of Experimental Social Psychology, 15,* 295–303. (p. 627)

**Freeman, W. J.** (1991, February). The physiology of perception. *Scientific American,* pp. 78–85. (p. 164)

**Freud, S.** (1931; reprinted 1961). Female sexuality. In J. Strachey (Trans.), *The standard edition of the complete psychological works of Sigmund Freud.* London: Hogarth Press. (pp. 464–465)

**Freud, S.** (1933). *New introductory lectures on psycho-analysis.* New York: Carlton House. (p. 464)

**Freud, S.** (1935; reprinted 1960). *A general introduction to psychoanalysis.* New York: Washington Square Press. (p. 140)

**Friedman, H. S.** (1991). *The self-healing personality: Why some people achieve health and others succumb to illness.* New York: Holt. (p. 589)

**Friedman, H. S., & DiMatteo, M. R.** (1989). *Health psychology.* Englewood Cliffs, NJ: Prentice-Hall. (p. 590)

**Friedman, M., & Ulmer, D.** (1984). *Treating Type A behavior—and your heart.* New York: Knopf. (pp. 581, 596)

**Friedrich, O.** (1987, December 7). New age harmonies. *Time,* pp. 62–72. (p. 501)

**Frieze, I. H., Parsons, J. E., Johnson, P. B., Ruble, D. N., & Zellman, G. L.** (1978). *Women and sex roles: A social psychological perspective.* New York: Norton. (p. 470)

**Frijda, N. H.** (1988). The laws of emotion. *American Psychologist, 43,* 349–358. (p. 451)

**Fritsch, G., & Hitzig, E.** (1870; reprinted 1960). On the electrical excitability of the cerebrum. In G. Von Bonin (Trans.), *Some papers on the cerebral cortex.* Springfield, IL: Charles C. Thomas. (p. 60)

**Fromkin, V., & Rodman, R.** (1983). *An introduction to language* (3rd ed.). New York: Holt, Rinehart & Winston. (pp. 341, 344)

**Fulker, D. W., DeFries, J. C., & Plomin, R.** (1988). Genetic influence on general mental ability increases between infancy and middle childhood. *Nature, 336,* 767–769. (p. 385)

**Fuller, M. J., & Downs, A. C.** (1990). Spermarche is a salient biological marker in men's development. Poster presented at the American Psychological Society convention. (p. 118)

**Funder, D. C.** (1987). Errors and mistakes: Evaluating the accuracy of social judgment. *Psychological Bulletin, 101,* 75–90. (p. 338)

**Funder, D. C.** (1991). Global traits: A neo-Allportian approach to personality. *Psychological Science, 2,* 31–39. (p. 477)

**Funder, D. C., & Block, J.** (1989). The role of ego-control, ego-resiliency, and IQ in delay of gratification in adolescence. *Journal of Personality and Social Psychology, 57,* 1041–1050. (p. 122)

**Furnham, A.** (1982). Explanations for unemployment in Britain. *European Journal of Social Psychology, 12,* 335–352. (p. 615)

**Furnham, A.** (1993). A comparison between psychology and nonpsychology students' misperceptions of the subject. *Journal of Social Behavior and Personality, 8,* 311–322. (p. 235)

**Furnham, A., & Baguma, P.** (1994). Cross-cultural differences in the evaluation of male and female body shapes. *International Journal of Eating Disorders, 15,* 81–89. (p. 604)

**Furnham, A., & Taylor, L.** (1990). Lay theories of homosexuality: Aetiology, behaviours, and `cures.' *British Journal of Social Psychology, 29,* 135–147. (p. 416)

**Furstenberg, F. F., Jr., Moore, K. A., & Peterson, J. L.** (1985). Sex education and sexual experience among adolescents. *American Journal of Public Health, 75,* 1331–1332. (p. 417)

**Gabarino, J.** (1991). *No place to be a child: Growing up in a war zone.* Lexington, MA: Lexington Books. (p. 579)

**Gabarino, J.** (1992). *Children in danger: Coping with the consequences of community violence.* San Francisco: Jossey-Bass. (p. 579)

**Gabbay, F. H.** (1992). Behavior-genetic strategies in the study of emotion. *Psychological Science, 3*, 50–55. (p. 98)

**Gaertner, S. L., Mann, J., Murrell, A., & Dovidio, J. F.** (1989). Reducing intergroup bias: The benefits of recategorization. *Journal of Personality and Social Psychology, 57*, 239–249. (p. 688)

**Galambos, N. L.** (1992). Parent-adolescent relations. *Current Directions in Psychological Science, 1*, 146–149. (p. 125)

**Galanter, E.** (1962). Contemporary psychophysics. In R. Brown, E. Galanter, E. H. Hess, & G. Mandler (Eds.), *New directions in psychology*. New York: Holt, Rinehart & Winston. (p. 153)

**Gallagher, M.** (1990). Functional consequences of brain aging: The good news and the bad news. Address to the American Psychological Society convention. (p. 135)

**Gallant, S. J., Popiel, D. A., Hoffman, D. M., Chakraborty, P. K., and Hamilton, J. A.** (1992). Using daily ratings to confirm premenstrual syndrome/late luteal phase disorder. Part I. Effects of demand characteristics and expectations. *Psychosomatic Medicine, 54*, 149–166. (p. 591)

**Gallant, S. J., Popiel, D. A., Hoffman, D. M., Chakraborty, P. K., and Hamilton, J. A.** (1992). Using daily ratings to confirm premenstrual syndrome/late luteal phase dysphoric disorder. Part II. What makes a "real" difference? *Psychosomatic Medicine, 54*, 167–181. (p. 591)

**Gallatin, J.** (1980). Political thinking in adolescence. In J. Adelson (Ed.), *Handbook of adolescent psychology*. New York: Wiley. (p. 125)

**Gallup, G., Jr., & Newport, F.** (1990, December). Americans now drinking less alcohol. *Gallup Poll Monthly*, pp. 2–6. (p. 210)

**Gallup, G., Jr.** (1982). *Adventures in immortality*. New York: McGraw-Hill. (p. 251)

**Gallup, G., Jr., & O'Connell, G.** (1986). *Who do Americans say that I am?* Philadelphia, PA: Westminster Press. (p. 251)

**Gallup, G., Jr., & Suarez, S. D.** (1985). Alternatives to the use of animals in psychological research. *American Psychologist, 40*, 1104–1111. (p. 34)

**Gallup, G., Jr., & Suarez, S. D.** (1986). Self-awareness and the emergence of mind in humans and other primates. In J. Suls & A. G. Greenwald (Eds.), *Psychological perspectives on the self* (Vol. 3.). Hillsdale, NJ: Erlbaum. (p. 104)

**Gallup, G. H.** (1972). *The Gallup poll: Public opinion 1935–1971* (Vol. 3). New York: Random House. (p. 687)

**Gallup Organization.** (1988). *America's youth 1977–1988*. Princeton, NJ. (p. 125)

**Gallup Organization.** (1993). Other hemispheres may think our religion is alien and exotic. *PRRC Emerging Trends, 15*, 1–3. (p. 562)

***Gallup Poll Monthly*** (1991, January). Fear of dying. pp. 51–59. (p. 237)

***Gallup Poll Monthly*** (1992, October). The first presidential debate: Perot makes best impression; Bush falls short. p. 11. (p. 206)

***Gallup Poll Monthly*** (1993, July). Americans feel threatened by new immigrants. pp. 2–16. (p. 683)

***Gallup Poll Monthly*** (1993, October). Americans now more likely to say: Women have it harder than men. pp. 11–18. (p. 667)

***Gallup Poll Monthly*** (1993, September). The Gallup Poll of teenagers. p. 42. (pp. 125, 640)

***Gallup Report.*** (1989, March/April). Commercial aviation. pp. 32–33. (p. 333)

***Gallup Report.*** (1989, March/April). Importance of social values (self-image). p. 42. (p. 486)

**Galton, F.** (1874). *English men of science: Their nature and nurture*. London: Cass. (p. 78)

**Galton, F.** (1892). *Hereditary genius* (2nd ed.). London: Macmillan. (p. 360)

**Garcia, J., & Koelling, R. A.** (1966). Relation of cue to consequence in avoidance learning. *Psychonomic Science, 4*, 123–124. (p. 264)

**Gardner, H.** (1983). *Frames of mind: The theory of multiple intelligences*. New York: Basic Books. (p. 373)

**Gardner, H.** (1993). Multiple intelligences: The theory in practice. New York: Basic Books. (p. 373)

**Gardner, J. W.** (1984). *Excellence: Can we be equal and excellent too?* New York: Norton. (p. 141, 424)

**Gardner, J. W.** (1988, February). *The task of motivating*. Leadership Papers/9. Washington, DC: Independent Sector. (p. 390)

**Gardner, M.** (1983). Lessons of a landmark PK hoax. *The Skeptical Inquirer, 7*, 16–19. (p. 212)

**Gardner, R. A., & Gardner, B. I.** (1969). Teaching sign language to a chimpanzee. *Science, 165*, 664–672. (p. 348)

**Garfield, C.** (1986). *Peak performers: The new heroes of American business*. New York: Morrow. (p. 354)

**Garner, D. M., & Wooley, S. C.** (1991). Confronting the failure of behavioral and dietary treatments for obesity. *Clinical Psychology Review, 11*, 729–780. (p. 607)

**Garnets, L., & Kimmel, D.** (1990). Lesbian and gay dimensions in the psychological study of human diversity. Master lecture, American Psychological Association convention. (p. 413)

**Gash, D. M., Notter, M. F. D., Okawara, S. H., Kraus, A. L., & Joynt, R. J.** (1986). Amniotic neuroblastoma cells used for neural implants in monkeys. *Science, 233*, 1420–1421. (p. 134)

**Gastil, J.** (1990). Generic pronouns and sexist language: The oxymoronic character of masculine generics. *Sex Roles, 23*, 629–643. (p. 353)

**Gawin, F. H.** (1991). Cocaine addiction: Psychology and neurophysiology. *Science, 251*, 1580–1586. (p. 244)

**Gazzaniga, M. S.** (1967, August). The split brain in man. *Scientific American*, pp. 24–29. (p. 65)

**Gazzaniga, M. S.** (1983). Right hemisphere language following brain bisection: A 20-year perspective. *American Psychologist, 38*, 525–537. (p. 66)

**Gazzaniga, M. S.** (1985, November). The social brain. *Psychology Today*, pp. 29–38. (p. 66)

**Gazzaniga, M. S.** (1988). *Mind matters: How mind and brain interact to create our conscious lives*. Boston: Houghton Mifflin. (p. 66)

**Gazzaniga, M. S.** (1988). Organization of the human brain. *Science, 245*, 947–952. (p. 246)

**Gazzaniga, M. S.** (1992). *Nature's mind: The biological roots of thinking, emotions, sexuality, language, and intelligence*. New York: Basic Books. (pp. 86, 112)

**Gebhardt, D. L., & Crump, C. E.** (1990). Employee fitness and wellness programs in the workplace. *American Psychologist, 45,* 262–272. (p. 599)

**Geen, R. G.** (1984). Human motivation: New perspectives on old problems. In A. M. Rogers & C. J. Scheirer (Eds.), *The G. Stanley Hall Lecture Series* (Vol. 4). Washington, DC: American Psychological Association. (p. 419)

**Geen, R. G., & Gange, J. J.** (1983). Social facilitation: Drive theory and beyond. In H. H. Blumberg, A. P. Hare, V. Kent, & M. Davies (Eds.), *Small groups and social interaction* (Vol. 1). New York: Wiley. (p. 627)

**Geen, R. G., & Quanty, M. B.** (1977). The catharsis of aggression: An evaluation of a hypothesis. In L. Berkowitz (Ed.), *Advances in experimental social psychology* (Vol. 10). New York: Academic Press. (p. 446)

**Geen, R. G., & Thomas, S. L.** (1986). The immediate effects of media violence on behavior. *Journal of Social Issues, 42*(3), 7–28. (p. 637)

**Geiwitz, J.** (1980). *Psychology: Looking at ourselves* (2nd ed.). Boston: Little, Brown. (p. 136)

**Geldard, F. A.** (1972). *The human senses* (2nd ed.). New York: Wiley. (p. 165)

**Gelman, D.** (1989, May 15). Voyages to the unknown. *Newsweek,* pp. 66–69. (p. 440)

**Gelman, R.** (1979). Preschool thought. *American Psychologist, 34,* 900–905. (p. 93)

**Geranios, N. K.** (1993, September 26). Chimps learn to sign, and in the process, teach humans a little. Associated Press release in *Grand Rapids Press,* p. A18. (p. 348)

**Gerard, R. W.** (1953, September). What is memory? *Scientific American,* pp. 118–126. (p. 303)

**Gerbner, G.** (1985). Dreams that hurt: Mental illness in the mass media. Keynote address to the First Rosalynn Carter Symposium on Mental Health Policy, Emory University School of Medicine, Atlanta. (p. 534)

**Gerbner, G.** (1990). Stories that hurt: Tobacco, alcohol, and other drugs in the mass media. In H. Resnik (Ed.), *Youth and drugs: Society's mixed messages.* Rockville, MD: Office for Substance Abuse Prevention, U.S. Department of Health and Human Services. (p. 250)

**Gerbner, G.** (1993, June). Women and minorities on television: A study in casting and fate (Report to the Screen Actors Guild and the American Federation of Radio and Television Artists). (p. 636)

**Gerbner, G., Morgan, M., & Signorielli, N.** (1993). *Television violence profile no. 16: The turning point from research to action.* Annenberg School for Communication, University of Pennsylvania. (pp. 636–637, 640)

**Gershuny, J.** (1989). Time budgets as social indicators. *Journal of Public Policy, 9,* 419–424. (p. 679)

**Geschwind, N.** (1979, September). Specializations of the human brain. *Scientific American,* pp. 180–199. (p. 63–64)

**Geschwind, N., & Behan, P. O.** (1984). Laterality, hormones, and immunity. In N. Geschwind & A. M. Galaburda (Eds.), *Cerebral dominance: The biological foundations.* Cambridge, MA: Harvard University Press. (pp. 68, 667)

**Gfeller, J. D., Lynn, S. J., & Pribble, W. E.** (1987). Enhancing hypnotic susceptibility: Interpersonal and rapport factors. *Journal of Personality and Social Psychology, 52,* 586–595. (p. 238)

**Giambra, L. M.** (1974). Daydreaming across the life span: Late adolescent to senior citizen. *Aging and Human Development, 5,* 115–140. (p. 231)

**Gibbons, A.** (1992). Chimps: More diverse than a barrel of monkeys. *Science, 255,* 287–288. (p. 328)

**Gibbons, A.** (1992). Databasing the brain. *Science, 258,* 1872–1873. (p. 55)

**Gibbons, F. X.** (1986). Social comparison and depression: Company's effect on misery. *Journal of Personality and Social Psychology, 51,* 140–148. (p. 452)

**Gibson, E. J., & Walk, R. D.** (1960, April). The "visual cliff." *Scientific American,* pp. 64–71. (p. 193)

**Gibson, H. B.** (1979). The `Royal Nonesuch' of parapsychology. *Bulletin of the British Psychological Society, 32,* 65–67. (p. 212)

**Giles, T. R.** (1983). Probable superiority of behavioral interventions—II: Empirical status of the equivalence of therapies hypothesis. *Journal of Behavior Therapy and Experimental Psychiatry, 14,* 189–196. (p. 560)

**Gilligan, C.** (1982). *In a different voice: Psychological theory and women's development.* Cambridge, MA: Harvard University Press. (pp. 125, 138, 668)

**Gilligan, C., Lyons, N. P., & Hanmer, T. J.** (Eds.). (1990). *Making connections: The relational worlds of adolescent girls at Emma Willard School.* Cambridge, MA: Harvard University Press. (pp. 125, 668)

**Gilling, D., & Brightwell, R.** (1982). *The human brain.* New York: Facts on File. (p. 548)

**Gilovich, T.** (1991). *How we know what isn't so: The fallibility of human reason in everyday life.* New York: Free Press. (p. 22)

**Gilovich, T., Vallone, R., & Tversky, A.** (1985). The hot hand in basketball: On the misperception of random sequences. *Cognitive Psychology, 17,* 295–314. (p. 24)

**Gist, R., & Welch, Q. B.** (1989). Certification change versus actual behavior change in teenage suicide rates, 1955–1979. *Suicide and Life Threatening Behavior, 19,* 277–288. (p. 517)

**Gjerde, P. F.** (1983). Attentional capacity dysfunction and arousal in schizophrenia. *Psychological Bulletin, 93,* 57–72. (p. 524)

**Gladue, B. A.** (1990). Hormones and neuroendocrine factors in atypical human sexual behavior. In J. R. Feierman (Ed.), *Pedophilia: Biosocial dimensions.* New York: Springer-Verlag. (p. 416)

**Gladue, B. A., Boechler, M., & McCaul, K. D.** (1989). Hormonal response to competition in human males. *Aggressive Behavior, 15,* 409–422. (p. 633)

**Glass, D. C., & Singer, J. E.** (1972). *Urban stress.* New York: Academic Press. (p. 170)

**Glenn, N. D.** (1975). Psychological well-being in the postparental stage: Some evidence from national surveys. *Journal of Marriage and the Family, 37,* 105–110. (p. 141)

**Glick, P., Gottesman, D., & Jolton, J.** (1989). The fault is not in the stars: Susceptibility of skeptics and believers in astrology to the Barnum effect. *Personality and Social Psychology Bulletin, 15,* 572–583. (p. 492)

**Godden, D. R., & Baddeley, A. D.** (1975). Context-dependent memory in two natural environments: On land and underwater. *British Journal of Psychology, 66,* 325–331. (p. 309)

**Goff, D. C.** (1993). Reply to Dr. Armstrong. *Journal of Nervous and Mental Disease, 181,* 604–605. (p. 513)

**Goff, D. C., & Simms, C. A.** (1993). Has multiple personality disorder remained consistent over time? *Journal of Nervous and Mental Disease, 181,* 595–600. (pp. 513–514)

**Gold, M., & Yanof, D. S.** (1985). Mothers, daughters, and girlfriends. *Journal of Personality and Social Psychology, 49,* 654–659. (p. 125)

**Gold, P. E.** (1987). Sweet memories. *American Scientist, 75,* 151–155. (p. 304)

**Gold, P. E.** (1992). A proposed neurobiological basis for regulating memory storage for significant events. In E. Winograd & U. Neisser (Eds.), *Affect and accuracy in recall: Studies of "flashbulb" memories.* New York: Cambridge University Press. (p. 304)

**Goldberg, J., True, W. R., Eisen, S. A., & Henderson, W. G.** (1990). A twin study of the effects of the Vietnam War on posttraumatic stress disorder. *Journal of the American Medical Association, 263,* 1227–1232. (p. 579)

**Goldberg, L. R.** (1993). The structure of phenotypic personality traits. *American Psychologist, 48,* 26–34. (p. 475)

**Goldfried, M. R., & Padawer, W.** (1982). Current status and future directions in psychotherapy. In M. R. Goldfried (Ed.), *Converging themes in psychotherapy: Trends in psychodynamic, humanistic, and behavioral practice.* New York: Springer. (p. 560)

**Goldstein, A. P., & Glick, B.** (in press). Aggression replacement training: Curriculum and evaluation. *Simulation and Gaming.* (p. 635)

**Goleman, D.** (1980, February). 1,528 little geniuses and how they grew. *Psychology Today,* pp. 28–53. (p. 380, 420)

**Goleman, D.** (1990, September 16). Asian-Americans using education to escape prejudices. *Grand Rapids Press (The New York Times),* p. F8. (p. 388)

**Golomb, J., de Leon, M. J., Kluger, A., George, A. E., Tarshish, C., & Ferris, S. H.** (1993). Hippocampal atrophy in normal aging: An association with recent memory impairment. *Archives of Neurology, 50,* 967–973. (p. 306)

**Golomb, J., Kluger, A., de Leon, M. J., Ferris, S. H., Convit, A., Mittelman, M. S., Cohen, J., Rusinek, H., De Santi, S., & George, A. E.** (1994). Hippocampal formation size in normal human aging: A correlate of delayed secondary memory performance. *Learning & Memory, 1,* 45–54. (p. 306)

**Golub, S.** (1983). *Menarche: The transition from girl to woman.* Lexington, MA: Lexington Books. (p. 118)

**Gonsiorek, J. C.** (1982). Summary and conclusions. In W. Paul, J. D. Weinrich, J. C. Gonsiorek, & M. E. Hotvedt (Eds.), *Homosexuality: Social, psychological, and biological issues.* Beverly Hills, CA: Sage. (p. 414)

**Goodall, J.** (1968). The behaviour of free-living chimpanzees in the Gombe Stream Reserve. *Animal Behaviour Monographs, 1,* 161–311. (p. 111)

**Goodall, J.** (1986). *The chimpanzees of Gombe: Patterns of behavior.* Cambridge, MA: Harvard University Press. (p. 685)

**Goodchilds, J.** (1987, September 27). Quoted in Carol Tavris, Old age is not what it used to be. *The New York Times Magazine: Good Health Magazine,* pp. 24–25, 91–92. (p. 130)

**Goodhart, D. E.** (1986). The effects of positive and negative thinking on performance in an achievement situation. *Journal of Personality and Social Psychology, 51,* 117–124. (p. 491)

**Goodman, L. A., Koss, M. P., & Russo, N. F.** (1993). Violence against women: Mental health effects. Part II. Conceptualizations of posttraumatic stress. *Applied & Preventive Psychology, 2,* 123–130. (p. 579)

**Goodman, T. R., & Koenig, L. J.** (1992). Sex differences in depression: Explaining the absence in college populations. Paper presented to the American Psychological Association convention. (p. 517)

**Gopnik, A., & Meltzoff, A. N.** (1986). Relations between semantic and cognitive development in the one-word stage: The specificity hypothesis. *Child Development, 57,* 1040–1053. (p. 353)

**Goranson, R. E.** (1978). *The hindsight effect in problem solving.* Unpublished manuscript, cited by G. Wood (1984), Research methodology: A decision-making perspective. In A. M. Rogers & C. J. Scheirer (Eds.), *The G. Stanley Hall Lecture Series* (Vol. 4). Washington, DC: American Psychological Association. (p. 15)

**Gore, A., Jr.** (1992). *Earth in the balance: Ecology and the human spirit.* Boston: Houghton Mifflin. (pp. 279, 334)

**Gorsuch, R. L.** (1988). Psychology of religion. *Annual Review of Psychology, 39,* 201–222. (p. 422)

**Gortmaker, S. L., Must, A., Perrin, J. M., Sobol, A. M., & Dietz, W. H.** (1993). Social and economic consequences of overweight in adolescence and young adulthood. *New England Journal of Medicine, 329,* 1008–1012. (p. 604)

**Gotlib, I. H.** (1992). Interpersonal and cognitive aspects of depression. *Current Directions in Psychological Science, 1,* 149–154. (p. 485)

**Gotlib, I. H., & Hammen, C. L.** (1992). *Psychological aspects of depression: Toward a cognitive-interpersonal integration.* New York: Wiley. (p. 521)

**Gottesman, I. I.** (1991). *Schizophrenia genesis: The origins of madness.* New York: Freeman. (p. 527)

**Gottesman, I. I.** (1993). The origins of schizophrenia: Past as prologue. In R. Plomin & G. E. McClearn (Eds.), *Nature, nurture, and psychology.* Washington, DC: American Psychological Association. (p. 528)

**Gottfredson, L.** (1985). Education as a valid but fallible signal of worker quality: Reorienting an old debate about the functional basis of the occupational hierarchy. In A. C. Kerckhoff (Ed.), *Research in sociology of education and socialization* (Vol. 5). Greenwich, CT: JAI Press. (p. 374)

**Gottfredson, L. S.** (1986). Intelligence versus training: Job performance and black-white occupational inequality. Paper presented at a symposium on crime and employment: Two non-educational consequences of group IQ differences, American Psychological Association convention. (p. 388)

**Gottman, J., & Silver, N.** (1994). *Why marriages succeed or fail.* New York: Simon & Schuster. (p. 140)

**Gould, M. S., & Shaffer, D.** (1986). The impact of suicide in television movies: Evidence of imitation. *New England Journal of Medicine, 315,* 690–694. (p. 620)

**Gould, S. J.** (1977). *Ever since Darwin: Reflections in nautral history.* New York: Norton. (p. 211)

**Gould, S. J.** (1980). *The panda's thumb: More reflections in natural history.* New York: Norton. (p. 383).

**Gould, S. J.** (1981). *The mismeasure of man.* New York: Norton. (pp. 213, 363)

**Graf, P.** (1990). Life-span changes in implicit and explicit memory. *Bulletin of the Psychonomic Society, 28,* 353–358. (p. 135)

**Graham, J. W., Marks, G., & Hansen, W. B.** (1991). Social influence processes affecting adolescent substance use. *Journal of Applied Psychology, 76,* 291–298. (p. 250)

**Gray-Little, B., & Burks, N.** (1983). Power and satisfaction in marriage: A review and critique. *Psychological Bulletin, 93,* 513–538. (p. 649)

**Greeley, A. M.** (1991). *Faithful attraction.* New York: Tor Books. (pp. 20, 409, 417)

**Green, G., & Shane, H. C.** (1993, December). Facilitated communication: The claims versus the evidence. *Harvard Mental Health Letter,* pp. 4–5. (p. 626)

**Green, S. K., & Sandos, P.** (1983). Perceptions of male and female initiators of relationships. *Sex Roles, 9,* 849–852. (p. 677)

**Greenberg, R. P., Bornstein, R. F., Greenberg, M. D., & Fisher, S.** (1992). A meta-analysis of antidepressant outcome under "blinder" conditions. *Journal of Consulting and Clinical Psychology, 60,* 664–669. (p. 567)

**Greene, R. L.** (1987). Effects of maintenance rehearsal on human memory. *Psychological Bulletin, 102,* 403–413. (p. 293)

**Greenough, W. T., Black, J. E., & Wallace, C. S.** (1987). Experience and brain development. *Child Development, 58,* 539–559. (p. 85)

**Greenwald, A. G.** (1992). New look 3: Unconscious cognition reclaimed. *American Psychologist, 47,* 766–779. (p. 470)

**Greenwald, A. G.** (1992). Subliminal semantic activation and subliminal snake oil. Paper presented to the American Psychological Association Convention, Washington, DC. (p. 29)

**Greenwald, A. G., & Banaji, M. R.** (1995). Implicit social cognition: Attitudes, self-esteem, and stereotypes. *Psychological Review,* in press. (p. 220)

**Greenwald, A. G., Spangenberg, E. R., Pratkanis, A. R., & Eskenazi, J.** (1991). Double-blind tests of subliminal self-help audiotapes. *Psychological Science, 2,* 119–122. (p. 28)

**Greenwood, M. R. C.** (1989). Sexual dimorphism and obesity. In A. J. Stunkard & A. Baum (Eds.). *Perspectives in behavioral medicine: Eating, sleeping, and sex.* Hillsdale, NJ: Erlbaum. (p. 604)

**Greer, G.** (1984, April). The uses of chastity and other paths to sexual pleasures. *MS,* pp. 53–60, 96. (p. 411)

**Gregory, R. L.** (1978). *Eye and brain: The psychology of seeing* (3rd ed.). New York: McGraw-Hill. (p. 203)

**Gregory, W. L., Cialdini, R. B., & Carpenter, K. M.** (1982). Self-relevant scenarios as mediators of likelihood estimates and compliance: Does imagining make it so? *Journal of Personality and Social Psychology, 43,* 89–99. (p. 334)

**Greif, E. B., & Ulman, K. J.** (1982). The psychological impact of menarche on early adolescent females: A review of the literature. *Child Development, 53,* 1413–1430. (p. 118)

**Griffin, D. R.** (1984). Animal thinking. *American Scientist, 72,* 456–464. (p. 339)

**Grilo, C. M., & Pogue-Geile, M. F.** (1991). The nature of environmental influences on weight and obesity: A behavior genetic analysis. *Psychological Bulletin, 110,* 520–537. (p. 606)

**Grobstein, C.** (1979, June). External human fertilization. *Scientific American,* pp. 57–67. (p. 81)

**Grolnick, W. S., & Ryan, R. M.** (1987). Autonomy in children's learning: An experimental and individual difference investigation. *Journal of Personality and Social Psychology, 52,* 890–898. (p. 276)

**Grosof, D. H., Shapley, R. M., & Hawken, M. J.** (1993). Macaque V1 neurons can signal `illusory' contours. *Nature, 365,* 550–552. (p. 191)

**Gross, A. E., & Crofton, C.** (1977). What is good is beautiful. *Sociometry, 40,* 85–90. (p. 647)

**Grossman, M., & Wood, W.** (1993). Sex differences in intensity of emotional experience: A social role interpretation. *Journal of Personality and Social Psychology, 65,* 1010–1022. (p. 670)

**Gruder, C. L.** (1977). Choice of comparison persons in evaluating oneself. In J. M. Suls & R. L. Miller (Eds.), *Social comparison processes.* New York: Hemisphere. (p. 452)

**Guerin, B.** (1986). Mere presence effects in humans: A review. *Journal of Personality and Social Psychology, 22,* 38–77. (p. 627)

**Guion, R. M.** (1992). Science, pseudoscience, and silly science in applied psychology. Paper presented to the American Psychological Association convention. (p. 23)

**Gulevich, G., Dement, W., & Johnson, L.** (1966). Psychiatric and EEG observations on a case of prolonged (264 hours) wakefulness. *Archives of General Psychiatry, 15,* 29–35. (p. 225)

**Gur, R. E., Mozley, D., Resnick, S. M., Shtasel, D., Kohn, M., Zimmerman, R., Herman, G., Atlas, S., Grossman, R., Erwin, R., Gur, R. C.** (1991). Magnetic resonance imaging in schizophrenia. *Archives of General Psychiatry, 48,* 407–412. (p. 526)

**Gustavson, C. R., Garcia, J., Hankins, W. G., & Rusiniak, K. W.** (1974). Coyote predation control by aversive conditioning. *Science, 184,* 581–583. (p. 265)

**Gustavson, C. R., Kelly, D. J., & Sweeney, M.** (1976). Prey-lithium aversions I: Coyotes and wolves. *Behavioral Biology, 17,* 61–72. (p. 265)

**Gutierres, S. E., Kenrick, D. T., & Goldberg, L.** (1985). *Adverse influence on exposure to popular erotica: Effects on judgments of others and judgments of one's spouse.* Paper presented at the meeting of the Midwestern Psychological Association. (p. 412)

**Gutmann, D.** (1977). The cross-cultural perspective: Notes toward a comparative psychology of aging. In J. E. Birren & K. Warner Schaie (Eds.), *Handbook of the psychology of aging.* New York: Van Nostrand Reinhold. (p. 672)

**Haber, R. N.** (1970, May). How we remember what we see. *Scientific American,* pp. 104–112. (p. 288)

**Hackel, L. S., & Ruble, D. N.** (1992). Changes in the marital relationship after the first baby is born: Predicting the impact of expectancy disconfirmation. *Journal of Personality and Social Psychology, 62,* 944–957. (p. 141)

**Hackenberg, T. D., & Hineline, P. N.** (1990). Discrimination, symbolic behavior, and the origins of awareness. Unpublished manuscript, Temple University, Philadelphia. (p. 269)

**Haddock, G., & Zanna, M. P.** (1994). Preferring "housewives" to "feminists." *Psychology of Women Quarterly, 18,* 25–52. (p. 668)

**Hafner, H., & Schmidtke, A.** (1989). Do televised fictional suicide models produce suicides? In D. R. Pfeffer (Ed.), *Suicide among youth: Perspectives on risk and prevention.* Washington, DC: American Psychiatric Press. (p. 620)

**Haier, R. J.** (1993). Cerebral glucose metabolism and intelligence. In P. A. Vernon (Ed.), *Biologic approaches to the study of human intelligence.* Norwood, NJ: Ablex. (p. 376)

**Hall, C. S.** (1984). "A ubiquitous sex difference in dreams" revisited. *Journal of Personality and Social Psychology, 46,* 1109–1117. (p. 228)

**Hall, C. S., Dornhoff, W., Blick, K. A., & Weesner, K. E.** (1982). The dreams of college men and women in 1950 and 1980: A comparison of dream contents and sex differences. *Sleep, 5,* 188–194. (p. 228)

**Hall, C. S., & Lindzey, G.** (1978). *Theories of personality* (2nd ed.). New York: Wiley. (p. 471)

**Hall, C. S., & Van de Castle, R. L.** (1966). *The content analysis of dreams.* New York: Appleton-Century-Crofts. (p. 227)

**Hall, G. S.** (1904). *Adolescence: Its psychology and its relations to physiology, anthropology, sex, crime, religion and education* (Vol. I). New York: Appleton-Century-Crofts. (p. 118)

**Hall, J. A.** (1987). On explaining gender differences: The case of nonverbal communication. In P. Shaver & C. Hendrick (Eds.), *Review of Personality and Social Psychology, 7,* 177–200. (pp. 670–671)

**Hall, N. R., & Goldstein, A. L.** (1986, March/April). Thinking well: The chemical links between emotions and health. *The Sciences,* pp. 34–40. (p. 585)

**Hall, T.** (1987, September 27). Cravings: Does your body know what it needs? *The New York Times Magazine: Good Health Magazine,* pp. 23, 62–65. (p. 402)

**Halpern, D. F.** (1986). *Sex differences in cognitive abilities.* Hillsdale, NJ: Erlbaum. (p. 667)

**Halpern, D. F.** (1991). *Cognitive sex differences: Why diversity is a critical research issue.* Paper presented to the American Psychological Association convention. (p. 667)

**Halpern, D. F., & Coren, S.** (1988). Do right-handers live longer? *Nature, 333,* 213. (p. 586)

**Halpern, D. F., & Coren, S.** (1990). Laterality and longevity: Is left-handedness associated with a younger age at death? In S. Coren (Ed.), *Left-handedness: Behavioral implications and anomalies.* Amsterdam: North Holland Publishers. (p. 68)

**Halpern, D. F., & Coren, S.** (1991). Lateral preference and life span. *New England Journal of Medicine, 324,* 998. (p. 586)

**Halpern, D.F., & Coren, S.** (1993). Left-handedness and life span: A reply to Harris. *Psychological Bulletin, 114,* 235–241. (p. 586)

**Hamer, D. H., Hu, S., Magnuson, V. L., Hu, N., & Pattatucci, A. M. L.** (1993). A linkage between DNA markers on the X chromosome and male sexual orientation. *Science, 261,* 321–327. (p. 415)

**Hamid, A.** (1992). The developmental cycle of a drug epidemic: The cocaine smoking epidemic of 1981–1991. *Journal of Psychoactive Drugs, 24,* 337–348. (p. 243)

**Hamill, R., Wilson, T. D., & Nisbett, R. E.** (1980). Insensitivity to sample bias: Generalizing from atypical cases. *Journal of Personality and Social Psychology, 39,* 578–589. (p. 334)

**Hamilton, M. C.** (1988). Using masculine generics: Does generic "he" increase male bias in the user's imagery? *Sex Roles, 19,* 785–799. (p. 353)

**Hamilton, V. L., Hoffman, W. S., Broman, C. L., & Rauma, D.** (1993). Unemployment, distress, and coping: A panel study of autoworkers. *Journal of Personality and Social Psychology, 65,* 234–247. (p. 521)

**Hammersmith, S. K.** (1982, August). *Sexual preference: An empirical study from the Alfred C. Kinsey Institute for Sex Research.* Paper presented at the meeting of the American Psychological Association, Washington, DC. (p. 414)

**Hansel, C. E. M.** (1980). *ESP and parapsychology: A critical reevaluation.* Buffalo, NY: Prometheus Books. (p. 470)

**Hansen, C. H., & Hansen, R. D.** (1988). Finding the face-in-the-crowd: An anger superiority effect. *Journal of Personality and Social Psychology, 54,* 917–924. (p. 438)

**Hardin, C., & Banaji, M. R.** (1993). The influence of language on thought. *Social Cognition, 11,* 277–308. (p. 352)

**Hare, R. D.** (1975). Psychophysiological studies of psychopathy. In D. C. Fowles (Ed.), *Clinical applications of psychophysiology.* New York: Columbia University Press. (p. 531)

**Harkins, S. G., & Szymanski, K.** (1989). Social loafing and group evaluation. *Journal of Personality and Social Psychology, 56,* 934–941. (p. 628)

**Harlow, H. F., Harlow, M. K., & Suomi, S. J.** (1971). From thought to therapy: Lessons from a primate laboratory. *American Scientist, 59,* 538–549. (p. 96)

**Harrington, D. M., Block, J. H., & Block, J.** (1987). Testing aspects of Carl Rogers's theory of creative environments: Child-rearing antecedents of creative potential in young adolescents. *Journal of Personality and Social Psychology, 52,* 851–856. (p. 481)

**Harris, B.** (1979). Whatever happened to Little Albert? *American Psychologist, 34,* 151–160. (p. 266)

**Harris, L.** (1987). *Inside America.* New York: Random House. (pp. 579)

**Harris, L. J.** (1978). Sex differences in spatial ability: Possible environmental, genetic, and neurological factors. In M. Kinsbourne (Ed.), *The asymmetrical function of the brain.* New York: Cambridge University Press. (p. 680)

**Harris, L. J.** (1993). Do left-handers die sooner than right-handers? Commentary on Coren and Halpern's (1991) "Left-handedness: A marker for decreased survival fitness." *Psychological Bulletin, 114,* 203–234. (p. 587)

**Harris, R. J.** (1994). The impact of sexually explicit media. In J. Brant & D. Zillmann (Eds.), *Media effects: Advances in theory and research.* Hillsdale, NJ: Erlbaum. (p. 638)

**Harriston, K. A.** (1993, December 24). 1 shakes, 1 snoozes; both win $45 million. *Washington Post* release in *Tacoma News Tribune,* p. A1, A2. (p. 494)

**Hart, D.** (1988). The development of personal identity in adolescence: A philosophical dilemma approach. *Merrill-Palmer Quarterly, 34,* 105–114. (p. 124)

**Hart, J. Jr., & Gordon, B.** (1992). Neural subsystems of object knowledge. *Nature, 359,* 60–64. (p. 306)

**Hartmann, E.** (1981, April). The strangest sleep disorder. *Psychology Today,* pp. 14, 16, 18. (p. 227)

**Hartshorne, H., & May, M. A.** (1928). *Studies in deceit.* New York: Macmillan. (p. 478)

**Hartup, W. W.** (1989). Social relationships and their developmental significance. *American Psychologist, 44,* 120–126. (p. 100)

**Harvey, S. M.** (1987). Female sexual behavior: Fluctuations during the menstrual cycle. *Journal of Psychosomatic Research, 31,* 101–110. (p. 410)

**Hasher, L., & Zacks, R. T.** (1979). Automatic and effortful processes in memory. *Journal of Experimental Psychology: General, 108,* 356–388. (p. 291)

**Hasher, L., & Zacks, R. T.** (1984). Automatic processing of fundamental information: The case of frequency of occurrence. *American Psychologist, 39,* 1372–1388. (p. 291)

**Haskins, R.** (1989). Beyond metaphor: The efficacy of early childhood education. *American Psychologist, 44,* 274–282. (p. 387)

**Hassan, R., & Carr, J.** (1989). Changing patterns of suicide in Australia. *Australian and New Zealand Journal of Psychiatry, 23,* 226–234 (p. 517)

**Hatfield, E.** (1988). Passionate and companionate love. In R. J. Sternberg & M. L. Barnes (Eds.), *The psychology of love.* New Haven, CT: Yale University Press. (p. 647)

**Hatfield, E., & Sprecher, S.** (1986). *Mirror, mirror . . . The importance of looks in everyday life.* Albany: State University of New York Press. (p. 645)

**Hathaway, S. R.** (1960). *An MMPI Handbook* (Vol. 1, Foreword). Minneapolis: University of Minnesota Press. (Revised edition, 1972). (p. 476)

**Hauser, M. D.** (1993). Right hemisphere dominance for the production of facial expression in monkeys. *Science, 261,* 475–477. (p. 66)

**Hayes, J. R.** (1981). *The complete problem solver.* Philadelphia: Franklin Institute Press. (p. 308)

**Hazan, C., & Shaver, P. R.** (1994). Attachment as an organizational framework for research on close relationships. *Psychological Inquiry, 5,* 1–22. (p. 101)

**Hazelrigg, M. D., Cooper, H. M., & Borduin, C. M.** (1987). Evaluating the effectiveness of family therapies: An integrative review and analysis. *Psychological Bulletin, 101,* 428–442. (p. 555)

**Hearold, S.** (1986). A synthesis of 1043 effects of television on social behavior. In G. Comstock (Ed.), *Public communication and behavior.* New York: Academic Press. (p. 636)

**Heath, A. C., Eaves, L. J., & Martin, N. G.** (1989). The genetic structure of personality: III. Multivariate genetic item analysis of the EPQ scales. *Personality and Individual Differences, 10,* 877–888. (p. 108)

**Heath, A. C., Jardine, R., Eaves, L. J., & Martin, N. G.** (1989). The genetic structure of personality: II. Genetic item analysis of the EPQ. *Personality and Individual Differences, 10,* 615–624. (p. 108)

**Heath, A. C., Jardine, R., & Martin, N. G.** (1989). Interactive effects of genotype and social environment on alcohol consumption in female twins. *Journal of Studies on Alcohol, 50,* 38–48. (p. 249)

**Heath, L., & Petraitis, J.** (1987). Television viewing and fear of crime: Where is the mean world? *Basic and Applied Social Psychology, 8,* 97–123. (p. 637)

**Heatherton, T. F., & Baumeister, R. F.** (1991). Binge eating as escape from self-awareness. *Psychological Bulletin, 110,* 86–108. (p. 406)

**Hebb, D. O.** (1980). *Essay on mind.* Hillsdale, NJ: Erlbaum. (pp. 259, 433)

**Heider, F.** (1958). *The psychology of interpersonal relations.* New York: Wiley. (p. 613)

**Heiman, J. R.** (1975, April). The physiology of erotica: Women's sexual arousal. *Psychology Today,* pp. 90–94. (p. 411)

**Heinrichs, R. W.** (1993). Schizophrenia and the brain: Conditions for a neuropsychology of madness. *American Psychologist, 48,* 221–233. (p. 526)

**Heller, W.** (1990, May/June). Of one mind: Second thoughts about the brain's dual nature. *The Sciences,* pp. 38–44. (p. 69)

**Hellige, J. B.** (1993). Unity of thought and action: Varieties of interaction between the left and right cerebral hemispheres. *Current Directions in Psychological Science, 2,* 21–25. (p. 70)

**Helmreich, W. B.** (1992). *Against all odds: Holocaust survivors and the successful lives they made in America.* New York: Simon & Schuster. (p. 319)

**Helmreich, W. B.** (1994). Personal communication. Department of Sociology, City University of New York. (p. 319)

**Helms, J. E.** (1992). Why is there no study of cultural equivalence in standardized cognitive ability testing? *American Psychologist, 47,* 1083–1101. (p. 392)

**Hembree, R.** (1988). Correlates, causes, effects, and treatment of test anxiety. *Review of Educational Research, 58,* 47–77. (p. 434)

**Hendrickson, A. E.** (1982). The biological basis of intelligence. In H. J. Eysenck (Ed.), *A model for intelligence.* New York: Springer-Verlag. (p. 376)

**Henley, N. M.** (1989). Molehill or mountain? What we know and don't know about sex bias in language. In M. Crawford & M. Gentry (Eds.), *Gender and thought: Psychological perspectives.* New York: Springer-Verlag. (p. 353)

**Henninger, P.** (1992). Conditional handedness: Handedness changes in multiple personality disordered subject reflect shift in hemispheric dominance. *Consciousness and Cognition, 1,* 265–287. (p. 513)

**Henry, J. P., & Stephens, P. M.** (1977). *Stress, health, and the social environment.* New York: Springer-Verlag. (p. 579)

**Hepper, P. G., Shahidullah, S., & White, R.** (1990). Origins of fetal handedness. *Nature, 347,* 431. (p. 68)

**Herbert, T. B., & Cohen, S.** (1993). Depression and immunity: A meta-analytic review. *Psychological Bulletin, 113,* 472–486. (p. 584)

**Herek, G. M.** (1989). Hate crimes against lesbians and gay men: Issues for research and policy. *American Psychologist, 44,* 948–955. (p. 683)

**Herek, G. M.** (1990). The context of anti-gay violence: Notes on cultural and psychological heterosexism. *Journal of Interpersonal Violence, 5,* 316–333. (p. 683)

**Herman, C. P., & Polivy, J.** (1980). Restrained eating. In A. J. Stunkard (Ed.), *Obesity.* Philadelphia: Saunders. (p. 609)

**Herman, C. P., Olmsted, M. P., & Polivy, J.** (1983). Obesity, externality, and susceptibility to social influence: An integrated analysis. *Journal of Personality and Social Psychology, 45,* 926–934. (p. 605)

**Heron, W.** (1957, January). The pathology of boredom. *Scientific American,* pp. 52–56. (p. 182)

**Herrmann, D.** (1982). Know thy memory: The use of questionnaires to assess and study memory. *Psychological Bulletin, 92,* 434–452. (p. 320)

**Herrnstein, R. J., & Loveland, D. H.** (1964). Complex visual concept in the pigeon. *Science, 146,* 549–551. (p. 269)

**Hershenson, M.** (1989). *The moon illusion.* Hillsdale, NJ: Erlbaum. (p. 198)

**Hesburg, T. M.** (1974). *The humane imperative: A challenge for the year 2000.* New Haven, CT: Yale University Press. (p. 691)

**Hess, D. J.** (1993). *Science in the new age: The paranormal, its defenders and debunkers, and American culture.* Madison: University of Wisconsin Press. (p. 213)

**Hess, E. H.** (1956, July). Space perception in the chick. *Scientific American,* pp. 71–80. (p. 204)

**Hetherington, E. M.** (1979). Divorce: A child's perspective. *American Psychologist, 34,* 851–858. (p. 105)

**Hetherington, E. M., & Clingempeel, W. G.** (1992). Coping with marital transitions: A family systems perspective. *Society for Research in Child Development Monographs, 57,* 1–242. (p. 102)

**Hetherington, E. M., Reiss, D., & Plomin, R.** (1993). *The separate social worlds of siblings: The impact of nonshared environment on development.* Hillsdale, NJ: Erlbaum. (p. 110)

**Hetherington, E. M., Stanley-Hagan, M., & Anderson, E. R.** (1989). Marital transitions: A child's perspective. *American Psychologist, 44,* 303–312. (p. 102)

**Hewlett, B. S.** (1991). *Intimate fathers.* Ann Arbor, MI: University of Michigan Press (cited in D. Popenoe, The fatherhood problem. Institute for American Values Working Paper No. 40, October, 1993). (p. 100)

**Hicks, R. A., & Pellegrini, R. J.** (1982). Sleep problems and Type A-B behavior in college students. *Psychological Reports, 51,* 196. (p. 582)

**Hicks, R. A., Kilcourse, J., & Sinnott, M. A.** (1983). Type A-B behavior and caffeine use in college students. *Psychological Reports, 52,* 338. (p. 582)

**Higgins, E. T.** (1987). Self-discrepancy: A theory relating self and affect. *Psychological Review, 94,* 319–340. (p. 483)

**Higgins, E. T., & Bargh, J. A.** (1987). Social cognition and social perception. *Annual Review of Psychology, 38,* 369–425. (p. 483)

**Hilgard, E. R.** (1986). *Divided consciousness: Multiple controls in human thought and action.* New York: Wiley. (p. 239, 251)

**Hilgard, E. R.** (1992). Dissociation and theories of hypnosis. In E. Fromm & M. R. Nash (Eds.), *Contemporary hypnosis research.* New York: Guilford Press. (p. 239)

**Hines, M.** (1990). Gonadal hormones and human cognitive development. In J. Balthazart (Ed.), *Hormones, brain and behaviour in vertebrates, I. Sexual differentiation, neuroanatomical aspects, neurotransmitters and neuropeptides.* Basel: Karger. (p. 674)

**Hines, M., & Green, R.** (1991). Human hormonal and neural correlates of sex-typed behaviors. *Review of Psychiatry, 10,* 536–555. (p. 673)

**Hintzman, D. L.** (1978). *The psychology of learning and memory.* San Francisco: Freeman. (p. 296)

**Hinz, L. D., & Williamson, D. A.** (1987). Bulimia and depression: A review of the affective variant hypothesis. *Psychological Bulletin, 102,* 150–158. (p. 406)

**Hirst, W., Neisser, U., & Spelke, E.** (1978, June). Divided attention. *Human Nature,* pp. 54–61. (p. 239)

**Hirt, E. R., Zillmann, D., Erickson, G. A., & Kennedy, C.** (1992). Costs and benefits of allegiance: Changes in fans' self-ascribed competencies after team victory versus defeat. *Journal of Personality and Social Psychology, 63,* 724–738. (p. 521)

**Hobfoll, S. E.** (1989). Conservation of resources: A new attempt at conceptualizing stress. *American Psychologist, 44,* 513–524. (p. 575)

**Hobfoll, S. E., Lomranz, J., Eyal, N., Bridges, A., & Tzemach, M.** (1989). Pulse of a nation: Depressive mood reactions of Israelis to the Israel-Lebanon war. *Journal of Personality and Social Psychology, 56,* 1002–1012. (p. 518)

**Hobson, J. A.** (1988). *The dreaming brain.* New York: Basic Books. (p. 229)

**Hobson, J. A.** (1989). *Sleep.* New York: Scientific American Library. (p. 229)

**Hodgkinson, V. A., & Weitzman, M. S.** (1992). *Giving and volunteering in the United States.* Washington, DC: Independent Sector. (p. 643)

**Hoebel, B. G., & Teitelbaum, P.** (1966). Effects of forcefeeding and starvation on food intake and body weight in a rat with ventromedial hypothalamic lesions. *Journal of Comparative and Physiological Psychology, 61,* 189–193. (p. 403)

**Hoffman, C., & Hurst, N.** (1990). Gender stereotypes: Perception or rationalization? *Journal of Personality and Social Psychology, 58,* 197–208. (p. 684)

**Hoffman, L. W.** (1989). Effects of maternal employment in the two-parent family. *American Psychologist, 44,* 283–292. (p. 101)

**Hoffman, L. W.** (1991). The influence of the family environment on personality: Accounting for sibling differences. *Psychological Bulletin, 110,* 187–203. (p. 110)

**Hofstede, G.** (1980). *Culture's consequences: International differences in work-related values.* Beverly Hills, CA: Sage. (p. 424)

**Hogan, J.** (1989). Personality correlates of physical fitness. *Journal of Personality and Social Psychology, 56*, 284–288. (p. 593)

**Hohmann, G. W.** (1966). Some effects of spinal cord lesions on experienced emotional feelings. *Psychophysiology, 3*, 143–156. (p. 455)

**Hokanson, J. E., & Edelman, R.** (1966). Effects of three social responses on vascular processes. *Journal of Personality and Social Psychology, 3*, 442–447. (p. 446)

**Holden, C.** (1980a). Identical twins reared apart. *Science, 207*, 1323–1325. (p. 109)

**Holden, C.** (1980b, November). Twins reunited. *Science 80*, 55–59. (p. 109)

**Holden, C.** (1986a). Days may be numbered for polygraphs in the private sector. *Science, 232*, 705. (p. 436)

**Holden, C.** (1986b). Researchers grapple with problems of updating classic psychological test. *Science, 233*, 1249–1251. (p. 486)

**Holden, C.** (1990). Head Start enters adulthood. *Science, 247*, 1400–1402. (p. 387)

**Holden, C.** (1991). Alcoholism gene: Coming or going? *Science, 254*, 200. (p. 249)

**Holden, C.** (1991). New center to study therapies and ethnicity. *Science, 251*, 748. (pp. 504, 565)

**Holden, C.** (1993). Wake-up call for sleep research. *Science, 259*, 305. (p. 225)

**Holing, D.** (1988, October). Dolphin defense. *Discover*, pp. 70–74. (p. 279)

**Hollon, S. D., DeRubeis, R. J., & Seligman, M. E. P.** (1992). Cognitive therapy and the prevention of depression. *Applied & Preventive Psychology, 1*, 89–95. (p. 553)

**Holmes, D.** (1990). The evidence for repression: An examination of sixty years of research. In J. Singer (Ed.), *Repression and dissociation: Implications for personality theory, psychopathology, and health.* Chicago: University of Chicago Press. (p. 319)

**Holmes, D. S.** (1978). Projection as a defense mechanism. *Psychological Bulletin, 85*, 677–688. (p. 470)

**Holmes, D. S.** (1981). Existence of classical projection and the stress-reducing function of attributive projection: A reply to Sherwood. *Psychological Bulletin, 90*, 460–466. (p. 470)

**Holmes, D. S.** (1994). Is there evidence for repression? No. (Unexpurgated version on an article which was rewritten by the *Harvard Mental Health Letter* and published as "Is there evidence for repression? Doubtful," June, 1994, pp. 4–6.) (pp. 317, 319, 470)

**Holtgraves, T., & Skeel, J.** (1992). Cognitive biases in playing the lottery: Estimating the odds and choosing the numbers. *Journal of Applied Social Psychology, 22*, 934–952. (p. 22)

**Holzman, P. S., & Matthysse, S.** (1990). The genetics of schizophrenia: A review. *Psychological Science, 1*, 279–286. (p. 156)

**Hooper, J., & Teresi, D.** (1986). *The three-pound universe.* New York: Macmillan. (p. 59)

**Hooykaas, R.** (1972). *Religion and the rise of modern science.* Grand Rapids, MI: Eerdmans. (p. 12)

**Horn, J. L.** (1982). The aging of human abilities. In J. Wolman (Ed.), *Handbook of developmental psychology.* Englewood Cliffs, NJ: Prentice-Hall. (p. 137)

**Horne, J. A.** (1989). Sleep loss and "divergent" thinking ability. *Sleep, 11*, 528–536. (p. 225)

**Horney, K.** (1945). *Our inner conflicts: A constructive theory of neurosis.* New York: Norton. (p. 558)

**House, J. S., Landis, K. R., & Umberson, D.** (1988). Social relationships and health. *Science, 241*, 540–545. (p. 597)

**House, R. J., & Singh, J. V.** (1987). Organizational behavior: Some new directions for I/O psychology. *Annual Review of Psychology, 38*, 669–718. (p. 425)

**Howe, M. L., & Courage, M. L.** (1993). On resolving the enigma of infantile amnesia. *Psychological Bulletin, 113*, 305–326. (p. 84)

**Hoyer, G., & Lund, E.** (1993). Suicide among women related to number of children in marriage. *Archives of General Psychiatry, 50*, 134–137. (p. 516)

**Hsu, F. L. K.** (1953). *Americans and Chinese: Two ways of life.* New York: Schuman. Quoted in M. W. Morris, R. E. Nisbett, & K. Peng (in press), G. Lewis, D. Premack, & D. Sperber (Eds.), *Causal understandings in cognition and culture.* New York: Oxford. (p. 658)

**Hubel, D. H.** (1979, September). The brain. *Scientific American*, pp. 45–53. (p. 156)

**Hubel, D. H., & Wiesel, T. N.** (1979, September). Brian mechanisms of vision. *Scientific American*, pp. 150–162. (pp. 56, 163)

**Hucker, S. J., & Bain, J.** (1990). Androgenic hormones and sexual assault. In W. Marshall, R. Law, & H. Barbaree (Eds.), *The handbook on sexual assault.* New York: Plenum. (p. 411)

**Hugick, L.** (1989, July). Women play the leading role in keeping modern families close. *Gallup Report*, No. 286, pp. 27–34. (p. 669)

**Hugo, G.** (1987). Aging in the third world. *Social Science, 72*, 57–60. (p. 131)

**Hui, C. H.** (1990). West meets East: Individualism versus collectivism in North America and Asia. Invited address, Hope College. (p. 662)

**Hull, J. G., & Bond, C. F., Jr.** (1986). Social and behavioral consequences of alcohol consumption and expectancy: A meta-analysis. *Psychological Bulletin, 99*, 347–360. (p. 242)

**Humphrey, N., & Dennett, D. C.** (1989, Summer). Speaking for ourselves: An assessment of multiple personality disorder. *Raritan: A Quarterly Review, 9*, 68–98. (p. 513)

**Humphreys, L. G., & Davey, T. C.** (1988). Continuity in intellectual growth from 12 months to 9 years. *Intelligence, 12*, 183–197. (p. 378)

**Hunt, E.** (1983). On the nature of intelligence. *Science, 219*, 141–146. (p. 375)

**Hunt, J. M.** (1982). Toward equalizing the developmental opportunities of infants and preschool children. *Journal of Social Issues, 38*(4), 163–191. (p. 386)

**Hunt, M.** (1974). *Sexual behavior in the 1970s.* Chicago: Playboy Press. (p. 412)

**Hunt, M.** (1982). *The universe within.* New York: Simon & Schuster. (pp. 336, 338)

**Hunt, M.** (1990). *The compassionate beast: What science is discovering about the humane side of humankind.* New York: Morrow. (p. 7)

**Hunt, M.** (1993). *The story of psychology.* New York: Doubleday. (pp. 2, 41, 121, 123, 266, 380)

**Hunter, S., & Sundel, M.** (Eds.). (1989). *Midlife myths: Issues, findings, and practice implications.* Newbury Park, CA: Sage. (p. 138)

**Hurt, S. W., Schnurr, P. P., Severino, S. K., Freeman, E. W., Gise, L. H., Rivera-Tovar, A., & Steege, J. F.** (1992). Late luteal phase dysphoric disorder in 670 women evaluated for premenstrual complaints. *American Journal of Psychiatry, 149,* 525–530. (p. 591)

**Hurtado, S., Dey, E. L., & Trevino, J. G.** (1994). Exclusion or self-segregation? Interaction across racial/ethnic groups on college campuses. Paper presented at the American Educational Research Association annual meeting. (p. 683)

**Huston, A. C., Donnerstein, E., Fairchild, H., Feshbach, N. D., Katz, P. A., & Murray, J. P.** (1992). *Big world, small screen: The role of television in American society.* Lincoln: University of Nebraska Press. (p. 636)

**Hutnik, N.** (1985). Aspects of identity in a multi-ethnic society. *New Community, 12,* 298–309. (p. 664)

**Hyde, J. S.** (1983, November). *Bem's gender schema theory.* Paper presented at GLCA Women's Studies Conference, Rochester, IN. (p. 311)

**Hyde, J. S.** (1984, July). Children's understanding of sexist language. *Developmental Psychology, 20*(4), 697–706. (p. 353)

**Hyde, J. S.** (1986). Gender differences in aggression. In J. S. Hyde & M. C. Linn (Eds.), *The psychology of gender: Advances through meta-analysis.* Baltimore: Johns Hopkins University Press. (p. 671)

**Hyde, J. S., Fennema, E., & Lamon, S. J.** (1990). Gender differences in mathematics performance: A meta-analysis. *Psychological Bulletin, 107,* 139–155. (p. 667)

**Hyde, J. S., & Linn, M. C.** (1988). Gender differences in verbal ability: A meta-analysis. *Psychological Bulletin, 104,* 53–69. (p. 667)

**Hyler, S., Gabbard, G. O., & Schneider, I.** (1991). Homicidal maniacs and narcissistic parasites: Stigmatization of mentally ill persons in the movies. *Hospital and Community Psychiatry, 42,* 1044–1048. (p. 534)

**Hyman, R.** (1981). Cold reading: How to convince strangers that you know all about them. In K. Frazier (Ed.), *Paranormal borderlands of science.* Buffalo, NY: Prometheus Books. (p. 492)

**Hyman, R.** (1986). Maimonides dream-telepathy experiments. *Skeptical Inquirer, 11,* 91–92. (p. 213)

**Hyman, R.** (1994). Anomaly or artifact? Comments on Bem and Honorton. *Psychological Bulletin, 115,* 19–24. (p. 214)

**Iacono, W. G., & Grove, W. M.** (1993). Schizophrenia reviewed: Toward an integrative genetic model. *Psychological Science, 4,* 273–276. (p. 525)

**Idler, E. I., & Kasl, S. V.** (1992). Religion, disability, depression, and the timing of death. *American Journal of Sociology, 97,* 1052–1079. (p. 598)

**Ingham, A. G., Levinger, G., Graves, J., & Peckham, V.** (1974). The Ringelmann effect: Studies of group size and group performance. *Journal of Experimental Social Psychology, 10,* 371–384. (p. 628)

**Inglehart, M. R., Markus, H., & Brown, D.R.** (1989). The effects of possible selves on academic achievement—A panel study. In J. P. Forgas & J. M. Innes (Eds.), *Recent advances in social psychology: An international perspective.* New York: Elsevier Science Publishers. (p. 482)

**Inglehart, R.** (1990). *Culture shift in advanced industrial society.* Princeton, NJ: Princeton University Press. (pp. 140, 142–143, 428, 449, 490)

**Insel, P. M., & Roth, W. T.** (1976). *Health in a changing society.* Palo Alto, CA: Mayfield. (p. 129)

**Intons-Peterson, M. J., Roskos-Ewoldsen, B., Thomas, L., Shirley, M., & Blut, D.** (1989). Will educational materials reduce negative effects of exposure to sexual violence? *Journal of Social and Clinical Psychology, 8,* 256–275. (p. 640)

**Isen, A. M., & Means, B.** (1983). The influence of positive affect on decision-making strategy. *Social Cognition, 2,* 28–31. (p. 447)

**Isham, W. P., & Kamin, L. J.** (1993). Blackness, deafness, IQ, and g. *Intelligence, 17,* 37–46. (p. 354)

**Iyer, P.** (1993, Fall). The global village finally arrives. *Time,* pp. 86–87. (p. 655)

**Izard, C. E.** (1977). *Human emotions.* New York: Plenum Press. (pp. 440, 444)

**Izard, C. E.** (1994). Innate and universal facial expressions: Evidence from developmental and cross-cultural research. *Psychological Bulletin, 115,* 288–299. (p. 440)

**Jackson, D., & Rothstein, M.** (1993). Evaluating personality testing in personnel selection. *The Psychologist: Bulletin of the British Psychological Society, 6,* 8–11. (p. 478)

**Jackson, J. M., & Williams, K. D.** (1988). Social loafing: A review and theoretical analysis. Unpublished manuscript, Fordham University, New York. (p. 628)

**Jackson, S. W.** (1992). The listening healer in the history of psychological healing. *American Journal Psychiatry, 149,* 1623–1632. (p. 560)

**Jacobs, B. L.** (1987). How hallucinogenic drugs work. *American Scientist, 75,* 386–392. (p. 245)

**Jacobs, W. J., & Nadel, L.** (1985). Stress-induced recovery of fears and phobias. *Psychological Bulletin, 92,* 512–531. (p. 509)

**Jacobson, R. L.** (1986, September 3). Number of blacks taking SAT drops 5 pct. in 5 years. *Chronicle of Higher Education,* p. 108. (p. 388)

**James, W.** (1890). *The principles of psychology* (Vol. 2). New York: Holt. (pp. 50, 145, 174, 239, 297, 442, 454, 482, 619, 659)

**James, W.** (1902/1958). *Varieties of religious experience.* New York: Mentor Books. (p. 447)

**Jameson, D.** (1985). Opponent-colors theory in light of physiological findings. In D. Ottoson & S. Zeki (Eds.), *Central and peripheral mechanisms of color vision.* New York: Macmillan. (p. 167)

**Jamison, K. R.** (1993). *Touched with fire: Manic-depressive illness and the artistic temperament.* New York: Free Press. (p. 515)

**Janis, I. L.** (1982). *Groupthink: Psychological studies of policy decisions and fiascoes.* Boston: Houghton Mifflin. (p. 629)

**Janis, I. L.** (1986). Problems of international crisis management in the nuclear age. *Journal of Social Issues, 42*(2), 201–220. (p. 331)

**Janis, I. L.** (1989). *Crucial decisions: Leadership in policymaking and crisis management*. New York: Free Press. (p. 330)

**Janoff-Bulman, R., Timko, C., & Carli, L. L.** (1985). Cognitive biases in blaming the victim. *Journal of Experimental Social Psychology, 21*, 161–177. (p. 686)

**Jarvik, L. F.** (1975). Thoughts on the psychobiology of aging. *American Psychologist, 30*, 576–583. (p. 133)

**Jeffrey, R. W., & Wing, R. R.** (1983). Recidivism and self-cure of smoking and obesity: Data from population studies. *American Psychologist, 38*, 852. (p. 608)

**Jelicic, M., De Roode, A., Bovill, J. G., & Bonke, B.** (1992). Unconscious learning during anaesthesia. *Anaesthesia, 47*, 835–837. (p. 251)

**Jemmott, J. B., III, & Locke, S. E.** (1984). Psychosocial factors, immunologic mediation, and human susceptibility to infectious diseases: How much do we know? *Psychological Bulletin, 95*, 78–108. (p. 583)

**Jemmott, J. B., III, & Magloire, K.** (1988). Academic stress, social support, and secretory immunoglobulin A. *Journal of Personality and Social Psychology, 55*, 803–810. (p. 584)

**Jenish, D.** (1993, October 11). The king of porn. *Maclean's*, pp. 52–64. (p. 672)

**Jenkins, J. G., & Dallenbach, K. M.** (1924). Obliviscence during sleep and waking. *American Journal of Psychology, 35*, 605–612. (p. 315)

**Jensen, A. R.** (1980). *Bias in mental testing*. New York: Free Press (p. 368)

**Jensen, A. R.** (1983, August). *The nature of the black-white difference on various psychometric tests: Spearman's hypothesis*. Paper presented at the meeting of the American Psychological Association, Anaheim, CA. (p. 392)

**Jensen, A. R.** (1989). New findings on the intellectually gifted. *New Horizons, 30*, 73–80. (p. 375)

**Jensen, A. R.** (1993). Psychometric *g* and achievement. In B. R. Gifford (Ed.), *Policy perspectives on educational testing*. Boston: Kluwer. (p. 374)

**Jensen, A. R.** (1993). Spearman's hypothesis tested with chronometric information-processing tasks. *Intelligence, 17*, 47–77. (p. 388)

**Jensen, A. R., & Johnson, F. W.** (1994). Race and sex differences in head size and IQ. *Intelligence, 18*, in press. (p. 375)

**Jensen, J. P., & Bergin, A. E.** (1988). Mental health values of professional therapists: A national interdisciplinary survey. *Professional Psychology: Research and Practice, 19*, 290–297. (p. 562)

**Jepson, C., Krantz, D. H., & Nisbett, R. E.** (1983). Inductive reasoning: Competence or skill. *The Behavioral and Brain Sciences, 3*, 494–501. (p. A–7)

**Jervis, R.** (1985, April 2). Quoted in D. Goleman, Political forces come under new scrutiny of psychology. *The New York Times*, pp. C1, C4. (p. 337)

**John, O. P.** (1990). The "big five" factor taxonomy: Dimensions of personality in the natural language and in questionnaires. In L. A. Pervin (Ed.), *Handbook of personality: Theory and research*. New York: Guilford Press. (p. 475)

**Johnson, C. B., Stockdale, M. S., & Saal, F. E.** (1991). Persistence of men's misperceptions of friendly cues across a variety of interpersonal encounters. *Psychology of Women Quarterly, 15*, 463–475. (p. 673)

**Johnson, D.** (1990). Animal rights and human lives: Time for scientists to right the balance. *Psychological Science, 1*, 213–214. (p. 35)

**Johnson, D., & Drenick, E. J.** (1977). Therapeutic fasting in morbid obesity. Long-term follow-up. *Archives of Internal Medicine, 137*, 1381–1382. (p. 607)

**Johnson, D. W., & Johnson, R. T.** (1989). *Cooperation and competition: Theory and research*. Edina, MN: Interaction Books. (p. 689)

**Johnson, D. W., & Johnson, R. T.** (1994). Constructive conflict in the schools. *Journal of Social Issues, 50*(1), 117–137. (p. 689)

**Johnson, E. J., & Tversky, A.** (1983). Affect, generalization, and the perception of risk. *Journal of Personality and Social Psychology, 45*, 20–31. (p. 447)

**Johnson, J. S., & Newport, E. L.** (1989). Critical period effects in second language learning: The influence of maturational state on the acquisition of English as a second language. *Cognitive Psychology, 21*, 60–99. (p. 346)

**Johnson, M. H.** (1992). Imprinting and the development of face recognition: From chick to man. *Current Directions in Psychological Science, 1*, 52–55. (p. 97)

**Johnston, L. D., O'Malley, P., & Bachman, J.** (1994, January 27). Drug use rises among American teen-agers. Ann Arbor: News and Information Services, University of Michigan. (pp. 243, 248–250)

**Jones, E. E., Cumming, J. D., & Horowitz, M. J.** (1988). Another look at the nonspecific hypothesis of therapeutic effectiveness. *Journal of Consulting and Clinical Psychology, 56*, 48–55. (p. 560)

**Jones, J. M.** (1988). Piercing the veil: Bi-cultural strategies for coping with prejudice and racism. Invited address, national conference, "Opening doors: An appraisal of race relations in America," University of Alabama. (p. 663)

**Jones, J. M.** (1990). Promoting diversity in an individualistic society. Keynote address, Great Lakes College Association conference, "Multiculturalism transforming the 21st century." (pp. 656, 663)

**Jones, L.** (1985–86). CSICOP's international conference in London: Investigation and belief, past lives and prizes. *Skeptical Inquirer, 10*, 98–104. (p. 213)

**Jones, M. C.** (1924). A laboratory study of fear: The case of Peter. *Journal of Genetic Psychology, 31*, 308–315. (p. 547)

**Jones, M. C.** (1957). The later careers of boys who were early or late maturing. *Child Development, 28*, 113–128. (p. 119)

**Jones, S. S., Collins, K., & Hong, H-W.** (1991). An audience effect on smile production in 10–month-old infants. *Psychological Science, 2*, 45–49. (p. 441)

**Jones, W. H., Carpenter, B. N., & Quintana, D.** (1985). Personality and interpersonal predictors of loneliness in two cultures. *Journal of Personality and Social Psychology, 48*, 1503–1511. (p. 32)

**Jorgenson, D. O., & Papciak, A. S.** (1981). The effects of communication, resource feedback, and identifiability on behavior in a simulated commons. *Journal of Experimental Social Psychology, 17*, 373–385. (p. 689)

**Jorm, A. F., Korten, A. E., & Henderson, A. S.** (1987). The prevalence of dementia: A quantitative integration of the literature. *Acta Psychiatrica Scandinavica, 76*, 465–479. (p. 133)

**Jose, W. S., II, & Anderson, D. R.** (1991). Control data's StayWell program: A health cost management strategy. In S. M. Weiss, J. E. Fielding, & A. Baum (Eds.), *Health at work*. Hillsdale, NJ: Erlbaum. (p. 599)

**Josephs, R. A., Markus, H. R., & Tafarodi, R. W.** (1992). Gender and self-esteem. *Journal of Personality and Social Psychology, 63*, 391–402. (pp. 668-669)

**Juster, F. T., & Stafford, F. P.** (1991). The allocation of time: Empirical findings, behavioral models, and problems of measurement. *Journal of Economic Literature, 29*, 471–522. (pp. 390, 679)

**Kagan, J.** (1976). Emergent themes in human development. *American Scientist, 64*, 186–196. (p. 98)

**Kagan, J.** (1984). *The nature of the child*. New York: Basic Books. (p. 95)

**Kagan, J.** (1989b). *Unstable ideas: Temperament, cognition, and self*. Cambridge, MA: Harvard University Press. (pp. 470, 473)

**Kagan, J.** (1990). Interview with M. V. Ellis & E. S. Robbins, In celebration of nature: A dialogue with Jerome Kagan. *Journal of Counseling and Development, 68*, 623–627. (p. 97)

**Kagan, J., Snidman, N., & Arcus, D. M.** (1992). Initial reactions to unfamiliarity. *Current Directions in Psychological Science, 1*, 171–174. (p. 98)

**Kahneman, D.** (1985, June). Quoted by K. McKean, Decisions, decisions. *Discover*, pp. 22–31. (p. A–6)

**Kahneman, D., Fredrickson, B. L., Schreiber, C. A., & Redelmeier, D. A.** (1993). When more pain is preferred to less: Adding a better end. *Psychological Science, 4*, 401–405. (p. 177)

**Kahneman, D., Knetsch, J. L., & Thaler, R.** (1986). Fairness as a constraint on profit seeking: Entitlements in the market. *American Economic Review, 76*, 728–741. (p. 336)

**Kahneman, D., & Tversky, A.** (1972). Subjective probability: A judgment of representativeness. *Cognitive Psychology, 3*, 430–454. (pp. 22, 334)

**Kail, R.** (1991). Developmental change in speed of processing during childhood and adolescence. *Psychological Bulletin, 109*, 490–501. (p. 133)

**Kalin, N. H.** (1993, May). The neurobiology of fear. *Scientific American*, pp. 94–101. (p. 435)

**Kamarck, T., & Jennings, J. R.** (1991). Biobehavioral factors in sudden cardiac death. *Psychological Bulletin, 109*, 42–75. (p. 582)

**Kamin, L.** (1974). *The science and politics of IQ*. New York: Wiley. (p. 384)

**Kaminer, W.** (1992). *I'm dysfunctional, you're dysfunctional: The recovery movement and other self-help fashions*. Reading, MA: Addison-Wesley. (p. 247)

**Kandel, D. B., & Raveis, V. H.** (1989). Cessation of illicit drug use in young adulthood. *Archives of General Psychiatry, 46*, 109–116. (p. 250)

**Kandel, E. R., & Schwartz, J. H.** (1982). Molecular biology of learning: Modulation of transmitter release. *Science, 218*, 433–443. (p. 303)

**Kanekar, S., & Nazareth, A.** (1988). Attributed rape victim's fault as a function of her attractiveness, physical hurt, and emotional disturbance. *Social Behaviour, 3*, 37–40. (p. 673)

**Kann, L., Warren, W., Collins, J. L., Ross, J., Collins, B., & Kolbe, L. J.** (1993). Results from the national school-based 1991 Youth Risk Behavior Survey and progress toward achieving related health objectives for the nation. U.S. Department of Health and Human Services, *Public Health Reports, 108* (Suppl. 1), 47–55. (pp. 126, 250)

**Kapitza, S.** (1991, August). Antiscience trends in the U.S.S.R. *Scientific American*, pp. 32–38. (p. 215)

**Kaplan, H. I., & Saddock, B. J.** (Eds.). (1989). *Comprehensive textbook of psychiatry* (Vol. V). Baltimore, MD: Williams & Wilkins. (p. 565)

**Kaplan, H. S.** (1979). *Disorders of sexual desire*. New York: Brunner/Mazel. (p. 410)

**Kaplan, R. M.** (1984). The connection between clinical health promotion and health status: A critical overview. *American Psychologist, 39*, 755–765. (p. 599)

**Kaprio, J., Koskenvu, M., & Rita, H.** (1987). Mortality after bereavement: A prospective study of 95,647 widowed persons. *American Journal of Public Health, 77*, 283–287. (p. 578)

**Kapur, S., & Mann, J. J.** (1993). Antidepressant action and the neurobiologic effects of ECT: Human studies. In C. E. Coffey (Ed.), *The clinical science of electroconvulsive therapy*. Washington, DC: American Psychiatric Press. (p. 567)

**Karacan, I., Goodenough, D. R., Shapiro, A., & Starker, S.** (1966). Erection cycle during sleep in relation to dream anxiety. *Archives of General Psychiatry, 15*, 183–189. (p. 224)

**Karau, S. J., & Williams, K. D.** (1993). Social loafing: A meta-analytic review and theoretical integration. *Journal of Personality and Social Psychology, 65*, 681–706. (p. 628)

**Karno, M., Golding, J. M., Sorenson, S. B., & Burnam, A.** (1988). The epidemiology of obsessive-compulsive disorder in five US communities. *Archives of General Psychiatry*, 45, 1094–1099. (p. 507)

**Karr, B.** (1993, March). Challenge awards. *Skeptical Briefs*, p. 6. (p. 213)

**Kashima, Y., Siegal, M., Tanaka, K., & Kashima, E. S.** (1992). Do people believe behaviours are consistent with attitudes? Towards a cultural psychology of attribution processes. *British Journal of Social Psychology, 31*, 111–124. (p. 660)

**Kato, P. S., & Ruble, D. N.** (1992). Toward an understanding of women's experience of menstrual cycle symptoms. In V. Adesso, D. Reddy, & R. Fleming (Eds.), *Psychological perspectives on women's health*. Washington, DC: Hemisphere. (p. 591)

**Kaufman, A. S., Reynolds, C. R., & McLean, J. E.** (1989). Age and WAIS-R intelligence in a national sample of adults in the 20– to 74–year age range: A cross-sectional analysis with educational level controlled. *Intelligence, 13*, 235–253. (p. 137)

**Kaufman, J., & Zigler, E.** (1987). Do abused children become abusive parents? *American Journal of Orthopsychiatry, 57*, 186–192. (p. 101)

**Kaufman, L., & Rock, I.** (1962). The moon illusion I. *Science, 136*, 953–961. (p. 198)

**Kaylor, J. A., King, D. W., & King, L. A.** (1987). Psychological effects of military service in Vietnam: A meta-analysis. *Psychological Bulletin, 102,* 257–271. (p. 579)

**Keesey, R. E., & Corbett, S. W.** (1983). Metabolic defense of the body weight set-point. In A. J. Stunkard & E. Stellar (Eds.), *Eating and its disorders.* New York: Raven Press. (p. 403)

**Kellerman, J., Lewis, J., & Laird, J. D.** (1989). Looking and loving: The effects of mutual gaze on feelings of romantic love. *Journal of Research in Personality, 23,* 145–161. (p. 438)

**Kellermann, A. L., Rivara, F. P., Rushforth, N. B., Banton, H. G., Feay, D. T., Francisco, J. T., Locci, A. B., Prodzinski, J., Hackman, B. B., & Somes, G.** (1993). Gun ownership as a risk factor for homicide in the home. *New England Journal of Medicine, 329,* 1084–1091. (p. 632)

**Kelling, S. T., & Halpern, B. P.** (1983). Taste flashes: Reaction times, intensity, and quality. *Science, 219,* 412–414. (p. 178)

**Kelly, I. W., Laverty, W. H., & Saklofske, D. H.** (1990). Geophysical variables and behavior: LXIV. An empirical investigation of the relationship between worldwide automobile traffic disasters and lunar cycles: No relationship. *Psychological Reports, 67,* 987–994. (p. 530)

**Kelly, T. A.** (1990). The role of values in psychotherapy: A critical review of process and outcome effects. *Clinical Psychology Review, 10,* 171–186. (p. 562)

**Kempe, R. S., & Kempe, C. C.** (1978). *Child abuse.* Cambridge, MA: Harvard University Press. (p. 99)

**Kendall-Tackett, K. A., Williams, L. M., & Finkelhor, D.** (1993). Impact of sexual abuse on children: A review and synthesis of recent empirical studies. *Psychological Bulletin, 113,* 164–180. (p. 101)

**Kendler, K. S., Neale, M. C., Kessler, R. C., Heath, A. C., & Eaves, L. J.** (1992). Generalized anxiety disorder in women: A population-based twin study. *Archives of General Psychiatry, 49,* 267–272. (p. 509)

**Kendler, K. S., Neale, M., Kessler, R., Heath, A., & Eaves, L.** (1993). A twin study of recent life events and difficulties. *Archives of General Psychiatry, 50,* 789–796. (pp. 108, 521)

**Kennedy, S., & Over, R.** (1990). Psychophysiological assessment of male sexual arousal following spinal cord injury. *Archives of Sexual Behavior, 19,* 15–27. (p. 50)

**Kennell, J. N., & Klaus, M.** (1982). *Parent-infant bonding.* St. Louis: Mosby. (p. 97)

**Kenrick, D. T.** (1987). Gender, genes, and the social environment. In P. C. Shaver & C. Hendrick (Eds.), *Review of Personality and Social Psychology, 8,* 14–43. (pp. 671, 679)

**Kenrick, D. T., & Funder, D. C.** (1988). Profiting from controversy: Lessons from the person-situation debate. *American Psychologist, 43,* 23–34. (p. 478)

**Kenrick, D. T., & Gutierres, S. E.** (1980). Contrast effects and judgments of physical attractiveness: When beauty becomes a social problem. *Journal of Personality and Social Psychology, 38,* 131–140. (p. 412)

**Kenrick, D. T., & Keefe, R. C.** (1992). Age preferencs in mates reflect sex differences in human reproductive strategies. *Behavioral and Brain Sciences, 15,* 75–133. (p. 676)

**Kenrick, D. T., & Trost, M. R.** (1987). A biosocial theory of heterosexual relationships. In K. Kelly (Ed.), *Females, males, and sexuality.* Albany: State University of New York Press. (p. 673)

**Kerr, N. L., & Bruun, S. E.** (1983). Dispensability of member effort and group motivation losses: Free-rider effects. *Journal of Personality and Social Psychology, 44,* 78–94. (p. 628)

**Kessler, M., & Albee, G.** (1975). Primary prevention. *Annual Review of Psychology, 26,* 557–591. (p. 569)

**Kessler, R. C., Foster, C., Joseph, J., Ostrow, D., Wortman, C., Phair, J., & Chmiel, J.** (1991). Stressful life events and symptom onset in HIV infection. *American Journal of Psychiatry, 148,* 733–738. (p. 586)

**Kessler, R. C., McGonagle, K. A., Zhao, S., Nelson, C. B., Hughes, M., Eshleman, S., Wittchen, H-U., & Kendler, K. S.** (1994). Lifetime and 12-month prevalence of *DSM-III-R* psychiatric disorders in the United States. *Archives of General Psychiatry, 51,* 8–19. (p. 532)

**Kestenbaum, R.** (1992). Feeling happy versus feeling good: The processing of discrete and global categories of emotional expressions by children and adults. *Developmental Psychology, 28,* 1132–1142. (p. 438)

**Keys, A., Brozek, J., Henschel, A., Mickelsen, O., & Taylor, H. L.** (1950). *The biology of human starvation.* Minneapolis: University of Minnesota Press. (p. 401)

**Kiecolt-Glaser, J. K., Malarkey, W. B., Chee, M., Newton, T., Cacioppo, J. T., Mao, H-Y., & Glaser, R.** (1993). Negative behavior during marital conflict is associated with immunological downregulation. *Psychosomatic Medicine, 55,* 395–409. (p. 584)

**Kihlstrom, J. F.** (1985). Hypnosis. *Annual Review of Psychology, 36,* 385–418. (pp. 233, 236)

**Kihlstrom, J. F.** (1987). The cognitive unconscious. *Science, 237,* 1445–1452. (p. 220)

**Kihlstrom, J. F.** (1990). Awareness, the psychological unconscious, and the self. Address to the American Psychological Association convention. (pp. 316, 470)

**Kihlstrom, J. F.** (1990). The psychological unconscious. In L. A. Pervin (Ed.), *Handbook of personality: Theory and research.* New York: Guilford Press. (p. 316, 470)

**Kihlstrom, J. F., & McConkey, K. M.** (1990). William James and hypnosis: A centennial reflection. *Psychological Science, 1,* 174–177. (p. 239)

**Kimball, M. M.** (1989). A new perspective on women's math achievement. *Psychological Bulletin, 105,* 198–214. (p. 667)

**Kimble, G. A.** (1956). *Principles of general psychology.* New York: Ronald Press. (p. 264)

**Kimble, G. A.** (1981). *Biological and cognitive constraints on learning.* In L. T. Benjamin, Jr. (Ed.), *The G. Stanley Hall Lecture Series* (Vol. 1). Washington, DC: American Psychological Association. (p. 264)

**Kimura, D.** (1989, November). How sex hormones boost—or cut—intellectual ability. *Psychology Today,* pp. 62–66. (p. 674)

**Kimzey, S. L.** (1975). The effects of extended spaceflight on hematologic and immunologic systems. *Journal of the American Medical Women's Association, 30*(5), 218–232. (p. 584)

**Kimzey, S. L., Johnson, P. C., Ritzman, S. E., & Mengel, C. E.** (1976, April). Hematology and immunology studies: The second manned *Skylab* mission. *Aviation, Space, and Environmental Medicine*, pp. 383–390. (p. 584)

**King, D. W., & King, L. A.** (1991). Validity issues in research on Vietnam veteran adjustment. *Psychological Bulletin, 109*, 107–124. (p. 579)

**King, N. J., & Montgomery, R. B.** (1980). Biofeedback-induced control of human peripheral temperature: A critical review of the literature. *Psychological Bulletin, 88*, 738–752. (p. 595)

**King, P.** (1991, March 18). Bawl players. *Sports Illustrated*, pp. 14–17. (p. 452)

**King, S.** (1990). High risk for schizophrenia: From conception to young adulthood. *Journal of Counseling and Development, 69*, 81–84. (p. 529)

**Kinsey, A. C., Pomeroy, W., & Martin, C.** (1948). *Sexual behavior in the human male*. Philadelphia: Saunders. (p. 408)

**Kinsey, A. C., Pomeroy, W., Martin, C., & Gebhard, P.** (1953). *Sexual behavior in the human female*. Philadelphia: Saunders. (p. 408)

**Kirchner, W. H., & Towne, W. F.** (1994, June). The sensory basis of the honeybee's dance language. *Scientific American*, pp. 74–80. (p. 347)

**Kirk, S. A., & Gallagher, J. J.** (1989). *Educating exceptional children*. Boston: Houghton Mifflin. (p. 173)

**Kirkpatrick, L. A.** (1994). The role of attachment in religious belief and behavior. *Advances in Personal Relationships, 5*, 239–265. (p. 96)

**Kisor, H.** (1990). *What's that pig outdoors*. New York: Hill & Wang. (p. 173)

**Kitayama, S., & Markus, H. R.** (in press). Construal of the self as cultural frame: Implications for internationalizing psychology. In J. D'Arms, R. G. Hastie, S. E. Hoelscher, & H. K. Jacobson (Eds.), *Becoming more international and global: Challenges for American higher education*. Ann Arbor: University of Michigan Press. (p. 660)

**Kite, M. E., & Johnson, B. T.** (1988). Attitudes toward older and younger adults: A meta-analysis. *Psychology and Aging, 3*, 233–244. (p. 134)

**Klasen, S.** (1994). "Missing women" reconsidered. *World Development, 22*, in press. (p. 684)

**Klayman, J., & Ha, Y-W.** (1987). Confirmation, disconfirmation, and information in hypothesis testing. *Psychological Review, 94*, 211–228. (p. 328)

**Kleinke, C. L.** (1986). Gaze and eye contact: A research review. *Psychological Bulletin, 100*, 78–100. (p. 438)

**Kleinmuntz, B., & Szucko, J. J.** (1984). A field study of the fallibility of polygraph lie detection. *Nature, 308*, 449–450. (p. 437)

**Kleitman, N.** (1960, November). Patterns of dreaming. *Scientific American*, pp. 82–88. (p. 222)

**Klemm, W. R.** (1990). Historical and introductory perspectives on brainstem-mediated behaviors. In W. R. Klemm & R. P. Vertes (Eds.), *Brainstem mechanisms of behavior*. New York: Wiley. (p. 56)

**Kline, D., & Schieber, F.** (1985). Vision and aging. In J. E. Birren & K. W. Schaie (Eds.), *Handbook of the psychology of aging*. New York: Van Nostrand Reinhold. (p. 132)

**Kline, N. S.** (1974). *From sad to glad*. New York: Ballantine Books. (p. 523)

**Klineberg, O.** (1938). Emotional expression in Chinese literature. *Journal of Abnormal and Social Psychology, 33*, 517–520. (p. 440)

**Klineberg, O.** (1984). Public opinion and nuclear war. *American Psychologist, 39*, 1245–1253. (p. 689)

**Kluft, R. P.** (1991). Multiple personality disorder. In A. Tasman & S. M. Goldfinger (Eds.), *Review of Psychiatry* (Vol. 10). Washington, DC: American Psychiatric Press. (pp. 513-514)

**Klüver, H., & Bucy, P. C.** (1939). Preliminary analysis of functions of the temporal lobes in monkeys. *Archives of Neurology and Psychiatry, 42*, 979–1000. (p. 57)

**Koch, C.** (1988, June 17). Quoted in W. F. Allman, How the brain really works its wonders. *U. S. News & World Report*, pp. 46–54. (p. 339)

**Koestner, R., Franz, C., & Weinberger, J.** (1990). The family origins of empathic concern: A 26–year longitudinal study. *Journal of Personality and Social Psychology, 58*, 709–717. (p. 100)

**Kohlberg, L.** (1981). *The philosophy of moral development: Essays on moral development* (Vol. I). San Francisco: Harper & Row. (p. 121)

**Kohlberg, L.** (1984). *The psychology of moral development: Essays on moral development* (Vol. II). San Francisco: Harper & Row. (p. 121)

**Kohler, I.** (1962, May). Experiments with goggles. *Scientific American*, pp. 62–72. (p. 205)

**Köhler, W.** (1925; reprinted 1957). *The mentality of apes*. London: Pelican. (p. 328)

**Kohn, A.** (1987, October). It's hard to get left out of a pair. *Psychology Today*, pp. 53–57. (p. 689)

**Kohn, P. M., & Macdonald, J. E.** (1992). The survey of recent life experiences: A decontaminated hassles scale for adults. *Journal of Behavioral Medicine, 15*, 221–236. (p. 578)

**Kolata, G.** (1986). Youth suicide: New research focuses on a growing social problem. *Science, 233*, 839–841. (p. 517)

**Kolata, G.** (1987). Metabolic catch-22 of exercise regimens. *Science, 236*, 146–147. (p. 609)

**Kolb, B.** (1989). Brain development, plasticity, and behavior. *American Psychologist, 44*, 1203–1212. (p. 86)

**Kolers, P. A.** (1975). Specificity of operations in sentence recognition. *Cognitive Psychology, 7*, 289–306. (p. 291)

**Kolominsky, Y., & Parkhomenko, V.** (1993). Realization of socio-psychological assistance to children and youth of Chernobyl in the Republic of Belarus. Unpublished manuscript, Byelorussian Research Institute for Education, 16 Karolya Street, Minsk. (p. 577)

**Koltz, C.** (1983, December). Scapegoating. *Psychology Today*, pp. 68–69. (p. 685)

**Konishi, M.** (1993, April). Listening with two ears. *Scientific American*, pp. 66–73. (p. 171)

**Koopman, P., Gubbay, J., Vivian, N., Goodfellow, P., & Lovell-Badge, R.** (1991). Male development of chromosomally female mice transgenic for *Sry*. *Nature, 351*, 117–121. (p. 80)

**Koslowsky, M., & Babkoff, H.** (1992). Meta-analysis of the relationship between total sleep deprivation and performance. *Chronobiology International, 9*, 132–136. (p. 225)

**Koss, M. P.** (1993). Rape: Scope, impact, interventions, and public policy responses. *American Psychologist, 48,* 1062–1069. (p. 637)

**Koss, M. P., & Burkhart, B. R.** (1989). A conceptual analysis of rape victimization. *Psychology of Women Quarterly, 13,* 27–40. (p. 637)

**Koss, M. P., Dinero, T. E., Seibel, C. A., & Cox, S. L.** (1988). Stranger and acquaintance rape: Are there differences in the victim's experience? *Psychology of Women Quarterly, 12,* 1–24. (p. 637)

**Koss, M. P., Gidycz, C. A., & Wisniewski, N.** (1987). The scope of rape: Incidence and prevalence of sexual aggression and victimization in a national sample of higher education students. *Journal of Consulting and Clinical Psychology, 55,* 162–170. (p. 637)

**Koss, M. P., Koss, P., & Woodruff, W. J.** (1990). Relation of criminal victimization to health perceptions among women medical patients. *Journal of Consulting and Clinical Psychology, 58,* 147–152. (p. 637)

**Kosslyn, S. M., & Koenig, O.** (1992). *Wet mind: The new cognitive neuroscience.* New York: Free Press. (pp. 51, 137, 163, 220)

**Kotva, H. J., & Schneider, H. G.** (1990). Those "talks"—general and sexual communication between mothers and daughters. *Journal of Social Behavior and Personality, 5,* 603–613. (p. 126)

**Kraft, C.** (1978). A psychophysical approach to air safety: Simulator studies of visual illusions in night approaches. In H. L. Pick, H. W. Leibowitz, J. E. Singer, A. Steinschneider, & H. W. Stevenson (Eds.), *Psychology: From research to practice.* New York: Plenum Press. (p. 209)

**Kramer, M.** (1993, March 8). Getting smart about Head Start. *Time,* p. 43. (p. 387)

**Kraus, S. J.** (1991). Attitudes and the prediction of behavior. Unpublished doctoral dissertation, Harvard University, Cambridge, MA. (p. 615)

**Kraut, R. E., & Johnston, R. E.** (1979). Social and emotional messages of smiling: An ethological approach. *Journal of Personality and Social Psychology, 37,* 1539–1553. (p. 441)

**Krauthammer, C.** (1993, July 24–25). Science ought to stay out of the gay-rights fight. *International Herald Tribune,* p. 6. (p. 416)

**Krech, D.** (1978). Quoted in M. C. Diamond, The aging brain: Some enlightening and optimistic results. *American Scientist, 66,* 66–71. (pp. 85, 136)

**Kreitner, R.** (1992). *Management* (5th ed.) Boston: Houghton Mifflin. (p. 382)

**Kristof, N.** (1993, July 22). China faces huge surplus of males as scans hold key to missing girls. *The Guardian* (England), p. 22. (p. 684)

**Krosnick, J. A., & Alwin, D. F.** (1989). Aging and susceptibility to attitude change. *Journal of Personality and Social Psychology, 57,* 416–425. (p. 147)

**Krosnick, J. A., Betz, A. L., Jussim, L. J., & Lynn, A. R.** (1992). Subliminal conditioning of attitudes. *Personality and Social Psychology Bulletin, 18,* 152–162. (p. 155)

**Krupa, D. J., Thompson, J. K., & Thompson, R. F.** (1993). Localization of a memory trace in the mammalian brain. *Science, 260,* 989–991. (pp. 306–307)

**Kübler-Ross, E.** (1969). *On death and dying.* New York: Macmillan. (p. 143)

**Kuhl, P. K., & Meltzoff, A. N.** (1982). The bimodal perception of speech in infancy. *Science, 218,* 1138–1141. (p. 343)

**Kuiper, N.A., & Rogers, T. B.** (1979). Encoding of personal information: Self-other differences. *Journal of Personality and Social Psychology, 37,* 499–514. (p. 294)

**Kulik, J. A., Bangert-Drowns, R. L., & Kulik, C-L. C.** (1984). Effectiveness of coaching for aptitude tests. *Psychological Bulletin, 95,* 179–188. (p. 369)

**Kulik, J. A., Kulik, C. C., & Bangert-Drowns, R. L.** (1985). Effectiveness of computer-based education in elementary schools. *Computers in Human Behavior, 1,* 59–74. (p. 278)

**Kulik, J. A., Kulik, C. C., & Cohen, P. A.** (1980). Effectiveness of computer-based college teaching: A meta-analysis of findings. *Review of Educational Research, 50,* 525–544. (p. 278)

**Kurtz, P.** (1983, Spring). Stars, planets, and people. *The Skeptical Inquirer,* pp. 65–68. (p. 492)

**Kutas, M.** (1990). Event-related brain potential (ERP) studies of cognition during sleep: Is it more than a dream? In R. R. Bootzin, J. F. Kihlstrom, & D. Schacter (Eds.), *Sleep and cognition.* Washington, DC: American Psychological Association. (p. 223)

**Kwong, K. K.** and 12 others (1992). Dynamic magnetic resonance imagine of human brain activity during primary sensory stimulation. *Proceedings of the National Academy of Sciences, 89,* 5675–5679. (p. 55)

**Labouvie-Vief, G., & Schell, D. A.** (1982). Learning and memory in later life. In B. B. Wolman (Ed.), *Handbook of developmental psychology.* Englewood Cliffs, NJ: Prentice-Hall. (p. 135)

**Ladd, G. T.** (1887). *Elements of physiological psychology.* New York: Scribner's. (p. 219)

**LaFromboise, T., Coleman, H. L. K., & Gerton, J.** (1993). Psychological impact of biculturalism: Evidence and theory. *Psychological Bulletin, 114,* 395–412. (p. 664)

**Lagerspetz, K.** (1979). Modification of aggressiveness in mice. In S. Feshbach & A. Fraczek (Eds.), *Aggression & behavior change: Biological & social processes.* New York: Praeger. (p. 632)

**Lagerweij, E., Nelis, P. C., van Ree, J. M., & Wiegant, V. M.** (1984). The twitch in horses: A variant of acupuncture. *Science, 225,* 1172–1174. (p. 46)

**Laird, J. D.** (1974). Self-attribution of emotion: The effects of expressive behavior on the quality of emotional experience. *Journal of Personality and Social Psychology, 29,* 475–486. (p. 441)

**Laird, J. D.** (1984). The real role of facial response in the experience of emotion: A reply to Tourangeau and Ellsworth, and others. *Journal of Personality and Social Psychology, 47,* 909–917. (p. 441)

**Laird, J. D., Cuniff, M., Sheehan, K., Shulman, D., & Strum, G.** (1989). Emotion specific effects of facial expressions on memory for life events. *Journal of Social Behavior and Personality, 4,* 87–98. (p. 441)

**Lambert, W. E.** (1992). Challenging established views on social issues: The power and limitations of research. *American Psychologist, 47,* 533–542. (p. 353)

**Lambert, W. E., Genesee, F., Holobow, N., & Chartrand, L.** (1993). Bilingual education for majority English-speaking children. *European Journal of Psychology of Education, 8,* 3–22. (p. 353)

**Lancioni, G.** (1980). Infant operant conditioning and its implications for early intervention. *Psychological Bulletin, 88,* 516–534. (p. 83)

**Landauer, T. K.** (1986). How much do people remember? Some estimates of the quantity of learned information in long-term memory. *Cognitive Science, 10,* 477–493. (p. 301)

**Landers, A.** (1969, April 8). Syndicated newspaper column. Cited by L. Berkowitz, The case for bottling up rage. *Psychology Today,* September, 1973, pp. 24–31. (p. 446)

**Landers, S.** (1986, December). Judge reiterates IQ test ban. *APA Monitor,* p. 18. (p. 359)

**Landfield, P., Cadwallader, L. B., & Vinsant, S.** (1988). Quantitative changes in hippocampal structure following long-term exposure to Delta-9–tetrahydrocannabinol: Possible mediation by glucocorticoid systems. *Brain Research, 443,* 47–62. (p. 247)

**Langer, E. J.** (1983). *The psychology of control.* Beverly Hills, CA: Sage. (p. 490)

**Langer, E. J., & Abelson, R. P.** (1974). A patient by any other name . . . : Clinician group differences in labeling bias. *Journal of Consulting and Clinical Psychology, 42,* 4–9. (p. 534)

**Langer, E. J., & Imber, L.** (1980). The role of mindlessness in the perception of deviance. *Journal of Personality and Social Psychology, 39,* 360–367. (p. 534)

**Langlois, J. H., & Roggman, L. A.** (1990). Attractive faces are only average. *Psychological Science, 1,* 115–121. (p. 646)

**Langlois, J. H., Roggman, L. A., Casey, R. J., Ritter, J. M., Rieser-Danner, L. A., & Jenkins, V. Y.** (1987). Infant preferences for attractive faces: Rudiments of a stereotype? *Developmental Psychology, 23,* 363–369. (p. 645)

**Larrance, D. T., & Twentyman, C. T.** (1983). Maternal attributions and child abuse. *Journal of Abnormal Psychology, 92,* 449–457. (p. 93)

**Larsen, R. J., & Diener, E.** (1987). Affect intensity as an individual difference characteristic: A review. *Journal of Research in Personality, 21,* 1–39. (p. 98)

**Larsen, R. J., Diener, E., & Cropanzano, R. S.** (1987). Cognitive operations associated with individual differences in affect intensity. *Journal of Personality and Social Psychology, 53,* 767–774. (p. 457)

**Larsen, R. J., Kasimatis, M., & Frey, K.** (1992). Facilitating the furrowed brow: An unobtrusive test of the facial feedback hypothesis applied to unpleasant affect. *Cognition and Emotion, 6,* 321–338. (p. 442)

**Larson, R. W., & Bradney, N.** (1988). Precious moments with family members and friends. In R. M. Milardo (Ed.), *Families and social networks.* Newbury Park, CA: Sage. (p. 125)

**Lashley, K. S.** (1950). In search of the engram. In *Symposium of the Society for Experimental Biology* (Vol. 4). New York: Cambridge University Press. (p. 303)

**Lassiter, G. D., & Irvine, A. A.** (1986). Video-taped confessions: The impact of camera point of view on judgments of coercion. *Journal of Personality and Social Psychology, 16,* 268–276. (p. 614)

**Latané, B.** (1981). The psychology of social impact. *American Psychologist, 36,* 343–356. (p. 628)

**Latané, B., & Dabbs, J. M., Jr.** (1975). Sex, group size and helping in three cities. *Sociometry, 38,* 180–194. (p. 641)

**Lau, S., & Gruen, G. E.** (1992). The social stigma of loneliness: Effect of target person's and perceiver's sex. *Personality and Social Psychology Bulletin, 18,* 182–189. (p. 522)

**Laudenslager, M. L., & Reite, M. L.** (1984). Losses and separations: Immunological consequences and health implications. *Review of Personality and Social Psychology, 5,* 285–312. (p. 580)

**Laurence, J-R., & Perry, C.** (1988). *Hypnosis, will and memory: A psycho-legal history.* New York: Guilford Press. (p. 235)

**Layton, B. D., & Turnbull, B.** (1975). Belief, evaluation, and performance on an ESP task. *Journal of Experimental Social Psychology, 11,* 166–179. (p. 211)

**Lazarus, R. S.** (1984). On the primacy of cognition. *American Psychologist, 39,* 124–129. (p. 457)

**Lazarus, R. S.** (1990). Theory-based stress measurement. *Psychological Inquiry, 1,* 3–13. (p. 578)

**Lazarus, R. S.** (1991). Progress on a cognitive-motivational-relational theory of emotion. *American Psychologist, 46,* 352–367. (p. 457)

**Leach, P.** (1993). Should parents hit their children? *The Psychologist: Bulletin of the British Psychological Society, 6,* 216–220. (p. 274)

**Leach, P.** (1994). *Children first.* New York: Knopf. (p. 274)

**Lebow, J.** (1982). Consumer satisfaction with mental health treatment. *Psychological Bulletin, 91,* 244–259. (p. 556)

**Lederer, R.** (1987). *Anguished English.* Charleston, SC: Wyrick & Co. (p. 658)

**LeDoux, J. E.** (1986). Sensory systems and emotions: A model of affective processing. *Integrative Psychiatry, 4,* 237–243. (p. 456)

**Lee, B. A., Lewis, D. W., & Jones, S. H.** (1990). Blaming the homeless: A test of two theories. Paper presented at the American Psychological Association convention. (p. 615)

**Lee, G. R., Seccombe, K., & Shehan, C. L.** (1991). Marital status and personal happiness: An analysis of trend data. *Journal of Marriage and the Family, 53,* 839–844. (p. 140)

**Lefcourt, H. M.** (1982). *Locus of control: Current trends in theory and research.* Hillsdale, NJ: Erlbaum. (p. 489)

**Lefcourt, H. M., & Davidson-Katz, K.** (1991). The role of humor and the self. In C. R. Snyder & D. R. Forsyth (Eds.), *Handbook of social and clinical psychology: The health perspective.* New York: Pergamon Press. (p. 596)

**Lehman, D. R., Lempert, R. O., & Nisbett, R. E.** (1988). The effects of graduate training on reasoning: Formal discipline and thinking about everyday-life events. *American Psychologist, 43,* 431–442. (p. 30)

**Lehman, D. R., & Nisbett, R. E.** (1985). Effects of higher education on inductive reasoning. Unpublished manuscript, University of Michigan. (p. 491)

**Lehman, D. R., Wortman, C. B., & Williams, A. F.** (1987). Long-term effects of losing a spouse or child in a motor vehicle crash. *Journal of Personality and Social Psychology, 52,* 218–231. (p. 143)

**Leibowitz, H. W.** (1985). Grade crossing accidents and human factors engineering. *American Scientist, 73,* 558–562. (p. 196)

**Leigh, B. C.** (1989). In search of the seven dwarves: Issues of measurement and meaning in alcohol expectancy research. *Psychological Bulletin, 105,* 361–373. (p. 242)

**Leigh, B. C., Temple, M. T., & Trocki, K. F.** (1993). The sexual behavior of US adults: Results from a national survey. *American Journal of Public Health, 83,* 1400–1408. (p. 409)

**Leikind, B., & McCarthy, W. J.** (1985). An investigation of firewalking. *The Skeptical Inquirer, 10,* 23–34. (p. 176)

**Leikind, B., & McCarthy, W. J.** (1988). Firewalking. *Experientia, 44,* 310–315. (p. 176)

**Lenzenweger, M. F., Dworkin, R. H., & Wethington, E.** (1989). Models of positive and negative symptoms in schizophrenia: An empirical evaluation of latent structures. *Journal of Abnormal Psychology, 98,* 62–70. (p. 565)

**Leo, J.** (1991, August 19). No-fault syntax. *U.S. News & World Report,* p. 17. (p. 247)

**Lepper, M. R., Ross, L., & Lau, R. R.** (1986). Persistence of inaccurate beliefs about the self: Perseverance effects in the classroom. *Journal of Personality and Social Psychology, 50,* 482–491. (p. 338)

**Lerner, M. J.** (1980). *The belief in a just world: A fundamental delusion.* New York: Plenum Press. (p. 686)

**Leshner, A. I.** (1992). *Outcasts on main street: Report of the federal task force on homelessness and severe mental illness.* Washington, DC: Interagency Council on the Homeless, Office of the Programs for the Homeless Mentally Ill, National Institute of Mental Health. (p. 565)

**LeVay, S.** (1991). A difference in hypothalamic structure between heterosexual and homosexual men. *Science, 253,* 1034–1037. (p. 415)

**LeVay, S.** (1994, March). Quoted in D. Nimmons, Sex and the brain. *Discover,* pp. 64–71. (p. 415)

**Levenson, R. W.** (1992). Autonomic nervous system differences among emotions. *Psychological Science, 3,* 23–27. (p. 435)

**Levenson, R. W., Ekman, P., Heider, K., & Friesen, W. V.** (1991). Emotion and autonomic nervous system activity in an Indonesian culture. Unpublished manuscript, University of California, Berkeley. (p. 435)

**Levenson, R. W., Ekman, P., Heider, K., & Friesen, W. V.** (1992). Emotion and autonomic nervous system activity in the Minangkabau of West Sumatra. *Journal of Personality and Social Psychology, 62,* 972–988. (p. 441)

**Lever, J.** (1978). Sex differences in the complexity of children's play and games. *American Sociological Review, 43,* 471–483. (p. 670)

**Levesque, M. J., & Kenny, D. A.** (1993). Accuracy of behavioral predictions at zero acquaintance: A social relations analysis. *Journal of Personality and Social Psychology, 65,* 1178–1187. (p. 479)

**Levin, I. P., & Gaeth, G. J.** (1988). How consumers are affected by the framing of attribute information before and after consuming the product. *Journal of Consumer Research, 15,* 374–378. (p. 335)

**Levin, I. P., Schnittjer, S. K., & Thee, S. L.** (1988). Information framing effects in social and personal decisions. *Journal of Experimental Social Psychology, 24,* 520–529. (p. 335)

**Levin, J. S., & Vanderpool, H. Y.** (1987). Is frequent religious attendance really conducive to better health? Toward an epidemiology of religion. *Social Science and Medicine, 14,* 589–600. (p. 598)

**Levine, A.** (1990, May 7). America's youthful bigots. *U.S. News & World Report,* pp. 59–60. (pp. 657, 683)

**Levine, B., Roehrs, T., Zorick, F., & Roth, T.** (1988). Daytime sleepiness in young adults. *Sleep, 11,* 39–46. (p. 224)

**Levine, I. S., & Rog, D. J.** (1990). Mental health services for homeless mentally ill persons: Federal initiatives and current service trends. *American Psychologist, 45,* 963–968. (p. 565)

**Levinger, G.** (1987). The limits of deterrence: An introduction. *Journal of Social Issues, 43*(4), 1–4. (p. 687)

**Levinson, D. J.** (1986). A conception of adult development. *American Psychologist, 41,* 3–13. (p. 138)

**Levinson, D. J., Darow, C. N., Klein, E. B., Levinson, M. H., & McKee, B.** (1978). *The seasons of a man's life.* New York: Knopf. (p. 138)

**Levitt, E. E.** (1986). Coercion, voluntariness, compliance and resistance: The essence of hypnosis twenty-seven years after Orne. Invited address to the American Psychological Association convention. (p. 236)

**Levy, B., & Langer, E.** (1992). Avoidance of the memory loss stereotype: Enhanced memory among the elderly deaf. American Psychological Association convention, Washington, DC. (p. 172)

**Levy, J.** (1985, May). Right brain, left brain: Fact and fiction. *Psychology Today,* pp. 38–44. (p. 70)

**Lewicki, P., Hill, T., & Czyzewska, M.** (1992). Nonconscious acquisition of information. *American Psychologist, 47,* 796–801. (p. 470)

**Lewinsohn, P. M., Hoberman, H., Teri, L., & Hautziner, M.** (1985). An integrative theory of depression. In S. Reiss & R. Bootzin (Eds.), *Theoretical issues in behavior therapy.* Orlando, FL: Academic Press. (pp. 516, 522)

**Lewinsohn, P. M., & Rosenbaum, M.** (1987). Recall of parental behavior by acute depressives, remitted depressives, and nondepressives. *Journal of Personality and Social Psychology, 52,* 611–619. (p. 310)

**Lewis, C. C.** (1981). The effects of parental firm control: A reinterpretation of findings. *Psychological Bulletin, 90,* 547–563. (p. 105)

**Lewis, C. S.** (1967). *Christian reflections.* Grand Rapids, MI: Eerdmans. (p. 298)

**Lewis, D. O., Pincus, J. H., Bard, B., Richardson, E., Prichep, L. S., Feldman, M., & Yeager, C.** (1988). Neuropsychiatric, psychoeducational, and family characteristics of 14 juveniles condemned to death in the United States. *American Journal of Psychiatry, 145,* 584–589. (p. 99)

**Lewis, D. O., Pincus, J. H., Feldman, M., Jackson, L., & Bard, B.** (1986). Psychiatric, neurological, and psychoeducational characteristics of 15 death row inmates in the United States. *American Journal of Psychiatry, 143,* 838–845. (p. 633)

**Lewis, M.** (1992). Commentary. *Human Development, 35,* 44–51. (p. 310)

**Lewontin, R.** (1976). Race and intelligence. In N. J. Block & G. Dworkin (Eds.), *The IQ controversy: Critical readings.* New York: Pantheon. (p. 389)

**Lewontin, R.** (1982). *Human diversity.* New York: Scientific American Library. (p. 654)

**Libet, B.** (1985). Unconscious cerebral initiative and the role of conscious will in voluntary action. *Behavioral and Brain Sciences, 12,* 181–187. (p. 220)

**Licata, A., Taylor, S., Berman, M., & Cranston, J.** (1993). Effects of cocaine on human aggression. *Pharmacology Biochemistry and Behavior, 45,* 549–552. (p. 244)

**Lichtman, S. W., Pisarska, K., Berman, E. R., Pestone, M., Dowling, H., Offenbacher, E., Weisel, H., Heshka, S., Matthews, D. E., & Heymsfield, S. B.** (1992). Discrepancy between self-reported and actual caloric intake and exercise in obese subjects. *New England Journal of Medicine, 327,* 1893–1898. (p. 606)

*Life* (1991, January). Barbie fashon doll proportions. p. 78. (p. 407)

**Lifton, R. J.** (1986). *The Nazi doctors.* New York: Basic Books. (p. 242)

**Light, K. C., Koepke, J. P., Obrist, P. A., & Willis, P. W., Jr.** (1983). Psychological stress induces sodium and fluid retention in men at high risk for hypertension. *Science, 220,* 429–431. (p. 583)

**Linder, D.** (1982). Social trap analogs: The tragedy of the commons in the laboratory. In V. J. Derlega & J. Grzelak (Eds.), *Cooperative and helping behavior: Theories and research.* New York: Academic Press. (p. 687)

**Lindskold, S.** (1978). Trust development, the GRIT proposal, and the effects of conciliatory acts on conflict and cooperation. *Psychological Bulletin, 85,* 772–793. (p. 690)

**Lindskold, S.** (1986). GRIT: Reducing distrust through carefully introduced conciliation. In S. Worchel & W. G. Austin (Eds.), *Psychology of intergroup relations* (2nd ed.). Chicago: Nelson-Hall. (p. 690)

**Lindskold, S., & Han, G.** (1988). GRIT as a foundation for integrative bargaining. *Personality and Social Psychology Bulletin, 14,* 335–345. (p. 690)

**Lindskold, S., Han, G., & Betz, B.** (1986). Repeated persuasion in interpersonal conflict. *Journal of Personality and Social Psychology, 51,* 1183–1188. (p. 690)

**Lindskold, S., Walters, P. S., & Koutsourais, H.** (1983). Cooperators, competitors, and response to GRIT. *Journal of Conflict Resolution, 27,* 521–532. (p. 690)

**Linn, M. C., & Hyde, J. S.** (1991). Trends in cognitive and psychosocial gender differences. In R. M. Lerner, A. C. Petersen, & J. Brooks-Gunn (Eds.), *The encyclopedia of adolescence.* New York: Garland. (p. 668)

**Linn, M. C., & Peterson, A. C.** (1986). A meta-analysis of gender differences in spatial ability: Implications for mathematics and science achievement. In J. S. Hyde & M. C. Linn (Eds.), *The psychology of gender: Advances through meta-analysis.* Baltimore: Johns Hopkins University Press. (p. 667)

**Linville, P. W., Fischer, G. W., & Fischhoff, B.** (1992). AIDS risk perceptions and decision biases. In J. B. Pryor & G. D. Reeder (Eds.), *The social psychology of HIV infection.* Hillsdale, NJ: Erlbaum. (p. 336)

**Linz, D., & Donnerstein, E.** (1989). The effects of counter-information on the acceptance of rape myths. In D. Zillmann & J. Bryant (Eds.), *Pornography: Research advances and policy considerations.* Hillsdale, NJ: Erlbaum. (p. 640)

**Lippman, J.** (1992, October 25). Global village is characterized by a television in every home. *Grand Rapids Press* (*Los Angeles Times Syndicate*), p. F9. (p. 636)

**Lipsey, M. W., & Wilson, D. B.** (1993). The efficacy of psychological, educational, and behavioral treatment: Confirmation from meta-analyses. *American Psychologist, 48,* 1181–1209. (pp. 381, 558)

**Lissner, L., Odell, P. M., D'Agostino, R. B., Stokes, J., III, Kreger, B. E., Belanger, A. J., & Brownell, K. D.** (1991). Variability of body weight and health outcomes in the Framingham population. *New England Journal of Medicine, 324,* 1839–1844. (p. 607)

**Livingstone, M., & Hubel, D.** (1988). Segregation of form, color, movement, and depth: Anatomy, physiology, and perception. *Science, 240,* 740–749. (p. 163)

**Lock, M., Kaufert, P., & Gilbert, P.** (1988). Cultural construction of the menopausal syndrome: The Japanese case. *Maturitas, 10,* 317–332. (p. 130)

**Locke, E. A., & Latham, G. P.** (1990). Work motivation and satisfaction: Light at the end of the tunnel. *Psychological Science, 1,* 240–246. (p. 424)

**Loehlin, J. C.** (1989). Partitioning environmental and genetic contributions to behavioral development. *American Psychologist, 44,* 1285–1292. (p. 384)

**Loehlin, J. C., Horn, J. M., & Willerman, L.** (1989). Modeling IQ change: Evidence from the Texas adoption project. *Child Development, 60,* 993–1004. (p. 385)

**Loehlin, J. C., Lindzey, G., & Spuhler, J. N.** (1975). *Race differences in intelligence.* San Francisco: Freeman. (p. 388)

**Loehlin, J. C., & Nichols, R. C.** (1976). *Heredity, environment, and personality.* Austin: University of Texas Press. (pp. 108, 384)

**Loewenstein, G., & Furstenberg, F.** (1991). Is teenage sexual behavior rational? *Journal of Applied Social Psychology, 21,* 957–986. (p. 271)

**Loftus, E. F.** (1979). The malleability of human memory. *American Scientist, 67,* 313–320. (p. 311)

**Loftus, E. F.** (1980). *Memory: Surprising new insights into how we remember and why we forget.* Reading, MA: Addison-Wesley. (p. 235)

**Loftus, E. F.** (1992). When a lie becomes memory's truth: Memory distortion after exposure to misinformation. *Current Directions in Psychological Science, 1,* 121–123. (p. 312)

**Loftus, E. F.** (1993). The reality of repressed memories. *American Psychologist, 48,* 518–537. (p. 319)

**Loftus, E. F., & Coan, D.** (in press). The construction of childhood memories. In D. Peters (Ed.), *The child witness in context: Cognitive, social and legal perspectives.* New York: Kluwer. (pp. 318–319)

**Loftus, E. F., Donders, K., Hoffman, H. G., & Schooler, J. W.** (1989). Creating new memories that are quickly accessed and confidently held. *Memory and Cognition, 17,* 607–616. (p. 312)

**Loftus, E. F., & Kaufman, L.** (1992). Why do traumatic experiences sometimes produce good memory (flashbulbs) and sometimes no memory (repression)? In E. Winograd & U. Neisser (Eds.), *Affect and accuracy in recall: Studies of "flashbulb" memories.* New York: Cambridge University Press. (p. 85)

**Loftus, E. F., Levidow, B., & Duensing, S.** (1992). Who remembers best? Individual differences in memory for events that occurred in a science museum. *Applied Cognitive Psychology, 6,* 93–107. (p. 313)

**Loftus, E. F., & Loftus, G. R.** (1980). On the permanence of stored information in the human brain. *American Psychologist, 35,* 409–420. (p. 302)

**Loftus, E. F., & Palmer, J. C.** (1974). Reconstruction of automobile destruction: An example of the interaction between language and memory. *Journal of Verbal Learning and Verbal Behavior, 13,* 585–589. (p. 311)

**Logothetis, N. K., & Schall, J. D.** (1989). Neuronal correlates of subjective visual perception. *Science, 245,* 761–763. (p. 163)

**Logue, M. B., Sher, K. J., & Frensch, P. A.** (1992). Purported characteristics of adult children of alcoholics: A possible "Barnum effect." *Professional Psychology: Research and Practice, 23,* 226–232. (p. 493)

**London, P.** (1970). The rescuers: Motivational hypotheses about Christians who saved Jews from the Nazis. In J. Macaulay & L. Berkowitz (Eds.), *Altruism and helping behavior.* New York: Academic Press. (pp. 282, 643)

**LoPiccolo, J. L., & Stock, W. E.** (1986). Treatment of sexual dysfunction. *Journal of Consulting and Clinical Psychology, 54,* 158–167. (p. 413)

**Lord, C. G., Lepper, M. R., & Preston, E.** (1984). Considering the opposite: A corrective strategy for social judgment. *Journal of Personality and Social Psychology, 47,* 1231–1247. (p. 337)

**Lord, C. G., Ross, L., & Lepper, M.** (1979). Biased assimilation and attitude polarization: The effects of prior theories on subsequently considered evidence. *Journal of Personality and Social Psychology, 37,* 2098–2109. (p. 337)

**Lorenz, K.** (1937). The companion in the bird's world. *Auk, 54,* 245–273. (p. 96)

**Lovaas, O. I.** (1987). Behavioral treatment and normal educational and intellectual functioning in young autistic children. *Journal of Consulting and Clinical Psychology, 55,* 3–9. (p. 549)

**Lozoff, B.** (1989). Nutrition and behavior. *American Psychologist, 44,* 231–236. (p. 603)

**Lu, Z.-L., Williamson, S. J., & Kaufman, L.** (1992). Behavioral lifetime of human auditory sensory memory predicted by physiological measures. *Science, 258,* 1668–1670. (p. 300)

**Lubart, T. I.** (1990). Creativity and cross-cultural variation. *International Journal of Psychology, 25,* 39–59. (p. 381)

**Lubin, B., Larsen, R. M., & Matarazzo, J. D.** (1984). Patterns of psychological test usage in the United States: 1935–1982. *American Psychologist, 39,* 451–454. (p. 469)

**Lubinski, D., & Benbow, C. P.** (1992). Gender differences in abilities and preferences among the gifted: Implications for the math-science pipeline. *Current Directions in Psychological Science, 1,* 61–66. (p. 667)

**Luchins, A. S.** (1946). Classroom experiments on mental set. *American Journal of Psychology, 59,* 295–298. (pp. 329–330)

**Lukoff, D., Lu, F., & Turner, R.** (1992). Toward a more culturally sensitive DSM-IV: Psychoreligious and psychospiritual problems. *Journal of Nervous and Mental Disease, 180,* 673–682. (p. 562)

**Lull, J.** (Ed.). (1988). *World families watch television.* Newbury Park, CA: Sage. (p. 636)

**Lummis, M., & Stevenson, H. W.** (1990). Gender differences in beliefs and achievement: A cross-cultural study. *Developmental Psychology, 26,* 254–263. (p. 667)

**Lumsden, C. J., & Wilson, E. O.** (1983). *Promethean fire: Reflections on the origin of mind.* Cambridge, MA: Harvard University Press. (p. 445)

**Luria, A. M.** (1968). In L. Solotaroff (Trans.), *The mind of a mnemonist.* New York: Basic Books. (p. 287)

**Lykken, D. T.** (1982, September). Fearlessness: Its carefree charm and deadly risks. *Psychology Today,* pp. 20–28. (pp. 445, 531)

**Lykken, D. T.** (1983, April). Polygraph prejudice. *APA Monitor,* p. 4. (pp. 437)

**Lykken, D. T.** (1991). Science, lies, and controversy: An epitaph for the polygraph. Invited address upon receipt of the Senior Career award for Distinguished Contribution to Psychology in the Public Interest, American Psychological Association convention. (pp. 436, 437)

**Lykken, D. T., & Tellegen, A.** (1993) Is human mating adventitious or the result of lawful choice? A twin study of mate selection. *Journal of Personality and Social Psychology, 65,* 56–68. (p. 139)

**Lykken, D. T., Bouchard, T. J., Jr., McGue, M., & Tellegen, A.** (1993). Heritability of interests: A twin study. *Journal of Applied Psychology, 78,* 649–661. (p. 109)

**Lykken, D. T., McGue, M., Tellegen, A., & Bouchard, T. J., Jr.** (1992). Emergenesis: Genetic traits that may not run in families. *American Psychologist, 47,* 1565–1577. (p. 110)

**Lynch, G.** (1992, October 12). Quoted in L. Joyce, Disciplines converge in probe of memory and learning. *The Scientist,* pp. 16–17. (p. 304)

**Lynch, G., & Staubli, U.** (1991). Possible contributions of long-term potentiation to the encoding and organization of memory. *Brain Research Reviews, 16,* 204–206. (p. 304)

**Lyness, S. A.** (1993). Predictors of differences between Type A and B individuals in heart rate and blood pressure reactivity. *Psychological Bulletin, 114,* 266–295. (p. 582)

**Lynn, M.** (1988). The effects of alcohol consumption on restaurant tipping. *Personality and Social Psychology Bulletin, 14,* 87–91. (p. 241)

**Lynn, R.** (1982). IQ in Japan and the United States shows a growing disparity. *Nature, 297,* 222–223. (p. 388)

**Lynn, R.** (1983). Lynn replies. *Nature, 306,* 292. (p. 388)

**Lynn, R.** (1987). Japan: Land of the rising IQ. A reply to Flynn. *Bulletin of the British Psychological Society, 40,* 464–468. (p. 389)

**Lynn, R.** (1991). The evolution of racial differences in intelligence. *The Mankind Quarterly, 32,* 99–145. (p. 388)

**Lynn, S. J., & Rhue, J. W.** (1986). The fantasy-prone person: Hypnosis, imagination, and creativity. *Journal of Personality and Social Psychology, 51,* 404–408. (p. 234)

**Lynn, S. J., Rhue, J. W., & Weekes, J. R.** (1990). Hypnotic involuntariness: A social cognitive analysis. *Psychological Review, 97,* 169–184. (p. 238)

**Lyon, D., & Greenberg, J.** (1991). Evidence of codependency in women with an alcoholic parent: Helping out Mr. Wrong. *Journal of Personality and Social Psychology, 61,* 435–439. (p. 247)

**Lytton, H., & Romney, D. M.** (1991). Parents' differential socialization of boys and girls: A meta-analysis. *Psychological Bulletin, 109,* 267–296. (p. 676)

**Lyubomirsky, S., & Nolen-Hoeksema, S.** (1994). The effects of depressive rumination on thinking and problem solving. Unpublished manuscript, Stanford University, Stanford, CA. (p. 551)

**Macaskill, P., Pierce, J. P., Simpson, J. M., & Lyle, D. M.** (1992). Mass media-led antismoking campaign can remove the education gap in quitting behavior. *American Journal of Public Health, 82,* 96–98. (p. 602)

**Maccoby, E.** (1980). *Social development: Psychological growth and the parent-child relationship.* New York: Harcourt Brace Jovanovich. (pp. 104, 666)

**Maccoby, E. E.** (1990). Gender and relationships: A developmental account. *American Psychologist, 45,* 513–520. (p. 670)

**MacDonald, N.** (1960). Living with schizophrenia. *Canadian Medical Association Journal, 82,* 218–221. (p. 524)

**MacFarlane, A.** (1978, February). What a baby knows. *Human Nature,* pp. 74–81. (p. 83)

**Macfarlane, J. W.** (1964). Perspectives on personality consistency and change from the guidance study. *Vita Humana, 7,* 115–126. (pp. 118, 146)

**MacKay, D. G.** (1983). Prescriptive grammar and the pronoun problem. In B. Thorne, C. Kramarae, & N. Henley (Eds.), *Language, gender and society.* Rowley, MA: Newbury House. (p. 353)

**Mackenzie, B.** (1984). Explaining race differences in IQ: The logic, the methodology, and the evidence. *American Psychologist, 39,* 1214–1233. (p. 391)

**MacKinnon, D. W., & Hall, W. B.** (1972). Intelligence and creativity. *Proceedings, XVIIth International Congress of Applied Psychology* (Vol. 2, pp. 1883–1888). Brussels: Editest. (p. 381)

**MacLeod, C., & Campbell, L.** (1992). Memory accessibility and probability judgments: An experimental evaluation of the availability heuristic. *Journal of Personality and Social Psychology, 63,* 890–902. (p. 332)

**Maehr, M. L., & Braskamp, L. A.** (1986). *The motivation factor: A theory of personal investment.* Lexington, MA: Lexington Books. (p. 423)

**Magno, J. B.** (1989, April 15). The hospice concept of care: Facing the 1990's. Keynote address to the Association for Death Education and Counseling. (p. 144)

**Magnusson, D.** (1990). Personality research—challenges for the future. *European Journal of Personality, 4,* 1–17. (p. 531)

**Magnusson, D., & Bergman, L. R.** (1990). A pattern approach to the study of pathways from childhood to adulthood. In L. N. Robins & M. Rutter (Eds.), *Straight and devious pathways from childhood to adulthood.* Cambridge, England: Cambridge University Press. (p. 146)

**Mahoney, M. J.** (1989). Sport psychology. In I. S. Cohen (Ed.), *G. Stanley Hall Lecture Series* (Vol. 9). Washington, DC: American Psychological Association. (p. 80)

**Major, B.** (1987). Gender, justice, and the psychology of entitlement. In P. Shaver & C. Hendrick (Eds.), *Sex and gender.* Beverly Hills, CA: Sage. (p. 671)

**Major, B., Carrington, P. I., & Carnevale, P. J. D.** (1984). Physical attractiveness and self-esteem: Attribution for praise from an other-sex evaluator. *Personality and Social Psychology Bulletin, 10,* 43–50. (p. 645)

**Major, B., Cozzarelli, C., Sciacchitano, A. M., Cooper, M. L., Testa, M., & Mueller, P. M.** (1990). Perceived social support, self-efficacy, and adjustment to abortion. *Journal of Personality and Social Psychology, 59,* 452–463. (p. 578)

**Major, B., Schmidlin, A. M., & Williams, L.** (1990). Gender patterns in social touch: The impact of setting and age. *Journal of Personality and Social Psychology, 58,* 634–643. (p. 671)

**Malamuth, N. M., & Check, J. V. P.** (1981). The effects of media exposure on acceptance of violence against women: A field experiment. *Journal of Research in Personality, 15,* 436–446. (p. 638)

**Malamuth, N. M., Sockloskie, R. J., Koss, M. P., & Tanaka, J. S.** (1991). Characteristics of aggressors against women: Testing a model using a national sample of college students. *Journal of Consulting and Clinical Psychology, 59,* 670–681. (p. 638)

**Malan, D. H.** (1978). The case of the secretary with the violent father. In H. Davanloo (Ed.), *Basic principles and techniques in short-term dynamic psychotherapy.* New York: Spectrum. (p. 542)

**Malinosky-Rummell, R., & Hansen, D. J.** (1993). Long-term consequences of childhood physical abuse. *Psychological Bulletin, 114,* 68–79. (p. 99)

**Malkiel, B.** (1985). *A random walk down Wall Street* (4th ed.). New York: Norton. (p. 334)

**Malkiel, B. G.** (1989). Is the stock market efficient? *Science, 243,* 1313–1318. (p. 24)

**Malmquist, C. P.** (1986). Children who witness parental murder: Post-traumatic aspects. *Journal of the American Academy of Child Psychiatry, 25,* 320–325. (p. 319)

**Malone, T. W., & Lepper, M. R.** (1986). Making learning fun: A taxonomy of intrinsic motivations for learning. In R. E. Snow & M. J. Farr (Eds.), *Aptitude, learning, and instruction: Vol. III. Cognitive and affective process analysis.* Hillsdale, NJ: Erlbaum. (p. 423)

**Mandel, D.** (1983, March 13). One man's holocaust: Part II. The story of David Mandel's journey through hell as told to David Kagan. *Wonderland Magazine (Grand Rapids Press),* pp. 2–7. (p. 397)

**Manning, W. G., Keefer, E. B., Newhouse, J. P., Sloss, E. M., & Wasserman, J.** (1989). The taxes of sin: Do smokers and drinkers pay their way? *Journal of the American Medical Association, 261,* 1604–1609. (p. 600)

**Mansnerus, L.** (1992, October 4). Smoking: Is it a habit or is it genetic? *New York Times Magazine,* Part 2. (p. 601)

**Marcel, A.** (1983). Conscious and unconscious perception: Experiments on visual masking and word recognition. *Cognitive Psychology, 15,* 197–237. (p. 155)

**Marcus, A. C., & Siegel, J. M.** (1982). Sex differences in the use of physician services: A preliminary test of the fixed role hypothesis. *Journal of Health and Social Behavior, 23,* 186–197. (p. 592)

**Marino, L. A., Reiss, D., & Gallup, G. G., Jr.** (in press). Mirror self-recognition in Bottlenose dolphins: Implications for comparative investigations of highly dissimilar species. In S. Parker, R. Mitchell, & M. Boccia (Eds.), *Self-awareness in humans and nonhumans.* New York: Cambridge University. (p. 104)

**Mark, V., & Ervin, F.** (1970). *Violence and the brain.* New York: Harper & Row. (p. 58)

**Marks, D. F.** (1986). Investigating the paranormal. *Nature, 320,* 119–124. (p. 213)

**Markus, H., & Kitayama, S.** (1991). Culture and the self: Implications for cognition, emotion, and motivation. *Psychological Review, 98,* 224–253. (pp. 352, 441, 446, 660, 662, 671)

**Markus, H., & Nurius, P.** (1986). Possible selves. *American Psychologist, 41,* 954–969. (p. 482)

**Markus, H., & Wurf, E.** (1987). The dynamic self-concept: A social psychological perspective. *Annual Review of Psychology, 38,* 299–337. (p. 483)

**Marlatt, G. A.** (1991). Substance abuse: Etiology, prevention, and treatment issues. Master lecture, American Psychological Association convention. (pp. 242, 271)

**Marr, D.** (1982). *Vision.* San Francisco: W. H. Freeman. (p. 163)

**Marschark, M., Richman, C. L., Yuille, J. C., & Hunt, R. R.** (1987). The role of imagery in memory: On shared and distinctive information. *Psychological Bulletin, 102,* 28–41. (p. 295)

**Marsh, H. W., & Parker, J. W.** (1984). Determinants of student self-concept: Is it better to be a relatively large fish in a small pond even if you don't learn to swim as well? *Journal of Personality and Social Psychology, 47,* 213–231. (p. 452)

**Marshall, J. C., & Halligan, P. W.** (1988). Blindsight and insight in visuo-spatial neglect. *Nature, 336,* 766–767. (p. 164)

**Marshall, W. L.** (1989). Pornography and sex offenders. In D. Zillmann & J. Bryant (Eds.), *Pornography: Research advances and policy considerations.* Hillsdale, NJ: Erlbaum. (p. 638)

**Marteau, T. M.** (1989). Framing of information: Its influences upon decisions of doctors and patients. *British Journal of Social Psychology, 28,* 89–94. (p. 335)

**Martin, R. J., White, B. D., & Hulsey, M. G.** (1991). The regulation of body weight. *American Scientist, 79,* 528–541. (p. 403)

**Martin, S. J., Kelly, I. W., & Saklofske, D. H.** (1992). Suicide and lunar cycles: A critical review over 28 years. *Psychological Reports, 71,* 787–795. (p. 530)

**Martinez, J. L., Jr., Schulteis, G., & Weinberger, S. B.** (1991). How to increase and decrease the strength of memory traces. In J. L. Martinez, Jr., & R. P. Kesner (Eds.), *Learning and memory* (2nd ed). San Diego, CA: Academic Press. (p. 304)

**Martinsen, E. W.** (1987). The role of aerobic exercise in the treatment of depression. *Stress Medicine, 3,* 93–100. (p. 594)

**Martyna, W.** (1978). What does "he" mean? Use of generic masculine. *Journal of Communication, 28*(1), 131–138. (p. 353)

**Marx, J.** (1992). Familial Alzheimer's linked to chromosome 14 gene. *Science, 258,* p. 550. (p. 134)

**Maslach, C.** (1982). *Burnout: The cost of caring.* Englewood Cliffs, NJ: Prentice-Hall. (p. 580)

**Maslow, A. H.** (1970). *Motivation and personality* (2nd ed.). New York: Harper & Row. (pp. 400, 480)

**Maslow, A. H.** (1971). *The farther reaches of human nature.* New York: Viking Press. (p. 400)

**Masters, W. H., & Johnson, V. E.** (1966). *Human sexual response.* Boston: Little, Brown. (p. 409)

**Matarazzo, J. D.** (1983). Computerized psychological testing. *Science, 221,* 323. (p. 477)

**Matarazzo, J. D.** (1992). Psychological testing and assessment in the 21st century. *American Psychologist, 47,* 1007–1018. (p. 375)

**Matsumoto, D.** (1994). *People: Psychology from a cultural perspective.* Pacific Grove, CA: Brooks/Cole. (p. 352)

**Matsumoto, D., Kudoh, T., Scherer, K., & Wallbott, H.** (1988). Antecedents of and reactions to emotions in the United States and Japan. *Journal of Cross-Cultural Psychology, 19,* 267–286. (pp. 441, 443)

**Matt, G. E., Vazquez, C., & Campbell, W. K.** (1992). Mood-congruent recall of affectively toned stimuli: A meta-analytic review. *Clinical Psychology Review, 12,* 227–255. (p. 310)

**Matthews, K. A.** (1988). CHD and Type A behaviors: Update on and alternative to the Booth-Kewley and Friedman quantitative review. *Psychological Bulletin, 104,* 373–380. (p. 582)

**Matthews, K. A.** (1992). Myths and realities of the menopause. *Psychosomatic Medicine, 54,* 1–9. (p. 130)

**Maurer, D., & Maurer, C.** (1988). *The world of the newborn.* New York: Basic Books. (pp. 83, 115)

**May, C. P., Hasher, L., & Stoltzfus, E. R.** (1993). Optimal time of day and the magnitude of age differences in memory. *Psychological Science, 4,* 326–330. (p. 135)

**May, P. A.** (1986). Alcohol and drug misuse prevention programs for American Indians: Needs and opportunities. *Journal of Studies on Alcohol, 47,* 187–195. (p. 502)

**May, R.** (1982). The problem of evil: An open letter to Carl Rogers. *Journal of Humanistic Psychology, 22,* 10–21. (p. 487)

**McAdams, D. P.** (1992). The five-factor model *in* personality: A critical appraisal. *Journal of Personality, 60,* 329–361. (p. 475)

**McAlister, A., Perry, C., Killen, J., Slinkard, L. A., & Maccoby, N.** (1980). Pilot study of smoking, alcohol and drug abuse prevention. *American Journal of Public Health, 70,* 719–721. (p. 602)

**McBurney, D. H., & Collings, V. B.** (1984). *Introduction to sensation and perception* (2nd ed.). Englewood Cliffs, NJ: Prentice-Hall. (pp. 201–202)

**McBurney, D. H., & Gent, J. F.** (1979). On the nature of taste qualities. *Psychological Bulletin, 86,* 151–167. (p. 177)

**McCall, R. B.** (1994). Academic underachievers. *Current Directions in Psychological Science, 3,* 15–19. (p. 419)

**McCall, R. B., & Carriger, M. S.** (1993). A meta-analysis of infant habituation and recognition memory performance as predictors of later IQ. *Child Development, 64,* 57–79. (p. 378)

**McCall, R. B., Evahn, C., & Kratzer, L.** (1992). *High school underachievers.* Newbury Park, CA: Sage. (p. 667)

**McCann, I. L., & Holmes, D. S.** (1984). Influence of aerobic exercise on depression. *Journal of Personality and Social Psychology, 46,* 1142–1147. (p. 593)

**McCarron, D. A., Morris, C. D., Henry, H. J., & Stanton, J. L.** (1984). Blood pressure and nutrient intake in the United States. *Science, 225,* 1392–1398. (p. 603)

**McCarthy, C.** (1988, December 31). Koop versus booze. *Washington Post,* p. A19. (p. 242)

**McCarthy, P.** (1986, July). Scent: The tie that binds? *Psychology Today,* pp. 6, 10. (p. 179)

**McCartney, K., Harris, M. J., & Bernieri, F.** (1990). Growing up and growing apart: A developmental meta-analysis of twin studies. *Psychological Bulletin, 107,* 226–237. (p. 110)

**McCarty, D., Argeriou, M., Huebner, R. B., & Lubran, B.** (1991). Alcoholism, drug abuse, and the homeless. *American Psychologist, 46,* 1139–1148. (p. 565)

**McCaul, K. D., & Malott, J. M.** (1984). Distraction and coping with pain. *Psychological Bulletin, 95,* 516–533. (p. 177)

**McCauley, C. R., & Segal, M. E.** (1987). Social psychology of terrorist groups. In C. Hendrick (Ed.), *Group processes and intergroup relations.* Beverly Hills, CA: Sage. (p. 629)

**McClelland, D. C.** (1978). Managing motivation to expand human freedom. *American Psychologist, 33,* 201–210. (p. 420)

**McClelland, J. L., & Rumelhart, D. E.** (1988). *Explorations in parallel distributed processing: A handbook of models, programs, and exercises.* Cambridge, MA: MIT Press. (p. 340)

**McCloskey, M., Wible, C. G., & Cohen, N. J.** (1988). Is there a special flashbulb-memory mechanism? *Journal of Experimental Psychology: General, 117,* 171–181. (p. 288)

**McConkey, K. M.** (1992). The effects of hypnotic procedures on remembering: The experimental findings and their implications for forensic hypnosis. In E. Fromm & M. R. Nash (Eds.), *Contemporary hypnosis research.* New York: Guilford Press. (p. 235)

**McConnell, R. A.** (1991). National Academy of Sciences opinion on parapsychology. *Journal of the American Society for Psychical Research, 85,* 333–365. (p. 211)

**McCord, J.** (1978). A thirty-year follow-up on treatment effects. *American Psychologist, 33,* 284–289. (p. 557)

**McCord, J.** (1979). Following up on Cambridge-Somerville. *American Psychologist, 34,* 727. (p. 557)

**McCormick, C. M., & Witelson, S. F.** (1991). A cognitive profile of homosexual men compared to heterosexual men and women. *Psychoneuroendocrinology, 16,* 459–473. (p. 416)

**McCrae, R. R., & Costa, P. T., Jr.** (1982). Self-concept and the stability of personality: Cross-sectional comparisons of self-reports and ratings. *Journal of Personality and Social Psychology, 43,* 1282–1292. (p. 146)

**McCrae, R. R., & Costa, P. T., Jr.** (1986). Clinical assessment can benefit from recent advances in personality psychology. *American Psychologist, 41,* 1001–1003. (p. 475)

**McCrae, R. R., & Costa, P. T., Jr.** (1990). *Personality in adulthood.* New York: Guilford Press. (pp. 138–139)

**McEvoy, G. M., & Cascio, W. F.** (1989). Cumulative evidence of the relationship between employee age and job performance. *Journal of Applied Psychology, 74,* 11–17. (p. 133)

**McFarland, C., & Ross, M.** (1987). The relation between current impressions and memories of self and dating partners. *Psychological Bulletin, 13,* 228–238. (p. 312)

**McFarland, C., Ross, M., & DeVourville, N.** (1989). Women's theories of menstruation and biases in recall of menstrual symptoms. *Journal of Personality and Social Psychology, 57,* 522–531. (p. 591)

**McGarry-Roberts, P. A., Stelmack, R. M., & Campbell, K. B.** (1992). Intelligence, reaction time, and event-related potentials. *Intelligence, 16,* 289–313. (p. 376)

**McGhee, P. E.** (1976). Children's appreciation of humor: A test of the cognitive congruency principle. *Child Development, 47,* 420–426. (p. 94)

**McGrath, J., Welham, J., & Pemberton, M.** (1994). Month of birth, hemisphere of birth and schizophrenia. Unpublished (submitted) manuscript, Wolston Park Hospital, Brisbane, Australia. (p. 526)

**McGrath, M. J., & Cohen, D. G.** (1978). REM sleep facilitation of adaptive waking behavior: A review of the literature. *Psychological Bulletin, 85,* 24–57. (p. 229)

**McGregor, D.** (1960). *The human side of enterprise.* New York: McGraw-Hill. (p. 425)

**McGue, M., & Lykken, D. T.** (1992). Genetic influence on risk of divorce. *Psychological Science, 3,* 368–373. (p. 108)

**McGue, M., Bouchard, T. J., Jr., Iacono, W. G., & Lykken, D. T.** (1993). Behavioral genetics of cognitive ability: A life-span perspective. In R. Plomin & G. E. McClearn (Eds.), *Nature, nurture and psychology.* Washington, DC: American Psychological Association. (p. 385)

**McGue, M., Pickens, R. W., & Svikis, D. S.** (1992). Sex and age effects on the inheritance of alcohol problems: A twin study. *Journal of Abnormal Psychology, 202,* 3–17. (p. 249)

**McGuire, W. J.** (1986). The myth of massive media impact: Savings and salvagings. In G. Comstock (Ed.), *Public communication and behavior.* Orlando, FL: Academic Press. (p. 636)

**McGuire, W. J., McGuire, C. V., & Winton, W.** (1979). Effects of household sex composition on the salience of one's gender in the spontaneous self-concept. *Journal of Experimental Social Psychology, 15,* 77–90. (p. 663)

**McGuire, W. J., & Padawer-Singer, A.** (1978). Trait salience in the spontaneous self-concept. *Journal of Personality and Social Psychology, 33,* 743–754. (p. 663)

**McHugh, P. R., & Moran, T. H.** (1978). Accuracy of the regulation of caloric ingestion in the rhesus monkey. *American Journal of Physiology, 235,* R29–34. (p. 402)

**McKinlay, J. B., McKinlay, S. M., & Brambilla, D. J.** (1987a). Health status and utilization behavior associated with menopause. *American Journal of Epidemiology, 125,* 110–121. (p. 130)

**McKinlay, J. B., McKinlay, S. M., & Brambilla, D.** (1987b). The relative contributions of endocrine changes and social circumstances to depression in mid-aged women. *Journal of Health and Social Behavior, 28,* 345–363. (p. 130)

**McMillen, D. L., Smith, S. M., & Wells-Parker, E.** (1989). The effects of alcohol, expectancy, and sensation seeking on driving risk taking. *Addictive Behaviors, 14,* 477–483. (p. 242)

**McNally, R. J.** (1987). Preparedness and phobias: A review. *Psychological Bulletin, 101,* 283–303. (p. 445)

**Meador, B. D., & Rogers, C. R.** (1984). Person-centered therapy. In R. J. Corsini (Ed.), *Current psychotherapies* (3rd ed.). Itasca, IL: Peacock. (p. 545)

**Meaney, M. J., Aitken, D. H., Van Berkel, C., Bhatnagar, S., & Sapolsky, R. M.** (1988). Effect of neonatal handling on age-related impairments associated with the hippocampus. *Science, 239,* 766–768. (p. 85)

**Medawar, P.** (1982). *Pluto's republic.* New York: Oxford University Press. (p. 471)

**Mednick, S. A., Huttunen, M. O., & Machon, R. A.** (1994). Prenatal influenza infections and adult schizophrenia. *Schizophrenia Bulletin, 20,* 263–267. (p. 526)

**Meichenbaum, D.** (1977). *Cognitive-behavior modification: An integrative approach.* New York: Plenum Press. (p. 553)

**Meichenbaum, D.** (1985). *Stress inoculation training.* New York: Pergamon. (p. 553)

**Meier, R. P.** (1991). Language acquisition by deaf children. *American Scientist, 79,* 60–70. (pp. 173, 346)

**Meltzoff, A. N.** (1988a). Infant imitation and memory: Nine-month-olds in immediate and deferred tests. *Child Development, 59,* 217–225. (p. 281)

**Meltzoff, A. N.** (1988b). Infant imitation after a 1–week delay: Long-term memory for novel acts and multiple stimuli. *Developmental Psychology, 24,* 470–476. (p. 281)

**Meltzoff, A. N.** (1988c). Imitation of televised models by infants. *Child Development, 59,* 1221–1229. (p. 281)

**Melzack, R.** (1984). The myth of painless childbirth. *Pain, 19,* 321–337. (p. 177)

**Melzack, R.** (1990, February). The tragedy of needless pain. *Scientific American,* pp. 27–33. (p. 246)

**Melzack, R.** (1992, April). Phantom limbs. *Scientific American,* pp. 120–126. (p. 175)

**Melzack, R., & Wall, P. D.** (1965). Pain mechanisms: A new theory. *Science, 150,* 971–979. (p. 175)

**Melzack, R., & Wall, P. D.** (1983). *The challenge of pain.* New York: Basic Books. (p. 175)

**Mendolia, M., & Kleck, R. E.** (1993). Effects of talking about a stressful event on arousal: Does what we talk about make a difference? *Journal of Personality and Social Psychology, 64,* 283–292. (p. 598)

**Mento, A. J., Steel, R. P., & Karren, R. J.** (1987). A meta-analytic study of the effects of goal setting on task performance: 1966–1984. *Organizational Behavior and Human Decision Processes, 39,* 52–83. (p. 424)

**Merskey, H.** (1992). The manufacture of personalities: The production of multiple personality disorder. *British Journal of Psychiatry, 160,* 327–340. (p. 513)

**Merton, R. K.** (1938; reprinted 1970). *Science, technology and society in seventeenth-century England.* New York: Fertig. (p. 12)

**Merton, R. K., & Kitt, A. S.** (1950). Contributions to the theory of reference group behavior. In R. K. Merton & P. F. Lazarsfeld (Eds.), *Continuities in social research: Studies in the scope and method of the American soldier.* Glencoe, IL: Free Press. (p. 452)

**Merton, T.** (1957). *The silent life,* New York: Farrar, Straus & Cudahy. (p. 182)

**Mesquita, B., & Frijda, N. H.** (1992). Cultural variations in emotions: A review. *Psychological Bulletin, 112,* 179–204. (p. 441)

**Messer, W. S., & Griggs, R. A.** (1989). Student belief and involvement in the paranormal and performance in introductory psychology. *Teaching of Psychology, 16,* 187–191. (p. 213)

**Messick, S., & Jungeblut, A.** (1981). Time and method in coaching for the SAT. *Psychological Bulletin, 89,* 191–216. (p. 369)

**Metalsky, G. I., Joiner, T. E., Jr., , Hardin, T. S., & Abramson, L. Y.** (1993). Depressive reactions to failure in a naturalistic setting: A test of the hopelessness and self-esteem theories of depression. *Journal of Abnormal Psychology, 102,* 101–109. (p. 521)

**Meuwissen, I., & Over, R.** (1992). Sexual arousal across phases of the human menstrual cycle. *Archives of Sexual Behavior, 21,* 101–119. (p. 410)

**Michaels, J. W., Bloomel, J. M., Brocato, R. M., Linkous, R. A., & Rowe, J. S.** (1982). Social facilitation and inhibition in a natural setting. *Replications in Social Psychology, 2,* 21–24. (p. 627)

**Michaelson, R.** (1993, August). Behavior gets big billing in medical schools today. *The APA Monitor,* p. 56. (p. 573)

**Michel, G. F.** (1981). Right-handedness: A consequence of infant supine head-orientation preference? *Science, 212,* 685–687. (p. 68)

**Middlebrooks, J. C., & Green, D. M.** (1991). Sound localization by human listeners. *Annual Review of Psychology, 42,* 135–159. (p. 171)

**Mikulincer, M., Babkoff, H., Caspy, T., & Sing, H.** (1989). The effects of 72 hours of sleep loss on psychological variables. *British Journal of Psychology, 80,* 145–162. (p. 225)

**Milan, R. J., Jr., & Kilmann, P. R.** (1987). Interpersonal factors in premarital contraception. *Journal of Sex Research, 23,* 289–321. (p. 126)

**Milgram, S.** (1974). *Obedience to authority.* New York: Harper & Row. (pp. 622, 625)

**Miller, G. A.** (1956). The magical number seven, plus or minus two: Some limits on our capacity for processing information. *Psychological Review, 63,* 81–97. (p. 300)

**Miller, G. A., & Gildea, P. M.** (1987, September). How children learn words. *Scientific American,* pp. 94–99. (p. 342)

**Miller, J. B.** (1986). *Toward a new psychology of women* (2nd ed.). Boston, MA: Beacon Press. (p. 668)

**Miller, J. G.** (1984). Culture and the development of everyday social explanation. *Journal of Personality and Social Psychology, 46,* 961–978. (p. 661)

**Miller, J. G., Bersoff, D. M., & Harwood, R. L.** (1990). Perceptions of social responsibilities in India and in the United States: Moral imperatives or personal decisions? *Journal of Personality and Social Psychology, 58,* 33–47. (p. 643)

**Miller, K. I., & Monge, P. R.** (1986). Participation, satisfaction, and productivity: A meta-analytic review. *Academy of Management Journal, 29,* 727–753. (p. 490)

**Miller, N., & Maruyama, G.** (1976). Ordinal position and peer popularity. *Journal of Personality and Social Psychology, 33,* 123–131. (p. 420)

**Miller, N. E.** (1983). Value and ethics of research on animals. Paper presented at the meeting of the American Psychological Association. (p. 34)

**Miller, N. E.** (1985, February). Rx: Biofeedback. *Psychology Today,* pp. 54–59. (pp. 34, 595)

**Miller, N. E., & Brucker, B. S.** (1979). A learned visceral response apparently independent of skeletal ones in patients paralyzed by spinal lesions. In N. Birbaumer & H. D. Kimmel (Eds.), *Biofeedback and self-regulation.* Hillsdale, NJ: Erlbaum. (p. 594)

**Miller, P. C., Lefcourt, H. M., Holmes, J. G., Ware, E. E., & Saleh, W. E.** (1986). Marital locus of control and marital problem solving. *Journal of Personality and Social Psychology, 51,* 161–169. (p. 489)

**Miller, S. D., Blackburn, T., Scholes, G., White, G. L., & Mamalis, N.** (1991). Optical differences in multiple personality disorder: A second look. *Journal of Nervous and Mental Disease, 179,* 132–135. (p. 513)

**Mills, M., & Melhuish, E.** (1974). Recognition of mother's voice in early infancy. *Nature, 252,* 123–124. (p. 83)

**Mineka, S.** (1985). The frightful complexity of the origins of fears. In F. R. Brush & J. B. Overmier (Eds.), *Affect, conditioning and cognition: Essays on the determinants of behavior.* Hillsdale, NJ: Erlbaum. (p. 445)

**Mineka, S., & Suomi, S. J.** (1978). Social separation in monkeys. *Psychological Bulletin, 85,* 1376–1400. (p. 101)

**Mineka, S., & Sutton, S. K.** (1992). Cognitive biases and the emotional disorders. *Psychological Science, 3,* 65–69. (pp. 445, 508)

**Mintz, L. B., & Betz, N. E.** (1986). Sex differences in the nature, realism, and correlates of body image. *Sex Roles, 15,* 185–195. (p. 407)

**Mirin, S. M., & Weiss, R. D.** (1989). Genetic factors in the development of alcoholism. *Psychiatric Annals, 19,* 239–242. (p. 249)

**Mischel, W.** (1968). *Personality and assessment.* New York: Wiley. (p. 478)

**Mischel, W.** (1981). Current issues and challenges in personality. In L. T. Benjamin, Jr. (Ed.), *The G. Stanley Hall Lecture Series* (Vol. 1). Washington, DC: American Psychological Association. (p. 493)

**Mischel, W.** (1984). Convergences and challenges in the search for consistency. *American Psychologist, 39,* 351–364. (p. 478)

**Mischel, W., Shoda, Y., & Peake, P. K.** (1988). The nature of adolescent competencies predicted by preschool delay of gratification. *Journal of Personality and Social Psychology, 54,* 687–696. (pp. 122, 271)

**Mischel, W., Shoda, Y., & Rodriguez, M. L.** (1989). Delay of gratification in children. *Science, 244,* 933–938. (pp. 122, 271)

**Monaghan, P.** (1992, September 23). Professor of psychology stokes a controversy on the reliability and repression of memory. *Chronicle of Higher Education,* pp. A9–A10. (p. 319)

**Monahan, J.** (1992). Mental disorder and violent behavior: Perceptions and evidence. *American Psychologist, 47,* 511–521. (p. 534)

**Money, J.** (1987). Sin, sickness, or status? Homosexual gender identity and psychoneuroendocrinology. *American Psychologist, 42,* 384–399. (pp. 414–415)

**Money, J.** (1988). *Gay, straight, and in-between.* New York: Oxford University Press. (p. 638)

**Money, J., Berlin, F. S., Falck, A., & Stein, M.** (1983). *Antiandrogenic and counseling treatment of sex offenders.* Baltimore: Department of Psychiatry and Behavioral Sciences, The Johns Hopkins University School of Medicine. (p. 411)

**Moody, R.** (1976). *Life after life.* Harrisburg, PA: Stackpole Books. (p. 251)

**Mook, D. G.** (1983). In defense of external invalidity. *American Psychologist, 38,* 379–387. (p. 31)

**Moorcroft, W.** (1993). *Sleep, dreaming, and sleep disorders: An introduction* (2nd ed.). Lanham, MD: University Press of America. (pp. 222, 225)

**Moore, D. L., & Baron, R. S.** (1983). Social facilitation: A physiological analysis. In J. T. Cacioppo & R. Petty (Eds.), *Social psychophysiology.* New York: Guilford Press. (p. 627)

**Moore, D. W.** (1993, April). Public polarized on gay issue. *Gallup Poll Monthly,* pp. 30–34. (p. 416)

**Moore, T. E.** (1988). The case against subliminal manipulation. *Psychology and Marketing, 5,* 297–316. (p. 155)

**Moreland, R. L., & Beach, S. R.** (1992). Exposure effects in the classroom: The development of affinity among students. *Journal of Experimental Social Psychology, 28,* 255–276. (p. 644)

**Moreland, R. L., & Zajonc, R. B.** (1982). Exposure effects in person perception: Familiarity, similarity, and attraction. *Journal of Experimental Social Psychology, 18,* 395–415. (p. 644)

**Morelli, G. A., Rogoff, B., Oppenheim, D., & Goldsmith, D.** (1992). Cultural variation in infants' sleeping arrangements: Questions of independence. *Developmental Psychology, 26,* 604–613. (p. 106)

**Morris, N. M., & Udry, J. R.** (1978). Pheromonal influences on human sexual behavior: An experimental search. *Journal of Biosocial Science, 10,* 147–157. (p. 411)

**Morris, N. M., Udry, J. R., Kahn-Dawood, F., & Dawood, M. Y.** (1987). Marital sex frequency and midcycle female testosterone. *Archives of Sexual Behavior, 16,* 27–37. (p. 410)

**Morrison, D. C.** (1988). Marine mammals join the Navy. *Science,* 242, 1503–1504. (p. 279)

**Morrison, D. M.** (1985). Adolescent contraceptive behavior: A review. *Psychological Bulletin, 98,* 538–568. (p. 126)

**Morton, G. E.** (1994). Personal communication, 525 E. Mission, Spokane, Washington 99202. (p. 17)

**Moruzzi, G., & Magoun, H. W.** (1949). Brain stem reticular formation and activation of the EEG. *Electroencephalography and Clinical Neurophysiology, 1,* 455–473. (p. 56)

**Moser, P. W.** (1987, May). Are cats smart? Yes, at being cats. *Discover,* pp. 77–88. (p. 161)

**Mosher, D. L., & Anderson, R. D.** (1986). Macho personality, sexual aggression, and reactions to guided imagery of realistic rape. *Journal of Research in Personality, 20,* 77–94. (p. 241)

**Moss, A. J., Allen, K. F., Giovino, G. A., & Mills, S. L.** (1992, December 2). Recent trends in adolescent smoking, smoking-update correlates, and expectations about the future. *Advance Data* No. 221 (from Vital and Health Statistics of the Centers for Disease Control and Prevention). (p. 600)

**Moss, H. A., & Susman, E. J.** (1980). Longitudinal study of personality development. In O. G. Brim, Jr., & J. Kagan (Eds.), *Constancy and change in human development.* Cambridge, MA: Harvard University Press. (p. 147)

**Mott, F. L.** (1991). Developmental effects of infant care: The mediating role of gender and health. *Journal of Social Issues, 47*(2), 139–158. (p. 101)

**Moyer, K. E.** (1983). The physiology of motivation: Aggression as a model. In C. J. Scheier & A. M. Rogers (Eds.), *G. Stanley Hall Lecture Series* (Vol. 3). Washington, DC: American Psychological Association. (p. 632)

**Muehlenhard, C. L.** (1988). Misinterpreted dating behaviors and the risk of date rape. *Journal of Social and Clinical Psychology, 6,* 20–37. (p. 673)

**Murphy, G. E., & Wetzel, R. D.** (1990). The lifetime risk of suicide in alcoholism. *Archives of General Psychiatry, 47,* 383–392. (p. 517)

**Murphy, S. T., & Zajonc, R. B.** (1993). Affect, cognition, and awareness: Affective priming with optimal and suboptimal stimulus exposures. *Journal of Personality and Social Psychology, 64,* 723–739. (p. 155)

**Murphy, T. N.** (1982). Pain: Its assessment and management. In R. J. Gatchel, A. Baum, & J. E. Singer (Eds.), *Handbook of psychology and health: Vol. I. Clinical psychology and behavioral medicine: Overlapping disciplines.* Hillsdale, NJ: Erlbaum. (p. 176)

**Murray, C., & Herrnstein, R. J.** (1992, Winter). What's really behind the SAT-score decline? *Public Interest,* pp. 32–56. (p. 367)

**Murray, D. M., Johnson, C. A., Luepker, R. V., & Mittelmark, M. B.** (1984). The prevention of cigarette smoking in children: A comparison of four strategies. *Journal of Applied Social Psychology, 14,* 274–288. (p. 602)

**Murray, D. M., Pirie, P., Luepker, R. V., & Pallonen, U.** (1989). Five- and six-year follow-up results from four seventh-grade smoking prevention strategies. *Journal of Behavioral Medicine, 12,* 207–218. (p. 602)

**Murray, H.** (1938). *Explorations in personality.* New York: Oxford University Press. (p. 419)

**Murray, H. A.** (1933). The effect of fear upon estimates of the maliciousness of other personalities. *Journal of Social Psychology, 4,* 310–329. (p. 468)

**Murray, H. A., & Wheeler, D. R.** (1937). A note on the possible clairvoyance of dreams. *Journal of Psychology, 3,* 309–313. (p. 213)

**Murray, L., & Trevarthen, C.** (1986). The infant's role in mother-infant communications. *Journal of Child Language, 13,* 15–29. (p. 95)

**Murray, R., Jones, P., O'Callaghan, E., Takei, N., & Sham, P.** (1992). Genes, viruses, and neurodevelopmental schizophrenia. *Journal of Psychiatric Research, 26,* 225–235. (p. 526)

**Murstein, B. L.** (1986). *Paths to marriage.* Newbury Park, CA: Sage. (p. 645)

**Myers, D. G.** (1993). *The pursuit of happiness.* New York: Avon Books. (pp. 447, 453, 484)

**Myers, D. G.** (1993). *Social psychology* (4th ed.). New York: McGraw-Hill. (p. 484)

**Myers, D. G.** (1994). Society in the balance: America's social recession and renewal. Unpublished manuscript, Hope College, Holland, MI. (p. 127)

**Myers, D. G., & Bishop, G. D.** (1970). Discussion effects on racial attitudes. *Science, 169,* 778–779. (p. 629)

**Myers, I. B.** (1987). *Introduction to type: A description of the theory and applications of the Myers-Briggs Type Indicator.* Palo Alto, CA: Consulting Psychologists Press. (p. 473)

**Napolitan, D. A., & Goethals, G. R.** (1979). The attribution of friendliness. *Journal of Experimental Social Psychology, 15,* 105–113. (p. 613)

**Nash, M.** (1987). What, if anything, is regressed about hypnotic age regression? A review of the empirical literature. *Psychological Bulletin, 102,* 42–52. (p. 235)

**National Academy of Sciences.** (1984). *Bereavement: Reactions, consequences, and cure.* Washington, DC: National Academy Press. (pp. 583–584)

**National Academy of Sciences.** (1991). *Science, medicine, and animals.* Washington, DC: National Academy Press. (p. 33)

**National Academy of Sciences, Institute of Medicine.** (1982). *Marijuana and health.* Washington, DC: National Academy Press. (pp. 245, 573)

**National Center for Health Statistics.** (1990, October 1). Child care arrangements. *Advance data from vital and health statistics of the National Center for Health Statistics,* Report No. 187. (p. 101)

**National Center for Health Statistics.** (1990). *Health, United States, 1989.* Washington, DC: U.S. Department of Health and Human Services. (p. 133)

**National Center for Health Statistics.** (1991). Family structure and children's health: United States, 1988. *Vital and health statistics,* Series 10, No. 178, DHHS Publication No. PHS 91–1506 by Deborah A. Dawson. (p. 103)

**National Center for Health Statistics.** (1992, May). *Health United States 1991.* Hyattsville, MD: Department of Health and Human Services Pub. No. (PHS) 92–1232, Table 27. (p. 131)

**National Council on the Aging.** (1976). *The myth and reality of aging in America.* Washington, DC. (p. 133)

**National Institute of Mental Health.** (1982). *Television and behavior: Ten years of scientific progress and implications for the eighties.* Washington, DC: U.S. Government Printing Office. (p. 636)

**National Institute on Aging.** (1993). *In search of the secrets of aging.* Washington, DC: Superintendent of Documents. (p. 131)

**National Institute on Drug Abuse.** (1991). *National household survey on drug abuse: Population estimates 1991.* Rockville, MD: Alcohol, Drug Abuse, and Mental Health Administration. (p. 248)

**National Institute on Drug Abuse.** (1992). *National household survey on drug abuse: Population estimates 1991* (February 27, 1992 replacement pages). Rockville, MD: Alcohol, Drug Abuse, and Mental Health Administration. (p. 243)

**National Research Council.** (1987). *Risking the future: Adolescent sexuality, pregnancy, and childbearing.* Washington, DC: National Academy Press. (p. 126)

**National Research Council.** (1990). *Human factors research needs for an aging population.* Washington, DC: National Academy Press. (p. 132)

**National Safety Council.** (1991). *Accident facts.* Chicago: National Safety Council. (p. 333)

**National Victim Center and Crime Victims Research and Treatment Center.** (1992). *Rape in America: A report to the nation.* Arlington, VA: National Victim Center. (p. 637)

**Naveh-Benjamin, M.** (1990). Coding of temporal order information: An automatic process? *Journal of Experimental Psychology: Learning, Memory, and Cognition, 16,* 117–126. (p. 291)

**Naylor, T. H.** (1990). Redefining corporate motivation, Swedish style. *Christian Century, 107,* 566–570. (p. 426)

**NCTV News.** (1987, July-August). More research links harmful effects to non-violent porn. National Coalition on Television Violence, p. 12. (p. 637)

**Needles, D. J., & Abramson, L. Y.** (1990). Positive life events, attributional style, and hopefulness: Testing a model of recovery from depression. *Journal of Abnormal Psychology, 99,* 156–165. (p. 521)

**Neese, R. M.** (1991, November/December). What good is feeling bad? The evolutionary benefits of psychic pain. *The Sciences,* pp. 30–37. (pp. 175, 264, 515)

**Neisser, U.** (1979). The control of information pickup in selective looking. In A. D. Pick (Ed.), *Perception and its development: A tribute to Eleanor J. Gibson.* Hillsdale, NJ: Erlbaum. (p. 188)

**Neisser, U.** (1981). John Dean's memory: A case study. *Cognition, 9,* 1–22. (pp. 288, 309)

**Neisser, U.** (1982). Memorists. In U. Neisser (Ed.), *Memory observed: Remembering in natural contexts.* San Francisco: Freeman. (p. 287)

**Neisser, U., & Harsch, N.** (1992). Phantom flashbulbs: False recollections of hearing the news about *Challenger.* In E. Winograd & U. Neisser (Eds.), *Affect and accuracy in recall: Studies of "flashbulb" memories.* New York: Cambridge University Press. (p. 288)

**Neisser, U., Winograd, E., & Weldon, M. S.** (1991). Remembering the earthquake: "What I experienced" vs. "How I heard the news." Paper presented to the Psychonomic Society convention. (p. 304)

**Neitz, J., Geist, T., & Jacobs, G. H.** (1989). Color vision in the dog. *Visual Neuroscience, 3,* 119–125. (p. 165)

**Nelson, K.** (1973). Structure and strategy in learning to talk. *Monographs of the Society for Research in Child Development, 38*(1 & 2, Serial No. 149). (p. 344)

**Nelson, K.** (1993). The psychological and social origins of autobiographical memory. *Psychological Science, 4,* 7–13. (p. 84)

**Nelson, N.** (1988). *A meta-analysis of the life-event/health paradigm: The influence of social support.* Unpublished doctoral dissertation, Temple University, Philadelphia. (p. 597)

**Neugarten, B. L.** (1974). The roles we play. In American Medical Association, *Quality of life: The middle years.* Acton, MA: Publishing Sciences Group. (p. 141)

**Neugarten, B. L.** (1979). Time, age and the life cycle. *American Journal of Psychiatry, 136,* 887–894. (p. 139)

**Neugarten, B. L.** (1980, February). Must everything be a midlife crisis? *Prime Time,* pp. 45–48. (pp. 139, 146)

**Neugarten, B. L., Wood, V., Kraines, R. J., & Loomis, B.** (1963). Women's attitudes toward the menopause. *Vita Humana, 6, 140–151.* (p. 130)

**Nevin, J. A.** (1988). Behavioral momentum and the partial reinforcement effect. *Psychological Bulletin, 103,* 44–56. (p. 272)

**Newcomb, M. D., & Bentler, P. M.** (1988). Impact of adolescent drug use and social support on problems of young adults: A longitudinal study. *Journal of Abnormal Psychology, 97,* 64–75. (p. 247)

**Newcomb, M. D., & Harlow, L. L.** (1986). Life events and substance use among adolescents: Mediating effects of perceived loss of control and meaninglessness in life. *Journal of Personality and Social Psychology, 51,* 564–577. (p. 249)

**Newell, A.** (1988, March 9). Quoted in D. L. Wheeler, From years of work in psychology and computer science, scientists build theories of thinking and learning. *Chronicle of Higher Education,* pp. A4, A6. (p. 17)

**Newport, E. L.** (1990). Maturational constraints on language learning. *Cognitive Science, 14,* 11–28. (p. 346)

**Nezu, A. M., Nezu, C. M., & Blissett, S. E.** (1988). Sense of humor as a moderator of the relation between stressful events and psychological distress: A prospective analysis. *Journal of Personality and Social Psychology, 54,* 520–525. (p. 596)

**Ng, S. H.** (1990). Androcentric coding of *man* and *his* in memory by language users. *Journal of Experimental Social Psychology, 26,* 455–464. (p. 353)

**Nicholi, A. M., Jr.** (1987). Psychiatric consultation in professional football. *New England Journal of Medicine, 316,* 1095–1100. (p. 354)

**Nickerson, R. S., & Adams, M. J.** (1979). Long-term memory for a common object. *Cognitive Psychology, 11,* 287–307. (pp. 298–299)

**Nicol, S. E., & Gottesman, I. I.** (1983). Clues to the genetics and neurobiology of schizophrenia. *American Scientist, 71,* 398–404. (p. 527)

**Nicolaus, L. K., Cassel, J. F., Carlson, R. B., & Gustavson, C. R.** (1983). Taste-aversion conditioning of crows to control predation on eggs. *Science, 220,* 212–214. (p. 264)

**Niemi, R. G., Mueller, J., & Smith, T. W.** (1989). *Trends in public opinion: A compendium of survey data.* New York: Greenwood Press. (pp. 449, 600, 679)

**Nigro, G.** (1984). Cited in U. Neisser, The role of invariant structures in the control of movement. In M. Frese & J. Sabini (Eds.), *Goal directed behavior: The concept of action in psychology.* Hillsdale, NJ: Erlbaum. (p. 354)

**Nisbett, R., & Ross, L.** (1991). *The person and the situation.* New York: McGraw-Hill. (p. 426)

**Nisbett, R. E.** (1993). Violence and U.S. regional culture. *American Psychologist, 48,* 441–449. (p. 635)

**Nisbett, R. E., & Borgida, E.** (1975). Attribution and the psychology of prediction. *Journal of Personality and Social Psychology, 32,* 932–943. (p. 338)

**Nisbett, R. E., & Ross, L.** (1980). *Human inference: Strategies and shortcomings of social judgment.* Englewood Cliffs, NJ: Prentice-Hall. (p. 331)

**Noble, E. P.** (1993). The D2 dopamine receptor gene: A review of association studies in alcoholism. *Behavior Genetics, 23,* 119–129. (p. 249)

**Noel, J. G., Forsyth, D. R., & Kelley, K. N.** (1987). Improving the performance of failing students by overcoming their self-serving attributional biases. *Basic and Applied Social Psychology, 8,* 151–162. (p. 491)

**Nolen-Hoeksema, S.** (1990). *Sex differences in depression.* Stanford, CA: Stanford University Press. (p. 517)

**Nolen-Hoeksema, S., & Morrow, J.** (1991). A prospective study of depression and post-traumatic stress symptoms following a natural disaster: The 1989 Loma Prieta earthquake. *Journal of Personality and Social Psychology, 61,* 115–121. (p. 521)

**Noller, P., Law, H., & Comrey, A. L.** (1987). Cattell, Comrey, and Eysenck personality factors compared: More evidence for the five robus factors? *Journal of Personality and Social Psychology, 53,* 1208–1217. (p. 475)

**NORC.** (1993, March/April). National Opinion Research Center surveys on homosexuality reported in *American Enterprise,* pp. 82–83. (p. 416)

**Norman, D. A.** (1988). *The psychology of everyday things.* New York: Basic Books. (p. 209)

**Norris, P. A.** (1986). On the status of biofeedback and clinical practice. *American Psychologist, 41,* 1009–1010. (p. 594)

**Notarius, C., & Markman, H.** (1993). *We can work it out.* New York: Putnam. (p. 141)

**Nowak, R.** (1994). Nicotine scrutinized as FDA seeks to regulate cigarettes. *Science, 263,* 1555–1556. (p. 601)

**Nuttin, J. M., Jr.** (1987). Affective consequences of mere ownership: The name letter effect in twelve European languages. *European Journal of Social Psychology, 17,* 381–402. (p. 644)

**Oakhill, J., Garnham, A., & Johnson-Laird, P. N.** (1990). Belief bias effects in syllogistic reasoning. In D. J. Gilhooly, M. T. G. Keane, R. H. Logie, & G. Erdos (Eds.), *Lines of thinking* (Vol. 1). Chichester, England: Wiley. (p. 337)

**Oakhill, J. V., Johnson-Laird, P. N., & Garnham, A.** (1989). Believability and syllogistic reasoning. *Cognition, 31,* 117–140. (p. 336)

**O'Connor, P., & Brown, G. W.** (1984). Supportive relationships: Fact or fancy? *Journal of Social and Personal Relationships, 1,* 159–175. (p. 562)

**Oetting, E. R., & Beauvais, F.** (1987). Peer cluster theory, socialization characteristics, and adolescent drug use: A path analysis. *Journal of Counseling Psychology, 34,* 205–213. (pp. 122, 250)

**Oetting, E. R., & Beauvais, F.** (1990). Adolescent drug use: Findings of national and local surveys. *Journal of Consulting and Clinical Psychology, 58,* 385–394. (p. 250)

**Oettingen, G., & Seligman, M. E. P.** (1990). Pessimism and behavioural signs of depression in East versus West Berlin. *European Journal of Social Psychology, 20,* 207–220. (p. 490)

**Offer, D., Ostrov, E., Howard, K. I., & Atkinson, R.** (1988). *The teenage world: Adolescents' self-image in ten countries.* New York: Plenum. (p. 125)

**Ogloff, J. R. P., Roberts, C. F., & Roesch, R.** (1993). The insanity defense: Legal standards and clinical assessment. *Applied and Preventive Psychology, 2,* 163–178. (p. 503)

**Olds, J.** (1958). Self-stimulation of the brain. *Science, 127,* 315–324. (p. 59)

**Olds, J.** (1975). Mapping the mind onto the brain. In F. G. Worden, J. P. Swazey, & G. Adelman (Eds.), *The neurosciences: Paths of discovery.* Cambridge, MA: MIT Press. (p. 58)

**Olds, J., & Milner, P.** (1954). Positive reinforcement produced by electrical stimulation of the septal area and other regions of rat brain. *Journal of Comparative and Physiological Psychology, 47,* 419–427. (p. 58)

**O'Leary, A.** (1990). Stress, emotion, and human immune function. *Psychological Bulletin, 108,* 363–382. (p. 585)

**Oliner, S. P., & Oliner, P. M.** (1988). *The altruistic personality: Rescuers of Jews in Nazi Europe.* New York: Free Press. (pp. 122, 282, 643)

**Oliver, M. B., & Hyde, J. S.** (1993). Gender differences in sexuality: A meta-analysis. *Psychological Bulletin, 114,* 29–51. (p. 672)

**Olshansky, S. J., Carnes, B. A., & Cassel, C. K.** (1993, April). The aging of the human species. *Scientific American,* pp. 46–52. (pp. 131–132)

**Olweus, D., Mattsson, A., Schalling, D., & Low, H.** (1988). Circulating testosterone levels and aggression in adolescent males: A causal analysis. *Psychosomatic Medicine, 50,* 261–272. (p. 633)

**O'Malley, P. M., & Bachman, J. G.** (1983). Self-esteem: Change and stability between ages 13 and 23. *Developmental Psychology, 19,* 257–268. (p. 124)

**O'Neill, M. J.** (1993). The relationship between privacy, control, and stress responses in office workers. Paper presented to the Human Factors and Ergonomics Society convention. (p. 580)

**Opton, E., Jr.** (1979, December). A psychologist takes a closer look at the recent landmark Larry P. opinion. *APA Monitor,* pp. 1, 4. (p. 359)

**Orne, M. T.** (1982, April 28). Affidavit submitted to State of Pennsylvania. (p. 237)

**Orne, M. T., & Evans, F. J.** (1965). Social control in the psychological experiment: Antisocial behavior and hypnosis. *Journal of Personality and Social Psychology, 1,* 189–200. (p. 235)

**Ornstein, R. E.** (1991). *The evolution of consciousness: Of Darwin, Freud, and cranial fire.* Englewood Cliffs, NJ: Prentice-Hall. (p. 60)

**Osgood, C. E.** (1962). *An alternative to war or surrender.* Urbana: University of Illinois Press. (p. 690)

**Osgood, C. E.** (1980). *GRIT: A strategy for survival in mankind's nuclear age?* Paper presented at the Pugwash Conference on New Directions in Disarmament. (p. 690)

**OSS Assessment Staff.** (1948). *The assessment of men.* New York: Rinehart. (p. 492)

**Ostfeld, A. M., Kasl, S. V., D'Atri, D. A., & Fitzgerald, E. F.** (1987). *Stress, crowding, and blood pressure in prison.* Hillsdale, NJ: Erlbaum. (p. 581)

**Padgett, V. R.** (1989). Predicting organizational violence: An application of 11 powerful principles of obedience. Paper presented to the American Psychological Association convention. (p. 624)

**Paffenbarger, R. S., Jr., Hyde, R. T., Wing, A. L., & Hsieh, C-C.** (1986). Physical activity, all-cause mortality, and longevity of college alumni. *New England Journal of Medicine, 314,* 605–612. (p. 593)

**Page, S.** (1977). Effects of the mental illness label in attempts to obtain accommodation. *Canadian Journal of Behavioral Science, 9,* 84–90. (p. 534)

**Paikoff, R. L., & Brooks-Gunn, J.** (1991). Do parent-child relationships change during puberty? *Psychological Bulletin, 110,* 47–66. (p. 125)

**Paivio, A.** (1986). *Mental representations: A dual coding approach.* New York: Oxford University Press. (p. 295)

**Palace, E. M., & Gorzalka, B. B.** (1990). The enhancing effects of anxiety on arousal in sexually dysfunctional and functional women. *Journal of Abnormal Psychology, 99,* 403–411. (p. 456)

**Palladino, J. J., & Carducci, B. J.** (1983). *"Things that go bump in the night": Students' knowledge of sleep and dreams.* Paper presented at the meeting of the Southeastern Psychological Association. (p. 221)

**Palmer, S., Schreiber, C., & Box, C.** (1991). Remembering the earthquake: "Flashbulb" memory for experienced vs. reported events. Paper presented to the Psychonomic Society convention. (p. 304)

**Palumbo, S. R.** (1978). *Dreaming and memory: A new information-processing model.* New York: Basic Books. (p. 229)

**Pandey, J., Sinha, Y., Prakash, A., & Tripathi, R. C.** (1982). Right-left political ideologies and attribution of the causes of poverty. *European Journal of Social Psychology, 12,* 327–331. (p. 615)

**Panksepp, J.** (1982). Toward a general psychobiological theory of emotions. *Behavioral and Brain Sciences, 5,* 407–467. (p. 435)

**Parducci, A.** (in press). *Happiness: A contextual theory of pleasure and pain.* New York: Oxford University Press. (p. 451)

**Park, D. C.** (1992). Applied cognitive aging research. In F. I. M. Craik & T. A. Salthouse (Eds.), *The handbook of aging and cognition.* Hillsdale, NJ: Erlbaum. (p. 138)

**Parke, R. D.** (1981). *Fathers.* Cambridge, MA: Harvard University Press. (p. 100)

**Parker, G., Roy, K., Hadzi, P. D., & Pedic, F.** (1992). Psychotic (delusional) depression: A meta-analyis of physical treatments. *Journal of Affective Disorders, 24,* 17–24. (p. 567)

**Parks, R. W., Loewenstein, D. A., Dodrill, K. L., Barker, W. W., Yoshi, F., Chang, J. Y., Emran, A., Apicella, A., Shermata, W. A., & Duara, R.** (1988). Cerebral metabolic effects of a verbal fluency test: A PET scan study. *Journal of Clinical and Experimental Neuropsychology, 10,* 565–575. (p. 376)

**Parloff, M. B.** (1987, February). Psychotherapy: An import from Japan. *Psychology Today,* pp. 74–75. (p. 540)

**Passell, P.** (1993, March 9). Like a new drug, social programs are put to the test. *New York Times,* pp. C1, C10. (p. 30)

**Passons, W. R.** (1975). *Gestalt approaches to counseling.* New York: Holt, Rinehart & Winston. (pp. 545–546)

**Pate, J. E., Pumariega, A. J., Hester, C., & Garner, D. M.** (1992). Cross-cultural patterns in eating disorders: A review. *Journal of the American Academy of Child and Adolescent Psychiatry, 31,* 802–809. (p. 406)

**Paton, D.** (1992). Disaster research: The Scottish dimension. *The Psychologist: Bulletin of the British Psychological Society, 5,* 535–538. (p. 577)

**Patrick, C. J., & Iacono, W. G.** (1991). Validity of the control question polygraph test: The problem of sampling bias. *Journal of Applied Psychology, 76,* 229–238. (p. 437)

**Patterson, F.** (1978, October). Conversations with a gorilla. *National Geographic,* pp. 438–465. (p. 348)

**Patterson, G. R., Chamberlain, P., & Reid, J. B.** (1982). A comparative evaluation of parent training procedures. *Behavior Therapy, 13,* 638–650. (p. 635)

**Patterson, R.** (1951). *The riddle of Emily Dickinson.* Boston: Houghton Mifflin. (p. 523)

**Pauls, D. L., Morton, L. A., & Egeland, J. A.** (1992). Risks of affective illness among first-degree relatives of bipolar I old-order Amish probands. *Archives of General Psychiatry, 49,* 703–708. (p. 518)

**Pavlov, I. P.** (1927). In G. V. Anrep (Trans.), *Conditioned reflexes.* London: Oxford University Press. (pp. 260, 263)

**Pedersen, N. L., Plomin, R., McClearn, G. E., & Friberg, L.** (1988). Neuroticism, extraversion, and related traits in adult twins reared apart and reared together. *Journal of Personality and Social Psychology, 55,* 950–957. (p. 109)

**Pekkanen, J.** (1982, June). Why do we sleep? *Science, 82,* p. 86. (p. 225)

**Pelham, B. W.** (1993). On the highly positive thoughts of the highly depressed. In R. F. Baumeister (Ed.), *Self-esteem: The puzzle of low self-regard.* New York: Plenum. (p. 483)

**Pellegrino, J. W.** (1985, October). Anatomy of analogy. *Psychology Today,* pp. 49–54. (p. 375)

**Penfield, W.** (1969). Consciousness, memory, and man's conditioned reflexes. In K. Pigram (Ed.), *On the biology of learning.* New York: Harcourt, Brace & World. (p. 302)

**Penfield, W.** (1975). *The mystery of the mind.* Princeton, NJ: Princeton University Press. (p. 252)

**Pennebaker, J.** (1990). *Opening up: The healing power of confiding in others.* New York: W. Morrow. (p. 598)

**Pennebaker, J. W.** (1982). *The psychology of physical symptoms.* New York: Springer-Verlag. (p. 590)

**Pennebaker, J. W., Barger, S. D., & Tiebout, J.** (1989). Disclosure of traumas and health among Holocaust survivors. *Psychosomatic Medicine, 51,* 577–589. (p. 598)

**Pennebaker, J. W., & Harber, K. D.** (1993). A social stage model of collective coping: The Loma Prieta earthquake and the Persian Gulf war. *Journal of Social Issues, 49,* 125–145. (p. 598)

**Pennebaker, J. W., & O'Heeron, R. C.** (1984). Confiding in others and illness rate among spouses of suicide and accidental death victims. *Journal of Abnormal Psychology, 93,* 473–476. (p. 598)

**Peplau, L. A.** (1982). Research on homosexual couples: An overview. *Journal of Homosexuality, 8*(2), 3–8. (p. 414)

**Peplau, L. A., & Gordon, S. L.** (1985). Women and men in love: Gender differences in close heterosexual relationships. In V. E. O'Leary, R. K. Unger, & B. S. Wallston (Eds.), *Women, gender, and social psychology.* Hillsdale, NJ: Erlbaum. (p. 20)

**Perkins, K. A., Dubbert, P. M., Martin, J. E., Faulstich, M. E., & Harris, J. K.** (1986). Cardiovascular reactivity to psychological stress in aerobically trained versus untrained mild hypertensives and normotensives. *Health Psychology, 5,* 407–421. (p. 593)

**Perlman, D.** (1991). *Age difference in loneliness: A meta analysis.* Vancouver, BC: University of British Columbia. (ERIC Document Reproduction Service No. ED 326767.) (p. 522)

**Perlmutter, M.** (1983). Learning and memory through adulthood. In M. W. Riley, B. B. Hess, & K. Bond (Eds.), *Aging in society: Selected reviews of recent research.* Hillsdale, NJ: Erlbaum. (p. 135)

**Perls, F. S.** (1969). *Ego, hunger and aggression: The beginning of Gestalt therapy.* New York: Random House. (p. 545)

**Perls, F. S.** (1970). Four lectures. In J. Fagan & I. L. Shepherd, *Gestalt therapy now.* Palo Alto, CA: Science and Behavior Books. (p. 545)

**Perls, F. S.** (1972). Gestalt therapy [interview]. In A. Bry (Ed.), *Inside psychotherapy.* New York: Basic Books. (p. 659)

**Perrett, D. I., Harries, M., Misflin, A. J., & Chitty, A. J.** (1988). Three stages in the classification of body movements by visual neurons. In H. B. Barlow, C. Blakemore, & M. Weston Smith (Eds.), *Images and understanding.* Cambridge, England: Cambridge University Press. (p. 163)

**Perris, E. E., Myers, N. A., & Clifton, R. K.** (1990). Long-term memory for a single infancy experience. *Child Development, 61,* 1796–1807. (p. 84)

**Persky, V. W., Kempthorne-Rawson, J., & Shekelle, R. B.** (1987). Personality and risk of cancer: 20-year follow-up of the Western Electric study. *Psychosomatic Medicine, 49,* 435–449. (p. 584)

**Persons, J. B.** (1986). The advantages of studying psychological phenomena rather than psychiatric diagnoses. *American Psychologist, 41,* 1252–1260. (p. 533)

**Pert, C.** (1986). Quoted in J. Hooper & D. Teresi, *The three-pound universe.* New York: Macmillan. (pp. 59, 69)

**Pert, C. B.** (1986, Summer). The wisdom of the receptors: Neuropeptides, the emotions, and bodymind. *Advances* (Institute for the Advancement of Health), *3,* 8–16. (p. 52)

**Pert, C. B., & Snyder, S. H.** (1973). Opiate receptor: Demonstration in nervous tissue. *Science, 179,* 1011–1014. (p. 46)

**Peschel, E. R., & Peschel, R. E.** (1987). Medical insights into the castrati in opera. *American Scientist, 75,* 578–583. (pp. 410–411)

**Peters, T. J., & Waterman, R. H., Jr.** (1982). *In search of excellence: Lessons from America's best-run companies.* New York: Harper & Row. (p. 279)

**Petersen, A. C.** (1987, September). Those gangly years. *Psychology Today,* pp. 28–34. (p. 119)

**Peterson, C., & Barrett, L. C.** (1987). Explanatory style and academic performance among university freshmen. *Journal of Personality and Social Psychology, 53,* 603–607. (p. 491)

**Peterson, C., Peterson, J., & Skevington, S.** (1986). Heated argument and adolescent development. *Journal of Social and Personal Relationships, 3,* 229–240. (p. 120)

**Peterson, L. R., & Peterson, M. J.** (1959). Short-term retention of individual verbal items. *Journal of Experimental Psychology, 58,* 193–198. (p. 300)

**Peterson, R.** (1978). Review of the Rorschach. In O. K. Buros (Ed.), *The eighth mental measurements yearbook* (Vol. I). Highland Park, NJ: Gryphon Press. (p. 468)

**Petitto, L. A., & Marentette, P. F.** (1991). Babbling in the manual mode: Evidence for the ontogeny of language. *Science, 251,* 1493–1496. (pp. 343, 346)

**Peto, R., Lopez, A. D., Boreham, J., Thun, M., & Heath, C., Jr.** (1992). Mortality from tobacco in developed countries: Indirect estimation from national vital statistics. *Lancet, 339,* 1268–1278. (p. 600)

**Petruzzello, S. J., Landers, D. M., Hatfield, B. D., Kubitz, K. A., & Salazar, W.** (1991). A meta-analysis on the anxiety-reducing effects of acute and chronic exercise. *Sports Medicine, 11,* 143–182. (p. 593)

**Pettegrew, J. W., Keshavan, M. S., & Minshew, N. J.** (1993). 31P nuclear magnetic resonance spectroscopy: Neurodevelopment and schizophrenia. *Schizophrenia Bulletin, 19,* 35–53. (p. 526)

**Pettigrew, T. F.** (1969). Racially separate or together? *Journal of Social Issues, 25,* 43–69. (p. 688)

**Pettingale, K. W., Morris, T., Greer, S., & Haybittle, J. L.** (1985, March 30). Mental attitudes to cancer: An additional prognostic factor. *Lancet,* p. 750. (p. 585)

**Pfeiffer, E.** (1977). Sexual behavior in old age. In E. W. Busse & E. Pfeiffer (Eds.), *Behavior and adaptation in late life* (2nd ed.). Boston: Little, Brown. (p. 133)

**Phares, V., & Compas, B. E.** (1992). The role of fathers in child and adolescent psychopathology: Make room for Daddy. *Psychological Bulletin, 111,* 387–412. (p. 100)

**Phillips, D., & Stipek, D.** (1993). Early formal schooling: Are we promoting achievement or anxiety? *Applied and Preventive Psychology, 2,* 141–150. (p. 386)

**Phillips, D. P.** (1982). The impact of fictional television stories on U.S. adult fatalities: New evidence on the effect of the mass media on violence. *American Journal of Sociology,* 87, 1340–1359. (p. 620)

**Phillips, D. P.** (1985). Natural experiments on the effects of mass media violence on fatal aggression: Strengths and weaknesses of a new approach. In L. Berkowitz (Ed.), *Advances in experimental social psychology* (Vol. 19). Orlando, FL: Academic Press. (p. 620)

**Phillips, D. P., Carstensen, L. L., & Paight, D. J.** (1989). Effects of mass media news stories on suicide, with new evidence on the role of story content. In D. R. Pfeffer (Ed.), *Suicide among youth: Perspectives on risk and prevention.* Washington, DC: American Psychiatric Press. (p. 620)

**Phillips, J. L.** (1969). *Origins of intellect: Piaget's theory.* San Francisco: Freeman. (p. 92)

**Phillips, M. R., Wolf, A. S., & Coons, D. J.** (1988). Psychiatry and the criminal justice system: Testing the myths. *American Journal of Psychiatry, 145,* 605–610. (p. 534)

**Phinney, J. S.** (1990). Ethnic identity in adolescents and adults: Review of research. *Psychological Bulletin, 108,* 499–514. (pp. 663–664)

**Piaget, J.** (1930). *The child's conception of physical causality.* London: Routledge & Kegan Paul. (p. 88)

**Piaget, J.** (1932). *The moral judgment of the child.* New York: Harcourt, Brace & World. (p. 92)

**Piaget, J.** (1972). Intellectual evolution from adolescence to adulthood. *Human Development, 15,* 1–12. (p. 120)

**Piccione, C., Hilgard, E. R., & Zimbardo, P. G.** (1989). On the degree of stability of measured hypnotizability over a 25-year period. *Journal of Personality and Social Psychology, 56,* 289–295. (p. 234)

**Pickar, D., Labarca, R., Linnoila, M., Roy, A., Hommer, D., Everett, D., & Payl, S. M.** (1984). Neuroleptic-induced decrease in plasma homovanillic acid and antipsychotic activity in schizophrenic patients. *Science, 225,* 954–957. (p. 565)

**Pike, K. M., & Rodin, J.** (1991). Mothers, daughters, and disordered eating. *Journal of Abnormal Psychology, 100,* 198–204. (p. 406)

**Pinel, J. P. J.** (1993). *Biopsychology* (2nd ed.). Boston: Allyn & Bacon. (p. 403)

**Pinker, S.** (1990, September-October). Quoted in J. de Cuevas, "No, she holded them loosely." *Harvard Magazine*, pp. 60–67. (p. 341)

**Piotrowski, C., & Keller, J. W.** (1989). Psychological testing in outpatient mental health facilities: A national study. *Professional Psychology: Research and Practice, 20*, 423–425. (pp. 469, 477)

**Pittman, T. S., Davey, M. E., Alafat, K. A., Vetherill, K. V., & Kramer, N. A.** (1980). Informational versus controlling verbal rewards. *Personality and Social Psychology Bulletin, 6*, 228–233. (p. 423)

**Pleck, J. H., Sonenstein, F. L., & Ku, L. C.** (1993). Masculinity ideology: Its impact on adolescent males' heterosexual relationships. *Journal of Social Issues, 49*, 11–29. (p. 672)

**Pliner, P.** (1982). The effects of mere exposure on liking for edible substances. *Appetite: Journal for Intake Research, 3*, 283–290. (p. 405)

**Pliner, P., & Pelchat, M. L.** (1991). Neophobia in humans and the special status of foods of animal origin. *Appetite, 16*, 205–218. (p. 405)

**Pliner, P., Pelchat, M., & Grabski, M.** (1993). Reduction of neophobia in humans by exposure to novel foods. *Appetite, 20*, 111–123. (p. 405)

**Plomin, R.** (1990a). The role of inheritance in behavior. *Science, 248*, 183–188. (p. 109)

**Plomin, R., & Bergeman, C. S.** (1991). The nature of nurture: Genetic influence on "environmental" measures. *Behavioral and Brain Sciences, 14*, 373–427. (p. 113)

**Plomin, R., & Daniels, D.** (1987). Why are children in the same family so different from one another? *Behavioral and Brain Sciences, 10*, 1–60. (p. 112)

**Plomin, R., McClearn, G. E., Pedersen, N. L., Nesselroade, J. R., & Bergeman, C. S.** (1988). Genetic influence on childhood family environment perceived retrospectively from the last half of the life span. *Developmental Psychology, 24*, 37–45. (p. 113)

**Plomin, R., McClearn, G. E., Smith, D. L., Vignetti, S., Chorney, M. J., Chorney, K., Venditti, C. P., Kasarda, S., Thompson, L. A., Detterman, D. K., Daniels, J., Owen, M., & McGuffin, P.** (1994). DNA markers associated with high versus low IQ: The IQ QTL project. *Behavior Genetics*, in press. (p. 383)

**Plomin, R., Reiss, D., Hetherington, E. M., & Howe, G. W.** (1994). Nature and nurture: Genetic contributions to measures of the family environment. *Developmental Psychology, 30*, 32–43. (p. 113)

**Plomin, R., & Rende, R.** (1991). Human behavioral genetics. *Annual Review of Psychology, 42*, 161–190. (p. 384)

**Plous, S.** (1993). Psychological mechanisms in the human use of animals. *Journal of Social Issues, 49*(1), 11–52. (p. 34)

**Plous, S.** (1993). The nuclear arms race: Prisoner's dilemma or perceptual dilemma? *Journal of Peace Research, 30*, 163–179. (p. 688)

**Polich, J., Pollock, V. E., & Bloom, F. E.** (1994). Meta-analysis of P300 amplitude from males at risk for alcoholism. *Psychological Bulletin, 115*, 55–73. (p. 249)

**Polivy, J., & Herman, C. P.** (1985). Dieting and binging: A causal analysis. *American Psychologist, 40*, 193–201. (p. 609)

**Polivy, J., & Herman, C. P.** (1987). Diagnosis and treatment of normal eating. *Journal of Personality and Social Psychology, 55*, 635–644. (pp. 607, 609)

**Pollard, R.** (1992). 100 years in psychology and deafness: A centennial retrospective. Invited address to the American Psychological Association convention, Washington, DC. (p. 353)

**Pomerleau, O. F., Collins, A. C., Shiffman, S., & Pomerleau, C. S.** (1993). Why some people smoke and others do not: New perspectives. *Journal of Consulting and Clinical Psychology, 61*, 723–731. (p. 601)

**Pomeroy, W. B.** (1972). *Dr. Kinsey and the Institute for Sex Research.* New York: Harper & Row. (p. 408)

**Pons, T. P., Garraghty, P. E., Ommaya, A. K., Kaas, J. H., Taub, E., & Mishkin, M.** (1991). Massive cortical reorganization after sensory deafferentation in adult macaques. *Science, 252*, 1857–1860. (p. 86)

**Poole, D. A., Lindsay, D. S., Memon, A., & Bull, R.** (1994). Psychotherapy and the recovery of memories of childhood sexual abuse: U.S. and British practitioners' opinions, practices, and experiences. Unpublished manuscript, Central Michigan University. (p. 318)

**Poon, L. W.** (1987). Myths and truisms: Beyond extant analyses of speed of behavior and age. Address to the Eastern Psychological Association convention. (p. 133)

**Popenoe, D.** (1993). The evolution of marriage and the problem of stepfamilies: A biosocial perspective. Paper presented at the National Symposium on Stepfamilies, Pennsylvania State University. (p. 660)

**Porter, D., & Neuringer, A.** (1984). Music discriminations by pigeons. *Journal of Experimental Psychology: Animal Behavior Processes, 10*, 138–148. (p. 269)

**Posner, M. I., & Carr, T. H.** (1992). Lexical access and the brain: Anatomical constraints on cognitive models of word recognition. *American Journal of Psychology, 105*, 1–26. (p. 64)

**Powell, J.** (1989). *Happiness is an inside job.* Valencia, CA: Tabor. (p. 484)

**Powell, K. E., Thompson, P. D., Caspersen, C. J., & Kendrick, J. S.** (1987). Physical activity and the incidence of coronary heart disease. *Annual Review of Public Health, 8*, 253–287. (p. 593)

**Powell, M. C., & Fazio, R. H.** (1984). Attitude accessibility as a function of repeated attitudinal expression. *Personality and Social Psychology Bulletin, 10*, 139–148. (p. 616)

**Powers, D. E.** (1986). Relations of test item characteristics to test preparation/test practice effects: A quantitative summary. *Psychological Bulletin, 100*, 67–77. (p. 369)

**Pratkanis, A. R.** (1992). The cargo-cult science of subliminal persuasion. *Skeptical Inquirer, 16*, 260–272. (p. 153)

**Pratkanis, A. R., & Greenwald, A. G.** (1988). Recent perspectives on unconscious processing: Still no marketing applications. *Psychology and Marketing, 5*, 337–353. (p. 155)

**Pratt, M. W., Pancer, M., Hunsberger, B., & Manchester, J.** (1990). Reasoning about the self and relationships in maturity: An integrative complexity analysis of individual differences. *Journal of Personality and Social Psychology, 59*, 575–581. (p. 672)

**Premack, D.** (1983). The codes of man and beasts. *The Behavioral and Brain Sciences, 6*, 125–167. (p. 353)

**Prentice, D. A., & Miller, D. T.** (1993). Pluralistic ignorance and alcohol use on campus: Some consequences of misperceiving the social norm. *Journal of Personality and Social Psychology, 64,* 243–256. (p. 250)

**Presley, C. A., & Meilman, P. W.** (1992). *Alcohol and drugs on American college campuses: Report to college presidents.* Carbondale, IL: Student Health Program, Southern Illinois University. (p. 242)

**Prioleau, L., Murdock, M., & Brody, N.** (1983). An analysis of psychotherapy versus placebo studies. *The Behavioral and Brain Sciences, 6,* 275–310. (p. 560)

**Pritchard, R. M.** (1961, June). Stabilized images on the retina. *Scientific American,* pp. 72–78. (p. 157)

**Project on Redefining the Meaning and Purpose of Baccalaureate Degrees.** (1985). *Integrity in the college curriculum.* Washington, DC: Association of American Colleges. (p. 30)

**Prothrow-Stith, D.** (1991). *Deadly consequences.* New York: HarperCollins. (p. 635)

**Psychic Abscam.** (1983, March). *Discover,* p. 10. (p. 212)

***Public Opinion.*** (1984, August/September). Phears and Phobias, p. 32. (p. 506)

***Public Opinion.*** (1984, August/September). Tradeoffs, p. 36. (p. 19)

***Public Opinion.*** (1985, February/March). Defining woman's place, p. 40. (p. 19)

***Public Opinion.*** (1987, May/June). Teen angels (report of University of Michigan survey), p. 32. (p. 118)

**Pugh, G. E.,** (1977). *The biological origin of human values.* New York: Basic Books (p. 69)

**Pulver, A. E., Liang, K-Y., Brown, C. H., Wolyniec, P., McGrath, J., Adler, L., Tam, D., Carpenter, W. T., & Childs, B.** (1992). Risk factors in schizophrenia: Season of birth, gender, and familial risk. *British Journal of Psychiatry, 160,* 65–71. (p. 526)

**Putnam, F. W.** (1991). Recent research on multiple personality disorder. *Psychiatric Clinics of North America, 14,* 489–502. (p. 513)

**Pyszczynski, T., Hamilton, J. C., Greenberg, J., & Becker, S. E.** (1991). Self-awareness and psychological dysfunction. In C. R. Snyder & D. O. Forsyth (Eds.), *Handbook of social and clinical psychology: The health perspective.* New York: Pergamon. (p. 521)

**Qualls, P. J., & Sheehan, P. W.** (1981). Electromyograph biofeedback as a relaxation technique: A critical appraisal and reassessment. *Psychological Bulletin, 90,* 21–42. (p. 595)

**Quasha, S.** (1980). *Albert Einstein: An intimate portrait.* New York: Forest. (p. 378)

**Rabin, A. S., Kaslow, N. J., & Rehm, L. P.** (1986). Aggregate outcome and follow-up results following self-control therapy for depression. Paper presented at the American Psychological Association convention. (p. 553)

**Radecki, T.** (1989, February-March). On picking good television and film entertainment. *NCTV News, 10*(1–2), p. 5. (p. 636)

**Ramey, S. L., & Ramey, C. T.** (1992). Early educational intervention with disadvantaged children—To what effect? *Applied and Preventive Psychology, 1,* 131–140. (pp. 86, 386)

**Rand, C. S. W., & Macgregor, A. M. C.** (1990). Morbidly obese patients' perceptions of social discrimination before and after surgery for obesity. *Southern Medical Journal, 83,* 1390–1395. (p. 604)

**Rand, C. S. W., & Macgregor, A. M. C.** (1991). Successful weight loss following obesity surgery and the perceived liability or morbid obesity. *Internal Journal of Obesity, 15,* 577–579. (p. 604)

**Randi, J.** (1983a, Summer). The Project Alpha experiment: Part 1. The first two years. *The Skeptical Inquirer,* pp. 24–33. (p. 212)

**Randi, J.** (1983b, Fall). The Project Alpha experiment: Part 2. Beyond the laboratory. *The Skeptical Inquirer,* pp. 36–45. (pp. 12, 212)

**Rapoport, J. L.** (1989, March). The biology of obsessions and compulsions. *Scientific American,* pp. 83–89. (pp. 507, 509)

**Raskin, D. C.** (1982). University of Utah, as shown in *Science '82,* June, 24-27. (p. 436)

**Rauch, S. L., & Jenike, M. A.** (1993). Neurobiological models of obsessive-compulsive disorder. *Psychomatics, 34,* 20–32. (p. 509)

**Razran, G. H. S.** (1940). Conditioned response changes in rating and appraising sociopolitical solutions. *Psychological Bulletin, 37,* 481. (p. 267)

**Reagan, N., & Libby, B.** (1980). *Nancy.* New York: Morrow. (p. 139)

**Reagan, R.** (1988, December 21). Television interview with David Brinkley, broadcast December 22, and reported by wire services on December 23. (p. 615)

**Reason, J.** (1987). The Chernobyl errors. *Bulletin of the British Psychological Society, 40,* 201–206. (p. 629)

**Reason, J., & Mycielska, K.** (1982). *Absent-minded? The psychology of mental lapses and everyday errors.* Englewood Cliffs, NJ: Prentice-Hall. (p. 206)

**Reed, T. E., & Jensen, A. R.** (1992). Conduction velocity in a brain nerve pathway of normal adults correlates with intelligence level. *Intelligence, 16,* 259–272. (p. 376)

**Regier, D. A., Narrow, W. E., Rae, D. S., Manderscheid, R. W., Locke, B. Z., & Goodwin, F. K.** (1993). The de facto U.S. mental and addictive disorders service system: Epidemiologic catchment area prospective 1-year prevalence rates of disorders and services. *Archives of General Psychiatry, 50,* 85–94. (p. 556)

**Reisenzein, R.** (1983). The Schachter theory of emotion: Two decades later. *Psychological Bulletin, 94,* 239–264. (p. 456)

**Reiser, M.** (1982). *Police psychology.* Los Angeles: LEHI. (p. 212)

**Reiss, A. J., Jr., & Roth, J. A.** (Eds.) (1993). *Understanding and preventing violence.* Washington, DC: National Academy Press. (p. 633)

**Remley, A.** (1988, October). From obedience to independence. *Psychology Today,* pp. 56–59. (p. 105)

**Renner, M. J., & Rosenzweig, M. R.** (1987). Enriched and impoverished environments: Effects on brain and behavior. New York: Springer-Verlag. (p. 85)

**Rescorla, R. A.** (1988). Pavlovian conditioning: It's not what you think it is. *American Psychologist, 43,* 151–160. (p. 263)

**Rescorla, R. A., & Wagner, A. R.** (1972). A theory of Pavlovian conditioning: Variations in the effectiveness of reinforcement and nonreinforcement. In A. H. Black & W. F. Perokasy (Eds.), *Classical conditioning II: Current theory.* New York: Appleton-Century-Crofts. (p. 263)

**Resnick, S. M.** (1992). Positron emission tomography in psychiatric illness. *Current Directions in Psychological Science, 1,* 92–98. (p. 509)

**Ressler, R. K., Burgess, A. W., & Douglas, J. E.** (1988). *Sexual homicide patterns.* Boston: Lexington Books. (p. 638)

**Retterstol, N.** (1993). *Suicide: A European perspective.* New York: Cambridge University Press. (p. 516)

**Reveen, P. J.** (1987–88). Fantasizing under hypnosis: Some experimental evidence. *The Skeptical Inquirer, 12,* 181–183. (p. 237)

**Reynolds, D. K.** (1982). *The quiet therapies.* Honolulu: University of Hawaii Press. (p. 182)

**Reynolds, D. K.** (1986). *Even in summer the ice doesn't melt: Japan's Morita Therapy.* New York: Morrow (Quill paperback). (p. 182)

**Rheingold, H. L.** (1985). Development as the acquisition of familiarity. *Annual Review of Psychology, 36,* 1–17. (p. 96)

**Rhodes, S. R.** (1983). Age-related differences in work attitudes and behavior: A review and conceptual analysis. *Psychological Bulletin, 93,* 328–367. (p. 133)

**Rice, B.** (1985, September). Performance review: The job nobody likes. *Psychology Today,* pp. 30–36. (p. 615)

**Rice, M. E., & Grusec, J. E.** (1975). Saying and doing: Effects on observer performance. *Journal of Personality and Social Psychology, 32,* 584–593. (p. 282)

**Richardson, J.** (1993). The curious case of coins: Remembering the appearance of familiar objects. *The Psychologist: Bulletin of the British Psychological Society, 6,* 360–366. (p. 298)

**Richardson, J. T. E.** (1990). Questionnaire studies of paramenstrual symptoms. *Psychology of Women Quarterly, 14,* 15–42. (p. 591)

**Richardson, J. T. E.** (1993). The premenstrual syndrome: A brief history. Paper presented to the Annual Conference of the British Psychological Society. (p. 591)

**Richardson, J. T. E., & Zucco, G. M.** (1989). Cognition and olfaction: A review. *Psychological Bulletin, 105,* 352–360. (p. 180)

**Rieff, P.** (1979). *Freud: The mind of a moralist* (3rd ed.). Chicago: University of Chicago Press. (p. 471)

**Ring, K.** (1980). *Life at death: A scientific investigation of the near-death experience.* New York: Coward, McCann & Geoghegan. (p. 251)

**Ring, K.** (1992). *The omega project: Near death experiences, UFO encounters, and mind at large.* New York: Morrow. (p. 252)

**Riskind, J. H., Beck, A. T., Berchick, R. J., Brown, G., & Steer, R. A.** (1987). Reliability of DSM-III diagnoses for major depression and generalized anxiety disorder using the structured clinical interview for DSM-III. *Archives of General Psychiatry, 44,* 817–820. (p. 504)

**Roberts, L.** (1988). Beyond Noah's ark: What do we need to know? *Science, 242,* 1247. (p. 581)

**Roberts, M., & Harris, T. G.** (1989). Wellness at work. *Psychology Today,* pp. 54–58. (p. 599)

**Roberts, T-A.** (1991). Gender and the influence of evaluations on self-assessments in achievement settings. *Psychological Bulletin, 109,* 297–308. (p. 670)

**Robins, L., & Regier, D.** (Eds.). (1991). *Psychiatric disorders in America.* New York: Free Press. (pp. 499, 532)

**Robins, L. N., Davis, D. H., & Goodwin, D. W.** (1974). Drug use by U.S. Army enlisted men in Vietnam: A follow-up on their return home. *American Journal of Epidemiology, 99,* 235–249. (p. 246)

**Robinson, J. L., Kagan, J., Reznick, J. S., & Corley, R.** (1992). The heritability of inhibited and uninhibited behavior: A twin study. *Developmental Psychology, 28,* 1030–1037. (p. 98)

**Robinson, V. M.** (1983). Humor and health. In P. E. McGhee & J. H. Goldstein (Eds.), *Handbook of humor research: Vol. II. Applied studies.* New York: Springer-Verlag. (p. 596)

**Rochat, F.** (1993). How did they resist authority? Protecting refugees in Le Chambon during World War II. Paper presented at the American Psychological Association convention. (p. 625)

**Rock, I., & Palmer, S.** (1990, December). The legacy of Gestalt psychology. *Scientific American,* pp. 84–90. (pp. 190, 192)

**Rodin, J.** (1979). *Obesity theory and behavior therapy: An uneasy couple?* Paper presented at the meeting of the Association for the Advancement of Behavior Therapy. (p. 609)

**Rodin, J.** (1984, December). A sense of control [interview]. *Psychology Today,* pp. 38–45. (p. 405)

**Rodin, J.** (1985). Insulin levels, hunger and food intake: An example of feedback loops in body weight regulation. *Health Psychology, 4,* 1–18. (p. 609)

**Rodin, J.** (1986). Aging and health: Effects of the sense of control. *Science, 233,* 1271–1276. (pp. 490, 580–581)

**Rodin, J., & Slochower, J.** (1976). Externality in the non-obese: Effects of environmental responsiveness on weight. *Journal of Personality and Social Psychology, 33,* 338–344. (p. 405)

**Rodin, M.** (1992). The social construction of premenstrual syndrome. *Social Science and Medicine, 35,* 49–56. (p. 591)

**Roediger, H. L., III, Wheeler, M. A., & Rajaram, S.** (1993). Remembering, knowing, and reconstructing the past. In D. L. Medin (Ed.), *The psychology of learning and motivation: Advances in research and theory* (Vol. 30). Orlando, FL: Academic Press. (p. 312)

**Roemer, M. I.** (1991). *National health systems of the world: Vol. I.The countries.* New York: Oxford University Press. (p. 599)

**Roger, L. H., Cortes, D. E., & Malgady, R. B.** (1991). Acculturation and mental health status among Hispanics: Convergence and new directions for research. *American Psychologist, 46,* 585–597. (p. 664)

**Rogers, C. R.** (1958). Reinhold Niebuhr's *The self and the dramas of history:* A criticism. *Pastoral Psychology, 9,* 15–17. (p. 483)

**Rogers, C. R.** (1961). *On becoming a person: A therapist's view of psychotherapy.* Boston: Houghton Mifflin. (p. 543)

**Rogers, C. R.** (1970). *Carl Rogers on encounter groups.* New York: Harper & Row. (p. 554)

**Rogers, C. R.** (1980). *A way of being.* Boston: Houghton Mifflin. (pp. 480–481, 543)

**Rogers, C. R.** (1981). Notes on Rollo May. *Perspectives, 2*(1), 16. (p. 487)

**Rogers, S.** (1992–1993, Winter). How a publicity blitz created the myth of subliminal advertising. *Public Relations Quarterly,* pp. 12–17. (p. 154)

**Rogers, S.** (1994). Subliminal advertising: Grand scam of the 20th century. Paper presented to the American Academy of Advertising convention. (pp. 154, 197)

**Rogers, S. M., & Turner, C. F.** (1991). Male-male sexual contact in the U.S.A.: Findings from five sample surveys, 1970–1990. *Journal of Sex Research, 28,* 491–519. (p. 413)

**Rogerson, P. A.** (1994). On the relationship between handedness and longevity. *Social Biology, 40,* 283–287. (p. 587)

**Rohner, R. P.** (1986). *The warmth dimension: Foundations of parental acceptance-rejection theory.* Newbury Park, CA: Sage. (p. 106)

**Rohner, R. P.** (1994). Patterns of parenting: The warmth dimension in worldwide perspective. In W. J. Lonner & R. Malpass (Eds.), *Psychology and culture.* Boston: Allyn & Bacon. (p. 104)

**Rook, K. S.** (1984). Promoting social bonding: Strategies for helping the lonely and socially isolated. *American Psychologist, 39,* 1389–1407. (p. 522)

**Rook, K. S.** (1987). Social support versus companionship: Effects on life stress, loneliness, and evaluations by others. *Journal of Personality and Social Psychology, 52,* 1132–1147. (p. 598)

**Rosch, E.** (1974). Linguistic relativity. In A. Silverstein (Ed.), *Human communication: Theoretical perspectives.* New York: Halsted Press. (p. 352)

**Rosch, E.** (1978). Principles of categorization. In E. Rosch & B. L. Lloyd (Eds.), *Cognition and categorization.* Hillsdale, NJ: Erlbaum. (p. 326)

**Rose, G. A., & Williams, R. T.** (1961). Metabolic studies on large and small eaters. *British Journal of Nutrition, 1,* 1–9. (p. 606)

**Rose, R. J., Koskenvuo, M., Kaprio, J., Sarna, S., & Langinvainio, H.** (1988). Shared genes, shared experiences, and similarity of personality: Data from 14,228 adult Finnish co-twins. *Journal of Personality and Social Psychology, 54,* 161–171. (p. 108)

**Rose, S.** (1983). *The conscious brain.* New York: Knopf. (p. 63)

**Rosenbaum, M.** (1986). The repulsion hypothesis: On the nondevelopment of relationships. *Journal of Personality and Social Psychology,* 51, 1156–1166. (p. 647)

**Rosenberg, R.** (1984). Leta Hollingworth: Toward a sexless intelligence. In M. Lewin (Ed.), *In the shadow of the past: Psychology portrays the sexes.* New York: Columbia University Press. (p. 591)

**Rosenfeld, S. P.** (1987, March 29). Insanity defense is riskier now and can turn winners to losers. Associated Press release (*Grand Rapids Press,* p. A17). (p. 503)

**Rosenhan, D. L.** (1973). On being sane in insane places. *Science, 179,* 250–258. (p. 533)

**Rosenstein, M. J., Milazzo-Sayre, L. J., & Manderscheid, R. W.** (1989). Care of persons with schizophrenia: A statistical profile. *Schizophrenia Bulletin, 15,* 45–58. (p. 499)

**Rosenthal, D. A., & Feldman, S. S.** (1992). The nature and stability of ethnic identity in Chinese youth: Effects of length of residence in two cultural contexts. *Journal of Cross-Cultural Psychology, 23,* 214–227. (p. 664)

**Rosenthal, R., Hall, J. A., Archer, D., DiMatteo, M. R., & Rogers, P. L.** (1979). The PONS test: Measuring sensitivity to nonverbal cues. In S. Weitz (Ed.), *Nonverbal communication* (2nd ed.). New York: Oxford University Press. (p. 438)

**Rosenzweig, M. R.** (1984). Experience, memory, and the brain. *American Psychologist, 39,* 365–376. (p. 85)

**Rosenzweig, M. R.** (1992). Psychological science around the world. *American Psychologist, 47,* 718–722. (p. 2)

**Ross, H.** (1975, June 19). Mist, murk, and visual perception. *New Scientist,* pp. 658–660. (p. 190)

**Ross, L., Greene, D., & House, P.** (1977). The false consensus effect: An egocentric bias in social perception and attribution process. *Journal of Experimental Social Psychology, 13,* 279–301. (p. 19)

**Ross, L., & Stillinger, C.** (1991). Barriers to conflict resolution. *Negotiation Journal, 7,* 389–404. (p. 690)

**Ross, M., McFarland, C., & Fletcher, G. J. O.** (1981). The effect of attitude on the recall of personal histories. *Journal of Personality and Social Psychology, 40,* 627–634. (p. 316)

**Rosser, P. L., & Randolph, S. M.** (1989). Black American infants: The Howard University normative study. In J. K. Nuegent, B. M. Lester, & T. B. Brazelton (Eds.), *The cultural context of infancy: Vol. 1. Biology, culture, and infant development.* Norwood, NJ: Ablex. (p. 87)

**Rossi, A. S., & Rossi, P. H.** (1993). *Of human bonding: Parent-child relations across the life course.* Hawthorne, NY: Aldine de Gruyter. (p. 669)

**Rossi, P. J.** (1968). Adaptation and negative aftereffect to lateral optical displacement in newly hatched chicks. *Science, 160,* 430–432. (p. 204)

**Roth, T., Roehrs, T., Zwyghuizen-Doorenbos, A., Stpeanski, E., & Witting, R.** (1988). Sleep and memory. In I. Hindmarch & H. Ott (Eds.), *Benzodiazepine receptor ligans, memory and information processing.* New York: Springer-Verlag. (p. 228)

**Rothbart, M., Fulero, S., Jensen, C., Howard, J., & Birrell, P.** (1978). From individual to group impressions: Availability heuristics in stereotype formation. *Journal of Experimental Social Psychology, 14,* 237–255. (p. 685)

**Rothblum, E. D.** (1990). Women and weight: Fad and fiction. *Journal of Psychology, 124,* 5–24. (p. 607)

**Rothstein, W. G.** (1980). The significance of occupations in work careers: An empirical and theoretical review. *Journal of Vocational Behavior, 17,* 328–343. (p. 141)

**Rotton, J., & Kelly, I. W.** (1985). Much ado about the full moon: A meta-analysis of lunar-lunacy research. *Psychological Bulletin, 97,* 286–306. (p. 530)

**Rovee-Collier, C.** (1993). The capacity for long-term memory in infancy. *Current Directions in Psychological Science, 2,* 130–135. (p. 309)

**Roviaro, S., Holmes, D. S., & Holmsten, R. D.** (1984). Influence of a cardiac rehabilitation program on the cardiovascular, psychological, and social functioning of cardiac patients. *Journal of Behavioral Medicine, 7,* 61–81. (p. 593)

**Rowe, D. C.** (1990). As the twig is bent? The myth of child-rearing influences on personality development. *Journal of Counseling and Development, 68,* 606–611. (p. 110)

**Rowe, D. C., Vazsonyi, A. T., & Flannery, D. J.** (1994). No more than skin deep: Ethnic and racial similarity in developmental process. *Psychological Review, 101,* 396–413. (pp. 106, 392)

**Rozee, P. D.** (1993). Forbidden or forgiven: Rape in cross-cultural perspective. *Psychology of Women Quarterly, 17,* 499–514. (p. 637)

**Rozin, P.** (1976). The selection of food by rats, humans and other animals. In J. Rosenblatt, R. A. Hinde, C. Beer, & E. Shaw (Eds.), *Advances in the study of behavior* (Vol. 6). New York: Academic Press. (p. 405)

**Rozin, P., Millman, L., & Nemeroff, C.** (1986). Operation of the laws of sympathetic magic in disgust and other domains. *Journal of Personality and Social Psychology, 50,* 703–712. (p. 263)

**Ruback, R. B., Carr, T. S., & Hopper, C. H.** (1986). Perceived control in prison: Its relation to reported crowding, stress, and symptoms. *Journal of Applied Social Psychology, 16,* 375–386. (p. 490)

**Rubin, J. Z., Pruitt, D. G., & Kim, S. H.** (1994). *Social conflict: Escalation, stalemate, and settlement.* New York: McGraw-Hill. (p. 689)

**Rubin, L. B.** (1985). *Just friends: The role of friendship in our lives.* New York: Harper & Row. (p. 670)

**Rubin, Z.** (1970). Measurement of romantic love. *Journal of Personality and Social Psychology, 16,* 265–273. (p. 438)

**Rubonis, A. V., & Bickman, L.** (1991). Psychological impairment in the wake of disaster: The disaster-psychopathology relationship. *Psychological Bulletin, 109,* 384–399. (p. 577)

**Ruchlis, H.** (1990). *Clear thinking: A practical introduction.* Buffalo, NY: Prometheus Books. (p. 327)

**Rule, B. G., & Ferguson, T. J.** (1986). The effects of media violence on attitudes, emotions, and cognitions. *Journal of Social Issues, 42*(3), 29–50. (p. 637)

**Rumbaugh, D. M.** (1977). *Language learning by a chimpanzee: The Lana project.* New York: Academic Press. (p. 348)

**Rumbaugh, D. M.** (1985). Comparative psychology: Patterns in adaptation. In A. M. Rogers & C. J. Scheirer (Eds.), *The G. Stanley Hall Lecture Series* (Vol. 5). Washington, DC: American Psychological Association. (p. 350)

**Rumbaugh, D. M.** (1987, September 17). Personal communication. (p. 350)

**Rumbaugh, D. M.** (1994, February 15). Remarks on "Nova: Can chimps talk?" Public Broadcasting Service. (p. 350)

**Rumbaugh, D. M., & Savage-Rumbaugh, S.** (1978). Chimpanzee language research: Status and potential. *Behavior Research Methods & Instrumentation, 10,* 119–131. (p. 350)

**Rumbaugh, D. M., & Savage-Rumbaugh, S.** (1986). Reasoning and language in chimpanzees. In R. J. Hoage & L. Goldman (Eds.), *Animal intelligence.* Washington, DC: Smithsonian Institution Press. (pp. 328, 350)

**Rumbaugh, D. M., & Savage-Rumbaugh, S.** (1994, January/February). Language and apes. *Psychology Teacher Network,* pp. 2–5, 9. (p. 350)

**Rumelhart, D. E.** (1989). The architecture of mind: A connectionist approach. In M. Posner (Ed.), *Foundations of cognitive science.* Cambridge, MA: MIT Press. (p. 163)

**Rushton, J. P.** (1975). Generosity in children: Immediate and long-term effects of modeling, preaching, and moral judgment. *Journal of Personality and Social Psychology, 31,* 459–466. (p. 282)

**Rushton, J. P.** (1989). Genetic similarity, human altruism, and group selection. *Behavioral and Brain Sciences, 12,* 503–559. (p. 643)

**Rushton, J. P.** (1990). Race differences, r/K theory, and a reply to Flynn. *The Psychologist: Bulletin of the British Psychological Society, 5,* 195–198. (p. 388)

**Rushton, J. P., Fulker, D. W., Neale, M. C., Nias, D. K. B., & Eysenck, H. J.** (1986). Altruism and aggression: The heritability of individual differences. *Journal of Personality and Social Psychology, 50,* 1192–1198. (p. 632)

**Russell, B.** (1930/1985). *The conquest of happiness.* London: Unwin Paperbacks. (p. 452)

**Russell, J. A.** (1991). Culture and the categorization of emotions. *Psychological Bulletin, 110,* 426–450. (p. 441)

**Russell, J. A., Lewicka, M., & Niit, T.** (1989). A cross-cultural study of a circumplex model of affect. *Journal of Personality and Social Psychology, 57,* 848–856. (p. 443)

**Russo, N. F.** (1992). Abortion, childbearing, and women's well-being. *Professional Psychology: Research and Practice, 23,* 269–280. (p. 578)

**Rutter, M.** (1979). Maternal deprivation, 1972–1978: New findings, new concepts, new approaches. *Child Development, 50,* 283–305. (p. 99)

**Ryan, E. D.** (1980). Attribution, intrinsic motivation, and athletics: A replication and extension. In C. H. Nadeau, W. R. Halliwell, K. M. Newell, & G. C. Roberts (Eds.), *Psychology of motor behavior and sport—1979.* Champaign, IL: Human Kinetics Press. (p. 422)

**Ryckman, R. M., Robbins, M. A., Kaczor, L. M., & Gold J. A.** (1989). Male and female raters' stereotyping of male and female physiques. *Personality and Social Psychology Bulletin, 15,* 244–251. (p. 604)

**Rymer, R.** (1993). *Genie: An abused child's flight from silence.* New York: HarperCollins. (p. 346)

**Rzewnicki, R., & Forgays, D. G.** (1987). Recidivism and self-cure of smoking and obesity: An attempt to replicate. *American Psychologist, 42,* 97–100. (p. 608)

**Sacks, O.** (1985). *The man who mistook his wife for a hat.* New York: Summit Books. (pp. 304, 65, 181)

**Sacks, O.** (1990). *Seeing voices: A journey into the world of the deaf.* New York: HarperCollins. (p. 353)

**Sagan, C.** (1979a). *Broca's brain.* New York: Random House. (p. 53)

**Sagan, C.** (1979b). *Dragons of Eden.* New York: Random House. (p. 500)

**Sagan, C.** (1980). *Cosmos.* New York: Random House. (p. 680)

**Sagan, C.** (1987, February 1). The fine art of baloney detection. *Parade.* (p. 213)

**Sagan, C., & Druyan, A.** (1992). *Shadows of forgotten ancestors: A search for who we are.* New York: Random House. (p. 348)

**Salive, M. E., Guralnik, J. M., & Glynn, R. J.** (1993). Left-handedness and mortality. *American Journal of Public Health, 83,* 265–267. (p. 587)

**Salovey, P.** (1990, January/February). Interview. *American Scientist,* pp. 25–29. (p. 447)

**Salovey, P., & Birnbaum, D.** (1989). Influence of mood on health-relevant cognitions. *Journal of Personality and Social Psychology, 57,* 539–551. (pp. 311, 608)

**Salthouse, T. A.** (1992). *Mechanisms of age-cognition relations in adulthood.* Hillsdale, NJ: Erlbaum. (p. 133)

**Samuels, S., & McCabe, G.** (1989). Quoted in P. Diaconis & F. Mosteller, Methods for studying coincidences. *Journal of the American Statistical Association, 84,* 853–861. (p. 23)

**Sandberg, G. G., Jackson, T. L., & Petretic-Jackson, P.** (1985). *Sexual aggression and courtship violence in dating relationships.* Paper presented at the meeting of the Midwestern Psychological Association. (p. 637)

**Sanders, B., & Soares, M. P.** (1986). Sexual maturation and spatial ability in college students. *Developmental Psychology, 22,* 199–203. (p. 667)

**Sapadin, L. A.** (1988). Friendship and gender: Perspectives of professional men and women. *Journal of Social and Personal Relationships, 5,* 387–403. (p. 670)

**Sapolsky, B. S., & Tabarlet, J. O.** (1991). Sex in primetime television: 1979 versus 1989. *Journal of Broadcasting and Electronic Media, 35,* 505–516. (pp. 126, 639)

**Sapolsky, R. M., & Finch, C. E.** (1991, March/April). On growing old. *The Sciences,* pp. 30–38. (p. 132)

**Sarawathi, T. S., & Dutta, R.** (1988). *Invisible boundaries: Grooming for adult roles.* New Delhi: Northern Book Centre. Cited by R. Larson & M. H. Richards (1989). Introduction: The changing life space of early adolescence. *Journal of Youth and Adolescence, 18,* 501–509. (p. 678)

**Sarnoff, I., & Sarnoff, S.** (1989). *Love-centered marriage in a self-centered world.* New York: Hemisphere. (p. 410)

**Sartorius, N. R.** (1994). Description of WHO's mental health programme. In W. J. Lonner & R. Malpass (Eds.), *Psychology and culture.* Boston: Allyn & Bacon. (pp. 499, 574)

**Sato, K.** (1987). Distribution of the cost of maintaining common resources. *Journal of Experimental Social Psychology, 23,* 19–31. (p. 687)

**Savage-Rumbaugh, E. S., Murphy, J., Sevcik, R. A., Brakke, K. E., Williams, S. L., & Rumbaugh, D. M., with commentary by Bates, E.** (1993). Language comprehension in ape and child. *Monographs of the Society for Research in Child Development, 58* (no. 233), 1–254. (p. 350)

**Savitsky, J. C., & Lindblom, W. D.** (1986). The impact of the guilty but mentally ill verdict on juror decisions: An empirical analysis. *Journal of Applied Social Psychology, 16,* 686–701. (p. 503)

**Sayre, R. F.** (1979). The parents' last lessons. In D. D. Van Tassel (Ed.), *Aging, death, and the completion of being.* Philadelphia: University of Pennsylvania Press. (p. 133)

**Scarr, S.** (1984, May). What's a parent to do? [Conversation with E. Hall.] *Psychology Today,* pp. 58–63. (p. 386)

**Scarr, S.** (1986). *Mother care/other care.* New York: Basic Books. (pp. 101, 115, 387)

**Scarr, S.** (1988). Race and gender as psychological variables: Social and ethical issues. *American Psychologist, 43,* 56–59. (p. 668)

**Scarr, S.** (1989). Protecting general intelligence: Constructs and consequences for interventions. In R. J. Linn (Ed.), *Intelligence: Measurement, theory, and public policy.* Champaign: University of Illinois Press. (pp. 374, 385)

**Scarr, S.** (1990). Back cover comments on J. Dunn & R. Plomin (1990). *Separate lives: Why siblings are so different.* New York: Basic Books. (p. 113)

**Scarr, S.** (1993, May/June). Quoted in *Psychology Today,* Nature's thumbprint: So long, superparents, p. 16. (p. 112)

**Scarr, S., Pakstis, A. J., Katz, S. H., & Barker, W. B.** (1977). The absence of a relationship between degree of white ancestry and intellectual skills within a black population. *Human Genetics, 39,* 69–86. (p. 391)

**Scarr, S., Phillips, D., & McCartney, K.** (1990). Facts, fantasies and the future of child care in the United States. *Psychological Science, 1,* 26–35. (p. 102)

**Scarr, S., Webber, P. L., Weinberg, R. A., & Wittig, M. A.** (1981). Personality resemblance among adolescents and their parents in biologically related and adoptive families. *Journal of Personality and Social Psychology, 40,* 885–898. (p. 110)

**Scarr, S., & Weinberg, R. A.** (1976). IQ test performance of black children adopted by white families. *American Psychologist, 31,* 726–739. (p. 390)

**Scarr, S., & Weinberg, R. A.** (1986). The early childhood enterprise: Care and education of the young. *American Psychologist, 41,* 1140–1146. (p. 101)

**Schab, F. R.** (1990). Odors and the remembrance of things past. *Journal of Experimental Psychology: Learning, Memory, and Cognition, 16,* 648–655. (p. 180)

**Schab, F. R.** (1991). Odor memory: Taking stock. *Psychological Bulletin, 109,* 242–251. (p. 180)

**Schachter, S.** (1982). Recidivism and self-cure of smoking and obesity. *American Psychologist, 37,* 436–444. (p. 608)

**Schachter, S., & Singer, J. E.** (1962). Cognitive, social and physiological determinants of emotional state. *Psychological Review, 69,* 379–399. (p. 456)

**Schacter, D. L.** (1992). Understanding implicit memory: A cognitive neuroscience approach. *American Psychologist, 47,* 559–569. (p. 305)

**Schaie, K. W.** (1987). Old dogs can learn new tricks: Intellectual decline and its remediation in later adulthood. Address to the Eastern Psychological Association convention. (p. 136)

**Schaie, K. W.** (1989). Perceptual speed in adulthood: Cross-sectional and longitudinal studies. *Psychology and Aging, 4,* 443–453. (p. 133)

**Schaie, K. W.** (1994). The life course of adult intellectual abilities. *American Psychologist, 49,* 304–313. (p. 136)

**Schaie, K. W., & Geiwitz, J.** (1982). *Adult development and aging.* Boston: Little, Brown. (p. 136)

**Scheerer, M.** (1963, April). Problem solving. *Scientific American,* pp. 118–128. (pp. 329–330)

**Scheier, M. F., & Carver, C. S.** (1992). Effects of optimism on psychological and physical well-being: Theoretical overview and empirical update. *Cognitive Therapy and Research, 16,* 201–228. (p. 580)

**Schein, E. H.** (1956). The Chinese indoctrination program for prisoners of war: A study of attempted brainwashing. *Psychiatry, 19,* 149–172. (p. 617)

**Schelling, T. C.** (1992). Addictive drugs: The cigarette experience. *Science, 255,* 430–433. (p. 601)

**Schiavi, R. C., & Schreiner-Engel, P.** (1988). Nocturnal penile tumescence in healthy aging men. *Journal of Gerontology: Medical Sciences, 43,* M146–150. (p. 224)

**Schiffenbauer, A., & Schiavo, R. S.** (1976). Physical distance and attraction: An intensification effect. *Journal of Experimental Social Psychology, 12,* 274–282. (p. 627)

**Schleifer, S. J., Keller, S. E., McKegney, F. P., & Stein, M.** (1979). *The influence of stress and other psychosocial factors on human immunity.* Paper presented at the 36th annual meeting of the American Psychosomatic Society. (p. 584)

**Schlesinger, A. M., Jr.** (1965). *A thousand days.* Boston: Houghton Mifflin. (p. 629)

**Schmidt, F. L., & Hunter, J. E.** (1993). Tacit knowledge, practical intelligence, general mental ability, and job knowledge. *Current Directions in Psychological Science, 2,* 8–9. (p. 374)

**Schnaper, N.** (1980). Comments germane to the paper entitled "The reality of death experiences" by Ernst Rodin. *Journal of Nervous and Mental Disease, 168,* 268–270. (p. 251)

**Schneiderman, N., Chesney, M. A., & Krantz, D. S.** (1989). Biobehavioral aspects of cardiovascular disease: Progress and prospects. *Health Psychology, 8,* 649–676. (p. 582)

**Schnitzer, B.** (1984, May). Repunctuated message. *Games,* pp. 57, 62. (p. 339)

**Schoeneman, T. J.** (1994). *Individualism.* In V. S. Ramachandran (Ed.), *Encyclopedia of Human Behavior*. San Diego: Academic Press. (pp. 486, 660)

**Schofield, J. W.** (1986). Black-white contact in desegregated schools. In M. Hewstone & R. Brown (Eds.), *Contact and conflict in intergroup encounters.* Oxford: Blackwell. (p. 688)

**Schonfield, D., & Robertson, B. A.** (1966). Memory storage and aging. *Canadian Journal of Psychology, 20,* 228–236. (p. 135)

**Schooler, J. W., Gerhard, D., & Loftus, E. F.** (1986). Qualities of the unreal. *Journal of Experimental Psychology: Learning, Memory, and Cognition, 12,* 171–181. (p. 312)

**Schuckit, M. A.** (1994). Low level of response to alcohol as a predictor of future alcoholism. *American Journal of Psychiatry, 151,* 184–189. (p. 249)

**Schuerger, J. M., Zarrella, K. L., & Hotz, A. S.** (1989). Factors that influence the temporal stability of personality by questionnaire. *Journal of Personality and Social Psychology, 56,* 777–783. (p. 147)

**Schwartz, B.** (1984). *Psychology of learning and behavior* (2nd ed.). New York: Norton. (pp. 265, 508)

**Schwarz, N., & Clore, G. L.** (1983). Mood, misattribution, and judgments of well-being: Informative and directive functions of affective states. *Journal of Personality and Social Psychology, 45,* 513–523. (p. 447)

**Schwarz, N., Strack, F., Kommer, D., & Wagner, D.** (1987). Soccer, rooms, and the quality of your life: Mood effects on judgments of satisfaction with life in general and with specific domains. *European Journal of Social Psychology, 17,* 69–79. (p. 310)

**Scott, C., & Pepperell, P.** (1992). Exercise and depression: A meta-analysis. Paper presented at the Southwestern Psychological Association convention. (p. 593)

**Scott, W. A., Scott, R., & McCabe, M.** (1991). Family relationships and children's personality: A cross-cultural, cross-source comparison. *British Journal of Social Psychology, 30,* 1–20. (p. 106)

**Scribner, S.** (1977). Modes of thinking and ways of speaking: Culture and logic reconsidered. In P. N. Johnson-Laird & P. C. Wason (Eds.), *Thinking: Readings in cognitive science.* New York: Cambridge University Press. (p. 120)

**Seeman, P., Guan, H-C., & Van Tol, H. H. M.** (1993). Dopamine D4 receptors elevated in schizophrenia. *Nature, 365,* 441–445. (p. 526)

**Segall, M. H., Dasen, P. R., Berry, J. W., & Poortinga, Y. H.** (1990). *Human behavior in global perspective: An introduction to cross-cultural psychology.* New York: Pergamon. (pp. 94, 200, 672, 678, 685)

**Segerstrom, S. C., McCarthy, W. J., Caskey, N. H., Gross, T. D., & Jarvik, M. E.** (1993). Optimistic bias among cigarette smokers. *Journal of Applied Social Psychology, 23,* 1606–1618. (p. 491)

**Seginer, R., Karayanni, M., & Mar'i, M. M.** (1990). Adolescents' attitudes toward women's roles. *Psychology of Women Quarterly, 14,* 119–133. (p. 678)

**Segrin, C., & Dillard, J. P.** (1992). The interactional theory of depresion: A meta-analysis of the research literature. *Journal of Social and Clinical Psychology, 11,* 43–70. (p. 521)

**Seibert, P. S., & Ellis, H. C.** (1991). Irrelevant thoughts, emotional mood states, and cognitive task performance. *Memory and Cognition, 19,* 507–513. (p. 311)

**Seligman, M. E. P.** (1974, May). Submissive death: Giving up on life. *Psychology Today,* pp. 80–85. (p. 434)

**Seligman, M. E. P.** (1975). *Helplessness: On depression, development and death.* San Francisco: Freeman. (p. 490)

**Seligman, M. E. P.** (1988, October). Boomer blues. *Psychology Today,* pp. 50–55. (p. 660)

**Seligman, M. E. P.** (1989). Explanatory style: Predicting depression, achievement, and health. In M. D. Yapko (Ed.), *Brief therapy approaches to treating anxiety and depression.* New York: Brunner/Mazel. (p. 553)

**Seligman, M. E. P.** (1991). *Learned optimism.* New York: Knopf. (pp. 219, 490, 520–521)

**Seligman, M. E. P., & Schulman, P.** (1986). Explanatory style as a predictor of productivity and quitting among life insurance sales agents. *Journal of Personality and Social Psychology, 50,* 832–838. (p. 491)

**Seligman, M. E. P., & Yellen, A.** (1987). What is a dream? *Behavior Research and Therapy, 25,* 1–24. (pp. 222, 229)

**Selye, H.** (1936). A syndrome produced by diverse nocuous agents. *Nature, 138,* 32. (p. 575)

**Selye, H.** (1976). *The stress of life.* New York: McGraw-Hill. (p. 575)

**Serpell, R.** (1994). The cultural construction of intelligence. In W. J. Lonner & R. Malpass (Eds.), *Psychology and culture.* Boston: Allyn & Bacon. (p. 372)

**Shadish, W. R., Jr.** (1992). Do family and marital psychotherapies change what people do? A meta-analysis of behavioral outcomes. In T. D. Cook, H. Cooper, D. S. Cordray, H. Hartmann, L. V. Hedges, R. J. Light, T. A. Louis, & F. Mosteller (Eds.), *Meta-analysis for explanation: A casebook.* New York: Russell Sage Foundation. (p. 555)

**Shamir, B., House, R. J., & Arthur, M. B.** (1993). The motivational effects of charismatic leadership: A self-concept based theory. *Organizational Science,* in press. (p. 425)

**Shanks, D.** (1993, 30 January). Breaking Chomsky's rules. *New Scientist,* pp. 26–29. (p. 346)

**Shapiro, D. A., & Shapiro, D.** (1982). Meta-analysis of comparative therapy outcome studies: A replication and refinement. *Psychological Bulletin, 92,* 581–604. (p. 560)

**Shaughnessy, J., & Zechmeister, E.** (1992). Memory monitoring accuracy as influenced by the distribution of retrieval practice. *Bulletin of the Psychonomic Society, 30,* 125–128. (p. 321)

**Shaver, P. R., & Hazan, C.** (1993). Adult romantic attachment: Theory and evidence. In D. Perlman & W. Jones (Eds.), *Advances in personal relationships* (Vol. 4). Greenwich, CT: JAI Press. (p. 99)

**Shaw, H. L.** (1989–90). Comprehension of the spoken word and ASL translation by chimpanzees (Pan troglodytes). *Friends of Washoe, 9*(1/2), 8–19. (p. 350)

**Shea, M. T., Elkin, I., Imber, S. D., Sotsky, S. M., Watkins, J. T., Collins, J. F., Pilkonis, P. A., Beckham, E., Glass, D. R., Dolan, R. T., & Parloff, M. B.** (1992). Course of depressive symptoms over follow-up: Findings from the National Institute of Mental Health Treatment of Depression Collaborative Research Program. *Archives of General Psychiatry, 49,* 782–787. (p. 559)

**Shedler, J., & Block, J.** (1990). Adolescent drug use and psychological health: A longitudinal inquiry. *American Psychologist, 45,* 612–630. (p. 249)

**Sheehan, S.** (1982). *Is there no place on earth for me?* Boston: Houghton Mifflin. (p. 523)

**Sheldon, W. H.** (1954). *Atlas of man: A guide for somatotyping the adult male of all ages.* New York: Harper & Row. (p. 473)

**Shenon, P.** (1994, May 15). The world: Asia's having one huge nicotine fit. *New York Times,* p. 1. (p. 602)

**Shenton, M. E., Kiknis, R., Jolesz, F. A., & others** (1992). Abnormalities of the left temporal lobe and thought disorder in schizophrenia: A quantitative magnetic resonance imaging study. *New England Journal of Medicine, 327,* 604–612. (p. 526)

**Shepard, R. N.** (1990). *Mind sights.* New York: Freeman. (p. 36)

**Shepherd, C., Kohut, J. J., & Sweet, R.** (1990). *More news of the weird.* New York: Penguin/Plume Books. (p. 531)

**Shepperd, J. A.** (1993). Student derogation of the Scholastic Aptitude Test: Biases in perceptions and presentations of College Board scores. *Basic and Applied Social Psychology, 14,* 455–473. (p. 484)

**Sherif, M.** (1937). An experimental approach to the study of attitudes. *Sociometry, 1,* 90–98. (p. 620)

**Sherif, M.** (1966). *In common predicament: Social psychology of intergroup conflict and cooperation.* Boston: Houghton Mifflin. (p. 688)

**Sherman, L. W.** (1992). The influence of criminology on criminal law: Evaluating arrests for misdemeanor domestic violence. *Journal of Criminal Law and Criminology, 83,* 1–45. (p. 275)

**Sherman, L. W., & Berk, R. A.** (1984). The specific deterrent effects of arrest for domestic assault. *American Sociological Review, 49,* 261–272. (p. 275)

**Sherry, D., & Vaccarino, A. L.** (1989). Hippocampus and memory for food caches in black-capped chickadees. *Behavioral Neuroscience, 103,* 308–318. (p. 306)

**Shettleworth, S. J.** (1973). Food reinforcement and the organization of behavior in golden hamsters. In R. A. Hinde & J. Stevenson-Hinde (Eds.), *Constraints on learning.* London: Academic Press. (p. 277)

**Shneidman, E.** (1987, March). At the point of no return. *Psychology Today,* pp. 54–58. (p. 517)

**Shontz, F. C., & Green, P.** (1992). Trends in research on the Rorschach: Review and recommendations. *Applied and Preventive Psychology, 1,* 149–156. (p. 469)

**Shotland, L.** (1984, March 12). Quoted in Maureen Dowd, 20 years after the murder of Kitty Genovese, the question remains: Why? *The New York Times,* p. B1. (p. 640)

**Shotland, R. L.** (1989). A model of the causes of date rape in developing and close relationships. In C. Hendrick (Ed.), *Review of Personality and Social Psychology* (Vol. 10). Newbury Park, CA: Sage. (p. 673)

**Showers, C.** (1992). The motivational and emotional consequences of considering positive or negative possibilities for an upcoming event. *Journal of Personality and Social Psychology, 63,* 474–484. (p. 491)

**Shrout, P. E., Link, B. G., Dohrenwend, B. P., Skodol, A. E., Stueve, A., & Mirotznik, J.** (1989). Characterizing life events as risk factors for depression: The role of fateful loss events. *Journal of Abnormal Psychology, 98,* 460–467. (p. 518)

**Shulruff, L. I.** (1990, August 10). In sex case, focus is on multiple personalities. *New York Times.* (p. 513)

**Siegel, J. M.** (1990). Stressful life events and use of physician services among the elderly: The moderating role of pet ownership. *Journal of Personality and Social Psychology,* 58, 1081–1086. (p. 597)

**Siegel, L. S., & Hodkin, B.** (1982). The garden path to the understanding of cognitive development: Has Piaget led us into the poison ivy? In S. Modgil & C. Modgil (Eds.), *Jean Piaget: Consensus and controversy.* New York: Praeger. (p. 93)

**Siegel, R. K.** (1977, October). Hallucinations. *Scientific American,* pp. 132–140. (p. 251)

**Siegel, R. K.** (1980). The psychology of life after death. *American Psychologist, 35,* 911–931. (p. 252)

**Siegel, R. K.** (1984, March 15). Personal communication. (p. 244)

**Siegel, R. K.** (1990). *Intoxication.* New York: Pocket Books. (pp. 242–243, 246, 248)

**Siegel, R. K.** (1982, October). Quoted in J. Hooper, Mind tripping. *Omni,* pp. 72–82, 159–160. (p. 245)

**Sigmon, B. A.** (1993). Physical anthropology in socialist Europe. *American Scientist, 81,* 130–139. (p. 363)

**Silva, A. J., Stevens, C. F., Tonegawa, S., & Wang, Y.** (1992). Deficient hippocampal long-term potentiation in alpha-calcium-calmodulin kinase II mutant mice. *Science, 257,* 201–206. (p. 304)

**Silva, C. E., & Kirsch, I.** (1992). Interpretive sets, expectancy, fantasy proneness, and dissociation as predictors of hypnotic response. *Journal of Personality and Social Psychology, 63,* 847–856. (p. 234)

**Silver, M., & Geller, D.** (1978). On the irrelevance of evil: The organization and individual action. *Journal of Social Issues, 34,* 125–136. (p. 625)

**Silverman, K., Evans, S. M., Strain, E. C., & Griffiths, R. R.** (1992). Withdrawal syndrome after the double-blind cessation of caffeine consumption. *New England Journal of Medicine, 327,* 1109–1114. (p. 243)

**Silverman, P. S., & Retzlaff, P. D.** (1986). Cognitive stage regression through hypnosis: Are earlier cognitive stages retrievable? *International Journal of Clinical and Experimental Hypnosis, 34,* 192–204. (p. 235)

**Silverton, L.** (1988). Crime and the schizophrenia spectrum: A study of three Danish cohorts. In T. E. Moffitt & S. A. Mednick (Eds.), *Biological contributions to crime causation.* New York: Martinus Nijhoff. (p. 534)

**Simek, T. C., & O'Brien, R. M.** (1981). *Total golf: A behavioral approach to lowering your score and getting more out of your game.* Huntington, NY: B-MOD Associates. (p. 278)

**Simek, T. C., & O'Brien, R. M.** (1988). A chaining-mastery, discrimination training program to teach Little Leaguers to hit a baseball. *Human Performance, 1,* 73–84. (p. 278)

**Simmons, R. G., & Blyth, D. A.** (1987). *Moving into adolescence: The impact of pubertal change and school context.* New York: Aldine De Gruyter. (p. 119)

**Simons, E. L.** (1989). Human origins. *Science, 245,* 1343–1350. (p. 653)

**Simonton, D. K.** (1988). Age and outstanding achievement: What do we know after a century of research? *Psychological Bulletin, 104,* 251–267. (p. 138)

**Simonton, D. K.** (1990). Creativity in the later years: Optimistic prospects for achievement. *The Gerontologist, 30,* 626–631. (p. 138)

**Simonton, D. K.** (1992). The social context of career success and course for 2,026 scientists and inventors. *Personality and Social Psychology Bulletin, 18,* 452–463. (p. 382)

**Simpson, J. A., Rholes, W. S., & Nelligan, J. S.** (1992). Support seeking and support giving within couples in an anxiety-provoking situation: The role of attachment styles. *Journal of Personality and Social Psychology, 62,* 434–446. (p. 99)

**Sinclair, R. C., Hoffman, C., Mark, M. M., Martin, L. L., & Pickering, T. L.** (1994). Construct accessibility and the misattribution of arousal: Schachter and Singer revisited. *Psychological Science, 5,* 15–18. (p. 456)

**Singer, J. L.** (1975). Navigating the stream of consciousness: Research in daydreaming and related inner experience. *American Psychologist, 30,* 727–738. (p. 231)

**Singer, J. L.** (1976, July). Fantasy: The foundation of serenity. *Psychology Today,* pp. 32–37. (p. 232)

**Singer, J. L.** (1981). Clinical intervention: New developments in methods and evaluation. In L. T. Benjamin, Jr. (Ed.), *The G. Stanley Hall Lecture Series* (Vol. 1). Washington, DC: American Psychological Association. (p. 559)

**Singer, J. L.** (1986). Is television bad for children? *Social Science, 71,* 178–182. (p. 232)

**Singer, J. L., & Singer, D. G.** (1986). Family experiences and television viewing as predictors of children's imagination, restlessness, and aggression. *Journal of Social Issues, 42*(3), 7–28. (p. 637)

**Singh, D.** (1993). Adaptive significance of female physical attractiveness: Role of waist-to-hip ratio. *Journal of Personality and Social Psychology, 65,* 293–307. (p. 646)

**Sjostrom, L.** (1980). Fat cells and body weight. In A. J. Stunkard (Ed.), *Obesity.* Philadelphia: Saunders. (p. 605)

**Skinner, B. F.** (1953). *Science and human behavior.* New York: Macmillan. (p. 272)

**Skinner, B. F.** (1956). A case history in scientific method. *American Psychologist, 11,* 221–233. (p. 273)

**Skinner, B. F.** (1957). *Verbal behavior.* Englewood Cliffs, NJ: Prentice-Hall. (p. 344)

**Skinner, B. F.** (1961, November). Teaching machines. *Scientific American,* pp. 91–102. (p. 272)

**Skinner, B. F.** (1983, September). Origins of a behaviorist. *Psychology Today,* pp. 22–33. (pp. 278, 520)

**Skinner, B. F.** (1985). *Cognitive science and behaviorism.* Unpublished manuscript, Harvard University, Cambridge, MA. (p. 344)

**Skinner, B. F.** (1986). What is wrong with daily life in the Western world? *American Psychologist, 41,* 568–574. (p. 278)

**Skinner, B. F.** (1988). The school of the future. Address to the American Psychological Association convention. (p. 278)

**Skinner, B. F.** (1989). Teaching machines. *Science, 243,* 1535. (p. 278)

**Skinner, B. F.** (1990). Address to the American Psychological Association convention. (p. 275)

**Skinner, M., & Mullen, B.** (1991). Facial asymmetry in emotional expression: A meta-analysis of research. *British Journal of Social Psychology, 30,* 113–124. (p. 66)

**Sklar, L. S., & Anisman, H.** (1981). Stress and cancer. *Psychological Bulletin, 89,* 369–406. (p. 584)

**Skov, R. B., & Sherman, S. J.** (1986). Information-gathering processes: Diagnosticity, hypothesis-confirmatory strategies, and perceived hypothesis confirmation. *Journal of Experimental Social Psychology, 22,* 93–121. (p. 328)

**Slater, A.** (1994, February 15). Personal communication. (p. 91)

**Slater, A., Morison, V., & Somers, M.** (1988). Orientation discrimination and cortical function in the human newborn. *Perception, 17,* 597–602. (p. 91)

**Slavin, R. E.** (1989). Cooperative learning and student achievement. In R. E. Slavin (Ed.), *School and classroom organization.* Hillsdale, NJ: Erlbaum. (p. 689)

**Slavin, R. E., & Braddock, J. H., III** (1993, Summer). Ability grouping: On the wrong track. *The College Board Review,* pp. 11–18. (p. 381)

**Sleek, S.** (1994, April). Could Prozac replace demand for therapy? *APA Monitor,* p. 28. (p. 566)

**Slovic, P.** (1987). Perception of risk. *Science, 236,* 280–285. (p. 333)

**Slovic, P., & Fischhoff, B.** (1977). On the psychology of experimental surprises. *Journal of Experimental Psychology: Human Perception and Performance, 3,* 544–551. (p. 14)

**Small, G. W., Propper, M. W., Randolph, E. T., & Eth, S.** (1991). Mass hysteria among student performers: Social relationship as a symptom predictor. *American Journal of Psychiatry, 148,* 1200–1205. (p. 591)

**Small, M. F.** (1991, July). Sperm wars. *Discover,* pp. 48–53. (p. 674)

**Smart, R. G., Adlaf, E. M., & Walsh, G. W.** (1991). The Ontario student drug use survey: Trends between 1977 and 1991. Toronto: Addiction Research Foundation. (p. 248)

**Smith, A.** (1983). Personal communication. (p. 526)

**Smith, A.** (1987). Personal communication. (p. 87)

**Smith, A., & Sugar, O.** (1975). Development of above normal language and intelligence 21 years after left hemispherectomy. *Neurology, 25,* 813–818. (p. 87)

**Smith, D.** (1982). Trends in counseling and psychotherapy. *American Psychologist, 37,* 802–809. (p. 540)

**Smith, M. B.** (1978). Psychology and values. *Journal of Social Issues, 34,* 181–199. (p. 486)

**Smith, M. L., & Glass, G. V.** (1977). Meta-analysis of psychotherapy outcome studies. *American Psychologist, 32,* 752–760. (p. 560)

**Smith, M. L., Glass, G. V., & Miller, R. L.** (1980). *The benefits of psychotherapy.* Baltimore: Johns Hopkins University Press. (pp. 558–560)

**Smith, P. B., & Tayeb, M.** (1989). Organizational structure and processes. In M. Bond (Ed.), *The cross-cultural challenge to social psychology.* Newbury Park, CA: Sage. (p. 425)

**Smith, T. W.** (1990). *Adult sexual behavior in 1989: Number of partners, frequency, and risk.* (General Social Survey Topic Report No. 18). National Opinion Research Center, University of Chicago. (p. 409)

**Smith, T. W.** (1994). Attitudes towards sexual permissiveness: Trends and correlates. In A. S. Rossi (Ed.), *Sexuality across the life course.* Chicago: University of Chicago Press. (p. 409)

**Smith, T. W.** (1994). Personal communication. Data from General Social Survey, National Opinion Research Center, University of Chicago. (pp. 409, 449, 683)

**Snarey, J.** (1987, June). A question of morality. *Psychology Today,* pp. 6–7. (p. 122)

**Snarey, J. R.** (1985). Cross-cultural universality of social-moral development: A critical review of Kohlbergian research. *Psychological Bulletin, 97,* 202–233. (p. 122)

**Snodgrass, M. A.** (1987). The relationships of differential loneliness, intimacy and characterological attributional style to duration of loneliness. *Journal of Social Behavior and Personality, 2,* 173–186. (p. 522)

**Snodgrass, S. E., Higgins, J. G., & Todisco, L.** (1986). The effects of walking behavior on mood. Paper presented at the American Psychological Association convention. (p. 443)

**Snyder, M.** (1984). When belief creates reality. In L. Berkowitz (Ed.), *Advances in experimental social psychology* (Vol. 18). New York: Academic Press. (p. 534)

**Snyder, M., Tanke, E. D., & Berscheid, E.** (1977). Social perception and interpersonal behavior: On the self-fulfilling nature of social stereotypes. *Journal of Personality and Social Psychology, 35,* 656–666. (p. 630)

**Snyder, S. H.** (1984). Neurosciences: An integrative discipline. *Science, 225,* 1255–1257. (pp. 45, 565)

**Snyder, S. H.** (1986). *Drugs and the brain.* New York: Scientific American Library. (p. 567)

**Snyderman, M., & Rothman, S.** (1987). Survey of expert opinion on intelligence and aptitude testing. *American Psychologist, 42,* 137–144. (p. 389)

**Sobel, D. S.** (1993). Mind matters, money matters. *Mental Medicine Update Special Report,* pp. 1–8. (p. 599)

**Sokhadze, E. M., & Shtark, M. B.** (1991). Scientific and clinical biofeedback in the USSR. *Biofeedback and Self-Regulation, 16,* 253–260. (p. 595)

**Sokoll, G. R., & Mynatt, C. R.** (1984). *Arousal and free throw shooting.* Paper presented at the meeting of the Midwestern Psychological Association. (p. 434)

**Solomon, M.** (1987, December). Standard issue. *Psychology Today,* pp. 30–31. (p. 645)

**Solomon, R. L.** (1980). The opponent-process theory of acquired motivation: The costs of pleasure and the benefits of pain. *American Psychologist, 35,* 691–712. (p. 450)

**Solomon, S., Greenberg, J., & Pyszczynski, T.** (1991). A terror management theory of social behavior: The psychological functions of self-esteem and cultural world-views. *Advances in Experimental Social Psychology, 24,* 93–159. (p. 470)

**Solomon, Z.** (1990). Does the war end when the shooting stops? The psychological toll of war. *Journal of Applied Social Psychology, 20,* 1733–1745. (p. 529)

**Sommer, B.** (1992). Cognitive performance and the menstrual cycle. In J. T. Richardson (Ed.), *Cognition and the menstrual cycle: Research, theory, and culture.* New York: Springer-Verlag. (p. 591)

**Sommer, R.** (1969). *Personal space.* Englewood Cliffs, NJ: Prentice-Hall. (p. 657)

**Sonenstein, F. L.** (1992). Condom use. *Science, 257,* 861. (p. 126)

**Sontag, S.** (1978). *Illness as metaphor.* New York: Farrar, Straus, & Giroux. (p. 586)

**Sowell, T.** (1991, May/June). Cultural diversity: A world view. *American Enterprise,* pp. 44–55. (p. 690)

**Spanos, N. P.** (1982). A social psychological approach to hypnotic behavior. In G. Weary & H. L. Mirels (Eds.), *Integrations of clinical and social psychology.* New York: Oxford University Press. (p. 236)

**Spanos, N. P.** (1986). Hypnosis, nonvolitional responding, and multiple personality: A social psychological perspective. *Progress in Experimental Personality Research, 14,* 1–62. (p. 513)

**Spanos, N. P.** (1987–88). Past-life hypnotic regression: A critical view. *The Skeptical Inquirer, 12,* 174–180. (p. 237)

**Spanos, N. P.** (1991). Hypnosis, hypnotizability, and hypnotherapy. In C. R. Snyder & D. R. Forsyth (Eds.), *Handbook of social and clinical psychology: The health perspective.* New York: Pergamon Press. (p. 236)

**Spanos, N. P.** (1994). Multiple identity enactments and multiple personality disorder: A sociocognitive perspective. *Psychological Bulletin, 116,* 143–165. (p. 238)

**Spanos, N. P., & Coe, W. C.** (1992). A social-psychological approach to hypnosis. In E. Fromm & M. R. Nash (Eds.), *Contemporary hypnosis research.* New York: Guilford Press. (p. 238)

**Spanos, N. P., Menary, E., Gabora, N. J., DuBreuil, S. C., & Dewhirst, B.** (1991). Secondary identity enactments during hypnotic past-life regression: A sociocognitive perspective. *Journal of Personality and Social Psychology, 61,* 308–320. (p. 237)

**Spanos, N. P., Radtke, L., & Bertrand, L. D.** (1985). Hypnotic amnesia as a strategic enactment: Breaching amnesia in highly susceptible subjects. *Journal of Personality and Social Psychology, 47,* 1155–1169. (p. 233)

**Spector, P. E.** (1986). Perceived control by employees: A meta-analysis of studies concerning autonomy and participation at work. *Human Relations, 39,* 1005–1016. (p. 425)

**Spelke, E. S., Breinlinger, K., Macomber, J., & Jacobson, K.** (1992). Origins of knowledge. *Psychological Review, 99,* 605–632. (p. 92)

**Sperling, G.** (1960). The information available in brief visual presentations. *Psychological Monographs, 74* (Whole No. 498). (p. 299)

**Sperry, R. W.** (1956, May). The eye and the brain. *Scientific American,* pp. 48–52. (p. 204)

**Sperry, R. W.** (1964). *Problems outstanding in the evolution of brain function.* James Arthur Lecture, American Museum of Natural History, New York. Cited by R. Ornstein (1977), *The psychology of consciousness* (2nd ed.). New York: Harcourt Brace Jovanovich. (p. 67)

**Sperry, R. W.** (1968). Hemisphere deconnection and unity in conscious awareness. *American Psychologist, 23,* 723–733. (p. 66)

**Sperry, R. W.** (1982). Some effects of disconnecting the cerebral hemispheres. *Science, 217,* 1223–1226. (p. 70)

**Sperry, R. W.** (1985). Changed concepts of brain and consciousness: Some value implications. *Zygon, 20,* 41–57. (pp. 164, 252)

**Spiegel, D.** (1993). Social support: How friends, family, and groups can help. In D. Goleman & J. Gurin (Eds.), *Mind-body medicine: How to use your mind for better health.* Yonkers, NY: Consumer Reports Books. (p. 585)

**Spiegel, D., Bloom, J. R., Kraemer, H. C., & Gottheil, E.** (1989, October 14). Effect of psychosocial treatment on survival of patients with metastatic breast cancer. *The Lancet,* pp. 888–891. (p. 585)

**Spielberger, C., & London, P.** (1982). Rage boomerangs. *American Health, 1,* 52–56. (p. 582)

**Spiess, W. F. J., Greer, J. H., & O'Donohue, W. T.** (1984). Premature ejaculation: Investigation of factors in ejaculatory latency. *Journal of Abnormal Psychology, 93,* 242–245. (p. 412)

**Spitzberg, B. H., & Hurt, H. T.** (1987). The relationship of interpersonal competence and skill to reported loneliness across time. *Journal of Social Behavior and Personality, 2,* 157–172. (p. 522)

**Spitzer, R. L.** (1975). On pseudoscience in science, logic in remission, and psychiatric diagnosis: A critique of Rosenhan's "On being sane in insane places." *Journal of Abnormal Psychology, 84,* 442–452. (p. 534)

**Spitzer, R. L., Gibbon, M., Skodol, A. E., Williams, J. B. W., & First, M. B.** (1989). *DSM-III-R casebook.* Washington, DC: American Psychiatric Press. (p. 510)

**Spradley, J. P., & Phillips, M.** (1972). Culture and stress: A quantitative analysis. *American Anthropologist, 74,* 518–529. (p. 657)

**Sprecher, S.** (1989). The importance to males and females of physical attractiveness, earning potential, and expressiveness in initial attraction. *Sex Roles, 21,* 591–607. (p. 645)

**Sprecher, S., & Sedikides, C.** (1993). Gender differences in perceptions of emotionality: The case of close heterosexual relationships. *Sex Roles, 28,* 511–530. (p. 670)

**Spring, B.** (1988). Foods, brain and behavior: New links. *Harvard Medical School Mental Health Letter, 4*(7), 4–6. (p. 603)

**Spring, B., Chiodo, J., & Bowen, D. J.** (1987). Carbohydrates, tryptophan, and behavior: A methodological review. *Psychological Bulletin, 102,* 234–256. (p. 603)

**Spring, B., Pingitore, R., Bourgeois, M., Kessler, K. H., & Bruckner, E.** (1992). The effects and non-effects of skipping breakfast: Results of three studies. Paper presented at the American Psychological Association convention. (p. 603)

**Springer, S. P., & Deutsch, G.** (1985). *Left brain, right brain.* San Francisco: Freeman. (p. 68, 75)

**Squire, L.** (1990). Memory and brain systems. Invited address to the American Psychological Society convention. (p. 305)

**Squire, L., & Zola-Morgan, S.** (1991). The medial temporal lobe memory system. *Science, 253,* 1380–1386. (p. 306)

**Squire, L. R.** (1987). *Memory and brain.* New York: Oxford University Press. (p. 305)

**Squire, L. R., & Ojemann, J. G.** (1992). Activation of the hippocampus in normal humans: A functional anatomical study of memory. *Proceedings of the National Academy of Sciences, 89,* 1837–1841. (p. 306)

**Squire, S.** (1987, November 22). Shock therapy's return to respectability. *The New York Times Magazine,* pp. 78–89. (p. 304)

**Sroufe, L. A., Fox, N. E., & Pancake, V. R.** (1983). Attachment and dependency in developmental perspective. *Child Development, 54,* 1615–1627. (p. 99)

**Stack, S.** (1992). Marriage, family, religion, and suicide. In R. Maris, A. Berman, J. Maltsberger, & R. Yufit (Eds.), *Assessment and prediction of suicide.* New York: Guilford Press. (p. 516)

**Stake, J. E.** (1992). Gender differences and similarities in self-concept within everyday life contexts. *Psychology of Women Quarterly, 16,* 349–363. (p. 669)

**Stattin, H., & Magnusson, D.** (1990). *Pubertal maturation in female development.* Hillsdale, NJ: Erlbaum. (p. 119)

**Staub, E.** (1989). *The roots of evil: The psychological and cultural sources of genocide.* New York: Cambridge University Press. (p. 618)

**Staub, E.** (1992). Transforming the bystanders: Altruism, caring, and social responsibility. In H. Fein (Ed.), *Genocide watch.* New Haven, CT: Yale University Press. (p. 643)

**Staub, E.** (1993). Societal-cultural, familial and psychological origins of youth violence. Paper presented at the American Psychological Association convention. (p. 635)

**Steele, C.** (1990a, May). A conversation with Claude Steele. *APS Observer,* pp. 11–17. (pp. 388, 390)

**Steele, C. M.** (1992, April). Race and the schooling of black Americans. *Atlantic Monthly,* pp. 68–78. (p. 390)

**Steele, C. M., & Josephs, R. A.** (1990). Alcohol myopia: Its prized and dangerous effects. *American Psychologist, 45,* 921–933. (p. 242)

**Steele, S.** (1990). *The content of our character: A new vision of race in America.* New York: St. Martin's Press. (p. 653)

**Stein, J. A., Newcomb, M. D., & Bentler, P. M.** (1986). Stability and change in personality: A longitudinal study from early adolescence to young adulthood. *Journal of Research In Personality, 20,* 276–291. (p. 147)

**Steinberg, L.** (1987, September). Bound to bicker. *Psychology Today,* pp. 36–39. (p. 125)

**Steinberg, N.** (1993, February). Astonishing love stories (from an earlier United Press International report). *Games,* p. 47. (p. 645)

**Stellar, E.** (1985). Hunger in animals and humans. Distinguished lecture to the Eastern Psychological Association convention. (p. 404)

**Stengel, E.** (1981). Suicide. In *The new encyclopaedia britannica, macropaedia* (Vol. 17, pp. 777–782). Chicago: Encyclopaedia Britannica. (p. 516)

**Stern, M., & Karraker, K. H.** (1989). Sex stereotyping of infants: A review of gender labeling studies. *Sex Roles, 20,* 501–522. (p. 210)

**Sternberg, R. J.** (1984). Testing intelligence without IQ tests. *Phi Delta Kappan, 65*(10), 694–698. (p. 375)

**Sternberg, R. J.** (1985). *Beyond IQ: A triarchic theory of human intelligence.* New York: Cambridge University Press. (p. 375)

**Sternberg, R. J.** (1988). Applying cognitive theory to the testing and teaching of intelligence. *Applied Cognitive Psychology, 2,* 231–255. (p. 381)

**Sternberg, R. J., & Grajek, S.** (1984). The nature of love. *Journal of Personality and Social Psychology, 47,* 312–329. (p. 649)

**Sternberg, R. J., & Lubart, T. I.** (1991). An investment theory of creativity and its development. *Human Development,* 1–31. (p. 381)

**Sternberg, R. J., & Lubart, T. I.** (1992). Buy low and sell high: An investment approach to creativity. *Psychological Science, 1,* 1–5. (p. 381)

**Sternberg, R. J., & Salter, W.** (1982). Conceptions of intelligence. In R. J. Sternberg (Ed.), *Handbook of human intelligence.* New York: Cambridge University Press. (p. 371)

**Sternberg, R. J., & Wagner, R. K.** (1987). Tacit knowledge: An unspoken key to managerial success. (p. 374)

**Sternberg, R. J., & Wagner, R. K.** (1993). The *g*-ocentric view of intelligence and job performance is wrong. *Current Directions in Psychological Science, 2,* 1–5. (p. 374)

**Stevenson, H. W.** (1992, December). Learning from Asian schools. *Scientific American,* pp. 70–76. (pp. 388–389)

**Stevenson, H. W., & Lee, S-Y.** (1990). Contexts of achievement: A study of American, Chinese, and Japanese children. *Monographs of the Society for Research in Child Development, 55* (Serial No. 221, Nos. 1–2). (pp. 381, 389)

**Stevenson, H. W., Lee, S. Y., & Stigler, J. W.** (1986). Mathematics achievement of Chinese, Japanese, and American children. *Science, 231,* 693–699. (p. 389–390)

**Stevenson, H. W., Lummis, M., Lee, S-Y., & Stigler, J. W.** (1990). *Making the grade in mathematics: Elementary school mathematics in the United States, Taiwan, and Japan.* Reston, VA: National Council of Teachers of Mathematics. (p. 389)

**Stiles, D. A., Gibbons, J. L., & Schnellmann, J. D. G.** (1990). Opposite-sex ideal in the U.S.A. and Mexico as perceived by young adolescents. *Journal of Cross-Cultural Psychology, 21,* 180–199. (p. 678)

**Stiles, W. B., Shapiro, D. A., & Elliott, R.** (1986). Are all psychotherapies equivalent? *American Psychologist, 41,* 165–180. (p. 560)

**Stock, W. A., Okun, M. A., Haring, M. J., & Witter, R. A.** (1983). Age and subjective well-being: A meta-analysis. In R. J. Light (Ed.), *Evaluation studies: Review annual* (Vol. 8). Beverly Hills, CA: Sage. (p. 142)

**Stockton, M. C., & Murnen, S. K.** (1992). Gender and sexual arousal in response to sexual stimuli: A meta-analytic review. Paper presented at the American Psychological Society convention. (p. 411)

**Stoll, A. L., Tohen, M., & Baldessarini, R. J.** (1992). Increasing frequency of the diagnosis of obsessive-compulsive disorder. *American Journal of Psychiatry, 149,* 638–640. (p. 508)

**Stoll, A. L., Tohen, M., Baldessarini, R. J., Goodwin, D. C., Stein, S., Katz, S., Geenens, D., Swinson, R. P., Goethe, J. W., & McGlashan, T.** (1993). Shifts in diagnostic frequencies of schizophrenia and major affective disorders at six North American psychiatric hospitals, 1972–1988. *American Journal of Psychiatry, 150,* 1668–1673. (p. 518)

**Stone, A. A., & Neale, J. M.** (1984). Effects of severe daily events on mood. *Journal of Personality and Social Psychology, 46,* 137–144. (p. 448)

**Stone, A. A., Cox, D. S., Valdimarsdottir, H., Jandor, L., & Neale, J. M.** (1987). Evidence that secretory IgA antibody is associated with daily mood. *Journal of Personality and Social Psychology, 52,* 988–993. (p. 584)

**Stopes-Roe, M., & Cochrane, R.** (1990). The child-rearing values of Asian and British parents and young people: An inter-ethnic and inter-generational comparison in the evaluation of Kohn's 13 qualities. *British Journal of Social Psychology, 29,* 149–160. (p. 106)

**Stoppard, J. M., & Gruchy, C. D. G.** (1993). Gender, context, and expression of positive emotion. *Personality and Social Psychology Bulletin, 19,* 143–150. (p. 670)

**Storms, M. D.** (1973). Videotape and the attribution process: Reversing actors' and observers' points of view. *Journal of Personality and Social Psychology, 27,* 165–175. (p. 614)

**Storms, M. D.** (1981). A theory of erotic orientation development. *Psychological Review, 88,* 340–353. (p. 414)

**Storms, M. D.** (1983). *Development of sexual orientation.* Washington, DC: Office of Social and Ethical Responsibility, American Psychological Association. (p. 414)

**Storms, M. D., & Thomas, G. C.** (1977). Reactions to physical closeness. *Journal of Personality and Social Psychology, 35,* 412–418. (p. 627)

**Strack, F., Martin, L., & Stepper, S.** (1988). Inhibiting and facilitating conditions of the human smile: A nonobtrusive test of the facial feedback hypothesis. *Journal of Personality and Social Psychology, 54,* 768–777. (p. 442)

**Strack, S., & Coyne, J. C.** (1983). Social confirmation of dysphoria: Shared and private reactions to depression. *Journal of Personality and Social Behavior, 44,* 798–806. (p. 521)

**Strange, S. L., & Forsyth, D. R.** (1993). Long-term benefits of adolescent peer groups. Paper presented at the Eastern Psychological Association convention. (p. 124)

**Stratton, G. M.** (1896). Some preliminary experiments on vision without inversion of the retinal image. *Psychological Review, 3,* 611–617. (p. 204)

**Straub, R. O., Seidenberg, M. S., Bever, T. G., & Terrace, H. S.** (1979). Serial learning in the pigeon. *Journal of the Experimental Analysis of Behavior, 32,* 137–148. (p. 349)

**Strauman, T. J., Vookles, J., Berenstein, V., Chaiken, S., & Higgins, E. T.** (1991). Self-discrepancies and vulnerability to body dissatisfaction and disordered eating. *Journal of Personality and Social Psychology, 61,* 946–956. (p. 407)

**Straus, M. A., & Gelles, R. J.** (1980). *Behind closed doors: Violence in the American family.* New York: Anchor/Doubleday. (p. 273)

**Streissguth, A. P.** (1993). *Fetal alcohol fact sheet.* Fetal Alcohol & Drug Unit, University of Washington, School of Medicine. (p. 82)

**Streissguth, A. P., LaDue, R. A., & Randels, S. P.** (1988). *A manual on adolescents and adults with fetal alcohol syndrome with special reference to American Indians.* Department of Psychiatry and Behavioral Sciences, University of Washington. (p. 82)

**Strentz, H.** (1986, January 1). Become a psychic and amaze your friends! *Atlanta Journal,* p. 15A. (p. 212)

**Strickland, B.** (1992, February 20). Gender differences in health and illness. Sigma Xi national lecture delivered at Hope College. (p. 131)

**Striegel-Moore, R. H., Silberstein, L. R., & Rodin, J.** (1993). The social self in bulimia nervosa: Public self-consciousness, social anxiety, and perceived fraudulence. *Journal of Abnormal Psychology, 102,* 297–303. (p. 406)

**Striegel-Moore, R. H., Silberstein, L. R., & Rodin, J.** (1986). Toward an understanding of risk factors for bulimia. *American Psychologist, 41,* 246–263. (p. 407)

**Stringer, C. B.** (1990, December). The emergence of modern humans. *Scientific American,* pp. 98–104. (p. 653)

**Strupp, H. H.** (1986). Psychotherapy: Research, practice, and public policy (How to avoid dead ends). *American Psychologist, 41,* 120–130. (p. 560)

**Stunkard, A. J., Harris, J. R., Pedersen, N. L., & McClearn, G. E.** (1990). A separated twin study of the body mass index. *New England Journal of Medicine, 322,* 1483–1487. (p. 606)

**Sue, D. W.** (1990). Culture-specific strategies in counseling: A conceptual framework. *Professional Psychology: Research and Practice, 21,* 424–433. (p. 563)

**Suedfeld, P.** (1980). *Restricted environmental stimulation: Research and clinical applications.* New York: Wiley. (p. 182)

**Suedfeld, P., & Kristeller, J. L.** (1982). Stimulus reduction as a technique in health psychology. *Health Psychology, 1,* 337–357. (p. 182)

**Suedfeld, P., & Mocellin, J. S. P.** (1987). The "sensed presence" in unusual environments. *Environment and Behavior, 19,* 33–52. (p. 252)

**Suinn, R. M.** (1986). *Seven steps to peak performance.* Toronto: Hogrefe. (p. 354)

**Sulloway, F. J.** (1990). Orthodoxy and innovation in science: The influence of birth order in a multivariate context. Paper delivered at the American Association for the Advancement of Science annual meeting. (p. 421)

**Suls, J. M., & Tesch, F.** (1978). Students' preferences for information about their test performance: A social comparison study. *Journal of Experimental Social Psychology, 8,* 189–197. (p. 452)

**Sundstrom, E., De Meuse, K. P., & Futrell, D.** (1990). Work teams: Applications and effectiveness. *American Psychologist, 45,* 120–133. (p. 426)

**Suomi, S. J.** (1986). Anxiety-like disorders in young nonhuman primates. In R. Gettleman (Ed.), *Anxiety disorders of childhood.* New York: Guilford Press. (p. 509)

**Suomi, S. J.** (1987). Genetic and maternal contributions to individual differences in rhesus monkey biobehavioral development. In N. A. Krasnegor & others (Eds.), *Perinatal development: A psychobiological perspective.* Orlando, FL: Academic Press. (pp. 98, 466)

**Suppes, P.** (1982). Quoted by R. H. Ennis. Children's ability to handle Piaget's propositional logic: A conceptual critique. In S. Modgil & C. Modgil (Eds.), *Jean Piaget: Consensus and controversy.* New York: Praeger. (p. 94)

**Surgeon General.** (1986). *The Surgeon General's workshop on pornography and public health,* June 22–24. Report prepared by E. P. Mulvey & J. L. Haugaard and released by Office of the Surgeon General on August 4, 1986. (p. 638)

**Swann, W. B., Jr., & Miller, L. C.** (1982). Why never forgetting a face matters: Visual imagery and social memory. *Journal of Personality and Social Psychology, 43,* 475–480. (p. 295)

**Sweat, J. A., & Durm, M. W.** (1993). Psychics: Do police departments really use them? *Skeptical Inquirer, 17,* 148–158. (p. 212)

**Swerdlow, N. R., & Koob, G. F.** (1987). Dopamine, schizophrenia, mania, and depression: Toward a unified hypothesis of cortico-stiato-pallido-thalamic function (with commentary). *Behavioral and Brain Sciences, 10,* 197–246. (p. 526)

**Swim, J. K.** (1994). Perceived versus meta-analytic effect sizes: An assessment of the accuracy of gender stereotypes. *Journal of Personality and Social Psychology, 66,* 21–36. (p. 668)

**Szasz, T.** (1984). *The therapeutic state: Psychiatry in the mirror of current events.* Buffalo, NY: Prometheus Books. (p. 502)

**Szasz, T.** (1987). *Insanity: The idea and its consequences.* New York: Wiley. (p. 502)

**Taha, F. A.** (1972). A comparative study of how sighted and blind perceive the manifest content of dreams. *National Review of Social Sciences, 9*(3), 28. (p. 227)

**Tajfel, H.** (Ed.). (1982). *Social identity and intergroup relations.* New York: Cambridge University Press. (p. 684)

**Tang, S-H., & Hall, V. C.** (1994). The overjustification effect: A meta-analysis. *Applied Cognitive Psychology,* in press. (p. 276)

**Tannen, D.** (1990). *You just don't understand: Women and men in conversation.* New York: Morrow. (pp. 32, 669)

**Tanner, J. M.** (1978). *Fetus into man: Physical growth from conception to maturity.* Cambridge, MA: Harvard University Press. (p. 118)

**Tassinary, L. G., & Cacioppo, J. T.** (1992). Unobservable facial actions and emotion. *Psychological Science, 3,* 28–33. (p. 439)

**Tatarkiewicz, W.** (1976). *Analysis of happiness.* The Hague: Martinus Nijhoff. (p. 448)

**Tavris, C.** (1982, November). Anger defused. *Psychology Today,* pp. 25–35. (p. 447)

**Tavris, C.** (1992). *The mismeasure of woman.* New York: Simon & Schuster. (p. 591)

**Tavris, C.** (1993, January 3). Beware the incest-survivor machine. *New York Times Book Review,* pp. 1, 16–18. (p. 318)

**Taylor, S. E.** (1987). The process and prospects of health psychology: Tasks of a maturing discipline. *Health Psychology, 6,* 73–87. (p. 599)

**Taylor, S. E.** (1989). *Positive illusions.* New York: Basic Books. (pp. 335, 485, 596)

**Taylor, S. P., & Chermack, S. T.** (1993). Alcohol, drugs and human physical aggression. *Journal of Studies on Alcohol,* Suppl. No. 11, 78–88. (p. 633)

**Teevan, R. C., & McGhee, P. E.** (1972). Childhood development of fear of failure motivation. *Journal of Personality and Social Psychology, 21,* 345–348. (p. 420)

**Teghtsoonian, R.** (1971). On the exponents in Stevens' law and the constant in Ekman's law. *Psychological Review, 78,* 71–80. (p. 156)

**Temoshok, L.** (1992). *The Type C connection: The behavioral links to cancer and your health.* New York: Random House. (p. 585)

**Terman, L. M.** (1916). *The measurement of intelligence.* Boston: Houghton Mifflin. (p. 362–363)

**Terrace, H. S.** (1979, November). How Nim Chimpsky changed my mind. *Psychology Today,* pp. 65–76. (p. 349)

**Tetlock, P. E.** (1988). Monitoring the integrative complexity of American and Soviet policy rhetoric: What can be learned? *Journal of Social Issues, 44,* 101–131. (p. 690)

**Thatcher, R. W., Walker, R. A., & Giudice, S.** (1987). Human cerebral hemispheres develop at different rates and ages. *Science, 236,* 1110–1113. (pp. 88, 145)

**Thayer, R. E.** (1987). Energy, tiredness, and tension effects of a sugar snack versus moderate exercise. *Journal of Personality and Social Psychology, 52,* 119–125. (p. 593)

**Thayer, R. E.** (1993). Mood and behavior (smoking and sugar snacking) following moderate exercise: A partial test of self-regulation theory. *Personality and Individual Differences, 14,* 97–104. (p. 593)

**Thomas, A., & Chess, S.** (1986). The New York Longitudinal Study: From infancy to early adult life. In R. Plomin & J. Dunn (Eds.), *The study of temperament: Changes, continuities, and challenges.* Hillsdale, NJ: Erlbaum. (p. 146)

**Thomas, G. V., & Blackman, D.** (1991). Are animal experiments on the way out? *The Psychologist, 14,* 208–212. (p. 34)

**Thomas, L.** (1974). *The lives of a cell.* New York: Viking Press. (p. 180)

**Thomas, L.** (1983). *The youngest science: Notes of a medicine watcher.* New York: Viking Press. (p. 47)

**Thomas, L.** (1992). *The fragile species.* New York: Maxwell Macmillan. (p. 558)

**Thompson, C. P., Frieman, J., & Cowan, T.** (1993). Rajan's memory. Paper presented to the American Psychological Society convention. (p. 301)

**Thompson, J. K.** (1986, April). Larger than life. *Psychology Today,* pp. 38–44. (p. 407)

**Thompson, J. K., Jarvie, G. J., Lahey, B. B., & Cureton, K. J.** (1982). Exercise and obesity: Etiology, physiology, and intervention. *Psychological Bulletin, 91,* 55–79. (p. 609)

**Thompson, L.** (1992). Fetal transplants show promise. *Science, 257,* 868–870. See also technical articles in the *New England Journal of Medicine,* November 26, 1992. (p. 134)

**Thompson, L. A., Detterman, D. K., & Plomin, R.** (1991). Associations between cognitive abilities and scholastic achievement: Genetic overlap but environmental differences. *Psychological Science, 2,* 158–165. (p. 386)

**Thompson, P.** (1980). Margaret Thatcher: A new illusion. *Perception, 9,* 483–484. (p. 207)

**Thorndike, A. L., & Hagen, E. P.** (1977). *Measurement and evaluation in psychology and education.* New York: Macmillan. (p. 364)

**Thornton, B., & Moore, S.** (1993). Physical attractiveness contrast effect: Implications for self-esteem and evaluations of the social self. *Personality and Social Psychology Bulletin, 19,* 474–480. (p. 645)

**Tiggemann, M., & Rothblum, E. D.** (1988). Gender differences in social consequences of perceived overweight in the United States and Australia. *Sex Roles, 18,* 75–86. (p. 607)

**Timberlake, W., & Farmer-Dougan, V. A.** (1991). Reinforcement in applied settings: Figuring out ahead of time what will work. *Psychological Bulletin, 110,* 379–391. (p. 270)

**Timmer, S. G., Eccles, J., & O'Brien, K.** (1985–1986, Winter). How families use time. *ISR Newsletter* (University of Michigan), pp. 3–4. (p. 102)

**Tinbergen, N.** (1951). *The study of instinct.* Oxford: Clarendon. (p. 398)

**Tirrell, M. E.** (1990). Personal communication. (p. 261–262)

**Todd, J., Friedman, A., & Kariuki, P. W.** (1990). Women growing stronger with age: The effect of status in the United States and Kenya. *Psychology of Women Quarterly, 14,* 567–577. (p. 672)

**Tolchin, M.** (1994, April 17). Major airlines go two years without a fatality. *New York Times* report in *Grand Rapids Press,* p. A10. (p. 333)

**Tolman, E. C., & Honzik, C. H.** (1930). Introduction and removal of reward, and maze performance in rats. *University of California Publications in Psychology, 4,* 257–275. (p. 276)

**Tolstoy, L.** (1904). *My confessions.* Boston: Dana Estes. (p. 5)

**Tornstam, L.** (1992). Loneliness in marriage. *Journal of Social and Personal Relationships, 9,* 197–217. (p. 669)

**Torrey, E. F.** (1986). *Witchdoctors and psychiatrists.* New York: Harper & Row. (p. 561)

**Torrey, E. F., Bowler, A. E., Rawlings, R., & Terrazas, A.** (1993). Seasonality of schizophrenia and stillbirths. *Schizophrenia Bulletin, 19,* 557–562. (p. 526)

**Torrey, E. F., Torrey, B. B., & Peterson, M. A.** (1977). Seasonality of schizophrenic births in the United States. *Archives of General Psychiatry, 34,* 1065–1070. (p. 526)

**Toufexis, A.** (1993, May 24). Sex has many accents. *Time,* p. 66. (p. 126)

**Towler, G.** (1986). From zero to one hundred: Coaction in a natural setting. *Perceptual and Motor Skills, 62,* 377–378. (p. 627)

**Tramontana, M. G., Hooper, S. R., & Selzer, S. C.** (1988). Research on the preschool prediction of later academic achievement: A review. *Developmental Review, 8,* 89–146. (p. 378)

**Treisman, A.** (1987). Properties, parts, and objects. In K. R. Boff, L. Kaufman, & J. P. Thomas (Eds.), *Handbook of perception and human performance.* New York: Wiley. (p. 192)

**Triandis, H. C.** (1981). Some dimensions of intercultural variation and their implications for interpersonal behavior. Paper presented at the American Psychological Association convention. (p. 657)

**Triandis, H. C.** (1989a). The self and social behavior in differing cultural contexts. *Psychological Review, 96,* 506–520. (p. 659)

**Triandis, H. C.** (1989b). Cross-cultural studies of individualism and collectivism. In J. J. Berman (Ed.), *Nebraska symposium on motivation 1989* (Vol. 37). Lincoln: University of Nebraska Press. (p. 659)

**Triandis, H. C.** (1994). *Culture and social behavior.* New York: McGraw-Hill. (pp. 106, 342, 441, 490, 635, 657–660, 663, 678)

**Triandis, H. C., Bontempo, R., Villareal, M. J., Asai, M., & Lucca, N.** (1988). Individualism and collectivism: Cross-cultural perspectives on self-ingroup relationships. *Journal of Personality and Social Psychology, 54,* 323–338. (p. 660)

**Triandis, H. C., Brislin, R., & Hui, C. H.** (1988). Cross-cultural training across the individualism-collectivism divide. *International Journal of Intercultural Relations, 12,* 269–289. (p. 661)

**Trickett, P. K., & Putnam, F. W.** (1993). Impact of child sexual abuse on females: Toward a developmental, psychobiological integration. *Psychological Science, 4,* 81–87. (p. 313)

**Trimble, J. E.** (1994). Cultural variations in the use of alcohol and drugs. In W. J. Lonner & R. Malpass (Eds.), *Psychology and culture.* Boston: Allyn & Bacon. (p. 249)

**Triplett, N.** (1898). The dynamogenic factors in pacemaking and competition. *American Journal of Psychology, 9,* 507–533. (p. 627)

**Trolier, T. K., & Hamilton, D. L.** (1986). Variables influencing judgments of correlational relations. *Journal of Personality and Social Psychology, 50,* 879–888. (p. 22)

**Troll, L. E.** (1987). Mother-daughter relationships through the life span. In S. Oskamp (Ed.), *Family processes and problems: A social psychological analysis.* Newbury Park, CA: Sage. (p. 669)

**True, R. M.** (1949). Experimental control in hypnotic age regression states. *Science, 110,* 583–584. (p. 237)

**Tsang, Y. C.** (1938). Hunger motivation in gastrectomized rats. *Journal of Comparative Psychology, 26,* 1–17. (p. 402)

**Tsuang, M. T., & Faraone, S. V.** (1990). *The genetics of mood disorders.* Baltimore, MD: Johns Hopkins University Press. (p. 519)

**Tubbs, M. E.** (1986). Goal setting: A meta-analytic examination of the empirical evidence. *Journal of Applied Psychology, 71,* 474–483. (p. 424)

**Tucker, L. A.** (1983). Muscular strength and mental health. *Journal of Personality and Social Psychology, 45,* 1355–1360. (p. 473)

**Tulving, E., & Thomson, D. M.** (1973). Encoding specificity and retrieval processes in episodic memory. *Psychological Review, 80,* 352–373. (p. 309)

**Turk, D. C., Meichenbaum, D. H., & Berman, W. H.** (1979). Application of biofeedback for the regulation of pain: A critical review. *Psychological Bulletin, 86,* 1322–1338. (p. 595)

**Turkheimer, E.** (1991). Individual and group differences in adoption studies of IQ. *Psychological Bulletin, 110,* 392–405. (p. 385)

**Turkington, C.** (1987, August). Help for the worried well. *Psychology Today,* pp. 44–48. (p. 559)

**Turnbull, C.** (1961). *The forest people.* New York: Simon & Schuster. (p. 200)

**Turnbull, W. W.** (1986). *Student change, program change: Why SAT scores kept falling.* College Board Publications, Box 886, New York City 10101. (p. 367)

**Turner, C. W., Hesse, B. W., & Peterson-Lewis, S.** (1986). Naturalistic studies of the long-term effects of television violence. *Journal of Social Issues, 42*(3), 7–28. (p. 636)

**Turner, J. C.** (1987). *Rediscovering the social group: A self-categorization theory.* New York: Blackwell. (p. 664)

**Tversky, A.** (1985, June). Quoted in K. McKean, Decisions, decisions. *Discover,* pp. 22–31. (p. 332)

**Tversky, A., & Gati, I.** (1978). Studies of similarity. In E. Rosch & B. Lloyd (Eds.), *Cognition and categorization.* Hillsdale, NJ: Erlbaum. Reported by T. Gilovich (1991), *How we know what isn't so: The fallibility of human reason in everyday life.* New York: Free Press. (p. 16)

**Tversky, A., & Kahneman, D.** (1974). Judgment under uncertainty: Heuristics and biases. *Science, 185,* 1124–1131. (pp. 331, A–6)

**Tversky, A., & Kahneman, D.** (1983). Extensional versus intuitive reasoning: The conjunction fallacy in probability judgment. *Psychological Review, 90,* 293–315. (p. 332)

**Twiss, C., Tabb, S., & Crosby, F.** (1989). Affirmative action and aggregate data: The importance of patterns in the perception of discrimination. In F. Blanchard & F. Crosby (Eds.), *Affirmative action: Social psychological perspectives.* New York: Springer-Verlag. (p. A–5)

**U.S. Congress, Office of Technology Assessment.** (1983, November). *Scientific validity of polygraph testing: A research review and evaluation—A technical memorandum.* Washington, DC: U.S. Government Printing Office. (p. 437)

**Ulrich, R. E.** (1991). Animal rights, animal wrongs and the question of balance. *Psychological Science, 2,* 197–201. (p. 33)

**Ulrich, R. S.** (1984). View through a window may influence recovery from surgery. *Science, 224,* 420–421. (p. 177)

**Underwood, B. J.** (1957). Interference and forgetting. *Psychological Review, 64,* 49–60. (p. 315)

**United Nations** (1991). *The world's women 1970–1990: Trends and statistics.* New York: United Nations. (pp. 671, 683)

**United Nations** (1992). *1991 demographic yearbook.* New York: United Nations. (pp. 139, 632)

**United Nations** (1993). Children: A basic focus in IYF. *The Family,* No. 3., pp. 1–2. (p. 683)

**University of California** (1993, December). The new American body. *University of California at Berkeley Wellness Letter,* pp. 1–2. (p. 606)

**Urbany, J. E., Bearden, W. O., & Weilbaker, D. C.** (1988). The effect of plausible and exaggerated reference prices on consumer perceptions and price search. *Journal of Consumer Research, 15,* 95–110. (336)

**Usher, J. M.** (1992). Research and theory related to female reproduction: Implications for clinical psychology. *British Journal of Clinical Psychology, 31,* 129–151. (p. 591)

**Valenstein, E. S.** (1986). *Great and desperate cures: The rise and decline of psychosurgery.* New York: Basic Books. (pp. 58, 568)

**Vallone, R. P., Griffin, D. W., Lin, S., & Ross, L.** (1990). Overconfident prediction of future actions and outcomes by self and others. *Journal of Personality and Social Psychology, 58,* 582–592. (p. 15)

**Vance, E. B., & Wagner, N. N.** (1976). Written descriptions of orgasm: A study of sex differences. *Archives of Sexual Behavior, 5,* 87–98. (p. 410)

**Vandenberg, S. G., & Krause, A. R.** (1978). Mental rotations, a group test of three-dimensional spatial visualization. *Perceptual and Motor Skills, 47,* 599–604. (p. 667)

**van den Boom, D.** (1990). Preventive intervention and the quality of mother-infant interaction and infant exploration in irritable infants. In W. Koops, H. J. G. Soppe, J. L. van der Linden, P. C. M. Molenaar, & J. J. F. Schroots (Eds.), *Developmental psychology behind the dikes: An outline of developmental psychology research in The Netherlands.* The Netherlands: Uitgeverij Eburon. Cited by C. Hazan & P. R. Shaver (1994). Deeper into attachment theory. *Psychological Inquiry, 5,* 68–79. (p. 98)

**VanderStoep, S. W., & Shaughnessy, J. J.** (1991). The effects of a course in research methods in psychology on everyday scientific reasoning. Paper presented at the American Psychological Association convention. (p. 30)

**Van Dyke, C., & Byck, R.** (1982, March). Cocaine. *Scientific American,* pp. 128–141. (p. 244)

**Van Horn, J. D., & McManus, I. C.** (1992). Ventricular enlargement in schizophrenia: A meta-analysis of studies of the ventricular:brain ratio (VBR). *British Journal of Psychiatry, 160,* 687–697. (p. 526)

**van IJzendoorn, M. H., & Kroonenberg, P. M.** (1988). Cross-cultural patterns of attachment: A meta-analysis of the strange situation. *Child Development, 59,* 147–156. (p. 97)

**Van Leeuwen, M. S.** (1978). A cross-cultural examination of psychological differentiation in males and females. *International Journal of Psychology, 13,* 87–122. (p. 678)

**Van Leeuwen, M. S.** (1982). IQism and the just society: Historical background. *Journal of the American Scientific Affiliation, 34,* 193–201. (p. 366)

**VanTassel-Baska, J.** (1983). Profiles of precocity: The 1982 Midwest Talent Search finalists. *Gifted Child Quarterly, 27,* 139–145. (p. 378)

**Van Yperen, N. W., & Buunk, B. P.** (1990). A longitudinal study of equity and satisfaction in intimate relationships. *European Journal of Social Psychology, 20,* 287–309. (p. 649)

**Vaughn, K. B., & Lanzetta, J. T.** (1981). The effect of modification of expressive displays on vicarious emotional arousal. *Journal of Experimental Social Psychology, 17,* 16–30. (p. 433)

**Vaux, A.** (1988). Social and personal factors in loneliness. *Journal of Social and Clinical Psychology, 6,* 462–471. (p. 522)

**Vekassy, L.** (1977). Dreams of the blind. *Magyar Pszichologiai Szemle, 34,* 478–491. (p. 227)

**Vemer, E., Coleman, M., Ganong, L. H., & Cooper, H.** (1989). Marital satisfaction in remarriage: A meta-analysis. *Journal of Marriage and the Family, 51,* 713–725. (p. 140)

**Venn, J.** (1986). Hypnosis and the Lamaze method: A reply to Wideman and Singer. *American Psychologist, 41,* 475–476. (p. 238)

**Verbrugge, L. M., & Gruber-Baldini, A. L.** (1993). Age differences and aging changes in activities (Baltimore Longitudinal Study of Aging). Unpublished manuscript, Institute of Gerontology, University of Michigan. (p. 679)

**Vernon, P. A.** (1983). Speed of information processing and general intelligence. *Intelligence, 7,* 53–70. (p. 377)

**Vetter, B. M.** (1989, July 7). Manpower data need an overhaul. *AAAS Observer,* p. 10 (presents NSF estimate of 254,000 psychologists and Bureau of Labor Statistics estimate of 165,000). (p. 2)

**Vokey, J. R., & Read, J. D.** (1985). Subliminal messages: Between the devil and the media. *American Psychologist, 40,* 1231–1239. (pp. 154, 206)

**von Békésy, G.** (1957, August). The ear. *Scientific American,* pp. 66–78. (p. 169)

**von Frisch, K.** (1950). *Bees: Their vision, chemical senses, and language.* Ithaca, NY: Cornell University Press. (p. 347)

**von Frisch, K.** (1974). Decoding the language of the bee. *Science, 185,* 663–668. (p. 347)

**von Senden, M.,** (1932; reprinted 1960). In P. Heath (Trans.), *Space and sight: The perception of space and shape in the congenitally blind before and after operation.* Glencoe, IL: Free Press. (p. 203)

**Vygotsky, L. S.** (1932, reprinted 1962). *Thought and language* (E. Haufmann & G. Vaker, Eds. & Trans.). Cambridge, MA: MIT Press. (pp. 78, 93)

**Waddington, J. L.** (1993). Neurodynamics of abnormalities in cerebral metabolism and structure in schizophrenia. *Schizophrenia Bulletin, 19,* 55–69. (p. 526)

**Wagstaff, G.** (1982). Attitudes to rape: The "just world" strikes again? *Bulletin of the British Psychological Society, 13,* 275–283. (p. 615)

**Wahl, O. F.** (1992). Mass media images of mental illness: A review of the literature. *Journal of Community Psychology, 20,* 343–352. (p. 534)

**Wakefield, J. C.** (1987). The semantics of success: Do masturbation exercises lead to partner orgasm? *Journal of Sex and Marital Therapy, 13,* 3–14. (p. 413)

**Wakefield, J. C.** (1992). The concept of mental disorder: On the boundary between biological facts and social values. *American Psychologist, 47,* 373–388. (p. 500)

**Waldrop, M. M.** (1987). The workings of working memory. *Science, 237,* 1564–1567. (p. 297)

**Waldrop, M. M.** (1988). National Academy looks at computing's future. *Science, 241,* 1436. (p. 340)

**Wallach, M. A., & Wallach, L.** (1983). *Psychology's sanction for selfishness: The error of egoism in theory and therapy.* New York: Freeman. (p. 486)

**Wallach, M. A., & Wallach, L.** (1985, February). How psychology sanctions the cult of the self. *Washington Monthly,* pp. 46–56. (p. 486)

**Wallbott, H. G.** (1988). In and out of context: Influences of facial expression and context information on emotion attributions. *British Journal of Social Psychology, 27,* 357–369. (p. 208)

**Wallerstein, J. S.** (1991). The long-term effects of divorce on children: A review. *Journal of the American Academy of Child and Adolescent Psychiatry, 30,* 349–360. (p. 103)

**Wallis, C.** (1983, June 6). Stress: Can we cope? *Time,* pp. 48–54. (p. 578)

**Wallis, C.** (1987, October 12). Back off, buddy: A new Hite report stirs up a furor over sex and love in the '80s. *Time,* pp. 68–73. (p. 20)

**Wallis, C.** (1989, December 4). Onward, women! *Time,* pp. 80–89. (p. 679)

**Walster (Hatfield), E., Aronson, V., Abrahams, D., & Rottman, L.** (1966). Importance of physical attractiveness in dating behavior. *Journal of Personality and Social Psychology, 4,* 508–516. (p. 645)

**Warchol, M. E., Lambert, P. R., Goldstein, B. J., Forge, A., & Corwin, J. T.** (1993). Regenerative proliferation in inner ear sensory epithelia from adult guinea pigs and humans. *Science, 259,* 1619–1622. (p. 172)

**Ward, C.** (1994). Culture and altered states of consciousness. In W. J. Lonner & R. Malpass (Eds.), *Psychology and culture.* Boston: Allyn & Bacon. (p. 242)

**Ward, W. C., & Jenkins, H. M.** (1965). The display of information and the judgment of contingency. *Canadian Journal of Psychology, 19,* 231–241. (p. 22)

**Warm, J. S., & Dember, W. N.** (1986, April). Awake at the switch. *Psychology Today,* pp. 46–53. (p. 153)

**Warr, P., & Payne, R.** (1982). Experiences of strain and pleasure among British adults. *Social Science and Medicine, 16,* 1691–1697. (p. 597)

**Wason, P. C.** (1960). On the failure to eliminate hypotheses in a conceptual task. *Quarterly Journal of Experimental Psychology, 12,* 129–140. (p. 328)

**Wason, P. C.** (1981). The importance of cognitive illusions. *The Behavioral and Brain Sciences, 4,* 356. (p. 16)

**Wass, H., Christian, M., Myers, J., & Murphey, M.** (1978–1979). Similarities and dissimilarities in attitudes toward death in a population of older persons. *Omega, 9,* 337–354. (p. 143)

**Wasserman, E. A.** (1993). Comparative cognition: Toward a general understanding of cognition in behavior. *Psychological Science, 4,* 156–161. (p. 269)

**Waterhouse, R.** (1993, July 19). Income for 62 percent is below average pay. *The Independent,* p. 4. (p. A–2)

**Waterman, A. S.** (1988). Identity status theory and Erikson's theory: Commonalities and differences. *Developmental Review, 8,* 185–208. (p. 124)

**Watkins, J. G.** (1984). The Bianchi (L. A. Hillside Strangler) case: Sociopath or multiple personality? *International Journal of Clinical and Experimental Hypnosis, 32,* 67–101. (p. 512)

**Watson, J. B.** (1913). Psychology as the behaviorist views it. *Psychological Review, 20,* 158–177. (pp. 219, 259)

**Watson, J. B.** (1924). *Behaviorism.* New York: Norton. (p. 266)

**Watson, J. B., & Rayner, R.** (1920). Conditioned emotional reactions. *Journal of Experimental Psychology, 3,* 1–14. (p. 266)

**Watson, R. I., Jr.** (1973). Investigation into deindividuation using a cross-cultural survey technique. *Journal of Personality and Social Psychology, 25,* 342–345. (p. 628)

**Weaver, J. B., Masland, J. L., & Zillmann, D.** (1984). Effect of erotica on young men's aesthetic perception of their female sexual partners. *Perceptual and Motor Skills, 58,* 929–930. (p. 412)

**Webb, W. B.** (1992). *Sleep: The gentle tyrant.* Bolton, MA: Anker Publishing. (pp. 224, 226)

**Webb, W. B., & Campbell, S. S.** (1983). Relationships in sleep characteristics of identical and fraternal twins. *Archives of General Psychiatry, 40,* 1093–1095. (p. 226)

**Weinberg, M. S., & Williams, C.** (1974). *Male homosexuals: Their problems and adaptations.* New York: Oxford University Press. (p. 414)

**Weinberg, R., Scarr, S., & Waldman, I.** (1990). The Minnesota transracial adoption study: A follow-up of IQ test performance at adolescence. Paper presented at the American Psychological Society convention. (p. 390)

**Weiner, B.** (1985). An attributional theory of achievement motivation and emotion. *Psychological Review, 92,* 548–573. (p. 457)

**Weingartner, H., Rudorfer, M. V., Buchsbaum, M. S., & Linnoila, M.** (1983). Effects of serotonin on memory impairments produced by ethanol. *Science, 221,* 472–473. (p. 304)

**Weinstein, N. D.** (1980). Unrealistic optimism about future life events. *Journal of Personality and Social Psychology, 39,* 806–820. (p. 491)

**Weinstein, N. D.** (1982). Unrealistic optimism about susceptibility to health problems. *Journal of Behavioral Medicine, 5,* 441–460. (p. 491)

**Weinstein, N. D.** (1987). Unrealistic optimism about susceptibility to health problems: Conclusions from a community-wide sample. *Journal of Behavioral Medicine, 10,* 481–500. (p. 608)

**Weiss, J. M.** (1977). Psychological and behavioral influences on gastrointestinal lesions in animal models. In J. D. Maser & M. E. P. Seligman (Eds.), *Psychopathology: Experimental models.* San Francisco: Freeman. (p. 580)

**Weisse, C. S.** (1992). Depression and immunocompetence: A review of the literature. *Psychological Bulletin, 111,* 475–489. (p. 584)

**Weissman, M. M., Merikangas, K. R., Wickramaratne, P., Kidd, K. K., Prusoff, B. A., Leckman, J. F., & Pauls, D. L.** (1986). Understanding the clinical heterogeneity of major depression using family data. *Archives of General Psychiatry, 43,* 430–434. (p. 518)

**Weisz, J. R., Rothbaum, F. M., & Blackburn, T. C.** (1984). Standing out and standing in: The psychology of control in America and Japan. *American Psychologist, 39,* 955–969. (p. 656)

**Wellman, H. M., & Gelman, S. A.** (1992). Cognitive development: Foundational theories of core domains. *Annual Review of Psychology, 43,* 337–375. (p. 92)

**Wells, B. L.** (1986). Predictors of female nocturnal orgasms: A multivariate analysis. *Journal of Sex Research, 22,* 421–437. (p. 412)

**Wells, C.** (1983, March). Teaching the brain new tricks. *Esquire,* pp. 49–57. (p. 297)

**Wells, G., & Murray, D. M.** (1984). Eyewitness confidence. In G. L. Wells & E. F. Loftus (Eds.), *Eyewitness testimony: Psychological perspectives.* New York: Cambridge University Press. (p. 312)

**Wells, G. L.** (1981). Lay analyses of causal forces on behavior. In J. Harvey (Ed.), *Cognition, social behavior and the environment.* Hillsdale, NJ: Erlbaum. (p. 258)

**Wender, P. H., Kety, S. S., Rosenthal, D., Schulsinger, F., Ortmann, J., & Lunde, I.** (1986). Psychiatric disorders in the biological and adoptive families of adopted individuals with affective disorders. *Archives of General Psychiatry, 43,* 923–929. (p. 519)

**Wenderoth, P.** (1992). Perceptual illusions. *Australian Journal of Psychology, 44,* 147–151. (p. 191)

**Wener, R., Frazier, W., & Farbstein, J.** (1987, June). Building better jails. *Psychology Today,* pp. 40–49. (p. 490)

**Werker, J. F.** (1989). Becoming a native listener. *American Scientist, 77,* 54–59. (p. 343)

**West, P. D. B., & Evans, E. F.** (1990). Early detection of hearing damage in young listeners resulting from exposure to amplified music. *British Journal of Audiology, 24,* 89–103. (p. 170)

**Westefeld, J. S., & Furr, S. R.** (1987). Suicide and depression among college students. *Professional Psychology: Research and Practice, 18,* 119–123. (p. 516)

**Wever, E. G.** (1949). *Theory of hearing.* New York: Wiley. (p. 171)

**Wheeler, D. L., Jacobson, D. L., Paglieri, R. A., & Schwartz, A. A.** (1993). An experimental assessment of facilitated communication. *Mental Retardation, 31,* 49–60. (p. 626)

**Wheeler, L., Reis, H. T., & Bond, M. H.** (1989). Collectivism-individualism in everyday social life: The middle kingdom and the melting pot. *Journal of Personality and Social Psychology, 57,* 79–86. (p. 659)

**Whelan, J. P., Mahoney, M. J., & Meyers, A. W.** (1991). Performance enhancement in sport: A cognitive behavioral domain. *Behavior Therapy, 22,* 307–327. (p. 354)

**Whitbourne, S. K., Zuschlag, M. K., Elliot, L. B., & Waterman, A. S.** (1992). Psychosocial development in adulthood: A 22-year sequential study. *Journal of Personality and Social Psychology, 63,* 260–271. (p. 146)

**White, G. L., & Kight, T. D.** (1984). Misattribution of arousal and attraction: Effects of salience of explanations for arousal. *Journal of Experimental Social Psychology, 20,* 55–64. (p. 647)

**White, H. R., Brick, J., & Hansell, S.** (1993). A longitudinal investigation of alcohol use and aggression in adolescence. *Journal of Studies on Alcohol,* Supplement No. 11, 62–77. (p. 633)

**White, K. M.** (1983). Young adults and their parents: Individuation to mutuality. *New Directions for Child Development, 22,* 61–76. (p. 125)

**White, L., & Edwards, J.** (1990). Emptying the nest and parental well-being: An analysis of national panel data. *American Sociological Review, 55,* 235–242. (p. 141)

**Whitehead, B. D.** (1993, April). Dan Quayle was right. *The Atlantic,* pp. 47–84. (p. 100)

**Whiten, A., & Byrne, R. W.** (1988). Tactical deception in primates. *Behavioral and Brain Sciences, 11,* 233–244, 267–273. (p. 21)

**Whiting, B. B., & Edwards, C. P.** (1988). *Children of different worlds: The formation of social behavior.* Cambridge, MA: Harvard University Press. (p. 106)

**Whitley, B. E., Jr.** (1990). The relationships of heterosexuals' attributions for the causes of homosexuality to attitudes toward lesbians and gay men. *Personality and Social Psychology Bulletin, 16,* 369–377. (p. 416)

**Whorf, B. L.** (1956). Science and linguistics. In J. B. Carroll (Ed.), *Language, thought, and reality: Selected writings of Benjamin Lee Whorf.* Cambridge, MA: MIT Press. (p. 352)

**Wickelgren, W. A.** (1977). *Learning and memory.* Englewood Cliffs, NJ: Prentice-Hall. (p. 294)

**Wicker, A. W.** (1971). An examination of the "other variables" explanation of attitude-behavior inconsistency. *Journal of Personality and Social Psychology, 19,* 18–30. (p. 615)

**Wickless, C., & Kirsch, I.** (1989). Effects of verbal and experiential expectancy manipulations on hypnotic susceptibility. *Journal of Personality and Social Psychology, 57,* 762–768. (p. 234)

**Widom, C. S.** (1989a). Does violence beget violence? A critical examination of the literature. *Psychological Bulletin, 106,* 3–28. (p. 101)

**Widom, C. S.** (1989b). The cycle of violence. *Science, 244,* 160–166. (p. 101)

**Wiens, A. N., & Menustik, C. E.** (1983). Treatment outcome and patient characteristics in an aversion therapy program for alcoholism. *American Psychologist, 38,* 1089–1096. (p. 549)

**Wierzbicki, M.** (1993). Psychological adjustment of adoptees: A meta-analysis. *Journal of Clinical Child Psychology, 22,* 447–454. (p. 111)

**Wiesel, T. N.** (1982). Postnatal development of the visual cortex and the influence of environment. *Nature, 299,* 583–591. (p. 203)

**Wigdor, A. K., & Garner, W. R.** (1982). *Ability testing: Uses, consequences, and controversies.* Washington, DC: National Academy Press. (p. 392)

**Wilder, D. A.** (1981). Perceiving persons as a group: Categorization and intergroup relations. In D. L. Hamilton (Ed.), *Cognitive processes in stereotyping and intergroup behavior.* Hillsdale, NJ: Erlbaum. (p. 684)

**Willerman, L., Schultz, R., Rutledge, J. N., & Bigler, E. D.** (1991). *In vivo* brain size and intelligence. *Intelligence, 15* 223–228. (p. 376)

**Williams, C. L.** (1989). *Gender differences at work: Women and men in nontraditional occupations.* Berkeley: University of California Press. (p. 678)

**Williams, C. L., & Berry, J. W.** (1991). Primary prevention of acculturative stress among refugees. *American Psychologist, 46,* 632–641. (p. 578)

**Williams, J. E.** (1992). Culture and behavior: Sense and nonsense. Presidential address to the Southeastern Psychological Association convention. (p. 26)

**Williams, J. E., & Best, D. L.** (1990). *Measuring sex stereotypes: A multination study.* Newbury Park, CA: Sage. (p. 671)

**Williams, L. M.** (in press). Recall of childhood trauma: A prospective study of women's memories of child sexual abuse. *Journal of Consulting and Clinical Psychology.* (p. 318)

**Williams, R.** (1989). *The trusting heart: Great news about Type A behavior.* New York: Random House. (p. 582)

**Williams, R.** (1993). *Anger kills.* New York: Times Books. (p. 582)

**Williams, R. B., Barefoot, J. C., Califf, R. M., Haney, T. L., Saunders, W. B., Pryor, D. B., Hlatky, M. A., Siegler, I. C., & Mark, D. B.** (1992). Prognostic importance of social and economic resources among medically treated patients with angiographically documented coronary artery disease. *Journal of the American Medical Association, 267,* 520–524. (p. 597)

**Williams, S. L.** (1987). Self-efficacy and mastery-oriented treatment for severe phobias. Paper presented to the American Psychological Association convention. (p. 547).

**Willingham, W. W., Lewis, C., Morgan, R., & Ramist, L.** (1990). *Predicting college grades: An analysis of institutional trends over two decades.* Princeton, NJ: Educational Testing Service. (p. 368)

**Willmuth, M. E.** (1987). Sexuality after spinal cord injury: A critical review. *Clinical Psychology Review, 7,* 389–412. (p. 412)

**Wilson, J. P., Harel, Z., & Kahana, B.** (1988). *Human adaptation to extreme stress: From the Holocaust to Vietnam.* New York: Plenum Press. (p. 579)

**Wilson, J. Q., & Herrnstein, R. J.** (1985). *Crime and human nature.* New York: Simon & Schuster. (p. 633)

**Wilson, R. C., Gaft, J. G., Dienst, E. R., Wood, L., & Bavry, J. L.** (1975). *College professors and their impact on students.* New York: Wiley. (p. 629)

**Wilson, R. S.** (1978). Synchronies in mental development: An epigenetic perspective. *Science, 202,* 939–948. (p. 87)

**Wilson, R. S.** (1979). Analysis of longitudinal twin data: Basic model and applications to physical growth measures. *Acta Geneticae medicae et Gemellologiae, 28,* 93–105. (p. 87)

**Wilson, R. S., & Matheny, A. P., Jr.** (1986). Behavior-genetics research in infant temperament: The Louisville twin study. In R. Plomin & J. Dunn (Eds.), *The study of temperament: Changes, continuities, and challenges.* Hillsdale, NJ: Erlbaum. (p. 97)

**Wilson, S. C., & Barber, T. X.** (1983). The fantasy-prone personality: Implications for understanding imagery, hypnosis, and parapsychological phenomena. In A. A. Sheikh (Ed.), *Imagery: Current theory, research, and applications.* New York: Wiley. (pp. 231, 252)

**Wilson, W. R.** (1979). Feeling more than we can know: Exposure effects without learning. *Journal of Personality and Social Psychology, 37,* 811–821. (p. 188)

**Winckelgren, I.** (1992). How the brain `sees' borders where there are none. *Science, 256,* 1520–1521. (p. 191)

**Windholz, G.** (1989, April-June). The discovery of the principles of reinforcement, extinction, generalization, and differentiation of conditional reflexes in Pavlov's laboratories. *Pavlovian Journal of Biological Science, 26,* 64–74. (p. 262)

**Wing, R. R., & Jeffrey, R. W.** (1979). Outpatient treatments of obesity: A comparison of methodology and clinical results. *International Journal of Obesity, 3,* 261–279. (p. 607)

**Wingert, P., & Kantrowitz, B.** (1990, Winter/Spring). The day care generation. *Newsweek special edition: The 21st century family,* pp. 86–92. (p. 102)

**Winkelstein, W., Jr., Samuel, M., Padian, N. S., & Wiley, J. A.** (1987). Selected sexual practices of San Francisco heterosexual men and risk of infection by the human immunodeficiency virus. *Journal of the American Medical Association, 257,* 1470. (p. 413)

**Witelson, S. F.** (1985). The brain connection: The corpus callosum is larger in left-handers. *Science, 229,* 665–667. (p. 68)

**Witelson, S. F., & McCulloch, P. B.** (1991). Premortem and postmorten measurement to study structure with function: A human brain collection. *Schizophrenia Bulletin, 17,* 583–591. (p. 376)

**Wixted, J. T., & Ebbesen, E. B.** (1991). On the form of forgetting. *Psychological Science, 2,* 409–415. (p. 301)

**Woehr, D. J., & Cavell, T. A.** (1993). Self-report measures of ability, effort, and nonacademic activity as predictors of introductory psychology test scores. *Teaching of Psychology, 20,* 156–160. (p. 8)

**Wolf, N.** (1991). *The beauty myth: How images of beauty are used against women.* New York: Morrow. (p. 606)

**Woll, S.** (1986). So many to choose from: Decision strategies in videodating. *Journal of Social and Personal Relationships, 3,* 43–52. (p. 645)

**Wolpe, J.** (1958). *Psychotherapy by reciprocal inhibition.* Stanford, CA: Stanford University Press. (p. 547)

**Wolpe, J.** (1982). *The practice of behavior therapy.* New York: Pergamon. (p. 547)

**Wong, D. F., & associates.** (1986). Positron emission tomography reveals elevated D2 dopamine receptors in drug-naive schizophrenics. *Science, 234,* 1588–1563. (p. 526)

**Wong, M. M., & Csikszentmihalyi, M.** (1991). Affiliation motivation and daily experience: Some issues on gender differences. *Journal of Personality and Social Psychology, 60,* 154–164. (p. 670)

**Wood, C. J, & Aggleton, J. P.** (1989). Handedness in "fast ball" sports: Do left-handers have an innate advantage? *British Journal of Psychology, 80,* 227–240. (p. 68)

**Wood, G.** (1979). The knew-it-all-along effect. *Journal of Experimental Psychology: Human Perception and Performance, 4,* 345–353. (p. 14)

**Wood, J. M., Bootzin, R. R., Kihlstrom, J. F., & Schacter, D. L.** (1992). Implicit and explicit memory for verbal information presented during sleep. *Psychological Science, 3,* 236–239. (p. 292)

**Wood, J. M., Bootzin, R. R., Rosenhan, D., Nolen-Hoeksema, S., & Jourden, F.** (1992). Effects of the 1989 San Francisco earthquake on frequency and content of nightmares. *Journal of Abnormal Psychology, 101,* 219–224. (p. 228)

**Wood, J. V., Saltzberg, J. A., & Goldsamt, L. A.** (1990). Does affect induce self-focused attention? *Journal of Personality and Social Psychology, 58,* 899–908. (pp. 311, 521)

**Wood, J. V., Saltzberg, J. A., Neale, J. M., Stone, A. A., & Rachmiel, T. B.** (1990). Self-focused attention, coping responses, and distressed mood in everyday life. *Journal of Personality and Social Psychology, 58,* 1027–1036. (p. 521)

**Wood, W.** (1987). Meta-analytic review of sex differences in group performance. *Psychological Bulletin, 102,* 53–71. (p. 671)

**Wood, W., Lundgren, S., Ouellette, J. A., Busceme, S., & Blackstone, T.** (1994). Minority influence: A meta-analytic review of social influence processes. *Psychological Bulletin, 115,* 323–345. (p. 630)

**Wood, W., Wong, F. Y., & Chachere, J. G.** (1991). Effects of media violence on viewers' aggression in unconstrained social interaction. *Psychological Bulletin, 109,* 371–383. (p. 636)

**Woodruff-Pak, D. S.** (1989). Aging and intelligence: Changing perspectives in the twentieth century. *Journal of Aging Studies, 3,* 91–118. (p. 136)

**Woods, N. F., Dery, G. K., & Most, A.** (1983). Recollections of menarche, current menstrual attitudes, and premenstrual symptoms. In S. Golub (Ed.), *Menarche: The transition from girl to woman.* Lexington, MA: Lexington Books. (p. 118)

**Wooley, S., & Wooley, O.** (1983). Should obesity be treated at all? *Psychiatric Annals, 13*(11), 884–885, 888. (p. 406)

**World Health Organization.**(1979). *Schizophrenia: An international follow-up study.* Chicester, England: Wiley. (p. 525)

**Worobey, J., & Blajda, V. M.** (1989). Temperament ratings at 2 weeks, 2 months, and 1 year: Differential stability of activity and emotionality. *Developmental Psychology, 25,* 257–263. (p. 97)

**Worthington, E. L., Jr.** (1989). Religious faith across the life span: Implications for counseling and research. *The Counseling Psychologist, 17,* 555–612. (p. 120)

**Worthington, E. L., Jr., Martin, G. A., Shumate, M., & Carpenter, J.** (1983). The effect of brief Lamaze training and social encouragement on pain endurance in a cold pressor tank. *Journal of Applied Social Psychology, 13,* 223–233. (p. 177)

**Wortman, C. B., & Silver, R. C.** (1989). The myths of coping with loss. *Journal of Consulting and Clinical Psychology, 57,* 349–357. (p. 143)

**Wright, P., & Murray, R. M.** (1993). Schizophrenia: Prenatal influenza and autoimmunity. *Annals of Medicine, 25,* 497–502. (p. 526)

**Wu, T-C., Tashkin, D. P., Djahed, B., & Rose, J. E.** (1988). Pulmonary hazards of smoking marijuana as compared with tobacco. *New England Journal of Medicine, 318,* 347–351. (p. 247)

**Wulff, D.** (1991). *The psychology of religion.* New York: Wiley. (p. 422)

**Wyatt, J. K., & Bootzin, R. R.** (1994). Cognitive processing and sleep: Implications for enhancing job performance. *Human Performance, 7,* 119–139. (pp. 228, 292)

**Wynn, K.** (1992). Addition and subtraction by human infants. *Nature, 358,* 749–759. (p. 92)

**Wysocki, C. J., & Gilbert, A. N.** (1989). *National Geographic* survey: Effects of age are heterogeneous. *Annals of the New York Academy of Sciences, 561,* 12–28. (p. 180)

**Yalom, I. D.** (1985). *The theory and practice of group psychotherapy* (3rd ed.). New York: Basic Books. (p. 554)

**Yang, K., & Bond, M. H.** (1990). Exploring implicit personality theories with indigenous or imported constructs: The Chinese case. *Journal of Personality and Social Psychology, 58,* 1087–1095. (p. 475)

**Yang, N., & Linz, D.** (1990). Movie ratings and the content of adult videos: The sex-violence ratio. *Journal of Communication, 40*(2), 28–42. (p. 637)

**Yarmey, A. D.** (1991). Voice identification over the telephone. *Journal of Applied Social Psychology, 21,* 1868–1876. (p. 312)

**Yarnell, P. R., & Lynch, S.** (1970, April 25). Retrograde memory immediately after concussion. *Lancet,* pp. 863–865. (p. 304)

**Yarrow, L. J., Goodwin, M. S., Manheimer, H., & Milowe, I. D.** (1973). Infancy experience and cognitive and personality development at ten years. In L. J. Stone, H. T. Smith, & L. B. Murphy (Eds.), *The competent infant.* New York: Basic Books. (p. 101)

**Yates, A.** (1989). Current perspectives on the eating disorders: I. History, psychological and biological aspects. *Journal of the American Academy of Child and Adolescent Psychiatry, 28,* 813–828. (p. 406)

**Yates, A.** (1990). Current perspectives on the eating disorders: II. Treatment, outcome, and research directions. *Journal of the American Academy of Child and Adolescent Psychiatry, 29,* 1–9. (p. 406)

**Zajonc, R. B.** (1965). Social facilitation. *Science, 149,* 269–274. (p. 627)

**Zajonc, R. B.** (1980). Feeling and thinking: Preferences need no inferences. *American Psychologist, 35,* 151–175. (p. 456)

**Zajonc, R. B.** (1984a). On the primacy of affect. *American Psychologist, 39,* 117–123. (p. 456)

**Zajonc, R. B.** (1984b, July 22). Quoted in D. Goleman, Rethinking IQ tests and their value. *The New York Times,* p. D22. (p. 362)

**Zajonc, R. B., & Markus, G. B.** (1975). Birth order and intellectual development. *Psychological Review, 82,* 74–88. (p. A–8)

**Zajonc, R. B., Murphy, S. T., & Inglehart, M.** (1989). Feeling and facial efference: Implications of the vascular theory of emotions. *Psychological Review, 96,* 395–416. (p. 442)

**Zanna, M. P., & Pack, S. J.** (1975). On the self-fulfilling nature of apparent sex differences in behavior. *Journal of Experimental Social Psychology, 11,* 583–591. (p. 677)

**Zaslow, M. J.** (1991). Variation in child care quality and its implications for children. *Journal of Social Issues, 47*(2), 125–138. (p. 101)

**Zebrowitz-McArthur, L.** (1988). Person perception in cross-cultural perspective. In M. H. Bond (Ed.), *The cross-cultural challenge to social psychology.* Newbury Park, CA: Sage. (p. 661)

**Zechmeister, E. B., & Johnson, J. E.** (1992). *Critical thinking: A functional approach.* Pacific Grove, CA: Brooks/Cole. (p. 693)

**Zeidner, M.** (1990). Perceptions of ethnic group modal intelligence: Reflections of cultural stereotypes or intelligence test scores? *Journal of Cross-Cultural Psychology, 21,* 214–231. (p. 388)

**Zelnick, M., & Kim, Y. J.** (1982). Sex education and its association with teenage sexual activity, pregnancy, and contraceptive use. *Family Planning Perspectives, 14*(3), 117–126. (p. 417)

**Zigler, E. F.** (1986, February). Quoted in D. Meredith, Day care: The nine-to-five dilemma. *Psychology Today,* pp. 36–39, 42–44. (p. 101)

**Zigler, E. F.** (1987). Formal schooling for four-year-olds? No. *American Psychologist, 42,* 254–260. (p. 386)

**Zigler, E. F.** (1990). Letter. *Science, 248,* 1176. (p. 387)

**Zigler, E. F., & Muenchow, S.** (1992). *Head Start: The inside story of a great American experiment*. New York: Basic Books. (p. 387)

**Zilbergeld, B.** (1983). *The shrinking of America: Myths of psychological change.* Boston: Little, Brown. (pp. 557, 559)

**Zillmann, D.** (1986). *Effects of prolonged consumption of pornography.* Background paper for The Surgeon General's Workshop on Pornography and Public Health, June 22–24. Report prepared by E. P. Mulvey & J. L. Haugaard and released by Office of the Surgeon General on August 4, 1986. (pp. 435, 456)

**Zillmann, D.** (1989). Effects of prolonged consumption of pornography. In D. Zillmann & J. Bryant (Eds.), *Pornography: Research advances and policy considerations.* Hillsdale, NJ: Erlbaum. (pp. 412, 638)

**Zillmann, D., & Bryant, J.** (1984). Effects of massive exposure to pornography. In N. Malamuth & E. Donnerstein (Eds.), *Pornography and sexual aggression.* Orlando, FL: Academic Press. (p. 638)

**Zimbardo, P. G.** (1970). The human choice: Individuation, reason, and order versus deindividuation, impulse, and chaos. In W. J. Arnold & D. Levine (Eds.), *Nebraska Symposium on Motivation, 1969.* Lincoln, NE: University of Nebraska Press. (p. 628)

**Zimbardo, P. G.** (1972, April). Pathology of imprisonment. *Transaction/Society*, pp. 4–8. (p. 618)

**Zinbarg, R. E., Barlow, D. H., Brown, T. A., & Hertz, R. M.** (1992). Cognitive-behavioral approaches to the nature and treatment of anxiety disorders. *Annual Review of Psychology, 43,* 235–267. (p. 553)

**Zoglin, R.** (1992, November 23). Can anybody work this thing? *Time,* p. 67. (p. 209)

**Zucker, G. S., & Weiner, B.** (1993). Conservatism and perceptions of poverty: An attributional analysis. *Journal of Applied Social Psychology, 23,* 925–943. (p. 615)

**Zuckerman, M.** (1979). *Sensation seeking: Beyond the optimal level of arousal.* Hillsdale, NJ: Erlbaum. (p. 399)

**Zuckerman, M.** (1990). Some dubious premises in research and theory on racial differences: Scientific, social, and ethical issues. *American Psychologist, 45,* 1297–1303. (p. 662)

# Illustration Credits

INTRODUCTION

**Opener** Santi Visalli/The Image Bank **p. 4** (*top and bottom*) Laura Dwight **p. 6** (*left*) Richard Howard (*center and right*) Treë

CHAPTER **1**

**Opener p. 10** Rick Friedman/Black Star **p. 12** Rob Kinmonth **p. 14** AP/World Wide Photos **p. 18** Susan Kuklin/Photo Researchers **p. 19** Elsa Peterson/Design Conceptions **p. 21** Courtesy of David S. Wilkie **Fig. 1–3** Reprinted by permission of The Free Press, an imprint of Simon & Schuster from *How We Know What Isn't So: The Fallibility of Human Reason in Everyday Life* by Thomas Gilovich. Copyright © 1991 Thomas Gilovich. **Fig. 1–4** Barry Ross/Copyright © 1987 *Discover Magazine* **p. 26** Movie Still Archives **Fig. 1–6** Frank, M. G., & Gilovich, T. (1988). The dark side of self and social perception: Black uniforms and aggression in professional sports. *Journal of Personality and Social Psychology, 54,* 74–85. Copyright © 1988 American Psychological Association. Reprinted by permission. **p. 32** Mark S. Wexler/Woodfin Camp & Associates **p. 33** Jim Amos/Science Source/Photo Researchers **p. 36** From *Mind Sights* by Roger N. Shepard. Copyright © 1990 Roger N. Shepard. Reprinted by permission of W. H. Freeman and Company.

CHAPTER **2**

**Opener p. 40** Bradley E. Clift **p. 53** A. Glauberman/Photo Researchers **Fig. 2–10** Alexander Tsiaras/Stock, Boston **Fig. 2–11** Hank Morgan/Rainbow **Fig. 2–12** Daniel R. Weinberger, M.D., CBDB, NIMH **p. 58** (*top*) Frank Siteman/Stock, Boston (*bottom*) Pix*ELATION from Fran Heyl Associates **Fig. 2–16** Adapted from Gazzaniga, M. S., Steen, D., & Volpe, B. T. (1979). *Functional neuroscience* (p. 278). New York: Harper & Row. Copyright © 1979 Harper & Row Publishers, Inc. Reprinted by permission of HarperCollins Publishers, Inc. **Fig. 2–20** Courtesy of Drs. Jack Belliveau and Bruce Rosen, Massachusetts General Hospital, NMR Center **Fig. 2–22** Rose, S. (1983). *The conscious brain*. New York: Alfred A. Knopf. Copyright © 1973 by Steven Rose. Reprinted by permission of Alfred A. Knopf, Inc. **p. 63** Courtesy of Marcus Raichle, MD, Mallinckrodt Institute of Radiology, St. Louis, MO **Fig. 2–23** Adapted from Specialization of the human brain by N. Geschwind. Copyright © 1979 Scientific American, Inc. All rights reserved. **Fig. 2–24** Martin M. Rotker **Figs. 2–26, 2–27** Gazzaniga, M. S. (1983). Right hemisphere language following brain bisection: A 20-year perspective. *American Psychologist, 38,* 525–537. **p. 69** Courtesy of Drs. Michael E. Phelps and John Mazziotta, UCLA School of Medicine

CHAPTER **3**

**Opener p. 76** Don & Liysa King/Lightwaves/The Image Bank **p. 79** Ralph Dominguez/Globe Photos **Fig. 3–1** Per Sundstrom/Gamma-Liaison **Fig. 3–3a, b, c** Petit Format/Science Source/Photo Researchers **Fig. 3–3d** Donald Yeager/Camera MD Studios **p. 83** Enrico Ferorelli **Fig. 3–4** Conel, J. L. (1939–1963). *The postnatal development of the human cerebral cortex* (Vols. I–IV). Cambridge, MA: Harvard University Press. Reprinted by permission. **Fig. 3–5** Courtesy of Carolyn Rovee-Collier, Rutgers University **Fig. 3–6** From Brain changes in response to experience by M. R. Rosenzweig, E. L. Bennett, and M. C. Diamond. Copyright © 1972 Scientific American, Inc. All rights reserved. **p. 87** Laura Dwight **p. 88** Bill Anderson/Monkmeyer **p. 89** (*top and bottom*) Robert Doisneau/Rapho/Black Star **p. 90** (*top left*) David M. Grossman (*top right*) Patti Putnam/The Stock Market (*bottom left, center, and right*) Doug Goodman/Monkmeyer **Fig. 3–9** Wynn, K. (1992). Addition and subtraction by human infants. *Nature, 358,* 749–759. Reprinted by permission of *Nature*. Copyright © 1922 Macmillan Magazines Limited. **p. 93** (*left and right*) Ontario Science Centre **Figs. 3–10, 3–11** Harlow Primate Laboratory, University of Wisconsin **Fig. 3–12** Kagan, J. (1976). Emergent themes in human development. *American Scientist, 64,* 186–196. Reprinted by permission of *American Scientist*, Journal of Sigma XI, The Scientific Research Society. **p. 100** Laura Dwight **p. 102** Carol Palmer/The Picture Cube **p. 104** Sybil Shackman/Monkmeyer **p. 105** John Coletti/The Picture Cube **p. 106** Sybil Shackman/Monkmeyer **p. 109** Bob Sacha **p. 111** Kathleen Marie Menke/Crystal Images/Monkmeyer

CHAPTER **4**

**Opener p. 116** Joe Rodriguez/Black Star **Fig. 4–1** Tanner, J. M. (1978). *Fetus into man: Physical growth from conception to maturity*. Cambridge, MA: Harvard University Press. Reprinted by permission. **p. 119** J. Gerard Smith/Monkmeyer **p. 120** (*left*) Charles Harbutt/Actuality (*right*) Bob Daemmrich/The Image Works **p. 121** UPI/Bettmann Newsphotos **p. 124** (*left*) Mug Shots/The Stock Market (*right*) Richard Hutchings/Info Edit **p. 125** Joel Gordon **Fig. 4–4** Johnston, L. D., & Bachman, J. G. (1980), and Bachman, J. G., Johnston, L. D., & O'Malley, P. M. (1987). *Monitoring the future: Questionnaire responses from the nation's high school seniors*. Ann Arbor, MI: Institute for Social Research, The University of Michigan. **p. 129** Peter Southwick/Stock, Boston **Fig. 4–6** Adapted from Insel, P. M., & Roth, W. T. (1976). *Health in a changing society* (p. 98). Mountain View, CA: Mayfield. **Fig. 4–7** Olshansky, S. J., Carnes, B. A., & Cassel, C. K. (1993, April). The aging of the human species. *Scientific American*, pp. 46–52. Copyright © 1993 Scientific American, Inc. All rights reserved. **Fig. 4–8** Adapted from Doty, R. L., et al. (1984). Smell identification ability: Changes with age. *Science, 226,* 1441–1443. Copyright © 1984 the American Association for the Advancement of Science. **p. 133** David Wells/The Image Works **Fig. 4–9** Jorm, A. F., Korten, A. E., & Henderson, A. S. (1987). The prevalence of dementia: A quantitative integration of the literature. *Acta Psychiatrica Scandinivica, 76,* 465–479. Copyright © 1987 Munksgaard International Publishers Ltd., Copenhagen, Denmark. **Fig. 4-10** Data from Crook, P. H., & West, R. L. (1990). Name and recall performance across the adult life-span. *British Journal of Psychology, 81,*

335–349. **Fig. 4–11** From Schonfield, D., & Robertson, B. A. (1966). Memory storage and aging. *Canadian Journal of Psychology, 20*, 228–236. Copyright © 1966 Canadian Psychological Association. **p. 135** Gale Zucker/New York Times Pictures **Fig. 4–12** Geiwitz, J. (1980). *Psychology: Looking at ourselves*. Boston: Little, Brown, & Co. **Fig. 4–13** Adapted from Schaie, K. W. (1994). The life course of adult intellectual abilities. *American Psychologist, 49*, 304–313. Copyright © 1994 American Psychological Association. Adapted by permission. **Fig. 4–14** Adapted from Kaufman, A. S., Reynolds, C. R., & McLean, J. E. (1989). Age and WAIS-R intelligence in a national sample of adults in the 20 to 74 year age range: A cross-sectional analysis with educational level controlled. *Intelligence, 13*, 235–253. **p. 138** Henley & Savage/Stock, Boston **Fig. 4–15** McCrae, R. R., & Costa, P. T., Jr. (1990). *Personality in adulthood* (Fig. 6, p. 149). New York: Guilford Press. Copyright © 1990 Guilford Press. **p. 141** (*top*) Joe McNally (*center*) Bob Daemmrich/The Image Works (*bottom*) Charles Harbutt/Actuality **p. 142** Charles Harbutt/Actuality **Fig. 4–16** Data from Ingelhart, R. (1990). *Culture shift in advanced industrial society*. Princeton, NJ: Princeton University Press. **Fig. 4–17** Adapted from Eron, L., & Huesman, R. (1984). The control of aggressive behavior by changes in attitudes, values, and the conditions of learning. In R. J. Blanchard & C. Blanchard (Eds.), *Advances in the study of aggression* (Vol. I). Orlando, FL: Academic Press.

## CHAPTER 5

**Opener p. 150** Tim Bieber/The Image Bank **p. 152** Detail "The Forest Has Eyes" by Bev Doolittle © The Greenwich Workshop, Inc., Trumbull, CT **p. 153** (*left and right*) Thomas Eisner **p. 156** Marcia Weinstein **Fig. 5–2** Stabilized images on the retina by R. M. Pritchard. Copyright © 1961 Scientific American, Inc. All rights reserved. **p. 160** E. R. Lewis, Y. Y. Zeevi, and F. S. Werblin, 1969. **Fig. 5–8** Adapted from Frisby, J. P. (1980). *Seeing: Illusion, brain and mind* (p. 157). London: Roxby Press. Reprinted by permission of the publisher. **Fig. 5–9** Fritz Goro, LIFE Magazine ©1971 Time Warner, Inc. **p. 164** Edward S. Gazsi © National Geographic Society **Fig. 5–11** Fritz Goro, LIFE Magazine ©1944 Time Warner, Inc. **Fig. 5–12** From Richmond Products, Boca Raton, FL **Fig. 5–14** From Albers, J. (1975). *The interaction of color* (revised pocket edition) (Plate VI-3). New Haven, CT: Yale University Press. Photo courtesy of the Josef Albers Foundation. **p. 168** Nilsson, L. (1974). *Behold man*. Boston: Little, Brown. Photo courtesy of Bonnier Fakta **p. 171** Stan Schroeder/Animals Animals **Fig. 5-17** Wever, E. G. (1949). *Theory of hearing*. New York: Wiley. **p. 172** Dave Schlabowske/Time Magazine, Time Warner, Inc. **p. 173** Jill Levine **p. 174** James Carroll **p. 176** Community News, Christchurch, New Zealand. Photo courtesy of *The Skeptical Inquirer* **Fig. 5–20** Wysocki, C. J., & Gilbert, A. N. (1989). In C. Murphy & W. S. Cain (Eds.), *Proceedings of the conference on nutrition and the chemical senses in aging* (Annals of the New York Academy of Sciences) (Vol. 561). New York: New York Academy of Sciences. **p. 181** Joseph McNally/Sygma

## CHAPTER 6

**Opener p. 186** Angelo Lomeo/The Image Bank **Fig. 6–1** Bradley, D. R., et al. (1976). Reply to Cavonius. *Nature, 261*, 78. Reprinted by permission of *Nature*. Copyright © 1976 by Macmillan Journals Limited. **p. 188** Will and Deni McIntyre/Photo Researchers **Fig. 6–2** Neisser, U. (1979). The control of information pickup in selective looking. In A. D. Pick (Ed.), *Perception and its development: A tribute to Eleanor J. Gibson*. Hillsdale, NJ: Lawrence Erlbaum. Copyright © 1979 by Lawrence Erlbaum Associates, Inc. **p. 189** (*left and right*) S. Schwartzenberg/The Exploratorium **p. 190** (*top*) Rick Friedman/Black Star (*bottom left and right*) Photos courtesy of Helen E. Ross, from Ross, H. E., (1975). Mist, murk and visual perception. *New Scientist, 66*, 658–660. **Fig. 6–4** Kaiser Porcelain, Ltd. **Fig. 6–5** Photo by Walter Wick **Fig. 6–6b** Enrico Ferorelli **p. 194** Otto Greule, Jr./Allsport USA **p. 195** (*top*) Ron Watts/Black Star (*bottom*) David de Lossy/The Image Bank **p. 196** (*left*) Rainer Grosskopf/Tony Stone Worldwide (*right*) From Perceiving shape from shading by Vilayanur S. Ramachandran. Copyright © 1988 Scientific American, Inc., Photo copyright © George V. Kelvin. All rights reserved. **Fig. 6–8** City Art Gallery, Bristol/The Bridgeman Art Library, Superstock **Fig. 6–9** Shepard, R. N. (1981). Psychophysical complementarity. In M. Kubovky & J. R. Pomerantz (Eds.), *Perceptual organization* (pp. 279–341). Hillsdale, NJ: Lawrence Erlbaum. Copyright © 1981 Lawrence Erlbaum Associates. **Fig. 6–11a** From *Mind Sights* by Roger N. Shepard. Copyright © 1990 by Roger N. Shepard. Reprinted by permission of W. H. Freeman and Company. **Fig. 6–11b** Alan Choisnet/The Image Bank **Fig. 6–12** Day, R. H. (1984). The nature of perceptual illusions. *Interdisciplinary Science Reviews, 9*, 47–58. **p. 200** Adapted from Pictorial perception and culture by Jean B. Deregowski. Copyright © 1972 Scientific American, Inc. All rights reserved. **Fig. 6–13** S. Schwartzenberg/The Exploratorium **Fig. 6–15** Blakemore, C. R., & Cooper, G. F. (1970). Development of the brain depends on the visual environment. *Nature, 228*, 447–448. Reprinted by permission of *Nature*. Copyright © 1970 Macmillan Journals Limited. **p. 204** Courtesy of Hubert Dolezal **Fig 6–16** From *Mind Sights* by Roger N. Shepard. Copyright © 1990 by Roger N. Shepard. Reprinted by permission by W. H. Freeman and Company. **Fig. 6–17a** Frank Searle, photo supplied by Steuart Campbell. **Fig. 6–17b** Dick Ruhl **Fig. 6–19a, b** E. Adams/Sygma **Fig 6–20** From *Mind Sights* by Roger N. Shepard. Copyright © 1990 Roger N. Shepard. Reprinted by permission of W. H. Freeman and Company. **p. 208** Adapted from Gregory, R. L., & Gombrich, E. H. (Eds.). (1974). *Illusion in nature and art*. New York: Charles Scribner's Sons. Copyright © 1973 C. Blakemore, J. D. Deregowski, E. H. Gombrich, R. L. Gregory, H. P. Hinton, and R. Primrose. Reprinted by permission of Charles Scribner's Sons. **p. 209** Norman, D. (1988). *The psychology of everyday things*. New York: Basic Books. Reprinted by permission of Basic Books, Inc., a division of HarperCollins Publishers. **p. 210** Photo by Walter Wick **Fig. 6–21** Kraft, C. (1978). A psychological approach to air safety: Simulator studies of visual illusions in night approaches. In H. L. Pick, H. W. Leibowitz, J. E. Singer, A. Steinschneider, & H. W. Stevenson (Eds.), *Psychology: From research to practice*. New York: Plenum Press. **p. 214** Alva Bernadine

## CHAPTER 7

**Opener p. 218** Joel Gordon **p. 221** Hank Morgan/Rainbow **Figs 7–1, 7–2** Reproduced from Some must watch while some must sleep by William C. Dement. Copyright © 1972, 1974, 1976 William C. Dement and the Stanford Alumni Association, Stanford, CA. **Fig. 7–4** Webb, W. B. (1992). *Sleep: The gentle tyrant*. Bolton, MA: Anker Publishing. **Fig. 7–5** Hartmann, E. (1984). *The nightmare: The psychology and biology of terrifying dreams*. New York: Basic Books. Copyright © 1984 Ernest Hartmann. Reprinted by permission of Basic Books, Inc., a division of HarperCollins Publishers. **p. 228** National Gallery of Art, Washington, Rosenwald Collection **Fig. 7–6** From Snyder, F., & Scott, J. (1972). The psychophysiology of sleep. In N.S. Greenfield & R.A. Sternbach (Eds.), *Handbook of psychophysiology*. New York: Holt, Rinehart & Winston. **p. 231** Peter Turnley/Black Star **p. 233** James Wilson/Woodfin Camp & Associates **p. 234** Mimi Forsyth/Monkmeyer **p. 238** Joel Gordon **p. 239** Courtesy of Ernest Hilgard **p. 242** MADD, Minnesota State Office and Clarity Coverdale Rueff, Minneapolis **Fig. 7–9** Ronald K. Siegel **Fig. 7–10** Johnston, L. D., O'Malley, P. M., & Bachman, J. G. (1991). Drug use among American high school seniors, college students and young adults, 1975–1990 (Vol. 1). (Dhhs Pub. No. (ADM) 91–1813.) Washington, DC: Government Printing Office. **Fig. 7–11** From Hallucinations by R. K. Siegel. Copyright © 1977 Scientific American, Inc. All rights reserved.

## CHAPTER 8

**Opener p. 256** George White/Location Photography **p. 259** Lawrence Migdale/Stock, Boston **p. 260** Sovfoto **Fig. 8–1** Adapted from Goodwin, C. J. (1991). Misportraying Pavlov's apparatus. *American Journal of Psychology, 104*, 135–141. **p. 264** Courtesy of UCLA Media **p. 266**

Brown Brothers **Fig. 8–5** Richard Wood/The Picture Cube **p. 269** (*bottom*) Fred Bavendam/Peter Arnold, Inc. **p. 270** Bob Daemmrich **Fig. 8–6** Adapted from Teaching machines by B. F. Skinner. Copyright © 1961 Scientific American, Inc. All rights reserved. **p. 274** Joan Liftin/Actuality **Fig. 8–7** Tolman, E. C., & Honzik, C. H. (1930). Introduction and removal of reward, and maze performance in rats. *University of California Publications in Psychology, 4*, 257–275. Reprinted by permission of the University of California Press. **p. 277** Courtesy of Animal Behavior Enterprises **p. 278** Joe McNally **p. 281** Courtesy of Albert Bandura, Stanford University **p. 282** (*top*) From Meltzoff, A. N. (1988). Imitation of televised models by infants. *Child Development, 59*, 1221–1229. Photos Courtesy of A. N. Meltzoff and M. Hanak (*bottom*) Bob Daemmrich/The Image Works

## CHAPTER 9

**Opener p. 286** Ken Robert Buck/The Picture Cube **p. 287** Courtesy of Hersh & Treadgold, Inc., Desktop Paging Software, Inc., and NEC, Inc. **p. 289** Fred Ward/Black Star **p. 291** (*left*) Erika Stone (*right*) Bob Daemmrich/Stock, Boston **Fig. 9–2** Data from H. Ebbinghaus, 1885. Graph from Baddeley, A. D. (1982). *Your memory: A user's guide*. New York: Macmillan. Copyright © 1982 Macmillan Publishing Co., Inc. Reprinted by permission. **Fig. 9–3** Craik, F. I. M., & Watkins, M. J. (1973). The role of rehearsal in short-term memory. *Journal of Verbal Learning and Verbal Behavior, 12*, 599–607. **Fig. 9–4** Craik, F. I. M., & Tulving, E. (1975). Depth of processing and the retention of words in episodic memory. *Journal of Experimental Psychology: General, 104*, 268–294. Copyright © 1975 American Psychological Association. Reprinted with the permission of the authors. **Fig. 9–5** From *The psychology of learning and memory* by Douglas L. Hintzman. Copyright © 1978 W. H. Freeman and Company. Reprinted by permission of W. H. Freeman and Company. **Fig. 9–8** Nickerson, R. S., & Adams, M. J. (1979). Long-term memory for a common object. *Cognitive Psychology, 11*, 287–307. **Fig. 9–10** Peterson, L. R., & Peterson, M. J. (1959). Short-term retention of individual verbal items. *Journal of Experimental Psychology, 58*, 193–198. Copyright © 1959 American Psychological Association. Reprinted by permission of the authors. **p. 301** R.J. Erwin/Photo Researchers **Fig. 9–11** Adapted from *Human memory: Structures and processes* by R. Klatzky. Copyright © 1980 W. H. Freeman and Company. Reprinted by permission of W. H. Freeman and Company. **Fig. 9–12** Adapted from Bahrick, H. P (1984). Semantic memory content in permastore: 50 years of memory for Spanish learned in school. *Journal of Experimental Psychology: General, 113*, 1–29. Copyright © 1984 American Psychological Association. Adapted by permission. **p. 304** Lynn Johnson/Black Star **Fig. 9–14b** From Learning and Memory, 1994. Copyright © Cold Spring Harbour Laboratories, Courtesy of James Golomb, M.D., Department of Neurology, NYU School of Medicine. **p. 308** (*top and bottom*) Seth Poppel/Yearbook Archives **Fig. 9–15** Adapted from Bower, G. H. (1986). Prime time in cognitive psychology. In P. Eelen (Ed.), *Cognitive research and behavior therapy: Beyond the conditioning paradigm*. Amsterdam: North Holland Publishers. **Fig. 9–16** Adapted from Godden, D. R., & Baddeley, A. D. (1975). Context-dependent memory in two natural environments: On land and under water. *British Journal of Psychology, 66*, 325–331. **Fig. 9–17a, b** Courtesy of Carolyn Rovee-Collier, Rutgers University **Fig. 9–18** Loftus, E. F. (1979). The malleability of human memory: *American Scientist, 67*, 313–320. Reprinted by permission of *American Scientist*, Journal of Sigma Xi, The Scientific Research Society. **Fig. 9–19** Jenkins, J. G., & Dallenbach, K. M. (1924). Obliviscence during sleep and waking. *American Journal of Psychology, 35*, 605–612. Copyright © 1924 Board of Trustees and the University of Illinois. Reprinted by permission of the University of Illinois Press. **p. 319** Courtesy of Elizabeth Loftus, University of Washington **p. 321** Hugh Rogers/Monkmeyer

## CHAPTER 10

**Opener p. 324** Antony Edgeworth/The Stock Market **p. 327** (*top left*) Ron Sanford/Black Star (*top right*) J. Messerschmidt/The Picture Cube **p. 328** Based on illustration by Vichai Makilul modified by Richard Swartz in Rumbaugh, D. M., & Savage-Rumbaugh, S. (1986). Reasoning and language in chimpanzees. In R. J. Hoage & L. Goldman (Eds.), *Animal intelligence*. Washington, DC: Smithsonian Institution Press. **Fig. 10–1** From Problem solving by M. Scheerer. Copyright © 1963 Scientific American, Inc. All rights reserved. **Fig. 10–2** Adapted from Luchins, A. S. (1946). Classroom experiments on mental set. *American Journal of Psychology, 59*, 295–298. Copyright © 1946 Board of Trustees of the University of Illinois. Reprinted by permission of the University of Illinois Press. **Fig. 10–3** Duncker, K. (1945). On problem-solving. *Psychological Monographs, 58* (Whole no. 270). **Fig. 10–4** From Problem solving by M. Scheerer. Copyright © 1963 Scientific American, Inc. All rights reserved. **Fig. 10-5** Adapted from Luchins, A. S. (1946). Classroom experiments on mental set. *American Journal of Psychology, 59*, 295–298. Copyright © 1946 Board of Trustees of the University of Illinois. Reprinted by permission of the University of Illinois Press. **Fig. 10-6** Duncker, K. (1945). On problem-solving. *Psychological Monographs, 58* (Whole no. 270). **p. 333** Diedra Laird/*The Charlotte Observer* **p. 337** Stanley Rowin/The Picture Cube **p. 341** M. & E. Bernheim/Woodfin Camp & Associates **Fig. 10–7** Adapted from Werker, J. F. (1989). Becoming a native listener. *American Scientist, 77*, 54–59. Reprinted by permission of *American Scientist*, Journal of Sigma Xi, The Scientific Research Society. Photos courtesy of Peter McLeod, Acadia University **p. 345** Elizabeth Crews **Fig. 10–8** Johnson, J. S., & Newport, E. L. (1989). Critical period effects in second language learning: The influence of maturational state on the acquisition of English as a second language. *Cognitive Psychology, 21*, 60–99. **p. 346** George Ancona in Ancona, G., & Beth, M. (1989). *The Handtalk Zoo*. New York: Macmillan Publishing Company. **Fig. 10–9** von Frisch, K. (1974). Decoding the language of the bee. *Science, 185*, 663–668. Copyright © The Nobel Foundation 1974. **p. 348** (*center*) Paul Fusco/Magnum Photos (*bottom left*) Language Research Center, Yerkes Regional Primate Research Center **Fig. 10–10** From Savage-Rumbaugh, E. S., Murphy, J., Sevcik, R. A., Brakke, K. E., Williams, S. L., & Rumbaugh, D. M., with commentary by Bates, E. (1993). *Language comprehension in ape and child*. Monographs of the Society for Research in Child Development, 58 (no. 233), 1-254. **p. 352** Elizabeth Crews/The Image Works **p. 353** Stephen Dunn/Allsport **p. 354** Tony Freeman/Photo Edit

## CHAPTER 11

**Opener p. 358** Gregory Edwards/International Stock Photo **p. 360 & p. 361** National Library of Medicine **p. 362** News Service, Stanford University **p. 363** (*top*) Will & Deni McIntyre/Photo Researchers (*bottom*) Lew Merrim/Monkmeyer **Fig. 11–1** From Thorndike, A. L., & Hagen, E. P. (1977). *Measurement and evaluation in psychology and education*. New York: Macmillan. Reprinted by permission of Macmillan Publishing Company. Photo of dog © Russ Kinne/Comstock **Fig. 11–2** College Entrance Examination Board. (1983, 1990). *Sample SAT questions from 10 SATs*. Princeton, NJ: Educational Testing Service. Copyrights © 1983, 1990 Educational Testing Service, Princeton, NJ. Reprinted by permission. **p. 371** (*left*) Victor Englebert/Photo Researchers (*right*) George Ancona/International Stock Photo **Fig. 11–7** From Wiltshire, S. (1991). *Floating cities*. London: Michael Joseph Ltd. **p. 378** Courtesy of Joseph F. Fagan III, Infantest Corporation **Table 11–1** American Psychiatric Association (1994). *Diagnostic and statistical manual of mental disorders* (4th ed.). Washington, DC: American Psychiatric Association. **p. 380** (*top*) Tony Mendoza/The Picture Cube (*bottom*) Michael O'Neill **Fig. 11–8** Bouchard, T. J., Jr. (1982). Twins—Nature's twice-told tale. In *1983 Yearbook of Science and the Future*. Chicago: Encyclopaedia Britannica Copyright © 1982 Encyclopaedia Britannica, Inc. Reprinted by permission of Encyclopaedia Britannica, Inc. **Fig. 11–9** Fulker, D. W., DeFries, J. C., & Plomin, R. (1988). Genetic influence on general mental ability increases between infancy and middle childhood. *Nature, 336*, 767–769. Reprinted by permission of *Nature*. Copyright © 1988 Macmillan Magazines Limited. **p. 387** (*left*) Jacques Chenet/Woodfin Camp & Associates (*right*) Susan Lapides/Design Conceptions **Fig. 11–10** Lewontin, R. (1976). Race and intelligence. In N. J. Block & G. Dworken (Eds.), *The IQ controversy: Critical readings*. New York: Pantheon. Copyright © 1976 N. J. Block & G. Dworken. Reprinted by permission. **Fig. 11–11** Adapted from Stevenson, H. W., et al. (1986). Mathematics achievement in Chinese,

Japanese, and American children. *Science, 231,* 639–699. Copyright © 1986 American Association for the Advancement of Science. **p. 390** Jason Goltz

## CHAPTER 12

**Opener p. 396** Scott Markewitz/FPG **p. 398** (*top*) Bob Daemmrich/The Image Works (*bottom*) Tony Brandenburg/Bruce Coleman, Inc. **p. 399** (*left*) George Ancona/International Stock Photo (*right*) Harlow Primate Laboratory, University of Wisconsin **Fig. 12–1** Maslow, A. H. (1970). *Motivation and personality* (2nd ed.). New York: Harper & Row. Copyright © 1954 Harper & Row Publishers, Inc. Copyright © 1970 by Abraham H. Maslow. Reprinted by permission of HarperCollins Publishers, Inc. **Fig. 12–2** Adapted from Cannon, W. B. (1929). *Bodily changes in pain, hunger, fear, and rage.* New York: Branford. **Fig. 12–3** Pix*ELATION from Fran Heyl Associates **p. 403** (*bottom*) Richard Howard **p. 404** Richard Olsenius/Black Star **p. 406** Tony Freeman/Photo Edit **Fig. 12–4** Stunkard, A., Sorenson, T., & Schulsinger, F. (1980). Use of the Danish Adoption Register for the study of obesity and thinness. In S. Kety (Ed.), *The Genetics of Neurological and Psychiatric Disorders* (p. 119). New York: Raven Press. Copyright © 1983 Raven Press. **p. 408** Photo by Dellenbeck reprinted by permission of the Kinsey Institute for Research in Sex, Gender, and Reproduction, Inc. **Fig. 12–5** Byrne, D. (1982). Predicting human sexual behavior. In A. G. Kraut, *The G. Stanley Hall Lecture Series* (Vol. 2). Washington, DC: American Psychological Association. Copyright © 1982 American Psychological Association. Reprinted by permission of the author. **p. 414** Cynthia Johnson/Time Magazine **p. 416** Nathaniel Antman/The Image Works **p. 417** Bumpass, L. L., & Sweet, J. A. (1989). National estimates of cohabitation. *Demography, 26,* 615–625. **p. 419** (*top*) Rob Nelson/Black Star **Fig. 12–6** McClelland, D.C., et al. (1953). *The achievement motive.* New York: Appleton-Century-Crofts. Reprinted by permission of Irvington Publishers, New York **p. 422** UPI/Bettmann Archives **p. 424** Fujifotos/The Image Works **p. 426** Ted Thai/Time Magazine

## CHAPTER 13

**Opener p. 432** Bob Daemmrich/Stock, Boston **p. 436** Courtesy of David Raskin, University of Utah, as shown in *Science* '82, June, pp. 24–27. **p. 437** Bernard Gottfryd/Woodfin Camp & Associates **Fig. 13–3** Kleinmuntz, B., & Szucko, J. J. (1984). A field study of the fallibility of polygraph lie detection. *Nature, 308,* 449–450. Reprinted by permission of *Nature.* Copyright © 1984 Macmillan Journals Limited. **Fig. 13–4** Dr. Paul Ekman, University of California at San Francisco **p. 439** (*bottom*) Culver Pictures **Fig. 13–5** Courtesy of Dr. Paul Ekman from Ekman, P., & Friesen, W. V. (1984). *Unmasking the face* (reprint ed.). Palo Alto, CA: Consulting Psychologists Press **Fig. 13–6** Courtesy of Louis Schakel **p. 442** (*bottom left and right*) Michael Kausman/The New York Times Pictures **Fig. 13–7** Courtesy of Carroll Izard, University of Delaware **p. 447** Wolfgang Kaehler **Fig. 13–9** Astin, A., Korn, W. S., & Riggs, E. R. (1993). *The American freshman: National norms for Fall 1993.* Los Angeles: Higher Education Research Institute, Graduate School of Education, UCLA; Dey, E. L., et al. (1991). *The American freshman: Twenty-five year trends.* Los Angeles: Higher Education Research Institute, UCLA. **Fig. 13–11** Adapted from Solomon, R. L. (1980). The opponent-process theory of acquired motivation: The costs of pleasure and the benefits of pain. *American Psychologist, 35,* 691–712. Copyright © 1980 American Psychological Association. Reprinted by permission of the author. **p. 451** William Johnson/Stock, Boston **p. 453** Robert Deutsch/*USA Today*

## CHAPTER 14

**Opener p. 460** Dede Hatch/The Picture Cube **p. 462** Culver Pictures **p. 463** Edmund Engelman **Fig. 14–1** Adapted from Freud, S. (1933). *New introductory lectures on psychoanalysis* (p. 111). New York: Carlton House. **p. 466** (*left*) Rick Friedman/Black Star (*right*) Harlow Primate Laboratory, University of Wisconsin **p. 467** (*top*) National Library of Medicine (*bottom*) The Bettmann Archive **p. 468** Archives of the History of American Psychology **p. 469** (*left and right*) Lew Merrim/Monkmeyer **p. 473** AP/Wide World Photos **Fig. 14–2** Eysenck, S. B. G., & Eysenck, H. J. (1963). The validity of questionnaire and rating assessments of extraversion and neuroticism, and their factorial stability. *British Journal of Psychology, 54,* 51–62 (Fig. 1). **Table 14-2** Adapted from McCrae, R. & Costa, R. T., Jr. (1986). Clinical assessment can benefit from recent advances in personality psychology. *American Psychologist, 41,* 1002. **Fig. 14–3** Adapted from Butcher, J. N. (1990). *The MMPI-2 in psychological treatment* (Figs 1–3 and 1–4, pp. 13–14). New York: Oxford University Press. **p. 480** Ted Polumbaum/Life Magazine © 1968 Time Warner, Inc. **p. 481** Mark Antman/The Image Works **p. 482** Sybil Shackman/Monkmeyer **Fig. 14–4** Adapted from Bandura, A. (1978). The self-system in reciprocal determinism. *American Psychologist, 33,* 344–358. Copyright © 1978 American Psychological Association. Adapted by permission. **p. 489** Stephen Wade/Allsport USA **p. 490** Joe McNally

## CHAPTER 15

**Opener p. 498** Comstock **p. 500** Tony Ray Jones/Magnum Photos **Fig. 15–1** J. Otis Wheelock; courtesy of Department of Library Services, American Museum of Natural History **p. 503** AP/World Wide Photos **Fig. 15–2.** Phears and phobias. (1984, August/September). *Public Opinion,* p. 32. Washington, DC: American Enterprise Institute for Public Policy Research. Reprinted by permission of the American Enterprise Institute for Public Policy Research. **Table 15-1** Adapted from The biology of obsessions and compulsions by J. L. Rapoport. Copyright © 1989 Scientific American, Inc. All rights reserved. **p. 509** (*top*) Paul Fusco/Magnum Photos **Fig. 15–3** Baxter, L. R., et al. (1987). Local cerebral glucose metabolic rates in obsessive-compulsive disorder. *Archives of General Psychology, 44*(3), 211–218. Copyright © 1987 American Medical Association. **p. 510** Punch/Rothco **p. 512** AP/Wide World Photos **p. 518** (*top*) AP/Wide World Photos (*bottom*) Stephen P. Allen/Gamma Liaison **Fig. 15–6a, b, & c** Courtesy of Drs. Lewis Baxter and Michael E. Phelps, UCLA School of Medicine **Fig. 15–8** Forgas, J. P., et al. (1984). The influence of mood on perceptions of social interactions. *Journal of Experimental and Social Psychology, 20,* 497–513. **Fig. 15–9** Perlman, D. (1990). Age differences in loneliness: A meta-analysis. Paper presented to the American Psychological Association convention. **Fig. 15–10** Adapted from Lewinsohn, P. M., et al. (1985). An integrative theory of depression. In S. Reiss & R. Bootzin (Eds.), *Theoretical issues in behavior therapy.* Orlando, FL: Academic Press. **p. 524** (*left*) Berthold, L., *Untitled.* The Prinzhorn Collection, University of Heidelberg (*right*) August Natterer, *Witch's Head.* The Prinzhorn Collection, University of Heidelberg. Photos: Krannert Museum, University of Illinois at Urbana-Champaign **p. 528** (*top*) From Suddath, Richard L., et al. (1990). Anatomical abnormalities in the brains of monozygotic twins discordant for schizophrenia. *The New England Journal of Medicine, 322,* 12. ©1990 by the Massachusetts Medical Society. Photo courtesy of Daniel R. Weinberger, M.D., NIH-NIMH/NSC. (*bottom*) Courtesy of Genain Family **Fig. 15-12** Adapted from Magnusson, D. (1990). Personality research—challenges for the future. *European Journal of Personality, 4,* 1–17.

## CHAPTER 16

**Opener p. 538** Treë **p. 539** (*left*) The Granger Collection (*right*) The Bettmann Archive **p. 540** Culver Pictures **p. 541** Paul Meredith/TSW, Click Chicago Ltd. **p. 542** Steve Goldberg/Monkmeyer **p. 543** Michael Rougier, Life Magazine, © Time Warner, Inc. **Fig. 16–1** Gilling, D., & Brightwell, R. (1982). *The human brain.* New York: Facts on File. Copyright © 1982 D. Gilling and R. Brightwell. Reprinted by permission of Facts on File, Inc., New York. **Fig. 16–4** Rabin, A. S., et al. (1986). Aggregate outcome and follow-up results following self-control therapy for depression. Paper presented at the American Psychological Association convention. **p. 554** Stacy Pick/Stock, Boston **Fig. 16–6** Adapted from Smith, M. L., et al. (1980). *The benefits of psychotherapy* (p. 88). Baltimore, MD: Johns Hopkins University Press. Reprinted by permission. **p. 561** Mark

Antman/The Image Works **Fig. 16–7** Lee Snider/The Image Works **p. 565** Lynn Johnson/Black Star **p. 567** James Wilson/Woodfin Camp & Associates

## CHAPTER 17

**Opener p. 572** Michael Heron/Monkmeyer **p. 574** (*left*) Arlene Collins/Monkmeyer (*right*) Andy Levin/Photo Researchers **Fig. 17–5** Adams, P. R., & Adams, G. R. (1984). Mount St. Helens ashfall: Evidence for a disaster stress reaction. *American Psychologist, 29*, 252–260. Copyright © 1984 American Psychological Association. Reprinted by permission of the authors. **p. 578** Peter Glass/Monkmeyer **Fig. 17–6** Adapted from Weiss, J. M. (1977). Psychological and behavioral influences on gastrointestinal lesions in animal models. In *Psychopathology: Experimental models* by Maser and Seigelman (Eds.). Copyright © 1977 W. H. Freeman and Company. Reprinted by permission of W. H. Freeman and Company. **p. 583** Lennart Nilsson/Boehringer Ingelheim International GmbH **p. 585** Paul Fusco/Magnum Photos **Fig. 17–7** Adapted from Coren, S. (1993). *The left-hander syndrome: The causes and consequences of left-handedness*. New York: Vintage Books. **Fig. 17–10** Adapted from Safer, M. A., et al. (1979). Determinants of three stages of delay in seeking care at a medical clinic. *Medical Care, 17*(1), 11–28. Reprinted by permission of the publisher. **Fig. 17–11** McFarland, C., Ross, M., & Decourville, N. (1989). Women's theories of menstruation and the biases in recall of menstrual symptoms. *Journal of Personality and Social Psychology, 57*, 522–531. Copyright © 1989 American Psychological Association. Reprinted by permission of the authors. **Fig. 17–12** Adapted from McCann, I. L., & Holmes, D. S. (1984). Influence of aerobic exercise on depression. *Journal of Personality and Social Psychology, 46*, 1142–1147. Copyright © 1984 American Psychological Association. Reprinted by permission of the authors. **Fig. 17–13** Dan McCoy/Rainbow **p. 595** Steve Liss/Time Magazine **Fig. 17–14** Friedman, M., & Ulmer, D. (1984). *Treating type A behavior—and your heart*. New York: Alfred A. Knopf, Inc. Copyright © 1984 by Meyer Friedman. Reprinted by permission of Alfred A. Knopf, Inc. **p. 598** Bob Krist/Black Star **p. 600** Joel Gordon **Fig. 17–18** Brown, L. B., Hane, H., & Ayres, E. (1993). *Vital signs: The trends that are shaping our future*. New York: Norton. Reprinted by permission of the Non-Smokers' Rights Association of Canada, Ottawa. **p. 604** Lincoln Russell/Stock, Boston **Fig. 17–19** Bray, G. A. (1969). Effect of caloric restriction on energy expenditure in obese patients. *Lancet, 2*, 397–398. Copyright © 1969 The Lancet Ltd. **p. 606** Joseph Neumayer/Design Conceptions **Fig. 17–20** Brownwell, K. D., & Jeffrey, R. W. (1987). Improving long-term weight loss: Pushing the limits of treatment. *Behavior Therapy, 18*, 353–374. Copyright © 1987 Association for the Advancement of Behavior Therapy. Reprinted by permission of the publisher and the authors. **Fig. 17–21** Dietz, W. H., Jr., & Gortmaker, S. L. (1985). Do we fatten our children at the television set? Obesity and television viewing children and adolescents. *Pediatrics, 75*, 807–812. Copyright © 1985. Reproduced by permission of *Pediatrics*.

## CHAPTER 18

**Opener p. 612** David Madison **p. 616** AP/Wide World Photos **p. 618** Thomas Hopker/Magnum Photos **Fig. 18–2** Philips, D. P. (1974). The influence of suggestion on suicide: Substantive and theoretical implications of the Werther effect. *American Sociological Review, 39*, 340–354 (Fig. 1, p. 343). Reprinted by permission of the American Sociological Association. **Fig. 18–3** William Vandivert/*Scientific American* **Fig. 18–4** Adapted from Fein, S., Goethals, G. R., Kassin, S. M., & Cross, J. (1993). Social influence and presidential debates. Paper presented at the American Psychological Association convention. **p. 623** Courtesy of CUNY Graduate School and University Center **p. 625** AP/Wide World Photos **Fig. 18–6** Adapted from Wheeler, D. L., Jacobsen, D. L., Paglieri, R. A., & Schwartz, A. A. (1993). An experimental assessment of facilitated communication. *Mental Retardation, 31*, 49–60. **p. 627** Focus on Sports **p. 628** Bob Daemmrich/Sygma **p. 631** Margaret Bourke-White, Life Magazine. Copyright © 1946 Time Warner, Inc. **p. 633** Presse-Sports **p. 634** Serge de Sazo/Rapho/Photo Researchers **Fig. 18-8** Anderson, C. A., & Anderson, D. C. (1984). Ambient temperature and violent crime: Tests on the linear and curvilinear hypotheses. *Journal of Personality and Social Psychology, 46*, 91–97. Copyright © 1984 American Psychological Association. Reprinted by permission of the authors. **Fig. 18–9** Adapted from Malamuth, N. M. (1989). Sexually violent media, thought patterns, and anti-social behavior. In G. Comstock (Ed.), *Public communication and behavior* (Vol. 2). San Diego, CA: Academic Press. **Fig. 18–10** Darley, J. M., & Latané, B. (1968, December). When will people help in a crisis? *Psychology Today*, pp. 54–57, 70–71. Copyright © 1968 Sussex Publishers, Inc. Reprinted by permission of *Psychology Today*. **Fig. 18–11** Darley, J. M., & Latané, B. (1968). Bystander intervention in emergencies: Diffusion of responsibility. *Journal of Personality and Social Psychology, 8*, 377–383. Copyright © 1968 American Psychological Association. Reprinted by permission of the authors. **p. 642** (*top*) Akos Szilvasi/Stock, Boston (*bottom*) Joel Gordon **p. 643** Brian A. Potts **p. 644** (*top*) Rex USA (*bottom left and right*) Cynthia Johnson/The Gamma Liaison Network **p. 645** James Kamp/Black Star **p. 646** (*left*) Margaret Gowan/Tony Stone Worldwide (*center*) Victor Englebert/Photo Researchers (*right*) Nancy Brown/The Image Bank **p. 648** (*bottom left*) Henri Cartier-Bresson/Magnum Photos (*bottom right*) Renee Lynn/Photo Researchers

## CHAPTER 19

**Opener p. 652** Photo Researchers **p. 654** (*left*) Joe Carini/The Image Works (*center*) Robert Caputo/Stock, Boston (*right*) Brett Froomer/The Image Bank **p. 655** (*left*) Willie L. Hill, Jr./Stock, Boston (*center*) Sally Cassidy/The Picture Cube (*top right*) Lawrence Migdale/Stock, Boston (*right*) Sally Cassidy/The Picture Cube (*bottom right*) Owen Franken/Stock, Boston **p. 656** Fujifotos/The Image Works **p. 657** Gary Rogers/The Image Bank **p. 658** D. Cannon/Allsport USA **Table 19-1** Schoeneman, T. J. (1994). Individualism. In V. S. Ramachandran (Ed.), *Encyclopedia of human behavior*. San Diego, CA: Academic Press; Triandis, H. C. (1994). *Culture and social behavior*. New York: McGraw-Hill. Reproduced by permission of the publisher **p. 662** Bob Daemmrich/The Image Works **p. 663** (*top*) Courtesy of James Jones (*bottom*) David Austen/Stock, Boston **p. 664** Jonathan Wenk/Black Star **Fig. 19–2** Vandenberg, S. G., & Kuse, A. R. (1978). Mental rotations, a group test of three-dimensional spacial visualization. *Perceptual and Motor Skills, 47*, 599–604 (Fig. 1). Copyright © 1978 *Perceptual and Motor Skills*. Reprinted by permission of the authors and the publisher. **p. 668** Bob Daemmrich/Stock, Boston **Fig. 19–3** Tornstam, L. (1992). Loneliness in marriage. *Journal of Social and Personal Relationships, 9*, 197–217. Copyright © 1992 Sage Publications Ltd. Reprinted by permission of the author. **p. 670** (*left*) Jerry Howard/Stock, Boston (*right*) Myrleen Ferguson/Photo Edit **Fig. 19-4** Buss, D. (1994). *The evolution of desire*. New York: Basic Books. Copyright © 1994 by David M. Buss. Reprinted by permission of BasicBooks, a division of HarperCollins Publishers, Inc. **p. 676** (*left*) Lindsay Hebberd/Woodfin Camp & Associates (*right*) L. Townshend/The Picture Cube **Fig. 19–6** Stiles, D. A., Gibbons, J. L., & Schellmann, J. G. (1990). Opposite-sex ideal in the U.S.A. and Mexico as perceived by young adolescents. *Journal of Cross-Cultural Psychology, 21*(2), 180–199. Reprinted by permission of Sage Publications, Inc. **p. 679** David Butow/Black Star **Fig. 19–7** Astin, A., Korn, W. S., & Riggs, E. R. (1993). *The American freshman: National norms for fall 1993*. Los Angeles: Higher Education Research Institute, Graduate School of Education, UCLA; Dey, E. L., et al. (1991). *The American freshman: Twenty-five year trends*. Los Angeles: Higher Education Research Institute, UCLA. **p. 681** Elsa Peterson/Design Conceptions **p. 682** Mario Ruiz/Picture Group **Fig. 19–8** Niemi, R. G., Moeller, J., & Smith, T. W. (1989). *Trends in public opinion: A compendium of survey data*. New York: Greenwood Press. Reprinted with permission of Greenwood Publishing Group, Inc., Westport, CT.; Smith, T. W. (1994). Personal communication. Data from General Social Survey, National Opinion Research Center, University of Chicago. **p. 685** Michael S. Yamashita/Woodfin Camp & Associates **p. 687** Keith Gosse/The *Evening Telegram* **p. 689** Bob Daemmrich/Stock, Boston

# Name Index

# Subject Index